D1726606

LIVES
THAT SHAPED YOUR LIFE

PROTEUS

LIVES
THAT SHAPED YOUR LIFE

COMPILED BY BOB BRECHER

PROTEUS

PROTEUS BOOKS is an imprint of
The Proteus Publishing Group

United Kingdom
PROTEUS (PUBLISHING) LIMITED
Bremar House,
Sale Place,
London, W2 1PT

United States
PROTEUS PUBLISHING COMPANY
distributed by:
LIPPINCOTT & CROWELL PUBLISHERS, INC.
521 Fifth Avenue,
New York, NY 10017

ISBN 0 906071 13 5 hardback

First published in UK February 1980
First published in US May 1980
© 1980 Proteus Publishing Group
All rights reserved.

Printed and bound
in Hong Kong by
South China Printing Co.

Contents

Introduction & Acknowledgment

Some two and a half years ago I was approached to work on a book about prominent people. The brief was very vague, intentionally leaving much to my interpretation and imagination. My publishers' only imperatives were that I produce a book of general reference for a wide readership, particularly among young and middle-teen students, that I imbue it with a strong sense of history, and that I deliver it ... quickly!

As to the latter demand, I am afraid I have proved a great disappointment. Two projected publication dates have come and gone, and as I write these words a third — which I am determined to meet — is too close for comfort.

My problems began immediately, in trying to decide how to interpret the word "prominent". I could have played safe and treated it as a synonym for "famous", but I soon realised that there are any number of current celebrities — movie, television, sports and political personalities, for instance — whose names are better known than perhaps two-thirds of those featured in this book. Yet no more than a handful are destined to stand even the most cursory test of time. History itself teaches us a quirky lesson in this regard. Many of the great men and women who people the following pages were underestimated or even overlooked in their own life-times, and it is only with the benefit of the passage of time that their lasting contributions to our way of life can be appreciated.

In the end, then, I chose a title for the book which the publishers considered "snappy" and I considered stimulating, and let it dictate the editorial policy. I would argue that each of the more than 360 LIVES that follow *did* shape — and by their achievements continue to shape — our lives, or at least the lives of many of us, in some way. Obviously, the reader with no enthusiasm for horseracing will not feel especially grateful to the twelfth earl of Derby, who did so much to promote and sponsor equestrian sport in the early nineteenth century; the reader with no sense of adventure may find the success of a Donald Campbell or the exploits of Blondin, the legendary ropewalker, absurd and pointless. But whether they righted wrongs, made life more convenient and enjoyable by practical invention, moved the spirit (for good or evil) by example, or merely entertained, all the people I have chosen have had an affect on society generally which has lasted, for more than two centuries in some cases, and seems likely to last quite a while yet.

To give the book a historical "feel", I decided to use the medium of contemporary newspaper articles, usually obituaries or biographical notes. Editorial (and typographical) styles vary immensely, of course, from publication to publication and from era to era, but I hope the reader will share my belief that the stylistic hazards of an eighteenth century account of, say, George Washington still make a refreshing change from the kind of sterile rehashes of the great lives that fill modern encyclopaedias and history books. How a person's contemporaries viewed him or her can be just as revealing and as fascinating as the biographical details themselves.

Having settled on this approach, I scoured through almost 50 English-language periodicals in libraries in London, New York, Washington D.C. and elsewhere. Inevitably, there has been a tendency to concentrate on certain papers: The Times, Daily Telegraph and the Standard in London, the Manchester Guardian, the Glasgow Herald, the New York Times, Herald and Tribune, the San Francisco Chronicle and the Chicago Tribune. This is not through any preconceived bias, but simply a reflection of the fact that some periodicals have always, or at times in their history, given greater editorial prominence to obituaries and personal notes than others, particularly in the early years covered by this book. One of the curious pieces of information I acquired in the course of research is that the "craze" for obituaries, like that for crosswords, is a fairly recent phenomenon. Before the 1890s, it seems, they were just not popular reading.

Finally, a word on selection. Much of the delay in completion of the book was due to the arduous task of selection, and even now I am confident that I have not got it exactly right. From a working list of about 5,000 names, compiled by committee and with the aid of specialists in certain fields about which I was rather too ignorant, I researched over 2,000, finally reducing the number of entries to about 365. The process of elimination was slow, painful and hesitant: many that appear were reprieved from exclusion at the eleventh hour, many that do not were strong candidates to the last. I do not believe that anybody who really *has* to be in has been omitted, but I know that any reader will be able to make a good case for replacing at least one entry a page with another.

It would be pointless to apologize for my selection (and, indeed, for my categorisation, which some may find eccentric in places!), and therefore I do not.

* * * * * *

It has to be said that this book is essentially the work of many people. It is the work of all the correspondents, reporters, editors and proprietors (many of whose names I will regretfully never know) of the journals from which the material emanates. It is the work of the superintendents, staff and facilities of the various libraries I used, particularly the British Library Newspaper Reading Room in Colindale, the New York Public Library Newspaper Annexe in Manhattan and the Library of Congress in Washington D.C. And it is the work of my editor, who helped immensely on background research, selection and organisation of material. To all, my sincere thanks.

The principal periodicals consulted were (in alphabetical order):

Chicago (Daily) Tribune;
Columbia Centinel, of Boston;
Daily Express,
Daily Herald,
Daily Mail,
Daily Mirror,
Daily News, and
Daily, Telegraph, all of London;
Dictionary of National Biography;
Gentleman's Magazine, of London;
Glasgow Herald;
Los Angeles Times;
Manchester Guardian;
Massachussetts Mercury, of Boston;
Newsweek magazine;
New York Evening Post;
New York Herald;
New York Times;
The Observer, of London;
St. Louis Post-Dispatch;
San Francisco Chronicle;
San Francisco Examiner;
The Standard,
The Star, and
The Sun, of London;
Time magazine.;
The Times, of London;
The Times Picayne, of New Orleans;
The Tribune, and
The World, of New York.

B.B.

Adventure

Adventurers are those whose exploits fire the imagination. What they have done may not in itself be important (like **Houdini**'s escapology); what matters is the doing of it. The danger braved, the risk taken, just because the challenge is there: **Louis Blériot**, first to fly the Channel, or **Amelia Earhart**, the first woman to fly round the world (with apologies to fans of Charles Lindbergh). Or perhaps taking a walk on a tightrope across the Niagara Falls, like **Blondin**. In the military field there is the example of **Lawrence of Arabia**, who turned a small-scale assignment into a crusade which inspired millions. Some pit themselves against a barrier, just because it is there – they risk, and often come to lose, their lives for the sake of a few extra inches or miles per hour, like **Donald Campbell** and **Henry Segrave**, representing here all those eccentric yet inspired achievers who push themselves to the limit and beyond for the sake of a record. Still others, like the **Montgolfier** brothers, themselves grow into symbols – in this case, like that of Icarus, rather too early to include here, of man's aspiration to fly. Perhaps the most famous adventurer of the past two hundred years not to have an obituary is Fletcher Christian, whose mutiny on *The Bounty* in 1789 came to have an enormous impact on our folklore, but whose family at the time of his return to England in the 1790's ignored his disgraceful presence, and who died quite anonymously. In his place, **William Bligh**, of whom he got rather the better, and some of his fellow mutineers have to do duty for him.

Eccentricity, of course, is the keynote of adventure, and a few of our choices in this section are included to represent the spectrum from oddity to obsession that the more sedate in spirit find difficult to understand. What compels a **Joselito** to face the bull time and again: a death wish? Why are the **Captain Webbs** and **Bobby Leaches** of this world driven to try their bizarre tests of courage? Are braving the Niagara Falls on a tightrope, in a barrel or swimming really as absurd and pointless as they seem?

Finally, the quintessential adventurer. **David Crockett** may have broken no records, attempted no feats of insane daring, but he lived his whole life as an enterprise, by design rather than circumstance, and rightly deserves his place in the heart and soul of everyone moved by the spirit of adventure.

The Herald
12th April 1836

TEXAS.—SAD NEWS.—The following is extracted from a New Orleans paper of the 28th ult. Will it not rouse the nation?

HIGHLY IMPORTANT FROM TEXAS.—We learn by the passengers of the schr. Camanche, 8 days from Texas, that the War has assumed a serious character—on the 25th Feb. the Texian Garrison in Bexar of 150 men, commanded by Lt. Col. B. Travis was attacked by the advance division of Gen. Sea. Anna's army consisting of 2000 men who were repulsed with the loss of many killed between 500 to 800 men, without the loss of one man of the Texians—about the same time Col. Johnson with a party of 70 men while recoonoitering the westward of San Patricio was surrounded in the night by a large body of Mexican troops—in the morning the demand of a surrender was made by the Mexican Commander unconditionally, which was refused; but an offer of surrender was made as prisoners of war, which was acceded to by the Mexicans. But no sooner had the Texians marched out of their quarters and stacked their arms, than a general fire was opened upon them by the whole Mexican force—the Texians attempted to escape but only three of them succeeded; one of whom was Col. Johnson.

Between the 25th February and 2d March the Mexicans were employed in forming entrenchments around the Alamo and Bombarding the place; on the 2d March Col. Travis wrote that 200 shells had been thrown into the Alamo without injuring a man. On the 1st March the Garrison of Alamo received a reinforcement of 32 Texians from Gonzales having forced their way thro' the enemies lines, making the number in the Alamo consisting of 182 men.

On the 6th March about midnight the Alamo was surrounded by the whole force of the Mexican army commanded by San. Anna in person—the battle was desperate until day light when only 7 men belonging to the Texian Garrison were found alive who cried for quarters, but were told that there was no mercy for them—they then continued fighting until the whole were butchered. One woman, Mrs. Dickinson, and a negro of Col. Travis were the only persons whose lives were spared. We regret to say, that Col. David Crocket and companion, Mr. Benton and Col. Bonham, of S. C., were among the number slain. Gen. Cowie was murdered in his bed sick and helpless. Gen. Cos on entering the Fort ordered the servant of Col. Travis to point out the body of his master; he did so, when Cos drew his sword and mangled the face and limbs with the malignant feeling of a Camanche savage. The bodies of the slain were thrown into a mass in the centre of the Alamo and burned. The loss of the Mexicans in storming the place was not less than 1000 killed and mortally wounded, and as many wounded, making with their loss in the first assault between 2 and 3000 men.

The flag used by the Mexicans was a blood-red one, in place of the constitutional one. Immediately after the capture, Gen. San. Anna sent Mrs. Dickinson and the servant to General Houston's camp, accompanied by a Mexican with a flag, who was bearer of a note from San. Anna, offering the Texians peace and general amnesty, if they would lay down their arms and submit to his government. Gen. Houston's reply was, "True sir, you have succeeded in killing some of our brave men, but the Texians are not yet conquered." The effect of the fall of Bexar throughout Texas was electrical. Every man who could use the rifle and was in a condition to take field, marched forthwith to the seat of war. It is believed that not less than 4000 rifemen were on their way to the army when the Camanche smiled, determined to wreak their revenge on the Mexicans.

Gen. Houston had burnt Gonzales, and fallen back on the Collorado with about 1000 men. Col. Fanning was in the Fort at Goliad, a very strong position, well supplied with munitions and provisions, with 4 or 500 men.

The general determination of the people of Texas is to abandon all their occupations and pursuits of peace, and continue in arms until every Mexican east of the Rio del Norte shall be extirminated.

TEXAS.

About four hundred and eighty years before the Christian æra, a man, palsied with fear crossed the Eurotas, and entered breathless the ancient city of Sparta. He soon collected around him a group of old men, women, and children. Spartan taciturnity was unbroken—their looks of surprise put the question, "I am from Thermopylæ, your king Leonidas is slain—I am the only survivor—three hundred Spartans held at bay the whole Persian army, for ten days—they fell to a man, covered with wounds, defending the liberty of Greece—I only am left to tell—look at this wound—rouse Spartans, rouse." The news of that disastrous day, flew like lightning from Mount Athos to the remotest shores of Peloponnesus. Thebes, Athens, Corinth, all were in consternation. But what of it? Did they despair? Did they despond? The barbarous massacre of Leonidas only roused to deeper vengeance and higher daring the whole people of Greece. Athenians, Thebans, Corinthians, Spartans, Achaians, and all, forgot their local feuds—cast to the winds their private quarrels, and united to a man in resisting the military tyranny of Persia, the countless hosts of Xerxes—the myriads of ignorant barbarians who dared to invade the classic soil of Hellas. They assembled at Platea—they fought—they conquered—they drove the invader back to his jungles and his forests. Greece was triumphant—liberty secure—and civilization unscathed.

Such is a brief view of the crisis through which Greece—beautiful enchanting Greece passed and for the first time established the principle that courage guarantees freedom—and, the blood of the devoted patriot only waters more freely the tree of liberty.

What Thermopylæ was to ancient Greece—what Bunker-hill has been to the United States—so will Bexar be to Texas.

The bloody, brutal massacre of the gallant little garrison of Bexar or San Antonio, will raise a spirit of noble vengeance throughout the United States, only to be paralleled by the sensation produced in ancient Greece, on the fall of Leonidas being known throughout her smiling land. Alas! poor Davie Crockett! where be thy sarcasms now! thy shrewd remarks! thy pointed absurdities! thy cunning stories whose very vanity made thee a delightful study to the philosopher!—all gone—all chopfallen—all lost but in the recollection of those who knew thee!

It is utterly impossible at this distance from the scene of action, to realize the horrors of the bloody massacre perpetrated by the Mexicans at San Antonio, against bone of our bone and flesh of our flesh.

The sensation realized at New Orleans, at Mobile, at every town on our western and south western frontier, is without a parallel in the history of human excitement, since the fatal day of Bunker Hill, when the blood of freemen flowed freely for a similar cause. It is idle—utterly so—futile—completely so, to enter into an examination of miserable technical points, in the affairs between Mexico and Texas. Under the form of a legitimate war, Santa Anna has perpetrated deeds more atrocious than those of the pirate on the high seas—of the wandering, houseless Arab of the desert. Not content with overwhelming the gallant little band of 187 patriots commanded by Col. Travis, by forty times their number, their very remains are mutilated—their hallowed ashes are scattered to the four winds—by those fiends actuated by the spirit of demons, and spirited on by the vengeance of hell itself.

Is it possible to hold terms at all with such a race of miscreants as these Mexicans have proved themselves to be? No—never. The period of vengeance has arrived—the cup of wickedness is running over. Let the people of the United States rouse as one man—let them demand of their government the instant recognition of the independence of Texas—let the Mexican embassy be drummed out of the country. They only represent a band of savages worse than the Seminoles. Not a moment is to lost. The blood of our murdered brethren in Alemo, cries to high heaven for instant and immediate vengeance. The inhuman monster, Santa Anna, has thrown his last cast. The government in Mexico is toppling to its foundation. He cannot conquer Texas—he may retard its peace—its prosperity—its independence—but he never can reduce that beautiful land of the brave and the free, if the people of the United States still retain the slightest throb resembling that which animated the hearts of their glorious ancestors.

Let a meeting be instantly called in the largest hall in New York. The Commissioners of Texas are now among us. Let us hear what they have to say—let us organize—let us act.

Daily Telegraph
27th July 1911

OVER NIAGARA FALLS.

TRIP IN A STEEL BARREL.

GRAPHIC STORY.

From Our Own Correspondent.

NEW YORK, Wednesday.

Old Bobby Leach, 69 years of age, who leaped Niagara Falls yesterday afternoon in a steel barrel, was out of doors again to-day, and the hero of the holiday throngs—chiefly honeymoon couples—now flocking to the famous resort. He told interviewers that he had achieved the greatest ambition of his life, and although bruised from head to foot, with arms and legs sprained and forehead cut, he is the happiest man alive. Leach is an Englishman by birth, and several times, encased in a barrel, he has braved the rapids of Niagara, always reserving the falls for the last great event of his adventurous career.

Leach keeps a restaurant at Niagara Falls, and to-day, in the centre of his dining hall, surrounded by trophies and English, Canadian, and American flags, was the famous barrel, 7ft long, made of tin steel plates, in which the leap was made. Inside was the rope hammock, strongly lashed to the ends, in which Leach was tied from the moment the barrel entered the Niagara River, a mile above the falls, until he was fished out twenty-five minutes later from the whirlpool, within a stone's-throw of the mighty avalanche.

The strongest feature about Leach is his patriotic instinct, which seems to have been nurtured by perpetual contact with American and Canadian visitors to the Niagara Falls. He told interviewers this afternoon that he had not been able to do much for England, but his great trip in the barrel, witnessed by many thousands of spectators on either bank, would, he knew, be "put to England's credit."

A GAMBLE WITH LIFE.

Leach certainly gambled with his life. He came down the upper rapids at a terrific rate, leaping, diving, hurry-scurrying, sometimes bashed against the rocks, at other times disappearing beneath the frenzied waters, until he entered the relatively deep, even flow, which, like the calm before a storm, leads to the stupendous cataract.

"I took a firmer grip of the sides of my hammock," said Leach, "and just waited. The diameter of the barrel is only 3ft, and water leaked through the airholes. 'England expects every man to do his duty,' says I, and over we went. The wooden ends of my barrel had been smashed by collision with the rocks, and I wondered how I should feel when the barrel touched bottom and thousands of tons of water were charging over me. I seemed to pause an instant on the brink, then plunged down. That's about all I recollect; but I'm all right again to-day. No, I shan't repeat the performance."

Within thirty seconds the steel barrel, tossing about like a cork, reappeared at the bottom of the falls, and then, with a tremendous impetus towards the Canadian shore, shot away down the river. A boat with friends was in waiting, and Frank Bender, a fine swimmer, with a rope about his waist, dived in the foaming water and secured a hold on the barrel, which was promptly hauled ashore and opened. With the exception of a gash over the forehead, Leach was not badly injured. He was dosed first with brandy and then with oxygen. Leach soon recovered consciousness. "No more Niagara," was his first exclamation.

He described the trip through the Upper Rapids as frightful. It seemed as though the barrel turned over a million times, and once, when he struck a rock, and water poured in, he was prepared to die.

The Times
20th May 1935

From a drawing by Mr. Augustus John, R.A., reproduced in "The Seven Pillars of Wisdom."

LAWRENCE OF ARABIA

A GENIUS OF WAR AND LETTERS

THE DESERT REVOLT

By Captain B. H. Liddell Hart

If a tragic waste, it was none the less a fitting way in which T. E. Lawrence met his end. It was, I imagine, the way he would have chosen. For it was on his motor-cycle that he seemed to find his outlet from harassing thought and sense of futility: to him the sensation of speed was the one that never palled, seeming to free the spirit from the bondage of human limitations.

THE ARAB REVIVAL

"Lawrence of Arabia" he was christened when he burst into fame, and in spite of his own protests the title stayed fast—fixed by its aptness. The most significant territorial titles have not been based on the mere possession of land, but have sprung from the association of a career with a country or place. While it is true that Lawrence's campaigns only touched parts of Arabia, the ripples went far wider. From the time when opportunity, in the guise of the Arab revolt, came to him in 1916, his purpose was two-fold— to relieve Britain's clouded fortunes in the East by creating a new Arab lever in aid of her strategy; to free the Arabs from the Turkish yoke and to give them a fair chance of fulfilling their own aspirations. That dual purpose he brilliantly fulfilled. The ever-extending operations of the Arabs, directed by Lawrence, went far to free the British movements from past stagnation and to paralyse the Turkish. They were a vital factor in the overthrow of the Turkish armies and the British conquest of Palestine. And the tide of the Arab revolt, carried a thousand miles from Mecca to Damascus, ended in the establishment of an Arab State in Syria.

It was overthrown by the French after the War, a breach of faith which Lawrence was powerless to avert, though it weighed on his mind. But in 1921, emerging from his Oxford retreat, he inspired and guided policy to such effect that Feisal, robbed of one kingdom, was given another in Iraq by the British, while his brother was also placed at the head of a new Arab State in Transjordan. After the lapse of centuries the Arabs had again become a factor with which the world, and its politics, must reckon. In the historical sense it is, above all, because of this fresh impact of the Arab upon the European peoples that the man who was the propelling agent is rightly styled "Lawrence of Arabia."

MILITARY LEADERSHIP
THE TOOLS OF COMMAND

Perhaps his greatest personal triumph was not in inspiring the Arabs but in impressing his powers as a military leader upon the British regular officers with whom he came in close contact. Nothing is more astonishing that the way these, his seniors, were ready to follow his lead— although several were themselves outstanding men. In part, that influence may be explained by applying to him the words with which Voltaire depicted Marlborough: "He had to a degree above all other generals of his time that calm courage in the midst of tumult, that serenity of soul in danger, which the English call a cool head . . . the greatest gift of nature for command." But there was something more.

The radiance of Lawrence's personality has obscured, even from some who subconsciously responded to it, the deeper power that his knowledge gave him. In this lies the message that his War achievement bears. He was more deeply steeped in knowledge of war than any general. Although at first sight this comment may seem startling, it is essentially matter of fact. Many certainly knew more about the workings of the military machine than Lawrence, but in all else that counted he had the advantage. His youth helped him. They had spent so many years in rising to command that, naturally, they could not hope to have his intimate experience in using the weapons upon which tactics are based. The machine-gun which dominated the battlefields of 1914-1918 was a development since their youth, and the light automatic, scarcely less important in its influence, had only been introduced since the War began. All these he mastered, showing an aptitude rare even in receptive youth, and adding something of his own to their tactical use. Aircraft were another novelty that he came to understand through actual flying experience that no other commander of land forces enjoyed. He also overrode the barriers that in former days prevented infantry and cavalry soldiers from intruding into the sapper's or gunner's field; thus he added to his equipment an expert grasp of demolition and a working grasp of gunnery.

This first-hand knowledge of the tools of command, if not essential, was at least invaluable. The great commanders of old, when weapons were simple and slow-changing, built up their strategic plans on a personal knowledge of the groundwork, which their successors by force of circumstance lacked. The increasing specialization of warfare has been largely responsible for the sterilization of generalship; it can only be overcome by wide thought and hard work. But of few can we expect the prodigious capacity for both which Lawrence revealed, helped by a remarkable ability to free himself from social distractions.

THEORY AND PRACTICE

It was through this in youth that he had acquired his knowledge of history and higher theory of war—I have never known a general who had read as widely. As an undergraduate he traced for himself the sources of the Napoleonic system of warfare at a time when they were unknown to most military students, and when only a few of the more profound Napoleonic students were on the right track. Yet this exploration of military history was merely an offshoot of Lawrence's self-imposed course of reading, which covered most fields of human knowledge. As a youth he thought nothing of reading half through the night, lying on a rug or mattress, a habit that had the convenience of allowing him to go to sleep where he lay. By habit, too, he developed the faculty of "sensing" a subject, as a bee draws in the nectar as it flits from flower to flower. It was always the unexpected, the undiscovered, or the inaccessible sources that he sought—"Originals and sidelights, not compilations." Thus it did not take him long to cover the realm of military literature.

This historical knowledge, enriched by a general knowledge of many subjects that indirectly concerned war, formed an intellectual equipment such, perhaps, as no other commander of his time possessed. When checked by personal experience it gave him a theoretical mastery of war that was also unique—and his personality transmuted this into a practical mastery. His power of command overcame handicaps such as no famous commander has suffered. He exercised command without being in command. He had to give directions under the disguise of advice. He had to deal not merely with allies, but with a multitude of allies. He had not only to make bricks without straw—or with little compared with what he had set out to create—but to make a conquering force out of men of straw.

The post-War suggestion that Lawrence "backed the wrong horse" is the most foolishly irrelevant criticism—because it ignores the time factor. Lawrence, indeed, only appeared on the scene after Ibn Sa'ud had suffered temporary eclipse; he had been a junior member of the Intelligence Service in Egypt and was still awaiting formal sanction for his transfer to the new Arab Bureau in Cairo when, in October, 1916, he paid a visit to the Hejaz coast and made a contact with the Arab leaders that led to his returning there shortly after as liaison officer with and adviser to Feisal. When he appeared the Sherif of Mecca had been in revolt against the Turks since June and we were committed to his support—for our own sakes. Faced with the actual circumstances of 1916, and the need to ease Britain's awkward situation, Lawrence had no choice but to use the instruments that were at hand, the Sheriffian allies who were already actively engaged against the common foe. No one was more conscious of their frailty—for the good reason that he had a closer view than anyone else.

THE TURKISH DEFEAT
TACTICAL ARTISTRY

But the facts of the next two years form one of the most astonishing feats in history. The revolt in the Hejaz was triumphantly consolidated and the Turkish occupation reduced to one beleaguered garrison, which eventually fell like a ripe apple. Carried northward by Lawrence "off his own bat," the Arab movement produced a dramatic *coup* by the capture of Aqaba. This success was not only an offset to the double British failure before Gaza but removed all danger to the communications of the British Army in Palestine. Also to the sea communications of the British Empire through the Suez Canal. But the spread, and spreading, success of the revolt did more than cancel debits. A larger number of Turks were now pinned down along the Hejaz railway and south of it than faced the British Army.

In the next stage, when the British occupied Jerusalem and Jericho after breaking through the incompletely defended front between Gaza and Beersheba, the Arabs served as a shield to Allenby's flank and a lever on the Turks'. It began with a northward extension of the railway demolitions, which led the admiring Arabs to christen Lawrence "Destroyer of Engines"—in view of the fact that the Turks had scantier reserves of material than of men, "killing engines" was a more deadly strategy than "killing Turks." The Arabs cut off the supplies which the Turks were drawing from the corn-belt east of the Dead Sea—here Lawrence added a fresh touch of novelty to his strategy by capturing a grain-fleet with a detachment of horsemen. This was the sequel to the one "battle" he fought—in January, 1918, at Tafila, where he first arrested and then routed a Turkish counter-invasion. His own mockery of his achievement cannot hide the fact that he here displayed a tactical artistry, based on consummate calculation and *coup d'œil*, in the purest classical tradition.

1918

By such widespread interference and by the widening ripples of unrest it created, Lawrence helped to distract the Turks' attention during the first half of 1918, when Allenby was drained of troops to repair the losses in France. Further, this "intangible ghost" forbade the enemy to reknit their power of resistance by withdrawing to a rearward line near the Sea of Galilee, and so forestalling Allenby's attack. Liman von Sanders himself confessed that his main reason for giving up the idea was "because we could no longer have stopped the progress of the Arab insurrection in rear of our army."

At last, in September, Allenby was ready to strike. Nearly half the Turkish forces south of Damascus were kept away from the British front by the elusive threats of a few thousand Arabs, directed by Lawrence. As a result Allenby, from his army of 250,000 men, was able to concentrate odds of over five to one against the sector chosen for his decisive blow. During the previous month Lawrence wove a web of feints and fictions to persuade the Turkish command that Allenby's attack was coming east towards Amman instead of north to Galilee. During the final three days of preparation, the Arabs emerged from the desert and cut the railway north, south, and west of Deraa junction—the focal point of the enemy's communications. This triple stroke went far to hamstring the Turkish armies just as Allenby was about to jump upon them. The two armies between the Jordan and the Mediterranean coast were swiftly crushed, the flocks of fugitives being rounded up by the British cavalry or pulverized by the British aircraft. Only the Fourth Army, which yet had been the strongest of the three, remained—east of the Jordan. Lawrence, with an Arab detachment, audaciously moved across its line of retreat. It soon degenerated into a foot-slogging, footsore collection of crumbling units, shrinking hourly under the privations of the march and the pin-pricks of the Beduin. The last large fragment was headed off and destroyed just short of Damascus by the Arabs, who crowned their military achievement by slipping into Damascus ahead of the British.

A NEW STRATEGY

The arrival in Damascus was the vindication not only of the Arab rising but of the course of Lawrence's thought. It was the culmination not only of a campaign but of a theory of war—which he had evolved and applied. It was an inversion of orthodox strategy; one that was born of his early studies, especially of Saxe, but developed by reflection upon the conditions of the Arab campaign. It was designed to turn the weakness of the Arabs into an asset and the very strength of the Turks into a debit—by forcing them to spread as widely as possible in order to check a flame of revolt which was extended to wherever they were not, while the Arabs, striking at the materials of which the Turks were short, avoided engagement with the men of whom the Turks had plenty—until they were forced to extend too widely. By this strategy the Arabs inflicted the maximum damage with the minimum loss, and so with the maximum encouragement, to themselves. With cheap success their confidence grew and the rebel numbers swelled; with vain chase the Turks grew exhausted and depressed. For the orthodox principle of concentration, Lawrence substituted dispersion; for battle, he substituted a creeping paralysis produced by an intangible

Continued

ubiquity. And in this kind of warfare he gave to the old principles of mobility and surprise a new application as well as a heightened power.

The very completeness of this inversion may suggest that it widens the past gulf between regular and irregular warfare. But on reflection one can see that its success turned on new material conditions which are even more marked in modern regular warfare. No civilized nation can maintain itself long without the railway, or maintain war without munitions. What the Arabs did yesterday the Air Force may do to-morrow, yet more swiftly. Moreover, this new exploitation of the changed "biological" conditions of war may be coupled with a more calculated exploitation of the psychological conditions—to which Lawrence also showed the way. To disarm is more potent than to kill. This fact, by bringing him into relation with the whole of war, gives a new meaning to his exploits in Arabia and Syria. Military history cannot dismiss him as merely a successful leader of irregulars. He is seen to be more than a guerrilla genius—rather does he appear a strategist of genius who had the vision to anticipate the guerrilla trend of the civilized warfare that arises from the growing dependence of nations on industrial resources.

CHARACTER AND PERSONALITY
"THE SEVEN PILLARS"

Lawrence himself was fully aware of this application. It had no small influence on the part he played in securing the Air Force its opportunity in the Middle East after the War, and also on his action in joining it himself—the utilization of the air, as he remarked, was "the one big thing left for our generation to do." Other factors, however, prompted the second step. He had a sense of fulfilment, reinforced by a sense of futility. It may be near the truth to say that he enlisted in the Air Force for the same reason that thoughtful men in the Middle Ages entered a monastery. A further impulse was his own awareness that he had strained his balance—as much by the excitement generated in writing his great book "The Seven Pillars of Wisdom" as by his War effort. He had begun this book early in 1919, and was helped to continue it by election to a research Fellowship at All Souls. On a journey from London to Oxford he lost the bulk of the manuscript, but at Hogarth's insistence renewed and completed the task in a few months, although several more years were spent in perfecting the prose and production. Then in 1921 he was called to the Colonial Office as Political Adviser on affairs in the Middle East, which had become in a dangerous tangle. On completing a year's service, a year which had seen far-reaching arrangements, he felt that the settlement justified his release—upon which he insisted.

A few months later he enlisted in the ranks of the Air Force, taking the name of Ross. The public discovery of his presence there produced a commotion which caused his discharge, whereupon he enlisted in the Tank Corps and formally adopted the name of Shaw. In 1925 his transfer back to the Air Force was arranged, and after a spell at Cranwell, and another in India, he came back to more interesting duty with flying boats, and to an ostensibly humble connexion with the Schneider Trophy Race arrangements of 1929. If scrupulously correct in demeanour, in accord with his status as an aircraftman, he found many ways of exerting an influence for the good of the Service, without and within.

The earlier years of humdrum service were years of restoration—it was a healthier man, physically and mentally, who took his discharge this last March; a man who looked much less than his 46 years and radiated an air of contentment, whatever the unease that might lie deeper in one who saw all things too clearly. In the later years of his service his interest revived and his gifts were better utilized—although still insisting on the lowest rank, he gave invaluable aid in the development of high-speed motorboats for the assistance of seaplanes, and of target-boats for bombing experiments. As his service drew to an end he insisted that he intended to rusticate in his cottage, but there were moments when he spoke of re-emergence, and once, not long ago, he even suggested that his neap-tide might still lie ahead.

LAPSED AMBITIONS

As a youth Lawrence certainly had ambition—an ambition so immense that it embraced the idea of attaining equal greatness in action and in reflection. But experience taught him their incompatibility. Although the range of his travel in the one sphere was the means of carrying him far in the other his course stopped with a jerk—as if the brakes of reflection had locked the wheels of action. At 26, when he made his plunge into the War, he resolved to become a general and to be knighted by the time he was 30. Long before this he had shed such desires—as soon, indeed, as they were within his reach. The ambition that survived was merely for achievement. This in turn lapsed when Damascus was reached. For three days he ruled it; on the fourth he left—driven forth by his own perception of the danger to his wisdom, and the freedom this implies. Ambition was almost the last fetter on his spiritual freedom that needed removal to make release complete.

A whim of Nature had sent him into the world apparently devoid of the normal man's appetites. From the competitive instinct also he had always been free; throughout his career he strove only to reach a standard raised in his own mind, not to outreach other men. Thus he eliminated one of the fundamental sources of human friction. More common still, yet more subtle, is the possessive instinct; never strong in Lawrence, he sought to remove its tendrils wherever perceived. This proved difficult even for

him. Although through deficiency or difference of tastes he succeeded in reducing his material wants to a level which amused even his friends and astonished others, he could not rid himself of all possessions without in some degree sterilizing his spiritual desires —they cropped up in a book, a binding, or a fragment of music. Wisdom itself interferes with freedom. Although he came nearer to complete freedom than any man I have known, he could not attain it. Being incarnate, he must still be tied, even though it was by strands invisible to the normal eye.

The extent of his differences from the normal, accentuated by an impish humour, was often baffling and sometimes exasperating even to friends. But to those who knew him, so far as any could, he was a message of the wisdom that comes along the path of freedom. That message cannot die.

Glasgow Herald
5th January 1967

LAST BLUEBIRD

DONALD CAMPBELL fitted uncomfortably into the nineteen sixties. Certainly his greatest triumph, the breaking of both the land and water speed records in 1964, took place in this decade. But, in a world of moon satellites and astronauts, his dream of moving faster and faster on land or water at a speed slower than that travelled by air passengers on their way to the holiday beaches seemed curiously outdated. It seemed closer to the 'thirties when the triumph of a Bluebird could not be dwarfed by the speed and technical sophistication of more advanced technology.

Of course Campbell was a special case. His family's name was linked with speed. He followed in his father's footsteps, surpassing even Sir Malcolm's records. Perhaps it was because he felt he only took swifter strides than his father and not different steps that he was never satisfied with breaking both records once but tried to push himself —and his luck—faster and faster along the same path until yesterday.

His courage was never outdated although the way he showed it may have been. The mixture of determination, stubbornness, and patriotism which made him persist in his attempts to break a record, no matter the time wasted in waiting for saltbeds to dry or lake winds to drop, are qualities which are hard to find. They led some to call him aloof and irascible; but they stamped him as an individual unafraid to turn away from the comfortable life he might have led towards the dangers of the Bluebird.

His record is likely to remain unbroken for a long time. Men as brave as he have turned away to conquer other elements. Men less adventurous than he have settled in their armchairs and spent their admiration and awe on more novel exploits. The professional backers lost much of their interest a long time ago. Technical advances derived from building a Bluebird, whether for land or water, became smaller. Motor manufacturers and oil companies are unlikely to give an aspiring record breaker the finance and support they were increasingly unwilling to give to Campbell. Some one may try it from time to time. But without much backing, public enthusiasm, or a father's memory to give encouragement such attempts may well falter. The sport or challenge made famous by Sir Malcolm Campbell probably died yesterday on Coniston Water with his son.

The Daily Mail
14th June 1930

Sir Henry Segrave's speed-boat, Miss England II., floating upside down just after her plunge beneath the surface which caused the death of Sir Henry and one of his mechanics.

The Times
26th July 1883

Matthew Webb, who was drowned on Tuesday in attempting to swim through the whirlpool and rapids at the foot of the Falls of Niagara, was born at Irongate, near Dawley, in Shropshire, on the 18th of January, 1848. He was 5ft. 8in. in height, measured 43in. round the chest, and weighed about 14½ stone. He learnt to swim when seven years of age, and was trained as a sailor on board the Conway training ship in the Mersey, where he saved the life of a fellow seaman. In 1870 he dived under his ship in the Suez Canal and cleared a foul hawser, and on the 23d of April, 1873, when serving on board the Cunard steamer Russia, jumped overboard to save the life of a hand who had fallen from aloft, but failed, and it was an hour before he was picked up almost exhausted. For this he received a gold and other medals. He became captain of a merchant ship, but he soon afterwards relinquished the sea and devoted himself to the sport of swimming. At long distance swimming in salt water he was *facile princeps*, but he did not show to such advantage in fresh water. In June, 1874, he swam from Dover to the North-East Varne Buoy, a distance of 9½ nautical, or about 11 statute, miles. On July 3, 1875, he swam from Blackwall Pier to Gravesend Town Pier, nearly 18 statute miles, in 4 hours 52 minutes, and on the 19th of the same month he swam from Dover to Ramsgate, 19¼ statute miles, in 8 hours 45 minutes. On August 12, 1875, he made an unsuccessful attempt to swim across the Channel from England to France, but failed in consequence of the heavy sea, although, as he had succeeded in compassing the distance from Dover to the South Sand Head, 15¼ statute miles, in 6 hours 48 minutes, he determined to make another attempt. After waiting some days for a favourable opportunity the weather became more suitable and the sea calmer. Accordingly, on the 24th of August he started on his adventurous journey. Having dived off the Admiralty Pier at Dover, he at once proceeded with the powerful breast stroke for which he has been noted. He was steered at the start south-east by south-half-south, and this course was retained for the entire distance. Webb was revived with a little brandy after having been in the water for an hour and three-quarters. The average number of strokes was 20 per minute. Beef-tea was the principal nourishment of which the swimmer partook. Some little anxiety was apparently felt by Webb after he had been in the water for a few hours, but this with great perseverance he soon mastered. When within about seven miles of the French coast the south-west stream was so strong that it seemed almost doubtful whether he would be able to reach it. He declined much refreshment, and throughout the night kept on his way in a most energetic manner. At half-past 8 in the morning some evidence of weakness was shown, as he swam short and was much quicker in his strokes, and an hour and ten minutes later he had increased them still more. Yet this was only a natural result of such continuous exertion, and this exhaustion it was feared would increase. This, however, did not turn out to be the case, and he reached the French coast at Calais at 20 minutes to 11. He was immersed for 21 hours 44min. 55sec., and had swum over 39 miles, or, according to another calculation, about 45½ miles, without having touched a boat or artificial support of any kind. On the conclusion of the feat he was driven to an hotel and at once put to bed, with a medical man in attendance. He slept for three hours, and then awoke with apparently nothing further to trouble him than weakness and hunger. He thus beat the time taken by Captain Boyton, who with paddle and sails, and in an inflated dress, had crossed the Channel a few weeks previously in 22½ hours. This feat of skill and endurance excited an enthusiasm in England which it is difficult now to realize, and which extended far beyond the comparatively narrow circle of proficients in swimming. Webb, on his return from Calais, was greeted as a worthy representative of English manhood, and for many weeks he remained the hero of the hour. A few days after his arrival in London he happened to stroll into the Stock Exchange, and being recognized was quickly encircled by a crowd of enthusiastic brokers, each man striving to press the hand of the hero of the Channel swim.

Webb had frequently appeared in public subsequently to his great performance in the Channel, having swum against Beckwith and other noted swimmers at the Westminster Aquarium and elsewhere, but these exhibitions failed to evoke much popular enthusiasm. In the year 1880 he won a six days' swimming race at the Lambeth Baths, beating W. Beckwith and other swimmers easily. In March, 1880, Webb remained in the tank of the Westminster Aquarium for a period of 60 hours, with the exception of an interval of 21min. 30sec. In August of the same year Webb eclipsed his Aquarium swim by remaining in the tank of the Scarborough Aquarium for 74 hours, excepting four minutes' interval. Subsequently, in the following year, Webb was defeated by W. Beckwith in a six days' swim of ten hours a day at the Westminster Aquarium; but on October 1, 1881, at Hollingworth Lake, Lancashire, he defeated Mr. A. Jennings in a five hours' swim, accomplishing a distance of 5 miles 660 yards. Last year, in America, Webb remained in the water 128¾ hours, minus 94 minutes, in a tank at the Horticultural Hall Building, Boston, Massachusetts, commencing October 9, 1882. Previous to leaving England for America this year Webb was defeated by Beckwith in a six days' swim, being compelled from congestion of the lungs to relinquish his efforts. Of late his health had been so impaired as to cause considerable anxiety to his friends. Indeed before he left England, it was quite evident that the vigorous constitution he at one time possessed had undergone a great change, and it is strange that he should have entertained the idea of swimming over the most difficult river in the world in such a condition. He was married about three years ago, and leaves a widow and two children. It was, we understand, to obtain money for the support of his family that he risked his life in this last fatal attempt.

Daily Telegraph & Morning Post
30ᵗʰ September 1952

JOHN COBB HAD ONE FEAR

RISK OF WATER BEING THROWN INTO ENGINE

By W. A. McKENZIE,
Daily Telegraph Motoring Correspondent

John Cobb had one fear about the jet-powered Crusader in which he lost his life on Loch Ness yesterday. In the last talk I had with him during trials on the loch he told me what it was.

From the eye-witness reports of the crash it appears that the thing he feared took place. "At high speed," he said, "one kicks up a lot of water in front. There's always a risk that it will get thrown into the intake orifice of the engine, and—put the fire out . . . ."

The emphasis he gave the last words, and the pause which followed them, were eloquent of what the result might be if the power were suddenly to be cut off.

I saw the death, 22 years ago, of Sir Henry Segrave, who also died attacking the world's marine speed record on Windermere. The two men's lives were as similar as the circumstances of their death.

Both were old Etonians. Both had seen service in the R.A.F. Both, when they died on the water, were holding the world's land speed record, and no man has lived to hold both records.

MR. JOHN COBB

The Times
11ᵗʰ December 1815

On the 7th instant, in Bond-street, Vice-Admiral William Bligh, F.R.S. of Farningham house, Kent, aged 63.

A Court Martial is now sitting on board the DUKE, at Portsmouth, on the *Mutineers* of the BOUNTY—Lord HOOD is the President—it commenced on Wednesday last, and, we believe, will be over this day.

The Times
17ᵗʰ July 1810.

The *Moniteur* of the 9th inst. mentions the death of the celebrated MONTGOLFIER, (the first who discovered the principles of aerostation and ascended in a balloon,) at E durac, where he went for the benefit of the baths, on the 26th of June, in the 70th year of his age.

The Times
20th July 1937

MISS EARHART

A PILOT OF COURAGE AND SKILL

Hope has now been officially abandoned that Miss Earhart (Mrs. G. P. Putnam) can have survived her last adventurous flight, after being missing for over a fortnight.

Miss Earhart left Miami, Florida, on June 1 to fly round the world from west to east, with Captain Fred Noonan as navigator. Her machine was a Lockheed Electra, which was called the "Flying Laboratory" from its equipment of instruments and experimental apparatus. She arrived at Dumdum aerodrome, Calcutta, from Karachi on June 17, having covered about 15,000 miles, more than half her journey, at an average of 900 miles a day. From that point she had been working along the British air mail route. She arrived at Port Darwin on June 28, and started at 10 a.m. on July 2 from Lae, New Guinea, for Howland Island on the most hazardous part of her flight. Although signals for help are reported to have been received from her, she was never seen again, and prolonged searches by sea and air have failed to discover any traces of her machine.

Miss Earhart first became famous in June, 1928, when she crossed the Atlantic as a passenger, but afterwards, in 1932, she made a solo flight from Newfoundland to Ireland. In each case she was the first woman to accomplish the feat—if sitting in an aeroplane as a passenger can be called a feat. She was, however, a pilot of more than average ability, and at a time when sensational flights were constantly being made to advertise the name of the pilot, her modesty and her refusal to use her fame for commercial purposes made her very popular. In this she resembled Colonel Lindbergh, whom she was also supposed to resemble in features. In America she was popularly known as "Lady Lindy."

Amelia Earhart came from Atchison, Kansas, where she was born on July 24, 1898. During the War she served with the Canadian Red Cross, and afterwards entered Columbia University. She then learnt to fly, but her occupation in life was social welfare work among children in Boston. She was 30 years of age when she made her first crossing of the Atlantic by air. Mrs. F. E. Guest, wife of the former Secretary of State for Air, and herself an American by birth, financed the flight to the extent of £8,000, and intended to fly in the machine herself. Finally she was persuaded to give her place to Miss Earhart. The machine was a Fokker with three 200-h.p. Wright Whirlwind engines, and was a twin-float seaplane. In the previous year, 1927, which had seen the greatest number of Atlantic flights, the successes of Lindbergh, Chamberlin, Byrd, and Brock, and also a regrettable number of fatal accidents, the three-engined Fokker had never failed its passengers on an ocean flight. The fitting of floats for wheels was an additional safeguard, and the machine also carried wireless. There were three on board—Commander Wilmer Stultz, the pilot, Mr. Gordon, the mechanic, and Miss Earhart. The machine was named "Friendship." She left Newfoundland on June 17, 1928, and 21 hours later came down in Burry Port harbour in South Wales.

Not much was heard of Miss Earhart for a couple of years, but on April 8, 1931, she set up an autogiro altitude record, by reaching a height of about 19,000ft. in a machine of that type with a 300-h.p. engine. She was also credited with two other aeroplane records for carrying certain weights at certain speeds.

It was not until after her marriage, on February 7, 1931, to Mr. G. P. Putnam, of the famous publishing house, that she was able to gratify her ambition of flying the Atlantic as a solo pilot, and being the first woman to do so. She was quite frank about her feelings. She did not profess that the flight would do any good to anyone or anything. "I did it really for fun," she said, "not to set up any records or anything like that." This time she chose a fast single-engined aeroplane, a Lockheed Vega with Pratt and Whitney 420 h.p. Wasp engine.

On May 20, 1932, she set off from Harbour Grace, Newfoundland, and after 13½ hours she made landfall off Donegal. This was the fastest Atlantic flight to date. She had trouble with various instruments and accessories on the machine during her flight, but she was then an experienced pilot, and doubtless her previous crossing stood her in good stead. When she was four hours out one section of the heavy exhaust manifold on the engine began to leak. At the same time she met bad weather and had to begin blind flying, and soon afterwards her altimeter failed her. She told our Aeronautical Correspondent that she then climbed up into the clouds until the tachometer (engine revolutions counter) froze, "and then I knew I couldn't be near the sea." She thought she went up to 12,000ft., but ice began to form on the wings and the clouds were still heavy above her. Meanwhile the intense heat at the leaking exhaust began to burn away the metal. She looked over at it and wished she hadn't as she saw the flames coming out, and it worried her all night. Other parts began to work loose and serious vibration was set up. The engine also "began to run rough," petrol leaked into the cockpit from the petrol gauge, and there was the danger lest petrol fumes should reach the exhaust manifold and be exploded by the flames that poured from the gap. At last she made Ireland as she guessed, but could not be sure, and without an altimeter could not go high enough through the clouds to be sure of clearing the hills. So she turned north until she saw the hills above the river mouth west of Londonderry. Following the railway track, she made an almost perfect landing on a farm two miles from Londonderry, and was hospitably entertained by the farmer and his wife.

When she arrived in London she was given a great welcome. Afterwards she crossed to France, where her husband joined her, and was fêted and decorated there, as well as in Belgium and Italy, and the United States conferred a flying decoration on her.

In September, 1932, Miss Earhart set up another record for women by flying non-stop and solo across the United States from Los Angeles to Newark, New Jersey, in 19 hours 4 minutes, which was only 1 hour 25 minutes longer than the best time by a man pilot (Frank Hawks) over that route.

In January, 1935, Miss Earhart flew alone in her Lockheed Vega monoplane from Honolulu to Oakland, California, 2,408 miles, in 18 hours 15 minutes; and in the following May she made a non-stop flight from Mexico City to New York, 2,100 miles, in 14 hours 18 minutes. She had to cross mountains 10,000ft. high.

On March 17 of the present year she left Oakland, California, on a flight round the world, but crashed at Honolulu on March 21. As the fuselage struck the ground a tongue of flame was seen to shoot from it, and it was believed that only Miss Earhart's prompt action in turning off the ignition saved the lives of herself and her two companions.

The Times
9th May 1920

THE DEAD BULLFIGHTER

SPAIN'S GRIEF.

The news of the death of the matador Joselito, or "el Gallito" (the Cockerel), has affected the whole country to-day. It appears that he was about to dispatch his fifth bull when he was gored, and he died in half an hour. He had been wounded in seven previous bull-fights. The evening newspapers devote columns to the accident and to the life of Joselito.

Joselito was engaged to Señorita Consuelo Hidalgo, a singer at the Queen Victoria Theatre in Madrid.

He will be buried at Sevilla, his native town. Hundreds of wreaths and thousands of telegrams of condolence have reached his relatives from all parts of the country. To-night while the coffin is in Madrid a strong force of police has been necessary to keep back the crowds which has wanted to pass round it.

JOSE GOMEZ.

(FROM A SPANISH CORRESPONDENT.)

The "aficion" (a word which is to bullfighting what "The Turf" is to horseracing) has to deplore a severe loss in the death of José Gómez alias Joselito, and sometimes Gallito. A slender, graceful boy of 17, he began his career eight years ago in the wake of his elder brother, Rafael (El Gallo), a great though unequal artist of the bullring.

"The Gallos," (the Cocks) as the two brothers were known, came from a Sevillan gypsy family, and were both, particularly the elder, fine types of that race, rich in physical distinction and that instinct for harmonious movements which the true "aficionado" never fails to appreciate. Joselito, though not so beautifully masculine as his brother, surpassed him in steadiness, in quickness, and in that unfailing science which enabled him to produce the maximum effect with the minimum of danger. The youth became the idol of the "aficion," and he would have been the most popular man in Spain but for Belmonte.

"The aficion" never gives herself to one man, but divides her favours between two rivals. Thus, the history of bullfighting is a series of rival wars between Lagartijo and Frascuelo, then Espartero and Guerrita, then Bombita and Machaquito, and, until yesterday, Joselito and Belmonte. Passion and opinion are keen, and Gallistas and Belmontistas are irreconcilable enemies. Partly, this division is in the nature of all sport. But it corresponds also to something deeper, which can only be understood when it is realized that bullfighting is a fine art.

There are two schools of bullfighting. The one tends towards developing its technique. It prides itself on the close knowledge of the characteristics of each kind of bull. It is also given to ability and adornment. The other relies more on inspiration, impulse, rhythm. The first is connected with rhetoric and efficiency, and that excellency of execution which seeks the obstacle and the *tour de force*. The other is more of a kind with music and poetry, and it is simple and sober in its methods, though direct and effective in its appeal. Joselito was a master of the first school. Belmonte is the present master of the second. Joselito was the idol of the philistine. Belmonte that of artists and of the people.

One of the most acute of Spanish contemporary minds, Ramón Pérez de Ayala, once, during the war, explained to the writer that he always could find whether a man was pro-German or pro-Ally. If he liked Joselito then he was for efficiency, he was for autocracy, and a pro-German. If he liked Belmonte, then he was for impulse; he was for liberty; he was pro-Ally. And the most curious thing about this original test is that it worked!

Manchester Guardian
21st February 1897

AN EXCITING SCENE.

M. Blondin's Feat at Niagara Falls.
From the Buffalo Republic, July 1.

Yesterday was the day announced by Mons. Blondin for his daring attempt to cross the Niagara River, on a rope extended from bank to bank. As a consequence, train after train left here the whole day to convey visitors to the scene, and the steamer Arrow went down twice loaded down with human freight. As a matter of choice we preferred to adopt the Canada side as the best from which to witness the great feat, and so went down on the Arrow, Capt. Raymond, which left at 9½ o'clock yesterday morning. The boat was quite full of ladies and gentlemen, all bound to witness the sight, and among the passengers several individuals who were endeavoring to turn an honest penny by sweat cloths, a slight turn at faro, &c., while a rusty young man made a bank of the steam chest forward, and with a confederate was endeavoring to swindle some one into betting on three-card monte. If the crowd had not been from Buffalo, it is probable that the rusty young man might have made his expenses; but under the circumstances he didn't accomplish his liquor bill. An institution in a Fez cap, incomprehensible coat, and exaggerated trowsers, with a grim face covered with sandy hair, was traveling among the crowd with a combination of agonies in the shape of a bass drum, violin, jumping jack, bells and cymbals, which he put in operation by firing off his boots periodically and spasmodically. We scarcely thought this individual realized anything extraordinary either.

Persons who went on the boat were under the impression that there was a band on board, half of whom were composed of negroes and half of Germans. They commenced playing something when the boat started, and in such an original style, that while dozens were under the impression they were "doing" Hail Columbia, all the rest on board would have sworn it was the "Other Side of Jordan." The reader can imagine the style of this band. They kept on playing all the way down, until everybody was exasperated. They were remonstrated and expostulated with; prayers and entreaties availed not, and it was not until the passengers left the cars at Clifton that they were allowed some liberty of hearing. A gentleman intimated that heavy swearing would be quite a relief from such strains.

Arrived, the visitors scattered themselves to the different hotels, and to stroll over the beautiful grounds, many taking a trip down to the rope to examine that as far as possible, and settle their minds as to the probability of the crossing being accomplished. We took a trip down there with others, and owing to the kindness of Mr. Colcord, the agent of M. Blondin, were made acquainted with everything pertaining to the means and the attempt of the great great feat. The rope is stretched across the gorge of the river, at a point about three-quarters of a mile below the Clifton House, and extends to White's Pleasure Grounds on the opposite side. At this point the river is about eleven hundred and fifty feet wide, the banks being high and precipitous—the Canadian bank being one hundred and eighty one, and the American one hundred and sixty-five feet in height. The abyss is a frightful one, and no one could contemplate the perilous undertaking announced without a shudder. The entire length of the rope stretched is thirteen hundred feet. To sustain this stiffly in its position, nearly forty thousand feet of small rope was used in the shape of guys, fifty-seven of which are on each side of the rope, and are fastened to the banks. In consequence of the weight of the rope, there is a curve in it, from bank to bank, of about fifty feet, which gives quite a horizontal line for two or three hundred feet in the centre, from which t ere is a gradual ascent to each bank. The rope, with its guys, looked like a spider's web, and far too flimsey to sustain itself, or hang together, not to speak of its capacity to sustain M. Blondin. At this time (noon) there were hundreds of people examining the rope, and, with scarcely an exception, they all declared the inability of M. Blondin to perform the feat, the incapacity of the rope to sustain him, and that he deserved to be dashed to atoms for his desperate foolhardiness.

Continued

14

All about the point mentioned, on the Canada-side, a number of comfortable stagings had been built, where seats rose one above the other, as in an amphitheater, while booths were scattered in every direction, at which the weary-stomached visitor could satisfy himself with anything from buck-shot whisky up to tartaric acid lemonade, for four glasses of which latter pleasant fiction we disbursed $1. (This would bring tartaric acid up to $400 or $500 per pound.) Where the rope ended a staging had been built, with a table containing glasses, and surrounded with seats, for the members of the Press. On the American side, quite as excellent arrangements were made, and the peculiarities mentioned in respect to the whisky and other refreshments, we presume, were quite as marked. We did not go over to the American side, but we take it for granted that everybody's experience at the Falls will bear us out.

At about 3 o'clock the banks along the river, for great distances, were crowded with people, determined to have a good sight. Some were pic nicking on the grass; others imagining they were eating dinners at the different booths; and the rest either eating at the hotels, or waiting a chance at the *second* tables.

As the hour of 4 o'clock drew near, crowds commenced rushing from all directions towards the scene of the great exploit, and by 4½ o'clock the banks on both sides were fairly black with people, who crowded every available position for a mile on each side of the river. At this time the sight was a very gay one. The grounds on the American side were decorated with flags, banners and streamers of many colors; the banks lined with ladies, gentlemen and children; the gleaming instruments of the different brass bands, their inspiring strains, and the occasional shouts that went up, all went to make the scene very lively and very exciting. A train of cars, filled with passengers, had stopped upon the track, almost overlooking the rope, and formed a substantial background to a portion of the picture.

On the Canada side things were a jam, and people who had thought of cushioned seats and high backed chairs, hesitated not at roosting upon the fence palings, or sitting down in two inches of dust. Faro dealers and sweat-cloths plied their trade manfully, until 5 o'clock, when their operations were suspended by the music of the band on the American side announcing the appearance of M. BLONDIN and his great feat.

THE CROSSING.

At a few minutes before 5, M. BLONDIN could be seen standing on the American side, dressed in tights and covered with spangles, upon which the sun shone, making him appear as if clothed in light. He appeared scarcely the size of a year old infant, at that distance, and the rope upon which he was standing a mere thread over an awful abyss. At 5 o'clock precisely, he started from the American side. Without hesitation he balanced his pole in his hands, and with a calmer and less fluttering heart than could have been found in that vast audience, he commenced his terrible walk. The slightest misstep, the merest dizziness, the least uncertainty, would cast him at once into the perdition beneath, and the crowd held their breaths in amazement as he went on and on over the frightful chasm. On his part, however, there was not the slightest irresoluteness. Calmly he tread the rope, which scarcely trembled or swayed with his weight, and at about 550 feet from the shore he cooly sat down on the rope, perched nearly 200 feet above the water, waved his hands to his friends, and beckoned to the little steamer the *Maid of the Mist*, lying in the river below, to come up beneath the rope. He then laid down on the rope full length with his balance pole across his chest, with the same disregard and carelessness that a person would have reclined upon a lounge.

After some little time the steamer came beneath, when M. BLONDIN, throwing down a line, drew up from the deck of the steamer a bottle of wine, which having disposed of, threw back the bottle, rose to his feet with the same certainty that had marked all his previous operations, and continued his performance. For about two hundred feet further he went steadily along, when, having arrived at that part of the rope which hung nearly in a horizontal line, he started on a fast run. At this time he was just over the centre of the raging torrent beneath, and there was scarcely a person within sight of him who did not shrink from the sight and shudder at his peril.

After the nearly horizontal portion of the rope had been passed, he reduced his speed as he came to the ascent on the Canada side. With the hot sun blazing full in his face, and bearing a heavy pole, the operation was not only of marvelous intrepidity and daring, but full of toil and fatigue. He came slowly up the ascent on the Canada side, amid the crash of "Sweet Home" from brass bands, and the cheers upon cheers that went up from thousands of throats, celebrating the success of this most wonderful of all human feats, requiring the utmost skill, expertness and clear-headedness, besides a miraculous courage and nerves of adamant.

As he came within about fifty feet of the shore, Mr. Colcoad the agent, went part of the way out to meet him, and as he ascended the platform, hundreds of hands reached a hearty shake of gratification at his success, and admiration of his courage. When he got upon the staging he was received by several members of the Press, and Mr. KAVANAGH, of the Great Western Hotel, at Clifton, who had provided some excellent champagne to celebrate M. BLONDIN's success, of which M. BLONDIN partook. He appeared very much fatigued on arriving, and was bathed from head to foot with perspiration.

As soon as he could get in a carriage which was provided for him, he was called upon for a speech, and getting up in the carriage, amid thundering cheers, he said, in broken English:

"MY FRENS: I have got safely over. I see you are very glad, and so am I. I hope you will remember me. I cannot speak very good English, but it is all right. I shall go back again soon."

A large amount of money was soon subscribed in the most liberal style, and it was handed to M. BLONDIN, who returned his thanks.

At a few minutes past 6 o'clock, M. BLONDIN, apparently perfectly refreshed, and entirely confident, appeared upon the stand, and amid cheers and the music of the band—"Other Side of Jordan"—he commenced his return, with the same coolness, determination and indifference that had marked his first successful attempt. He walked the descent much faster, and when he came to the horizontal position rope, ran more rapidly than before, and passed safely across in six minutes. The first crossing, including stoppages, was made in a few seconds over seventeen minutes.

Arrived on this side, he was received with shouts and cheers, the music of bands, and the screams and whistles of several locomotives, which were on the track in sight of the river, and for a time it seemed as though Pandemonium, in the way of noises, had

... and with ...
... among the crowd, ...
... such at the wonderful ... of this
... performer.

He was borne to his carriage in this manner, and from it returned his thanks to the eager crowd, stating that he had felt not the slightest trepidation or alarm during the performance of the feat, and that his only concern was the feelings of his friends, who had been extremely anxious lest some accident should occur. M. BLONDIN then returned to his hotel, after announcing that he should repeat the feat on the Fourth of July—Monday next.

Everything passed off charmingly throughout the day. The weather was just cool enough to be delightful, and we are happy, as well as surprised, to say that we heard of not the slightest accident during the day. Where so many were assembled together, this is a matter of astonishment, and probably unparalleled.

WHEN M. BLONDIN—"that fool of a Frenchman going to commit suicide"—startled the world by crossing the Falls of Niagara on a tight-rope in 1859 no one would have believed that he was destined to die in his bed, like any other man, at the ripe age of 73. But BLONDIN did more than simply walk straight across the Falls: he crossed them on stilts, he crossed them blindfold, and he crossed them carrying a man on his back, to whom, according to the story, he remarked, about midway across, "If you don't sit quiet I shall have to put you down." Finally he stood upon his head half-way across, surrounded by a display of fireworks. The name BLONDIN has for many years been a household word, and the most famous rope-walker who has ever lived will always be

The Times
4th November 1926

The Handcuff King.

Modern slang gives us many kings—oil kings, cocoa kings, and others—but the men who have deserved the title of king by being the best in the world at a certain job are very few. HARRY HOUDINI, whose death in New York has been reported this week, was one of them. He was, by all consent, unmatched at freeing himself from handcuffs, ropes, strait-waistcoats, boxes, locked doors, any instrument of confinement which anyone chose to put about him in any manner. In his books (which are more amusing than he meant them to be, because at writing English he was not a king) he gives instances of rash rivals, who challenged or misrepresented him, and suffered at his hands deserved ignominy on public stages. But HOUDINI was truly at his kingliest not on the public stage, but in a private house, a newspaper office, a prison, anywhere where there was no possibility of aid from delusion. In such places his only means were knowledge, dexterity, strength, and endurance. When he writes very grandly :— " I shall not delve into the very deep intricacies " of some of the great modern feats of handcuff " manipulations, and jail-breaking, as accom- " plished by myself," he does not mean that he is withholding secrets which would make his feats possible without knowledge, dexterity, strength, and endurance. He had taken the trouble to learn the mechanism of every lock and handcuff in the world. He had practised till his dexterity was consummate. And as for strength and endurance, he records the " pain, " torture, agony, and misery of mind " which he endured during the one hour and twenty-nine minutes which it took him to get out of the strait-jacket used for the murderous insane in the prison at Hanover. These were his secrets. It was with these alone that he performed his incredible feats. If he has taken them with him into his present existence, how hardly will the keepers of the gates confine him to the place decreed for him !

It is impossible not to respect a man who worked so hard and so wisely at his job, even though that job served no purpose beyond entertainment, and in Germany at least was held to be too dangerous to have its methods divulged. And it is impossible not to envy a man whose job is one in which he may come very near to perfection. It would have been just for HOUDINI to say that there was no lock, rope, handcuff in the world that he could not defeat ; and it would be just for MR. CINQUEVALLI to claim that there is no feat of balancing that he has not mastered or could not master. These kings are absolute monarchs in their enchanting little realms. But to most people such mastery is denied, not by reason of their lack of skill, but because of the variability or the very greatness of their material. The surgeons, to whose marvellous dexterity we cheerfully entrust our bodies, know that their dexterity is not marvellous enough to put beyond possibility of doubt its effect upon a thing so subtle and so strange as the human frame. The writer, who believes that he has perfectly, and in perfect language, expressed his meaning, betrays himself a coxcomb. The musician, who has given his life to the mastery of an instrument, sees perfection ever farther and farther ahead of him. With a HOUDINI or a CINQUEVALLI the technique is everything. He knows that his aim can be achieved and that he can achieve it. Many a statesman, a philanthropist, a reformer, knows not only that he himself cannot achieve the end towards which he is working, but that his end is unachievable. As such men struggle by faith along a path that they know to be unending, they must often be tempted to envy the man who can assure himself of perfection, however humble his aim may be. But they will not the less respect the good qualities which enable here and there a man to become king at a job in which, after all, a good many other students remain duffers.

remembered not perhaps as a mere acrobat, but, if one may legitimately make the distinction, as the man who first exhibited the many possibilities of the art of balance. Blondin declared that a rope-walker, like a poet, was born, not made. " Sir," he once remarked, with the deliberateness of Dr. JOHNSON, " I have never felt fear—no, not even " when crossing Niagara. I was a rope-walker at " four." It is, we believe, a fact that he was able to ride his grooved-wheel bicycle safely across the rope before he had even attempted to master the difficulties of riding an ordinary bicycle upon the road. And his skill seems always to have secured for him a natural and prescriptive exemption from the use of nets and other safeguards which are required in the case of less convincing performers. " Fall? " his agent once remarked with indignation. " He can't ! "

Glasgow Herald
3rd August 1936

DEATH OF LOUIS BLERIOT

First Man to Fly the Channel

PIONEER FRENCH AVIATOR

M. Louis Bleriot, the pioneer aviator and the first airman to fly across the English Channel, died yesterday following a heart attack at his home in Paris. He was 64 years of age.

Louis Bleriot was the Lindbergh of his day. His pioneer flight across the Channel was as daring a feat in 1909 as was Colonel Lindbergh's Transatlantic trip through the air in 1927. By being the first to accomplish the seemingly impossible feat of their respective times, each was responsible for a direct move in the progress of aviation.

Born at Cambrai on July 1, 1872, Bleriot was the son of a manufacturer, and thus came into contact with mechanics from his boyhood. He went to a technical school and took a degree in engineering. After his military service, spent for the most part as a second lieutenant of artillery at Tarbes, he became interested in automobiles.

FIRST AEROPLANE FACTORY IN FRANCE

After several years of experimental work he invented the motor car searchlight in 1896. Four years later the sight of the famous flying machine built by Ader and exhibited in Paris turned his attention towards the then infantile science of aviation.

Year in and year out Bleriot studied the problem of making a practicable aeroplane. He conducted dozens of experiments and lost most of the fortune he had made with his motor car searchlight. In 1906, aided by two friends, he founded the first aeroplane factory in France. Finally on September 17, 1907, his wildest dreams came true. He flew 186 metres in a monoplane built by his own hands.

THE CHANNEL FLIGHT

On October 31, 1908, he startled the world by making the first cross-country flight on record. With one stop he flew a distance of about 60 miles. At that time the idea that anyone would leave the ground again in one of those "wild contraptions" after having landed safely was almost unbelievable.

Then Bleriot caused a sensation with his announcement that he intended to fly across the English Channel. He accomplished the feat on July 25, 1909, flying from Calais to Dover.

The destroyer Escopette was assigned to steer a course. Apparently the idea that Bleriot's machine might move faster than a destroyer never entered anyone's head.

At first Bleriot's machine moved above the vessel, then, seemingly bothered by the smoke from the destroyer's stacks, it steered slightly away. Little by little it pulled away, and in exactly 38 minutes the 'plane covered the 23.5 miles between France and England. Bleriot by his feat won a prize of £1000 offered by a London newspaper for the first flight across the Channel. He was acclaimed everywhere he went in England, and was greeted by a characteristic French demonstration on his return to Paris. He was congratulated by the Government and made an officer of the Legion of Honour.

LEADING DESIGNER

Bleriot immediately devoted himself to aircraft construction. His 'planes were used by the French Army during the war, and he was soon regarded as one of the world's leading designers. After the war he began his campaign for the introduction of the monoplane as both a fighting and commercial machine, and he was destined to see his viewpoint accepted by the whole world.

In August, 1926, he flew the Channel again for the first time since his historic crossing of 1909. He had just designed a huge monoplane capable of making a non-stop Transatlantic flight with 30 passengers carried in cabins within the hollow wings. This machine, including the research work, was to cost nearly £50,000 and was to be driven by four Bristol-Jupiter engines. In July, 1929, he marked the 20th anniversary of his epoch-making flight across the Channel by repeating it and afterwards taking part in the English celebrations. His trip was made in one of his giant 'planes, thus illustrating the great progress made by aviation. The spot where he landed near Dover in 1909 had been marked by a monument.

His factories near Paris were the scene of a stay-in strike during the recent French labour disputes, and he expressed himself in favour of the Government taking over control.

M. Bleriot remained an active airman to the end of his life, and in June, 1934, flew to London to attend a special display given in his honour. He was made a life member of the Royal Aero Club. M. Bleriot was married and leaves two sons.

THE LATE M. LOUIS BLERIOT.

Architecture & Design

The architects and designers of the past two hundred years have shaped our lives quite literally. Our surroundings, whether in terms of the buildings we use or the furniture and household bits and pieces we surround ourselves with, probably exert a far greater influence over the sort of people we are, both individually and as a society, than we might at first suppose. The great engineers, represented here by **Isambard Kingdom Brunel** and **Ferdinand de Lesseps**, have determined how we move both ourselves and our goods. Brunel's *SS. Great Britain*, the first iron steamship, his suspension bridge over the River Avon, and many of his other engineering feats provide the model for our industrial society, as do de Lesseps' Panama and Suez Canals. Likewise **Josiah Wedgwood**'s pottery, both artistically and technically. **William Morris**'s furnishings have recently inspired a whole host of imitators, while **Walter Gropius's** *Bauhaus* of the 1920's saw the birth of a vast variety of everyday objects which are still with us, having been designed on a then revolutionary principle, now a watchword for design – functionalism. Strangely enough, the death in 1944 of that other great fore-runner of functional, machine-inspired design, the Italian Marinetti, whose Manifesto of 1909 initiated Futurism, went unrecorded in the British press. Representing architecture, we have **Robert Adam**, who along with John Nash created what is now regarded as the epitome of civilized elegance; and **Frank Lloyd Wright** and **Le Corbusier**, who between them stand for all that is most exciting in modern building, inspiring – for better or worse – a whole generation. **Louis Sullivan**, curiously enough, who has as much claim as anyone to the dubious honour of having designed the first real skyscraper, appears to have received comparatively scant notice, in sharp contrast to M. **Eiffel** whose monument continues to cause traffic jams in the heart of Paris.

New York Times
10th April 1959

ICONOCLAST NOTED FOR STRONG IDEAS

Believed Form In Building Should Follow Function— Once Foe of Skyscrapers

Special to The New York Times.

PHOENIX, Ariz., April 9— Frank Lloyd Wright, regarded by many as the greatest architect of the twentieth century, died early today in St. Joseph's Hospital. He was 89 years old

Mr. Wright, who had considered himself to be "the greatest living- architect," was admitted to the hospital Monday night for emergency surgery to remove an intestinal obstruction. His physician said he was "getting along satisfactorily and then suddenly died."

From his estate, Taliesin West, northeast of Phoenix, Mr. Wright designed a new Capitol for Arizona. He proposed an "oasis in the desert, its fountains and greenery contrasting with the sand and rocks around it." The plan created a controversy, but was rejected.

When a group of architects proposed a skyscraper type of building for a Capitol, Mr. Wright looked at the drawing and described it as "a sidewalk-happy chimneypot with a derby hat on top, a poor version of a poor original—the United Nations Building in New York."

This was typical of Mr. Wright's comments, for which he was almost as well known as his buildings. He condemned retiring at 60 as a "murderous custom" and pleaded for a curb to America's "lust for ugliness."

A gradual change in the architect's fame, fortune and attitude might have been marked on May 28; 1953, when he received the Gold Medal Award of the National Institute of Arts and Letters. He then said:

"A shadow falls; I feel coming on me a strange disease— humility."

From Radical to Leader

During his lifetime Mr. Wright was in turn the great radical of American architecture and the acknowledged leader of a flourishing modern school of building.

This change in status of the white - haired iconoclast of American architecture did not evolve through any relaxation of his uncompromising theory that form in building should follow function, but rather in the public's gradual acceptance of his doctrine and deviations.

Hailed in Europe in his early years as the creator of an American architecture, he did not so readily gain acceptance in his own country, where the skyscraper was king. Although trained by Louis Sullivan, who was known as the "father of the skyscraper," Mr. Wright was strong in his condemnation of that peculiarly American architectural phenomenon.

Mr. Wright scathingly condemned the topless towers of New York. He had no use for the great steel and stone cities; he denounced the "box" house in this country, declaring that "a box is more of a coffin for the human spirit than an inspiration."

His own philosophy of architecture was enunciated in low terrain-conforming homes that became known as "prairie architecture"; in functional office buildings of modest height utilizing such materials as concrete slabs, glass bricks and tubing; in such monumental structures as the Imperial Hotel in Tokyo that withstood the great earthquake of 1923.

From the very beginning, his designs were different from anything that had been built before—"designed-for-living" bungalows. He built the first one for himself. It was the home for his bride, the former Catherine Tobin, whom he married when he was 21. She was 19. They met at a church social, married and went to live at Oak Park, a Chicago suburb noted for its many churches. There the Wrights's six children were born: Lloyd and John, who became architects; Catherine, David, Frances and Llewellyn

The architect's Oak Park houses were low bungalows, free of fancy woodwork, dormer windows, corner towers or towering chimneys. The horizontal planes of the structures were accentuated. They "hugged the earth."

Among architects the houses created a sensation. Soon Mr. Wright's designs became known in this country as "prairie architecture" because they fitted so snugly into the flat landscape for which they were made. In Europe they were widely hailed and in Germany several books were written about them and a portfolio of them was published. America, for the most part, still chose to ignore both the builder and his creations.

Suddenly Mr. Wright gained fame, not through his already substantial contribution to modern American architecture, but through scandal and tragedy. In 1909 he went to Germany to arrange for publication of the portfolio of his work and some essays on architecture he had written. A short time before, he had built a house for E. H. Cheney, a neighbor at Oak Park. When the architect sailed for Germany, Mrs. Cheney went with him.

When they returned, Mr. Wright built perhaps his most famous structure, his own home, Taliesin ("Shining brow" in his ancestral Welsh), in Spring Green, Wis. He built his country home on a commanding site overlooking the Wisconsin River. It was to be a "refuge" for Mrs. Cheney, whose husband had divorced her.

On Aug. 15, 1914, tragedy struck Taliesin. Mrs. Cheney, her two children and four other persons were killed by a crazed servant, who also burned the house to the ground. Mr. Wright later rebuilt Taliesin, determined, as he said "to wipe the scar from the hill."

Meanwhile, publication in Germany of Mr. Wright's work had come to the attention of the Emperor of Japan, who, in the fall of 1915 sent a delegation of officials and architects to see him and to ask him to submit plans for a $4,500,000 hotel the Emperor hoped to build in Tokyo. The architect made sketches, which were accepted, and he went to Japan to superintend the building of the hotel.

His greatest problem was to foil the earthquakes that periodically brought destruction and death to Japan. The brilliance with which he solved his problem ... onstrated twice --once before the hotel was completed, when a minor quake shook Tokyo, and again when it had been up for two years.

The Imperial Hotel was an elastic structure, the walls and floors having a sliding quality never before attained. Its plumbing was designed so that pipes would not break and the electric wiring was placed so that temblors would not cause short circuits and charge the building with high-voltage death.

It was completed in 1922. A year later fierce quakes rocked Tokyo and Yokohama. Nearly 100,000 persons died under collapsing walls and falling roofs or were burned to death in the holocaust that followed. Days later, when communication between Tokyo and the outside world was re-established, word went out that the Imperial Hotel was the only large structure that had survived the disaster.

In the next few years domestic trouble continued to harass the architect. He had been estranged from his first wife, who finally consented to divorce him after his return from Tokyo. His second marriage, to Miriam Noel, a sculptor, was brief. They were married in 1923 and divorced in 1927. The next year Mr. Wright married Olga Lazovich. They had a daughter, Iovanna.

In 1927, when he lost Taliesin by foreclosure of a mortgage, Mr. Wright called in his friends, many of them wealthy business men, and incorporated himself under Wisconsin laws, selling stock on his earning power.

He regained Taliesin, built

several houses and planned extensive projects, most of which were too "visionary" and did not materialize. In 1929 he incorporated himself again and established the Taliesin Fellowship Foundation, where he trained many apprentice architects.

had received many prizes and honors, including election to the American Academy of Art and Letters, the white-haired individualist was still capable of stirring up the critics.

Mr. Wright was the author of many books, including "Modern Architecture" and "Two Lectures on Architecture," 1931; "An Autobiography," and "The Disappearing City," 1932; "An Organic Architecture," 1939; "When Democracy Builds," 1945; "Genius and Mobocracy," 1949; "An American Architecture," 1955, and "A Testament," 1957.

Through controversy and criticism the architect rose steadily while his critics declared he was not only ahead of his time, but also ahead of all time, and his disciples and admirers made extravagant claims for his work. In 1940, when a comprehensive exhibition of Mr. Wright's work was shown in New York, he was reckoned as a great force in American architecture, but not as the last word.

Gradually he began to gain vogue and commissions. Among the structures for which the architect became famous were the Midway Gardens in Chicago, the Larkin Company administration building in Buffalo, the S. C. Johnson Company building at Racine, Wis.; the Falling Water House of Edgar J. Kaufmann at Bear Run, Pa., which he built above a waterfall, and the Price Tower at Bartlesville, Okla.

There also was the circular Friedman house near Pleasantville, N. Y., in a cooperative development known as Usonia Houses. Usonia was the descriptive word used by Mr. Wright to typify what he considered to be the ideal American architectural style.

Taliesin West Added

He added Taliesin West, his own home in Phoenix, Ariz., to the rapidly growing list of Wright showplaces throughout the nation. This home, situated in Paradise Valley, he used as he did Taliesin East, as headquarters for his foundation teaching program. Approximately forty young apprentice architects yearly spent the term from April through November in the Wisconsin Taliesin and from December through March in the Arizona home.

One of Mr. Wright's largest commissions was the $10,000,000 campus of Florida Southern College in Lakewood. The project was begun in 1936 and sixteen structures were to be completed by 1960. Again Mr. Wright received mixed reactions for one of the edifices—a modern chapel building.

Even as an octogenarian who

Only Commission in New York Was Guggenheim Art Museum

After more than a half-century of renown Frank Lloyd Wright received in 1945 his first commission in New York—the new home of the Solomon R. Guggenheim Museum on Fifth Avenue between Eighty-eighth and Eighty-ninth Streets. He did not live to see it completed.

When the dean of architecture received the commission, a project involving more than $2,000,000, he said:

"For the first time art will be seen as if through an open window, and, of all places, in New York. It astounds me."

One of Mr. Wright's favorite targets for caustic comment and criticism was New York's forest of skyscrapers. An exponent of what he called "organic" architecture, a term that baffled many, he devised a museum building he saw as a "little temple in a park."

When the design of his initial venture here was published, an avalanche of cheers and derision was loosed. The "little temple" was hailed by Wright partisans, by others it was called variously, a "washing machine," a "hot cross bun," a "marshmallow."

Even some of the staunchest supporters of the gifted architect "shuddered" to envision the museum cylindrical in shape—in its environment of staid, decades-old apartment buildings. Mr. Wright was imperturbable.

When he submitted plans for his six-story building to the city authorities in 1953, the Department of Housing and Building refused to grant a license. It said the structure would violate building codes. With an elasticity that infrequently characterized his reaction to criticism, Mr. Wright complied with the request to make a few alterations.

He stood firm on other disputed specifications, such as a plexiglass dome for the building and glass doors. The plans to start building were delayed several times but, finally, the museum was in construction in 1956. It is expected to be completed in a month or two.

Criticism came from a new source. Mr. Wright planned a continuous gallery in the form of a spiraling ramp from ground floor to the top. The pictures wouldn't hang right, the artists complained. Mr. Wright was adamant—the artists were wrong, he said. The grade of the ramp was no steeper than the grade of a sidewalk from building line to curb.

It was an open secret, too, that the museum staff was bitter about the ramp, and found serious fault with Mr. Wright's lack of adequate provision for art storage and overlooking space for a restoration laboratory.

The Times
19th September 1859

ISAMBARD KINGDOM BRUNEL.

Our columns of Saturday last contained the ordinary record of the death of one of our most eminent engineers, Mr. I. K. Brunel. The loss of a man whose name has now for two generations, from the commencement of this century to the present time, been identified with the progress and the application of mechanical and engineering science, claims the notice due to those who have done the State some service. This country is largely indebted to her many eminent civil engineers for her wealth and strength, and Mr. Brunel will take a high rank among them when the variety and magnitude of his works are considered, and the original genius he displayed in accomplishing them. He was, as it were, born an engineer, about the time his father had completed the block machinery at Portsmouth, then one of the most celebrated and remarkable works of the day, and which remains efficient and useful. Those who recollect him as a boy recollect full well how rapidly, almost intuitively, indeed, he entered into and identified himself with all his father's plans and pursuits. He was very early distinguished for his powers of mental calculation, and not less so for his rapidity and accuracy as a draughtsman. His power in this respect was not confined to professional or mechanical drawings only. He displayed an artist-like feeling for and a love of art, which in later days never deserted him. He enjoyed and promoted it to the last, and the only limits to the delight it afforded him were his engrossing occupations and his failing health.

The bent of his mind when young was clearly seen by his father and by all who knew him. His education was therefore directed to qualify him for that profession in which he afterwards distinguished himself. His father was his first, and, perhaps, his best tutor. When he was about 14 he was sent to Paris, where he was placed under the care of M. Masson, previous to entering the college of Henri Quartre, where he remained two years. He then returned to England, and it may be said that, in fact, he then commenced his professional career under his father, Sir I. Brunel, and in which he rendered him important assistance—devoting himself from that time forward to his profession exclusively and ardently. He displayed even then the resources, not only of a trained and educated mind, but great, original, and inventive power. He possessed the advantage of being able to express or draw clearly and accurately whatever he had matured in his own mind. But not only that; he could work out with his own hands, if he pleased, the models of his own designs, whether in wood or iron. As a mere workman he would have excelled. Even at this early period steam navigation may be said to have occupied his mind, for he made the model of a boat, and worked it with locomotive contrivances of his own. Everything he did, he did with all his might and strength, and he did it well. The same energy, thoughtfulness, and accuracy, the same thorough conception and mastery of whatever he undertook distinguished him in all minor things, whether working as a tyro in his father's office, or as the engineer of the Great Western Railway Company, or, later, in the conception and design in all its details of the Great Eastern. Soon after his return to England his father was occupied, among other things, with plans for the formation of a tunnel under the Thames. In 1825 this work was commenced, and Brunel took an active part in the work under his father. There are many of his fellow labourers now living who well know the energy and ability he displayed in that great scientific struggle against physical difficulties and obstacles of no ordinary magnitude, and it may be said that at this time the anxiety and fatigue he underwent, and an accident he met with, laid the foundation of future weakness and illness. Upon the stoppage of that undertaking by the irruption of the river in 1828, he became employed on his own account upon various works. Docks at Sunderland and Bristol were constructed by him, and when it was proposed to throw a suspension bridge across the Avon at Clifton, his design and plan was approved by Mr. Telford, then one of the most eminent engineers of the day. This work was never completed. He thus became known, however, in Bristol, and when a railway was in contemplation between London and Bristol, and a company formed, he was appointed their engineer. He had previously been employed, however, as a railway engineer in connexion with the Bristol and Glocestershire and the Merthyr and Cardiff tramways. In these works his mind was first turned to the construction of railways, and when he became engineer of the Great Western Railway Company he recommended and introduced what is popularly called the broad guage, and the battle of the guages began. This is not the place or the time to say one word upon this controversy. No account of Mr. Brunel's labours, however, would be complete without mentioning so important a circumstance in his life. Considering the Great Western Railway as an engineering work alone, it may challenge a comparison with any other railway in the world for the general perfection of its details, and the speed and ease of travelling upon it. Many of its structures, such as the viaduct at Hanwell, the Maidenhead-bridge, which has the flattest arch of such large dimensions ever attempted in brickwork, the Box-tunnel, which, at the date of its construction, was the longest in the world, and the bridges and tunnels between Bath and Bristol deserve the attention of the professional student. They are all more or less remarkable and original works.

In the South Devon and Cornish railways there are also works of great magnitude and importance. The sea wall of the South Devon Railway, and, above all, the bridge over the Tamar, called the Albert-bridge from the interest taken in it by the Prince Consort, deserve to be specially mentioned, together with the bridge over the Wye at Chepstow, as works which do honour to the genius of the engineer and the country too. It was on the South Devon Railway that he adopted the plan which had been previously tried on the London and Croydon line,—viz., of propelling the carriages by atmospheric pressure. This plan failed, but he entertained a strong opinion that this power would be found hereafter capable of adoption for locomotive purposes. It is impossible, in such a rapid sketch as this of his energetic and professional life, to do more than notice, or rather catalogue, his works. It was in connexion with the interests of the Great Western Railway that he first conceived the idea of building a steamship to run between England and America. The Great Western was built accordingly. The power and tonnage of this vessel was about double that of the largest ship afloat at the time of her construction. Subsequently, as the public know, the Great Britain was designed and built under Mr. Brunel's superintendence. This ship, the result, as regards magnitude, of a few years' experience in iron shipbuilding, was not only more than double the tonnage of the Great Western, and by far the largest ship in existence, but she was more than twice as large as the Great Northern, the largest iron ship which at that time had been attempted. While others hesitated about extending the use of iron in the construction of ships, Mr. Brunel saw that it was the only material in which a very great increase of dimensions could safely be attempted. The very accident which befel the Great Britain upon the rocks in Dundrum Bay showed conclusively the skill he had then attained in the adaptation of iron to the purposes of shipbuilding. The means taken under his immediate direction to protect the vessel from the injury of winds and waves attracted at the time much attention, and they proved successful, for the vessel was again floated, and is still afloat.

While noticing those great efforts to improve the art of shipbuilding, it must not be forgotten that Mr. Brunel, we believe, was the first man of eminence in his profession who perceived the capabilities of the screw as a propeller. He was brave enough to stake a great reputation upon the soundness of the reasoning upon which he had based his conclusions. From his experiments on a small scale in the Archimedes he saw his way clearly to the adoption of that method of propulsion which he afterwards adopted in the Great Britain. And in the report to his directors in which he recommended it, he conveyed his views with so much clearness and conclusiveness that when, with their approbation, he submitted it to the Admiralty he succeeded in persuading them to give it a trial in Her Majesty's navy, under his direction. In the progress of this trial he was much thwarted; but the Rattler, the ship which was at length placed at his disposal, and fitted under his direction with engines and screw by Messrs. Maudslay and Field, gave results which justified his expectations under somewhat adverse circumstances. She was the first screw ship which the British navy possessed, and it must be added, to the credit of Brunel, that though she had originally been built for a paddle ship, her performance with a screw was so satisfactory that numerous screw ships have since been added to the navy. Thus prepared by experience and much personal devotion to the subject of steam navigation by means of large ships, he, in the latter part of 1851 and the beginning of 1852, began to work out the idea he had long entertained—that to make long voyages economically and speedily by steam required that the vessels should be large enough to carry the coal for the entire voyage outwards, and, unless the facilities for obtaining coal were very great at the outport, then for the return voyage also ; and that vessels much larger than any then built could be navigated with great advantages from the mere effects of size. Hence originated the Great Eastern. The history of this great work is before the public, and its success in a nautical point of view is admitted, as well as the strength and stability of the construction of the vessel. More than this cursory notice of this last memorial of his skill cannot now be given. All the circumstances attending the construction, the launching, the trial of this great ship are before the public. It would hardly be just, however, to the memory of this distinguished engineer if we were to conclude this notice with-

out an allusion to his private character and worth. Few men were more free from that bane of professional life—professional jealousy. He was always ready to assist others, and to do justice to their merits. It is a remarkable circumstance that in the early part of his career he was brought into frequent conflict with Robert Stephenson, as Stephenson was with him, and that, nevertheless, their mutual regard and respect were never impaired. Brunel was ever ready to give his advice and assistance whenever Stephenson desired it, and the public will recollect how earnestly and cordially during the launch of the Great Eastern Stephenson gave his assistance and lent the weight of his authority to his now deceased friend. Such rivalry and such unbroken friendship as theirs are rare, and are honourable to both.

The death of Mr. Brunel was hastened by the fatigue and mental strain caused by his efforts to superintend the completion of the Great Eastern, and in those efforts his last days were spent. But we must not forbear to mention that for several years past Mr. Brunel had been suffering from ill-health brought on by over exertion. Nevertheless he allowed himself no relaxation from his professional labours, and it was during the period of bodily pain and weakness that his greatest difficulties were surmounted and some of his greatest works achieved. Possessing a mind strong in the consciousness of rectitude, he pursued, in single hearted truthfulness, what he believed to be the course of duty, and in his love of and devotion to his profession he accomplished, both at home and abroad, on the continent and in India, works, the history of which will be the best monument to his memory. With an intellect singularly powerful and acute, for nothing escaped his observation in any branch of science which could be made available in his own pursuits, yet it was accompanied by humility and a kindliness of heart which endeared him to all who knew him and enjoyed his friendship. The very boldness and originality of his works, of which he was never known to boast, while it added to his fame, added no little to his anxiety, and not unfrequently encompassed him with difficulty—

"Great was the glory, but greater was the strife,"

which told ultimately upon his health and strength, and finally closed his life when he was little more than 53 years of age. We have left unnoticed many of his works, and many that deserve the attention and study of the young engineer. They will find their record in professional works, and in them his works will hereafter be fully described and considered. Mr. Brunel was a member of the Royal Society, having been elected at the early age of 26. In 1857 he was admitted by the University of Oxford to the honorary degree of Doctor of Civil Laws, a distinction of which he was justly proud.

The Gentleman's Magazine
3rd March 1792 Vol 62

The Times
29th December 1923

At his house in Albemarle-street, Robert Adam, esq. architect, fellow of the Royal and Antiquarian Societies of London and Edinburgh. His death was occasioned by the bursting of a blood-vessel in his stomach. The many elegant buildings, public and private, erected in various parts of the kingdom by Mr. Adam, will remain lasting monuments of his taste and genius; and the natural suavity of his manners, joined to the excellence of his moral character, had endeared him to a numerous circle of friends, who will long lament his death.—Mr A. was born in 1728, at Kirkaldy, in the county of Fife, the same place that gave birth to Mr. Adam Smith, author of "The Wealth of Nations." He was the second son of Mr. A. esq. of Maryburgh, an architect of distinguished merit. He received his education at the University of Edinburgh. The friendships he formed were with men who have since eminently distinguished themselves by their literary productions; amongst whom were Mr. David Hume, Dr. Robertson, Mr. Adam Smith, Dr. Adam Ferguson, and Mr. John Home. At a more advanced time of life he had the good fortune to enjoy the friendship and society of Archibald Duke of Argyle, the late Mr. Charles Townshend, the Earl of Mansfield, and several others of the most illustrious men of the age.—Mr. Adam, after his return from Italy, was appointed architect to his Majesty, in the year 1762, which office, being incompatible with a seat in parliament, he resigned in 1768, on his being elected to represent the county of Kinross. It is somewhat remarkable that the Arts should be deprived at the same time of two of their greatest ornaments, Sir Joshua Reynolds and Mr. Adam; and it is difficult to say which of them excelled most in his particular profession. Sir Joshua introduced a new and superior style of portrait-painting. It is equally true that Mr. Adam produced a total change in the architecture of this country; and his fertile genius in elegant ornament was not confined to the decoration of buildings, but has been diffused into almost every branch of manufacture. His talents extended beyond the line of his own profession; he displayed in his numerous drawings a landscape a luxuriance of composition, and an effect of light and shadow, which have scarcely ever been equaled. The loss of Mr. Adam at this time must be peculiarly felt, as the new University of Edinburgh, and other great public works, both in that city and in Glasgow, were erecting from his design, and under his direction.—To the last period of his life, Mr. Adam displayed an increasing vigour of genius and refinement of taste; for, in the space of one year preceding his death, he designed 8 great public works, beside 25 private buildings, so various in their style, and so beautiful in their composition, that they have been allowed, by the best judges, sufficient of themselves to establish his fame unrivalled as an artist.—On the 10th instant, his remains were interred in the South aisle of Westminster Abbey. The funeral was private, being attended only by a select number of his friends, who esteemed him while living, and wished to bestow this last mark of their regard. The pall was supported by the Duke of Buccleugh, the Earl of Coventry, the Earl of Lauderdale, Lord Viscount Stormont, Lord Frederick Campbell, and Mr. Pulteney.

M. EIFFEL DEAD.

A GREAT ENGINEER.

(FROM OUR OWN CORRESPONDENT.)

PARIS, DEC. 29.

The death has occurred in Paris of M. Gustave Eiffel, designer of the tower which bears his name. He was 91 years old.

M. Eiffel was born at Dijon, and he was educated as an engineer. At the time when his career opened, metallic construction was beginning its modern development, and M. Eiffel studied it thoroughly. His first important work of this kind was the building of the railway bridge over the Garonne at Bordeaux in 1858, for which the piers were placed, by means of compressed air, at a depth of 80ft. below the river surface. Years later he devised improved methods in the construction of a bridge over the Douro at Oporto. He built several bridges in France and other countries, including Hungary, and also designed the railway station at Budapest. M. Eiffel was charged with the construction of locks in the first Panama Canal undertaking, which was interrupted by the financial crisis.

In 1886 M. Eiffel offered on his own responsibility to build the Eiffel Tower, and finished the work for the exhibition of 1889. After 20 years of private ownership the tower became the property of the City of Paris. It is now used as a wireless station, for which purpose its height of nearly 1,000ft. makes it admirably suitable. In all this purely engineering work M. Eiffel used new forms of pier construction for arches of great width. Among other works, the construction of the cupola of the Grand Equatorial at Nice is an interesting example of his methods. From 1900 until the war began M. Eiffel occupied himself with meteorological observation and research and for some years published an annual "Atlas Météorologique."

In 1907 he published his "Recherches expérimentales sur la Résistance de l'air, exécutées à la Tour Eiffel." When aeroplanes became practicable, he began to apply these researches for the benefit of the new art of flying. In 1910 he published a book describing his experiments, and this was translated into English and German. Further researches in aerodynamics made at his laboratory at Auteuil were described in a book published in 1914, on the eve of the war. Throughout the war his aero-dynamical experiments continued, and he published a report on them in 1919, and many practical suggestions made by him about the design of aeroplanes, propellers, and projectiles were adopted. The Technical Section of the Aeronautical Department still makes use of his laboratory. M. Eiffel continued his work until 1920, when he published his "L'Hélice Aérienne."

Le Corbusier Dies While Swimming

ARCHITECT OF "RADIANT CITIES"

ROQUEBRUNE.
French Riviera, Friday.

Le Corbusier, the French architect whose controversial designs won him world fame as a creator of twentieth century architecture, died to-day while swimming in the Mediterranean. He was 77.

He had a heart attack 50 yards from shore and was dead when other swimmers pulled him from the sea, according to the police.

The man, once hailed by French Culture Minister M. Andre Malraux, as "the world's greatest architect" had been holidaying here for the past fortnight.

Le Corbusier was born at Chaux de Fonds, Switzerland, but became a naturalised Frenchman after moving to Paris at the age of 28. His real name was Charles Edouart Jeanneret-Gris.

Le Corbusier became a familiar name around the world from the time he launched his "radiant city" conception for towns composed of "living units" with open spaces between tall blocks of methodically geometrical buildings.

When le Corbusier built a 14-storey "radiant city" living unit in Marseilles after the econd World War, however, the Society for the General Aesthetics of France sued him for damages on a technical point, claiming that it wanted to "fight these deep warts which dishonour France."

Many Books

The architect emerged triumphant from the suit. Many Governments brought him in to plan new towns or improve old ones and his "radiant cities" turned into and architectural revolution.

Le Corbusier was also an accomplished painter, sculptor, and designer of tapestries, though his works in these fields often startled the traditionalists and brought new controversy.

He wrote so many books on architecture that Lloyd Wright, the American architect, was reported once to have refused to see him on the ground that he never received journalists.

Le Corbusier built on what he called the "modular," a system basing the proportions of his buildings on those of the human body, and was often very down-to-earth in his thinking.— Reuter.

LOUIS HENRI SULLIVAN.

Architect Who Designed Many Notable Buildings Dies in Chicago.

CHICAGO, April 15.—Louis Henri Sullivan, known as the Dean of American architects, died here yesterday. Mr. Sullivan was born in Boston in 1856 and educated at the Massachusetts Institute of Technology and the Ecole des Beaux Arts, Paris. Among the buildings he designed are the Transportation Building for the Chicago World's Fair, the Condict Building, New York; the Prudential Building, Buffalo; the Wainwright Building and Union Trust Building, St. Louis.

Mr. Sullivan had written many articles on architecture for technical journals. He produced several notable examples of skyscraper construction, his work in that field illustrating his dictum that "form follows function." In a passage often quoted he wrote: "The loftiness of a tall building is the very open organ tone of its appeal. It must be in turn the dominant chord in the architect's expression. The force and power of altitude must be in it. It must be every inch a proud and soaring thing, rising in such sheer exultation that from bottom to top it is a unit without a single dissenting line—the new, the unexpected, the eloquent peroration of the most bold, the most sinister, the most forbidding conditions."

The Times
5th October 1896

DEATH OF MR. WILLIAM MORRIS.

The death of Mr. William Morris, which, we regret to say, took place shortly after 11 o'clock on Saturday morning at Kelmscott House, Hammersmith, after a long illness, removes from the world a man whom we do not hesitate to call a great artist. A poet, and one of our half dozen best poets, even when Tennyson and Browning were alive; an artist whose influence is visible almost everywhere; a craftsman who devoted himself, in a commercial age, to the union of arts and crafts, it may be said of him, with little or no exaggeration, that he adorned all that he touched. And, if another famous epitaph may be allowed to suggest itself, we should say that, while his best work—a poem of his own, or a volume from the Kelmscott Press—is often present on our bookshelves, most of us find something in the nature of a monument to Mr. Morris in the better taste of our domestic surroundings. It is seldom, indeed, that an Englishman is an artist of this type. True, Mr. Morris was neither a painter nor a sculptor. He studied painting for a time, but preferred to give his energies to the more practical arts with which his name has been so long associated, and to the poems some of which, we do not doubt, will live long after him. No one who has witnessed the Arts and Crafts Exhibitions, which he helped to promote—and which are renewed this year in an exhibition opened for a private view on the day of his death—will deny that he possessed and effectively used a remarkable diversity of gifts. To these he added a strenuous and outspoken English nature, such as rarely combines with the typical artistic temperament.

Of Mr. Morris's poems, important as they are, we need not speak at any length. They have been before the world for a long time, and the world at once made up its mind that their author, if not a poet of the first rank, was an earnest and sweet singer, who did not fritter away his genius on fugitive pieces and newspaper lyrics, but had enough industry and ambition for large subjects. The "Earthly Paradise," a series of 24 romances told by travellers who take their way, not to Canterbury, but towards an imaginary Utopia in the West, is probably Mr. Morris's best known work. It had been preceded in 1858 by the "Defence of Guenevere, and other poems," and in 1867 by the "Life and Death of Jason," a great poem in more senses than one, in 17 books. The "Earthly Paradise" was the work of the years 1868-70; or perhaps it would be more correct to say that those were the years in which its various parts were published. Then came "Love is Enough; or, the Freeing of Pharamond—a Morality," in 1873, and this was followed a few years later by translations in verse—and often in poetry—of the Æneid and the Odyssey, and "Poems by the Way," in 1892. Surely no poet can have worked harder, or, considering the extent of his work, with greater success. Nor should his prose romances be forgotten, "A Dream of John Bull" (1888), "News from Nowhere" (1891), and others. The latest of them "The Well at the World's End," was only issued just before his death. Besides these were "The Story of Grettir the Strong" and "The Story of the Volsungs and the Niblungs," translations from the ancient Icelandic Sagas undertaken in collaboration with Mr. Eiríkr Magnússon, and a translation, in 1895, of the famous Anglo-Saxon epic of Beowulf. Criticism, especially of well-known work, is out of place in an obituary notice. As regards these translations, we may adhere to what we said of them at the time—that their English is "a marvel in these days of novel and newspaper." But this is true also of all that Morris wrote or did. He never omitted to be thorough—never forgot that he was a craftsman as well as an artist. His English, indeed, was always singularly pure, and made up in simplicity what it may have lacked in vigour. If his verse, with its weak rhymes, is sometimes a little cloying, a little hyper-Lydian —though this is never the fault of his Virgil— his descriptions are often so vivid that one hardly knows where the real ends and the ideal begins. The following seven lines, taken nearly at random from the "Earthly Paradise," will serve as an example :—

> Dusky and dim, though rich with gems and gold,
> The house of Venus was; high in the dome
> The burning sunlight you might now behold,
> From nowhere else the light of day might come
> To curse the Shame-faced Mother's lovely home;
> A long way off the shrine the fresh sea-breeze,
> Now just arising, brushed the myrtle-trees.

William Morris's birthplace was neither a library nor a studio. He was born in Walthamstow, of that commercial class whose characteristics he so little admired in after life. His father, a substantial merchant, died in 1844, leaving, we believe, a considerable property. Young Morris was educated first at Forest School, Walthamstow, and then at the recently founded Marlborough College, whence he passed to Exeter College, Oxford. It was in the early days of the Pre-Raphaelites, to some of whom Oxford furnished a congenial home. Given the Pre-Raphaelite movement on the one hand, and a residence at Oxford on the other, it is easy to understand the forces that influenced an artistic undergraduate in those days. For a long time after 1856, the year of his degree, he and his friends, Rossetti among them, left behind them a material memento of their Oxford life in the shape of the eight or ten frescoes of Arthurian subjects, since hopelessly ruined and at last removed, that used to decorate the debating-room of the Union. More lately, unless we are mistaken, some of Mr Morris's handiwork has adorned the chapel of his old college, of which he was elected an honorary Fellow, with Sir E. Burne-Jones, in 1882. It was in 1863 that he established, with partners in the undertaking, the factory for the production of artistic glass, tiles, wall-paper, and the like, for which his name has long been famous ; and it was in consequence of this unusual combination of manufacture and literature that he seemed to have a sort of dual existence in the eyes of the public. His poems were " by Morris, the wall-paper maker," his wall-papers " by Morris, the poet."

We have referred to his poems as his best work, and might justify the epithet on the ground that they are *ære perennius*, while the concrete productions of his factory must needs perish in process of time, or be debased by the imitations of inferior art. But we do not know that Morris himself would have taken this view of the fruits of his life. One cannot read his poems without feeling that their easy music, not hammered out, but flowing free, must have been a source of pleasure to the writer ; yet his sense of beauty and his energy perhaps found a still keener gratification in the material things produced by his hand and under his direction. Enlarging on whatever Mr. Ruskin has said of the nobility of honest work, and utterly despising the notion that an artist should plan and design, but, save in the finest of fine art, not execute, Morris held not only that executive handicraft was within the province of an artist, but that all crafts demanded artistic treatment. This principle he preached and practised with a good deal of enthusiasm, we wish we could add with an equal degree of success. It was of " us handicraftsmen " that he spoke to the Trades' Guilds ; and it was as a " common fellow " that he addressed a gathering of Birmingham artists and workmen. His cardinal principle was " Art made by the people, and for the people, as a joy to the maker and the user." " I do not want art for a few any more than education for a few, or freedom for a few." " You," he said, " you whose hands make those things that should be works of art, you must be all artists, and good artists too, before the public at large can take real interest in such things ; and when you have become so, I promise you that you shall lead the fashion ; fashion shall follow your hands obediently enough." That, he went on to say, is better than " working helplessly among the crowd of those who are ridiculously called manufacturers, that is, handicraftsmen, though the more part of them never did a stroke of hand-work in their lives, and are nothing better than capitalists and salesmen." It was the gospel of handiwork, its aims, methods, and rewards ; taught, indeed, by a fellow-workman, but by one whom fortune permitted to exhort and to lead. There can be no doubt of the hopefulness with which Morris

taught and followed his opinions. If they led him, as they have led other generous men before him, towards Socialism, the world can afford to judge him indulgently, as not apprehending much danger from his rhetoric. We do not desire to enlarge on the unpractical extremes to which his industrial and political opinions tended ; they are only the results of a warm heart and a mistaken enthusiasm ; they indicate, not the strength of the man, but his weakness, and are as nothing compared with the lasting work of his better genius. It is to be feared that his ideals and aspirations for art will never approach realization. Here and there his example will continue to animate individuals ; but no human power, even if the economic relations between consumers and producers, between users and makers, could change at his bidding, would give the mass of our workers a love or a knowledge of art. Our national nature, and the inevitable laws of economy, will not yield to persuasion, or promises, or dreams. Until they do so, only those who are willing to cry in the wilderness will prophesy the artistic millennium.

It must be allowed, however, that Morris's actual work was far more practical than his doctrine. The factory that he established more than 30 years ago in conjunction with such artists and kindred spirits as D. G. Rossetti, E. Burne-Jones, and Ford Madox Brown, was at first an experiment, but soon became a commercial success, and ultimately worked something like a domestic revolution. It may be suspected that fashion had as much share in the result as the latent æstheticism of the British public ; and fashionable Mr. Morris's work certainly became, greatly to the improvement of our houses, and possibly of our taste also. To say that a thing, no matter what, was " designed by Morris " was to pass a final verdict in its favour. Whether this improved state of things is permanent or not, and whether Mr. Morris's admirers and customers followed him with much conviction and intelligence, may be left as open questions. What is evident is that we are not at one with our fathers in matters of taste, and that our present ideas on such subjects have been mainly influenced by Mr. Morris and his school. Into the more serious issues that underlie his principles, and those of all real artists, it is not our business to enter. We record only work done, and only indicate the intention that inspired it ; we say, in one word, that Morris's death has taken from us an original and singularly sincere artist, who worked hard to make the world a little more beautiful and a little more honest. His book on Socialism is nothing. It is always the expert in one subject who desires eminence in another. It is not the political visionary, but the delightful poet, the thorough craftsman, the subtle designer, the sumptuous printer, the many-sided man himself, whom we shall remember.

DR WALTER GROPIUS
Influential modern architectural philosopher

Dr. Walter Gropius, the architect, who died in Boston at the age of 86, had been for many years one of the major world forces working towards an architecture that acknowledged and exploited modern technology. With his master, Peter Behrens, with Le Corbusier in France, Aalto in Finland, and Frank Lloyd Wright in the United States he may be classed as one of the most influential architects of modern times; and his influence was spread not only by example but by precept issuing from the Bauhaus at Dessau, that great institution which combined all the crafts in one philosophic unity and brought the work of the artist into the closest association with industry.

Gropius was nevertheless always on his guard against abstract terms like "functionalism" (which he did not scruple to call "catchwords"), and deprecated the propaganda which would make the new architecture a fashion "as snobbish as any of the older academic fashions which it aims to displace". His attitude was based not only on the frank acceptance and full exploitation of steel, glass, and reinforced concrete but on the realization that the day of the individual craftsman was done. He regarded the craftsman's role, in the modern industrial age, as that of creating well conceived and serviceable building components capable of being multiplied in quantity by mass production.

This great architectural philosopher and teacher was driven from his own country by the Nazi regime. Germany's loss might have been England's gain, for Gropius lived and worked among us for three years, but in the end it was America which offered him a post consonant with his status, the Chair of Architecture at Harvard.

Walter Gropius was born in Berlin on May 18, 1883, the son of an architect, Walter Adolf Gropius, and his wife Manon Scharnweber. From his formative years he determined to follow his father's profession; and after studying at the technical highschools at Charlottenburg and Munich he worked as assistant to Peter Behrens, one of the fathers of modern architecture, and it was in this period that his originality and far sightedness began to emerge.

In 1910 Gropius set up his own office; and in the following year, working with Adolf Meyer, produced one of the most remarkable industrial buildings of prewar years. This was the Fagus shoe-last factory at Alfeld-an-der-Leine, which had the forthright cubic outline and the huge areas of glass which were later to become associated with modern factory architecture. In 1914 he designed the Hall of Machinery for the Cologne exhibition of the Deutscher Werkbund, and (with Adolf Meyer) the Administrative Building at the same exhibition. From August, 1914, he served for some three years and a half as an air observer in the war, winning the Iron Cross of the first class and being shot down on one occasion by the French. Meanwhile, in 1915, he had been granted leave to discuss with the Grand Duke of Saxe-Weimar his taking control of the Saxon Academy of Arts and Crafts from the Belgian architect Henry van de Velde, who had himself suggested Gropius as his successor.

After the war Gropius took over two schools, the Grossherzogliche Sächsische Kunstgewerbeschule and the Grossherzogliche Sächsische Hochschule für Bildende Kunst, combining these institutions in 1919 as the Staatliches Bauhaus, at Weimar. Here he gathered round him a brilliant group of instructors and began to put into effect his theories about the relationship of design to industry. But he was severely hampered by the obscurantist attitude of the Government of Thuringia, and in April, 1925, left Weimar to start afresh in the smaller town of Dessau.

Now began a fruitful period of teaching, experimentation, craftwork and building that was to have incalculably beneficial effects on architecture in every civilized country. The Bauhaus at Dessau has been described as "the one school in the world where modern problems of design were approached realistically in a modern atmosphere". A distinguished team of professors included Johannes Itten, Oskar Schlemmer, Wassily Kandinsky, László Moholy-Nagy, and Paul Klee.

The Bauhaus building itself, began in autumn, 1925, and finished in December 1926, was a triumphant vindication of the principles of its architect and of the lines on which he had educated the students who worked on it. The whole of its interior decorations and fittings were produced in its own workshops.

At Dessau, as at Weimar, Gropius encountered vigorous and often ill-informed criticism from official bodies, craft organizations and so forth, and the press was full of controversy. Though he had forbidden any kind of political activity in the school it was constantly urged by his enemies that the Bauhaus was a centre of "bolshevism"; and in 1928 Gropius gave up the struggle.

Meanwhile Gropius had continued with his private practice. In 1926 he designed two houses for the Weissenhof permanent housing exhibition at Stuttgart, to which several of the most famous European architects contributed designs. In 1929 he won first prize in the Spandau-Haselhorst housing competition, and although the design was never executed it exerted considerable influence.

His most noteworthy designs of this kind in Germany actually carried out were those for the large Siemensstadt estate near Berlin. Gropius was the supervising architect for the scheme in which several others collaborated, and he was responsible for two of the blocks. In this scheme he was able to put many of his theories into practice. Among the best in Europe at the time it was designed and served as a model for much subsequent work.

The rise of Nazi power brought with it hard times and hard words for modern minded artists, and in 1934 Gropius left Germany for London, along with several other architects who had become refugees from Nazi persecution. These included the late Erich Mendelsohn and the

Hungarian-born Marcel Breuer, who had taught under Gropius at the Bauhaus and was later to become Gropius's partner in America. Gropius set up in practice in London in partnership with Mr. E. Maxwell Fry. He stayed for three years, and during that period he and Fry made several interesting projects, including an influential and prophetic one for high flats in a park-like setting at Windsor, and they were the architects of several buildings including Impington Village College, Cambridgeshire (1936), which was one of the four village colleges erected by the county council in support of the late Henry Morris's educational ideas with which Gropius found himself in close sympathy. A one-storey building with single depth classrooms, fan-shaped hall and club amenities, it serves the dual purpose of a secondary school, library and local community centre.

Early in 1937 Gropius was appointed Senior Professor of Architecture at Harvard University, and the following year he became Chairman of the Department of Architecture. He quickly began work on a house for his own occupation. A modern version of the traditional New England house, it has much of the classic serenity of the houses that he had designed for himself and the Bauhaus teachers in 1926.

For the first four years after his arrival he entered into partnership with Marcel Breuer, who had followed him from England. Between 1943 and 1948 Gropius resumed his experiments with standardized building elements for mass-produced housing which he had begun in Germany in 1932. His new experiments, chiefly with houses composed of timber panels based on a module both horizontally and vertically of 40 inches, were made in collaboration with Konrad Wachsmann in Long Island, and examples were erected on a considerable scale in California.

In 1945 Gropius went into partnership with several architects of the younger generation forming a team of eight under the name of " The Architects, Collaborative ". In this enterprise Gropius was the guide and leading spirit. That he was able to work enthusiastically with so large a group demonstrates his great belief in the value of team work, which he had always felt to be necessary in modern building. Buildings for which the team has been responsible include the Harvard University Graduate Centre, Cambridge, Massachusetts (1949-50), the McCormick office buildings in Chicago (1953), and the United States embassy building in Athens (1961). In recent years Gropius's name reappeared on English building sites as a result of his agreeing to become consulting architect for several big property developments, notably that of the (still vacant) Monico site in Piccadilly Circus.

Gropius's work as a designer of buildings however, though necessary to him as a means of keeping him in touch with the practical problems of a rapidly changing profession, was not as outstanding as his great reputation might suggest; only his Bauhaus building at Dessau can claim a place among the significant buildings of this century. His reputation was due to his vision as an architectural philosopher, his understanding—far in advance of his time—of the nature of architecture's place in the industrialized world of today and his dedication and integrity as a teacher. The whole essence of the challenge that the twentieth-century architect must face was contained in the ideas he spent his life expounding, and the reason why, in the past few years, his name was less frequently than hitherto on the younger architects' lips was simply that those ideas—through Gropius's efforts—had become widely accepted and were no longer revolutionary. Nevertheless, the opportunities the younger generation of architects now enjoys it owes to him more than to anyone else.

Gropius was an honorary F.R.I.B.A., vice-president of the Congrès Internationaux de l'Architecture Moderne (at whose conferences he was a revered and influential figure) and an Honorary R.D.I. In 1956 he was awarded the Royal Gold Medal for Architecture. He presided over numerous international committees including those responsible for appointing and briefing the architects of the Uno building, New York, and the Unesco building, Paris. His writings include *Staatliches Bauhaus* (1923), *Internationale Architektur* (1924), *Bauhaus Bauten* (1933), *The New Architecture and the Bauhaus* (1935) and *Bauhaus 1919-28* (1939) this last edited with his wife Ilse Frank and Herbert Bayer.

The Times
8th December 1884

DEATH OF M. DE LESSEPS.

PARIS, DEC. 7.

I had telegraphed to-day for news of M. de Lesseps to La Chesnaye, his country house, where he has been living for some time. I know that his family had of late been considerably alarmed as to the state of his health. This evening at 6 o'clock I received in reply a telegram dated five minutes past 4 saying :— " Your telegram arrives at the very moment when M. Ferdinand de Lesseps succumbs after a brief illness."

Thus disappears in a distant and almost unknown corner of the country the man of whom his fellow-countrymen had shown themselves so proud, " the great Frenchman," who, with M. Pasteur, has been among the greatest glories of contemporary France. It was his indomitable ardour, his irresistible desire to endow the world with another short cut between oceans, his ambition to add one more ray of glory to the aureole of the engineering genius of his country that drew him into the impossible Panama undertaking. The insatiable tribe of unscrupulous men who are always on the look-out for a stroke of business laid in the way of his impetuous inexperience all sorts of snares, into which he fell. He thought to dominate the waters of the Chagres and the rock of the Culebra as he had done the sands of the desert ; and, up to the last moment, so convinced was he that it was with the greatest difficulty he was induced to accept the canal with locks. Such a compromise he considered as unworthy of his conception, as incomplete, and as humiliating for modern engineering genius. He used to say :—" The dredges have never deceived me ; they have always fulfilled the task demanded of them, and they always will do so. The Culebra will disappear ; we shall give the waters of the Chagres 20 different beds ; we shall scatter it over the plain, and the tamed river will carry our peaceful fleets, in the passage of which the Culebra will no longer place any obstacles."

And up to the very last, in spite of all opposition, he remained unalterably convinced as to the feasibility of a canal at sea level uniting the Atlantic and the Pacific. In this the engineer and the contractor may have conceived a mad design, but the man had cherished a grand dream. As The Times said yesterday, " Some men cannot get on without a pet aversion." Upon such men, capable of such jealousy and such hate, the glory of a De Lesseps weighs heavily. They are satisfied only when they have succeeded in throwing mud upon this glory, and so this passion for delation, which rages here so violently at certain times, which furnished thousands of victims to the executioner of the Revolution, which breeds the anonymous letter-writer, which fans the flame of each fresh scandal, which finds its home in the columns of a certain sort of newspaper, demanding the dishonour of one man, the expulsion of another, and the arrest of a third—this shameful passion for delation burst forth with a savage glee indiscriminately against Ferdinand de Lesseps and against all connected with him. But posterity will doubtless recognize that he succumbed not to the lust of riches, but to the glorious temptation of once more rendering a service to humanity and civilization. From Suez remained to him one founders' share bought with his wife's dowry. From Panama he emerged by selling that founders' share in order to pay to the liquidator 675,000f. as final amends for his mistake. Up to the very last, with a blindness which is his supreme justification, he placed all his savings, as well as those of his wife and children, in Panama bonds ; and he would now have left his family quite without resources if the Suez Canal Company had not set apart for them a sum which saves them from destitution. —Our Own Correspondent.

The Times
8th January 1795

On Saturday last, at his seat in Staffordshire, Mr. Wedgwood, so well known for his great improvement in Staffordshire ware. His death was in consequence of a decayed tooth, which caused a mortification.

Manchester Guardian
22nd November 1898

Sir John Fowler, Bart., a famous engineer, died on Sunday night. One of the greatest of his works—which he carried out in conjunction with Sir B. Baker—was the stupendous Forth Bridge.

Art

Some of what is now looked upon as rubbish will no doubt come to be regarded as masterpieces of the twentieth century – perhaps even some of what is now looked upon at all only by its author. Presumably it is for reasons to do with this sort of time-lag that painters who have revolutionized our ideas about painting, who have shown us how to see the world in a new way, went quite unrecognized at the time of their deaths. Neither Goya, Cézanne, nor van Gogh, for instance, were recorded. **Kandinsky**, the Expressionist, **Constable** and **Turner**, by contrast, were given all due recognition, as was **Millais**, our chosen pre-Raphaelite – who was suitably notorious as well as popular, creating, together with Rosetti and Hunt, an image of the painter as a bohemian which still has force. From the Impressionists, who more than anyone in the nineteenth century painted an altogether new world, there is **Monet**, doing duty, of course, for a host of others. **Toulouse-Lautrec**, with his insistence on and obsession with simple and primitive forms, did much to set the twentieth century scene, as did **Renoir**. **Munch**, the Norwegian who began painting directly what others felt rather than what he himself saw, epitomises the interiorisation of modern painting, and together with **Picasso**, whose name is of course synonymous with modernism, will surely be remembered even if all the others should eventually be pushed into the background. **Pollock** stands here for the Action Painters of the fifties, dripping paint onto canvas, riding bicycles over it, and generally causing some to wonder at how the frontiers of art were being pushed back, and others most perhaps at the extent to which self-indulgence could pass for art. No such reservations will ever greet the work of **Rodin**, who sculpted classical beauty out of stone, or that of **Mathew Brady**, the legendary American mid-nineteenth century photographer, who helped turn a new-fangled gimmick into an art-form.

New York Times
14th August 1896

SIR JOHN MILLAIS DEAD

PRESIDENT OF THE ENGLISH ROYAL ACADEMY DIES AT LONDON.

The End of a Long Battle with Disease—A Painter from Boyhood, He Achieved Many Successes Early in Life—Shunned the Beaten Paths and Pictured Nature as He Saw It—Some of His Most Famous Creations.

LONDON, Aug. 13.—Sir John E. Millais died to-day, after a long illness, of cancer of the throat.

He underwent the operation of tracheotomy for the relief of cancer of the throat May 16, and never fully rallied from its effects, which immediately caused his death.

It was on Feb. 20 of the present year that Sir John Everett Millais rounded out his artistic career by becoming President of the Royal Academy of England. The attainment of that position was the logical result of his talents and of the use he had made of them. This statement is highest eulogy

Sir J. E. Millais, R. A.,
Who Died in London Yesterday.

or severest criticism, according to the view which one takes of art and its aims and ends, according to the weight which one attaches to popular approval and material success, and according to the opinion which one holds as to the present status of the Royal Academy. There are room and reason for wide difference of belief on all these points, and an obituary is hardly the place in which to do more than intimate that the artistic principles and practice of its subject were not on the plane deemed loftiest by not a few even of those critics who recognize most cordially his high ability.

A typical Briton in appearance and character it was not by accident that the painter's name is distinctly French. Though born at Southampton, (in 1829,) Millais came of a Jersey family that is said to have been prominent among the island's lesser landlords long prior to the Norman conquest, and which is still represented there.

Millais's vocation was clear at a very early age. From boyhood, almost from infancy, he was a painter. When nine years old he was a pupil in the Sass Academy at London, and won a medal from the Society of Arts with a drawing from the antique; when eleven he became a student in the Royal Academy, and within twelve months was composing intricate arrangements of figures and horses that would have been creditable suggestions for a man of thirty. At fourteen he took the Academy silver medal, and at eighteen a gold medal, the school's highest honor.

Notwithstanding his early successes, perhaps on account of them, Millais revolted against the routine conventions of academic teaching, and in connection with Dante Gabriel Rossetti, Holman Hunt, and others—they were seven in all—he helped to found the "Pre-Raphaelite Brotherhood," a curious organization, whose motto was "Truth," and whose aim was to generalize nothing, but to paint nature as it appeared to themselves, not as it appeared in "the antique." For a short time these young artists tried to explain their views by means of the pen as well as the brush, and published a periodical called The Germ; or, Art and Poetry. The principal works executed by Millais while under the pre-Raphaelite influence were "Christ in the House of His Parents" and "Ferdinand Lured by Ariel," in 1850; "Mariana in the Moated Grange" and "The Woodman's Daughter," in 1851; in 1852, "The Huguenot" and "Ophelia," and in 1853, "The Order of Release," the last enjoying the distinction of being protected at the Royal Academy by a rail to keep back the crowds of people that thronged about it.

Millais was elected an Associate of the Royal Academy in 1853, and became a full member in December, 1863. He exhibited "The Proscribed Royalist" in 1853, "The Rescue" in 1855, "Peace Concluded," "Autumn Leaves," and "L'Enfant du Regiment" in 1856; "A Dream of the Past—Sir Isumbras at the Ford" in 1857; "The Heretic" in 1858, "Vale of Rest" and "Spring Flowers" in 1860, "The Black Brunswicker" in 1861, "My First Sermon" in 1863, "My Second Sermon" and "Charlie Is My

Darling" in 1864, "Joan of Arc" and "The Romans Leaving Britain" in 1865, and "Sleeping," "Waking," and "Jephthah" in 1867; "Sisters Rosalind and Celia," "Stella," "Pilgrims to St. Paul's," and "Souvenir of Velasquez" (his diploma work) in 1868; "The Gambler's Wife," "Vanessa," "The End of the Chapter," and "A Dream at Dawn" in 1869; "A Flood," "The Knight Errant," "The Boyhood of Raleigh," and "A Widow's Mite" in 1870; "Chill October," "Joshua Fighting with Amelek," "A Somnambulist," and "Yes or No" in 1871; "Flowing to the River" and "Flowing to the Sea" in 1872; "Early Days," "New-Laid Eggs," and "Lalla Rookh" in 1873; "Scotch Firs," "Winter Fuel," "The Picture of Health," "The Northwest Passage," "Still for a Moment," and "A Day Dream" in 1874; "The Fringe of the Moor," "The Crown of Love," and "No!" in 1875; "Forbidden Fruit," "Over the Hills and Far Away," and "Getting Better" in 1876; "A Yeoman of the Guard," "The Sound of Many Waters," and "Yes!" in 1877; "The Princes in the Tower," "A Jersey Lily," (Mrs. Langtry,) and "St. Martin's Summer" in 1878. In 1878 Millais also exhibited "A Good Resolve" in the Grosvenor Gallery, and "The Bride of Lammermoor" in King Street, St. James's.

He exhibited at the Royal Academy "The Tower of Strength" and a portrait of Gladstone in 1879; a portrait of himself (painted by invitation) for the collection of portraits of artists painted by themselves, in the Uffizi Gallery, Florence; "Cuckoo" and a portrait of Mr. Bright in 1880; portrait of Principal Caird, D. D.; "Cinderella," and portraits of the Earl of Beaconsfield and of Dr. Fraser, Bishop of Salisbury, and "Forget-Me-Not" in 1883. A large number of these, as well as some later pictures, were brought together in the exhibition of the artist's work held at the Grosvenor Gallery in the early months of 1886.

Manchester, in 1881; a portrait of Cardinal Newman in 1882; "Une Grande Dame," "The Grey Lady," a portrait of the Marquis of Salisbury, and "Forget-Me-Not" "Mercy," "Lilac," and a portrait of Lord Rosebery were his chief pictures in 1887. In 1890 he exhibited in the Royal Academy "The Moon Is Up and Yet It Is Not Night," and portraits of "The Right Hon. W. E. Gladstone and His Grandson." In 1893 he exhibited a portrait of John Hare and "The Girlhood of Saint Theresa," but showed nothing in 1894. He was decorated with the ribbon of the Legion of Honor in 1878. In 1881 he was appointed a Trustee of the National Portrait Gallery, in the place of the late Dean Stanley, and in 1882 he was elected a Foreign Associate of the Académie des Beaux-Arts, in place of the Italian sculptor, Dupre.

In 1885 Millais was knighted by the Queen; in 1883 he had been elected a member of the Institute of France. He was also a member of the Academies of Edinburgh, Antwerp, Madrid, and Rome. He married the divorced wife of John Ruskin, and leaves a family of several children. One daughter married Lieut. William Thompson of the army, and one son is an occasional writer on art topics in the English magazines. Mrs. Lester Wallack is a sister of Millais.

Up to very recently Millais was a man of splendid physique and robust health. Even at the time of his election as President of the Royal Academy, however, he had begun to fail, and there were doubts if he could long perform the duties of the office, which, socially at least, are somewhat onerous. The immediate cause of death was a cancer of the throat. It took the form of a growth on the vocal cords, and for some months was not regarded as serious. The disease suddenly became malignant. Several operations, including that of tracheotomy, were performed during the last ten days, but it was known that no permanent good effects could result from them. Sir John died in his magnificent house in Palace Gate, Kensington, London, where it had been his custom to entertain lavishly the most prominent people of the city, and where royalty was very often his guest.

New York Times
12th August 1956

8 Killed in 2 L. I. Auto Crashes; Jackson Pollock Among Victims

Special to The New York Times.

SOUTHAMPTON, L. I., Aug. 11 — Eight persons were killed and at least four others were injured in two separate automobile accidents near here tonight.

One of the dead was identified as Jackson Pollock, abstract painter. He was 44 years old.

A head-on collision on Montauk Highway at 10:43 P. M., four miles west of Southampton village, took the lives of six persons and injured three others.

The accident occurred when eastbound and westbound automobiles crashed at a curve on the two-lane highway in the Shinnecock Hills section of Southampton Town.

Mr. Pollock's convertible turned over three miles north of East Hampton, according to witnesses. The accident occurred shortly after 10 P. M. on Fireplace Road.

A woman riding in the car was killed and another woman, identified by Southampton hospital authorities as Ruth Kligman, was injured. The police were unable to determine the cause of the accident, but said the automobile had smashed into an embankment.

Three ambulances from Southampton Hospital were sent to the scene of the two-car crash. One of the injured died shortly after arriving at the hospital. He was identified as Walter Smith Jr. of Riverhead.

Two other dead were identified as Victor E. Prusinowski Jr., 29, and his wife, Vera, 26. The police were not able to identify three dead women. Three other injured were Mr. Smith's wife, and his brother and sister-in-law, Mr. and Mrs. Joseph Smith.

Traffic on the highway, also known as Route 27, was backed up for half a mile in both directions and was tied up for an hour and a half.

Technique Was Unorthodox

Mr. Pollock became known for an unorthodox painting technique of putting his canvas flat on the floor and dripping paint onto it. Some critics praised his paintings as "the most original art among the painters of his generation," while others dismissed his work as "unorganized explosions of random energy."

Once a student of Thomas Hart Benton, Mr. Pollock turned away from his teacher's "American Scene" realism and developed his own abstract style. After his one-man show in 1943, he had ten solo exhibitions in New York within eleven years, and won recognition in Europe as a leading abstract expressionist.

Mr. Pollock was married to Lee Krasner, an established painter in her own right. Acquaintances here said that she was now in Europe. For the last ten years the couple had been living near East Hampton, where Mr. Pollock converted a near-by barn into a studio.

Mr. Pollock was born in 1912 on his father's farm near Cody, Wyo. He grew up in Wyoming, Arizona and California. Showing an aptitude for painting, he left Los Angeles High School at 17 to travel to New York, where he studied at the Art Students League for two years.

It was there, Mr. Pollock once said, that Benton gave him the "only formal instruction" he ever had.

In the early Forties he reacted against his earlier naturalistic approach and began painting in a semi-abstract, experssionist idiom.

By 1947 he had evolved the "dripped paint" technique that characterized the best-known period of his work.

A retrospective show covering eighteen years of his work opened at the Sidney Janis Gallery in November, 1955. The exhibtion comprised sixteen canvases representing the artist's different artistic periods.

The New York Times critic commented at the time on "the ruthless steps he has taken to shatter the conventions of art and introduce, for the first time in art, raw and naked, the elemental and largely subconscious promptings of his creative nature".

Daily Telegraph
11th September 1901

The death under distressing circumstances is reported to-day of one of the finest and most original contemporary black and white artists, Toulouse Lautrec. He was only thirty-five, but for three years past had suffered from mental disease, to which, after repeated rallies, followed by relapses, he has succumbed. He was one of the originators of the modern artistic poster, and Dudley Hardy may be said to belong to his school. His style inclined to the grotesque, but his satirical pictures of odd bits and bizarre, sometimes sordid, scenes of Parisian life were always strongly characteristic and spiritedly vigorous in treatment.

The Times
4th December 1919

A FAMOUS IMPRESSIONIST.

DEATH OF M. AUGUSTE RENOIR.
(FROM OUR OWN CORRESPONDENT.)

The death is announced, on the Riviera at the age of 78, of the Impressionist painter Auguste Renoir, some of whose happiest canvases are to be seen in the Luxembourg Gallery. Renoir began life as a porcelain painter at Limoges, where he was born. He came to Paris towards the end of the Second Empire, and soon fell under the influence of the Impressionists. The life of Montmartre and the Quartier Latin, open air scenes, and portraits were all alike treated by him with a fascinating freshness of heart and eye which eventually won recognition.

The Times
23rd December 1851

DEATH OF J. M. W. TURNER, Esq., R. A.

The fine arts in this country have not produced a more remarkable man than Joseph Mallord William Turner, whose death it was yesterday our duty to record; and although it would here be out of place to revive the discussions occasioned by the peculiarities of Mr. Turner's style in his later years, he has left behind him sufficient proofs of the variety and fertility of his genius to establish an undoubted claim to a prominent rank among the painters of England. His life had been extended to the verge of human existence; for, although he was fond of throwing mystery over his precise age, we believe that he was born in Maiden-lane, Covent-garden, in the year 1775, and was consequently, in his 76th or 77th year. Of humble origin, he enjoyed the advantages of an accurate rather than a liberal education. His first studies, some of which are still in existence, were in architectural design; and few of those who have been astonished or enchanted by the profusion and caprice of form and colour in his mature pictures would have guessed the minute and scientific precision with which he had cultivated the arts of linear drawing and perspective. His early manhood was spent partly on the coast, where he imbibed his inexhaustible attachment for marine scenery and his acquaintance with the wild and varied aspect of the ocean. Somewhat later he repaired to Oxford, where he contributed for several years the drawing to the *University Almanac*. But his genius was rapidly breaking through all obstacles, and even the repugnance of public opinion; for, before he had completed his 30th year he was on the high road to fame. As early as 1790 he exhibited his first work, a watercoloured drawing of the entrance to Lambeth, at the exhibition of the Academy; and in 1793 his first oil painting. In November, 1799, he was elected an associate, and in February, 1802, he attained the rank of a Royal Academician. We shall not here attempt to trace the vast series of his paintings from his earlier productions, such as the "Wreck," in Lord Yarborough's collection, the "Italian Landscape," in the same gallery, the *pendant* to Lord Ellesmere's Vanderwelde, or Mr. Munro's "Venus and Adonis," in the Titianesque manner, to the more obscure, original, and, as some think, unapproachable productions of his later years, such as the "Rome," the "Venice," the "Golden Bough," the "Téméraire," and the "Tusculum." But while these great works proceeded rapidly from his palette, his powers of design were no less actively engaged in the exquisite water-coloured drawings that have formed the basis of the modern school of "illustration." The "Liber studiorum" had been commenced in 1807 in imitation of Claude's "Liber veritatis," and was etched, if we are not mistaken, by Turner's own hand. The titlepage was engraved and altered half-a-dozen times from his singular and even nervous attention to the most trifling details. But this volume was only the precursor of an immense series of drawings and sketches, embracing the topography of this country in the "River Scenery" and the "Southern Coast"—the scenery of the Alps, of Italy, and great part of Europe—and the ideal creations of our greatest poets, from Milton to Scott and Rogers, all imbued with the brilliancy of a genius which seemed to address itself more peculiarly to the world at large when it adopted the popular form of engraving. These drawings are now widely diffused in England, and form the basis of several important collections, such as those of Petworth, of Mr. Windus, Mr. Fawkes, and Mr. Munro. So great is the value of them that 120 guineas have not unfrequently been paid for a small sketch in water-colours; and a sketchbook, containing chalk drawings of one of Turner's river tours on the continent, has lately fetched the enormous sum of 600 guineas. The prices of his more finished oil paintings have ranged in the last few years from 700 to 1,200 or 1,400 guineas. All his works may now be said to have acquired triple or quadruple the value originally paid for them. Mr. Turner undoubtedly realized a very large fortune, and great curiosity will be felt to ascertain the posthumous use he has made of it. His personal habits were peculiar, and even penurious, but in all that related to his art he was generous to munificence, and we are not without hope that his last intentions were for the benefit of the nation, and the preservation of his own fame. He was never married, he was not known to have any relations, and his wants were limited to the strictest simplicity. The only ornaments of his house in Queen Anne-street were the pictures by his own hand, which he had constantly refused to part with at any price, among which the "Rise and Fall of Carthage" and the "Crossing the Brook" rank among the choicest specimens of his finest manner.

Mr. Turner seldom took much part in society, and only displayed in the closest intimacy the shrewdness of his observation and the playfulness of his wit. Everywhere he kept back much of what was in him, and while the keenest intelligence, mingled with a strong tinge of satire, animated his brisk countenance, it seemed to amuse him to be but half understood. His nearest social ties were those formed in the Royal Academy, of which he was by far the oldest member, and to whose interests he was most warmly attached. He filled at one time the chair of Professor of Perspective, but without conspicuous success, and that science has since been taught in the Academy by means better suited to promote it than a course of lectures. In the composition and execution of his works Mr. Turner was jealously sensitive of all interference or supervision. He loved to deal in the secrets and mysteries of his art, and many of his peculiar effects are produced by means which it would not be easy to discover or to imitate.

We hope that the Society of Arts or the British Gallery will take an early opportunity of commemorating the genius of this great artist, and of reminding the public of the prodigious range of his pencil, by forming a general exhibition of his principal works, if, indeed, they are not permanently gathered in a nobler repository. Such an exhibition will serve far better than any observations of ours to demonstrate that it is not by those deviations from established rules which arrest the most superficial criticism that Mr. Turner's fame or merit are to be estimated. For nearly 60 years Mr. Turner contributed largely to the arts of this country. He lived long enough to see his greatest productions rise to uncontested supremacy, however imperfectly they were understood when they first appeared in the earlier years of this century; and, though in his later works and in advanced age, force and precision of execution have not accompanied his vivacity of conception, public opinion has gradually and steadily advanced to a more just appreciation of his power. He is the Shelley of English painting—the poet and the painter both alike veiling their own creations in the dazzling splendour of the imagery with which they are surrounded, mastering every mode of expression, combining scientific labour with an air of negligent profusion, and producing in the end works in which colour and language are but the vestments of poetry. Of such minds it may be said in the words of Alastor:—

" " Nature's most secret steps
" He, like her shadow, has pursued, where'er
" The red volcano overcanopies
" Its fields of snow and pinnacles of ice
" With burning smoke ; or where the starry domes
" Of diamond and of gold expand above
" Numberless and immeasurable halls,
" Frequent with crystal column and clear shrines
" Of pearl, and thrones radiant with chrysolite.
" Nor had that scene of ampler majesty
" Than gems or gold—the varying roof of heaven
" And the green earth—lost in his heart its claims
" To love and wonder . . . . . . "

It will devolve on our contemporaries, more exclusively devoted than ourselves to the history of the fine arts to record with greater fulness and precision the works of Mr. Turner's long and active life; but in these hasty recollections we have endeavoured to pay a slight tribute to the memory of a painter who possessed many of the gifts of his art in extraordinary abundance, and who certainly in dying leaves not his like behind. He will be buried, by his own desire, in St. Paul's Cathedral, by the side of Sir Joshua Reynolds.

The Times
29th January 1944

HR. EDVARD MUNCH

NORWEGIAN EXPRESSIONIST PAINTER

Hr. Edvard Munch, who died in Oslo on January 23, was the best-known of modern Norwegian painters.

Munch was born at Loten, Norway, on December 12, 1863, son of Christian Munch, a doctor of medicine. In 1882 he became an art student in Christiania and in 1889 he settled for a while in Paris, where he made contact with impressionists like Monet and Pissarro, and took a special interest in the *pointillisme* of Seurat. Moving to Berlin in 1892, he exhibited that year by invitation at the Verein Berliner Künstler, and his canvases caused such controversy that the show was closed. His characteristic style, comprehending rough colour, and dramatic, swirling compositions of grim subjects, was crystallized about this time. After periods of work in Berlin and Paris, with the summers spent in Norway, at Aasgaardstrand, came his great " Frieze of Life " in 1907. This was sold in 1912 and distributed between museums in Berlin, Lubeck, and Oslo. About this time his style showed extensive changes, and lines of colour criss-crossing vertically and horizontally displayed the mark of neo-impressionism.

From 1912 onwards Munch travelled extensively, in Germany, France, Switzerland, and Italy, often in connexion with exhibitions of his work. The most important of these was in Berlin, in 1927, where nearly 250 works were shown. Considerable historical importance must attach to the painting of Munch, in that he was virtually the founder of the German movement that became known as Expressionism. Round him there formed a group which called itself *die Brücke*, and its various members spread the style which dominated German art before the 1914-18 war and in the ensuing years until the Hitler régime brought about an enforced reorientation.

New York Times
19th December 1944

KANDINSKY, LEADER IN MODERN ART, 78

Internationally Known Dean of Non-Objective Painters Dead —Works Displayed Here

Wassily Kandinsky, internationally known dean of non-objective painters whose works were widely exhibited in this country, died Sunday in Paris, it was announced here yesterday by the Solomon R. Guggenheim Foundation. He was 78 years old.

Noted for the gaiety, lyric feeling and brilliant color of his oils and water-colors, Mr. Kandinsky had been engaged since the start of the century in non-objective painting—the presentation of color compositions without obvious picturization. His love for his work was demonstrated in Paris three years ago, under Nazi occupation, when he continued to paint although he had to wear gloves, a hat and an overcoat because of the lack of heat due to the rigors of war.

Born in Moscow, Mr. Kandinsky spent his childhood in Italy, attended the University of Odessa and as a young man was invited to assume the professorship of law and economics at the University of Dorpat in Russia. However, he preferred to work as an artist, and studied in Munich, Paris and Berlin.

His increasing interest in non-objective art led Mr. Kandinsky to write "Upon the Spiritual in Art," a work on his theories of art. In 1912 he and Franz Marc founded in Munich the international artistic movement known as The Blue Rider, which was also the title of a book published by the group.

During the first World War Mr. Kandinsky returned to his native Russia from Germany. After the war he became associated with the Moscow Academy and was director of the Museum of Pictorial Culture in Moscow. He helped found other museums in various parts of Russia. In 1920 he served as Professor of Art at the University of Moscow. The next year he founded the Russian Academy of Artistic Sciences.

In 1922-32 he was Professor of Art at the Bauhaus, which was located first at Weimar and subsequently at another German city, Dessau. Since 1934 Mr. Kandinsky had been working in Paris.

His works can be found in this country at the Museum of Non-Objective Paintings of the Solomon R. Guggenheim Foundation, in the private collection of Miss Peggy Guggenheim, in the Museum of Modern Art in New York and in the Chicago Art Institute.

The Gentleman's Magazine
June 1837 Vol 7

JOHN CONSTABLE, ESQ. R.A.
April 1. In Charlotte st. Fitzroy sq. John Constable, esq. R.A.

Mr. Constable was the son of a miller, near Woodbridge, in Suffolk. Early in life he showed so strong a passion for the arts that it could not be controlled, and his friends placed him under an instructor. Mr. Farringdon, R.A. was his master for some time, and he became a student of the Royal Academy; his improvement was rapid, and he commenced portrait painter, which line he followed with much success for some years, but his taste was decidedly for landscape painting, and he finally abandoned the more lucrative walk of portraiture for the agreeable and congenial one of which he was so fond.

His mode of painting was peculiar, but it embodied much truth and sound principles of art, which will render his works lasting, and far more valuable hereafter than they are at present, though highly esteemed by the best judges.

There is a light and sunny freshness about his pictures which imparts an interest to subjects even so simple as those he was accustomed to paint. He was perhaps more skilled in the real composition and qualities of colours than any other of his brethren in art : and had so far studied the effects, which time and exposure have upon them, that it is well known to his friends that he generally painted his pictures more with a view to their future effect after the lapse of some years, than to their original appearance. The dashes of white with which many of his latter pictures have been so strangely sprinkled, will hereafter (as he contemplated) became far less conspicuous, and the whole effect be harmoniously mellowed.

Mr. Constable was elected a Royal Academician about twelve years ago, from among numerous competitors. He was much under 60 years of age, very active, and not subject to any attacks of illness, and his constitution was considered very sound. He had attended the general assembly of the Royal Academy on the previous evening, in their new edifice, went through the duties with his usual alacrity, and did not complain, or appear at all ailing. He died on the following night of an affection of the heart. Mr. Constable published a few years ago a work on English Landscape. In 1831 appeared a pair of his best landscapes, a view in Suffolk, and another in Essex, engraved in mezzotinto by D. Lucas, 20½ in. by 26.

In private life Mr. Constable was much esteemed by those who were intimate with him. He had inherited from his father a respectable competence. He has left several children to deplore their bereavement; and they are now complete orphans, having lost their mother about six years ago. One of his sons is a youth serving in the navy.

The Sun
9th April 1973

Now a family row over his £20m fortune

PABLO PICASSO, the controversial artist with an unquenchable thirst for painting, women and drink, died yesterday, aged 91.

The extrovert genius — the most famous and influential artist of the century, who once lived by selling his paintings for peanuts and keeping warm by burning his unsold canvasses —left £20million.

He died in his fortress-like villa at Mougins, near Nice, in the South of France, only a month before what would have been his greatest exhibition of paintings.

And only hours after his death from a heart attack, a family row was brewing over who gets his fortune.

EXILED

The Spanish-born Communist, whose Dove of Peace became a world famous symbol, lived in France in self-imposed exile because of his hatred of General Franco's regime.

Picasso, an amazingly prolific one-man art factory, could turn out as many as seven canvasses a day.

Experts believe his genius lay more in the fantastic creative energy than in technical ability, but nobody denies he was also the "inventor" of modern painting.

Picasso's famous "blue period" in Paris in the early 190Js was due to the fact that blue paint was the cheapest available.

Although the master rarely ventured from his villa in the past three years, living happily with his 47-year-old wife Jacqueline, his greater love life was a series of tempestuous affairs.

He had an enormous appetite for women. He had seven mistresses altogether and married two of them.

There was Fernande Olivier and her friend Marcelle Humbert, whom he threw over to wed a Russian ballerina Olga Kokhlova.

Other mistresses followed including Francoise Gilot who bore him two illegitimate children. Then he met and married Jacqueline.

HEIR

Jacqueline should inherit most of the artist's vast wealth but there is bound to be a row because of his complicated love life.

There is a son, Paulo, born to Olga Kokhlova in 1921, who along with Jacqueline is a legal heir. They were with him when he died.

Three years ago, Claude Ruiz - Picasso, born of Picasso' association with Francoise Gilot, tried unsuccessfully in the French courts to establish a claim.

The New York Times
19th January 1896

DEATH OF MATTHEW B. BRADY

The Famous Photographer of War Times Succumbs to Misfortunes at the Presbyterian Hospital.

Matthew B. Brady, the famous war photographer, died at the Presbyterian Hospital Wednesday night, alone and unnoticed. The hospital books state that he died from Bright's disease, but his death was really due to the misfortunes which have befallen him in recent years. He was seventy-two years old.

Matthew Brady has a double claim to remembrance. He was one of the earliest and for many years the leading photographer of this country.

When the Prince of Wales visited the United States, in 1860, as a slim and handsome youth of nineteen, Mr. Brady photographed him. A copy of this photograph was forwarded two years ago to the Prince, who acknowledged the receipt in kindly terms.

Bayard Taylor spoke of Mr. Brady in the days before the war as the "Court photographer."

During the war Mr. Brady engaged a number of photographers, who took upward of 30,000 pictures of battle scenes, showing famous battlefields as they appeared before and after some of the greatest conflicts of the war. Nearly every important paper and illustrated magazine published during war times made use of these photographs.

He hoped the Government would purchase the complete collection, and, although the War Department took the bulk of them, the photographer was never repaid for the time and money he spent.

When he became old and nearly blind, and finally had the additional misfortune to meet with a carriage accident, Mr. Brady became practically dependent upon the kindness of his friends.

He was a veteran of the Seventh Regiment, and was cared for by members of that organization and the Artist's Fund Society. It was through their efforts that he was admitted to the Presbyterian Hospital.

Among those whose photographs Mr. Brady took were Webster, Clay, Calhoun, Benton, the two Van Burens, Lincoln, Seward, Chase, "Dolly" Madison, Mrs. Hamilton, ... ane.

New York Times
18th November 1917

RODIN, FAMOUS SCULPTOR, DEAD

Frenchman Distinguished for His Realism Dies at His Villa Near Paris at 77.

FOUGHT CRITICS 50 YEARS

His "La France" Presented by France to America—"The Thinker" in Metropolitan Museum.

PARIS, Nov. 17.—Auguste Rodin, the famous sculptor, died in his villa at Meudon, in the outskirts of Paris, after an illness of a few days.

Had he lived, M. Rodin would have been elected a member of the Academy of Fine Arts by almost a unanimous vote a week from today.

Paul Laurens, the painter, said of Auguste Rodin: "He belongs to the race of those men who march alone."

And for most of the seventy-seven years of his life the great sculptor marched alone, first battling his way against the adversities of relentless poverty and hostile criticism and, in the latter years of his life, alone at the head of an international army of enthusiastic admirers.

When Rodin presented one of his early pieces to the Academy of Fine Arts he was told that his work did not "exhibit any evidence of talent," and some fifty years or so later critics in many places were hailing him as the greatest sculptor of the world—save Michael Angelo—since Pheidias and Praxiteles. He faced starvation in his youth because he could not sell his statues, and in October, 1916, the French Chamber of Deputies accepted his gift of his works and art collections, valued at $400,000, and gave him for life the use of the Biron mansion in Paris, which became known through the Parliamentary act as the Rodin Museum.

François Auguste Rodin was born in Paris on Nov. 12, 1840, of wretchedly poor parents. He entered a free drawing school in the Latin Quarter at the age of 14 and, after several years of study, made a model in clay of one of his companions, with which he tried to win entrance to the Academy of Fine Arts. He failed. Some time later he tried again, and again was denied. A third attempt resulted in the third failure.

His First Masterpiece.

Rodin was not discouraged by his failures at the Academy of Fine Arts. He had no means, and was obliged to consort with the very poorest in Paris, yet he struggled on and submitted his work at every public examination that was held, always without success. Fortunately he came at last under the notice of Barye, the painter and sculptor of animals, who carried his artistic education to the point from which Rodin could pursue it alone. At the age of 23, before embarking on a determined struggle to fame and fortune, the future sculptor married. This move served as an incentive, and spurred him on in his task, for in less than twelve months he had produced his first masterpiece, entitled "L'homme au nez cassé." This was submitted to the judges at the Salon in 1864 and promptly refused; he took it home and treasured it carefully. One of his first cares when, in after years his countrymen had recognized his talent, was to have this bust cast in bronze, in which form it crossed the Channel, and was shown at the Grosvenor Gallery in 1881.

After the Franco-German war, during which he was forced to endure the siege of Paris, Rodin migrated to Brussels, where he executed a great deal of work, besides sending two busts to the Paris Salon; both were accepted, and were placed on exhibition in 1875. Two years later the master was further recognized with the "Age d'Airain," or "Primeval Man," which represents one of the first inhabitants of our world, physically perfect, but in the infancy of comprehension. The claims of this amazing statue could not be overlooked by the Salon committee when Rodin brought the work to Paris. So realistic, indeed, was it that some of the sculptor's critics hinted that the figure must have been molded from the living model.

He Aimed for Realism.

But Rodin was not yet free from harsh criticism and ridicule. The school of orthodoxy in sculpture was as hostile to him as were the orthodox musicians to Wagner. Rodin did not idealize his subjects, but aimed for realism, going to nature for his inspiration. To him all nature was life, and, life was art. He saw in the shaking form of an old man or woman, with bowed head and bent and twisted limbs, something as worthy of artistic expression as a Venus or Apollo. And he was a worker in mass, producing his subjects in detail only so far as would bring out his dominating conception. His work, therefore, had less of finished form than that of the conventional artists, and his recognition by them was, therefore, delayed until by the very power of his work he forced himself upon them.

Even after he had won fame Rodin's work was sometimes ridiculed. His statue of Balzac, for example, was received with jest and gibe. It was an extraordinary and unconventional conception of the great novelist, which Rodin executed upon commission from the Society of Men of Letters. The Parisian public became so worked up over the merits of the monument that the controversy for the time eclipsed interest even in the sensational Dreyfus trial. Balzac was represented in a voluminous dressing gown, the features and figure roughly sketched. Critics exclaimed that it was "an enormous porpoise standing upright, draped in a thick bath wrapper." They called it grotesque, huge, and flippant; while, on the other side, there were those who saw in it "the incarnation of the great writer's soul." The society which had ordered it, however, held the majority view that the work was incomprehensible, if not ridiculous, and it gave the commission to the sculptor Falguière, who executed a more conventional work in the following year. Rodin's Victor Hugo was received with more appreciation, and by many is considered one of his masterpieces.

A Tireless Worker.

The sculptor was a tireless worker, the quantity of his work being as amazing as its quality. His greatest output in one year was in 1889. No less than thirty-one pieces of sculpture were put on view at the Georges Petit Gallery in that year, among them being some of the best of Rodin's life-work, such as "Ugolino," "The Danaid," "The Thinker," "Bastien Lepage," and "The Bourgeois of Calais." For quality, quantity, and quickness the production was unique.

For years after the Balzac controversy Rodin devoted himself to a great decorative composition some twenty feet high, "The Portal of Hell," for the Museum of Decorative Arts. This work was inspired mainly by Dante's Inferno, the poet himself being seated at the top, while at his feet is the writhing of passion and anguish of despair. The figure of "The Thinker," which is one of Rodin's best-known works in America, has been exhibited in cast for several years at the Metropolitan Museum of Fine Arts in New York, and at various other places. It is one of the figures designed for this titanic representation of "The Portal of Hell."

His Bust of "La France"

A bronze bust of "La France" by Rodin was presented to the United States by the people of France during the tercentenary celebration of the discovery of Lake Champlain, and has since been mounted on a monument to Champlain at Crown Point, N. Y. In addition M. Rodin had executed busts for a number of wealthy Americans, and the Metropolitan Museum of Art through a gift of $25,000 by Thomas Fortune Ryan, has obtained the largest single collection of the works of Rodin outside the artist's own studios. There are forty examples of his works in the New York Museum.

Rodin in his later life received many [...] M. Whistler he sent a collection of his works to England as a token of admiration of the British troops, and later he executed a deed of gift to the French Government of the entire collection of his own works, other art objects he had acquired, and the Hotel Biron in which they were assembled for a museum.

Rodin's drawings are almost as wonderful as his sculptor work. A valuable album containing over a hundred plates, with an aggregate of 142 drawings, was published some years ago by Messrs. Goupil. In more recent times the experiments made by the great sculptor with his pencil were on behalf of personal friends. He illustrated Bergerat's "Enguerrande," Octave Mirabeau's "Jardin des Supplices," and ornamented a copy of Baudelaire's "Fleurs du Mal."

New York Herald Tribune
6th December 1926

Claude Monet, Noted Nature Painter, Dies

Father of Impressionism and Dean of Modern School of Artists Succumbs in 86th Year at Home in France

Clemenceau at Bedside

Former Premier Overcome at End of Life - Long Friend Helped in War

From the Herald Tribune Paris Bureau
Copyright, 1926, New York Tribune Inc.
PARIS, Dec. 5.—Claude Monet, world famous painter and intimate friend of Georges Clemenceau, died at 10 o'clock this morning at his home in the artists' colony at Giverny, in the Eure Department. M. Clemenceau was at his bedside. The former Premier was overcome by death of his lifelong friend, who had been an inspiration in war time.

The artist, who had recently celebrated his eighty-fifth birthday, had been seriously ill for several weeks and failed slowly during the last week. The funeral will be held on Wednesday, according to advices reaching here to-night.

Pioneer of His School

The last of the famous "Impressionists" of French pictorial art in the nineteenth century might in a direct sense be called also the first of them, for it was he who gave them their name. In 1874 he exhibited a painting called "Impression — Rising Sun," which attracted much attention and was hailed as the harbinger of a new school of art, which thereafter became known as Impressionist. This pioneer, Claude Monet, was born in Paris on November 14 1840. When he was five years old his family moved to Havre, where he passed his boyhood. He led a most irregular life, neglecting school and devoting his time there in filling his textbooks with caricatures and drawings.

"My youth," he has said, "was essentially that of a vagabond. I made wreaths on the margins of my books; I decorated the blue paper of my copy-books with ultra-fantastical ornaments. At fifteen I was known all over Havre as a caricaturist. My reputation was so well established, that I was sought on all sides and asked for caricature portraits. The abundance of orders and the insufficiency of the subsidies derived from maternal generosity inspired me with a bold resolve which naturally scandalized my family. I took money for my portraits. According to the appearance of my clients, I charged 15 to 20 francs for each portrait, and the scheme worked beautifully. In a month my patrons had doubled in number. I was now able to charge 20 francs in all cases without lessening the number of orders. If I had kept on I would to-day be a millionaire.

"At sixteen one feels rich with 2,000 francs. I obtained from several picture lovers who protected Boudin and who had relations with Monginot, with Troyon, with Amand Gautier, some letters of introduction and set out post haste for Paris.

"It took me some little time at first to decide on my line of action. I called on the artists to whom I had letters. I received from them excellent advice; I received also some very bad advice. Did not Troyon want me to enter the studio of Couture? It is needless to tell you how decided was my refusal to do so. I admit even that it cooled me, temporarily at least, in my esteem for Troyon."

At the age of twenty he enlisted in the army and at his own insistent request was assigned to a regiment in Algeria, where he spent two years. Sent home as an invalid, he lived for a time with Toulmouche, the painter, who had married one of his cousins and who recommended him to study under Gleyre. But Gleyre was a conventional Classicist, who criticized his pupil's work because he painted his models as they were, and not as they should have been. So Monet left him, along with Renoir, Sisley and others, to follow his own bent.

Jongkind His Real Master

He next fell in with Jongkind, who, he has said, was thereafter his real master and to whom he owed the final education of his eyes. Three years later he exhibited at the Salon two marine views, which were hung on the line and received much praise. Thereupon, along with Degas, Cezanne and Duranty, he "went back to nature" in open-air painting.

When the war of 1870 broke out he went to England, where Daubigny befriended him by introducing him to Durand-Ruel, who put his works on exhibition in his well known gallery. This was the beginning of his prosperity, though he still had years of struggle before him. For a score of years he had to contend with hostile criticism and ridicule, but these never swerved him from the course he had adopted. He spent much time in Holland, England and Italy, before finally establishing himself at Giverny, in France.

Before his use of the word "Impression" in 1874 he had produced many pictures of varied types, such as "The Breakfast," "Camille," "Fontainebleau Forest," "Vessels Leaving Havre" and numerous landscapes. Some of these are in the Louvre, and the Luxembourg Gallery. There followed, in 1874 and later, a remarkable series of studies of cathedrals, particularly of that of Rouen—variations of the same theme, in different conditions of light. One of these represents him in the Metropoli-

tan Museum of Art—a loan from the late Theodore M. Davis.

In the closing years of his productive life he maintained his fondness for pictures of cathedrals, and also painted many sea and suncoast views. In the early years of the present century he busied himself with a notable series of views in London. The late M. Caillebotte purchased a number of his works and bequeathed them to the Luxembourg Museum in Paris. The latest years of his activity were spent at his home at Giverny, making numerous studies of the same scenes in different lights and at different seasons of the year. Of some subjects he thus made as many as a dozen completed studies each.

When he approached the age of fourscore he began to be troubled with cataract, and was thus much hampered in his work. In February, 1923, he was twice operated upon. The first operation was performed at his own home at Giverny, with his dearest friend, the "old Tiger" Clemenceau, by his side to encourage him and to aid the surgeon. The second operation took place a fortnight later at the clinic at Neuilly, again with Clemenceau present. Unfortunately, neither the admonitions of the surgeons nor the strenuous commands of Clemenceau could restrain him from resuming work too soon, and less than six months later a third operation was performed, at Giverny, with both Clemenceau and Pierre Bonnard at hand, to compel him to remain quiet. In that they succeeded, and after a sufficient interval Monet was able to resume work on a great mural design of water lilies which he intended as a gift to the French government, to be hung in the Orangerie at the Tuileries Gardens. This great gallery was in 1922 established by the French government, at a cost of millions of francs, to be a permanent museum of Monet's works.

The American public first became acquainted with the works of Monet through an exhibition of his cathedral paintings, in this city in 1896. Three years later there was an exhibition of twenty-two of his miscellaneous works at the Lotos Club arranged by the late John Eldkerin which attracted much attention and elicited much comment both favorable and unfavorable.) At that time "impressionism" was still on trial with most Americans. In January, 1920, however, there was no more doubt about him when twenty-seven of his paintings, of the first class, formed the very cream of one of the finest sale exhibitions of old masters and modern painters that this city has seen. These included scenes in Venice, and on the Thames; in the poppy fields of France, and along the Mediterranean coast; perhaps above all in his own exquisite gardens at Giverny; but all marking him beyond doubt or cavil as a master in draftsmanship and composition and, above all, a supreme master of atmosphere and color in pictorial art.

Business & Commerce

The death in 1849 of **Meyer Rothschild** one of the five brothers who created a dynasty may be said to the end of the beginning of the grand financiers of the modern world. Due recognition was also given to **Alfred Krupp**, in 1887; and all those who have since benefited from the international arms trade have reason to be grateful for his example. Those who owe a debt of gratitude to Messrs. Levi and Strauss, on the other hand — and there must be few who do not — will be interested to know that their deaths went unmarked. **Lord Leverhulme** represents here the power of marketing: for the energy that goes into the selling of soap powder is perhaps the *reductio ad absurdum* of our consumer society. **Ivar Kreugar** reminds us of the power-wielding possibilities of the magnate, and **Helena Rubinstein** of what people will pay for a veneer of glamour. Mr. **Woolworth** has the honour of starting what has become what must be the world's best-known chain store, showing on just how vast a scale it is possible to operate. For all their flamboyance and mystery respectively, neither Aristotle Onassis nor Howard Hughes can quite match the sheer obtrusiveness of Woolworth. **Gordon Selfridge** may be considered Woolworth's single department-store counterpart, the founder of an emporium that still acts as a focal point in London's West End. **Rockefeller** and **Howard Hughes** are two all-American heroes of rather different breeds; the one founded a dynasty combining philanthropy and finance, the other turned his hand to just about anything, and turned just about anything into gold. Like Ivar Kreugar, though, nothing in his life quite matched Hughes' sad leaving of it. **Conrad Hilton** and **Charles Atlas** have each given the international language a new word.

What is there to say about **Henry Ford**? His methods, the production-line, and his company, perhaps the first of the great multi-nationals, speak for themselves — for better or worse. **John Cadbury**, Quaker and founder of the confectionery empire, represents the acceptable face of capitalism. And so to Mr **Alphonse Capone**, a hard, not to say somewhat ruthless businessman, whose ultimate failure was brought about only by his insistence on using unconventional, or perhaps just over-explicit, methods.

Daily Telegraph
4ᵗʰ May 1937

FROM FARMER'S SON TO WORLD'S RICHEST MAN

MR. J. D. ROCKEFELLER'S £200,000,000

Mr. John Davison Rockefeller, who amassed a fortune which, at its peak, reached £200,000,000, died yesterday at the age of 97.

No business man in history has ever attracted greater attention. When he retired, more than a quarter of a century ago, he was in control of seven-eighths of the oil industry of the United States. He had created a gigantic organisation which represented an empire of its own, connected by land and sea, by air and pipe-line not only throughout America but the world.

But for a long period he was fiercely reviled and in danger of his life because of the hostility aroused by the relentless business methods associated with him. A remarkable change in the public attitude occurred in recent years and he has died as the greatest philanthropist of his age, whose gifts staggered the imagination.

After his 90th birthday Mr. Rockefeller made a remarkable resolve. He determined to ensure, so far as it was humanly possible, that he should live to be 100.

To this end he devoted himself with as determined a purpose and as businesslike a method as he had applied in accumulating his enormous fortune. The preservation of his life became his greatest concern.

His conviction was that he could conserve his bodily resources by avoiding the slightest excitement or unnecessary exertion, and by being protected from anything that might cause him irritation.

SILENCE AND SUNSHINE

To ensure still further peacefulness at night on his 3,000 acres estate near New York—from which he had already removed a railway line and a road—he directed that his retinue of servants should retire beyond the gates at sundown. The 70 negro guards remaining had their shoes soled with an inch of rubber so that there would not be any crunching sound on the gravel paths.

The whole estate was surrounded by a barbed wire fence 12ft high. Neighbours' houses in the distance were acquired in order that they might be demolished. If any legal rights delayed demolition the houses had to have their sides painted green, in an attempt to achieve an effect that harmonised with the landscape.

When, at 93, he found it inadvisable to travel to his estate in Florida where he had had a hill levelled and a little village removed because they were in the way—Mr. Rockefeller had the sunshine brought to him. A special sun-room was built.

He reduced exercise to a minimum, took abundant rest, and was scrupulously careful over his frugal diet.

END OF HIS AMBITION

Yet within the past year or so he had lost his great ambition to be a centenarian. He came to the conclusion that the achievement was of no importance. Why should he go on living merely to make a millionaire's record?

It simply meant that by means of all the resources of science and medicine he would be able to extend the ritual of living one day exactly like the next—the feeble and more or less lifeless occupant of a bed or a chair.

He had lost all his old business associates, he had given up all recreations, he received no visitors, he spent the hours in waiting for the end. And no further effort was necessary. His dynasty of dollars was secure.

The full extent of his riches is impossible to estimate with accuracy, but it was estimated three years ago that, after his colossal benefactions, it had shrunk to £30,000,000.

Mainly responsible was the stock market crash of 1929, which made enormous inroads on his possessions.

Almost as difficult to estimate is the extent of the Rockefeller benefactions.

GIFTS FOR "GOOD OF MANKIND"

£150,000,000 BENEFACTIONS

According to calculations made last year, the Rockefeller money that has been devoted "to the good of mankind" reaches the stupendous total of £150,000,000. Some of the gifts which have been made are as follows:

Rockefeller Foundation	£37,000,000
General Education Board	£25,000,000
Rockefeller Institute	£11,000,000

The original endowment of the Rockefeller Foundation was with £20,000,000, the largest single gift ever made.

John D. Rockefeller's habit of philanthropy had started modestly. As a boy of 16 he was taught by his father to keep a little account book and to enter in it a record of all his receipts and expenditure, however trifling. This book, which he called "Ledger A," remains a prized possession of his family. In it are included entries of a few cents for the poor or for church collections.

During the war Mr. Rockefeller began his plan of transferring the vast bulk of his fortune to his son, and by 1921 the main operation had been completed. Since then Mr. Rockefeller, jun., has had full control, and the magnitude and diversity of the interests represented are astonishing. Apart from other great endowments and gifts, Rockefeller millions have been distributed as follows:

Religion	£5,700,000
National Parks	£5,400,000
Education	£5,000,000
Reconstruction projects	£4,000,000
Arts and Letters	£3,150,000
International Gifts	£2,850,000
Miscellaneous	£1,220,000
Bureau of Social Hygiene	£1,160,000

One gift from the Rockefeller millions was of £400,000 to the League of Nations, but an offer made to the Egyptian Government of £2,000,000 for the building and endowment of a museum and school of archæology at Cairo was rejected because of the insistence that the institution should be directed not merely by Egyptians, but by competent archæologists.

He was not 21 when he embarked on his first enterprise of any importance. With £400, some of it borrowed from his father, he entered into a partnership which took him to the oilfields.

Then, with another man, named Andrews, he opened a small oil refinery in Cleveland. Andrews attended to the technical side; Rockefeller to salesmanship and finance.

The biggest development came when they began to acquire rival concerns. If they could not succeed in buying them they drove them out.

When it was discovered that it was cheaper to refine the oil on the sea coast, big factories were set up at the chief seaside cities. Mr. Rockefeller brought in his brother William, and established him as the agent of the business in New York. Means were discovered also of diminishing enormously the cost of production.

Casks which in 1872 had cost 9s. 5d. each were, in the course of a few years, manufactured for 5s., and as 3,500,000 barrels were used every year this saving alone came to £800,000. On cans over a million sterling was saved.

By 1877 their capital had risen to £700,000; Cleveland, their headquarters, was splendidly situated on Lake Erie for shipments, but the oil had to be brought by rail, and to give them an advantage over all rivals Rockefeller managed to get concessions from the railway companies for lower rates of transportation than were charged to any other traders.

These transactions were undoubtedly illegal—contrary to the laws of the States through which the railways passed. The effects were disastrous to the smaller competitors, and ultimately to all others. They sold or leased their plants to the great monopolists, and as the years went by the Standard Oil men had wiped out practically all competition.

Nothing the Trust did so embittered the people of the United States against it as the secret agreements with the railways, and the ruthless manner in which all rivals were ruined, at whatever cost. Mr. Rockefeller and his partners played for an immense stake. Supremacy in Pennsylvania meant practically monopoly over the United States. Neither money nor legality was allowed to stand in the way. They won, and so founded the most lucrative corporation in the world.

"HAPPIEST MAN"

Yet with all his wealth his habits were sparing. He took lunch on a bun and a cup of milk; he dressed simply; he did not smoke; he did not drink; he never was seen at a ball or any other social amusement; of all the life of the New York "Four Hundred" he knew nothing. His one enjoyment, apart from the love of trees and country life, was golf.

Mr. Rockefeller retired in 1911, and he occupied himself in developing, with the aid of his son, his enormous benefactions.

In his 80th year he declared: "I am the happiest man in the world—it seems to me that I have just begun to live"; and ten years later he stated that he was "in perfect health and full of hope and cheer for the future."

"I believe," he said once, "it is a religious duty to get all the money you can, to keep all you can, and to give away all you can."

The Guardian
10th November 1849

THE LATE MR. ROTHSCHILD.—By his own report, Nathan Meyer Rothschild came to Manchester because Frankfort was too small for the operations of the brothers, although the immediate cause was some offence to a customer; and it is characteristic of the intrepidity of the man that, with scarcely any hesitation, and with an absolute ignorance of the English language, he came to the country in which he realised such great results. On Tuesday he told his father he would go to England, and on Thursday he started. With £20,000 he commenced his career, and in a short time his capital was trebled. At Manchester he soon saw there were three profits to be made, in the raw material, the dyeing, and the manufacturing. It need hardly be added that his great mind had stomach for them all, and that, having secured the three, he sold goods cheaper than any one else. This was the foundation of that colossal fortune which afterwards passed into a proverb; and, in 1800, finding Manchester too small for the mind which could grapple with three profits, Rothschild came to London. It was the period when such a man was sure to make progress, as, clear and comprehensive in his commercial views, he was also rapid and decisive in working out the ideas which presented themselves. Business was plentiful, the entire continent formed our customers, and Rothschild reaped a rich reward. From bargain to bargain, from profit to profit, the Hebrew financier went on and prospered. Gifted with a fine perception, he never hesitated in action. Having bought some bills of the Duke of Wellington at a discount, his next operation was to buy the gold which was necessary to pay them, and, when he had purchased it, was, as he expected, informed that "government required it." Government had it, but doubtless paid for the accommodation. "It was the best business I ever had," he exclaimed triumphantly; and he added, that, when the government had got it, it was of no service to them until he had undertaken to convey it to Portugal. In 1812 Meyer Anselm, the head of the house, died at Frankfort. A princely inheritance, unbounded credit, and solemn advice never to separate were left to his four sons. From this period Nathan Meyer Rothschild was regarded as the head, though not the elder of the family, and skilfully did he support and spread the credit of the name. Previous to the advent of Mr. Rothschild foreign loans were somewhat unpopular in England, as the interest was receivable abroad, subject to the rate of exchange, liable to foreign caprice and payable in foreign coin. He introduced the payment of the dividends in England, and fixed it in sterling money, one great cause of the success of these loans in 1825. Although Mr. Rothschild was commonly termed a merchant, his most important transactions were in connection with the Stock Exchange. It was here that his great decision, his skilful combinations, and his unequalled energy made him remarkable. At a time when the funds were constantly varying the temptation was too great for a capitalist like Mr. Rothschild to withstand. His operations were soon noticed; and, when the money market was left without an acknowledged head by the deaths of Sir Francis Baring and Abraham Goldsmidt,—for the affairs of the latter were wound up and the successors of the former did not aim at the autocracy of the money market,—the name of Nathan Meyer Rothschild was in the mouths of all city men as a prodigy of success. Cautiously, however, did the capitalist proceed, until he had made a fortune as great as his future reputation. He revived all the arts of an older period. He employed brokers to depress or raise the market for his benefit, and is said in one day to have purchased to the extent of four millions. The name of Rothschild as contractor for an English loan made its first public appearance in 1819. But the twelve millions for which he then became responsible went to a discount. It was said, however, that Mr. Rothschild had relieved himself from all liability before the calamity could reach him. From this year his transactions pervaded the entire globe. The old and the new world alike bore witness to his skill; and with the profits of a single loan he purchased an estate which cost £150,000. Minor capitalists, like parasitical plants, clung to him, and were always ready to advance their money in speculations at his bidding. Nothing seemed too gigantic for his grasp; nothing too minute for his notice. His mind was as capable of calculating a loan for millions as of calculating the lowest possible amount on which a clerk could exist. Like too many great merchants whose profits were counted by thousands, he paid his assistants the smallest amount for which he could procure them. He became the high priest of the temple of Janus, and the coupons raised by the capitalist for a despotic state were more than a match for the cannon of the revolutionist. From most of the speculations of 1824 and 1825 Mr. Rothschild kept wisely aloof. The Alliance Life and Fire Assurance Company,

Continued

Chicago Sunday Tribune
26th January 1947

Al Capone Dies in Florida Villa

Heart Fails After Stroke of Apoplexy

Miami Beach, Jan. 25 (*Æ*)—Scarface Al Capone, Chicago prohibition era mobster, died in his villa here at 6:25 [Chicago time] tonight. He was 48.

"Death came very suddenly," said Dr. Kenneth S. Phillips, who has been attending the ex-gang leader since he was stricken with apoplexy last Tuesday.

"All the family was present. His wife, Mae, collapsed and is in very serious condition."

Dr. Phillips said death was caused by heart failure.

Announced by Doctor

Dr. Phillips emerged from the Capone home about 7:30 p. m. and announced the death to newsmen.

Dozens of persons, none of them identified, were admitted to the estate. A block long line of sleek, black limousines was parked outside.

Tourists and the curious also flocked to the island. A virtual promenade of rubberneckers strolled by or stood around, chatting, some laughing.

A hearse pulled thru the gates and soon afterward took the body of Capone to a funeral home.

[*Louis Rago, undertaker at 624 N. Western av., Chicago, left for Miami Beach by plane last night to take charge of arrangements for Capone's funeral. The body will be brought to Chicago, arriving Tuesday or Wednesday. It was understood that Capone's mother expressed the desire that both the funeral and the burial be in Chicago. The family has a plot in Mount Olivet cemetery.*]

An apoplectic stroke hit Capone Jan. 21 and swept him so close to death that the Rt. Rev. William Barry administered the last rites of the Roman Catholic church.

Pneumonia Sets In

More than 16 hours later the onetime gang overlord rallied and came out of his coma to talk with his wife and son, Alfred.

He was out of danger for a time, then pneumonia developed and with this complication his heart weakened.

At his Palm Island home when he died were his wife and son, his mother, Theresa; his father, Ermio; a sister, Mrs. Mafalda Mariotote, and two brothers, Ralph and Matthew.

TYPICAL OF ERA

Alphonse Capone personified an era. For the greater part of a decade he was Chicago's most publicized criminal: the figurehead universally chosen to illustrate the breakdown of law and order that followed the effort to legislate alcoholic beverages out of America.

He was head of a huge ring of alcohol cookers, illegal brewers, vice resort managers, gambling house keepers, whisky warehouse raiders, and hired gunmen that gave Chicago a reputation as a city of lawlessness in the roaring 1920s. He had rivals, of course, but few of them ever got rich and many of them perished by gunfire which, if he did not order it, was at least in his interest.

Fantastic Tales About Capone

In the days of his power there were fantastic tales about him. His "syndicate" was credited with doing a business of 25 million dollars a year and he was reputedly many times a millionaire; there was even a story that he had personally lost $7,500,000 in a few years of gambling. With awe, it was related that the armored car in which he rode weighed 7½ tons and that he went about always with at least a dozen "torpedoes" [armed bodyguards] to protect his life.

Dozens of murders were attributed to him and his gang; murders for which no one was ever tried. There were many accusations, most of which no one troubled to deny, that he and his cohorts practiced bribery of public officials and policemen on a large scale. Capone was astute enough to realize the great money-making possibilities in labor rackets, and some of his underlings were still prospering in them long after he retired. He began toward the end of his sovereignty to understand the power of the ballot, and there were territories in which only his candidates could be elected.

which owes its origin to this period, was, however, produced under his auspices; and its great success is a proof of his forethought. None of the loans with which he was connected were ever repudiated; and when the crash of that sad period came, the great Hebrew looked coldly and calmly on, and congratulated himself on his caution. At his counting-house a fair price might be procured for any amount of stock which at a critical time, would have depressed the public market; and it was no uncommon circumstance for brokers to apply at the office of Mr. Rothschild instead of going in the Stock Exchange. He has, however, occasionally been surpassed in cunning; and on one occasion a great banker lent Rothschild a million and a half on the security of consols, the price of which was then 84. The terms on which the money was lent were simple. If the price reached 74, the banker might claim the stock at 70; but Rothschild felt satisfied that, with so large a sum out of the market, the bargain was tolerably safe. The banker, however, as much a Jew as Rothschild, had a plan of his own. He immediately began selling the Consols received from the latter, together with a similar amount in his own possession. The funds dropped; the Stock Exchange grew alarmed; other circumstances tended to depress it; the fatal price of 74 was reached; and the Christian banker had the satisfaction of outwitting the Hebrew loanmonger. But, if sometimes outwitted himself, there is little doubt he made others pay for it; and on one occasion, it is reported that his finesse proved too great for the authorities of the Bank of England. Mr. Rothschild was in want of bullion, and went to the governor to procure on loan a portion of the superfluous store. His wishes were met; the terms were agreed on; the period was named for its return; and the affair finished for the time. The gold was used by the financier; his end was answered, and the day arrived on which he was to return the borrowed metal. Punctual to the time appointed, Mr. Rothschild entered; and those who remember his personal appearance may imagine the cunning twinkle of his small, quick eye as, ushered into the presence of the governor, he handed the borrowed amount in bank notes. He was reminded of his agreement, and the necessity of bullion was urged. His reply was worthy a commercial Talleyrand. "Very well, gentlemen. Give me the notes. I dare say your cashier will .... with gold from your vaults, and then I can re......... In such a speech, the only worthy re............—*Francis's Chronicles of the Stock Exchange.*

Even Language Tainted.

Out of his operations grew a new slang: A thousand dollar bill was a "grand"; a man slain had been "put on the spot," or "taken for a ride," or "rubbed out." A gang was a "mob" and an identification was a "finger." A partner was one who "owned a piece" of a business. The business itself was a "racket."

The best information available shows Capone was born in Naples, Italy, in 1899, and was brought to the United States as a small child. He grew up in Brooklyn and became a member of the notorious Five Points gang there. He was a protege of John Torrio, earlier a prominent Chicago dealer in vice. Torrio brought him to Chicago about 1919 and got him a job as a guard for James Colosimo, who was slain a couple of years later in his south side restaurant.

Husky in Physique.

Capone was big and husky. Tales that he was a soldier in the World war were never corroborated. A scar on his left cheek was a souvenir of a gang fight and won him the nickname "Scarface Al," a pseudonym he resented.

He and Torrio had organizing ability. They made prostitution pay in south side resorts and, later, in extensions to the suburb. The prohibition rackets were just starting up and they went into them energetically. Other desperate men did the same, and a war of extermination soon began. After a few murders had been accomplished, Torrio was severely wounded by rival gangsters, lost his nerve, and went away from Chicago. Capone became his heir. This was in late 1924.

Capone knew how to make himself safe. He paid his "torpedoes" well. He set up headquarters in a Cicero hotel and thereby gave a good suburb an undeserved notoriety. The alcohol wars became intensified. The Capone syndicate's enemies began to disappear or were absorbed. The millions rolled in. Capone branched out into dog racing tracks and other ventures; he bought a magnificent home at Miami Beach, Fla.

Slayings of Capone Type.

The slaying in 1925 of William McSwiggin, an assistant state's attorney, shocked the conscience of Chicago. So, too, did the Valentine day massacre—seven men of a north side gang were lined up in a Clark street garage and machine gunned to death in 1929. Their leader, George [Bugs] Moran, who escaped, said: "Only Capone kills like that."

These crimes were never solved, and Capone was never arrested in connection with them, or with any other slayings. He seemed to be too big for the law in Chicago. In 1928, he had been arrested in Philadelphia, Pa., as a gun toting vagrant and sentenced to a year in jail, but on his release took up his Chicago career again without being molested.

However, Capone failed to pay his income tax. Agents of the federal government traced the operations by which he had become wealthy. In 1931, he was indicted in federal District court for failing to report a million of his "take" in the years 1924-'29, the period of his greatest power. On July 30, 1931, he pleaded guilty, explaining that, in return for the plea, it had been agreed he would be sentenced only to two and a half years in prison. Judge James H. Wilkerson refused to be bound by any agreement and the plea was changed to not guilty.

A huge mass of evidence, introduced by the government at the trial which began on Oct. 6, 1931, exposed the workings of the underworld kingdom of Capone. The presentation required nearly two weeks and the trial resulted in a verdict of guilty. Judge Wilkerson sentenced the gang leader to five years in prison and a $10,000 fine on each of three counts and a year in jail and a fine of $20,000 on other counts.

Two of the five year sentences were served concurrently and the total of his punishment was 10 years in prison, one year in jail, and $50,000 in fines.

The prosecutor in the case, whose work was most important in bringing the heavy hand of justice upon Capone, was Dwight H. Green, now governor of Illinois.

Six months later, all legal resources being exhausted, Capone was taken to the federal prison in Atlanta, Ga. Later he was transferred to the stronger penitentiary on Alcatraz Island, where he lived under strict discipline and apparently obeyed rules. In January, 1939, having satisfied the prison sentence, counting time off for good behavior, Capone was transferred to the more pleasant prison at Terminal Island, near San Pedro, Cal. It was reported then that the former gang chief was suffering from paresis.

Released in 1939.

He was released by federal authorities on Nov. 16, 1939, and at the request of his family taken by them to a hospital in Baltimore, Md. He was described then as a mere shell of his former self. The way to his freedom was opened only after the $50,000 in fines and more than $7,000 in costs had been paid by his relatives.

In July, 1942, Capone and several associates, among them his brother Ralph, settled for $30,000 a $250,000 demand for taxes on beer handled by the syndicate.

As his paresis advanced, Capone was described as becoming more and more child-like. Dr. Joseph Moore of Baltimore, Md., who examined him, said he had "the mentality of a 12 year old," while Jack [Greasy Thumb] Guzik, who was one of the top men in the "syndicate," snorted last July that Capone was "as nutty as a fruitcake."

The Times
25th October 1922

MR. GEORGE CADBURY.

BUSINESS MAN AND SOCIAL WORKER.

Mr. George Cadbury, whose death is announced on another page, not only built up the great cocoa manufacturing business of Cadbury Brothers, Limited, but was also a very religious man, a philanthropist, and a social reformer. At one time he was chief proprietor of the *Daily News*, but had transferred his interests to his sons.

Mr. Cadbury, who was born on September 19, 1839, came of an old Quaker family, and was educated at the Friends' School at Edgbaston. His father, John Cadbury, traded in Birmingham in a small way as a cocoa and chocolate manufacturer. George Cadbury was 22, and his brother Richard, who died many years ago, was 25, when, in 1861, they took over the cocoa works, which at that time hardly employed a score of workpeople. Cocoa was not then the popular beverage that it is to-day, nor had the taste for chocolate been developed. The young men had an uphill struggle, but industry and business aptitude were rewarded. At that time chocolate makers used various processes to "counteract the fats"; George Cadbury had the simple idea of eliminating the fats, which resulted in a better article at less cost. He did pioneer work by travelling for the firm, but the week-end always found him at home, and on Sundays he conducted for over fifty years an early morning Bible class, first for youths and later for men. By 1864 the fortunes of the firm were assured, and by 1879 extension had become imperative. It was then that Cadbury decided to move the factory from Birmingham to the country at Bournville. He planned the village himself on garden city lines, and it now houses over nine thousand workpeople. He advanced the money for house building at 2½ per cent., the Bournville Village Trust being from the beginning entirely separate from the cocoa works. In 1891 the whole property, now valued at over £150,000, was made over to a trust under the Charity Commissioners, which was charged to devote the whole of the income to the settlement of other villages on like lines.

All his life Mr. Cadbury was firm in his attachment to the Society of Friends. He established a settlement on inter-denominational lines at Woodbrooke, his old family house, and he was one of the early promoters of co-operation among the Free Churches, which resulted in the formation of the Free Church Council. For housing and social reform he was zealous; but though a warm supporter of the Liberal Party, he could never be induced to stand for Parliament. Honours he refused, notably the offer of a Privy Councillorship from Lord Rosebery. Many years ago he sat on the Birmingham Town Council, and later he was elected to the Worcestershire County Council. In 1891 he bought four papers in the Birmingham district, and ten years later he was persuaded by Mr. Lloyd George and others to become part-proprietor of the *Daily News*. Ultimately he assumed the sole responsibility for the paper, but afterwards transferred his interests to a trust administered by his sons. During his control the paper organized a Sweating Exhibition, which led to the passing of the Trade Boards Act. Mr. Cadbury was also one of the founders of the National Old Age Pensions Society, and took a practical interest in various institutions for the benefit of children.

In 1872 Mr. Cadbury married Mary Tylor, who died in 1887, leaving three sons and two daughters. In 1888 he married Elsie Mary Taylor, O.B.E., who survives him with three sons and three daughters.

The Daily Telegraph & Morning Post
9th April 1947

HENRY FORD: THE MECHANIC GIFTED WITH GENIUS

IT was not the ambition to be a mere moneymaker that led Henry Ford to become one of the wealthiest men who ever lived.

As a patient mechanic with the determination to excel, he had such a great fund of imagination, technical skill, and enterprise that in the end he could not help himself. He has died leaving, it has been said, a personal fortune of well over £50,000,000, while the fortune he made for his family probably reached the dimension of not less than £450,000,000.

Son of a Cork farmer who left Ireland for America a century ago, Ford found himself, as a boy, working so hard in the fields that the experience remained a vivid memory throughout his life.

His main concern seems to have been the amount of physical fatigue that had to be endured, and he gradually convinced himself that the whole system was wrong. "I hated the gruelling grind of farm work," he once declared, "Twenty-five days a year is all that it ought to take for a man to get his living from the soil."

Horseless Vehicles

At the age of 11 he came upon the first mechanically propelled vehicle he had seen. It was primitive enough—a portable steam engine and boiler mounted on wheels, with a water tank and a coal cart behind—but it excited his imagination when he learned that it was designed to simplify the operation of sawing wood or threshing. Why could there not be a widespread use of machinery like this for farming?

Five years later Ford ran away from home. He had decided after much youthful thought that what farms needed were horseless vehicles instead of slow and cumbersome one-horse-power hay motors. As he knew nothing about mechanics, he found employment for himself in an electrical factory. The wages were about 7s 6d a week.

The useful experience he gained there was supplemented later by working in a watchmaker's shop, and elaborating on the merits of producing watches in such enormous numbers that they could be sold at a very cheap price.

Here, indeed, may be traced the origins of that gift for mass production methods of which, on a far vaster scale, he was to be such a past-master in later years. But meanwhile, as no one encouraged him, he went back to sift his ideas on the subject of horseless farm vehicles.

"The Thing Worked"

After laborious effort he achieved his first success—a steam vehicle with a paraffin-heated boiler that could be neatly controlled. The boiler, however, was much too dangerous, and for the next two years he tried to find one that would be more satisfactory. Finally, he abandoned the steam method and turned his attention to the internal combustion engine.

Months passed, and then, as the product of nightly work in a large shed alongside his home, he was able to emerge and chug-chug down the street in his first car, its wheezy two-cylinder engine mounted on a buggy frame and with four bicycle wheels that had been refitted with strong tyres.

The contraption was noisy, it spluttered out clouds of black smoke, and it caused some derision, but to Ford it was enough that "the darned thing actually worked."

It was his success in matching the little "flivver," and winning with it, against an unbeaten racing car, that marked the real beginning of his remarkable business career. So much attention was attracted in America by his exploit that there was no difficulty in establishing the Ford Motor Company with a capital of £20,000.

A dozen men, including a coal dealer, a candy maker and a pair of lawyers took stock. Ford's own contribution was the car he had made, and with an allotment of 255 shares he became vice-president, designer and master mechanic at a salary of £10 a week. That was in 1903.

Sixteen years later, when Ford's son Edsel bought up all the stock to bring the whole business into the hands of the family, he paid some extraordinarily large amounts for the shares.

Senator James Couzens, at one time one of Ford's clerks, had paid £625 for 24 shares, and ultimately received £7,500,000 in 1919. It cost the Fords £50,000 to buy in one share that a Mrs. Hauss had originally bought for £20 as a speculation. It is said that eight of the 13 original investors became dollar millionaires.

Assembly Line Ideas

In the intervening years Ford had been developing his business to astonishing proportions. Later progress was at such a rate that by 1931 the 20,000,000th Ford car had been made. Such was the commanding success of what was, officially, the T Model, though it was perhaps better known to the multitude as the "Tin Lizzie."

In 1936 Ford is said to have refused an offer of £250,000,000 for his property, and it was calculated that, on this valuation, his income at 6 per cent. worked out at £23 a minute.

Meanwhile the great business, which had begun in an unpretentious two-storey building in Detroit, was reaching out to Europe. A great factory was set up at Trafford Park, Manchester, and another at Cork. Plans went forward in 1929 for the establishment of a still greater one at Dagenham in Essex. Ford companies were springing up in several other countries as well.

Coincident with all this activity, the remarkable Henry Ford was establishing great enterprises that embraced iron mines, blast furnaces, ships, rubber plantations, and aircraft works, and even banking. He became the second largest maker of glass in America.

He developed mass production methods to an extent that had never previously been attempted. Ford was in particular a pioneer of the "assembly line" now so common a feature in all big factories. It enabled him to build cars much faster than any cars were built elsewhere.

He embarked in 1914 on high rates of pay for his workers that attracted world attention, and he proclaimed boldly the day was coming when work would be no more than five hours a day, with long holidays too.

Yet Ford had his failures that were as startling as some of his successes. To a large extent these were a product of the autocratic spirit that he developed. In a minor way he had asserted this when he once ordered that all the married men in his works in America were to grow enough vegetables to support their winter needs, and when he declared that he would, if necessary, make his factory at Dagenham "dry."

It was when he persisted in directing ideas of this kind on the largest scale against the trade unions and even the Government that he lost heavily.

Ford Peace Ship

Eventually his obstinate refusal in 1933-34 to agree to the State enforcing rules in business led to his great fight against President Roosevelt's New Deal, to legal actions, and to a boycott of his manufactures until his eventual capitulation. Similarly, his hostility to the trade unions, and the determined manner in which he sought to conquer opposition, greatly hindered his business until in 1938 he made his peace with them.

It was perhaps inevitable that a man of such forceful personality should do some futile things. One of his most spectacular mistakes was his hope to bring the 1914-18 war to an end by means of his "peace ship." Into this vessel he had acquired he crowded cranks, pacifists and intellectuals as "peacemakers" who were to hurl "bombs loaded with faith" on Europe and "bring the men out of the trenches."

Alas! the voyagers found it impossible to keep peace even among themselves, and the entire enterprise foundered in ridicule. That happened in 1915. Not long afterwards the United States became a belligerent and then the Ford concern played a notable part.

In his later years he had ample opportunity for gratifying a taste for expensive hobbies. He collected many things, particularly after visits to Britain. He established an "English village" by purchasing, among other buildings, a cottage that had once been the home of Anne Boleyn, and an ancient Cotswold smithy which he re-erected on his estate. But he failed to do the same kind of thing with a City church.

Willow Run Bombers

His son Edsel succeeded him as president of the Company in 1919. When he died in 1943, Henry Ford resumed office at the age of 80, and he finally retired at the end of hostilities with Japan. During the war he not only made aeroplanes, but was the world's largest producer of engines of all kinds, for jeeps and other vehicles as well as aircraft. His Willow Run plant, capable of turning out one Constellation bomber an hour, was almost fantastic in its size and a model of organisation. The machines went in at one end as raw material and left at the other end as powerful warcraft.

Some years ago Ford announced his determination to live to the age of 100, and to be of service to himself and mankind until he was 85. Now he has died in his 84th year. He was a mechanic of genius, but still a mechanic.

New York Times
9th April 1919

F. W. WOOLWORTH LEAVES $65,000,000

Owner of 1,050 Five and Ten Cent Stores Dies Suddenly at His Glen Cove Home.

BUILT HIGHEST BUILDING

Merchant's Success Came After His First Store Opened in Utica in 1879, Had Failed—Dies at 66.

Frank Winfield Woolworth, founder of the chain of five and ten cent stores in this country and in England bearing his name, and builder of the Woolworth Building in this city, which is the highest building in the world, died early yesterday morning at his country home, Winfield Hall, at Glen Cove, L. I., in his sixty-seventh year. He had been in declining health for some time, and left his town home, 990 Fifth Avenue, last Friday, believing that the change would benefit him. Mrs. Woolworth is dangerously ill, and she was not able to go with her husband to their country home.

Besides his widow, Mrs. Jennie Creighton Woolworth, he is survived by two daughters, Mrs. Charles E. F. McCann and Mrs. James P. Donahue of this city, who were with him when he died, and a brother, C. S. Woolworth of Scranton, Penn. Mr. Woolworth became suddenly worse Monday afternoon, and soon after the arrival of Dr. W. H. Zabriskie of Glen Cove, who was summoned, he lost consciousness and grew steadily worse until the end.

The funeral services will be held at his home in the city tomorrow morning at 11 o'clock. Interment will be in Woodlawn Cemetery.

Born on a farm at Great Bend, Jefferson County, N. Y., the son of John H. and Fanny McBrier Woolworth, Mr. Woolworth lived with his parents and worked on the farm until he was 21 years old. For two Winters before he was 21 he got his first commercial experience helping in a grocery store at Great Bend. There was no salary attached to the work, and all Mr. Woolworth asked was the experience. After much effort, he finally obtained a job with Augsbury & Moore, merchants, of Watertown, N. Y., who took him on a six months' trial. The first three months he worked for nothing and the second three months he received $3.50 a week, which was the amount he paid for board. At the end of the six months he received an increase of fifty cents a week. In time he was getting $10 a week, and in the Spring of 1878 he got his first inkling of the five-cent business. It came about through the introduction of a five-cent counter in the store in which he was working in Watertown.

Purchasing $350 worth of goods on a note indorsed by his father, Mr. Woolworth on Feb. 22, 1879, opened his first store in Utica, N. Y. The venture proved a failure, and the store was closed in three months. In June of the same year he opened another store in Lancaster, Penn., which proved a success from the start, and has continued to the present time. Other stores were established. Several of them were failures at the beginning, while others thrived. He had different partners at different times in his ventures, and, in 1912, when the F. W. Woolworth Company was formed, they had 596 stores. The number continued to grow each year, until now the company, of which Mr. Woolworth was the President, owns and controls 1,050 five and ten cent stores in the United States and Canada. The business last year was more than $107,000,000. The Woolworth fortune, which was built out of nickels and dimes, is estimated at $65,000,000.

In addition to his connection with the Woolworth corporation, Mr. Woolworth was one of the largest stockholders and a Director of the Irving National Bank and the Irving Trust Company, President and largest stockholder of the Broadway-Park Place Company, which owns the Woolworth Building, which cost $13,000,000, and other properties in this city.

Mr. Woolworth was a member of the Chamber of Commerce of New York, the Union League Club, Lotos Club, and Hardware Club and a Director of the Pennsylvania Society.

The Times
11th December 1972

CHARLES ATLAS

Charles Atlas, the 97-pound weakling who turned himself into the strong man whose physique always got him the girl has died at the age of 80.

He was born Angelo Siciliano, and went to the United States as a skinny 12-year-old in 1904. A bully kicked sand in his face at the beach one day, and Atlas resolved to build up his body through his own personal system of "dynamic tension". He won a national contest as the world's most perfectly developed man in 1922 and 1923 and a few years later founded a muscle-building correspondence course.

The Times
15th July 1887

A telegram received through Reuter's Agency and dated Essen, July 14, informs us that Herr Alfred Krupp, the proprietor of the celebrated steel works and gun foundry, died yesterday evening at his villa near Essen. Herr Krupp was born on April 11, 1810, at Essen, where his father, Frederick Charles Krupp, had set up a small foundry. When his father died Herr Krupp and his brother carried on the business in partnership with their mother until 1848, when Alfred became sole possessor of it and (preserving the firm's old style of "Friedrich Krupp") developed it into the greatest steel-casting industry in the world. After patient and long-continued experiments and countless failures he succeeded in making steel in huge blocks. In the London Exhibition of 1851 he showed a block of cast steel of 45 centners, whereas previously one of 20 centners had been considered a marvel. Herr Krupp's great achievements in this branch of industry were honourably attested by his exhibits at Munich (1854) and Paris (1855) and still more remarkably in the Universal Exhibitions of London (1862), Paris (1867), Vienna (1873), and Philadelphia (1876), and others still more recently held. The Krupp steel foundry a few years ago covered an area of 500 hectares, and employed 10,600 workmen, in addition to the 5,000 men employed in other undertakings of the firm. No fewer than 77 steam-hammers were constantly at work. Railway lines connected the works with the railway system of the country; and the establishment included a chemical laboratory, a photographing and lithographing house, and book printing and binding workshops. The articles produced included axles, wheels, machinery of various kinds, cannon, and shells and other missiles; some of the cannon rivalling in size and power the most tremendous productions of Whitworth and Armstrong. The Krupp cannon are, as is well known, loaded at the breech; and their merit has always consisted quite as much in the use of the finest, strongest, and purest metal as in the peculiarity of their construction or "building." These cannon have been found to possess almost unsurpassable durability, accuracy, and range; and it may be mentioned that the plentiful shell fire which harassed Lord Wolseley's forces at Kassassin was delivered from Krupp cannon purchased by the Egyptian Government at Essen. Up to 1876 Herr Krupp had delivered to different Governments 15,000 cannon, mostly equipped with carrriages and ammunition. After the terrible conflict of 1870-1 had been ended the German army was supplied throughout with the perfected field-piece of Herr Krupp, and the whole of the German coasts are defended by battery guns of his design and construction. The firm possesses for its experimental practice a strip of land seven miles long, fitted up as a cannon-range, near Dülmen, in Westphalia. The firm also carries on extensive mining and smelting works, and owns much land, rich in iron-ore, in Northern Spain, employing four steamers in the conveyance of the metal to Germany. Herr Krupp's genius came opportunely to the aid of his countrymen in the crisis brought on by Prince Bismarck's resolute efforts to attain German unity. The effect of the massing of numerous batteries of his latest and perfected cannon, with their concentrated fire directed on an attacking force, has yet, however, to be witnessed—it is to be hoped, at a very distant day. His achievements in the course of a long and active career have more than once been rewarded by his Sovereign and by foreign princes, and some time ago it was announced that the Emperor had conferred upon him the rank of baron. The late Lord Lytton humorously contended that when the means of destruction had been improved so as to be instantaneously fatal to the largest opposing force wars would become absurd and impossible, as involving certain death to all concerned. If there be any truth in this theory much commendation will certainly be due to the deceased cannon-founder.

The *Academy* announces the death of Professor Pott, of Halle, in his 85th year, "the last of the triumvirs who founded the study of comparative philology—Bopp, Grimm, and Pott."

The Times
14th March 1932

The Death of M. Kreuger

On Saturday the news reached Sweden that M. IVAR KREUGER, head of a great group of match-manufacturing companies and of a financial corporation with ramifications in every part of the civilized world, had died in Paris by his own hand. Almost at once a Cabinet Council was summoned, and within a few hours the Riksdag had been called together to pass the precautionary legislation—a task completed during last night—which seems to be demanded. Such is the impact of one man's death upon the stability of his huge concerns. From all that is known of the state of the immense international enterprise of which M. KREUGER was the initiatory and controlling brain there is reason to accept the undoubted emergency, partly signalled and partly created by his death, without panic. The man who was driven on Saturday to this last act was no common adventurer caught up and cornered at last by the self-defeating ingenuity of his devices. He may have made mistakes. Some of his operations have been criticized from time to time as over-confident. But it is clear that he was the victim, not so much of faults in the huge system which he had built up within a brief twenty years, as of a world-condition simultaneously affecting and afflicting every industrialist and every financier in greater or less degree. The simpler truth would seem to be, not that M. KREUGER has taken the way of suicide out of irretrievable ruin, moral and financial, but that the unimaginable strain of conducting from week to week an immense international business, beset and hampered by every difficulty that the helpless unwisdom and disorganization of these times have put in its way, exhausted his courage, broke down his nervous resistance, and left him with no more power to fight or even to live.

The work of M. KREUGER's hands was regarded, and justly, by the world as a structure of great solidity in the main. Fundamentally, like his own career, it was of simple design. He built on two parallels. He was a manufacturer of matches and he sought the markets necessary for his product. He sought, what every industrialist seeks, the economies of stability in demand and supply, stability in price. He obtained it by the rapid and logical enlargement of his control over supplies. He put his faith in the internationality of industry in the new age and, when the world has been once more made safe for trade, he may well come to be regarded as a pioneer ahead of his time. While he extended his control through one company after another over the manufacture of matches in many countries, he simultaneously provided for his output by securing from the Governments of a dozen or more countries the monopoly of their national markets. He paid for these acquisitions in loans, and, while a few of these may have been improvidently granted, the whole system was well-knit and could have been counted on to withstand any but the conjunction of natural adversity and human interference character-istic of the present depression. But debts have grown intolerable as prices have fallen. Debtor Governments with their restrictions upon ex-change have maintained their credit, it might be said, at the expense of their creditors A concern like M. KREUGER's, dependent before all upon the free financial flow, found its own circulation impeded and grown sluggish and illiquid. The final task which broke M. KREUGER down was the raising of a loan to replace assets no longer free and the produce of loans from debtors who had frozen them-selves in. It is primarily a financial predica-ment. The great businesses are there, the trade is there. The commercial organization and control are intact. These essential elements of reconstruction survive, and their persistence must moderate and limit the anxieties which have inevitably filled the week-end.

The grievous conclusion of a strange career is deeply to be deplored for various reasons. First, it is a shock to confidence which the financial centres, with much already to unnerve them, with much unsettled and doubtful, would pray to have been spared. A few days will show how much genuine loss and strain needs to be met. In the meantime from Sweden itself, most heavily committed of all countries to the Kreuger fortunes, come not unhopeful reports, while punctual steps have been taken to stay and discipline alarm. Rational judgment will await a fuller disclosure and will refuse to increase voluntarily the mischiefs of the time. In the next place it is evi-dence, not new as such but deeply to be regretted, of the war which international inaction and indecision are waging against the interests of manufacture and commerce. It is another warning to Governments that time does

not wait. Apart from these considerations of broader effect, it is impossible not to think in individual and human terms of the life that ended on Saturday. "When beggars die there "are no comets seen." But all the world is astir and a Parliament is in session because the career of a Swedish industrialist is suddenly over. Fiction itself would not lightly dare a parallel to it. A man of ambition but of no vanity, M. KREUGER seems to have had no weakness of the kind that brings weaker timber to wreck. He set about his undertakings because he had the vision and the courage to conceive of them as necessary. He began as venturously as other great industrialists have begun, but his con-ceptions, though huge, were sober. He remained modest and clear-headed, and though he dealt in the course of business—a sufficient tribute to its scale—with nearly a score of Govern-ments, he had no aspiration for any personal role. He was, first and fore-most, an industrialist and as such ranked among the half-dozen greatest organizers of his kind to-day. He was a financier by force of

circumstances. He was not born or trained to finance, and where he came short it was, perhaps, on the side of caution. At the moment of failure it is a matter of credit to him and of reassurance to the public mind that its causes are reasonably well known and that the blame is not chiefly his. Least of all does personal sus-picion light upon him in his last day. No such career has been known in our time, and, but for mental collapse under an intolerable load, it is possible that the man who bore it might have lived to steer his course and all that depended on him into a calmer age.

The Times
9th May 1947

RETAIL STORE TRADE IN BRITAIN

Mr. H. Gordon Selfridge died yesterday at his home at Putney Heath in his ninety-first year. A man of bound-less energy and unflagging optimism, he looked upon retail trade in domestic com-modities as something far more than the handing of goods over a counter for a stated price.

Henry Gordon Selfridge came of pure New England stock on both sides of the family, but was born in the West, at Ripon, Wisconsin, the only son of Robert O. Selfridge, who had fought for the North in the Civil War, and who died soon after the birth of his child. His mother moved to Jackson, Michigan, and the young Selfridge left school at 14 to work in a bank, where he remained as a junior for two years. There followed a brief period as book-keeper in a factory and an attempt to enter the United States Navy, but he was rejected because he was too small. In 1879 he went to the trading firm of Field, Leiter, and Co., a concern specializing in the mail order business from Chicago, and he had a chance of advance-ment elsewhere in 1881, but Marshall Field perceived his ability, and retained him as manager of his department.

Selfridge was to go forward to prosperity during the next 23 years with the renamed firm of Marshall Field. When he was about 22 he drew new ideas from the catalogues of a Boston " dry goods " house, obtained permis-sion to visit Boston, Philadelphia, and New York, and returned with innumerable fresh notions which earned him a rise in salary. He began to specialize in the retail side of the busi-ness and showed something like a genius for organization. He made further and longer journeys, to London, Paris, and other Euro-pean capitals. Once back in America he felt strongly inclined to start in business for him-self, but Field raised his salary at one bound from $5,000 to $20,000 a year, and he re-mained. In 1892 he was made a junior partner, controlling a retail department which employed 10,000 persons. He made efforts to persuade Field to open up business in New York, Paris, and London, without success, and in 1903, having accumulated a fortune of some £300,000, he decided to retire from business and to devote himself to travel, reading, and the cultivation of his orchids But to a man of Selfridge's combative and restless temperament, retirement in the prime of life proved impossible.

Visiting London in 1906, he considered opening a store there, and before long decided to do so, and began to make his plans. There were many prophets of gloom who tried to persuade him that London was already well served, or more than served, with large retail shops and that he was courting disaster. But he persisted, bought his site on the north side of Oxford Street, and proceeded with the erec-tion of a great building which took the labours of some 1,500 workmen over 10 months and cost some £400,000. The business opened in March, 1909, with 130 departments and a capital of £1,000,000. Libraries, rest rooms, writing rooms, and a roof garden added to its amenities, and a sustained and highly skilful adver ing campaign kept all these activities prom ntly in the public eye. How finished was Selfridge advertising technique was demon trated by the diversity of its appeal. Reade of *The Times*, in particular, will not n d to be reminded of the p lished little p dosophical and moral essays which appeared in these columns under the signature of Callisthenes.

With his rapidly growing staff Selfridge pre-served the happiest relationships. Believing in tru t and encouragement, he eschewed pater-nalism, and though the Selfridge employees were given ample facilities for sport and social life they managed these affairs them-selves. Selfridge expected from his assistants the same enthusiasm, energy, and intelligence which he displayed; but he believed in quick rewards for merit, and used to say that if one of his young men was not promoted within three years " there is something wrong with him—or with us." He was particularly keen to avoid exaggeration and over-statement in his advertisements, and initiated a scheme whereby any assistant pointing out an error of fact in an advertisement from the house won a monetary prize for his vigilance.

Selfridge remained an American citizen for most of his long life, and it was not until 1937 that he applied for British naturalization papers. He warmly believed in the desirability of closer co-operation between the two nations, and wrote at length on the subject in the New York *Sun* in 1916. Apart from orchids his chief private interest was in bookbindings, of which he had a fine and sumptuous collection. In October, 1939, Selfridge retired from the board of his company, with the title of presi-dent. He married, in 1890, Rose Buckingham, of Chicago, who died in 1918, and there were four children of the marriage—a son and three daughters.

The Times
7th April 1976

Mr Howard Hughes, the American millionaire business man, film producer, pilot, aircraft designer and formerly majority shareholder of Trans World Airlines, died on April 5 at the age of 70.

A man whose considerable talents, urge for novelty, and endless financial success kept him constantly in the public eye, Hughes considered himself accountable to no one for his conduct of his own business. When he climbed out of his aircraft after breaking an air speed record before the war he said to a reporter: "Well, I said I'd do it and I've done it. What else would you expect me to say?" In his last years his deliberate avoidance of publicity became obsessive, and more was said and written about it than about the man himself.

Many theories were advanced for his being a recluse who had shunned all public appearances for nearly two decades. Some said that his bacteriophobia allowed him no contact with the "diseased" outside world; others claimed that he was no longer alive or had been kidnapped and that only a mythical presence kept his empire going. Even the Nevada State Gaming Commission failed to provoke Hughes to prove his existence: he sent it a handwritten letter with fingerprints instead.

Born in Houston, Texas, on December 24, 1905, Hughes was the son of a Harvard lawyer, a flamboyant, pushful man who invented the Hughes oil drill and left his son an actual fortune of nearly a million dollars and a potential fortune infinitely greater. "He never asked me whether I liked things, he just shoved them down my throat", the son said afterwards in a rare, expansive moment. "But he was a terrifically loved man."

Young Hughes had a conventionally expensive education and went to law to win control of his fortune while still a minor. He turned over the Hughes Tool Company to professional managers at once, ran away with an heiress in 1925, and went into the film business. In 1928 with *Hell's Angels* (starring Ben Lyon and Jean Harlow) he successfully married his twin interest in aviation and the cinema, in one of the most profitable films about flying ever made. At least two other pictures he produced achieved a good reputation: *The Front Page*, which was about newspapers an starred Adolphe Menjou and Pat O'Brien; and *Scarface*, a gangster tale in which Paul Muni had the leading part.

During the next 20 years he divorced his first wife, Ella Rice, in 1928, "discovered" Jean Harlow and Jane Russell, broke the world air speed record, the California-New York transcontinental record, and the round-the-world record in successive years from 1935 to 1937, and founded a pioneer electronics company (Hughes Aircraft). He bought himself into TWA with 600 shares in 1939. Jack Frye, then president of TWA, needed $15m to buy new aircraft and Hughes was persuaded to use the resources of his tool company to buy the aircraft and lease them to the airline. He designed several aircraft himself, including the celebrated plywood craft to carry 700 passengers and save metal which he and the Federal Government developed during the war. It flew once, in 1947, and has been laid up ever since.

He amassed a fortune of over $2,000m, was involved in a series of spectacular incidents like the plane crash in 1947 which nearly killed him while he was testing one of his own designs. The next day he was conducting business in his bed. Before he left hospital he had a working bed specially designed by himself. He was constantly reported in the company of rising young women in Hollywood but evaded all but the barest publicity about his affairs. Occasionally he made brief incursions into public affairs, like the Congressional hearing in 1946 which broke the career of Senator Owen Brewster, but more and more he avoided public accountability for his actions.

A perfectionist, he laboured endlessly to satisfy himself about the virtues of a course of action before following it. He delayed the use of jet aircraft by TWA until long after other airlines had adopted them. He is reported to have brought design managers of aircraft manufacturing concerns to the point of nervous collapse.

This was not the only legal action he was embroiled in. TWA's action against Hughes resulted in a judgment against him for $142m; TWA had alleged that Hughes had used his position as a 75 per cent stockholder to damage the airline by failing to buy jets for its fleet. His second wife, Jean Peters, whom he married in 1957, divorced him in 1971. He was sued by Los Angeles Airways; by Mr Robert Maheu (who formerly ran his gambling operations in Nevada) and by Dr Robert Buckley (his former personal physician).

In 1971 Hughes had moved to the Bahamas from Nevada where he had lived as a hermit since 1966 on the top floor of a Las Vegas hotel. From there he had bought other hotels, casinos, land and mining claims after he divested himself of his interest in TWA.

A tall, lanky man, 6ft 3in in height and for many years less than 10st, Hughes was curiously unanimated for a man with such a taste for violent novelty. He was said to be hard of hearing. In his later years he put on a couple of stone, but became more pinched and severe in the face. He had no children.

Those who had dealings with him in his later years reported his manner as relaxed but remote. Although he seldom wore a tie, the stories of his sloppy clothing were exaggerated. But he did like to conduct business in the informality of a car seat or on board a train or aircraft in a peripatetic life from one of his half-dozen establishments to another. He had a predilection for night work and considered his staff fair game for telephone calls at all hours. Outsiders he normally telephoned during the day. He was said on occasion to work for more than 24 hours continuously, and then go to bed no matter what time it was and sleep until he was rested.

He was stubborn and inordinately suspicious of business partners, never regarding a verbal discussion as anything more than an indication of what might eventually be hammered out in writing. For some 20 years before he died his affairs were protected from inquisition by a battery of confidential assistants and the negative services of a public relations company. He allowed the day-to-day conduct of his companies to go entirely to his managers, and vested a large part of his fortune in a medical foundation. When TWA eventually sued him in a squabble over company policy and control, he simply disappeared for weeks. After five years he eventually sold his majority interest for more than $500m. It was only many months later that a study of the markets in California indicated that he had put most of the money in short-term government bonds.

In a final step in his defence against publicity, Hughes vested all copyright in publications concerning himself in a company he controlled. But this measure did not protect him. In 1972, McGraw-Hill, a New York publishing company, announced it was about to publish his autobiography, based, so the claim went, on a series of interviews Hughes had given to the author Clifford Irving. Hughes broke a 13-year silence in a long distance telephone call from the Bahamas to deny the authenticity of the "autobiography". He said he had never met Clifford Irving. This led to a complicated series of court hearings both in the United States and Switzerland, and the disposal of $650,000 deposited by the publishers in a Swiss bank as advance payment for the book. Irving himself was later convicted of fraud and jailed, as was his wife Edith, who had used the name Helga Hughes to deposit the advances in Switzerland.

The Daily Telegraph
4th January 1979

Hilton, the man who gave English a new word, dies at 91

By HENRY MILLER in New York

CONRAD Hilton, the hotel magnate who learned the business carrying bags from a railway station to a small inn that his Norwegian-immigrant father ran in San Antonio, New Mexico, has died in California, aged 91.

From a modest 5,000-dollar investment in his first hotel in Cisco, Texas, in 1919, he built a corporation that boasts 188 Hiltons in America and 54 others elsewhere.

Mr Jacques Cosse, a spokesman for corporation said: "The word Hilton means hotel. People say 'take me to the Hilton' — not the Hilton Hotel. That is how he will be remembered, for a new word — Hilton."

One of Mr Hilton's mottos was: "Be big. Think big. Act big. Dream big." By doing so, he became America's best-known hotel owner.

Work was said to be his great love and his devotion to it was partly responsible for the break-up of his first two marriages, to Mary Barron and actres Zsa Zsa Gabor. He married his third wife, Mary Kelly, two years ago.

Dance of luck

Ballroom dancing was one of his recreations and at nearly every Hilton hotel opening the spotlight would be trained on Mr Hilton and some pretty young companion. They would perform an old European dance called the Varsoviana which he considered a ceremonial dance of good luck.

Boyish, candid and trusting, Mr Hilton had a hard streak of practicality and the ability to make a shrewd deal. He credited his success mainly to opportunities he saw lying in front of people who were looking elsewhere.

Whenever he bought a hotel, his slogan was "Dig for gold."

At one time or another, the Hilton group included the Waldorf-Astoria and Plaza hotels in New York, the Sir Francis Drake in San Francisco the Mayflower in Washington and the Palmer House in Chicago.

Mr Hilton was an eternal optimist and did not want to listen to bad news. "Don't bother me with that," he would say.

He ran his empire with the help of his two sons by his first wife, Barron and Eric Michael. A third son, "Micky" Hilton, who was Elizabeth Taylor's first husband, died of a heart attack in 1969, aged 42. Mr Hilton also had a daughter, Francesca, by Zsa Zsa Gabor.

Daily Herald
8th May 1925

DEATH OF LORD LEVERHULME

HIS SOAP COUPS

William Hesketh Lever, chairman of Lever Bros., Ltd., and founder of Port Sunlight, was born at Bolton in 1851.

Both for artistic effect and for the edification of the young, it was essential that Lord Leverhulme, the strenuous apostle of Samuel Smiles, should have himself been a self-made man, rising by his own endeavours from poverty to fantastic wealth, a living example of how the glittering prizes of Capitalism are within the reach of every boy who eschews drink, idleness, and nonsensical (!) ideas about Socialism.

Therefore, you will find it everywhere recorded that he began his career as an apprentice in a grocer's shop, packing sardines and prophetic bars of soap. And that is, indeed, true. Only—a fact usually omitted from the record—the grocer's shop happened to be the property of his father, and his father's firm one of the most flourishing in the North of England. It fetched £60,000 when sold.

William Lever, then, did not start from scratch. A man of intense energy and superb self-confidence, completely devoted to work, an early riser, a teetotaller, a non-smoker, a devout Methodist. But, above all, a man of intense energy, which was bound to make its mark in any field.

SOAP CONQUESTS

He chose money-making as his career, and, looking round him, saw possibilities in soap.

He began with "Lever's Honey Soap," but it was "Sunlight" which made him known.

The conquest of soap completed, he began restlessly to push into other spheres—the fish trade is the most familiar example. He played tempestuously with politics as a Liberal. He became a tempestuous patron of the arts.

His moral earnestness and his shrewd business instinct taught him that the wise capitalist seeks to propitiate his workers. Hence his model village at Port Sunlight. Hence the profit-sharing scheme of which he was so proud. Of the £5,000,000 profits made by his company last year, no less than £200,000 was divided among the workers as an object lesson of the blessings of Capitalism and the follies of trade unions.

Philanthropist and profiteer, devout Christian and hard egoist, a toiling slave to his own ambitions, his career, glitteringly successful on the surface, is a tragic contradiction underneath. It was not his fault that this was the natural and approved outlet in these days for his abilities and his dynamic energy. The gods which he worshipped were the gods of Capitalism: let it at least be said for him that he worshipped them with all his might.

Daily Mirror
2nd April 1965

OTHER WOMEN'S FACES MADE HER A FORTUNE

WOMEN who get to the top are usually distinguished more for their drive and energy than their friendliness and charm.

Helena Rubinstein, head of a £350,000,000 cosmetics industry, who died in New York yesterday, managed to maintain an endearing air of simplicity which delighted those who met her for the first time.

She looked, and often souried, more like a Jewish granny than a tough tycoon.

Careful about money, as are so many of the world's richest people, she owned no car, and she always travelled tourist.

But she spent lavishly on exotic jewellery, clothes from the top Paris couturiers, modern paintings and art treasures from all over the world.

Her homes in New York, London, and Paris were more like beautiful museums than places where "Madame," as her staff called her, could put her feet up and enjoy her favourite dining-alone dish —tripe and black bread.

Helena was born in Cracow, Poland. One of eight daughters, she ran away to Australia in order to avoid an arranged marriage.

Requests

Her beautiful complexion led to compliments from the locals. The compliments were followed by requests for some of her face cream, which had been made in Poland for her mother.

She borrowed £250, imported the cream in quantity and the Rubinstein Empire grew until today it employs 30,000 people in fourteen countries.

She had two marriages The first, to a young Australian writer, Edward Titus, ended in a divorce in 1937 after twenty-five years

There were two sons of this marriage. One of them, Roy Titus, is in New York and will continue to run the Rubinstein beauty empire.

Just before World War II, Helena Rubinstein met her second husband, Prince Gourielli, in New York.

He died in 1955, and Helena never remarried.

Courage is not something Helena Rubinstein lacked.

Last May gunmen entered her New York home. They threatened to kill her if she didn't hand over the keys to her jewels.

"All right," she said. "Go ahead and kill me. I'm an old woman and I've lived my life. You can kill me—but you're not going to rob me."

One thing that Helena guarded all her life was the secret of her age.

Now the secret is out. She was ninety-four.

No one could even have suggested that Helena Rubinstein's face was her fortune. But she died a rich and brilliant woman, having made a fortune out of other women's faces.

Causes Célèbres

Occasionally, when people come to feel that someone has been treated by society as a scapegoat, their indignation is aroused and the case becomes a *cause célèbre*. The victim comes to be seen as something of a martyr, sometimes by choice, sometimes by accident. Often the victim is a political one: **Dreyfus**, framed on a charge of treason in a wave of anti-semitism in France; **Sacco** and **Vanzetti**, the avowed anarchists executed in the United States; or **Sir Roger Casement**, an Irish national executed for treason by the British. The Tolpuddle Martyrs, unfortunately, although some were rehabilitated two years after being transported to Australia, appear to have merited no obituaries. Sometimes the scapegoat is chosen not so much on account of who he is, but because he merely happens to be convenient; so the Nazis executed a young Dutchman, **van der Lubbe**, on a trumped-up charge of having started the Reichstag fire. Then there are those ruined by false accusation, represented here by **Fatty Arbuckle**; or those who, like **Oscar Wilde**, are accused by reason of their prominence to serve as an example. Still others come by sheer chance to symbolize the harshness or injustice of contemporary punishment: **Caryl Chessman**, and **Timothy Evans** in England, both victims of capital punishment and probably innocent; or **Oscar Slater**, who spent twenty years in jail, was found to have been wrongly convicted, and given a free pardon and £6000. **Derek Bentley** and **Julius** and **Ethel Rosenberg** aroused a depth of feeling about the propriety of the death penalty that has never since been equalled, both in the same year (1953). Coincidence, or a true sign of the times? **John Garfield** is a reminder that oppression in the twentieth century is not a phenomenon limited to Iron Curtain countries and banana republics.

The vast majority, however, die unsung. Nobody except themselves, their families, and their friends even know of their persecution. The few included here must stand as tribute to them all.

Jan Masaryk, **George Archer-Shee** (the real-life "Winslow boy") and the **Tichborne Claimant** are all different breeds of the other, endlessly fascinating branch of the classic *cause célèbre*: the did-they/didn't-they? were-they/weren't-they? group. Well, did they or didn't they? Were they or weren't they? I hope we never find out!

The Glasgow Herald
11th January 1934

VAN DER LUBBE EXECUTED

Guillotined in Presence of His Judges

APATHETIC TO THE LAST

"Honourable" Death for Reichstag Incendiary

Van der Lubbe, the young Dutchman who was sentenced to death for having set fire to the Reichstag building, was executed in Leipzig yesterday morning.

He was executed on the guillotine instead of being hanged, it being explained at National Socialist headquarters that "while hanging is an ignominious penalty reserved or traitors and such like, Lubbe committed his crime out of conviction."

The execution, in accordance with German law, was carried out in presence of the Judges who had sentenced him. Lubbe remained apathetic to the end.

While it is not expected that it will make any official protest to Germany, the Dutch Government is understood to be "very disappointed" at the execution.

PRESIDENT REFUSES A PARDON

Van der Lubbe, the young Dutchman who was found guilty of setting fire to the Reichstag on February 27 last year, was given the honour—according to the Nazis—of execution on the guillotine instead of the gallows at 7.30 this morning.

At the Nazi headquarters it was explained that van der Lubbe was guillotined instead of hanged, because, "while hanging is an ignominious penalty reserved for traitors and such like, Lubbe committed his crime out of conviction." It was pointed out that decapitation should not be interpreted as a milder form of execution than hanging.

It was late last night when van der Lubbe was informed by Dr Werner, the Reich Prosecutor, that President von Hindenburg declined to make use of his privilege to pardon him, and that the execution would take place the following morning.

STILL APATHETIC.

Lubbe listened with the same apathy he showed during the trial. He gave no reply to the question whether he wanted a clergyman to attend him on his last walk to the guillotine, nor did he express any special wishes which are generally granted to people on the eve of their execution.

The guillotine was erected during the night by the executioner and his attendant in the prison yard of the Leipzig District Court, and everything was ready when the clock sounded the hour of execution. At 7.25 the feeble peals of the prison bells announced to the outer world that a man was paying the penalty for his crime.

Nobody, however, knew that this man was van der Lubbe, the man sentenced to death by Germany's Supreme Court, for burning the Reichstag. There was no indication yesterday that President von Hindenburg had declined to pardon him.

At six o'clock this morning a warder entered Lubbe's cell and told him that his last hour had come. Lubbe did not say a word. He rose, and after he had been shaved the Governor of the prison arrived to lead his prisoner into the courtyard.

JUDGES PRESENT.

When Lubbe entered the courtyard in the dim light this morning the State Prosecutor (Dr Werner) awaited him, attended by the Assistant Prosecutor (Dr Parrisius), the President of the Supreme Court (Dr Bunger), and three Judges of the Supreme Court. Twelve councillors of the State of Leipzig, the Prison Governor, the District Governor, a doctor, and a clergyman were also present in accordance with the law.

The press was not admitted to see the grim spectacle of the execution.

Without showing any signs of emotion Lubbe, with head down, listened to the death sentence being again read by Dr Bunger. The Dutchman shook his head when asked whether he wanted to make a statement.

When the State Prosecutor (Dr Werner) said, "And now I hand you to the executioner," the latter (Engelhardt, of Magdeburg), clad in evening dress and wearing white gloves, laid his hand on the prisoner. Willingly Lubbe followed Engelhardt to the scaffold, where he was tied to a plank.

Engelhardt pressed a button, and Lubbe's head rolled into a basket filled with sawdust. The execution itself lasted 30 seconds only, and before the clergyman had finished his prayers the executioner said, "Justice has been done."

The doctor attested to the death, and while those who attended the execution were signing a document van der Lubbe's body was carried away in a simple black coffin. Yesterday evening Lubbe was examined as to his sanity, and was pronounced sane.—Reuter.

DUTCH GOVERNMENT " VERY DISAPPOINTED "

OFFICIAL PROTEST NOT EXPECTED

THE HAGUE, Wednesday.

Reuter is officially informed that the Dutch Government is "very disappointed" at the execution of van der Lubbe. It is stated that the Government had done all possible to have the death sentence commuted to life imprisonment.

The Dutch Consul at Leipzig has been informed that the body of van der Lubbe will be at the disposal of his family in Holland. This information will be communicated to the members of van der Lubbe's family by the burgomasters of the communities in which they are resident.

The news of the execution of van der Lubbe made a deep impression here. In Government and Parliamentary circles especially surprise was felt at the rapid action of the German Government.

It was generally believed that van der Lubbe's sentence would be commuted to life imprisonment, and in view of the fact that van der Lubbe was believed to be no longer of sound mind his execution was considered unthinkable on these grounds.

—It is not expected that the Dutch Government will protest against the execution after the formal steps already taken. Among the Radical Parliamentary groups the execution has aroused great indignation, as also amongst the population, and large crowds have gathered to read the latest news in front of the newspaper offices.

Only the Dutch National Socialists and Fascist groups approve the death sentence.

The only official statement is one confirming that the Dutch Minister in Berlin was informed of the impending execution last night.—Reuter.

AN UNSOLVED MYSTERY

VAN DER LUBBE MAINTAINS SILENCE

BERLIN, Wednesday.

With the death of van der Lubbe under the guillotine all prospect of solving the riddle of the Reichstag fire appears to have vanished for ever. For the impassive Dutchman maintained his silence to the end, and died without betraying any of the accomplices which the trial revealed he must have had.

All the eye-witnesses of the final scene are pledged to secrecy, but it is known that van der Lubbe showed complete indifference to his fate, and mounted the guillotine with head bowed even lower than usual and arms pinioned behind him, without uttering a sound.

The whole of the proceedings, which took place in the dim light of dawn, only lasted five minutes, and the actual execution 30 seconds. Van der Lubbe's body lies in the coffin pending the receipt of an intimation whether his relatives wish it to be transported to Holland at their own expense. If not, it will be most probably handed over to the Leipzig University for anatomical purposes.

The German press, on instructions, has only published the official announcement of the execution, and has no comment to make on it.

Another man was executed at the same time as van der Lubbe this morning, but in Hamburg Jail and by the axe. He was Ernst Lindau, who two years ago shot a policeman to gain possession of his revolver.—Reuter.

New York Times
22nd May 1952

JOHN GARFIELD DIES AT HOME OF FRIEND

Actor, 39, Famed for 'Tough' Roles on Stage and Screen, Had Cardiac Ailment

John Garfield, stage and screen actor noted for his portrayal of tough characters, died of a heart ailment in the apartment of a friend, Miss Iris Whitney, at 3 Gramercy Park yesterday morning. He was 39 years old.

Miss Whitney, an actress and interior decorator, said Mr. Garfield had visited her Tuesday night and had become ill. She let him stay overnight in the bedroom, while she slept in the living room, she added. After trying vainly to waken him in the morning, she telephoned Dr. Charles H. Nammack, a private physician, who pronounced the actor dead at 9 A. M. The Medical Examiner's office ascribed Mr. Garfield's death to a cardiac condition and said there was "nothing suspicious" about it.

The actor had starred recently in a successful nine-week revival of Clifford Odets' play "Golden Boy." It was in a smaller role in this same play in 1937 that Mr. Garfield gained the prominence that led to Hollywood roles.

His husky physique, shock of dark hair and his truculent manner made him a natural choice for "type casting" as gangster, criminal or "grown-up Dead-End kid."

After the death of his mother when he was 7 years old, the future actor played hookey so often that he was expelled from several schools. Finally he was sent to Public School 45, the Bronx, of which Angelo Patri, who was noted for his rehabilitation of problem pupils, was principal.

"That was the beginning of everything for me." Mr. Garfield said. With Mr. Patri's encouragement, he took up boxing, in which he attained sufficient prowess to rank as a semi-finalist in a Golden Gloves tournament, and studied oratory and dramatics. He attended the Heckscher Foundation dramatic school on a scholarship. To pay his expenses, he earned $6 a week as a newsboy and received $5 more from Mr. Patri.

Aided by Angelo Patri

Born Julius Garfinkle in New York, he was the son of David and Hannah Garfinkle. "My father," he said, "was a presser in a factory during the week, but a cantor on weekends and holidays." Later . . . . into the Bronx.

With the Heckscher Theatre group he appeared in "A Midsummer Night's Dream" and other plays while attending Roosevelt High School. He also studied for the theatre under Mme. Maria Ouspenskaya and Richard Boleslavsky. Next he joined Eva Le Gallienne's Civic Repertory group, where he played minor roles.

Later, as Jules Garfield—the first change in his name—he became associated with the Group Theatre Acting Company, which had been formed in 1930-31. As an apprentice he worked with the regular company at Ellenville, N. Y., where the group's plays were prepared for the stage.

Won Lead in 'Wonderful Time'

His first chance was as a member of the road company of "Counselor at Law," with Otto Kruger. Later he played in the Broadway production, starring Paul Muni. Then he was offered the lead in Marc Connelly's production of Arthur Kober's "Having a Wonderful Time."

The play was a hit, but Mr. Garfield, feeling obligated to the Group Theatre, left his $300-a-week role to accept a $40 bit part in "Golden Boy." "It seemed to me," he said, "that in the Group lay the future of American drama." He appeared in such plays as "Waiting for Lefty," "Awake and Sing," "Weep for the Virgins" and "Peace on Earth."

Mr. Garfield signed a contract with Warner Brothers in 1938 but specified that he be allowed to do one stage play a year. His first assignment was in "Four Daughters." Much of the credit for the success of the picture went to John Garfield—as Warner's had renamed him.

His protests about pictures with prison atmosphere and suspensions from scheduled roles led to better parts in "Juarez," "Saturday's Children," "The Sea Wolf" and "Out of the Fog," and "Tortilla Flat."

More recent pictures include "The Postman Always Rings Twice," "Gentleman's Agreement" and "Body and Soul."

During the war he went on many overseas tours to entertain troops and was a leader in the Hollywood Canteen, West Coast center for servicemen.

In 1951 Mr. Garfield testified before the House Committee on Un-American Activities as "a cooperative" witness, "I am no Red," he insisted. "I am no pink. I am no fellow traveler." He described himself as a Democratic party member and a political liberal and said Communist front organizations that had used his name had done so without his authorization.

In 1948 he won the La Guardia Award for stage and screen, established by the Non-Sectarian Anti-Nazi League to Champion Human Rights.

The Times
11th March 1948

JAN MASARYK'S SUICIDE IN PRAGUE

◆

JUMP FROM APARTMENT WINDOW

CZECH MINISTER'S REQUEST TO SECURITY COUNCIL

It was announced in Prague yesterday that a State funeral would be given to Mr. Jan Masaryk, the Foreign Minister of Czechoslovakia, who had committed suicide by jumping from the window of his apartment in the Foreign Office.

Mr. Nosek, the Minister of the Interior, stated in the National Assembly that Mr. Masaryk must have been suffering from depression, which had been " increased by recriminations from the west " for his part in the crisis.

A formal request by the Czechoslovak Minister at United Nations headquarters for an investigation of events in his country by the Security Council has been declined on the ground that it is a nongovernmental communication.

MR. JAN MASARYK

Mr. Jan Masaryk, whose tragic death in Prague is reported on another page, was the distinguished son of a famous father whose single-minded devotion to his people was the major factor in the creation of modern Czechoslovakia out of the ancient lands of Bohemia and Moravia.

Jan Garrigue Masaryk was born in 1886 in Prague and educated there. He emigrated to the United States in 1907, but when the Czech Republic came into being in 1918 he entered its Ministry of Foreign Affairs. The next year he went for a time to Washington as Chargé d'Affaires. Counsellor at the London Legation from 1921 to 1922, he returned for a time to his own country as secretary to the Minister of Foreign Affairs and in 1925 he returned to London as Minister to Great Britain, a post which he was to hold until the end of 1938.

Then came the time of reconstruction. In August he flew to London to take part in the discussions of the Unrra council and remained to participate in the conference of the preparatory committee of the United Nations organization. On the vexed question of minorities he was uncompromising in his view that the Sudeten Germans should leave Czechoslovakia, but declared that the transfer would be carried out with humanity. He was also unwilling to give way to Poland on the longstanding dispute over Teschen. Towards the end of 1946 he was nominated, against Roman Catholic opposition, as head of the Czechoslovak delegation to the United Nations Assembly.

Though by upbringing and inclination he inclined more to the west than to the east, he made great efforts after the liberation of his country to get each side to understand the point of view of the other. This was strikingly demonstrated in his speech as president of the World Federation of the United Nations Associations which took place at Marianski Lazne last August. If he failed, it was a noble failure.

and, in spite of the *Gestapo*, numbers of his fellow-countrymen managed to hear him. Employing an appealing colloquial style, and thoroughly understanding his own people, his influence over them was very great. At first the Germans sought to ignore it, but then they were forced into attempts to discount the effect he created. In December there appeared in these columns a letter from him which sought to expose the German attempt to fix the blame for bloodshed in Bohemia and Moravia on well known Czechoslovaks who enjoyed the hospitality of other countries ; and pointed to the long-premeditated German plan to eradicate the culture of his nation.

In July, 1940, Masaryk was appointed Minister of Foreign Affairs in the Czechoslovak provisional Government and in 1941 Deputy Prime Minister as well. Late in the latter year he went for eight months to the United States, where he had discussions with President Roosevelt and members of his administration, and also gave many lectures and had conferences with the Czechoslovak colony there. Returning to Great Britain in July, 1942, he continued to play a prominent part in the conferences between the various provisional Governments which had their headquarters in London during the war, and his broadly European point of view more than once brought a harmony to the discussions when, had it not been for his tact, discord might have reigned. In spite of increasing pressure of business he continued his broadcasts, though less regularly than before. Nevertheless, the embarrassment of the Germans was not appreciably lessened.

The Munich agreement was a severe personal blow to him and after its conclusion he felt the need to conclude his mission to London. First, however, he went to the United States and undertook an extended lecture tour. Opening it at Columbia University he said that the partitioning of Czechoslovakia would be worth while if it brought peace, but expressed some doubt whether it had in fact done so. He was no longer, he said, interested in saving frontiers but rather in saving Europe. In July, 1939, he was back in London, and stated that he intended to devote the remaining years of his life to trying to bring humanity back again. On September 8 he introduced the first news bulletin in the Czech language to be broadcast from the B.B.C. He declared that his national programme was a free Czechoslovakia in a free Europe. He was to prove much the most popular broadcaster Czechoslovakia had ever known. He went regularly to the microphone.

Manchester Guardian
28th January 1953

DEATH SENTENCE

There is a very strong case for the abolition of capital punishment in this country, and the execution of Derek Bentley will make it still stronger. There is no case, while capital punishment remains the normal penalty for murder, for exempting Bentley from it. He has been fairly tried and sentenced, his appeal has failed, the Home Secretary has decided that he cannot advise the Queen to use her royal prerogative of mercy in his favour. The arguments advanced for special consideration make a powerful appeal to the emotions, and in so tragic a story it is right that they should. But to yield to the appeal would be to set aside two vital principles of our law. It is said to be unfair that Craig, on whom the greater burden of responsibility for the crime falls, should escape death because of his youth while his subordinate is to die. But to ignore the existing distinction between older and younger criminals —and if it is done in this instance it will be done in others—is to throw into confusion the whole principle on which the treatment of youthful criminals is founded. Does anyone who now calls for the reprieve of Bentley suggest that the distinction made between criminals over and under eighteen is a wrong one? Again, it is said that if there are degrees of guilt there ought to be degrees of punishment, and Bentley's should be the lighter. But it is well established that where two men are engaged together on an enterprise which ends in murder it is not only the man who strikes the blow who is guilty. In many murders where more than one man is concerned there are degrees of guilt ; one man is the ringleader, the others follow his lead ; yet all are guilty and all subject to the same penalty. If Craig had been of the same age as Bentley he too would have been condemned to death also ; the contrast between their sentences would disappear, and with it the force of humane emotion which makes Bentley appear to be unfairly treated. Yet would Bentley's share of the guilt have been any less if his companion had been older?

Does not this argument put a premium on the employment of at least one youthful member in any criminal enterprise which may end fatally? If it is true that Bentley's sentence ought to be lighter than Craig's that is a strong point against the death sentence, which admits of no degrees, and in favour of substituting long terms of imprisonment, which can be modified in detail. It is not a ground for making exceptions to the law as it now stands.

In the Commons yesterday Mr Silverman advanced a doctrine which at first sight seems even more perilous than departure from the legal principles just discussed. This is that the Home Secretary is answerable to Parliament for the advice he gives the Sovereign on the exercise of the royal prerogative, in just the same way as he is for any other of his duties in office, and that Parliament is entitled to tell him what advice he should give. One can easily see what the acceptance of this doctrine would lead to. Every murderer has friends or kinsmen who would feel bound to press his M.P. to take up his case ; few members would not shrink from the invidious decision to refuse ; soon numerous murders would become matters for debate in Parliament, which would become in effect a final court of appeal, without the judicial qualifications and with all the political disqualifications for such a duty. It is no doubt for this reason that Parliament has in the past steadfastly followed the rule that the Home Secretary's advice in this sole respect cannot be questioned until after it has taken effect. This may seem paradoxical, but it is wise. There is something in Mr Bevan's argument that the Speaker should have let Mr Silverman's motion go on the order-paper and then ruled it out of order. But Mr Silverman's main position cannot be maintained, or can be maintained only with

possibly disastrous consequences. That he has been able to carry with him in this argument so many members of distinction and experience is one more illustration of the difficulty of considering dispassionately any question of which the death sentence makes part, and one more argument for abolishing it, not in Bentley's case but in all cases. We hope the members who have acted with Mr Silverman will give solid support to the long-debated reform of the law. But the need is to reform the law, not to whittle it away by making exceptions to it.

New York Times
30th June 1933

FATTY ARBUCKLE DIES IN HIS SLEEP

Film Comedian, Central Figure in Coast Tragedy in 1921, Long Barred From Screen.

ON EVE OF HIS 'COME-BACK'

Succumbs at 46 After He and Wife Had Celebrated Their First Wedding Anniversary.

Roscoe C. (Fatty) Arbuckle, film comedian, died of a heart attack at 3 o'clock yesterday morning as he slept in his suite in the Park Central Hotel. A few hours before he and his third wife, Mrs. Addie McPhail Arbuckle, had celebrated their first wedding anniversary. He was 46 years old.

The comedian and Mrs. Arbuckle went to bed about midnight. She awoke three hours later and spoke to him. She got no answer. A few minutes later the house physician had pronounced Arbuckle dead.

"Only yesterday," said Macklin Megley, a friend of the actor, "he finished the last of a series of shorts for Warner Brothers. He came off the set in the studio in Astoria and said to Ray McCarey, the director, 'Do you mind if I knock off for a few minutes? I can't get my breath; I want a breath of fresh air.'"

He finished the picture, however, and came home to prepare with Mrs. Arbuckle, for the party. At dinner they were the guests of William La Hiff, restaurant owner, along with Johnny Dundee and Johnny Walker, prizefighters, and other Broadway folk. From the dinner they returned to their suite.

Continued

Called It His "Happiest Day."

Joseph Rivkin, Arbuckle's manager,. seemed broken up over the news. "He said to me only yesterday, 'This is the happiest day of my life, Joe; it's a second honeymoon.'"

Megley and other friends spoke with some bitterness of "the bad break" that put Arbuckle out of the films at the height of his career, when he was making $1,000 a day.

The body was moved to the Campbell Funeral Church at Sixty-sixth Street and Broadway. It will lie in state in the Gold Room of the establishment in a gray cloth casket until the funeral service is held to-morrow (Saturday) afternoon at 1 o'clock. Rudolph Valentino, Jeanne Eagels and June Matthews occupied the same room in death.

Falstaffian in size, if not in subtlety, Fatty Arbuckle had figured in many minor escapades before the fatal party at which he was host in the St. Francis Hotel, San Francisco, on Sept. 5, 1921. It was one of his specialties to e arrested for speeding; he was known the world over by his nickname, but every police court appearance added more publicity and the public laughed indulgently.

His popularity was universal, specially with the children. Arbuckle went to Paris and was much fêted on the boulevards. He placed a wreath on the Tomb of the Unknown Soldier beneath the Arc de Triomphe. He returned to this country in triumph, hailed as a sort of fat, funny man of good, clean fun.

Held $3,000,000 Contract.

Arbuckle's last contract in 1921 called for twenty-two films for which he was to receive $3,000,000. Some of the pictures had been completed, but were scrapped by Paramount Pictures Corporation after the San Francisco affair.

Virginia Rappe, young actress and model, died as the result of injuries she received during that drinking party and Arbuckle was arrested and charged with murder on Sept. 10. After he had spent eighteen days in a death cell, the grand jury passed an indictment for manslaughter, and Arbuckle was tried three times. Twice juries disagreed upon the verdict; the third trial resulted in an acquittal.

Then came long years of Fatty Arbuckle's trial before public opinion. His efforts at rehabilitation were entirely unsuccessful until quite recently, when he had been working hard on four comedy "shorts" for Warner Brothers. The Arbuckle affair resulted in his pictures being banned everywhere.

Roscoe Conkling Arbuckle was born at Smith Centre, Kan., on March 24, 1887.

In 1913 he was very fat and comparatively affluent. Then he met Mack Sennett of bathing beauty fame, and he played in comedy films with the late Mabel Normand, Charles Chaplin, Chester Conklin, Ford Sterling and others. In 1917 he formed a partnership with Joseph M. Schenck for the release of his comedies through Famous Players Lasky Corporation.

Arbuckle is reputed to have made $1,000 a day in his heyday. He returned to the stage in 1927 as Jimmy Jenks in "Baby Mine," and was tolerably well received at Chanin's Theatre in this city. Later he made several vaudeville appearances.

The comedian was married three times. Aminta Durfee Arbuckle, his early vaudeville partner, after standing by him for two years after the tragedy, sued for divorce in 1923. His second wife, Doris Deane Arbuckle, obtained a divorce in 1929. He married Addie Oakley Dukes McPhail last year.

The Times
2nd April 1898

ARTHUR ORTON.

Arthur Orton, better known as the Tichborne Claimant, died suddenly yesterday morning at his lodgings in Shouldham-street, Marylebone. The cause of death is supposed to have been heart disease. Orton came to Shouldham-street, where he occupied the second floor at No. 21, about two months ago with his wife, who is still a comparatively young woman, and his appearance was well known in the neighbourhood. He had been in very poor health for some time past, but so needy were his circumstances that he had to get parish medical relief and had even been advised by the parish doctor to enter the infirmary. About 6 o'clock yesterday morning his wife, alarmed at his appearance as he lay in bed, sent for a doctor, who pronounced life to be extinct.

The death of Arthur Orton recalls the story of one of the most famous impostors and certainly of the longest trials in the annals of our history. Of pretenders who have sought to support fictitious claims by pertinacious and unscrupulous lying, there had, of course, been many before Orton; but it was left for him to work out the lie circumstantial in such a way as to divide the country for years into two great parties—those who "believed" in the Claimant, and those who did not; while for a long time, even after his eventual conviction and sentence, there were still thousands of people full of sympathy for the "unfortunate nobleman" who was "languishing" in prison instead of enjoying the possession of "his estates." But his "Full Confession," given to the world in 1895, removed any doubt that may have been still lingering in the mind of the most fervent of his supporters as to the real character of the claims which had caused an intensity of public excitement that only those who actually lived through it can now adequately realize.

It was in 1866 that the first was heard of these claims. Arthur Orton, the son of a shipping butcher, of Wapping, and then about 31 years of age, was following the business of a slaughterman at Wagga Wagga, New South Wales, and he saw in an Australian paper an advertisement in which Lady Tichborne set forth that she had heard that her son, Roger Charles, was alive in Australia, and she begged him to communicate with her. This Roger, the son of Sir Charles and Lady Tichborne, and heir to the Tichborne estates, was born in 1829, and was educated in France till about 1843. He entered the Army in 1849, proposed marriage to his cousin, Miss Kate Doughty, in January, 1852, but was refused, and sailed from Havre for Valparaiso in 1853. In April, 1854, he left Valparaiso in the Bella, but the vessel foundered at sea, and nothing more was heard of him afterwards. Lady Tichborne, however, clung to the idea that he was still living, and it was in response to her advertisements that Orton, leaving Wagga Wagga in June, 1866, turned up at Sydney, and announced that he was the missing son, he and eight of the crew having been saved from the wreck of the Bella. He reached England at the end of 1866, in order to further his claim to the Tichborne estates, valued at something like £24,000 a year, and, though the claim was resisted on behalf of Sir Henry (minor), son of Sir Alfred Tichborne, the fact that Lady Tichborne herself "recognized" the Claimant as her son, and believed in him up to the time of her death, told enormously in his favour. He had, too, plenty of time in which to work up his case, as it was not until May 11, 1871, that the hearing of his action began before Chief Justice Bovill in the Court of Common Pleas. It lasted 103 days, and in the result the jury expressed themselves satisfied that the Claimant was not Sir Roger Tichborne. He was thereupon arrested for perjury and forgery, but was released on bail three weeks afterwards. His trial on these charges began before Chief Justice Cockburn and Justices Mellor and Lush on April 23, 1873, and did not close until February 28, 1874, the Claimant being found guilty and sentenced to 14 years' penal servitude. The actual number of days occupied by his trial had been no fewer than 188, while it was remarkable not only for its

inordinate length but also for the extraordinary scenes by which it was characterized. For these scenes the person chiefly responsible was Dr. Kenealy, who, in April, 1873, succeeded Serjeant Sleigh as leading counsel for the defence, and conducted the case in such a manner that the Lord Chief Justice was led to denounce in his summing up, "the torrent of undisguised and unlimited abuse in which the learned counsel for the defence had thought fit to indulge," and to declare that "there never was in the history of jurisprudence a case in which such an amount of imputation and invective had been used before." After the trial was over Dr. Kenealy tried to turn the Claimant's "wrongs" into a national question by publishing a virulent print called the Englishman; while, undeterred by his being disbenched and disbarred, he started the Magna Charta Association, and also went about the country delivering the most extravagant speeches concerning the trial. Elected M.P. for Stoke in February, 1875, he moved for a commission of inquiry into the conduct of the Tichborne case, but obtained only one vote in addition to that of himself and co-teller, while there were 433 against him.

Futile as this agitation was, so far as Arthur Orton was concerned, it had the effect of maintaining public interest in a subject which had already been more or less before the country since 1866, and, it may be added, of keeping up a still widespread belief that the Claimant was the genuine Sir Roger after all. There was, too, a certain revival of interest in the matter after the release of the Claimant in October, 1884, on ticket-of-leave, he having completed nearly 11 years of his sentence. An attempt was then made to reopen the question, but the novelty of Orton's lectures and of his appearances at music-halls and publichouses as the ill-used baronet who still yearned for his estates soon wore off, and in 1895 he played his last card by publishing his "confessions." These appeared in the People, and were certainly interesting reading as showing the way in which an imposition that had deceived so many thousands of persons, and had cost the Tichborne estate £92,000, had originated and been carried out. In them Orton related with considerable detail how his attention was called to Lady Tichborne's advertisement, and how, merely for a "lark" at first, he assumed a mysterious air and allowed his friends at Wagga Wagga, who declared that he "answered the description," to think that he was the person in question. Hard up for money, and finding people ready enough to advance some to him when they thought he was Sir Roger Tichborne, he left them under that delusion, hoping to raise sufficient to enable him to get to Panama, where he had a brother, and there settle down. At Sydney he met Bogle, Gilfoyle, and many other persons acquainted with the Tichborne family, and proceeded, as he termed it, to "suck their brains." Being a good listener and having a retentive memory he speedily secured a large fund of information about the Tichbornes, and was then able to "recall" to various more or less gullible persons a variety of bygone events in such a way as to convince them of the truth of his story. He was thus able to raise some hundreds of pounds, and he then set off for Panama with the intention of there letting the whole thing drop. But, as he could not get rid of some of his newly-made friends, he found himself forced to come on to England and act up to the character he had already assumed. He again resorted to his former tactics of "sucking the brains" of people who could tell him about the Tichbornes, and bit by bit "the story really built itself" and "grew so large that he really could not get out of it." His worst experience in the working up of his case seems to have been the first meeting with Lady Tichborne in Paris, the very prospect of which made him ill; but the remarkable fact that she "recognized" him as her son was, of course, of the greatest assistance to him in his scheme, and thenceforward he had plenty of support, financial and otherwise. Then, as people got "infatuated" with him and persisted in calling him "Sir Roger," he forgot, as he said who he was, and his mind was so thoroughly worked ... that by degrees he began to believe that he really was the rightful owner of the estates." But his story, though most elaborately concocted, broke down under the extremely rigorous investigations to which it was subjected, and Orton himself was, no doubt, fully cured of his delusion as to his own identity long before his sentence came to an end.

On the failure of his health Orton had to give up lecturing, and he then took a tobacconist's shop, but for the past few months he is said to have got a living by " showing " himself in various publichouses at Kilburn at receptions got up for his benefit.

Personally, the chief characteristic of Arthur Orton during the days when he was still known as the Claimant was his remarkable bulk. As it happened, however, he began to assume his massive proportions only when he started on his career of imposture. At the time of his leaving Wagga Wagga, in June, 1866, he was quite slim, and, according to his " confessions," only 10st. 8lb. During his few months' stay at Sydney he increased to 18st., and when, in January, 1867, Lady Tichborne " recognized " him in Paris as the missing Sir Roger, he was 21st. He still kept putting

on flesh until, by the time of his conviction, he weighed no less than 25st. When, however, he regained his freedom in 1884, at the end of his ten years and eight months' imprisonment, he weighed, as he himself represented, only 10st. 6lb., or 2lb. less than in the summer of 1866 ; but at the time of his death he is said to have weighed 18st.

It is a singular coincidence that so recently (as Thursday last) there was offered for sale by Messrs. Knight, Frank, and Rutley, at their galleries in Conduit-street, a collection of legal and other documents relating to the Tichborne trial. Besides voluminous briefs, letters, and documents, it comprised a complete file of the *Tichborne Gazette* from June 11, 1872, to November, 1874, some volumes of Dr. Kenealy's paper, the *Englishman*, a large number of photographs, and an assortment of the posters by which, when the Claimant was touring the country, the British public were called upon to come to his aid and help him to regain his " rights." It was, perhaps, only in accordance with the Claimant's fall from his previous notoriety that the entire collection of relics should have realized only £7 17s. 6d.

The Times
4th August 1916

EXECUTION OF CASEMENT.

A TRAITOR'S RECORD.

IRISH BRIGADE FOR EGYPT.

Roger David Casement, sentenced to death for high treason, was hanged in Pentonville Prison at 9 o'clock yesterday morning. Shortly before execution he was received into the Roman Catholic Church.

By 8 o'clock a crowd had begun to assemble in Caledonian-road, which runs in front of the gaol, but it was never very large. About 150 people, chiefly women and children from the immediate neighbourhood, stood on the footpath and fixed their gaze on the prison walls, and when the breakfast hour at the various local works arrived, probably another 100 spectators put in an appearance. Many of these were munition workers. The tramway and omnibus traffic was in no way impeded. The passengers, like the crowd, turned their eyes towards the prison buildings. The only intimation to the outside world that the execution had taken place was by the striking of the minute bell, but the street noise was so loud that its first note was not generally heard. It reached the women munition workers, however, for they at once rushed off to work again. Near to where they had stood was a group of workmen, who on hearing the bell raised a cheer. Five minutes afterwards the crowd had disappeared, and the street resumed its normal appearance.

About half an hour after the sentence had been carried out, the usual official notices were posted outside the main doors of the prison. The first was a " Declaration of the Sheriff and others," that judgment of death was executed on Roger David Casement in their presence, and it was signed by R. Kynaston Metcalfe, Acting Under-Sheriff of London ; O. E. M. Davies, governor of the prison ; and James McCarroll, Roman Catholic priest of the prison. A second was in like terms, but it was signed by A. R. Preston, Under-Sheriff of Middlesex. A third notice was the certificate of the surgeon, P. R. Mander, that he had examined the body and found that Roger David Casement was dead.

THE DISPOSAL OF THE BODY.

The inquest on Casement's body was held by Mr. Walter Schroder, in the prison, shortly before noon.

Mr. Gavan Duffy, who appeared on behalf of the relatives, formally identified the body, and said that he could not state Casement's age exactly, but he was between 50 and 60. His general health was sometimes very bad. Asked what was his last known address in this country, the witness said he preferred not to make it public. He therefore wrote it down and handed it to the Coroner.

Mr. Duffy then asked if he might make a statement in reference to the burial.

The CORONER.—The order for the burial is issued by me and handed to the governor. As to any matter in reference to the burial of the body beyond that, any application must be made to the authorities.

Mr. Duffy.— I appreciate that, sir. I have applied to the Home Office for permission to have his body. I consider it a monstrous act of indecency to refuse it.

The CORONER.—On that I cannot express any opinion.

Mr. O. E. M. Davies, governor of the prison, and Mr. J. F. Style, acting chief warder, gave evidence of the execution of the sentence. The former, in reply to Mr. Duffy, said that Roman Catholic priests were present, and they performed the rites of burial of their Church.

Dr. P. R. Mander, senior medical officer of the prison, said that death was instantaneous.

Mr. Duffy. I understand that the doctor has had the prisoner under observation for a month, and I want him to say whether, as a result of the observation, he can say whether there is any truth in the suggestion of insanity which has been made in the Press.

The witness.—I saw no evidence of insanity.

The jury then returned a formal verdict of " Death due to execution."

The Times
24th August 1927

SACCO-VANZETTI TRIAL.

HISTORY OF THE CASE.

The case of Sacco and Vanzetti, who were executed for murder just after midnight on Monday, has dragged on for over six years.

Nicola Sacco and Bartolomeo Vanzetti, Italians who had never been naturalized in the United States, were tried at Dedham, Massachusetts, in 1921 on a charge of murdering the paymaster and guard of a shoe company in South Braintree in the previous year. The murder was accompanied by a robbery of $15,000 (£3,000). After 59 witnesses had testified for the prosecution and 99 for the defence, both prisoners were convicted. Vanzetti was also convicted on a charge of attempting to shoot a paymaster at Bridgewater in 1919.

The defence offered in the case of each defendant was an *alibi*. Vanzetti said that he was in Plymouth selling fish at the time of the murder, and Sacco that he was in Boston trying to get a *visa* for a passport. There was a great mass of confused evidence. They were, however, convicted.

At once Communist organizations all over the world started an outcry. They declared that the two men had been denied a fair trial and that they had been tried less for murder than for Communism. It happened that at the time of their arrest the authorities all over America were conducting a strong campaign against the "Reds," and the Department of Justice was arresting and deporting Communists in great numbers. It was known that Sacco and Vanzetti, who had fled to Mexico during the war in the mistaken belief that they were liable for conscription, had returned to Massachusetts to foment industrial unrest and class war.

When the case had been reviewed by a higher Court and a new trial refused there was a further outcry, and violent anti-American demonstrations—including the explosion of a bomb at the door of the United States Embassy in Paris—took place all over Europe. There were other demonstrations in Bordeaux, Marseilles, Lyons, Vera Cruz, and Algiers, and also in London. In Lisbon an attempt was made to blow up the American Consulate.

Others besides Communists came to believe that the two men had not had a fair trial and took up their case. Large funds were raised by public subscription, and two attempts to reopen the case were made but failed. Further demonstrations followed on each occasion, and more bombs were exploded, this time in Argentina and Uruguay.

On July 16, 1926, immediately after the second refusal of the Court to grant a new trial—this application and the various other applications for a new trial had to be made before Judge Thayer, who tried the case in the first instance—counsel for the defence filed affidavits supporting a new motion on the ground that entirely new evidence had reached him. This evidence was an alleged confession by a Portuguese named Madeiros, who was in Dedham gaol under sentence of death for another murder.

This evidence was not substantiated in the eyes of the authorities, and Sacco and Vanzetti were sentenced at Dedham on April 9 of this year to death by electrocution in the second week in July. After a petition for an investigation into the case had been sent to Mr. Fuller, Governor of Massachusetts, by the "Sacco-Vanzetti Defence Committee," Mr. Fuller appointed a committee of three—Dr. Lowell, of Harvard, Dr. Samuel W. Stratton, and ex-Judge Robert Grant—to advise him in his inquiry, and a 30 days' stay of sentence was granted. This committee came to a unanimous decision that there was no evidence of any miscarriage of justice, and that the sentence should stand.

THE COMMITTEE'S REPORT.

In their report on the case the committee, headed by Dr. Lowell, said :—

The committee have seen no evidence to make them believe that the trial was unfair. On the contrary, they are of opinion that the Judge endeavoured, and endeavoured successfully, to secure for the defendants a fair trial ; that the District Attorney was not in any way guilty of unprofessional behaviour ; that he conducted the prosecution vigorously, but not improperly ; and that the jury, a capable, impartial, and unprejudiced body, did, as they were instructed, " well and truly try and true deliverance make." . . . To us the reading of the stenographic report of the trial gives the impression that the Judge tried to be scrupulously fair.

The committee, however, added :—

From all that has come to us we are forced to conclude that the Judge was indiscreet in conversation with outsiders during the trial. He ought not to have talked about the case off the bench, and doing so was a grave breach of official decorum. But we do not believe that he used some of the expressions attributed to him, and we think that there is exaggeration in what the persons to whom he spoke remember. Furthermore, we believe that such indiscretions in conversation did not affect his conduct at the trial or the opinions of the jury, who, indeed, so stated to the committee.

The report says that in the case of Sacco the chief circumstances are as follow :—

He looks so much like one of the gang who committed the murder that a number of witnesses are sure that he is the man. Others disagree. But at least his general appearance is admitted, even by many of those who deny the identity, to resemble one of the men who took part in the affair. Then a cap is found on the ground near the body of the man he is accused of killing which bears a resemblance in colour and general appearance to those he was in the habit of wearing. And when tried on in Court it fitted—that is, his head was the size of one of the men who did the shooting. Then there is the fact that a pistol that Berardelli [one of the murdered men] had been in the habit of carrying, and which there is no sufficient reason to suppose was not in his possession at the time of the murder, disappeared, and a pistol of the same kind was found in the possession of Vanzetti when he and Sacco were arrested together, and of which no satisfactory explanation is given. It is difficult to suppose that Berardelli was not carrying his pistol at the time he was guarding the paymaster with the pay-roll, and no pistol was found upon his person after his death. It is natural, also, if the bandits saw his pistol, they should carry it off, for fear of someone shooting at them as they escaped.

Of the alleged confession of Madeiros the report says :—

The impression has gone abroad that Madeiros confessed committing the murder at South Braintree. Strangely enough, this is not really the case. He confesses to being present, but not to being guilty of the murder. He says that he, as a youth of 18, was influenced to go with the others without knowing where he was going or what was to be done, save that there was to be a hold-up which would not involve killing, and that he took no part in what was done. In short, if he were tried his own confession, if wholly believed, would not be sufficient for a verdict of murder in the first degree. His ignorance of what happened is extraordinary, and much of it cannot be attributed to a desire to shield his associates, for it had no connexion therewith.

Dealing with the statement of Madeiros that the shooting brought on an epileptic fit which showed itself by a failure of memory, the report continues :—

In his whole testimony there is only one fact that can be checked up as showing a personal knowledge of what really happened, and that was his statement after the murder that the car stopped to ask the way at the house of Mrs. Hewins, at the corner of Oak and Orchard streets in Randolph. As this house was not far from the place on a near-by road where Madeiros subsequently lived, he might well have heard the fact mentioned. If the Government were to try to convict him of this offence and he were to say that the whole thing was a fabrication to help Sacco and Vanzetti, he certainly could not be convicted on his own confession, and probably could not even be indicted.

During the trial there was a good deal of disagreement between the expert witnesses about the bullet which killed Berardelli. The committee decided that the evidence for the prosecution was right, and that the bullet was fired from a pistol such as that in the possession of Sacco at the time of his arrest. This bullet was of a type so obsolete that a search failed to reveal any of that type. Bullets of this description, however, were found on Sacco when he was arrested. A revolver found on Vanzetti was similar to one known to have been carried by the murdered man but not found on the body. Finally, the committee stated :—

It has been urged that a crime of this kind must have been committed by professionals, and it is for well-known criminal gangs that one must look. But to the committee both this crime and the one at Bridgewater do not seem to bear the marks of professionals, but of men inexpert in such crimes.

FURTHER BOMB OUTRAGES.

On August 4 Governor Fuller made public his decision that there was no justification for intervention in the case, after an inquiry which had lasted eight weeks. This decision was followed by further protests and demonstrations in Union-square, New York, and in Paris and London, where a Sunday meeting in Trafalgar-square was followed by a procession to the American Embassy. After further bomb outrages in New York, where two bombs exploded in railway subways, and in Philadelphia, Baltimore, and Argentina, where a general strike was proclaimed, the next step in the case came on August 9, when the pleas for revocation of the death sentence, or, alternatively, for a stay of execution, were dismissed by Judge Thayer. Shortly before midnight on August 10, however, the time at which the execution was due to take place, Mr. Fuller announced a respite, to extend until August 22.

On the same night there was a demonstration in Hyde Park, attended by about 10,000 people, who subsequently marched to the American Embassy. Police charges were necessary to break up the crowd. During the following days there were bomb explosions at the home of one of the jurors in the case, on Boston Common, and at Buenos Aires, and another protest meeting took place in Boston. On August 15 Sacco was reported to have ended a hunger strike which had lasted 29 days.

On Tuesday, August 16, a new appeal, embodying three pleas of the defence, came before the Supreme Court of Massachusetts, which, on August 19, gave judgment against all three pleas. Various pleas for a stay of execution were then made to the Judges of the Supreme Court individually and were refused in turn by Federal District Judge J. M. Morton and by Justices Holmes, Brandeis, Stone, and Chief Justice Taft.

The Times
2nd February 1948

DEATH OF OSCAR SLATER

Oscar Slater, who was wrongfully convicted of murder in 1909 and was vindicated after he had spent nearly 19 years in prison, died on Saturday at Ayr. He was 75. Slater was tried at Edinburgh for the murder of Marion Gilchrist, of Glasgow, on December 21, 1908. After his arrest in America Miss Gilchrist's maid, Helen Lambie, said that she identified him as a man she saw leaving Miss Gilchrist's flat. Slater was sentenced to death, but on the eve of execution the sentence was commuted to penal servitude for life. He was released in 1927.

The late Sir Arthur Conan Doyle and others worked to establish his innocence. In 1928 the Scottish Court of Criminal Appeal set aside the conviction, and in the same year Slater accepted £6,000 from the Government as an ex gratia payment for his wrongful conviction.

The Times
1st December 1900

A Reuter telegram from Paris states that OSCAR WILDE died there yesterday afternoon from meningitis. The melancholy end to a career which once promised so well is stated to have come in an obscure hotel of the Latin Quarter. Here the once brilliant man of letters was living, exiled from his country and from the society of his countrymen. The verdict that a jury passed upon his conduct at the Old Bailey in May, 1895, destroyed for ever his reputation, and condemned him to ignoble obscurity for the remainder of his days. When he had served his sentence of two years' imprisonment, he was broken in health as well as bankrupt in fame and fortune. Death has soon ended what must have been a life of wretchedness and unavailing regret. Wilde was the son of the late Sir William Wilde, an eminent Irish surgeon. His mother was a graceful writer, both in prose and verse. He had a brilliant career at Oxford, where he took a first-class both in classical moderations and in Lit. Hum., and also won the Newdigate Prize for English verse for a poem on Ravenna. Even before he left the University in 1878 Wilde had become known as one of the most affected of the professors of the æsthetic craze and for several years it was as the typical æsthete that he kept himself before the notice of the public. At the same time he was a man of far greater originality and power of mind than many of the apostles of æstheticism. As his Oxford career showed, he had undoubted talents in many directions, talents which might have been brought to fruition had it not been for his craving after notoriety. He was known as a poet of graceful diction; as an essayist of wit and distinction; later on as a playwright of skill and subtle humour. A novel of his, "The Picture of Dorian Gray," attracted much attention, and his sayings passed from mouth to mouth as those of one of the professed wits of the age. When he became a dramatist his plays had all the characteristics of his conversation. His first piece, Lady Windermere's Fan, was produced in 1892. A Woman of no Importance followed in 1893. An Ideal Husband and The Importance of Being Earnest were both running at the time of their author's disappearance from English life. All these pieces had the same qualities—a paradoxical humour and a perverted outlook on life being the most prominent. They were packed with witty sayings, and the author's cleverness gave him at once a position in the dramatic world. The revelations of the criminal trial in 1895 naturally made them impossible for some years. Recently, however, one of them was revived, though not at a West-end theatre. After his release in 1897, Wilde published "The Ballad of Reading Gaol," a poem of considerable but unequal power. He also appeared in print as a critic of our prison system, against the results of which he entered a passionate protest. For the last three years he has lived abroad. It is stated on the authority of the Dublin Evening Mail that he was recently received into the Roman Catholic Church. Mrs. Oscar Wilde died not long ago, leaving two children.

New York Times
3rd May 1960

Caryl Chessman Executed; Denies His Guilt to the End

Kidnapper Goes Calmly to Death After Appeals in Last Hours to California High Court and Justice Douglas

SAN FRANCISCO, Calif., May 2—Caryl Chessman was executed today.

After a series of last-hour legal maneuvers in state and Federal courts on opposite sides of the country, the convict-author kept his ninth scheduled appointment in the gas chamber at San Quentin Prison. He had lived nearly twelve years in the prison's death row.

[The execution of Caryl Chessman set off a wave of revulsion in many parts of the world, according to United Press International. Several anti-American demonstrations were reported.]

Chessman was escorted into the little octagonal steel room, with its dark green walls, and strapped into the right hand one of two chairs just after 10 A. M., Pacific Coast time (1 P. M. New York time).

At 10:03:15, cyanide pellets were dropped from a container under the chair into a basin of sulphuric acid solution. At 10:12, prison doctors said Chessman was dead of the resulting acid fumes.

Warden Fred Dickson said Chessman's last request to him had been "to specifically state that he was not the red-light bandit" for whose crimes he was paying the penalty.

Chessman, 38 years old, was convicted in 1948 on numerous felony counts growing out of depredations against parked couples in lonely places around Los Angeles. The counts invoking the death penalty included kidnapping, "with bodily harm."

An hour and fifty-five minutes ahead of the scheduled execution hour the seven-justice State Supreme Court began discussion in near-by San Francisco of a petition filed on Saturday afternoon. The petition had sought a writ of habeas corpus.

At 9:10 A. M. the court ruled, 4 to 3, against the first request. Fifteen minutes later George T. Davis of Chessman counsel asked for a stay so that the decision might be appealed to the United States Supreme Court.

This was denied at 9:50 by the same vote.

Five minutes later Mr. Davis and Miss Rosalie Asher, co-counsel, were in the chamber of Federal District Judge Louis E. Goodman. They wanted a brief stay, time enough to argue on a request to petition the United States Supreme Court for a writ of review.

At almost the same time Associate Justice William O. Douglas of the Supreme Court had sent word of his denial of a plea for a stay of execution. The papers had been airmailed to him in Washington.

Judge Goodman listened to Mr. Davis and Miss Asher, then sent his clerk, Edward Evansen, to ask Miss Celeste Hickey, his secretary, to put a phone call through to the warden at San Quentin at 10:03.

The prison number was passed along to Miss Hickey orally through several persons and somehow, in the noise and tension, a digit was dropped. She had to dial again after having verified the number. Associate Warden Louis Nelson told her that the cyanide pellets had just been dropped.

Miss Asher emerged, weeping, from the judge's chambers.

Wanted an Hour's Stay

Judge Goodman told reporters he had planned to ask the warden to stay the execution one hour.

At Sacramento, Gov. Edmund G. Brown received the news of the execution as he sat in his private study in his Capitol office. Outside the Capitol, a group of pickets was marching. Its leader, Dr. Isadore Ziferstein, a Los Angeles psychiatrist, called the Governor "the hangman of California."

Other pickets had marched outside the prison all night.

As Chessman was led into the gas chamber, sixty witnesses, about two-thirds of them newspaper, radio and television reporters, were crowded into a first-floor room in the death house. Set into one side of this room was the gas chamber.

Five guards sat on a bench outside, one for every window through which the witnesses watched.

Chessman, in white shirt, new blue jeans and stockings, walked into the chamber without show of emotion, accompanied by four guards. Two of them strapped him into the chair. All walked out.

At that moment Chessman looked to his right and saw two reporters with whom he had often talked. He moved his lips carefully to shape the words:

"Tell Rosalie [his attorney and executrix] I said good-by. It's all right."

A woman reporter made a circle with her thumb and forefinger to show she understood. The other reporter nodded. Chessman half smiled.

A moment later the cyanide pellets were released. Later the physicians estimated he had been conscious for thirty-two seconds.

Warden Dickson told a news conference after the execution that Chessman had been "hopeful until ten minutes to ten," when the warden informed him of the State Supreme Court's refusal to grant a stay.

He said that Chessman had stayed awake all night writing letters and had left seven with him for delivery. Prison chaplains had stopped by but Chessman, an agnostic, had requested no last rites.

Mr. Davis, reflective and solemn, said afterward in his San Francisco office that perhaps his client's "greatest flaw, his greatest lack of character, was his unrelenting unwillingness to believe in something greater and bigger than himself."

"He almost prided himself on the fact that he remained an agnostic to the end," the attorney said.

Funeral Set For Today

SAN FRANCISCO, May 2 (UPI) — Caryl Chessman had made his own funeral arrangements with the Harry M. Williams funeral home in near-by San Rafael.

"He signed all the papers himself," said Mr. Williams.

The body will be cremated without ceremony, tomorrow at Mount Tamalpais cemetery in San Rafael.

Mr. Williams said he understood that Chessman's mother was buried there. Chessman had told him he had no living relatives.

12-Year Court Fight Helped Stir Pleas To Save Chessman

Special to The New York Times.

SAN FRANCISCO, May 2—Caryl Whittier Chessman's death today in San Quentin's gas chamber ended a twelve-year battle for survival — a largely single-handed battle that stirred world-wide controversy.

Probably not since the Sacco-Vanzetti case in the nineteen twenties had a capital offense created such an international furor.

Protests came from all strata of society. Millions signed petitions in Brazil, thousands in Switzerland. The Queen of Belgium pleaded for his life, as did Dr. Albert Schweitzer, Aldous Huxley, and Pablo Casals. So did the Vatican, through its newspaper, L'Osservatore Romano.

Today's appointment with the executioner was the ninth for Chessman, a fact that in itself generated intense feeling. Adding to the mounting intensity of those feelings was the picture of the condemned man, expertly tutoring himself in the law while living in the prison's death row—and time and again staving off his scheduled execution.

Sentence Called Cruel

"Cruel and inhuman punishment" was a phrase used by those protesting Chessman's pending execution after so many years in prison. Many noted he had been doomed to die without having taken another life.

In January, 1948, Chessman, then 27 years old, had been on parole for only six weeks from California's Folsom Prison when he was arrested in Los Angeles as the suspected "red-light bandit" who had been marauding lonely spots. The marauder had approached his parked victims, usually couples, with a red light resembling that of a police car.

The police said he had confessed, but Chessman insisted that the admission had been extracted by torture. He was charged with eighteen counts of robbery, kidnapping, sexual abuses and attempted rape.

During his two-week trial in June, Chessman acted as his own counsel, with a court-appointed public defender as legal adviser. The jury deliberated thirty hours. It returned a verdict of guilty on seventeen counts, without recommendation for mercy, thus making the death penalty mandatory on two counts.

The two counts derived from California's "Little Lindbergh" law, enacted in 1933 as an aftermath of the Lindbergh kidnapping case and providing death for kidnapping "with bodily harm."

Chessman was sent to San Quentin's condemned row to await an appeal to the State Supreme Court, automatic in capital punishment cases. The conviction and sentence were upheld, and Chessman's first execution date was set for March 28, 1952.

Then began the almost incredible activity in Cell 2455 Death Row. That prison's address became the title of a book that sold a half million copies and was translated into a dozen languages. It was one of four books Chessman wrote in the cell. At times he ingeniously smuggled out manuscripts after he had been forbidden to publish any more.

One book, "The Kid Was a Killer," was published today.

Chessman also, as he put it, "read or skimmed 10,000 law books." The legal briefs subsequently addressed to state and Federal courts from 2455, were widely acknowledged as expert in style and logic.

After the success of his first book, Chessman retained a group of attorneys to help him with the increasingly difficult judicial maneuvers.

During those years Chessman's appeals centered principally on a plea of denial of due process of law because of an allegedly faulty trial transcript. At the start of his trial he had moved, unsuccessfully, for a daily transcript of the testimony.

The trial's court reporter died of a heart attack before he had transcribed more than a third of the record. The reporter had used an old-style shorthand script. Chessman contended that this was not wholly familiar to the reporter appointed by the court to complete the transcription.

Various courts, however, rejected Chessman's attacks on the trial transcript.

In all, Chessman carried his appeals twice to the Superior Court of Marin County, in which San Quentin is situated; once to the State Appellate Court; eleven times to the California Supreme Court; seven times to the U. S. District Court; five times to the United States Court of Appeals for the Ninth Circuit, and sixteen times to the United States Supreme Court.

In his latest appeals to the courts, Chessman argued through counsel that he had been subjected to "cruel and unusual" punishment in violation of the Constitution. In this argument he cited a last-minute reprieve granted to him in February by Gov. Edmund G. Brown, following receipt of a message from the State Department.

The Governor was said to have acted partly to spare President Eisenhower possible embarrassment on his goodwill trip to South America. Uruguayans had threatened to demonstrate against the President if Chessman were executed.

Of late, Chessman's lawyers also offered evidence that they said showed that Chessman was not the "red-light bandit." However, the courts rejected further petitions for a writ of habeas corpus, and this evidence never received a judicial review.

Daily Graphic
30th July 1910

CADET VINDICATED.

ADMIRALTY'S WITHDRAWAL OF THE CHARGE.

COMMONS REFERENCES.

George Archer-Shee, the cadet who was dismissed from Osborne Naval College, was yesterday completely vindicated. The Admiralty unreservedly withdrew the charge against him—namely, that on October 7th, 1908, when he was thirteen, he stole a 5s. postal order from another cadet, Terence Back.

The announcement was made with unexpected suddenness soon after the hearing of the petition of right by the boy's father, Mr. Martin Archer-Shee, was resumed in the King's Bench Division before Mr. Justice Phillimore and a special jury. Sir Rufus Isaacs, the Solicitor-General, said on behalf of the Admiralty that with regard to the issues of fact the Court would not be further troubled with this case. As the result of the investigation that had taken place, he wished to say that he accepted the statement made in evidence by George Archer-Shee that he did not write the name on the postal order, and did not cash it, and consequently that the boy was innocent. He made this statement without reserve of any description. On the other hand, his learned friend Sir Edward Carson (for the petitioner), would also accept his statement with regard to the action of the Admiralty that those responsible for what had happened acted bona-fide and with a reasonable belief in the truth of the statements made to them.

The Times
13th July 1935

ALFRED DREYFUS

THE GREAT "AFFAIRE"

More than a generation has passed away since the storm which raged for years round the unfortunate Captain Dreyfus, whose death is recorded on another page, rent the French nation, almost in twain, poisoned the political atmosphere of France, undermined successive Ministries, swept at times through the Presidential gates of the Elysée itself, and threw its lengthening shadow even over international relations.

The origin of the *affaire Dreyfus* touches the grotesque, for it arose out of the activities of a wretched charwoman, employed by the French Secret Service to collect scraps from the waste-paper basket of Colonel von Schwarzkoppen, the Military Attaché of the German Embassy, in the hope of discovering the channel through which ever since 1892 military secrets had been leaking out from the French War Office. The only clue hitherto obtained was a reference in a note of Schwarzkoppen to information received from *ce* (*sic*) *canaille de D.* (who subsequently turned out to be an obscure German agent of the name of Dubois), when one day in the summer of 1894 some bits of paper were brought to the War Office which, when pasted together, enumerated five documents of considerable importance that the writer promised to obtain for delivery to Germany. This was the famous *bordereau* which played a damning part in the case. There was clearly a traitor, and a well-informed traitor, at work. Who could it be?

In spite of the ignominious collapse of Boulangisme in 1889, a strong reactionary party still existed in France, which, though composed of several different and discordant factions, still hoped to overthrow the Parliamentary Republican form of government. Indignation at the Panama scandal fostered the campaign against the Jewish "hidden hand."

Nowhere were political reaction and anti-Semitism so firmly entrenched as in the Army, which, not without some reason, regarded the squalid and corrupt intrigues of Republican politicians as dangerously harmful both to the dignity of France and to the supreme exigencies of national defence. General Mercier, then Minister of War, and most of the highest authorities in the War Office, shared these sentiments. So when, with only the initial D of one of Schwarzkoppen's agents to guide them, they explored the list of officers of the General Staff who might have been in a position to know the secrets which the author of the *bordereau* had promised to deliver to Germany, they at once fastened on to the name of Captain Dreyfus. It began with a D. He was presumed to possess knowledge of the documents mentioned in the *bordereau*. There was a considerable similarity between his handwriting and that of the *bordereau*. Above all, he was a Jew, and therefore obviously a potential traitor.

ARREST AND SENTENCE

The arrest took place on October 15, 1894, and du Paty de Clam, to whom the task was entrusted, carried it out in his own melodramatic fashion. He told Dreyfus to write out portions of the *bordereau* in his presence, but without giving him any information as to its nature or as to the immediate purpose. It was a cold day and a cold room, and at one moment Dreyfus shivered and his hand shook. "Ah, you tremble!" exclaimed du Paty de Clam in an ominous voice. "No," replied the still unsuspecting Dreyfus: "only my fingers are chilled." When the copy was finished, du Paty shouted at him, "You are the traitor! I arrest you!" and pointed at the same time to a revolver which he had laid on the table, expecting the unfortunate man to make away with himself as soon as he realized that his crime had been found out.

Dreyfus protested indignantly his innocence, but to no purpose. He was sent to the military gaol, and thence brought before a Court-martial. Though a minority of the five experts produced by the War Office denied the identity of handwriting, a secret *dossier*, which subsequently turned out to consist of forged documents, which were never communicated to him, was submitted to the Court, and he was convicted of treacherously supplying a foreign Government with French military secrets, and sentenced to degradation and lifelong imprisonment in a fortress. He bore with extraordinary stoicism the terrible ordeal of public degradation inflicted upon him in Paris, in January, 1895, and he was shipped off shortly afterwards to the Ile du Diable, on the coast of French Guiana, where he was to be subjected to a long series of moral tortures far worse than all the physical hardships of solitary detention in a pestilential climate, and sometimes in heavy chains.

There was a growing minority of distinguished and courageous Frenchmen whose conscience would not allow them to remain silent when they were once convinced that there had been an appalling miscarriage of justice. In September, 1897, Scheurer-Kestner, the Vice-President of the Senate, threw all his great influence into the scales in favour of revision of the proceedings of 1894. Jaurès, the Socialist leader, asked searching questions in Parliament. The anti-Dreyfus Press was full of vitriolic abuse. Even the more intelligent public opinion was still largely apathetic, and at the General Election of May, 189 , most of Dreyfus's Parliamentary supporters were thrown out. The new Brisson Cabinet began by setting its face as firmly as had its predecessors against revision, and the civilian War Minister, Cavaignac, professed to possess fresh evidence of Dreyfus's guilt in a super-*dossier* full of the most extravagant fabrications.

THE TURNING OF THE TIDE

Picquart, however, once more resumed the offensive. Almost simultaneously with the appearance of Zola's impassioned manifesto "J'accuse" Picquart wrote and published a letter to the Prime Minister in which he gave Cavaignac the lie and set forth once more the whole overwhelming case in support of revision.

The tide had at last turned. M. Brisson intimated that the Government had now determined to take steps to secure a revision. Cavaignac resigned. The Brisson Cabinet was, indeed, overthrown by a vote of the Chamber censuring Ministers for their failure to protect the Army against attacks, and another was formed under M. Dupuis, with M. de Freycinet as War Minister. Only then the Court of Cassation declared the claim put forward by Mme Dreyfus for revision to be "formally admissible."

At that very moment, the sudden death of M. Félix Faure, who was believed to have always shared the views of the Army chiefs, brought a very different type of man to the Elysée in the person of M. Loubet. The anti-Dreyfusards organized public demonstrations against the new President. There were stormy debates in the Chamber and fresh Ministerial crises. But the Court of Cassation on June 3, 1899, annulled the judgment passed on Captain Dreyfus in 1894 and ordered a fresh Court-martial to be held at Rennes. On the very day before this decision Esterhazy had admitted that he was the author of the *bordereau*, but declared that he had acted under the orders of high officials of the War Office.

THE RENNES COURT-MARTIAL

Dreyfus was brought back from the Ile du Diable, where he had no inkling of the long campaign conducted by his friends to get his case reopened, and had indeed been tortured by vile reports that his wife had renounced him. But the iron had entered too deep into his soul, and, always a proud and rather hard man, he was too weary and too embittered to do justice to himself when he appeared before the Court at Rennes.

Still, even if the personal impression which he made upon his Judges was not favourable, the facts including the damning evidence that the notorious *bordereau* had been deliberately ante-dated spoke far more powerfully than he or even his able advocates, Demange and Labori, could do for his innocence. Yet at the end of the long-drawn trial, which, ushered in by a dastardly attempt to shoot Labori on his way to the Court, was throughout a mockery of the forms of justice, the military Judges, by five against two, found him again guilty of treason and sentenced him to 10 years' detention. But, with an inconsistency which at once vitiated their finding, they admitted extenuating circumstances for a crime so heinous that nothing could extenuate it.

The President and the French nation, except a fanatical section past redemption, realized that it was no longer the honour of Dreyfus, but of French justice and of France herself, that was at stake, for the Rennes verdict had sent a thrill of horror and indignation throughout the civilized world.

Von Schwartzkoppen, it may be noted, declared on his death-bed in 1917, " Dreyfus is innocent it was all lies and forgeries." Von Schwartzkoppen's memoirs fully bear out the innocence of Dreyfus and the guilt of Esterhazy.

On September 19 Dreyfus received a free pardon from M. Loubet and was set at liberty. Not for another seven years, however, was complete justice done to him. In June, 1906, when France had finally recovered her balance and the first Morocco crisis had tested and purified the real patriotism of the French people, the full chambers of the Court of Cassation were summoned together to reconsider the case, and in the following month recorded their judgment, quashing all previous proceedings and declaring the innocence of Captain Dreyfus to be clearly established. He was gazetted back into the Army a few days later, and on the same spot on which he had undergone his degradation in 1894 he was publicly invested with the Legion of Honour. At the same time Colonel Picquart was appointed general in command of the 10th Division in Paris.

Besides an unsuccessful attempt on Dreyfus's life when he attended the translation of Zola's remains to the Pantheon, there was to be yet another and finer epilogue to the drama when the War broke out in 1914. Dreyfus, who had meanwhile retired from the Army, volunteered for active service, and, besides taking part with his battery in the battle of the Ourcq, when the Germans threatened Paris in the first month of the War, he had the satisfaction of seeing his eldest son promoted on the battlefield. After the War Alfred Dreyfus passed finally out of the public eye into the privacy of a serene old age.

The Times
10th March 1950

MURDERER HANGED

Timothy John Evans, 25, lorry driver, of Rillington Place, Notting Hill, W., was executed yesterday at Pentonville, for the murder of Geraldine, his 14-months-old daughter, on December 2. Evans was sentenced to death at the Central Criminal Court on January 13.

The Times
15th July 1953

Misgivings Relieved

The swift but thorough inquiry conducted by MR. SCOTT HENDERSON has disposed of the shadow of suspicion that justice might have miscarried when TIMOTHY JOHN EVANS was hanged in 1949 for the murder of his child, having been also charged with that of his wife. Concerning the death of MRS. EVANS, three different stories have been told by two murderers, the second being JOHN REGINALD CHRISTIE, whose execution for another murder has been appointed for to-day. EVANS, on being arrested, said that he had strangled his wife. At his trial he withdrew this confession and said that CHRISTIE had killed her in attempting to induce abortion. CHRISTIE, last month, giving evidence in support of his plea of insanity when charged with a later murder, said that he had murdered MRS. EVANS by gas poisoning. Of these three stories, the second and third are totally incompatible with the condition of the body when found. EVANS's original confession, on the other hand, tallied with it in detail; and his confession of how he strangled the baby—the offence of which he was actually convicted—corresponded as closely to the condition of the child's body as discovered by the police. There is other evidence, from much less tainted sources, which amply confirms the finding of the jury; but these are the essential facts required to set public misgivings at rest.

The inquiry has served a most valuable purpose. These misgivings, though they now prove unfounded, were real. They needed and deserved to be allayed. They were more than an accidental by-product of the peculiarly nauseous exploitation of a very sordid case. Very many people, accustomed to discounting the effects of such sensationalism upon clear thought, were still perturbed by the unembroidered fact at the heart of the case—the coincidence that, if the verdict was correct, there were two murderers living in 1949 in one squalid little house in Rillington Place. If the police had known, as they know now, that CHRISTIE in 1949 had already killed two women, their investigation of the deaths of MRS. EVANS and her child would have taken a different course, as would the trial of EVANS. But MR. HENDERSON has shown that the same conclusions would have been inevitably reached.

It is now possible to face again the great question of capital punishment unhaunted by the dreadful suspicion that an innocent man has lately been hanged. The issue of its abolition is sure to be raised when the long-awaited Report of the Gowers Commission is published, though this was not included in their terms of reference. The case for the death penalty has not been strengthened by these two trials and executions; neither has it been weakened.

New York Times
20ᵗʰ June 1953

SPY CASE A STORY OF LEGAL BATTLES

Rosenbergs' Death Sentences Signaled Court Maneuvers Exceeding Two Years

---

CLIMAX BY 'INTERLOPERS'

Plea to Douglas Raised Point That Kaufman Had Barred —Clemency Twice Denied

When Julius and Ethel Rosenberg were put to death last night two years, two months and fourteen days had passed since they were sentenced to die for betraying their country.

The death sentence was pronounced by Judge Irving R. Kaufman on April 5, 1951, and the next day the first notice of appeal was taken. Thus was signaled the beginning of a legal battle waged untiringly on behalf of the convicted atom spies. The arguments were taken from the District Court here to the Circuit Court of Appeals and to the United States Supreme Court.

In addition, the condemned couple appealed twice to the President of the United States for clemency, but both times, once in February and again yesterday, President Eisenhower refused.

Three times scheduled executions were stayed to permit the hearing of appeals and further argument. Even so, the Rosenbergs lived a day beyond the fourth date for the execution of their sentences.

"Interlopers" Gain a Stay

This extraordinary circumstance came about through the granting of a stay by Associate Justice William O. Douglas at the behest of two attorneys, Fyke Farmer of Nashville, Tenn., and Daniel G. Marshall of Los Angeles, who two days earlier had been termed "intruders" and "interlopers" by Judge Kaufman.

Newly entering the case, they presented to Justice Douglas, as they had attempted unsuccessfully to offer to Judge Kaufman, the contention that the General Espionage Act of 1917, under which the Rosenbergs were sentenced, had been superseded by the 1946 Atomic Energy Act. This latter act provides that the death penalty or imprisonment for life may be imposed in espionage cases only upon recommendation of the jury. The Rosenberg jury had not made such a recommendation.

The argument of the two attorneys was upheld by Justice Douglas at the special session of the recalled Supreme Court yesterday, but its applicability was rejected by a majority of the court 6 to 3. Justice Douglas' stay, under which the Rosenbergs had obtained an extra day of life, was vacated by this decision. A final appeal for executive clemency was denied by the President, and the doom of the Rosenbergs was sealed.

The couple became the first United States civilians to be put to death for espionage. Although the record of espionage in this country goes back to the British Major John André, put to death by the Continental Army for dealing with Benedict Arnold, the crime was not formally defined until the 1917 Act. It was under this act, as amended, that the Rosenbergs were tried and convicted.

Trial Opened in March, 1951

A jury of eleven men and a Bronx housewife in Federal Court here convicted the couple on March 29, 1951. The jury found that the 35-year-old electrical engineer and his 37-year-old wife had funneled vital information on the atomic bomb to the Soviet Union in the war years of 1944 and 1945.

The trial opened March 6, 1951, before Judge Kaufman. Irving H. Saypol, then United States Attorney for the Southern District of New York and now a Justice of the State Supreme Court, told the jury that the pair had conspired to steal and deliver to the Soviet Union "the one weapon that might well hold the key to the survival of this nation and the peace of the world—the atomic bomb." He branded the Rosenbergs as "traitorous Americans" worshiping and owing allegiance to the Soviet Union and to world communism.

Testimony at the trial disclosed that the Rosenbergs were part of an international spy apparatus that operated so effectively the Soviet Union obtained vital information enabling her to produce an atomic bomb years before her own scientists could have solved the secrets of nuclear fission. There is evidence that just a month after the bomb was dropped on Nagasaki a sketch and detailed description of the terrible weapon was in the hands of the Russians.

In passing sentence, Judge Kaufman said the crime of the Rosenbergs was "worse than murder." He expressed the belief that the placing of this weapon in the hands of the Russians had precipitated Communist aggression in Korea.

"By your betrayal," Judge Kaufman told the Rosenbergs, "you undoubtedly have altered the course of history to the disadvantage of your country. We have evidence of your treachery around us every day—for the civilian defense activities throughout the nation are aimed at preparing us for an atom bomb attack."

The Rosenbergs maintained their innocence to the end, but the evidence against them was damning. It was provided chiefly by David Greenglass, Mrs. Rosenberg's brother. He testified that his sister and his brother-in-law had recruited him to steal atomic bomb secrets, among them a rough sketch of the detonating device and other details of a bomb similar to that which was dropped on Nagasaki, Japan, in 1945, when he was an Army sergeant acting as foreman of an atomic assembly plant at Los Alamos, N. M.

Dr. Walter Koski, nuclear physicist, testified that the information revealed in sketches made by Greenglass was sufficient to disclose to any foreign power expert the atomic research experiments then in progress at the atom bomb center.

The Rosenbergs, evidence showed, turned over the stolen atomic secrets to Anatoli A. Yakovlev, at that time the Soviet vice consul in New York. He was indicted with the Rosenbergs, but had left the country long before they were arrested.

The trial established links between the Rosenbergs and Harry Gold, a Philadelphia chemist, who confessed he was the contact man and courier for two Soviet agents. The agents were Alan Nunn May, British scientist, and Dr. Klaus Fuchs, German-born British-naturalized atomic physicist who was present at the birth of the atomic bomb at Los Alamos in 1945. Both scientists admitted their espionage activities and received prison terms. Gold is serving a thirty-year term in the United States, as is Morton Sobell, an electronics engineer convicted with the Rosenbergs. Greenglass was sentenced to fifteen years for his part in the conspiracy.

The Rosenbergs were natives of this city and were educated in New York schools. Both attended Seward Park High School, although they did not meet until several years after they had been graduated.

Rosenberg received a Bachelor of Science degree in Electrical Engineering at City College in February, 1939. He then worked for several engineering concerns and eventually was employed as a junior engineer in the signal service of the War Department's general depot in Brooklyn.

He transferred later to the Signal Corps, working his way up to the position of associated engineering inspector. He held that post until Feb. 9, 1945, when he was suspended on the recommendation of his commanding officer, who said he had received information that Rosenberg was a member of the Communist party.

From then until his arrest on July 17, 1950, Rosenberg was active as a partner in several private businesses dealing in surplus and engineering products.

Ethel Rosenberg, like her husband, grew up on New York's lower East Side. As a young girl she was interested in singing, the piano, dancing and dramatics. She was graduated from high school at the age of 15 and became the youngest member of the Schola Cantorum after having taken voice lessons.

She was employed at various times as a stenographer and typist. In 1940, she worked for three months as a temporary clerk in the Bureau of the Census in Washington.

Crime & the Law

No list of (in)famous criminals could omit Dr. **Crippen**, the archetypal felon on the run and the first to be caught by modern technology, namely radio; or **Landru**, more affectionately known as Bluebeard, a true "murderer by trade". **Herschel**, the inventor of fingerprinting, and **Bertillon**, who has some claim to being the greatest detective we have known, stand for the other side of the business, while **J. Edgar Hoover** might be regarded by some as being the outstanding all-rounder. The American Romantic tradition is epitomized in **Jesse James**, the original great train robber, standing for outlaws and gangsters the world over, from Ned Kelly to Dick Turpin and **John Dillinger**, a ruthless yet romantic character in an unromantic age. **"Pancho" Villa** is remembered as the good-natured bandit, though his early tendencies to Robin Hoodery had turned to terrorism by the time of his murder in 1923. Wyatt Earp, on the other hand, stands here as the archetypal lawman.

After Livy and Cicero, Lord **Halsbury** is one of the greatest, and certainly one of the most influential, of legal minds, happily sharing the honours with his American near contemporary, the great **Oliver Wendell Holmes**. **Napoleon Buonaparte**, the Corsican maestro whose notice appears elsewhere in this book, may be better known for his general-ship, but he is also responsible for the basis of most of Europe's legal systems, the Code Napoléon: and who is to say that this is not his most powerful and lasting legacy? **Clarence Darrow** is, of course, the defence counsel whose example surpasses all others, and but for whom writers of American TV series might have to search considerably wider for inspiration. **Nathan Leopold**, probably Darrow's most famous client, originated the concept of "murder for kicks", and must share with the Birdman of Alcatraz (obituary elsewhere) the honour of keeping alive human faith in rehabilitation. **Adolf Eichmann** is here to remind us, should we need reminding, not only of the scale crime can assume, but also of the apparent fineness of the line between crimes against humanity and the performance of duty.

Jack the Ripper endures as a giant of crime folklore and as the epitome of obsessional mass murder, though his tally of six was quite modest by the standards of some of his (or her) modern American cousins, who seem to be vying for a place in the Guinness Book of Records. **Albert Anastasia** represents business-suited felons everywhere and, one is tempted to suggest, the getter of "just deserts".

Finally we feature two criminals whose exploits prompted major changes in the law. Incredible as it may seem, kidnapping for ransom was a novelty in 1932 when aviator Charles Lindbergh's infant son was stolen from his New Jersey cot and slain. It took the police three years to track down **Bruno Richard Hauptmann**, the ultimately convicted perpetuator, and the resultant "Little Lindbergh Law" as it was known, recognized kidnapping as a federal offence in America for the first time. **Daniel M'Naghten** tried to assassinate then British prime minister Sir Robert Peel, shooting instead the statesman's political secretary. The discussion in the House of Lords that followed M'Naghten's trial crystallized the notion of insanity as a legal defence, and has become a yardstick for many of the world's legal systems ever since.

The Telegraph
31st August 1971

U.S. 'KILLER FOR THRILL' DIES AT 66

By Our New York Staff

NATHAN LEOPOLD, who horrified the world in 1924 when he and a friend killed a boy for thrills, has died of a heart attack in hospital in San Juan, Puerto Rico, aged 66. He left his eyes to a local school of medicine.

In recent years Leopold, who was paroled from prison in 1958 after serving 33½ years, has tried to atone by becoming a guinea pig for medical research.

In 1924 Leopold, then 19, and Richard Loeb, 18, both students from wealthy families, killed Bobby Frank, 14, to "test their reactions."

Clarence Darrow, one of the greatest American lawyers at the time fought successfully to save them from execution. They were sentenced to life imprisonment for murder and 99 years for kidnapping.

Judge John Caverly recommended that they never be paroled.

Loeb was killed in a fight with another prisoner in 1936.

27 languages

In prison, Leopold reorganised the prison library, learned 27 languages and became an authority on ornithology and mathematics.

In 1949, Mr Adlai Stevenson, Governor of Illinois, commuted his 99-year kidnapping sentence to 85 years for his work as a guinea pig in tests of new drugs against malaria.

This made him eligible for parole in 1953. It was denied him then and again in 1955 and 1956, but he was eventually released in 1958.

Leopold went to Puerto Rico as a $10 (£4) a month laboratory technician in a missionary hospital.

In 1959 he entered the University of Puerto Rico, took a master's degree in social medicine and later worked for the Puerto Rican Health Department.

In 1961 he married the widow of a San Juan doctor.

Forfeited every chance

When he left prison, Leopold was asked if he felt he had paid his debt to society.

He replied: "Atonement, expiation, that's impossible for me to say. I don't know how to measure punishment.

"I have forfeited every chance for happiness. Now whether that's enough, I don't know."

In a recent interview, Leopold said: "The crime is definitely still in the central part of my consciousness. Very often it occupies the forefront of my attention and I can think of nothing else.

In a classic denunciation of capital punishment which saved Leopold and Loeb from execution, Clarence Darrow told Judge Caverly: "Your honour stands between the past and the future.

"You may hang these boys, you may hang them by the neck till they are dead. But in doing so, you will turn your face to the past.

"In doing it, you are making it harder for every other boy who, in ignorance and darkness, must grope for the future, for a time when hatred and cruelty will not control the hearts of men . . . when we can learn that all life is worth saving, and that mercy is the highest attribute of man."

The brilliant killer who wiped the slate clean

IN 1924 two brilliant, wealthy young students shocked the world by kidnapping and brutally murdering a boy—just for the thrill of it.

At their famous trial 14 - year - old Bobby Frank's killers said they wanted to test their reaction to the experience.

They were sentenced to life imprisonment for murder and 99 years for kidnapping.

One of them, Richard Loeb, died in jail in 1936. The other, Nathan Leopold, died last night—still trying to atone for his guilt as he had done for the last 47 years.

ON HIS DEATH BED Leopold insisted that his body be used for research. He gave his eyes to medicine.

IN JAIL he offered himself as a guinea pig for gruelling malaria tests.

He learned 27 languages and became an authority on several sciences.

For his work on malaria his 99-year kidnap sentence was commuted to 85 years.

This made him eligible for parole. In 1958 he was turned loose.

He worked as a laboratory technician in a missionary hospital.

Then he took a degree in social medicine and went to work for the Puerto Rican Health Department.

Leopold had entered prison a slim young man. He came out balding, flabby and sick with diabetes.

Asked once if he felt he had paid his debt to society, he said :—

"I have forfeited every chance of happiness. Other people will have to decide if that's enough."

LEOPOLD IN 1924   **LEOPOLD IN 1963**

New York Times
23rd July 1934

DILLINGER SLAIN IN CHICAGO; SHOT DEAD BY FEDERAL MEN IN FRONT OF MOVIE THEATRE

CHICAGO, July 22.—John Dillinger, America's Public Enemy No. 1 and the most notorious criminal of recent times, was shot and killed at 10:40 o'clock tonight by Federal agents a few seconds after he had left the Biograph Theatre at 2.433 Lincoln Avenue, on Chicago's North Side.

DILLINGER DEFIED CAPTURE FOR YEAR

Nation's Most-Feared Criminal, He Was Hunted by Army of Police and Federal Agents.

John Dillinger, the mid-West outlaw who, in the space of a year became one of the country's most notorious bad men, a killer of the old frontier tradition, had left a trail of dead and wounded across several States and of terror through the Northwest.

A small army had been on his trail, and several times he had been ambushed. But each time he was able to shoot his way out and flee. Each time, except when he achieved the daring exploit of walking out of the heavily guarded and supposedly escape-proof Lake County jail at Crown Point, Ind., last March 4.

Then, a prisoner facing a long list of charges, he cowed guards and other inmates with a two-ounce piece of wood whittled to resemble a pistol and stained with shoe blacking.

Only last Fall did his exploits begin to attract attention. He had been sentenced in 1924, a farm boy who had committed an amateur hold-up in his home town, to six years in the Indiana State Prison for robbing a grocery in Groveton.

Met Band in Prison.

The prison schooled him in the ways of the outlaw. There he met most of the criminals who later formed his band.

Released in 1930, he resumed his career of crime. His hold-ups, carried out in a sensational, almost flamboyant manner, won for him and his mob the reputation of being super-criminals.

On the request of his father, the family's minister and the grocer he had held up, he was released from jurisdiction by the parole board in May, 1933. This, although he had been in trouble since the very beginning of his term, having "hid out" in the machine shop to which he was first assigned, sawed through the bars of his cell door and made his way into an adjoining cell block, fought with another inmate, destroyed prison property and given all round evidence of being incorrigible. The Governor revoked the board's decision, however, and he was declared a delinquent patrolist.

Scoffing at the revocation of his parole, Dillinger, free in spite of the Governor, never did return. The old charges became back numbers. He resumed his career of crime. His hold-ups, carried out in a sensational, almost flamboyant manner, won for him and his mob the reputation of being super-criminals.

In the late Summer he staged three robberies, in one of them holding up the girl cashier of a small-town bank, obtaining $25,000 in all. A fellow-inmate of reformatory days was with him. But he wandered into Ohio, was captured and held there as a bank robber.

Engineered Prison Break.

From that time on Dillinger grew to his present stature, to which fact and fable have contributed. While he was being held at Lima, Ohio, he engineered a plot by which Harry Pierpont, Russell Clark, John Hamilton and Charles Makley, who had come to know the daring with which he planned for those he dominated at Michigan City penitentiary, escaped from the prison. Six others fled with them.

Hamilton, Makley and Pierpont came to Lima. Working exactly as if they were following well-laid plans, they raided the jail and released their chief. Sheriff Jess Sarber of Allen County resisted. They shot and killed him. That was on Oct. 12.

Dillinger gave an indication of the bravado which was later to attract the attention—and the comment—of London, Paris and Berlin as well as the United States when he next appeared in Chicago. The police got wind of it.

A trap was set for him by the Chicago police as he visited a doctor's office on Nov. 16. Dillinger adopted a device that later was to insure his death by violence, but his escape until then. He shot his way out.

Federal Reward Offered.

Events followed swiftly after that, multiplying until his name became a by-word for outlawry, his existence a political shibboleth, his career a reason for the passage of laws in Congress and the posting of a $10,000 reward by the United States Government for his capture.

Only four days after he had walked from the trap he appeared at Racine, Wis., at the head of his lawless band. They raided the American Bank and Trust Company, obtained more than $10,000 and escaped.

Spectacular in the way he staged his lawless escapades, devil-may-care in his encounters with the law, he nevertheless brought every possible modern facility into play in his skirmishes. He used fast cars. He had bullet-proof vests. His men used machine guns.

And when, with Hamilton and Makley, he took possession of the safe deposit vault of the Unity Trust and Savings Bank in Chicago on Dec. 13, he reached his loot with electric torches. A haul of $8,700 and a large amount of jewelry, placed in the heavily guarded, time-locked protected vault for security against his kind, was netted.

John Hamilton, Dillinger's lieutenant, and probably others of the gang, remained behind in Chicago. The following day the police picked up Hamilton's trail. Police Sergeant William T. Shanley set a trap for him. Hamilton, following his chief's cue, shot his way out, killing Shanley. A second victim lay dead on the Dillinger trail.

Six days later another Dillinger group fell afoul the police at Paris, Ill. Edward Shouse, an aide of the outlaw, was captured. But in the gun battle, Eugene Teague, an Indiana State policeman, was killed; the third victim.

Dillinger was traced to a North Side apartment. The Chicago police closed in on Dec. 21. This time the casualties were on Dillinger's side. Lewis Katzewitz of Streator, Sam Ginsburg, an escaped Michigan prisoner, and Charles Tilden, who had broken out of an Illinois prison, were slain.

Ten days later the battle was declared to be a fight to the finish. The Chicago police received orders to shoot members of the gang on sight. But that very same night, Dillinger declared his defiance by staging a hold-up of the Beverly Gardens, a resort, wounding two highway policemen in escaping.

On Jan. 6, 1934, the police picked up the trail of Jack Klutas, a gang leader affiliated with Dillinger, in Bellwood, a Chicago suburb. He was shot and killed battling for escape, and five were dead.

Then another policeman fell, mortally wounded, before a Dillinger onslaught. He, Hamilton and another member of the mob held up the First National Bank of East Chicago. In escaping with more than $20,000, the careening Dillinger automobile passed Policeman William P. O'Malley, who was talking with a friend. Before the policeman could become aware of his antagonist, shots burst out and the policeman was dead.

Captured by "Hick Cops."

Dillinger was captured on Jan. 25. He, Makley, Clark and Pierpont appeared quietly in Tucson, Ariz., all but Pierpont in the company of women. They had considerable luggage and their hotel caught fire. They offered large rewards for the rescue of the luggage and obtained it.

One of the firemen read a detective story magazine and saw Dillinger's picture. He told the local police. One by one the members of the gang were captured before they could resort to arms. The luggage held a miniature arsenal. Dillinger was chagrined at his capture by what he called "hick cops."

Under heavy guard, Pierpont, Makley and Clark were sent to Ohio. Pierpont and Makley were sentenced to death for the Sarber murder, Clark to life imprisonment. Dillinger was taken to the Crown Point Jail.

The desperado announced to his fellow prisoners that he intended to break jail. They guffawed. In his cell, from a block of wood, he fashioned what looked like an automatic pistol. The morning of March 3 he held up a guard and the warden, cowed other guards, robbed thirty-three persons of $15 "for expenses" and helped himself to two of the jail's machine guns.

Stealing the automobile of the woman Sheriff, he drove away with a murder, Herbert Youngblood, a Negro. He carried with him a deputy sheriff and a garage attendant as hostages, throwing them out later on.

A nation-wide search was started for him. The Indiana officials were criticized by Attorney General Cummings, the prosecutor of Lake County lost his campaign for renomination. Dillinger picked up where he had left off.

Ten days later he raided the Mason City, Iowa, bank. He was wounded in the shoulder. He forced a physician in St. Paul to treat him, and was able to continue. But on March 16, two more deaths marked his trail.

Youngblood turned up in Port Huron, Mich., and boasted of his successful jailbreak. The police heard of it. In the ensuing battle Youngblood and Under-Sheriff Charles Cavanaugh were killed.

Dillinger himself was trapped on March 31 in St. Paul. Government operatives had thrown a cordon about him then. Confronted in an apartment with Eugene Green and a woman companion, he made his way to freedom behind a barrage of bullets. He and Green were wounded.

Green died of his wounds and others he received a few days later, on April 11. Dillinger, with pistol leveled, forced Dr. Clayton E. May of Minneapolis and a nurse to treat him and he lived to survive a more spectacular ambuscade. The doctor was fined and imprisoned because, terror-stricken, he had not informed the authorities.

Then the outlaw's exploits became unbelievable. He visited his father, John Sr., at the latter's homestead near Mooresville, Ind., and the neighbors marked the visit by petitioning the Governor for a pardon for the killer.

Raided a Police Station.

With posses on his trail, he and a companion raided a police station at Warsaw, Ind., stealing two bullet-proof vests and two pistols from the arsenal, and made contact again with Hamilton by visiting the criminal's sister in Michigan.

Although the Federal authorities were massing agents against him, he and his gang decided on a holiday in the Wisconsin woods. They motored to a resort near Mercer, mixed among the guests, practiced target shooting and enjoyed restful card games.

The Federal agents got wind of the hideout. Reinforcements sped to the scene by airplane. The resort was surrounded. But dogs barked the alarm and a battle began. Two Civilian Conservation Corps members and a local resident were fired on, and Eugene Boisenau, one of the CCC men, was killed.

Terrific battles were fought about the resort, in which W. Carter Baum, a Federal agent, was killed and a constable, a Federal agent and two civilians were wounded, but Dillinger and his men stole cars and escaped to St. Paul.

There they fought a running gun battle with Sheriff's deputies and escaped. But the gang was scattered. A small army was marshaled to close in on him. Congress was stirred. Ten anti-crime bills were passed by the House and his name resounded in debate.

But for three months he eluded pursuers. He had been wounded in the battle around mercer. He was taken to another doctor for treatment, seriously hurt. Albert Reilly, one of his aides, was captured in Minneapolis and said his chief was dead. But Dillinger's father exhibited a letter from the son in denial.

Two detectives were shot to death in East Chicago on May 24. Dillinger was suspected. The kidnaping of Edward Bremer, St. Paul banker, was laid to a plot kindled by her fertile, twisted brain. By that time the legend began outrunning the story.

The amount of his thefts has been estimated at $5,000,000. Gunmen copied his methods, however, and fact became inseparable from fiction. But the deaths he caused directly totaled about a score, including police, Federal agents, bystanders and the thugs who had allied themselves with him.

New York Times
14th January 1929

NOTED GUN FIGHTER OF OLD WEST DEAD

End Comes to Wyatt Earp at Los Angeles After Life of Battling "Bad Men."

DEFEATED CLANTON GANG

As Referee With a Pistol at Sharkey-Fitzsimmons Fight, His Decision Stood.

LOS ANGELES, Jan. 13 (P).—The West lost another of its few remaining frontier gun fighters today with the death here of Wyatt Earp, once a peace officer at Dodge City, Kan., and at Tombstone, Ariz. Mr. Earp's colorful career led him through a dozen fatal conflicts with "bad men" of the Old West. He was 78 years old.

Earp and three brothers, Virgil, Morgan and Jim, together with Doc Holliday, were principal figures in the stormy days of Cochise County, Ariz., where Tombstone is located. Their conflict with the Clanton gang of cowboys, shortly after which Morgan Earp was killed from ambush, and during which two famous gunmen died, was followed by an investigation.

The Earps, led by Wyatt, then a Deputy United States Marshal, were exonerated on the ground that they had acted as peace officers.

Wyatt Earp gained further public notice when he was chosen as referee of the Tom Sharkey-Bob Fitzsimmons fight in San Francisco. He wore a six-shooter in the ring, and no protests were made at the time, although many were heard later.

Among the friends of Earp were Bat Masterson, Wild Bill Hickok and other famous figures of the early West. In Alaska, during the gold rush, Earp met Bill Hart, the motion-picture actor; Wilson Mizner, playwright, and the late Tex Rickard, all of whom were close friends.

Earp had been ill for some time. He left his bed the day before Rickard died to send a telegram to his sick friend in Florida. The exertion caused a relapse.

Earp left a widow and a niece. The funeral will be held Tuesday.

The Guardian
20th April 1882

THE MURDERED ROBBER.

HIS DEATH THE RESULT OF AN UNDERSTANDING WITH THE GOVERNOR.

THE CORONER'S INQUEST AND THE BODY IDENTIFIED—A SENSATIONAL SCENE—THE MOTHER'S CURSE.

ST. JOSEPH, Mo., April 4—At the Coroner's inquest Mrs. Samuels, mother of Jesse James, testified that it was her son Jesse. Considerable excitement was created by her denunciation of the treachery of Dick Little. Gov. Crittenden has just arrived here. It is unknown at present what will be done with the body, but the Governor has ordered it to be turned over to his relations.

A dispatch from Kansas City says: It is now known that the taking of Jesse James was the fulfillment of an agreement between Gov. Crittenden and Bob Ford, and that Ford was to receive one-fourth of the reward and immunity.

In an interview with Dick Little and a reporter, on Sunday night last, the scheme was foreshadowed, but Little said it was not to have been accomplished before Wednesday or Thursday, and only then, if it was found impossible for Timberlake to capture the bandit leader alive.

Gov. Crittenden stated here to-day that his first meeting with Ford at the St. James Hotel, in this city, was on February 22 when arrangements by which Jesse James was to be either captured or killed were consummated. He met Little a few days later. He was non-committal as to the disposition to be made of Ford and Little, but admitted that their ultimate pardon was not improbable.

Sheriff Timberlake, Dick Little and Mrs. Samuels, mother of the dead bandit, passed through this place last night, en route to St. Joseph, where they have since identified the body under oath. The double confession of Dick Little is still a mystery and officers are endeavoring to solve it and learn which is correct.

The trial of the Blue Cut robbers is in progress at Independence, and the utmost efforts of counsel are directed toward proving an alibi.

Mattie Collins, wife of Dick Little, recently showed a correspondent a letter received from Jesse James, in which he stated that he would stay in this country until he had killed Dick Little, and that then he and his brother Frank and their families would put the Atlantic Ocean between them and the United States.

Gov. Crittenden, who arrived at Kansas City this morning, asserts positively that the body is that of Jesse James, and that his death was the result of an understanding between the authorities and Bob Ford, who killed him, and Dick Little, who surrendered to Sheriff Timberlake at the same time Ford did.

The inquest was concluded at noon to-day. Mrs. Samuels (the mother of Jesse James), his wife, Dick Little and Sheriff Timberlake identified the body, and during the proceedings Mrs. James and Mrs. Samuels made a highly sensational scene, attacking Little and calling all manner of curses down upon him for having conspired to betray his leader.

The Coroner's jury returned a verdict of murder in the first degree against Ford, and the authorities of Buchanan county refuse to give him up.

The body of James will probably be taken to the old farm near Kearney, Clay county, for burial.

The confirmation of James's death has created a profound sensation in Western Missouri, and farmers near this place and Independence, who have not been in this place for years, rode in town this morning in order to investigate the rumor. Some denounce Ford as an assassin, whose only object was blood money, while others excuse him upon the ground of expediency.

The Governor will return to Jefferson City to-night, where some steps will be taken to protect Ford, who is thought to be in some danger from the friends of the dead robber. "Cracker-Neck" was upon horseback this morning, and some threats of vengeance are said to have been made against the lives of Ford and Little. The Ford brothers reside on a farm about two miles from Richmond, the county seat of Ray County, in this State. Robert, who did the shooting, is only about twenty years old. The house is said to have been the rendezvous of some of the James gang, and it was there that Dick Little killed Wood Hite, brother of Clarence Hite, who was recently sentenced to twenty-five years in the penitentiary and is now in prison. It is said both belonged to the James gang at one time, but this statement does not seem to be verified. The family came from Virginia fifteen years ago, and has always been considered very respectable. For sometime past both brothers are believed to have been in the detective service, and specially engaged in hunting out members of the James gang.

At the inquest on the body of Jesse James to-day, H. H. Craig, Police Commissioner of Kansas City, testified: I know the Fords; Robert Ford assisted Sheriff Timberlake and myself. Ford was not commissioned; Robert Ford acted through our instructions, and Charles was not acting under our instructions.

Mrs. Samuels, mother of Jesse James, took the stand. She is large, with kindly face and eyes and rather prominent nose. Her hair is black, sprinkled with gray. When she took the stand her face had a resolute appearance, but as the examination progressed that disappeared, and she was very much affected. She testified that she was the mother of Jesse James and she had seen the body but a moment before.

"Is that the body of your son?" asked the Coroner.

"It is," she answered, and then sobbed out. "Would to God it was not."

Placing her hands upon the heads of the little son and daughter of Jesse James, who were standing just in front of her, she continued: "And these are his orphan children."

As she said this she was moved to tears.

When Mrs. Samuels retired from the court room, Dick Little was standing near the door. Her eyes rested on him a moment and then she turned upon him with the fierceness of a tiger. "Traitor! traitor! traitor!" she exclaimed excitedly. God will send vengeance on you for this. You are the cause of all this. Oh, you villain; I would rather be in my poor boy's place than in yours.

The jury found a verdict that James came to his death from a pistol-shot at the hands of Robert Ford.

The Ford brothers are confined in jail charged with murder, under a warrant sworn out by Mrs. James. They will not be interviewed, and the Sheriff refuses admittance to all comers. Robert Ford, who did the shooting, is 22 years old, and Charley is 20.

New York Times
14th February 1914

BERTILLON, NOTED CRIMINOLOGIST, DIES

Creator of Identification by Measurements in Use by Police of the World.

FAMOUS ANTHROPOLOGIST

Director in Paris Police Department Was Handwriting Expert in Dreyfus Trial—His Works.

PARIS, Feb. 13.—The death occurred here to-day of Alphonse Bertillon, creator of the system of criminal identification, which made his name known throughout the world. He was in his sixty-first year.

M. Bertillon was a distinguished anthropologist and was the author of many works on ethnography, anthropometry, and criminal photography.

By Marconi Transatlantic Wireless Telegraph to The New York Times.

LONDON, Saturday, Feb. 14.—The London Times Paris correspondent says:

"Curiously enough, Bertillon himself was one of the few persons against whom the weapon of identification which he invented would have been of no avail. I happened to be at the Prefecture of Police when the news of his death arrived. I asked to be shown marks of his thumbs and fingers, but was told that the surface of his skin was so irregular that he never succeeded in making a good imprint."

Dr. Alphonse Bertillon, director of the Anthropometric Department of the Paris police, the creator of the system of measurement now in use by police of cities the world over, was in his sixty-first year. He was born in Paris on April 22, 1853. His father before him was a noted anthropologist, and he was reared as a boy in a home where discussions of scientific subjects were common. He himself developed an interest in anthropology very early in life, and began its study systematically in connection with his father. He studied medicine also, and was admitted to practice.

It was through his studies in medicine and anthropology that his attention was presently centred on the subject of identification by exact physical measurements, and in 1880 he announced his system of absolute identification by measurements. The idea was at first received with incredulous jeers in the scientific world, but the young scientist persisted and finally induced the Paris police to allow him to make demonstrations.

He proved his case, and was quickly recognized as the most valuable man in the police department. He was put at the head of the Bureau of Identification by the Prefect of Police, and he maintained that position for thirty years to the time of his death. In that time he perfected his system, until it was almost universally adopted and became a terror to the criminals of the world.

For his discovery and its subsequent perfection Dr. Bertillon was made a Chevalier of the Legion of Honor. He continued his interest in anthropology and in the period between 1883 and 1900 wrote many authoritative works on that subject, ethnography, anthropometry, and criminal photography. He was the author also of several works on identification through handwriting and graphic work.

It was as a handwriting expert that Dr. Bertillon figured in the famous Dreyfus trial. The guilt or innocence of Capt. Dreyfus of the charge of treason hinged upon the identification of his handwriting with that of the infamous bordereau, the treasonable correspondence between the traitor in the French Army, and the German authorities to whom he promised to make his betrayal. Lieut. Col. Du Patty de Clam, in whose hands the investigation had been entrusted, thought he saw a resemblance to the handwriting of the bordereau in letters he had obtained from the young Capt. Dreyfus. He submitted samples of both to Bertillon, and so impressed the expert with his eloquent presentation of his own views, that Bertillon finally declared the writer of the bordereau and of the letters one and the same man.

Bertillon subsequently testified at the trial of Dreyfus, as one of three experts on handwriting called by the Government. Two of these declared Dreyfus the author of the bordereau; one declared he was not. Two experts called by the defense testified that Dreyfus was not the author of the treasonable document. At that trial Dreyfus was adjudged guilty, and condemned to life imprisonment on Devil's Island, where he remained five years until his case was reversed.

Dr. Bertillon had been ill for some time, suffering from anemia, complicated with other maladies. He was operated on in October last, when blood was transfused into his veins from those of his brother. At the time the operation was pronounced a success.

Anastasia slain in Park Sheraton Hotel Barber shop....

New York Times
26th October 1957

ANASTASIA SLAIN IN A HOTEL HERE; LED MURDER, INC.

TWO FIRE 10 SHOTS

Masked Killers Escape —11 Witness Attack in Barber Shop

By MEYER BERGER

Death took The Executioner yesterday. Umberto (called Albert) Anastasia, master killer for Murder, Inc., a homicidal gangster troop that plagued the city from 1931 to 1940, was murdered by two gunmen. They approached him from behind at 10:20 A. M. as he sat for a haircut in the Park Sheraton Hotel barber shop at Seventh Avenue and Fifty-fifth Street.

The trigger-men fired ten shots. Five took effect. The first two caught Anastasia's left hand and left wrist. One tore into his right hip. The fourth got him in the back after he had come out of the chair and had stumbled into the mirror he had been facing as the barber worked. The fifth bullet caught him in the back of the head.

Both killers had scarves over the lower part of their faces. They got away.

Two Weapons Are Found

The pistols used in the killing were dropped right after they were used. One was found a few minutes later in a vestibule just outside the barber shop that opens into Fifty-fifth Street. The other was dropped into a trash basket at the Fifty-fifth Street end of the Fifty-seventh Street BMT subway station. A porter who was emptying the bins found it.

Eleven persons besides Anastasia were in the shop when the gunmen entered—five barbers, two other customers, two shoeshine men, a valet and a manicurist. They, and persons just outside the shop, fled screaming and shouting into the street, with the killers among them or right behind them. Where the killers went no one noticed.

The police tonight issued a thirteen-state alarm for two men in the murder. One was described as about 40 years old, 5 feet 8 inches tall, weighing 180 pounds, sallow complexion, wearing a gray suit, dark gray fedora with three-inch brim and dark-green aviator-type glasses. The other was said to be about 30, about 5 feet 5 inches, weighing 150 pounds, light complexion, thin black pencil moustache, wearing a dark brown suit, lighter brown fedora with three-inch brim and dark-green glasses.

Although 100 detectives were thrown into the case immediately by Chief of Detectives James B. Leggett, the police had no positive motive for the killing. There was talk that Anastasia was trying to reorganize the remnants of old racket groups in town, and that the younger hoodlums would have none of his leadership.

In addition, countless underworld figures had scores to settle with Anastasia. For 36 of his 55 years he had plotted gang killings, or had seen to them himself. Of Murder, Inc.'s sixty-three assassinations, thirty-one are supposed to have been Anastasia's handiwork.

The police were quick to throw guards around all persons they questioned in the Anastasia murder yesterday—the barber shop crew, a hotel elevator boy, several men and women who might have brushed shoulders with the fleeing gunmen as they left; owners of near-by shops that give upon the barber shop.

The dead man's kin were guarded, too, against their wishes, among them Anthony (Tough Tony), Anastasia, 50-year-old brother. He is a vice president of the International Longshoremen's Association and business manager for Local 1814 of that organization. He lives at 8220 Eleventh Avenue, in Brooklyn's Dyker Heights district.

Lived Behind Fence

Umberto Anastasia lived in rather splendid fashion behind a seven-foot barbed-wire fence at 75 Bluff Road, in the Palisade section of Fort Lee, N. J. Great Doberman pinschers roamed his lawns like sleek dark shadows at night. They would give tongue when strangers went by.

Anastasia drove away from the house at 7 o'clock yesterday morning in a blue 1957 Oldsmobile hardtop sedan registered in the name of his current driver and bodyguard, Anthony Coppola. He parked it at the Corvan Garage, 124 West Fifty-fourth Street, at 9:28 A. M.

An hour-and-a-half later, the 49-year-old bodyguard drove it back to his own home at 450 Park Avenue, Fairview, N. J. Later, a friend drove the car to a parking lot on Centre Street—across from the Criminal Courts Building. The police took it from there to the West Fifty-fourth Street police station.

At 6:30 P. M. the last of the many drivers and bodyguards Anastasia had kept close to him walked into police headquarters here and said he was ready for questioning.

Detectives took him at once to West Fifty-fourth Street, where all the other witnesses had been taken. Mike Mirante, another long-time Anastasia associate, had turned up about a half hour before. Detectives took him for questioning too.

The police would not disclose what they had learned from those questioned.

By midnight, the detectives had questioned fifty witnesses, and ten more were waiting their turns. One of the first group was Harry Stasser, 58, of 30 Ocean Parkway, Brooklyn, for ten years Anastasia's partner in the Madison Dress Company. The concern does about a $150,000 annual gross.

How It Happened

Anastasia strolled into the hotel barber shop at about 10:15 and called greetings to the help. Joseph Bocchino who holds down Chair 4, facing Fifty-fifth Street, gave the chair a few swipes while Anastasia hung up his topcoat and stripped open his white shirt. He was dressed all in brown—brown shoes with rather an amateur polish, brown suit, a rather untidy brown tie.

"Haircut," he said, and he seemed to need one. His hair was thin in front, but thick and lush over-all, especially down the back. He sat upright, a broad-chested, broad-shouldered fellow with fleshy nose, round but firm chin.

The barber draped a cloth around the gangster's neck, swirled the sheet into place, and got out the electric clippers for the back of the neck. No one in the shop was jogged out of morning dreaminess.

The room, 35 by 28 feet, was filled with customary hum. The recessed overhead fluorescents lighted the place well, but not with glare. Arthur Grasso, the shop owner, was at the cashier's stand near one of the doors leading from a hotel corridor.

ASSASSINS ESCAPE IN ENSUING PANIC

11 Witness the Killing—31 Murders Laid to Victim, Called the Executioner

A minute or two later, as Mr. Bocchino plied the clippers from Anastasia's left side, the door opened. The gunmen stepped in. They were middle-sized men, dark and rather broad. Their weapons came out as they crossed the threshold.

One of the two men spoke through his scarf. He told Mr. Grasso: "Keep your mouth shut if you don't want your head blown off." The shopowner's jaw fell. Then his lips compressed. The two trigger-men moved swiftly behind Anastasia's chair. If his heavy-lidded eyes had been open—apparently they were not—he might have seen them in the mirror, but he sat, relaxed, with no notion that death was close.

Both men seemed to open fire at once. The shots came in short spurts. One gun roared, and stopped. The other gun roared and stopped. The sound had a weird cadence.

Anastasia leaped forward with the first report. His heavy feet kicked at the foot rest and tore it away. He landed on his feet, weaving. He did not turn around to face the killers. He lunged further forward, still facing the mirror. The second spurt of bullets threw him against the glass shelving in front of the mirror. He grabbed for the shelving and brought a glass of bay rum to the tiles with a shattering crash. He took two further shots. Then the last shot—so the police figure it—took him back of the head.

The heavy body turned. Anastasia fell to the floor two chairs away. He fell on his left side. One pudgy hand was outstretched. The fluorescent lights kicked fire from the diamonds in his fat finger ring. He lay still.

The gunmen had said no word after their quiet warning to Mr. Grasso. They did not speak as they strode to the door, guns still in hand. Which way they turned no man seemed to notice. People who had heard the cannonade had dropped to corridor floors, or had fled, some directly ahead of the killers.

Constantine Alexis who runs a hotel flower shop alongside the barber's, watched the crowd fleeing past his window. He remembered later that there were four or five men in one group heading for a Fifty-fifth Street exit. Someone was hollering: "Somebody's gone crazy in there." The florist dialed frantically for the police.

Police radio cars converged on the barbershop in a matter of minutes. Traffic policemen rushed through the doors. Dr. Robert Cestari came from nearby St. Clare's Hospital and kneeled over Anastasia between the chairs.

He applied a stethoscope, looked up and said: "He's dead."

Apparently the bullet at the back of the head had ended Anastasia's life immediately.

Word of Shooting Spreads

Word of the shooting spread swiftly across the city. The radio blared it. Before that, though, a newspaper office had telephoned the story to one of its reporters at Police Headquarters in Brooklyn. He called Anthony Anastasia in the I. L. A. office at 341 Court Street.

The reporter said, "Tony, you know what just happened to Albert?" and Anthony said "No, what happened?" The reporter told him: "Albert was just knocked off over in the Park Sheraton Hotel. Just a couple of minutes ago." The union boss's voice broke. "No," he cried, "no, no." He started to say something more, but his voice failed. He hung up.

Longshoremen sitting in the office sat white-faced at the news. They raced downstairs behind Anthony, one got behind the wheel of his Chevrolet, and they raced for Manhattan. They made it in almost record time.

When Anthony hurried into the barbershop, a detective held the sheeting aside. The union chief stared at his brother's face as if in disbelief. He spoke no word, but he shook with sobbing.

One of his men touched him on the shoulder. He got up and let them lead him back to the car. He had them drive them to the West Fifty-fourth Street police station. Detectives kept him only a little while. Assistant District Attorney Alexander Herman of the Homicide Division told reporters later, "He was completely cooperative. That's all we can tell you now."

Even before Anthony identified the body, the police had the first of the two murder weapons. It was a .38-caliber Colt revolver, with only one of it's six bullets unfired. The gunman had dropped it in a glassed-in vestibule on his way out to Fifty-fifth Street.

The fact that the second weapon, a .32 with five shots discharged, was found in the subway, seemed fair indication that both killers had run out of the vestibule in the panicky rush that followed the shooting.

The subway entrance in Fifty-fifth Street is only a few steps away. Both weapons, incidentally, were originally sold by dealers out of town; the .32 thirty-seven years ago, the other in 1934. Detectives did not tell in what town they were bought. The guns were turned over to ballistics experts and to fingerprint men.

A few hours later, after an autopsy, Umberto Anastasia Jr., son of the dead executioner, came to identify his father. He looked at the figure for only a moment, and turned away. Then he left with Robert Anastasio (Anastasio was the original spelling of the family name and some branches still use it), a nephew of the old gang boss who lives in Brooklyn, original stamping ground of the clan.

Feared By Racketeers

Detectives expressed no sorrow over the passing of Umberto Anastasia. He had been the most notorious hoodlum in New York —probably in the East—for better than twenty years and had managed to cover his tracks every time. It was common knowledge that he fancied himself as The Executioner. Even the fact that he had spent some time in the Sing Sing Prison death house himself thirty-six years ago did not seem to lessen his appetite for violence.

Even the underworld "big shots" who moved in The Executioner's private circle stood in deathly fear of him. They included the late Louis (Lepke) Buchalter, chief of rackets in New York City that brought in millions. Frank Costello, Joe Adonis and Augie Pisano, men of might in gambling and nightclub operations on both shores of the Hudson, were never easy in his company.

The late Willie Moretti, a mob boss on the New Jersey side, stood in mortal fear of Umberto. He was boxed in, one night in October, 1951, in a dark little inn in Cliffside Park, N. J., and shot to death by four gunmen.

Yet, Anastasia, who managed a peaceful garment factory in Hazelton, Pa., on the side, could seem pleasant, genial and generous.

'Nice to Deal With'

The men in the Park Sheraton barber shop exclaimed over his tips. So did all the other hired hands there. Douglas du Lac, owner of a toy shop in the hotel, had always thought of him as "very much the gentleman, nice to deal with, a man with a real love for kids."

Anastasia seemed to buy toys about twice a month, which was about as often as he came to the barber shop. "Always big expensive toys, too," Mr. du Lac recalled.

He might have had a spending spree in mind even yesterday, though he never got around to it. When detectives went through his pockets they came up with, roughly, $1,900 in cash, in notes ranging from $1 to $100. He had no weapon on him.

The detectives were not too happy over the murder in one way. They have apparently made no headway into the motives for the attempted murder, last May, of Frank Costello, an associate of Anastasia.

A gunman stepped up to

Costello one spring evening in the lobby of his apartment house on Central Park West and cut loose, at fairly close range, with several shots. The gambler got a burning wound, but quickly recovered. He insisted that he knew no reason for the attempt on his life. The police were left baffled.

The Anastasia shooting yesterday was the second of its kind in the hotel in twenty-nine years. Arnold Rothstein, the gambler, who lived there when it was the Park Central Hotel, was shot within its walls on Nov. 4, 1928. He lingered in a hospital a few days after the shooting before dying.

The police acknowledged last night that they were closely guarding not only innocent bystanders in the Anastasia case, but members of the Anastasia family, too, and the homes of Anastasia associates brought in for questioning.

'Special Attention' Detail

When they threw men around Anthony Anastasia's place in Dyker Heights last night, they termed the move "special attention," a gesture that Anthony has resented on past occasions. Men in radio cars in the neighborhood also had orders to tour by the home once every fifteen minutes.

The District Attorney's office in the Bronx heard of The Executioner's killing with some regret. He was wanted in the Bronx for questioning about the murder of Vincento Macri of 4499 Henry Hudson Parkway, found shot to death and stuffed in a trunk in the spring of 1952. The district attorney thought he might shed some light on the disappearance of Benedetto Macri, Vincenzo's brother, whose blood-stained automobile turned up ten days later on a lonely road in Harrison, N. J. Benedetto's body was never found.

Chief of Detectives Leggett, wearied with work on the Anastasia case last night, finally snapped back a bit bitterly at an innocent who asked: "Why do you think they killed him, Chief?" His answer was: "Maybe somebody didn't like him."

Senate Inquiry Planned To Summon Anastasia

Special to The New York Times.

WASHINGTON, Oct. 24.— Senate investigators said tonight they had planned to call Albert Anastasia to testify on labor racketeering in the New York area.

However, they declared that they had "no evidence" that there was any connection between his slaying today and the committee's plans.

Robert F. Kennedy, counsel of the Senate Select Committee on Improper Activities in the Labor or Management Field, said Anastasia had appeared before Senate investigators in May, 1956. At that time, he said, Anastasia testified behind closed doors before the Senate Permanent Investigations Subcommittee, which laid some of the groundwork for the current inquiry.

Anastasia was then questioned about the alleged racketeer domination of companies that held contracts to produce or ship military uniforms.

Mr. Kennedy tonight, however, would not say why the select committee had wanted to question Anastasia.

He said that while no date had been set for his appearance, the committee did expect to call him.

Mr. Kennedy said the select committee had issued a subpoena for Anastasia earlier this year. This was not served, he said, because Anastasia's attorney had told the committee that Anastasia would appear voluntarily.

Chicago Tribune
3rd May 1972

Director Molded FBI Into Great Law Agency

Hoover: 48 Years Fighting Crime

The Federal Bureau of Investigation, under J. Edgar Hoover, ended the era of notorious gangsterism and kidnaping in the United States during the 1930s, then threw its protecting arm about national security.

It captured Nazi spies during World War II and Communist spies in the cold war. It was the FBI that discovered that the secret of the atom bomb had been stolen and given to Russia. Evidence collected by this scientific crime detecting organization sent Julius and Ethel Rosenberg to the electric chair for espionage and others to prison.

Blazing guns of college-educated government agents brought death to one "public enemy" after another. Among these was John Dillinger, probably the most brazen outlaw since Jesse James. His killing was the FBI's first big triumph in its drive on killerbank robbers who terrorized Midwestern communities.

Ten murders were among the many crimes attributed to Dillinger and his gang in their foray of less than a year.

Woman Betrayed Him

Dillinger was betrayed to the FBI by the "woman in red" who had gone to a Sunday night movie with him in 1934. Agents shot him to death in a Chicago alley while he was trying to draw a pistol.

Gangsters George [Baby Face] Nelson, Charles [Pretty Boy] Floyd and "Ma" and Fred Barker were killed, and Alvin Karpis and George [Machine Gun] Kelly drew long prison sentences.

Nelson had killed three FBI agents before he in turn was killed by agents in a furious gun battle at Barrington, Ill. Floyd and the Barkers also had elected to shoot it out with agents rather than surrender.

The "G-men" proved they could outsmart and outfight "rats"—Hoover's term for criminals.

The FBI had an important part in solving the kidnap-murder of Charles Augustus Lindbergh Jr., one of the most shocking crimes of all. It was the coordinator of all federal investigative agencies that aided New Jersey officials. Bruno Richard Hauptmann was arrested as the abductor-killer and executed.

At Hauptmann's trial the public learned a lot about science in crime detection as various wonders from the FBI laboratory were unfolded.

Before the 1930s ended, Hoover was able to say that not one organized crime gang was operating.

The FBI in War

Then came World War II and much greater responsibilities for the FBI. It put the heat on likely saboteurs so fast after Pearl Harbor that not a single case of foreign-directed sabotage occurred during the entire war. A great number of enemy aliens were jailed immediately.

Hoover's men also swooped down on enemy premises and seized secret arsenals, explosives, and other materials. They recommended security measures for more than 2,000 war plants and captured a number of spies. Sometimes the enemy espionage agents were persuaded to doublecross Adolf Hitler.

In one such case, the FBI constructed a radio station that a German spy had been instructed to build on Long Island. For two years this man, working under strict surveillance, sent misleading information to Germany that the FBI supplied.

The FBI's most spectacular wartime feat was the capture of eight German spies and saboteurs who landed from submarines on the coasts of Florida and Long Island in 1942. All were seized within a few days after their landing.

Atomic Spying Discovered

Hoover personally assisted the attorney general in their prosecution. Six were executed. The other two were spared that fate because they helped to prepare the case against their fellows. One was sentenced to life imprisonment and the other to 30 years. Both were deported to Germany after the war.

In the fall of 1944 two more spies landed from a German submarine on the coast of Maine and were caught almost at once. A military commission sentenced them to hang but the President commuted their punishment to life imprisonment.

Others Rounded Up

Fuchs' arrest set off a spy hunt that sent the Rosenbergs to the chair and others to prison.

During the 1949 trial in New York of 11 top American Communist leaders on charges of advocating the violent overthrow of the government, it developed that FBI agents had infiltrated the Communist ranks. Seven testified against the defendants. They had been planted for long periods as undercover agents. Their testimony came as a complete surprise.

Communists were left in the dark as to how many other FBI men were watching them from the inside.

Testifying before a Congressional committee on one occasion, Hoover declared that the Communist Party in this country was a fifth column far better organized than were Nazi fifth columns in Europe prior to the war.

"Communism in reality is not a political party," he continued. "It is a way of life—an evil and malignant way of life. It reveals a condition akin to disease that spreads like an epidemic and, like an epidemic, quarantine is necessary to keep it from infecting the nation."

Hoover gave a warning against Communism in America—and made an appeal to Americans for alertness to the danger—in a 1958 book he wrote entitled "Masters of Deceit."

Big Robbery Solved

The FBI also was concerned with robberies of banks in which there were government-insured funds, transportation of stolen automobiles across state lines and other crimes that violated federal laws.

In 1956 the FBI announced that the $2,775,395.12 Brink's robbery in Boston had been solved after a six-year investigation. Eleven men were named by the FBI as participants. Of the loot, $1,218,211.29 was in cash—then the biggest cash haul in the nation's history.

The FBI was not immediately involved in the assassination of President Kennedy in Dallas Nov. 22, 1963, because Lee Harvey Oswald, the assassin, was captured so quickly, but it then delved into any possible conspiratorial overtones.

When the Warren Commission, which investigated the assassination, suggested the the FBI was negligent in not advising the Secret Service that Oswald was in Dallas at the time of Kennedy's visit, Hoover contended there was nothing in the record to suggest that Oswald was dangerous.

He had worked during the war at Los Alamos, N.M., where the first atomic bomb was assembled, and at Harwell, the center of British atomic research. A congressional committee rated him as the deadliest spy in all history.

Communism and American morale were constant concerns of Hoover.

He observed his 40th anniversary as director of the FBI in May, 1964, by warning of Communist attempts to penetrate the civil rights movement. But after Negro riots spread across the country that summer he asserted the disturbances were neither race riots nor the work of Communists or other extremists organizations.

Instead, he said, they represented "a senseless attack on all constituted authority without purpose or object."

In his 40th anniversary interview Hoover asserted "Communism remains today as it has always been—a serious threat to our nation . . . two areas in which it has been enjoying a measure of success are with its youth programs and its work among minority groups."

He said, "The party is now avidly attempting to infiltrate the present civil rights movement in order to manipulate it and control it for the sole benefit of Communistic objectvies.

"This callous exploitation should be a matter of concern

for all of us, for no one will win if the Communists are successful in turning the legitimate grievances of our Negro citizens into a debilitating class struggle."

In testimony before a House appropriations subcommittee Feb. 23, 1968, Hoover said black nationalist groups and students of the new Left posed a threat to the nation's security. He named the Student Nonviolent Coordinating Committee, the Black Muslims, and the Revolutionary Action Movement.

Retirement Waived

Hoover's mandatory retirement age of 70 was waived by President Johnson before his 70th birthday Jan. 1, 1965. President Nixon waived it again. But soon after his 74th birthday in 1969, it was reported the man who symbolized the FBI would retire at 75.

It was Hoover who raised the FBI from a hack-ridden government bureau to the nation's top law enforcement agency. The road wasn't easy and criticism was plentiful. Politicians went after his scalp. Sections of the press sometimes were critical, and so, too, were some judges.

But whatever the criticism, Hoover seemed always to emerge unscathed. He served under eight Presidents and numerous attorney generals.

During those years he molded the FBI into a model for law inforcement agencies not only in the United States but abroad. He created methods systems and institutions which reformed and revitalized all forms of police work.

Political patronage was abolished. High standards for FBI agents were set up, both physical and educational. They had to be lawyers or accountants and were required to have ability and aggressiveness. They had to keep fit and keep their shooting eye sharpened thru constant practice.

The director established the FBI National Academy for training selected officers in scientific law enforcement. He constantly warned them against using third degree or other illegal methods of getting evidence. "The test · tube is mightier than the rubber hose," he observed.

Hoover started from scratch and built up the valuable fingerprint file.

The National Crime Laboratory, another Hoover creation, worked with scraps of evidence.

Such accomplishments brought many awards.

These included the President's award for "exceptionally meritorious civilian service" to the government that President Eisenhower bestowed on him in 1958. The accompanying citation said his "brilliant leadership has contributed immeasurably to the preservation and strength of the nation, its Constitution, and laws."

President Truman personally presented the Medal of Merit to Hoover. The citation with it said:

"Under his able leadership, the Federal Bureau of Investigation not only has become a powerful instrument of law enforcement in peacetime, but thruout the war years safeguarded the internal security of the United States, rendering ineffective espionage and preventing sabotage."

Turned Down Lucrative Offers

After the war, King George VI appointed Hoover an honorary Knight Commander of the civil division of the Most Excellent Order of the British Empire. That was in recognition of his "outstanding contribution to the Allied victory in the field of intelligence and security."

In 1954 Atty. Gen. Herbert Brownell Jr. awarded Hoover a Certificate of Merit in recognition of his 30 years' service as FBI director. That same year, for "outstanding service to his country," he received the Cardinal Gibbons Medal from the National Alumni Association of the Catholic University of America.

Hoover was the recipient of many other awards—honorary degrees, gold medals, citations and plaques. The work of the FBI was the subject of a book, movie scenarios, and radio programs.

There were offers of higher-paying positions, too. As FBI director, Hoover's salary rose to $42,500.

It was reported in 1951 that he had been offered the post of commissioner of baseball, which carries a $75,000 annual salary. Two years later he turned down an offer of $100,000 a year for 10 years to become head of the International Boxing Club. New York City invited him in 1955 to be police commissioner at $25,000. He declined.

John Edgar Hoover was born Jan. 1, 1895, in Washington, about five blocks from the Capitol. His father was an official of the Coast and Geodetic Survey and his mother was a grand-niece of a one-time Swiss Consul General to the U.S.

While attending high school, young Hoover worked as a $30-a-month messenger in the Library of Congress. That was the start of his government career that was to last for many years.

All his life he liked sports. Once in a baseball game he missed a fly ball and that error was permanently recorded in a flat nose.

Won Scholastic Honors

He wanted to play football, but the coach wouldn't even give him a tryout—he only weighed around 100 pounds. Hoover then took up debating and led his team to four championships.

He also went in for military training and became a captain of cadets. His company won the best rating of the corps. He was graduated as valedictorian of his class in 1913. Classmates called him "Speed" because he liked to get things done in a hurry. As an adult he was 5 feet 11 inches tall and weighed 180 pounds.

Origin of "G-Man"

Hoover entered George Washington University, where he received his Bachelor of Laws degree in 1916 and his Master of Laws in 1917. He was an honor student.

It was in 1917 that he first got a job with the Department of Justice, a clerkship. His rise was rapid.

Within two years Atty. Gen. A. Mitchell Palmer picked him to prosecute a large number of aliens seized in roundups of suspected subversives. He personally conducted Emma Goldman, the anarchist, to the ship when she and others were deported in 1919.

A reporter who watched him described the future FBI head as "that slender bundle of high-charged electric wire."

While working as a special attorney in the Justice Department, Hoover began signing his name J. Edgar instead of John E. That was to avoid confusion with a fellow employe.

In 1921 Hoover became assistant director of the FBI and on May 10, 1924, at the age of 29, was promoted to director. The bureau then had 657 employes. A quarter of a century later there were more than 14,-000.

It was an underworld character, "Machine Gun" Kelly, one of the kidnapers of Charles Urschel, wealthy oil man, who gave the name "G-men" to FBI agents.

When an FBI agent cornered Kelly in his Memphis hideout, the gangster pleaded:

"Don't shoot, G-man."

"Don't shoot, what?" asked the agent.

"G-man, Government man," Kelly explained.

The name stuck.

Hoover Directed Big Cases

To Hoover, a major violation of a Federal law was a personal challenge. With high-strung energy, he himself directed most big cases.

There was much praise for Hoover's accomplishments, but the record showed some criticism, too.

Sen. Kenneth D. McKellar [D., Tenn.] was a severe critic at one time. He called the FBI director a swivel chair detective who left it to his men to make arrests and risk their lives. He was particularly caustic at the Congressional committee hearing in 1936. It was brought out that Hoover had never made an arrest personally.

Tass Briefly Notes Death of Hoover

MOSCOW, May 2 (UPI)—The official Soviet Tass news agency today reported briefly and without comment the death of FBI Director J. Edgar Hoover. "Edgar Hoover, who headed the U.S. Federal Bureau of Investigation since 1924, died in Washington at the age of 77," a dispatch from New York said.

Chicago Daily Tribune
6th March 1935

OLIVER WENDELL HOLMES DIES

Would Have Reached Age 94 on Friday.

Noted Liberal of High Court for Many Years

(Picture on Page 6)

Washington, D. C., March 6 [Wednesday].—(P)—Oliver Wendell Holmes died here early this morning.

The death was announced by the "great dissenter's" former secretary, Mark Howe, who announced that it occurred at 2:15 a. m. eastern standard time.

Death was caused by bronchial pneumonia. It ended a public service which began with years of soldiering in the civil war and included 78 years spent as an associate justice of the Supreme court, where by almost universal accord he was known as the "great liberal." He retired in January, 1932.

Nearly 94 Years Old.

Mr. Holmes would have reached 94 Friday.

The illness which caused the death of the age-weakened jurist developed from a cold contracted after an automobile ride Feb. 23. Almost to the last Mr. Holmes retained the irrepressible spirit that characterized his active years.

Despite the strain of pneumonia, which required frequent administration of oxygen to enable him to breathe, he made light of the concern his illness occasioned and delighted at times in joshing his nurses and doctors.

Calls It "Foolery."

One of his last comments, referring to the extreme care given him, was that "this is a lot of damn foolery." Again, in mock impudence, he smilingly thumbed his nose at his old friend, Felix Frankfurter, Harvard law professor, as the latter passed his sick bed.

An aged domestic, who had been Justice Holmes' housekeeper when he first came to Washington to take his seat on the Supreme court more than 30 years ago, refused until the last to give up hope for his recovery. She was Margaret Cottingham, who was convinced her aged employer would "pull through" because he was "such a marvelous man."

The eminent jurist was in an oxygen tent in the second floor bedroom of his home. A policeman was stationed in front of the house to keep traffic moving and to attempt to keep noises at a minimum.

Nephew Nearest Relative.

At the bedside when Mr. Holmes died were his nearest relative, Edward J. Holmes of Boston, a nephew, and Mrs. Holmes; Prof. Frankfurter; James Rowe, present secretary of Mr. Holmes; Thomas Corcoran, reconstruction corporation counsel; John G. Palfrey of Boston, and Mary Donnellan, a faithful servant.

Howe issued a prepared statement which said:

"The funeral will be at All Souls church, 16th and Harvard streets, Washington, Friday, March 8, at noon.

"Honorary pallbearers will be the chief justice and the associate justices of the United States Supreme court. Mr. Holmes will be given private military burial at Arlington National cemetery."

Howe said the reason Friday was selected because it would have been his 94th birthday.

Native of Boston.

Justice Holmes was born in Boston March 8, 1841, and obtained the foundation of his education in the public schools of that city. He was the son of the noted American poet, whose full name he bore, and a daughter of a chief justice of the Massachusetts Supreme court. He entered Harvard and was in his senior year when the civil war began. He enlisted a short time before the graduation ceremonies, wrote the class poem in camp, and was given his degree sometime later.

He entered the service of his country as a lieutenant in the Massachusetts infantry, was promoted to a captaincy and retired with the rank of colonel. At one time he acted as the aide-de-camp to Brig. Gen. H. G. Wright. He was wounded at Ball Bluff, Va., near Washington; again at the battle of Antietam, and a third time at Fredericksburg.

Gets Degree in Law.

He returned to his studies when the war was ended, at which time he was 23 years old, and obtained his law degree from Harvard two years later. He immediately began the private practice of law. He was a member of the firm of Shattuck, Holmes and Monroe until he was elevated to the Supreme court of Massachusetts in 1882.

He was married at the age of 31 to Miss Fanny Dixwell of Cambridge, Mass. She died April 30, 1929. The couple had no children.

After serving continuously as justice of Massachusetts Supreme court, of which he was chief justice, three years, he was elevated to the United States Supreme court in December, 1902, by President Roosevelt. On the high bench he maintained an enviable record for attendance, and it was not until 1922, when he was 81 years old, that his health became impaired, primarily, it was said, as a result of his war wounds.

Vigorous for His Age.

After submitting to two major operations he returned to the bench, apparently given a new lease on life. Even with his ninetieth birthday approaching he showed few marks of his advanced age, other than a slight stoop of the shoulders and his whitened hair. Well over 6 feet tall, with a military mustache and a pink complexion, no trace of baldness marring his snow white hair, the justice was an imposing figure during the final years of service.

It was a momentous occasion when Justice Holmes read his last opinion in January, 1932. In a low, husky voice, on occasion having trouble with his speech, he read the opinion through. The first intimation his associates had that he no more would engage in their deliberations came the next day when President Hoover announced he had received the justice's resignation.

Lived in Seclusion.

After his resignation Justice Holmes lived in comparative seclusion in his Washington home. A few of his friends remained in close contact with him, and he frequently made tours of the surrounding country in a hired automobile, but he did little or no entertaining and almost never left his home in the evening.

Although in retirement, habits of a lifetime were not broken. He left Washington when the members of the Supreme court left for their vacations and returned to his town home when the court resumed sessions. One of his greatest pleasures during the last few years had been quiet reading in his own home or in the library of congress, and visits to the museums in Washington.

Oldest on Supreme Bench.

On Oct. 4, 1928, when he was 87 years 6 months and 29 days old, he became the oldest man ever to sit on the bench of the Supreme court. His length of office on the bench of the high court, however, was exceeded by Chief Justice Marshall and Associate Justices Field and Harlan, but none equaled the complete judicial career of more than 49 years established by Holmes.

HOLMES LONG FRIEND OF BRANDEIS; NAMES LINKED IN OPINIONS

Washington, D. C., March 6.—[Special.]—In his later years former Justice Oliver Wendell Holmes' closest friend was Justice Louis D. Brandeis whose name was linked so often with his in judicial opinions that the phrase "Holmes and Brandeis dissent" became a legal byword.

They appeared inseparable both on and off the bench. Often they came to court arm in arm and left the same way. Following Mr. Holmes' retirement in 1932, Brandeis frequently called on him at the red brick home where the aged man became almost a recluse.

The two friends were a familiar sight walking side by side.

Used Homely Maxims in His Decisions

HOLMES' VIEWS SUMMED UP ON 91ST BIRTHDAY

Washington, D. C., March 6.—(P)—In typically chaste prose, Oliver Wendell Holmes summed up his philosophy on his 91st birthday.

He made his only radio address then in responding to tributes paid him by Chief Justice Hughes, Dean Charles E. Clark of the Yale law school, and Charles A. Boston, president of the American Bar association. Justice Holmes said:

"In this symposium my part is only to sit in silence. To express one's feelings as the end draws near is too intimate a task.

"But I may mention one thought that comes to me as a listener-in. The riders in a race do not stop short when they reach the goal. There is a little finishing canter before coming to a standstill. There is time to hear the kind voice of friends and to say to oneself: 'The work is done.' But just as one says that the answer comes: 'The race is over, but the work is never done while the power to work remains.' The canter that brings you to a standstill need not be only coming to rest. It cannot be while you still live. For to live is to function. That is all there is in living.

"And so I end with a line from a Latin poet who uttered the message more than 1,500 years ago:

"'Death plucks my ear and says, Live—I am coming.'"

Justice Holmes was almost 90 when he procured a copy of Thucydides in the original Greek.

Night after night he pored over it in his library at home. Some one asked him why at his age he had chosen such a task.

"Because no gentleman should go to his grave without first having read Thucydides in the original."

Washington, D. C., March 6.—(P)—In his decisions Justice Oliver Wendell Holmes eschewed formal legal language except where it was necessary and used instead homely maxims. Some were:

A horse car cannot be handled like a rapier.

A man cannot shift his misfortunes to his neighbor's shoulders.

Most differences are merely differences of degree when nicely analyzed.

Every calling is great when greatly pursued.

The notion that with socialized property we should have women free and a piano for everybody seems to me an empty humbug.

There is no general policy in favor of allowing a man to do harm to his neighbor for the sole pleasure of doing harm.

One of the eternal conflicts out of which life is made up is that between the efforts of every man to get most he can for his services and that of society disguised under the name of capital to get his services for the least possible return.

Free competition is worth more to society than it costs.

Nature has but one judgment on wrong conduct—the judgment of death. If you waste too much food you starve; too much fuel, you freeze; too much nerve, you collapse.

Those traveling the road of life have at their command one and only one rule to success, to bring to their work a mighty heart.

The man of action has the present, but the thinker controls the future.

Man must face the loneliness of original work.

We cannot live our dreams. We are lucky enough if we can give a sample of our best and if in our hearts we can feel that it has been nobly done.

Life is action; the use of one's powers. As to use them to their height is our joy and duty, so it is the one end that justifies itself.

Life is an end in itself, and the only question as to whether it is worth living is whether you have had enough of it.

There is in all men a demand for the superlative, so much so that the poor devil who has no other way of reaching it attains it by getting drunk.

We are all fighting to make the kind of a world that we should like. Others will fight and die to make a different world with equal sincerity and belief.

The life of the law has not been logic; it has been experience.

The constitution is an experiment as all life is an experiment.

Great constitutional provisions must be administered with caution. Some play must be allowed for the joints of the machine.

Legislatures are ultimate guardians of the liberty and welfare of the people in quite as great a degree as the courts.

The word "right" is one of the most deceptive of pitfalls—most rights are qualified.

Congress certainly cannot forbid all efforts to change the mind of the country.

The best test of truth is the power of the thought to get itself accepted.

We should be eternally vigilant against attempts to check the expression of opinions that we loathe.

LIFE ROMANTIC, WAS PHILOSOPHY OF O. W. HOLMES

Washington, D. C., March 6.—(P)—Oliver Wendell Holmes' epigrammatic summary of living is framed on the office wall of Oswald Ryan, general counsel of the federal power commission.

Ryan received the philosophical letter in the beloved justice's handwriting after his graduation from Harvard. It said:

"Life is a romantic business. It is painting a picture, not doing a sum; but you have to make the romance, and it will come to the question how much fire you have in your belly."

The Times
13th March 1843

The murderer of Mr. Drummond was on Saturday night acquitted on the ground of insanity. We have too much respect for the administration of justice, and for the magistrates by whom justice is administered, to dispute the propriety of this acquittal, although to us it is unsatisfactory; but we owe it to truth to say that it *is unsatisfactory*, and it is due to ourselves and to our readers to explain the grounds of our dissatisfaction. There were two questions involved in the inquiry. First, did the prisoner know what he was doing when he killed Mr. Drummond? Secondly, if he did, was he properly responsible for the act? The first question seems to have been answered in the affirmative, or conceded affirmatively on all sides. It has not been pretended that when he the murderer fired upon his lamented victim, he could doubt that it was a human being upon whom he was firing. No one has suggested that he thought he was shooting at a hare or a partridge, or an inanimate mark; neither has it been surmised that the murderer was unconscious of the effect of his act, as if he believed that the pistol would spirt rose-water, or produce any other harmless effect. The point conceded is that when M'Naughten fired upon Mr. Drummond, *he knew he was about to put a human being to death*, he having at the time received no *immmediate provocation*, and being subjected to no *immediate danger*, real or imaginary.

These concessions would, by the law of England, as it was known and understood by lawyers up to the 4th day of March, 1843, command a verdict of guilty. Nor did the law of England stand unsupported by high authority in attaching such responsibility to such actions as are committed with a full knowledge of their object and of their effect. " Moral depravity, though it grow to uncontrol- " able passion," says the father of moral philo- " sophy, does not constitute that involuntariness " which excuses guilt."—*Nicomachean Ethics, Lib. ;, c. I.* And again—"It is by bad habits that men " become depraved; but by depravity men become " wicked beyond their own control; such involuntari- " ness is, however, no excuse."—*Eudemion Ethics, Lib. 2, c. VIII.* All the other authorities run in a uniform current—all concur in affirming that man is responsible for all the acts which he knowingly commits, and of which he knows the consequences—there is no consideration admitted as to the degree of his intelligence if these requisites be fulfilled. It is upon this principle that in various countries, Jacques Clement, Ravaillac, Felton, Ankerstrom, Bellingham, and a hundred other assassins, have been made to atone on the scaffold for the crime of murder, though every one of them might have as good a plea of insanity as the murderer acquitted on Saturday. What, in effect, were the proofs of insanity advanced by this wretch? He was a Socialist, an Infidel, a miser; and he suspected that the world was in a conspiracy to destroy him. Is not this the very case of self-depravation supposed by Aristotle? Socialism and Infidelity prepared him for destroying the intellectual and moral senses, and avarice directed the particular means. The complaint of the miser, that the world is in a conspiracy to ruin him, has been a common-place of the drama from Aristophanes to Moliere. But this madman—mad in what concerned his duties to Heaven and to his fellow-creatures—was shrewd as regarded himself. He saved seven or eight hundred pounds from a petty trade in a few years, and cast about with uncommon skill and caution to make the utmost profit of these savings. Nay, when he was minded to commit a murder, he

prepared his pistols carefully and skilfully, reconnoitred the ground diligently for a week before, and, as it appears, made the best efforts to escape after the completion of his crime, at first by a bodily struggle, and subsequently by craft, which there is reason to fear has had too much to do with his acquittal. But those learned persons who think they have made a great discovery as often as they can produce a new sample of jargon, say that M'Naughten is a "*monomaniac.*" What is *a monomaniac?* A person who is not, upon one particular subject, governed by the rules of right reason. Why, if this absence of rational self-government take the direction of crime, this monomaniac, is the self-depraved wretch of whom Aristotle speaks, is if possible more than others responsible. Saul, the odious King of Israel, was a monomaniac of this description: he abandoned his duty to his Creator, and "an evil spirit from the Lord fell upon him." Not the less judicially did the visitation overtake him because it came, as experience shows, by a natural process. Saul was a monomaniac, but Saul was held responsible; and the responsibility was continued to be exacted from his bloody house after he had gone to his own place. *Monomania*, which in plain language means absurd extravagance upon one particular point, may be innocent, as in the case of the illustrious Pascall, one of "the wisest, best, and brightest of "mankind." Pascall fancied that he was in constant danger of falling into a pit; and when it is innocent, human laws have no concern with it. But monomania may be also vicious and dangerous; and where it is, woe be to those who shall treat it as an excuse for crime. Heaven did not so treat it in the case of Saul, and man cannot so treat it with safety to society. If you have any delicacy in punishing the crime of the *monomaniac*, punish the *monomania* when it is plainly the result of self-depravation, as, if a criminal *monomaniac*, it must be. The Malay who "*runs a muck*, and strikes at all "he meets," is merely a *monomaniac*; yet it is found convenient to knock him in the head when he is seen rushing with his "kreese" bared, and nobody has ever pitied him more than a mad dog. Something, it is plain, must now be done to protect society from this neologically described class of murders. It would seem as if there is really no law upon the subject. On Saturday, indeed, the whole process of a criminal trial appeared to have been inverted. The mad doctors, who attended in the modest character of witnesses, were really the persons who charged the Court and the jury, laying down the law of moral responsibility to both, and the judge it was who returned the verdict, under the direction of these mad doctors. We may think that this was yielding too much to the mad doctors. Even upon the question of insanity we should hesitate to admit their authority as conclusive, for as we never met a healer of bodily ills who acknowledged any person to be in the enjoyment of perfect physical health, we question whether a mad doctor, pressed home upon the point, will give any man in England credit for perfect mental health. The reason will be found in Charles the Fifth's complaint of the watches, no two of which would keep exact time. Each has a certain standard which he calls health of body or of mind, as the case may be, and the least departure from that standard is, in his opinion, a deviation from health; but, if the mad doctor's evidence upon the existence and degree of insanity is to be received with suspicion, we respectfully submit that, upon the question of responsibility, his evidence is not to be received at all. That is a question for the law, and the law was clear until the *verdict*, of Saturday. Of that *verdict* we shall say nothing, for a reason already given, and also because to expatiate upon the terrible consequences which such a verdict seems to threaten, might be to promote them.

PLEA OF INSANITY IN CRIMINAL CASES.

The LORD CHANCELLOR then rose and said—My lords, I have felt anxious at the earliest possible day to call your lordships' attention to the subject of the notice I gave on a former occasion with reference to a late trial. The circumstances connected with that trial have created a deep sensation among your lordships, and also in the public mind; and, say lords, I am not surprised at this. A gentleman in the vigour of life, of most amiable character (hear, hear), incapable of giving offence or doing an injury to any individual, was murdered in the streets of this metropolis in open day. The assassin was secured—was committed for trial: that trial has taken place, and he has escaped with impunity. Your lordships will not be surprised that this circumstance should have created a deep feeling in the public mind, and that many persons should, on the first impression, be disposed to think that there is some great defect in the laws of the country with reference to this subject, and that there should be a full revision of those laws, in order that a repetition of such outrages may be prevented. My lords, I felt it my duty, in consequence of some suggestions of your lordships, to consider, in consultation with others, this interesting and important subject, with the view of ascertaining not only what the law is with reference to it, but for the purpose of ascertaining, if there should turn out to be a defect, what practical remedies should be applied, and what the nature of those remedies should be. You must be aware, my lords, that this is a most difficult and delicate subject, because all persons who have directed their attention to these inquiries—all persons who are best informed upon them, concur in stating that the subject of insanity is but imperfectly understood. I am not now speaking of general and complete mental alienation, but I am speaking of that description of insanity which consists in a delusion directed to one or more subjects, or one or more persons; and those who are acquainted with the subject know how difficult it is to decide to what extent the moral senses and the moral feelings that guide men's actions are influenced by delusions of this description. We all know that persons who labour under a mental delusion with respect to one or more subjects are entirely—or apparently entirely—rational with respect to others. They are frequently very intelligent, frequently very acute; it is often extremely difficult to discover the existence of this concealed malady, and persons who labour under it are uncommonly astute in defeating all endeavours to detect its existence. My lords, we almost all of us know and recollect the statement made by Lord Erskine in his eloquent defence of Hatfield with respect to the acuteness with which persons who labour under infirmities of this description defeat the skill, sagacity, and intellect of the most experienced persons. He tells us of an instance of a prosecution having been directed by a person who had been confined in a lunatic asylum against his brother and the keeper of that asylum for false imprisonment and duress. Lord Erskine was counsel for the defence. He says he was informed in his brief and instructions that the man was undoubtedly insane, but the particular infirmity of his mind was not disclosed to him. The prosecutor was himself a witness in support of the indictment; he was put into the box and examined, and when Lord Erskine came to cross-examine him he found his evidence, clear, distinct, collected, and rational. He tried to discover some lurking alienation of mind. During a cross-examination, conducted with all the skill and sagacity of that eminent advocate, for a period, as he says, of nearly an hour, all his endeavours were foiled. The answers were perfectly rational—there was not the slightest appearance of any mental alienation. A gentleman came into court who had been accidentally detained, and whispered in Lord Erskine's ear that the witness thought he was the Saviour of mankind. The moment Lord Erskine had that hint, he made a low bow to the witness, addressed him in terms of great reverence, respectfully begged to apologise for the unceremonious manner in which he had treated a person of his sacred character, and called him by the term of Christ. The man immediately said, "Thou hast spoken truly : I am the Christ" (hear, hear). A similar circumstance is mentioned in the French work of M. Pinel, with respect to a person confined in the Bicetre. A commission was appointed to visit that prison for the purpose of liberating those persons who were confined there as being of unsound mind, but who were not labouring under that calamity. M. Pinel states, that he examined one particular patient repeatedly upon many successive days, and, though he was a person experienced in those inquiries and a man of considerable learning and sagacity, all his endeavours to prove the man insane were frustrated and foiled. The result was, he ordered a certificate to be prepared for his liberation. It was necessary, before the man was liberated, that he should himself sign the certificate. It was placed before him, and he signed "Jesus Christ." Of course the certificate decided the question, and the man was not liberated. My lords, I could mention a great variety of instances to show you the different shapes and forms which insanity of this description takes, collected from medical writers and jurists of this country, France, and Germany, where the subject has been much and deeply investigated. The result would be, that your lordships would be satisfied that any attempt at a definition or description of this particular disease would

be altogether futile; and the only course we can pursue is to lay down some general comprehensive rule, and to leave those who have to administer the laws of the country to apply that rule to the different cases according to their discretion. Now, my lords, the question for our consideration is, what is actually the law of the country with respect to crimes committed by persons labouring under infirmities and diseases of this description? I apprehend, when you come to consider it, there is no doubt with respect to the law (hear, hear)—that it is clear, that it is distinct, that it is defined; and I think the result will be upon your mind, that it will be impossible beneficially to alter that law, or render it better in that respect, than the law as at present shaped actually exists. My lords, for this purpose I wish to be as clear and as perspicuous as possible. It is a subject of great importance; it is one in which the public take a deep interest, and everything, therefore, connected with it ought to be laid before the public through your lordships with the utmost possible precaution. I think it is not necessary, my lords, to quote any text-writers upon this subject. I shall go to the fountain-head, and state to your lordships what learned judges have said in the course of their administration of justice applicable to this subject, and the law they have laid down for the guidance of those who have to decide on the criminality or innocence of persons charged before them. The first authority to which I shall beg leave to refer is the authority of a most learned and most accurate judge. I speak in the presence of noble and learned friends who recollect that learned judge, and who will concur with me in saying that he never was exceeded by any person who has had to administer justice in this country in the accurate and sound views which he took of the law,—I mean Mr. Justice Le Blanc. I shall state to your lordships how the law was laid down by that learned judge, in a case that was tried before him at the Old Bailey in the year 1812, a few months after the trial of Bellingham. The circumstances of that case, as far as are necessary for me to introduce the judgment, were shortly these:—The prisoner had entertained a great antipathy for a person named Burrowes. There was no foundation for it—in fact, he had never given him the slightest cause for offence. With great deliberation he loaded a blunderbuss and shot him. Fortunately, however, the man was not killed. He was tried under the act for shooting—a capital offence. The defence set up was insanity; he had epileptic fits, which not unfrequently do produce that infirmity of mind. He had, about a month before, had a commission of lunacy issued against him; a jury was impanelled, and found a verdict of insanity. Mr. Warburton, the keeper of a lunatic asylum, a man of great experience in these matters, gave judgment that in his opinion he was insane, and said that insanity of that description often led to creating and harbouring the strongest antipathies without any cause against particular individuals. This was the substance of the case presented to the jury. The learned judge, with respect to the main point, summed up in these words: "It is for you to determine whether the prisoner, when he committed the offence with which he stands charged, was or was not incapable of distinguishing right from wrong whether he was under the influence of an illusion with respect to the prosecutor which rendered his mind at the moment insensible of the nature of the act he was about to commit, since in that case he would not be legally responsible for his conduct. On the other hand, provided you shall be of opinion that when he committed the offence he was capable of distinguishing right from wrong, and not under the influence of such an illusion as disabled him from distinguishing that he was doing

a wrong act, he would be answerable to the justice of his country and guilty in the eye of the law." The prisoner was afterwards found guilty, and I believe executed. That, my lords, is the law of the land, so far as relates to men labouring under some delusion; and, while it is upon them, acting under its influence—if it be so powerful as to render them incapable of distinguishing right from wrong, or knowing that they are doing wrong in murdering their fellow-creatures—in such cases they cannot be considered responsible in law for their actions. All the decisions show this to be the law. The next case which I shall mention is that of Bellingham, who was tried before Lord Chief Justice (Sir James) Mansfield. I thought it important in this case, in consequence of different observations that have been made upon it, to request the Solicitor of the Treasury to search for any shorthand-writer's notes of the proceedings ; and I have received the following as the substance of the summing up, as far as it is connected with this subject. The facts must be fresh in your lordships' recollection, notwithstanding the lapse of time. The Chief Justice, after some remarks on the cases of men who are utterly and totally deprived of reason, said, "There are other species of insanity, where people take particular fancies into their heads, who are perfectly sane and sound upon all other topics; but that is not a species of insanity that can excuse any person who has committed a crime, unless it so affects his mind at the particular period when he commits

continued

a crime as to disable him from distinguishing between right and wrong, or the just consequences of his actions;" and subsequently he put it to the jury thus—"The question is, whether you are satisfied that the prisoner had a sufficient degree of capacity to distinguish between good and evil at the time when he was committing this act ? In that case you will find him guilty." So that, although the expressions in some instances vary, the substance of the two judgments is, I apprehend, exactly the same—that if the party at the time when he committed a crime was in such a state of mind as not to know he was doing a wrongful act, he is not to be held legally responsible. My lords, there was an earlier case to which I will call your attention; that of Hatfield. Mr. Erskine, in his eloquent and powerful defence on that occasion, stated what he conceived the law to be in cases of this description—"Where a man is labouring under a delusion, if the jury are satisfied that this existed at the time of the offence, and that the act done was committed with that delusion, and done under its influence, he will not be considered as guilty in the eye of the law." That was, in eloquent expressions, alleged to be the law in cases of this sort; and Lord Kenyon, who, with the rest of the judges of the Queen's Bench (it being a trial at bar), presided, interrupted the defence, and said, "Mr. Attorney General, can you call any witnesses to controvert these facts ? With regard to the law, as it has been laid down, there can be no doubt whatever. If a man be in a deranged state of mind at the time of committing an act, he is not criminally answerable; the material part of the case is whether, at the very time, his mind was sane." And, after other observations, his lordship said, "His insanity must be made out to the satisfaction of a moral man meeting the case with fortitude of mind, and knowing the anxious duty he has to discharge; yet, if the scales hang tremulously, throw in a certain proportion of mercy in favour of the prisoner." In that case, then, my lords, which preceded the others, Lord Kenyon and the rest of the judges of the Queen's Bench agreed with the law as laid down by Mr. Erskine—that if a man committing a crime be labouring under such a delusion at the time as not to know right from wrong, he cannot be made the subject of a criminal proceeding. My lords, no departure has been made from that law, as thus laid down, not by single judges alone, but in conjunction with others of their brethren, who must be taken to have concurred with them. No alteration has taken place in that law, or in the way in which the judges administered it who presided at the late trials. In Oxford's case, Lord Chief Justice Denman laid down precisely the same law; and in order that there might be no mistake, it being a subject of such deep importance and interest, he consulted with two other learned judges associated with him (Mr. Justice Patteson and Mr. Baron Alderson), who concurred in a written note of the law upon the subject, which was read to the jury by the Lord Chief Justice. My lords, I take the law there to be distinctly settled; and, if it be so, the next question for your consideration is, whether there is any reason, or even any possibility, of altering it? Can you say, that if a man at the time when he commits a crime be under the influence of a delusion and insanity, so as not to know right from wrong, or the character of the act he is committing, is it possible, my lords, that you should, by any legislative provision, declare that such a man ought to be the subject of punishment, and lose his life in cases in which the capital penalty applies ? My lords, it is impossible (hear, hear). You might pass such a law, for your lordships have the power to do it; but when you come for the first time to put that law into execution the common sense and common feeling of men would revolt against it (hear, hear), and you would be compelled to retrace your steps, and to repeal the law, which in a moment of feeling you had passed, under the influence of recent powerful impressions and contrary to what you would have deemed wise under the sway of sober and steady reason (hear, hear). Lord Coke says, that to execute an insane person is murder, a course contrary to all law and all reason, and alien from all the principles of justice (hear). My lords, if you entertain any doubts upon the law, you can summon the judges of the land and hear their opinion upon it (as it is a subject of great importance), and thus have the law laid down under their united authority, to operate in all time, for the guidance of courts of justice, and to direct, with more force than is attained by the influence of a single judge, the verdicts of juries. It is for your lordships to determine whether you will feel it necessary to resort to such a measure. But perhaps, my lords, you will ask, with some anxiety and curiosity, what the law of other countries is upon this subject? My lords, the law of other countries corresponds (as of necessity it must) with our own upon this subject. As for the law of Scotland, I quote from a learned writer, Mr. Alison (in his "Criminal Law")—"To amount to a complete bar as to punishment the insanity, at the time of committing an act, must have been of such a kind as entirely to deprive the man of the use of his reason as applied to the act in question, and prevent him from knowing whether he was doing wrong." And if your lordships refer to the learned treatises (on the criminal law) of Mr. Baron Hume, you will find, that (though more expansively treated and more loosely worded) the law is deduced to an effect substantially the same; and, further, I can call your lordships' attention to a case cited by Mr. Alison on the subject. A man was indicted for the murder of another by shooting

him; having pursued him over a moor he shot him dead. The defence was insanity, under the delusion that the man murdered was an evil spirit whom the prisoner had been commanded by God to destroy. No one doubted that if the facts necessary to support the defence had been made out to the satisfaction of the jury, the judges (it is clear from the way in which the case was conducted) would have considered it a substantial defence; but the facts were not made out, and the man was found guilty from the defect in the evidence, the jury being of opinion, under the direction of the Court, that there was not sufficient evidence to show that at the time the man committed the act he really was labouring under that delusion. My lords, to pass from Scotland to France, in the "Code Napoleon" (the criminal code not less of ancient than of modern France) the French law on the subject is thus laid down:—"With respect to every crime, and every misdemeanour, no man can be made accountable who, at the time he does the act, is under alienation of mind." And though, my lords, I have no particular text-writer to quote as to the law of Germany on the subject, I have read many German treatises upon it, in which cases are cited satisfying me that the law of Germany in this respect corresponds with the law of France, the law of Scotland, and our own. The question then is, whether we can, under these circumstances, attempt to vary the law? Is it practicable? Is it possible? and, allowing it to be even practicable, would it be judicious (hear, hear) ? My lords, some persons say, "Define precisely what the law is." I say, to attempt to define upon a subject with which we are as yet only partially acquainted would be difficult and dangerous (hear, hear). Let us leave the general law as it stands, and let the judges, before whom prisoners are arraigned and tried, apply the particular facts to the law so laid down (hear, hear). My lords, I have heard it said (it is an argument I have heard in the streets), "The object of punishment is the prevention of crime: you do not punish by way of retribution, or in a spirit of vengeance, but to prevent others from committing similar offences; and, therefore" (it is said), "although a man may be under the influence of an insane delusion at the time when he commits an offence, if he knew the effect he was about to produce—if he knew, for instance, when he fired the pistol that the result would be the death of the party fired at, there is a sufficient ground for carrying the law into execution against him, because we punish to prevent others from imitating the offence." My lords, I should have dealt summarily with this position if I had not found it supported in the writings of a most rev. prelate, not a member of your lordships' house. [The noble and learned lord referred to Archbishop Whately, who, he was here informed, was a member of the House of Peers]—at least had I known that he was, I would have certainly sent him a note upon the subject. That most rev. prelate stated the position precisely as I have just described it, and gives, by way of illustration, the case of a dog habituated to the worrying of sheep, "who has no moral sense, but who, nevertheless, is punished," for the purpose of correction. This, my lords, is the illustration presented of the position founded professedly on the theory that the object of punishment is not retribution, but prevention—by example deterring others from committing similar offences. But by whom is the example to be presented ? By persons incapable of committing crimes ? Do you punish a person guilty of no offence ? one who is not the subject of punishment ? No, my lords, he must, in the first instance, deserve the punishment—if you are to inflict penalties, not in the spirit of retribution, but of prevention (hear, hear). My lords, I am surprised that a person of such sagacity, ability, and learning, as the most rev. prelate should commit what (with the highest deference for him) I must call such a logical absurdity (a laugh). But then as to the illustration. You punish the dog, my lords, not as an example to other dogs (laughter), but for his own correction (hear, hear); so that the illustration is as inapplicable and extravagant as the theory is incorrect and unfounded (hear, hear). My lords, if you should be satisfied, then, that the law is as I have stated it, and that no change can with propriety be made in that law, the next question is, whether any alteration can beneficially be made in the mode of administering the law. I apprehend, my lords, that this is equally impracticable. A man charged with a crime has a right to be tried by a jury, he has a right to have counsel assigned to him for his defence, he has a right to summon such witnesses as he may think proper for the purpose of his defence; his counsel has the right—nay, it is his duty, to make such observations on the case (both as to the law and as to the facts) as he may think available for the interests of his client; the jury are to decide upon the question of fact: and, my lords, over the whole presides a learned judge, whose duty it is to decide on the admissibility and inadmissibility of evidence—whose duty it is to state the law to the jury—whose duty it is to give a practical commentary upon the law with reference to the facts, leaving the general question of fact to the determination of the jury—the constitutional tribunal of the country. That, my lords, is the form and mode of proceeding in this, as in every other criminal case. How can you change it? Is it practicable? If practicable, is it advisable (hear)? No man can entertain a doubt upon this point (hear). If, then, my lords, the rule of law be right, if the mode of administering the law be right, what room is there for legislation? You may say, that in a particular instance the law has not been well administered—that the jury have drawn an improper conclusion of fact from the testimony, that witnesses may have stated opinions not warranted by science, and that the result has been unfortunate. My lords, it is a misfortune you must submit to, because it is not to be remedied by legislation. I do not say this is the case in the present instance, but as it is supposed and asserted by some to be, and I say if it be so, my lords, there is no ground for your interference—you cannot remedy the evil; legislation cannot reach it. My lords, let me say a few words as to the late trial. It lasted two days. The prosecution was conducted by an hon. and learned friend of mine (the Solicitor General), holding a high office, and as distinguished in that office by his talents as an advocate, and his learning as a lawyer (hear), as any man who ever preceded him in it (hear, hear). The learned judges who presided—three in number, were among the most eminent and most enlightened of all who adorned the bench (hear, hear). There were the Lord Chief Justice of the Common Pleas and two judges of the Court of Queen's Bench—all men of admitted learning, of great talent, of long experience, of conscientious character and conduct (hear, hear). What was the case laid down by Lord Chief Justice Tindal? Precisely, my lords, what I have stated to you as the law on the subject. I have procured the shorthand-writer's notes of the charge, which I will read from, in order to be certain of the precise words used:—" The point which will at last be submitted to you will be, whether on the evidence you have heard you are satisfied that at the time the prisoner committed the act of which he stands charged he had a competent use of his understanding to know he was doing, with respect to the very act itself, a wicked and a wrongful thing—a thing which he knew to be wicked and wrongful; for if at the time he did it he was not sensible that he was violating the law of God or man, undoubtedly he is not a person responsible for this act, or liable to any punishment whatever; but if, on balancing the evidence in your minds as it has been brought before you, you should think he was a person capable of distinguishing between right and wrong with respect to this act, he is then a responsible agent, liable to all the penalties of the law imposed upon such acts." That being, then, my lords, the law as it was laid down by the learned judge, the only question is, whether the jury have drawn a right conclusion from the facts or evidence? It has been objected, "why did the learned judges interpose, and not suffer the trial to take its course to the very end?" In considering the circumstances, and the great feeling excited, it would have been better had this course been pursued (hear). But I do not believe, for a moment, that it would have made the slightest alteration in the issue (hear, hear). The reason why I think so is, that while medical men, experienced in the subject, had been summoned on the part of the prisoner, two medical men of eminence on the part of the Crown, and who themselves had examined the prisoner with a view to the conclusion whether or not he was sane at the time of committing the act, were sitting, during the trial, in court, and were not called on the part of the prosecution, and (not being called) the necessary inference was that their evidence would have corroborated that adduced for the prisoner. I knew from positive information upon the subject, that it was impossible that the verdict could have been different from what it was. In Hatfield's case, where the trial was at bar before the four judges of the King's Bench, there the Chief Justice, in like manner to the Chief Justice of the Common Pleas, interposed and asked the prosecuting counsel whether he had the means of contradicting the evidence given by the witnesses for the defence?—and, on being replied to in the negative, he said at once " It is impossible to doubt as to the verdict of the jury." Precisely the same course was pursued by my learned friend the Chief Justice of the Common Pleas, and I can assure your lordships that it is quite impossible for any one to judge of the propriety of the course unless he were actually present in court during the whole period of the trial. My lords, I have thought it right to address these few observations to your lordships upon this case. I have only obtained my knowledge of the case from the newspapers. I have yet received no report of the evidence, and therefore I feel myself incapable of forming a judgment upon it; but knowing the great powers and legal ability of my learned friend, the Solicitor General, who conducted the prosecution, knowing also the high and unspotted character of the judges who presided, I cannot doubt but that justice was fairly and properly administered. Then, my lords, what are the conclusions I draw from these premises? First, that no alteration in the law is practicable, and that we are not called upon to alter the code in which the law is administered. The only thing left then, my lords,

is to see whether, by way of legislation, any measures of precaution, stronger than those at present existing, can be adopted for preventing the recurrence of such evils (hear). I am not at present prepared to introduce any bill for that purpose, but I trust in a few days I shall be able to lay one on your lordships' table having that object in view. Of course it is impossible for me, or any man to say, that something of the kind may not occur again. They are events which have happened in all times, not only in this country but in France, and every other civilised country; however, by legislation, I trust that we may render it more seldom than it has yet been. With respect to the general law upon the subject, probably your lordships might think it advisable to have the opinions of the judges (hear, hear); some of your lordships may think it better that we should legislate upon such a subject upon the united opinion and authority of that learned and venerable body. Should such be the pleasure of your lordships, I will request their attendance upon this house. As I before stated, I am not now in a condition to propose any measure; but, I hope, in the course of two or three days to be able to lay the bill, of which I now give notice, on your lordships' table.

Lord CAMPBELL said he should be sorry, for the sake of the character of the administration of justice in this country, if any doubt should be thrown upon the verdict lately given in the Central Criminal Court, and it seemed not to be the intention of his noble and learned friend to throw any doubt upon it. He had no doubt that M'Naughten was properly acquitted; but he agreed that it would have been more satisfactory if the trial had gone to a conclusion, and a reply had been heard from the Solicitor General, and there had been a summing-up by the judge. His noble and learned friend had said that the law was correctly laid down by the learned judge; but what signified how the law was laid down when the trial was stopped? when the judge asked the Solicitor General if he could rebut the evidence, and the Solicitor General said he could not, and would not press the case further? Let it not be supposed that he (Lord Campbell) meant the slightest reflection upon the learned judge who so highly adorned the bench; but he did regret that he should have been so impressed with the evidence of the medical witnesses, because the impression made upon the public mind was, that if a certain number of medical men said that a person under trial was insane, the trial must be stopped, and cadit quæstio. He contended that the question ought not to have been put; that was for the jury, not for witnesses to decide the point. It would be dangerous if it should go abroad that the opinion of medical men could acquit. He knew that Dr. Haslam was of opinion that all persons were insane. The case of Hatfield differed from that of M'Naughten. In that case it was proved, not by medical witnesses, but by persons who knew the facts, that he had been in the army and received a severe wound in the head, that he had been discharged from the military hospital as insane, that within three days of his committing the act he declared he had had an interview with the Supreme Being, and that he had made an attempt upon the life of his own child, whom he tenderly loved, within a few hours of his committing the act for which he was tried. He (Lord Campbell) thought the law required no alteration, since by the law as it stood partial insanity gave no immunity. He would read a short extract from Lord Hale:—" And this is the condition of very many, especially melancholy persons, who for the most part discover their defect in excessive fears and griefs, and yet are not wholly destitute of the use of reason; and this partial insanity seems not to excuse them in the committing of any offence for its matter capital; for doubtless most persons that are felons of themselves and others are under a degree of partial insanity when they commit these offences; it is very difficult to define the indivisible line that divides perfect and partial insanity; but it must rest upon circumstances duly to be weighed and considered both by the judge and jury, lest on the one side there be a kind of inhumanity towards the defects of human nature, or on the other side too great an indulgence given to great crimes." So that it was necessary to consider the state the person was in at the moment, and whether he could distinguish between right and wrong. He much wished that there should be a more authoritative declaration of the law on the subject than had hitherto existed, and he rejoiced that his noble and learned friend had suggested to the house to take the opinion of the judges, in order that the profession and the public might know what question was to be put to the jury. The public were now inundated with medical works on the subject of insanity, and on the responsibility incurred by insane persons. Those books were read by persons, and their minds became filled with discussions about homicidal tendencies and homicidal propensities, and men but too readily caught up the idea that persons very prone to homicide were in a state of insanity. Alison's observations on that subject were not unworthy of their lordships' attention; he said, that few men read about other persons, or about things in general, and, though mad as regarded themselves and their own affairs, they still understood the difference between right and wrong: the delusion which they laboured under merely incapacitating them for applying any moral rules to their own conduct; but their mental alienation was too great to allow of their being held

Continued

responsible for their actions. That writer further observed, that amongst madmen few were aware that murder was a crime, for they generally appeared to think themselves nowise blameable, and to justify their conduct on the ground that their victims were in a conspiracy against them, or were their mortal enemies. If the doctrine of that writer were sound any man in a fit of jealousy might murder the person who he thought injured him; wherever there was a suspicion of injury revenge might be gratified with impunity. He, therefore, wished that the law might be authoritatively laid down. Looking to the direction of the judges in the cases of Arnold, of Lord Ferrers, of Bellingham, of Oxford, of Francis, and of M'Naughten, he must be allowed to say that there was a wide difference both in meaning and in words. He would repeat, therefore, that an authoritative statement of the law would be highly desirable, and, if necessary, a declaratory act should be passed. Lord Mansfield narrated the circumstances under which a man named Wood indicted parties for conspiracy and false imprisonment. They took him from Westminster to London and confined him in a lunatic asylum. At the first trial in Westminster Hall, Wood being examined as a witness in support of the indictment, for a whole hour baffled the cross-examination of counsel; at length a string was touched which disclosed the nature of his malady. He subsequently preferred a fresh indictment, and, remembering what had occurred on the previous occasion, became more guarded, and, notwithstanding all the ingenuity of the defendants' counsel, they must have been found guilty, if the shorthand-writer who took notes of the preceding trial had not been produced to read the evidence then given by the witness, when he stated that he was "the Saviour of mankind." With respect to the unhappy persons acquitted on the plea of insanity, the present practice apeared to him to be most mischievous. Unfortunately, it so happened that persons acquitted under those circumstances at once became public characters. To hundreds and thousands they became objects not only of curiosity, but of courtesy and respect; they were the envy of many who were confined in the same places, often enjoying more comforts and indulgence than their companions in confinement. It was quite his opinion that such persons should be removed from the public eye, that they should be heard of as little as possible; that the treatment they received should render the example effective upon the public mind, deterring others from like offences. With these observations, he should leave the matter wholly in their lordships' hands, and he sincerely rejoiced that his noble and learned friend had taken it up.

The LORD CHANCELLOR said, that as to the place or mode of confinement, persons so acquitted might be disposed of in any manner which her Majesty directed. The attention of government had certainly been directed to the subject, and in future such persons would not be so confined as that no one should have access to them; but it would not be permitted to make public spectacles of them. If it were their lordships' pleasure to require the opinion of the judges, he should take the earliest possible opportunity to carry that object into effect.

Their lordships then adjourned.

The Times
1st December 1921

LANDRU'S TRIAL TO-DAY.

CHARGED WITH 11 MURDERS.

(FROM OUR OWN CORRESPONDENT.)

PARIS, Nov. 6.

They say that when in 1899 the great trial at Rennes was agitating all France and half Europe, there was found in Paris a signalman who had never heard the name of Captain Dreyfus. Could there be produced to-day, one wonders, a solitary Frenchman who had never heard of Landru? For Landru, though the crimes alleged against him are merely brutal and sordid, flashed into fame in 1919 and for a time in the columns of the Paris Press almost rivalled the Peace Conference, and has since become a gigantic and legendary figure in the annals of crime.

To-morrow, in the Palais de Justice, Versailles, before a jury which will be composed of the whole reading population of France, Henri Désiré Landru—this strangely appropriate second name for this strange being, whom so many have desired and who has possessed so many, seems to lend a further bizarre touch to a case which is compounded of strangeness—stands his trial for his life. The crimes now alleged against him of murder, theft, and fraud reach the imposing total of 26, while the prosecution will seek to prove that he killed and burnt in a furnace in his remote little villa at Gambais, near the forest of Rambouillet, 10 women and one man.

The murders charged against Landru are alleged to have begun with those of the widow Cuchet and her son André early in 1915, and only to have ended with that of Marie Thérèse Marchadier in January, 1919. All these 11 persons, whose names have been found inscribed in the luminous notebook kept by Landru, have disappeared. All the efforts of the prosecution to trace a single one of them have failed, and evidence will be brought that several of them had been seen by trustworthy witnesses staying with Landru.

But even supposing that Landru is guilty of these murders, it is difficult to realize the vast interest and queer fascination the career of this master Bluebeard has aroused. It is not as if Landru holds the "record" for murder; it is not as if he showed remarkable originality in the method whereby he disposed of the remains of his victims. Bloch, of Chicago, killed his 26 as against Landru's alleged 11, while the method of disposing of the bodies by incinerating them in the kitchen fire was inspired by the case famous in its day of Pell, of Montreuil, in 1885.

A man on his trial for life under the French system of justice has a terrible and protracted series of ordeals to face. He is unable to take refuge in solemn silence and has to submit to persistent remorseless interrogations by the Judge of First Instance. He has to undergo the ordeal of being conducted in person to the scenes of his alleged crimes and there to be an eye witness of the ghoulish processes of their reconstruction. Never, during an interrogatory which lasted from his arrest in April, 1919, to well into last year did Landru falter before the persistent M. Bonin, Juge d'Instruction, whose fame Bluebeard sardonically claims he has made. His ready wit and his perverse but brilliant humour are legendary.

One of his methods of fencing with the prosecution is to affect the discretion of "a man of honour." Asked where the victim is or where she went, he smiles sardonically and inquires how he can decently be asked as a gentleman to reveal the secrets of his association with a lady. For his victims—the police have discovered that he was in association or in intimate correspondence with no fewer than 283 deluded women—he appears to have exercised something of the fascination of a serpent for a bird. "Give up Landru? Never. He is sublime," was the recorded remark of one of his victims to the solicitations of her friends.

The trial is expected to last several weeks. Me. Godefroy, Advocate-General, leads for the prosecution, while the accused will be defended by perhaps the most brilliant and celebrated leader of the French Criminal Bar, Me. de Moro-Giafferi.

The line of defence naturally is not as yet fully disclosed, but it is believed from statements he has made that the defender of Caillaux and Humbert will chiefly lay stress on the inability of the prosecution to prove the death of any single one of the alleged victims of Gambais. The chief legal and dialectical tussle is likely to take place when, after the examination in chief of Landru has been concluded, medical and scientific witnesses come forward to give their testimony. There are hints of dramatic surprises, and in some quarters it is suggested that the trial may be yet further postponed. One may recall that even if Landru is acquitted he will not walk out of the court a free man. He has already been condemned to a sentence of five years' penal servitude for frauds in connexion with the motor-cycle business he once possessed, so that if he is acquitted of murder on a wholesale scale he will have at all events to serve a term in the penal settlement in French Guiana.

To-morrow's proceedings are unlikely to get beyond the selection of jurymen.

The "Bluebeard of Gambais."

The man who has been described for two years or so as the "Bluebeard of Gambais" was found guilty of murder yesterday in the Assize Court at Versailles. His trial lasted long, and it was marked by procedure and by incidents which are foreign to this country; but few people will doubt that the result was in accordance with justice. The Court day by day was thronged with emotional persons, mainly women, who gesticulated excitedly and laughed loudly during the hearing of evidence, and it appears that the prisoner was permitted to rebuke them from the dock. The interest in the case drew attention away from many important public matters; but the mysterious disappearance of ten women who had been associated with a plausible and, indeed, a witty murderer was bound to provoke curiosity among a large class. The indictment took about two hours to read, and it was stated that the prosecution had 4,500 documents in its *dossier*. The evidence was purely circumstantial. It showed that LANDRU took a villa at Gambais and that some of the 283 women with whom he had become acquainted in his extraordinary career went there as his guests and were never seen again. The allegation was that he had killed them, in most cases to obtain money, and had incinerated their bodies in an oven. The police found human bones and fragments of clothing in the garden. The case for the prosecution was mainly *vestigia nulla retrorsum*, and to support it there was evidence that LANDRU did not take return tickets for his guests. The property of some of the missing women was produced in Court, but the prisoner said that he had bought it and that he had taken them to his villa merely to transact business. The evidence, which was not strong in individual cases, was conclusive in the view of the jury in its cumulative effect.

It was not only the number of the victims which caused public wonder. There was the character of the man and his demeanour in the dock on the capital charge. He had been detained awaiting trial for more than two years, and yet to the last, with perhaps a moment of physical exhaustion or melancholy, he retained his self-possession. It seemed at times as though he had resolved to base a good part of his defence on M. ANATOLE FRANCE'S "Les Sept Femmes de la Barbe-Bleue." He was the *bon seigneur — cet honnête gentilhomme*, but he had not at the Gambais villa even that pardonable *cabinet des princesses infortunées*. "Show me the corpses," he exclaimed, at the same time chiding the police with their incompetence in finding "an innocent Landru"—*un bon seigneur*. How could any chivalrous host, he asked, insult his guests by handing to them return tickets; how could an *honnête gentilhomme* disclose the secrets of his meetings with ladies and wrongly compromise their *fiancées*? He had even taken one of them to Mass, because he gloried in "liberty of conscience." He had obliged another by hanging her dogs, whose skeletons were found in the garden at Gambais. No murderer was ever so dramatic and audacious in the dock. Chivalry, mockery, humility, humour, sarcasm, equanimity — these were the words used to describe his demeanour. There was an artistry of villainy in his conduct which will make his trial memorable enough to require a new and more horrible edition of the children's fairy tale, when his fate as a man is forgotten and a righteous indignation has subsided by the lapse of time.

The Times
14th March 1938

MR. CLARENCE DARROW

A FAMOUS AMERICAN COUNSEL

Mr. Clarence Darrow, of Chicago, whose death at the age of 80 is announced to-day, was for many years the best-known criminal lawyer in the United States. During a career at the Bar extending over more than 50 years he appeared in a great number of celebrated trials in different parts of the country. He was generally to be found on the side of the defendant.

He had a ready sympathy, which was at times unreasoning, with the man whom he regarded as the underdog, and sometimes when he heard of someone being prosecuted in a distant part of the country he would throw everything else aside and set out to conduct the defence throughout a long trial. He told the story of his life in an autobiography which was published in 1932, after he had retired from regular practice. Unlike most leading barristers in America, he never entered political life, though from the outset his sympathies lay with the Democratic party, among whose leaders he had then a close friend in William Jennings Bryan. Gradually his views on political and social questions became more and more advanced and radical and more and more sympathetic to those of the Socialist group, small in numbers and influence.

Born at Kinsman, a country town in Ohio, on April 18, 1857, of well-to-do parents, he was called to the Bar in 1878 and began to practise in Chicago. Before long he was in a high position in the legal department of the city, but did not remain there long, and when he left he showed at once that stern resistance to constituted authority which became rather his foible. He was usually retained by the labour organizations to represent them in most of the big legal cases in which they were involved, and Labour was then just fighting its way to recognition and often came into serious conflict with the law.

Among them the chief was the trial of Eugene Debs, on many occasions Socialist candidate for the Presidency, after the riotous strikes at West Pullman in 1894. Darrow took a part in the arbitration over the anthracite coal strike of 1902, in the settlement of which President Theodore Roosevelt had a considerable share. He also appeared for the Macnamara brothers, two prominent labour leaders who were charged in connexion with the dynamite outrage at the offices of the Los Angeles *Times*, in which more than 20 persons were killed, in 1911. The whole labour world was shocked when the brothers pleaded "Guilty" after one of their colleagues had turned State's evidence. In 1924 Darrow appeared as counsel for the defence in the Loeb-Leopold murder case in Chicago, where two young men, boys almost, belonging to wealthy families, were charged with a brutal and senseless murder. Many points of interest were argued, including the most recent theories of psycho-analysis and criminal responsibility. That they escaped the capital sentence was due to Darrow's brilliant tactical move in entering a plea of "Guilty" as well as to his burning eloquence.

Most notable of all his cases perhaps was his appearance in defence of Mr. J. T. Scopes, a Tennessee schoolmaster, who was tried at Dayton, Tennessee, in 1925, on a charge of teaching the doctrine of evolution to his pupils contrary to the laws of the State. Darrow was opposed to those champions of the strict interpretation of the Bible, the Fundamentalists, including his old friend, Bryan, and the two argued the case at great length over many days, while reporters from all corners of the country telegraphed long messages far and wide, and crowds flocked to the town from far and near as to a great fair. In the end the decision went against Darrow's client after a trial which had attracted world-wide attention.

Darrow was much interested in criminology, of which he had made a specially close study, and in social and economic questions. His views were most advanced on every topic, no matter what it might be. He seemed to pride himself on being in advance of his times. He wrote a book on "Crime, Its Cause and Treatment," and a large number of pamphlets and short stories. He was twice married and had one son by his first wife.

The Times
12th December 1921

LORD HALSBURY.

THE LAWYER AND THE MAN.

A CHANCELLOR WHO NEVER DOUBTED.

In Lord Halsbury passes away not merely a great lawyer, but a man in the fullest sense of that word. His career at the Bar, in the House of Commons, and in the House of Lords is known to all who know anything of our public men.

No one would have expected that "Giffard, Hardinge, S., 26, Chancery-lane, S. Wales Circuit, Glamorgan and Middlesex Sessions, C.C.C."—his description in the Law List in the fifties—would attain to the topmost point of his profession.

As early as 1865, when he took silk, he was a successful counsel; but even then his friends would not have predicted that he would one day be Lord Chancellor. A few years later he was much in request in actions in which an impressive speech and skill in cross-examining were required. By-and-by he appeared frequently in election petitions. His clients were always certain that his advocacy would be vigorous, his cross-examination powerful, and that he would conduct his case in a robust, business-like fashion, even if, trusting too much to his powers of rapid comprehension, he refused to burn the midnight oil in the work of preparation. Probably his first great triumph was achieved in 1867, when, as counsel for Governor Eyre, he was opposed to the late Mr. Justice Stephen, and persuaded the magistrates at Market Drayton to refuse to commit his client on a charge of murder. The memory of Giffard's speech still lingers. In the opinion of no mean judges it was comparable to any speech delivered in a Court of justice in recent times. In less memorable cases much the same from time to time occurred. Many were the murmurs by his juniors in "Salter's" robing-room at Westminster over Giffard's indolence; they were varied by enthusiastic expression of admiration at some powerful, masterly speech which he had delivered. At the end of the 'sixties and the beginning of the 'seventies he was seen much at Guildhall in commercial actions; he was engaged in almost all the great common law cases, including the Tichborne, and he was sure to be included in every important election petition.

IN THE HOUSE OF COMMONS.

Always an ardent party politician, he was not very successful on the hustings. After being appointed Solicitor-General in 1875 he met with one electoral rebuff after another. At last, in 1877, he was returned for Launceston, for which he sat for many years. Never esteemed a great debater in Parliament, he was ready, fluent, resourceful, and faithful to party ties, except, indeed, when the policy of his party was too Liberal for his temperament. He distinguished himself by the virulence of his attacks on Mr. Gladstone. In truth, the characters of the two men were radically antipathetic. Giffard hated the *finesse* displayed in the appointment to the Ewelme rectory and the like too much to do justice to the virtues or talents of one who seemed to him a demagogue. Fortune strongly favoured his advance. In 1870 it would have appeared to his admirers that his chances of sitting on the Woolsack were small as compared with those of the brilliant Sir John Karslake or that consummate advocate Sir John Holker. But they fell out of the race; the former worn out mentally and physically by activity too strenuous and varied; the latter forced by disease to accept a Lord Justiceship, which he held with manifest consciousness of his approaching end. By a chapter of accidents, rarely, if ever, paralleled, Giffard became Chancellor in 1885. He held that office until January, 1886. It was afterwards his rare fortune to be Chancellor from July, 1886, to August, 1892, and from June, 1895, to 1905. Altogether he held the seals for a longer period than any other Lord Chancellor or Lord Keeper except Lord Eldon.

HIS WORK AS CHANCELLOR.

To be candid, the expectations as to the manner in which he would discharge the duties of that office were not very high. They were, however, signally falsified. Though not a close student of law, he absorbed it rapidly; he took a broad view of facts and formed a commonsense judgment upon them; and, sitting with Judges of rare ability—Watson, Herschell, Selborne, Bramwell—he held his own with any of them. His ascendancy, in spite of his advanced age, became more and more marked. It was to equity lawyers a mystery that he, who had given little attention to their special science, should not be in any way led by Judges, such as Lord Davey or Lord Macnaghten, who had given their lives to its study. Whether the matter before the House was a Scottish appeal turning on a question of feudal law or a point of equity; whether he was sitting to determine in the Privy Council a question of French law, he was sure to dominate his colleagues. When once he had committed himself to an opinion as to a case it was almost hopeless for the side against which he had pronounced to snatch victory from his strong grasp. And with the disappearance of Lord Herschell and one or two other Law Lords this ascendancy grew instead of being weakened. Only his colleagues knew to the full what a powerful personality he was in counsel. His influence, it was suggested, was shaken when, in 1897, he found himself in a minority in the case of Allen v. Flood. But how strong it was appeared in Quinn v. Leathem, when he induced the House to modify—some say overrule—the expressions of certain of his colleagues in the former. Some of the innermost of his convictions were expressed in his declaration that it would be a disgrace to the jurisprudence of our country if it afforded no remedy for the conduct disclosed in Quinn v. Leathem.

His judgments filled for many years a large part of the reports of the House of Lords and Privy Council. They will rarely be consulted for accurate and concise expositions of the law. He was too fond of disposing of a case in the easiest and shortest way and of taking "a broad view"—to use his favourite expression—which shirked difficulties. In the Taff Vale case he was content to say ditto to Mr. Justice Farwell's judgment. In an appeal to the Privy Council which excited much attention in South Africa, and involved delicate questions as to the binding effect of concessions made by a chief whose territory was annexed, he disappointed lawyers by basing his decision on reasons which excluded a full discussion of the problems involved. The controversy over the Marnis case was caused mainly from his citing on the hearing a case which was really irrelevant—a case not relied upon in the considered judgment. His view of the development of law is revealed in his famous dictum in Quinn v. Leathem:—

A case is only an authority for what it actually decides. I entirely deny that it can be quoted for a proposition that may seem to follow logically such a mode of reasoning assumes that the law is necessarily a logical code, whereas every lawyer must acknowledge that the law is not always logical at all.

A dictum subversive of all legal reasoning. Speaking in the same mood, he once described history as "a string of names and dates." He once astonished the world by stating that he thought cheques under £2 were illegal.

MODELS OF LUCIDITY.

All the same, his judgments were marked by robust good sense or keen perception of essentials; they showed the capacity to master and marshal facts which had distinguished him at the Bar, and they were expressed in clear and vigorous language. As an example of his strong, decisive way of dealing with questions may be cited his judgment in Walter v. Lane. As examples of his lucid presentment of legal arguments might be instanced his judgment in De Nicols v. Curlier, Powell v. Kempton Park Race Course Company, and in the Driefontein Mining Gold Mines case. His judgment in the first of these three cases, dealing with an interesting point of private international law, is a model of lucid statement. His judgment in the last-named case was a masterly examination of the authorities. Perhaps, to be candid, he fell in later years into a vein of dogmatism, and approached decisions brought under review with an unconscious prejudice against them, the result being that, while the Court of Appeal was never stronger than in the later years of his life, the percentage of reversals remarkably increased. Nor did he care to express himself with deference as to the opinions of Judges at least his equals as lawyers. He had made practically the whole Bench. He had been an eminent and successful advocate when most of them were children, and he was not particular as to his words when he overruled them. Thus, in a case as to the construction of a will, he prefaced his judgment with the remark, "I have not been able to entertain the smallest doubt as to what is the true solution of the question. . . .

It is, to my mind, absolutely amazing that anyone can entertain the smallest doubt as to what these words mean "—though the Court of Appeal had held them to mean that which he did not. "It is exceedingly clear that the judgment of the Court of Appeal must be reversed." "I think the contention hardly admits of plausible statement." "I am bewildered by the absurdity of such a suggestion." "I confess I have not been able to entertain any doubt." Similar phrases often recur in his later judgments. "It seems to me *luce clarius* that the appellants are entitled to succeed." He will go down to history as the Chancellor who never doubted.

He was supposed to be no great friend of legal reforms. He was opposed to several principles embodied in the Judicature Acts. He was averse to the extension of the County Court jurisdiction. Nor did he favour proposals to inquire into the working of our judicial system. He was indifferent, if not hostile, to the Commercial Court. He came down to the Parliament of his own Inn to persuade it not to join with the other three Inns in supporting the then Attorney-General's scheme for a law school, a scheme distasteful to him, who belonged to the pre-scientific ages. And yet as a Judge and a legislator he was a party to many innovations. Witness his decision in what is called the Clitheroe case, in which, reversing a well-known decision always quoted in the books, he refused a writ of *habeas corpus* to a husband claiming to take possession of his wife. Nor can a Chancellor who passed the Land Transfer Act and several other measures scarcely less important be said to have done nothing as a law reformer. As his friend, Sir Harry Poland, once said, his name will always be connected with one of the greatest of reforms, that which enabled accused persons to go into the witness-box and give evidence. His patriotism and good sense, shocked at the consequences of decisions which permitted alien enemies to trade in this country under cover of the Joint Stock Companies Acts, led him to bring in a Bill to amend the law as laid down by the Court of Appeal.

"THE LAWS OF ENGLAND."

One of his achievements, wonderful considering his age, was to plan and superintend the publication of "The Laws of England "—an attempt to carry out by private enterprise the scheme propounded in 1860 by a Commission for preparing a complete digest of our laws. He was often a wise counsellor to his party—in the view of Lord Salisbury an unequalled exponent of safe, common-sense opinion.

On January 25, 1920, he celebrated the 70th anniversary of his call to the Bar, and attended that day the morning service in the Temple Church, having received the day before an eloquent and graceful address of congratulation, on behalf of the Bench and the Bar, from Lord Birkenhead.

The Bar admired "the grand old man" of their profession: his vigour of intellect, his force of character, his courage, his abiding youth, his high sense of the aims and place of law in the community. When far advanced in years he sat for a short time in the Court of Appeal, and his quickness, incisiveness, and capacity of settling on the centre of a case were never more conspicuous. As late as June, 1916, he delivered a judgment in the House of Lords in the case of a German company. Not a great orator or a debater of the first order, he was always, and never more than in his later years, clear in argument and forcible in expression. In congenial company, and especially in addressing younger members of the Bar, he revealed a vein of humour which did not come to light in his political speeches. Another attraction was his love of their profession. Asked why, with all the work incident to a large practice, he never aged in it, his answer was, "I never wanted to be up there" (pointing to the Bench).

During his terms of office it fell to him to appoint almost all the members of the Supreme Court and most of the County Court Judges. His choice was often criticized, and not without reason. What may be said in extenuation is that his mistakes were due mainly to good-nature, and that, at all events, he did not reserve the best appointments for those whose claims were solely political. In this, as in other matters, his indolence permitted things to be done which were not conducive to his influence.

A GREAT POLITICAL FIGURE.

To describe fully his political career would be to write the history of the last 40 or 50 years. In all the events of that period he has had a share—in the last 20 a large share. In office and in Opposition, in the House of Commons and in the House of Lords, he has always been the consistent adversary of every measure subversive of the Constitution. Combative and courageous, direct in speech and always intelligible, he was the out and out opponent of such measures as the Parliament Act or Welsh Church Disestablishment. He was a party man; but if his party was weak or wavering, Lord Halsbury was the first to reprove it. Disdaining subtleties and half measures, he often found himself the spokesman of many of his countrymen who admired frank, courageous speech.

To statesmen in the highest place he was notoriously a most valued counsellor, and surely never in the long line of the Chancellors of England was found a man more fitted to be Keeper of the Conscience of the King.

Greater forces in public life there doubtless are—men more in harmony with public opinion, more careful to catch the wavering wind. And yet a friend may say with truth :—

He was a *man* ; take him for all in all,
I shall not look upon his like again.

Daily Telegraph
26ᵗʰ October 1917

SIR W. J. HERSCHEL

The death has taken place, at the age of 84, of Sir William James Herschel, Bt., a distinguished Indian civil servant from 1853 to 1878. His services included those of Secretary to the Board of Revenue, Calcutta, and Commissioner of Cooch Behar. He was educated at Haileybury and Oxford, and was well known as the discoverer of the use of finger-prints for identification purposes. When Sir Francis Galton issued "Finger-Print Directories," in 1895, he inscribed the volume to Sir William Herschel in the following terms: "I do myself the pleasure of dedicating this book to you, in recognition of your initiative in employing finger-prints as official signatures nearly forty years ago, and in grateful remembrance of the invaluable help you freely gave me when I began to study them." Since the early discoveries in this field in the magistrates' court at Jungipoor, on the upper reaches of the Hoogbly, there have been many masterful developments of its original applications, to which Herschel, Galton, and Sir Edward Henry have contributed, so that finger-prints, to use Sir William's own words, have now become "a weapon of penetrating certainty for the sterner needs of justice."

Sir William is succeeded in the baronetcy by his son, the Rev. John Charles William Herschel, vicar of Braywood since 1914.

New York Times
4th April 1936

HAUPTMANN PUT TO DEATH FOR KILLING LINDBERGH BABY; REMAINS SILENT TO THE END

WALKS CALMLY TO CHAIR

Execution Is Delayed 40 Minutes to Permit Any Final Move.

PRISONER HOPES TO LAST

Repeatedly Denies All Guilt While Counsel Fight Losing Battle to Save Life.

WIFE IN FUTILE EFFORT

Signs a Formal Complaint Accusing Wendel of Crime as Hauck Fails to Act.

By RUSSELL B. PORTER
Special to The New York Times.

TRENTON, April 3.—Silent to the end except for renewed declarations of his innocence, Bruno Richard Hauptmann was put to death by the State of New Jersey tonight for the murder of Charles A. Lindbergh Jr.

He walked into the execution chamber and, without saying a word, stepped quickly to the electric chair as his two spiritual advisers read to him from the Bible in German. The current was turned on at 8:44 P. M. He was pronounced dead at exactly 8:47½ o'clock after a thorough examination by several physicians.

More than fifty official witnesses and newspaper men watched the execution in the small, brightly lighted execution chamber with its smudged white-washed brick walls, its high ceiling with a skylight, and its rows of wooden chairs in one-half of the room.

The witnesses sat in these chairs behind a three-foot-high canvas barrier which separated them from the prison officials, the executioners, the condemned man and the others in the same section as the electric chair.

Back of the witnesses was the door through which they had entered from the prison yard. At their left was a gray, iron grilled door leading to the cells in the death house. To the right behind the electric chair was the door to the autopsy room.

Set in the wall behind the electric chair was a cabinet whose open doors displayed a large wheel and an instrument board. Robert Elliott, the gray-haired official executioner, with his lined, weather-beaten face and his gray suit and colored shirt and tie, stood behind the chair. Across the arms of the chair lay a long wooden board with large bulbs, which had been used in testing it.

Witnesses Are Warned

Colonel Mark O. Kimberling, principal keeper in charge of the New Jersey State prison, ordered the witnesses to button up their coats and not put their hands into their pockets or make any suspicious motions during the execution. He instructed the guard to hold up a large clock by which the execution could be timed.

The warden then instructed another guard to telephone the central office and find out whether "there is any message for us." This was a last effort to see whether any legal move might still prevent the execution. In a moment the guard returned with the word that there was no message.

Elliot, who had been testing the electric chair, notified Colonel Kimberling that everything was in order and the colonel ordered that Hauptmann be brought in from his adjoining death cell.

There was an absolute hush in the death chamber. No one said a word or made a sound. Then men could be heard breathing. Several coughed.

The door from the death house swung inward and Hauptmann walked into the room behind a keeper. His two spiritual advisers, the Rev. John Matthiesen of Trenton and the Rev. D. G. Werner of the Bronx, both in black, followed him. Other keepers came in after them.

Hauptmann's face was more yellow than white, but it was absolutely composed. He barely glanced around the room, then turning toward his left, saw the electric chair walked toward it and sat down in it so rapidly that he almost seemed to leap into it. He seized the arms with his hands and sat

there quietly. For a moment there appeared to be a fleeting attempt at a smile on his features, but it passed immediately and he sat there in the same apathetic, stoical manner that he exhibited in the witness chair at Flemington.

His head was shaved close and one leg of his khaki trousers with dark stripes along the side was slit. He wore a gray shirt and brown slippers.

As soon as he had entered the room, one of the ministers could be heard reading from the Bible in German. Hauptmann did not respond to the reading.

The guards placed the black mask over Hauptmann's face, strapped his arms, feet and chest to the chair, and attached the electrodes. While first Mr. Werner and then Mr. Mathiesen continued to read from the Bible, Colonel Kimberling, who kept his hat and coat on during the execution, nodded toward Elliott from his place alongside of the chair. Behind the chair, the executioner turned on the current.

Three shocks were given so closely together that they seemed like one. The first shock was given at 8:44, and the third at 8:45.

As soon as the current was turned off the straps were loosened and the physicians applied stethoscopes to the body. Dr. Howard Wiesler, prison physician, said, "This man is dead!" at 8:47½.

The ministers continued reading until this moment.

Guards then carried the body into the autopsy room in the rear, but no autopsy was performed, the

State having dropped this procedure six or seven years ago.

During the day, in which futile last-minute efforts were made by his wife and counsel to further delay the execution, already postponed once this week and twice previously, Hauptmann constantly repeated his assurance to his keepers and spiritual advisers that he had told the truth and had nothing more to say.

Although the execution was scheduled for 8 o'clock, Colonel Kimberling delayed it for forty minutes waiting for any eleventh-hour developments in the long legal fight that Hauptmann has waged to escape execution.

The witnesses, including about thirty newspaper men, six physicians, several members of the New Jersey Legislature, representatives of Governor Hoffman, and officers of the State police, began to gather in the warden's office of the State Prison well before 7 o'clock. This was in accordance with Colonel Kimberling's instructions for every one to be in his office at 7:15 o'clock.

At this hour Governor Hoffman and Attorney General Wilentz were still in conference at the State House on the defense plea for a reprieve, and neither the prison officials nor the witnesses knew whether the execution would actually take place.

When the witnesses passed through the police lines surrounding the prison, they found a considerably smaller crowd than on Tuesday night, when the execution was postponed exactly at 8 o'clock, the hour appointed for it. This was partly because of uncertainty as to whether it would really be carried out tonight.

Another reason was the weather. It was dark, chilly and blustery in the streets outside the prison.

While heavy clouds hung over the long, rambling lines of prison buildings with their high walls of stone, brick and concrete surmounted by sentry boxes, floodlights from the top of the death house, great flares from the sound-reel trucks, and bright flashes from camera bulbs, illuminated the scene with weird blue and yellow effects.

The witnesses passed through an aisle formed by two rows of State troopers in their bright blue and yellow uniforms up the steps into the gloomy, century-old, brownstone Administration Building, which is of Egyptian architecture with hieroglyphics and carvings of winged serpents and animals in the stone above the gate.

At the top of the steps each witness was searched by a prison guard looking for concealed weapons or cameras. Inside the heavy barred gate the witnesses were more thoroughly searched by other guards in a little room just inside the wall. This search looked into the linings of hats and coats, pockets and their contents, wallets, papers and other articles worn or carried. Each witness was then escorted into the warden's office, where women secretaries checked his official invitation with the official list.

Colonel George Selby, deputy principal keeper, next required each one to sign an affidavit that he had not smuggled deadly weapons, cameras, drugs or other contraband into the prison.

Searched again in another room, the witnesses were taken into a double grill with iron bars on both sides, in which they were searched again, in groups of three. Then they were admitted to the center, inside the main prison building, with aisles radiating from it into the cell blocks like spokes of a wheel.

Here there was a long wait, with the witnesses at first smoking cigarettes and talking, but later falling silent and looking about with strained, nervous expressions as the clock on the wall slowly pointed toward 8 o'clock, the hour fixed for the execution. At 7:50 o'clock they learned with the arrival of Albert B. Hermann, clerk of the Board of Pardons, who was a witness, that Governor Hoffman had denied a reprieve.

The Warden Is Searched

Colonel Selby entered the center at 7:58 o'clock and ordered the witnesses to line up in a double row, the physicians first. There was a long wait until 8:15, when Colonel Kimberling came in, being searched by the guards as he entered from his office.

The principal keeper announced that the execution would be carried out soon. Then he said that he had heard rumors that an effort would be made to take photographs of the execution or to make some sort of a "demonstration" in the death house. For these reasons, he added, every one would be searched just before entering the execution chamber. He said that he would submit to a search first, and any one who did not wish to submit to the same search could not witness the execution. Then he added:

"If Hauptmann wants to say anything, I'm warden of this prison and will handle it. No police officer, no press and no one else will have anything to do with it but listen to it. Everybody is to remain seated until the execution is over. If there is any demonstration, the person making it will be removed from the chamber."

Colonel Kimberling led the way from the center, starting at 8:20 o'clock. In a double line 100 feet long, the witnesses marched through iron barred gates into the middle cell block, then through the dimly lighted mess hall and kitchen corridors, out into the open prison yard, where the moon and stars could be seen in a sky which had cleared within an hour, shining down between the rows of prison buildings.

Enter the Death House

The witnesses walked for several hundred feet, through the yard to the new brick building which constitutes the death house. Folding doors slid open to admit them to the courtyard. Here, as they were searched just outside the death chamber door, they could see keepers with rifles and bayonets pacing up and down above them on the roof of the building, and could hear the murmur of the crowd in the street, not far away.

After this final search, the witnesses were admitted to the execution chamber, the first ones entering just about 8:30 o'clock. A few minutes after the execution, the witnesses filed out, and left the prison by a gate only a few feet from the death house.

C. Lloyd Fisher, chief defense counsel, visited Hauptmann in the death house at 7:20 o'clock tonight. He was the prisoner's last visitor except for his spiritual advisers, who returned this evening and stayed with him until the end.

Condon Has No Comment; Gets the News by Phone

Dr. John F. (Jafsie) Condon, the intermediary who paid the $50,000 Lindbergh ransom money four years ago and who was an important State witness in the trial which ended in the conviction of Bruno Richard Hauptmann, received the news of Hauptmann's execution last night without comment.

Gregory Coleman, a friend of Dr. Condon, told newspaper men that the former educator had first received the news by telephone from another friend whose identity was not disclosed.

Daily Telegraph
21st July 1923

DRAMATIC END
OF
MEXICAN BANDIT.

GENERAL VILLA SHOT.

CHIHUAHUA CITY (Mexico), Friday.

The rebel Villa was killed at 8.30 this morning on his ranch at Canutillo by his secretary, Miguel Trillo, who, in his turn, was shot down a few minutes later by Villa's supporters.

A general battle ensued between the men on Trillo's side and those loyal to Villa, about 800 men being involved. It is reported that the men were dissatisfied because they had not been paid.

It appears that Trillo fired at Villa without warning in a sudden fit of anger. The general died almost immediately. There were about 100 casualties in the battle that followed.—Reuter.

MEXICO CITY, Friday.

An official statement issued here says that Villa was killed in an ambush this morning near Parral, Chihuahua. President Obregon has ordered that Villa's funeral shall be accorded full military honours. The announcement states that Villa, with his personal secretary, Trillo, and an escort, was ambushed on his way from his ranch at Canutillo to Parral. Villa was instantly killed, together with Trillo and three members of the escort.—Reuter.

VILLA'S CAREER.

The death of Villa robs Mexico of a very picturesque figure, but it is not likely that anyone beyond his immediate followers will regret the passing of the bloodstained guerilla leader. Francisco Villa, whose real name was Doroteo Orango, was born at Las Nieves (Durango) in 1868. He never was educated, being almost completely illiterate all his life, and began his career of crime when only 14, when he served his first sentence for cattle-lifting. He was scarcely out of prison when he was re-arrested for homicide and returned again to his cell. Released for the second time, he took to the hills, and at the head of a band of outlaws terrorised the whole State of Durango.

The exploits of the bandit soon gave him more than local celebrity. There was the notorious murder in the open street at Chihuahua of his partner, the murder of the factory-owner, Mr. Soto, and the theft of over $10,000 from the latter's daughter. Thanks to this successful coup he increased his band, and, entering into politics in 1911, joined Madero's revolutionists. In six months he terrorised Chihuahua State by murders and outrages, and at the triumph of the revolution resumed with greatly enhanced prestige his old trade of bandit.

Within a few months he was arrested, but Madero saved his life and he fled over the border. In February of 1913 Huerta seized power, and once more Villa took the field, nominally in support of Carranza, Huerta's chief rival, really for his own hand. He soon distinguished himself by his usual type of exploit. In May, 1913, he carried out a daring train robbery at Baeza, and raided and plundered the town of San Andres. The next victim was the town of Sta. Rosalia, which he sacked, murdering or torturing most of the inhabitants. In July, 1913, Casas Grandes felt his hand, where eighty peaceful citizens were shot out of hand, and two months later he carried San Andres a second time, against a garrison of Federal troops, and left over 300 corpses

Continued

behind him, many of the victims being burned alive. Federal columns were sent against him without success. On Sept. 29 he surprised a superior force at Aviles, murdered all his prisoners, and, capturing Torréon, butchered prominent citizens and exacted from the survivors $3,000,000. Two months later he took Juarez by surprise, and on Dec. 8 entered Chihuahua in triumph.

THE BENTON MURDER.

In Chihuahua Villa established a regular reign of terror, an incident in which in February, 1914, assumed international proportions. This was the murder of W. F. Benton, a ranchowner and British subject, who had ventured to remonstrate with him on his disregard for the elementary rights of property. The murder was, according to the account of The Daily Telegraph Special Correspondent, Signor Luigi Barzini, peculiarly brutal. Unarmed, Mr. Benton rode into Villa's camp to protest against the seizure of his cattle. " I have not stolen anything from you," Villa replied. " Not you," said Benton, " but your men." " I can do nothing for you," Villa exclaimed, adding vulgar insults. " Get out." Perfectly calm, Benton went on: " I am a British citizen. If you will not do me justice, I shall appeal to the authorities of my country." He then turned to leave. As he was crossing the threshold Villa aimed his revolver and fired. One of his aides-de-camp followed suit, and Benton fell on his face—dead.

This and other outrages led to the American landing at Vera Cruz on April 21, and to diplomatic action which caused Huerta's withdrawal from Mexico in August, and left Carranza, Zapata, and Villa in control. Villa pursued his usual savagery in establishing the " Constitutionalist " position, and succeeded in capturing Mexico City on April 2. The allies quarrelled, however, and a convention was called to choose a provisional president, and under Villa's guns resolved to eliminate Carranza. It chose General Gutierrez as president, and charged Villa with the task of driving the Carranzanists from the capital.

That accomplished, Villa was a real power in Mexican politics, and diplomacy saw fit to forget his crimes and treat with him. Obviously a man of energy and skill and a capable soldier, he was ruling northern Mexico, if ruthlessly, at least fairly efficiently, and a mission was sent by President Wilson to his headquarters. Before anything could be accomplished, however, Carranza's cause recovered, and in April, 1915, under the leadership of Obregon, his troops defeated Villa at Celaya, and Leon recaptured Torréon. Negotiations by the American Powers dragged on, and finally, in September, they declared they would recognise the leader who should show the greatest success during three weeks in maintaining order. Obregon again defeated Villa, and on Oct. 19 Carranza was recognised de facto by the American Powers.

RAID INTO AMERICA.

Now an outlaw, Villa still succeeded in maintaining himself in the north, and bent on provoking intervention, raided across the American border and murdered American citizens. On March 9, 1916, he crossed the border in force, and captured Columbus (New Mexico). He was driven out by American troops, and a punitive expedition under General Pershing entered Mexico and maintained a " dead or alive " pursuit of Villa, which lasted nine months, and cost the United States $100,000,000. In a battle at Parral American troops were ambushed, and a number of them killed. On March 31, however, the bandit's followers were defeated at Guerrero. The Americans were successful in a number of other skirmishes, and penetrated so far south as to meet Carranza's troops, who were also in pursuit of the renegade leader. Villa, wounded, but always eluding his pursuers, lived in a Chihuahua mountain cave for five weeks, and on the American army's withdrawal from Mexico renewed his depredations. On March 11, 1917, Carranza was elected President.

From that date Villa went back to frank brigandage, taking advantage of any civil strife to raid and murder. Government troops failed to subdue him, though his chief lieutenant, Angeles, was captured and executed in November, 1919. Early in 1920 the Obregon revolt brought him back as a revolutionary leader, and on May 27, 1920, three Federal forces started out to capture him. In July, as 8,000 men were closing in on him, he agreed to an armistice and surrendered to General Eugenio Martinez at Sabinas. He declared his adherence to Obregon, later elected President, and was granted by the Mexican Government one year's pay and a small farm for each of his men, a grant equal to £100,000. In August he solemnly declared that he had ended his career of outlawry, when, at the head of 900 followers, he entered San Pedro, Coahuila, and announced his intention of accepting the amnesty an' ------ing down as a farmer. But the temptation to robbery was too strong, and Villa until his death was still leader of an outlaw gang.

The Glasgow Herald 26th July 1910

CRIPPEN ARRESTED.

STRONG ACTION BY SHIP'S CAPTAIN.

DRAMATIC SCENE ON BOARD THE MONTROSE.

The " Daily Express " of this morning says :—On Saturday Captain Kendall, using the almost absolute power of the commander of a ship at sea, decided to arrest the couple. Crippen and Miss Le Neve were confronted by Captain Kendall, the chief officer, and the purser. Crippen was immediately searched and deprived of a revolver, a number of cartridges, and a penknife, while Miss Le Neve burst into tears. Crippen at once demanded to know what offence he was charged with, and was told that he had contravened the law by representing that the woman with whom he was travelling was a boy, and by giving a false name in the papers which he had signed. He could have freed himself by proving that the woman was his wife and offering evidence of his identity. He failed, however, to produce a marriage certificate or any document bearing out his assertion that his name was Robinson. On this technical charge he and Miss Le Neve were immediately placed under close arrest in separate cabins. Crippen is watched day and night by an officer of the ship and a seaman, while a stewardess and a seaman keep similar guard over the woman. Miss Le Neve is in a distressing condition of collapse, and has expressed her willingness to make a statement to a police official as soon as possible. Crippen declares that he can prove his innocence.

Miss Le Neve appeared to be ill during the voyage and rarely left her cabin. Sympathetic inquiries were made, and Crippen explained that the " boy " was in delicate health. Suspicions were soon aroused by her appearance, but no confirmation was obtained until Friday last, when the couple were overheard talking together about their escape. Captain Kendall, the commander of the Montrose, was at once informed, and communicated by means of wireless telegraphy with Mr A. Piers, manager of the steamship lines of the Canadian Pacific Company.

STORY OF THE FLIGHT.

In consequence of the conflicting statements that have been published respecting the movements of Dr Crippen and Miss Le Neve, the London office of the Canadian Pacific Railway communicated with the Antwerp representative of that company. A reply was received yesterday to the effect that two passengers booked there under the names of Mr and Master Robinson for Montreal by the Canadian Pacific Railway steamer Montrose. As these people are, in the opinion of the officers of the Montrose, undoubtedly Dr Crippen and Miss Le Neve, the arrest of the alleged murderer may be looked forward to with some confidence.

The report that the fugitives were on board the Allan liner Sardinian has now to be discarded for the later and more circumstantial story that they are on board the C.P.R. steamer Montrose. The Montrose left Antwerp for Montreal on the 20th inst., and, according to the story, Scotland Yard was advised by wireless telegraphy by the captain of the vessel on Friday the 22nd that he believed he had on board his ship Dr Crippen and Miss Le Neve; that the woman, who was dressed in male attire, exactly answered the description of Le Neve; and that the other person, except in his disguise, answered the description of Dr Crippen. He asked for instructions. On receipt of this message Scotland Yard decided to act, and, as stated yesterday, despatched Inspector Dew in pursuit of the fugitives.

The story of how the missing couple (assuming they are the persons wanted) were discovered is interesting. The Montrose is a second class boat and carries no first class passengers. A few hours before she sailed from Antwerp a gentleman in semi-clerical attire, accompanied by a young man, booked passages for Montreal, giving the names of " Mr Robinson and son." They were not long on board, however, till a stewardess had her suspicions aroused regarding the " son." The general deportment and the speech of this person were decidedly more like those of a woman than a man, and the stewardess, after careful observation of the unusual passenger, communicated her suspicions to the captain. " Mr Robinson and son " were thereafter closely watched, and the captain being convinced that he had on board these much-wanted persons Crippen and Le Neve, communicated with the shore as stated above. Such is the latest story of the missing couple.

Although the Montrose is not a mail boat, she will, the Central News learns, on this occasion, at the request of the Scotland Yard authorities, call at Rimouski, on the River St Lawrence, where the Canadian mails are usually landed, and between which place and Montreal there is direct railway communication. Inspector Dew will board the Montrose at Rimouski, and if he identifies the fugitives as those wanted in connection with the murder of Mrs Crippen he will forthwith take them into custody and probably bring them back.

The White Star liner Laurentic, on which Inspector Dew is travelling, does the trip between Liverpool and Montreal in seven days. She left Liverpool on Saturday last, and is therefore due at Montreal on Saturday night next. The Montrose, on the other hand, usually takes 11 days. As she left Antwerp on the 20th, she is due to arrive on or about Sunday the 31st, so that Inspector Dew should be in time to welcome the suspects.

CRIPPEN

continued

6th October 1888

POLICE THE ILLUSTRATED NEWS
LAW COURTS AND WEEKLY RECORD

SISTER OF VICTIM

FIFTH VICTIM

MORTUARY

THE BERNER ST VICTIM.

INSPECTOR REID

INQUEST ON FIFTH VICTIM AT ST GEORES IN THE EAST

TWO MORE WHITECHAPEL HORRORS. WHEN WILL THE MURDERER BE CAPTURED?

BACK OF BERNER STREET

FIRST DISCOVERY OF THE CRIME

GOING TO HER DOOM

POLICE CONSTABLE WATKINS SIGNALLING FOR ASSISTANCE

FINDING THE BODY IN MITRE SQUARE

MITRE SQUARE ALDGATE

THE FATAL SPOT

THE SCENE ON SUNDAY IN BERNER STREET

EXTERIOR OF THE GATE

THE FIFTH VICTIM OF THE WHITECHAPEL FIEND.

FINDING THE MUTILATED BODY IN MITRE SQARE.

Newsweek
25th December 1961

EICHMANN TRIAL:

The Nether Hell

Rain fell in blinding sheets, and the first fierce winds of winter whined around the Beth Haahm courtroom in Jerusalem where Adolf Eichmann awaited his judgment.

Meticulously, the former SS colonel went through his familiar gestures. He hitched up his belt, adjusted the microphone before him in his bulletproof glass box. He did not look at those in the courtroom audience—soldiers in khaki uniforms, men in open-throated sports shirts, old ladies wearing babushkas. They scarcely moved, and they made no sound. They just watched Eichmann.

The hour was 9 on the morning of Dec. 15—248 days after the Eichmann trial began and seventeen years after he had ordered the last of some 6 million Jews shipped to Hitler's concentration camps. Three days before, the three presiding judges had found Eichmann guilty on all fifteen counts against him. Twelve of these carried the death penalty for crimes against humanity and against the Jewish people.

"The accused well knew that the order for the physical extermination of the Jews was manifestly unlawful," the three judges had declared in their 175-page verdict, "and that by carrying out this order he was committing criminal acts on an enormous scale."

The judges also rejected Eichmann's main defense, that he had acted only as a small cog in a powerful machine. "The accused," they said, "closed his ears to the voice of conscience [and] thus he sank from one depth to another until, in the implementations of the 'final solution [of the Jewish problem],' he reached the nether hell."

No Monster? Eichmann had clung to this defense in his own final statement however, claiming: "I am not the monster I am made out to be.

"Today of my own free will, I would ask the Jewish people for pardon," he said, "and would confess that I am bowed down with shame at the thought of the iniquities committed against the Jews and the injustices done them, but . . . this would, in all probability, be construed as hypocrisy."

In the courtroom, the moment for pronouncing the judgment had now arrived. But the minutes ticked away . . . one . . . five . . . ten . . . While tension mounted steadily, seventeen minutes passed before the judges entered.

First on his feet to greet them was Eichmann, standing at rigid attention. He remained impassive as Chief Judge Moshe Landau pronounced the six Hebrew words that sealed his doom—"*Beith din ze dan otcha l'mita*" (The court sentences you to death). He walked from the courtroom without bowing to the judges or uttering a word.

Under Israeli law, Eichmann can appeal to the Supreme Court; if that fails, he can seek clemency from Israel's President Yizhak Ben-Zvi. Both are considered forlorn hopes, although the appeals at least will delay Eichmann's hanging until next spring. Until then, Eichmann, dressed in red prison garb, will be kept in the high-security Ramleh prison near Tel Aviv.

In his last days, Defense Attorney Robert Servatius said, Eichmann wanted to "talk to someone trained in religious questions . . . But then he decided against it, saying: 'They'll try to convert me, and this will lead to differences of opinion, and I am too tired . . .'"

The Daily Graphic
30ᵗʰ July 1910

"CRIPPEN" CHASE ENDING.

CAPTAIN'S STORY OF LIFE ON THE MONTROSE.

INSPECTOR DEW LANDS.

The Transatlantic chase after " Dr." Crippen and Miss Le Neve is almost at an end. Yesterday afternoon the steamer Laurentic, with Inspector Dew on board, reached Father Point, Quebec, and the Montrose, with the man who is believed to be Crippen, and his companion reached Belle Isle. The two vessels were therefore yesterday 600 miles apart, and the Montrose is expected at Father Point to-morrow.

There the fugitives, if identified by the inspector, will be arrested, a proceeding which will come to them as a complete surprise, for they are unaware that suspicion attaches to them on the steamer.

Inspector Dew landed at Father Point last night and went to a boarding-house where the provincial police are staying. He will board the Montrose to-morrow with the police.

The Montrose and the Laurentic have been in wireless communication on several occasions, a fact of which advantage was taken by Inspector Dew to communicate at length with Captain Kendall and complete his arrangements for the arrest of the suspects. The ships did not sight each other, the object of keeping apart being not to arouse Crippen's suspicion.

MESSAGES FROM THE MONTROSE.

An early wireless message yesterday from the Montrose received in New York was, reports Reuter, as follows:—

Suspected persons answering police description Crippen and Le Neve aboard. No arrests made. Other passengers ignorant situation.—(Signed) Marconi Operator.

The operator added that he was forbidden to give further information. The telegram was despatched when the Montrose was 150 miles east of Belle Isle.

Later the following statement was despatched by wireless by Captain Kendall to the " Montreal Star ":—

I am confident that they are Crippen and Le Neve. The man continues to shave his upper lip, and is growing a beard. He has no suspicions, and the passengers also are ignorant of the real situation. Le Neve refrains from talking.

They have no baggage with them. The couple cannot be parted and are very reticent. The man has evidently travelled much. He is generally busy reading books, and appears to be very sleepless.

The first clue was obtained two hours after we left Antwerp. The man says he is taking the boy to California for his health. He spends much of his time in his room. The boy appears bright at times, but shows signs of worry. The man booked as a merchant; the boy as a student.

In another telegram received from the Montrose yesterday aftesrnoon, Captain Kendall reiterates his statement that Crippen is quite unconscious of the fact of his identity being known. " He thinks he is safe," says the captain, "and therefore there is no danger of his attempting anything desperate."

Inspector Dew will await the Montrose at Father Point. He will join Mr. McCarthy, chief of the Quebec police, who is accompanied by Mr. Denis, formerly police chief at Point Levis, and Mr. Charles Gauvreau, representing the Dominion Government. His duty will merely be to identify the suspects, the actual arrests, if found to be justified, being performed by his Canadian confreres.

The prisoners will be taken to Quebec, and, according to a Central News message, will probably return to England on board the Royal George, which sails on Wednesday or Thursday.

The couple will be separated immediately they are taken into custody, and there are expectations that Miss Le Neve will make a confession.

Excitement in Quebec is running high, says Reuter, in anticipation of the arrival of Mr. Dew and his quarry. Detectives and plain clothes police are swarming around all boats arriving. Several mysterious persons supposed to be connections of Dr. Crippen are being watched.

Doubt is expressed whether Dr. Crippen will allow himself to be taken alive.

AT SCOTLAND YARD.

Notwithstanding the news given above, it is possible that Crippen and his companion will not be brought to England for a considerable time. It is stated that when news of the arrest reaches Scotland Yard an officer will be despatched to Canada in connection with the hearing of the case for extradition there. This, it is said, will proceed slowly, and therefore it is considered likely that Inspector Dew will not arrive in England with the prisoners until after August.

Dissent

The figures in this section are widely different and yet have one thing in common: they are all people who have insisted on standing out for their beliefs, and who by doing so, have inspired others. **George Washington**'s insistence, like that of the leader of the Boston Tea Party, Sam Adams, whose death the newspapers did not record, bore rather considerable consequences, as did that of **Jefferson Davis** and – by contrast – **Geronimo** both of them shaping a large part of the attitude of modern America. **Che Guevara**'s vision of a new world, on the other hand, remains just that; but his death in the Bolivian jungle has come to serve as a rallying-point for revolutionaries the world over. **Emiliano Zapata** exemplifies revolutionaries who inspire entire nations. The act of **Jan Palach** in burning himself to death in Wenceslas Square (the first European to follow the Vietnamese Buddhists' example) was a desperate gesture to cement the resolve of a nation. **Woody Guthrie**, **Paul Robeson**, and **Lenny Bruce** all fought to change the morality of society by altogether different means, simply by carrying on their professions – writing and singing songs, the great inspiration of the sixties; insisting on being treated with the respect due to him as a performer; and getting people to laugh about things which prevailing morality thought beyond laughter.

William Cobbett, horrified by the conditions around him in early nineteenth-century Britain saw, reported, and argued – the first investigative reporter, perhaps. **Simon Bolivar** liberated much of Latin America in the early nineteenth century, while **Steve Biko** obstinately refused to leave the conscience of white South Africa and the world alone in the late 1970s. **Charles Bradlaugh** insisted on his atheism at a time when public figures like himself could no more be atheists than they could ten years ago have been homosexuals. **Leon Trotsky**, like **Marat** and **Rosa Luxemburg** before him, was assassinated for insisting on what he saw as the truth, against its corruption by Stalin. Of such stuff, dreams are made.

Washington Post
4th October 1967

Woody Guthrie Dies of Muscular Illness; Wrote Songs, Sang About Poor People

Woody Guthrie, who sang his songs in saloons and bars, picket lines and concert halls, migrant camps and Madison Square Garden, died in Creedmore State Hospital, Queens, N.Y., yesterday.

The 55-year-old folk singer and composer, who has been described as "a national possession, like Yellowstone and Yosemite," had been doomed for 15 years by Huntington's chorea, the disease that killed his mother when he was a boy. It destroys muscle coordination, and Mr. Guthrie had been helpless for years. At the end, only his eyelids moved.

But before all that happened to him, he had been a traveling man, roaming the country for more than 20 years. He wouldn't give up the road. Even when fame and a chance for big money finally came, he avoided comfort like the plague and kept on wandering.

When he became the star of a radio show in the early 1940s, he bought a Chrysler after the first four programs and fled New York. He gave the Chrysler to a Farmers Union organizer in Oklahoma City, and kept on going with his guitar.

From 1932 to 1952, he is believed to have written more than 1000 folk-type songs (he wrote 26 to celebrate the building of the Grand Coulee and Bonneville Dams) and everybody, from Frank Sinatra to the long-haired boys twanging guitars in Dupont Circle, sings them.

Many of the songs are gone, but some are part of every folk singer's repertoire, and concert halls, night clubs, bars and kindergartens are filled with the sound of his music.

The best known, of course, are "Hard Travelin'," "So Long, It's Been Good to know You," and "This Land Is Your Land."

Mr. Guthrie was a poet of the down-trodden, the poor and the lost. He had grown up in hard times and had a hard life. He remembered the Okies vividly, the dust bowl and the refugees from their own homes. He sought out the poor.

Much of his work was filled with anger and outrage at what man had done and kept doing to man, but there was no despair. His lyrics contained wit, humor and tenderness.

"I am out," he said "to sing songs that will prove to you that this is your world and that if it has hit you pretty hard and knocked you for a dozen loops . . . no matter what color, what size you are, how you are built, I am out to sing the songs that make you take pride in yourself and in your work . . . I hate a song that make you think you're not any good. I hate a song that makes you think you are just born to lose. . ."

It was Clifton Fadiman, writing in the New Yorker magazine in the 1940s, who proclaimed Mr. Guthrie "a national possession, like Yellowstone or Yosemite, and part of the best stuff this country has to show the world." In 1966, Secretary of the Interior Stewart L. Udall awarded him the Conservation Service Award and called him a poet of the American landscape. Mr. Guthrie couldn't attend the ceremony. He was bed-ridden, able only to move his eyelids and a hand, feebly. He could hear, but he couldn't talk.

Born in Okemah, Okla., one of five children, he learned blues and folk songs from monica. But, it was a hard childhood. A sister died in a fire, his mother in an insane asylum. His father committed suicide after bankruptcy.

Mr. Guthrie was on the road at 17, singing and playing his guitar and composing songs all over the Southwest and California.

The plight of the Okies, the dispossessed families of the dust bowl and the Depression, he saw them at first hand and the memory stayed with him.

He made art of the experience. As Nat Hentoff wrote in The Reporter magazine several years ago, "Guthrie wrote songs that have outlasted the Okies—'Talkin' Dust Bowl Blues', 'I Ain't Got No Home in This World', and 'Dust Bowl Refugee."

He wrote poems, short stories, articles and letters. His autobiography, "Bound for Glory," was much-praised in the 1940s, and there have been plans to publish much of his other writing.

Short and lean, with a solemn, weather beaten face and wiry, bushy hair. He looked like the man of the people he insisted on being. He never got rich, though he could have.

Mr. Guthrie was married and divorced three times and had seven children, one of whom, a girl, died in a fire. He is survived by three daughters and three sons, one of whom, Arlo, is a folk singer.

New York Times
12th April 1919

CARRANZA TROOPS KILL GEN. ZAPATA

Body of Mexican Rebel Chieftain Is Produced as Evidence by Soldiers.

TRAPPED IN MOUNTAINS

Leader of Indians Thrice Led Followers Into Mexico City— Once Villa Ally.

MEXICO CITY, April 11. (Associated Press.)—General Emiliano Zapata, the rebel leader in Southern Mexico, has been killed by Government troops, according to an announcement made by the Mexican War Department tonight. The announcement confirmed an earlier newspaper report of Zapata's death from Cuatitla, in the State of Morelos.

The announcement says that a part of the 50th Regiment serving under General Pablo Gonzalez of the Carranza army returned to Cuautla, General Gonzalez's headquarters, tonight with the body of the dead rebel chief.

Later the Mexican Government received an official bulletin confirming the press report of Zapata's death.

Advices from Morelos say that the death of Zapata was brought about by strategy. Zapata, with his followers, had been hiding in an inaccessible mountain region since the Government troops had pacified the State of Morelos, which had been the stronghold of Zapata since he began his revolt in 1909.

The rebel chief is said to have been killed in an unnamed part of the mountains of Southern Morelos by troops under command of Colonel Guajardo. The War Department has promoted the Colonel to a Generalship for his feat.

Special Cable to THE NEW YORK TIMES.

MEXICO CITY, April 11.—Zapata rebelled in 1910 under a plan which was guaranteed to give land rights to the

The Times
23rd August 1940

THE BOLSHEVIST REVOLUTION

Leon Trotsky, Lenin's principal associate in the Bolshevist Revolution, and the organizer of the Red Army, died at Mexico City on Wednesday night, telegraphs our New York Correspondent, of the effects of the murderous attack made on him on Tuesday.

Lev Davidovitch Bronstein, later known as Trotsky, was born in a small town in South Russia in 1879 and educated in Odessa. At the age of 19 he was arrested as a member of a Marxist group and sent to Siberia. He escaped in 1902, joined Lenin in London, worked and then broke with him, and in the famous split in the party adhered to the Menshevik wing. He returned to Russia in the 1905 revolution, became President of the first Soviet in St. Petersburg, and was once more imprisoned and exiled to Siberia. Escaping a second time, he led the wandering life of a revolutionary refugee in Austria, Switzerland, and France, editing more than one revolutionary journal and contributing to many others, besides being the author of numerous pamphlets.

When war broke out in 1914 Trotsky, who had by this time broken with the Mensheviks, moved to Paris, and conducted a vigorous anti-war campaign. At the Zimmerwald Conference he once more drew nearer to Lenin, and was expelled from France in 1916. From Spain he went to New York, where he won popularity among the Russian Jews and the International Workers of the World. After the March Revolution in 1917 he started off for Russia, breathing out threats to the American Government. On his way he was arrested by the British authorities at Halifax, Nova Scotia, as a dangerous revolutionary, but was ultimately released at the request of the Russian Provisional Government and allowed to continue his journey. On his return to Russia he was made a member of the Petrograd Soviet. He now joined the Bolshevist Party, took part in the abortive July revolt, and with Lenin was mainly responsible for organizing the successful revolution of November 7.

As Commissar for Foreign Affairs in Lenin's Government it fell to Trotsky to conduct the negotiations with the Germans that culminated in the peace of Brest-Litovsk. He tried to evade the crushing demands of the Germans, but his speeches and his revolutionary proclamations availed nothing against the mailed fist. The Bolshevists had to accept humiliating terms, and Tchitcherin was sent to conclude the negotiations. The war with Germany was over and the civil war began. Trotsky was appointed Commissar for War, and he brought a new Red Army into being. Communist discipline was enforced by propaganda and by that system of universal political espionage and terror on which the Bolshevist Government relied. Since Trotsky's fall, official historians have done everything to belittle his role. But at the time his name was coupled everywhere with that of Lenin. His resource and driving power were made use of to the full by the inner circle of Communists, but, as a late-comer to the party, he was never completely trusted.

In 1923 rumours spread that he was suffering from some illness. The death of Lenin was a fatal blow to his influence. For years a long and obscure struggle had raged between Stalin, who had under his control the machinery of the Communist Party, and Trotsky, who had a much greater personal prestige inside and outside Russia. Step by step Trotsky was ejected from all his posts. In January, 1925, he ceased to be Commissar for War; and Stalin steadily and skilfully contrived to remove all Trotsky's adherents from prominent posts in the Government. In October, 1926, Stalin even ventured to eject Trotsky himself from the Politbureau. In the summer of 1927 the three Soviet diplomats—Krestinsky, Rakovsky, and Kameneff—joined the Opposition, and at the Party Congress in November 1927, Trotsky and his followers were expelled from the party. Trotsky was sent into exile to Central Asia. He was under a strict surveillance by the Ogpu, and any communication with the outer world became very difficult.

But Trotsky could not be silent. A violent attack on Stalin, published in Germany under the title "The True Situation in Russia" and containing letters in which Lenin foresaw the Stalin-Trotsky feud and warned his colleagues against Stalin's autocratic ambition, caused a rift in the party abroad and determined Stalin to expel his rival from Russia. In 1929 Trotsky was sent to Constantinople, where for some years he dwelt on Prinkipo Island. He continued to agitate and intrigue, and vainly asked permission to repair to England. His "History of the Russian Revolution" did not endear him the more to his rival, and he finally left Turkey for France. But Stalin's hostility, his own inability to refrain from political activities, and his dangerous interest in world revolution made no country willing to keep him for long. He was requested to leave France in 1935, after being accused by Moscow of complicity in the Kiroff murder. His old associates were "liquidated," and in the following year the Russian Government asked for his expulsion from Norway, where he had taken refuge. Early in 1937 he found asylum in Mexico. There, after he had been condemned to death in absence by a Soviet Court, he figured in an "unofficial inquiry" into his alleged guilt, conducted by a committee of prominent Americans, and disposed of some of the circumstantial evidence produced at the Moscow trials. He was in constant danger from Russian agents, and last May he narrowly escaped from an armed band who attacked his villa near Mexico City.

Trotsky was emotional and vain, energetic and ruthless, capable of rapid decision in moments of danger, but far inferior to Lenin in judgment and foresight. Of medium height, with a high forehead, from which was brushed back a big mane of black hair, with strongly marked Jewish features and grey eyes that peered sharply through pince-nez, he was not an attractive personality. In his later years he became the natural focus of those Communists who opposed the opportunistic policy of Stalin. But he remained a name rather than the leader of a party and had little gift for inspiring the loyalty and devotion of his disciples. His literary abilities were outstanding; and his autobiography and his "History of the Russian Revolution," both of which have appeared in English translations, are the most readable writings of any of the Russian revolutionaries.

The Gentleman's Magazine
31st July 1793 Vol 63

Indian. He was known as the Attila of the South. With his brother, Eufemio, who was killed last year, he terrorized all the southern States. Morelos, where Zapata was born, once a flourishing agricultural State and noted for its sugar-production, is now in ruins. Where sugar mills which cost millions once gave work to hundreds of Indians only mounds of bricks remain.

Zapata's famous specialty was to raid small towns in States near Morelos and steal young women for his harem. He is known to have had over fifty young women in his harem. In spite of Zapata's program of land for the Indians, they got none. Reports from the State of Morelos say the Indians are starving and practically naked.

Cuernavaca, famous as a health resort and used by Maximilian when he was Emperor as a summer home, is practically destroyed. A large church containing a number of old Spanish masters is in ruins, and the old paintings have been destroyed by the bandits, who used them for clothing.

At the height of his power several years ago General Zapata figured as one of the possible heads of the Mexican Government. At three different times during the last ten years his followers were in control of Mexico City for brief periods.

After the downfall of Porfirio Diaz, Zapata and Francisco Villa, in southern and northern Mexico respectively, have been the sources of unending trouble for the various Governments of Mexico. Zapata, the first to raise the standard of revolt, is the first to fall. Villa, still is active in the north, although not on as extensive a scale as formerly.

For ten years Zapata had ravaged southern Mexico. Starting with a small force in 1909, he was able by 1911 to defeat Government forces sent against him, and during the Huerta régime held sway over several States in addition to Morelos, where he began and ended his career. For a short time in 1914 Zapata and Villa worked together against Huerta, but the southern leader soon disagreed with the northern rebel chief and withdrew again to the mountains south of Mexico City.

Marat, that infamous regicide, who lately fell beneath the affaffin's dagger, and who fo juftly merited the fate he has met with, is thus deferibed. He was a little man, of a cadaverous complexion, and a countenance exceedingly expreffive of the bloody difpofition of his mind. To a painter of maffacre, he would have afforded a fine portrait for the chief murderer. His head would be ineftimable for fuch a fubject. His eyes refembled thofe of the tiger-cat, and there was a kind of ferocioufnefs in his looks that corresponded with the favage fiercenefs of that animal. The only artifice he ufed a favour of thofe lineaments of the breaft was that of wearing a round hat, fo far pulled down before, as to hide a great part of his countenance.

Chicago Tribune
6th December 1889

JEFF DAVIS IS DEAD.

The Leader of the Confederacy Passes Away at New Orleans.

LAST HOURS OF THE VETERAN.

His Physicians Had Been Hopeful of His Ultimate Recovery.

LAST NIGHT HE BECAME DELIRIOUS

Death Soon Came to End His Long and Eventful Career.

BRIEF SKETCH OF MR. DAVIS' LIFE.

NEW ORLEANS, La., Dec. 6.—[Special.]—Jefferson Davis died at 12:45 this morning. Up to yesterday the improvement in his condition had been steady, and his physicians and friends were encouraged to hope that he might soon be removed to his estate at Beauvoir. Late yesterday afternoon, however, Mr. Davis' condition changed suddenly for the worse and a high fever manifested itself. Mr. Davis became delirious, and Drs. Bickham and Chaille were summoned to his bedside, where they remained up to the time of his death.

Jefferson Davis

Shortly before 6 o'clock in the evening Mr. Davis was attacked by a severe congestive chill, followed by high fever. The attack was sudden, and up to that moment Mr. Davis was no worse than he had been at any time during the last week or ten days. In the height of his fever he passed into unconsciousness, and though Mrs. Davis, who watched over him with the greatest solicitude, fancied at times that he responded to her words by a faint pressure of the hand, not a word passed his lips. Justice and Mrs. Fenner, the Payne family, Drs. Chaille and Bickham, and a number of the relations and connections of Mr. and Mrs. Davis were present in the chamber of death when the end came. All arrangements for interment, etc., will be attended to later in the day.

JEFF DAVIS' CAREER.

Jefferson Davis was born June 3 1808, in that part of Christian County, Kentucky, which now forms Todd County. His father was Samuel Davis, and he had served in the Georgia cavalry during the Revolution. When Jefferson was but an infant the family moved to a place near Woodville, Miss., where young Davis began his education, later entering the Transylvania College, Kentucky. In 1824 he was appointed by President Monroe to the United States Military Academy, from which he graduated in 1828, and was assigned to the First Infantry. He served in the Black Hawk war of 1831-'32, and March 4, 1833, was promoted to be First Lieutenant of Dragoons.

June 30, 1835, after more service against the Indians, he resigned, eloped with the daughter of Zachary Taylor, then a Colonel in the army, and settled near Vicksburg, Miss., as a cotton planter. He remained here quietly until 1843, when he entered politics and made a reputation as a popular speaker. In 1845 he was sent to Congress, where he at once took an active part in debate, especially with reference to the preparations for the war with Mexico. In June, 1846, he resigned his seat in the House to accept the Colonelcy of the First Mississippi Volunteers, and at once moved to reinforce Gen. Taylor in the Rio Grande. His record in this war was an excellent one. He charged a fort at Monterey without bayonets and led his command through the streets nearly to the Grand Plaza. In repulsing a charge at Buena Vista he was severely wounded, and was complimented for his bravery.

May 27, 1847, his regiment was ordered home and he was made a Brigadier-General by President Polk, but declined the honor. In August he went to the Senate, where he became a zealous advocate of State rights. In 1851 he resigned his seat to become candidate for Governor of Mississippi, but was defeated at the polls. A year later he supported Franklin Pierce for the Presidency, and as a reward for his labors was made Secretary of War. He increased the standing army, improved the equipment, and made many changes in the tactics.

HE BECOMES A REBEL.

At the close of President Pierce's term he was again sent to the Senate and became the Democratic leader. Many of his speeches during this time contained strong Union sentiments, but Dec. 10, 1860, he made a speech in which he carefully distinguished between "the independence which the States had achieved at great cost" and the Union, which had cost "little time, little money, and no blood," thus taking his old State-rights position. Jan. 10, 1861, he made another speech, asserting the right of secession and urging that the garrison be withdrawn from Fort Sumter.

Jan. 21, being officially informed that Mississippi had seceded Jan. 9, he withdrew from the Senate and went to his home. He was at once appointed Commander-in-Chief of the army of Mississippi, but Feb. 18, 1861, he resigned that office to accept the Presidency of the Confederate States. In his inaugural address he said that "necessity not choice" had led to secession. In his first message, April 29, he condemned as illegal and absurd President Lincoln's proclamation calling for troops and announcing a blockade of the Southern ports. Soon after this the Capital was removed from Montgomery to Richmond, and Mr. Davis removed thither. July 20, after delivering his second message, he went to Manassas and saw the close of the battle of Bull Run and the victory of the Confederate troops. Then followed a season of inactivity for which he was severely blamed; but, nevertheless, Nov. 10,

1861, he was formally elected President for six years and was duly inaugurated Feb. 22, 1862. Before this he had held the office by virtue of appointment by the Provisional Congress.

OPPOSITION TO DAVIS.

The reverses of the year 1862, including the fall of Forts Henry and Donelson and the capture of New Orleans, began to tell, however, in a growing opposition to his Administration. One of the first acts of the Congress had been to pass a sweeping conscription law, to which Mr. Davis assented, and this was stoutly resisted in some quarters. Dec. 23, 1862, he issued a proclamation in retaliation for the emancipation proclamation of President Lincoln. In this he declared that Gen. B. F. Butler was a felon, and ordered that all commissioned officers serving under him, as well as all serving with slaves, should be treated as "robbers and criminals deserving death." In his message of January, 1863, he proposed turning over all Union prisoners to the State courts to be tried as the abettors of a servile insurrection, but the proposition was rejected by the Congress.

The disasters of July—Gettysburg and Vicksburg—and the state of the currency emboldened the opposition to fiercely assail the Administration. Food, too, was scarce, and the army was on half rations, and this added to the clamor. The removal July 17, 1864, of Gen. Joseph E. Johnston from command of the army that opposed Sherman gave additional cause for complaint, it being alleged that he did it from purely personal reasons. When Atlanta was evacuated Sept. 1, 1864, Mr. Davis visited Georgia and tried to raise the spirits of the people there, but without much success.

In January, 1865, he sent three Commissioners to treat with the United States Government, but their mission was unsuccessful. There was a temporary outburst of enthusiasm, but it soon died away; as the Union armies continued to advance, and more and more dissatisfaction was expressed. In his last message to the Congress —March 13, 1865—Mr. Davis asserted that the Confederacy had ample means to meet the emergency, and April 2, less than a month later, he was obliged to evacuate Richmond. April 5 he issued a proclamation from Danville, asserting that the army was now "free to move from point to point, and strike the enemy in detail far from his base," and in less than a week he had to retire from Danville.

HIS CAPTURE.

He was captured near Irwinsville, Ga., May 10, and taken to Fort Monroe. May 8, 1866, he was indicted for treason by a grand jury in the United States District Court for Virginia, sitting at Norfolk under Judge Underwood. May 13, 1867, he was admitted to bail in the sum of $100,000. He was never brought to trial, a nolle prosequi being entered by the Government December, 1868. After being given an enthusiastic reception in the South, his imprisonment having silenced all opponents, he went to Canada and then to England. Returning he became President of a life-insurance company in Memphis. In 1879 Mrs. Dorsey of Beauvoir, Miss., bequeathed him her estate, and there he has since resided, occasionally appearing to make a speech in some Southern city. He was excepted from a bill restoring political rights to those who took part in the Rebellion and excepted from a bill pensioning veterans of the Mexican war, it being charged that he was responsible for the horrors of Andersonville.

New York Times
4th August 1966

Lenny Bruce, Uninhibited Comic, Found Dead in Hollywood Home

His Nightclub Acts Blended Satire With Scatology and Led to Arrests

Special to The New York Times

HOLLYWOOD, Aug. 3 (AP) —Lenny Bruce, the controversial nightclub comedian whose acts were sprinkled with four-letter words and pungent social satire, died tonight in his home on Hollywood Boulevard. He was 40 years old.

The police said narcotics paraphernalia were found near his half-clad body, and the coroner's office listed an overdose of narcotics as probable cause of death. An autopsy will be performed tomorrow.

Mr. Bruce's real name was Leonard Alfred Schneider and he was born in Mineola, L. I. His parents were divorced when he was 5 years old, and he went to live with relatives. He entered the Navy at the age of 16, and was discharged in 1946. He then took on the various jobs that sustained him until he came to Hollywood to study acting under the G.I. Bill.

He landed his first job as a comic in a Brooklyn nightspot. In Baltimore he met and married Honey Harlow, a striptease dancer. They were divorced in 1957.

Meantime, he had appeared on the Arthur Godfrey Show and gained something of a national reputation. He then returned to Hollywood, where he worked at nightclubs and on a local television show.

Last October the United States District Court in San Francisco, in support of a bankruptcy action, declared him a pauper.

'Radically Relevant'

There were those who listened to Lenny Bruce's series of staccato jokes on religion, motherhood, politics and the law, carefully embellished with scatology, who agreed with one estimate that he was "the most radically relevant of all contemporary social satirists."

There were others who said he was "obscene."

Whatever his significance, Lenny Bruce was controversial.

Since he first attracted public attention about six years ago, he had angered and amused people here and abroad with his biting, sardonic, introspective free-form patter that often was a form of shock therapy for his listeners.

He was denounced in Sydney, Australia, for what was called a blasphemous account of the Crucifixion and a steady stream of dirty words, and his show closed the day after it opened.

He was arrested by the police in April, 1964, after an appearance in a Greenwich Village nightclub and later convicted for giving an obscene performance. But nearly 100 persons prominent in the arts and other fields, including Prof. Lionel Trilling of Columbia, Norman Mailer, James Jones, Robert Lowell, and Dr. Reinhold Neibuhr, rallied to his defense and signed a statement that described him as a social satirist "in the tradition of Swift, Rabelais and Twain."

His controversial stage performances at first attracted big audiences, but later his financial rewards dwindled. He once noted that in 1960, before he was ever taken to court, he had earned $108,000, but in 1964 he expected to earn only $6,000.

A lean, intense man, Mr. Bruce regarded the nightclub stage as

"the last frontier" of uninhibited entertainment. Although he seemed to be doing his utmost at times to antagonize his audiences, he also displayed an air of morality beneath his brashness that some felt made his lapses in taste often forgiveable and sometimes necessary.

He became known as one of the early "sick" comedians because he often carried his sharp comments to their naked and personal conclusion. Sanctity was hardly a word he knew. He even had an unkind word for Smoky the Bear.

True, Smoky doesn't set forest fires, Mr. Bruce said, but he eats Boy Scouts for their hats.

He would express relief at what he said was a trend of "people leaving the church and going back to God."

Always on familiar terms with history and psychology, Mr. Bruce would illustrate his concern with integration with the example of the early Romans, who thought there was "something dirty" about the Christians. He had one Roman ask another:

"Would you want your sister to marry one?"

His concern with issues of the day was more than an onstage feeling. He once noted:

"I was just thinking this morning that I'd never slept over at a colored person's house. I've never had dinner in a Negro home. There's a big foreign country in my country that I know very little about. And more than that, when whites talk about riots, we really lose our perspective completely. A man from Mars could see what's really happening—convicts rioting in a corrupt prison."

His humor on the stage rarely evoked a comfortable belly laugh. It required concentration, and then often produced a wry smile and perhaps a fighting gleam in the eye. There were also spells of total confusion as Mr. Bruce rambled in a stream-of-consciousness fashion.

The many adults who found his humor obscene agreed with two Criminal Court judges here who found in 1964 that Mr. Bruce's performances "patently offensive to the average person in the community, as judged by present-day standards."

In addition to his several arrests for narcotics and obscenity, the comedian was deported from Britain three years ago, got back in by way of Ireland and was deported again.

His autobiography was published in 1965. It was titled, "How to Talk Dirty and Influence People."

Washington Post
24ᵗʰ June 1970

Paul Robeson:
Renaissance Man of the Arts

Unusual in this century was a voice like Paul Robeson's. In the ability of his songs to evoke empathy and stir memories, his was in the tradition of Feodor Chaliapin and Enrico Caruso.

His luminous bass-baritone, his role as a leading early developer of black music and his songs of many peoples in many languages, mark him as a significant influence on American culture, and on world culture, too.

But the range of his talent extended beyond his musical voice. In his numerous stage and screen roles, from his portrayal of the haunted Brutus Jones in Eugene O'Neill's "The Emperor Jones," to "Othello" in the longest run of any Shakespeare play in Broadway history, his performances were called by some critics the tours de force of a great actor.

In the years before he developed as an artist, his achievements as an athlete (he had twice been named an end on Walter Camp's All-America football team) and a scholar (he was Rutgers University's class valedictorian, Phi Beta Kappa, and held a law degree from Columbia University), marked him as a man of extraordinary versatility.

But he was more than a concert artist, stage and screen actor, athlete and scholar. He was a passionate humanitarian.

When, in 1957, he began his book, "Here I Stand," with the words, "I am a Negro," and stated six paragraphs later, "I am an American," these seemingly redundant declarations were no mere empty words. For while Robeson's blackness, indeed even his militance long before it was either chic or safe, is unquestioned, that the white establishment cast aspersions on his patriotism is the central fact of the final decade of his career.

An early victim of Sen. Joseph McCarthy's Communist hunting in the early '50s, Robeson's brilliant career was painted over with the dull brush of political innuendo.

But it was a tarnish from which Robeson was never to recover. His punishment was the lifting of his passport for eight years, canceling of numerous concerts, and a cloak of silence over his brilliant career, which only began to be lifted in the 1970s, 10 years after he had retired because he was too sick to resume his career.

Robeson was a man of deep principles who stuck by them even when it became clear that it would result in professional disaster. While contemporary historians and Robeson point out he was not a member of the Communist Party, he refused to disavow his admiration for the Russian people, a stand then criticized by some blacks as well as many whites.

He stood, too, for liberation of colonized Africans, all of which made him, in the eyes of some, doubly dangerous—a dangerous black and a dangerous Red.

Once, because he had commented that in Russia "I felt for the first time like a full human being—no color prejudice like in Mississippi, no color prejudice like in Washington," one of the members of the House Un-American Activities Committee angrily demanded: "Why did you not stay in Russia?"

"Because my father was a slave," Robeson retorted, "and my people died to build this country, and I am going to stay right here and have a part of it, just like you. And no fascist-minded people will drive me from it. Is that clear?"

He said in 1957: ". . . I care . . . less than nothing about what the lords of the land, the big white folks, think of me and my ideas . . . But I do care—and deeply—about the America of the common people . . . the working men and women whose picket lines I've joined, auto workers, seamen, cooks and stewards, furriers, miners, steel workers and the foreign-born, the various nationality groups, the Jewish people with whom I have been close, and the middle-class progressives . . . the people of the arts and sciences, the students—all of that America of which I sang in the 'Ballad for Americans' . . . that do the work."

Robeson was a man ahead of his time, voicing utterances in the '30s and '40s that were controversial for any man.

Robeson's personal odyssey was inseparable from the life and struggles of black Americans and common people around the globe to whom he felt closest.

He was born on April 9, 1898, in Princeton, N.J., which Robeson later called a "humiliating" Southern town transplanted to the North. His father was William Drew Robeson, a minister; his mother, Maria Louisa Bustill Robeson, a schoolteacher.

The elder Robeson escaped from slavery in North Carolina when he was 15, and worked his way through Lincoln University. Robeson worshiped him. "He was the glory of my boyhood years," he said. "How proudly . . . I walked at his side, my hand in his, as he moved among the people." His mother died when he was 5. By then a blind, semi-invalid, she was burned to death when a coal from a stove fell on her long-skirted dress.

After attending elementary and high school in small New Jersey towns, he won, through academic competition, a four-year scholarship to Rutgers and entered in 1915, the school's third black student.

Unlike, say, a Picasso, who could draw from the time he was old enough to grasp a pencil, Robeson's magnificent voice did not dominate his early life. He sang in church, and did occasional concerts while he was at Rutgers. But the glee club did not want him because of the social affairs that followed its concerts.

When he tried to make the football team, he was slugged in the face, smashed in the nose and had his shoulder dislocated. He was 17.

He went on to be selected as first-team All-America end for two years—1917 and 1918. He also was elected to Phi Beta Kappa, was class valedictorian and debating champion. He then entered Columbia University law school.

Driven by high aspirations, he assumed law would help "raise my people, the black people of the world." During his second year, he met and married Eslanda Cardozo Goode, a vivacious young woman who was the first black analytical chemist at Columbia Medical Center. She died in 1965.

He played professional football on weekends to help pay his way through law school and turned to acting for the same reason. Offered a chance to tour England in "Voodoo," in which he had first appeared in an amateur production at the Harlem Y, he accepted.

After graduation he got a job writing briefs for a downtown law office. He was not permitted to appear in court, and when a white secretary refused to take his dictation, the frustration and bitterness came crashing down—he walked out.

He needed money, and prodded by his wife, he turned to drama, which was a growing interest for her and for Harlem in that period of cultural flowering known as the Harlem Renaissance.

His first major role was in Eugene O'Neill's new play, "All God's Chillun Got Wings," to be followed by a revival of "The Emperor Jones," the role first created by the black actor Charles Gilpin.

Robeson's performance in these plays made an instant impact on theatergoers and critics alike.

Reviewing it in the American Mercury, George Jean Nathan said: "Robeson, with relatively little experience and with no training to speak of, is one of the most thoroughly eloquent, impressive and convincing actors that I have looked at and listened to in almost 20 years of professional theatergoing."

He emerged as a leading developer of black music in 1925, when he began his singing career with a concert in New York. It was the first concert ever given that consisted solely of Negro music. Together with Lawrence Brown, his accompanist for many years, who had been working on special arrangements of Negro spirituals, he took the Negro spiritual as an art form to a foremost position on concert stages.

The audience at the Greenwich Village Theater simply sat and clamored for encores, and the critics went wild.

"All of those who listened last night to the first concert in this country made entirely of Negro music," said the New York World critic, "may have been present at a turning point, one of those thin points of time in which a star is born and not yet visible—the first appearance of this folk wealth to be made without deference or apology. Paul Robeson's voice is difficult to describe. It is a voice in which deep bells ring . . ."

For the next 35 years, Robeson's singing was to earn him worldwide fame, and for most of the 1930s and '40s, was one of the world's leading concert singers.

Jerome Kern wrote "Ol' Man River" with Robeson in mind, but because of a delay in the premiere of "Show Boat" he didn't get his chance to appear in it until the London production in 1928. He gave Sunday afternoon concerts at Drury Lane, for which Lawrence Brown came over from Paris.

Robeson starred in films and more than 11 major plays in this country and England. In 1930 he played "Othello" with Peggy Ashcroft, Sybil Thorndike and Maurice Brown.

Announcement of Robeson as Othello prompted joy and outrage. A black in the role would violate every Shakespearean concept, said some; the most natural thing in the world, said others. Stage historians knew an American Negro had played Othello in the past—Ira Aldrich, a native of Maryland, appeared successfully in the role in Europe in the last century. (The theater at Howard University is named in Aldrich's honor.)

The highlight of Robeson's theater career was to come 13 years later when he played "Othello" on Broadway for 296 consecutive performances, setting the all-time record for any Shakespeare play on Broadway.

From 1927 to 1939, Robeson made England his home base, touring most of Europe and crisscrossing the Atlantic to make films and perform concerts.

Robeson made his first trip to Russia in 1934, partly to talk about making a film with the great Sergei Eisenstein. Stopping in Berlin en route, he was nearly mobbed by stormtroopers, an event that left him deeply shaken.

When he left he told Eisenstein: "I hesitated to come . . . I feel like a human being for the first time since I grew up. Here I am not a Negro but a human being . . . Here, for the first time in my life I walk in full human dignity. You cannot imagine what that means to me as a Negro."

As fascism raged in Europe, Robeson felt it his duty to sing, and he sang in Barcelona where he witnessed the ravages of the Spanish Civil War and in besieged Madrid.

He returned to America in 1939, the same year as the beginning of World War II. He said he felt he was evading his full responsibility by living in England. The New Deal made this country seem a more hopeful place than when he left. One of his first acts was to refuse any engagements where blacks were segregated. In the South, this meant he sang only at black colleges and universities but many whites came.

That same year, at the peak of his career, he retired from making films, and denounced Hollywood. "I thought I could so something for the Negro race in films—show the truth about them and about other people, too . . . The industry is not prepared to permit me to portray the life or express the living interests, hopes and aspirations of the struggling people from whom I come . . . You bet they will never let me play a part in a film in which a Negro is on top."

He made the famous recording, "Ballad for Americans," in 1939, which became a rallying cry for Americans to make them proud of their heritage. No run-of-the-mill patriotic song, it sang of the man-in-the-street in terms as starkly truthful as shiningly faithful, and was subsequently performed around the country.

.."Who are you?
.."Well, I'm everybody who's nobody.
.."I'm the nobody who's everybody ....
...... "I'm just an Irish, Negro, Jewish,
..Italian, French, and English,
..Spanish, Russian, Chinese,
..Polish, Scotch, Hungarian,
..Litvak, Swedish, Finnish,
..Canadian, Greek and Turk,
..And Czech and double-check American .....
...... Man in white skin can never be free
..While his black brother is in slavery ....."

He gave concerts from New York to Los Angeles, and was also in demand as a speaker. He collected an array of awards that ranged from the Spingarn Medal of the NAACP to the coveted Diction Award of the American Academy of Arts and Sciences, which had only been given nine times in the 20 years it had existed.

In 1941, he joined in founding the Council on African Affairs.

Robeson's career began to suffer from political innuendo beginning in 1946.

In 1947, a congressman asked a star anti-Communist witness how he identified Communists. His criteria: applauding at a Robeson concert or owning a Robeson record.

In 1948 Robeson was called before the Senate Judiciary Committee and asked whether or not he was a Communist. He refused to answer because the question was "an invasion of my right to secret ballot."

During a 1949 tour at the height of the Cold War he caused an uproar in the United States when he told the World Peace Congress in Paris, "It is unthinkable that American Negroes could go to war on behalf of those who have oppressed them for generations against the Soviet Union, which in one generation has raised our people to full human dignity."

In 1949, Robeson took part in peaceful protests against the conviction of U.S. Communist leaders, and subsequently two of his concerts were thrown into an uproar when they were invaded by anti-Communist elements.

The 1950 Peekskill riots culminated anti-Robeson sentiment. They occurred when the American Legion in that upstate New York town led a demonstration in an effort to prevent one of his concerts and violence ensued. After that, he found closed concert halls and groups afraid to sponsor him.

The State Department took away his passport in 1950 on the grounds that his trips abroad possibly "would not be in the interest of the U.S."

In the meantime a number of books dropped references to Robeson. College Football, published in 1940, listed a 10-man All-America team for 1918, the only 10-man team in All-America history. Paul Robeson, end, was the missing man.

Until the 1970s, most major bookstores or libraries, or books on concert singers published after 1949, failed to include him in the index, or mentioned him only in passing, or only once.

Most newsreel and film footage of the major movies in which he starred vanished. When the American Film Institute wanted to show "The Emperor Jones" in 1973, all existing 35 m.m. prints and negatives appeared to have been destroyed, so the AFI uncovered some 300 bits and pieces of 16 m.m. material and painstakingly made up a complete print of the film for showing at the Kennedy Center.

In his major political statement, "Here I Stand," published in 1957, Robeson commented on the popularly held belief that he was politically naive and courted by the Communists so they could gain through him a foothold among American blacks.

"It has been alleged that I am part of some kind of 'international conspiracy.'

"The truth is I am not and never have been involved in any international conspiracy or any other kind, and do now know anyone who is ...

".. In 1946, at a legislative hearing in California, I testified under oath that I was not a member of the Communist Party, but since that I have refused to give testimony or to sign affidavits as to that fact. There is no mystery involved in this refusal ... I have made it a matter of principle ... (because that) infringes upon the constitutional rights of all Americans ..."

In 1952, he was awarded the Stalin Peace Prize.

It took eight years, a worldwide campaign and a Supreme Court ruling to have his passport restored in 1958.

A "long, standing ovation" in the words of the New York Times greeted Robeson when he gave his first Carnegie Hall recital in 11 years, on May 9, 1958.

Then he went abroad to fulfill concert, television and theater engagements in Europe, New Zealand and Australia. He returned home in 1963, in poor health, and retired.

Intimates dispute the rumors that Robeson was in his last years a bitter, tragic figure who had changed his mind about his controversial political stands. "Nothing," said his son, Paul, "could be further from the truth."

From the statement Robeson issued in 1963, it appears simply that the times have caught up with his ideas.

"The power of Negro action of which I wrote in my book has changed from an idea to reality ... The concept of mass militancy, or mass action, is no longer deemed 'too radical' in Negro life."

On his 75th birthday in 1973, a near-capacity crowd, including a galaxy of stars, flocked to Carnegie Hall for a three-hour celebration, and greetings arrived from heads of state around the world. Robeson's jubilant son said the day tore to shreds "the curtain that has surrounded my father."

It was called a cultural celebration, and the program carried a statement Robeson made in 1937, but which seemed prophetically to foresee the consequences of his passion:

"The artist must elect to fight for freedom or for slavery. I have made my choice. I had no alternative."

The Times
17th January 1790

AMERICA.

The following is the Answer of the President of the United States to the Address of the Senate on the death of General WASHINGTON:—

"GENTLEMEN OF THE SENATE,

"I receive with respectful and affectionate sentiments, in this impressive Address, the obliging expressions of your regret for the loss our country has sustained, in the death of her most esteemed, beloved, and admired Citizen.

"In the multitude of my thoughts and recollections on this melancholy event, you will permit me only to say, that I have seen him in the days of adversity, in some of the scenes of his deepest distress and most trying perplexities: I have also attended him in his highest elevation and most prosperous felicity; with uniform admiration of his wisdom, moderation, and constancy.

"Among all our original associates in that memorable league of the Continent in 1774, which first expressed the sovereign will of a free nation in America, he was the only one remaining in the general Government. Although, with a constitution more enfeebled than his, at an age when he thought it necessary to prepare for retirement, I feel myself alone bereaved of my last brother, yet I derive a strong consolation from the unanimous disposition which appears in all ages and classes, to mingle their sorrows with mine, on this common calamity to the world.

"The life of our Washington cannot suffer by a comparison with other countries, who have been most celebrated and exalted by fame. The attributes and decorations of Royalty, could have only served to eclipse the majesty of those virtues, which made him, from being a modest citizen, a more resplendent luminary. Misfortune, had he lived, could hereafter have sullied his glory only with those superficial minds, who, believing that characters and actions are marked by success alone, rarely deserve to enjoy it. Malice could never have blasted his honour; and envy made him a singular exception to her universal rule. For himself he had lived enough, to life and to glory. For his fellow-citizens, if their prayers could have been answered, he would have been immortal. For me, his departure is at a most unfortunate moment. Trusting, however, in the wise and righteous dominion of Providence over the passions of men, and results of their councils and actions, as well as over their lives, nothing remains for me but humble resignation.

"His example is now compleat, and it will teach wisdom and virtue to magistrates, citizens, and men, not only in the present age, but in future generations, as long as our history shall be read. If a *Trajan* found a *Pliny*, a *Marcus Aurelius* can never want biographers, eulogists, or historians.

"JOHN ADAMS.

The Guardian
14th September 1977

Biko might have led a black South Africa

An intellectual and charismatic leader, Bantu Stephen Biko was the 21st black political detainee to die in detention in South Africa since June 1976. He was, perhaps, the only South African leader who could claim to have the mass support of the young radical urban blacks, a force which is playing an increasingly significant role since the Soweto uprisings last year.

Internationally, Steve Biko has been hailed as one of South Africa's most important and astute politicians. Visiting American congressmen, Western diplomats, academics, and newsmen seldom left South Africa without paying him a call.

Andrew Young, the US Ambassador to the United Nations, yesterday described Biko's death as a major loss to the future of South Africa. " No nation can afford to lose its most dedicated and creative leadership and yet prosper," Mr Young said.

" I know personally how much the United States suffered nationally as a result of the similarly tragic deaths of President John Kennedy, Dr Martin Luther King Jr, and Senator Robert Kennedy. These losses cost us nearly a decade of progress."

Mr Biko began his career as a medical student in the mid-1960s at the University of Durban-Westville, and took part in the activities of the white-led National Union of South African Students. In 1968, he spearheaded and argued the need to create a separate organisation for black students which would help black people to regain their identity and self-respect, as well as provide political direction.

The South African students organisation came into being the following year, with Steve Biko as president. Since then, he had been the moving force behind the creation of numerous other Black Consciousness organisations, including the Black Peoples Convention and community self-help programmes in Kingwilliamstown, in the Eastern Cape, where he lived under banning orders.

Detained and arrested several times, and banned in 1973, Mr Biko proved a painful thorn in the side of the South African Government—one which was difficult to remove because of his immense stature and following.

South Africa's account of Mr Biko's death was quickly derided by those in Britain who knew him. Lady Birley, wife of the former headmaster of Eton who lectured in South Africa for many years, said that the idea that Mr Biko committed suicide was absolute nonsense.

Lord Birley, who is in hospital, believed that Biko was a potential Prime Minister of South Africa. The Rev Paul Oestreicher, chairman of the British Section of Amnesty International, said that people did not die of hunger strikes so quickly. " I would like to see the medical evidence," he said.

Praise for Mr Biko's personality as a leader of Black Consciousness has also come from Christian Concern for Southern Africa, the Black People's Convention, and the Catholic Institute for International Relations.

Mr Donald Woods, the white editor of the Daily Dispatch of East London, a close friend of Mr Biko's, called him " the greatest man I have ever met." Mr Woods once wrote an article in which he speculated Mr Biko might become the first Prime Minister of a future South Africa under a black government.

When news of Mr Biko's death was broadcast by Radio South Africa, about 400 blacks and whites gathered for a spontaneous memorial service at the Dikonia Hall, in Braamfontein, near the centre of Johannesburg.

At the close, the crowd sang the anthem of black nationalism, Nkosi Sikelele Afrika (God Bless Africa), and gave the Black Power clenched fist salute.

The British Labour Party last night expressed " extreme disquiet and shock " at Mr Biko's death.

New York Times
18th February 1909

OLD APACHE CHIEF GERONIMO IS DEAD

Captured by Late Gen. Lawton in 1886 After a Long and Bloody Career.

SINCE PRISONER OF WAR

Old Indian Had Been Repeatedly Captured and as Often Returned to Warpath.

Special to The New York Times.

LAWTON, Okla., Feb. 17.—Geronimo, the Apache Indian chief, died of pneumonia to-day in the hospital at Fort Sill. He was nearly 90 years of age, and had been held at the Fort as a prisoner of war for many years. He will be buried in the Indian Cemetery to-morrow by the missionaries, the old chief having professed religion three years ago.

As the leader of the warring Apaches of the Southwestern territories in pioneer days, Geronimo gained a reputation for cruelty and cunning never surpassed by that of any other American Indian chief. For more than twenty years he and his men were the terror of the country, always leaving a trail of bloodshed and devastation. The old chief was captured many times, but always got away again, until his final capture, in 1886, by a small command of infantry scouts under Capt. H. W. Lawton, who, as Major General, was killed at the head of his command in the Philippines, and Assistant Surgeon Leonard Wood, to-day in command of the Department of the East, with headquarters at Governors Island.

The capture was made in the Summer, after a long and very trying campaign of many months, in which Lawton and Wood gained a reputation which will be long remembered in the annals of the army. Geronimo was at first sent to Fort Pickens, but was later transferred to Fort Sill. Until a few years ago he did not give up the hope of some day returning to the leadership of the tribes of the Southwest, and in the early years of his imprisonment he made several attempts to escape.

Geronimo was a Chiricahua Apache, the son of Chal-o-Row of Mangus-Colorado, the war chief of the Warm Spring Apaches, whose career of murder and devastation through Arizona, New Mexico, and Northern Mexico in his day almost equaled that of his terrible son. According to stories told by the old Indian during his last days, he was crowned war chief of his tribe at the early age of 16. For many years he followed the lead of old Cochise, the hereditary chief of the Apaches, who died in 1875 and was succeeded by Natchez, his son, who, however, was soon displaced by Geronimo with his superior cunning and genius for the Indian method of warfare.

After trailing the band led by Geronimo for more than ten years Gen. Crook would probably have captured him in 1875 had he not been transferred to duty among the Utes just as success seemed to be near at hand. For seven years after this the situation in the Southwest was the worst ever faced by the settlers. Crook was sent back in 1883. A large body of troops was placed at his disposal, and in a month he had succeeded in driving Geronimo back to his reservation, capturing him and his men on the Mexican border.

The Times
19ᵗʰ February 1831

In 1885 Geronimo broke out again, and this time was surrounded by Crook in the Cañon de los Embidos. But the Indians succeded in slipping away, and Crook was removed and Nelson A. Miles placed in command. Miles had already gained a reputation as an Indian fighter, and while he did not exactly cut the field wires behind him to prevent interference from Washington, stories are told of the frequent disregard of troublesome messages.

Lawton and Wood were placed in command of the scouts late in the Summer of 1885. They asked permission to take a picked body of men into the hostile territory and endeavor to run down Geronimo. Gen. Miles finally sent them off with many misgivings. There followed months of privation and hardships which were never forgotten by the men who went with the two young officers. They were gone nearly a year. Gen. Miles often not knowing even where they were or whether or not they had been destroyed by the enemy. On the night of Aug. 20, 1886, the General was sitting at the telegraph instrument in the office at Wilcox, Ariz., waiting for dispatches, when the key suddenly clicked off the news that Geronimo and his men had been surrounded at the junction of the San Bernardino and Baische Rivers, near the Mexican border. Miles hastened there and met the chief on his way north under guard of Lawton. The old warrior was surrounded by about 400 bucks, squaws, papooses, and dogs. They had little else than their blankets and tent poles, and as Gen. Miles afterward stated in his memoirs, "The wily old chief had evidently decided to give up warfare for a time and live on the Government until his tribes gained sufficient strength to return to the warpath."

Gen. Miles writes: "Every one at Washington had now become convinced that there was no good in the old chief, and he was, in fact, one of the lowest and most cruel of the savages of the American continent." The people of the West demanded that he be not allowed to go back to the reservation. He and his bucks were accordingly sent to Fort Pickens and the squaws and papooses to Fort Marion, Florida. It was finally decided to keep Geronimo confined as a prisoner of war. His desire to get back to the West was so pitiful, however, that he was transferred to Fort Sill, where he spent the remainder of his days.

Gen. Wood tells an interesting anecdote of an incident which occurred one afternoon when he was guarding the old chief while Lawton went in search of his command, the location of which he had lost soon after the surrender: "About 2 o'clock in the afternoon the old Indian came to me and asked to see my rifle. It was a Hotchkiss, and he said he had never seen its mechanism. When he asked me for the gun and some ammunition I must confess I felt a little nervous, for I thought it might be a device to get hold of one of our weapons. I made no objection, however, and let him have it, showing him how to use it. He fired at a mark, just missing one of his own men who was passing. This he regarded as a great joke, rolling on the ground and laughing heartily and shouting, 'Good gun.' "

Gen. Miles, in his memoirs, describes his first impression of Geronimo when he was brought into camp by Lawton, thus: "He was one of the brightest, most resolute, determined-looking men that I have ever encountered. He had the clearest, sharpest dark eye I think I have ever seen, unless it was that of Gen. Sherman."

There now seems no doubt of the death of BOLIVAR, the liberator of Colombia. He expired on the 17th of December last, in the neighbourhood of Santa Martha, in the government of Carthagena, after a lingering illness.

Some years ago the death of this eminent individual would have created a sensation both in the old and the new world. Every accident that happened to him would have been reckoned a political event,—the bulletin of his health would have spread through two hemispheres,—and his abandonment of the political stage would have left a grand part of the drama of American independence without an actor. Now his exit will scarcely compose an article in the common obituary of warriors or statesmen; and instead of leaving a continent in tears at his loss, as he might once have done, he was obliged to complain, on his death-bed, of the ingratitude which had " brought " him to his grave."

This change of interest and opinion respecting a distinguished individual has partly, no doubt, arisen from the altered situation, not only of America, but of Europe; and partly from new views of the Liberator's character.

When he first made his appearance on the political stage, the Spanish colony to which he belonged was struggling with the mother country for independence. Being a man of great capacity, and of considerable fortune—having more knowledge than the rest of his brethren brought up in the same colonial bondage, and probably more ambition than knowledge, he soon gained an ascendancy among the revolutionary or independent party. The sympathies of the Old and New World were in favour of his cause; adventurers from Europe flocked to his standard; the political arrangements which he made, being in accordance with the most approved system of modern constitutional freedom, were hailed as evidences of transcendent wisdom; and, without knowing much about American warfare, people imagined that the victories announced over the Spaniards were proofs of great military talents and experience.

The liberation of the extensive provinces composing the republic of Colombia,—the union of these provinces into one state,—the organization of its Government,—and the establishment of its political relations with the rest of the world, were no doubt, in a great measure, the work of BOLIVAR. He had likewise the merit of seeing that his Colombian institutions could not be safe while a Spanish corporal's guard remained west of the Atlantic, and therefore resolved to assist the other provinces of Spanish America to throw off the yoke from which his country had been freed. Hence under his auspices, if not by his personal conduct, the Spaniards were pursued towards the south,—hence his troops, after a tedious but glorious campaign, compelled their enemy to capitulate after a tyranny of 300 years,—hence he became the liberator of Peru, and had a portion of the ancient vice-royalty called Bolivia, after his name. Wherever his arms extended, his command over the minds of the civil classes of the population was more striking than his victories, and free institutions were planted on the footsteps of conquest.

It would probably have been impossible for the most skilful political architect to have constructed a permanent edifice of social order and freedom with such materials as were placed in the hands of BOLIVAR; but whatever could be done he accomplished, and whatever good exists in the present arrangements of Colombia and Peru may be traced to his superior knowledge and capacity. When compared with WASHINGTON, we immediately recognize the great distance between the liberator of South and North America,—a distance, however, not greater perhaps than between the colonists of England and Spain, with whom they had respectively to deal; but let us measure him by the SAN MARTINS, SANTANDERS, and the other chiefs who have obtained supreme power on their way to exile, and we shall be sensible of the vast superiority of BOLIVAR.

It is a misfortune for his fame that he continued so long to retain power as the head of the army or as President of the Republic. Latterly, the disorganization of the provinces—the necessity of frequent changes in the fundamental laws—the separation of the maritime and interior districts from each other—and the frequent intrigues or rebellions against his authority, have conspired to strip him of the administrative reputation which he at first acquired. In this country we can never pardon a Government which contracts debts without paying dividends; and on the Stock Exchange we are afraid that the glory of the Liberator is now at a discount.

Independently of the blame attached to his conduct, in circumstances which he could not control, two charges have been brought against his character, which probably a more intimate acquaintance with it might show to be groundless. He has been accused of attempts to make himself a Sovereign, and of being destitute of personal courage. The former charge, which lost him the admiration of the French liberals before the revolution of July, is supported by no evidence. His ambition was too enlightened to seek for the absurd gratification of being an upstart king, on a continent where kings are not in fashion; and we have seen that he repeatedly declined the presidency for life, when the President's chair might have been converted into a regal throne. On his personal bravery in the field we can say nothing; but if he did not possess a quality which is, of all others, the most vulgar in a soldier, he at least had acquired the art of directing the courage of his troops, and overcoming that of his enemies.

The Times
18th January 1919

LIEBKNECHT SHOT DEAD.

ROSA LUXEMBURG KILLED BY THE MOB.

BERLIN CRIME.

(FROM OUR OWN CORRESPONDENT.)

STOCKHOLM, JAN. 17.

Karl Liebknecht and Rosa Luxemburg, the leaders of the Spartacists, were killed in Berlin on Wednesday night. A Berlin telegram gives the following account of the tragedy :—

Liebknecht was arrested by soldiers yesterday [Wednesday] morning, and taken to the local military headquarters at the Hotel Eden. After the preliminary examination Liebknecht was being conducted in an automobile to Moabit police station when he attempted to escape near the Neuer See as the car was driving through the Tiergarten. The guards summoned him to stop, or otherwise they would fire. As he disobeyed the summons and continued running, the escort fired, and Liebknecht fell dead, shot between the shoulders.

Rosa Luxemburg, who was arrested at the same time as Liebknecht, was also conducted to the Hotel Eden. When led out from the hotel to be taken to Moabit she was recognized by the crowd, which surrounded the vehicle in which she was placed, and dragged her out. Violently handled by the infuriated mob, she was finally shot in the back by someone in the crowd. Led away dying she expired shortly afterwards.

OFFICIAL VERSION.

The following report was transmitted yesterday through the wireless stations of the German Government :—

The already reported arrest of Liebknecht led, on the same evening, to his death by shooting whilst he was trying to escape. The report of the arrest of Rosa Luxemburg has since been confirmed. She also, so far as is known, lost her life.

Karl Liebknecht and Rosa Luxemburg were separated after their arrest in the house of a relative of Liebknecht named Markussohn. Liebknecht was afterwards being transferred to the quarters of the Staff of the Guard Cavalry Defence Division in the Eden Hotel near the Zoological Gardens. The news of their arrest spread very quickly, so that a large crowd assembled before the Eden Hotel, part of it hostile, and this element penetrated into the front room of the hotel.

After the prisoners had been indisputably identified, Liebknecht was taken by a side exit to an automobile which was to take him to the prison for inquiry. In spite of the greatest possible haste of the motor driver, Liebknecht received a heavy blow over the head from someone in the crowd, and he bled profusely.

To shake off the crowds, the motor drove through the Tiergarten instead of going through the busy streets, but it broke down on the way and this necessitated a stop for a long time. As Liebknecht, in spite of the severe handling which he had undergone, felt sufficiently strong, the motor driver urged him to proceed on foot so that they might find another motor-car on the way. They had not gone more than 50 paces when Liebknecht ran away. As, in spite of repeated challenges, he continued to run, several of the men in charge of him fired, and a shot hit him in the back. Liebknecht fell in a heap, apparently dead.

In order to be able to take Rosa Luxemburg away in safety, news was spread from the Eden Hotel to the effect that she had already been taken away, whereupon the crowd commenced to disperse. The motor-car, which apparently had moved away, turned back in order to pick up Rosa Luxemburg. She left the hotel behind the motor driver and surrounded by the men in charge. In a few seconds, however, the hostile crowd had again assembled, and it succeeded in pressing forward near Rosa Luxemburg. She was beaten by the crowd and fell down unconscious in the motor-car, which moved off at the greatest possible speed.

On the bridge the motor driver was loudly called upon to stop. As a result of the present measures for secluding extensive portions of Berlin, numerous bridges are occupied by guard posts who hold up every vehicle and search it for arms. Thinking that it was such a guard post with whom he had to deal, the motor driver stopped. The next moment a crowd of people jumped into the motor-car and brought out of it the body of Rosa Luxemburg. It is feared that Rosa Luxemburg was already killed.

The Government at once ordered a strict inquiry, and has temporarily arrested the two motor-car drivers. Although the body of Rosa Luxemburg had not been recovered up to the afternoon hours, the Press takes the death of the Spartacist leaderess for granted and also treats as certain the death of Liebknecht.—*Wireless Press.*

ROSA LUXEMBURG.

Rosa Luxemburg has for years been recognized as the most extreme of all German Socialists. She was a Jewess of obscure origin, apparently between 50 and 60 years of age. She was an extraordinarily eloquent speaker, and equally fearless in criticism of her " comrades " and in conflicts with the authorities.

In 1906 Rosa Luxemburg, already in alliance with Karl Liebknecht, argued the doctrine of the general strike against Bebel at the Jena Congress of the German Socialist Party ; throughout her career she was always for " direct action " and what she called " seizure of power." Her speech at Jena led to her first imprisonment—a sentence of two months for " incitement to violence." Since then she has often been in prison, and at the outbreak of the war she served a long sentence on conviction of making, early in 1914, defamatory accusations against officers and non-commissioned officers of the German Army, whom she accused of brutality towards subordinates. She was released early in 1916, but was soon put under " preventive arrest " and treated with extreme severity. Since the Revolution Rosa Luxemburg had been more Bolshevist even than the German Spartacists, and at one moment seemed to be quarrelling with Liebknecht because he was not absolutely opposed to any sort of participation in the elections to the National Assembly.

A correspondent, who saw and heard Rosa Luxemburg at former International Socialist Congresses, describes her as a most extraordinary woman. A cripple, waddling in her movements, and standing hardly 5ft. high, she was full of fire, vigour and hatred. She always expounded most extreme views, which gained her on the Continent the name of " Red Rosa." Although she was supposed to have come from a Polish *bourgeois* family, she hated the *bourgeoisie* even more than either Lenin or Trotsky. Although belonging herself to the intellectuals, she frankly despised them. The mob, the proletariat, the lowest of the low, always appeared to her most, and she could sway them with her outpouring of hatred for the *bourgeoisie*. She was an *enfant terrible* at all Socialist congresses. She seemed to delight in creating stormy scenes. With her remarkable flow of words, she could not be silenced. Her shrill voice pierced any uproar. She always dreamed of a social revolution of the most sanguinary kind. Had power in Germany fallen into her hands, she would have surpassed the reign of terror of the Russian Bolshevists.

The Guardian
11th October 1967

Che Guevara, Marxist architect of revolution

By RICHARD BOURNE

The death of Ernesto "Che" Guevara in a small clash in South-east Bolivia is somewhat ironic. A man hailed as the master guerrilla strategist of the Cuban revolution has met his death at the hands of the ill considered troops of a Bolivian dictatorship.

In his 1960 guerrilla manual, Guevara wrote: "Given suitable operating terrain, land hunger, enemy injustices, etc., a hard core of thirty to fifty men is, in my opinion, enough to initiate armed revolutions in any Latin-American country."

Born in 1928 in Rosario, Argentina, Guevara opted early for a life of adventure and took up sport in an effort to overcome his enduring asthma. His father —who told me in July in Buenos Aires that he had no idea of his son's whereabouts—found that they were both independently involved in anti-Perón conspiracies in the early 1950s. By then Guevara had already qualified as a doctor and had travelled through Chile and Peru and had been thrown out of Colombia and Venezuela for his political activism.

Sought refuge

Forced to flee from Argentina by Perón's secret police, Guevara was compromised in a revolt in La Paz, Bolivia, and moved to Guatemala, which was then being governed by the Popular Front President, Arbenz Guzmán. He took refuge in the Argentine Embassy when the CIA-sponsored coup by Castillo Armas overthrew Arbenz and the experience undoubtedly ripened his anti-Americanism. In Mexico City he was introduced to Fidel Castro through Castro's brother, Raúl.

On December 2, 1956, Guevara landed with Castro's expedition on the shores of Batista's Cuba and the happiest period of his life commenced. Starting simply as the party's doctor, he gradually became its ideologist, tactician, and Castro's indispensable lieutenant.

He was the strategist of the battle of Santa Clara, which precipitated Batista's flight, and was put in charge of the fortress of Havana after its capture. Later he was named Chief of Education in the Revolutionary Army and in November, 1959, he became President of the National Bank and subsequently Minister of Industry.

Among his books are "Guerrilla Warfare" (1960), accepted as a classic, and "Passages of Revolutionary War" (1963), which contains his personal impressions of the Sierra Maestra. In his writing he concentrated on the moral requirements of a revolutionary and .loped that Cuba would see the dawn of a "new man" such as was dreamt of in 1917.

Rumours of disagreements with Castro grew. After months of mystery Castro announced that Guevara, who was known to have a garibaldian yearning to liberate the entire Latin American land mass, had resigned Cuban citizenship and left for "a new field of battle in the struggle against imperialism."

Like an elusive Pimpernel Guevara was thereafter reported anywhere from the Congo to Santo Domingo via Vietnam.

His presence with the Bolivian guerrillas was affirmed by Régis Debray and first denied then affirmed by the Bolivian Government. He had written his own epitaph: "Wherever death may surprise us, let it be welcome, provided that this our battle cry may have reached some receptive ear and another hand may be extended to wield our weapons . . ."

The Times
20th June 1835

THE LATE WILLIAM COBBETT. — Clifford's-inn, Friday Morning, June 19.—It is my mournful duty to state, that the forebodings above are realized, and that the hand which has guided this work for 33 years has ceased to move! The readers of the *Register* will, of course, look to this number for some particulars of the close of my poor father's life; but they will, I am sure, be forgiving if they find them shortly stated. A great inclination to inflammation of the throat had caused him annoyance from time to time, for several years, and, as he got older, it enfeebled him more. He was suffering from one of these attacks during the late spring, and it will be recollected, that when the Marquis of Chandos brought on his motion for the repeal of the malt-tax, my father attempted to speak, but could not make his voice audible beyond the few members who sat round him. He remained to vote on that motion, and increased his ailment; but on the voting of supplies on the nights of Friday, the 15th, and Monday, the 18th of May, he exerted himself so much, and sat so late, that he laid himself up. He determined, nevertheless, to attend the House again on the evening of the Marquis of Chandos's motion on agricultural distress, on the 25th of May, and the exertion of speaking and remaining late to vote on that occasion were too much for one already severely unwell. He went down to his farm early on the morning after this last debate, and had resolved to rest himself thoroughly, and get rid of his hoarseness and inflammation. On Thursday night last he felt unusually well, and imprudently drank tea in the open air; but he went to bed apparently in better health. In the early part of the night he was taken violently ill, and on Friday and Saturday was considered in a dangerous state by the medical attendant. On Sunday he revived again, and on Monday gave us hope that he would yet be well. He talked feebly, but in the most collected and sprightly manner, upon politics and farming; wished for "four days' rain," for the Cobbet-corn and root crops; and on Wednesday he could remain no longer shut up from the fields, but desired to be carried round the farm; which being done, he criticized the work that had been going on in his absence, and detected some little deviation from his orders, with all the quickness that was so remarkable in him. On Wednesday night he grew more and more feeble, and was evidently sinking; but he continued to answer with perfect clearness every question that was put to him. In the last half-hour his eyes became dim; and at 10 minutes after 1 p.m., he leaned back, closed them as if to sleep, and died without a gasp. He was 73 years old; but, as he never appeared to us to be certain of his own age, we had some time ago procured an extract from the register of Farnham parish, in which it appears that the four sons of my grandfather, George, Thomas, William, and Anthony, were christened on the 1st of April, 1763, and, as Anthony was the younger son, and William was the third, we infer that he was born one year before he was christened, that is, on the 9th of March, 1762. He might, therefore, have been older, but not much.—JOHN M. COBBETT.

The hay harvest has already commenced in the neighbourhood of Lincoln; the crops in general are heavy.—*Boston Herald*.

Continued

Of WILLIAM COBBETT, whose almost sudden decease we announced in *The Times* of yesterday, no fact can be told that has not long been known. His origin and progress in the world—his habits and character, public as well as private—his errors, contradictions, prejudices, hatreds, unblushing effrontery, shameless disregard of truth for its own sake, and matchless power of illustrating or confounding it, as might suit the temper of the moment—all these have for a quarter of a century been so familiar to the minds of men, that long before his death they had ceased to inspire any lively interest, or to draw any active attention.

Against COBBETT's moral character in domestic life, as we have no exact knowledge, we do not feel ourselves justified in saying anything. Of his management on points of honour and fair dealing between man and man, it has been reported that others besides Sir FRANCIS BURDETT were qualified to speak with more certainty than we can pretend to.

But take this self-taught peasant for all in all, he was perhaps in some respects a more extraordinary Englishman than any other of his time. "*Nitor in* "*adversum*" was a motto to which none could lay equal claim with WILLIAM COBBETT. Birth, station, employment, ignorance, temper, character, in early life were all against him. But he emerged from, and overcame them all. By masculine force of genius, and the lever of a proud, confident, and determined *will*, he pushed aside a mass of obstacles of which the least and slightest would have repelled the boldest or most ambitious of ordinary men. He ended by bursting that formidable barrier which separates the class of English gentlemen from all beneath them, and died a member of Parliament, representing a large constituency which had chosen him twice.

COBBETT was by far the most voluminous writer that has lived for centuries. He has worked with incessant industry for more than 40 years, without, we verily believe, the interruption of so much as a single week from languor of spirit, or even from physical weakness.

The first general characteristic of his style is, perspicuity unequalled and inimitable. A second is homely, muscular vigour. A third is purity, always simple, and raciness often elegant. His argument is an example of acute, yet apparently natural, nay involuntary, logic, smoothed in its progress and cemented in its parts by a mingled stream of torturing sarcasm, contemptuous jocularity, and fierce and slaughtering invective. His faults are coarseness, brutality, and tedious repetition. We must add, that the matter of this most forcible of writers rarely shows much inventive faculty; though his active and observing mind supplied abundance of illustration to his argument; and, when he happens to present an original view of any subject, it is almost invariably more eccentric and ingenious than just.

But as a political reasoner, considered with reference to a series of publications throughout successive years, if we admit COBBETT to be the most copious and diligent of writers, it is only to pronounce him by far the most inconstant and faithless that ever appeared before his countrymen. He never was, in the proper sense, a party man; that we acknowledge. His fluctuating praise, therefore, or blame of individuals, being incidental to his support or condemnation of certain doctrines, is not a ground whereon it would be reasonable to reproach him. But for the doctrines themselves, for the principles, the opinions, the measures, which from year to year he alternately wrote up, and reprobated—we speak not of the men,—in this point of view it is, that COBBETT's pretensions to common consistency, or common honesty, or common decency, seem altogether not so much untenable as laughable. The man wrote as if he was wholly unconscious of having ever written anything before. He not only repeated himself, which was his custom, but repeated, with grave contempt for mankind, his contradictions of himself as earnestly and vehemently as he had at first repeated the opinions which he was now busy in abandoning. This, with his strange and solitary perverseness on particular questions, affixed a levity to his name and character which long ago destroyed all the influence his unquestioned abilities must otherwise have infallibly procured him, and the same spirit betraying itself after he got into Parliament prevented his acquiring any weight or credit there at all proportionate to the strength and vivacity of his intellect, if he had not so mischievously abused it.

But we take leave of COBBETT. For years this journal was the favourite weekly victim of an animosity which we suspect to have been on his part more affected than real. We never deliberately injured him, as he must have known, and in his grave we should be sorry to offer him any injustice. He was a man whom England alone could have produced and nurtured up to such maturity of unpatronized and self-generated power. Nevertheless, though a vigilant observer of the age, and a strenuous actor in it, he lay upon the earth as a loose and isolated substance. He was incorporated with no portion of our political or social frame. He belonged neither to principles, to parties, nor to classes. He and his writings formed a remarkable phenomenon. He was an

MR. BRADLAUGH.

Yesterday died Charles Bradlaugh, the junior member for Northampton. In his robust frame had been sown long ago the seeds of disease. In the Session of 1889 it had become painfully apparent that he had lost his old vigour and elasticity. A visit to India appeared for a time to restore him to health ; but the recovery was only partial. His friends have for a long time been aware that his public work was over. He became seriously ill a week or two ago, and had not been in full possession of his senses since Friday evening last week. On Thursday there was thought to be a possibility of his recovery, owing to the continuance of a slight improvement which had appeared in his condition on the previous evening ; but he became worse later on, and passed away peacefully and quietly at half-past 6 o'clock yesterday morning.

Charles Bradlaugh was born September 26, 1833, at Hoxton. His father was a lawyer's clerk, and, according to the testimony of his son William Bradlaugh, "one of the kindest, noblest, and best men that ever lived." His son Charles was, for a time, employed in the same office as his father. He subsequently acted as a wharf clerk, and in the course of his many employments he was successively a coal merchant and a traveller for a manufacturer of buckskin laces. He was precociously intelligent, and at a very early age he was an active Sunday-school teacher under the Rev. Mr. Packer, of St. Peter's, Hackney-road. He fell under the influence of the friends and disciples of Richard Carlile, the once famous editor of the *Republican and Prompter,* and the hero of half a dozen prosecutions for blasphemy and sedition ; and by 19 Bradlaugh had become known on Hackney-downs and in Victoria Park as a fluent advocate of freethought. He did not prosper in business, and he gladly availed himself for some months of the hospitality of Mrs. Carlile, the widow of Richard Carlile. In his distress he decided to enlist as a soldier, and the 7th Dragoon Guards welcomed the tall, stalwart recruit. About this part of Mr. Bradlaugh's life, and, in fact, about many passages in his early years, there is obscurity —his own accounts of them are not always quite consistent. There are traditions that while with his regiment in Kildare and Dublin he read much, that once at least he distinguished himself as a pugilist, that he was an earnest advocate of teetotalism, and a champion of popular rights. What is certain is that he became orderly clerk, that he disliked soldiering, and that he managed to purchase in 1853 his discharge, taking with him a good character from his colonel. He returned to London, and again got, apparently with some difficulty, employment as a lawyer's clerk. The first of the Common Law Procedure Acts was then coming into operation ; in the applications made at Chambers there was an opportunity for adroitness and astuteness; and Bradlaugh was quick to profit by the chance. At all events, he picked up that knowledge of legal forms and processes of which he made effective use in later years. While in the office of Mr. Rogers, of Fenchurch-street, and other solicitors, he lectured on religious subjects. In a few years he ceased to be a lawyer's clerk, and as "Iconoclast," the representative of pugnacious, aggressive atheism, he began that career of pamphleteering and lecturing which made his name repulsive to the majority of his countrymen. From town to town he travelled preaching freethought, and was the chief figure in little-edifying platform encounters, in which well-meaning, ill-advised advocates of orthodoxy were persuaded to take part. He aspired to the place which Paine, Richard Carlile, Robert Taylor, and Charles Southwell had successively occupied; and he succeeded. He possessed considerable powers of speech, and the courage needed to face an angry mob or a hostile audience. The hard, reckless way in which he touched sacred themes, his arrogance and ever present egotism, made him offensive even to many who thought as he did. But he won platform victories ; and he elicited a certain admiration by his ingenuity in his far from few legal difficulties—for example, when he foiled the Devonport authorities by lecturing from a boat moored in deep water only a few yards from a large audience ranged along the shore. In the Hall of Science and the pages of the *National Reformer* he advocated Republicanism and Secularism, and

inflamed the not inconsiderable number of his followers with hopes of what he would accomplish when he entered the House. Several times he tried, without success, to get a seat. At last, in April, 1880, he was returned for Northampton.

Then began a long course of litigation, which had the effect of making Mr. Bradlaugh known to those who had scarcely heard of "Iconoclast." He had always been prone to show his legal acumen. He sued in 1861 the superintendent of police at Devonport for interfering with his lectures, but recovered only a farthing damages, and for the first time figured in the law reports—wherein his name was afterwards so prominent—by moving unsuccessfully in the Court of Common Pleas for a new trial. He was more successful in defying the Inland Revenue in an attempt to enforce an obsolete Act against the *National Reformer*. In 1877 he and Mrs. Besant were indicted for publishing an obscene book, "The Fruits of Philosophy," and they were sentenced to six months' imprisonment and a fine of £200. The conviction, however, was ultimately quashed on technical grounds ; the pleader had omitted to set out in the indictment the entire book, or so much of it as was complained of. While in Parliament Mr. Bradlaugh spent most of his time for several Sessions in trying to remove the barrier opposed to his taking his seat by the form of the oath of allegiance. When elected he claimed to be entitled to affirm under the Parliamentary Oaths Act, 1866, and the Evidence Acts, 1869 and 1870. A Select Committee, by a majority of one, reported against his claim. Then, to the amazement of his friends, he claimed on May 21 the right to take the oath. A Select Committee decided against his competence, and the House proceeded to pass a resolution denying his right either to take the oath or to affirm. Refusing to recognize the authority of the House, he was removed by the Serjeant-at-Arms. An action for enormous penalties, for having sat and voted without having first taken the oath, was begun. It is unnecessary to recall all the subsequent intricate steps of the struggle waged from 1880 to 1885, the athletic performances in the House of Commons whereby he sought to secure his seat, or the memorable 21st of February, 1882, whereon, before an amazed House, he stepped to the table, drew a Testament from his pocket, and administered the oath to himself. Successively excluded by the House and invariably re-elected by his constituents, he was allowed in 1886 to take the oath, and two Sessions afterwards the principles for which he had contended triumphed by the passing of the Oaths Act. In that interval Mr. Bradlaugh was rarely out of litigation, which he conducted with rare skill, but with a clever layman's weakness for dwelling *inter apices juris* and for pushing technicalities to extremes. In "The Queen v. Bradlaugh," "Clarke v. Bradlaugh," "Bradlaugh v. Erskine," and "Bradlaugh v. Gosset" he showed remarkable acuteness. The decision of the House of Lords in "Clarke v. Bradlaugh" was that the writs against him were so much waste paper. A scarcely less important victory was that which he achieved in the action which he brought with success against Mr. Newdegate for maintenance.

Since he was permitted to take his seat Mr. Bradlaugh has been less heard of. But the part of his life to be regarded with most satisfaction was the last. The junior member for Northampton had little resemblance to "Iconoclast," the lecturer of the Hall of Science, or the Republican editor of the *National Reformer*. Of late, and especially since his visit to India, he sought to become the champion of Hindoo claims for representation ; and if his advocacy of this cause showed no great knowledge, it was conducted with no needless acrimony. To one of his last speeches of importance in the House of Commons, on the report of the Select Committee on Perpetual Pensions—his favourite theme of denunciation—no exception could be reasonably taken. He grew in moderation and decorousness. He kept his irreligious opinions in the background. He learned perhaps to understand much of what he had scoffed at ; and more than once he set an example to those who ought to have known better. With Socialism he had no sympathy, and he declined to purchase support by flattering it. He showed by his conduct in regard to the Employers' Liability Bill, and, more recently, in regard to the Eight Hours Movement, that he dared risk his popularity. His Parliamentary achievements, in a time unfavourable to the efforts of private members, were considerable, and they were due to the qualities wherein his strength lay—a dogged perseverance and an eminently practical bent of mind—together with the respect which he succeeded in extorting from all parties in the House and which grew rapidly in the last few years. This feeling culminated in the unopposed motion carried on Tuesday last, whereby the House decided to expunge the resolution of June 22, 1880, which refused him permission to take the oath or to affirm. It was a pathetic circumstance that when the news of this arrived Mr. Bradlaugh had already passed into unconsciousness. Mr. Bradlaugh was not even a Wilkes, far less a Danton, as his flatterers told him. Nor was he the mediocrity which his many enemies among working men described him. He was a remarkable figure of a somewhat obsolete type.

The Times
28th January 1969

Jan Palach

BY his terrible act of self-martyrdom, 21-year-old Jan Palach has focused the eyes of the world on the agony of his country.

A poster in Prague's Wenceslas Square, where Palach set himself on fire, asks: "What are we to say about a time in which the light of the future must be brought by burning sacrifice?"

One day the Russians may also ask themselves that.

Jan Palach died in the name of freedom, the freedom that the Russians have taken away.

For those who live, the awful dilemma of the Czechoslovak people remains:

To compromise, to try to gain time, and hope for a lesser servitude; or to resist more vigorously and risk an explosion which could bring the full, brutal weight of Soviet reprisals.

PATIENCE

Mr. Dubcek and the other leaders have chosen compromise. They believe that by patience they may save a little and perhaps in time win back more.

What choice had they? Could they in conscience have led their people into hopeless bloodshed? Nobody could have brought them help.

Yet, inevitably, as compromise seems more and more like surrender, the mood of desperation will grow.

"Better," says another Prague poster, "to die standing up than to live on your knees."

For an individual to choose death can be the course of courage. It can give inspiration to others.

But nations do not die. They must endure whatever their suffering. A desperate revolt now could only increase that suffering and result in even less liberty.

Wreaths and candles are placed at the foot of the St. Wenceslas monument in Prague during a mass march yesterday in memory of Jan Palach, the student who set himself on fire and died.

Education & Child Welfare

Included here are a number of people all of who, in their different ways, have helped to create the modern phenomenon, hardly known before the industrial revolution, of childhood. **Thomas Arnold**, headmaster of Rugby, was the effective founder of the Public School, an institution which by means of the indelible stamp put on all those who pass through it, determined, and some would say still determines, the nature of British public life. By contrast, **Maria Montessori** represents child-centred education in practice, although her nineteenth-century predecessor in nursery education, Froebel, went unrecognized by the British press; and **John Dewey**, the American pragmatist philosopher, its theory. The nerve of the teacher is symbolized by Mr. **Scopes**, who managed to have himself prosecuted a mere fifty years ago for daring to teach the Darwinian view of evolution. The privilege – or if you agree with Ivan Illich, the terrible curse – of compulsory education is here given its due in the shape of **W. E. Forster**, the initiator of the 1870 Education Act. Contemporary concern with inner-city problems, from Brooklyn to Deptford, is represented by **Margaret Macmillan**, who with her sister, Rachel, was among the first to establish a nursery school in the rough end of town. **Thomas Barnardo** is here, and so is **Pestalozzi**. **Helen Keller** taught the world by example that scarcely any disability cannot be overcome.

On a different note, and to provide a counterweight to the seriousness of the educators, we may read about **Hans Christian Andersen**, unfailingly delightful, and the **Grimm** brothers. Englishness must of course be here: and, (with apologies to Winnie-the-Pooh fans), it is so in the person of **Charles Dodgson**, the Oxford mathematician, better known as **Lewis Carroll**. Finally, and perhaps a little whimsically, the death is recorded of Lord **Baden-Powell**.

The Times
21st September 1905

DEATH OF DR. BARNARDO.

We regret to announce the death of Mr. Thomas John Barnardo, F.R.C.S.Edin., the founder and director of " The National Incorporated Association for the Reclamation of Destitute Waif Children," more familiarly known as Dr. Barnardo's Homes. His death took place at his home, St. Leonards-lodge, Surbiton, at 6 o'clock on Tuesday evening, of *angina pectoris*. Dr. Barnardo had been in a precarious state of health for some time, and while at Nauheim, where he had gone for his health, he had two severe attacks of *angina*, and at his earnest request was brought home. As soon as his condition would permit, this was done by easy stages, and he arrived last Thursday evening. After his return he had several more severe attacks, during which his sufferings were very intense. He so far rallied from these attacks as to give great hopes ; but, when apparently his condition was improving, he suddenly passed away.

The Daily Telegraph & Morning Post
7th May 1952

FOUNDER OF NEW TEACHING THEORY

Dr. Maria Montessori, whose kindergarten system of education, founded in Italy in 1908, subsequently gained favour in many parts of the world, has died, aged 81.

The first woman to secure a medical degree from the University of Rome, she was concerned at the beginning of her career with the care of mentally defective children. Her experiences at this work convinced her that the normal child would develop more quickly if allowed a great deal of freedom in the classroom.

She was repelled by the sight of children kept immobile behind their desks " like butterflies transfixed with a pin." This, she declared, " annihilated " the children instead of disciplining them. She introduced small, comfortable desks and chairs, and low windows from which the children could see the world outside.

Her small pupils enjoyed a liberty of choice in the subjects they were to study which shocked contemporary educationists. Children, she argued, learn first with their hands. She gave them knots to untie and stoppers to fit into bottlenecks; they learned the alphabet by feeling cardboard letters as much as by seeing them, and when they tired of a subject it was dropped.

INNOVATIONS DISPUTED

Some of her innovations are still the subject of dispute. Attention was quickly drawn to the perils inherent in their application to all children without regard to important factors. Punishments and rewards were alike banished, and fairy-stories had no part in the curriculum; these were replaced by true stories of mankind and of the animal world.

Children, she decided, could assimilate knowledge much more quickly than had generally been supposed, provided that the dividing line between work and play was eliminated. Consequently she taught arithmetic at three-and-a-half, and algebra at five. Extension of some of these principles by inexperienced and over-enthusiastic disciples has, in the opinion of some authorities, done more harm than good.

Dr. Montessori's theories, however, gained ground in the face of objections. " Children's Houses " were opened all over the Continent, and spread to England and America. There are now 300 in Britain alone, and countless other schools have adopted her principles in part.

MATHEMATICAL PRODIGY

Born near Ancona on Aug. 30, 1870, Maria Montessori was a " progressive " from early youth. She shocked contemporaries in Rome by dispensing with a chaperone, and was something of a mathematical prodigy. She was diverted from her original intention of becoming an engineer by the sight of a maimed and bleeding beggar in the street.

Mussolini was not slow to realise the value of the Montessori schools with a view to the training of future Fascists, but Dr. Montessori was hardly less quick in realising the dangers of his sponsorship. She left Italy in 1932, and four years later her schools there were banned. In India when war broke out, she was interned as an enemy alien, but allowed to continue her activities.

Dr. Montessori was the author of several books which described her methods. She was unmarried.

Dr. Barnardo was the ninth son of the late Mr. John M. Barnardo, a gentleman of Spanish origin, but born in Germany ; and it is remarkable that his famous son, who was born and brought up in Ireland, should have come to be so intrepid a benefactor of poor English children. It is perhaps still more remarkable that one who was by race a Spaniard and by birth-place an Irishman should have been withal a keen Protestant ; but young Barnardo grew up among Protestants, and in early life came to have strong religious convictions. He was born in 1845, and was educated privately, and entered as a student at the London Hospital, proceeding in due course to Edinburgh and Paris. His idea was to qualify for medical mission work in China ; but as a medical student he found philanthropic interests in the East-end, some work that he undertook during a cholera epidemic opening his eyes to the needs of the neighbourhood. He procured a room in which he began to teach the rough, ragged boys of the district. Dr. Barnardo owed much of his success to his powers of vivid description ; and in his book, " My First Arab ; or, How I began my Life-work," he told the story of the way in which he realized how many London children were absolutely homeless and always " slept out." What he now began to do came to the ears of Lord Shaftesbury and others, who went down East under his guidance to satisfy themselves about the facts. The result was that instead of going to China, Barnardo was urged to give himself to this work, and the " Homes " were started in a small way in 1866. It need not be added that the headquarters of the undertaking have in process of time developed into the small town whose address is Stepney-causeway. It would take too long to describe all the various uses to which the buildings are put ; and, indeed, the plentiful supply of literature which he put out in explanation of the work makes it unnecessary. His principle was never to refuse any deserving case, and when this was once accepted he was committed to making suitable provision for the immense variety of cases that he was liable to receive. So he had a home for destitute boys, all-night refuges for homeless boys and girls, an infirmary, a crèche, a labour house for destitute youths, an industrial home for girls, a home for deaf and dumb girls, a shoe-black brigade home, and children's free lodging-houses. Nor did London content him. He had institutions of various sorts—to name a few—at Stockton-on-Tees, Birkdale, Middlesbrough, Bradford, Exeter, Brighton, and Jersey. It is some time since he could say that 55,000 children had passed in and out of his Homes, of whom the great majority had done well in after life.

For it is in this respect that the credit of his work stands or falls. He professed always to legislate for the future. For many years he had organized the emigration of his young hopefuls to Canada, where he had emigration depôts in Ontario for girls, and in Toronto and in Winnipeg for boys, while he took a farm of some thousands of acres in Manitoba, where he set the elder boys to work. He went on the principle that Canada was large enough to receive all that he could send, and that it was at once good for Canada and good for the children that they should go. His output in this particular was from 1,000 to 1,500 yearly ; and he believed and stated that only two per cent. failed to give satisfactory proof of the care that had been bestowed upon them. At home, two characteristic developments of his energy deserve notice. One is the Girls' Village Homes at Barkingside, near Ilford, the first cottage being built at the expense of one who was a stranger to Dr. Barnardo and had merely seen an appeal of his for help. The one cottage has multiplied into nearly 60. The village has a church, a day school, a school of cookery, and a residence for his workers, the gift of some admirer of his activity. The village has frequently been visited by Poor Law officials and by foreign philanthropists, and the girls are trained for domestic service and other occupations. In 1901 he was enabled, by the generosity of Mr. E. H. Watts and his family, to take over the premises of the Norfolk County School at North Elmham near Norwich, as a training school for the Navy and the mercantile marine, to which likely lads are drafted from his other homes.

It need not be said that Dr. Barnardo's religious convictions continued to play a large part in the daily life of his various institutions. He remained throughout of the type that for want of a better word is called undenominational. But the growing importance of the Church of England Waifs and Strays Society showed him that nothing was to be gained by displaying any hostility to the Church of England. He continued to maintain at the " Edinburgh Castle," Limehouse, where there is a hall holding 3,000 people, his mission work among adults, without connecting that work with any definite system of religious teaching ; but at the Ilford Girls' Homes the congregation was ministered to by a Church of England chaplain, who was in some way recognized by the Bishop of the diocese. Even here the Doctor held himself free to invite Nonconformists or laymen to occupy the pulpit, so that the dread of some of his Nonconformist supporters that Dr. Barnardo was going over with all his great following to the Church of England had no foundation in fact. He was most in his element at the great gatherings at the Albert Hall, when the various objects of his care, especially the most pitiable, were brought out on exhibition with the benevolent Doctor as showman. Considering that he had long suffered from a serious affection of the heart requiring occasional treatment at Nauheim, his activity and his excitable energy were really marvellous ; and it will indeed be difficult for his successor, if he is to have one, to maintain the multifarious work of the incorporated homes now that their founder has gone.

With all his ill-health, he died as he would have wished—in harness. Only in July we published an appeal, to which a large number of influential names were attached, with a view to a national contribution to the Homes in celebration of the Doctor's 60th birthday. The fact that the signatories included the Bishop of London and Sir John Kennaway, Mr. Samuel Smith and the Bishop of Stepney, Lord Roberts and Mr. Stead, is a sufficient indication of the various minds and interests to which the work appealed, while at the subsequent meeting at the Mansion-house Dr. Barnardo was able to read out a message from Queen Alexandra wishing him God-speed in his work. At that meeting mention was made of proposals to get grants for the Homes from the great City Guilds and even from the County Council, so that the " Founder " leaves his beloved work at a critical stage, when it can perhaps hardly continue as a merely philanthropic venture, but must be acknowledged as the national concern that it really is.

Dr. Barnardo married in 1873 the only daughter of Mr. William Elmslie, of " Lloyds " and Richmond.

The Times
16th June 1842

THE LATE DR. ARNOLD.

We do not like to pass without marked notice the sad and most unexpected death of Dr. Arnold, of Rugby—a loss which will be felt with no ordinary acuteness by that large circle of pupils and friends whom he possessed certainly no ordinary powers of attaching to himself. We need hardly say, that with many of his opinions, political and theological, we can have little sympathy ; yet we should, indeed, be sorry if such differences blinded us to the talent and industry—the earnest and active uprightness with which he devoted himself, and that as a religious duty, to his calling as a writer and a teacher—and to that genuine zeal in matters of right and wrong, of truth and falsehood, which, if it may have tempted him at times to an over-warmth of feeling and expression, we can yet honour as noble in itself and most honourably opposed to the indifferentism not only of the day, but of many of those with whom his abstract political opinions would more particularly and naturally have connected him. Both in the valuable historical works which bear Dr. Arnold's name, and in the influence he has exerted over the moral characters of those intrusted to his immediate care—an influence traceable, we believe, less to his unquestionable talent than to its union with single-minded and unselfish integrity—he has left behind that kind of memorial which is most befitting him, and which, perhaps, he would most have wished.

New York Times
23rd October 1970

Scopes of 'Monkey Trial' Is Dead at 70

By The Associated Press

SHREVEPORT, La., Oct. 22— John T. Scopes, whose teaching of evolution led to the "monkey trial" of 1925, died of cancer yesterday at the age of 70.

Mr. Scopes outlived all the other principal figures in the celebrated trial. William Jennings Bryan, the prosecutor, died five days after he won Mr. Scopes's conviction. The colorful defender, Clarence Darrow, died in 1938.

Overshadowed by Counsel

By ALDEN WHITMAN

An obscure 24 - year - old schoolteacher in the summer of 1925, John Thomas Scopes became the prinicpal in a courtroom drama that occupied the nation and most of the civilized world. In the trial, which involved questions of academic freedom, the defendant was overshadowed by the special counsel who waged the case.

For the defense were Clarence Darrow, the Chicago criminal lawyer and civil libertarian; Arthur Garfield Hays of the American Civil Liberties Union, and Dudley Field Malone, also a civil libertarian. For the State of Tennessee there was William Jennings Bryan, "the Great Commoner" and silver-tongued orator who had thrice been the Democratic Presidential candidate.

The central issue in Dayton, Tenn., was the right to teach a version of biology that differed from that expounded in the Bible. It pitted Mr. Bryan, a defender of Fundamentalism, against Mr. Darrow, who upheld Darwinian evolutionary theory in a withering examination of Mr. Bryan's Bible literalism.

Mr. Scopes a shy, clean-cut young man, who never uttered a word at the trial, was overwhelmed in the carnival-like circumstances under which it was held. The end result was anticlimactic. He was convicted and fined $100. On appeal, the verdict was upset on a technicality; the case was never retried. In 1967, the statute he was accused of breaching was repealed.

The trial had its origins in a fervor of Fundamentalism in Tennessee. A legislator named John Washington Butler, clerk of the Round Lick Association of Primitive Baptists, framed a bill early in 1925 to outlaw the teaching in the public schools of "any theory that denies the story of the Divine Creation of man as taught in the Bible, and to teach instead that man has descended from a lower order of animals."

When the bill was signed into law, Gov. Austin Peay suggested that it would probably never be "an active statute." In New York, however, the fledgling American Civil Liberties Union, searching for a Tennessee biology teacher who would agree to test the law, ran an advertisement in The Chattanooga News. There was also a news article in The Chattanooga Times.

A group of loungers in a Dayton drugstore, seeking a way to put their town of 1,500 population on the map, saw its opportunity. A boy was sent to fetch Mr. Scopes, who was known around town as an opponent of the law.

Story Got Instant Notice

Fresh from the University of Kentucky, he had been hired as an athletic coach and teacher by the Dayton school system the previous September at $150 a month. He was a believer in absolute freedom of discussion in the schoolroom, and he agreed to take part in a test case. But he had not taught biology. He had, however, conducted a short review of the subject during the regular teacher's illness, and he had made use of a state-approved textbook that mentioned evolution favorably.

Mr. Scopes submitted to immediate arrest by the local police, and the loungers quickly notified the papers in nearby Chattanooga as well as The Associated Press, which flashed the story across the nation.

The teacher was indicted and his trial set for July 10. Mr. Bryan announced he would help the prosecution and, meanwhile the A.C.L.U. had engaged Mr. Darrow, Mr. Hays and Mr. Malone.

Describing the atmosphere in Dayton, Bynum Shaw, magazine writer, wrote recently that the town "became a circus," adding:

"Pullman cars were ordered for railroad sidings to accommodate guests. A barbecue pit was dug on the courthouse lawn, and bleachers erected for the convenience of itinerant evangelists. Stores displayed monkey signs and waved huge banners; J. R. Darwin, a Dayton haberdasher, found a gold mine in his name.

"The press arrived, more than 100 reporters and photographers, 30 of them sleeping on cots in a store loft and sharing one tap and a single outdoor privy. Most famous of the writers was H. L. Mencken."

A jury ("unanimously hot for Genesis," in Mr. Mencken's celebrated gibe) was chosen. It included one man who could not read. The presiding judge was John T. Raulston, who announced that "I'm jist a re'lar mountaineer jedge."

The courtroom was insufferably hot, so the trial, each session of which opened with a prayer, was moved outdoors. Mr. Bryan appeared in shirtsleeves and suspenders and cooled himself with a palm-leaf fan. Mr. Darrow, also in shirtsleeves, wore purple suspenders.

The undoubted high point of the trial came when Mr. Darrow (he was addressed throughout as "Colonel") called Mr. Bryan as a defense witness and relentlessly questioned him on the Bible story of Creation and other Scriptural incidents.

Jonah and the Whale

One memorable part of Mr. Darrow's examination had to do with Jonah and the whale. Did Mr. Bryan believe, he was asked, that Jonah had remained three days in the belly of the whale, as recounted in Elizabethan English in the King James translation of Holy Writ. Mr. Bryan replied:

"I believe in a God who can make a whale and can make a man and make both do what He pleases."

Was this whale just an ordinary big fish, or had God created him especially for this purpose? Mr. Darrow pursued.

"The Bible does not say," replied Mr. Bryan, "therefore do not know."

"But," Mr. Darrow retorted, "do you believe He made them —that He made such a fish and that it was big enough to swallow Jonah?"

"Yes, sir," responded Mr. Bryan. "Let me add: One miracle is just as easy to believe as another."

When the case got to the jury, after eight days, it took eight minutes to return a guilty verdict. Mr. Scopes's fine was paid by Mr. Mencken, whose trial reportage displayed his contempt for what he called "the yokels" of the Bible Belt. Mr. Scopes who had received mail by the sackful, quickly slipped into obscurity.

Born in Kentucky

He was born Aug. 3, 1900, in Paducah, Ky., the fifth child and only son of Thomas and Mary Scopes. He attended the University of Illinois, and then the University of Kentucky, from which he was graduated in 1924. His only teaching experience was eight months in Dayton.

He left the town and the state after his conviction to study geology at the University of Chicago, and later worked as a geologist for Gulf Oil of South America and for the United Gas Company in Texas and Louisiana.

Interest in his case languished until 1955, when the trial was re-created on Broadway in "Inherit the Wind," starring Paul Muni as Clarence Darrow and Ed Begley as William Jennings Bryan. The play was made into a movie with Spencer Tracy and Fredric March.

Three years ago, after Mr. Scopes had retired, he was the author (with James Presley) of "Center of the Storm," a reminiscence of his life and the trial. In it he wrote:

"Today, over 40 years from the trial, it seems incredible that the Dayton controversy rose to such an emotional peak. The war cries of the Fundamentalists sound archaic. Yet they were very serious. The trial itself was a test and a defense of the fundamental freedom of religion. At stake was the principle of separation of church and state. If the state is allowed to dictate that a teacher must teach a subject in accordance with the beliefs of one particular religion, then the state can also force schools to teach the beliefs of the person in power, which can lead to the oppression of all personal and religious liberties."

Mr. Scopes is survived by his widow, Mrs. Mildred Walker Scopes; two sons, John Thomas Jr. and William C.; and his four sisters. He will be buried in Paducah.

A Roman Catholic funeral was planned today for Mr. Scopes in Shreveport, La. He was converted at the time of his marriage.

The Daily Telegraph
3rd June 1968

Helen Keller beat deafness and blindness

MISS HELEN KELLER, who died at Westport, Connecticut, on Saturday, aged 87, was one of the world's most remarkable women. Mark Twain described her as one of the two most interesting characters of the 19th century, the other being Napoleon.

Despite total blindness and deafness, with consequent dumbness, in infancy, she lived to become a cultured and charming personality. She worked unselfishly all her life for her afflicted fellow-creatures.

Although she lived for so long in a darkened and silent world of ideas and ideals, based only on touch, taste and smell, she graduated from college with a B.A. degree, could read four languages and was a distinguished author.

She " listened " by placing her hand gently on the throat or lips of the speaker and while she could speak slowly and gutterally, she usually preferred to transmit her thoughts by the quick flutterings of her fingers.

Her other senses became more highly developed with the passage of time. She could eventually recognise what part of London or New York she was in by the distinctive odours, and " smell " the trade of people introduced to her such as farmers, painters, or mechanics.

She could quickly distinguish between white and mauve lilac by the difference in fragrance.

She learned to feel vibrations through her feet. Sitting in a hotel lounge, she liked to assess the character and personality of passers-by by their manner of walking. In the words of one of her friends, she demonstrated the " almost illimitable power " of the human will.

LOVING COMPANION
Miss Sullivan's work

Born at Tuscumbia, Alabama, the daughter of a Confederate officer, Helen Adams Keller was 19 months old when an illness deprived her of sight and hearing. As she had previously only uttered childish exclamations, she was also, for all practical purposes, dumb.

When she was six her parents engaged a young woman, Miss Anne Sullivan, in an attempt to train her. Thus began a loving companionship which lasted for 50 years, although at first the terribly handicapped child was completely intractable.

Miss Sullivan finally attracted her interest by teaching her the names of objects which she touched in the manual alphabet. From this she graduated to Braille and then to writing. At the age of 10 she learned how to speak orally although at this not unnaturally, she was never completely successful.

Miss Sullivan remained her constant guide and companion through school and college, patiently interpreting by means of the manual alphabet the various lectures and the contents of textbooks.

WROTE BEST-SELLER
Swimming as hobby

In 1902, before she graduated, Miss Keller wrote an autobiography, " The Story of My Life," which became a best-seller when published.

An expert typist, she used a Braille machine first, and then copied the manuscript on an ordinary typewriter. In this way she wrote a dozen books, including " The World I Live In," and "Helen Keller's Journal," and contributed regularly to magazines. Her hobbies were swimming and horse-back riding.

In 1914 another girl, Miss Polly Thompson, had joined her as helper, and when Miss Sullivan, who became Mrs. Macy, herself began to suffer from failing eyesight, Miss Thompson assumed the role of visual and oral interpreter. She died in 1960. Miss Sullivan had died in 1936.

TRAVELLED WIDELY
Trips to Europe

Miss Keller, who was associated with many organisations concerned with the welfare of the deaf and blind, travelled widely in her efforts on behalf of her fellow-sufferers, even when she was over 70.

She made several trips to Europe, during which she met the late King George V and Queen Mary. In 1946 she had a long audience with the Queen, now Queen Elizabeth the Queen Mother. In 1955 she met Sir Winston Churchill.

The Broadway success, " The Miracle Worker," the story of Helen Keller and Anne Sullivan, came to London in 1961. It also became a film.

In 1965 Helen Keller was named one of the 10 greatest living American women for the Women's Hall of Fame at the New York World's Fair.

HELEN KELLER

The Times
14th August 1875

HANS CHRISTIAN ANDERSEN.

Hans Andersen, who died the other day at the age of 70, and has been buried by his countrymen with national mourning and honours, deserves something more than a passing notice. If the Danes were so proud of him, it was very much because his fame was cosmopolitan and he had made himself friends all the world over. There had been strong men in Denmark before Agamemnon, and among his immediate predecessors, even among his earlier contemporaries, it could boast of poets and novelists who excelled him in the more exalted attributes of literary genius. In depth and power, for example, he yielded decidedly to Oehlenschläger, as he would have been ready to acknowledge, for his complacent pride in his great success was free from all unworthy jealousy. Yet Oehlenschläger and others pay the penalty of having written in the language of an inconsiderable people, while Andersen's name is become a household word in drawing-rooms and nurseries in America as in Europe. The causes of his exceptional popularity are easy enough to discover. They are to be found in the broad range of his sympathies, and the quick susceptibility of his emotional mind to seize upon novel impressions in their most picturesque aspects. Wherever he went he found a new country, and his mind, changing its hues like the chameleon, was tinged at once with the local colouring and reflected the finer lights and shades of the innermost spirit of the people he sojourned among. Even in the extravagances of his flights of romance, he remained essentially a citizen of the world. If some of his Danish poems and stories take high rank among his works, it was because the scenery and legends of his Fatherland lent themselves to his peculiar tastes and gifts. There is much that is wildly picturesque in the scenery of the Peninsula and its islands, with its blasted heather, glorious beech forests, and channels frozen over in the winter. They abound in those stirring legends of Heathendom and Mediæval chivalry with which he had enriched his fancy and fired his genius; the kindly family life of people was eminently congenial to his more tranquil moods. But those Danish works of his come behind the Italian "Improvisatore," because his native country had never inspired him as Italy did. He had no lack of imagination, although even in the most fantastic and far-fetched of his fairy tales we often find that the leading ideas are borrowed; he could multiply images and illustrations at will, till his pages were almost overcharged with them. But he arrested the attention of his readers and won upon their affections by the conscientiousness with which he clung to Nature. It was Nature he drew upon for his abounding images, although he showed them to you refined and idealized through his own poetical medium. He idealized each shifting scene as he saw it without losing sight of its distinctive features; then, with a marvellous facility of tenacious memory and ingenious fancy, he reproduced them again and again for his purposes, so that they should strike keys corresponding to associations with those who had the best right to recognize them. He had the art of etherealizing prosaic elements without letting the pictures suffer in their realism. He expressed with grace and power what others felt and failed to express, or else expressed imperfectly. So that, independently of any parade of sentiment, the books in which he lays his scenes abroad have a singular pathos for people with whom he had nothing in common in race or speech, in habits or education.

As he went to Nature for his scenery, and to actual life for his characters, so his books are pervaded by a strong self-consciousness, which he scarcely takes the trouble to conceal. You have the story of the development of his poetical genius in his "Improvisatore," as we shall take occasion to show by-and-by. But his slightest stories abound in allusions to his own individuality. As for his famous "Ugly Duckling," that is literally an allegorical biography, and if you look to the notices of his own life you discover the original of each separate incident. It is the secret of the apparently inexplicable popularity of the tale that, under a quaint and almost trivial disguise, it is a record of deep and bitter personal experiences. The duckling was bitten by the mother duck, beaten by the chickens, and kicked by the girl who fed the poultry. It was quite melancholy because it was ugly and scoffed at by the whole yard, and when it tried to hide itself and its sorrows among the bushes the small birds were scared and flew up in a fright. Little Andersen was mocked at, bullied, and beaten by the other boys when he first attended the village school, and afterwards when he tried an apprenticeship to tailoring. The duckling was conscious that it swam strongly and well, though the fastidious critics of the pond jeered at its awkwardness, and even its mother treated her offspring harshly, although her maternal partiality admitted some merits invisible to others. Andersen began to write poems and plays when a mere child, but the neighbours laughed at his juvenile efforts, and his mother threatened to beat him for crying over his failures. He had no playfellows, and his pleasures lay in devouring all the books he could get hold of and taking long solitary walks in the woods. Like the duck, he took flight from home in hopes of some change for the happier before he could well use his wings. When only 14, the boy came to Copenhagen with a few dollars in his pocket and an introduction to the leading theatre. The manager declined his services because he was too thin, and then for years he struggled on through various vicissitudes, among people who could not at all understand him. It was the story of the duckling's refuge in the old woman's cottage, with the hen and the tom-cat for companions, who always said "'we and the world,' because they thought they were half the world, and by far the better half." The hen would acknowledge neither use nor ornament in any one who could not lay eggs; the tomcat placed the chief ends of existence in purring, curving one's back, and giving out sparks. But, finally, the false duckling, mounting its youthful plumage, is welcomed by its noble kindred, and exults in its own glorious image reflected in the clear water; and the children exclaim, "This one, so young and so handsome, is the most beautiful of all!"

No doubt it was to those early trials of his, to his repeated disappointments, and the weary bitterness of hopes deferred, that we may attribute much of the pathos in Andersen's writings as well as the touches of sarcastic bitterness. His tastes or instincts were too pronounced to be stifled; with profound self-confidence they tided him over everything, and amid his many rebuffs and sorrows he found friends enough to keep him continually vibrating between the extremes of hope and despondency. Experiences of the sort were sure to go far in moulding and influencing a temperament so impressionable. If he could hold out doggedly against trouble, he was singularly susceptible to elation. Like the young swan, he attained to literary distinction, social consideration, and comparative ease just as his powers had reached their maturity, and he takes no pains to conceal his complacency. In his "Improvisatore" he expresses discontent with the comparative obscurity of his lot, and murmurs against the adventitious distinctions of those who are his superiors by birth and fortune. His later writings have a very different tone. Then, he was a welcome guest in the highest society at home, and his name was a letter of introduction abroad, wherever literature was held in regard. In his "Poets' Bazaar," for instance, he relates with naive exultation how he attended a concert of Liszt's in the Stadt London at Hamburg; and how, although he arrived late, they had reserved him the place of honour among all the wealthy merchants and financiers. Partial successes, with the harsh strictures of jealous critics, had served to stimulate him; an assured position and universal flattery and deference helped to spoil him. The quickness of his fancy and the easy fluency of his pen had conspired to make him somewhat careless in his best days. Now these faults grew upon him, nor did he write anything subsequently that quite equalled the "Improvisatore." That was the novel that made him, and as its double theme was especially congenial to him, so the book had a double charm for his readers. It was a study of his own inner nature, a revelation of the course of feelings generated in his early struggles, transplanted from Scandinavia to those Italian scenes he had always dreamt of as realms of enchantment. All the artist comes out in him, and he excels himself in exuberant force of description. We know no book, not even "Childe Harold," Hawthorne's "Transformation," "the Roba di Roma," or "Tolla," that so vividly recalls Rome and the surrounding Campagna. We believe him when he tells us, "that whenever my mind goes back to the Tiber, I see it ever before me as upon this evening; the thick yellow water lit up by the moonbeams, the black stone pillars of the old ruinous bridge, which with strong shadow lifted itself out of the stream where the great mill wheel rushed round." The pages are covered with pictures of the kind, taken in the country and the city as well as with vivid studies of genre; church interiors and crumbling temples, tombs turned to huts, and well-grown aqueducts, buffaloes and brigands, lakes lying among the woodlands of the Sabine-hills, half-naked peasants, half-crazed sybils, and gorgeous banquets in the palaces of the Roman nobles. He never misses an opportunity of confounding realism with invention. His Improvisatore is nephew to no less a person than Beppo, the notorious old beggar, of the Pincian Steps; the Improvisatore's patron is of the house of Borghese, and he makes his début as singer in the very room where some of Andersen's readers may have danced or dined. The account of his life under the roof of the Palazzo Borghese reads like a page from Rousseau's "Confessions," and goes a long way towards helping us to understand his books, and interpret the spirit and allusions of his poems. "Excellenza lamented my want of the fundamental principles of knowledge. It mattered not how much I might read, it was nothing but the sweet honey which was to serve for my trade that I sucked out of books." "The beautiful and the noble in everything seized upon me and attracted me. In tranquil moments I often thought on my education, and it seemed to me that they existed in the whole of nature." "People pointed always to my faults," he complains. "Was there, then, nothing at all intellectual, no good points in me?" "I who with my whole soul had clung to manhood, was now changed like Lot's wife into a pillar of salt. . . . There were moments when my spiritual consciousness raised itself up in fetters, and became a devil of highmindedness, which looked down upon the folly of my prudent teachers and whispered into my ear." But he always consoles himself with the thought that, "Thy name will live and be remembered when all theirs are forgotten, or are only remembered through thee, as the refuse and the bitter drops which fell into thy life's cup." As for his manner of composing, we have it set before us, we cannot doubt, in his account of his improvising at the San Carlo Theatre in Naples, the difference being that in reality he used a pen instead of pouring out his thoughts to music. He rejects unhesitatingly the subjects that do not fall within the range of his likings and personal knowledge; as for the rest, the choice is indifferent to him when he finds himself in the vein. When the note has once been struck, his ideas enchain themselves in a natural sequence, and he spins his plots out of those light materials his lively memory supplies in profusion. "Capri" is suggested, and he will none of it, as he knows no more of it than the outlines he has seen across the Bay. But "the Catacombs" stimulate him at once; he has not only visited them, but been lost and has nearly perished there. The "Fata Morgana" are equally attractive, for although he had never seen the resplendent phenomenon, it suggested the dream world he lived so much in, and he could people it with forms of Italian beauty luxuriating in Italian summer scenery. As for "Tasso," that again was the history of his own aspirations and achievements, and the passion with which he sung "the death of Sappho" was inspired by an unfortunate attachment of his own.

We have endeavoured hastily to trace the connexions between Andersen's personal history and the display of his talents from his indications in his most characteristic works. There is much in the "Improvisatore" to give it a prospect of living when his other books for adults may have been forgotten; but it is his children's stories, his legends, and his fairy tales that offer him his best chance of immortality. When he sets himself to tell his marvellous tales he brings himself down to the level of his little listener, and not the least wonderful thing in each of them is the art with which the author conceals his art. He writes with an engaging simplicity that almost deceives those to whom, in the words of Mrs. Gamp, "the wickedness of this world is print." You may lose something when you dispel the illusion; but when your attention is turned that way, you become aware of the undercurrent of earnestness and experience which invariably underlies the obvious meaning, and occasionally flashes up to the surface in some bright or stinging *double entendre*. The happy use of some epithet or qualifying adjective often gives point or turn to the whole of a tale, or there comes a touch of irony or a dash of sarcasm to remind you that there are sermons or morals to be found in his stories, and lessons of life in the vagaries of his exuberant humour. Perhaps nothing proved more conclusively the versatility of his natural gifts than the circumstances under which he received a Royal pension to send him on a journey abroad while his light was still under a bushel. The pension was given him on the recommendation of five of the foremost men in the Danish world of letters, and each of these distinguished authorities recommended him on account of a different merit. It is to Mary Howitt we are indebted for the incident, and it would be unjust to end any notice of Andersen without adverting to his singular good fortune in having been so admirably interpreted in English. Mrs. Howitt in particular has caught his spirit and style so thoroughly, and entered so entirely into his meaning, that books depending so greatly on their spirit and style, strange to say, have scarcely lost in translation.

The Gentleman's Magazine
27th February 1827 Vol.97

M. PESTALOZZI.

Feb. 17. At Neuhof, in Switzerland, aged 82, M. Pestalozzi, a " benefactor of the human race."

Pestalozzi was born at Zurich, in 1746. Having lost his father at an early age, he was brought up by his mother, who procured for him the advantages of a good education. His intention was to have devoted himself to the bar; but becoming deeply interested in the various plans which were agitated in Zurich for bettering the condition of the lower orders, he abandoned the study of the law; and was afterwards induced to undertake a manufacturing speculation, with a view of entering into closer contact with the poor. His plan seems to have been somewhat similar to that pursued by Mr. Owen at Lanark; so far, at least, as connecting the instruction of the young with the labours of their parents.

But a series of unfortunate circumstances ruined his establishment. In the retirement that ensued on his failure, he composed his Tale of Léonard and Gertrude, a work which may vie in popularity with the Pilgrim's Progress, or Robinson Crusoe. It became popular in Germany as well as in Switzerland, and the author was encouraged to renew his exertions. Between the years 1781 and 1797, he published his Weekly Journal for Country Folks, Letters on the Education of the Children of indigent Parents, Reflections on the March of Nature in the Education of the Human Race, &c.

After the abolition of the ancient Swiss Governments, and the meeting of the Helvetic Legislative Council at Aran, M. Pestalozzi addressed to the Council a tract, entitled " Reflections on the Wants of the Country, and principally on the Education and Relief of the Poor." He was appointed principal editor of the Helvetic Journal, a paper devoted to the moral and religious interests of the people. In 1799 he was nominated director of an orphan institution, which the Government had established at Stantz. This appointment enabled him to reduce some of his theories to practice; at Stantz, he became at once the teacher, steward, and father of the institution; and there he formed the plan of interrogative education, which has since been known throughout Europe by his name. " I wished to prove," writes he to his friend Gessner, " by the essay I was about to make, that public education is of value, only as far as it resembles private. Every system of education, which is not carried on in the spirit of domestic relations, tends to demoralize man. The instructor should live among his pupils, as in the bosom of his own family. This turn of mind I felt within myself, and I wished that my pupils should discover from every word, action, and look, that I loved them with all my heart, that their pleasures were my pleasures, and that their happiness constituted mine." After struggling with the difficulties of his position for several months, Pestalozzi was enabled to discern the fruits of his labours. Many of his pupils announced good abilities, and in a short time were seen above seventy children, taken almost all from a state of poverty, living together in peace and friendship, full of affection for one another, and with the cordiality of brothers and sisters. He had just succeeded in introducing some manual employment into his school, when the thread of his labours was rudely snapped by political changes; and exhausted in mind and body, he sought to recruit his powers by retirement and relaxation. After an interval of repose, Pestalozzi, under the patronage of the Swiss government, resumed his labours at Burgdorf, in the canton of Berne. At this period he was joined by several men of various degrees of talent and attainment; and the patronage of the Swiss government augmented his pecuniary resources, and furnished him with a locale for his exertions. But political changes once more broke up the rising institution.

The next period of Pestalozzi's career commences with the formation of two separate establishments, consisting, for the most part, of his former pupils. The children of the poorer class took up their abode at Munch Buchsee, a little village about five miles distant from Berne. Here Pestalozzi was much aided by M. de Fellenberg, who has since applied his principles of education, with some important modifications, to the instruction of both rich and poor. At Yverdun, in the canton de Vaud, Pestalozzi resumed his labours for the instruction of the higher and middle ranks of society. The fame of his method was now very generally spread through Switzerland and Germany. Many young men assembled under his paternal roof to act as instructors, and pupils from every part of Europe constituted one happy family around him. Each class had at its head an instructor, who lived with his scholars, and joined in their amusements as well as their studies; and thus, connecting himself not only with their duties, but with their pleasures, was enabled to win their affections, and gently mould them to his purpose. The character of Pestalozzi was the bond that united them; the kindness with which their masters treated them, and which overflowed in every word and action of Pestalozzi himself, contributed to impart a character of good humour and benevolence to the whole groupe. At Yverdun the principles of the method were applied to other branches of instruction, and the former plans were materially improved. A committee of masters watched over the moral and intellectual welfare of the institution, and drew up essays, or arranged exercises, for the approbation of the whole body. This may be dated as the most flourishing period of Pestalozzi's undertaking, though his pecuniary resources were by no means free from embarrassment. This circumstance co-operated with other causes to introduce divisions among the masters; a separation took place; and from that moment the institution at Yverdun declined. Disputes and dissensions between some of the individuals who had been connected with his establishment, much embittered Pestalozzi's declining years; and, by withdrawing his attention from the school itself, diminished its usefulness, and hastened its dissolution. In 1825 Pestalozzi left the canton de Vaud, and retired to his little estate at Neuhof, in the canton of Argau, where he occupied himself till his death in preparing elementary works. His last production was entitled : " Advice to my Contemporaries."

In 1803 M. Pestalozzi was one of the deputation which Buonaparte summoned from the Swiss Cantons, to deliberate on the means of restoring tranquillity to Switzerland; but he returned home before any arrangement could be effected.

Benevolence was the prevailing feature in Pestalozzi's character. It burned in him with the intensity of a passion, and needed sometimes the sober restraints of judgment. It was as discernible in the affectionate simplicity of his ordinary manners, as in the persevering exertions, and disinterested sacrifices, which marked his long life of trial and suffering. His genius was original, profound, and fertile, rising superior to the most overwhelming difficulties, but too frequently negligent of ordinary resources. The style of his writings is vigorous, pathetic, and piquant, but unpolished and irregular; in his philosophical works heavy, involved, and obscure. His conversation was particularly animated, playful, and entertaining, abounding in unexpected turns of thought, with an occasional felicity of expression that made an indelible impression on the hearer's mind.

Glasgow Herald
30th March 1931

CHILD EDUCATION PIONEER

DEATH OF MISS MARGARET M'MILLAN

HER INFLUENCE ON SCHOOL METHODS

Miss Margaret M'Millan, C.B.E., the nursery school pioneer, who was made a Companion of Honour in June last, died early yesterday in a nursing home at Harrow, where she had been seriously ill for several days.

Margaret M'Millan was a pioneer, and, like every pioneer, had a certain amount of rough weather to meet, but, unlike most of the clan, she had the happiness of seeing her ideas carried into effect during her lifetime. She had all the insight of genius, coupled with a wide culture, thoughtful mind, and passionate appreciation of the beautiful. See her books—"The Camp School," "Education through the Imagination"—for proof of these statements.

But she was above all an educationist; one who never stopped growing herself, and who never shut her eyes to nor hesitated to acknowledge the inadequacy of her most darling project if practical experience proved it so.

She fought and laboured for school clinics—school clinics that were to cure at least the physical ills of the children of the poor. And at last she got her clinic. Got, too, the best service possible—medical, dental, nursing—and, after a faithful trial, was forced to admit that its benefits were at the best temporary, and that by itself it was but a waste of time. It was a bitter disillusionment. But she knew now from first-hand experience, not only that prevention is better than cure, but in a sense the only real cure. She knew, too, what the real cure was, and, undaunted, began to advocate it.

SCOTTISH ASSOCIATIONS.

Miss M'Millan was born in New York, her parents being James and Jean Cameron M'Millan. Her father died when she was a child, and she was brought up with her grandparents in Inverness. She went to school first at Inverness Academy and later at Geneva. After that she went to live in Bradford, and in 1894 was elected to the School Board, serving on that body for eight years, fighting always to improve the physical condition of the school children.

She wanted medical inspection, and never stopped agitating till she got it. She wanted school baths, and a leaflet on hygiene and cleanliness was sent out into the schools. England at that time ignored the proposals, but Germany had the leaflet translated and circulated in all her schools, and started at once to build baths by the thousand.

After the clinic experience had demonstrated that doctoring alone was practically useless, that fresh air, cleanliness, and good food were absolutely vital, she worked harder than ever to get these. In 1904 the late Mr Joseph Fels, of land reform fame, offered Miss M'Millan £5000 to start a Health Centre, the scheme for which she had already drawn up. Miss M'Millan, wishing to work in with the authorities, induced Mr Fels to offer both money and scheme to the L.C.C. The scheme was turned down, and never again was £5000 offered to her!

EVELYN HOUSE.

Camps for boys and girls were next started. Mr John Evelyn gave Miss M'Millan a house with an acre of garden rent free, and all future experiments were centred round this house. By and by more ground was acquired. The boys and girls slept out summer and winter (the camps were separate), had simple but nourishing meals, the best teaching, and the best medical attention

The fame of the camps spread abroad, and many people, including foreigners, began to visit them. Dr Paul Herz, Chief Medical Officer of the Danish Schools, wrote in "School Hygiene" :—"In spite of poor equipment and the poor area, no open-air school children in England or elsewhere can compare with the camp children in physique and bearing." But Miss M'Millan was still not satisfied. To get absolutely perfect results they must be taken in hand sooner.

BABY CAMP.

The Baby Camp was started in 1914, and, from the first, was a phenomenal success, though the means at Miss M'Millan's disposal were far from adequate. The L.C.C., however, which at first had been so discouraging, had begun to pay grants. Grants were also given by the Ogilvie Trust, and later by the Board of Education. But until the death of Mr Fels in 1914, when the income of £400 a year which he allowed Miss M'Millan died with him, the money that came from him was her chief mainstay.

Then came the war. Evelyn House was in the Zeppelin area, and what the camps suffered those years is beyond telling. Out-door sleeping had to be given up, but otherwise "carry on" was the order of the day there as elsewhere. In 1917 Margaret M'Millan suffered an irreparable loss in the death of her sister Rachel. She called the Baby Camp the Rachel M'Millan Baby Camp, and the nurses who receive there a highly specialised training the Rachel M'Millan nurses.

Gradually she began to see all her ideas realised, even though only partially, and the Government recognised her services to the country by conferring upon her the C.B.E. The Fisher Education Act authorised the establishment of nursery schools by local authorities. The Nursery School Association came into being, and Miss M'Millan continued to lecture on the need for more nursery schools. Her own pioneer one at Deptford was always the shining example, for one of the worst slums in London had been made to blossom as the rose.

The Times
9th January 1941

FOUNDER OF THE BOY SCOUTS

We deeply regret to record that Lieutenant-General Lord Baden-Powell, O.M., who was famous throughout the world as the founder of the organization of Boy Scouts and Girl Guides, died early yesterday morning at Nyeri, Kenya, as reported by our Nairobi Correspondent on another page. He was 83 years old, and had been critically ill with heart trouble last November.

Robert Stephenson Smyth Baden-Powell was born in London on February 22, 1857. He was the seventh son of the Rev. Baden Powell, F.R.S., Savilian Professor of Geometry at Oxford, and came of pure English stock on both sides of the family, his mother being the daughter of Admiral Smyth. He was sent in 1871 to Charterhouse, then situated in London, though shortly afterwards moved to Godalming. There he remained for five years under Dr. Haig Brown, and distinguished himself at football, shooting, and theatricals. During the holidays he acquired much useful knowledge in yachting and small boat sailing with his brothers.

EARLY SOLDIERING

Baden-Powell intended going up to Oxford, and even went there, but, hearing that there was an examination just coming on for commissions in the Army, he entered mainly with the idea of seeing what the examination was like. He passed fifth, however, and as there was rather a dearth of officers at the time, those passing high obtained their commissions direct without having to go through Sandhurst. Accordingly, on September 11, 1876, he was gazetted lieutenant in the 13th Hussars, and shortly after left to join his regiment in India. The regiment was ordered up to Afghanistan, but was too late to take part in any actions. He was promoted captain in 1883, in which year he won the Kadir pig-sticking cup from a field of 54 horses. In 1884 the regiment went to Natal, and in the same year Baden-Powell published a small book entitled " Reconnaissance and Scouting," and two years later " Cavalry Instruction," a manual for the use of officers. In 1887 he was appointed Assistant Military Secretary to his uncle, General Sir Henry Smyth, Commanding the Forces at the Cape; soon after he joined in an expedition to Zululand, and later went with a Commission to Swaziland under Sir F. de Winton, where he met and conferred with the Boer generals Joubert and Smit. He also went on a sporting trip to Portuguese East Africa. In 1890 Sir Henry Smyth was appointed Governor of Malta, and Captain Baden-Powell went with him again as Assistant Military Secretary; he was promoted major in 1892.

When, in November, 1895, Colonel Sir Francis Scott was sent with an expedition to depose King Prempeh in Ashanti, Major Baden-Powell was ordered to organize a native levy to act as a covering force to the expedition. The operations were brought to a satisfactory conclusion and Baden-Powell, besides receiving the star, was promoted brevet lieutenant-colonel. He afterwards described the expedition in a book entitled " The Downfall of Prempeh." After he had rejoined his regiment in Ireland he was offered by General Sir Frederick Carrington the post of Chief Staff Officer to a force being formed to operate in Matabeleland. The rising of the Matabele, largely due to the absence of the constabulary who had been taken in the Jameson Raid, had begun in March, 1896, and over 150 farmers with women and children had been massacred within a week; all the Englishmen in the country were organized in troops, while relief columns were sent up from neighbouring colonies. Lieutenant-Colonel Plumer raised a force in Kimberley and Mafeking and marched over the country in which, four years afterwards, he had so hard a time in trying to relieve Mafeking. The capital, Bulawayo, was threatened with attack, and then the natives in Mashonaland also rose. Baden-Powell went reconnoitring by himself and in September was given command of a column operating in the Somabula Forest. He attacked the stronghold of Wedza, captured it, and, after clearing the frontier in Mashonaland, returned home in January, 1897. Besides the medal, he received a brevet colonelcy, and was shortly afterwards transferred from the 13th Hussars to command the 5th Dragoon Guards in India.

SIEGE OF MAFEKING
BADEN-POWELL'S COMMAND

When, in 1899, the situation in South Africa was becoming intolerable, Colonel Baden-Powell was one of the special officers sent out to investigate, report, and organize defences. In July he left England with orders to organize the allotment of troops for the defence of Rhodesia and Bechuanaland. Two regiments were specially raised to prevent incursions—the Rhodesian Regiment to watch the northern frontier, under Plumer, and the Protectorate Regiment, under Lieutenant-Colonel Hore, to guard the Bechuanaland frontier. The headquarters of the latter were at Mafeking, and it soon became evident that this centre, where large supplies were stored and which was the one point of importance between Kimberley and Bulawayo, would form an alluring bait for the Boers. Baden-Powell left the Transvaal frontier to Plumer and went himself to Mafeking.

On October 9 the Boers sent their ultimatum, demanding the withdrawal of our troops from the frontiers, and on the 12th the first blood of the war was spilt, when an armoured train bringing guns to Mafeking was derailed and captured at Kraaipan, some 40 miles to the south. Immediately afterwards the enemy surrounded the town, and the memorable siege began. The garrison consisted of about 700 trained men and 300 armed townsmen, while by October 20 there were 5,000 Boers under General Cronje around the place. " B. P." was the life and soul of the defence and innumerable tales are still told of his resource and ingenuity. At last on May 17, 1900, Colonel Mahon engaged the enemy some eight miles from the town, defeated him and relieved the garrison. On the Queen's Birthday, seven days after, the first train with stores entered the town.

This siege, one of the longest on record, conducted by a handful of defenders against heavy odds with hardly a mistake, brought great credit to the commander. One of the first messages to get through was from Queen Victoria, congratulating him and making him major-general and a C.B., and the news of the relief of Mafeking was received in England with much jubilation.

As soon as possible Baden-Powell pushed forward into the Transvaal, with a large force composed of the Mafeking garrison and relief force, and, after seeing to the defence of Rustenberg, joined in a combined movement against De Wet. In August, 1900, he was invalided home suffering from a general breakdown. When the war seemed to be dying down it was decided, in order to pacify the country, to form a large body of armed constabulary to be dispersed over the whole of the newly acquired territory in South Africa; and the organization of it was entrusted to Baden-Powell. The men were got together largely from Canada and Australia, and by May, 1901, a force of fine smart men, dependable and keen, were fully equipped and at work on their duties; and before the end of the war the force numbered 9,500 men. They formed a most useful addition to the forces in suppressing the final flickerings of the war, and when peace was at last declared they did much to pacify the country and reinstate civil authority.

In 1903 General Baden-Powell was appointed Inspector-General of Cavalry and returned to England to take up that post, which he continued to hold for four years, during which time many changes were introduced into the cavalry training as a result of the experience gained during the war. In June, 1907, he was promoted lieutenant-general, and in the following year was given the command of the Northumbrian Territorial District, to superintend the introduction of the new system. In October, 1909, King Edward gave him a knighthood of the Victorian Order, and soon afterwards he was made a K.C.B.

THE BOY SCOUTS

ORIGIN AND GROWTH OF THE MOVEMENT

In May, 1910, recognizing that he had been making for himself an occupation which might prove of more importance to the nation than the holding of an ordinary military command, Baden-Powell retired from the Army, although he might well have risen to the rank of field-marshal. He had asked the advice of King Edward VII, who had said " Stick to the Scouts."

The origin of the Boy Scout movement, though it has been a matter of some controversy, is simple enough. Always fond of boys and interested in their welfare, and having raised a small corps of boy messengers in Mafeking, Baden-Powell on his return to England became much in request to inspect various schools' cadet corps and boys' brigades. Having some years before written " Aids to Scouting " for the instruction of soldiers, it was natural that when addressing these boys he should have suggested that they might well study the subjects contained therein. His own scouting adventures appealed to them, the book was eagerly read by numbers of boys, and the author decided to compile a book specially for their use.

He then recognized that, while mere scouting might form an attractive amusement, the subject might well be extended and developed both into a pastime and into a serious system of education. By such means real discipline could be instilled, and with this could be combined the principles of chivalry and patriotism. But to make it attractive to young minds it was necessary to combine such ideals with games and sham adventure. Red Indians and backwoodsmen always have a fascination for boys; accordingly tracking, hunting, camping, and so on, were made to form the basis of this educational system. Another idea which had much to do with the success of the movement was that of dressing the boys in a distinctive uniform, which was at once practical, picturesque, and yet cheap; and the system was adopted of giving badges as certificates of competency in various subjects.

On January 16, 1908, *The Times* reviewed a pamphlet outlining " Scouting for Boys," and early in the same year a work was published with the same title and rapidly ran through many editions. But meanwhile the " Chief Scout " had organized a small corps of " Boys Scouts," and in July, 1907, had taken them to camp on Brownsea Island, in Poole Harbour. So successful did this experiment prove to be, and so salutary to the boys, that more extended operations were decided upon. It was now evident that much good might come of this movement. The original idea grew into something more grand and ambitious. From merely being a pastime it became a means of enlarging the minds of the boys. They learnt to make themselves useful, not only to themselves but to others. They were shown how to develop themselves physically and morally. It became a system of chivalry, almost a religion. So keenly did all classes of boys take the matter up that it has become a source of incalculable good to the nation, and later to other nations all over the world.

RAPID DEVELOPMENT

Within a few years the movement had developed in an extraordinary way. Thousands of boys flocked to the standard. Hundreds of keen men, realizing the good that was in it, enrolled themselves as Scoutmasters and Commissioners, and an efficient headquarter staff was formed, generals and other officers of the Army unselfishly throwing in their lot. King Edward VII too' a keen interest in the organization, and had promised to hold a great review of the Scouts; but this was only very shortly before the nation had to mourn his loss. In July, 1911, however, King George V carried out the wish of his father, and attended a great rally of some 30,000 Scouts in Windsor Park.

But meanwhile numbers of girls begged to be enrolled, and were eventually banded as " Girl Guides " in 1910. Miss Baden-Powell, the Chief Scout's sister, gave to her brother invaluable help in establishing the Girl Guides, for her enthusiasm and organizing ability played a great part in ensuring the success of the new branch. Later Lady Baden-Powell took on the post of Chief Guide. In 1917 the Chief Scout published " Girl Guiding." The scouting movement rapidly extended to other parts of the world, almost every civilized country having organized some system based on the Chief Scout's book. In order to encourage this progress and gain experience of the methods prevailing abroad, he started on a world tour in January, 1912. Going outward through the United States, he visited Japan, thence going to Australia and New Zealand, and home *via* Natal and other parts of South Africa.

REORGANIZATION

JAMBOREES AND TOURS

During the last War the Scouts did excellent service. After the War great changes were made. So many of the older boys and Scoutmasters had laid down their lives that the whole movement required reorganization. In July, 1920, was held a great Jamboree at Olympia. Scouts from all over the world attended this function, which was a most inspiring display of the efficiency of the reorganized constitution. Another Jamboree was held at Birkenhead in 1929.

There was much concern in 1934 when the Chief Scout had to undergo an internal operation, but he recovered, and after a cruise in the Mediterranean went on a world tour with the chief object of attending the Australian Jamboree at Christmas. His next tour was to Africa in 1936, and in December of that year he went to Paris for the twenty-fifth anniversary of the movement. He went to India in 1937 to attend the Jamboree at Delhi, and his visit he described in a special article in *The Times* on April 24 of that year. The year 1937 brought the Waterler Peace Prize to him, and a silver wedding gift subscribed to by boys and girls all over the world which was presented to him at a dinner in London at which the Princess Royal presided. Then he planned an African tour, but his health necessitated him staying in Kenya. On coming back to England in 1938 he went on a cruise to Northern Europe. He was back in Kenya when the war broke out, and he offered to return to England " to lend a hand," but Lord Somers, Deputy Chief Scout, urged him not to undertake the journey.

In 1929 the Chief Scout was raised to the peerage as Lord Baden-Powell, of Gilwell. He had been made a baronet in 1922, a G.C.V.O. in 1923, and a G.C.M.G. in 1927, and in 1937 received the Order of Merit. He also held many foreign decorations, was Colonel-in-Chief of the 13th/18th Hussars, and had received honorary degrees from Oxford, Cambridge, and other universities. He married, in October, 1912, Olave, daughter of Mr. Harold Soames, and had two daughters and a son, the Hon. Arthur Robert Peter Baden-Powell, born in 1913, who succeeds to the title. Lady Baden-Powell was made a G.B.E. in 1932, and she has the Order of the White Rose of Finland.

As an artist and caricaturist, Lord Baden-Powell was quite above the ordinary, and numbers of his sketches, drawn with the left hand, adorn his many books. Among these may be mentioned " Pig Sticking," " Sport in War," " Sketches in Mafeking and East Africa," " My Adventures as a Spy," " Indian Memories," " Lessons from the 'Varsity of Life," and " More Sketches of Kenya," published last year. He also did some sculpture, and his bust of Captain John Smith was exhibited in the Royal Academy. He was a member of the Mercers' Company, of which he was Master in 1913.

Chicago Daily Tribune
2nd June 1952

JOHN DEWEY, 92, PHILOSOFER AND EDUCATOR, DIES

Succumbs to Pneumonia After Injury in Fall

New York, June 1 (AP) — John Dewey, 92, the philosofer, who switched education's emphasis from subject matter to the child, died tonight of an attack of pneumonia.

Dewey became ill yesterday, a few days after he was reported recovering from a broken hip suffered in a fall last November.

He failed quickly, his widow said, and died quietly in his home.

Fell Playing with Children

The hip injury was suffered when he fell in his apartment while playing with his two adopted children, Adrienne, 12, and John Jr., 9.

Dewey was born on Oct. 20, 1859, in Burlington, Vt., the son of a farmer turned grocer.

He was graduated from the University of Vermont in 1879 and took his Ph.D. degree from Johns Hopkins in Baltimore in 1884. In the meantime he began his teaching career which continued for about 50 years.

After receiving his doctorate, he taught philosofy at the University of Minnesota and he spent many years in the middle west.

Finally he returned to the east and remained at Columbia university for a quarter of a century before retiring in 1930. He was the author of a number of books.

Launched Experiment Here

It was about 1900 at the University of Chicago, where he was director of the school of education, that Dewey first put his philosofical ideas to work. He initiated an experimental school there. Years of controversy followed.

Basically he believed in "learning by doing." Instead of stuffing a child's mind with facts, he would have the pupil learn thru scientific inquiry.

The educator's 90th birthday was marked by a testimonial dinner here. Approximately 1,500 persons attended, while elsewhere in this country and abroad meetings were held in his honor.

Dewey married Alice Chipman in 1886, and they had six children, of whom four survive. Mrs. Dewey died in 1927.

In 1946 Dewey was married to Mrs. Roberta Lowitz Grant, and they adopted two children.

The Standard
6th April 1886

MR. W. E. FORSTER.

We regret to announce the death of Mr. W. E. Forster, which occurred yesterday afternoon, at his residence, Eccleston-square. On Saturday it was stated that his convalescence had sufficiently advanced to enable him to go out for a drive on the previous day. The next morning, however, between nine and ten o'clock, he had a serious relapse, and fell into a state of unconsciousness, which continued until the end, shortly before one o'clock yesterday. Shortly before Mr. Forster's death his medical attendant, Dr. Mackenzie, was summoned and was present, and at his death Mrs. Forster and their two adopted sons and two adopted daughters were by the bedside. Many telegrams and letters have been received at Eccleston-square expressing sympathy with the bereaved family, including a message from the Queen. At present no date has been fixed for the funeral.

Mr. Forster's last public appearance was in St. George's Hall, Bradford, where, in August, he addressed his Constituents. Shortly afterwards he went to the Continent to recruit his health, and there, while staying at Baden-Baden, he was exposed to the malaria from an open drain, or cesspool, which sowed the seeds of his fatal illness. From the first attack he recovered sufficiently to return to England, and proceeded to Torquay, where he remained up to a few weeks ago, when he came back to London.

The Right Hon. W. E. Forster was born of a Quaker family, at Bradpole, in Dorsetshire, on the 18th July, 1818. His father was a distinguished member and minister of the Society of Friends, and his son retained through life the bias of his early education. He was educated at the Quakers' school at Tottenham, and on the completion of his education went into business at Bradford. In 1850 he married a daughter of Dr. Arnold, the famous head master of Rugby School. He commenced his public life by standing for the borough of Leeds at the General Election of 1859, but did not succeed in obtaining a seat in the House of Commons till 1861, when he was returned at a bye-election for Bradford. During the remainder of Lord Palmerston's Administration he acted with that section of Ministerialists who sat below the gangway, and distinguished himself sufficiently to earn a place in the Government of Lord John Russell which took office in the Autumn of 1865. From November of that year to the following June he was Under Secretary for the Colonies, and after the resignation of the Ministry continued to act with his Party against the Conservative Reform Bill, though his name is not specially connected with any particular feature of that famous controversy. In 1869 he was appointed Vice President of the Council, and now his Parliamentary career began in earnest.

Next to the disestablishment and disendowment of the Irish Church, the most important measure passed by Mr. Gladstone's first Government was the Education Act of 1870, the successful carriage of which was due almost exclusively to the tact, temper, and moderation of the new Vice President. His path was surrounded by enemies. He had, on the one hand, the Church Party, which believed, perhaps justly, that the measure was a covert attack on the parochial influence of the clergy, intended to prepare the people's minds for depriving them of their position altogether. He had, on the other, the whole religious party in Parliament, represented by Churchmen and Dissenters equally, who dreaded even the partial exclusion of Scriptural teaching from the new curriculum; and he had, at the same time, the extreme Secularists to deal with, who clamoured against the admission of it. Here were evidently the elements of a formidable coalition, which would certainly have taken definite shape and form had the measure fallen into other hands. But Mr. Forster contrived to disarm his opponents in detail, and he did it the more readily that his sincerity and earnestness were beyond dispute, and all that he asserted was believed. He conciliated the Dissenters by appealing to his "Puritan blood," which made him cling to the teaching of the Bible. He reassured Churchmen by declaring that he fully recognised the immense services which the Church of England had rendered to education, and that the new system was meant only to supplement, and not to supersede, the old one. We entertain no doubt that Mr. Forster meant what he said; and it is probable that nothing but confidence in his statements upon this head would have enabled him to pass the measure. But the history of the Education Question during the last fifteen years only shows us how impossible it is for Statesmen to impose limits on their own measures, and therefore with what extreme caution such promises should always be received. The same may be said of Mr. Forster's pledge that the education rate would never exceed threepence in the pound. It has already reached four times that amount. But all these things were not foreseen at the time, and the Radicals being propitiated by the compulsory element in the Bill, it was allowed to pass, if not amid general satisfaction, at least without creating much alarm.

The Ballot followed in 1872, and here again the powerful assistance of Mr. Forster was of great use to the Government, for the measure was not popular, and the energy of a few enthusiasts would hardly have prevailed against the lukewarmness of the Liberals and the open hostility of the Conservatives had it not been vigorously supported from the Treasury Bench. Mr. Gladstone's Ministry, however, had now spent its force. No more triumphs were in store for it; and in the following year came the defeat on the Irish University Bill, followed by the General Election of 1874, which once more consigned Mr. Forster to the ranks of Opposition.

Piqued at his defeat, Mr. Gladstone acted as he had done in 1867, and threw up the leadership of the Party, as far at least as the House of Commons was concerned. It then became necessary to appoint a successor, and it was seen at once that the choice of the Party lay between Mr. Forster and Lord Hartington. Mr. Forster declared publicly that if elected he should not accept the office, as he did not believe that he could command an undivided allegiance. But had no such declaration been made, Lord Hartington would equally have been selected, and events justified the choice. He made one of the very best leaders which the House of Commons had ever seen; and he had what Mr. Forster, had not, and what Radicals and Liberals alike know the value of—an hereditary political position, which, though worthless nowadays, without corresponding talents, carries great weight in combination with them. Mr. Forster served his new leader loyally, and distinguished himself by his opposition, not only to the Foreign Policy of Lord Beaconsfield, but also to two important measures affecting his own previous Administration—we mean the Education Act Amendment Act of 1876, and the Contagious Diseases (Animals) Act of 1878. In his resistance to these he displayed, perhaps for the only time in his life, a warmth and want of candour which can only be attributed to the heated atmosphere which he breathed on the Opposition benches, where an attitude towards the Government benches was fast being developed to which the House of Commons had long been a stranger. The repeal of a Clause which pressed heavily on denominational schools, and the introduction of a new Clause providing for the dis-

solution of School Boards where they were no longer necessary, were the two points most hotly contested. By the Clause now repealed the Parliamentary grant was never to exceed the amount of the school income derived either from rates, fees, or voluntary subscriptions. And as by this provision all Voluntary Schools were heavily handicapped, the denominationalists had never ceased to protest against it. As, however, the majority of Voluntary Schools were Church Schools, the Liberal Party turned a deaf ear to the appeal, and it was only with great difficulty that the Conservative Government succeeded in redressing the injustice. Why School Boards should continue to cumber the ground when there was no work for them to do it is difficult to understand. But the Liberals, and Mr. Forster among them, declared that Government was "stifling" the Act. The Cattle Bill of 1878 was also resisted with extraordinary pertinacity, Mr. Forster being among the foremost assailants. On this point we think it must be allowed that his usual frankness and perspicacity deserted him, and that he allowed himself to become the tool of a faction. He seems, indeed, to have persuaded himself that it was really a nefarious attempt to keep up the price of English stock, in the interest of the graziers and butchers, instead of being, as it really was, the surest means of ultimately lowering it.

When it was understood that Parliament would be dissolved early in 1880, Mr. Forster was not among those who took a sanguine view of the position. He believed that the Tory Party would still secure a majority, though probably a reduced one, and that another seven years of Opposition awaited the Liberals. He may have lived to wish that such had really been the case, for what followed was disastrous alike to his country, to his Party, and to himself. Mr.

Gladstone, "cursed with granted prayers," was returned to power at the head of an immense majority, and Mr. Forster accepted the onerous position of Chief Secretary for Ireland.

How far the resolution of the new Government to dispense with the precautionary measures which Lord Beaconsfield was preparing to renew for the security of life and property in Ireland received the approval of Mr. Forster we have yet to learn. But he was soon made to feel the effects of that ostentatious contempt for the policy of his predecessor which in every department of Government was displayed by Mr. Gladstone. Ireland became practically unmanageable. The reign of terror began, and still the Government refused to adopt coercive measures. In March, 1881, the Protection to Person and Property Bill was passed. But it did not seem to produce very much effect; nor did the imprisonment of Mr. Parnell and his accomplices have that discouraging influence on the operations of the Land League which the Government anticipated. The Ministry was at its wits' end. Something must be done to pacify Ireland, or their credit was gone for ever. In an evil hour communications were opened with the Prisoners at Kilmainham, and an agreement was made that if they would undertake to use their influence for the pacification of Ireland they should be at once set free. Mr. Forster promptly refused to be a party to any arrangement of the kind, and immediately resigned his post. It was dangerous to the public peace, he said, to release these men without either some better guarantee for their good conduct than we were likely to obtain, or without first arming the Executive with further powers adequate to cope with the consequences. His advice was rejected; The "suspects" were released; and the first fruits of the bargain was the murder of Mr. Forster's successor, Lord Frederick Cavendish, within bowshot of the Castle. Mr. Forster

very gallantly offered his services to the Government till a new Chief Secretary could be found, but the vacancy was filled up by Mr. Trevelyan, and Mr. Forster's connection with the late Administration was at an end.

As the Radical element in the Government grew bolder and bolder every day, and theories began to be broached on the subject of English land tenure which pointed directly to confiscation, the distance between Mr. Forster and his former associates grew wider and wider. So also in regard to Foreign and Colonial affairs Mr. Forster was less and less satisfied with the policy of the Government. On the progress of the Egyptian Question, the bombardment of Alexandria, and the Soudan War he thought what all men thought who were not blinded by partisanship. Of our policy at the Cape, our submission to the Boers, and our desertion of the allies who had trusted us he spoke in the severest terms of shame and indignation; nor was he much better pleased with the methods which the Radicals were adopting for securing a victory at the elections. He would have nothing to say to the Caucus, and told his constituents at Bradford that he, for one, would be indebted to no such machinery for the honour of their votes. He did his best to encourage the connection between England and her Colonies; and was always weighing the possibility of a great Colonial Confederation. In short, he had no sympathy whatever with the Modern Radical School in their views either of property or of liberty, either of the interests or the honour of Great Britain, or of the moral and physical qualities which have made her what she now is.

Under the influence of convictions so irreconcilable with those with which the dominant Liberalism was animated, the probable accession of Mr. Forster to the ranks of the Conservatives was a frequent subject of speculation. In private society he made no secret of his contempt and dislike for the last Liberal Government as a whole, and often spoke of their follies and blunders as freely and as strongly as if he had been one of their opponents. But he shared very strongly in the sentiment which makes Party men cling to an old name, and would have disliked exceedingly being obliged to call himself a Conservative, though he had agreed with them more closely than he did. If the Conservative Party could only change its name, he has been heard to say, there would be no difficulty; and he used to talk of the possibility of building up a great Constitutional Party in the next House of Commons to resist the progress of Radicalism. He became, in fact, before his death the type of a Party. When men spoke of "Moderate Liberals," they thought of Mr. Forster and Mr. Goschen—men who represented the Liberalism of the Reform epoch, not the Socialism of the Radical epoch. He was very well fitted to form the nucleus of a new Party; for, though not, perhaps, born to be a leader, he was eminently the kind of man whose example is readily followed, and whose influence is greater than their authority. He was always ready to talk on political subjects, even with strangers; and his openness and accessibility lent a charm to his conversation, in spite of a little roughness of demeanour which clung to him to the last. He is a great loss to the House of Commons and to the Party of Conservative progress, for he was thoroughly trusted and respected, and no change of sides which he might have thought it proper to make would ever have been attributed to any but the worthiest of motives.

The news of Mr. Forster's death coming so shortly after the favourable reports of the past few days caused considerable excitement in Bradford, and it being market day and the Exchange crowded with merchants and manufacturers from all parts of the West Riding, the loss to the borough and the nation formed the chief topic of conversation. Sympathy and sorrow were expressed alike amongst political foes and friends. The Town Hall bell tolled, and all the public buildings and clubs hoisted their flags at half-mast.

The Times
15th January 1898

"LEWIS CARROLL."

We regret to announce the death of the Rev. Charles Lutwidge Dodgson, better known as "Lewis Carroll," the delightful author of "Alice in Wonderland," and other books of an exquisitely whimsical humour. He died yesterday at The Chestnuts, Guildford, the residence of his sisters, in his 66th year. He was educated at Christ Church, Oxford, and distinguished himself in the Schools, taking a first class in Mathematical and a second in Classical Moderations, and a first in the Final Mathematical School, and a third in *Literæ Humaniores*. He became a Senior Student of Christ Church in 1861 and in the same year mathematical lecturer, a post which he continued to fill for 20 years. In 1861 he was also ordained. He began his literary career in 1860 by the publication of "A Syllabus of Plane Algebraical Geometry," which was followed the next year by "The Formulæ of Plane Trigonometry." "A Guide to the Mathematical Student in Reading, Reviewing, and Writing Examples" made its appearance in 1864, and in 1865 "The Adventures of Alice in Wonderland" burst upon an astonished world. Few would have imagined that the quiet, reserved mathematician, a bachelor, who all his life was remarkable for his shyness and dislike of publicity, possessed the qualities necessary to produce a work which has stood the test of more than 30 years, and still captivates young and old alike by its quaint and original genius. This was the first, or one of the first, of those entertaining books, since become numerous, which afford almost equal enjoyment to boys and girls and to those children of a larger growth who, although years have rubbed off the bloom of their youthful illusions, yet preserve their love of innocent laughter and nonsense. "Alice in Wonderland" was originally written to amuse one of Dean Liddell's daughters. The author was an intimate friend of the Dean and Mrs. Liddell, and took infinite pleasure in the society of their little girls. It was in order to beguile her hours of playtime that these diverting fancies were woven for one of the children. The success of the book was never in doubt, and the story is current, though we cannot vouch for its authenticity, that the Queen herself on reading it was so much delighted that she commanded the author to send his next work to Windsor. He did so, and her Majesty was almost as bewildered as Alice on finding that it consisted of "An Elementary Treatise on Determinants"!

It is curious to notice how frequently "Alice in Wonderland" is quoted in reference to public affairs, as well as to the ordinary matters of every day life. Hardly a week passes without the employment of its whimsicalities to point a moral or adorn a tale, and only yesterday a letter from a correspondent was published in *The Times* in which the Dreyfus-Esterhazy case was paralleled, with an aptness which was really surprising, from Lewis Carroll's immortal story. Some years ago Alice made her appearance on the London stage in a graceful dramatic version of the book, and delighted the children home for the Christmas holidays, for whose especial benefit ocular demonstration was given of her surprising experiences. In 1869 Lewis Carroll published "Phantasmagoria and other poems"; in 1870 "Songs from 'Alice's Adventures in Wonderland,'" in 1871 "Through the Looking-Glass and What Alice Found There,"—a continuation which obtained almost the success of the original work—and in the same year "Facts, Figures, and Fancies relating to the Elections to the Hebdomadal Council." "Euclid, Book V., Proved Algebraically," made its appearance in 1874, to be followed two years later by another example of the author's versatility in "The Hunting of the Snark, an Agony in Eight Fits." His subsequent works include "Doublets: a Word Puzzle," 1879; "Rhyme? and Reason?" 1883; "A Tangled Tale," 1885; "Alice's Adventures Underground," 1886; "The Game of Logic," 1887; "Curiosa Mathematica, Part I.—A New Theory of Parallels," 1888; and "Symbolic Logic," 1896.

Although, as is abundantly evident from this list of his works, Lewis Carroll was a serious and hardworking mathematician, there can be no doubt that his chief title to fame will always rest on those *jeux d'esprit* which have won for him so secure a place in the affections of readers for whom mathematics are, as a rule, the reverse of attractive. In many a home and many a schoolroom there will be genuine sorrow to-day when it is announced that the author of "Alice in Wonderland" and "Through the Looking-Glass" has passed away.

The Times
25th September 1863

DEATH OF JACOB GRIMM.

This celebrated German writer, who, in conjunction with his late brother William, has been so long well known, not only in Germany, but throughout all Europe, died on Sunday evening last at Berlin, after a short illness. He was born on the 4th of January, 1785, and had therefore reached his 79th year. Although he sought comparative retirement after the death of his brother he was indefatigable up to his last moment in carrying out the objects to which he had devoted his long and useful life; and with patriotic self-devotion his last hours were spent, not in earning new fame by the continuation of those works which were so peculiarly his own, but in the preparation of his great German dictionary. Jacob Grimm, like many others, had difficulties to contend with in the outset of his career. When he commenced the profession of authorship, Augustus William Schlegel looked upon ancient German literature as in some degree his own domain, and did not treat the young beginner with any degree of friendship, regarding him almost as an usurper, and finding terrible fault with his etymology. But a change soon came over the feelings of Schlegel as to his countryman, for afterwards he never spoke or wrote of him without expressing the highest opinion of his talents; and he once said, "I cannot name him without expressing my admiration of his greatness." His loss will be irreparable in more than one sense, for he was honoured and esteemed in Germany not less as a man than as a scholar, and the tranquil spirit by which he was actuated manifested itself in the kindly nature of his writings. In politics he took the Liberal side, and his loss will be felt by many German journals, with the conductors of which he was on terms of valued amity. It is to be regretted that the great national German dictionary on which he was engaged has not reached beyond the word "Fromm"; but, from the ample materials left by the deceased, there is every hope that the work will be concluded in as satisfactory a manner as that in which it was commenced.

Entertainment

Perhaps one of the first great mass entertainers was **Mme. Tussaud**, whose brilliant creations have their imitators the world over. In the area of light reading, **Bram Stoker's Dracula**, even more than Mary Shelley's *Frankenstein*, set the scene for the whole horror genre, which was to overflow into the cinema early in the next century. Similarly, **Arthur Conan Doyle's** extraordinarily atmospheric creation, Sherlock Holmes, initiated what is today almost certainly the most popular form of light fiction, the detective story, later brought to its undoubted perfection by **Agatha Christie**, whose Poirot and Miss Marple between them epitomise the two qualities which any self-respecting detective must have: eccentricity and ordinariness. Where would Gardner, Chandler, and the rest be without them? The mystery story itself, the beginning of the long line of which the above are honourable members, was of course given its modern form by **Wilkie Collins.** **Edgar Allan Poe** and **Alisteir Crowley** created bizarre genres of entertainment which frighten yet fascinate. The highlight of popular culture, with whose decline are associated many disasters, the English music hall, is here acknowledged by **Marie Lloyd**; its most elegant and sophisticated relation by Himself, **Noel Coward**; and its second cousin once or twice removed by **Gypsy Rose Lee. P. T. Barnum** was the original great impresario of curiosities and latterly the circus. "**General Tom Thumb**", Barnum's original star attraction, and **Joseph Grimaldi**, the modern clown *par excellence*, are two whose names live on. **Walt Disney**'s Mickey Mouse, Bugs Bunny, and the rest need no introduction; but he is also here for his stunning contribution to the vulgarization of entertainment, Disneyland and its imitations. Radio humour, and its later development into TV comedy, with its unique ability to present the individual and his nightmare, is here represented by **Tony Hancock**, whose sad end is perhaps the classic two-life tale of inspired talent torn by self-doubt. Equally obsessive was the determination that drove **Karl Wallenda**, compulsive showman and patriarchal circus entertainer, ultimately to a death that seemed almost inevitable.

The act of **Laurel** and **Hardy** and **Cecil B. de Mille** transcends the silver screen which was their principal medium and their names are ever associated with a certain style. **Cole Porter** wrote popular songs that the masses are still humming half a century later, and **Maurice Chevalier**, perhaps because he was the last international star of his kind, will always epitomise the wistfulness of continental cabaret entertainment.

National Biographies

GRIMALDI, JOSEPH (1779–1837), actor and pantomimist, born 18 Dec. 1779 in Stanhope Street, Clare Market, came of a family of dancers and clowns. His grandfather, Giovanni Battista Grimaldi, was known in Italy and France, and his father, Giuseppe Grimaldi (d. 23 March 1788, aged 75), is said to have acted at the Théâtres de la Foire in France, to have first appeared in London at the King's Theatre in the Haymarket, and to have played at Drury Lane in 1758-9, and subsequently at Sadler's Wells. During the Lord George Gordon riots he wrote, instead of 'No Popery,' 'No Religion' on his door. Grimaldi's mother, a Mrs. Rebecca Brooker, danced and played utility parts at the last-named theatres. The first appearance of 'Joe' Grimaldi was at Sadler's Wells, 16 April 1781, as an infant dancer, and he took part in the pantomime of 1781, or that of 1782, at Drury Lane. In the intervals between his engagements at the two theatres he went to a boarding-school at Putney, kept by a Mr. Ford. In successive pantomimes at Drury Lane and Sadler's Wells he acquired mastery of his profession. A list of the pieces in which he appeared is valueless, and his adventures, though they furnish material for a volume, are to a great extent imaginary, or consist of accidents such as are to be expected in his occupation. After his father's death he was allowed to act at the two houses—Drury Lane and Sadler's Wells—on the same night, and had to run from one to the other. His boyish amusements consisted in breeding pigeons and collecting insects. He is said to have collected with great patience four thousand specimens of flies. In 1798 he married Maria Hughes, the eldest daughter of one of the proprietors of Sadler's Wells. His work at this time was arduous, and his earnings were considerable. He was, however, through life imprudent or unlucky in his investments, and rarely succeeded in keeping the money he made. His health, moreover, suffered from his pursuits. In 1799 his first wife died, and in 1802 he married Miss Bristow, an actress at Drury Lane. In 1803 his brother John Baptist, who had gone to sea, turned up for a single occasion, and then disappeared in a manner that gave rise to strong presumption that he had been murdered. At this time Grimaldi is credited in the 'Memoirs' with having played some parts in the regular drama. Aminadab in 'A Bold Stroke for a Wife' is advanced as one. No such part, however, occurs in the comedy of that name. He sometimes played parts in melodrama, and once, for his benefit at Covent Garden, Bob Acres in the 'Rivals.' A quarrel with the management at Drury Lane was followed by a visit to Dublin, where he acted under Thomas and Charles Dibdin at Astley's Theatre, and subsequently in Crow Street. On 9 Oct. 1806, as Orson in Thomas Dibdin's 'Valentine and Orson,' he made his first appearance at Covent Garden. During the O.P. riots Grimaldi went on in his favourite character of Scaramouch, and effected a temporary lull in the storm. His visits to country towns—Manchester, Liverpool, Bath, Bristol, &c.—developed into a remunerative speculation. As Squire Bugle, and then as clown in the pantomime of 'Mother Goose,' Covent Garden, 26 Dec. 1806, he obtained his greatest success. This pantomime was constantly revived. In 1816 Grimaldi quitted Sadler's Wells and played in the country, but returned in 1818, having purchased an eighth share of the theatre. In this and following years his health began to decline. From 1822 his health grew steadily worse, and he was unable to fulfil his engagements at Covent Garden. In 1825 he was engaged as assistant manager at Sadler's Wells, at a salary of 4l. a week, subsequently diminished by one half. On Monday, 17 March 1828, he took a benefit at Sadler's Wells. On 27 June of the same year, at Drury Lane, he took a second benefit, and made his last appearance in public. On this occasion he played a scene as Harlequin Hoax, seated through weakness on a chair, sang a song, and delivered a short speech. His second wife died in 1835, and on 31 May 1837 he died in Southampton Street, Pentonville. He was interred on 6 June in the burial-ground of St. James's Chapel, Pentonville Hill, in the next grave to that of his friend Charles Dibdin. As a clown Grimaldi is held to have had no equal. His grimace was inexpressibly mirth-moving; his singing of 'Tippety Witchet,' 'Hot Codlins,' and other similar ditties, roused the wildest enthusiasm, and with him the days of genuine pantomime drollery are held to have expired. He was a sober man, of good estimation, and all that is known of him is to his credit. Pictures of Grimaldi in character are numerous. One by De Wilde, as clown, is in the Mathews Collection at the Garrick Club. A series of sixteen coloured engravings, representing the principal scenes in 'Mother Goose,' was published by John Wallis in 1808. A picture of him in ordinary dress, by S. Raven, is in an edition of the 'Memoirs,' in which are, of course, many celebrated pictures in character by George Cruikshank. The manuscript of Grimaldi's 'Memoirs,' of which a small portion only has been printed, was in the possession of Henry Stevens. Many residences in London are associated with Grimaldi, the best known being 8 Exmouth Street, Spa Fields, Clerkenwell, where he lived in 1822.

In 1814, in 'Robinson Crusoe,' his son, JOSEPH S. GRIMALDI, made, as Friday, a very successful début, and began thus an ill-disciplined and calamitous career, during which he was engaged at Covent Garden and elsewhere. He took for a while his father's position, but died in 1832 of delirium, aged 30.

The Times
3rd January 1972

M Maurice Chevalier, the French comedian and actor, died on Saturday night. He was 83.

When Mistinguett died in 1956 a part of Paris died with her. She was the incomparable " Miss "—a symbol of a gaiety and warmth that had its origin in a little flower-seller from *Les Halles*.

Now Maurice Chevalier is dead, and Paris has lost another part of its history and its legend. He, too, represented the warmth and the gaiety of shabby little back streets, and the heart and soul of a great city. Age meant nothing to him. He was the same personality in youth as he was as a veteran actor. His popularity did not depend on his voice, or his style or his charm. It had nothing to do with sex appeal.

Mistinguett used to say of him " Il a le fluide ", and when challenged to define this could only shrug her shoulders in perplexity. Yet to her, it was his supreme quality. By it she meant that he had the power to abolish the footlights and the orchestra pit, and to become one with his audience. They were united with him in a strange bond of intimacy. It is an undefinable quality, possessed only by a few great artists.

Chevalier was born at Menilmontant, a poor district outside Paris, on September 12, 1888, the son of Victor Charles Chevalier, a house painter, and Sophie Josephine, a lace-maker. The family were poor, and when Maurice was eight his father deserted them. Two years were then spent in a children's home (Chaplin was placed in an orphanage when he was five), and he went to work when still very young, earning a pittance in a number of trades. But the stage called him, as it called Chaplin, and his gaiety and friendliness soon won him a small niche as an entertainer. The music-hall was his obvious destination, and by the time he had reached his teens he was appearing at the Eldorado in Paris in a show aptly named *Le Beau Gosse*.

The turning point in his career occurred when he became Mistinguett's dancing partner at the *Folies Bergère* in 1910. It was sometimes said of him later that Mistinguett made him, but she herself always denied this. After all, for her he had *le fluide* and it was only necessary to teach him the technique of their trade, and to help him to become a true artist and professional. They worked together, on and off, for 10 years ; and together they captured Paris. They became as much a part of it as the Eiffel Tower.

Chevalier joined the French army in 1914, but was wounded and taken prisoner in his first engagement with the enemy, and spent more than two years in a prisoner-of-war camp. But in 1918 he was able to return to the Paris music-halls, and took up the threads of his career once again. He was soon back at the *Folies Bergère*, and he made his first appearance on the London stage at the Palace Theatre, in February, 1919, in *Hullo, America*.

MAURICE CHEVALIER

Comedian popular for his warmth and gaiety

The coming of sound in the cinema found him at the peak of his career ; and his was exactly the type of personality of which the new talking pictures of Hollywood were so urgently in need. He could sing, dance and act reasonably well, but above all he had the power to project his personality from the screen. His casual, intimate style and seemingly effortless technique were in sharp contrast to the over-acting and over-talking approach of so many of the existing film players.

It was now that his luck, which had changed so notably once he had left the misfortunes of his childhood behind, was once again to give him exactly the opportunity he needed. It was Jesse Lasky who was generally considered to have started Chevalier on his American film career, but in fact it was MGM's most talented producer, Irving Thalberg, who first realized his potentialities and gave him a film test in Paris in 1928. Lasky saw the test, and later saw Chevalier at the Casino de Paris, where he was the darling of an audience composed largely of American and British tourists. Lasky quickly put him under contract and took him to New York, where he allowed Florenz Ziegfeld to use him for a few weeks in his *Midnight Frolic* on the New Amsterdam Roof before whisking him away to Hollywood.

His first picture was *Innocents of Paris*, which was made in haste and did not amount to very much, but which was an instant success, partly on account of Chevalier's personality, and partly because of his singing of its theme song, " Louise ", which was to become a part of his repertoire for the remainder of his life.

Hollywood was now about to enter its golden era of musicals. It had the best song writers in the world, and most of the best directors. Not all took kindly to the new and specialized technique of filming musicals, but there was one man who revealed an exceptional flair for them. This was the German, Ernst Lubitsch, and it was Chevalier's supreme good fortune to be directed in his second picture, *The Love Parade*, by this master craftsman. Lubitsch had

style, elegance, wit—and a Continental sophistication which was rare in Hollywood.

Lasky chose a new young singer from Broadway called Jeanette MacDonald to play opposite Chevalier in *The Love Parade*, and as a team they fitted perfectly into the Lubitsch pattern. The film was a triumphant success. From then on Chevalier had only to stay on in Hollywood to make himself a fortune and to become a film star known throughout the world. His pre-war American films included *Paramount on Parade*, *The Big Pond*, *The Playboy of Paris*, *The Smiling Lieutenant*, *One Hour With You*, *Love Me Tonight*, *A Bedtime Story*, *The Way to Love*, *The Merry Widow* and *The Man from the Folies Bergère*. He also made two British pictures, *The Beloved Vagabond* and *Break the News*.

During this time he did not forsake the stage, and continued to appear in Paris, New York and London.

During the Second World War he remained in France, performed in Paris from time to time and paid at least one professional visit to prisoner-of-war camps in Germany. Certainly the Germans made many attempts to exploit him, and after the war he was obliged to answer charges of collaboration. Of these he was acquitted and in 1946 resumed his career, making a film under René Clair's direction called *Le Silence est d'Or*. This, though successful enough, was a long way from the opulent musicals of his hey-day in America ; it seemed in the 1950s that his career as an international film star might be ended, although he continued to appear on the stage throughout the world.

Then in 1958 he made *Gigi* with Leslie Caron, and suddenly it seemed as though all the old magic was back again. Here was an elderly man looking back over his shoulder nostalgically to a romantic past, and serenading the beauty of woman as he had serenaded it all his life. The twinkle was still there in his eye, the charm and the roguishness ; but above all there remained the power to achieve that complete personal intimacy with his audience. Chevalier was home again, against his native background. The *gamin* had grown up into a *boulevardier*, bu he was still a carefree youth at heart.

He will be remembered in many ways and in many parts, but always and above all with his straw hat tilted down over his nose and his lower lip pouting a little like a naughty schoolboy as he confided in his audience with that easy intimacy which made them feel that they were sitting opposite him on the other side of his fireplace, and sharing with him his confidences about life, about love and about women.

Chevalier was a holder of the Croix de Guerre and an officer of the Legion of Honour.

He was married in 1927 to Yvonne Vallée, the singer and dancer, but this marriage was dissolved in 1935.

Daily Telegraph
13th January 1976

LIKE POIROT, AGATHA CHRISTIE'S LAST CASE IS OVER

DAME AGATHA CHRISTIE died yesterday aged 85, her undisputed world wide reign as the Queen of the Crime Novel at last ended. Millions of people who read her books or paid their money at theatre or cinema box offices will feel they have lost a close and dear friend.

No other author in this century had the same sort of personal relationship through the printed word with readers as did Agatha Christie, who was made D B E in 1971.

Any book with her name on it was certain to be the best of " reads."

When at the end the reader found himself bamboozled by her clever handling of the plot it was with joy and affection that he acknowledged her mastery.

Statistics about her sales do not really give the measure of her success. She wrote more than 80 books, indeed the 80th was published on her 80th birthday, and these had sold more than 300 million throughout the world.

Copyrights sold for £1m

At one time she sold her copyrights to the M G M film corporation for more than £1 million, but later bought them back. She later sold them to Booker McConnell.

Her income from books and plays was said to have been about £100,000 for several years. A principal contribution was the phenomenal success of " The Mousetrap," which opened at the Ambassadors Theatre in November, 1952. It is still running, but at the St. Martins.

What was the secret of her success? Surely the answer must be consistency. Yet paradoxically it was her very refusal to be consistent, to play by the rules, that made her supreme.

When she started writing there were severe conventions that governed the writing of the detective story. Her first effort in this genre, " The Mysterious Affair at Styles" (1920), which introduced Hercule Poirot to his adoring public, was a good example of the orthodox story.

Rules broken

But soon she was breaking these over-rigid rules, yet at the same time was always playing fair with her readers. The most exciting of these innovations was " The Murder of Roger Ackroyd " (1926), where the murderer proved to be the narrator of the story.

Later there was a novel in which the " murder" proved to have been a natural death; and another, recently a triumphantly successful film, " The Murder on the Orient Express," when all the suspects turn out to be the murderers.

Then later, in " Ten Little Niggers" (1939), all the suspects are killed. The true consistency lay in the ingenuity with which she manipulated the basic elements which made up the whodunnit formula.

Poirot set aside

Most detective-story writers who had created a character as successful as Poirot would have stuck to him.

With his gallicisms and his " little grey cells," it looked as if he would rival Sherlock Holmes; but Dame Agatha regularly set him on one side to write with other central figures, mostly the more homely Miss Marples, but also others.

Sometimes she abandoned the detective figure and even on one occasion dabbled on the edges of science fiction.

At first she fought shy of turning her stories into plays. She let others try, but later said that she was never wholly happy with their work.

After the success of " The Mousetrap " she wrote her own scripts, with greatest success in " Witness for the Prosecution " (1953), which ended with a last-act twist far more theatrically stunning than " The Mousetrap."

Trained as musician

Quite simply in her crime writing she was the supreme professional. Her other novels, romantic in tone, written under the name Mary Westmacott, were never so satisfying and her poems, though neat enough, always lacked the imaginative power that characterised her crime novels.

Dame Agatha was born in Torquay, the daughter of an American father, Frederick Alvah Miller, and an English mother.

She was educated privately, principally as a musician, and her first ambition was to be a concert singer. She felt, however, that she was too nervous ever to be able to appear in public and abandoned the idea.

In 1914 she married Col Archibald Christie and while her husband was in the Army served as a V A D nurse, gaining knowledge of medical matters that was later to serve her in good stead.

She wrote her first novel when she was convalescing after an illness. A regular flow of books followed almost every year after the success of the first.

Soon after the publication of " Roger Ackroyd " she was involved in a real-life mystery, which afterwards she never liked to talk about. Indeed on the rare occasion that she gave interviews the reporter would have to give a guarantee in advance that he would not bring the matter up.

One day, she vanished from her Berkshire home and her car was found abandoned in Surrey. An over-imaginative assistant chief constable made several alarmist statements and some newspapers hired other detective story writers to air their theories about the causes of her disappearance.

The headlines persisted until she turned up some days later at a hotel in Harrogate, having suffered loss of memory.

The incident was never satisfactorily explained, though psychiatrists might speculate on the reason that she chose to register at the Harrogate hotel in the name of the woman who was later to be cited when Dame Agatha divorced Col Christie in 1928.

Second marriage

Col Christie died in 1962. There was one daughter of the marriage and it is her son who will inherit most of Dame Agatha's fortune.

In 1930 Dame Agatha married the archaeologist, Sir Max Mallowan, and accompanied him to many of his excavations in the Middle East, thus exploring the background for some of her novels—" Murder in Mesopotamia" and " Murder on the Nile " for instance.

She wrote about her experiences as an archaeologist's wife in "Come Tell Me How You Live," originally published in 1947, but re-issued in a new edition last week.

She disliked, however, those who patronised her work, particularly "The Mousetrap." She was prepared to admit that she was surprised as anyone at its unending success, but she insisted that "it was not at all a bad play."

Dame Agatha never sought publicity. She remained shy and liked the privacy of her homes in Devon and Berkshire. Yet she never made a fetish of privacy and, once she had agreed to meet someone, showed that she possessed great charm and a happy sense of humour.

It may have started as an advertising gimmick, but the presence of "A Christie for Christmas" was an essential part of the autumn publishing scene. Every year a new work appeared. It was with some alarm that "Curtain: Poirot's Last Case" was received last year.

This was the story that Dame Agatha had written just after the 1939-45 war, describing the death of Hercule Poirot, and had left to be published after her own death.

So as not to disappoint those who waited so faithfully for their "Christie for Christmas" it was issued a couple of months ago. This proved, indeed, to be the herald of Dame Agatha's own final curtain.

No one would claim that she was the most ingenious of plotters; no one would claim she was the best stylist; but quite simply she was the best all-rounder.

The detective story will go on, but no one will ever again occupy the same place that Agatha Christie held in the hearts of her readers.

Highlights of Dame Agatha Christie's celebrated career as a thriller writer. With the Queen at the London premiere in November, 1974, of the film, "Murder on the Orient Express," and (below) at a party with the actress Mary Law after the 1,998th performance of "The Mousetrap," in September 1957, when it became the longest-running straight play in the history of the British theatre.

New York Times
16th October 1964

Cole Porter Is Dead; Songwriter Was 72

By The Associated Press

SANTA MONICA, Calif., Oct. 15 — Cole Porter, the world-famed composer and lyricist died at 11:05 P.M. today at a Santa Monica hospital, where he underwent kidney surgery last Tuesday. He was 72 years old.

Mr. Porter wrote the lyrics and music for his songs, and in both he brought such an individuality of style that a genre known as "the Cole Porter song" became recognized.

The hallmarks of a typical Porter song were lyrics that were urbane or witty and a melody with a sinuous, brooding quality. Some of his best-known songs in this vein were "What Is This Thing Called Love," "Night and Day," "Love for Sale" and "Begin the Beguine."

But an equally typical and equally recognizable Porter song would have a simple, bouncy melody and a lyric based on a long and entertaining list of similarities, opposite or contrasts. "Let's Do It" ticked off the amiable amatory habits of birds, flowers, crustacea, fish, insects, animals and various types of humans, while "You're the Top" was an exercise in the creation of superlatives that included such items as "the nimble tread of the feet of Fred Astaire," "Garbo's salary" and "Mickey Mouse."

Still a third type of Porter song was exclamatory in both lyrics and melody. "Just One of Those Things," "From This Moment On" and "It's All Right With Me" were instances.

Reflected His Living

The glossy opulence of the scores Mr. Porter wrote for Broadway and Hollywood was a valid reflection of his own manner of living. Between World Wars he and his wife, the former Linda Lee of Louisville, Ky., were active in a gay international set that gathered at Paris, the Riviera and Venice.

Their home on the Left Bank in Paris had platinum wallpaper and chairs upholstered in zebra skin. Mr. Porter once hired the entire Monte Carlo Ballet to entertain his house guests. For a party in Venice, where he rented the Palazzo Rezzonico for $4,000 a month, he hired 50 gondoliers to act as footmen and had a troupe of high-rope walkers perform in a blaze of lights.

Most of Mr. Porter's songs were written far from Broadway. His score for "Anything Goes," which included "I Get a Kick Out of You," "You're the Top," "All Through the Night" and the title song, was com-

posed while he was cruising down the Rhine. He wrote the songs for "Jubilee" ("Begin the Beguine," "Just One of Those Things" and "Why Shouldn't I?" among others) during a round-the-world cruise with the show's librettist, Moss Hart.

But Mr. Porter was no dilettante composer. Not even the rigors of his busy social rounds interfered with his creativity.

"I've done lots of work at dinner, sitting between two bores," he once said. "I can feign listening beautifully. I can work anywhere."

Praised by Rodgers

He was a careful craftsman whose work won the admiration of his peers. Richard Rodgers has said, "Few people realize how architecturally excellent his music is. There's a foundation, a structure and an embellishment. Then you add the emotion he's put in and the result is Cole Porter."

Mr. Porter himself could not characterize his songs.

"I don't know how my music gets that way," he said when he was asked to make the effort. "I simply can't analyze it. I can't analyze the music of others. The word for Dick Rodgers's melodies, I think, is holy. For Jerome Kern, sentimental. For Irving Berlin, simplicity. For my own, I don't know."

Mr. Porter was a trim, slight, dark man, groomed in subdued, elegant taste. He usually sported a boutonniere in the lapel of his well-tailored suits. His speech was quiet, reserved, almost clipped.

He was born on a 750-acre farm in Peru, Ind., on June 9, 1892, the son of Samuel Fenwick Porter, a fruit grower, and the former Kate Cole. He could play the violin when he was 6, and the piano when he was 8. At the age of 10 he composed a song, "The Bobolink Waltz," that pleased his mother so much

that she had it published in Chicago.

Despite the boy's musical leanings, his maternal grandfather, J. O. Cole, who had made a fortune in the lumber business, wanted him to be a lawyer. To this ostensible end, young Porter was sent to Worcester Academy in Massachusetts and to Yale, where he wrote two of the most famous of all college songs, "Bingo Eli Yale" and the "Yale Bulldog Song."

He continued his studies at the Harvard Law School but, at the suggestion of the dean, transferred to the School of Music. With a fellow student, T. Lawrason Riggs, he wrote a show, "See America First," which was produced on Broadway in 1916 with a cast that included Clifton Webb. It was a failure. Mr. Porter then joined the French Foreign Legion where he had a specially constructed portable piano made for him so that he could carry it on his back and entertain the troops in their bivouacs.

In 1919 he married Mrs. Linda Lee Thomas, widow of E. R. Thomas, a banker and publisher, and settled in Paris.

Mr. Porter made casual contributions to two revues during the early 1920's, "Hitchy-Koo" and "Greenwich Village Follies of 1924," but he was not induced to write a Broadway score again until 1928, where contributed the songs to "Paris," a play with incidental music that starred Irene Bordoni. Only five of Mr. Porter's songs were used in the final production, but one was the provocatively amusing "Let's Do It."

During the intervening years, he had been writing and performing songs for the amusement of his friends, but the reception accorded "Let's Do It" apparently convinced him that he could communicate pleasurably to a broader audience. As a result, a steady series of Porter show scores and a wide variety of memorable songs followed during the next 15 years.

Among these shows and songs were "Fifty Million Frenchmen" in 1929 ("You Do Something To Me"), "Wake Up and Dream," also 1929 ("What Is This Thing Called Love"); "The New Yorkers" in 1930 ("Love for Sale"); "Gay Divorce" in 1932 with Fred Astaire ("Night and Day"); "Anything Goes" with Ethel Merman, Victor Moore and William Gaxton in 1934 ("You're the Top," "I Get a Kick Out of You"); "Jubilee" in 1935 ("Begin the Beguine," "Just One of Those Things"); "Red, Hot and Blue" with Miss Merman, Jimmy Durante and Bob Hope in 1936 ("It's Delovely," "Down in the Depths on the 6th Floor").

Also, "Leave It to Me" in 1938 in which Mary Martin made her Broadway debut singing "My Heart Belongs to Daddy"; "Dubarry Was a Lady" with Miss Merman and Bert Lahr in 1939 ("Friendship"); "Panama Hattie" with Miss Merman in 1940 ("Make It Another Old Fashioned, Please"); "Let's Face It" in which Danny Kaye sang "Melody in 4F" in 1941; "Something for the Boys" with Miss Merman in 1943 and "Mexican Hayride" with Bobby Clark in 1944.

While Mr. Porter was horseback riding in the summer of 1937, his horse slipped, threw him and fell on top of him, breaking both his legs and damaging his nervous system. One result of Mr. Porter's accident was chronic osteomyelitis, a bone disease. In attempts to alleviate this, he was subjected to more than 30 operations during the next 20 years but, despite this, his right leg had to be amputated in 1958. For the rest of his life, Mr. Porter lived under the constant pressure of pain and, reversing his previously gay social life, became a virtual recluse.

Worked in Wheel Chair

Still he continued to turn out his songs. The score for "Leave It to Me," written shortly after his accident, was composed while he was almost completely bedridden. In order to continue his work, he had his piano placed on blocks so that he could roll up to the keyboard in his wheel chair.

At the end of World War II, Mr. Porter hit what seemed to be a dry period. Two successive shows—"Seven Lively Arts" in 1944 and "Around the World in 80 Days" in 1946—were failures. But in 1948 he came back with his biggest artistic and commercial success, "Kiss Me, Kate," a musical treatment of "The Taming of the Shrew."

In this score, Mr. Porter was not only at his Porterian best with such songs as "Too Darn Hot," "Always True to You in My Fashion" and "So in Love," but he also revealed a remarkable talent for blending the idioms of both Porter and Shakespeare in "I've Come to Wive It Wealthily in Padua," "I Am Ashamed that Women Are So Simple," "I Hate Men" (which Brooks Atkinson called "the perfect musical sublimation of Shakespeare's evil-tempered Kate") and the kind of grammatical challenge that Mr. Porter relished, a song written entirely in the subjunctive, "Were Thine That Special Face."

Other Musicals

Mr. Porter's later Broadway scores included "Out of This World" (1950), "Can-Can" (1953) and "Silk Stockings" (1955).

For films he wrote "I've Got You Under My Skin" and "Easy to Love" for "Born to Dance" in 1936; "Rosalie" and "In the Still of the Night" for "Rosalie" in 1937; "I Concentrate on You" for "Broadway Melody" in 1940 and "You'd Be So Nice to Come Home To" for "Something to Shout About" in 1943.

Mr. Porter's wife died in 1954. During his last years he lived in a nine-room, memorabilia-filled apartment in the Waldorf Towers. On weekends he was driven to a 350-acre estate in the Berkshires and in the summers he lived in California.

He rarely saw anyone except intimate friends. A 90-minute television program honoring him was presented in 1960, and a party celebrating his 70th birthday was given in 1962, but he was unwilling to attend either event. When Yale University wished to confer an honorary degree of Doctor of Humane Letters on him in 1960, Mr. Porter accepted on condition that the presentation be made in his apartment.

Daily Telegraph
22nd April 1912

DEATH OF
MR. BRAM STOKER.

SIR H. IRVING'S MANAGER.

We regret to announce the death of Mr. Bram Stoker, which occurred on Saturday evening, at his residence in St. George's-square, after a long illness. He was 65 years of age.

Mr. Bram Stoker was well known by reason of his long association with Sir Henry Irving, as acting manager of the Lyceum Theatre, and by his remarkable novels. But his career contained many other activities which, had he pursued them, might have brought him fame. His versatility is indicated by the fact that, as a student at Trinity College, Dublin, where he entered in 1866, he took honours in pure mathematics, was president of the Philosophical Society, auditor of the Historical Society, and athletic champion of the University. From his great height and fine physique it was not difficult to infer his capacity for athletic distinction.

His father was the late Mr. Abraham Stoker, who held a position in the Chief Secretary's Office, Dublin Castle, and in the case of the son the baptismal name became abbreviated into the strangely-sounding syllable "Bram." It appears that the you man's professional career began in his University days, for in 1866 he entered the Irish Civil Service as Registrar of the Petty Sessions Clerk's Department of the Chief Secretary's office. He became Inspector of Petty Sessions in 1877, and retired from the service in the following year. At the University he had won silver medals in history and composition, and as a Civil servant he found time to practise his literary talent. To various newspapers he acted as literary, art, and dramatic critic, and he even contrived to combine public duties with the editing of an evening newspaper.

THE MEETING WITH IRVING

It was in 1878 that he quitted Ireland and became manager for Henry Irving, whom he had already met and written about when the great actor was appearing in Dublin. Their first meeting was in 1876, when Stoker was in his 30th year. He was so impressed by hearing Irving recite that, strong man as he was, he fell into a condition approaching hysteria. A great friendship was struck between the two men and lasted until Irving's death nearly thirty years later. Having completed his book on "The Duties of Petty Sessions Clerks," having served long enough in the Civil Service to be qualified for a pension in case of retirement from ill-health, and having in this eventful year also married Florence Anne Lemon, daughter of the late Lieut.-Colonel Balcombe, Bram Stoker joined Irving in December at Birmingham. One of the heaviest of his new duties was the correspondence. From the first day of his association with the famous actor until the latter's death Stoker seldom wrote less than fifty letters a day, and during the whole period he estimated that he wrote in Irving's name letters not far short of half a million. When they arrived in London Stoker found his toil and anxieties greatly increased. The Lyceum, which was to be opened, was in a state of chaos—a mass of poles and platforms within and without. But "Hamlet" was being hurried on. Irving was beginning his management practically without capital, and that was an added source of embarrassment.

On the second night of the performance of "Hamlet" the Chinese Ambassador and Sir Halliday Macartney came to see Irving in his dressing-room, and presently the Ambassador, who was, Stoker narrated, wearing magnificent robes of Mandarin yellow, wandered off in the direction of the stage. He was close to the edge of the arch at the back of the scene, where Ophelia had made her entrance and would make her exit. Stoker jumped for him, and just succeeded in catching him before he had passed into the blaze of the limelight. I could fancy the sudden amazement of the audience and the wild roar of laughter that would follow when, in the midst of this most sad and pathetic of scenes, would enter unheralded this gorgeous anachronism." Stoker confessed that he was tempted to let the splendid accident occur. "Its unique grotesqueness would have ensured a widespread publicity not to be acquired by ordinary forms of advertisement." But it would have been rather hard on Ophelia, who was no one less than Ellen Terry. On another occasion a very different and very painful contretemps actually did occur. The actor who took the part of Polonius on entering gave his first line with so strange an intonation that Irving at once signed to the prompter to let fall the act-drop, came forward and apologised to the audience, and restarted the play from the beginning of the Act 1, scene 3—with a new Polonius.

"WITHOUT THE PRINCE."

Stoker's affection for Irving may be gathered from a little entry in his diary for March 27 of 1879, when Irving, having a serious cold, was unable to play:

Stage very dismal. Ellen Terry met me in the passage, and began to cry. I felt very like joining her.

One of Stoker's manifold duties was to supervise the production of scenery for new pieces, and the late Hawes Craven, one of the most famous exponents of the intricate art of scene-painting, who did much work for Irving, was one of his intimates. It happened in 1887-8 that Irving, then about to leave for America, arranged for the production of "Faust" on his return, and commissioned Keeley Halswelle to make the designs for the scenery. The great paint-rooms of Covent-garden Opera House were engaged for the painter's use. Questions as to his progress bore no fruit, and at last Stoker paid a visit of inspection. "To my surprise and horror, I found the acres of white untouched even to the extent of a charcoal outline. The superb painter of pictures, untutored in stage art and perspective, had found himself powerless before those solitudes."

AUTHOR OF "DRACULA."

During his career as Irving's manager, Bram Stoker continued his literary pursuits, and was also called to the Bar at the Inner Temple. The best-known and strangest of all his books was the novel "Dracula," which he published in 1897. Written largely in the form of letters, this story achieved a triumph in the bizarre. Its author had a genius for the extreme of improbability, to which he lent an air of weird fascination that gave some of his books the atmosphere of a dream, or rather of a nightmare. He delighted in introducing into human drama such dubious but terrible creatures of imagination as vampires and human snakes. He also produced another type of fiction in which the supernatural played no part. Of this kind was his successful novel "The Man," a story of the sea. All his stories were essentially original. In 1906 and 1907 he issued his "Personal Reminiscences of Henry Irving," and had since that date produced several novels. A man of extremely genial nature and of wide experience and travel, he had hosts of friends, and was always a welcome speaker at public dinners, where drama, literature, or any other of the many topics in which he interested himself were under discussion.

Daily Telegraph
12ᵗʰ March 1973

Noel Coward, master craftsman of theatre

DURING the latter part of his career, it became a habit with some people to speak of Sir Noel Coward, who has died, aged 73, as "The Master."

The appellation carried a curious mixture of faint irony and genuine admiration.

It also conveyed perhaps a slight amusement that one who had started as an *enfant terrible* and continued as a young rebel should have become at last a pillar of the theatrical establishment.

However the title was earned, nobody could have deserved it better. Coward was indeed a master craftsman in almost every department of the theatre.

As actor, dramatist, composer, director, his eye was sure and his hand steady; and if his singing voice was nothing to boast about, nobody could have used it more skilfully to put over those songs of his, whether explaining how none but mad dogs and Englishmen went out in the midday sun or adjuring Mrs. Worthington not to put her daughter on the stage.

Natural talent

This all-round expertise had its roots, of course, in natural talent; but its extremely early efflorescence can be put down with some certainty to his stage training as a child, especially at the hands of Italia Conti.

He was a professional actor at the age of 11, and by the time he acted in his own first play, "I'll Leave it to You" (New Theatre, July, 1920) he already had a considerable and varied experience.

In September he was at the Duke of York's in a popular revue, "London Calling," of which he was part-author besides composing the music.

This ran nearly a year and in the autumn of 1924 he scored a resounding success both as actor and as author in "The Vortex," which was staged first at the Everyman in Hampstead and was removed to the Royalty, where it ran for 224 performances.

He then went with the play to New York and saw it succeed again.

It was in 1923 that he began to make his real mark as an all-round man of the theatre.

In February of that year he appeared at the Savoy in his own play, "The Young Idea," which he described as a comedy of youth, and which was intended as (and quite successfully was) a rude gesture in the faces of the conventional-minded stuffies.

Sir Noel Coward, who died at his home in Jamaica yesterday. He was 73.

More harm

He was still not quite 25 when "The Vortex" was staged in London, and it is possible to argue that its success did him more harm than good.

It was a highly emotional piece, and his first attempt at anything more ambitious than light entertainment. If it had failed, he might have put off any further attempts to make a name as a serious dramatist until later on, when he had gained a wider experience of life outside the over-sophisticated world of the theatre and the entertainment world generally.

As things were, he was tempted to try to repeat the success of "The Vortex" with similar pieces less happily conceived, and the outcome was a number of plays in which the writing was serious but the characters were essentially trivial.

Coward had to endure the galling experience that while his light pieces such as "Hay Fever" (1925) continued to be received with acclaim, his weightier work met with little respect from critics or public.

This phase of Coward's career was brought to a climax when, in 1926, the Censor banned the most seriously-intended of all his plays, "This Was a Man."

Coward uttered a scream of youthful indignation (matched almost exactly, many years later in a similar situation, by John Osborne), declaring his intention of shaking from his feet the dust of an unappreciative London, and writing in future for a more liberal-minded New York.

This threat fell rather flat when New York, having seen "This Was a Man" staged, decided that the solemnity of the approach was not justified by the flimsiness of the material.

It seems probable that Coward, maturing as he neared his thirties, came to realise that there had been something wrong with his social values.

At any rate, from that time onwards, there was no more striving after achievements outside his range, no more mistaking tinsel for something precious.

New confidence

"Bitter Sweet" in 1929 "Private Lives" in 1930, and "Cavalcade" in 1931 all bore witness to a newly justified confidence in his own powers.

How great, and how well justified, this confidence was can be judged from an incident in the casting of "Private Lives." Coward himself and Gertrude Lawrence were to play the chief parts, of a divorced couple who, meeting again by chance, abandoned their new partners and went off together, quarrelling happily.

He offered the part of the other man to Laurence Olivier, who had had the frustrating experience of a run of good parts in plays which failed. Olivier thought the character a dull one and refused it: but Coward swept the refusal aside.

"Look, young man," he said firmly. "You'd better be in a success for a change."

This was not said arrogantly. One of the strongest strands in Coward's character was his ability to remain unspoiled by success. "The bigger he gets, the nicer he is," a close friend said of him once.

The remark to Olivier was made as a piece of friendly and practical advice, and in the outcome it proved sage and timely.

"Private Lives" succeeded completely in both London and New York, and it changed Olivier's luck for him.

His variety

Happiness, they say, has no history; and the same is true of continuous and predictable success such as Coward was now enjoying. A mere catalogue of his achievements during the 'thirties and World War Two would make dull reading; it is the variety of those achievements that makes them interesting.

In "Bitter Sweet" he brought originality and style into the convention-ridden field of the British musical play.

In "Design for Living" (1932) he returned to his sophisticated high-comedy style, incidentally demonstrating his increasing concern with America by setting the piece in New York.

In "Conversation Piece" (1934) he was all period elegance and in "Tonight at 8.30" (written in 1935 but not seen in London till January, 1936) he showed a remarkable increase of range.

Some of the nine one-act plays in which he and Gertrude Lawrence enjoyed a triumph which they were to repeat in New York at the end of the same year showed an understanding of and sympathy for simple people which had been absent from his work hitherto, though there had been an approach to it in "Cavalcade."

"Blithe Spirit"

With the outbreak of the 1939-45 war all theatres in Britain were closed, and Coward worked in Paris on propaganda for the Allies until the fall of France. Later he visited various fronts, doing valuable work entertaining the troops.

When, in 1941, the German air attacks had been contained to the point which allowed London theatres to function again, he wrote "Blithe Spirit" in a matter of a few days.

It was presented at the Piccadilly, in July, 1941, and nobody who was at its first performance is likely to forget the exhilaration that the occasion gave to its war-battered audience. It had a record-breaking run of 1,997 performances.

Coward followed this up in 1942 with "Present Laughter" and "This Happy Breed," and then, in 1943, broke yet one more kind of new ground with a film, "In Which We Serve," a fine and dignified tribute to the Royal Navy.

Signs of staleness

In the after-war period, Coward's powers as a dramatist began to show slight signs of staleness. He was still greatly successful by most people's standards, but not by his own.

A big musical, "Pacific, 1860," failed at Drury Lane in 1946, and of his next batch of plays only "Relative Values" (1951) had a really long run.

Such small signs of decline gave the young writers of the "new wave" of dramatists, when they arrived later in the 50's, an excuse to treat him as a spent force.

As an actor, Coward now rarely appeared except in his own pieces; but in 1953 he gave his versatility yet another airing by acting King Magnus in a revival of Shaw's "The Apple Cart."

Coward's real genius was for more intimate playing; as a cabaret entertainer in America he is said to have commanded a salary equivalent to £13,000 a week.

Proofs that he was still a more formidable dramatist than the young men thought. "Nude with Violin" (1957) was not a negligible production, neither was "Waiting in the Wings" (1960), which was his 50th play.

Several of his light comedies—"Private Lives," "Present Laughter," "Hay Fever"—had popular revivals; and the last-named was particularly gratifying. Presented at the National Theatre, it was acclaimed with delight, was found to have lost hardly anything of its gaiety or point, and took rank as a minor classic.

That Noël Coward was a great man of the theatre there can be no doubt at all. One looks in vain for a match to his versatility in all our stage's history.

As a literary man he did not stand so high. His work always seemed to lose point when printed.

Lodging house

His life was lived so much in the public eye that his early years of obscurity seem hardly relevant.

He was born in comparatively humble circumstances at Teddington, his parents being Arthur Coward and his wife Violet (née Veitch).

One of the endearing points in his character was the fact that in the first years of triumph he still kept on his rooms in a lodging-house in Ebury Street run by his father. Later he went to live in Bermuda then Montreux, Switzerland, and Jamaica. He never married.

A knighthood was conferred on Coward in the 1970 New Year Honours. His 70th birthday had been marked by an extensive presentation of his works on BBC television.

Time Magazine
3rd April 1978

When Karl Wallenda was a boy in Germany, the story goes, he answered an ad asking for someone who could do a handstand. The ad did not say just where the handstand was to be done.

The prospective employer, a circus performer named Louis Weitzman, agreed to try the boy out. He led him up a ladder to a platform 40 ft. in the air. "Just walk behind me," said Weitzman as he started out on the high wire, "and when I bend a little, you get up and do a handstand on my shoulders."

Karl Wallenda looked down.

"I can't," he said.

"You do it," said Weitzman, "or I'll shake you off the wire."

So Karl Wallenda did a handstand on Weitzman's shoulders. So Karl Wallenda became a high-wire stunt man. Probably it was in his blood all along. His father was a catcher in a wandering troupe of aerialists; his mother performed with the troupe too. But when Wallenda first began performing his own high-wire act, he soon showed the daring that was to make him the greatest of his strange breed. He not only walked the wire but rode a bicycle on it—with his brother Herman on his shoulders. He invented an act that had never before been performed, the pyramid—Karl and Herman and another man all teetering across the slender cable. The act premiered in Milan in 1925 and proved a sensation. John Ringling hired Wallenda to bring the act to New York City, and there the first performance won a 15-minute ovation.

There were no safety nets underneath: Karl Wallenda did not believe in them. "*Gott* give us the courage and gift of talent to do our acts," he once told an interviewer, "and when he be ready to take us, he will."

In 1947 Wallenda devised a more complicated form of his pyramid—seven people in three tiers, six men connected by shoulder bars and one young woman perched on top on a chair, all swaying at the edge of the void, preserved only by their incredible combination of skill, balance and courage. Old Karl billed them as "the Great Wallendas," and he did his best to keep the act in the family.

Dieter Schepp, a nephew recently arrived from East Germany, was making his first appearance in the great pyramid in Detroit on the night of Jan. 30, 1962, when he suddenly began losing his grip on the balance pole. There came a terrible cry: "*Ich kann nicht mehr halten*" (I can't hold on any more). Then the pole slipped, Dieter fell, and the whole pyramid of Wallendas came apart in mid-air, some clinging to the wire, others plunging to the concrete floor. Dieter and another man died there; Karl's adopted son Mario was paralyzed from the waist down.

Karl Wallenda, the patriarch, would not give up. "It is our pride," he said. "I feel better if I go up again. Down here on the ground I break all to pieces." Some of his partners were less determined. "I'm scared silly every time I go on," said Gunther Wallenda, a nephew. Karl's second wife Helen, who once performed in the act, refused even to watch it any longer. "I always sit in a back room and pray," she said. Wallenda was adamant. "The rest of life," he said, "is just time to fill in between doing the act."

"The wind is my worst enemy," Wallenda once said of his outdoor performances. Last week, as he prepared to walk a wire strung 300 ft. between two beachfront hotels in San Juan, P.R., he was warned that the winds blowing in off the sea were tricky. There was a steady breeze of 12 m.p.h., but with gusts up to 23 m.p.h.

"Don't worry about it," said Karl as he checked the wire at the tenth-floor window, some 100 ft. above the sidewalk. "The wind is stronger on the street than up here."

Karl Wallenda was 73 by now, but still strong, hard-muscled, his eyes a bright blue, his gray hair tufted around his ears. He had said he would make the walk, and so he would. There were 200 people watching. Among them was his granddaughter Rietta, 17, the only relative then performing in his act.

Wallenda had no sooner started than a gust of wind made the cable vibrate. Wallenda stopped, steadied himself. A hush fell over the crowd.

He started again, crossed a little more than halfway. The cable began to sway. Wallenda leaned forward to keep his balance. One young member of his troupe, waiting on the roof at the far end of the wire, warned him to crouch down for better balance.

"Sit down, Poppy, sit down!" the youth cried.

Wallenda started to crouch. A gust of wind suddenly jarred him. Then, as the horrified crowd watched, he started to fall, very slowly at first. He reached out for the cable with one hand, but he was still holding the balancing bar and could not get a grip on the cable. Down he went, still holding onto the pole. Ten stories below, he landed on the roof of a taxi and bounced off onto the sidewalk. At the hospital, he was pronounced dead of massive internal injuries.

Five hours later, two of the old man's protégés joined Rietta Wallenda in doing the high-wire act under the big top in San Juan. The crowd gave her a standing ovation. She bowed and smiled. Tears streamed down her cheeks.

"Sit Down, Poppy, Sit Down!"

A last warning before Karl Wallenda fell to his death

**Karl Wallenda crouches in wind; tries to grip
the cable; falls past the cable; hurtles toward
ground, still clutching balancing pole**

The Daily Telegraph
8th July 1930

SHERLOCK HOLMES'S CREATOR

CONAN DOYLE'S VARIED CAREER

NOVELIST WHO BEGAN AS DOCTOR

CATHOLIC, AGNOSTIC AND SPIRITUALIST

By the Late T. P. O'CONNOR

Sir Arthur Conan Doyle (whose death is reported on another page) was famous as the creator of Sherlock Holmes, one of the few living and permanent figures in the gallery of detective fiction.

Trained for the medical profession, Sir Arthur was in turn writer of fiction, war correspondent, playwright, historian of the South African campaign, and the sturdy champion of England in the Great War, a Roman Catholic who turned agnostic and afterwards became a strenuous advocate of spiritualism, and the man who did more than anyone to secure the release, after eighteen years' imprisonment, of Oscar Slater, who had been sentenced to death for the murder of a woman in Glasgow.

He came of Irish stock, his uncle being "Dicky" Doyle, the famous artist of *Punch.* His father was a public official in Edinburgh, where Conan Doyle was born on May 22, 1859. The family being strictly Roman Catholic, young Doyle was sent to Stonyhurst, and then came a year in Germany, and five years as a medical student in Edinburgh. During those student days his real education as a man of letters began, by studying the characters of some of the remarkable men who were professors in the medical school. One of them, Dr. Rutherford, stood for Professor Challenger; another, Dr. Joseph Bell, was the original of Sherlock Holmes.

Bell had a wonderful power of diagnosis of ailments and character.

"Well, my man, you've served in the Army?" he said to a civilian patient. "Aye, sir." "Not long discharged?" "No, sir." "A Highland regiment?" "Aye, sir." "A non-com. officer?" "Aye, sir." "Stationed at Barbados?" "Aye, sir."

"You see, gentlemen," he would explain, "the man was a respectful man, but did not remove his hat. They do not in the Army, but he would have learned civilian ways had he been long discharged. He has an air of authority, and he is obviously Scottish. As to Barbados, his complaint is elephantiasis, which is West Indian, and not British."

EARLY LITERARY EFFORTS

Conan Doyle had not long been in the medical school before the literary ferment was working in him; his allowance for his lunch was two pence, the price of a mutton pie; he often spent the two pence at a second-hand bookstall, and went fasting. A friend who had been impressed by the vividness of style in Doyle's letters to him, suggested that he had a talent for writing, and under this encouragement Doyle wrote his first published tale, which was accepted by *Chamber's Journal,* and brought a fee of three guineas.

He got the post of medical man on a small vessel trading to West Africa, and had many wanderings and adventures. He fell a victim to a fever that nearly killed him. On his return he definitely started his career as a medical man at Southsea. He had only £10 as capital; he was a complete stranger. He had to pick up bits of furniture so as to make at least one room presentable for the patients who might come; he cleaned up his own plate and did, in short, all the domestic work of a servant. He kept his small allowance of food in a trunk; and the trunk also had to serve as his dining table; and he did his own cooking on a gas stove.

Doyle seemed in danger of settling down to the sedate and uninteresting life as a family doctor when literature began at last to hold out some brighter prospects. James Payn accepted a story for the "Cornhill," and gave him a fee of £30. Doyle also stormed the impregnable fortress of "Blackwood." But he felt that he was not getting "forrader," and that until he had produced a book he could not hope for large recognition. He was not quite satisfied with the marvellous M. Dupin, the greatest detective in Gaboriau. He thought the type of detective in fiction could be improved on, **and then he bethought himself of Dr. Bell,** who became Sherlock Holmes. And so began the now famous stories.

While Doyle was awaiting the publication of the first "Sherlock Holmes" book he spent much time and labour on a historical novel, which tried to reproduce the Puritans of the Cromwellian period. It was rejected by several publishers, but Andrew Lang finally got it taken by Longmans. Then he wrote his two historical novels, "The White Company" and "Sir Nigel," both dealing with English history of the period of Edward III. In after years Sir Arthur said that these two books, in his personal judgment, constituted his best literary work.

MEDICINE ABANDONED

In spite of these successes, and being, as he insisted, always a man of simple tastes and small wants, he might, in spite of growing success as a man of letters, have remained in Southsea but for a family incident —the threat of consumption to a little daughter. Koch had just been announced as the discoverer of a new and certain cure for consumption.

Acquaintance with Sir Malcolm Morris, the celebrated surgeon, helped to mature the germ already in Doyle's mind of trying his chances in London. Acting on the advice of Morris, he resolved to become an eye specialist, and went to Vienna to get intensive training. He took rooms in Montagu-street, and waited there for hours every day for patients who did not come; which in the end helped, for these idle hours gave him the opportunity of writing. It was thus he began the series of short stories in which Sherlock Holmes was the chief figure. While he was starting on this new departure, a fit of influenza threw him back on himself; and then, with a feeling of exultation, he made the big refusal, threw physic to the dogs, and started as a writer pure and simple. From this time forward he lived entirely by his pen.

BOXING ADEPT

A great misfortune fell upon him in the illness of his wife, which was diagnosed as consumption. He devoted years to her relief. Shut up with her in the solitude of Davos, he was enabled to devote himself entirely to literary work, and there began the "Brigadier Gerard" series. On his return from a lecture visit to America, he went to Egypt, where he became a war correspondent with the Expedition to the Soudan. He made the acquaintance of Kitchener, but turned back before the final advance to Khartoum. Returning to his literary work, Doyle found his next theme in a study of the big prize-fighters of the past; it was then he wrote "Rodney Stone" —one of his most popular works and one of his best written.

In most that he attempted Doyle succeeded, but one ambition eluded him—a seat in the House of Commons. He fought Central Edinburgh as a Liberal Unionist, and then Hawick Burghs as a Tariff Reformer, but in neither case was he successful.

No sketch of Doyle would be complete which did not mention his great love of sport, including riding, shooting, ski-ing, and boxing. At boxing he was something of an adept, always ready for a bout in gloves with a friend; once, indeed, he fought another man while they were both in evening dress after a party where they had both been guests. One of the offers which amused him was from an American newspaper which cabled him to come over and describe the fight between Jeffries and Johnson. His knowledge of prize-fighting and of boxing generally proved to be very useful; it accounts for the simplicity and the strength of the boxing scenes in "Rodney Stone"; the best descriptions of such feats since the days of George Borrow.

The last phase in the life and adventures of Doyle must be dealt with very summarily. His religious creeds indeed showed throughout his life a curious mutability; for, beginning as a Roman Catholic, he went on to agnosticism, and ultimately turned to spiritualism.

EDALJI CASE

Mention has been made of the efforts of Sir Arthur to secure the release of Oscar Slater. Another convicted man whose cause he championed was G. E. T. Edalji, the Parsee, who in October, 1903, was sentenced to seven years' penal servitude for cattle maiming. Sir Arthur became convinced that there had been a miscarriage of justice, and he devoted the powerful advocacy of his pen to securing a reversal of the sentence. In January, 1907, THE DAILY TELEGRAPH published an article in which Sir Arthur gave the results of his investigations into the case, and it was largely as a consequence of his efforts that at the end of three years' confinement, Edalji was released and pardoned.

Sir Arthur also took part in the agitation which resulted in the release of Adolph Beck.

Such, then, was Conan Doyle—a manly man, a tender man, a little rough-hewn in mind and in body; the inventor of a being almost as popular as Robinson Crusoe, and the author of much innocent delight to his generation and perhaps of generations to come.

Sir Arthur was twice married—first to Louise, daughter of Mr. J. Hawkins, of Minsterworth, and secondly to Jean, daughter of Mr. J. B. Leckie.

Reproduced above is a facsimile of the last letter written by Sir Arthur Conan Doyle, which was published yesterday in the correspondence columns of THE DAILY TELEGRAPH.

Continued

The Times
8th July 1930

SIR ARTHUR CONAN DOYLE

THE CREATOR OF "SHERLOCK HOLMES"

Sir Arthur Conan Doyle, novelist, patriot, and in his later years ardent spiritualist, whose death in his seventy-second year we announce this morning, came of a family well known in the world of art and humour. His grandfather was John Doyle, the portrait painter and lithographer, who, under the signature of "H. B.," produced the still well-remembered caricatures of the Duke of Wellington and other great men of his day. Of the sons of John Doyle one was the yet more famous Richard ("Dicky") Doyle, who designed "the best known picture in the world," the present cover of *Punch*, and worked much for that journal until his religious convictions—the family being Irish and Roman Catholic—compelled him to sever his connexion with a paper that attacked the Pope. Another son was Charles Doyle, also an artist, who settled in Edinburgh.

Arthur Conan Doyle was the eldest son, born on May 22, 1859, of this Charles Doyle. He received his education at Stonyhurst and at Edinburgh University, and adopted the profession of medicine, practising at Southsea from 1882 to 1890. Though it is not to medicine that he owed his fame, his knowledge and experience were of service to him in more than one way. He introduced the subject again and again into his novels, and not only into the specifically medical stories, such as "Round the Red Lamp"; and, always patriotic and keenly interested in the work and fortunes of the British Empire, he put himself at the disposal of his country during the South African War and served as senior physician to the field hospital equipped and maintained by Sir (then Mr.) John Langman.

One result of this experience was an important pamphlet (following a book on "The Great Boer War") entitled "The Cause and Conduct of the War," which was translated into 12 European languages, and given away by thousands. The object of the pamphlet was to put the facts of the case fairly and temperately before the peoples of Europe, and to disabuse them of some, at least, of the erroneous ideas that had been industriously spread on the subject of our political morality and our methods of warfare. It was doubtless in recognition of these services, no less than of those he rendered in fiction, that in 1902 he received the honour of knighthood. His public career also included two unsuccessful contests for a seat in Parliament, the first for Central Edinburgh in the Liberal Unionist interest in 1900, the second for the Hawick Burghs as a Tariff Reformer in 1906.

It is, however, as a writer of fiction that Sir Arthur Conan Doyle was most widely known. The stories which his name brings instantaneously to the mind are those of which Sherlock Holmes is the central figure. The personality of the eccentric amateur detective—with his fiddle, his dressing-gown, his strong tobacco, his courage and resource, and his genius for the unravelling of mysteries which no mere professional detective could hope to possess—was well fitted to catch the popular imagination. And his creator made use of him with an ingenuity which was none the less remarkable because he knew each secret to start with, and worked backwards from it. And it cannot have been wholly by luck or accident (though it may have been by inspiration) that the character of Holmes's friend, Dr. Watson, has become no less famous and even more beloved than Holmes himself. Besides this remarkable success in rejuvenating detective fiction to the great advantage of his successors, Conan Doyle achieved sterling results in the long list of historical romances that sprang from his fertile brain, from 1887, when he published his first book, "A Study in Scarlet," for some half a century onward. The tales of the Napoleonic era concerning Brigadier Gerard; "Micah Clarke," "The White Company," "Sir Nigel"—these and others are still popular, and deserve to be. But none of them, nothing else that Doyle ever wrote, equals "Rodney Stone," which contains, incidentally, the best exposition of the author's passion for pugilism.

His work for the stage was less successful than his books. Only one of his plays achieved a great vogue: the little *Story of Waterloo*, which provided Sir Henry Irving with one of his favourite and most effective characters, that of the very old soldier, Corporal Gregory Brewster.

In his later years Sir Arthur Conan Doyle gave himself up more and more to the enthusiasms which his quick sympathies aroused in a generous nature. These included Home Rule for Ireland, prison reform, divorce, and especially spiritualism. Always fond of travelling, he visited Australia in 1921 and South Africa when he was 70, in the interests of the beliefs to which he had been converted from the sheer materialism of his early manhood. He wrote a history of spiritualism; and his views on the evidence for it and on evidence in general coloured much of his later fiction. Among his many exploits in defence of what he believed to be truth and justice was his long and finally successful struggle for the release of Oscar Slater. In this he showed himself as keen and generous a sportsman as he did in the hunting-field (it took a weight-carrier to bear the massive frame of him), on the cricket-field, on the golf links, and in all the relations of life.

Doyle was twice married, first to Miss Louisa Hawkins, of Minsterworth, Gloucestershire, who died in 1906; and secondly, to Jean, daughter of Mr. J. B. Leckie, of Crowborough.

New York Times
21st September 1889

WILKIE COLLINS.

Every one who has felt his flesh creep over that fat villain Count Fosco and his white mice will be sorry to learn that WILKIE COLLINS is dead. While "Blind Love" is running in the *Illustrated London News* its versatile author has succumbed to a second attack of the acute malady which formerly beset him. His great successes were made so long ago that many people thought of him as passed away with THACKERAY and DICKENS until the news of his sickness recalled his existence or some announcement caught the eye which showed that notwithstanding his sixty-odd years there was no end to the resources of his ingenuity. Yet COLLINS was a contemporary of DICKENS and ANTHONY TROLLOPE and stood in intimate literary relations with the former in the editing of *Household Words* and *All the Year Round*. He suffered somewhat from overshadowing, but his methods were so different from those of DICKENS and his books were so strongly popular that he established a following of his own and pursued his way independent of his greater comrade.

WILKIE COLLINS was in some respects a British ALEXANDRE DUMAS. He gave great attention to the plot, as a general thing, and was not so much careless as perhaps naturally deficient in filling up the skeleton in such a way as to produce the best results. As a rule, his novels are well knit and hang together; the reader is led on by curiosity, even if he be fastidious enough to shake his head at the style, which is too apt to be dry and thin, giving to the characters an unnatural air of self-assertion and consciousness. He did not form himself on DICKENS, although there are points of resemblance between the two which are the result of similar sides to their natures and similar environment. It was rather France whose novelists suggested to COLLINS the popularity of a good strong plot, the outcome of which should be concealed from the reader and his attention gradually wrought up to the catastrophe. "The Woman in White" (1859) is the best-known novel of this kind, though "The Moonstone" (1868) was almost equally popular, and "Man and Wife" (1870) more satisfactory to critical readers. "The Moonstone" will be remembered as bringing in a good deal of the occult lore of India, which at the time had not been so much written about in English, and was particularly fresh for novels.

Notwithstanding his prolific pen, we must rank WILKIE COLLINS below CHARLES READE as an artist in novel writing, and in some respects, quiet humor for instance, hardly on the level of TROLLOPE. He has a certain relationship with Miss BRADDON in the somewhat hard sensationalism of his novels. An author who paid so much attention to the structure of his plot was easily persuaded to attempt the stage, and his success was far beyond that of ordinary novelists who attempt to adapt their work for the boards. A short story called "The Frozen Deep," which may be remembered in the readings WILKIE COLLINS gave during his visit to the United States in 1873, was placed on the stage, and then came the turn of the most popular of his novels. "The New Magdalen," a novel with a purpose after the way of DICKENS and READE, was unexpectedly successful when dramatized, and it is not out of the reckoning that it should hold the stage still.

Though the great popularity of WILKIE COLLINS declined about fifteen years ago, he must be still very widely read, for the HARPERS' edition of seventeen volumes, illustrated, is a permanent feature of the advertising lists, not to speak of the unauthorized reprints about the country. While some readers have somewhat wearied, then, of the mysteries and ingenious detective plots of WILKIE COLLINS, there must be a steady demand for his romances from those who are less exacting as to the quality of the light literature they consume. Personally he was an attractive character, and had warm friends. His round, ruddy face, with beard and spectacles, and his slight, round-shouldered figure, gave him a somewhat professional look when in this country last. He read selections from his own works well, and made an excellent impression. Those who only saw and heard him recite will join his friends in regrets for his death at an age when many writers of England and America are still vigorous.

New York Times
2nd December 1947

ALEISTER CROWLEY

LONDON, Dec. 1 (Reuters)— Edward Alexander Crowley, better known as Aleister Crowley, author and poet, who was an alleged practitioner of "black magic" and blood sacrifice, died today in Hastings at the age of 72.

The Times
9th October 1922

DEATH OF MARIE LLOYD.

A GREAT COMEDIENNE.

We regret to announce the death of Miss Marie Lloyd, the famous variety actress and singer, which occurred early on Saturday morning at her residence at Golders Green. In her the public loses, not only a vivid personality whose range and extremely broad humour as a character actress were extraordinary, but also one of the few remaining links with the old music-hall stage of the last century.

Mr. Leon Pollock, the manager of the Edmonton Empire, thus describes her last appearance on any stage:—" This was on Tuesday last at the second house here. She gave her first performance almost as brightly as of old, although it was obvious she was not very well. I was called to her dressing room afterwards and found that she was very ill indeed. A doctor was sent for and he very strongly advised her not to go on a second time. 'You ought to go home immediately,' he said, but Marie would not listen to him, and when she went on she could hardly stand. Throughout the hall none of the audience thought that she was ill. It was the *Pagliacci* business again. Herself and myself alone knew the tragedy that was being enacted. Her last song was 'A Ruin that Cromwell knocked about a bit,' in which she had to imitate the staggerings and clumsy buffonery of a drunken woman. Her weakness was mistaken by the audience for fine comic acting, and they shrieked with laughter as she fell." She had had a serious illness some time ago, but recovered sufficiently to appear at the Alhambra last month. The audience on that occasion were extraordinarily enthusiastic. Repeatedly they "called" and she made a brief speech of thanks. She was due to return to the Alhambra on October 16.

Born in 1870, the daughter of John Wood and his wife Matilda (Archer), she made her first appearance, under the name of Bella Delmere, at the Eagle Music Hall, on May 9, 1885. Six weeks later she sang under her own name at the same hall. The music-halls of the East End—the old Falstaff, Old-street, Belmont's Sebright, and the Star, Bermondsey—were a valuable experience for her, and led the way to the Bedford and the Middlesex, Drury-lane. It was at the latter hall—the site of which is now covered by the Winter Garden Theatre—that she made her first step in that popularity which never deserted her, with "The Boy that I love sits up in the Gallery." Her next engagement was at the Oxford, where she was in the bill for twelve consecutive months. Tours in the provinces, in the United States, South Africa, and Australia preceded an engagement as "principal girl" at Drury Lane, in the pantomime of *Humpty Dumpty*, in 1891. In the two following seasons at "Old Drury" she appeared in *Little Bo-Peep* and *Robinson Crusoe*. In 1898 she went on tour in a musical play, *The A.B.C., or Flossie the Frivolous*, written for her by Mr. H. Chance Newton. Of the fifty songs which were, at one time or another, immense favourites with her public, "Everything in the garden's lovely," "Oh, Mr. Porter, what shall I do?" "Then you wink the other eye," and "Tiddley-om-Pom," are perhaps the best remembered.

It is a great tribute to her powers that she maintained her popularity to the end, being indeed "booked up" for some years ahead. But she did not presume on her fame, for she was a very hard worker, always studying touches from real life wherewith to build up her inimitable impersonations. Her rewards were considerable : for a long time she made from £250 to £300 a week, and when she appeared on "sharing terms" she drew as much as £800. But her generosity, both public and private, was open-handed. To the Variety Artistes' Benevolent Fund she was a constant donor, as well as to other charities of the profession ; she was also ever ready to appear in the cause of charity. Her private beneficence to the less fortunate members of the profession was equally generous. It is also remembered that in the music-hall strike of 1907 she came out with the others and worked with success as a "picket." She was married three times, first to Percy Courtney, then to Alec Hurley, the singer of coster songs, who died in 1913, and lastly to Bernard Dillon, the jockey. In 1908, annoyed at some misstatements which had appeared about her, she issued the following characteristic advertisement :—

MISS MARIE LLOYD.
NOTICE TO ALL.
Miss Marie Lloyd has ONE Daughter—and she is NOT on the Stage.

In answer to all enquiries :—
Marie Lloyd ... Born February 12, 1870.
[Then followed the names and dates of birth of her brothers and sisters, eight in number.]
THIS IS FINAL. Will anyone disputing this, kindly apply to Somerset House ?
Wood is the family name ; Lloyd, stage ditto.

New York Times
16th July 1883

GEN. TOM THUMB.

Charles Heywood Stratton, "Gen. Tom Thumb," the most famous of the little family of lilliputians introduced by P. T. Barnum to the sight-seeing world more than 40 years ago, died at his late residence in Middleboro, Mass., yesterday morning, of apoplexy. He had been ill for several days, but no serious results were anticipated. The "General" was born in Bridgeport, Conn., on Jan. 4, 1838, and was the third of four children, all excepting himself being of ordinary stature. He was first exhibited by Mr. Barnum, 41 years ago, when he was only 4 years old. At that time he was said to be 11 years old on the show-bills, which story he adhered to for more than 20 years. On Jan. 18, 1844, he was taken to Europe. On this visit he was given the title by which he was always known by Queen Victoria, who dubbed him a "General" upon his presentation at Court. He weighed at that time only 20 pounds. As he grew older he increased in weight and height, and at the time of his death he weighed 75 pounds and was 40 inches in height. He returned from his European trip in 1847. In 1862 he again entered Mr. Barnum's service, and, together with "Commodore" Nutt, was exhibited in this City at the old museum. In 1863, on Feb. 10, he was married with great pomp and ceremony in Grace Church, this City, to Miss Lavinia Warren Bump, herself a midget, who was his constant companion, both on and off the stage, until his death. She survives him. In 1869 the "General," Mrs. Stratton, her sister, the late Minnie Warren, and "Commodore" Nutt made a trip around the world, the incidents of which are almost historic. It lasted three years. In 1872 the family moved into the General's residence in Middleboro, which was erected for him during his absence from home, where they have lived ever since. It is a large building, in which everything excepting one sleeping apartment is of the ordinary size. In this chamber, however, the furniture is small enough for a doll's house. The "General" was a hospitable host, a generous neighbor, and was highly esteemed by those who knew him intimately. His married life was very happy. He had one child, born in Brooklyn 14 years ago, who only lived two years. It was of ordinary size. He was a very enthusiastic Freemason, and was probably the most diminutive Knight Templar in the world. He was exhibited at Coney Island in the Summer of 1881. His body will be taken to Bridgeport for interment. The time of the funeral will be decided on upon the arrival of his widow from Cincinnati.

New York Times
16th December 1966

Walt Disney, Who Built Entertainment Empire on a Mouse, Dies

Walt Disney, who built his whimsical cartoon world of Mickey Mouse, Donald Duck and Snow White and the Seven Dwarfs into a $100-million-a-year entertainment empire, died in St. Joseph's Hospital here this morning. He was 65 years old.

His death, at 9:35 A.M., was attributed to acute circulatory collapse. He had undergone surgery at the hospital a month ago for the removal of a lung tumor that was discovered after he entered the hospital for treatment of an old neck injury received in a polo match.

Just before his last illness, Mr. Disney was supervising the construction of a new Disneyland in Florida, a ski resort in Sequoia National Forest and the renovation of the 10-year-old Disneyland at Anaheim. His motion-picture studio was turning out six new productions and several television shows and he was spearheading the development of the vast University of the Arts, called Cal Art, now under construction here.

Although Mr. Disney held no formal title at Walt Disney Productions, he was in direct charge of the company and was deeply involved in all its operations. Indeed, with the recent decision of Jack L. Warner to sell his interest in the Warner Brothers studio, Mr. Disney was the last of Hollywood's veteran moviemakers who remained in personal control of a major studio.

Weaver of Fantasies

From his fertile imagination and industrious factory of drawing boards, Walt Elias Disney fashioned the most popular movie stars ever to come from Hollywood and created one of the most fantastic entertainment empires in history.

In return for the happiness he supplied, the world lavished wealth and tributes upon him. He was probably the only man in Hollywood to have been praised by both the American Legion and the Soviet Union.

Where any other Hollywood producer would have been happy to get one Academy Award—the highest honor in American movies—Mr. Disney smashed all records by accumulating 29 Oscars.

David Low, the late British political cartoonist, called him "the most significant figure in graphic arts since Leonardo."

Mr. Disney went from seven-minute animated cartoons to become the first man to mix animation with live action, and he pioneered in making feature-length cartoons. His nature films were almost as popular as his cartoons, and eventually he expanded into feature-length movies using only live actors.

From a small garage-studio, the Disney enterprise grew into one of the most modern movie studios in the world, with four sound stages on 51 acres. Mr. Disney acquired a 420-acre ranch that was used for shooting exterior shots for his movies and television productions. Among the lucrative byproducts of his output were many comic scripts and enormous royalties paid to him by toy-makers who used his characters.

Mr. Disney's restless mind created one of the nation's greatest tourist attractions, Disneyland, a 300-acre tract of amusement rides, fantasy spectacles and re-created Americana that cost $50.1-million.

By last year, when Disneyland observed its 10th birthday, it had been visited by some 50 million people. Its international fame was emphasized in 1959 by the then Soviet Premier, Nikita S. Khrushchev, who protested, when visiting Hollywood, that he had been unable to see Disneyland. Security arrangements could not be made in time for Mr. Khrushchev's visit.

Even after Disneyland had proven itself, Mr. Disney declined to consider suggestions that he had better leave well enough alone:

"Disneyland will never be completed as long as there is imagination left in the world."

Ideas Met Skepticism

Repeatedly, as Mr. Disney came up with new ideas he encountered considerable skepticism. For Mickey Mouse, the foundation of his realm, Mr. Disney had to pawn and sell almost everything because most exhibitors looked upon it as just another cartoon. But when the public had a chance to see speak, the noble-hearted mouse with the high-pitched voice, red pants, yellow shoes and white gloves became the most beloved of Hollywood stars.

When Mr. Disney decided to make the first feature-length cartoon—"Snow White and the Seven Dwarfs"—many Hollywood experts scoffed that no audience would sit through such a long animation. It became one of the biggest money-makers in movie history.

Mr. Disney was thought a fool when he became the first important movie producer to make films for television. His detractors, once again, were proven wrong.

He was, however, the only major movie producer who refused to release his movies to television. He contended, with a good deal of profitable evidence, that each seven years there would be another generation that would flock to the movie theaters to see his old films.

Mickey Mouse would have been fame enough for most men. In France he was known as Michel Souris; in Italy, Topolino; in Japan, Miki Kuchi; in Spain, Miguel Ratoncito; in Latin America, El Raton Miguelito; in Sweden, Muse Pigg, and in Russia, Mikki Maus. On D-Day during World War II Mickey Mouse was the pass-word of Allied Supreme Headquarters in Europe.

But Mickey Mouse was not enough for Mr. Disney. He created Donald Duck, Pluto and Goofy. He dug into books for Dumbo, Bambi, Peter Pan, The Three Little Pigs, Ferdinand the Bull, Cinderella, the Sleeping Beauty, Brer Rabbit, Pinocchio. In "Fantasia," he blended cartoon stories with classical music.

His cartoon creatures were often surrounded with lovely songs. Thus, Snow White had "Some Day My Prince Will Come" and the dwarfs had "Whistle While You Work." From his version of "The Three Little Pigs," his most successful cartoon short, came another international hit, "Who's Afraid of the Big Bad Wolf?" Cliff Edwards as Jiminy Cricket sang "When You Wish Upon a Star" for "Pinocchio." More recently, "Mary Poppins" introduced "Supercalifragilisticexpialidocious."

Exhibition at Museum

Mr. Disney seemed to have had an almost superstitious fear of considering his movies as art, though an exhibition of some of his leading cartoon characters was once held in the Metropolitan Museum of Art in New York. "I've never called this art," he said. "It's show business."

One day, when Mr. Disney was approaching 60 and his black hair and neatly trimmed mustache were gray, he was asked to reduce his success to a formula.

"I don't really know," he said. "I guess I'm an optimist. I'm not in business to make unhappy pictures. I love comedy too much. I've always loved comedy. Another thing. Maybe it's because I can still be amazed at the wonders of the world.

"Sometimes I've tried to figure out why Mickey appealed to the whole world. Everybody's tried to figure it out. So far as I know, nobody has. He's a pretty nice fellow who never does anybody any harm, who gets into scrapes through no fault of his own, but always manages to come up grinning. Why Mickey's even been faithful to one girl, Minnie, all his life. Mickey is so simple and uncomplicated, so easy to understand that you can't help liking him.

But when Dwight D. Eisenhower was President, he found words for Mr. Disney. He called him a "genius as a creator of folklore" and said his "sympathetic attitude toward life has helped our children develop a clean and cheerful view of humanity, with all its frailties and possibilities for good."

By the end of his career, the list of 700 awards and honors that Mr. Disney received from many nations filled 29 typewritten pages, and included 29 Oscars, four Emmys and the Presidential Freedom Medal.

There were tributes of a different nature. Toys in the shape of Disney characters sold by the many millions. Paris couturiers and expensive jewelers both used Disney patterns. One of the most astounding exhibitions of popular devotion came in the wake of Mr. Disney's films about Davy Crockett. In a matter of months, youngsters all over the country who would balk at wearing a hat in winter, were adorned in coonskin caps in midsummer.

Walt Disney was born in Chicago on Dec. 5, 1901. His family moved to Marceline, Mo., when he was a child and he spent most of his boyhood on a farm.

He recalled that he enjoyed sketching animals on the farm. Later, when his family moved back to Chicago, he went to high school and studied cartoon drawing at night at the Academy of Fine Arts. He did illustrations for the school paper.

New York Times
22nd January 1959

When the United States entered World War I he was turned down by the Army and Navy because he was too young. So he went to France as an ambulance driver for the Red Cross. He decorated the sides of his ambulance with cartoons and had his work published in Stars and Stripes.

After the war the young man worked as a cartoonist for advertising agencies. But he was always looking for something better.

When Mr. Disney got a job doing cartoons for advertisements that were shown in theaters between movies, he was determined that that was to be his future. He would say to friends, "This is the most marvelous thing that has ever happened."

In 1920 he organized his own company to make cartoons about fairy tales. He made about a dozen but could not sell them. He was so determined to continue in this field that at times he had no money for food and lived with Mr. Iwerks.

In 1923 Mr. Disney decided to leave Kansas City. He went to Hollywood, where he formed a small company and did a series of film cartoons called "Alice in Cartoonland."

After two years of "Alice in Cartoonland," Mr. Disney dropped it in favor of a series about "Oswald the Rabbit." In 1928 most of his artists decided to break with him and do their own Oswald. Mr. Disney went to New York to try to keep the series but failed. When he returned, he, his wife, his brother Roy and Mr. Iwerks tried to think of a character for a new series, but failed. They decided on a mouse. Mrs. Disney named it Mickey.

Added Sound to Cartoon

The first Mickey Mouse cartoon, "Plane Crazy," was taken to New York by Mr. Disney. But the distributors were apathetic. "Felix, the Cat" was ruler of the cartoon field, and they saw nothing unusual in a mouse.

When Mr. Disney returned from New York he decided that sound had a future in movies. He made a second Mickey Mouse, this one with sound, called "Steamboat Bill." In October, 1928, the cartoon opened at the Colony Theater in New York. Success was immediate and the Disney empire began.

Cecil De Mille, 77, Pioneer of Movies, Dead in Hollywood

—Cecil B. De Mille died of a heart ailment today in his home on De Mille Drive here. He was 77 years old.

Although confined to his home since last Saturday, Mr. De Mille continued to work. He was preparing to start filming "On My Honor," a history of the Boy Scout movement and its founder, the late Lord Baden-Powell.

Barnum of the Movies

Cecil Blount De Mille was the Phineas T. Barnum of the movies—a showman extraordinary.

A pioneer in the industry, he used the broad medium of the screen to interpret in "colossal" and "stupendous" spectacles the story of the Bible, the splendor that was Egypt, the glory that was Rome. He dreamed in terms of millions, marble pillars, golden bathtubs and mass drama; spent enormous sums to produce the rich effects for which he became famous.

During his lifetime, Mr. De Mille produced more than seventy major films, noted for their weight and mass rather than for subtlety or finely shaded artistry.

In 1953 he won an Academy Award for "The Greatest Show on Earth," which had been released a year earlier. Previously he had won neither an Oscar nor the New York Film Critics annual award.

Won Box-office Awards

The fact that his first Oscar did not come until forty years after he had produced one of the earliest four-reel feature films, "The Squaw Man," was brushed off with a characteristic De Millean gesture:

"I win my awards at the box office."

This was true. His pageants and colossals awed the urban, suburban and backwoods audiences. By 1946 his personal fortune, despite his regal spending habits, was estimated at $8,000,-000.

The producer basked in publicity's intense glare in late 1944-45 when he made a heroic issue of a demand by the union of which he was a member that he pay a $1 contribution to its political action fund. He had been in radio about a decade by that time, staging shows for a soap company at a reported salary of $5,000 a week.

Mr. De Mille carried the fee fight to the courts, was defeated, and then went on a one-man campaign against political assessments by unions. He later sought reinstatement in the union, but failed to get it.

Mr. De Mille was born at De Mille Corners, a backwoods crossroads in Ashfield, Mass., on Aug. 12, 1881, while his parents were touring New England with a stock company. His father, Henry Churchill De Mille, was of French-Dutch ancestry; his mother, the former Matilda Beatrice Samuel, of English stock.

At 17 he went on the stage. He played in "Lord Chumley," "The Warrens of Virginia" (which he adapted to the screen later), "The Prince Chap" and "Hearts Are Trumps."

In the cast of "Hearts Are Trumps," was Constance Adams, daughter of a New Jersey judge, engaged in a small part. They were married Aug. 16, 1902, four days after Mr. De Mille's twenty-first birthday.

In 1913 he was having lunch with Jesse Lasky when the talk turned to movies. Mr. De Mille threw in his lot with the ambitious Lasky and with a newcomer in the theatre, Sam Goldwyn. All three reached the top rung in the movie world, though finally along separate paths.

The first product of the new movie company—The Jesse L. Lasky Feature Play Company—was a screen version of "The Squaw Man." It was turned out in an abandoned stable in Los Angeles with crude equipment, but it bore Mr. De Mille's mark.

He was credited with many motion picture innovations. Indoor lighting was first tried out on an actor in "The Squaw Man." This picture, besides being the screen's first epic, was also the first to publicize the names of its stars.

On his first day as head of the Lasky-Goldwyn-De Mille combine, Mr. De Mille signed three unknowns—a $5 cowpoke named Hal Roach, an oil-field hand named Bill (Hopalong Cassidy) Boyd and a thin-nosed teenager who called herself Gloria Swanson. This was the nucleus around which he built his galaxy of screen stars.

To Mr. De Mille was attributed the inspiration for doing different versions of a popular picture, a possibility everyone else had overlooked. He is also supposed to have conceived of opening films with a printed cast of characters. The so-called "sneak preview"—showing a film to a test audience—was another contribution.

Switched to Americana

The first "Ten Commandments," produced in 1923 at a cost of $1,400,000, made money. From that time on Mr. De Mille wallowed in extravagant props and super-gorgeous sets. It was a good formula. It worked in "The Crusades," "The Sign of the Cross," "King of Kings," "Cleopatra" and a long list of other De Mille spectaculars.

In the latter part of his career Mr. De Mille switched from Scriptural subjects to the American scene. He turned out flamboyant chunks of Americana in "The Plainsman," taken from the lives of Wild Bill Hickok and Buffalo Bill; "The Buccaneer," a dramatic account of the life of the pirate Jean Lafitte; "Union Pacific," and "Reap the Wild Wind," a story about Key West.

"The Buccaneer," originally produced in 1937, was remade last year, with Mr. De Mille acting in a supervisory role. Unlike the new "The Ten Commandments," "The Buccaneer" was what the trade called a "remake."

"The Ten Commandments," however, was a completely new version of the Bible story and differed greatly from his first film of that title. "The Ten Commandments," issued in 1956, had grossed a reported $60,000,-000 here and abroad by last fall.

Other expensive pictures Mr. De Mille produced were "Unconquered," in 1947, and "The Greatest Show on Earth," which cost an estimated total of $4,000,000 each. In 1949 he produced "Samson and Delilah" for about $3,000,000. During that same year he was named chairman of the Motion Picture Industry Council.

In June, 1958, he learned that plans to place translations of the hieroglyphics on the Egyptian obelisk in Central Park were being put aside for lack of funds. He offered to pay the cost of erecting four bronze plaques at the base of "Cleopatra's Needle," saying:

"As a boy, I used to look upon the hieroglyphics as so many wonderful pictures."

Two weeks ago, the Department of Parks announced that Mr. De Mille had donated $3,760 for the project.

The Times
29th April 1970

GYPSY ROSE LEE
Queen of burlesque

Gypsy Rose Lee the sophisticated stripper who disapproved of nudity, died in Los Angeles on Sunday night. She was 56.

Miss Lee outgrew an "ugly duckling" childhood to become the undisputed queen of burlesque, a peculiarly American phenomenon that is now on its own deathbed. She was not even old enough to attend school when she joined her mother and sister June —later to become June Havoc, the film star—on the ruthless vaudeville circuit in an act called "Dainty June and her Newsboy Songsters."

At 16, she encountered Tessie the Tassel-Twirler at Kansas City's old Missouri theatre Dainty June and her Newsboy Songsters were out of work and the only job going was a burlesque turn. Rose grabbed it because "I was tired of starving". Tessie the Tassel-Twirler gave Rose her first lessons in the fine art of stripping, and the future duchess of striptease never forgot Tessie's early advice: "In burlesque, you've gotta leave 'em hungry for more. You don't dump the whole roast on the platter". Gypsy never did. She regarded striptease as an art form spicing her act with heady quotations from such austere thinkers as Aldous Huxley and Spinoza. And she later found the theatre's trend towards nudity not at all to her liking.

By the time she was 17 she was a star at Billy Minsky's Republic theatre in New York. She quickly moved into Ziegfeld's Follies. She went to Hollywood— to star, among others, as the Bible-thumping gospeller Aimee Semple McPherson—and in May 1937, at the pinnacle of her fame, announced her retirement from the skin game. That year she married the first of her three husbands—in a bouncing motorboat off the California coast.

Gypsy, by now an American folk heroine, turned her considerable energies to writing: she published such best-selling thrillers as *G-String Murders*, *Mother Finds a Body* and finally *Gypsy*, an autobiography that

later became a Broadway musical and a Hollywood film.

It may seem pretentious to speak of artistry in relation to her act, but it was certainly a form of entertainment which required a high degree of professionalism, in just the same way as the work of the great music-hall comedians from Dan Leno to Max Miller required an equal skill and knowledge. Of Gypsy Rose Lee it could perhaps be said that she never really took very much off except her competitors whom she knew to be vastly inferior to herself.

There was no real place for her in the cinema, and least of all in the rather prudish era of Hollywood in the 1930s, although she did make a few minor and rather halfhearted appearances, and she was seen as late as 1952 in *Babes of Baghdad*. Thus she remained for most filmgoers of the period, on both sides of the Atlantic, as little more than a naughty legend, suggestive of a union between the Folies Bérgères and the honky-tonk saloons of the old West. What made her distinctive was not only her style and professionalism, but also her poise, her intelligence and her sense of humour.

Her real name was Rose Louise Hovick and she was born in Seattle, Washington, in 1914.

The Times
8th April 1891

MR. P. T. BARNUM.

A Reuter telegram from Bridgeport, Connecticut, states that Mr. PHINEAS T. BARNUM died yesterday afternoon. This world-famous showman, was born at Bethel, Connecticut, on July 5, 1810. He entered into business at the early age of 14, and for upwards of 65 years he was before the public in various capacities, as manager, lecturer, author, newspaper editor, and banker. He was also for some time Mayor of Bridgeport, Connecticut, and he made no empty boast when he declared himself to be the proprietor of the "greatest show on earth." America has had many great private shows, collections, and museums, but Barnum's was undoubtedly the mammoth exhibition. For some time Mr. Barnum was a general merchant in his native town, and at 21 years of age he was editor and proprietor of the *Herald of Freedom* in Danbury, Connecticut. In 1834 he removed to New York, and in the course of a few years he owned and managed several successful museums and shows. In 1841 he purchased the American Museum, by which, in a few years, he acquired a fortune. In 1842 he brought out Charles S. Stratton, the dwarf, better known throughout the world as General Tom Thumb. Mr. Barnum and the "General" had the honour of being twice received by the Queen, the Prince Consort, and the Royal Family at Buckingham Palace. The "General" caused her Majesty and the Royal children the liveliest amusement, and the readiness he showed in making himself friendly with the heir to the British Crown excited much laughter. In 1855 Mr. Barnum took up his residence at Bridgeport, where he engaged largely in real estate and manufacturing enterprises. These were unsuccessful, however, and he became bankrupt. Having effected a compromise with his creditors, he resumed the management of the museum, and soon retrieved his fortunes. In 1856 he engaged Jenny Lind (Madame Goldschmidt) to visit America to give 150 concerts, but the engagement was cancelled when 93 performances had been given. At the age of 48 Mr. Barnum again visited England, and lectured at St. James's-hall, London, and also in other large cities and towns. His lectures were full of wit, and as a *raconteur* he was almost unrivalled. He was not afraid to bring out what told against himself, as well as those things which demonstrated his marvellous Yankee shrewdness and ingenuity. At the age of 55 he was elected to the Connecticut Legislature, and was thrice re-elected. At 65 he was elected Mayor of Bridgeport. During his earliest engagements in the show business he was twice burnt out—once in 1865 and again in 1868, when he announced his retirement from business. The instinct of the showman, however, was far too strong for him, and after a few years he re-entered the field upon a larger scale than ever. One of his later strokes of business was the purchase of the celebrated elephant Jumbo from the Zoological Society in 1881 for the sum of £2,000. The tragic fate of the animal will be remembered by our readers; it was killed in 1885 under sad circumstances. On yet a third occasion Barnum suffered great loss, for in November, 1887, his entire menagerie was destroyed by fire. But nothing could daunt the restless spirit of the man, and after disasters which appeared to others hopelessly irreparable, he came up smiling and marked by greater courage than ever. The "greatest show on earth" required 100 railway cars for its conveyance, and in 1879 it was estimated that the number of Barnum's patrons up to date reached the enormous figure of 90,000,000. In 1882 a day's receipts for his great show in Boston amounted to over £3,000, and in ten days to upwards of £21,000. For his hippodrome in New York he purchased for £33,000 from Messrs. Sanger, of London, a duplicate of the whole plant for the splendid pageant of the "Congress of Monarchs." Mr. Barnum was a candidate for the American Congress in 1866, but was defeated by his Democratic opponent. His visit with his show to London in 1889 will be fresh in the memory of our readers. Besides lecturing on temperance and other subjects, Mr. Barnum published several books. His "Life," written by himself, appeared in 1855, and it was afterwards greatly enlarged. This autobiography has at least the merit of frankness, Mr. Barnum entering with much detail into the record of his unsuccessful as well as his successful ventures. In 1865 he published "The Humbugs of the World;" in 1869, "Struggles and Triumphs;" in 1883, "Money-Getting;" and in 1890 a collection of "Stories." Deceased made many large donations to public charities, notably one of $100,000 for a Natural History Museum in Tuff's College, Boston. Mr. Barnum was received by many crowned heads and a number of the most distinguished men of the time, all of whom were anxious to see a man who was unique of his class.

New York Times 24th February 1965

STAN LAUREL DIES, MOVIE COMEDIAN

Teamed With Oliver Hardy in 200 Slapstick Films— Played 'Simple' Foil

Stan Laurel, the sad-faced, scalp-scratching fall guy of the movie comedy team of Laurel and Hardy, died of a heart attack today in his apartment. He was 74 years old.

His partner of more than 200 slapstick films, Oliver Hardy, died in 1957. Mr. Laurel had been retired since 1955 when he suffered a stroke. He had declined to appear in public after Mr. Hardy's death.

A Screen Favorite

Laurel and Hardy were often acclaimed as masters of the careful slapstick, geniuses of a woman-dominated society. Critics placed them close to, but not quite on a par with, Charlie Chaplin, Buster Keaton and others who gained fame as comic singles. Yet their doubles act was the highlight of many a Saturday afternoon at the movies, not to mention the rest of the week, during the late nineteen-twenties and through the thirties.

On the screen, Mr. Laurel, who was 5 feet, 9 inches tall, blue-eyed, and had sandy-brown hair, spoke in a querulous voice that made everyone tremble for his survival vis à vis the 250-pound, 6-foot 1-inch, aggressive Hardy. Yet it was Laurel who often came out the winner. While Hardy was being soundly thrashed by his screen wife, a weepy Laurel would be getting the sympathetic caresses of his movie helpmeet.

The pair had such a vogue that they often did not have time to hammer out stories.

"Nobody ever thinks of giving us a plot," Mr. Laurel once said. "All they do is tell us how funny we are and then push us in front of a camera. We go into the front office and beef and the producers slap down a long list of figures that say we were smash hits at the box office. So they want to know, why do we want to bother with writing our own stuff?"

The pair dressed somberly on screen, as though they were an ill-assorted butler duo. The bowler was their hallmark and they used it as their main prop. Their comedy was frantic on the whole but careful in part. A fight would start with a slap, move to a slow return slap, followed by another slap and so on as a graceful prologue to a full-scale brawl and headlong flight.

Hardy was the idea man, the fellow with plans for a night out, for a get-rich-quick scheme. Laurel was the sidekick, honest and simple, who inevitably thwarted the deal and plunged the two into catastrophe.

Became a Team in '26

The drawling Lancashire-born Laurel and the high-pitched Georgia-born Hardy teamed up in 1926. They were always anxious for their two and three-reelers to be polished pieces of work.

"We had a rough idea of schedule," Mr. Laurel was quoted as saying in John McCabe's biography "Mr. Laurel and Mr. Hardy." "But our prime worry was whether or not the picture was going to be good.

"We would start out with an idea, go along working on it as we were shooting. If something went wrong with what we were doing, we'd just 'cut' and laugh about it. It was damned fine fun and damned hard work in those days when we were making ourselves a well-known team. Come to think of it, it was always fun."

Arthur Stanley Jefferson (Stan Laurel) was born in the little English town of Ulverson on June 16, 1890. He was born into show business. "My family were all theatrical," he once explained.

He followed the trouper's traditional route — circuses, musicals, vaudeville. He arrived in the United States at the age of 20, a member of the Karno "Night in the English Music Hall" troupe. Another British actor in the cast was Charlie Chaplin. At times, Mr. Laurel was his understudy and he said later, "I don't think there's any greater in the business or ever will be."

Mr. Laurel barnstormed for a bit before settling in Hollywood. He found it was tougher to get jobs as a comic than it was to write comedy. In 1917, he joined Hal Roach's studio and wrote, produced and directed.

The big break came in 1926 by accident, one that befell Mr. Hardy, whom Mr. Laurel was directing in a movie. Mr. Hardy, a trencherman and gourmet, burned his arm while cooking a leg of lamb at home.

"We tried to get someone else for the part but nobody was available," Mr. Laurel recalled. "Mr. Roach then asked me to play Hardy's part. Of course we had to rewrite it, but when the picture was finished, Roach liked it, and he asked me to write myself into the next one. By then Hardy was ready to go into the next picture and I appeared with him in it."

They made other films, but not as partners. Mr. Roach observed that they were supplementing each other in fine style and suggested that the movies be called Laurel and Hardy comedies.

The team had tremendous success. There were two million people enrolled in European fan clubs. They had their imitators, too, but none stood up for very long.

Their antics made for a hard day's work. What with the pummeling and the running, they should have been winded when the quitting whistle blew. According to Mr. Laurel, Mr. Hardy was more of a "playboy" who enjoyed going out or playing golf, while Mr. Laurel took care of the editing and the team's business affairs. He said that they did not see too much of each other off the job.

The team was among the few who made the jump from silents to sound.

"We had decided we weren't talking comedians and, of course, preferred to do pantomime, like in our silents," Mr. Laurel said. "So we said as little as possible—only what was necessary to motivate the things we were doing. If there was any plot to be told, we generally would have somebody else tell it. After a while we really liked sound, because it emphasized the gags, and, as time went on, we became a little more accustomed, and did more talking than we first intended."

Hancock in his new series for Australian T.V. Only three episodes had been made.

The Sun
26th June 1968

DON'T blame Tony Hancock, the sublime and friendly comedian, for the forlorn, infuriating and empty drama of his death in a hotel room with a bottle of tablets nearby.

His life through his last few months in Sydney—in spite of the handshakes the grins and the cheerful hellos he found on every street—was anything but funny.

Last Sunday he watched from my home a British ship steaming out of Sydney harbour and said with that wan quizzical sadness that used to look so appealing on TV: "What's ahead for me but work, work, work?"

Twice he asked that. And then he added another question that seems somehow relevant now: "Do Australian newspapers print summaries of divorce court evidence?"

While other guests around him called for Scotch or beer or gin, Tony drank tomato juice.

He made little quips about spartan self-discipline, but nobody laughed very much. For his tiny band of special Australian friends were only too aware of the secret and vicious battles he was waging against himself.

We could all list his inner enemies without knowing then that two days later they would all gang up to strike him dead.

In order, these enemies were self-doubt, an illogical but overweening feeling of rejection, an incosolable loneliness, the conviction that nobody but his mother really loved him and a goading temptation to drink himself insensible every day.

REVEALING

Australian strangers could never know of these conflicts, for outwardly Tony was the impeccably polite and cheerful British chap, calmly tolerant of most of the oddities of the American way of Australian life.

I never saw him irritated or put out. Only at times, such as last Sunday, inexpressibly sad.

The things he secretly longed for emerged only through relaxed conversations in quiet moments—simple revealing British things like wet streets outside the London Palladium and a packed crowd at Lord's cricket ground.

To selected friends he talked of great nights in the theatre when men and women stars—never himself—won their audiences by talent and guts.

One of these friends, my son Rusty, who worked with him on his London television shows and was his constant companion here, helped him every day to hide away from well-wishers who sought to give him celebrity treatment.

For the grim jest is that the man who died partly from loneliness could have called on limitless numbers of admiring Australians to crowd into his life. For him just to walk down a Sydney street was to set people smiling.

DISCIPLINE

To go with him to a fashionable Sydney club was to see the manager at once beg him to accept honorary membership. Yet he preferred the quiet company of a few men from the T V production crew who worked with him.

The word had gone out: "The new TV series Hancock is making with Sydney's Channel Seven is brilliant. It will sell around the world. Tony is funnier than ever."

But only three episodes had been completed up to this morning when the star left the cast forever. Scrawled on the back of the script of episode four found near his body was a halting farewell note: "Love to my mother. Tell her the soul lives on..."

Only tragic destiny now has the laugh on Tony Hancock, the loveable tormented comic who could not believe in himself and lost his greatest personal battle the very moment he had it won.

National Biographies

TUSSAUD, MARIE, Madame Tussaud (1760–1850), founder of the waxwork exhibition known by her name, born at Berne in 1760, was the posthumous daughter of Joseph Gresholtz, a soldier who had served on the staff of General Wurmser in the seven years' war, by his wife Marie, the widow of a Swiss pastor named Walther. In 1766 she was adopted by her maternal uncle, Johann Wilhelm Christoph Kurtz or Creutz (he subsequently latinised his name into Curtius), under whose auspices she was taken to Paris and taught wax modelling, an art in which she became proficient. Curtius, a German Swiss (though during the revolution from prudential motives he gave himself out to be an Alsatian), migrated to Paris in 1770, and ten years later started a 'Cabinet de Cire' in the Palais Royal. The business was extended in 1783 by the creation of a 'Caverne des grands voleurs' (the nucleus of the 'Chamber of Horrors') in the Boulevard du Temple, in a house formerly occupied by Foulon. Curtius seems to have been a man of taste and conviviality; a mania for modelling in wax was fashionable in Paris, and the 'ceroplastic studio' of M. Curtius in the 'Palais,' owing largely no doubt to its central position, became for a time a popular rendezvous for Parisian notabilities. There as a child Marie Tussaud was spoken to by Voltaire, Rousseau, Franklin, Diderot, Condorcet, and other famous men, and she was even sent for to Versailles to give lessons in flower-modelling to Madame Elisabeth, Louis XVI's sister. On 12 July 1789 a crowd of well-dressed persons obtained from the exhibition in the Palais Royal the busts of Necker and Philippe d'Orléans, and carried the effigies through the city dressed in crape. Two days later Curtius proved his patriotism by taking part in the 'storming' of the Bastille. At the close of the year, as one of the 'vainqueurs de la Bastille,' he was presented by the municipality with an inscribed musket (still preserved at Madame Tussaud's). Three brothers and two uncles of Marie Tussaud were in the Swiss guard, and all perished bravely in defending the Tuileries on 10 Aug. 1792. The safety of Marie and her uncle was ensured by the powerful protection of Collot d'Herbois, from whom Curtius is said to have received some employment under the committee of public safety. He was certainly called upon to model the lifeless heads of a number of victims of the Terror, and of this repulsive work his niece would appear to have had more than her fair share. Marie is said to have been imprisoned for a short time under the Terror, and to have had as a fellow-captive Joséphine de Beauharnais. Her uncle (after 9 Thermidor, 28 July 1794) came under suspicion as a partisan of the organisers of the Terror, and met his death under strong suspicion of poison.

In the meantime Marie had married M. Tussaud, the son of a well-to-do wine grower from Mâcon, and for six years with varying fortune they seem to have carried on the Cabinet de Cire under the name of Curtius. About 1800 she separated from her husband, and in 1802 she got a passport from Fouché and transferred her cero-plastic museum to England. At the outset she planted herself at the Lyceum in the Strand, and her exhibition soon eclipsed the notorious old waxwork of Mrs. Salmon, under whose name four rooms of tableaux in the style of Mrs. Jarley were shown near St. Dunstan's, Fleet Street, from early in the eighteenth century down to 1812 (cf. *Spectator*, No. 28; *Harl. MS.* 5931; *Brit. Mus. Cat.*) Subsequently Madame Tussaud removed her 'Museum' to Blackheath, and later her figures were displayed in all the large towns of the United Kingdom. Many of them were submerged on one occasion in the Irish Channel, and in the Bristol riots of October 1831 her show was within an ace of being burned to the ground. One of her first catalogues, dated Bristol 1823, is headed 'Biographical and Descriptive Sketches of the whole-length composition Figures and other works of Art forming the Unrivalled Exhibition of Mme. Tussaud (niece to the celebrated Courcis of Paris), and artist to Her late Royal Highness Mme. Elizabeth, sister to Louis XVIII' (Brit. Mus.; an edition of 1827 is described in *Notes and Queries*, 7th ser. xii.) Among the figures stated to have been taken from life are George III (1809), Napoleon (1815), Josephine (1796), Louis XVIII (1814), Voltaire (March 1778), Robespierre, 'taken immediately after his execution by order of the General Assembly,' Marat, Carrier, Fouquier Tinville, and Hébert. In 1833 the exhibition found a settled home in Baker Street, London. Madame Tussaud's remarkable collection of relics, already including the bloodstained shirt in which Henry IV was assassinated (purchased by Curtius at the Mazarin sale) and the knife and lunette of one of the early guillotines, was greatly enhanced in value in 1842 by the purchase of Napoleon's travelling carriage, built at Brussels for the Moscow campaign in 1812, and captured at Jemappes after the battle of Waterloo ('The Military Carriage of Napoleon,' 1843). Marie Tussaud retained her faculties to the last, and distinguished visitors to the exhibition, from the Duke of Wellington downwards, were entertained by her recollections. When she was over eighty she divided all she possessed between her two sons, Joseph and François (grandfather of John Theodore Tussaud, the present modeller to the exhibition). She died at Baker Street on 16 April 1850, and her remains were placed in the vaults of the Roman catholic chapel in the Fulham Road. A wax model of the old lady is shown in the Marylebone Road, whither the exhibition (now the property of a company) was removed from Baker Street in 1884

New York Times
8th August 1957

Oliver Hardy of Film Team Dies;
Co-Star of 200 Slapstick Movies

Portly Master of the Withering Look and 'Slow Burn'— Features Popular on TV

—Oliver Hardy, the fat, always frustrated partner of the famous movie comedy team — Laurel and Hardy, died early today at the North Hollywood home of his mother-in-law, Mrs. Monnie L. Jones. Mr. Hardy, who was 65 years old, suffered a paralytic stroke last Sept. 12.

His widow, Lucille, who had worked as a script girl on his movies before their marriage in 1940, said Mr. Hardy never regained the power of speech after the stroke and required constant nursing care.

Stan Laurel, the frail, sad-looking member of the team, said today: "What's there to say. It's shocking, of course. Ollie was like a brother. That's the end of the history of Laurel and Hardy." Mr. Laurel suffered a stroke in June, 1955, but reported that he was steadily regaining strength.

Found New Audience

In recent years Mr. Hardy had found an entirely new audience through the appearance of the old Laurel and Hardy films on television. In particular, "Babes in Toyland" has become a regular offering during the Christmas season.

Scripts meant little in Laurel and Hardy comedies, as much of the plot and byplay were improvised as the shooting proceeded. The team was among the first to slow the unnaturally fast pace so characteristic of the early comedy movies.

Mr. Hardy made his first picture at the age of 21 in Jacksonville, Fla. His displacement, well on the way to its eventual 300 pounds, happened to catch the eye of a Lubin Film Company unit on location there.

At the time he had just finished four years with a stock company in Atlanta, where he was born in 1892. He had drifted into the profession by performing on showboats and in vaudeville during vacations from his law studies at the University of Georgia.

The Jacksonville role was followed two years later, in 1915, by a series of comic films with the Pathé Studios, then situated in Ithaca, N. Y. From 1918 until 1925, when it was bought by Warner Brothers, Mr. Hardy worked at Vitagraph as a director, often with Larry Semon, who later went on to earn $100,000 a year for stopping custard pies with his face.

Their joint career, begun in 1926 by a chance appearance in a silent two-reeler, spanned nearly 200 films. At one time their movies for Hal Roach were filmed in English, German, French, Spanish and Italian to keep pace with an expanding world audience.

Sound was only incidental to Mr. Hardy's comedy. His actions were essentially pantomime, based on the Mack Sennett silent vocabulary of the delayed and double takes. He was a master of the tailspin, the slow burn, or—when surveying the disasters wrought by his well-meaning partner—the withering look.

Although the team concentrated on feature-length films such as "The Devil's Brother," "Swiss Miss" or "Blockheads" in later years, most critics felt that the two-reelers were a more suitable mold for their hectic efforts.

New York Tribune
9th October 1849

Death of Edgar A. Poe.

EDGAR ALLAN POE is dead. He died in Baltimore the day before yesterday. This announcement will startle many, but few will be grieved by it. The poet was known, personally or by reputation, in all this country; he had readers in England, and in several of the states of Continental Europe; but he had few or no friends; and the regrets for his death will be suggested principally by the consideration that in him literary art has lost one of its most brilliant but erratic stars.

The character of Mr. Poe we cannot attempt to describe in this very hastily written article. We can but allude to some of its more striking phases.

His conversation was at times almost supra-mortal in its eloquence. His voice was modulated with astonishing skill, and his large and variably expressive eyes looked repose or shot fiery tumult into theirs who listened, while his own face glowed, or was changeless in pallor, as his imagination quickened his blood or drew it back frozen to his heart. His imagery was from the worlds which no mortals can see but with the vision of genius. Suddenly starting from a proposition exactly and sharply defined in terms of utmost simplicity and clearness, he rejected the forms of customary logic, and by a crystalline process of accretion, built up his occular demonstrations in forms of gloomiest and ghastliest grandeur, or in those of the most airy and delicious beauty—so minutely, and distinctly, yet so rapidly, that the attention which was yielded to him was chained till it stood among his wonderful creations—till he himself dissolved the spell, and brought his hearers back to common and base existence, by vulgar fancies or exhibitions of the ignoblest passion.

He was at all times a dreamer—dwelling in ideal realms—in heaven or hell—peopled with the creatures and the accidents of his brain. He walked the streets, in madness or melancholy, with lips moving in indistinct curses, or with eyes upturned in passionate prayer, (never for himself, for he felt, or professed to feel, that he was already damned,) but for their happiness who at the moment were objects of his idolatry;—or, with his glances introverted to a heart gnawed with anguish, and with a face shrouded in gloom, he would brave the wildest storms; and all night, with drenched garments and arms beating the winds and rains, would

speak as if to spirits that at such times only could be evoked by him from the Aidenn close by whose portals his disturbed soul sought to forget the ills to which his constitution subjected him—close by the Aidenn where were those he loved—the Aidenn which he might never see, but in fitful glimpses, as its gates opened to receive the less fiery and more happy natures whose destiny to sin did not involve the doom of death.

He seemed, except when some fitful pursuit subjugated his will and engrossed his faculties, always to bear the memory of some controlling sorrow. The remarkable poem of The Raven was probably much more nearly than has been supposed, even by those who were very intimate with him, a reflexion and an echo of his own history. He was that bird's

> —Unhappy master,
> Whom unmerciful disaster
> Followed fast and followed faster,
> Till his songs the burden bore—
> Till the dirges of his hope, the
> Melancholy burden bore
> Of " Nevermore," of " Nevermore."

Every genuine author in a greater or less degree leaves in his works, whatever their design, traces of his personal character : elements of his immortal being, in which the individual survives the person. While we read the pages of the Fall of the House of Usher, or of Mesmeric Revelations, we see in the solemn and stately gloom which invests one, and in the subtle metaphysical analysis of both, indications of the idiosyncracies, —of what was most remarkable and peculiar—in the author's intellectual nature. But we see here only the better phases of this nature, only the symbols of his juster action, for his harsh experience had deprived him of all faith, in man or woman. He had made up his mind upon the numberless complexities of the social world, and the whole system with him was an imposure. This conviction gave a direction to his shrewd and naturally unamiable character. Still, though he regarded society as composed altogether of villains, the sharpness of his intellect was not of that kind which enabled him to cope with villainy, while it continually caused him by overshots to fail of the success of honesty. He was in many respects like Francis Vivian in Bulwer's novel of " The Caxtons." " Passion, in him, comprehended many of the worst emotions which militate against human happiness. You could not contradict him, but you raised quick choler; you could not speak of wealth, but his check paled with gnawing envy. The astonishing natural advantages of this poor boy—his beauty, his readiness, the daring spirit that breathed around him like a fiery atmosphere—had raised his constitutional self-confidence into an arrogance that turned his very claims to admiration into prejudices against him. Irascible, envious—had enough, but not the worst, for these salient angles were all varnished over with a cold repellent cynicism, his passions vented themselves in sneers. There seemed to him no moral susceptibility ; and, what was more remarkable in a proud nature, little or nothing of the true point of honor. He had, to a morbid excess, that desire to rise which is vulgarly called ambition, but no wish for the esteem or the love of his species; only the hard wish to succeed—not shine, not serve—succeed, that he might have the right to despise a world which galled his self conceit."

We must omit any particular criticism of Mr. Poe's works. As a writer of tales it will be admitted generally, that he was scarcely surpassed in ingenuity of construction or effective painting. As a critic, he was more remarkable as a dissector of sentences than as a commenter upon ideas : he was little better than a carping grammarian. As a poet, he will retain a most honorable rank.

In poetry, a prose, he was most successful in the metaphysical treatment of the passions. His poems are constructed with wonderful ingenuity, and finished with consummate art. They illustrate a morbid sensitiveness of feeling, a shadowy and gloomy imagination, and a taste almost faultless in the apprehension of that sort of beauty most agreeable to his temper.

Exploration

The spirit of discovery is thought by many to be an integral part of human nature: from the child going outside the front door for the first time to **Yuri Gagarin**, the first spaceman, man is forever searching beyond his immediate boundaries. In these days when the heights and depths of the earth seem all to have been visited by man, it seems strange to recall that little more than a hundred years ago **Edward Whymper** caused a sensation by reaching the summit of the Matterhorn, and that only 50 years ago **Mallory** and **Irvine** could still disappear forever into exploring legend on Everest. Often the attempt ends in death: **James Cook** on a Pacific beach; **Robert Scott** in the isolation of the Antarctic, having just been beaten to the South Pole by **Roald Amundsen**. For the sake of balance, **Robert Peary** is also included, having been first to reach the North Pole. Perhaps the most romantic story of all, however, is that of **John Franklin** and his search for the fabled North-West Passage round the northern shores of Canada to the Pacific. After his failure to return, thirty nine expeditions went in search of some trace of him before, thirteen years later, his remains were finally found. The tradition of the lone eccentric is represented here by **Dr. Livingstone**, the epitome of the European trekking through nineteenth-century Africa in search of the crock of gold, or of souls to be saved: and by **Richard Burton**, who, having become probably the first European to set foot in Mecca, found, with John Speke, Lake Tanganyika; failed to find the source of the Nile (later discovered by Speke and Grant); and returned home to the Foreign Service, scholarship, and translation of the *Kama Sutra*.

The contemporary interest in civilisations of the past – hoping perhaps to learn from them? – is given its due in the person of **Hermann Schliemann**, who, having once made up his mind to discover Homer's Troy, moved heaven and earth to do so, and, having removed seven layers of the latter, finally succeeded: and in that of **Howard Carter**, who ought perhaps to be known as Mr. Tutenkhamun.

The Sun & New York Herald
21st February 1920

Explorer Dies in Washingon Home.

ROB'T E. PEARY, DISCOVERER OF POLE, IS DEAD

Succumbs After Long Illness and Many Operations for Blood Transfusion.

FAMILY AT HIS BEDSIDE

Stood "on Top of Earth" in Ninth Attempt—Made Rear Admiral.

Admiral Peary's Career.

In the history of the world's 300 years of effort at polar achievement the name of Robert Edwin Peary, American, stands out preeminent. And perhaps nowhere in the world's history is there a more conspicuous example of the indissoluble association of a name with an ambition.

Small wonder then that the American people thrilled, paused and applauded when on the afternoon of September 6, 1909, two years after his Lotus Club speech, the following laconic message was received by the Associated Press by wireless and telegraph from Peary:

"INDIAN HARBOR, via Cape Ray N. E., Sept. 6.—Stars and Stripes nailed to the north pole. PEARY."

Peary's actual attainment of the pole had been just five months before, on April 6. It had taken those five months for the explorer to get within hailing distance of civilization, and when he did his short announcement opened the floodgates of one of the bitterest scientific and personal public controversies of recent times.

Unknown to Peary when his first announcement of achievement reached civilization the world for four days had been celebrating the supposed success of Dr. Frederick A. Cook. Cook, on board a Danish steamship bound for Copenagen, had telegraphed on September 2 that he reached the pole on April 21, 1908, nearly a year before Peary.

While the claim of the Brooklyn physician had been questioned from the first he had many ardent supporters, and pending proof to the contrary had for four days been hailed as the discoverer of the Pole, the conqueror of the uncharted northland. Then came Peary's famous message that Cook had "handed the world a gold brick," followed by this more explanatory statement which reached New York by way of Indian Harbor, Labrador, on the afternoon of September 8:

"I have nailed the Stars and Stripes to the North Pole. This is authoritative and correct. Cook's story should not be taken too seriously. The two Eskimos who accompanied him say he went no distance north and not out of sight of land. Other members of the tribe corroborate their story."

Obtaining leave from the naval service he first led an expedition to Greenland for the purpose of determining the extent of this little known territory. He discovered and named many points that since have become familiar names, such as Independence Bay, Melville Land and Heilprin Land. In one of his later voyages to Greenland he discovered the famous meteorites, one of which may be seen in the New York Museum of Natural History.

Between these voyages Peary took to the lecture platform in an effort to raise funds for further exploration. The earnestness with which he threw himself into this task is evidenced by the fact that on one tour he delivered 168 lectures in ninety-six days, raising $13,000.

The explorer's seventh voyage into the Arctic had to be given up when both his feet became frozen. Although he had reached the most northerly land in the world, the tip of Greenland, which he named Cape Morris K. Jessup, and had attained a latitude of 84.17, then the record of achievement in the Western Hemisphere, Peary wrote in his diary:

"The game is off. My dream of sixteen years is ended. I have made the best fight I knew. I believe it was a good one. But I cannot accomplish the impossible."

Dr. Fridtjof Nansen, in his ship the Fram, reached 86 degrees and 14 minutes north latitude in 1896, and in 1900 the Duke of the Abruzzi reached 86.33, the best record at the time.

These achievements prompted Peary to try again. Accordingly on July 26, 1905, he set sail from North Sydney, C. B., on his eighth attempt to reach the Pole. He and his party were aboard the specially designed ship Roosevelt, a stout sailing vessel with reinforced stem and bows and auxiliary engines. With him were his veteran navigator, Capt. Bob Bartlett; Dr. Wolff, Charles Percy, steward; Matthew A. Henson, Chief Engineer George A. Wardwell, Prof. Ross G. Marvin and others.

"Only an Empty Bauble."

He reached 87 degrees 6 minutes, and wrote:

"I thanked God with as good grace as possible for what I had been able to accomplish, though it was only an empty bauble compared with the splendid jewel for which I was straining my life.

"My flags were put out from the summit of the highest pinnacle near us and a hundred feet or so beyond this I left a bottle containing a brief record and a piece of the flag which six years before I had carried around the northern end of Greenland. Then we started to return."

Peary was 52 years old when in July, 1908, he set out from New York on his ninth and successful attempt to reach the pole. The personnel of his party was, with one or two exceptions, the same as that which accompanied him on his eighth attempt.

Proceeding northward through Robeson Channel to the Kane Basin Peary established a winter base at Cape Sheridan on the Lincoln Sea on September 5. It was determined there to approach the pole in five detachments. This method was followed until the eighty-eighth parallel was reached, when Peary, with the negro Matt Henson left Capt. Bartlett, who was in charge of the fourth detachment, and accompanied by four Eskimos made the last dash of 135 miles afoot in five days, reaching the pole April 6.

"Prize of Three Centuries."

"The first thing I did," wrote Peary in his own story of his achievement,

"was to write these words in my diary:

'The pole at last. The prize of three centuries. My dream and goal for twenty years cannot bring myself to realize it. It seems all so simple and commonplace.'"

Peary and his companions spent thirty hours in the vicinity of the Pole, which was found to be a great tract of frozen sea and not of land. The weather during the time was cloudless, the temperature varying from 13 to 33 degrees below zero. In the open places where soundings were taken the 9,000 feet of wire which Peary had with him failed to touch bottom.

Hoists American Flag.

Records of the occasion were deposited and photographs made and the Stars and Stripes hoisted for any to see who might in future years attempt to duplicate Peary's feat by air or otherwise. That was in accordance with the explorer's code, although there is, of course, small likelihood of the records or other evidence remaining in place on account of the continuous movement of the ice.

Scientists examined all of Peary's data, compared his observations and decided finally that he actually reached a point one mile and one-sixteenth from the mathematical top of the earth. For all scientific purposes Peary had achieved his ambition and so far is the only white man who truthfully could declare that he had stood on the top of the world.

On his return home Peary placed his proofs before the House Committee on Naval Affairs, which in concurrence with the Senate on March 4, 1911, voted him the thanks of Congress, raised him to the rank of Rear Admiral of the United States Navy and retired him on pay. Decorations, medals and awards of many kinds were showered on him before and after ultimate recognition of his achievement had been made by his own Government.

Following his lecture tours Admiral Peary spent some time in rest with his family on Eagle Island, off the coast of Maine. During this period he worked on two books, "The North Pole" and "Secrets of Polar Travel."

With the outbreak of the European war Admiral Peary's professional instincts forced him into more active channels and he accepted the chairmanship of the National Aerial Coast Patrol Commission. From time to time he warned against the likelihood of a raid on the Atlantic coast by submarine or aircraft and took the lead in an agitation looking toward the establishment of an American naval base in Greenland.

In 1916 Admiral Peary made his first and only essay towards a political career. He became a candidate on a preparedness platform to succeed the late United States Senator Edwin C. Burleigh of Maine, but after a week withdrew, saying that he felt he was unskilled in politics and not temperamentally suited to a career that he thought would necessitate frequent attacks upon his friends.

Admiral Peary was married in 1888 to Miss Josephine Diebitsch of Washington, who frequently accompanied him on his Arctic trips. It was on one of these that his daughter, Marie Ahnighito Peary, was born. She has the distinction of having been born farther north than any other white child and became popularly known as "The Snow Baby."

Admiral Peary was a member of all the principal geographical societies of the world and held decorations from many foreign Governments. He was a member of Phi Beta Kappa and Delta Kappa Epsilon fraternities and of Kane Lodge F. and A. M., named for Elisha Kent Kane, another American explorer of Arctic fame.

The Gentleman's Magazine
11th January 1780 Vol 50

Tuesday 11.

Admiralty-Office. Capt. Clerke, of his Majesty's sloop the Resolution, in a letter to Mr. Stephens, dated the 8th of June, 1779, in the harbour of St. Peter and St. Paul, Kamptschatka, gives the melancholy account of the celebrated Capt. Cooke, late commander of that sloop, with four of his private mariners, having been killed, on the 14th of February last, at the island of O'why'he, one of a group of new-discovered islands, in the 22d degree of north latitude, in an affray with a numerous and tumultuous body of the natives.

Capt. Clerke adds, that he had received every friendly supply from the Russian government; and that as the companies of the Resolution, and her consort the Discovery, were in perfect health, and the two sloops had twelve months stores and provisions on board, he was preparing to make another attempt to explore a northern passage to Europe. [*Gazette.*]

It is said, that having been a considerable time at the island where Capt. Cook met with his fate, and all the while very friendly with the inhabitants, upon sailing from thence he met with an accident in the mast of his ship, and returned there to repair it. The people then shewed a different disposition, and took away one of his boats, which they would not again part with; upon which the captain, with a lieutenant and nine marines, went on shore to compel them to deliver the boat; they seemed very riotous and rude, particularly one man, whom the captain ordered to be fired on with small shot; which they not regarding, he ordered bullets to be fired, which killed the most daring man and another; upon which they rushed in upon the captain and his people with large clubs, and killed the captain and three men; the lieutenant and the four others escaped.

Capt. Cook was born at Marton, near Great Ayton in Yorkshire, in 1728; had been at sea from his youth, and passed through all the stations, from an apprentice-boy in the coal trade to a post captain in the royal navy, where his character was calculated to command love and respect, being equally brave, modest, and intelligent in his profession. He was first appointed captain of the Endeavour, and sailed from Deptford July the 30th, 1768, and arrived at Otaheite the 13th of April following. He continued in the South Seas till March 1770, and returned by way of Batavia to England, July 12, 1771. In this voyage he was accompanied by Mr. Banks and Dr. Solander. Nov. 28, 1771, he was appointed commander of the Resolution; and in June 1772, made his second voyage for the discovery of the Southern Hemisphere, when having sailed into as high a southern latitude as 71, and met with nothing but islands of ice, which interrupted his passage, these obliged him to return, and on the 20th of July, 1775, he arrived at Plymouth. In July, 1776, Capt. Cook sailed from Plymouth a third time, on the same discovery, of whom nothing had been heard after his departure from the Cape of Good Hope till the unfortunate account of his death brought by way of Russia. It is almost incredible, that in the second voyage the captain established such a system of diet and cleanliness, that (to use his own words) under the Divine Favour, Capt. Cook, with a company of one hundred and eighteen men, performed a voyage of three years and eighteen days, throughout all the climates from 52 degrees North to 71 degrees South, with the loss of only one man by distemper, and this man is supposed to have had a disorder upon his lungs when he went on board, which probably occasioned his death. When a very young man, he was sollicited to be godfather to a female child of a friend, which he consented to; and after the ceremony was over, said sportively to her father, that he intended her for his wife. This resolution, however unlikely to be carried into execution at that time, he lived to perform; and from the mutual affection which subsisted between him and his consort, he seemed to have insured to himself a fund of domestick happiness to chear

Gent. Mag. Jan. 1780.

the latter part of his life. The spirit of enterprise was, however, too strong in him to resist the call of his sovereign. He accepted the command offered him to make further discoveries with alacrity, and fell a victim to that intrepid disposition, which, until this fatal voyage, had brought him home safe, to the satisfaction of all his friends, who now have only to regret his loss.

His journal, to the time of his death, with all his papers relative to the voyage, are received at the Admiralty Office.

It is observable that the famous Magellan, after discovering the straits that bear his name, met with a similar fate, being slain in battle by the natives of Mathan, one of the Philippine islands, in 1521, before he had compleated his circumnavigation: but in this he widely differed from our great countryman, that he was the aggressor, in endeavouring to extort tribute for his master the King of Spain; but Capt. Cook, on the defensive, and in this, as a voyager, was almost singular, that he never knowingly injured, but always studied to benefit the savages whom he visited. Thus at Otaheite, where he was best known, he was looked upon as a kind of tutelar deity. The island O'why'he, where he lost his life, being in lat. 22 deg. N. long. 200 deg. E. of Greenwich, must lie in the great South Sea, near the tropic of Cancer, about 30 deg. W. of Chiameten in Mexico. Being much to the north of Otaheite, Capt. Cook must have touched there first, and also, probably, explored the coasts of California, and was then proceeding in search of the N. E. passage, with the summer before him. Kamschatka lies in the Eastern ocean, in lat. 55 deg. N. long. 157 deg. E. of Greenwich. The passage (if any) from thence to Europe must be by the Northern ocean, to the N. of Siberia, Nova Zembla, &c. But as such a voyage can only be made in summer, and would take up no more than three months, Capt. Clerke's letter being dated in June last, we may conclude that he has not found it, and must therefore be now returning (we trust) by the Indian ocean and the Cape of Good Hope.

*The Times
21st October 1800*

SIR RICHARD BURTON.

We announce with much regret that Sir Richard Burton, the eminent Eastern traveller and Orientalist, who has held the post of British Consul at Trieste since 1872, died there yesterday morning, at the age of 69. In him there has passed away one of the most remarkable and cosmopolitan, and at the same time one of the most scholarly, explorers of our time. Sir Richard Burton's name is in popular estimation associated with Africa, and rightly so, for there he did his most valuable and most original work. His discovery of Lake Tanganyika, especially when combined with that of the Victoria Nyanza by his companion Speke, deserves to rank with Stanley's memorable journeys. He and his companions were lions in their day, and if the excitement then was less than it has been over Mr. Stanley's recent expedition, it was not due to the fact that the geographical work they did was less important or accomplished with less hazard. The conditions which fan excitement and nurse enthusiasm had not reached the development 30 years ago which they have attained now.

Richard Francis Burton was born on March 19, 1821, at Barham-house, Herts, the son of Colonel Netterville Burton, of the 36th Regiment, and his wife Martha Baker. Richard's grandfather was rector of Tuam, in Ireland, and his granduncle Bishop of Killala. They were the first of the family to settle in Ireland, and belonged to the Burtons of Barker-hill, near Shap, Westmorland, who, again, are connected with some of the leading Burton families all over the kingdom. Much of Richard Burton's eccentricity was inherited both on the father's and mother's side. Most of his boyhood and youth was spent at Tours and in wandering with his restless father over the Continent, from one temporary place of residence to another. Burton's training and education were thus of an irregular and spasmodic character, ill-fitted to qualify him for the routine of an official career. It, however, fostered his powers of observation, and gave him ample opportunity of exercising his wonderful faculty for the acquisition of languages. The Burton children were left very much to themselves, so that Richard's innate wayward disposition had little check. At last, in 1840, the family returned to England, and young Burton was entered at Oxford, going into residence at Trinity College in the Michaelmas Term of that year. His previous training was not conducive to compliance with Oxford ways. He was leader in the wildest pranks of his time ; in Latin and Greek he made little headway, but he quickly mastered Arabic. Burton soon got disgusted with University life and resolved to quit it. This he did by deliberately attending a race meeting against orders, and was of course " sent down." This was precisely what he wanted. When he arrived suddenly in London (in 1842), he told his friends that he had been allowed an extra vacation for taking a double first-class with the very highest honours. Of course the truth was soon discovered, and in the end he obtained a commission in the East India Company's service. He sailed from England on June 18, 1842, his only companion being a bull-terrier of the Oxford breed. He landed at Bombay on October 28, and was posted as ensign to the 18th Regiment, Bombay Native Infantry, which he joined at Baroda. He soon became master of Hindustani and fencing, and astonished his fellow officers and displeased his superiors by the eccentricities of his conduct. Nevertheless in 1843 he was made regimental interpreter, and succeeded in indulging his wandering propensities by expeditions to various parts of India. Burton's career as an explorer,

however, may be said to have begun in 1852, when he undertook, in the disguise of a Pathan, that journey to Medina and Mecca the description of which forms one of the most interesting of his many narratives. His life thenceforth, until he settled down as Consul at Trieste, was an almost uninterrupted series of exploring expeditions. Before this (1851) he had published a volume on " Scinde," giving the results of his observations while resident in the " unhappy valley," and in the same year a volume on " Goa and the Blue Mountains."

Burton's next expedition was to Somaliland, even now but little known, and then full of dangers. The expedition was undertaken by the Directors of the East India Company, and Burton was accompanied by Lieutenant Speke. The expedition left Aden at the end of 1854, and Burton alone, again in disguise, succeeded, amid the greatest risks, in entering the sacred city of Harrar. Returning again to Berbera in the beginning of 1855, Burton intended to penetrate to the Nile, but shortly after landing the expedition was attacked, Burton and Speke being wounded, and narrowly escaping with their lives. The narrative of this hazardous expedition was published in 1856, under the title of " First Footsteps in East Africa." After a run to Constantinople in 1856, in the vain hope of being employed in the war against Russia, Burton returned to England still more disgusted with officialism, and still more determined to distinguish himself as an African explorer. He now undertook, after a trial trip to Zanzibar and other coast towns, the expedition into the heart of Africa on which his fame will mainly rest. For years rumours had been reaching the coast of great lakes in the interior ; and Krapf and Rebmann, two missionaries, had actually seen a snow-covered mountain just under the Equator. Livingstone had made his great journey across the continent (he arrived in England in December, 1856), and had aroused an interest in Africa which has been increasing in intensity ever since. We have heard much recently of the great lakes and rivers and mountains which covered the old maps of Africa, but which D'Anville rightly swept away. A great lake was reported to exist in the Zanzibar interior, and it was to find this that Burton and his companion Speke left Zanzibar in June, 1857, under the auspices of the Royal Geographical Society. For the first time the route which has now become a well-trodden highway, from Bagamoyo to Ujiji, was traversed by the feet of white men. After more than the usual trouble, a final start was made, and through many trials and sufferings Ujiji was reached on February 14, 1858, about eight months from leaving Bagamoyo. Thus the first of those great lakes of Central Africa which probably form its most remarkable feature found its place on the map. Moreover, the expedition went over hundreds of miles of new country, and in addition Speke made a run to the north to find that other great lake, Victoria Nyanza, around which English and German interests have of late been mainly centred. Altogether this may be regarded as one of the most notable of African expeditions, and Burton was rightly hailed on his return to England in 1859 as an explorer of the first rank. He well deserved the gold medal which the Royal Geographical Society awarded him and the many other honours which were showered upon him. He may justly be regarded as the pioneer in a region where subsequently splendid work was done by Livingstone, Cameron, and Stanley. To the unhappy dispute which followed between Burton and Speke, and which gave rise to so much bitter feeling, it is not necessary to do more than allude.

After a run to the United States in 1860, when Burton visited Salt Lake City and the West (about which he wrote in his " City of the Saints "), he was once more back in Africa. Meantime, January 22, 1861, he had married the lady who has been his loyal and helpful companion through life. Lady Burton belongs to the Arundells of Wardour. In August, 1861. Burton and his bride sailed for " the Foreign Office Grave," Fernando Po, to which he had been appointed Consul. His three years' stay here was spent in exploring the whole of the coast region round the Bight of Biafra, varied by a special mission to the King of Dahomey, the results of which are recorded in two separate works. Burton's excellent work in this unhealthy region brought him promotion, and in 1865 he went as British Consul to Sao Paulo, in Brazil. As usual, this born explorer could not rest. He traversed all his province, voyaged down the San Francisco, visited the La Plata States, and subsequently crossed the continent to Chili and Peru, returning by the Straits of Magellan. As usual the result was a big book, " The Highlands of Brazil " (1869).

From Brazil Burton was transferred to Damascus, where he landed in October, 1869. Damascus he made the basis of an exploration of Syria, but on the reduction of the Consulate he returned to

England in 1871. A visit to Iceland in 1872 resulted in an elaborate work on the island, one of the most complete in our language. In the same year Burton was appointed to the Consulship at Trieste, and that post he filled till the day of his death. But even there he could not rest. In 1876 and 1877-78 he made two visits to the Land of Midian to explore the old mines, the result being two works, too full of learning to be quite popular. In 1882, in company with Commander Cameron, Burton made an expedition to the interior of the Gold Coast for the purpose of prospecting the mines in that unhealthy region, but the only result was another book.

This may be regarded as Burton's last expedition. Since then his health began gradually to break down, and no wonder, considering the hardships he had had to endure from his boyhood upwards. But idleness with Burton meant unhappiness, and if he were not exploring, he was engaged in some scholarly investigation or some literary enterprise. His translation of Camoens (1880) is in itself a masterly performance, abounding with the most recondite and learned annotations. His literal translation of the " Arabian Nights " is the work of an accomplished Eastern scholar, who could treat the curious questions suggested by these stories of a comparatively primitive life with the frankness and some of the recklessness of science. Many memoirs and papers, besides the works we have mentioned, have come from Burton's busy hand, all of them marked by that keen research, frank criticism, and scholarly annotation which make his works a mine of knowledge, but which at the same time render them somewhat difficult reading.

Burton, as might have been expected, was never an official favourite, and his numerous friends are of opinion that his many services entitled him long ago to a handsome retiring pension ; but Government was inexorable, and his only reward was a K.C.M.G., bestowed in 1886. Notwithstanding the apparent brusqueness of his manner and the frankness of his talk, Burton had many warm friends. No man ever succeeded better with the natives either of Africa or Asia ; indeed, with barbarism he had almost more sympathy than with civilization. He was a man of real humanity and an unwavering friend. Like Livingstone and Stanley, he was one of those determined men of action who carry out their purpose through every obstacle. As an observer he was keen and accurate, and, in spite of his perplexingly allusive style, was clear and graphic in his descriptions. In many respects Richard Burton was one of the most remarkable men of his time ; but he will probably be longest remembered as the first pioneer in Central Africa, the discoverer of Lake Tanganyika.

Glasgow Herald
3rd August 1928

MYSTERY OF THE ARCTIC

AMUNDSEN'S FATE

CONFLICTING VIEWS

MOSCOW, Thursday.

Professor Vise, the leader of the Polar Relief Expedition on board the Soviet icebreaker Malyguin, and the aviator Babushkin arrived here to-day to report to the Rescue Committee.

Professor Vise said that he felt sure that Captain Amundsen and his companions were still alive, and he believed that they had landed in a region where both bears and reindeers were to be found. With his expert knowledge of Polar conditions, a man like Captain Amundsen could easily keep alive not only for a month but for a whole year.

The position of the Alessandri party was different, however, as it was composed of men unacquainted with Polar conditions. Nevertheless, they had firearms, and they ought to be able to exist for a considerable time.

On the other hand, M. Babushkin was of opinion that Captain Amundsen was dead, because he believed that the Latham seaplane came down on the water during a storm and that its occupants were drowned.—Reuter.

HOPE ABANDONED

OSLO, Thursday.

While the rescue expeditions are continuing their work, all hope of finding either Amundsen or the balloon party of the Italia alive has been abandoned here.

Experts are satisfied that Amundsen did not attempt to go straight to the rescue of the Nobile group, for the aeroplane was too heavily laden, but that he made for King's Bay, and that he aeroplane fell in the sea. When last seen the Latham seaplane was north-west of Bear Island, flying rather low, and in the last wireless message sent from the Latham Amundsen asked the wireless stations in North Norway about the weather and the landing conditions at King's Bay.

The last words Amundsen said at Bergen to Captain Wisting, who was to go on board the aeroplane at King's Bay, were—" Well, then, we meet at King's Bay."

The result of the inquiry which is to be held in Rome into the history of the expedition is eagerly awaited here, but some doubt is expressed as to whether the whole tragic story will be made public.—Reuter.

NOBILE INTERVIEWED

ROME, Thursday.

" Our expedition was worth all the suffering and sacrifices of wealth for the geographical and scientific research it will give the world," said General Nobile to-day in an exclusive interview.

" No Polar aerial expedition in history has ever accomplished so much scientifically as ours," he declared. " It has not been said we flew 245 hours, out of which we flew 134 over Polar regions. It has not been said that we encountered meteorological difficulties that tested the fibre of every man with us. We overcame a thousand difficulties, yet if we could have continued three hours more our entire programme would have been completed."—Exchange Telegram.

The Times
11th February 1913

THE POLAR DISASTER.

CAPTAIN SCOTT'S CAREER.

NAVAL OFFICER AND EXPLORER.

Captain Robert Falcon Scott, R.N., F.R.G.S., was a west countryman by birth. He was the eldest son of the late Mr. John Edward Scott, of Outlands, Devonport, where he was born on June 6, 1868. After being educated at Stubbington House, Fareham, he entered the Britannia as a naval cadet in the summer of 1881, sitting for his examination within a few days of his thirteenth birthday. Passing out two years later he served as a midshipman in the Boadicea, on the Cape Station, in the Monarch, in the Channel Squadron, and in the Rover, in the Training Squadron, and in August, 1887, he became an acting sub-lieutenant. He passed his examinations for the rank of lieutenant with credit, taking a first-class certificate in four out of the five subjects, and his commission in the rank was dated August 14, 1889, when he was serving in the Amphion, cruiser, on the Pacific Station, to which he had been appointed in the previous year. On returning home, he entered the Vernon schoolship in September, 1891, to qualify in torpedo duties, and his first appointment as a torpedo lieutenant was in 1893 to the Vulcan, then a new torpedo depôt-ship, under the command of Captain (now Admiral Sir) John Durnford. He left this ship to become a staff officer in the Defiance, torpedo school-ship at Devonport, of which the present Vice-Admiral Sir Henry Jackson, then a commander, was in command, and in August, 1896, he went to sea again as torpedo lieutenant of the battleship Empress of India in the Channel Squadron. After nearly a year in this vessel, he was transferred in a similar capacity to the Majestic, the flagship successively of Admirals Sir Henry F. Stephenson and Sir Harry H. Rawson, commanding the Channel Squadron. Sir Henry Stephenson, it may be noted, is an old Arctic explorer, having served in the expedition of 1875-6.

The flag-captain of the Majestic at this date was Prince Louis of Battenberg, now First Sea Lord, and Lieutenant Scott remained in her for nearly three years, part of this time as first lieutenant, until he was promoted to commander on June 30, 1900. For some six years afterwards he relinquished his active career in the Royal Navy to devote himself to Antarctic exploration.

HIS FIRST EXPEDITION.

On their return to England from the first expedition in 1904 Captain Scott and his men were given a reception which was enthusiastic beyond measure. The Royal Geographical Society held a great meeting in the Albert Hall at which Captain Scott was awarded not only a Royal medal, but a special Antarctic medal as well, copies of which in silver and bronze were presented to the officers and men of the expedition. He received medals and honours from many societies and universities, and King Edward created him a C.V.O. He was promoted by the Admiralty to the rank of captain in recognition of his services, but it was not until August, 1906, that he returned to sea duty. In that month he accompanied Rear-Admiral (now Admiral Sir) George Egerton, with whom he had been shipmate in the Vernon, to the battleship Victorious as flag-captain on Admiral Egerton's appointment as rear-admiral in the Atlantic Fleet. Captain Scott served in this post for 12 months, the Victorious being relieved by the Albemarle in January, 1907. From January to May, 1908, he was in command of the Essex, cruiser, in the Portsmouth Division of the Home Fleet, which he left to become flag-captain in the Bulwark to Rear-Admiral (now Vice-Admiral Sir) Stanley Colville, commanding the Nore Division of the Home Fleet. The Bulwark was transferred to the Channel Fleet in September, 1908, Scott remaining in command. In March, 1909, he went to the Admiralty as Naval Assistant to the Second Sea Lord at the time that Sir Francis Bridgeman succeeded Sir William May in that position. Captain Scott was the first holder of this appointment (the Second Sea Lord not having had a naval assistant before), and it was also the last appointment that he held under the Admiralty, for he resigned at the end of 1909 to prepare for his second expedition to the Antarctic.

Captain Scott, even if he had never rendered his great service to Antarctic discovery, was fairly certain by his scientific and other attainments of rising to distinction in his profession. Lord Goschen once said, in speaking of his qualifications for the command of an expedition, that he was relinquishing, at least for a time, a brilliant career in the Navy. Of high courage and endurance, he had proved himself a first-rate organizer and a born leader of men. He was a man of wide culture and extensive reading, interested in everything that concerns humanity. He was a man of genuine modesty, warm-hearted, with troops of friends in all ranks of life, and bright and entertaining as a companion, firm in his friendship and chivalrous in his conduct. In appearance he was thick-set, sturdily built, with a strong, clean-shaven face, tight determined lips, and keen blue eyes. His manner at first acquaintance gave little indication of the geniality, the keen enthusiasm, and the strenuous personal force which were traits of his character, and made him extremely popular among all with whom he came in contact.

Just after he took up his appointment in command of the Bulwark, Captain Scott was married to Miss Kathleen Bruce, a daughter of the late Canon Bruce. The bride's aunt, Mrs. Thompson, the widow of Dr. Thompson, Archbishop of York, had apartments in Prince Edward's Lodging, and the wedding, by permission of the King, took place at the Chapel Royal, Hampton Court Palace. The best man was Captain Henry H. Campbell, R.N. Miss Bruce had been a pupil of M. Rodin, the sculptor, and she had herself exhibited both in the Salon and the Royal Academy. She designed the special gold medal for Arctic exploration, which was presented by the Royal Geographical Society to Rear-Admiral Peary when he visited this country in May, 1910. Captain Scott's one son was born before he left England on his last expedition, and pictures of the little boy when two years old were sent as a Christmas card by his mother to reach the explorer in the Polar regions.

The Manchester Guardian
28th January 1834

LIVINGSTONE.

The despatch received at the Foreign Office from the Acting Consul at Zanzibar yesterday, it is to be feared, leaves no room for doubt that the news of the death of Dr. Livingstone, which we published yesterday under reserve, is too true.

Livingstone, born at Blantyre, near Glasgow, in or about the year 1817, was of humble parentage. His father, as the son informs us, was a small tea dealer, and, partly through his strict conscientiousness, he never rose to be anything more. In his case, however, virtue did not wholly miss its reward, for he lived long enough to see his son a distinguished man. In early life the future traveller was one of those typical Scotch lads who work at a handicraft during the summer months to enable them to study for a profession the rest of the year. From the first Livingstone seems to have made up his mind as to his career of missionary labour in Africa. At any rate, his studies soon began to take a direction suited to the work. He obtained a good knowledge of medicine, and we may judge that he was not unmindful of the necessary theological qualifications by his being ordained for the pastoral office. This happened in 1840. He had previously been in communication with the London Missionary Society, and the Society soon found him employment of the kind he sought, and he sailed for Port Natal. Here he made the acquaintance of his future wife, the daughter of the Rev. Robert Moffat. Livingstone's wife was his constant companion in all his travels until her death at Shupanga some twelve years ago. In the sixteen years following 1840 he was hard at work in Southern Africa, not wholly in converting natives, but in improving his and the world's knowledge of the Continent. In 1855 his merit was recognised by the bestowal of the Victoria gold medal of the Royal Geographical Society, for having "traversed South Africa from the Cape of Good Hope, by Lake Ugami to Linganti, and thence to the western coast in 10 degrees south latitude." In the same year we find him, with Linganti for his new starting point, following the Zambesi right down to the Indian Ocean. In the next year, 1856, he returned to England and received a splendid welcome from the Royal Geographical Society. Sir Roderick Murchison, who was the spokesman on this occasion, said that Livingstone, in his journey over eleven thousand miles of African territory, had made geographical discoveries of incalculable importance, "by his astronomical observations he had determined the sites of numerous places, hills, rivers, and lakes, nearly all of which had been hitherto unknown, while he had seized upon every opportunity of describing the physical features, climatology, and geological structure of the countries which he had explored, and had pointed out many new sources of commerce." In 1858 he returned to Africa with some assistance from Her Majesty's Government, and about three years later he entered Lake Nyassa. The expedition (Zambesi) was recalled in 1864. Livingstone again came to England, in the following year, to "refit," and again started for the African continent in 1865. For a long time nothing was heard of him, but in 1867 came a report of his death, and in the same year a search expedition started under the command of Mr. E. D. Young. In the April of the following year letters were received from Livingstone himself, announcing that he was in good health. In a subsequent letter printed here in 1869 he expressed his belief that the chief sources of the Nile—the discovery of which had been the main object of his later travels—arise between 10 and 12 degrees south latitude, or nearly in the position assigned to them by Ptolemy. Another letter received from him was dated Ujiji, May 1869. In the beginning of 1870 discredited but tolerably circumstantial reports of his murder by the Johanna tribe of negroes were received. In the June of the same year, however, Dr. Kirk reported his probable safety. To set all doubts at rest another expedition started in search of him in February, 1872. It was organised by the Royal Geographical Society and commanded by Lieutenant Dawson. In the two or three months following Livingstone's safety was several times reported, though from no authoritative quarter, but at length it was established beyond doubt by the expedition organised by Mr. Gordon Bennett of the *New York Herald.* Mr. Stanley, the special correspondent of the *Herald,* landed at Marseilles in July 23, 1872, and he lost no time in giving publicity to an account of one of the most extraordinary enterprises in the history of journalism. Mr. Stanley, after leaving Zanzibar, met with much opposition from the native chiefs, but at last he accidentally fell in with Livingstone at Ujiji in November, 1871, and remained with him till March, 1872, when he brought away the traveller's diary and other documents. Mr. Stanley reported that Livingstone had arrived at Ujiji in bad condition, having been robbed and deserted by his attendants. Lieutenant Dawson's expedition, hearing of Stanley's success, returned home, and severe censure fell on the chiefs. Much disappointment was felt, said Sir Henry Rawlinson, at this abrupt termination of an expedition which had been prepared with so much care and at so great an expense, and which promised so well both in regard to relieving Livingstone and advancing our geographical knowledge. In Livingstone's letters he spoke of the Nile springs being about 600 miles south of the most southerly part of Lake Victoria Nyanza, and also of about 700 miles of watershed in Central Africa, of which he had explored about 600; and of the convergence of the watershed first into four and then into two mighty rivers in what he termed the Great Nile Valley, between 10 deg. and 12 deg. south latitude. His main conclusions, however, were not accepted in England. The President of the Royal Geographical Society showed there were good reasons for the belief that this great water system of Central Africa belonged to the Congo and not to the Nile. "To Livingstone," Sir Henry Rawlinson added, "belongs the secondary honour—if, indeed, it be secondary—of having discovered and traced the upper course of the Congo, which is emphatically called by the natives 'the great river' of Africa." Some account of another expedition still on its way to the succour of the great traveller, and of the untimely end of Mr. Moffat, a nephew of Livingstone, and one of its leaders, was lately given in our columns. Dr. Livingstone was the author of "Travels and Researches in South Africa," published in 1857, and of "Expedition to the Zambesi and its Tributaries," which appeared in 1865.

Glasgow Herald
30th January 1922

HIS LAST VOYAGE

DEATH OF SIR ERNEST SHACKLETON

ON BOARD THE QUEST ON JANUARY 5

A Reuter telegram from Monte Video states that Sir Ernest Shackleton died on board the Quest on the fifth of this month from angina pectoris following an attack of influenza. Sir Ernest, it will be remembered, and his band of 18 sailor-explorers sailed from London on Saturday, September 21 of last year on a 30,000 miles voyage of exploration and scientific investigation in the Antarctic.

When Sir Ernest died the vessel was off Gritvicken. His body has been brought to Monte Video on board a Norwegian steamer, the Professor Grauvel, and will be transferred to another vessel for conveyance to England, whither it will be accompanied by Captain Hussey, who is a medical man and the meteorologist of the expedition.

The Expedition's projected itinerary after leaving South Georgia was as follows: Bouvet Island, Cape Town (to take in stores), Crozet Island, M'Donald Island, Heard Island. It was further proposed to take soundings on the way to New Zealand to discover the limits of the Continental shelf.

EXPEDITION TO CARRY ON

Command Frank Wild, the second in command, has taken charge of the Expedition, and proposes to carry on.

AN ADVENTUROUS LIFE

Since boyhood days Sir Ernest Shackleton's whole life has been filled with adventure. The son of a doctor, he was born in Ireland at Kilkea, County Kildare, on February 15, 1874, so that when he died he was in his forty-eighth year. His father moved from Ireland to the neighbourhood of London when Ernest was 11 years of age, and for five years the lad continued his education, first at a private school and then at Dulwich College. His father wanted him to enter the medical profession, but his own inclinations were towards a seafaring life. He was always of an ambitious and adventurous disposition, and early gave signs of being attracted to the southern hemisphere by starting to dig a hole in the back garden, with the object of finding a short cut to Australia! His father decided to let him go to sea, and he was apprenticed to the White Star Line, making his first voyage at the age of 16 on board the Hoghton Tower, bound for the Pacific Coast of South America. A terrific storm was encountered in rounding Cape Horn, and young Shackleton narrowly escaped serious injury from falling tackle, which did damage to several of his companions. Going ashore at one of the Chilean ports, he found himself in the midst of a local revolution, and had to run for his life before a band of infuriated armed men, only just escaping through the kindly offices of a British resident, who opened a window and afforded him refuge.

After serving his apprenticeship, Sir Ernest joined the Welsh Shire Line, and sailed more than once round the world. Then he entered the service of the Union-Castle Line, and was one of the officers of the Tintagal Castle while she was employed as a troopship during the South African War. It was at this time that he first came under public notice as the author of a book, "O.H.M.S.," giving a description of some of his experiences of transport work, with illustrations by a fellow-officer. Author and artist took the risk of bringing out the book at their own expense, and for once the procedure was justified, the book being, in a small way, quite a success. Sir Ernest was not ambitious for literary fame without some knowledge of his subject. He was passionately fond of the great poets, and while still a lad at sea used to employ his leisure moments in committing long passages to memory. This and other avocations, however, did not make him neglectful of his calling, and he both studied for and passed into the Royal Naval Reserve. This qualification, coupled with his native persistence and good record in the merchant service, gained for him the coveted honour of a place in the National Antarctic Expedition which was being fitted out on board the Discovery under Captain Robert Scott, R.N. On an enterprise of this kind Sir Ernest Shackleton's versatility stood him in good stead. He not only served as fourth officer of the ship but was quickly able to turn his hand to any scientific investigation in which his help was needed, and, moreover, contributed to the general entertainment of the company during the continuous night of the Antarctic winter by editing the "South Polar Times"—a typewritten magazine, of which the facsimile reproduction, including the beautiful drawings of Dr A. E. Wilson, is now a treasured possession of book collectors.

THE DISCOVERY EXPEDITION

When Captain Scott came to select his companions on the big march to the South, Dr Wilson and Sir Ernest Shackleton were the two on whom his choice finally fell, and they went with him to what was then the farthest point to which any explorers had penetrated within the Antarctic Circle—latitude 82 deg. 17 min. S. This point was reached on Ross's Great Ice Barrier, far to the south of New Zealand, on December 22, 1902. So far the journey had been accomplished without serious mishap, and on Christmas Day Sir Ernest Shackleton imparted a festive touch to the scanty menu by producing a miniature plum pudding, which he had managed to secrete in one of his socks. But the three explorers were all suffering from scurvy, and on the return journey Shackleton broke a blood vessel, and had to be hauled back to the ship by his companions. He was invalided home, much to his disappointment, but recovered so rapidly on the voyage that when he arrived in this country he had practically regained his normal health.

For his share in the Discovery expedition Sir Ernest Shackleton was awarded a copy in silver of the special gold medal awarded to Captain Scott by the Royal Geographical Society in 1904. Early in the same year he was appointed secretary of the Royal Scottish Geographical Society in succession to Colonel Bailey; married a daughter of the late Mr Charles Dorman, and settled down in Edinburgh. For two or three years the society pursued a somewhat exciting career of expansion under his energetic and unconventional management, but the old craving for adventure soon began to assert itself. At the General Election of 1906 he contested Dundee, unsuccessfully, in the Unionist interest, and then entered the service of a famous shipbuilding firm on the Clyde.

A FAMOUS JOURNEY

All this time he was planning a new expedition, and in 1907 he was able to announce his plans. The expedition started the same year on board the Nimrod, and won high praise from the best authorities for the careful attention to detail with which it was organised. This, indeed, was characteristic of Sir Ernest Shackleton's methods, and goes a long way to explain the success which he achieved. In the Antarctic summer of 1908-9 he made his famous journey south over the Ross Barrier, past the farthest south point reached in 1902, up the great Beardmore Glacier to the lofty plateau of South Victoria Land, and over the plateau to latitude 88 deg. 25 min. S.—less than a hundred geographical miles from the South Pole. On the return journey one of the members of the little party became seriously ill, and, leaving him in charge of a companion, Shackleton and Wild hurried on alone. Arrived at the base, Sir Ernest had a hasty meal and then set out again at once with help for his sick companion. In this way he travelled 93 miles in three days with scarcely any sleep—a feat in itself remarkable, coming as it did at the end of a journey in which he had travelled no fewer than 1700 miles in 120 days.

On his return to this country Sir Ernest Shackleton received the honour of knighthood from the King and lectured before the Royal Geographical Society at a great meeting in the Albert Hall, at which the Prince of Wales (now King George) presented him with a special gold medal on behalf of the Society. For a few years he remained at home, but presently he was planning another Antarctic expedition with the object of crossing the South Polar Continent from the Weddell Sea to the Ross Sea. The expedition was ready to start in August, 1914, just as war broke out. Sir Ernest at once offered his services and those of his companions to the Admiralty, but the offer was refused, and he was told to go ahead. The story of the expedition is still fresh in the public memory. How his ship was crushed in the ice of the Weddell Sea before a landing could be effected and how he brought every man of the party safely back after a series of adventures which is without parallel in the history of Antarctic exploration is one of the great epics of Polar travel. By this disaster, even more than by his earlier successes, Sir Ernest Shackleton stamped himself as one of the greatest of modern explorers.

THE FOURTH EXPEDITION

On the present expedition Sir Ernest proposed to circumnavigate the Southern Seas by a route for the most part outside of the Antarctic Circle, and call at several little-known islands to investigate the flora and fauna and geographical features of these fragmentary remains of what may once have been great land masses, forming connecting links with other parts of the world. In addition he proposed to penetrate the Antarctic ice in the Enderby Quadrant of the Antarctic regions and endeavour to locate the line of coast which, it is surmised, runs there, roughly east and west, but which has only once or twice been dimly sighted.

The expedition was unfortunate in its early experiences. When at last the Quest sailed from these shores she encountered extraordinarily heavy weather on the voyage to Lisbon. The body of the vessel stood the strain remarkably well. One of those on board said that he was satisfied after that experience that she could live through any sea. Unhappily, however, engine trouble developed, and though repairs were carried out at Lisbon Sir Ernest Shackleton was not satisfied. After calling at Madeira the Quest crossed the Atlantic to Rio de Janeiro, and there was put into dry dock. Alterations were made both in her engines and in her spread of canvas, and when the expedition left Rio, after receiving a great welcome and every possible assistance from the Brazilian authorities, great hopes were entertained that all would go well.

But the delay necessitated a change of programme. It was no longer possible to proceed direct to Cape Town and make that port the base of operations for the Antarctic campaign in the Enderby Quadrant. Instead, Sir Ernest decided to sail for South Georgia, take on board supplies of coal there, and push straight off to the Enderby Quadrant. Under this revised programme he expected to reach Cape Town at the end instead of the beginning of the Antarctic summer. All these hopes, alas, are now dashed to the ground. The news of Sir Ernest Shackleton's death from angina pectoris has come with the shock of a complete surprise. Sir John Scott Keltic, vice-president, and former secretary, of the Royal Geographical Society, when told the news last night by the London representative of " The Glasgow Herald," expressed himself as greatly grieved and shocked, and said that Sir Ernest Shackleton was the last man whom he would have expected to be carried off in that way.

SIR ERNEST'S HONOURS

Sir Ernest Shackleton's work gained for him many honours. In 1909 he was made C.V.O., and he was a Commander of Distinguished Orders of Denmark, Sweden, Norway, France, Prussia, Italy, and Russia. He was also a gold medallist of the Geographical Societies of Scotland, Denmark, Belgium, France, Italy, America, Russia, London, Antwerp, and Paris.

GLASGOW CONNECTIONS

On November 20, 1909, after his return from the Nimrod expedition, Sir Ernest Shackleton visited Glasgow, and told his triumphant story to a crowded audience in the St. Andrew's Hall. In characteristic fashion Sir Ernest made light of the terrible privations which he and his companions had often suffered. He told of one occasion when they were forced to eat the flesh of a horse that had lain dead for several days, with the result that all got dysentery. However, they all managed to keep cheerful, and staved off the pangs of hunger by talking of food all day long. A favourite pastime under such conditions, and one which always elicited laughter, was for each one to describe his own ideal of a sumptuous bill of fare.

In June, 1914, shortly before he set out on his third voyage, Glasgow University conferred the honorary LL.D. degree on the famous explorer. They desired, said the Dean of the Faculty in presenting the graduand, to associate this University with so brave a man and the leader of so great an enterprise. Nothing was too hard for mortals, yet labours such as his could only be undertaken in the spirit of Pompey when he said, " Necesse est ut eam, non ut vivam " (" That I should go is imperative; it is not imperative that I should survive ")

The Times
3rd March 1939

MR. HOWARD CARTER

DISCOVERY OF TOMB OF TUTANKHAMEN

Mr. Howard Carter, the great Egyptologist, who gained fame for his part in one of the most successful and exciting episodes in the annals of archaeology, the discovery and exploration of the tomb of Tutankhamen, died at his London home, Albert Court, S.W., yesterday.

After the War the fifth Earl of Carnarvon applied for and was granted a concession in the Valley of the Tombs of the Kings. It had been thought that all the mysteries of the famous valley had been disclosed. All former excavators had worked on the system of " sondages "—that is, making pits in rubbish in likely places in the hope of finding a tomb entrance. But Lord Carnarvon and Mr. Carter decided that they must excavate down to actual bedrock and that their best chance was to clear away former workers' rubbish, which had often been dumped down without previous search of the ground. About 150,000 to 200,000 tons of rubbish was removed, and though they came across much untouched ground, nothing save some alabaster vases and a few minor objects rewarded their perseverance until November 5, 1922, when Howard Carter came upon a step cut in the rock.

Thus Carter made a find rarely vouchsafed to the archaeologist. Even then it was only after years of toil. The step which was beneath the entrance of the tomb of Rameses VI proved to be the beginning of a stairway that led down to the tomb of Tutankhamen. Hardly daring to believe that the good fortune, so long deferred, had then come, Carter loyally waited until his friend and fellow-worker, Lord Carnarvon, could arrive from England to help him, and he filled in the stairway as a protection until the work could begin in earnest. When Lord Carnarvon arrived the way was again cleared of rubbish and he and Carter opened the first door, which revealed a descending passage leading to a second door. A little breach was made in it and a candle inserted into the dark hole, then gradually, his eyes becoming accustomed to the darkness, Carter saw " strange animals, statues, and gold —everywhere the glint of gold." And this was but a glimpse of the treasures which were eventually to be brought to light. To have found the tomb at all was a triumph, but to have found it intact was beyond the wildest dreams of Egyptologists, as Royal tombs had been so often the prey of the ancient robber. The discovery stirred the whole civilized world more perhaps than any other archaeological success had ever done.

Born at Swaffham, Norfolk, in 1873, Howard Carter was the youngest son of Mr. Samuel John Carter, animal painter. Owing to delicate health he was educated privately, but as a youth he showed great keenness and aptitude for archaeological work, and when 17 years of age he went to Egypt on the staff of the E.E.F. Archaeological Survey. He had the good fortune to receive his training in what was to be his life's work under Lord Amherst of Hackney, Professor Ll. Griffith, Professor Sir Flinders Petrie, Professor E. Naville, and Sir Gaston Maspero. In 1892 he assisted Professor Flinders Petrie in the excavation of Tel-el-Amarna on behalf of Lord Amherst, and from 1893 to 1899 he was draughtsman to the E.E.F. Staff, Deir-el Bahari campaign.

For the next 20 years and more he was engaged on many important investigations which seemed to lead him step by step to the crowning achievement of 1922, and there was probably no one richer in experience and knowledge or more competent than Howard Carter to be in charge of the treasures of the tomb. In the course of his career he served as Inspector-General of the Antiquities Department of the Egyptian Government ; he reorganized the antiquity administration for Upper Egypt under Sir William Garstin and Sir Gaston Maspero ; and he was responsible for the electric installation in the Tombs of the Kings and Abu Simbel. He discovered the Royal tomb of Mentuhetep ; started scientific investigation in the Valley of the Kings, and found the tomb of Hatshepsût (as king), the tomb of Thothmes IV, and private tombs on behalf of Mr. T. M. Davis. On behalf of the late Lord Carnarvon he carried out the exploration of the Theban Necropolis, and he discovered extensive private tombs, the valley-temple of Hatshepsût, the tomb of Amenhetep I, the cemetery of the eighteenth-dynasty queens, the cliff tomb of Queen Hatshepsût (as consort) and finally the sepulchre of Tutankhamen.

As was natural Howard Carter's widest read books were those volumes on " The Tomb of Tutankhamen," the first of which appeared in 1923, and the third in 1933. He had in addition published works entitled " The Tomb of Thothmes IV " ; " The Tomb of Hatshepsût " ; " Five Years' Explorations Thebes " (with A. C. Mace) ; and numerous communications and reports to archaeological journals. Mr. Carter made a number of successful lecture tours in different parts of the world, and in the United States often spoke to audiences of 3,000 and 4,000. Yale University conferred upon him the honorary degree of Sc.D. He was unmarried.

The Times

26th June 1924

Mr. A. C. Irvine, who, with Mr. Leigh Mallory, lost his life on Mount Everest, photographed in camp attending to the expedition's oxygen apparatus by aid of which he and his comrade hoped to reach the summit. He was a skilled mechanic.

MALLORY AND IRVINE'S FATE.

BASE CAMP, June 11.

With the deepest regret I add these few lines continuing the above dispatch. Mallory and Irvine perished on the mountain beyond all doubt. They were last seen by Odell from Camp Six going strong for the top. I have not yet seen Odell, but estimate that this was about 11 in the morning of the 8th, and that the point reached at that time by the climbers was about 28,000ft. Nothing has been seen or heard of them since. Odell returned to Camp Four that night, and until about noon on the 9th the absence of news occasioned only anxiety, as the climbers might well have passed the night in Camps Five and Six.

At noon on the 9th Odell and two porters started from Camp Four and spent the night at Camp Five. About 1 p.m. on the 10th Odell reached Camp Six, whence he signalled that there was no sign of the missing men. Camps Five and Six were under continuous observation by Hazard from Camp Four throughout. These were provided with magnesium flares for distress signals, and there is no doubt that the climbers did not return to them. This puts any possibility of their survival out of the question, for no one could spend two nights on the mountain under existing conditions except in one or other of the two high camps and live.

The only likely explanation of the tragedy is that there was a mountaineering accident, unconnected with questions of weather or the use of oxygen. This is borne out by my own observations four days previously of the nature of the ground they were crossing when last seen. I remained at Camp Three, directing operations by messenger, watching for a signal through the telescope, until 5.30 in the afternoon of the 10th, by which time I saw Odell reach Camp Four safely. My condition and that of Captain Bruce, the only climber with me, precluded our reaching Camp Four in time to be of any help, and, beyond a letter of instructions and the use of a system of signals, I had to give the supporting party in Camp Four a free hand. They appear to have done all that was humanly possible.

I should add that I myself forbade any reconnaissance beyond Camp Six, as the weather was extremely threatening and conditions on the mountain appeared to be as bad as they could be, and I had to consider the lives of the two British and three Himalayan members of the Expedition who were still at or above Camp Four. I shall, of course, give you all details in my next dispatch.

FATAL ASSAULT ON EVEREST.

21st June 1924

CLIMBING EVEREST.—Mr. G. Leigh-Mallory and Mr. A. C. Irvine have lost their lives in the attempt to climb to the summit of Mount Everest. Our photograph shows Mr. Mallory and Lt.-Col. Norton climbing Everest in the Expedition of 1922.

Manchester Guardian
29ᵗʰ December 1896

DR. SCHLIEMANN

Dr. Schliemann died at the Grand Hotel in Naples on Friday afternoon of abscess on the brain. In an obituary notice the *Standard* says:—Dr. Heinrich Schliemann, whose name is principally known to the world, in connection with a series of the most remarkable discoveries ever made of the relics of ancient Greece, was a man of varied talents and original character. Born on the 6th of January, 1822, at Neubuckow, in Mecklenburg-Schwerin, the son of a poor Lutheran pastor, young Schliemann attended school up to the age of 15, when, instead of being destined to a university career, he found himself, owing to the *res angusta domi*, compelled to accept the position of apprentice to a grocer in the neighbouring town of Fürstenberg. After five years thus spent, young Schliemann commenced his *Wanderjahre* by going as a common sailor on a Hamburg merchantman bound for Venezuela. The vessel, however, never reached its destination, as it had not gone further than the Dutch island of Texel, in the North Sea, when it was wrecked. Schliemann, who had to struggle against great privations, now made his way to Amsterdam, where he soon succeeded in finding occupation as a clerk. In this position he found time during the next few years to study and acquire all the chief languages of modern Europe, and in 1846 his principal, finding that he knew Russian, sent him as his agent to St. Petersburg.

After travelling in Syria and Egypt, he, in 1859, paid his first visit to Greece, the future scene of his archaeological triumphs. In 1864 he made a voyage round the world, and in 1866 settled in Paris, chiefly in order to study Greek antiquities, with a view to preparing himself to carry out the desire he had long cherished of investigating the sites of the most famous places in the history of ancient Hellas. After a visit to Ithaka, he proceeded to Asia Minor and commenced the work which ere long made his name known throughout the civilised world. Being convinced, from his familiarity with the Homeric poems, that the place called Hissarlik was the site of ancient Troy, he applied to Constantinople for permission to excavate the spot, and, having obtained the sanction of the Turkish authorities, he commenced operations in April, 1870, defraying the whole of the heavy expenditure out of his own pocket. With occasional interruptions in the hotter months, he continued his excavations at Ilium until the year 1882. During these years he was materially assisted by his wife, a Greek lady whom he had married on his second visit to Athens. The result of Dr. Schliemann's operations at Hissarlik was successful beyond all his expectations, and the work in which he told the story fairly astonished the learned world. At the same time, the best scholars by no means admitted all that the author claimed. From beneath a dense superincumbent mass, consisting of red cinders mixed with the scoriæ of copper and lead, the learned excavator had unquestionably unearthed a vast variety of very ancient objects. He had found old brick walls, numbers of ancient tools made of stone, ancient weapons of bronze, and numerous objects in terra-cotta, bone, and ivory, besides many vases, jewels, and other objects in gold, silver, and amber. In the latter he believed he had discovered the actual treasures of the old Trojan King Priam, as described in the "Iliad;" but in this, as in some other contentions as to the real character of the relics he had brought to light, the most eminent authorities in Germany and elsewhere were not able to agree with him. At the same time, no one questioned the value of Schliemann's discoveries as illustrations of the Homeric poems.

Troy was, however, not the only scene of Schliemann's successes in the way of archaeological research. At Mycenæ, the old capital of King Agamemnon, he began excavating in 1876, and succeeded in discovering in the ruins of the ancient citadel numerous precious articles of personal adornment and weapons, as well as skeletons, coming down from the most ancient period of Greek history. Many of the objects here found are in solid gold. They have been deposited in the Politechnikon at Athens. Dr. Schliemann carried out other excavations, most of them successful, in Ithaka and Tiryns and Orchomenos, where, as at Mycenæ, he brought to light some remarkable examples of the Cyclopean style of architecture. The Lion Gate and the so-called Treasury of Atreus at Mycenæ, the relics of a Cyclopean town on Mount Aetos, in Ithaka, the so-called Treasury of Minyas at Orchomenos, and the imposing remains of the Royal Palace at Tiryns are among the monuments of the most remote period of Hellenic art and history whose discovery we owe to the indefatigable labours of Dr. Schliemann.

The Times
4ᵗʰ December 1849

THE FATE OF SIR JOHN FRANKLIN.—The Arctic officers have just been summoned to the Admiralty to offer their joint advice as to the course which it seems most proper to pursue under the present condition of things with reference to the fate of Sir John Franklin. Sir John Richardson, in his report to the Admiralty, presents strong grounds of hope that the missing expedition may be shut up under circumstances that are compatible with its reappearance. According to him, the lands in the neighbourhood of which the lost expedition should most probably be looked for, abound in animals which might supply the failing stores on board the ships; and he thinks that should Sir John Franklin's provisions become so far reduced as to be inadequate, with this aid, to a winter's consumption, it is not likely that he would remain longer by his ships—but rather, it is probable, that in one body, or in several, the officers, and crews —with boats cut down so as to be light enough to drag over the ice, or built expressly for that purpose—would endeavour to make their way eastward to Lancaster Sound, or southward to the main land, according to the longitude in which the ships were arrested. Great stress is laid on the fact, that no trace of a wreck, or of any misfortune to the expedition, is found on any part of the path which they must have passed. For ourselves we think this argument tells both ways. We rejoice to know, however, that the search after the missing adventurers is to be renewed. The Enterprise and Investigator are to be immediately re-equipped and despatched at once to the Sandwich Islands—there to await further orders. From this it will be seen that the route by Behring's Straits is to be explored, and the westward coasts of Banks's and Parry's islands will, we presume, be carefully examined.—*Athenæum.*

The Glasgow Herald
18ᵗʰ September 1911

DEATH OF MR. E. WHYMPER.

MOUNTAINEERING DISASTER RECALLED

Reuter's correspondent at Chamonix announces that Mr Edward Whymper, the great mountaineer, explorer, and author, died there on Saturday.

Edward Whymper, perhaps the most distinguished and at all events the best known of British Alpinists, was born in London on April 27, 1840. He was the son of an artist, and was trained as a wood engraver. When only 20 years of age he was commissioned to make a series of sketches of Alpine scenery, and during his tour succeeded in reaching the summit of Mount Pelvoux, a peak hitherto deemed inaccessible. His ascent in 1864 of a neighbouring peak, now named Pointe des Ecrins—the highest summit in the French Alps next to Mont Blanc—was reckoned the most remarkable climbing feat up to that date. From 1861 to 1865 he made various ascents, many of them of a pioneering nature, in the Mont Blanc group and the Pennine Alps. Having made six unsuccessful attempts to scale the Matterhorn from the Italian side, he made up his mind to try the ascent from Zermatt, being convinced that its perpendicular appearance on that side was largely an optical illusion. His companions were Lord Francis William Douglas, brother of the Marquis of Queensberry; the Rev. Charles Hudson, an experienced mountaineer; Mr Robert Douglas Hadow, and four guides—Michael Croz, Peter Taugwalder, and his two sons. The ascent was begun on July 13, 1865, and by noon of the next day it had been safely achieved. During the descent Croz, who was leading, had stepped aside from helping Mr Hadow, when the latter slipped, fell on Croz, and knocked him over. Mr Hudson and Lord F. Douglas were dragged

off their feet by the rope which linked the party together. Mr Whymper and the older Taugwalder, who were above, stood their ground, "but the rope broke midway between Taugwalder and Lord F. Douglas. For two or three seconds, says Mr Whymper, in his "Scrambles Among the Alps," "we saw our unfortunate companions sliding downwards on their backs, and spreading out their hands endeavouring to save themselves; they then disappeared one by one, and fell from precipice to precipice on to the Matterhorn glacier below, a distance of nearly 4000 feet in height." All the bodies were found two days later except that of Lord Francis Douglas, only some portions of which have since been discovered.

In 1867 and 1872 Mr Whymper visited Greenland, where he made an important collection of fossil plants. In 1879-80, along with a Swiss guide named Carrel, he made what is perhaps his most memorable series of ascents, in the Andes of Ecuador; he was the first to reach the summit of Chimborazo, and he spent a night on the summit of Cotopaxi. His Andean adventures are graphically described in his largest and most important book, "Travels among the Great Andes of the Equator," published in 1892, which, besides purely mountaineering matter, contains interesting and quaint particulars about Ecuador and its inhabitants. He also made some useful investigations regarding mountain sickness. Between 1901 and 1905 he travelled in Canada and explored the mountains in the neighbourhood of the "Great Divide." Besides the two books mentioned, he published a book on the use of the aneroid barometer and two books on the Chamonix and Zermatt regions. His books were admirably illustrated by himself, and the Alpine volumes have gone into many editions.

Mr Whymper was an F.R.S.E., a Fellow and Patron's Medallist of the Royal Geographical Society, an hon. member of the Geographical Society of Paris, and of many mountaineering clubs. He leaves a widow and one child.

The New York Times
28th March 1968

'Yuri Gagarin Killed A Test Plane Falls'

MOSCOW, Thursday, March 28 — Yuri A. Gagarin, the world's first man in space, was killed yesterday in an air accident, the Moscow radio announced today.

The announcement said the crash occurred during a training flight and also killed Col. Vladimir S. Seryogin, described as chief of the detachment. Both victims will be buried in the Kremlin wall, the radio bulletin added. The radio said the cosmonaut, who was 34 years old, died while test-flying a new aircraft.

The official announcement as carried by Tass, the Soviet press agency, said:

"It is officially announced here that Hero of the Soviet Union Yuri Gagarin, the world's first cosmonaut, has perished during an air crash."

Colonel Gagarin made man's first flight in space on April 12, 1961, a one-orbit trip lasting 108 minutes.

Tass said the announcement of Colonel Gagarin's death had been made by the Communist party's Central Committee, the Presidium of the Supreme Soviet (Parliament), and the Soviet Council of Ministers.

From Obscurity to Renown

Until the morning of April 12, 1961, Yuri Alekseyevich Gagarin was no better known than any of the other 1,200 or so Gagarins living in the Moscow area.

But that morning, Yuri Gagarin, then 27 years old, sat cramped in the cockpit of a Vostok space capsule as it was launched from a pad at Baykonur, in Kazakhstan.

At 9:07 A.M., the capsule went into orbit around the earth and Yuri Gagarin became the world's first man in space. His flight represented an epochal scientific and technological achievement for the Russians.

In both the Soviet Union and the West, it was realized that Cosmonaut Gagarin had begun a new chapter in history, one in which man had dared cross the threshold of the universe.

Setback for U. S.

The Gagarin flight was a blow to those involved in the United States space program as well as a political and diplomatic setback, a fact underlined by the Soviet Union's trumpeting of the feat as evidence of "the genius of the Soviet people and the powerful force of socialism."

The formerly unknown test pilot was transformed into an international hero. Streets were named for him in many Soviet cities, monuments were erected, and Government officials pinned medals on his tunic. Premier Nikita Khrushchev publicly smothered him with kisses, compared him to Christopher Columbus, and named him a Hero of the Soviet Union.

Since that flight both Russian and American astronauts have gone on to greater achievements, including multimanned multiple-orbit flights. But Gagarin's was man's first flight in space, and history will remember him for it.

His heroism was applauded on an international tour and he rose in the ranks of the Communist Party, which he had joined in 1949. Colonel Gagarin served as chairman of the Soviet-Cuban Friendship Society, and as a delegate to the 22d Congress of the Communist Party. Since 1962 he had served as a deputy in the Supreme Soviet.

Yuri Gagarin was a rather quiet man, mild-spoken almost to a fault. He had intelligent, dark eyes and bushy eyebrows. His forehead was broad and his nose snubbed, and persons who knew him said he had the appearance and demeanor of "a typical Muskovite."

Daily Telegraph
28th January 1967

3 U.S. SPACEMEN DIE IN ROCKET FIRE

CAPE KENNEDY TEST PAD DISASTER

FLAMES TRAP APOLLO TEAM IN CAPSULE

Daily Telegraph
16th April 1967

A LONELY DEATH

COLONEL KOMAROV, a heroic pioneer in the terrifying new field which has been opened to exploration in the last 20 years, has died in the service of science. He is, so far as we can tell, the first cosmonaut to have lost his life during "operations." The three Americans who formed the first Apollo crew perished on the ground while testing their capsule last January.

The name of VLADIMIR KOMAROV thus becomes linked with those of so many others who have risked and found death while seeking to add to the world's treasure of knowledge. From the first experiments with balloons until the latest marvel of space travel, flight has claimed many victims. These have carried on a long story. Navigators who crossed uncharted oceans in cockleshells, the men who trekked into the heart of Africa, and those who battled their way towards the North and South Poles are among those who set the great tradition which Col. KOMAROV has followed.

In this kind of endeavour frontiers mean little. The world's sympathy goes out to Col. KOMAROV's family and to the Soviet Union now mourning one of its heroes. America, mindful of both Russia's casualties and her own, suggests co-operation in the manned exploration of space. Is this a field where frontiers might vanish altogether?

RUSSIAN INQUIRY INTO SPACE CRASH

ASTRONAUT'S RECORD OF HEART TROUBLE

MYSTERY OF FAILURE TO USE EJECTOR

Daily Telegraph
6th July 1971

SILENT TRAGEDY OF SOYUZ

3 cosmonauts die at controls

THE RECORD-BREAKING orbital flight of Russia's three Soyuz II cosmonauts ended in silent tragedy and mystery at dawn yesterday when the men were found dead in their seats after what was apparently a perfect soft landing in the steppes of Kazakhstan, Soviet Central Asia.

YURI GAGARIN

Humanities

Jean-Jacques Rousseau, whose ideas on the relation of the individual to the state, education, and the example of the Noble Savage have done so much to shape Western attitudes, failed to have his death recorded by the nascent British press, a distinction he shares with Immanuel Kant, the philosopher *par excellence* of modern Protestanism; with Georg Friedrich Wilhelm von Hegel, the outstandingly tortuous philosopher of non-commonsense; and with Auguste Comte, who among other, though less bizarre achievements, is the founder of sociology. Who was it who said the British were nothing if not intellectually insular? **Jeremy Bentham**, the theoretical lynchpin of the welfare state and theoretician-in-chief of the Industrial Revolution, was more fortunate, as was **John Stuart Mill**, the greatest of British liberals. In a somewhat different vein, **Matthew Arnold** stands for all who have upheld Culture against culture, from Lévy-Bruhl to F. R. Leavis to UNESCO. **Friedrich Nietzsche** both exemplifies all that is opposed to this Christian tradition and yet also shares its elitism in his impatience of the common man; by contrast to the bringer of the news that God was dead, **Pope John XXIII** symbolizes those who beg to differ – but without arrogance. **Dietrich Bonhoeffer**, a martyr to his cause of bringing Christianity to terms with its social responsibility, somehow combines the two, in a way reflecting the experience of many. The economists, whose machinations effect all our relationships, are represented by the founder of Capitalism as a doctrine, **Adam Smith**, and by **John Maynard Keynes**, who sought to mitigate some of its consequences. **Bertrand Russell** was perhaps the sole British thinker to approach the old ideal of the philosopher, the all-round intellectual activist. **Sigmund Freud**'s influence need hardly be detailed; whereas **Wilhelm Reich** rarely receives his due as the inspiration behind the – alleged? – sexual liberation of recent years. **Edith Covell** and Dr. **Schweitzer** both represent humanity in action, and **William Wilbeforce** a life dedicated to philanthropy.

The Times
22nd October 1915

MISS CAVELL'S DEATH.

The Execution of Miss Cavell.

The ordinary German mind is doubtless incapable of understanding the "horror and dis-"gust" which the military execution of MISS CAVELL will arouse throughout the civilized world. The papers issued this morning by the Government, despite the restraints of official correspondence, disclose something of the feelings which the deed excited in the members of the American and of the Spanish Legations in Brussels, who strove with chivalrous zeal to save our countrywoman's life. We shall be surprised if within the next few days the Press of all neutral lands does not re-echo these feelings with an intensity which will astonish the disciples of *Kultur*. Here we have in its highest development that boasted product of the Teutonic intelligence and the Teutonic heart. The very spirit of Zabern, but of Zabern in war-time, broods over the whole brutal and stupid story. There is not in Europe, outside Germany and her Allies, a man who can read it without the deepest emotions of pity and of shame. The victim was a lady who had devoted her life to the noblest and the most womanly work woman can do. She was the head of a great nursing institute which has trained numbers of nurses for Germany as well as for Belgium. She herself nursed many wounded Germans at the beginning of the war. She has been sentenced to death by their officers, and shot by their comrades. So is it that the Germans requite the charity of strangers. She had been guilty of a military offence—the offence of harbouring her own wounded countrymen and Belgians amongst whom she had lived and worked, and of getting them across the Dutch frontier. That was enough for the uniformed pedants who tried her, and for their civilian subordinates. She was perfectly straightforward and truthful with the Court. They sent her to her death upon her own admissions. They could not, even by their own harsh law, have convicted her without these admissions. Her frankness did not profit her any more than did her sex, her calling, or her services to the KAISER'S wounded troops. There was the fact ; she acknowledged certain acts which could be twisted into "conveying soldiers to the enemy," and the legal penalty for this offence under the German Military Code is death. That was enough for her Judges. They sentenced her on a Monday afternoon, and had her shot in the dark at 2 o'clock next morning. NAPOLEON ordered a similar "execution" in the ditch of Vincennes. It cost him and his Empire dear.

AMERICAN MINISTER applied for leave for his Councillor of Legation to visit the prisoner before trial. He was refused " on grounds "—unstated—" of principle." She was not even allowed to see a lawyer before she was tried. That measure of elementary justice, allowed to the meanest felon by the laws of civilized communities, is, it seems, not permitted by German Military tribunals. The counsel for the defence has to pick up the case as best he can in Court. The Councillor of the American Legation expressed his intention of being present so as to watch the case. MISS CAVELL'S lawyer, who declared that the Court was always perfectly fair, nevertheless begged him not to attend, as the Judges would resent his presence and it would greatly prejudice the accused. As soon as the American Legation heard that the prosecution asked for a death sentence, they put themselves into communication with the civil authorities. The chief business of BARON VON DER LANCKEN, the head of the *Politische Abteilung*, and of his staff appears to have been to mislead the AMERICAN MINISTER as to the jeopardy in which the prisoner stood, until their military accomplices could put her to death without embarrassing intervention. They did their work with characteristic thoroughness. The Americans were insistent. HERR CONRAD gave them positive assurances twice over that they would be informed of developments, and told them some time after the sentence that it had not been passed and probably would not be passed for a day or two. But the Legation learned the truth, and MR. GIBSON, on behalf of the MINISTER, who was ill, together with the SPANISH MINISTER, called on BARON VON DER LANCKEN to protest against the horror on which the military authorities were determined. The BARON said he did not believe sentence had been passed, and expressed his surprise that his visitors should trust unofficial information. Their story was " quite "improbable," and, even if it were true, the execution would not be immediate. They were firm, and compelled him to ascertain the facts—which were exactly as they had stated. They put before him with much force the reasons for not carrying out the sentence, pointing out the " fearful effect " a summary execution would have on opinion in Belgium and abroad, and urging that a delay could not possibly hurt Germany. The BARON answered that the matter rested with the MILITARY GOVERNOR, and, after a brief conference with this authority, told them that he was inexorable. He had acted " with "mature deliberation " and refused to accept any representations. The BARON actually declared that " even the Emperor himself could " not intervene." HIS MAJESTY, it will have been seen, has since intervened in the case of the other prisoners condemned to death by the same tribunal.

There is not much more to tell. The Councillor to the American Legation was refused permission to visit the prisoner after sentence, and a like refusal was at first given to the English clergyman, Mr. GAHAN. This last refusal, worthy of the Jacobins who refused a confessor to MARIE ANTOINETTE, was, however, not persisted in, and the doomed Englishwoman had the consolations of her own Church and received the Holy Communion from Mr. GAHAN's hands. He found her "admirably strong and "calm." She admitted again her guilt according to German military law, but assured him that "she was happy to die for her country." Her country with one voice acknowledges the claim. She did in very truth die for England, and England will not lightly forget her death. That she had committed a technical offence is undeniable, but so did ANDREAS HOFER, and other victims of Napoleonic tyranny whose doom patriotic Germans never cease to execrate. But hers was a case, if ever there has been one, where the commonest sense of expediency demanded that mercy should temper justice. The action of the EMPEROR proves that he at least is sensible of this. We do not know whether the hide-bound brutality of the military authorities or the lying trickery of the civilians is the more repulsive. Both were determined that Miss CAVELL should die, and they conspired together to shoot her before an appeal could be lodged. They have killed the English nurse, as NAPOLEON killed the Duc D'ENGHIEN, and by killing her they have immeasurably deepened the stain of infamy that degrades them in the eyes of the whole world. They could have done no deed better calculated to serve the British cause.

**The Times
31st July 1833**

DEATH OF WILLIAM WILBERFORCE, ESQ.—It is this day our melancholy duty to announce the death of William Wilberforce, a name with which there is probably associated more of love and veneration than ever fell to the lot of any single individual throughout the civilized globe. At one period the sad event would have been felt as a grievous national calamity, and even now the tidings of his departure will be heard with the deepest sorrow through every part of the empire. But he worked while it was called day, remembering the night was coming wherein no man may work. And he was not permitted to leave the scene of his labours till he beheld the great cause to which he had dedicated all the energies of his soul triumphant, and the fetters of the negro about to be struck off for ever. His warfare is accomplished; his course is finished; he kept the faith. Those who regard him merely as a philanthropist, in the worldly sense of that abused term, know but little of his character. His philanthropy took its origin in love to God; it was kindled at the sacred fire of divine love, and it burned with such bright and steady lustre only because it was daily replenished from its hallowed source. The sad event took place last night at the house of Mrs. Smith, in Cadogan-place. Mr. Wilberforce was in the 74th year of his age. We must reserve all particulars for our next. We understand Mr. Wilberforce has directed in his will that his funeral should be conducted without the smallest pomp, and that his body should be interred in the family vault of his brother-in-law in the churchyard of Stoke Newington, pursuant to a promise made to the late Mr. Stephen.

THE EDITH CAVELL MEMORIAL.

QUEEN ALEXANDRA'S WISH.

Queen Alexandra sent yesterday for Lord Knutsford, chairman of the London Hospital, and discussed with him the suggestion that the *Daily Mirror* Memorial Fund to Miss Cavell, the English nurse whom the Germans shot in Brussels, should be devoted to the extension of the Nursing Home at the hospital. Her Majesty informed him that it was her wish that the new Nurses' Home which is being built at the London Hospital, and to which she had given her name, should be called, instead of the "Alexandra Home," the "Edith Cavell Home." This she thought a more fitting memorial to Miss Cavell than the scheme first suggested, which was only that an addition should be made to an existing home.

The organizers of the fund have received the following telegram from Miss Cavell's mother:—

I think Lord Knutsford's proposal of Edith Cavell Home in the London Hospital very suitable, but leave the decision to him and other people of influence. Not a statue.

**Daily Express
22nd April 1946**

Keynes dies, his loan unpassed

WORN OUT AFTER CONFERENCE

Express Staff Reporter

WHILE the American Senate paused yesterday in its debate on the loan, Lord Keynes, the economist, whose brainchild it was, died after a heart attack at his home, Tilton, Ripe, near Lewes, Sussex. He was 62.

Only 10 days ago he appeared in sparkling health and form, though he had returned exhausted, a few days before, from a conference at Savannah, Georgia.

He died within three minutes of collapsing at 10 a.m. With him was his wife, the former ballerina, Lydia Lopokova.

At Savannah, Keynes skirmished with Mr. Fred Vinson, U.S. Secretary of the Treasury, about the administrative set-up of the Bretton Woods Monetary Fund and International Bank.

Keynes urged that the fund's fiscal year should begin, like Britain's, on April 1. "No," said Vinson, "July 1."

"Why?" asked Keynes. "Because," shouted Vinson, slamming the table, "it is just three days before July 4" (American Independence from Britain Day).

Keynes wanted the bank in New York, America's financial centre. The Americans chose Washington, the political centre.

Nevertheless, Keynes moved a vote of thanks to Vinson, and spoke of his "dignity, patience, firmness and fairness."

And of Lord Keynes, Mr. Vinson said last night: "In these chaotic days the world can ill afford to lose men of his stature."

He foreshadowed the disastrous effects to the world of the political plan to exact £6,000,000,000 of reparations from Germany.

Between the wars, as Cambridge professor, he was against the gold standard and advocated cheap money and a "managed" currency to cure depression.

He was opposed by Lord Norman, then Governor of the Bank of England, but after Britain was forced off gold in 1931, Keynes became again the Treasury's Chief Economic Adviser. And later a director of the Bank of England.

Mr. Attlee, the Prime Minister, said last night: "His services to the State as an adviser on economics and finance and as a negotiator were invaluable."

The Guardian
4th February 1970

Thinker in the grip of passions

IN 1921 the death of Bertrand Russell from acute pneumonia at the German Hospital, Peking, was reported by the Japan Advertiser.

Truth caught up with error in a day or two, but not before a shoal of disparaging biographical articles had rushed into print in British newspapers.

Nearly 50 years later the obituary tone will be less waspish and more understanding. In the interval Bertrand Russell had achieved great age and had come to be revered throughout the world as a sage and a philosopher.

Undoubtedly his motive was to fight evil. To some it may have seemed to have led him into strange quarters and some of his colleagues may not have been so well motivated. But he went to prison for his motives. He was dismissed from academic posts for them. He sat in the dust of the roadway, when almost 90, for them, to be hauled away, albeit gently, and sent to prison again.

His own summing up of his life, its urges, its ideals came in his three volumes of autobiography. In the first, published just before his 95th birthday, he wrote:

"Three passions, simple but overwhelmingly strong, have governed my life, the longing for love, the search for knowledge and unbearable pity for the suffering of mankind. These passions, like great winds, have blown me hither and thither over a deep ocean of anguish.

"I have sought love, first, because it brings ecstasy—ecstasy so great that I would often have sacrificed all the rest of life for a few hours of this joy.

Bertrand Russell's mother died when he was two, his father in the following year. He moved to the house of his grandfather, who had been the Lord John Russell of the Reform Bill — and who died three years later.

Bertrand's upbringing was undertaken by his pious grandmother "a Puritan with the moral rigidity of the Covenanters."

At fifteen, in spite of his grandmother's precautions, Bertrand lost his faith in religion. Happily he had (aged 11) found that he excelled in mathematics.

He described the discovery of Euclid — as dazzling as first love. I had not imagined that there was anything so delicious in the world.

He went to Cambridge, read Moral Science and in 1895 was elected to a lectureship at Trinity. In 1903 he published his Principles of Mathematics. Ten years later he and the philosopher A. N. Whitehead completed the three volumes of Principia Mathematica. It is on this work the inspiration of a new philosophical sect, the "logical positivists," that Russell's professional reputation as a philosopher rests.

It has had a profound and enduring influence and is acknowledged to be one of the outstanding works of the human mind.

The public, to whom such a book could mean nothing, judged Bertrand Russell by other criteria—and it judged him severely. He opposed the Boer War; disliked the Fabians for their authoritarian tendencies; advocated women's suffrage; during the 1914-18 war, pamphleteered against conscription (fined £100).

All this was bad enough, but in 1917 he wrote an article in which he said that the United States government had called out troops, not to fight the Germans, but to support capitalism; he was clapped in jail for six months and, for a time, lost his Cambridge lectureship.

At last, as he said ruefully, he had found the key to fame. He spent the time in prison writing The Introduction to Mathematical Philosophy, every page of which the bewildered prison governor was compelled by his duty, to read.

Up to the eve of the Second World War, Russell remained a believer in neutrality; in 1940 he publicly renounced pacifism. It was not the last of his renunciations. In 1948 he wanted to drop the A-bomb on Russia before Russia dropped it on us. By 1960 he had become a leading protagonist of unilateral nuclear disarmament.

Unlike the conventional notion of a philosopher, Russell had charm, gaiety, old-fashioned manners, an eighteenth century precision of speech; a "hyena" laugh; a liking for vigorous exercise; a gift for expressing himself lucidly.

"University life would be better, both intellectually and morally, if most university students had temporary, childless marriages," he once declared. "This would solve the sexual urge yet need not take up time which ought to be given to work."

It was, it must be pointed out, a view which he himself did not practise in his days at Cambridge. He came shyly and inexperienced to his first marriage, as he described it in his autobiography, taking four years to pluck up the courage to propose. He followed it with three more marriages and other less officially sanctioned affairs, which he himself described.

During his later years Russell was president of the Campaign for Nuclear Disarmament until he disagreed with the chairman, Canon Collins, over civil disobedience which he claimed was campaign policy. Then for a time he was chairman of the Committee of 100.

At the time of the Cuban missile crisis, when events seemed to be moving towards the third world war, he sent telegrams to all world leaders involved.

Those telegrams went from his hillside retreat in Penrhyndeudraeth, where he lived during his last years and conducted his affairs with the help of his wife and his American secretary.

Among the last of his brain children was the International War Crimes Tribunal on American actions in Vietnam, which eventually met in Stockholm in May, 1967.

It had been refused permission to hold sessions in Paris and Lord Russell said that plans to have a public session in London had to be abandoned because of the attitude of Prime Minister Harold Wilson.

While it was in session, Lord Russell celebrated his 95th birthday. Any doubts about his mental liveliness were dispelled by an exchange he had with the Oxford University Press over a paperback edition of his Problems of Philosophy.

The publishers wanted a cover showing a street photograph, slightly out of focus. "How clever is the photographer," commented the philosopher. "He makes abstract that which appears to be concrete."

As a philosopher, and as a writer, it was Bertrand Russell's genius to achieve the opposite effect.

Daily Telegraph
6th September 1955

DR. SCHWEITZER, A LIFE DEVOTED TO HUMANITY

'SAINT' OF LAMBARENE

DR. ALBERT SCHWEITZER, who has died aged 90, approached the almost unattainable ideal of the complete man, perhaps more than anyone in this modern age.

He was remarkable for his exceptional achievements in theology and music, and for putting his own interpretation of Christian ethics into practice with such single-mindedness and energy.

His saintliness was honoured by those who knew him personally. The world had for long been impressed by his decision, at the age of 30, to leave behind two great reputations, become a mission doctor and devote his whole life to the service of humanity.

YOUTH IN ALSACE
Three careers

In the little Alsatian village of Günsbach, where he grew up, his schoolmates looked upon him as a "sprig of the gentry," because he was a minister's son. To be set apart from the other boys was an agony to him; and he suffered many a beating rather than wear an overcoat, the badge of a "gentleman."

As Dr. Schweitzer grew up he came to believe that whatever he possessed more than other men he should not accept as a matter of course; he would live a life of more than average devotion.

When he was 21 he resolved to devote his life to science, philosophy and music until he was 30, and then to give himself to the service of humanity. For the next nine years he followed three simultaneous careers—theology, philosophy and music.

LEADING ORGANIST
Bach biography

He was recognised as one of Europe's leading organists; his biography of Bach was hailed as "a new revelation." As a Doctor of Philosophy he was known for his work on Kant, and as a theologian he had been appointed principal of Strasbourg's Theological College of St. Thomas.

During these years he often worked day and night, but he kept the secret of his vow. When he finally announced his intention to spend the rest of his life among the Africans, most of his friends were shocked and angry.

The next six years Dr. Schweitzer spent as a medical student. In addition he was preaching every Sunday and working on two major theological volumes.

When that struggle was over he married Helene Bresslau, the daughter of a Strasbourg University colleague, and on Good Friday, 1913, they set out together for the tiny settlement at Lambaréné in French Equatorial Africa, now the Republic of Gabon.

His first surgery at Lambaréné was a windowless hen-house with a broken roof. Patients came in hordes from as far as 200 miles away. In nine months he had treated nearly 2,000 patients. Most of them suffered from sleeping-sickness, others were lepers.

Dr. Schweitzer early realised that his accommodation was completely inadequate to deal with the hundreds of cases. Within a year, with native labour, he had cleared a patch in the jungle and created a hospital.

Year after year he struggled against lack of funds, plague and pestilence, against native ignorance and indifference, against one of the worst climates in the world.

But medicine was only part of his work. He preached the gospel on Sunday, and on almost every day of the week he served as architect, carpenter, judge or gang foreman.

NOBEL PRIZE WINNER
Order of Merit

This struggle was to last all his life. From time to time Dr. Schweitzer came to Europe to lecture and to give organ recitals to raise funds for his work. Always he returned

Honours were showered on him and he was awarded the Nobel Peace Prize for 1952. In 1955 he became an honorary member of the Order of Merit.

In 1957, in a message broadcast by Oslo radio, Dr. Schweitzer made the first of several appeals for the cessation of nuclear tests. He warned the world that radio-activity was "a catastrophe to the human race."

When he reached his 90th birthday last January he was still active despite his great age.

For some time then he had been a centre of controversy, being accused by some of resistance to medical progress in his hospitals. He was also accused of paternalist condescension towards Africans and of impatience with the advice of experts.

Dr. Schweitzer defended his concept of primitive medical treatment for primitive patients in his jungle hospital. "The simple African labourers convinced me that conditions are different here from those in Europe and necessities are different," he said. "So I built an African hospital for Africans."

Although he had lost faith in the 19th-century myth of progress, he never fell into the despair which despises reason, or turned away from life into learning and thought which feed only on themselves. The essence of Dr. Schweitzer's message was that he combined extreme intellectual scepticism with extreme reverence for life.

The remedy that he proposed for the restoration of civilisation was a return to the principles of Christianity as originally enunciated by its Founder.

His philosophy of "reverence for life" forms the central theme of the treatise on the "Philosophy of Civilisation," on which, during the intervals in his work of mercy, he had been writing for many years.

Morning Post
17ᵗʰ April 1888

Mr. MATTHEW ARNOLD had reached so high a position in the literature of his country that the news of his death will be felt with a pang of regret in every English-speaking household where the "Philistinism," against which he waged such unceasing war, is not still rampant. There are people, themselves, perhaps, well known among the leading writers of their country, who may be disposed to deny the name of a great man to the conspicuous figure just gone from us. Their number, however, we believe to be small, and their opinion to be based on too narrow and exclusive an interpretation of the epithet. There are degrees of greatness, as of everything else, and the lines which MATTHEW ARNOLD laid down for himself were scarcely broad enough for the traffic of the entire literary world to pass their way. The authority of "Culture and Anarchy" may be said to have marked an epoch, but it was an epoch in taste rather than one of the far greater and grander group which from time to time have dominated the ethical or intellectual progress of mankind. The work which he did was, as nearly as possible, perfect of its kind, and in his own purview it possessed a moral and mental efficacy far superior to many efforts of a very different and, as we are disposed to think, infinitely more enduring kind. It would, however, be needless and illogical to press this comparison when once it has been indicated. The talented specialists who strive to invent new systems of thought or conduct for the benefit of mankind, are best left to adjust their own differences, or, failing that, to present their own controversies to the world. Most people knew what Mr. MATTHEW ARNOLD thought about Mr. HERBERT SPENCER and Mr. FREDERIC HARRISON, as it is also known what these distinguished men think of each other's views, and what both again have thought of Mr. MATTHEW ARNOLD. There is an old Dutch proverb particularly applicable in literary matters which bids us " try all and "keep to the best." It should be quite possible to recognise that there are higher phases of speculative thought than are to be found even in the delicate and subtle criticism of MATTHEW ARNOLD. But it should be equally possible to recognise this without therefore denying him a place among the prophets, although the world at large still believes that he prophesied often of minor things. It seems to us that to assign to any man admittedly possessed of genius his right niche in the literary Pantheon, we must first ascertain in what the nature of genius itself consists. Speaking in the broad way alone possible within our present limits, it would appear that genius is displayed less in the subject matter with which an author deals than in the universality of his treatment. Apart from this distinguishing character few contemporary leaders of thought could have soared above a recognition based on mere agreement, varied by a condemnation caused by difference of opinion. It is easy to make this clear by almost any example. Cardinal NEWMAN is read with approbation and sympathy by the advocates of nearly every Christian denomination. The reason is that he is the universal exponent of Revelation, and touches chords which lie far beneath all differences. DARWIN'S great discovery has been welcomed by men of the most conflicting opinions, and he was laid to rest in Westminster Abbey amid a general demonstration of sympathy. The same high quality may be found in the epoch-making works of Mr. HERBERT SPENCER, with the result that his researches into the sociological conditions under which we lived are valued by many who re-

ward his more extreme opinions with emphatic distaste. In the same way it should be easy to see that MATTHEW ARNOLD, at his own level and from an absolutely different standpoint, makes the same universal appeal for a fair hearing of the literary gospel he has set forth, and this without in the least involving any acceptance of his more eccentric conclusions.

There is little doubt that the majority of men have found it much easier to sneer at the exponent of culture than to appreciate his mental attitude with any degree of accuracy. Such phrases as " lucidity," or the still more familiar "sweetness and light," have been divorced from their context and made the object of much cheap sneering about the "rose-"water " method of treating the difficulties of man's social improvement. None the less, they form part of a system entitled to be described as a coherent whole, with high and earnest aims. If MATTHEW ARNOLD erred in attributing too much of possibility to his doctrine of striving after perfection in matters of taste, as well as in those of judgment on more vital matters, he was never for one moment swayed by it to the exclusion of his own "lucidity." Nor has his work been without its decided fruits. Men and women no longer take a pride in their own narrowness and incapacity to find pleasure in the beautiful, and for this good result the fastidious critic of their habits of thought is much more responsible than he has ever been for those irrational votaries of blue china and sunflowers, who caught the letter and missed the spirit of his teaching. The very fact that MATTHEW ARNOLD dealt with matters so little tangible to the whole world that men of education will to-day be asking themselves what his precise province really was has caused his influence to be to a large extent unconscious. But none the less it has spread like oil upon the troubled waters of ugliness and bigotry, and the ideas of "totality" and " provinciality" as applied to thought will long survive any eccentric disquisitions on a modification of the Episcopacy as a prelude to an eirenicon between the Churches of England and Scotland. The doctrine of a conscious striving after a correct standard in all things is never likely to prove a panacea for the ills of society, until the critical faculty becomes universal, and art, morals, and literature have acquired a very different meaning in the eyes of men and women generally.

Of MATTHEW ARNOLD as a poet it is only now possible to speak in a perfunctory manner. Mr. SWINBURNE has placed on record his opinion that his best poems must live as long as any of their time, not because his generation " liked the prose less, but they "like the verses more." That this will ever be the case with a very wide circle we may permit ourselves to doubt. MATTHEW ARNOLD will be poeta poetarum rather than the popular favourite of the general reader of English poetry. The very points on which Mr. SWINBURNE has lovingly dwelt, to wit, "the per-"fection of work and the personality in the "workman," imply this by the nature of the case. But the critic and poet himself would scarcely have desired a reward for which he disdained to strive. His poetry will doubtless remain as the best exemplification of his theory, and the theory itself, with the constant inculcation of the endeavour to " grow towards "the light," will no more die with MATTHEW ARNOLD than it was born with him. In some shape or another it is insisted on by every teacher of good things, although not always with the same universality or originality, or perhaps it

may be added with the same eccentricity. But now that the eloquent pen is laid aside and the music of MATTHEW ARNOLD's style will no longer enrich the world of letters, the aggressive side of his method will probably be minimised, and the real good he has worked in a small circle will radiate more widely, with the result of upsetting much of the moral and mental narrowness and inconsistency that still remains with us. If he did not grasp the weighty social weapons he believed himself to wield, he yet directed them with a skill which forbids men again to despise them.

The Daily Mail
27ᵗʰ August 1900

THE MAD PHILOSOPHER AND THINKER OF GENIUS

The celebrated philosopher Friedrich Nietzsche died on Saturday at Weimar, where he had resided for the past few years in a state of mental obscuration. He was in his fifty-sixth year.

His death is a great event for the educated Liberal classes. He was the principal interpreter of their thirst for power and wealth and their opposition to religious dogmas and sentiments.

To the English taste his philosophy is unpalatable. He preached the doctrine that human progress must eventually produce a superhuman race. His incontestable genius was morbid throughout, and his failure of mind was heralded by characteristic passages in his later writings.

Nietzsche's literary style is reminiscent at once of Ibsen, Heine, and Schopenhauer. The dogmatism with which he enunciated his theories frequently partook of absolute ferocity, particularly so when he was attacking Christianity. His most notable and characteristic book, "Thus Spake Zarathustra," published only a few years ago, is full of savage onslaughts upon Philistinism and conventionalism.

The Times
25ᵗʰ July 1945

PASTOR D. BONHOEFFER

Pastor Dietrich Bonhoeffer, who was murdered by the S.S. in the Flossenburg concentration camp last April at the age of 39, was a son of the distinguished psychiatrist Professor C. Bonhoeffer. Educated in Berlin, Barcelona, Rome, and New York, he was lecturer in systematic theology in Berlin from 1930 to 1933, but resigned when Hitler came to power. He took a leading part in resisting Reich Bishop Müller and in founding the Pastors' Emergency League. From 1933 to 1935 he was pastor of two German congregations in London, returning to Germany in 1935 to direct an illegal Confessional Church training college in Pomerania. He was deeply involved in the early stages of the plot to destroy Hitler, which failed in July, 1944. The pastor, who had been arrested in 1943, was tried in the " People's Court " early this year and sentenced to death. Before execution could take place, however, his judge was killed in an air raid which necessitated further proceedings. Shortly before the Americans arrived at Flossenburg he and his brother, Dr. Klaus Bonhoeffer, aged 44, were murdered. There will be a memorial service for Pastor Bonhoeffer at Holy Trinity, Kingsway, on Friday, July 27, at 6 p.m.

Manchester Guardian
1st May 1873

JOHN STUART MILL.

Mr. John Stuart Mill, whose death at Avignon we record to-day, was born in 1806. Those who love to trace the qualities of distinguished men in their immediate ancestry will find their task easy in the present case. James Mill, the father of the subject of our memoir, was not only an historian but a philosopher, and something more than a philosophic historian. It has been said of him that no English writer since Locke has shown so much acuteness in the branch of metaphysics to which his inquiries were devoted. John Stuart Mill, like some other men who have risen to the highest intellectual eminence in our generation, was educated at home. In his case, indeed, no "happy ignorance" of some things generally known to those otherwise trained was the result of the process. With James Mill as the director of his studies, he was simply more regularly educated than those who at the public school or the university can only receive their fraction of attention from the most conscientious teacher. At the age of 17 Mill obtained a clerkship in the Hon. East India Company, in whose service his father held a high position. He remained in the East India Office the greater part of his life, rising step by step, until, in 1856, he was appointed Examiner of Indian Correspondence—James Mill's former post. In his father's company and among his father's friends, he was as it were nursed in philosophy. He was frequently brought into contact with Bentham, and the influence of that powerful mind may be traced in his earliest as in his latest speculations. At the comparatively early age of 21, indeed, Mill in some measure justified his title to the nickname of "Young First Principles," which Mr. Disraeli bestowed upon him, by editing and preparing from the author's manuscript Bentham's "Rationale of Judicial Evidence." Mill's name soon became known in the higher periodical literature. He may be said to have educated himself with his pen, though his earliest productions are strikingly free from any traces of the immaturity of his powers. In 1835 he began his editorial and proprietary connection with the London and Westminster Review. He was at first associated with Sir W. Molesworth in this undertaking, but he afterwards carried it on alone until 1840. To this publication he contributed some of the best of his shorter productions. In 1836 his name was so far identified with the particular branch of science in which he has earned much of his fame that he was elected a member of the Political Economy Club. For a period of about thirty years Mill's name appears frequently in the records of the Club. In 1843 we find him opening a discussion on the question "is political economy a science à priori, or what is commonly called a science of facts?" But in that year he showed the breadth and range of his powers by producing a masterpiece in another field of intellectual effort—his "System of Logic, Ratiocinative and Inductive." Here, not content with bold innovations of view in regard to the principles and grounds of syllogistic and deductive reasoning, he tried to reduce the inductive method to the strictest rule. In a concluding part of the work he showed the influence on his own train of thought of one of the most commanding minds of the age in the inquiry "whether moral and social phenomena are really exceptions to the general constancy and uniformity of the course of nature." In Mr. Bain's late contribution to literature, that gentleman, tilting against the philosophers generally, urges upon Mr. Herbert Spencer's attention the danger in view which in metaphysics are always placed of supposing that the investigation of the processes of thought will enable them to distinguish its forms; and he appears to think that a man having devoted a certain portion of his time to the question how thoughts and feelings are constructed might give the rest to the results of the construction; in other words, we presume, he would

quote, with a difference in favour of the objects of his peculiar aversion, Butler's—

"For all a rhetorician's rules
Teach nothing but to name his tools,"

and would have the philosophers occasionally employ the implements so curiously fashioned on those practical difficulties which are the stumbling-blocks of humbler minds. At a very early period Mr. Mill seems to have anticipated this recommendation, for his love of abstract science was mingled with an active interest in even the details of social and legislative questions. In 1844 he broke ground again in the old field of inquiry with his "Essays on the Unsettled Questions of Political Economy." But the unsettled questions were not to receive their settlement in that treatise, which was to find a further development in the "Principles of Political Economy, with some of their Applications to Social Philosophy" (1848). In political economy Mr. Mill was most completely successful. The logic, for all its great merits, might with the utmost advantage have been compressed. It is a great and memorable work, unrivalled as yet in our language, and the mature result of half a lifetime of thought and study. Moreover, its value is likely to endure, for the style and method of statement are admirably clear and the great body of the doctrine can scarcely be said to be in dispute. It is only where logic trenches upon the deeper problems of metaphysics that Mill's work becomes unsatisfactory and his method fails. But in the political economy the abstract character yet limited range of his subject is precisely suited to his genius. Here it is not a question so much of first principles as of rigorous deductions from these, and a lucid statement of results; and in both these processes Mr. Mill is unsurpassed. In 1851 his union with Mrs. Harriet Taylor, a widow, was destined, as he has so eloquently shown, to perpetuate an exalting influence on his career which a long friendship with the lady had already exercised. His brief dedication of the "Essay on Liberty" (published in 1859, and after her death) is her best biography. She is there spoken of as "the inspirer and in part the author of all that is best in my writings; the friend and wife, whose exalted sense of truth and right was my strongest incitement, and whose approbation was my chief reward." The volume he declares, "like all that I have written for years, belongs as much to her as to me; but the work, as it stands, has had in a very insufficient degree the inestimable advantage of her revision, some of the more important portions having been reserved for a more careful re-examination, which they are now never destined to receive. Were I but capable of interpreting to the world one half the great thoughts and noble feelings which are buried in her grave, I should be the medium of a greater benefit to it than is ever likely to arise from anything that I can write, unprompted and unassisted by her all but unrivalled wisdom."

A year before the publication of the essay on "Liberty," he had retired from the service of the East India Company on the transfer of the Indian Administration to the Government of the Queen, and he had declined the offer of a seat in the newly formed Indian Council. "Dissertations and Discussions," and "Thoughts on Parliamentary Reform," were published in the same year as the essay on "Liberty." In the year following he was elected a corresponding member of the French Academy. "Considerations on Representative Government" appeared in 1861, and "Utilitarianism" in the following year. As a philosopher, Mr. Mill belonged in metaphysics to what has been called "the school of experience," of which Bacon is regarded as the founder, and Hobbs, Locke, and Comte as champions. In ethics he was a devout disciple of the great Bentham, whose leading principle of "utility," or the greatest happiness of the greatest number, he adopted as the test of all right action. In his essay on "Utilitarianism," he endeavoured to expand this principle by distinguishing the quality as well as the quantity of pleasure, but though this enabled him to make his theory square better with known facts it nevertheless involved it in hopeless inconsistency, and so far as we are aware, no thinker of any note has followed him in this aberration. Mr. Mill was not an original, though he was a very clear, thinker. The complexion of his philosophic creed may be traced with perfect distinctness to the various influences of his

education. First, that of his father, James Mill (an acuter writer in some respects than his son), then of Hobbes and Hulme, and finally of Auguste Comté. This last influence happily came late, or it may safely be surmised that the "Political Economy" and the essay on "Liberty" would never have been written. In 1865 appeared "Auguste Comte and Positivism," and an "Examination of Sir W. Hamilton's Philosophy." This is not the time or place to enter into an elaborate discussion of Mr. Mill's speculative writings, nor shall we attempt to assign the palm between him and Sir William Hamilton, his great antagonist. His essay on Hamilton's writings is probably the most portentously lengthy review in existence, and its value is, in our judgment, by no means equal to its bulk. His capital work in the region of purely abstract speculation is unquestionably his "Logic." In 1865 he began a brief parliamentary career of three years by his election as one of the members for Westminster. The question whether he is to be considered successful or the reverse as a popular representative is one that would involve no little difficulty at the outset in the definition of terms. As a debater, Mr. Mill undoubtedly did not take high parliamentary rank, but to the last he was a "popular" member, for he showed that there was an identity of opinion between the very "fewest" few and the many which the latter, at least, had never suspected, and he gave a status to the Radicalism of the platform which has secured its introduction to the very best society of political beliefs. In the Reform debates of 1867 he showed his interest in a cause with which his name is especially identified by moving an amendment, the object of which was to enable women to vote at parliamentary elections. He did not, he said, claim the vote as an abstract right, but on the grounds of expediency and justice. The discussion assumed a jocular character; but even at that early stage of the agitation the amendment (supported by Mr. Fawcett, Mr. Denman, and Sir George Bowyer) counted 73 supporters against it of 196. At the general election of 1868 Mr. Mill lost his seat for Westminster, and there can be little doubt that he was glad of an opportunity of retiring with honour from a position in which his powers of public usefulness found no congenial employment. In the same year appeared "England and Ireland," and in the year following "The Subjection of Women." Mr. Mill was elected an Associate of the Belgian Académie Royale in 1870. His inaugural address on the occasion of his election to the Lord Rectorship of the University of St. Andrew was published in 1867.

The Times
26th July 1790

At Edinburgh, Adam Smith, Esq. LL. D. and F. R. S. of London and Edinburgh, one of the Commissioners of his Majesty's Customs in Scotland.

The Times
4th June 1963

A NEW IMPETUS IN ROMAN CATHOLICISM

His Holiness Pope John XXIII, who succeeded Pope Pius XII as Supreme Pontiff in 1958, died yesterday evening. He was 81.

He was in his seventy-seventh year when he took possession of the see of Rome, and there was some inclination to regard him as a " caretaker ", an elderly Pope destined to preside over the consolidation of the changes wrought by his predecessor. A reasonable judgment has seldom been more completely mistaken. His pontificate produced an immediate and sustained change of atmosphere inside and outside the Church, it promoted internal reform and external conciliation, and it restored to Catholicism a sense of historical movement, something which, by the nature of ecclesiastical institutions, is prone to become overlaid by a cautious conservatism.

The new impetus was derived from small acts, like the Pope's abatement of Vatican ceremonial, and great acts, like his convocation of a general council. Whether small or great they were part and parcel of his conception of the nature of his office. " Some hope to find in the Pope ", he said, preaching at his coronation Mass, " a skilled diplomat and statesman; others a scholar, an organizer of public affairs, or one whose mind is in touch with every kind of modern progress. . . . They are none of them on the right track . . . the new Pope has before his mind, more than all else, that wonderful picture which St. John gives, in the words of the Saviour himself, of the Good Shepherd."

INFORMAL APPROACH

It was as a shepherd of his people, as *servus servorum Dei*, that he sought to impress on the world the sacred obligations of his office, not by hieratic solemnity or the worldly dignity of a court. In this his appearance helped; the coarse strength of his peasant features was expressive of benignity and simple humanity. His personal actions too were suited to his purpose: visits to the sick in Rome and to the prisoners in the Regina Coeli, his eagerness to dispense with ceremony, and his informal encounters. Above all, his conception of his office issued in his teaching, which had a universality of reference matching, as has not always happened, the universality of papal diction.

The principal sources of his teaching are the two encyclicals, *Mater et Magistra* (1961) and *Pacem in Terris* (1963), and his homilies concerning the second Vatican Council. In the first of these encyclicals he extended the social teaching of his predecessors Leo XIII and Pius XI, enlarging on the duties owed by a society to the underprivileged within it and by prosperous nations to those which are not. He returned to the latter question in *Pacem in Terris* in which he declared that it is " vitally important that the wealthier states, in providing varied forms of assistance to the poorer, should respect the moral values and ethnic characteristics peculiar to each, and also that they should avoid any intention of political domination ".

In another passage the Pope extended the principle of subsidiarity, familiar in papal teaching on the state, to the field of international relations, arguing the necessity for " a public authority, having world-wide power and endowed with the proper means for the efficacious pursuit of its objective ". This authority would not supplant individual political communities but would exist to tackle economic, social or political problems which are " posed by the universal common good " and are too large or complex or urgent to be amenable to solution by individual states.

The part of the encyclical which attracted most attention concerned relations between Catholics and others in the pursuit of public goals. Having reminded the faithful that error is not to be confused with the erring person, and that false philosophies regarding man and the universe are not identical with their associated historical movements, in which there might be patches of good (a reference which was everywhere understood to embrace communism), he went on to say that " a drawing nearer together or a meeting for the attainment of some practical end, which was formerly deemed inopportune or unproductive, might now or in the future be considered opportune and useful ".

ECUMENICAL COUNCIL

Even this amber light signalling a more cooperative attitude (of which an illustration had been afforded a few weeks before by the Pope's reception in audience of Mr. Khrushchev's son-in-law) was too much for the more conservative spirits in the Curia and caused some embarrassment to the more zealous denunciators of communism and all its works; and there were not wanting those who attributed the electoral successes of the Italian Communist Party which followed to confusion sown in the minds of the faithful by the Pope's departure from rigidity.

It was, however, in his decision to summon an ecumenical council, and even more in the role he assigned to it, that the historical importance of his pontificate lay. His decision was both an initiative and a response within the quickening movement towards Christian unity. The context, that of unity, in which the decision was announced led to some initial confusion. It was thought possible that, like the fifteenth-century Council of Florence, the second Vatican Council might be concerned with formal overtures to separated hierarchies or with the preparation of doctrinal formulae to which other Churches might be found to subscribe. In fact, as the Pope was soon to make clear, the council was to be more immediately concerned with the unfinished business of the Vatican Council of 1870, and its approach to unity was to be along the only road giving any promise of lasting progress namely, the preparation of Christian minds and the removal of unnecessary obstructions erected by historical prejudices and by the ubiquitous ecclesiastical gift for defining and institutionalizing differences.

He gave the chief task of the council as being concerned with the spread of the Catholic faith, the renewal of right standards of morality, and the bringing of ecclesiastical discipline into closer accord with the needs and conditions of the times. The Italian word *aggiornamento* aptly signifies the process of adaptation that was to be undertaken; and it was to be pursued, not by the traditional method of condemning the errors of others but by presenting the life and teaching of the Catholic Church in a positive form. This was to be the council's task of preparation in the cause of Christian reunion. Although the Pope did not live to see this work carried through, his guidance during the preparatory and opening phases of the council meant that the work was well begun.

Angelo Giuseppe Roncalli was born at Sotto il Monte, some eight miles from Bergamo in the foothills of the Italian Alps, on November 25, 1881. The eldest son of Giovanni and Maria Roncalli, who had 12 other children, he came of a line that had farmed their own land near Bergamo for some five centuries, living frugal and independent lives.

FIRST APPOINTMENT

At the age of 11 he entered the junior seminary at Bergamo, proceeding to the major seminary and in 1900 to Rome where he took his degrees in theology. He was ordained in 1904 in Rome and said his first Mass in the Basilica of St. Peter, where in later years he sang his first Pontifical High Mass as Bishop and eventually was crowned as Pope.

The young priest's first appointment was as private secretary to Mgr. Radini-Tedeschi, newly consecrated Bishop of Bergamo, who had a profound influence on him and whom he described in later years as " the pole star of my priesthood ". A man of learning and saintly life, the Bishop was a pioneer in Catholic Action, particularly with regard to the promotion of Christian social principles.

In addition to his duties as secretary, Father Roncalli taught theology in the seminary where he had studied for the priesthood and devoted what time he could spare to research into the history of his native province. His interest in research was fostered by Bishop Radini, who, during a visit to Milan, introduced him to the Librarian of the Ambrosian Library, Mgr. Achille Ratti, the future Pope Pius XI. Thus he received special facilities for his studies, during which he came upon a mass of documents concerned with St. Charles Borromeo and his visits to Bergamo, which he used as the basis of a work extending over the years to six volumes, the last one appearing after his election as Pope.

Bishop Radini died in 1914. In the same year his secretary was conscribed for military service and became a sergeant in the medical corps. Subsequently as a lieutenant he was appointed chaplain to military hospitals.

During and after the 1914-18 War Fr. Roncalli developed plans for religious training in teachers' training colleges and in secular schools, and when the seminary at Bergamo reopened he played a considerable part in its spiritual direction, without resuming his former position on the faculty. His powers of organization and his increasing popularity as a preacher marked him out for advancement and in 1921 Pope Benedict XV, in the closing months of the pontificate, summoned him to Rome to become national director of the Association for the Propagation of the Faith. Four years later Pope Pius XI appointed him to the titular see of Areopolis and named him as Apostolic Visitor to Bulgaria.

His first experience in the diplomatic service of the Vatican gave him an opportunity to study the complex problems affecting the Eastern Churches, their relations with Rome, and the position of residents in Bulgaria who were of the Latin Rite. The knowledge he acquired in Bulgaria and later in Turkey and Greece served him throughout his life and inspired in him a longing for reunion between east and west. As later, in other countries, he travelled widely as his duties permitted, gained a working knowledge of the language, and in his dealings with the Bulgarian Government made continuous efforts to establish harmony.

DELICATE ROLE IN PARIS

He was transferred in November, 1934, to Istanbul as Apostolic Delegate to Turkey and Greece and as Administrator of the Latin Rite in Constantinople. His experience of ecclesiastical relations with eastern bodies was thus greatly enlarged. Over a period of 10 years he became very widely popular and he developed personal friendships both with members of the Turkish Government and with leading members of the Orthodox Church. In Greece his term of office was remembered particularly because of his successful efforts to relieve distress caused by the German occupation and the Allied blockade.

His recall from Turkey in 1944 was followed immediately by appointment as Papal Nuncio to France. The situation in Paris, to which the provisional Government had returned after the liberation of the city, was a particularly delicate one, because of the strained relations between leaders of the resistance movement and members of the hierarchy whom they thought had supported the puppet Government at Vichy or had appeared to collaborate with the German occupation. One of the first steps taken by the Government was to ask the Holy See to recall the then Nuncio and it was expected that further representations would be made for the removal of a number of bishops from their sees. The new Nuncio, therefore, was called to exercise tact and patience in examining complaints, the majority of which were withdrawn within a very short time after his arrival in Paris. The arrival itself was dramatic, for, reaching the city on New Year's Eve, he prepared hurriedly an address to General de Gaulle which he delivered the next day as dean of the diplomatic corps, the Russian Ambassador senior in time of office standing beside him and fingering the address he had expected himself to read.

In 1953, after the reception of the Red Hat, Pope Pius XII appointed him to the Patriarchate of Venice, where he instituted the custom of holding open times for any of his flock to visit him privately and began unexpected visits to churches and parishes. When Pope Pius XII died in 1958 and the Patriarch left Venice for the Conclave, someone reminded him jokingly that in 1903 Pius X had left Venice with a return ticket. The Patriarch smiled and made no reply; but it was clear from his speech to the Cardinals on his election as Pope that he knew that he was *papabile*.

It was in the eleventh ballot that Cardinal Roncalli, Patriarch of Venice, was elected, surprising the Conclavists by taking the name of John, which had been his father's name and the patronal title of the church in which he was baptized. But in stating that he would be John XXIII he assumed the title of a fifteenth-century Anti-Pope. Surprise was caused too by his immediate prolongation of the Conclave by a day in order that he might hold a private consistory before the Cardinals dispersed.

GREGARIOUS NATURE

His predecessor had reigned for 19 years and had been responsible for remarkable developments in the life of the Church, notably in the revision of the Holy Week liturgy, the introduction of Evening Mass, and the relaxation of the Eucharistic fast. His reign was marked also by administrative changes natural to his rather solitary temperament in the course of which he discontinued the routine audiences of Cardinals in Curia, dispensed for much of his pontificate with the services of a Cardinal Secretary of State and tended generally to keep the reins of government in his own hands.

The new Pope, gregarious rather than solitary by nature, had shown a strong belief, as Patriarch of Venice, in the delegation of duties to free him for more active pastoral work. He had expressed his view of government as being to see everything without seeming to see much, and to correct it without seeming to do so. While paying warm personal tribute to Pope Pius XII, going so far as to suggest a possible canonization, he immediately ordered the resumption of curial audiences and began a series of informal and unexpected visits to administrative offices in the Vatican. Immediately after his coronation, seven days after the election, he began his frequent appearances in the streets of Rome, thus clearing away the last vestiges of the conflict between the Holy See and the Italian state.

It was said at the time that these informal appearances by Pope John XXIII outside the Vatican were intended by him to emphasize his dual position as Supreme Pontiff and Bishop of Rome, a point emphasized by his convocation of a Synod of Rome and by alterations in the appointment of Cardinal Bishops to ensure the exercise of episcopal duties. Apart from the formal drive to take possession of his Basilica of St. John Lateran, he preached in 1959 from an open-air altar erected beneath the Arch of Constantine, made Christmas visits to the inmates of the Regina Coeli prison in Rome and to the sick and aged in hospitals and homes. In the same year he resumed the ancient practice by which the Pope in person took part in the lenten processions to churches named as "stations".

One of his first formal acts as Pope was the elevation of 23 new Cardinals to the Sacred College. They included the late Cardinal Godfrey, Archbishop of Westminster, and Cardinal Tardini, who thereupon received appointment as Secretary of State, and they enlarged the composition of the College to 74 members, four more than the normal complement. By 1962 he had enlarged the membership of the Sacred College by a further 12.

The Pope's natural geniality allied to his knowledge of protocol made notable the visits to him by heads of state and reigning sovereigns. Particularly notable was the visit in 1961 by Queen Elizabeth and the Duke of Edinburgh, as this was the first time that an English reigning Queen had visited the Pope since the Reformation. Equally significant, for another reason, was the visit in 1960 of the then Archbishop of Canterbury, Lord Fisher of Lambeth, a visit followed in the following year by the Moderator of the General Assembly of the Church of Scotland.

These two visits were regarded as being particularly important as evidence of the Pope's personal contribution to the spread of the ecumenical movement; and they occurred shortly after the proclamation of the outstanding event of the Pontificate, the holding in St. Peter's Basilica of the Second Vatican Council, which opened in October, 1962, and adjourned in December until the following September.

Three years were devoted to the preliminary work for the council, by specially created commissions, the Pope frequently presiding at sessions of the central commission. In addition the Pope created a separate secretariat for the promotion of Christian unity, headed by Cardinal Bea, who in 1962, visited England and lunched at Lambeth Palace with the Archbishop of Canterbury. The secretariat was responsible for the invitation to other churches to send representatives as observers at the council. That the Greek Orthodox Churches declined the invitation (although two observers came from the Russian Church) must have been a personal disappointment to Pope John.

The council had not been long in session when the Pope issued a gentle hint that the assembled fathers could with advantage speed up their deliberations and restrain their pious loquacity, and he gave the presidency new powers to control debate, which were promptly used. A more important intervention followed. The *schema* on "the sources of revelation", which had been prepared with a conservative emphasis on the distinction between Scripture and tradition and which was judged by some to pay too little regard to modern biblical scholarship, encountered strong criticism. The debate having reached deadlock a motion to postpone further discussion of the *schema* was supported by a large majority but technically defeated. Thereupon the Pope intervened in favour of the majority opinion and ordered that the document be redrafted by a commission with which Cardinal Bea's secretariat was to be associated. The intervention was welcomed, and not only by the more "liberal" prelates.

Towards the end of November the Pope was confined to his apartments by illness. An operation for a prostate disorder was rumoured. There was, however, sufficient recovery in his health to enable him to make a brief appearance at the council on the day of its adjournment until the following September; and he was soon able to fulfil his normal engagements. On May 22, however, reports of another set back were confirmed when he had to cancel his general audience in St. Peter's. Although he more than once rallied bravely his condition then declined rapidly.

The Times
7th June 1832

DEATH OF JEREMY BENTHAM.

The following account has come from a most respectable gentleman well acquainted with the deceased:—

"Died, yesterday, at his residence, in Queen-square-place, Westminster, Jeremy Bentham, in his 85th year. During the late unhealthy season, he had been subject to repeated attacks of bronchitis; but he had recovered from the first severe attacks with so much vigour, that it was considered by many that he would return to his former state of health, and he again received the visits of distinguished foreigners, and of public men, with whom he was in the habit of friendly intercourse; and it was believed that he would have been able to continue his labours for several years to come. Several days ago he had taken up the portion of his manuscripts for the third volume of his unpublished *Constitutional Code*, which is reputed by jurists who are acquainted with its progress, to be one of the most valuable of his productions, as it contains the principle for the formation of a judicial establishment, and a code of procedure. Another attack of his disorder, however, arrested his labours for ever. His death was singularly tranquil. Only a portion of his works have been printed, and of those printed, some which have been spoken of by eminent men as the most valuable, such as the "Essay on Judicial Establishments" have never in reality been published. Repeated proposals have been made to publish a complete edition of his works. A few weeks ago Prince Talleyrand, who at all times, in common with the leading spirits of the age, has professed his high admiration of the author, made proposals to get a complete edition of all his works, in French, published at Paris. A short time before his death he had projected a new work on language, and on mathematics. Amongst the unpublished works is one on the use of language, with a view to the giving certainty to the expression of the will of the legislature. Some, if not all, of these works, will, it is expected, be edited by gentlemen well conversant with the branches of science and art to which the works relate, and will at some future period be made public, in a complete and uniform shape. Besides those which were translated by the late M. Dumont, others of his works, which are little known in England, have great reputation on the continent of Europe and in North and South America. Mr. Bentham was a bencher of Lincoln's-inn, and was the father of the bar. In conformity with the desire of his father, he practised for a short time in equity, and was immediately remarked for the ability he displayed; but the death of his father left him with a moderate fortune and the free choice of his course of life, when he at once abandoned all prospects of professional emoluments and honours, and devoted the whole of his subsequent life to those labours which he believed would produce the greatest happiness to his fellow-creatures. His extreme benevolence and cheerfulness of disposition are highly spoken of by all who had the honour to be admitted to his society, which was much sought after, and also by his domestics and by his neighbours who were acquainted with his habits. The news of the Reform Bill having been carried greatly cheered his last hours. He has, we are informed, bequeathed his body to his medical friend, Dr. Southwood Smith, with a charge that he shall use it in an anatomical school for dissection, in illustration of a course of lectures.

The Times
25th September 1939

Professor Sigmund Freud, M.D., originator of the science of psycho-analysis, died at his son's London home at Hampstead on Saturday night at the age of 83. From 1902 until recently he was Professor of Neurology in the University of Vienna. When the Germans violated Austria last year he was compelled to fly to England, where he had lived ever since.

Freud was one of the most challenging figures in modern medicine. Indeed, though his work was primarily medical, there is something incongruous in speaking of him as a doctor. Rather he was a philosopher, using the methods of science to achieve therapeutic ends. Philosophy, science, and medicine all paid him the tributes of excessive admiration and excessive hostility.

The truth would seem to be that even at this late date the time has not yet arrived when a just estimate of psychoanalysis and its founder is possible. The atmosphere is too highly charged with controversy. Supporters and opponents are still in too bitter a mood. One can neither affirm that Freud's teaching will stand the test of time, nor deny that it may change permanently the whole conception of the operations of the human mind. Psycho-analysis, whatever it may have become in alien hands, possesses at least the merit of having been given to the world as a treatment of disease and not as a moral law. Freud, indeed, though he took great liberties with philosophy, though he was himself a philosopher *malgré lui*, always wrote and spoke as a man of science. He did not pretend to have invented his remarkable view of mental processes; he asserted that he had discovered it.

But Freud, the man, was clearly bigger than his detractors are usually ready to admit. His influence has pervaded the world within the space of but a few years. It can be discerned to-day in almost every branch of human thought, and notably in education, and some of his terms have become part of everyday language, "the inferiority complex" for example.

Misunderstanding dogged Freud's steps from the beginning. He spoke of sex in that large sense which includes the love of parents for their children, the love of children for their parents, the labours of a man to provide for his family, the tenderness of a grown man towards his mother, and so on : and immediately his intention was narrowed by his critics to their own partial view. They accused him of attempting to undermine the moral law. Again, he indicated his belief that natural impulses which have been suppressed have not, by that act, been annihilated. They remain in what he called the "unconscious mind," to vex and trouble their possessors. At once the cry was raised that this man preached a doctrine of unbridled libertinism. Those raising it overlooked the fact that Freud had placed side by side with his doctrine of repression his doctrine of "sublimation." We must not, he taught, regard a natural impulse as, of itself, wrong or unworthy. To do so is to abhor the law of Nature and so the order of the universe. Rather we must take that impulse and apply it to the noblest purposes of which we are capable.

This, it may be admitted, was a little like saying that a negative produces a positive, and that man owes his spiritual development to racial and social taboos. It was a doctrine which appealed strongly to Puritanical minds, with the result that Freud's supporters, like his opponents, included persons of the most diverse views. Psycho-analysis thus became not one but a dozen battle-grounds on which the combatants fought with the fierceness of zealots. There is indeed, in all Freud's writing, a haunting echo of theological controversy. His conception included under other names, many ancient doctrines and dogmas. Thus there is but little real distinction between "original sin" and the "natural impulse" of the Viennese professor. Freud, too, adjured his patients to recognize their human nature as the necessary first step to cure ; not merely the knowledge but the conviction of sin was essential to a change of heart. Again, he bade his followers know themselves by every means and devised astonishing new methods of self-knowledge or "self-analysis." Thus was the evil spirit of a suppressed emotion or desire unmasked and released to be transmuted into the good spirit serving as a mainspring of action.

The famous theory of dreams and the various "complexes" resolve themselves, when viewed as Freud meant them to be viewed, into observations of the activities of the "natural man" imprisoned and ignored yet always alive within us. This original sin, if denied, possesses, he believed, the power to "attach" itself to or "associate" itself with other, apparently good and innocent, thoughts, lending them, thereby, its own passionate energy. Hence the innumerable "anxieties" and fears ("phobias") of the mentally sick : hence their strange apings of physical disease, their perverted ideas, their unreasoning prejudices. To resurrect this natural man and yoke his powers to fresh and useful enterprises was the life-aim of the physician.

There are those, to-day, who deny the very existence of the "unconscious mind" though their numbers are diminishing. There are others who see in nervous ailments only the failure of will power, whereby, as they think, we hold our instincts in wholesome restraint. Finally, there are many who believe that an actual physical lesion, a disease of the body, underlies every abnormality of the mind. Freud's doctrine is anathema to all such. His doctrine, moreover, has been modified and changed, notably by Jung, who laid far less stress than Freud on the sexual character of emotional impulse. The controversy is apt to become a barren one.

Freud was born at Freiberg, in Moravia, on May 6, 1856, and studied in Vienna and at the Salpétrière in Paris, graduating M.D. in 1881. Most of his numerous works have been translated into English and other languages, and he was editor of *Internationale zeitschrift für Psychoanalyse* and of *Imago*, and director of the *International Journal of Psycho-Analysis*. Last year he was elected a Foreign Member of the Royal Society, and many years ago he received the honorary degree of LL.D. from Clark University, Worcester, Massachusetts. Professor Freud married in 1886, and had three sons and three daughters.

The Times
15th November 1957

Dr. Wilhelm Reich, a psycho-therapist and an early disciple of Freud, has died in the Lewisburg penitentiary in Pennsylvania, our Washington Correspondent reports. He had been in prison since early this year serving a two-year term for contempt of court, a conviction that arose from his persistence in promoting his "orgone energy accumulators" in defiance of a court injunction.

Reich was a director of the Seminar for Psycho-Analytic Therapy in Freud's clinic from 1924 to 1930 and was the author of a widely respected work on character analysis. He went to the United States before the last war and drew wide public notice when he propounded his theory of "orgone energy," which, he claimed, was a health-giving force which could be tapped by means of his orgone accumulators. Reich prescribed his "orgone boxes" or "blankets" for the cure of a number of serious diseases, and in 1954 these devices were listed as frauds by the food and drug administration, and he was forbidden to sell or lease them. He continued to do so, however, was convicted of criminal contempt in 1954, and his final appeal was rejected by the Supreme Court in February this year, after which he entered the Lewisburg penitentiary. The prison authorities stated that Reich's death was a result of a heart seizure.

Invention & Discovery

Many of the most important inventors are missing from the following pages, for their work went unrecognized in their lifetimes. To mention only a few of those without whom how we live would have been very different: James Sharp and Ferdinand Carré, who invented the gas cooker and fridge respectively; W. H. Carothers, who invented nylon; and W. L. Judson, without whom we would be without that most useful of devices, the zip. Even Charles Macadam, who has given his name to the tarmacadam without which we might have no petrol queues, died unremarked, as did Matthew Trevithick, the Cornishman who was probably the greatest mechanical genius of the Industrial Revolution. By contrast, the death of **Lord Sandwich**, credited with the invention of that most unpleasant of station buffet offerings, the triangle of dampish sponge enveloping a similarly shaped slice of yellow polystyrene, was duly noted, though not on that account. So was that of **King Gillette**, the inventor of the razor blade, representing here, along with **Clarence Birdseye**, who originated frozen food, the ordinary bits and pieces of our lives. The **Wright** brothers, **James Watt**, **Gottlieb Daimler**, **Gottfried Benz**, and **Thomas Edison** need no introduction. **Sir Henry Bessemer** may be regarded as marking the zenith of industrialization, for his efficient production of steel from pig-iron made possible the development of twentieth century heavy industry. For its computerized transformation, we are indebted to **Charles Babbage**, in effect the inventor of the computer. For that other symbol of the mid twentieth century we have **Leo Baekeland** to thank, the inventor of baekelite which was to become plastic. **Louis Daguerre** developed the daguerrotype, later the photograph, the memory device, both personal and social, which became an art form. **Bramah**'s name could hardly be omitted, even though the name of the inventor of the flushing toilet has not been immortalized in the same way as that of an early manufacturer, Thomas Crapper, unobituarized. Luckily he was soon followed by **Joseph Bazalgette**, the initiator of modern sanitation, who laid London's first proper sewers.

George Eastman must have been cursed countless times by the unphotogenic, for it was he who made the snapshot available to the masses through the development of the "Kodak" camera. That Teutonic duo Count **von Zeppelin** and **Wernher von Braun** turned their skills for making war machinery into peaceful post-war applications, but it remains to be seen whether rocketry will become as redundant as the airship as a mode of transport.

New York Times
9th March 1917

COUNT ZEPPELIN DIES OF PNEUMONIA AT 79

Inventor of the German War Dirigible Lost and Regained a Fortune by His Experiments.

ONCE REGARDED AS A CRANK

Long Series of Failures Preceded His Success—His Craft of Military Value Only as Scouts.

GENEVA, March 8. (via Paris.)— Count Ferdinand von Zeppelin died at Charlottenburg this morning of pneumonia.

Count Ferdinand von Zeppelin will go down in history as one of the most important figures of the great war. His dirigibles, known as "Zeppelins," have raided England forty-two times and left behind them more than 426 dead and 864 injured. In addition, their bombs caused property damage the amount of which has not been estimated. In 1916 seven Zeppelins raiding England were destroyed, and since the war began forty-one have been destroyed elsewhere.

Count von Zeppelin was born in Constance, Baden, in 1838. He was the son of a Court official of Württemberg and was brought up to be a soldier. His family is one of the oldest in Europe and belongs to the Mecklenburg "Uradel" or aristocracy, whose nobility dates back to the birth of modern history. They were Counts in the middle of the eighteenth century and had always been prominent in the various wars in which their country became embroiled. All the von Zeppelins were fighters. In 1899, Count Henry von Zeppelin, a nephew of the inventor, fell during the Boer war while fighting at the head of his commando.

Here During Civil War.

Count von Zeppelin was a Lieutenant of Cavalry at the age of 23, and two years later, in April, 1863, he was sent to this country as Prussian military attaché with the Union Army in the civil war. He was attached to the Army of the Mississippi, in which General Carl Schurz commanded a brigade. It was while acting as attaché with the Union Army that Count von Zeppelin had his first experience as an aeronaut. He went up in a captive balloon belonging to the corps to which he was attached and came down a convert to aerial observation and warfare.

On his return home Zeppelin returned to his regiment and took an active part in the Prussian campaign against Austria in 1866. Then came the Franco-Prussian war of 1870, when he became famous. On July 24, 1870, a few hours after the declaration of war, with four other young officers and seven troopers, Count von Zeppelin made a reconnoissance into France. He was said to have been the first German soldier to cross the line into France during that war and his report proved of great value to von Moltke. At the end of the war he was a Colonel and then received promotion until he reached the rank of General at the age of 42. During 1890 Count von Zeppelin was commandant of the fortress of Saarburg. Two years afterward he retired from the army and devoted his time to aeronautics.

His Fortune Swept Away.

Then began the struggle which cost him his fortune of more than $750,000 and caused him to be looked upon as a crank. Airship after airship, model after model he built, and all were failures. Most of them were right in theory, but would not fly. His fortune was finally exhausted and his credit gone. Driven to extremes for funds with which to prosecute his work, he appealed to the public through the newspapers.

Finally he made his supreme effort. He sacrificed all the property he and his family owned and built Zeppelin No. 3. With this crude dirigible he made six flights during the Summer and Fall of 1907. On Sept. 24, 1907, he made a three-hour trip in the vicinity of Lake Constance, during which he passed over five States and visited their capitals. This balloon was 420 feet long and held 11,000 cubic meters of gas.

Then, during 1908, he went up in the fifth airship he had built and sailed nearly 900 miles in about thirty-seven hours. This was his epochal performance and Emperor William and all Germany hailed him as "the conqueror of the air." More recently, during 1914, the Emperor proclaimed him "the greatest German of the twentieth century" and conferred on him the Order of the Black Eagle, the highest honor at his command.

His exploits during 1908 ended his financial difficulties also. Airship after [...] long of life, and with a monetary loss of not less than $300,000 for each vessel. The Emperor and his Government came to his aid several times and when one of his greatest Zeppelins was torn from its moorings and wrecked the German public came to his assistance and subscribed a fund of $1,000,000, of which the Crown Prince was President. In addition, several of his airships were bought by the German Army.

In August, 1909, Count von Zeppelin, in the Zeppelin III., flew from Bitterfeld to Berlin, where he was welcomed as a national hero. More than 2,000,000 people turned out to greet him, and when he landed at Tegel the Kaiser embraced him and presented him to the imperial family. The Burgomaster of Berlin read an address of welcome and then the Kaiser introduced Count von Zeppelin to Orville Wright, who had been invited to Tegel so that the two "masters of the air" should meet.

From the very beginning of his successful flights Count von Zeppelin planned to adapt his invention to military uses. As early as July, 1908, he flew for twelve hours without a stop, carrying fourteen men, two rapid-fire guns, a wireless outfit, and bombs.

Count von Zeppelin married the Russian Baroness Isabella von Wolff, who came from the German-speaking province of Livenia.

**COUNT FERDINAND
VON ZEPPELIN.**
Inventor of the airship, died 1917.

The Times
25th February 1944

DR. L. H. BAEKELAND

Dr. L. H. Baekeland, the scientist and inventor of "Bakelite," died in New York on Wednesday.

Born in Ghent in 1863, Leo Hendrik Baekeland graduated as a Doctor of Science at Ghent University in 1884, and, having married his Professor's daughter, emigrated to America. In 1893 he founded the Newara Chemical Society and manufactured "Velox" and other photographic papers, which were his invention. After selling his company to the Eastman Kodak Company he devoted his time to chemical research. He began his work as one of the pioneers of plastics when he became president of the Bakelite Corporation in 1910. Dr. Baekeland had received honorary degrees from the universities of Pittsburgh, Columbia, Brussels, and Edinburgh, and many medals and foreign awards, including the Legion of Honour and the Messel Medal of the Society of Chemical Industry.

The Times
16th July 1861

M. Daguerre, the inventor of the Daguerreotype, died at Petit Brie, near Paris, on the 10th inst.

New York Times
9th October 1956

Clarence Birdseye Is Dead at 69; Inventor of Frozen-Food Process

Developed Method for Quick Freezing and Also Devised System for Dehydrating

Clarence Birdseye, the inventor of a process for quick-freezing foods that made his name a household word in the United States, died Sunday night of a heart ailment in his residence at the Gramercy Park Hotel. He was 69 years old. He had a home also in Gloucester, Mass.

Mr. Birdseye developed his quick-freezing process after years of experimentation based on experiences as a fur trader in Labrador.

He also developed a new method for dehydrating foods—which he called the "anhydrous method"—and was responsible for many developments in the incandescent lighting field. He held nearly 300 United States and foreign patents.

The inventor was born in Brooklyn on Dec. 9, 1886, the son of Clarence Frank Birdseye, a lawyer, and Ada Underwood Birdseye.

During Mr. Birdseye's high school years, his family moved to Montclair, N. J. His lifelong interest in food came to light when he voluntarily attended the school's cooking class.

After graduation, Mr. Birdseye entered Amherst College with the class of 1910. He left to go to work without having been graduated, but the college presented an honorary degree to him in 1941.

During vacation times in his college years, and later, he worked as a naturalist for the United States Biological Survey. In 1912 he went to Labrador as a fur trader and became a friend of Sir Wilfred Grenfell, the medical missionary. Mr. Birdseye spent some time on Sir Wilfred's hospital ship, sailing along the coast and ministering to the fishermen.

In 1915 Mr. Birdseye married Eleanor Gannett of Washington. The next year they returned to Labrador, accompanied by their first child, then only a few weeks old.

Mr. Birdseye said later that it was the presence of his family in Labrador that first spurred his interest in frozen foods.

"Fresh food was a very urgent problem in Labrador," he recalled. "I found that foods frozen very quickly in the dead of winter kept their freshness as long as they were held at low temperature."

After his return home, Mr. Birdseye began the experiments that led to the development of his process. At the start, he could afford to spend only $7 for equipment, including an electric fan, ice and salt. Later, a friend lent him the corner of an ice house to carry on his work.

In 1924 Mr. Birdseye and three partners formed the General Seafoods Company in Gloucester. A year later the company marketed quick-frozen fish fillets—the first of a large variety of frozen packaged foods.

The development not only brought a fortune to Mr. Birdseye, but helped to revive the Massachusetts fishing industry.

Four years later the Postum Company, Inc., and Goldman Sachs Trading Corporation bought the rights to Mr. Birdseye's process for more than $22,000,000. Postum later bought out Goldman Sachs and changed its name to the General Foods Corporation.

Mr. Birdseye did not invent quick-freezing, nor was his company the first of its kind. The chief virtues of his method lay in its extremely rapid freezing and the fact that the foods were frozen in packages by pressing them between refrigerated metal plates.

Mr. Birdseye later invented the Birdseye reflector and infra-red heat lamps, widely used in industry. One of his hobbies, tracking whales, led him to perfect a kickless harpoon gun.

In 1949, he developed his anhydrous method of taking the water out of food. Four servings of food prepared in this manner can be carried in containers no larger than a cigarette package.

Three years ago, Mr. Birdseye began successful experiments in Peru to develop and perfect a continuous-flow process for converting crushed sugar cane into paper pulp.

Besides his widow, Mr. Birdseye is survived by two sons, Kellogg G. Birdseye of Closter, N. J., and Henry S. Birdseye of Albuquerque, N. M., and two daughters, Ruth of Gloucester and Mrs. Eleanor B. Talbot of Burlingame, Calif.

The Guardian
18th June 1977

Wernher von Braun, who died yesterday, aged 65, was head of Hitler's rocket research programme and mastermind of the V2. As Germany collapsed, he loaded his team into a fleet of trucks pumped full of rocket fuel, salvaged his experimental equipment, and headed for the American lines from the ruined V2 base at Peenemunde. Within a few weeks he was on his way to White Sands, New Mexico, philosophically explaining his defection in basic terms: "Next time I want to be on the winning side."

He was born in Weirsitz, East Prussia, in 1912, and was shaped by his family for a life of diplomacy or junker gentility. His decision to search for a more academic career baffled his father, Baron Magnus von Braun, but his mother encouraged his studies which led him to a course of advanced physics at the University of Berlin and a preoccupation with the newly developed interest in rocketry with its dreams of space travel.

In 1931, after firing several solid fuel rockets on an abandoned ammunition dump in Berlin, he was searching enthusiastically for financial backing and readily accepted an offer by the German Army to work on an artillery weapon which would not violate the Treaty of Versailles.

At 20 he was appointed head civilian specialist at the Army's rocket station at Kummersdorf. It was there, in 1934, that he met Hitler, who von Braun later described as giving the impression of being "a pretty dowdy type" on first meeting. "Later," von Braun said, "I began to see his brilliance, but you could also see his flaws."

He quickly perfected two successful liquid fuel rockets. These impressed Hitler who began to increase his demands for a military rocket and provided von Braun with a team of Germany's senior scientists and technicians based at Peenemunde in the Baltic marshes.

The first V2 exploded on the ground, the second failed within 30 seconds of takeoff. The third soared to a record height of 60 miles. Two years later, the first V2 fell on London. "I felt satisfaction," von Braun said. "I visited London twice after the war and I love the place. But I loved Berlin and the British were bombing hell out of it."

On his arrival in New Mexico at the White Sands rocket proving grounds, von Braun accomplished the transition from villain to hero beyond the wildest dreams of the American Government public relations machine. He began producing war missiles for his former enemies, then, in 1960, eclipsed all memory of the deathshead inventor by becoming chief of the National Aeronautics and Space Administration.

In 1958, he put America's first Explorer satellite, Jupiter C, into orbit but claimed that if the Pentagon had listened to his proposals two years earlier he could have beaten the Russian Sputnik.

The Gentleman's Magazine
9th December 1814 Vol 84

Dec. 9. At Pimlico, Joseph Bramah, esq. It is always a most gratifying task to have to place upon record the merits of those who have been in any degree distinguished for their useful talents or moral worth: but how to draw a just picture of his deserts, whose whole career (whether as regards his public or private actions) has been marked by an overflowing and laudable desire to be useful to his fellow-creatures, we confess ourselves to be at some loss. The name of Mr. Bramah, as an engineer and mechanist, is so well known to the whole world, as to render it almost a matter of supererogation to offer any comment upon the profound abilities which he has displayed in the line of his profession: suffice it to say, that the productions of his genius are duly appreciated, and will ever remain a theme for unqualified admiration and unbounded applause, while the Arts and Sciences are patronized and sought after. Intuitive talent in the way of invention and discovery, however, was not the sole distinguishing trait which belonged to Mr. B.: he had an acute, comprehensive, and discerning mind, which made him almost immediately master of the most difficult subjects; and he had a peculiar facility and force of expression, which gave him a vast superiority in all matters under discussion, however diffuse: thus gifted, his arguments seldom failed to convince; and his mode of reasoning being always liberal and unsophisticated, served to stamp them with a character of uncommon value. His integrity and love of principle were, perhaps, the strongest features which marked all his actions; and hence it followed that his society was courted by persons of the highest talent, and of all conditions. Of his religious habits we will briefly observe, that his practical piety and morality, his humanity and active benevolence, will always entitle him to a place in the hearts of good men, who must regard his loss as a public calamity. The deep affliction of his amiable widow and children will of itself speak for him as a husband and a father; and it is at once pleasing and consolatory to know that his death was as easy as his life had been exemplary, and that he sunk into eternity, serene and happy, loving and beloved, surrounded by his whole family, and sincerely lamented by a large and respectable circle of friends

The Times
20th October 1871

THE LATE MR. CHARLES BABBAGE, F.R.S.

Our obituary column on Saturday contained the name of one of the most active and original of original thinkers, and whose name has been known through the length and breadth of the kingdom for nearly half a century as a practical mathematician— we mean Mr. Charles Babbage. He died at his residence in Dorset-street, Marylebone, at the close of last week, at an age, spite of organ-grinding persecutors, little short of 80 years.

Little is known of Mr. Babbage's parentage and early youth, except that he was born on the 26th of December, 1792, and was educated privately. During the whole of his long life, even when he won for himself fame and reputation, he was always extremely reticent on that subject, and, in reply to questioners, he would uniformly express an opinion that the only biography of living personages was to be found, or, at all events, ought to be found, in the list of their published works. As this list, in Mr. Babbage's own case, extended to upwards of 80 productions, there ought to be no dearth of materials for the biographer; but these materials, after all, as a matter of fact, are scanty, in spite of an autobiographical work which he gave to the world about seven years ago, entitled *Passages in the Life of a Philosopher*.

At the usual age Mr. Babbage was entered at the University of Cambridge, and his name appears in the list of those who took their Bachelor's degree from Peterhouse in the year 1814. It does not, however, figure in the Mathematical Tripos, he preferring to be Captain of the Poll to any honours but the Senior Wranglership of which he believed Herschel to be sure. While, however, at Cambridge he was distinguished by his efforts, in conjunction with the late Sir John Herschel and Dean Peacock, to introduce into that University, and thereby among the scientific men of the country in general, a knowledge of the refined analytic methods of mathematical reasoning which had so long prevailed over the Continent, whereas we in our insular position, for the most part, were content with what has been styled "the cramped domain of the ancient synthesis." The youthful triumvirate, it must be owned, made a successful inroad on the prejudices and predilections which had prevailed up to that time. Keeping this object steadily in view, in the first place they translated and edited the smaller treatise on the Calculus by Lacroix, with notes of their own, and an Appendix (mainly, if not wholly, from the pen of Sir John Herschel) upon Finite Differences. They next published a solution of exercises on all parts of the Infinitesimal Calculus, a volume which is still of great service to the mathematical student, in spite of more recent works with a similar aim. To this publication Mr. Babbage contributed an independent essay on a subject at that time quite new, the solution of Functional Equations.

By steps and stages, of which the records at our command are scanty, these pursuits gradually led Mr. Babbage on to that practical application of mathematical studies which may justly be considered to be his crowning scientific effort—we mean, of course, the invention and partial construction of the famous calculating engine or machine which the world has associated with his name. As a writer in the *Dictionary of Universal Biography* remarks:—

"The possibility of constructing a piece of mechanism capable of performing certain operations on numbers is by no means new; it was thought of by Pascal and geometers, and more recently it has been reduced to practice by M. Thomas, of Colmar, in France, and by the Messrs. Schütz, of Sweden; but never before or since has any science so gigantic as that of Mr. Babbage been anywhere imagined."

His achievements here were twofold; he constructed what he called a Difference Engine, and he planned and demonstrated the practicability of an Analytical Engine also. It is difficult, perhaps, to make the nature of such abstruse inventions at all clear to the popular and untechnical reader, since Dr. Lardner, no unskilful hand at mechanical description, filled no less than twenty-five pages of the *Edinburgh Review* with but a partial account of its action, confessing that there were many features which it was hopeless to describe effectively without the aid of a mass of diagrams. All that can here be said of the machine is that the process of addition automatically performed is at the root of it. In nearly all tables of numbers there will be a law of order in the differences between each number and the next. For instance, in a column of square numbers—say, 9, 16, 25, 36, 49, 64, 81, &c.—the successive differences will be 7, 9, 11, 13, 15, 17, &c. These are differences of the first order. If, then, the process of differencing be repeated with those, we arrive at a remarkably simple series of numbers— to wit 2, 2, 2, 2, &c. And into some such simple series most tables resolve themselves when they are analyzed into orders of differences; an element— an atom, so to speak—is arrived at, from which by constant addition the numbers in the table may be formed. It was the function of Mr. Babbage's machine to perform this addition of differences by combinations of wheels acting upon each other in an order determined by a preliminary adjustment. This working by differences gave it the name of the "Difference Engine." It has been repeatedly stated that the construction of this machine was suddenly suspended, and that no reason was ever assigned for its suspension. But the writer in the *Dictionary* already quoted above thus solves the mystery in which the matter has hitherto been shrouded:—

"In spite of the favourable report of a Commission appointed to inquire into the matter, the Government were led by two circumstances to hesitate about proceeding further. Firstly, Mr. Clements, the engineer or machinist employed as his *collaborateur*, suddenly withdrew all his skilled workmen from the work, and, what was worse, removed all the valuable tools which had been employed upon it."

—an act which is justified as strictly legal by Mr. Weld in his *History of the Royal Society*, though a plain common-sense man of the world may reasonably doubt its equity, as the tools themselves had been made at the joint expense of Mr. Babbage and the Treasury. "Secondly," says the same authority, "the idea of an Analytical Engine—one that absorbed and contained as a small part of itself the Difference Engine—arose before Mr. Babbage." Of course he could not help the fact that "Alps upon Alps should arise" in such matters, and that, when one great victory was achieved, another and still greater battle remained to be faced and fought. But no sooner did Mr. Babbage, like an honest man, communicate the fact to the Government than the then Ministers, with Sir Robert Peel and Mr. H. Goulburn at the head of the Treasury, took alarm, and, scared at the prospect of untold expenses before them, resolved to abandon the enterprise. Mr. Babbage, apart from all help from the public purse, had spent upon his machine, as a pet hobby, no small part of his private fortune—a sum which has been variously estimated between 6,000l. and 17,000l. And so, having resolved on not going further into the matter, they offered Mr. Babbage, by way of compensation, that the Difference Engine as constructed should remain as his own property—an offer which the inventor very naturally declined to accept. The engine, together with the drawings of the machinery constructed and not constructed, and of many other contrivances connected with it, extending, it is said, to some 400 or 500 drawings and plans, was presented in 1843 to King's College, London, where we believe they are to be seen in the museum, bearing their silent witness to great hopes dashed down to the ground, or, at all events, to the indefinite postponement of their realization.

In speaking at this length of Mr. Babbage's celebrated machine, we have a little anticipated the order of events, and must return to our record of the leading facts of his life. In the year 1828 he was nominated to the Lucasian Professorship of Mathematics in his old University, occupying in that capacity a chair which had once been held by no less a man than Sir Isaac Newton. This chair he held during eleven years. It was while holding this Professorship, namely, at the general election of November, 1832—which followed on the passing of the first Reform Bill—that he was put forward as a candidate for the representation of the newly-formed borough of Finsbury, standing in the advanced Liberal interest, as a supporter not only of Parliamentary, financial, and fiscal reform, but also of "the Ballot, triennial Parliaments, and the abolition of all sinecure posts and offices." But the electors did not care to choose a philosopher; so he was unsuccessful, and we believe never again wooed the suffrages of either that or any other constituency.

We have mentioned the fact that Mr. Babbage was the author of published works to the extent of some 80 volumes. A full list of these, however, would not interest or edify the general reader, and those who wish to study their names can see them recorded at full length in the new library catalogue of the British Museum. Further information respecting them will be found in the 12th chapter of Mr. Weld's *History of the Royal Society*, which we have already quoted. One or two of them, however, we should specify. The best known of them all, perhaps, is his *Ninth Bridgewater Treatise*, a work designed by him at once to refute the opinion supposed to be implied and encouraged in the first volume of that learned series, that an ardent devotion to mathematical studies is unfavourable to a real religious faith, and also to give specimens of the defensive aid which the evidences of Christianity may receive from the science of numbers, if studied in a proper spirit.

Another of his works which has found a celebrity of its own is a volume called *The Decline of Science*, from the title and the contents of which give us reason to believe that its author looked somewhat despondingly on the scientific attainments of the present age. The same opinion was still further worked out by Mr. Babbage in a book on the first Great Exhibition, which he published just 20 years ago. Another of his works which deserve mention here is one on *The Economy of Manufactures*, which was one result of a tour of inspection which he made through England and upon the Continent in search of mechanical principles for the formation of Logarithmic Tables.

It is about 40 years since Mr. Babbage produced his Tables of Logarithms from 1 to 108,000, a work upon which he bestowed a vast amount of labour, and in the publication of which he paid great attention to the convenience of calculators, whose eyes, he well knew, must dwell for many hours at a time upon their pages. He was rewarded by the full appreciation of his work by the computers not only of his own, but of foreign countries; for in several of those countries editions from the stereotyped plates of the tables were published, with translations of the preface. Notwithstanding the numerous logarithmic tables which have since appeared, those of Mr. Babbage are still held in high esteem by all upon whom the laborious calculations of astronomy and mathematical science devolve.

Mr. Babbage was one of the oldest members of the Royal Society at the time of his death; he was also more than fifty years ago one of the founders of the Astronomical Society, and he and Sir John Herschel were the last survivors of that body. He was also an active and zealous member of many of the leading learned societies of London and Edinburgh, and in former years at least an extensive contributor to their published *Transactions*. His last important publication was the amusing and only too characteristic autobiographical work to which we have already referred as *Passages in the Life of a Philosopher*.

The Times
3rd September 1819

THE LATE JAMES WATT, Esq.—The following short biographical memoir of this useful man is from the *Birmingham Gazette*:—

"By the death of this truly great man our country is deprived of one of its most illustrious ornaments. Mr. Watt may justly be placed at the very head of those philosophers who have improved the condition of mankind by the application of science to the practical purposes of life. His steam-engine is probably the most perfect production of physical and mechanical skill which the world has yet seen; while in the variety, extent, and importance of its applications, it certainly far transcends every similar invention. So great was the activity and power of his mind, that he not only embraced the whole compass of science, but was deeply learned in many departments of literature; and such was the felicity of his memory, that it retained, without effort, all that was confided to it. He was still more distinguished, not only by that highest prerogative of genius, promptness and fertility of invention, but also by its rare and happy union with a calm and sagacious judgment, regulated and matured by those habits of patient attention and investigation, without which no great production of human art was ever carried to perfection. His manners were marked by the simplicity which generally characterises exalted merit; he was perfectly free from parade and affectation; and though he could not be unconscious either of the eminent rank he held among men of science, or of those powers of mind by which he had attained it, yet his character was not debased by the slightest taint of vanity or pride. He had for many years retired from business, but his mind continued actively employed on scientific improvements. He perfected an apparatus for the medical application of factitious airs; and the amusement of his latter days was the contrivance of a machine for imitating and multiplying statuary, which he brought to a considerable state of perfection. Happy in his domestic connexions, in the complete enjoyment of his extraordinary intellect, respected and beloved by the wise and good of every country, and having attained the great age of 84 years, his useful and honourable life was terminated, after an illness of short duration, rather of debility than of pain, by an easy and tranquil death. Mr. Watt was elected a Fellow of the Royal Society of Edinburgh in 1784; of the Royal Society of London in 1785; and a Member of the Batavian Society in 1787; in 1806 the honorary degree of Doctor of Laws was conferred upon him by the spontaneous and unanimous vote of the Senate of the University of Glasgow; and in 1808 he was elected a Member of the National Institute of France."

New York Herald Tribune
15th March 1932

George Eastman Kills Self, Saying 'My Work Is Done'

ROCHESTER, March 14.—George Eastman, founder and chairman of the board of the Eastman Kodak Company, killed himself at his home this afternoon by firing a pistol bullet into his heart. A bachelor, seventy-seven years old, he was Rochester's leading citizen and one of the most generous philanthropists in America. He built his company from nothing to a $200,000,000 corporation and gave between $75,000,000 and $90,000,000 to charitable and educational institutions.

In ill health for some time, it was said tonight by his intimates that Mr. Eastman had begun to fear that he might lose his reason. Just before 1 o'clock this afternoon he asked his personal physician, Dr. Audley W. Stewart, and the nurses who had been in attendance up him, to leave his bedroom.

"Work Is Done," He Says in Note

"I want to write a note," he told them. He lit a cigarette and wrote the note, nine monosyllabic words, to which he added his initials. Then, methodical as always, he screwed the cap back on his fountain pen, took off his glasses and placed them on the table, and carefully snuffed out his cigarette.

A moment later those in the house heard a shot. Rushing to Mr. Eastman's room, Dr. Stewart and the others found him lying dead on his bed. In his hand was the same pistol he had carried on various African hunting trips. On the table was this note of farewell:

"To my friends:

"My work is done. Why wait?

"G. E."

Eastman Gave Millions Away For Enjoyment

Opposed Hoarding Wealth for Future and Made Gifts of Nearly $90,000,000

Coined the Word 'Kodak'

George Eastman made millions from the kodak, and gave most of them away because he found it was fun to give money. In December, 1924, when he announced gifts of $12,500,000 to educational institutions, he said: "Two courses are open to the man of wealth. He can hoard his money for his heirs to administer or he can get it into action and have fun with it while he is still alive I prefer getting it into action and adapting it to human needs." In 1929, when he celebrated his seventy-fifth birthday, his gifts had reached $72,000,000—almost $1,000,000 for each of his years—and continued steadily. His donations were in four fields: to education, because he never had much himself; to improve the public health; to promote music, because he thought a machine age needed emotional outlet, and to his employees.

Coined Word "Kodak"

Eastman did not invent the camera, but he simplified it so that millions could use it. From a complicated, cumbersome machine which took an expert to operate it and a laboratory to develop its pictures, he made a compact device which children could use to perpetuate the things they saw. The word he coined, "kodak," has been in the dictionary both as verb and noun for many years. It has become a synonym for precise, accurate portrayal.

George Eastman was just such a precise individual as the pictures he produced. He came from old New England Yankee stock, dating back to Roger Eastman, of the Massachusetts Bay Colony, which came to America in 1638. His father was George Washington Eastman, who owned a fruit nursery at Waterville, N. Y., where George was born on July 12, 1854, and his mother, whom he adored, was Mary Kilbourn. The elder Eastman moved to Rochester when his son was six years old and set up a business college. He died a few months later. The boy attended public schools until he was fourteen, when his mother became ill. He went to work to help support her and his sisters. His first job, in an insurance office, paid $3 a week. Within fifteen years he had saved $3,000, the original capital of the Eastman Kodak Company.

Some years ago, telling of his career at the time he was working in a bank for $1,000 a year and experimenting in photography as a hobby, Mr. Eastman said:

"The world seemed a good place to me. I was keeping tab of my dollars and cents and enjoying my leisure time taking pictures and thinking up ways of improving them. My superior, whose assistant I was, left the bank. The thing that I expected was that I should naturally fall in line for promotion. I didn't get it. Some relative of a director of the bank was brought in and placed over me. It wasn't right. It wasn't fair. I stayed for a short time longer, then quit. I gave myself up entirely to the work of cultivating my hobby, photography."

And so an injustice which kept him from becoming a minor bank official made him take the step which produced the kodak, whose clicking shutter has missed no corner of the earth, and the flexible roll film, which made possible the motion picture.

His first interest in photography came with the purchase of a camera for a vacation trip. The machine was huge and awkward, so Eastman rebuilt it to make it more compact. He found also that it was necessary to prepare each plate as it was needed. That started him experimenting.

Worked for Days Without Sleep

He had read an article on dry plates in an English magazine, and succeeded in working out a process of his own. Before he left the bank Mr. Eastman had hired an assistant to carry on the routine work in a small laboratory during the day, and he worked himself at night. When he quit the bank he devoted himself in earnest to the work, laboring continuously for days on end without sleep, and making up with solid slumbers interrupted only for meals over the week end. He had succeeded in selling a few of his plates, and orders multiplied. The year he left the bank, 1881, he had a nice business started, but he had a severe setback when dealers began complaining that some of his plates were worthless. Discovering that the sensitiveness of film decreased with age he took back all the bad plates and sent out new stock, this time with printed warnings giving a final date for development. He needed capital, and took into partnership Henry A. Strong, a boarder in his mother's home. By this time competition had arisen in dry plate manufacture, and Mr. Eastman turned to experimenting again with the idea of eliminating the bulky glass plates from the photographer's equipment.

With the aid of William H. Walker, an employee, he succeeded in placing the dry-plate emulsion on a fine-grained paper, and thus began the era of the photo-film. The Royal Geographic Society of Great Britain recognized the achievement and gave the two men medals.

The first snapshot camera was developed in 1887, when Mr. Eastman devised a machine consisting of lens, instantaneous shutter and film roll. The roll comprised 100 exposures, and when these were used up the whole camera was returned to the factory and the pictures developed. "You press the button, and we do the rest," was the slogan of this Kodak No. 1, the forerunner of the pocket cameras which are an indispensable part of every outing today. The name was coined by the inventor—the "k" being in honor of his mother, whose maiden name was Kilbourn.

About this time another inventor who was tinkering with photography sent Eastman a money order for $2.50 to pay for fifty feet of film. The customer's name was Thomas A. Edison. He used the Eastman film in a motion picture machine. The "movies" were soon taking about half the output of the Eastman fact

In 1898, while he was in England attending to affairs of his foreign enterprises, Mr. Eastman discovered that he was worth $1,000,000. Exultantly he told his mother when he returned home. "Yes?" she said, only mildly interested. Perhaps it was the tone of her voice that made him realize that mere possession of money was nothing to brag about. At any rate, he began turning back some of his profits to his employees. In 19.. he inaugurated a system of wage dividends. In 1928 these amounted to more than $3,000,000. It was said then that the cash and stock gifts to employees during the preceding seventeen years had totaled more than $35,000,000. In 1925 he distributed 10,000 shares of his own stock among employees.

He could have doubled the wages of the workers, he explained, but the high wage would not have been stable and the employees would not have saved so much of their additional income.

Once when the men who polished the metal parts of cameras struck, the company set them up in a co-operative business of their own, giving one share of stock to each man. Their income was good, but they quarreled over the rates of pay and sold stock to one another until one man owned the business. After that Mr. Eastman did not consider turning over his business directly to the workers.

Although he gave so much to his employees, still his surplus wealth piled up. Kodak Park at Rochester, "the Kodak City," begun in 1890 as one building, and a dozen acres of land, expanded to 400 acres and seventy buildings where 19,000 people found employment. Nor had the laboratories stopped when the machines were turning out thousands of miles of film for amateurs to use at vacation time and motion picture companies to show in thousands of busy theaters. The portable motion-picture machine for amateurs, the autographic device and, finally, in 1928, the greatest triumph since the roll film—the color motion pictures for amateurs—were successively announced to the world.

Summary of His Gifts

The company's worth has been estimated at $250,000,000. Mr. Eastman's gifts, therefore, had to be increased if he was to get his maximum of fun. The following partial list of his major donations will indicate how he got it:

University of Rochester	$35,500,000
Mass. Institute of Technology	20,000,000
Tuskegee Institute	2,362,000
Hampton Institute	2,000,000
Kodak stock distributed to employees	6,000,000
Chamber of Commerce Building	1,350,000
War chest, 1918	500,000
Expense of war chest	100,000
General Hospital	500,000
Mechanics Institute	625,000
Y. M. C. A.	300,000
Red Cross, 1917	250,000
War relief	225,000
State and municipal research bureau	300,000
Highland Hospital	100,000
Genesee Hospital	75,000
Rochester parks	100,000
Stevens Institute of Technology	50,000
Friendly Home	50,000
S. P. C. C. shelter	45,000
Y. W. C. A. and Infants Hospital	$25,000
Musical instruments for public schools	15,000
Dental Clinic, Royal Free Hospital London, England	1,300,000
Eastman Visiting Professorship, Oxford	200,000
Waterville Memorial	50,000
Dental Dispensary, Rome	1,000,000
Dental Dispensary, Stockholm	1,000,000
Dental Dispensary, Paris	1,000,000
Dental Dispensary, Brussels	1,000,000

Although his gifts reached tremendous proportions, they were made without ostentation. Mr. Eastman gave $11,000,000 to the Massachusetts Institute of Technology under the name of "Mr. Smith," and admitted the gift reluctantly when it was traced to him. He later increased the amount.

His reticence was a part of his cool, cautious personality. He had been too busy to become famous until the world ferreted him out. A spare, gray little man, he was meticulous in all the things that he did. At seventy-four, he said: "The remaining years are very precious to me, and I am now doing what the movies call a fade-out." His chief joys were good health, extreme comfort, perfect food, which he sometimes cooked himself to be sure that it was good, flowers and music. His house was tastefully arranged, with a fireplace in each room.

Terry Ramsaye, the writer, once said that "if the whole of George Eastman's life were to be run through a white filter paper, there probably would not be a tint or trace of abandon or reck-lessness."

The Gentleman's Magazine 30th May 1792 Vol 62

At his house in Hertford-street, May-fair, of a diarrhœa, which had been two years in operation, the Right Hon. John Montagu, fourth Earl of Sandwich, Viscount Hinchinbrook, a governor of the Charter-house, the oldest of the elder brethren of the Trinity-house, of which he had enjoyed the honour and the patronage nearly 43 years (Sir Geo. Pocock, who died a short time before him, being the next upon the list). He was also the oldest general in the army, and recorder of Huntingdon and Godmanchester, F. R. and A. SS. His Lordship had all the advantages of an excellent genius, improved by foreign travel, in the course of which he visited Grand Cairo, Constantinople, Italy, and most of the Courts in Europe. In these travels he formed a valuable collection of coins, and other antiquities. Among the latter was that curious marble now in Trinity-college library, Cambridge, illustrated by Dr. Taylor, 1743, by the title of "Marmor Sandvicense;" and to the same college his Lordship also presented a mummy from Teneriffe. Soon after his return, he took his seat in the House of Lords, where he displayed uncommon talents as an orator, and a thorough knowledge of the real interests of his country. He was early engaged in public life. In 1744 he was second lord of the Admiralty, under the Duke of Bedford. In 1746 he was appointed minister-plenipotentiary to the States General, and afterwards at the treaty of Aix-la-Chapelle, in the year 1748, where he shewed such eminent abilities and talents for business as recommended him to Government well qualified to hold the first offices of state. He was one of the lords justices for the administration of government during his Majesty's absence, 1748 and 1750; joint vice-treasurer, receiver-general, and paymaster of Ireland, and treasurer at war there, in 1755. In 1763 he was nominated ambassador to Spain, but succeeded George Grenville at the head of the Admiralty in the same year. He was secretary of state 1763—1765, 1770—1771. He was at the head of the Board of Admiralty 1748, 1763, and 1771; and it is but barely doing him justice to say, that no man ever filled that high office with greater ability. It is chiefly owing to the great efforts and unwearied diligence of this Nobleman, during the last war, that the maritime force of Great Britain was kept up on such a respectable establishment that we were enabled to meet our numerous foes in every quarter of the globe with a superior force; and that such victories were gained by our Rodneys and other brave officers over the French, the Spaniards, and the Dutch. Few men in office have equaled Lord Sandwich in the regularity and dispatch of business; for whenever any officer made application to him, he was sure of receiving a speedy and decisive answer. He shone no less conspicuously in private life; his easy and engaging manners, chearfulness of temper, and conviviality of disposition, endearing him to all ranks and societies. He retained his faculties almost to the last, and spoke with great clearness and precision of the many singular public events which, in the term of 73 years, he had witnessed; though he believed they were not more new and extraordinary to his contemporaries than those in a former century must have been to those concerned with them. By his first lady, Judith, third daughter of Charles first Viscount Fane of the kingdom of Ireland, whom he married in 1740, he had issue three sons: 1. John, his successor, born 1743-4; 2. Edward, born 1745, died 1752; and William-Augustus, born 1752, died 1776; and one daughter, Mary, born 1747-8, died 1761.—His Lordship has left little personal property, and of that Miss Gordon will probably have a large share. The estates are worth 14,000l. a year. The families of the Duke of Somerset, of the Earl of Cork and Orrery, and of Mr. Popham the master in chancery, were related to his Lordship, next after his own children.

The Times
16th March 1891

DEATH OF SIR JOSEPH BAZAL-GETTE.

Less than two years have elapsed since the premature decease of the Metropolitan Board of Works—a body which, though its departure may have been unlamented, had done good work for London, and had deserved the gratitude of Londoners. And now we have to record the death of one whose name will always be linked with the greatest works carried out by the Metropolitan Board, Sir Joseph Bazalgette, who was their Chief Engineer for the whole period of 32 years during which the Board controlled the destinies of London at large. He died yesterday afternoon, at his residence, St. Mary's, Wimbledon-park. He was born in 1819, and married in 1845 Maria, daughter of Mr. Edward Kough, of Wexford. He entered the engineering profession in 1840, and was knighted—a well-deserved honour—in 1874. Londoners are probably as dissatisfied with their government to-day as they were 30 years ago. Perhaps it is just in consequence of this perennial dissatisfaction that that government has so enormously improved in the interval ; but imagination shrinks from transporting itself back to the time when the Metropolitan Board first came into office, when the Crimea and Sebastopol were the words that were foremost on every tongue. In those days some of the London water companies still drew their water from the Thames at Battersea-bridge, and one of them, though its directors were confident that the supply was of excellent quality, was responsible for 6,000 deaths from cholera in consequence. What drainage there was was the result of a number of independent sewer commissions, some of which, by the way, under Acts of Parliament dating back as far as the reign of Henry VIII., had the power to levy what recently has come to be known as a "betterment" rate upon the area which they served ; but the sewers one and all drained straight into the Thames, and their contents according to Sir John Simon, still ran at low tide "in a stream of some length across the mud of the retreating river."

It was the imperative need for a general drainage system which called the Metropolitan Board of Works into existence, and gave their Chief Engineer the opportunity of linking his name to all time with the monumental work of the Thames-embankment. On that work there is no need here to dwell. We hear not a little from time to time of "jerry-building," but when the New Zealander comes to London a thousand years hence to sketch the ruins of St. Paul's, the magnificent solidity and the faultless symmetry of the great granite blocks which form the wall of the Thames-embankment will still remain unmoved to testify that, in the reign of Victoria, "jerry-building" was at least not quite universal. Middle-aged Londoners can still remember how the mud swirled and stank at low tide beneath the basement of Somerset-house ; how the gardens of the Temple and Montague-house sloped down uninterrupted to the water's edge. Some of them may remember how one great nobleman only lately dead all but succeeded in preventing the execution of a work which affected the life and health of 3,000,000 Londoners, because the Embankment would cut off his town residence from access to the river. But of the great sewer that runs beneath Londoners know, as a rule, nothing, though the Registrar-General could tell them that its existence has added some 20 years to their chance of life.

Broadly speaking, the Metropolitan Main Drainage system, as designed and carried out by Sir Joseph Bazalgette, consists of three parallel sewers, a high level, a middle, and a low level sewer, all of which unite at Abbey Mills, not far from the Stratford Station on the Great Eastern Railway, and are thence carried down to the outfall at Barking, which is some distance below Woolwich. The high level sewer runs along the southern slopes of the Hampstead and Highgate hills ; the middle level along Oxford-street with a branch from Piccadilly ; while the low level commences at Chiswick, and, striking the river alongside the railway bridge at Battersea, is carried under the Embankment and up Queen Victoria-street through the heart of the City. Figures, when they come to eight or nine places, fail to touch the imagination from their very vastness, or we might get an idea of the magnitude of this system, which already, however, has been proved inadequate to its task, from the fact that the average flow of sewage is estimated at 180 million gallons per diem in dry weather ; but, inadequate though the system may be, in its main outlines, it has stood the test of time. Theorists have talked of separate systems of drainage, have lectured on the economic value of town sewage to agriculture have started companies without number for its commercial utilization ; but the experts stand to-day at the point where they stood a generation back and maintain that the best thing to do with town sewage is to get rid of it as quickly and as cheaply as possible. And the problem how best to do this on a scale which the world had not seen before and has hardly seen since was successfully grappled with and met by Sir Joseph Bazalgette. Of the later development of his system—of the precipitation tanks and the chemical treatment, with their thousands of tons of lime and protosulphate of iron, of the clarified effluent, and the sludge ships which carry the solid matter away out to sea—there is no need to speak here. Though there are two ships in active work, the Barking and the Bazalgette, matters have scarcely gone beyond the experimental stage ; and it is not as the eponymous hero of a sludge ship that Londoners ought to remember the name of Sir Joseph Bazalgette.

Little need be said of the work of the Chief Engineer of the Metropolitan Board in other directions. Except within the City limits he had charge of all the bridges crossing the Thames as far west as Hammersmith. For the design of the new Battersea-bridge the responsibility is his. Among his latest works in this direction may be mentioned the Woolwich Ferry, which has been successfully and gratuitously in operation for now almost two years, and has proved an enormous boon to the inhabitants of that thickly-populated district. He also was one of the earliest to appreciate the value of the Greathead shield-system of tunnelling for sub-aqueous work ; and if he and the Metropolitan Board had had their way the Blackwall Tunnel, which the County Council has only within the last few weeks resolved to construct, would before this have been on the highway to completion. For the new high level bridge at the Tower Sir Joseph also prepared designs, but the City asserted its claim to the sole control of the undertaking, and, as it backed its claim by an offer to bear the entire expense, not unnaturally that claim was permitted to prevail. One other branch of the work of the Engineer to the Metropolitan Board of Works deserves a word of notice. Hardly a year passes in which thirty or forty Bills for railway, gas, tramway, or waterworks affecting the metropolis are not introduced into Parliament and referred to committees upstairs. On each and all of them the Metropolitan Board had to enter an appearance. Here it was a question of interference with sewers ; there of compelling pipes to be placed in a subway to avoid breaking up the road ; elsewhere it was a question of the headway of a bridge, or of the rights of the public against the water companies. In the Parliamentary committee rooms there were few witnesses better known or more influential than Sir Joseph Bazalgette. Even since his retirement he was retained in not a few instances to give evidence on behalf of the London County Council in matters on which he could speak with unique authority. In the Session which for purposes of Private Bill legislation has only lately opened, with schemes to the fore for electric subways in all directions, and when the vast question of the water supply of London is apparently once more to be seriously considered, there are few witnesses, it may be added, who will be so much missed as the late Engineer of the Metropolitan Board of Works.

Manchester Guardian
17th March 1898

SIR HENRY BESSEMER

The death of Sir Henry Bessemer, which was briefly announced in our second edition yesterday morning, removes one of the creators of the age of steel.

He was born on January 13, 1813, at Charlton, in Herts, where his father, Mr. Anthony Bessemer, had established a typefoundry. The father was a man of inventive ability, whose mechanical and chemical devices were at once ingenious and practical. From these circumstances Bessemer was early habituated to the use of tools, which were the playthings of his childhood. He was as a youth a skilful turner and a dexterous modeller in clay. He went to school at Hitchin, and at eighteen began business life as a designer and modeller. He invented a perforating stamp for the Government Stamp Office, and on the suggestion of Miss Ann Allen, the lady who in 1833 became his wife, he made the date an integral part of the instrument. The device was adopted, but a promise of lucrative employment in the department was never fulfilled, greatly to the disappointment and indignation of the young inventor.

He turned his thoughts to other directions, made improvements in typefounding, devised a machine for producing figured Utrecht velvets, and discovered a profitable bronze powder. This was not patented but used in a secret process, and as the secret was well kept it was very profitable. He had his own ideas, which were in advance of the time, as to the construction of railway trains, and he made improvements in the manufacture of paints, oils, and varnishes. His centrifugal pump, his sugar separator, and his plate-glass polishing machine were among the notable exhibits of the Great Exhibition of 1851. He turned his attention to the problem of guns and projectiles, but the plans he submitted to the British War Office were rejected without a trial. Some time later he was on a visit to Lord James Hay at Paris, and there he met at dinner Prince Napoleon. After dinner the conversation turned on artillery, and Bessemer naturally mentioned his plan of firing elongated projectiles from smooth-bore guns. The Prince was struck with the idea, and at once arranged an interview between the inventor and the Emperor, who gave a *carte blanche* for experiments at Vincennes. The results were satisfactory, and as Bessemer and the French officers stood by the blazing wood fire in the quarters at Vincennes Commandant Minié, the inventor of the famous rifle, remarked that although the rotation of the shot was effected, yet unless they had something better to make guns of such heavy elongated projectiles could not be used with safety. This remark was the seed which, falling on suitable ground, bore fruit in the great invention which has identified the name of Bessemer with an industrial revolution. "My knowledge of metallurgy was at this time very limited," observed Bessemer, "but this was in one sense a great advantage to me, for I had very little to unlearn, and so could let my imagination have fuller scope." The first result of many experiments was the model of a little gun, which he presented to the Emperor of the French. The metal was "wonderfully tough for cast-iron, but wonderfully brittle if classed as malleable iron." Now Bessemer began to see that if he could succeed the improved metal would not only affect the construction of guns, but have a great commercial value for engineering purposes of almost every kind. But while carrying on with great ardour and at great expense the many laborious experiments that were necessary, he was anxious to take the opinion of someone of eminence in the world of practical science, for there are moments when even the most convinced inventor may wonder whether he is not living in an atmosphere of self-deception. Bessemer showed the results he had obtained to Mr. George Rennie, the president of the Mechanical Section of the British Association, who urged him to bring the discovery at once before the Cheltenham meeting of that Association." The paper "On the manufacture of malleable iron without fuel," which was read August 11, 1856, caused a profound sensation, and within a month he had received £27,000 for licences to use the process. But now there came great and unforeseen difficulties. Bessemer had used Blaenavon pig-iron with the result already named, but the manufacturers working under his licences and using various other brands were often unsuccessful. The Bessemer process was formally condemned by the ironmasters of Staffordshire and Worcestershire, and a fiasco seemed inevitable. Bessemer was still convinced that he was in the right, and many costly experiments were made. As the difficulties were chemical rather than mechanical, he fitted up a laboratory, and employed an expert authority on chemistry to make analyses of all the materials used in the experiments and to tabulate and classify the results obtained. Many paths were tried, only to find that they led nowhere. Six months of constant and expensive experiment had produced no result. There had been a great revulsion of feeling against the Bessemer process, and even his friends counselled him to give up a struggle which they feared could only end in disaster. But in a few more months he had produced from charcoal pig-iron that had cost £7 per ton a steel that was worth from £50 to £60 per ton. But not one single ironmaster in Great Britain was willing to adopt the system. Some steel bars made at his experimental workshop at St. Pancras were introduced into Galloway's foundry at Manchester, and in the two months' trial the workmen were without suspicion that any change had been made or that they were not using metal costing £60 a ton. The result was that the Galloways entered into partnership with Bessemer and others, and works were opened at Sheffield. The cheaper rate at which they could produce made them formidable competitors, and one by one the ironmasters obtained licences for the working of the Bessemer process. At the end of the fourteen years' term of partnership the works were sold for twenty-four times the amount of the whole subscribed capital of the firm, and each of the five partners retired with eighty-one times the amount of his subscribed capital. This was, of course, apart from the value of the patent itself. There was a fine show of the many uses to which the Bessemer steel might be applied at the great Exhibition of 1862. Soon after Mr. John Platt, M.P. for Oldham, with nine of his friends became interested in the patent rights. They left the control to the inventor, but were to receive a fourth of the royalties. Bessemer named £50,000 as the price, and within three weeks from the opening of the Exhibition Bessemer and the ten purchasers dined together at the Queen's Hotel in Manchester, and each of the ten handed him a roll of £5,000 in bank notes. A few years later Bessemer handed them half-yearly a gross sum equal to £260,000.

The most interesting parts of a man's life are those in which he is struggling to success or failure. Bessemer had now conquered fame and fortune. He received various foreign orders of chivalry, and in 1879 was knighted by the Queen. He was a member of many scientific societies at home and abroad. London and Hamburg gave him the freedom of those cities. Nine places in the United States have been named Bessemer. He has had long life in which to enjoy the fruits of his arduous labours, his remarkable genius for invention, and, not least, the indomitable will which enabled him to conquer the difficulties that would have been insuperable to most men.

New York Times
18ᵗʰ October 1931

EDISON, AT 10, BEGAN CAREER AS INVENTOR

Regarded Dull in School Days at Milan, Ohio, He Early Showed His Genius.

EDUCATED BY HIS MOTHER

He Started Fortune by Devices Revolutionizing the Telegraph Business While an Operator.

PROLIFIC IN NEW IDEAS

Reached Height of Career Early With Development of Trolleys, Electric Light, Phonograph, Kinetoscope.

Thomas Alva Edison was born at Milan, Ohio, on Feb. 11, 1847. He came of vigorous and independent-minded stock, originally coming to America from the Zayder Zee. His great-grandfather was Thomas Edison, a New York banker of prominence on the Tory side during the Revolutionary War. So much of a Loyalist was he that when the Colonies won their independence he went to Canada to live under the British flag. There his grandson, Samuel, became a rebel against the King, rose to the rank of Captain in Papineau's insurgent army in 1837 and fled to the States with a price on his head.

Samuel Edison settled at Milan, Ohio, where his son, Thomas Alva Edison, was born. Edison got most of his schooling there. He was always, as he remembered it later, at the foot of his class. In interviews he recalled his mother's indignation when one of his teachers told him that he was "addled," a fighting adjective in country districts. His mother, who had been a teacher, took him out of school and educated him herself. His early reading, like that of Abraham Lincoln, consisted of what the village afforded. At the age of 9 he had read or his mother had read to him "The Penn Encyclopedia," "Hume's History of England," a history of the Reformation; Gibbons's "Decline and Fall of the Roman Empire," and Sear's "History of the World."

Started Experimenting Early.

But the books which put the backward schoolboy of the tiny canal village on the way to become one of the greatest men of his time were popular works on electricity and chemistry. He and his mother performed some of the simple chemical experiments they found described in the books. That started Edison on his career as an experimenter, investigator and scientist. The first steps of his career are described as follows in a condensed biography by William H. Meadowcroft, for many years Edison's private secretary:

"At about 10 or 11 years of age Edison became greatly interested in chemistry and, having procured some books on the subject, persuaded his mother to allow him a space in her cellar for a laboratory. Here he experimented with such chemicals as he could procure at the local drug stores with his limited pocket money. He had gathered together about 200 bottles of various sizes and shapes to contain his chemicals, and labeled them all with the word 'Poison,' so that they would not be disturbed. At that early age, as later, he doubted the statements in books until he had proved them by experiment.

"Edison continued his chemical studies at home until he was between 12 and 13 years old, and then, finding that his pocket money was inadequate to purchase all the apparatus and chemicals he wanted, persuaded his father and mother to allow him to become a railroad newsboy, in order that he might earn money for his experiments. He received the necessary permission and thus came to sell newspapers, magazines, candy, &c., on one of the trains of the Grand Trunk Railway running between Port Huron and Detroit. Part of the baggage car was allowed him for his stock of goods, and into this space he moved his laboratory from his home on to the train and there continued to experiment, but on an enlarged scale. He also bought a printing press and some type and published on the train a weekly newspaper, which he called The Weekly Herald, of which he was proprietor, publisher, editor, compositor, pressman and distributor. The paper contained local, market and railway news, and had as many as 400 paid subscribers at one time. So far as is known, this was the first newspaper ever printed on a moving train, and by the youngest known editor in the world.

Conductor Boxed His Ears.

Edison continued along these lines of work between two and three years until one day a bottle containing phosphorus fell off a shelf and broke upon the floor. The phosphorus set fire to the car, which was with some difficulty saved from burning up, and the conductor put the boy and his belongings off the train and boxed his ears so soundly as to cause the beginning of the deafness with which he has ever since been afflicted.

"Some little time before this Edison had saved from death the child of a station agent along the line of the railway, and the father, in gratitude, offered to teach the boy telegraphy. This offer was eagerly accepted, and since that time Edison had assiduously studied the art, besides continuing his chemical and other studies. His career as a train newsboy being ended after the incident above related, he now sought and obtained employment as telegraph operator, and at about 15 years of age entered upon this phase of his career. He plunged into the art with great enthusiasm and worked as an operator in various telegraph offices in different parts of the United States. Having the ability of living with but a very few hours of sleep, he worked nearly twenty hours a day, and not only continued his chemical studies but also applied himself very closely to the study of electricity and the art of telegraphy. He was always willing to take the place of a skilled press operator and work through the night after working all day, in order to perfect his speed, and succeeded so well that he became one of the most rapid and efficient telegraphers of his day, and advanced to the position and pay of a first-class operator."

One of his first inventions caused

his discharge from his job. Young Edison had his mind so full of inventions and science that he did not have time to put in his full hours as operator. The circuit manager, suspecting that Edison might wander away from his telegraph instruments for an hour or so, required him to send the signal "six" every half hour while he was on duty. The outcome was the invention of a wheel with notches in it which automatically ticked off the required signal. The signals were given with such remarkable precision that suspicion was aroused. He was investigated, found out, and let go. The invention was the forerunner of the modern messenger boy "call box."

Edison had worked in a dozen cities before he became of age and had achieved a reputation as the operator who couldn't keep a job. He lost his job because his mind was too full of "duplex transmission," which has since revolutionized the telegraph business.

He invented in those early days a "repeater," which automatically picks up a feeble message at the end of a long wire.

He drifted to New York, but there were no jobs for him. He turned up at the offices of the Law Gold Reporting Company one afternoon when the crude ticker service they were operating for market reports had broken down. He repaired it and promptly got a mechanic's job at $300 a month. He was about 22 years old then, and from that time fortune began to smile on him. He worked out improvements in stock tickers and telegraph appliances and got $50,000 for one invention of a ticker.

It was this money that gave him the means to extend his experiments. During this period he had developed the multiple telegraph appliance into a six-fold transmission system, the carbon telephone transmitter, the microtasimeter for measuring the smallest changes in temperature, the megaphone, the incandescent lamp, the phonograph, the kinetoscope, the alkaline storage battery, the magnetic ore separator and the trolley car.

Questionnaire Became Famous.

Almost entirely self-educated, Edison never had the opportunity or the leisure to make himself a profound student of physics, mathematics and theoretical chemistry, but he had a rich equipment for an inventor. To an enormous practical grasp of physics and electricity he joined wide general experience, reading and intellectual activity. The scattering and unsystematic book learning which he had gathered as a boy at home he developed in the same discursive way throughout the rest of his life. He read books of every kind. He was a believer in vast and miscellaneous general information, as he demonstrated in 1921, when the Edison questionnaire became famous. He gave to his prospective employes the kind of an examination which he himself could have passed when he was a youth. He wanted to find men of his own type, men of intellectual curiosity and general knowledge. He recognized the necessity for specialists but he insisted that a great specialist needed a diffused intellectual background.

In talking about the questionnaire Edison's secretary said that his chief, then nearly 75, was still an omnivorous reader and devoured the whole magazine field from The Police Gazette to The Astrophysical Journal. His general experience and knowledge fed the inventor with ideas. His practical scientific knowledge, his original, penetrating mind and his invincible industry gave him the greatest output of invention of any living man.

An Invention Every Two Weeks.

In 1914 it was announced that the patent records at Washington showed that Edison had patented new ideas at the rate of one every two weeks for nearly forty years. He knew more about what the world needed and how to supply it than any other man of his time, if not of all time. Many of his inventions were failures. Some were good enough as inventions, but not commercial successes. Asked in one of his interviews what was his first electrical invention Edison replied:

"What was my first electrical invention? You would never guess. It was a machine to record votes in Congress. It was a mighty good invention. I had a lot of iron type, each member's name being set up in a line, and these lines were controlled by push buttons and electromagnets, so that each man could bring his name upon the 'yea' side or the 'nay' side as he pleased. I used chemically sensitized paper to record them, and the thing worked fine. A brother telegraph operator named Sam—I have forgotten the rest of his name—and myself were dead sure that we were going to make $50,000 out of it. He took the thing before a Congressional committee, and the first thing they told him was that if there was anything on earth the members of Congress did not want it was just that kind of thing, because the only right the minority had was to delay the game! After that experience, which was in 1869, I knew enough not to invent anything again until I was sure it was wanted."

Moves to Larger Shop.

When Edison was only 26 years old, in 1873, he made an agreement with the Western Union Telegraph Company to give them an option on all telegraph inventions that came out of his head. He then moved to Newark, N. J., into a bigger shop than his Manhattan working place. He completed an automatic telegraph, making possible the transmission of 1,000 words a minute, in all conditions of weather, between points as far distant as Washington and New York. He devised a Roman letter system of chemical telegraphy.

At the age of 29 Edison had become so famous that curious people crowded his workshop at Newark and he could not work satisfactorily. He moved further away from New York, to Menlo Park, N. J. At that time he had made $400,000 from his inventions.

Before that time he had already experimented on an incandescent electric light that would compare in size and expense with the ordinary gas jet and that might be handled as easily as gas. At the time the arc lamp was already in existence in public squares in this city. Backed by a syndicate with a capital of £300,-000, including men such as J. Pierpont Morgan, J. Hood Wright, Henry Villard, Grosvenor P. Lowery and Edward D. Adams, Edison extended his experiments.

His first accomplishment was a lamp with a platinum burner protected by a high vacuum in a glass globe. He continued his experiments with other substances and finally, in 1879,

he made the discovery which made the incandescent light a success. The incident was described as follows in a New York newspaper article, the accuracy of which was vouched for by Edison himself:

"Sitting one night in his laboratory, reflecting on some of the unfinished details, Edison began abstractedly rolling between his fingers a piece of compressed lampblack mixed with tar for use in his telephone. For several minutes his thoughts wandered far away, his fingers in the meantime mechanically rolling out the little piece of tarred lampblack until it became a slender filament. Happening to glance at it, the idea occurred to him that it might give good results as a burner if it were made incandescent. A few minutes later the experiment was tried, and to the inventor's gratification satisfactory though not surprising results were obtained. Further experiments were made with altered forms and compositions of the substance, each experiment demonstrating that the inventor was on the right track.

"A spool of cotton thread lay on the table in the laboratory. The inventor cut off a small piece, put it in a groove between two clamps of iron and placed the latter in the furnace. At the expiration of an hour he removed the iron mold containing the thread from the furnace and took out the delicate carbon framework of the thread—all that was left of it after its fiery ordeal. This slender filament he placed in a globe and connected it with the wires leading to the machine generating the electric current. Then he extracted the air from the globe and turned on the electricity.

Brilliant Light His Reward.

"Presto! A beautiful light greeted his eyes. He turned on more current, expecting the fragile filament immediately to fuse; but no. The only change was a more brilliant light. He turned on more current and still more, but the delicate thread remained intact. Then, with characteristic impetuosity, and wondering and marveling at the strength of the little filament, he turned on the full power of the machine and eagerly watched the consequences. For a minute or more the tender thread seemed to struggle with the intense heat passing through it—heat that would melt the diamond itself. Then at last it succumbed and all was darkness. The powerful current had broken it in twain, but not before it had emitted a light of several gas jets.

"Night and day, with scarcely rest enough to eat a hearty meal or to catch a brief repose, the inventor kept up his experiments, and from carbonizing pieces of thread he went to splinters of wood, straw, paper and many other substances never before used for that purpose. The result of his experiments showed that the substance best adapted for carbonization and the giving out of incandescent light was paper, preferably thick, like cardboard, but giving good results even when very thin."

Edison's discovery was embodied in Patent 223,898, filed Nov. 4, 1879. Improvements have since been made in the method of making the filament, but the incandescent lamps that light the world are like the lamps described in Patent 223,898. On Jan 1, 1880, the public was invited to go to Menlo Park and see the operation of the first lighting plant. Electricians, many of them, insisted that there was some trickery in the exhibition, but almost simultaneously the Edison lighting system spread all over civilization. Syndicates were formed all over the world.

Invention of Phonograph.

The fiftieth anniversary of the phonograph was celebrated at Edison's laboratories in 1927. It was invented by Edison in 1877 and publicly demonstrated in 1878. This invention came easy to him. An accident attracted his attention. His daring imagination and vast store of knowledge were instantly focussed on the accident, and the phonograph was born in his mind almost instantaneously. His story of the phonograph, told in the North American Review ten years after the invention, was as follows:

"To make the idea of the recording of sound more clear, let me remark one or two points. We have all been struck by the precision with which even the faintest sea waves impress upon the surface of the beach, the fine sinuous line which is formed by the rippling edge of their advance. Almost as familiar is the fact that grains of sand sprinkled on a smooth surface of glass or wood near a piano sift themselves into various lines and curves according to the vibrations of the melody played on the piano keys. These things indicate how easily the particles of solid matter may receive an imparted motion, or take an impression from delicate liquid waves, air waves, or waves of sound. Yet, well known though these phenomena were, they apparently never suggested until within a few years that the sound waves set going by human voice might be so directed as to trace an impression upon some solid substance with a nicety equal to that of the tide recording its flow upon the beach.

Discovery an Accident.

"My own discovery that this could be done came to me almost accidentally while I was busy with experiments having a different object in view. I was engaged upon a machine intended to repeat Morse characters which were recorded on paper by indentations that transferred their message to another circuit automatically when passed under a tracing point connected with a circuit-closing apparatus. In manipulating this machine I found that when the cylinder carrying the indented paper was turned with great swiftness, it gave off a humming noise from the indentations—a musical, rhythmic sound resembling that of human talk heard indistinctly. This led me to try fitting a diaphragm to the machine which would receive the vibrations or sound waves made by my voice when I talked to it and register these vibrations upon an impressible material placed on the cylinder.

"The material selected for immediate use was paraffined paper, and the results obtained were excellent. The indentations on the cylinder, when rapidly revolved, caused a repetition of the original vibrations to reach the ear through a recorder, just as if the machine itself was speaking. I saw at once that the problem of registering human speech so that it could be repeated by mechanical means as often as might be desired was solved."

The actual story of the making of the first phonograph is told in Francis Arthur Jones's biography of Edison as follows:

"When Edison had conceived the phonograph, he called Kruesi to him, showed him a rough sketch of the proposed machine and asked him to build the model as quickly as he could. In those days Edison's model makers worked by the piece and it was customary to mark the price on each model. In this instance the cost agreed upon was $8. Kruesi

CONTINUED

Ludwig Saw in Edison Our 'Uncrowned King'; Tells of His Pleasure at Crowd's Homage

was asked how long it would take him to complete the model and he replied that he couldn't tell, but he promised that he wouldn't rest until it was finished. This was in the Menlo Park days, when Edison was looked upon as a sleepless wonder. He was accustomed to his chief assistants working for him for two or three days without a rest, and no man showed more tireless energy than Krusei. He could do with as little repose as the inventor himself, and would become so absorbed in his work that fatigue was unfelt and time forgotten. The principles of the phonograph he absorbed with lightning rapidity, but it took him thirty hours to make the model—thirty hours without rest and very little food. At the end of that time he brought to Edison the historic machine which is now preserved in the South Kensington Museum. It was a large, clumsy affair; tinfoil was used as the material on which the indentations were to be made and the cylinder was revolved by hand.

"If Edison was in any way excited on receiving the first model of his invention for recording human speech, he did not show it, and those who were with him on that memorable occasion affirm that he regarded it at the time more in the light of a queer toy than that of a machine which would create any great sensation. Among those who were present when Krusei brought in his model was Carman, the foreman of the machine shop; and this man, unable to believe what he had been told, bet Edison a box of cigars that the machine wouldn't work. The inventor, with much good humor, accepted the wager and then, with a smile, born of absolute faith in his deductions, slowly turned the handle of the machine and spoke into the receiver the first verse of 'Mary Had a Little Lamb.' Then the cylinder was returned to the starting point and faint but distinct came back the words of that juvenile classic faithfully repeated in Edison's familiar tones. Those present were awed rather than astonished, and the tension was not broken until Carman, in accents of pretended disappointment and with assumed disgust, exclaimed, 'Well, I guess I've lost.'"

Edison invented the motion picture machine in 1887. The Zoetrope and other machines were then in existence for throwing pictures from transparencies on a screen one after another and giving the effect of action. It occurred to Edison that pictures could be taken in rapid succession by the camera and later used to synthesize motion. The question who was first in this field is a mooted one. Terry Ramsaye, after an exhaustive investigation, gives the credit to Edison, holding that he was first to produce the motion picture camera and to find a method of flashing the pictures successively on the eye so that they fused into a representation of the original action. Edison put his pictures on the market in the form of a peep-show. Put a nickel in the slot and you could see dances, prizefights, fencing matches and other bits of action.

Failed as a Prophet.

Here Edison, for all his powers of forecasting the future, made his major failure as a prophet. He did not foresee the future of the motion pictures. Open-minded as he often was, he could not be argued into believing that they had any future. For a long time he opposed the idea of projecting pictures on the screen. He thought that it would ruin the nickel-in-the-slot peepshow business. In spite of his creative imagination and his comprehensive genius, Edison seemed to have been lacking in showmanship. The one thing absent from his varied life was some contact with the stage or with the advertising business. He allowed others to anticipate him in actually throwing motion pictures on the screen.

Edison had the talking pictures in mind from the first. To put it more exactly, he regarded the motion picture as something which would be useful for illustrating the phonograph. Mr. Ramsaye records the statement of old employes of Mr. Edison that, back in 1888, when he returned from a trip to Europe, phonograph and motion pictures were brought into synchronization, so that a man stepped forward and bowed on the picture screen, while the voice on the phonograph croaked, "Welcome home, Mr. Edison," or a greeting to that effect. The inventor worked on the idea of talking pictures and sought to introduce them commercially in 1913, but they were a failure, because the phonograph had not then reached its present perfection.

Edison worked for a while on the airplane. James Gordon Bennett Jr. had offered a prize for the first flying machine. Edison had the idea of a helicopter. He tried to make an engine by using ticker tape soaked in dynamite. This tape was fed into the engine piecemeal and exploded. Something went wrong with the machine and a workman was nearly killed. The inventor decided that the dynamite-driven engine would not do.

His Contribution to Radio.

One of Edison's chance discoveries is the basis of radio. This is the so-called Edison effect. It was the discovery that a current of electricity is produced when a filament is heated in a vacuum. For many years this was a laboratory novelty. But at length other scientists found various uses for it. It is the basis of the radio tube of De Forest and the whole radio industry is founded on it. In the field of pure science, as apart from the field of applied science, the discovery of the Edison effect remains the inventor's greatest achievement.

During the latter years of his life Edison worked on many improvements on the phonograph, on improvements on batteries and other electrical equipment.

Edison was married twice, in 1873 to Miss Mary G. Stillwell, by whom he had three children, Marion Estelle, Thomas A. and William L. Edison, and in 1886 to Miss Mina Miller, who is the mother of Madeleine, Charles and Theodore Edison. The elder daughter is now Mrs. Marion Oser of Norwalk, Conn., and the younger is Mrs. John Eyre Sloane of West Orange.

A story indicating the strong hold Edison had on the popular imagination of America is related by Emil Ludwig, the German writer, in his forthcoming book, "Gifts of Life," which Little, Brown & Co. of Boston will publish next month. The incident deals with a trip which Mr. Ludwig enjoyed in the company of the famous inventor and Henry Ford to Florida. Mr. Ludwig, telling the story of the episode, writes:

"On the expedition to the south of Florida with Edison and Ford, we arrived late in one of those small new towns. Lunch was over, so we went into the café and ordered something. So as not to attract attention, Ford had a table laid quite at the back in semi-obscurity. Edison, who never takes lunch, stayed in the car, sitting in his usual place in front, for he sees better from there. He sent his chauffeur in to lunch with us. The car stood in the shade on the other side of the broad empty street, about ten yards from our café.

"Somebody had meanwhile spied the old man in his solitary car and probably called out his name, so he was done for! When, after a short time, I went to the window, the street was literally black with people, and I vainly tried to fight my way through to the car.

"There he sat, and every one was holding out a slip of paper, either to ask some stupid question or merely get his autograph; and he was writing on his little slips, nodding, laughing, waving to the people. When we, stranded as we were, asked him by gestures across the sea of human beings whether he wanted a lifeboat, and the crowd drew his attention to us, he looked over, nodded, laughed, and shouted:

"'Don't worry! It's all right!'

"Then he turned back to the throng with a friendly nod, and I thought to myself: 'There sits the uncrowned King of America.'"

The Times
2nd February 1948

MR. ORVILLE WRIGHT

PIONEER IN AVIATION

Mr. Orville Wright, who, with his brother, the late Mr. Wilbur Wright, mastered the design and control of the glider, equipped it with an engine, and thus raised it to the dignity of a true flying machine, died at Dayton, Ohio, on Friday night, at the age of 76.

On December 14, 1903, Orville and Wilbur Wright decided to make a flight from Kill Devil Hill, near Kitty Hawk, in North Carolina, in the machine they had built, and in which they had installed a 12 h.p. four-cylinder engine of their own design. This aircraft had no landing wheels, being launched by running it down the slope of the hill on rails. The brothers tossed for first flight, and Wilbur won. He started off down the hill, but the machine did not rise, and crashed, with slight damage. This took two days to repair, and on December 17 they prepared to try again. This time it was Orville's privilege to make the attempt. The machine rose in the air and actually flew for 12 seconds, covering 120 feet before it landed. Thus the first power-driven flight was accomplished, and the air became a new highway for mankind.

Though chance had given this distinction to Orville Wright, it is impossible to separate the credit due to the two brothers, for they worked absolutely in harmony. It would, however, be unjust to others to regard them as the originators of the aeroplane as it is known to-day. They did great work, but so did others. Without an engine an aeroplane is but a glider, and several men had made successful gliders. The principles of flight, which seem to have been grasped by Leonardo da Vinci, were set forth in detail by Sir George Cayley in the first decade of the nineteenth century. In 1848 John Stringfellow made a model which actually flew under its own power, and many gliding flights had been made by Otto Lilienthal, the German, and Pilcher, the Englishman. Though the mystery of flight had been mastered, its application awaited the production of an engine which was light in proportion to its power. The Wright brothers saw the need, and designed such an engine themselves. That, perhaps, was their greatest achievement.

Even so, it was not by much that they beat their competitors in the race to be the first to fly under power. Their contemporary compatriot, Professor Langley, had constructed a machine which would probably have lifted a man into the air had it not been wrecked in attempting to take off. Lack of money prevented Langley from carrying on his experiments, but afterwards others rebuilt his machine, modified it somewhat, and made a successful flight with it. In France the brothers Voisin, Henry Farman, and Louis Bleriot were on the point of success; while in England the greatest of all, Alliott Verdon Roe, was not far behind. The Wrights first flew in 1903. The Frenchmen succeeded two and a half years later, and Roe made his first flight in 1908. It can also fairly be said that the Wright design of an aeroplane was not the prototype of all flying machines. The tractor biplane, produced by A. V. Roe in 1912, set the fashion to the world for many years to come.

Orville Wright was born on August 19, 1871, at Dayton, Ohio, the son of Bishop Milton Wright. Wilbur was the third son and Orville the fourth. When they grew up the two younger brothers tried their hands at journalism and brought out a weekly paper, but later they started a bicycle business and became practical mechanics. Flying was a subject which always interested them, and they read all that they could find on the subject. In 1896 they heard that Lilienthal had been killed by a crash of his glider, and they made up their minds to carry on his work. After three years of study they went into camp at Kitty Hawk and commenced to experiment with gliders. It was a fairly simple matter to get a glider into the air. The difficulty was to control its flight. To this the careful and indefatigable brothers paid the greatest attention, every conceivable point being discussed and threshed out between them. They adopted the biplane principle and had an elevator out in front of the glider, but no tail or vertical rudder. They contrived to turn by banking the machine by means of the warp, and slowly they practised, gradually accustoming themselves to the feel of the machine and to working the controls in all directions. After three years of practice they designed their engine and had it made. Then they felt ready for a power-driven flight. On the day of Orville's first flight of 12sec., three other flights were made. Each was a little longer than the last, and the fourth flight by Wilbur covered 852ft. and lasted 59sec. Then as the machine lay on the ground a sudden gust blew it over and damaged it considerably. That machine was not rebuilt until Orville decided to lend it to the Science Museum, South Kensington, 2 years later, after a dispute with the Smithsonian Institute in Washington, where it had previously been displayed.

For five more years the brothers worked in comparative secrecy; in 1905 a flight of 24 miles was made, and in 1908, the year in which A. V. Roe made his first hops in his own aircraft, the Wrights decided to show their discovery to the world. Orville approached the Government, while Wilbur brought a machine to France, where the feats of Henry Farman and others had attracted much attention. The French speedily saw their master in Wilbur. Orville was not so fortunate. He gave a demonstration before the authorities at Fort Mayer, with Lieutenant Selfridge as passenger. One of the twin propellers fouled the steering gear and the machine crashed. Selfridge was killed and Orville broke a thigh. The United States authorities were not favourably impressed, and when Orville was able to get about again he and his sister joined Wilbur in France. From the French Government they received practical encouragement, and when they returned home their own country decided to honour its prophets. Washington was decorated in their honour and President Taft received the brothers at the White House.

New York Times
2nd June 1912

WILBUR WRIGHT IS BURIED.

Brother Announces Business Plans — Factory Reopens Monday.

DAYTON, Ohio, June 1.—The body of Wilbur Wright was buried in Woodland Cemetery here with simple ceremonies this afternoon. The body was viewed by 25,000 people as it lay in state from 10 to 1 o'clock, and the church from which the funeral was held was crowded almost to suffocation during the ceremonies which followed, beginning at 3 o'clock.

The services were in charge of Dr. Maurice E. Wilson of Dayton, a Presbyterian minister, and the funeral was conducted from the First Presbyterian Church, though the decedent had been reared in the United Brethren faith. He had no church affiliations at the time of his death, though his brother, Orville, is a member of one of the Dayton churches of the United Brethren denomination, and his father is a Bishop in that Church.

Following brief services at the church the body was conveyed to Woodland Cemetery, where the services were private.

During the time church services were being held all industry was stopped in Dayton. Street cars and telephone service were discontinued for three minutes, beginning at 3:30, while shops and stores closed from 3:30 until 4 o'clock.

The honorary pallbearers were Russell A. Alger of Detroit, Fred Alger of Detroit, both members of the Wright company; Robert J. Collier of New York, one of the closest personal friends of the Wrights; Charles J. Edwards, also representing the Wright company; Dr. Levi S. Pitler and Dr. D. B. Conklin of Dayton, the attending physicians; President John Patterson of the National Cash Register Company, and Congressman James M. Cox.

Plans of Wilbur Wright for the development of aviation will be carried on uninterruptedly by his brother Orville, according to a statement by Orville Wright to-night.

"The death of my brother has been an irreparable blow to all of us," he said. "Although I have given no thought to business affairs, the work started by him will be carried on. His death came as a fearful shock right when we were in the midst of plans for a bright future.

"Wilbur was President of the company, and I was the First Vice President. I cannot say at present whether I will become President, but my brother's ideas will be carried out. I do not know how his place at the factory will be filled. It will be the most difficult task we have undertaken yet."

It is understood the operation of the plant will be resumed Monday.

Morning Post
5th April 1929

PIONEER OF MOTOR CARS

DEATH OF KARL BENZ

DIFFERENTIAL GEAR INVENTOR

From Our Own Correspondent

BERLIN, April 4.

One of the pioneers in the construction of internal combustion motor engines has passed away in Dr. Karl Benz, the founder of the famous Benz motor works.

Born in 1844, he was the son of an engine driver, from whom he inherited the taste for things mechanical. Very early in life he devoted himself to the problem of inventing a mode of self-propulsion for street vehicles.

Whether or not he was the Father of the motor-car, a distinction claimed by various countries, he at any rate produced a two-stroke motor in 1878, and in 1885 a four-stroke tricar with 250 revolutions per minute and ⅔rds of a horse power which is now in the museum at Munich.

NO SUPPORT AT HOME

An improved model soon after achieved a speed of 10 m.p.h., and his exhibit at the Munich exhibition in 1888 won the gold medal. His invention nevertheless found no support in Germany and was left to be exploited in England and America.

When later the motor-car began to become a marketable commodity the firm of Benz at once took the lead in Germany, where it has retained a prominent share in the development of the industry ever since. In 1926 Benz was amalgamated with the Daimler motor firm, the combined capital standing at £2,500,000.

It may thus be truly said that Dr. Benz, who remained on the board of directors of the combined firms to the end, had lived through every stage of the development of the motor-car from its most primitive beginnings to its latest efflorescence.

Our Motoring Correspondent writes: Every motorist should be grateful to Karl Benz, as he was the inventor of the differential gear which allows one wheel of a car to go faster than the other when the vehicle is negotiating a corner and is one of the fundamental parts of the modern motor-car. He was also largely instrumental in introducing electric ignition for cars, and he produced a surface carburetter.

The Times
7th March 1900

A Reuter telegram states that HERR DAIMLER, the inventor of the Daimler motor-car, died at Cannstadt yesterday.

The Times
11th July 1932

MR. K. C. GILLETTE

The co-inventor of the Gillette safety razor, Mr. King Camp Gillette, died on Saturday night at his ranch near Los Angeles at the age of 77. He was born at Fond du Lac, Wisconsin, and was of French descent. His mother was the author of "The White House Cook Book." He was educated at public schools in Chicago, and set himself to invent and manufacture an article which would have a universal sale. He had a hard struggle, but the result was the Gillette safety razor and its blades; though it bore his name he only claimed to be the co-inventor, and always acknowledged the help he received from Mr. W. E. Nickerson. Mr. Gillette was a great traveller and was keenly interested in sociology and economics. His views are set out at length in a series of books which came from his pen, such as "Human Drift," "Gillette's Social Redemption," "Gillette's Industrial Solution," "The World Corporation," and "The People's Corporation." He was married and had one son.

Literature

Literature, here confined to the novel and poetry, is not an area in which we may reasonably expect any sort of agreement when it comes to picking out a dozen or so names to represent the achievement of the past two hundred years. Thus the Marquis de Sade, with whom pornography proper may be said first to have entered the realm of literature, received no suitable accolade; and even **Jane Austen** received only a brief mention. Amazingly, neither Dostoevsky nor Kafka, two writers who have shaped our vision of the world more than most, were sufficiently recognized when they died to be accorded so much as a brief mention in our newspapers. Nor was Wilfred Owen, perhaps the most influential of the war poets. **Charles Dickens**, by contrast, the recorder *par excellence* of the nineteenth century, did not die unnoticed. Nor did **William Wordsworth**, the gentle reveller in the delights of Nature whose work not only saved John Stuart Mill from a nervous breakdown or worse, but whose communion with the natural world shaped the sensibility of generations. So too with **T. S. Eliot**, whose work raised poetry from the status of mere insight to that of secret code, and who is recorded here in honour of all those who seek to protect Culture by making it impenetrable to all but the unelected. **Goethe** and **Tolstoy** are here as perhaps the greatest of the writers whose insight into human nature epitomises Art. **Ernest Hemingway** represents the great hero of literature, the individual who takes on allcomers; **D. H. Lawrence** the individual who takes on certain other individuals only, at whatever cost; and **F. Scott Fitzgerald** that great band of second-rank writers, like E. M. Forster, Henry James, and Herman Melville, who tell us, brilliantly, certain things about certain people only. **James Joyce**, like several others in these pages, represents himself alone. **Conrad**, **Stevenson** and Samuel Clemens, better known as **Mark Twain** produced highly stylised reading which will continue to entertain us for generations to come, while **Robert Frost**'s verse contrasts nicely with Eliot's in its approachability. **Thomas Mann** here represents several contemporary novelists whose ability to penetrate and dissect the human soul creates prose of timeless appeal.

The Times
25th April 1850

DEATH OF THE POET WORDSWORTH.

It is with feelings of much regret that we announce to-day the death of William Wordsworth. The illustrious poet breathed his last at noon on Tuesday by the side of that beautiful lake in Westmoreland which his residence and his verse had rendered famous. We are not called upon in his case to mourn over the untimely fate of genius snatched away in the first feverish struggles of development, or even in the noonday splendour of its mid career. Full of years, as of honours, the old man had time to accomplish all that he was capable of accomplishing ere he was called away. It may well be, that he had not carried out to completion many of his plans, but it is a natural incident to humanity that execution falls far short of design. What a man could not accomplish in something like half a century of a poetical career under all the favourable conditions of unbroken quiet, moderate but sufficient means, and vigorous health, may fairly be supposed to have been beyond his reach. Therefore, as far as concerns the legacy of song William Wordsworth has bequeathed to his country, we have nothing to regret. Removed by taste and temperament from the busy scenes of the world, his long life was spent in the conception and elaboration of his poetry in the midst of the sylvan solitudes to which he was so fondly attached. His length of days permitted him to act as the guardian of his own fame,—he could bring his maturer judgment to bear upon the first bursts of his youthful inspiration, as well as upon the more measured flow of his maturest compositions. Whatever now stands in the full collection of his works has received the final *imprimatur* from the poet's hand, sitting in judgment upon his own works under the influence of a generation later than his own. It is sufficiently characteristic of the man, that little has been altered, and still less condemned. Open at all times to the influences of external nature, he was singularly indifferent to the judgment of men, or rather so enamoured of his own judgment that he could brook no teacher. Nature was his book, he would admit no interpretation but his own. It was this which constituted the secret of his originality and his strength, at the same time that the abuse of the principle laid him open at times to strictures, the justice of which few persons but the unreasoning fanatics of his school would now be prepared to deny.

But we feel this is not a season for criticism. There is so much in the character, as well as in the works of William Wordsworth, to deserve hearty admiration, that we may indulge in the language most grateful to our feelings without overstepping the decent limits of propriety and plain sincerity. We would point out, in the first place, one of the great excellencies of the departed worthy. His life was as pure and spotless as his song. It is rendering a great service to humanity when a man exalted by intellectual capacities above his fellow-men holds out to them in his own person the example of a blameless life. As long as men are what they are it is well that the fashion of virtue should be set them by men whose rare abilities are objects of envy and emulation even to the most dissolute and unprincipled. If this be true of the statesman, of the warrior, of the man of science, it is so in a tenfold degree of the poet and the man of letters. Their works are in the hands of the young and inexperienced.

Their habits of life become insensibly mixed up with their compositions in the minds of their admirers. They spread the moral infection wider than other men, because those brought within their influence are singularly susceptible of contamination. The feelings, the passions, the imagination, which are busy with the compositions of the poet, are quickly interested in the fashion of his life. From " I would fain write so" to " I would fain live so" there is but a little step. Under this first head the English nation owes a deep debt of gratitude to William Wordsworth. Neither by the influence of his song, nor by the example of his life, has he corrupted or enervated our youth ; by one, as by the other, he has purified and elevated, not soiled and abased, humanity. If we may pass from this more general and important consideration to a more limited sphere of action, we would point out the example of the venerable old man who now lies sleeping by the side of the Westmoreland lake to the attention of all who aim at high literary distinction. To William Wordsworth his art was his all, and sufficed to him as its own rich reward. We do not find him trucking the inspirations of his genius for mere sums of money, nor aiming at political and social distinctions by prostituting the divine gift that was in him. He appears to have felt that in the successful cultivation of his art he was engaged in a laborious, if in a delightful occupation. Could he succeed, he was on the level of the greatest men of his age, although he might not have a single star or riband to hang up against the wall of his rustic cottage, nor a heavy balance at his banker's as evidence of his success. These things are but the evidence of one species of triumph,—the poet, the dramatist, the historian, should aim at distinctions of another kind.

If we think the present occasion an unfit one for cold criticism, we may without impropriety devote a few brief sentences to the excellences of the compositions of the Poet of Rydal Mount. There must be something essentially " English" in his inspirations, for while few poets have exercised greater influence in his own country, on the continent his works are little known even to students who have devoted much time and attention to English literature. In Germany, for example, you will find translations at the chief seats of literary society of the poetry of SCOTT, BYRON, MOORE, and SHELLEY : SOUTHEY and COLERIDGE are less known; the name of WORDSWORTH scarcely pronounced at all. Of France the same thing may with truth be said. In either country there may be rare instances of students of the highest order, of a GUIZOT, a MÉRIMÉE, a HUMBOLDT, a BUNSEN, who are well acquainted with the writings of Wordsworth, and share our insular admiration for his beauties, but such exceptions are few indeed. There must, therefore, be some development of " English" thought in Wordsworth which is the secret of his success amongst ourselves, as of his failure in securing an European reputation. It is certain that some of the great poets whose names we have mentioned have left it upon record that they are indebted for the idea of some of their most beautiful passages to the teaching and example of Wordsworth, and yet the scholars have charmed an audience which the master could not obtain. It is probably the case that in no country of Europe is the love for a country life so strongly developed as in England, and no man who could not linger out a summer day by the river bank or on the hill side is capable of appreciating Wordsworth's poetry.

The familiarity with sylvan scenes, and an habitual calm delight under the influence of nature, are indispensable requisites before the tendency of the song can be understood which works by catching a divine inspiration even from the dewy fragrance of the heatherbell and the murmur of the passing brook. It was not in Wordsworth's genius to people the air with phantoms, but to bring the human mind in harmony with the operations of nature, of which he stood forth the poet and the interpreter. We write with the full recollection of many lovely human impersonations of the departed poet present to our minds ; but his great aim appears to have been that which we have endeavoured to shadow out as distinctly as our limited space would permit.

Before concluding we would advert to a point which is perhaps more in keeping with the usual subjects of our columns than the humble tribute of admiration we have endeavoured to offer to the illustrious man who has just been called away. Let us hope that the office of Poet Laureate, which was dignified by its two last possessors, may never be conferred upon a person unworthy to succeed them. The title is no longer an honour, but a mere badge of ridicule, which can bring no credit to its wearer. It required the reputation of a Southey or a Wordsworth to carry them through an office so entirely removed from the ideas and habits of our time without injury to their fame. Let whatever emoluments go with the name be commuted into a pension, and let the pension be bestowed upon a deserving literary man without the ridiculous accompaniment of the bays. We know well enough that birthday odes have long since been exploded ; but why retain a nickname, not a title, which must be felt as a degradation rather than an honour by its wearer ? Having said thus much, we will leave the subject to the better judgment of those whose decision is operative in such matters. Assuredly, William Wordsworth needed no such Court distinctions or decorations. His name will live in English literature, and his funeral song be uttered, amidst the spots which he has so often celebrated, and by the rivers and hills which inspired his verse.

Daily Picayune
22nd April 1910

MARK TWAIN'S CAREER.

Story of the Life of the Famous Humorist and Author.

New York, April 21.—The mere chronology of Mark Twain's life is soon told. Like most dwellers in the imagination his significance to posterity lies not, as with men of action, in how he wrought upon events, but rather in how events wrought upon him; for from such reactions resulted his imaginative output—one of the most considerable of his time, and, as it now seems, one of the securest. Briefly, then, Mr. Twain was born Samuel Langhorne Clemens in Florida, Mo., on Nov. 30, 1835.

"My parents," he writes in his own burlesque autobiography, "were neither very poor nor conspicuously honest." The earliest ancestors the Twains have any record of was a friend of the family by the name of Higgins. The county chronicles have it that the eldest Clemens failed in business and died, leaving the son the ample world to make his fortune in.

Accordingly Mark Twain's acquaintance with literature began in putting words into type, not ideas into words. Educated only in the public schools he was apprenticed to a printer at 13, and worked at his trade in St. Louis, Cincinnati, Philadelphia and New York until at 18 he could gratify a boyish ambition to become cub to a Mississippi River pilot. Both these happenings reacted profoundly on his later life.

His knowledge of river life, acquired when he was a pilot, took form in Tom Sawyer, Huckleberry Finn and Life on the Mississippi, regarded abroad as his surest title to fame. It even suggested his pseudonym for "Mark Twain" is a linesman's cry to the pilot when the boat gets into shallow water. And his familiarity with printing turned him naturally first into newspaper work, then into creative writing and finally into the publishing business, wherein, like Sir Walter Scott, he suffered a bankruptcy disastrous to everything but his honor, and, like Sir Walter again, paid off by his pen debts not of his own making.

In due time Mark Twain became a full-fledged pilot. He tells the rest himself, in a chapter of life on the Mississippi.

"By and by the war came, commerce was suspended, my occupation was gone. I had to seek another livelihood. So I became a silver miner in Nevada; next a gold miner in California; next a reporter in San Francisco; next a special correspondent in the Sandwich Islands; next a roving correspondent in Europe and the East; next an instructional torch-bearer on the lecture platform, and finally I became a scribbler of books, and an immovable fixture among the rocks of New England."

This was in 1872, two years after he had married Miss Olivia L. Langdon, of Elmira, N. Y., who brought him an independent fortune. At that time his writings were in growing demand, he had an assured income—owned his home and seemed indeed a fixture. But in 1885 his popularity as an author and his acquaintance with the mechanics of the publishing trade—besides being a practical printer, he had been part owner of the Buffalo Express before his marriage, drew him into the firm of C. L. Webster & Co., publishers. The firm brought out the memoirs of General Grant and paid his widow $350,000, but its prosperity was short-lived, and it failed with liabilities of $96,000. The failure had already sucked in $65,000 of Mark Twain's cash, but he determined also to shoulder the debts and to pay them off. He undertook, in 1895-96, a lecture trip around the world.

Mark Twain was an inveterate smoker, and one of the most leisurely men in the world. An old pressman who was once printer and devil in an office where he was an editorial writer tells this anecdote of his habits of work.

"One of my duties was to sweep the room where the editors worked. Every day Mark would give me a nickel to get away from him. He would rather die in the dust than to uncross his legs. One day he gave me a nickel to dot the 'I' in his copy for him. He certainly did enjoy life, the man did. Yet this ... ... acquitted himself ... a ... ... deal of work."

in his life, and bound himself voluntarily to pay off debts that he could have discharged without hurt to his good name by passing through bankruptcy.

He did not practice as he preached. "It don't make no difference," he had Huck Finn say, "whether you do right or wrong, a person's conscience ain't got no sense, and just goes for him anyway. If I had a yaller dog that didn't know no more than a person's conscience did, I'd pizen him. It takes up more room than all the rest of a person's insides, and yet ain't no good no how."

With Mark Twain's lecture trip around the world began his international celebrity and his gradual rise into a figure taken in some sense to typify the American spirit. From humorist he became the kindly but mocking moralist and philosopher of Puddin' Head Wilson. His literary output became more occasional and, though written with more finesse, more critical and less creative, his public appearances grew more frequent, his whimsical utterances gained greater currency, and a whole literature of anecdotes about him grew up.

Yale gave him the degree of M.A. and later of LL.D. in 1901; the University of Missouri, his native state, followed with LL.D. in 1902, and in 1907 the University of Oxford, with great ceremony, made him Litt.D.

Indeed, serious appreciation of Mark Twain as an artist, and not a mere jokesmith, began abroad, but his true worth has long been recognized in this country.

"Mark Twain's humor," said William Dean Howells, "will live forever. He portrays and interprets real types, not only with exquisite appreciation and sympathy, but with a force and truth of drawing that make them permanent. He had the true humorist's tender heart and deep seriousness. Like Bret Harte, with whom he worked; like the great West that bred him, his most audacious sallies were terse and sternly grave. As a moralist, love of humanity, hatred of sham and the sense of duty formed his most ironic and debonair preachments."

Four children were born to Mark Twain, of whom two, a son and a daughter, died young.

One daughter, Jean, who had been an invalid for life, was found dead in her bathtub last fall in her home, at Redding, Conn. Her tragic death greatly saddened her father, who declined in health from that moment. A third daughter, Clara, is Mrs. Ossip Gabrilowitch, wife of the pianist, whom she married last year.

Mark Twain's first book was the "Jumping Frog." His best known in this country is possibly "Innocents Abroad."

His surest title to fame is generally believed to be "Tom Sawyer," and its companion volume, "The Adventures of Huckleberry Finn." In all, his books had a sale of more than 500,000 copies and were translated into six languages. Among the better known are: "A Tramp Abroad," "The Prince and the Pauper," "A Connecticut Yankee at the Court of King Arthur," "Puddin' Head Wilson" (dramatized), "Joan of Arc," "A Double-Barreled Detective Story" and "Eve's Diary."

He left an unfinished autobiography, portions of which had appeared serially.

New York Times
18th December 1894

DEATH OF R. L. STEVENSON

Apoplexy Carries Away the Master of Modern English Fiction.

BURIED ON PAA MOUNTAIN SUMMIT

Inspiring Career of a Writer in Whose Work Was Charmingly Reflected the Mind of a Great Artist.

LONDON, Dec. 17.—A dispatch to The Star, dated Apia, Samoa, Dec. 8, confirms the report that Robert Louis Stevenson, the novelist, died suddenly a few days ago from apoplexy. His body was buried on the summit of Paa Mountain, 1,300 feet high.

The Westminster Gazette, in an article on the death of Robert Louis Stevenson, says that, although Mr. Stevenson was anything but apoplectic, there is little doubt that his untimely end was due to apoplexy, induced by the heat of the climate. He left a new novel half completed. The Gazette says he was among the most lovable of modern writers, and the news of his death will be heard with the keenest regret. Perhaps no author of recent years has enlisted so much personal interest on the part of his readers.

The Pall Mall Gazette says that in letters recently written Mr. Stevenson said he had two novels practically completed, but could not be induced to part with them until they had received finishing touches. One is entitled "The Chief Justice's Clerk,"

R. L. Stevenson.

the plot of which was foreshadowed in "Catriona." Those who have read portions of this work regard it as his masterpiece. The other book, entitled "St. Ives," is the story of a French prisoner who made his escape from Edinburgh Castle and had stirring adventures in a romantic district of Scotland. Mr. Stevenson had many shorter tales sketched out. He loved Samoa better than any other place, except Scotland. His wife, interviewed recently, said: "We mean to live in Samoa always and leave our bones there."

Stevenson's Forty-three Years.

Robert Louis Stevenson's full name was Robert Louis Balfour Stevenson, but the Balfour he had ceased to use. He was a native of Edinburgh, Scotland, and the date of his birth was Nov. 13, 1850. His father, Thomas Stevenson, had eminence in connection with lighthouses. For many years Thomas Stevenson was an Inspector of Lighthouses, and retained his activity in that office until near the time of his death, in 1888. On the English coast he was connected with the building of several houses; in the arrangement of reflectors he made important improvements, and some of his knowledge on the subject went into a book which he published on lighthouse optics. When he died his son wrote a sketch of his life, and one of his son's books was dedicated to him, " by whose devices the great sea lights in every quarter of the globe shine out more brightly."

Thomas Stevenson, like most Scotchmen, had dabbled in theology. In 1877 he brought out " Christianity Confirmed by Jewish and Heathen Testimony, and the Deductions from Physical Science." The work went into a second edition in the following year. Thomas Stevenson's devotion to lighthouses came to him by inheritance. His father was that Robert Stevenson who, between 1795 and 1840, designed no fewer than eighteen lighthouses for the Scotch coast, the chief of which was the famous one on Bell Rock, in which he improved on the one Smeaton had built at Edystone.

Of his Scotch origin Louis Stevenson was always proud. He has said in one of his books that to be born a Scotchman is " the

Mrs. Stevenson.

happiest lot on earth." But it was a privilege one must pay for. " You have to learn," he said, " the paraphrases and the Shorter Catechism; you generally take to drink; your youth, so far as I can find out, is a time of louder war against society, of more outcry and tears and turmoil than if you were born, for instance, in England. But, somehow, life is warmer and closer, the hearth burns more redly, the lights of home shine softer on the rainy street, the very names endeared in verse and music cling nearer round our hearts."

Stevenson's father intended him for a lawyer, and with that end in view carefully educated him at private schools and at the University of Edinburgh. He went far enough with his legal studies to be entered at the Scottish bar, and then changed the whole course of his life. He began to travel for his health, and in this found such enjoyment that he took to writing of the things he saw. Then it was that he entered upon the literary career which has given him fame and honor wherever contemporary literature is read. Before his travels began he had probably made some attempts at authorship, for to an earlier period belong these contributions which Mr. P. G. Hamerton obtained from him for his Portfolio and Leslie Stephen for The Cornhill Magazine.

His first published books have date of 1878, when his " Inland Voyage " and " Edinburgh: Picturesque Notes " made their appearance. The first of these at once seized public attention. It was an account of travel in canoes by two friends, who took to Belgian and French waters. It was the author's style which captivated his readers. Some one described it as a compound of Sir Philip Sidney, Lord Bacon, George Herbert, Stern, and Blackmore. He was seen to have rare humor, great insight, refined feeling, and splendid powers of fresh description. Mr. Hamerton declared that he was " one of the most perfect writers living, one of the very few who may yet do something that will become classical." The book on Edinburgh naturally appealed to a narrower audience, but it was greatly liked wherever it was read. He was not wholly complimentary, having the ability to see things as they were, but his style and his effective descriptions charmed all.

Already had Mr. Stevenson begun to show his fondness for France. This was in part due to his uncertain health, but in part also to a genuine liking for the land and people. As early as 1876 he had spent a whole Summer there, and at Barbizon, Grez, and Fontainebleau American artists first made acquaintance with the brilliancy of his mind and the charm of his personality. Out of this Summer came part of the experience recorded in " An Inland Voyage," and two years later French travel—the region of the Covennes—yielded up his " Travels with a Donkey," through which, in this country, his rise to fame really began. Of actual scenes of travel and adventures the book contained a small amount. Not the occurrences of the journey so much as the way things were told made the value of this new piece of composition. Critics saw an improvement on former writings. As he was more natural, so was there a corresponding absence of premeditated art. His sympathies with men and women were as generous as ever, but his humanity was more healthy, and his fun sweeter and stronger.

Stevenson's next volume was his "Virginibus Puerisque and Other Papers," which appeared in 1881, and in the following year came his "Familiar Studies of Men and Books." Both contained matter that was repeated from the periodicals for which he had written—The Portfolio, The Cornhill, The New Quarterly, and Macmillan's. In 1882 he published his "New Arabian Nights," with which were included some short stories that originally were published in The Cornhill and Temple Bar. Of this volume, The Saturday Review remarked that there was little to be got from the stories but pleasure. It praised "their striking fertility of invention," their charming touch of chivalry, which is by no means too common, either in real life or in fiction, and that other quality of the author's, also by no means too common, of making his readers' cup full of horrors, and yet putting no offense in it."

When "Treasure Island" came out, in 1883, fame for Stevenson had already been achieved; but this work was to widen and deepen it everywhere. The book is said to have had its origin in a suggestion made to the author by a small boy, in whom he was interested, who repeatedly had asked him why he did not write something interesting like "Robinson Crusoe." Although especially a book for boys, this work gave quite as much pleasure to folks grown to man's estate, and to whom tales of prowess and daring in the Spanish Main have always been captivating. What The Saturday Review admired most in it was, as usual, the style. It said the book was "written in that crisp, choice, nervous English, of which he has the secret, with such a union of measure and farce as to be in its way a masterpiece of narrative."

Mr. Stevenson's first visit to America had been made before "Treasure Island" appeared. In the Summer of 1879 he determined to make a voyage from Liverpool to New-York in the steerage, and on arrival here he concluded to continue the journey on land in an immigrant car as far as San Francisco. It was an odd mode of travel for one with Stevenson's refinement and sensitive spirit, but with him love of adventure has ever been one of the strongest passions. We may, perhaps, call it an inherited taste—a survival in the tastes of the man of letters of what had been the daily habit and environment of his ancestors for two or more generations. Out of the American trip Mr. Stevenson got a series of magazine papers, and some years later a further fruit was seen in his book, "The Silverado Squatters; a Sketch from a California Mountain," which had to do with a deserted mining camp in the southern part of the State. Originally, the story was printed in The Century Magazine. Mr. Stevenson's charming collection of verse relating to the inner life of childhood followed next. It was appropriately called "A Child's Garland of Verse," and only two years ago an illustrated reprint of it awakened new praises.

Next, in 1885, came "Prince Otto: A Romance," in which he dealt with the morals of marriage, and in 1886 his "Strange Case of Dr. Jekyll and Mr. Hyde," which has enjoyed the double reputation of great success on the stage as well as in book and story form. Mr. Stevenson has declared that the principal incident was dreamed by him many years before he wrote the story. In his dream he saw Hyde rush into a mysterious recess, take a drug, and then, by the terror that followed, was awakened. Such was the impression the dream made on him that it haunted him for years before he made a story out of it.

In the same year was published "Kidnapped," which was described as the "Memoirs of the Adventures of David Balfour in the year 1751." It told of his being kidnapped and cast away on a desert island, where he had many sufferings, and from which he escaped to the west highlands of Scotland, there to meet Alan Breck Stewart "and other notorious highland Jacobites." Balfour suffered much at the hands of his "Uncle Ebenezer Balfour of Shawes, falsely so called." Balfour was declared to have written these memoirs himself, and the adventures end when the hero is scarcely more than a boy. Most readers were reminded of it by "Treasure Island." The workmanship was admired and the horrors were related with such charm and freshness, joined to refinement, that readers of fine taste found the work a source of genuine pleasure.

Books which now followed were "The Merry Men and Other Tales and Fables," "Underwoods," a volume of verse; a "Memoir of Fleming Jenkins," and "Memories and Portraits," all in 1887; "The Black Arrow: A Tale of the Two Roses," in 1888; "The Master of Ballantrae," 1889; "Ballads," including two long romances of South Sea life, and "The Wrong Box," (in which he had the assistance of Lloyd Osbourne,) in 1890; and since 1890, "The Wrecker," (also with the help of Mr. Osbourne,) "Across the Plains, with Other Memories and Essays," and then his book on Samoa, which he called "A Footnote to History. Eight Years of Trouble in Samoa." More recently have appeared "David Balfour," (1893,) and "Island Nights' Entertainments," (1893.) The long story "David Balfour," was widely read in the year of its appearance, and has been greatly admired.

Mr. Stevenson, after the years spent in France for his health, sought elsewhere for a better climate than Scotland afforded. At one time he fixed his abode at Bournemouth, in the south of England, at a country home, which he called Skerryvore. Again he came to New-York and spent a Winter and some additional months in the Adirondacks, and finally he pitched his tent in Samoa. Great was the surprise of the public when it learned that to this remote Pacific isle the brilliant author had gone for a stay that would be prolonged, and might be permanent. He was dwelling in Samoa when the quarrel among the European powers occurred, with the awful disaster by which such wreck was done to the war ships of three nations. In his "Footnote to History," these Samoan events find extended narration in which are mingled accounts of beggars and planters, the strife of consuls, the awful hurricane, the scene on the shore and in the harbor when the hurricane had passed, and the making and unmaking of Kings, with the sorrows of one of them named Laupepa.

Stevenson's marriage was as romantic as any tale he ever told. Lloyd Osbourne, who assisted him in writing two of his stories, was the son of his wife by a former marriage, and when Mrs. Osbourne became Mrs. Stevenson she was recently divorced from her husband, Samuel C. Osbourne. She and Osbourne had been married in Indiana in 1858. He maiden name was Vandergrift, and in 1861 the couple, with a son and daughter, started for Arizona with a few thousand dollars they had saved. Mr. Osbourne put his money in a mine, for which a few months later $100,000 was offered. Osbourne wished to sell, but his partner did not. They held on, and six months later the mine would not fetch a dollar.

Osbourne, with his family, then went to San Francisco, and he so prospered as a court reporter that he sent his wife to Europe to educate the children. In Paris Mrs. Osbourne, in 1883, met Stevenson, and fell in love with him. Returning to San Francisco she obtained a divorce, and arrangements were at once made for her marriage with Stevenson. Osbourne was invited to the wedding and accepted. On the appointed day he presented himself in faultless attire, with a lady on his arm, whom he introduced as Mrs. Osbourne. To this lady Osbourne had been quietly married as soon as the divorce was granted. Some newspaper stories have declared that the divorce broke Osbourne's heart, but his prompt second marriage hardly bears out the story. In any event, it is known that as Mr. and Mrs. Stevenson took up their abode in Samoa, so Mr. and Mrs. Osbourne took up theirs in Australia. Each couple went to a land where all the old ties might be forgotten.

New York Herald
3rd July 1961

Life of Hemingway; Works Controversial

A Literary Great to Some, But To Others an Anti-Intellectual

He called death a "defect" and safety a "fickle friend." And yesterday Ernest Hemingway was killed by a blast from one of his beloved hunting weapons—apparently by accident. The shotgun ended the long, violent and remarkable story of one of the century's major writers.

With the publication of his novel, "The Sun Also Rises," in 1926 when he was twenty-eight, Mr. Hemingway immediately established a wide reputation as a writer. In the years since then, as his novels, short stories and articles appeared, the quality of that reputation varied greatly.

There have been few other American writers of stature who have been the subject of so much conflicting critical opinion. To some critics Mr. Hemingway was one of the great American literary men; to others he was essentially an anti-intellectual preoccupied to the point of obsession with violence and death. The criticism was heard that a Hemingway character could not think —that he could only feel.

In 1954 Mr. Hemingway received the Nobel Prize for Literature, perhaps the highest recognition that can come to a writer.

Public Figure, Too

Mr. Hemingway was a public as well as a literary figure. To millions who never read his books, but read about him in newspapers and magazines, he was a hard-drinking hunter and fisherman, a man who could always be counted on to turn up in a correspondent's uniform and with a portable typewriter when there was a war to write about, a lover of bullfighting and a companion of Spanish bullfighters.

Toward the end of his life, he grew a beard because a slight skin cancer from exposure to the sun had made it painful to shave.

His wife and his friends took to calling him "Papa." His name frequently turned up in Broadway columns though he came to New York infrequently. Mostly his visits were quick ones, perhaps to buy some elephant guns for his next safari and to look at the El Grecos at the Metropolitan Museum, on his way abroad from his home in Cuba. He did not like New York and called it a phony town.

He was born in Oak Park, Ill., on July 21, 1899, one of six children.

His father was a physician who, ironically, shot himself to death. The father, Dr. Clarence E. Hemingway, was despondent over illness.

But before his health faded, the elder Hemingway took Ernest with him on long hunting and fishing trips into the woods of northern Michigan. It was the youngster's first contact with the life he loved—the life of the outdoors. In school the young man boxed and played football and generally avoided his studies. When he left school, without a degree of any kind, he started to loaf around the country. He continued "on the bum" for a year before deciding to get into the newspaper business.

After a short stretch as a reporter on "The Kansas City Star" Mr. Hemingway went to Italy in 1917 as an ambulance driver with an American unit. He transferred to the Italian infantry. He was wounded and was decorated by the Italian government.

Correspondent in Paris

After the war he was sent to Paris as correspondent for "The Toronto Star," and it was there that he produced his first famous books. Mr. Hemingway, like many other American writers in Paris in the '20s was well-known to Montparnasse, and spent a good deal of time at the literary cafes — the Select, the Rotonde and the Dome. But he was working, too, and he published three books in three years—"Three Stories and Ten Poems" (1923), "In Our Time" (1924) and "The Torrents of Spring" (1926).

When "The Sun Also Rises" was published, a few months after "Torrents of Spring," Mr. Hemingway became a hero to critics and the public alike. The public was taken with the picture of hard-boiled expatriates, living on the cafe terraces of Paris and Pamplona, Spain. The critics liked the unadorned and incisive prose. Scores of writers began to pay him the compliment of imitation. They still are paying it.

The profound impression created by "The Sun Also Rises" may have been due to the way it crystallized the disillusion and cynicism of the post-war era in which it was produced. "You are all a lost generation," Mr. Hemingway said.

In 1929, Mr. Hemingway embellished his reputation with "A Farewell to Arms," in which he turned his experience in Italy into what many critics regarded as one of the finest works of art ever to come from a war. Mr. Hemingway's vividly emotional descriptions of the Italian retreat at Caporetto and his hero and heroine's escape across Lake Como became modern literary classics.

Work in Gradual Decline

After the success of "A Farewell to Arms," Mr. Hemingway's work went into a gradual decline that ended only with "For Whom the Bell Tolls." Books such as "Death in the Afternoon" (1932), which was about bull-fighting, and "Green Hills of Africa" (1935), which was about hunting, fed the Hemingway legend of hard living, but added little to the Hemingway reputation of hard writing. Nor did "To Have and to Have Not" (1937), his first "American" novel, laid in Key West, Fla., impress many readers. Only in his short stories, such as "The Gambler, the Nun and the Radio," "Fathers and Sons," "The Snows of Kilimanjaro," and that consummate masterpiece of terror, "The Killers," did he indicate that he was marking time, not marching back.

Meanwhile, an inevitable reaction against the Hemingway legend, as exemplified in his "tough-guy" style of writing, had set in. Its most widely publicized manifestation took the form of a fist fight between Mr. Hemingway and Max Eastman in 1937. Mr. Eastman had accused Mr. Hemingway of begetting a literary style of "wearing false hair on the chest." Mr. Hemingway, who was 6 feet and weighed more than 200 pounds, met Mr. Eastman in the Scribners office shortly afterward, opened his shirt to exhibit a manly thatch, and bounced a copy of Mr. Eastman's offending book off its author's head. Both sides claimed victory in the ensuing tussle.

The compelling theme that Mr. Hemingway had lacked for a decade came with the Spanish Civil War of 1936-'37. Spain, Mr. Hemingway had once written, was the only country where he felt himself at home, and when Francisco Franco launched his rebellion against the republic, Mr. Hemingway went to Madrid. Living under bombardment in the Hotel Florida, he wrote newspaper articles, stories, and a play,

"The Fifth Column," which was first produced on Broadway in 1940, starring Franchot Tone and Lenore Ulric. It ran for eighty-seven performances. It was next produced last year, for television. But Spain also gave him the material for his most popular novel and perhaps his crowning literary achievement, "For Whom the Bell Tolls," published in 1940.

He had written of war before, but never of a war that he felt was necessary, even desirable. The knowledge of life and of death he had gained in Spanish bull rings, in African jungles, in his wanderings through a dozen countries seemed to fuse into a single testament to humanity.

In World War II, Mr. Hemingway went back to reporting, and served in Europe as a correspondent for "Collier's." He covered the D-Day invasion of France, and shortly afterward joined a fighting unit of the French Forces of the Interior and became a captain. Later he was a correspondent with the United States 1st Army and after the war received the War Department's Bronze Star Medal.

Mr. Hemingway always contended his private life was his own business, but his four marriages—to Hadley Richardson in 1921, Pauline Pfeiffer in 1927, Martha Gellhorn in 1940 and Mary Welsh in 1946—had a way of getting in the papers.

The closest Mr. Hemingway came to expressing a credo was in "For Whom the Bell Tolls." Here he took sides; he wrote about men fighting the good fight and dying a good death. The futility was not gone altogether; but it was at least tempered with hope that the act of death might contain within it the seeds of resurrection.

The very title Mr. Hemingway chose for his book showed a consciousness of the oneness of humanity in a man who was one of its most cynical observers. The title came from a passage—Mr. Hemingway made it famous—in the writings of John Donne, seventeenth-century British poet, metaphysician and clergyman. Mr. Hemingway gave it a new validity 300 years after it was written:

"No man is an Iland, intire of itselfe; every man is a peece of the Continent, a part of the Maine; if a Clod bee washed away by the Sea, Europe is the lesse, as well as if a Promontorie were, as well as if a Mannor of thy friends or of thine owne were; any man's death diminishes me, because I am involved in Mankinde; and therefore never send to know for whom the bell tolls; it tolls for thee."

Post-War II Novel

In 1950 Mr. Hemingway published his first novel in ten years, "Across the River and Into the Trees." Like "For Whom the Bell Tolls," it was about war—this time World War II—but it did little to enhance his reputation.

Three years later Mr. Hemingway won his first Pulitzer Prize with "The Old Man and the Sea," a short novel of a three-day fight by an old and luckless Cuban fisherman to land an enormous fish. Mr. Hemingway's Nobel Prize the next year was for his "style-making mastership as demonstrated in 'The Old Man and the Sea.'" He announced he would use $8,000 of his $35,000 prize money to pay off his debts.

For many years Mr. Hemingway and his wife lived in a big rambling country house called La Vigia (The Watchtower) ten miles southeast of Havana in the village of San Francisco de Paula. They lived in considerable style: there were nine in the household staff.

The author arose at six and began writing at 6:30 or 7. He usually worked until noon and then spent the rest of the day holding court for his many friends, or attending a cock fight, or just drinking at a bar in Havana.

Mr. Hemingway at one time had forty fighting cocks of his own. For many years he had a power cruiser called Pilar, after the matriarch of "For Whom the Bell Tolls." He was an indefatigable marlin fisherman.

The Hemingways spent much time in Spain watching bullfights and in Africa hunting game. In 1954 Mr. Hemingway went on safari with his wife to gather material for magazine articles and barely came back alive. The Hemingways were injured when a light plane in which they were riding made an emergency landing in the elephant country of Uganda. They took another plane and were injured again when it crashed and burned after a groundloop. Mr. Hemingway spent months at his Cuban farm recovering from a fractured spine and a ruptured kidney. His wife was not so severely hurt.

After reports of his death in the jungles had been circulated, the burly novelist had emerged from the brush with a bunch of bananas in one hand and a bottle of gin in the other. Before the true effects of his injuries were known, he cracked: "I feel wonderful."

Much of 1959 Mr. Hemingway spent in Spain traveling around after Antonio Ordonez, the reigning matador, and watching him work in the ring. Between fights Mr. Hemingway was writing, and announced on his return to Cuba that he had completed 40,000 words which he intended to be published as an appendix to "Death in the Afternoon," his book on bull fighting.

Visited by Alsop

After the rise of the regime of Fidel Castro, Herald Tribune columnist Joseph Alsop visited Mr. Hemingway at his home near Havana. It was in March of last year and Mr. Alsop wrote, after attending a cock fight with the author—during which a number of bearded revolutionaries came up to "Papa" to pay their respects:

"Possibly it does not matter that an individual American is much cherished in a land where the 'hate-America' cry is now heard on all sides. But it seemed to matter to me . . ."

A year or so ago Mr. Hemingway came back to live for a time in the United States for the first time in a decade. He rented a log house in the little Idaho town of Ketchum, one mile from Sun Valley. There he hunted game birds and worked on a new novel.

Many of Mr. Hemingway's novels and stories have been made into movies. In the case of at least one—"A Farewell to Arms"—two movies were made, the first in 1932, with Helen Hayes and Gary Cooper, and the second in 1957, with Jennifer Jones and Rock Hudson.

Mr. Hemingway took little pleasure in the treatment he got at the hands of Hollywood. For example, he had contempt for "The Snows of Kilimanjaro," in which Gregory Peck starred. "It should be called 'The Snows of Zanuck.'" he said. Darryl F. Zanuck was the producer.

Of recent years, many of Mr. Hemingway's writings have been adapted to television.

Daily Telegraph & Morning Post
13th August 1955

THOMAS MANN, AUTHOR WHO DEFIED NAZIS

DRIVEN INTO EXILE

The work of Thomas Mann, who has died aged 80, is assured of a permanent place in literature by the great sweep of his imaginative powers, the precision of his writing, and his analytical approach to a number of the problems which confront humanity.

He probed deeply into the antithesis of life and intellect, and, with acidity, into the position of the artist in the universal scheme.

While his writings betrayed considerable heart-searching, he rarely, if ever, offered any solution to the problems he propounded. The themes of decay and death attracted him, and featured prominently in much of his work, and many of his characters were notable for their abnormality.

Born in Lübeck in 1875 of an old Hanse family, Thomas Mann was the son of a merchant and senator, who died when his son was 15. Three years later the boy moved to Munich, where his mother had preceded him, and worked for a time in an insurance office. Quickly tiring of commercial life, he threw up his job to live in Rome, where he published his first novel.

MASTERPIECE AT 25

Some of his short stories had already attracted attention, but "Buddenbrooks," which appeared in 1901 when he was 25, was hailed as a masterpiece. Precursor of many family sagas it was largely autobiographical, and dealt with the decline, and final dissolution, of a middle-class family. Its sale to date exceeds 1,200,000 copies.

Mann returned to Munich, where he joined the staff of the satirical weekly Simplicissimus. "Death in Venice," considered by many his most perfect work, appeared in 1912, and "The Magic Mountain," the scene of which was laid in a sanatorium for consumptives at Davos, in 1924. He was awarded the Nobel prize for literature in 1929, and "Mario and the Magician" followed a year later.

Mann, who had been watching with growing alarm the rise of the Nazis, left Germany in 1933, the year Hitler became Chancellor. His outspoken condemnation of the new regime ended inevitably in the cancellation of his German citizenship, and the withdrawal of his Bonn University degree, three years later.

There followed several years of restless wandering in France, Switzerland and Czechoslovakia, and a period of financial difficulty. He accepted the offer of Czechoslovakian citizenship made by President Benes, but had to flee when the country fell.

AMERICAN CITIZEN

He became an American citizen in 1938, and was appointed Lecturer in Humanities at Princeton University. The first volume of "Joseph and his Brethren," an imposing and ambitious Biblical work, appeared in 1935, and was followed by two more.

In 1947, in the course of a visit to England, he expressed with emotion his admiration for Britain, without whose unique resistance in 1940, he said, it was very doubtful if there would have been left any form of civilisation. In 1949 he visited Germany for the first time since his exile, to lecture in honour of the 200th anniversary of the birth of Goethe. He also lectured in London, and at Oxford, where he received an honorary Degree of Doctor of Literature. In 1953 a Degree of Doctor of Letters was conferred on him at Cambridge.

Two of his later works were "Doctor Faustus," a vast political and theological biography of a fictional German composer published in 1949, and "The Holy Sinner," a story of the Middle Ages, 1952. He left America, where, he said, life had become "too complicated," in 1952 to live in Switzerland near Lake Zurich.

Thomas Mann married, in 1905, Miss Katja Pringsheim, who survives him, with two sons and three daughters. One daughter, Erika, is the wife of W. H. Auden, the poet.

The Times
10th June 1870

One whom young and old, wherever the English language is spoken, have been accustomed to regard as a personal friend is suddenly taken away from among us. CHARLES DICKENS is no more. The loss of such a man is an event which makes ordinary expressions of regret seem cold and conventional. It will be felt by millions as nothing less than a personal bereavement. Statesmen, men of science, philanthropists, the acknowledged benefactors of their race might pass away, and yet not leave the void which will be caused by the death of DICKENS. They may have earned the esteem of mankind; their days may have been passed in power, honour, and prosperity ; they may have been surrounded by troops of friends, but, however preeminent in station, ability, or public services, they will not have been, like our great and genial novelist, the intimate of every household. Indeed, such a position is attained not even by one man in an age. It needs an extraordinary combination of intellectual and moral qualities to gain the hearts of the public as DICKENS has gained them. Extraordinary and very original genius must be united with good sense, consummate skill, a wellbalanced mind, and the proofs of a noble and affectionate disposition before the world will consent to enthrone a man as their unassailable and enduring favourite. This is the position which Mr. DICKENS has occupied with the English and also with the American public for the third of a century. If we compare his reputation with that of the number of eminent men and women who have been his contemporaries, we have irresistible evidence of his surpassing merits. His is a department of literature in which ability in our time has been abundant to overflowing. As the genius of the Elizabethan age turned to the drama, so that of the reign of VICTORIA seeks expression in the novel. There is no more extraor-

dinary phenomenon than the number, the variety, and the generally high excellence of the works of fiction in our own day. Their inspirations are as many as the phases of thought and social life. They treat not only of love and marriage, but of things political and ecclesiastical, of social yearnings and sceptical disquietudes; they give us revelations from the empyrean of fashion and from the abysses of crime. Their authors have their admirers, their party, their public, but not the public of DICKENS. It has been his peculiar fortune to appeal to that which is common to all sorts and conditions of men, to excite the interest of the young and the uninstructed, without shocking the more refined taste of a higher class and a more mature age. Thus the news of his death will hardly meet the eye of an educated man or woman who has not read his works and who has not been accustomed to think of him with admiration and friendly regard.

To the survivors, at least, there is something terrible in sudden death, and when we hear that DICKENS is gone we cannot but recall how THACKERAY died before him, also in the vigour of age, and apparently in the fulness of health. DICKENS has lived longer than his great rival, for he was born only a year after, and he has survived him several years. But he has been cut off while still in what may be called middle age. He was born in February, 1812, and has consequently not long attained his fifty-eighth year. As men live and work now, this is an age which would give the hope of many years of successful exertion, to be succeeded by a period of honoured repose. But we have this consolation, that the life of DICKENS has been long enough to allow full scope for his genius, and to enable him not only to earn, but to enjoy his fame. In this respect his career has been extraordinary. He was one whose marvellous powers were developed early, and he attained the highest eminence in the first years of his literary career. It is certainly a wonderful phenomenon that a book like Pickwick, the pages of which overflow with humour, and are marked in every sentence with the keenest observation of men and things, should have been produced by a young man of 24. After the light but clever Sketches by Boz, DICKENS began Pickwick in 1836, and finished it in the course of the succeeding year. We are inclined to think that this, the first considerable work of the author, is his masterpiece ; but, whatever may be the world's decision on this point, it can hardly be doubted that the prize must be given to one of the group of fictions which he produced within the first ten or twelve years of his literary life. Nicholas Nickleby teems with wit, and the characters, with one or two exceptions, are life-like in the extreme. Oliver Twist everybody knows ; Martin Chuzzlewit is excellent, and the American portions are not only the most amusing satire that has been published in the present age, but fill us with wonder that the peculiarities of thought, manner, and diction of a people should be so surely seized and so inimitably expressed by a young writer who had been only a few months in the country.

In this marvellous precocity of genius DICKENS formed a contrast to some of those with whom a comparison naturally suggests itself. SCOTT was 34 years old before he published his first great poem, the Lay of the Last Minstrel, and it was nearly ten years afterwards, in 1814, that he made his experiment as a novelist with Waverley. So, too, THACKERAY, though known for some time in the field of literature, made his first great success with Vanity Fair, when no longer a young man. Of DICKENS it may be said, also, that his early books show no signs of juvenility. When young in years he showed the mental balance of an experienced writer. And yet what freshness and vigour there was in those wonderful serials which, about the time the present QUEEN came to the throne, changed the popular literature of the day ! When that young unknown author appeared on the field he was at once hailed as the new chief of popular fiction. It is a long time ago, but our older readers will remember the excitement caused by the Pickwick Papers. The shilling numbers of Boz carried everything before them. They were read here by tens of thousands, though the reading public thirty years ago was not what it is now ; and they were re-

Washington Post & City Life
30th January 1963

printed in every possible form in America. In fact, half the newspapers in the States transferred them to their columns bodily the day after their arrival. This popularity they fully deserved. They are among the few books of the kind that one can return to again and again; or having opened at any page can read straight on, carried forward by a sense of real enjoyment. The best characters stand out in real flesh and blood, and in this respect are superior to those of THACKERAY, which, though excellently designed, show too much the art of an able sketcher from artificial types. For this reason, THACKERAY, though he has always maintained his hold on the London world in which his personages figure, has never come near to DICKENS in popularity with the great mass of the people. The characters of DICKENS have been accepted by all men's discernment as the true reflection of human nature; not merely of manners or costume. SQUEERS is to everybody the low tyrannical schoolmaster; BUMBLE the representative of parochial pomposity; Mrs. GAMP is the type of her vulgar hardhearted sisterhood. Perhaps a more signal proof of the genius of DICKENS is the manner in which his style and diction have penetrated into the ordinary literature of the country. So much has become naturalized and is used quite unconsciously that it is only by re-reading those earlier works which most impressed his contemporaries that one becomes aware how great has been their influence.

We cannot conclude these remarks without paying a tribute to the moral influence of the writings of which we have spoken. Mr. DICKENS was a man of an eminently kindly nature, and full of sympathy for all around him. This, without being paraded, makes itself manifest in his works, and we have no doubt whatever that much of the active benevolence of the present day, the interest in humble persons and humble things, and the desire to seek out and relieve every form of misery is due to the influence of his works. We feel that we have lost one of the foremost Englishmen of the age. There are clever writers enough, but no one who will take the place, literary and social, that belonged to him. It was but the other day that at the Royal Academy Banquet he made the best speech of the evening, in matter, language, and manner. His powers as an actor are well known, though, of late years, they have been only exhibited in the narrower field of public readings. He was made to be popular, and, even irrespective of his literary genius, was an able and strong-minded man, who would have succeeded in almost any profession to which he devoted himself. We can but condole with the public on his sudden and premature loss.

By Harry Gabbett
Staff Reporter.

Robert Frost, undisputed poet laureate of the New Frontier (and of some old frontiers before it) died yesterday in Boston's Peter Bent Brigham Hospital.

He had lived 88 years and within the stark beauty of a single line or two he had managed time after time to transfix for posterity some central truth he had gleaned from almost every one of them.

Perhaps not since Ralph Waldo Emerson has an American poet been so widely acclaimed in his lifetime. It is highly probable, too, that no other American man of letters since Edgar Allan Poe so personified the poetry he produced.

Mr. Frost was born and spent the first 11 years of his life in San Francisco. It was with New England, however, that his prolific pen identified him so inextricably that countless of his admirers still find themselves hard put to reconcile the accident of his birth.

Man and a Half

By his own pixyish reckoning, "Mr. Frost matured quickly—into a man and a half. He was, he insisted, half poet, half teacher and half farmer. The "half" of him that was poet earned for him four Pulitzer Prizes.

He was in constant demand as an instructor (in the Humanities he grew to know so well) by schools of international repute on both sides of the Atlantic.

But eight generations of Frosts before him had wrung their living from New England's grudging soil—and so, perhaps, the biggest "half" of Mr. Frost was farmer.

William P. Frost, the poet's father, was a Harvard graduate who was working in San Francisco as a newspaperman when his son was born. He named him Robert Lee Frost, out of deference to his own sympathies in the War Between the States.

The elder Frost died when the boy was 11 and his mother lost no time in setting aright that geographical accident of her son's birth. She got back to New England with him in time for him to graduate from the high school at Lawrence, Mass., in 1892.

To Dartmouth, Harvard

Within the next five years, he had married Elinor M. White (she died in 1938), attended Dartmouth College for a few months and Harvard University for a couple of years. He graduated from neither, but over the ensuing years more than 40 colleges and universities were to shower him with honorary degrees. He also had got up

his first book of poems, "Twilight."

There were five poems in it and he succeeded in having copies of the collection printed. "Twilight," he was to say years later, "had no success and deserved none." But he has also said that "a few scattered lines in it are as much mine as any I was ever to write."

After the manner of the prophet, traditionally without honor in his own country, Mr. Frost sold his New Hampshire farm in 1912 and took his wife and their four children to England.

Already properly entombed as an American artist in a number of anthologies, he was published almost immediately in England. In 1913 two volumes of his poems—"A Boy's Will" and "North of Boston" —were published and two years later he returned to his native land with an established reputation.

He settled on a farm in Franconia, N. H., where he busied himself between his pen and his plow. In 1916 he brought out "Mountain Interval" and that same year began a 22-year association with Amherst College as an English teacher.

The first of his Pulitzer Prize-winners was "New Hampshire," published in 1923. Next was his "Collected Poems" (1930), followed by "A Further Range" (1936) and "A Witness Tree" (1942).

Ironically, he had won the big literary award all four times before he emerged as anything more than just another poet who had won a prize.

Stature Enhanced

Slowly, to be sure, but inexorably, Mr. Frost broke over the national scene about which he wrote as a personality in his own right. He was also, the country found to its delight, something of an epigrammatist—a very quick man with a very few words, all of which required very little explanation.

In becoming a character, however, he lost nothing of the mettle which had brought him greatness, and the ensuing decades of his public emergence served merely to enhance his stature.

A frequent visitor to Washington through the years, the poet's appearances here were climaxed with his selection by President John F. Kennedy as the honored poet of his inauguration in 1961.

Those who witnessed those swearing-in ceremonies on Capitol Hill will be more likely to forget which President took the oath of office before their sight of Mr. Frost fades from their memories of that cold, gusty day.

It was as though the very elements to which he had dedicated so many of his best-

loved lines were in conspiracy against his presence. Great swirls of wind watered his eyes, tousled his shaggy white hair, and tore from his grasp the typescript from which he tried to read his dedicatory remarks.

He surrendered gracefully, with a determined recital from memory of his "The Gift Outright," a 1943 creation to which he referred as his "most national" poem. It may well be the only well-known poem co-authored by a President of the United States.

Its closing lines read originally, ". . . to the land vaguely realizing westward/ But still unstoried artless unenhanced/Such as she was such as she would become." At President Kennedy's suggestion, Mr. Frost changed the next-to-last word to "will."

Poet's Explanation

Mr. Frost proved eminently quotable orally—a quality he just as successfully achieved in his verse.

"A poem," he explained once, "begins with a lump in the throat; a homesickness or lovesickness. It is a reaching out toward expression, an effort to find fulfillment. A complete poem is one where an emotion has found its thought and the thought has found the word."

Newsmen waited impatiently on his birthdays. He was good on such occasions for a column or more of good clean fun—the vein in which he chose to dispense much of his off-the-cuff horse sense.

A request for his idea of freedom might bring forth the observation that "you have freedom when you're easy in your harness."

Or to the where-do-we-go-from-here question: "I'm a little coy about where the human race is headed. As a matter of fact, whenever you can't pin me down on a specific point, it's due to my quality of uncatchability."

To what did he ascribe his eminence (on a 1960 visit here)? "At the age of 12," he explained, "I spent a summer with a mouthful of nails, helping to make shoes. I'm here because I didn't swallow any."

President's Quotation

President Kennedy probably did more than anyone else to popularize a couple of Mr Frost's lines. He closed out many a speaking engagement in his 1961 campaign tour of the country with this ending of a perennial favorite of the anthologists, "Stopping by Woods on a Snowy Evening":

But I have promises to keep,
And miles to go before I sleep.

It was his "Fire and Ice," however, which proved most ir-

Continued

resistible to the compilers of poetry collections who deigned to include Mr. Frost's work. It reads:

Some say the world will
end in fire,
Some say in ice.
From what I've tasted of
desire
I hold with those who
favor fire.

But if it had to perish
twice,
I think I know enough of
hate
To say that for destruction
ice
Is also great
And would suffice.

There probably is no phase of human experience on which Mr. Frost did not have a personal opinion—and he was not one to keep opinions to himself.

Realism Characterised

"There are two types of realists," he once assured an interviewer who probably had asked him about something else. "The one who offers a good deal of dirt with his potato to show that it is a real one; and the one who is satisfied with the potato brushed clean. To me, the thing that art does for life is to clean it, to strip it to form."

His running feud with his famous contemporary, Carl Sandburg, was so famous that one may be permitted to suspect it was contrived (after the manner of Jack Benny's disregard for Fred Allen).

"I would as soon write free verse," Mr. Frost confided to another interviewer, "as play tennis with the net down." Sandburg thought that one over and wrote an article proving that you could play better tennis with the net down."

Critics found his poetry lean, hungry, trite, stereotyped, great, poor, mediocre and in between. A casual follower of Mr. Frost's artistic development would have to call him changeless. Apparently he was born full-blown and he caught this quality himself in two lines he wrote in 1900:

They would not find me
changed from him
they knew.
Only more sure of all I
thought was true.

The lines applied at his death to Mr. Frost himself, and of such depth was his honesty he probably would be quick to admit it.

The volume that was destined to be his last was "In the Clearing," published in the spring of last year.

Four lines from that collection bespeak his awareness of his own approaching end. It was characteristic of the man that he could consider his death a tentative accomplishment—a transitory state in which the popular concepts of a hereafter would not obtain. The lines:

And I may return
If dissatisfied
With what I learn
From having died.

Daily Telegraph
21st November 1910

LATE COUNT TOLSTOY.

HIS LITERARY CAREER.

During his long and remarkable career Count Lyeff Tolstoy touched every extreme of opinion on all the principal questions which perplex men's minds and fire their hearts. He preached almost every doctrine for which proof or probability can be alleged; and he announced each of these conflicting views with the eagerness of the discoverer, the sincerity of the apostle, and the dogmatism of the master. But all the ordinary arms of the reformer—history, science, political economy, statistics, and even emotional impulse—he cast aside as needless or harmful, and appealed to the world on the strength of his own powerful but unaided word. Yet in ethics he has set before us but an epitome of the Gospel, with the life-giving personality of Christ left out, and, none the less, he confidently exclaims, "The time will come when men will be convinced of the truthfulness of my teaching." His theory of Art is, if possible, still more unsatisfactory, and no more complete refutation of it could possibly have been written than his own "War and Peace," "Anna Karenina," and the "Death of Ivan Ilyitch," the three undying monuments engraved upon which the name of Lyeff Tolstoy will go down to distant posterity. Tolstoy belonged to the very select class of literary men who awake and find themselves famous. His first books, however, were studies and sketches rather than finished productions; he was learning his trade, and he was known in his own country already for some years before he became known to Europe. It was to Turgenev, his countryman, contemporary, and friend, that he owed his first introduction to the public of France, as well as many other good things in his life. But once Tolstoy's writings began to be read his hold upon the lovers of good literature in all countries was assured, for even a slight sketch by him was sufficient to reveal his extraordinary powers of observation, description, analysis, and presentation of character.

Uneventful externally as his life was after his retirement from the Army, it was full of incident to him, of instruction, and "states of soul." He was a man to watch everything, to feel everything, and to combine keen observation and strong feeling in a curious way. Like Alphonse Daudet, who, when he uttered a great cry at the death of his father, wondered the next moment how the cry could be described, Tolstoy, when standing by the side of his dead mother or seeing his beloved brother's slow descent to death, was able to note everything he saw, everything he felt. When once he had got hold of his public, his productions began to be quick and fertile. His greatest triumph was "War and Peace." It would be wrong to say that this was the first really truthful picture of war—for Beyle in "Rouge et Noir" had given an account of the battle of Waterloo which has never been surpassed as a picture of war from the point of view of the private soldier and the mere individual; and the writings of Erckmann-Chatrian had also done much to bring home to the mind of the world what were the horrors of war in contradistinction to the old writers, who had known nothing of war but its romance and its glories. But Tolstoy worked on a broader, larger scale—on a vaster stage than any preceding writer, and in many respects he might claim thus to have been the creator of a new model of writers on his theme.

The novel which appealed to more general emotions, and which finally gave Tolstoy his hold on the imagination of the world, was "Anna Karenina." Here was a story of direct primordial human passion; with long and sometimes prolix divagations, it is true, but, on the whole, with very fair concentration on the central subject. It was the story of the love of a woman, married without her consent to a man to whom she is indifferent, in place of another, young, handsome, devoted. The theme, it will be seen, is not new; but Tolstoy invested it with such reality, such passion, such sombre and powerful light, that it was read with breathless interest from one end of Europe to the other, and most of the millions of readers who are to be found in the United States had read it even before it was well known in England. Many criticisms can be passed upon its treatment and its moral. "Vengeance is mine, I will repay"—this was the motto which Tolstoy affixed to the volume, and the story is intended to prove the truth of the Biblical text. It is, of course, but one side of a very difficult question, for there have been loves that were illicit, immoral according to all accepted standards, and yet some of them have been noble and a few of them successful. But the woman in Tolstoy's novel has to be sacrificed to the moral, and even at the moment when everything seems to point to the final triumph of her happiness, when she has proved the love of her lover and found it enduring, devoted, and worthy, she can find no other solution for the vexed problem of her life but suicide in the most agonised form, namely, by throwing herself under the wheels of a passing engine; and the man has to find in the battlefield escape from remorse and the sense of bereavement.

Some of Tolstoy's shorter stories were even more powerful and characteristic than the longer ones. Whoever wishes to get at once an idea of his style and to see into the depths of his soul and the core of his gospel, should read a little story called "The Death of Ivan Ilyitch." It is characteristic of the author that the story opens with what in most writers would be the climax and the end—namely, the death of the man whose story is being told. Ivan Ilvitch is presented to you as he lies a corpse on his bed in the very first page, with that look of curious reproach and of having done the right thing—to use Tolstoy's own quaint description—which the dead always seem to wear. But, though you know thus now the climax has ended from the very start, it does not in the least alter or even diminish the intensity of the interest with which you watch the illness through its every stage and its every emotion down to the final sigh in which the unhappy struggler gives up the conflict and welcomes the end. The grimness of the story—its sometimes awful revelation of all the horrors of mental and physical torture—all these things do not prevent you from following breathlessly page after page of the narrative; and there is not a scene in it which does not remain with you as vividly and as ineffaceably as if it had been the story of somebody's death who belonged to your own flesh and blood.

All these stories pointed to a gradual development in Tolstoy of the darker spirit of Puritanism—perhaps even of the brooding melancholia which argues the mind, if not diseased, at least disillusioned. And probably they owed their origin largely to temperament and to somewhat sad experiences. With a frankness that recalls the astounding self-revelations of Rousseau, Tolstoy told during his life the story of his youthful follies, escapades, disillusions. It is evident that even in the hours of youthful self-abandonment he had in him the germs of the sombre philosopher; he was never a man to do anything in entire self-forgetfulness—the brooding spirit of reflection always lay like a spectre above and around him. And when men of that temperament are dragged into the vortex of vicious self-indulgence—into drink and debauchery and fashionable frivolity—the final awakening is always the same. The most gloomy of all men is probably the man of imagination who leaves behind him the flesh-pots; he has not enjoyed them heartily during the hours of possession, and his disgust is overwhelming. So it was with Tolstoy, for the second half of his life was one long denial and, as he thought, renunciation and repentance of the first half. Like all reactions, it was both violent and extreme. In the end he who had once been the gay and light-o'-love young civilian, or the dashing young officer, and who, even in middle age, was the affectionate husband and the father of a huge family, arrived at ideas as to the relations of the sexes which lie at the roots of the Church that preaches the celibacy of the clergy and the holiness of virginity in man and woman. This new gospel was preached with extraordinary frankness in the "Kreutzer Sonata." It is the story of a marriage between two people who began by violently loving each other. The relations of the two are remorselessly pursued through their different stages until the marriage of love ends in the murder of the wife by the husband. Here was mere anarchy, and the fanaticism which in some sections of people—especially among the compatriots of Tolstoy—has led to unnatural horrors; indeed, it is difficult to understand how the gospel of pessimism could find a deeper depth of hopelessness.

Such, then, was this great writer: Slavonic to his finger-tips. He was Slavonic in the intensity of his emotions, in the extravagance of his methods and the merciless logic of his thoughts and acts; above all things Slavonic in the depths of melancholy despair to which his race seem condemned by the gloom of their climate, the spreading desolation of their steppes, the depths of their peasant poverty and ignorance and drunkenness, the combined helplessness and omnipotence of their Government, and a religion which appeals to the fears and the superstitions and has little hold on the consciences and the hearts of its votaries.

The Times
5th January 1965

THE MOST INFLUENTIAL ENGLISH POET OF HIS TIME

Mr. T. S. Eliot, O.M., and Nobel Prizeman, died yesterday at his home at the age of 76.

He was the most influential English poet of his time. His work had won him a high reputation, not only throughout the English-speaking world but in all countries where the European tradition, which he himself so faithfully upheld, still flourishes. His works in verse and prose have been translated into almost every European language and have been the subject of more books and articles than have ever before been published about an author during his lifetime.

Thomas Stearns Eliot came of a New England family which had emigrated in the seventeenth century from the Somerset village of East Coker—a village which gave its name to one of his most famous poems and will now give the shelter of its church to his ashes. He was born on September 26, 1888, at St. Louis, Missouri, United States, the younger son of Henry Ware Eliot and Charlotte Stearns. Apart from some schoolboy verses in the *Smith Academy Record*, the first of his poems to be printed appeared in the *Harvard Advocate* (May 24, 1907), a publication of which he was later an editor. At Harvard, Eliot was a contemporary of Ezra Pound, to whose poetic example he acknowledged a debt in the dedication of *The Waste Land*. After taking his degree, Eliot studied in the Graduate School of Philosophy, where his rare intellectual gifts were recognized by his appointment as Assistant in Philosophy (1912-13) and by his election later to the Sheldon Travelling Fellowship in Philosophy, which enabled him to spend an academic year at Merton College, Oxford, working under Bradley and Joachim. A period of study at the Sorbonne confirmed what was to be a life-long interest in French literature. Eliot then made his home in England and lived in London for the rest of his life. He had been a naturalized British subject since 1928.

His literary gifts began to be noticed by a discerning few of the " Bloomsbury Group "—among them Maynard Keynes and Virginia Woolf—during the 1914-18 War. At this period his activities included the assistant editorship of the *Egoist* (1917-19), teaching at Highgate Junior School, lecturing to L.C.C. evening classes, and reviewing; from 1919 onwards he contributed to *The Times Literary Supplement* a memorable series of articles on the Elizabethan and Jacobean dramatists. These and some earlier reviews were collected in *The Sacred Wood* (1920), a volume which marked him out as a critic well equipped and perspicuous, provocative if something " donnish " in manner. His position in the world of letters was thus assured. His first poems to appear in book form had been printed in Pound's *Catholic Anthology* (1915); *Prufrock* was issued separately in 1917; and in 1919 some 200 copies of *Poems* were hand-printed by Leonard and Virginia Woolf at the Hogarth Press.

IN LLOYDS BANK

After the war, which ended as he was about to be commissioned in the U.S. Navy, he was employed at Lloyds Bank in Cornhill, where it was his business to prepare the bank's monthly report on foreign affairs. His City career came to an end in 1922, when he was appointed the first editor of the *Criterion*, which he directed until it ceased publication in 1939. In its first issue appeared *The Waste Land*, which announced the arrival of a major poet and, by the mingled enthusiasm and execration with which it was received, the impact of an original talent. Its presentation of disillusionment and the disintegration of values, catching the mood of the time, made it the poetic gospel of the post-war intelligentsia; at the time, however, few either of its detractors or its admirers saw through the surface innovations and the language of despair to the deep respect for tradition and the keen moral sense which underlay them.

In 1925 he joined the board of Faber's, where he was responsible during the next 40 years for the publication of much of the most important poetry of our time, and was a source of counsel and encouragement to many younger poets. His own later works included *Ash Wednesday* (1930), *Four Quartets* (1943), the poetic dramas, *Murder in the Cathedral* (1935), *The Family Reunion* (1939), *The Cocktail Party* (1950), *The Confidential Clerk* (1954), and *The Elder Statesman* (1959), and several volumes of collected essays and addresses.

It was in one of these, *For Lancelot Andrewes* (1928), that Eliot had announced his allegiance to the Church of England. He at once became a leading and influential layman of the Anglo-Catholic persuasion, engaging in vigorous, but always closely reasoned, controversy upon matters of doctrine and ritual, especially after the Lambeth and Malvern conferences and during the contentions over Church Union in South India. Eliot's attitude in ecclesiastical affairs was dogmatically, even intransigently, conservative: there was perhaps a certain intolerance here in his zealous but uncompromising defence of tradition. He was a devoted churchwarden, and an active but discreet propagandist. His most imposing work of a purely religious character appeared in 1939 as *The Idea of a Christian Society*.

ANGLO-CATHOLIC TRADITION

Of the non-literary influences which most contributed to Eliot's poetic development his religion must be put first. The fastidiousness, the moral taste, and the intellectual severity, which were a legacy of his New England ancestors, merged with the Anglo-Catholic tradition to direct his poetry ever farther in the exploration of spiritual awareness, the search for spiritual values. From *The Waste Land* and *The Hollow Men*, through *Journey of the Magi* and *Ash Wednesday*, to the *Four Quartets* there ran a steady line of development towards the positive treatment of religious experience, so that he could say in the last-named work that " the poetry does not matter " while leaving the reader in no doubt as to its strictly poetic integrity. At the same time, a long-drawn-out private tragedy which darkened his middle years left a deep impression on his poetry: the rawness, the shuddering distaste, the sense of contagion, the dry despair which emerge from certain passages of *Ash Wednesday*, for instance, and *The Family Reunion*, are traces of it. But for this emotional wound, so long unhealed, his poetry might well have been more genial, less ascetic; but, equally, it might well have been less intense.

The Family Reunion (1939), the most wholly poetic of his plays, was the first of four dramas of modern domestic life whose basic theme is derived from Greek tragedy. It was also the first in which he perfected by a masterly use of the stressed line, an instrument which successfully captured the cadence and rhythm of everyday conversation in verse and passed, without breaking its own texture, from small talk to the statement of profundities. With this instrument he fashioned *The Cocktail Party*, which in 1949 and the following year had a remarkable success on both sides of the Atlantic. *The Cocktail Party* chatter, light, easy, amusing, was gaily decorated with the sprightly extravagances that make in the theatre the effect of wit; and at the same time the play told the story of four people, emotionally interlocked, who discover their appropriate forms of salvation after the impact of a shaking experience.

Not all Eliot's followers shared the public's enthusiasm. They felt that he had adhered all too closely to his self-imposed rule to avoid poetry which could not stand the test of dramatic utility. And even those who appreciated the practical value of the rule in the existing state of the theatre still hoped that the next play might more boldly seize new ground for the poetic drama. But in *The Confidential Clerk*, which came in 1953, Eliot seemed to have relinquished some of the ground he had won at least for dramatic poetry. The poetic overtones this time were fainter, for the comedy sought to hold audiences through laughter and surprise and there were lesser demands on feeling. The falling off went unchecked in his last play, *The Elder Statesman* (1959) which failed to hold the stage.

Yet no dramatist of our time has come more firmly to grips with the conditions which the theatre imposes on poetry. Verse and prose, he saw clearly, were but means to an end—the rendering whole of an imagined reality in terms of the stage. It may well be that *Murder in the Cathedral* will come in the end to have a longer life than the later experiments. But, in spite of their weaknesses of construction and characterization, there is the precision, the personal yet exquisite and unobtrusive rhythm, of the dialogue to keep them in mind and to offset the somewhat chill sense they give of moving in a kind of emotional twilight.

After the 1939-45 War Eliot's work outside the theatre was confined to the writing of lectures and addresses for various occasions at home and abroad, many of them in connexion with the bestowal of honorary degrees, prizes, and other official tributes. He was never revisited in his later years by the inspiration that produced *Four Quartets*, his greatest poetic achievement.

Eliot's chief literary influences were the French Symbolists and, above all, Dante. But, both as poet and critic he drew deep from the whole European tradition which, as editor of the *Criterion*, he had sought to preserve and reinvigorate. His poetry, each poem "a raid on the inarticulate", strove incessantly towards greater purity of utterance and wider integration of experience, just as it displayed an increasing mastery of those personal rhythms, sometimes colloquial, sometimes - hieratically formal, which he developed from the blank verse line. Technically, his influence over younger English poets was for many years marked and widespread. No English poet since Wordsworth had so constantly, so unequivocally or so openly insisted upon absolute self-dedication to the art, or approached it with greater humility. A critic truly said of him: "In struggling towards a discipline of spirit through a discipline of language, Eliot has reaffirmed in his own practice the value of poetry."

The quality of his writing was inseparable, to those who knew him, from the integrity of his character. In public Eliot, a stooping, sombre-clad figure, appeared to be shy and retiring, formal in his manner, which was courtly and attentive, but detached. The impertinence of the curious, the sometimes intemperate attentions of admirers, he kept alike at arm's length by a playful, evasive wit. With his intimate friends he enjoyed banter and jokes even, in earlier days, practical jokes. Although, in his earlier verse and prose, he often gave the impression of having been born middle-aged, he remained very youthful in some of his responses: children were devoted to "Old Possum", and relished his elaborate and agreeably mystifying fun, which found such ingenious and rhythmically diverse expression in *Old Possum's Book of Practical Cats*. He was, above all, a humble man; firm, even stubborn at times, but with no self-importance; quite unspoilt by fame; free from spiritual or intellectual pride.

POETIC DRAMA REVIVAL

Eliot's chief preoccupation since the mid-1930s was the revival of poetic drama. By precept and example he strove to restore to the English stage a form of writing without which, he believed, drama could never express the full range of human sensibility. His entry into the theatre was made with characteristic deliberation, step by step, each preparing for the next. His first experiment, in *Sweeney Agonistes* (1932) two brilliant "Fragments" of an Aristophanic melodrama—was never fully exploited. Its dramatic possibilities were barely explored in *The Rock* (1934), a commissioned work, something between a conventional pageant and an ecclesiastical revue and chiefly distinguished for its liturgical choruses. *Murder in the Cathedral*, first performed in the Chapter House at Canterbury in 1935, explored these possibilities to some purpose and became a theatrical success both here and in America and later (in translation) on the Continent. The play's effectiveness as drama is attested by the number of times it has been revived, but Eliot himself considered that its verse had only the negative merit of avoiding any echo of Shakespeare.

The Times
6th April 1832

GOETHE.—The veneration in which the memory of Goethe is held in Germany is not so universal and unqualified as some tourists and critics pretend. The admiration of his extraordinary powers as an author has not, it seems, been sufficient to overcome the objections to which his character is liable on political grounds. A letter from Frankfort, dated March 26, in the *Allgemeine Zeitung*, says—"The news of Goethe's death appears to have made very little impression on the majority of the inhabitants of this place. 'An old aristocrat the less,' was the expression to which the event gave utterance in a large mixed company. Goethe knew the opinion of his native city, and was of course far from being proud of it." The fact is, that Goethe lived among Princes, and shared their antipathies to popular rights and free institutions. The Government of Weimar, bepraised as it has been for the liberal encouragement of literature and the fine arts, is as forward as any of the petty despotisms of Germany in its decrees against the political liberty of the press. But the feeling which, according to the letter from Frankfort, appears to prevail in German society, is one of the signs of the times which should not escape observation. It shows that in the present age, the highest talents of any kind, military or literary, will not save the possessor from disrespect,—from the disrespect even of those who would, by a very natural prejudice, be most inclined to exalt him, if he declares hostility to the greatest interest of mankind—political improvement.

Chicago Daily Tribune
23rd December 1940

F. S. FITZGERALD, JAZZ AGE NOVEL WRITER, IS DEAD

Career of 'Great Gatsby' Author Ends at 44.

Dec. 22 (AP).— 44, novelist, short story writer and scenarist, died at his Hollywood home yesterday. Fitzgerald, author of "This Side of Paradise," and "Tales of the Jazz Age," came to Hollywood in 1937. He adapted his "The Great Gatsby" for the screen, did the scenario for Erich Remarque's "Three Comrades" and other film work. He suffered a heart attack three weeks ago.

Told of Hectic Period.

"This Side of Paradise" appeared in 1920 when Fitzgerald was 24, a year after he left the United States army. He had quit Princeton university in his senior year to go into service as a second lieutenant in the 45th infantry.

The hero, Amory Blaine, of "This Side of Paradise," was somewhat a composite of "All the Sad Young Men" of the unsettled postwar "flapper" era and the novel became a sort of social document, in critical estimation.

The term "All the Sad Young Men" was employed six years later as the title of a Fitzgerald short story collection.

Acclaimed for his first novel, Fitzgerald soon wrote "Flappers and Philosophers." Then came "The Beautiful and Damned" in 1922.

A critic described his early works as documentary "in their vivid presentations of adolescent life, its turbulent spirit, swift tempo, charged atmosphere, excesses and boldness, as well as its uncertain psychology and gropings to know itself in new and unadjusted conditions."

Wed Judge's Daughter.

Fitzgerald married Zelda Sayre, daughter of an Alabama Supreme court justice, in 1920. They have one daughter, Frances Scott Fitzgerald.

Fitzgerald was born in St. Paul, Minn., and christened Francis Scott Key Fitzgerald in honor of the composer of "The Star Spangled Banner," a maternal ancestor.

Fitzgerald had done little film work recently but turned out occasional short stories and worked on a play for the New York stage.

Funeral services will be held in Baltimore, Md.

The Times
4th August 1924

JOSEPH CONRAD.

A PHILOSOPHER OF THE SEA.

THE MERCHANT-SERVICE.

Mr. Joseph Conrad (whose death is announced on another page) must ever remain one of the most remarkable examples in literary history of a writer who has adorned a language that was not by birth or upbringing his own. His proper name was Joseph Conrad Korzeniowski, and he was born in the Ukraine in 1857 of a Polish landed family. His father, a man of letters who translated Shakespeare into Polish, became involved in the Polish rebellion of 1863, and was banished to Vologda. He returned, however, for the last year and a half of his life to Cracow, where his son Joseph passed his boyhood.

At an early age his passion for literature disclosed itself. "I was a reading boy," he recounted later in life; "I read, what did I not read!" But he not only read; he dreamed. His dreams were of the far spaces of the globe; there is a tale that he pointed, when he was ten, to the unmarked tracts in Central Africa on an atlas of the time, declaring, "When I grow up I will go there." But it was the sea that became an ever stronger lure as he approached manhood; he must be a sailor, and an English sailor, too. He was 19 when he found his way to Marseilles and made his first voyage to the Gulf of Mexico. He worked on two French ships, and then, having joined the crew of an English steamer on her voyage to the Azov Sea, came back with her to Lowestoft, and thus reached his second fatherland.

IN THE BRITISH SERVICE.

His grand aspiration was now to be realized. He became an A.B. on board a British ship and was raised to second officer. By 1884 he was a master in the British merchant service, and had reached the goal he had set himself. Before another ten years had passed he had tasted all the varieties of sea-life and steeped himself in the enchantments of the tropical lands that had haunted his imagination from childhood. Together with this hoarded knowledge, he had learned English seamanship and also, of necessity, the English language. Only the spark was needed now to fire in creative energy this triple acquisition. In some biographical notes that received his sanction he is said to have "dropped somewhat casually into the literary life, partly as a result of illness, partly through his friendship with John Galsworthy and the prompting of Edward Garnett." That "casually" can only refer to the occasion. It was, perhaps, a chance that this or that stimulus sent Conrad to pen and paper. But that there lay deep in him the compulsion to expend himself in writing he confessed in his book "Some Reminiscences," published in 1912. He speaks there of "a hidden, obscure necessity, a completely masked and unaccountable phenomenon"—a force as imperious and inexplicable, in short, as that which had drawn him to the sea and England. He speaks, too, revealingly of "a sentiment akin to piety which prompted me to render in words assembled with conscientious care the memory of things far distant and of men who had lived."

As these words remind us, his earliest books were made directly from the stuff of his sea-experience. The first story he published was "Almayer's Folly," in 1895. How it was written he has laconically noted:—

Commenced in September, 1889, in London, then laid aside during voyages to Congo and Australia. Taken up again in 1893, and finished on May 22, 1894. Submitted to T. F. Unwin on June 2, 1893. Accepted in August, same year. Published in May, 1895. The author worked at the manuscript at sea, and it was nearly lost in the wreck of a boat on the Congo.

The tragic hero of this tale of the Borneo coast had his original in the author's own observation. "I had seen him for the first time some four years before from the bridge of a steamer moored to a rickety little wharf forty miles up, more or less, a Bornean river." The manuscript, as it accompanied him on his wanderings, grew slowly, with the laborious effort that never came in one who found composition a toil and a strain. "Line by line," he recorded, "rather than page by page, was the growth of 'Almayer's Folly.'" It was the mental fruit of Conrad's experience as first officer of the Vidar, trading between Singapore, Borneo, Celebes, and Sumatra. When the book was finished, Edward Garnett kept its dubious author to his vocation by a skilful suggestion. "You have the style, you have the temperament; why not write another?" The modesty of the demand for just one more prevented Conrad (he has recorded) from feeling scared; and "another" came—"An Outcast of the Islands," in 1896, the scene of which is laid on the same coasts as "Almayer's Folly."

Glasgow Herald
14th January 1941

JAMES JOYCE

Distinguished Irish Author

STIR OVER "ULYSSES" RECALLED

We regret to announce the death of Mr James Joyce, the Irish author, which took place at Zurich early yesterday morning. Mr Joyce was 58 years old, and he is survived by his wife, a son, and a daughter.

Mr Joyce went to live in Switzerland recently from the French Riviera, where he and his family had been since the outbreak of war. On Friday Mr Joyce was taken ill, and after an intestinal operation, from which he was reported to have made a good recovery, he suffered a relapse.

Mr Joyce spent the greater part of his life on the Continent. Born in Dublin in 1882, he was educated at a Jesuit seminary and at the Royal University, where he graduated B.A. After writing some short stories, criticism, and verse, managing a cinema, and toying with the notion of going on the operatic stage (he had an excellent tenor voice), he left the Irish Capital in his early twenties for the Continent, where until his later years he lived by teaching English in Trieste, Zurich, Rome, and Paris.

Until 1925, when his famous and notorious novel, "Ulysses," was published in Paris (no British publisher being willing to invite the inevitable prosecution that its publication in this country would have invited), James Joyce was best known as the author of two books, "Dubliners" and "A Portrait of the Artist as a Young Man," the former a collection of short stories, the latter a novel. His other early writings were "Chamber Music" (poems in the Celtic Twilight vein), "Exiles" (a play), and an essay on Ibsen.

LIFE IN IRISH CAPITAL

"Dubliners" described various characters and ways of life in the Irish Capital, while "A Portrait of the Artist" was largely autobiographical, and was remarkable for the precision and delicacy with which the author described the mental states of a middle-class adolescent. In this novel James Joyce was associated with his hero, Stephen Dedalus, in an intense sensibility to the sound and shape of words. This preoccupation was later to become the dominating factor in Joyce's career as a novelist.

He had been at work on "Ulysses" for many years before its publication, and had lived in Paris working laboriously at this monumental novel, suffering from an affliction of the eyes which ultimately left him almost blind, and suffering, too, from poverty. In his later years he obtained assistance from a wealthy American patron.

When at last "Ulysses" appeared in a very ill-printed volume whose vagaries of English had surely tried the French compositors, it created a tremendous stir in high-brow literary circles here and in the United States. The stir communicated itself to the common reader when he learned that the book had been banned by the Customs as obscene, and a brisk trade soon developed in copies smuggled into Britain and sold at scarcity-value prices.

It was more than 10 years before an English publisher took his courage in his hands and brought out an edition of "Ulysses" in this country. It was permitted to appear. The price was three guineas, and the sales were small.

EXPERIMENT IN WORDS

Joyce had indeed very little to say to the common reader in "Ulysses" and even less in its successors. But that is not to ignore the importance of his work as a genuinely creative artist conducting a dual literary experiment—with words and with the now fashionable themes of time and space.

"THE NIGGER OF THE NARCISSUS."

After that there could be no real question of turning back. In 1897 appeared "The Nigger of the Narcissus," based on a voyage made by the author from Bombay to England in a sailing-ship: it is a study of sea-types from the British merchant service, and was, in its writer's opinion, "the story by which, as a creative artist, I stand or fall, and which, at any rate, no one else could have written." "Lord Jim" (1900), the tale of a young sailor who, after incurring disgrace as a seaman, becomes a wanderer in the East and a ruler in a savage Malayan village; "Typhoon" (1903), a collection of four short stories, with its sinister introductory storm-piece; and "Nostromo: a Tale of the Seaboard" (1904), with its picture of an imaginary State in South America, may be selected from the group of works that mark Conrad's first period, and find in "The Mirror of the Sea" (1906), with its blend of fable, reminiscence, and reflection, a kind of epilogue. Here we find the sea pictured as those only know it who have formed their manhood battling with it. "For all that has been said," writes Conrad, "of the love that certain natures (on shore) have professed to feel for it, for all the celebrations it had ever been the object of in prose and song, the sea has never been friendly to man." And again :—

It seems to me that no man born and truthful to himself could declare that he ever saw the sea looking young as the earth looks young in spring. But some of us, regarding the ocean with understanding and affection, have seen it looking old, as if the immemorial ages had been stirred up from the undisturbed bottom of ooze. For it is a gale of wind that makes the sea look old.

"The Secret Agent" (1907) opened up a different vein of memory and imagination. In this grim tale of the anarchist and criminal underworld (suggested by an attempt on Greenwich Observatory during the 'nineties) we are conscious of the son of an insurrectionary intellectual, who had seen at close quarters and felt the grip of Tsarist police methods. Yet here, as in the ghastly stories of crime and violence contained in "Within the Tides" (1915), we discern a harsh stoicism in facing the malignancies of life and Nature which leaves more room for irony than compassion. The year before, in "Chance," Conrad had painted in Mr. Smith, once known as "the great de Barral" of the "Orb Bank," the "Sceptre Trust," and other bubble enterprises, a subtle figure of the financial adventurer. In the same year as "Within the Tides" came "Victory," a return to the background of Celebes and Java; and in 1919 "The Arrow of Gold," a romantic fiction dated "about the middle years of the 'seventies, when Don Carlos de Bourbon, encouraged by the general reaction of all Europe against the excesses of Communistic Republicanism, made his attempt for the throne of Spain, arms in hand, among the hills and gorges of Guipuzcoa." Conrad's last novel, "The Rover," published last December, was also a historical tale, with its scene laid on the peninsula between Toulon and Hyères, and Nelson himself appearing for a moment.

In 1905 the Stage Society produced a play by Conrad entitled One Day More. It was described in these columns as "a heart-breaking little piece," but "the rugged strength and unflinching sincerity" of it were acknowledged. In 1919 "Victory" was dramatized by M. B. Macdonald Hastings, and in 1922 Conrad himself drew a play from "The Secret Agent," which just fell short of repeating the success of the novel. The year before a volume called "Notes on Life and Letters" revealed the rare critical capacity that accompanied Conrad's creative and imaginative power in letters.

About the same time appeared a book by Captain J. G. Sutherland, "At Sea with Joseph Conrad." The author had commanded a "Q" ship in 1916 for trapping submarines, and told how Conrad, who had been caught in Austrian Poland at the beginning of the war, and had already since then experimented with minesweeping and flying, sailed with him on what proved a disappointing voyage.

A LITERARY IDEAL.

In the work just mentioned, "Notes on Life and Letters," Conrad gives expression, in passing, to the ideal that ruled all his literary life. Readers of that book, he remarked, would find in it "Conrad literary, Conrad political, Conrad reminiscent, Conrad controversial." The one thing they would not find would be "Conrad en pantoufles." In fact, he never took his slippered ease with the language that he had been compelled to woo as a lover and had never romped with in the nursery. He never came to that point of familiarity with it that permitted neglect or disrespect :—

It is only through complete, unswerving devotion to the perfect blending of form and substance ; it is only through an unremitting, never-discouraged care for the shape and the ring of sentences that an approach can be made to plasticity, to colour ; and the light of magic suggestiveness may be brought to play for an evanescent instant over the commonplace surface of words: of the old, old words, worn thin, defaced by ages of careless usage. The sincere endeavour to accomplish that creative task, to go as far as that road as his strength will carry him, to go undeterred by faltering, weariness, or reproach, is the only valid justification for the worker in prose.

That was the strenuous and exacting creed that Conrad reaffirmed in every piece he published. It is, perhaps, the only creed that can be extracted from the long row of his volumes with their shifting glamour of mystery and beauty. The horror seems always close at hand, like the foul things crawling at the roots of the glowing jungle, or the swooping typhoon that ravages tropical calms. And Conrad was ready to accept the spectacle with the stubborn courage of the storm-beaten sailor :—

The ethical view of the universe involves us at last in so many cruel and absurd contradictions, when the last vestiges of faith, hope, charity, and even of reason itself, seem ready to perish, that I have come to suspect that the aim of creation cannot be ethical at all. I would fondly believe that its object is purely spectacular—a spectacle for awe, love, adoration, or hate, if you like, but, in this view—and in this view alone—never for despair ! Those visions, delicious or poignant, are a moral end in themselves. The rest is our affair—the laughter, the tears, the tenderness, the indignation, the high tranquillity of a steeled heart, the detached curiosity of a subtle mind—that's our affair.

"Ulysses" was principally an experiment in words, and the expression of the mind of a man for whom nothing was sacred and nothing private. It was a novel that profoundly shocked the conventional and many others who thought they were unshockable. Yet it was impossible to ignore Joyce's own objectivity in his treatment of a single day in the lives of two Dubliners, his original hero Stephen Dedalus, and the Jew, Leopold Bloom.

From the literary aspect, however, Joyce's frankness was less important than his use and creation of words as an instrument of thought and feeling. He took Carroll's Jabberwocky language and Lear's trick of making portmanteau words, added some creative invention of his own, and built up a language that for those who had the patience and the mental agility to master it gave them a full orchestra of sound and meaning in place of a thin piping of conventional English. To all this creative genius Joyce added as background and point of reference to his microscopic recording of a Dublin day the Homeric story.

SPURIOUS IMITATORS

As an experiment "Ulysses" was brilliantly successful, and it had the result of provoking many spurious imitations among young high-brow aspirants to literary fame. Most of them succeeded merely in being obscure. So, too, did Joyce himself in his later experiments, for when "Finnegans Wake" was published in 1939 it was seen that Joyce had carried his word-making several stages further into incomprehensibility, and had added to the reader's difficulties by employing the time-space theme.

"Finnegans Wake" recounts the dream and subconscious life of another Dubliner, H. C. Earwicker, ex-publican, ex-postman, ex-brewery employee. But there is not one background to the story but a thousand, and the scene is sometimes Dublin, sometimes New York, or Illium, or Tara, and the river when it is not the Liffey is the Scamander or the Mississippi.

There was the hint that Earwicker's dream-life was the expression of all history of all nations brought into one timeless history. But the experiment in word-making had been carried to the point where it may be doubted whether any but Joyce's immediate circle of disciples could comprehend the meaning of the nightmare language of distortion and verbal virtuosity he employed, and although the critics were respectful upon the book's appearance it was clear that it had given all of them a headache, and none of them a vision either of truth or of beauty.

Perhaps "Finnegans Wake" will become the infant-class primer of future generations when the experiments begun by Joyce have been brought to fruition. But, for the present generation it must be said that his greatness ended with "Ulysses"

The Guardian
4th March 1930
D. H. Lawrence.

It would be a rash prophecy to foretell the verdict of the next generation on the work of D. H. Lawrence, who has just died at what should have been the height of his power. Although he seemed to be always wrestling with an opposition, he really had his own time on his side. To decry the intellect is fashionable, and he decried it. Few people pretending to philosophy can ever have written more vigorous praise of the primitive than he. As a novelist he had shown an uncanny power of describing the atmosphere in which feeling and thought are fused. He drove into the nerves of his characters rather than into their minds, and later, when he had travelled widely on his strange wandering from Nottingham to New Mexico, he praised with an almost hysterical rapture the glory to be found in the savage and instinctive life. That suits the mode of the literary left wing, for whom balance and containment have ceased to be virtues. The general campaign against the sovereignty of reason has many fronts. The sceptic and the cynic snipe away from one corner, and the psycho-analyst saps and mines in another. Lawrence, who liked a bold image, cheerfully announced that the seat of reason was the abdomen and became ecstatic over the Red Indians, whose ceremonies delighted him with their massed sur-

render to a wild emotion. One can fairly surmise that this part of his work will be the least likely to endure. The age of reason will return again, and mankind will not for ever feel ashamed to be civilised. Lawrence's masterly portraiture of the human impulse in his fiction was another matter. It had strength and depth and was not merely stark for the look of the thing. His style was often jagged, and his vision of sex as a torturer had something of Strindberg's monomania. Even those who resent the vision must admire the rough-hewn result of the sculpture in words which Lawrence achieved. He tore at the rock of life with hand and implement that would not be broken or blunted. Perhaps his earliest work is most likely to endure. For then, with his memories of the Notts coalfield, he was working on mineral, and in "Sons and Lovers" he fashioned the hard substance of his place and people in memorable ways.

The Times
4th March 1930
MR. D. H. LAWRENCE

A WRITER OF GENIUS

David Herbert Lawrence, whose death is announced on another page, was born at Eastwood, near Nottingham, on September 11, 1885. His novel "Sons and Lovers" and his play The Widowing of Mrs. Holroyd are at least so far biographical as to tell the world that his father was a coalminer and his mother a woman of finer grain. At the age of 12 the boy won a county council scholarship; but the sum was scarcely enough to pay the fees at the Nottingham High School and the fares to and fro. At 16 he began to earn his living as a clerk. When his ill-health put an end to that, he taught in a school for miners' boys.

At 19 he won another scholarship, of which he could not avail himself, as he had no money to pay the necessary entrance fee; but at 21 he went to Nottingham University College, and after two years there he came to London and took up teaching again. It was in these years that he wrote, under the name of Lawrence H. Davidson, some books on history. He had begun also the writing of fiction, and his first novel, "The White Peacock," was published about a month after his mother's death had robbed him of his best and dearest friend.

"Sons and Lovers," published when he was 28, brought him fame. Many years of poverty were to pass before his work began to make him financially comfortable; and even then the collapse of a publishing firm in America deprived him of some of the fruits of his labours. But the revolt against society which fills his books had its counterpart in his life, in his travels, and especially in his attempt to found, in 1923, an intellectual and community settlement in New Mexico.

Undoubtedly he had genius. He could create characters which are even obtrusively real. His ruthless interpretation of certain sides of the nature of women was recognized by some women to be just. Every one of his novels, as well as his books of travel, contains passages of description so fine that they command the admiration of people whom much of his work disgusts. His powers range from a rich simplicity, a delicacy almost like that of Mr. W. H. Davies, to turbulent clangour, and from tenderness to savage irony and gross brutality. There was that in his intellect which might have made him one of England's greatest writers, and did indeed make him the writer of some things worthy of the best of English literature. But as time went on and his disease took firmer hold, his rage and his fear grew upon him. He confused decency with hypocrisy, and honesty with the free and public use of vulgar words. At once fascinated and horrified by physical passion, he paraded his disgust and fear in the trappings of a showy masculinity. And, not content with words, he turned to painting in order to exhibit more clearly still his contempt for all reticence.

It was inevitable (though it was regrettable) that such a man should come into conflict with the law over his novel "The Rainbow"; over some manuscripts sent through the post to his agent in London; and over an exhibition of his paintings. But a graver cause for regret is that the author of "Sons and Lovers," of "Amores," and the other

books of poems, of "Aaron's Rod," the short stories published as "The Prussian Officer," "Ladybird," and "Kangaroo" should have missed the place among the very best which his genius might have won.

In 1914 Lawrence married Frieda von Richthofen, who survives him. He left no children.

The Gentleman's Magazine
18th July 1817 Vol 87

At Winchester, Miss Jane Austen, youngest daughter of Rev. George Austen, Rector of Steventon, Hants, authoress of "Emma," "Mansfield Park," "Pride and Prejudice," and "Sense and Sensibility."

The Media & Communications

"Power comes from the barrel of a gun", Mao tse-Tung once said: and there was indeed a time when this was true. Today, however, it comes from control of the means of communication, whether these be newspapers, TV, radio, or other more specialised channels. New developments in communication once really did open up the world and make ordinary people's ideas more accessible to each other – **Rowland Hill**'s penny post, for instance, or **Louis Braille**'s script for the blind (though Braille's death went unrecorded in the English-language press and it was not until his centenary that he received proper recognition). Today's most important medium of communication, open to all, though often abused by Worldwide Telephone Tapping Inc., is of course **Alexander Bell**'s brain-child. Secretaries have **Isaac Pitman** to thank, while the aural counterpart of shorthand was presented to the world by **Stanley Morse**.

Those tools of communication which have by and large become the prerogative of institutions and/or governments are represented here by **William Randolph Hearst**, newspaper magnate *par excellence* and Alfred Harmsworth, **Lord Northcliffe**, who presided baronially over the largest newspaper empire the world has ever seen, together with the newspapers' valet *extraordinaire*, **Julius Reuter**. **Hedda Hopper**, the incomparable gossip columnist, is here, together with **Joseph Pulitzer**, the consummate journalist and **Jack London**, one of the early celebrity correspondents. **William Stead**, editor of the *Pall Mall Gazette*, represents campaigning journalism at its best, for his dogged work against child prostitution in turn-of-the-century London. Stead, incidentally, died with the Titanic in 1912. Sir **Allen Lane** pioneered paperback books and injected a new vigour into the arts of reading, writing and publishing. **Guglielmo Marconi** and **John Baird** are of course given their due. In a rather different vein, **Pope Pius IX** has found his way here, as symbol of the crucial first principle for all today's communicators – for it was he who, as recently as 1872, declared the Pope to be infallible. How appropriate that such a declaration should have been made just before the age of the professional media man. Finally we have **William Joyce**, here by virtue of his grand failure; and **Joseph Goebbels**, as a symbol of even greater success, a success hopefully to be neither repeated nor forgotten.

The Glasgow Herald
3rd August 1922

A PIONEER

DEATH OF INVENTOR OF TELEPHONE

DISTINGUISHED SCOTSMAN

From "The Glasgow Herald" and "The Daily Telegraph" Correspondent

Montreal, Wednesday. — Dr Alexander Graham Bell, the world famous inventor of the telephone and founder of the Bell telephone systems in Canada and the United States, died unexpectedly at five o'clock this morning at his summer residence, Beinn Bhreaugh, near Baddeck (Nova Scotia). Dr Bell's death came as a surprise, despite his advanced age. He had been in failing health for several months, although not confined to bed, but was able to enjoy drives around his Nova Scotian home. He became seriously ill at five o'clock on Tuesday afternoon, and was immediately attended by Dr Ker, of Washington, D.C., a cousin of his wife, who was a guest at his summer home, with Dr J. J. Roy, of Sydney, N.S. After the first attack Dr Bell never rallied and sank rapidly until his death early this morning. Dr Graham Bell was always regarded as a Canadian, although he was a Scotsman by birth, and had spent most of his life in the United States. He resided at Brantford, Ontario, for several years in the early seventies, where he continued his experiments in the development of the telephone, as a result of which Brantford has always since been known in Canada as "Telephone City." Dr Bell never lost touch with Canada. For many years past, since the development of the telephone brought him wealth, he spent the summer in Nova Scotia, and retained many warm friendships with scientists of the Dominion. His unexpected death has caused much sorrow. Mrs Bell was with the famous inventor when he died. It is understood that the remains will be removed to Washington for interment.

A NATIVE OF EDINBURGH

Mr Alexander Graham Bell, LL.D., Ph.D., D.Sc., M.D., was born in Edinburgh in 1847. He was the son of Mr Alexander Melville Bell, a well-known citizen of Edinburgh. He was educated at the Royal High School, Edinburgh University, and University College, London. In 1870 he went to Canada, and later became Professor of Vocal Physiology in Boston University. His achievements are amongst the foremost in modern science. He was responsible for the removal of the barriers which disease and distance alike presented to the transmission of human speech. He was the author of some of the chief developments in the methods of teaching the deaf and dumb. It was chiefly by the application of his father's system that Dr Bell did so much for the development of those institutions which sought to impart hearing to the deaf and the means of expression to the dumb. His achievements in that sphere no doubt suggested to him the importance of more general utility, and he was the first to solve the problem of the articulatory telephone. The first rudimentary telephone was constructed in 1861 by Philip Reiss, of Frankfort, but it was in 1876 that Dr Bell devised a practical instrument which was used both for transmitting and receiving messages. The transmitter devised by Professor D. E. Hughes in 1878 and Dr Bell's receiver are practically those in use to-day. Among other inventions which Dr Bell had to his credit were the photophone in 1880 and the graphophone in 1887. He investigated the laws of flight, and conducted important aeroplane tests in Nova Scotia. Among the many offices which he held were president of the American Association to Promote Teaching of Speech to the Deaf, president of the National Geographic Society, and Regent of the Smithsonian Institution.

A CIVIC HONOUR

Dr Bell revisited Edinburgh in November, 1920, after spending the greater part of his lifetime in America. The freedom of the city was conferred upon him by the Corporation of Edinburgh on the 30th of that month, "in recognition of his great achievement in the solution of the problem of telephonic communication, and of his brilliant and distinguished career as a scientist." The burgess ticket described him as "Doctor of Philosophy, Doctor of Laws, Doctor of Science, Doctor of Medicine, etc." Dr Bell was the first to receive the freedom of Greater Edinburgh, and the ceremony was the first occasion on which the enlarged Town Council appeared in the Council Chamber in their robes of office. The University of Heidelburg conferred upon him the degree of M.D. in recognition of his invention for discovering the position of various foreign substances, such as bullets, in the human body, an honour which was unique in the annals of that University. He was an officer of the French Legion of Honour, and was awarded the Volta Prix by the French Government. Among the numerous medals which he received was the Albert Medal, his name appearing immediately after that of King Edward VII. His publications include a Memoir on the Formation of Deaf Variety in the Human Race, Census Report on the Deaf of the United States, and lectures on the mechanism of speech.

PIONEER OF THE TELEPHONE

Dr Graham Bell, who was a tall, striking figure, with a grey beard, stated in an interview on the occasion of his last visit to Edinburgh, that it was in 1874 he hit upon the idea of transmitting the voice by the telephone. But it took constant experiment for more than a year to produce the voice well enough to be heard at the other end of the wire. "The voice," he said by way of describing the earliest stages, "might correspond to a pin-head blot in which, while the detail was there, you could not make it out. I had to keep on until the transmission had developed."

Then came the great centennial exhibition in Philadelphia in 1876, and with it his chance to let the world know the invention. Representative men of science were there to judge the inventions on exhibition, and they included in their number the late Lord Kelvin. But those examining scientists had a tiring day, and, by a strange fate, the last exhibit they decided to look at was the one immediately before Dr Bell's on the list. That was a heavy blow for the young inventor, for he had to leave that night for Boston, and his great chance seemed to have passed him. "But fate took a lucky turn for me," Dr Bell went on. "The Emperor of Brazil, Dom Pedro, who was then on a tour of the States, was in the exhibition, and he at once recognised me as the young man who some time before had shown him how deaf mutes were taught. He spoke to me, and I at once told him of my deep disappointment that my exhibit was not going to be seen. Dom Pedro made everything right for me. His word got the scientists to go one item further down the list, and they were introduced to the telephone. I went to another part of the building to speak through the instrument. The Emperor, who was given the first opportunity of listening put the receiver to his ear, and suddenly startled the group of scientists standing by with the exclamation, "My God, it speaks."

Discussing the future development of telephony, Dr Bell said they were probably just at the beginning. "Think of the marvels of the wireless telephone already. About a year ago he had a conversation between Arlington in the States and the Eiffel Tower in Paris, and a more remarkable thing still is that that conversation was tapped in Honolulu and was distinctly heard there. Now the 8000 miles between Honolulu away out in the Pacific and the Eiffel Tower covers a pretty big part of the globe, and we have therefore foreshadowed the possibility of one man talking to another anywhere else in the world and without wires at all."

During the war, as a private contribution to the preparations of America, Dr Graham Bell devoted his laboratory in Nova Scotia to perfecting a submarine chaser. The Armistice just obviated its use, for in the trials about that time it was travelling actually at 71 miles an hour.

PRESIDENT HARDING'S CONDOLENCES

Washington, Wednesday. — President Harding has telegraphed his condolences to Dr Graham Bell's widow, saying, "I have learned to revere him as one of the great benefactors of the race."—Exchange Telegram.

Halifax (N.S.), Wednesday.—Dr Graham Bell will be buried at the top of Mountain Bein Breagh, the site of his grave having been selected by himself.—Exchange Telegram.

THE COMING OF THE TELEPHONE

FROM A SPECIAL CORRESPONDENT

The invention of the telephone by Professor Graham Bell in 1876 has effected an influence in the daily life of everybody almost comparable with that of the locomotive. The telegraph has its uses, but the power to speak at once to anyone, to receive a prompt reply, and to carry on discussion in the free and sympathetic manner of a personal interview is a facility offered by the telephone only. Space is annihilated by a neat little apparatus which stands on the table and desk, or even at the bedside. Dwellers in town and country alike have installed the marvellous instrument, and straightway life is simplified, complications are smoothed out, delays and anxieties are removed. That this brings certain penalties in its train is but a proof of its power. The most dilatory correspondent, once he goes on the telephone system, is brought to book by its insistent call, and is compelled to answer inquiries. It is an autocrat which interrupts without apology and breaks in on privacy at any hour of the day or night.

A COMPLETE INVENTION

Bell's telephone was immediately successful in performance over short distances, and the receiving part of his instrument had been little changed since its inception. The ordinary long pattern differs only slightly from one of the early form used by him, and the small receiver is changed merely in the shape of the magnet. Few inventions have been designed with such finality and completeness, and the numerous alterations proposed by successive inventors have been no improvement.

The original sending instrument was the same as the receiver, and although this was perfect in its way, the power was very small and the possible distance correspondingly limited. The sending part obtained great additional power by the invention of Professor Hughes' microphone in 1878, while Edison was already developing much the same idea. Hughes' microphone was used for a long time in its original form, but Mr Hunning's form, with loose grains of carbon, invented soon after Hughes' publication of his work, gradually supplanted it, and now holds the field without rival.

For the last 40 years the sending and receiving instruments have defied essential improvement, but since the war an intermediate agent has been inserted, a relay or strengthener, by which far greater distances will no doubt be attained. This description ignores a vast amount of work spent on the problems of the connecting wires. The pandemonium of cross talk which early subscribers will remember vividly has been obviated. The attenuation caused by long distances has also yielded to the masterly mathematical work of Oliver Heaviside, and the vast problem of the central exchange is still open to other solutions. The next step appears to be the automatic exchange, whereby the speaker himself sets in motion a mechanical operator which connects him to the required number.

WIRELESS TELEPHONY

We are even assured that we may carry in our pockets a wireless set and call up the home from anywhere, but this may be taken at present with a pinch or two of salt. Nevertheless, wireless telephony is a well-accomplished fact, as everyone knows who has listened to the concerts at The Hague or Brussels while sitting here at home, and though some of the wild prophecies hazarded about this development are obviously unattainable on any large scale from the impossibility of excluding the messages of the other thousands of people who may all be trying to speak to each other, still in its sphere wireless telephony has a great field.

To attempt to describe all the applications of Bell's invention would occupy columns. In the war the telephone appeared everywhere. The underground miner was discovered, the submarine was located, it was used in surgery and in diagnosis by the physician; by its aid the deaf hear, for it is the case that in many forms of deafness the small voice of the telephone is more audible than the loud speech of the human. Both in the useful arts and in scientific research the little cup forms one of the most refined and searching of investigators. Indeed, simple as is its material form, it has been itself a scientific problem. Any handy boy can make one, but to explain precisely how it works and why it works so perfectly has taxed the brains of many learned men. No small part of the brilliance of the invention or of the combined inventions of Bell and Hughes consists in the undoubted fact that they work far more perfectly than anyone could possibly expect. Parts of the telephone systems do show at times imperfections, but the receiver and microphone are our faithful servants from year to year. Asking for no repairs, adjustments, or renewals, and costing for the essential parts only a few shillings, no wonder they have profoundly changed the world. "There is no speech nor language where their voice is not heard."

A PIONEER

DEATH OF INVENTOR OF TELEPHONE

DISTINGUISHED SCOTSMAN

A NATIVE OF EDINBURGH

Mr Alexander Graham Bell, LL.D., Ph.D., D.Sc., M.D., was born in Edinburgh in 1847. He was the son of Mr Alexander Melville Bell, a well known citizen of Edinburgh. He was educated at the Royal High School, Edinburgh University, and University College, London. In 1870 he went to Canada, and later became Professor of Vocal Physiology in Boston University. His achievements are amongst the foremost in modern science. He was responsible for the removal of the barriers which disease and distance alike presented to the transmission of human speech. He was the author of some of the chief developments in the methods of teaching the deaf and dumb. It was chiefly by the application of his father's system that Dr Bell did so much for the development of those institutions which sought to impart hearing to the deaf and the means of expression to the dumb. His achievements in that sphere no doubt suggested to him the importance of more general utility, and he was the first to solve the problem of the articulatory telephone. The first rudimentary telephone was constructed in 1861 by Philip Reiss, of Frankfort, but it was in 1876 that Dr Bell devised a practical instrument which was used both for transmitting and receiving messages. The transmitter devised by Professor D. E. Hughes in 1878 and Dr Bell's receiver are practically those in use to-day. Among other inventions which Dr Bell had to his credit were the photophone in 1880 and the graphophone in 1887. He investigated the laws of flight, and conducted important aeroplane tests in Nova Scotia. Among the many offices which he held were president of the American Association to Promote Teaching of Speech to the Deaf, president of the National Geographic Society, and Regent of the Smithsonian Institution.

A CIVIC HONOUR

Dr Bell revisited Edinburgh in November, 1920, after spending the greater part of his lifetime in America. The freedom of the city was conferred upon him by the Corporation of Edinburgh on the 30th of that month, "in recognition of his great achievement in the solution of the problem of telephonic communication, and of his brilliant and distinguished career as a scientist." The burgess ticket described him as "Doctor of Philosophy, Doctor of Laws, Doctor of Science, Doctor of Medicine, etc." Dr Bell was the first to receive the freedom of Greater Edinburgh, and the ceremony was the first occasion on which the enlarged Town Council appeared in the Council Chamber in their robes of office. The University of Heidelburg conferred upon him the degree of M.D. in recognition of his invention for discovering the position of various foreign substances, such as bullets, in the human body, an honour which was unique in the annals of that University. He was an officier of the French Legion of Honour, and was awarded the Volta Prix by the French Government. Among the numerous medals which he received was the Albert Medal, his name appearing immediately after that of King Edward VII. His publications include a Memoir on the Formation of Deaf Variety in the Human Race, Census Report on the Deaf of the United States, and lectures on the mechanism of speech.

PIONEER OF THE TELEPHONE

Dr Graham Bell, who was a tall, striking figure, with a grey beard, stated in an interview on the occasion of his last visit to Edinburgh, that it was in 1874 he hit upon the idea of transmitting the voice by the telephone. But it took constant experiment for more than a year to produce the voice well enough to be heard at the other end of the wire. "The voice," he said by way of describing the earliest stages, "might correspond to a pin-head blot in which, while the detail was there, you could not make it out. I had to keep on until the transmission had developed."

Then came the great centennial exhibition in Philadelphia in 1876, and with it his chance to let the world know the invention. Representative men of science were there to judge the inventions on exhibition, and they included in their number the late Lord Kelvin. But those examining scientists had a tiring day, and, by a strange fate, the last exhibit they decided to look at was the one immediately before Dr Bell's on the list. That was a heavy blow for the young inventor, for he had to leave that night for Boston, and his great chance seemed to have passed him. "But fate took a lucky turn for me," Dr Bell went on. "The Emperor of Brazil, Dom Pedro, who was then on a tour of the States, was in the exhibition, and he at once recognised me as the young man who some time before had shown him how deaf mutes were taught. He spoke to me, and I at once told him of my deep disappointment that my exhibit was not going to be seen. Dom Pedro made everything right for me. His word got the scientists to go one item further down the list, and they were introduced to the telephone. I went to another part of the building to speak through the instrument. The Emperor, who was given the first opportunity of listening put the receiver to his ear, and suddenly startled the group of scientists standing by with the exclamation, "My God, it speaks."

Discussing the future development of telephony, Dr Bell said they were probably just at the beginning. "Think of the marvels of the wireless telephone already. About a year ago he had a conversation between Arlington in the States and the Eiffel Tower in Paris, and a more remarkable thing still is that that conversation was tapped in Honolulu and was distinctly heard there. Now the 8000 miles between Honolulu away out in the Pacific and the Eiffel Tower covers a pretty big part of the globe, and we have therefore foreshadowed the possibility of one man talking to another anywhere else in the world and without wires at all."

During the war, as a private contribution to the preparations of America, Dr Graham Bell devoted his laboratory in Nova Scotia to perfecting a submarine chaser. The Armistice just obviated its use, for in the trials about that time it was travelling actually at 71 miles an hour.

The Times
15th June 1946

MR. J. L. BAIRD

PIONEER OF TELEVISION

Mr. J. L. Baird, the television pioneer, died at his home at Bexhill early yesterday morning at the age of 58, after an illness which began in February. Until then he had been actively engaged in research in his own company's laboratories. His company successfully showed the Victory parade by television at the Savoy Hotel last Saturday, but he was too ill to be present.

John Lodie Baird was born in 1888 at Helensburgh, Scotland, son of the minister of the West Parish Church. He was educated at Larchfield and the Royal Technical College, Glasgow, where he won an associate scholarship in electrical engineering. He was one of the outstanding inventors of his time, and well deserved the ultimate success which came to his experiments over so many years. As a young man he was fascinated by the possibility of "seeing by wireless," and at the age of 18, when indifferent health caused him to give up London business life, Baird went to Hastings, where he established a small laboratory and began his experiments. After some

months his primitive apparatus succeeded in reproducing objects in outline, and by 1926 he achieved true television and demonstrated before members of the Royal Institution the transmission of living human faces with light, shade, and detail. By this time Baird had moved his laboratory to an attic in Soho to continue his research, and full reward came to him in 1929 when television was broadcast first by the German Post Office, and two months later by the B.B.C. using his system. A year earlier Baird had been the first man to demonstrate transatlantic television and the transmission of images from this country to the Berengaria in mid-Atlantic.

Another step forward in television was made in 1931 when the modulated arc was used as the source of light, and it resulted in a far more brilliant picture than had been possible with the neon tube or a device known as the "Kerr cell," the only two forms of illumination previously used. Experiments were also being made with the cathode-ray tube about this time, and eventually it was adopted by Baird as the most successful method of providing a well-defined and brilliant picture. In 1937 the B.B.C. was transmitting both by Marconi-E.M.I. and Baird methods, but following a report by the Television Advisory Committee, it was decided that only the Marconi system should be used. Just before the war Baird

gave a demonstration of television in natural colour, using the cathode-ray tube and an arrangement of colour filters, which produced a satisfactory projection on a screen 2ft. 6in. by 2ft. He has also to his credit the invention of the "Noctovisor," an apparatus for seeing in the dark by invisible rays; and in April of this year Baird was reported to have completed his researches into a new phase of television which would enable audiences in special cinemas to see events as they occurred miles away. A bronze plaque in Queen's Avenue, Hastings, records that television was first demonstrated by John Lodie Baird from experiments started there in 1924—thus he had every claim to the title, "the father of television." Since 1941 Baird had been consulting technical adviser to Cable and Wireless, Limited.

He married Margaret Albu in 1931. There were one son and one daughter of the marriage.

Daily Telegraph
8th July 1970

Sir Allen Lane altered English reading habits

By DAVID HOLLOWAY

SIR ALLEN LANE, who died yesterday, aged 67, was the most remarkable figure among the publishers of his generation. It is not exaggerating to say that he changed the reading habits of the English-speaking world.

He did not, of course, invent the paperback; they had existed before he was born but he made them socially acceptable and, what is more, essential to life.

He did this partly by allowing young designers to make the first Penguins look attractive and by persuading hard-back publishers, who later admitted frankly that they thought he would fail, take some of their best titles at low prices so that he could establish a brilliant list.

Another of his triumphs was to persuade book sellers to handle his new fangled books.

Most of them were reluctant, but he was able to obtain a small show for them in one London store. By the afternoon of the first day Penguins were on display, the entire stock had been sold out—bought not by customers but by the staff of the store.

Now, of course, shops exist that sell nothing but Penguins and many more sell only paperbacks.

Several honours

He was an honorary Doctor of Laws at Manchester and Birmingham, an honorary Doctor of Letters of Oxford and Reading, and an honorary Fellow of the Royal College of Art. He was knighted in 1952.

In 1960 Penguin Books was found by an Old Bailey jury not guilty of publishing D. H. Lawrence's novel, "Lady Chatterley's Lover," as an obscene article contrary to the Obscene Publications Act, 1959. "This is a happy day for me," said Sir Allen.

Many people who now hold important positions in other publishing firms left Penguins, in some cases after sharp disagreement with Sir Allen. But this did not mean that he did not get on well with his staff. A devoted band of workers were with him for many years.

Although more than one hundred different firms in Britain now issue paperback editions, to the public at large a paperback is still a Penguin.

That is the measure of Allen Lane's achievement.

Misleading man

Those who knew Sir Allen only when he had achieved eminence would have difficulty in believing that he was a man who had rushed around selling his own books, or indeed early in his career had persuaded his uncle, John Lane, to publish James Joyce's "Ulysses" in this country.

In recent years he seemed a bland figure, more like a country squire than a tycoon but he was clearly not without a determined streak.

He allowed the many bright young men and women who worked for him over the years to have their heads but if he felt they went too far he would step in.

Sir Allen went to Bristol Grammar School and entered publishing in London as a youth. He married in 1941 Lettice, daughter of Sir Charles Orr, and had three daughters.

The Times
18th April 1912

MR. W. T. STEAD.

William Thomas Stead, whose "redoubtable journalistic career" (to use Lord Morley's phrase) has been abruptly closed by the wreck of the Titanic, was born in 1849, his father being a Congregational minister at Howdon-on-Tyne, a few miles from Newcastle. He received all the regular schooling he obtained at Silcoates (Wakefield), a school much frequented by the sons of Congregational ministers. He used to be fond of saying that he acquired there one distinction of much use to him in after life—he was known at school as the boy with the hardest shins. When 14 he was taken away from school in order to be apprenticed in a merchant's office at Newcastle. Here he remained, rising presently to the position of salaried clerk, for seven years. The firm had some dealings with Russia, and this was the origin of his special interest in that country. His real teachers were his father and himself. He was a true son of the manse; he was surrounded with a Puritan atmosphere, and Cromwell was the god of his idolatry. In after years he used to say that the greatest compliment he ever received was when Cardinal Manning said to him, "When I read the *Pall Mall* every night, it seems to me as if Oliver Cromwell had come to life again." One of the novelties which he promised the public in connexion with his short-lived *Daily Paper* was dramatic criticism by a man who up to that time had never set foot inside a playhouse. He dated his serious call from the appearance of Dick's "Penny Shakespeare." His pocket-money was 3d. a week, and the missionaries claimed a third of it—the rest all went in Shakespeare. It was his own early experience that led him in after years to produce a series of Penny Poets—one of his many publishing ventures. Even as a lad, he seems to have regarded himself as appointed to set the world to rights, for one of his favourite stories was of the following remark which his father once made to him :—"You would do much better, William, if you would occasionally leave God to manage His universe in His own way." He used laughingly to admit that he chose his telegraphic address to denote his vicegerency—"Vatican, London."

In 1871, when Mr. Stead was 22, there was a vacancy in the editorship of the *Northern Echo*, Darlington. He had long been an occasional (and unpaid) contributor to its columns ; the proprietor of the paper had detected in these letters and articles evidence of unusual vigour and ability, and he offered to the young merchant's clerk the post of editor-in-chief. Stead —perhaps for the last time in his life—felt great diffidence ; but the experiment proved a complete success. His great chance came with the Eastern Question and Mr. Gladstone's agitation over the atrocities in Bulgaria. He had by this time become a fast friend of Mme. de Novikoff, and the Bulgarian agitation appealed with compelling force to his ardent temperament and religious instincts. He came up to London in order to put himself in touch with the leaders of the crusade. He saw Carlyle among others, who used to speak of him as "that good man, Stead." His friendship with Canon Liddon dated from the same events. Presently, when Stead settled in London, he was the Canon's constant companion in afternoon walks upon the Embankment. Meanwhile his paper became the most powerful organ of the agitation in the North of England, and an "elector's catechism" which he printed in 1880—the first of many electoral sheets of the kind—had a very large circulation.

THE "PALL MALL GAZETTE."

The excellent service which Stead had rendered in the Press did not escape the notice of leading Liberals in London, and when Mr. Morley assumed the editorship of the *Pall Mall Gazette* in 1880 he selected Stead as his assistant-editor. The combination of the two men which ruled that journal for three years was a strong one. It was a union of classical severity with the rude vigour of a Goth. Mr. Morley was political director and wrote most of the leading articles. Stead looked after the rest of the paper, and was fertile in suggestions. Mr. Morley used to call Stead "the irrepressible," but in fact the assistant-editor was during these years successfully tamed. When there is a potent individuality at the head of a newspaper his instruments catch the dominant note ; and many an article in which outsiders supposed themselves to detect the style and temper of Mr. Morley was the work of Stead.

In 1883 Mr. Morley retired from the editorship, and Stead succeeded him. The six years that followed were those during which, as Stead used to say in his characteristic fashion, he was engaged in "running the British Empire from Northumberland-street." He undoubtedly made his paper a great political force, and, by a succession of shocks or spasms, rendered its daily doings the talk of the town. His first great political *coup* had far-reaching effects. To Stead, more than any other man, was due the sending of Gordon to the Sudan. Political memoirs record that on January 10, 1884, Lord Granville telegraphed to Sir Evelyn Baring asking whether Gordon might not be of use, but they omit to mention the impelling force under which the Foreign Secretary acted. This came from Stead. He had been seized with the idea of "Chinese Gordon for the Sudan," and acted upon his inspiration with characteristic vigour. On January 8 Gordon was at Southampton, on his way from Palestine to take charge of King Leopold's expedition to the head-waters of the Congo. Stead went down to see him, "interviewed" him at great length, and advocated his despatch to rescue the garrisons with much force and eloquence. The suggestion was warmly taken up in the Press, and the Government acted upon it.

Stead's assumption of the editorship of the *Pall Mall Gazette* coincided with the publication of Seeley's "Expansion of England," and he was in those days a persistent "Liberal Imperialist." He invented the phrases "Cut and Run !" and "Scuttle" to express his contempt for the policy of "Little Englanders." A younger generation should remember that there was no man who had done more in the Press to popularize the Imperial idea than Stead, the Pro-Boer of later days. Imperialism (as he conceived it) made him "a Home Ruler before Mr. Gladstone" ; and the Liberal leader, who had been stung and estranged by Stead's taunts about "the policy of scuttle," sent him a public message of reconciliation and approval at the time of the Home Rule "Kite." But Mr. Gladstone's satisfaction with his unruly follower was short-lived. Stead believed in Home Rule as a first step towards federation all round ; and from this point of view he was a fierce opponent of the exclusion of the Irish members from the Imperial Parliament as proposed in the Bill of 1886.

One direction in which Stead took his own line was towards a strong Navy. His "Truth about the Navy," though it appeared at a time when the agitation of 1884 about the Franchise was at its height, created a decisive impression, and compelled the

Continued

Government to introduce Supplementary Navy Estimates in the autumn Session of that year. The case had been presented with all the resources of journalistic emphasis, but Stead had behind him and behind the scenes the expert knowledge of naval officers who have since risen to high distinction. His crusade was a complete success because he was sure of all his facts. In the last few years he returned to the subject, and pressed for "Two keels to one" as against Germany.

The case was different in the next "sensation" with which Stead startled the town. This was the notorious series of "revelations" to which he gave the name "The Maiden Tribute of Modern Babylon." Long ago, at Darlington, he had taken a strong line against the Contagious Diseases Act, and he had formed friendships with Mrs. Josephine Butler and other Abolitionists. Early in 1885 information had been brought to him about the "white slave trade." What could he do to help the passage of the Criminal Law Amendment Bill then before the House of Commons, with very slender chances of becoming law that Session? He resolved to apply the same methods of personal inquiry and "sensational journalism" which had been successful in regard to the Navy. Impulsive, reckless, careless of his own reputation as he was in most respects, he took one precaution in the idle hope of protecting himself from subsequent misrepresentation; before entering into the labyrinth, he confided his purposes to the Archbishop of Canterbury, the Bishop of London, the Cardinal Archbishop of Westminster, and Lord Dalhousie. They warned him of the dangers, and, while witnesses of his *bona fides*, were in no way responsible for his methods. Having collected his information, Stead determined to publish it broadcast. He had convinced himself that nothing except an open appeal to the public conscience would suffice to carry the Bill and to create the public opinion necessary for its due enforcement. A storm of execration burst upon his head; the revelations, it was said, ought not to have been made if true, and besides they were "a pack of lies." One of the most shocking of the revelations was the story of a little girl who, it was alleged, had been sold by her parents. The editor of *Lloyd's News* presently discovered the facts, which were that the girl had been procured by an agent of Stead, and without the guilty knowledge of the parents. Stead was placed on trial for abduction. He had been deceived by his agents, and he had overstepped the limits of justifiable sensationalism by describing as a typical incident what was in fact an experiment of his own. He was sentenced by Mr. Justice Lopes at the Central Criminal Court on November 4, 1885, to three months' imprisonment. After a few days he was made a first-class misdemeanant, and he conducted his paper from a not incommodious cell in Holloway Gaol. He became a great friend of the Governor, who presented him, on liberation, with the suit of prison clothes which he had worn at Coldbath Fields. For many years Stead held a reception of his friends and admirers on the anniversary of his conviction, and on these occasions he always wore his Order of the Broad Arrow. Whatever may be thought of his methods, it cannot be denied that his crusade did in fact carry the Criminal Law Amendment Act and give impetus to international efforts towards checking the "white slave trade."

THE "REVIEW OF REVIEWS."

This episode in Stead's life brought him as many friends as enemies. He became one of the best-known personages of the day, and he made frequent appearances on the platform. He was looked to as a knight-errant, and the offices of his paper were the resort for some years of all who were in distress. Some were deserving, others were not. In 1889 he resigned the editorship of the *Pall Mall Gazette* in order to found the *Review of Reviews*. This gave Stead a powerful pulpit. He would probably have made an even greater political mark if he had not dabbled in spiritualism. His "Borderland" and "Letters from Julia" did much to undermine his influence; but here, again, he made as many adherents in one direction as he lost in another, and "Julia's Bureau" was besieged.

Of his political efforts not already mentioned, the most constant was an advocacy of a good understanding with Russia. In 1885 he had opposed the idea of fighting over the Penjdeh incident; his articles and pamphlets, in the compilation of which he was assisted by the late M. Lessar, contributed not a little to a friendly settlement. His "Truth about Russia" (1888) sought to correct many misunderstandings. The book (first published in the *Pall Mall Gazette*) was the result of a visit to Russia, during which he was received by Alexander III. In 1898 he again visited Russia in order to have audience of Nicholas II. Stead used to tell how after having had his full say to an exemplary listener he began to take leave, remarking that he would not detain the Tsar longer, as he was sure that his Majesty must wish to join his good wife and the children. The Tsar shook hands, saying with a good-natured smile that this was his first experience of being dismissed from an audience. It was after this talk with the Tsar that Stead embarked on the "Peace Crusade" which occupied much of his later years. He founded and edited a weekly paper, *War against War*. He attended The Hague Conferences and threw himself into Arbitration propaganda. This was probably a principal reason of his strong opposition to the South African War. He was the most militant and least compromising of all the Pro-Boers. His line was the more marked because of its apparent conflict with persons and policies in South Africa with which he had formerly been in sympathy. Lord Milner had been for some years his assistant on the *Pall Mall Gazette*, and Stead had proclaimed his confidence in his friend's judgment. He had, moreover, been an apologist for the Jameson Raid. He was also a great friend of Cecil Rhodes. Mowbray House, on the Thames Embankment, where the *Review of Reviews* had its offices, was always one of the first places to which Rhodes resorted on his visits to London, for the inspiration of a sympathetic and congenial mind. Stead was ever fertile in ideas, and the more grandiose the conception, the more it appealed to him. The will of Cecil Rhodes impressed everybody with its marks of originality and imagination; it is not so generally known that the ideas were in large measure Stead's, though it is on record that Rhodes at one time intended to appoint Stead his sole trustee.

Stead continued to conduct the *Review of Reviews* with great vigour. His "Character Sketches" and Chroniques of the Month had all the originality, force, and freshness which characterized his work as a daily journalist. He continued to go everywhere and see everybody, and the amount of miscellaneous work which he accomplished knew no diminution with the advance of years. He had founded also a very successful *American Review of Reviews*, and though in later years the control of this had passed into the hands of Dr. Albert Shaw, Stead retained a financial interest in it. He was deeply interested in American politics and problems, as was shown by his "If Christ came to Chicago," "The Labour War in the United States," and other works. He had joined the Titanic in order to address a meeting in New York on "The World's Peace" and to take part in the "Men and Religion Forward Movement."

HIS INFLUENCE ON JOURNALISM.

The influence of W. T. Stead on daily journalism in England was great. He struck the personal note. He acclimatized the "interview." He developed the "crossheads." He extended the scope of the special article and the signed contribution. He introduced pictorial illustration. All these were the outward signs of the current of fresh vigour and greater vividness of presentment which were an expression of his personality. His taste was not impeccable; but he had at command a wealth of allusion, and he was a master of nervous, vivid language. He had a most ingenious and fertile mind; he was a subtle dialectician; and his copiousness was prodigious. He was accessible to all-comers, though a notice at the bottom of the stairs used to run, "As callers are many and time is short, the former are asked to economize the latter." His correspondence was enormous and he kept all his letters. He did not write shorthand—an idle feat in one possessed of an unusually retentive memory. He was beloved by all who worked with him, for he was always helpful and indulgent and his flow of good spirits was unfailing. His conversation was apt to be monologue, but he was a brilliant and most entertaining talker—full of vivacity, spontaneity, and picturesque phrasing. He was frankly egotistical; but he had a keen sense of fun, he enjoyed nothing more than a laugh at himself, and those who knew the man at closest quarters liked him best. His generosity was unbounded, and his death will be mourned by a large number of persons of all sort and conditions whom he had befriended, encouraged, and stimulated. He married Emma L. Wilson in 1873. His eldest son, a young man of much charm and promise, died a few years ago; but he leaves a widow, daughters, and other sons.

Chicago Daily Tribune
23rd November 1916

Jack London Dies Suddenly at His California Home

Uremic Poisoning Kills Noted Author; Life Thrilling One.

Santa Rosa, Cal., Nov. 22.—Jack London, best known of California's authors, died at his Glen Ellen, Cal., ranch near here at 7:45 o'clock tonight, a victim of uremic poisoning. London was taken ill last night and was found unconscious early this morning by a servant who went to his room to awaken him.

His condition at first alarmed his sister, Mrs. Eliza Shepard, who summoned physicians from this city.

From the time London was found this morning he did not regain consciousness.

Besides his sister, Mrs. Shepard, London is survived by a daughter, who is a student at the University of California; his mother, who lives in Oakland, Cal., and his wife, Charmion London. Mrs. London was at her husband's side when death came.

London would have been 41 years old on Jan. 12.

Lived Like His Heroes.

Mr. and Mrs. London recently returned from a sojourn of several months in the Hawaiian islands and have been living on their Glen Ellen ranch, one of the most elaborately equipped in northern California.

Mr. London's life was as adventurous and strenuous as those of the heroes of whom he wrote. Born in San Francisco in Jan. 12, 1876, he was educated in the public schools there and entered the University of California, but left it to go to the Klondike.

Even before this he had gone to sea before the mast and worked up to a master's degree, journeyed to Japan and joined seal hunting expeditions in the Bering sea, and tramped throughout the United States and Canada to study sociological and economic problems.

Was Newspaper Man.

He was correspondent for American papers in the Russian-Japanese war and in half a dozen or so of the Central American revolutions. Between times he found the opportunity to make several visits to the South Sea islands.

It was the lands visited on his travels which formed the background for all of his novels. Two of his earlier stories, "The Call of the Wild" (1903) and "The Sea Wolf" (1904), have been pronounced the most virile of his writings. A few novels had preceded these, a dozen or more followed them, and scores of magazine stories flowed from his pen.

First Wife Got Divorce.

Mr. London was married to Miss Bessie Maddern of Oakland on April 7, 1900, and it was only a few years until she obtained a divorce, the evidence being based mostly on the famous "Kempton Wade letters," in which Mr. London was a collaborator with Miss Anna Strunsky.

His second marriage was the result of a speedy romance, culminating in a ceremony at 10 o'clock at night, by which Justice J. J. Grant united Mr. London and Miss Charmion Kittredge of Newton, Ia., in his courtroom in Chicago, on Nov. 19, 1905. The first Mrs. London had obtained her divorce only that morning.

The couple started on their honeymoon in a forty foot yawl, without crew. After two years of wandering the couple abandoned the voyage at Sydney, N. S. W., when Mr. London became ill.

New York Times
20th July 1937

MARCONI IS DEAD OF HEART ATTACK

Wireless Inventor Succumbs at His Home in Rome at the Age of 63

HIS CAREER STARTED AT 21

He Patented His System in 1896 and Then Went From Success to Success

By The Associated Press.

ROME, Tuesday, July 20.—Guglielmo Marconi, inventor of the wireless, died unexpectedly last night of a heart attack at his home here. He was 63 years old.

At 21 Took Up Wireless.

Guglielmo Marconi's father wanted him to study music in Bologna after he was graduated from the university there in 1895, but the young man had grown interested in the practical possibilities of certain invisible electric waves. He had seen them demonstrated in the physics laboratory as the latest scientific curiosity. They passed through free space and acted on a detector at the other side of the room.

He was then 21, and was convinced that these waves which had been discovered seven years previously by Heinrich Hertz, thirty-one years after Clerk Maxwell had predicted them mathematically, could be used to transmit telegraphic dots and dashes over a distance without the use of wires.

He was right from the very beginning.

In 1895, with a spark coil as a sender of Hertzian waves and with a receiver invented some years previously by Edouard Branley of France and known as a coherer, he established the first radio station in his father's home in Pontecchio, near Bologna, and sent telegraphic messages more than a mile without wires.

He patented his system next year in London and demonstrated it for the British Postoffice Department over distances up to nine miles. He had no difficulty in finding backers in London, who organized Marconi's Wireless Telegraph Company, Ltd., in 1897.

The signal was to be the letter "S," which in Marconi's code is made by three dots; and it was to be sent in a definite time pattern to avoid mistaking any electrical disturbance for the signals.

In a howling gale on Dec. 12, 1901, Marconi sent up a kite which raised 400 feet of bare copper wire into the air as the antenna to intercept the message which other engineers said he could not send around the curved earth, across 1,700 miles of ocean.

Transatlantic Attempt Wins.

The first attempt was a complete success. There was no doubt about it. But Marconi waited until the next day and repeated the test, with the same success, before announcing to the world that transatlantic wireless communication had come into existence.

On both sides of the Atlantic the general public accepted the announcement with little excitement, under the apparent impression that the transmission of signals not confined to wires, but broadcast to the infinite, would have little or no effect on their lives.

Since then the date of this first transatlantic message has been elevated into the opening of a new epoch in human history, in which the world has been brought within the instant sound of a man's voice, whether it be a King, a Pope, a President, a dictator or an explorer flying over the Pole.

The development was rapid. The first ocean daily newspaper which is now a regular equipment of all liners was published on the Campania in 1904. When Marconi in 1907 announced that he was ready to establish commercial wireless between America and Europe, there was a sharp drop in cable shares. In 1910 Congress ordered all vessels of more than fifty passengers to carry wireless apparatus for sending distress calls.

Meanwhile, electrical engineers were rapidly filling in the technical apparatus of radio communication, and with the development of the radio tube, wireless messages which had been confined to the dots and dashes of the telegraphic code, became commercial telephone conversations about 1912, and broadcasting took its start experimentally with the World War.

Pope Broadcasts Message.

Thirty years after the first transatlantic message, the Pope, in February, 1931, addressed a broadcast message in Latin and Italian to the entire world.

Even before the World War, radio was a new world industry, and the courts of every nation were busy deciding patent suits and complaints of investors who felt they had suffered in some way or other during the radio boom.

Marconi, however, remained personally absorbed in the engineering side of radio, proceeding like his friend Edison to deal with the broad problems still to be solved or the advances to be made, such as static and short-wave transmission; with the help of the technical resources of the world in which radio engineering had become a separate profession.

The backers regarded it as an opportunity such as had not appeared since the American inventor, Samuel F. B. Morse, with a similar practical turn of mind, had taken the electromagnet out of the physics laboratory and given the world a telegraph and cable system of communications.

From Success to Success.

With the backing of his company, Marconi's development of wireless telegraphy proceeded from success to success. In 1898 he established wireless communication across the English Channel with France; the wireless was used in naval manoeuvres over distances up to seventy-four miles; and it had its first application in the sending of a rescue call at sea when the English lightship East Goodwin was run down by a liner. The lightship, which had been equipped with an experimental wireless set to communicate with the South Foreland Lighthouse, was able to send a wireless message for help to the lighthouse in time to have lifeboats sent to the rescue.

Marconi's results so far had been regarded by scientists as interesting, but not surprising. To them Marconi was and always remained simply an engineer making practical use of electrical science. To engineers, on the other hand, Marconi in 1900 seemed to have reached the effective limit of wireless when he telegraphed without wires through a distance of 150 miles.

Since his Hertzian waves traveled at the speed of light, they were assumed to have the characteristics of light, which could not be sent over the horizon to reach a receiver on the other side of the world.

Nevertheless the Marconi Company built for him a powerful station at Poldhu in Cornwall in 1900, and Marconi crossed the ocean to St. John's, Nfld., in 1901 to listen for the first transatlantic wireless message.

Not Bound by Theory.

His attitude toward theorists who were sure they knew what could not be done practically with a natural phenomenon was expressed then and re-stated at various times during his life. "I do not think it wise to believe in the limitations indicated by purely theoretical considerations or even by calculations," he said. "As we have learned from experience, they are often based on insufficient knowledge of all the relevant factors. I believe, in spite of adverse forecasts, in trying new lines of research, however unpromising they may seem at first."

He was 27 when he established himself with his receiving apparatus and two technical assistants, G. S. Kent and P. W. Paget, on top of Signal Hill outside St. John's Harbor, and cabled to his operator at Poldhu to start sending a set of signals according to a prearranged program at 11:30 A. M. and 2:30 P. M., Newfoundland time.

In 1930 he was responsible for directing the attention of radio engineers to the use of ultra-short waves, which had been neglected on the ground that they were too close to light and could not travel around the horizon. Within a few years he had demonstrated that they could be transmitted five times further than might be assumed with light waves, and were little affected by fading and static.

Most of his work was done on his floating laboratory, the steam yacht Elettra, on which he could place himself on the face of the ocean in experimental positions with respect to land stations terrestrial obstruction, fogs or whatever he was attacking.

He remained an optimist about what could be done with radio. His prediction of transatlantic telephony was thirteen years ahead of the accomplishment. He expected television by 1926, and he expected that power would be transmitted eventually by a directed radio beam.

Promised New Surprise.

In April, 1934, he startled his associates in London with an unexplained promise: "I hope to surprise you in a year or two as I surprised you by transmission across the ocean in 1901."

Honours were heaped on him beyond enumeration during his lifetime. In 1909 the Nobel Prize in Physics was awarded to him, as well as the Albert Medal of the Royal Society of Arts, and in the United States, the Franklin Medal.

In 1914 the King of Italy appointed him a Senator, an honour reserved by his country for the highest achievement.

In 1931, fourteen nations of the world joined in a broadcast celebration of the thirtieth anniversary of the new epoch which began with his first transatlantic message.

Marconi's life was devoted to radio. According to his own explanation in 1934, he took everything else on faith.

"There is no doubt," he said then, "that from the time humanity began to think, it has occupied itself with its origin and its future, which undoubtedly is the problem of life. The inability of science to solve it is absolute. That would be terribly frightening were it not for faith."

Although he was born in Italy, at Bologna, on April 25, 1874, he was a citizen of the world through his travels. His father was an Italian banker and his mother was Anna Jameson, an Irish woman. He spoke English as perfectly as Italian.

In 1906 he married the Hon. Beatrice O'Brien in London, and in 1924 was divorced by her under the laws of Fiume. He had the marriage annulled in 1927 by the Rota of the Roman Catholic Church and immediately married Countess Marie Bezzi Scali. At this ceremony his best man was Mussolini.

**The Times
22nd April 1872**

PROFESSOR MORSE.—Samuel Finley Breese Morse has passed away from among us ; he died on Tuesday evening, the 2d of April, at the ripe age of 81. Professor Morse's name will be for ever so closely associated with the development of the electric telegraph that we feel it our duty to give some notice, though it be a brief one, of his life. He was the son of the Rev. Jedediah Morse, well known as a geographer, and was born in Charlestown, Massachusetts, on the 27th of April, 1791. Samuel Morse was educated at Yale College, but, having determined to become a painter, he came to England in 1811, formed a friendship with Leslie, whose portrait he painted, and in 1813 he exhibited at the Royal Academy a colossal picture of " The Dying Hercules." He returned to America and endeavoured to establish himself as a portrait painter, but without much success, until in 1822 he settled in New York, and painted for the corporation a full-length portrait of Lafayette, who was then on a visit to the United States. We find Mr. Morse again in England in 1829, remaining here until 1832, when he returned to his own country. His companion on this voyage was Professor Jackson, the eminent American chymist and geologist, who was then returning from Paris, where the question of the time occupied in the passage of the electric current through a good conducting wire was occupying the attention of scientific men. From Dr. Jackson Mr. Morse appears to have first learnt that the passage of the electric fluid was absolutely instantaneous, and it occurred to him that it might be used for conveying intelligence from one place to another. The friends of Professor Morse claim for him that during the voyage he had written out the general plan of his telegraphic arrangement. In 1835 he certainly placed in the New York University a model of his " Recording Electric Telegraph," and in 1837 he filed his caveat at the Patent Office in Washington. It was not, however, until 1840 that the patent was perfected, and then Professor Morse set about getting his telegraph used. Four years, however, passed away before he succeeded, the first electric telegraph completed in the United States being the line between Washington and Baltimore, which began to work in 1844. Since that time the recording electric telegraph of Morse has been adopted over the whole country, and at the time of his death there were not less than 20,000 miles of electric wires stretching over the States between the Atlantic and the Pacific Oceans. Mr. Morse's first telegraph was a chymical one, the electric current being used to decompose the acetate or carbonate of lead, or turmeric paper moistened with a solution of sulphate of soda. He, however, gave up this arrangement, and adopted the electro-magnetic system instead. This was, however, in his hands, a rather ponderous affair, his electro-magnet weighing 158lb., and the instrument was not sufficiently delicate for long distances. Experience enabled Mr. Morse to simplify his arrangements, and his " Simple Morse Circuit " was thought to be so complete that in 1857 the French Administration of Telegraphs adopted the Morse instrument before all others. The " Morse Code," the " Morse's Transmitting Plate," his " Embosser," and Morse's telegraph worked by induction currents are sufficient to show how completely the American artist has connected his name with the system of employing electricity to pass as the messenger from man to man, over earth and under the sea.—Athenæum.

ABOLITION OF PASSPORTS.—The new regulations abolishing passports came into operation at the Channel Ports of France last Saturday. Among the first to enjoy this privilege were the passengers by the South-Eastern Company's packet Lord Warden, which arrived at Boulogne from Folkestone shortly before 11 a.m. Immediately on the steamer going alongside the quay she was boarded by two commissaires of police carrying a register, wherein each passenger had to sign his name and state his ordinary place of residence. This is rather a slow mode of proceeding, and, unless several registers are adopted during the travelling season, will cause a serious loss of time ; though infinitely better than the troublesome passport, with the loss of time, money, and temper involved in obtaining it.

LORD DALLING.—Our Malta Correspondent, writing on the 12th inst., says :—" Lord Dalling and Bulwer arrived here to-day by the Peninsular and Oriental Company's packet from Alexandria, and intends, it is understood, to make a stay of some weeks in Malta to recruit his health, which is still very delicate.

**The Times
23rd June 1952**

BRAILLE CENTENARY

REMAINS TRANSFERRED TO THE PANTHÉON

FROM OUR OWN CORRESPONDENT

PARIS, JUNE 22

The centenary of the death of Louis Braille, the blind inventor of the alphabet for the blind, has been celebrated here in a number of ceremonies during the past days, leading to-day to the transfer of his remains to the Panthéon. Braille's remains, except his hands, were taken from the cemetery of Coupvraye, near Meaux, where he was born in 1809, and buried after his death, and were brought to Paris yesterday. The hands were put back in the grave at Coupvraye after a Mass read in the parish church in the presence of the Bishop of Meaux, the local authorities, representatives of institutes for the blind from France and other countries, and members of Braille's family.

At the Sorbonne yesterday a solemn ceremony was held in honour of Braille, at which M. Ribeyre, Minister of Health, awarded the Legion of Honour to Miss Helen Keller, the American, now 72 years old, who at an early age became blind, deaf, and dumb, but has learnt to speak. Messages were read from Mr. Trygve Lie, Secretary-General of the United Nations, and Señor Torres Bodet, Secretary-General of Unesco. Miss Keller was among those who spoke.

To-day the remains of Braille were taken in procession from the Institute for Young Blind Persons in Paris, where they were brought yesterday, to the Panthéon. The procession was composed principally of blind men and women of all ages, led by the children from the institute. The President of the Republic and all the highest personages in the State were present and heard M. Ribeyre pay tribute to the work of Braille.

The New York Times
3rd May 1945

GOEBBELS BUILT UP LURID NAZI DOGMA

Little Man Who Inflated Hitler Legend Devised Technique to Sway the German Masses

In the unholy trinity of nazidom, Hitler was the prophet and leader, Himmler, the executioner, and Paul Joseph Goebbels, the propagandist.

Hitler proclaimed the principle of falsification as a legitimate instrument for the achievement of power. The greater the lie and the more often it is repeated the more certain it is to be believed, he taught. Goebbels put that principle into effect for nearly twenty years, with no inconsiderable success.

Untold millions of Germans could not walk, talk or sleep without falling under the influence of the diminutive club-footed "herr doktor." The successes that came to the Nazi movement and the sweeping victories that made Nazi Germany for a period master of the European continent seemed to attest to the truth of the Hitler-Goebbels sanctification of the lie. Until almost the very last moment Goebbels continued to tell the German people that German victory was certain and to feed their dwindling hopes with promises of new and marvelous secret weapons with which Germany would yet snatch triumph out of ruin and defeat.

All this was but an added manifestation of the contempt that he exhibited for the intelligence of the mass. He lied Germany forward to many triumphs and ultimately to destruction.

Jobless After World War I

Goebbels was a typical product of that period of hopelessness and confusion that gripped Germany in the years after World War I. He belonged to the category of ambitious, jobless, shiftless intellectuals who, unable to find a place for themselves in society, struck out on the road of amoral political adventurism, that led them to the pinnacle of power but ultimately to catastrophe—for them and their country. Only in that catastrophe did their deceived followers discover that the totalitarian doctrine of the end justifying the means was, after all, tragically erroneous.

Whether Goebbels himself had come to understand this before his death will, of course, remain a secret. The fact is that in the last weeks of the war in Europe, when he could no longer conceal from the German people the débâcle that had befallen them, he continued to lie, to maintain that even in defeat Germany would yet triumph.

During the Ruhr occupation he returned to the Rhineland, and led groups of Nazi students in resistance to the French occupation in the Ruhr. For this he was expelled by the French in the autumn of 1924. He moved to Elberfeld, where he became the editor of a small newspaper, the Voelkische Freiheit, and attracted the attention of local Nazi leaders. He soon became a popular platform speaker, for which rôle he had a great natural gift, and went about the small towns of the northern Rhineland haranguing the populace against the Weimar Republic, the Versailles Treaty and the Allied powers.

His more intimate association with the Nazi movement began a year later, when he met the brothers Gregor and Otto Strasser, who at that time directed the Nazi party in northern Germany in an effort to compete with the Socialists and Communists for the attention of the working masses. Goebbels became editor of the Strasser paper, Nazionalsozialistische Briefe. In accordance with the ideas of the Strasser brothers, his leading articles preached a kind of national bolshevism and called for a Socialist dictatorship.

Unlike Hitler, the Strasser brothers, who supplied the left wing element of Nazi ideology, were not hostile to Soviet Russia but preached the application of communism in Germany within a patriotic, national framework. Goebbels was strongly inclined to this type of nazism, so much so that he barely escaped in the Nazi purge of June, 1934, in which Gregor Strasser perished with hundreds of other Nazis, headed by Capt. Ernest Roehm, who had insisted upon putting into effect the more radical social program of nazism, in opposition to the army and the industrialists behind Hitler. What saved Goebbels was his agility in the art of changing fronts at the last moment. Instead of finding himself among the Nazi corpses in the purge he continued to live and function as Hitler's chief propagandist and gauleiter of Berlin.

Goebbels met Hitler in 1926 and came completely under his spell. By that time he had moved a long way from his old left wing idealism to Nazi cynicism. His letters to Hitler were a long paean of adoration. Hitler and Goebbels complemented each other.

Under Hitler's influence he developed the sinister, Mephistophelian power and capacity for demagogy with which he later moved millions to Nazi delirium. He broke with his former friends, deserted the Strasser brothers—as he was later ready to desert Hitler—and, in 1927, founded his paper, the Angriff.

It was an entirely new Goebbels who wrote the leading articles in the Angriff. He abandoned the scholarly, heavy style of his editorials in the Nazionalsozialistische Briefe and developed a vicious, vulgar, venomous pen.

His oratory, too, enhanced by a magnificent metallic voice, gained in power and effectiveness. Ultimately he came to be recognized as a speaker even superior to Hitler in the ability to move multitudes to wild, fanatical enthusiasm.

His articles bristled with libel and vituperation. The vehemence and hatred he breathed in word and print left one speechless by their audacity. He was repeatedly fined for libel but always returned to his method and style.

Chosen Berlin Leader

It was then that Hitler perceived in him the ideal leader for the party in the capital. Goebbels was ordered to Berlin. There, at the end of 1926, his political career began in earnest. He was appointed district leader, first for Berlin, and later for the entire province of Brandenburg.

In 1928, Goebbels was elected to the Reichstag, where he agitated against the Young plan. In 1930 he obtained re-election as the Nazi flood began to rise, a result for which he received much of the credit because of his speeches, writings and organizing ability. Two years later he was in the forefront of the fight for "Red Berlin," when he organized the first Nazi shop-cells, which soon spread throughout the Reich and ultimately were united in the Nazi Labor Front.

In many instances he personally directed Nazi hoodlumism against shows and films that he regarded as inimical to the national interests of Germany.

This thundering little intellectual in the big trench coat, with loose parchment skin and burning black eyes, demoniac and lecherous, contributed every bit as much as did Hitler to infect Germany with the Nazi paranoia. Like Hitler he was governed by the mania of his own greatness, and his contempt for others extended to his associates on the Nazi Olympus—Goering, Himmler, Ribbentrop and the German generals.

To his mind they were essentially mediocrities, for their ambition was limited to the enslavement or destruction of human bodies. His aim, as he saw it, was greater: to pervert and subject to his will the mind and soul of man. Because of his sinister influence upon the intellect and spirit of millions he was feared and hated even in his own party.

It was he who conceived the spectacle of the Reichstag fire, kindled with the aid of Goering and others in February, 1933, on the eve of a national election that was designed to enable Hitler to cloak his usurpation of power with the mantle of legality.

It was his mind, too, that gave birth to the obscene idea of the burning of books, the funeral pyres on which Nazi hoodlums, after the advent of Hitler to power, consigned to destruction in thousands of volumes the works of thinkers and poets of Germany and other countries.

Goebbels was the father of the Nazi national press law, promulgated on Oct. 4, 1933. It provided rules for admission to the newspaper profession and created courts for supervision over the work of journalists. By this law journalism in Germany became a government function. Although newspapers remained ostensibly in private hands they were subject to rigid censorship, guidance and direction.

Assumed Control of Culture

In November, 1933, Goebbels extended his dictatorship to the entire cultural life of Germany with the inauguration of the National Kultur Chamber, of which he named himself president. This body embraced seven subdivisions covering music, the graphic arts, literature, sculpture and painting, the stage, motion pictures and radio. Artists and cultural workers who were not found acceptable were debarred from membership and prohibited from functioning in the Third Reich. Many of them found their way to concentration camps.

Goebbels was at Hitler's side on all important occasions affecting domestic and foreign policy. At each succeeding crisis, with each act of Nazi aggression that ultimately led to the war, Goebbels' talents for perversion of the facts and deception of the people were put into full force, and his voice resounded over the radio second only to Hitler's in efforts to convince the German people that black was white and vice versa.

"All the rules of warfare are obsolete and must be thrown overboard," he cried. "All means are fair and permissible in the struggle against the terrible foe."

Such was the Nazi doctrine of which Goebbels was so ingenious and eloquent an exponent.

History has decided otherwise.

The Times
27th February 1899

BARON DE REUTER.

A Reuter telegram from Nice states that Baron de Reuter died there on Saturday morning in his 83rd year.

Baron Paul Julius de Reuter was the founder of the great international telegraphic news agency which bears his name. He was born at Hesse-Cassel in 1816. Entering commercial life when only 13, he remained for some years in the office of his uncle, but during this time he made the acquaintance of the telegraphic experimentalist Professor Gauss, whose influence upon the young man was destined to have great results. In this manner young de Reuter became associated with the beginning of practical telegraphy, and when the first line on the Continent—that between Aix-la-Chapelle and Berlin—began operations in 1849, he opened an office in the former place for the collection and transmission of news by telegraph, thus starting in humble fashion the organization which now has agents in every portion of the world. Difficulties at first were, of course, numerous, but by steady persistence and indomitable energy de Reuter speedily overcame them. Means had to be devised in order to establish regular communication between places not already connected by telegraph, and swift couriers, carrier pigeons, and the services of the railways were among the agencies by means of which the news was sent from one centre to another. The Press censorship and vexatious laws, which at that period handicapped newspaper development on the Continent, naturally hampered the enterprising spirit of the late Baron, and the fact that Great Britain was alone among the European nations to enjoy a free Press, coupled with the laying of the Dover and Calais cable, in 1851, decided him to transfer his chief office to London, where it has ever since remained. At first his efforts were chiefly centred on commercial intelligence ; but the inadequacy and incompleteness of the foreign news then published by most of the English papers afforded de Reuter an excellent opportunity to utilize his organized system—as yet only a few years old—in order to remedy this deficiency, and in 1858 he undertook to supply some half-a-dozen London morning newspapers with foreign telegrams. This was the day of small things, but the extension of the telegraph system at home and abroad was followed by a corresponding enlargement in the scope and methods of Reuter's Agency. His *clientèle* gradually increased, and the public soon came to depend upon the agency for prompt and trustworthy information of occurrences all over the world. Among the earliest of de Reuter's " hits " was the telegraphic account of the momentous interview between Napoleon III. and the Austrian Ambassador which plainly indicated war between the two empires.

It is difficult to realize the days when all American news had to come by mail. At this time everything possible was done by de Reuter to accelerate the transmission. Fast sailing yachts met the incoming steamers off the Irish coast and received on board the despatches, packed in hermetically-sealed boxes, which were immediately conveyed to Crookhaven, the nearest point on the Irish coast. Thence the news was telegraphed by way of Cork over some 60 miles of wire laid down by de Reuter himself in order to obtain the most rapid transmission to London. When President Lincoln was assassinated by Booth the mail had already left New York, but Reuter's correspondent chartered a swift steamer, overtook the mail boat, and got the news on board. It was a Reuter telegram which first gave England the tidings of the disaster at Isandlhana in the Zulu war, and our defeat at Majuba Hill by the Boers was likewise first learnt in this country through the same agency. But, in addition to so extensively using the telegraph system, de Reuter was himself instrumental in laying new lines. In 1865 he obtained from the Hanoverian Government a concession for the construction of a submarine telegraph line between England and Germany which enabled a through telegraphic communication to be made direct between London and the principal towns of his native country. He also acquired from the French Government the right to construct and lay a cable between France and the United States. This was laid in 1865 and was worked in conjunction with the Anglo-American Telegraph Company. Twenty-four years ago Baron de Reuter converted his agency into a limited liability company, retaining, however, the managing directorship. In 1878 he retired from this position, though he still continued as an ordinary member of the board. He was succeeded in the post of managing-director of the company by his son, Mr. Herbert de Reuter, another son, Baron George de Reuter, having also a seat on the board.

The untiring energies of Baron de Reuter were not exhausted by his labours in connexion with the news agency. In 1872 he was granted an important concession by the Shah of Persia, which gave him the exclusive privilege of constructing railways, working mines and forests, and making use of all the other natural resources of that country, as well as of farming the Customs. The Baron endeavoured to make this gigantic monopoly subservient to British interests, though without excluding other nations, but in consequence of difficulties placed in his way as the result of various intrigues the British Government interposed in his favour and the concession was annulled, de Reuter receiving instead the concession of the Imperial Bank of Persia.

Baron de Reuter's title was conferred upon him in 1871 by the then Duke of Saxe-Coburg and Gotha, in recognition of his public services. He married, in 1845, Ida, daughter of Mr. S. M. Magnus, of Berlin.

The Washington Post
13th October 1911

J. PULITZER IS DEAD

Editor and Publisher Succumbs on Board His Yacht.

END COMES UNEXPECTEDLY

Wife and Younger Son at Bedside When Editor Expires.

Funeral Will Be Held in New York City. Penniless After Service in Civil War, He Amassed a Fortune Estimated at $20,000,000—Blind During Last 20 Years of His Life—Spent Much Time at Sea, but Kept in Touch With Papers.

New York, Oct. 30.—Late one afternoon, 22 years ago, Joseph Pulitzer, then but 42 years old, was leaning on the rail of a yacht as the boat was standing out of the Bosphorus and into the Black Sea looking toward the setting sun through eyes which for years had been strained.

"Has the sun set so soon?" Mr. Pulitzer asked suddenly of his secretary.

"Not quite, Mr. Pulitzer," was the answer.

"Yes it has," the editor insisted. "It has for me."

Up to that moment Mr. Pulitzer had been able vaguely to distinguish various objects before him, although each day the persistent haze before him had been growing thicker. Now he was able only to tell vaguely daylight from night. And for the past 20 years—almost up to the moment of his death—he kept in constant touch with the morning and evening editions of his New York World and his Post-Dispatch, of St. Louis, personally, during his short and infrequent visits to Manhattan, and by telegraph or cable while cruising here and abroad on his yacht.

Mr. Pulitzer was born at Budapest, on April 10, 1847. During his childhood in Hungary he received some instruction from a private tutor, which was the sum total of his schooling. Forty-seven years ago he landed at Boston. A tall, lean emigrant, more than 6 feet in height, he came to New York with a 20-franc piece as his sole belongings. At the time of his death his wealth is estimated at more than $20,000,000.

Sought Army Career.

Two of his mother's brothers had been officers in the Austrian army, and one of them fought under Maximilian, in Mexico. Not long before young Pulitzer decided to emigrate to America he had run away from home to Paris to enlist in the foreign legion, but was rejected because even then his sight was defective. Next he tried to enlist in London, but was again rejected. In America, however, in 1864 enlisting officers were not so particular. In September of that year he joined the Federal army as a private in the First New York cavalry, popularly known as the Lincoln cavalry. He served with the army of the Shenandoah until honorably discharged at the close of the civil war.

He returned to New York then, where he found things so bad that he half decided to tramp to New Bedford to ship on a whaling vessel. The youth, still in his teens, one day, in the old French's Hotel, at Frankfort street and Park row, got into trouble with a porter in the hotel, from which young Pulitzer arose with wrath in his heart against Manhattan, and he started toward St. Louis. Twenty-two years later Mr. Pulitzer was able to write out a check for $630,000 to buy the hotel and its contents—old French's stood on a part of the ground now occupied by the Pulitzer building, which in after years Mr. Pulitzer liked to refer to as "my monument."

He arrived in St. Louis in February, 1866, penniless, and first got a job at Jefferson barracks, where he took care of sixteen army mules. For two years he was fireman on a river boat running between St. Louis and New Orleans. When he was not working he was haunting the reading rooms and reference rooms of the St. Louis public library. His sole amusement was chess. One night, in a German saloon, he played chess against Dr. Emil Preetorius, one of the editors of the Westliche Post, a German newspaper of St. Louis, and beat the editor. In 1868 he got a job on the Westliche Post as a reporter.

The first public fight of note which the young reporter took up was a pen campaign against corruption in the St. Louis county court. He won his fight, the court was abolished and reorganized under a form of government which still prevails there. Mr. Pulitzer, in November, 1869, entered St. Louis politics and was elected a member of the lower house of Missouri's general assembly. When he went to the State capitol he took up his work there, not only as a legislator, but as a special correspondent of the Post as well. Some of the things he wrote about while a legislator angered a St. Louis contractor, and a few days later led to a dispute between the contractor and reporter in the corridor of the Schmidt Hotel. After the contractor had "dressed him down" Pulitzer went to his lodgings, pocketed a revolver, and returned to the hotel to demand an apology. The contractor struck at Pulitzer and Pulitzer shot the man in the leg. He was indicted, pleaded guilty, and was punished with a fine of $100. Mr. Pulitzer had become managing editor of the Westliche Post in 1871, or when the paper broke with Grant. The Post, which now was somewhat of a local power, threw its sympathies with the liberal Republican movement. A small inheritance added to his savings helped him at this time to become part owner of the paper.

Out of the liberal Republican movement grew a campaign that resulted in the convention at Cincinnati in the spring of 1872 and the nomination of Horace Greeley for President. Pulitzer is credited with the strategy which forced Carl Schurz into the chairmanship. The newspaper man had become so much a political power that the convention came to be popularly known as the "Bill and Joe convention," after its two leaders, Joseph Pulitzer and William Grosvenor, at that time editor of the Missouri Democrat.

Made Speeches in German.

Mr. Pulitzer stumped the middle West for Greeley during the campaign, and made more than 70 speeches, most of them in German. Four years later when Carl Schurz and the Republicans once more were at peace, Mr. Pulitzer's campaign speeches were remembered, and he was chosen by the Democratic party as Schurz's opponent in debate on the stump. Mr. Pulitzer now was a Democrat.

Political beliefs made it impossible for Mr. Pulitzer and Carl Schurz, who was interested in the Post, to continue their newspaper relations. In 1875 Pulitzer sold his interests in the Post to Schurz and Dr. Pretorius. The following year Charles A. Dana selected Mr. Pulitzer to go to Washington to report for the Sun the proceedings of the electoral commission which had to do with deciding the Tilden-Hayes presidential election.

While in Washington Mr. Pulitzer married Miss Katherine Davis, a relative of Jefferson Davis. After his marriage, Mr. Pulitzer, with his bride, went to Europe as a special correspondent of the Sun. Upon his return to this country in the winter of 1878 Mr. Pulitzer went back to St. Louis.

Buys Two Papers.

The following year he bought at public auction the St. Louis Evening Dispatch for $2,500. His purchase he soon found was almost a white elephant, inasmuch as the plant contained no fuel, the presses were almost useless, and there was no paper on which to bring out the publication. Nevertheless, on the evening of the first day Mr. Pulitzer was able to get out 1,000 copies of the paper. Principally because he needed a newspaper plant, Mr. Pulitzer, who had brought out his first edition of the Dispatch on December 10, 1879, got hold of the Evening Post one day later, and on the evening of December 12 on the streets appeared the first issue of the Post-Dispatch.

The new paper was successful, and Mr. Pulitzer began to look toward New York. On May 10, 1883, he bought the New York World from Jay Gould. A presidential campaign was looming ahead, and Mr. Pulitzer launched into the fight to elect Grover Cleveland. During the campaign he received the nomination for Congress from the Ninth New York district, and he was elected. During this campaign the editor made his last speech in German. He resigned his seat in Congress three months after his election, gave his salary to charity, and returned to his editorial work.

In 1886 he purchased the Park Row property where the Pulitzer building now stands. The building, at one time the tallest in the world, was not finished until after Mr. Pulitzer had become totally blind.

Lived Aboard Yacht.

Of late years he had spent most of his days aboard his yacht, surrounded by a corps of readers and secretaries, who read the newspapers to him carefully and then carried out his orders. It was an ordinary occurrence for him to wake up his staff aboard the yacht at 3 or 3 o'clock in the morning to aid him in some work he had suddenly thought of.

Mr. Pulitzer, in 1903, endowed Columbia University with $1,000,000 for the establishment of a school of journalism, and he gave large sums to charity during late years, contributing especially to charities to aid the blind.

He leaves, besides his wife, three sons and two daughters. His oldest son, Ralph, is married to a daughter of Dr. Seward Webb. His other sons are Joseph, jr., and Herbert, a lad of 14, and his daughters are Edith and Constance. The second of his six children, Lucille, died in 1896.

New York Times
2nd November 1911

JOSEPH PULITZER LAID IN WOODLAWN

Services in the Reopened St. Thomas's Church and at the Graveside.

LAST LOOK AT HIS FACE

Employes and Old Friends See Him in His Coffin at His Home, a Copy of His Newspaper in His Hand.

Funeral services for Joseph Pulitzer, owner of The New York World and St. Louis Post-Dispatch, who died suddenly on his yacht, the Liberty, last Sunday off Charleston, S. C., were held yesterday at St. Thomas's Church, Fifth Avenue and, Fifty-third Street, and just before the early dusk of yesterday afternoon his body was buried in the Pulitzer family plot in Woodlawn Cemetery. The grave is just off Poplar Avenue, in the northern section of the cemetery.

A special train took the funeral party to Woodlawn. Members of the family, including Mr. Pulitzer's widow and his three sons, were accompanied by the close friends of the dead publisher, members of his personal staff and heads of the staffs of The Morning and Evening World. At the grave the Rev. Dr. Stires of St. Thomas's Church read the short ritual of the Protestant Episcopal Church from an improvised pulpit of canvas. The mound over the grave was heaped with wreaths and flowers. During the service the booming of the guns of the fleet in the Hudson came across the hills in solemn repetition.

The services at St. Thomas's Church were attended by a great many public officials and newspaper workers. Editors and managers of The World followed the pallbearers up the aisle. A company of former members of The World staff attended in a body. From the Newspaper Publishers' Association a committee of prominent publishers was present. Every newspaper in the city was represented by from one to half a dozen of its executives. Among other prominent citizens at the services were Borough President McAneny, District Attorney Whitman, Supreme Court Justices Gerard and Giegerich, ex-Judge Alton B. Parker, and W. B. Hornblower, Congressman William Sulzer, Fire Commissioner Joseph H. Johnson, and John D. Crimmins.

The pallbearers were Nicholas Murray Butler, Lewis L. Clarke, Col. George Harvey, Gen. John B. Henderson, Frederick N. Judson, Seth Low, St. Clair McKelway, Dr. James W. McLane, George L. Rives, and J. Angus Shaw.

When the coffin, heaped with orchids and lilies of the valley, had been borne up the aisle of St. Thomas's, opened yesterday for the first time since its rebuilding, a choir of fifty voices sang " Abide with Me," one of Mr. Pulitzer's favorite hymns. Dr. Stires read the Episcopal burial service. There was no mention of the life and career of Mr. Pulitzer.

The choir chanted " Lord let me know mine end and the number of my days," and then the rector read Chapter XV. of the First Epistle to the Corinthians, beginning: " Now is Christ risen from the dead and become the first fruits of them that slept." A second hymn was sung, " Lead, Kindly Light." The minister brought two wreaths from the altar and placed them on the coffin and the funeral procession passed from the church as the choir sang the recessional, " Hark, Hark, My Soul."

At the moment the funeral services were begun all the work in The World offices, as well as in the plant of The St. Louis Post-Dispatch was stopped. For five minutes the course of Mr. Pulitzer's two enterprises was checked in honor of the last rites that were being paid to him.

Throughout the morning yesterday the body of Mr. Pulitzer lay in the library of his home at 7 East Seventy-third Street and was viewed by a host of his employes and friends. The room was filled with flowers and the walls covered with the wreaths from friends, too many to mention in detail. Mr. Pulitzer lay with his right hand across his chest, clasping a copy of his newspaper.

The Grand Army of the Republic, of which Mr. Pulitzer was a member, held a special service at noon at the Pulitzer home. This was led by Gen. George Loud. Following this the procession of carriages was formed at the house and drove down Fifth Avenue to Fifty-third Street. The church is undergoing extensive repairs, which made the handling of the crowd more difficult than usual at large funerals. Twenty-five policemen were on duty around the church.

Telegrams of condolence were received by Mrs. Pulitzer in great number yesterday. Messages came, among others, from Henry Watterson, editor of The Louisville Courier Journal; Whitelaw Reid, American Ambassador to Great Britain, and Clarence H. Mackay. Former Vice President Charles W. Fairbanks sent this telegram:

" The country has lost one of its greatest newspaper men and able citizens in Mr. Pulitzer. Pray accept my profound sympathy and sorrow."

The Times
8th February 1878

POPE PIUS IX.

The long sufferings of the Pope, Pius IX., are at last at an end. We have outlived the longest and one of the most eventful Pontificates on record. The name of Pius IX. will probably be the last in the roll of the Pope-Kings, but it will be added to the number of the Pope-Saints—a high compensation, for the canonization of Roman Pontiffs has been an extremely unfrequent occurrence during the long lapse of centuries since Peter's successors added to the Bishop's mitre a Monarch's diadem. Pius IX. will take his place among the Pope-Martyrs by the side of the many of his predecessors who underwent persecution, waged home and foreign wars, were the victims of conspiracy and rebellion, made experience of dethronement, restoration, exile, and captivity, of the various vicissitudes to which earthly sovereignty is liable—all calamities partly owing to the storms of the transitional period in which it was his lot to live, but partly, also, the consequences of the rashness and waywardness of his own physical and moral temperament, and of his attempts at unpractical and dangerous innovation. He lived " to see the years of Peter," an unprecedented distinction, and hailed as miraculous, violating a rule to which time had given almost the consistency of a destiny, and portending, a change which marked the close of an exploded system and laid open the prospect of a new order of things. It was only as head of a Church, not as ruler of an ecclesiastical State, that Pius IX. exceeded his allotted span of 25 years, and thus broke the spell of that fatal tradition. It was no longer a temporal sovereignty that he, in compliance with the solemn oath taken at his accession, was able to hand down " intact " to his successor, but merely a spiritual dominion, to which he endeavoured to give a worldwide extension, and which he exposed to contests the issue of which will long be doubtful. A failure

as a prince, Pius IX. aspired to achieve transcendant success as a priest. With a mind of no breadth, and a character of no real firmness, he flattered himself that he could crown the edifice of which the genius of Hildebrand had laid the foundation. It was only when the sceptre broke in his hand and the Royal mantle fell from his shoulders that he put forth his claims to the authority of a King of Kings. His ambition rose in the same measure as his territory dwindled ; his pretensions expanded in proportion as his sphere of activity was limited.

Naturally joyous and buoyant as was his disposition, the Pope was, however, subject to fits of sudden irritability, touchy and impatient, and above all things he was resentful of any presumption on his condescension, any approach to disrespect towards his person or dignity. He was easily ruffled by direct and frank contradiction. If it came to any divergence of views, who should know better than the Infallible ? His instincts tended to goodwill to all men, and in youth he had friends ; but there was something indiscriminate and somewhat instable in his affections, and, after his elevation, he was too full of himself to be capable of much expansion to other men. It was attested to his credit that he was free from the besetting sin of other Popes ; he was no Nepotist ; but it is well to observe that, after his return from Gaëta, it was not he who would not befriend and promote his relations ; the estrangement was owing to his brothers, who condemned his reactionary policy, and would not come near him. On the Throne Pius IX. found solitude. That same necessity of his position which compelled him to put up with men whom he feared, like Antonelli, closed his heart against those whom he might have felt prompted to love.

On the other hand, he was severe and even terrible to those who had justly or unjustly incurred his displeasure ; but it must be said, in justice to him, that the implacability of his enmity arose from his consciousness of his unerring judgment, and from the conviction that opposition to him was as unpardonable a sacrilege as rebellion to Heaven.

New York Times
24th January 1897

SIR ISAAC PITMAN'S CAREER

Life Work and Studies of the Great Originator of the System of Phonography.

HE WAS A TIRELESS WORKER.

His Devout Religious Feeling — A Clean and Orderly Printing Office — How He Cured His Indigestion — A Great Lover of Music.

Thousands of men and women in all parts of the world are to-day earning their livelihood through means furnished by the labors of Sir Isaac Pitman, the originator of phonography. Sir Isaac devoted his whole life to it, and, although he worked hard he made very little money.

Pitman was born at Trowbridge, in Wiltshire, on Jan. 4, 1813, and was the third child of a family of eleven children. He was educated at a small school in his native town, and left there to earn his own living when thirteen years of age. Isaac was a religiously disposed youth, and was brought up as a Baptist, his mother being a devout members of that denomination. Pitman's father took a great deal of interest in the studies of his children, and a good instructor was engaged to teach the four elder children music.

The piano was then beginning to supersede the harpsichord, and after acquiring some proficiency in fingering on the old-fashioned triangular harpsichord, the children were rewarded with a 5½ octave piano.

Thank Offering for a Piano.

Isaac was so overjoyed with the opportunity of playing on this instrument, which he regarded as a gift from Heaven, that he saved up his pocket money until it amounted to 5s., and dropped it in the collection box at Zion Chapel as a thank offering.

On leaving school Isaac became a junior clerk in the office of the factory of which his father was manager. He was at his desk at 6 o'clock every morning, and while there improved his mind by reading books on music and literature. One of his favorite books was Watts's "Improvement of the Mind," and he always believed that this work had a great influence in the formation of his habits and character. Another favorite work was Lennie's Grammar. When twelve years old he began to copy choice pieces of poetry and portions of Scripture into a little book which he kept in his pocket, for the purpose of committing them to memory. One book, dated May 31, 1825, contains extracts from Pope, Milton, Cowper, Montgomery, the Psalms, and Isaiah, interspersed with the Greek alphabet, the signs of the zodiac, arithmetical tables, and other items of useful information.

While he greatly increased his knowledge of books, he was at fault with regard to the pronounciation of words. He was conscious of this defect, and to correct it studied Walker's Dictionary. In this study he saw the scientific classification of the sounds of the language and discovered the defects of the common alphabet, and the glaring inconsistencies and absurdities of the current orthography, on which he was destined in after years to make so determined an onslaught.

In 1829 he studied Taylor's system of shorthand. That year he became a clerk for his father, who had gone into business for himself, and two years later gave up his clerkship for a position as schoolteacher at Barton-on-Humber.

Work of Bagster's Bible.

An incident occurred at Barton in 1835 which illustrated Pitman's industry and love of accuracy. While conducting the services at the Methodist Chapel, he borrowed a copy of Bagster's Comprehensive Bible, and he set himself the task of reading it carefully with all the marginal notes and references. He found fifteen errors in the references in the Old Testament, and wrote to Mr. Bagster, pointing out some of the mistakes. He told Mr. Bagster he made it a custom to read a portion of Scripture every morning and evening, and that if Mr. Bagster would let him have a copy of his Bible he would give him the benefit of the corrections and mistakes he might discover in reading it through. Mr. Bagster accepted the offer and sent the Bible. The magnitude of the task may be seen from the fact that the marginal references in Bagster's edition number 5,000. Pitman accomplished his task in three years.

He next devoted his studies to stenography, and at the suggestion of Mr. Bagster, instead of trying to improve the old systems, compiled a new one. His first manual was published in 1837, and in 1839 the first edition of 3,000 copies was exhausted.

The agitation for the penny post was then at its height. The Government offered a prize of £200 for the best method of collecting the fees for prepaid letters. Among the competitors was Isaac Pitman. In September, 1839, he submitted to the Lords of the Treasury a proposal to collect the postage by means of stamps.

Lectures on Shorthand.

Three years later Pitman began to lecture on his shorthand system. He had large and attentive audiences and made many converts. Very early in his crusade he proposed that the phonetic principle, a sign for a sound, should be also applied to the common reading alphabet, and that words be spelled as they are pronounced. The demand for Pitman's works increased so rapidly that in December, 1845, he moved his printing office from Bath to London. There at first he not only compiled the various works published, but often worked as a compositor, read all his proofs, kept his books, and conducted his own correspondence. His regular hours were from 6 A. M. until late at night. His habits were methodical in the extreme, and his mode of living was strictly temperate, if not abstemious. He rigidly abstained from intoxicants and from flesh diet, and never smoked. He gave his reasons for adopting vegetarianism in a letter which appeared in The London Times on Feb. 6, 1879. The letter was written and printed in reformed spelling. Mr. Pitman said: "Above forty years ago dyspepsia was carrying me to the grave. Medical advisers recommended animal food three times a day, and a glass of wine. I was nothing bettered, but rather grew worse. I avoided meat and wine gradually, recovered my digestive power, and have never since known, by any pain, that I have a stomach." Then he told of the active life he led and his custom of rising at 6 o'clock each morning, although sixty-six years of age; of never having taken a holiday until he was fifty, and having worked fourteen hours a day for several years. "I attribute my health and power of endurance," he concluded, "to abstinence from flesh meat and alcoholic drinks."

He Loved Music.

Mr. Pitman was a great lover of music, and in 1859 during the discussion on the subject of uniformity of musical pitch he drew up a table showing the number of vibrations of each note in comparison with every other note in the octave. In his youth he indulged his love of harmony so far as to compose a hymn tune and an anthem on Isaiah, xlix, 13-17. The day of cheap music had not arrived, and Pitman copied many musical works. His manuscript books still exist, and are models of neatness and accuracy.

His printing office was unlike any other known office. Everything in the room was scrupulously neat and everything had its place. Mr. Pitman occupied a desk in the middle of the room, and there wrote all his articles and conducted his correspondence. He always commenced his letters in the ancient style: "From Isaac Pitman to Mr. or Mrs. ——, or Miss ——," and closed the letter with the simple word, "Farewell." He was a strict disciplinarian. No talking was allowed in the office. He saw no company, seldom dined from home, or paid visits, and was first in his office in the morning and last to leave at night. He had no love for money, except for its uses in promoting his ends. He had a governing and despotic temper, and in all things took his own way.

Writing once on the advantages of shorthand and the trouble of reading bad writing, he said: "I find I can decipher writing made up of undercurves if the dots or jots are placed over i and j, but writing that consists of wider curves only is hopelessly illegible. As a bad servant is said to be the greatest plague of life domestic, so bad writing may be called the greatest plague of literary and commercial life. Not infrequently I receive letters the signatures of which I am utterly unable to decipher. In such cases I cut out the name, gum it on my reply, and hand over the puzzle to the Post Office."

He Made Little Money.

There was not much money in shorthand. When telling of his work in 1867, he said from 1887 to 1843 he gained nothing, but spent all the proceeds of his lectures in extending the circulation of his books. From 1843 to 1853 his income did not exceed £80 a year. It was £100 during the next five years and £150 for the next three.

In 1875 Pitman and other citizens of Bath formed themselves into a committee to establish a free library in the City of Bath. The effort was successful and a library of 9,000 volumes, of which 2,000 were presented by Mr. Pitman, was established. It did not last long, because the Burgesses would not raise the money for its maintenance.

The jubilee year of phonography was 1887 and an international congress of shorthand writers was held in London. The chief feature of this jubilee celebration was the unveiling of a bust of Pitman.

Isaac Pitman was knighted by the Queen in 1894 and was in his eighty-fifth year at the time of his death. He always thought he would live to be an old man. Speaking in 1848 in Nottingham, he said: "I am now thirty-five years old. I hope through the Divine mercy I may reach the age of eighty, and in the forty-five years of this period yet to come I fully expect to see phonetic printing so far established that a return to unphonetic spelling will be impossible."

New York Herald Tribune
2nd February 1966

Hedda Hopper At 75

The most famous don't-invite-'em pair in the history of female gossip columnists—to use a term coined by another columnist, Walter Winchell (male)—were known to millions as Louella Parsons and Hedda Hopper.

Their feud was almost as long-lasting and more understandable than the historic one of the mountaineer Hatfields and McCoys, which was lost in family obscurity.

Hedda and Louella didn't use guns; they used hatpins, which sometimes took on the proportions of harpoons. They aimed these weapons with malice and profit, less at each other than at the Hollywood colony, about whom they wrote trivia.

Both were indefatigable in collecting tittle-tattle about actors and actresses, ungrammatical in writing, and richly rewarded for their effort.

FEARED

Practically every member of the movie colony feared rather than respected both. Nobody dare give an item of gossip, quaintly called a "scoop" by the columnist, to one, for fear of incurring the wrath of the other.

Both got their professional name from husbands.

Hedda was married only once, to comedian De Wolf Hopper, who died in 1935. They had a son, Bill, who became an actor, as his mother was an actress before she turned Hollywood gossip columnist.

Louella was the senior in age and gossiping, and she gave up first. She retired last Dec. 1 at 82, after 40 years in the business.

But Louella outlived her younger rival. She was still living in a nursing home in California, when Hedda Hopper, 75, went to Cedars of Lebanon Hospital in Hollywood in a critical condition with pneumonia.

PNEUMONIA

Hedda, who worked to the last, died there yesterday of what was described as double pneumonia with heart complications. She had been taken ill on Friday.

Her death was announced by her son, who plays the part of private detective Paul Drake in the Perry Mason TV show. Also at the hospital at the time were a niece, Mrs. Jane Miller, and a few close friends.

The famous feud between the two columnists was more professional than personal, and was promoted by countless stories in magazines and other newspaper columns. Actually, though they didn't exactly like each other, they didn't hate each other and preserved the amenities, exchanging "hellos" when they rarely met.

BOOK

Life magazine reported in April, 1963, that when word got around Hollywood that Hedda Hopper was doing a book, Louella Parsons telephoned in a frenzy to ask what it would be about. "I'm just going to tell the truth," said Hedda. "That's exactly what I was afraid of," Louella said, and hung up.

After "The Whole Truth and Nothing But" came out (Hedda had previously written "From Under My Hat" in 1952), the author told Life: "I saw Louella after the book came out, quite by accident

coming out of Saks as she was coming up the steps on the arm of her nurse. I said, 'Hello, Louella,' and she looked straight ahead. 'Did you hear me, Louella?' I repeated, raising my voice. 'I heard you,' she said and continued walking. That's how I know she read the book."

Many of the millions of gossip gobblers had difficulty distinguishing between the two, except for one thing. Hedda was the one with the hats—magnificent, ridiculous, wholly undescribable hats. A favorite Hollywood gag was this alleged test of sobriety, repeating:

"Hedda Hopper has a horde of hooted hats; a horde of hooted hats has Hedda Hopper."

Also, Hedda was the one who did a weekly radio network show for years, and had a monthly screen magazine column (turned out by a ghost writer, unlike her newspaper column for the Chicago Tribune-New York News Syndicate).

The Saturday Evening Post reported eight years after Hedda started a column and was considered an upstart by the old-timer Louella (called "Lolly," in affection or derision, depending upon whether the nickname user was a friend or foe):

"Hedda Hopper is sometimes described as an actress trying to be a columnist . . . and Louella Parsons as a columnist trying to be an actress."

MOVIES

The writer concluded that the evidence seemed to favor the indomitable Miss Hopper, because in her few appearances in the movies Louella was a little shaky in the acting department, whereas Hedda "has tasted sweet success in both fields." Among her pictures were "Virtuous Wives," "Sherlock Holmes," "Don Juan," "Mona Lisa," "Life With Henry," "Reap the Wild Wind" and "Sunset Boulevard."

Born Elda Furry in Hollidaysburg, Pa., the daughter of a meat dealer, Hedda Hopper was never graduated from

grammar school. She came to New York and did a little of everything from appearing in an opera chorus to singing in a road version of a Broadway hit before her marriage to Mr. Hopper. She changed her first name to Hedda in an effort to disassociate herself from his four previous wives, named Ella, Ida, Edna and Nella.

She was "discovered" as a columnist by the late Alicia Patterson, long before the latter founded Long Island's Newsday. The publisher listened to Hedda talk at a party at the San Simeon ranch of another rival publisher, William Randolph Hearst, and concluded that anyone who could talk that glibly about Hollywood would make a good columnist. She offered her $50 for a weekly letter, but Hedda dropped it shortly when the rate of payment was dropped to $35 a week. She was offered a job by a small syndicate with 17 newspaper clients.

"But I can't spell," she protested.

"Get a secretary who can," the syndicate agent advised.

COLUMN

She did, and always dictated her column in a frenzied voice, as though she was broadcasting from a burning roof. She had a staff of five (including an editor who was permitted only to correct shaky grammar) by the time she was syndicated in less than 10 years to 110 metropolitan dailies and earning $200,000 a year.

She made many bloopers in her gossip items, some embarrassing (such as an expected birth by an actress not married) but she passed them off glibly and without apology.

She was fair to the movie industry after her fashion, never revealing trade secrets such as camera tricks, resisting pressure to give favorable publicity to bad pictures, being a sucker once but seldom twice to a press agent, and never paying for news tips.

The Times
28th August 1879

HOUSE OF LORDS.
WILLIAM JOYCE'S APPEAL DISMISSED
JOYCE v. DIRECTOR OF PUBLIC PROSECUTIONS

Before the LORD CHANCELLOR, LORD MACMILLAN, LORD WRIGHT, LORD PORTER, *and* LORD SIMONDS.

The House, by a majority of four to one, Lord Porter dissenting, dismissed the appeal of William Joyce from the judgment of the Court of Criminal Appeal dismissing his appeal against his conviction at the Central Criminal Court before Mr. Justice Tucker on September 19 on the third count of an indictment charging him with high treason.

The third count charged that Joyce, while a person owing allegiance to the Crown, was guilty of high treason by adhering to the King's enemies elsewhere than in the King's realm between September 18, 1939, and July 2, 1940, by broadcasting to the King's subjects propaganda on behalf of the said enemies, contrary to the Treason Act, 1351.

The first two counts were not proceeded with because they alleged that Joyce at the time of the offence charged was a British subject. After evidence on the question of nationality had been given Mr. Justice Tucker said that the evidence was overwhelming that Joyce was not a British subject.

Mr. G. O. Slade, K.C., Mr. Derek Curtis Bennett, K.C., and Mr. J. Burge appeared for Joyce ; the Attorney-General (Sir Hartley Shawcross, K.C.) and Mr. Gerald Howard for the Crown.

The LORD CHANCELLOR to-day said : I have come to the conclusion that the appeal should be dismissed. In common with the rest of your Lordships, I should propose to deliver my reasons at a later date.

LORD MACMILLAN.—I agree.

LORD WRIGHT.—I also agree.

LORD PORTER. In agreement with all your Lordships, I think that the renewal of his passport, which Joyce obtained on August 24, 1939, was evidence from which the jury might have inferred that he retained that document for use up to September 18 of that year, when he was proved to have first adhered to the King's enemies, and might therefore have inferred that he continued to owe allegiance to the Crown up to that date. As, however, in my view, the question whether he did so retain it was never left to the jury, but they were directed as a matter of law that his duty of allegiance was extended to the later date, and as your Lordships cannot send the case back for retrial, I would myself allow the appeal on that ground.

LORD SIMONDS.—I concur in the opinion given by my noble and learned friend on the Woolsack.

Solicitors. Messrs. Ludlow and Co. ; Director of Public Prosecutions.

The Times
15th August 1922

The death of LORD NORTHCLIFFE, which we record with deep sorrow this morning, is an event of more than national import. To the staff of this journal, of which he had been the chief proprietor for some fourteen years, it is a severe domestic bereavement ; but to tens of millions, in the British Empire and abroad, it implies a loss such as is felt only when a great human figure passes away. LORD NORTHCLIFFE'S greatness, and, indeed, his genius, are beyond question. To his personality none who came into touch with him could be indifferent. Many it attracted, some it repelled, but all felt its power. Yet his energy, his "drive," and, on occasion, his vehemence, were merely the most conspicuous of his many remarkable qualities. More truly characteristic of him was what he often called his "sixth sense," the faculty of divining the course of things, the instinctive insight that enabled him not only to apprehend but to feel, as present realities, events still in the making. Imagination he had, in unusual degree ; yet by no effort of imagination could he have realized, as he did realize, the growing German danger long before it was apparent to others, or have foreseen, as he foresaw, the fateful choice with which it would confront the British Empire.

To the Empire he was devoted heart and soul. The knowledge of Imperial questions and the keen interest in the welfare of the Dominions that he showed during his recent journey round the world, were the outcome of protracted inquiry and thought. Hardly less intense was his realization of the need for relations of the most cordial frankness between Great Britain and the United States. He knew the American Union from ocean to ocean and from North to South. In a score of visits, he had gained a personal knowledge of Americans which few Englishmen could rival. The secret of "getting on" with Americans he guessed instinctively. He liked them. They knew it, and returned his liking. His death severs a strong personal link between the public opinion of this country and that of the United States.

If, in Europe, he had a marked predilection for any country but his own, it was for France. Of Spain he was fond, and of Italy ; but France held an abiding place in his affections. The keenness of French minds appealed to him, while, in the first decade of this century, the vigour and dash of the French pioneers in motoring and in aviation aroused his eager admiration. It was this side of the French character that drew him to France, even before his growing realization that French and British political necessities are, in their larger aspects, identical, led him wholeheartedly to support the policy of the Entente.

His work in and for France, during the war and after, was but the expression of a deep, though by no means a blind, conviction that the welfare of France is inseparably bound up with that of Great Britain. In him France loses a tried friend.

Yet deepest and beyond compare was his passion for England. Scotland he esteemed and admired : Ireland, the country of his birth, he loved and understood, but England was the home of his heart. The patient, long-suffering, slow-witted Englishman, sure of instinct and sparing of speech, seemed to him the rock upon which the British Empire stands. The very differences between his own character and that of a typical Englishman did but enhance his appreciation of typical English qualities. He was one of those men who, while working for England to the best of their ability, understand that if England is to be in the future what she has been in the past, the insularity of the bulk of her sons needs constantly to be qualified by a wider vision than can be acquired in these islands, and by the inculcation upon the people of considerations and points of view which are not native to them. Few men, if any, knew as well as he how to impress the public. A born journalist, skilled in every detail of his craft, quick to grasp the essentials of any position and to express them in a few striking words, he divined the mental processes of a generation, mainly devoid of classical education ; and, in unconscious accordance with an old Scholastic principle, he fashioned the ideas he wished to propagate so that they might fit the shape of the intended recipient. If his first appeal was to the multitude rather than to an intellectual aristocracy, if he taught by iteration of simple formulas rather than by stately and measured argument, who shall gainsay the contention that these are, in modern circumstances, the least ineffective means of reaching the minds of the masses which, in the last resort, control democracies ? Of his own short-

comings he was often acutely conscious. To the end of his life he regretted that the circumstances of his impoverished youth, when he fought and won a very gallant struggle against adversity, should have deprived him of opportunities he might otherwise have enjoyed. His sense of humour, which was always keen, frequently prompted him to laugh at himself, not always slyly ; but, in his way, which was emphatically the way of a genius, he felt he had a mission, and, by the means which he thought best, he sought to fulfil it.

The struggles of his youth doubtless convinced him that poverty is best avoided. When, as the reward of enterprise and hard work, wealth came to him, he used his wealth not so much for himself as for the promotion of ends in which he believed. Weak as was the appeal which vague philanthropy made to him, firm as was his conviction that success is usually a sound test of the practical worth of ideas, he yet spent his wealth lavishly in the promotion of public interests and in the encouragement of tendencies that he thought useful to the nation. In every respect, his patriotism was intense. It was as passionate in regard to technical and special forms of progress as in relation to the more general aspects of public welfare. The early development of the motor-car and of aviation in this country was largely due to him. Thanks to his energy and vision, obstacles to progress were more speedily overcome than they could have been without the stimulus of his example and his outlay. He was among the first to perceive the potentialities of the submarine. Wireless telegraphy and telephony appealed to him both as useful discoveries in themselves and as marking fresh triumphs of human thought in the uncharted regions of space. For all his positiveness of mind, a sense of the mystery of the universe was ever with him. He believed in the reality of things unseen, however pertinaciously he concentrated his active attention upon things concrete and tangible.

Though his party politics were mainly Conservative, his tendencies were emphatically Liberal. His sympathy with the working classes was profound, and in a hundred practical directions he sought to raise the conditions of their lives and to remove restrictions upon the freedom of their development. Age matured some of his earlier opinions without changing the affectionate warmth of a very affectionate nature. While he appeared prone to impetuosity in action and sometimes impatient of arguments that ran counter to his instinctive perceptions, he acquired a degree of cautious and constructive wisdom that was rare among men of his dynamic temperament. Scornful of incompetence, contemptuous of those who attributed base or merely vindictive motives to him, pertinacious in the pursuit of policies but ever ready to consider new facts, he was often as incomprehensible to opponents as he was open-minded to his friends.

Not until the outbreak of the war did he give the full measure of his remarkable powers. He had long foreseen and foretold the struggle. He had done his utmost to prepare the country and the Empire against the day when they should have to defend in arms their very existence. When it came he threw himself into the war and into the waging of it with all the strength of his being. No effort was too strenuous, no fatigue too great for him. His impatience of men who did not " understand the " war " was often fierce, and found fierce expression ; but none who watched him close at hand, or who worked by his side during those years of strain and endeavour, could doubt that his one thought was how best to mobilize and organize the resources of the country and of the Empire for the supreme object of victory.

During his mission to the United States in the summer and autumn of 1917 he laboured with an intensity that undermined his constitution, and unquestionably shortened his days. He found our supply agencies in the United States in a chaotic condition, and left them organized. The anxiety he felt at the perilous shortage of oil supplies for the British Fleet and his successful efforts to obviate the danger told perceptibly upon him. When, at the beginning of 1918, he accepted the Directorate of Propaganda in Enemy Countries, after having declined suggestions that he should join the Cabinet, he devoted unsparingly his reserves of health to the supervision of the work carried out by an exiguous staff of experts whom he himself had selected. No account of the Great War and of the Allied Victory can be complete without reference to the important part he played in it as a patriotic citizen, a devoted public man, and a great journalist.

In the history of this journal his name can never be forgotten. One of the ambitions of his early life—no mean ambition—was to control it. He believed in it as a national institution of which the potency for good must in large measure depend upon its power to keep abreast of public movements and changes in current modes of thought. He sought, with a patience exemplary in a man of perceptions so quick and of impulses so strong, gradually to mould and adapt it rather than to revolutionize its traditions. With every phase of its growth he was intimately acquainted. Many an " innovation " was in reality a recession to practices and principles of an earlier day. He sought to widen its appeal, to increase its influence, and to maintain it as a pioneer rather than as a merely conservative element in British journalism. He respected the individuality and the traditional liberty of its Editors, with whom he conferred rather as an experienced colleague than as a proprietor. Of his success our readers may judge ; but neither they nor the nation at large can speak with full knowledge of LORD NORTHCLIFFE's devotion to *The Times*, or of the strength and sincerity of his desire that, when he should cease to control its fortunes, it should continue to stand in undiminished vigour as a main bulwark of independent opinion and of freedom of speech in a country whose institutions are based upon respect for both. Of him it may be said that, with his virtues and his faults, his achievements and his errors, he was a man in the full sense of the word, a man, moreover, animated by high public spirit, and inspired by a strong sense of public duty.

In bidding, with sorrowing hearts, a last farewell to LORD NORTHCLIFFE, their chief and friend, the staff of *The Times* extend deep sympathy to his aged mother, his devoted wife, and to his bereaved family. The memory of his work for the great journal they serve, and of his unremitting care for the public interests it seeks to foster, will be to them a standing injunction not to falter in the discharge of the duty they owe to themselves and, through *The Times*, to the nation and the Empire.

Chicago Daily Tribune
15th August 1951

HEARST'S SONS PLAN TO CARRY ON HIS EMPIRE

Publisher Dies at 88 in California Home

" The world has lost its greatest publisher-editor, and America has lost one of its most outstanding citizens and patriots," Mackay said. " His associates have lost a great leader, and a kindly and true friend. It will be a long time before we see his equal."

Tribute from Hoover

Many other tributes were paid to the publisher today. Former President Hoover said:

"William Randolph Hearst was the most powerful individual journalist in his day. His positive views, his trenchant expression, and his enormous circulation alone warrants that statement. He, however, was more, for he built a great newspaper empire that has endured and will continue to be the most potent force in American life."

Gen. Douglas MacArthur said:

"I have been shocked and deeply grieved to learn of the death of Mr. Hearst. His voice has for so long been a mighty one in defense of America's freedom that his loss is indeed national."

Newspapers published under the

Hearst banner are the Chicago Herald-American, the New York Journal-American, the New York Mirror, the Detroit Times, the Milwaukee Sentinel, the Boston American, the Boston Record, the Boston Sunday Advertiser, the Pittsburgh Sun-Telegraph, the Baltimore News-Post, the Baltimore Sunday American, the Los Angeles Examiner, the Los Angeles Herald and Express, the San Francisco Examiner, the San Francisco Call-Bulletin, the Albany Times-Union, the San Antonio Light, and the Seattle Post-Intelligencer.

The Hearst magazines are Cosmopolitan, Good Housekeeping, Harper's Bazaar, Town and Country, House Beautiful, Motor, Motor Boating, the American Druggist, and Connoisseur, a quarterly published in England.

The Hearst enterprises also operate the American Weekly, a Sunday newspaper supplement; the International News Service, a world wide news gathering and disseminating service; King Features Syndicate, and three radio stations.

At its peak prior to 1938, the Hearst publishing empire comprised 24 newspapers in 17 of the country's largest cities, and 13 magazines, including four published in England. Hearst had an estimated 38,000 persons on his payrolls in the 1920s and early 1930s.

Owned Huge Ranches

He owned huge ranch properties in California and Mexico and had large real estate holdings in New York. He owned the Homestake gold mine in South Dakota and other mines in Mexico and Peru. For years he was the biggest collector of art objects and antiques in the nation and amassed a collection on which he is estimated to have spent 35 million dollars.

Most of the art treasures Hearst spent half a lifetime collecting were sold at auctions here and abroad, many of them taken directly from warehouses where they had been stored after purchase. Among these was an 11th century Spanish monastery brought from Spain in 10,000 packing cases by special steamer in 1923 at a cost of more than $500,-000. This was sold for an undisclosed price after Hearst agents had offered to dispose of it for $19,000.

Hearst became a movie producer during the 1920s. He formed International Films to star Miss Davies in several feature pictures. Miss Davies, a former Ziegfeld Follies beauty and a model for Howard Chandler Christy, became one of the stars of the silent screen while working for Hearst.

The Hearst publishing interests climbed back to financial health in the early 40s. Hearst, who never relaxed editorial control of his properties, resumed business control under a regency arrangement set up by him from among his executives and advisers.

Hearst disposed of large portions of his real estate holdings but retained the glamorous parts of his palatial Wyntoon estate in California and his regal San Simeon ranch, a place of legendary splendor, in the same state.

Occupies 240,000 Acres

San Simeon occupies 240,000 acres overlooking the Pacific along a 50 mile crest of hills midway between Los Angeles and San Francisco. Bison, zebra, kangaroos, and other animals — a private zoo — roamed the hillsides. The manor house, which contains such treasures as the bed of Cardinal Richelieu and six Gobelin tapestries, has been valued at 15 million dollars.

Hearst took a deep interest in both national and international affairs. The latter subject preoccupied him to an increasing extent in the last two decades in his life. He was an uncompromising foe of internationalism and insisted on the United States keeping clear of foreign entanglements, including the United Nations.

He fought every proposal of American entry into a league of nations or for American adherence to a world court. He opposed every move to scale down or cancel the allied war debts of World War I., and his newspapers cried out against all of the steps which led the United States along the road to World War II. He hated communism and fought all manifestations of Russian influence in American life.

Expelled from France

Hearst was expelled from France on Sept. 1, 1930, while visiting Paris. The French ministry of the interior said the expulsion was ordered because of publication in Hearst newspapers two years before of a secret Anglo-French treaty on naval matters. Hearst also was accused of "hostility" to France.

Active personally in politics in earlier phases of his career, his greatest political triumph became, ironically, a source of one of his greatest regrets. This was the decisive part he played in bringing about the nomination of Franklin D. Roosevelt in 1932.

Hearst was a sponsor of John Nance Garner for the Presidential nomination in that year. At a critical stage of the Chicago convention, Hearst approved an alliance of his Garner forces with the California delegation of William Gibbs McAdoo which gave the combined Garner-McAdoo strength to Roosevelt, insuring his nomination. Garner got second place on the ticket which swept the country.

Breaks Quickly with F. D. R.

Shortly after Roosevelt went to the White House, however, the publisher broke with him and became one of his bitterest critics.

Hearst was born at San Francisco April 29, 1863, the only child of George and Phoebe Hearst. The elder Hearst was a United States senator and a wealthy man, with widespread mining and ranching interests. The son attended public schools in San Francisco and studied at Harvard university.

When he left school Hearst was offered a chance by his father to take over the management of a ranch, but the young man asked instead for control of one of the father's lesser properties, the San Francisco Examiner, a conservative newspaper with a circulation of about 24,000.

Staid Paper Blossoms

His father's acquiescense in this request launched Hearst on one of the most spectacular careers in the history of American journalism. The young editor demonstrated at once that he had strong convictions about how a newspaper should be run. The staid Examiner blossomed out with big headlines. Its reporters covered crime news with a thoroness San

Francisco had never known. The city was scandalized, but it bought the paper.

Circulation of the publication had doubled by the time of Sen. Hearst's death in 1891. Hearst inherited a lage share of the estate, estimated at 15 to 20 million dollars, and at once entered the eastern newspaper field, buying the moribund New York Journal.

Hearst's early career in New York was a battle with Joseph Pulitzer's New York World. Hearst hired Editor Arthur Brisbane away from Pulitzer. He bought color presses and gave a delighted public the Yellow Kid, Happy Hooligan, and the Katzenjammer Kids. The approach of the Spanish-American war gave Hearst full play in the use of headlines and sensational news stories.

When the Cuban insurrection began Hearst sent a staff of correspondents to Cuba to cover it and one of them rescued a Cuban woman prisoner from her cell and brought her to this country. When the United States declared war on Spain, Hearst became a war correspondent and snapped photografs of the battle of Santiago.

Firmly established in New York, Hearst founded the Chicago American in 1900, and thereafter added newspapers in Los Angeles, Boston, Baltimore, Washington, Atlanta, Milwaukee, Seattle, Syracuse, Rochester, Albany, and San Antonio.

Organizes News Services

He organized the International News Service and Universal Service, and entered the magazine field, his first venture being the magazine, Motor.

On April 28, 1903, he married Millicent Willson, daughter of George H. Willson of New York.

Hearst's active political career began in 1902 when he was elected to congress as a Democrat from New York's 11th district. He was re-elected in 1904.

During his service in the house he waged his first battle against Tammany Hall when in 1905 he was a candidate for mayor of New York on the ticket of the Municipal Ownership league. He demanded lower utility rates and transit fares and his papers campaigned for public ownership of utilities.

Candidate for Governor

The race was a close one and when the votes were counted his opponent was declared elected by a margin of 3,474 votes. Hearst always thought victory in this election was stolen from him by ballot frauds. The next year he organized the Independence league and became its candidate for governor. To avoid a three cornered gubernatorial race the Democratic party indorsed him for governor in return for the league's acceptance of the remainder of the Democratic ticket.

Charles Evans Hughes, later to become chief justice of the United States, was Hearst's Republican opponent in this contest. Hearst waged a bitter struggle but lost by 57,000 votes. He ran for mayor again in 1909 but was defeated by William J. Gaynor.

During Alfred E. Smith's first term as governor of New York in 1919, Hearst accused Smith in his papers of being in league with the so-called milk trust and failing to stop the distribution of impure milk in New York City. This led to a long political feud between Hearst and Smith. Smith blocked Democratic indorsement of Hearst for the United States senate in 1922, an act which 10 years later, according to some political observers, played a part in the Hearst pro-Roosevelt maneuver in the Democratic convention which ended Smith's hopes for nomination.

The Daily News
28th August 1879

The death of Sir Rowland Hill, which the daily announcements of his critical state have prepared the public to expect, took place yesterday morning at thirty-five minutes past four. He had been for some time past in failing health, and the prolongation of his life to his eighty-fourth year has taken place contrary to all the expectations of his family and friends. Though preserving to an extraordinary degree his intellectual acuteness and force of will, he has for some years lived in seclusion necessitated by physical weakness, and has lived entirely on one floor, furnished with a balcony, at his house at Hampstead. His last illness has been painful; but its close came without any struggle. He was unconscious through the whole of Tuesday, and passed away yesterday morning in his sleep.

Sir Rowland Hill was the third son of Mr. Thomas W. Hill, a schoolmaster. He was born December 3, 1795, at Kidderminster; and seven years later, when his father succeeded to a boarding-school at Birmingham, abode with him in that town. Trained with a view to the scholastic profession, he displayed in his youth great aptitude for practical mechanics, and constructed various scientific instruments, among others an electrical machine, after the lights of the time. While engaged in the work of practical teaching he devoted his spare time to learning the use of the theodolite, and executed a trigonometrical survey of the neighbourhood of Birmingham. At this period he tried his hand at administration, and framed a constitution for his father's school, which, by means of a committee elected by the whole body of scholars, proved a great help in preserving discipline. After seventeen years of tuition, Mr. Hill turned his attention to the schemes of colonisation then in vogue, and became the colleague of Mr. Edward Gibbon Wakefield. Thanks to the labours of these two gentlemen, the blunders which had been made in the attempt to colonise Western Australia were avoided, and the colonisation of South Australia proved completely successful. Another venture of Mr. Hill's —this time in the direction of mechanics—hardly turned out so well, but had the merit of acting as pioneer to the cylindrical system, on which all rapid printing is now performed. Mr. Hill, in common with other inventors striving in the same direction, saw clearly enough that the cylindrical system was the true one, but imagined that it was to be carried out by means of a cylinder armed with type. Wedge-shaped type to fit the exterior was thought to be the solution of the difficulty, and Mr. Hill invented a machine of this kind, consisting of a cylinder covered with wedge-shaped type, under which the paper was passed in long sheets or strips. As is now well-known, the problem was finally solved by the use of a papier-maché matrix, easily bent into cylindrical form, and metal castings taken from it.

Shortly afterwards Mr. Hill took up the subject of postage, just then exciting considerable attention. Parliamentary Committees and Royal Commissions had dealt with the subject, with the usual result of producing a heap of Blue Books. The reform, or rather reconstruction, of our postal system was effected so long ago that it is hardly to be wondered at that the renown which attended that achievement has an almost far-away ring to the ears of all but those well stricken in years. It is now thirty-nine years since the idea of an uniform rate of postage was carried into effect, not without meeting such strenuous opposition as appears at the present moment almost incredible. The idea of uniform charge for letters and messages has been so widely extended during the last few years that astonishment that it was not arrived at before the time of the venerable gentleman who has just concluded his long and useful career is the most prominent sentiment awakened in the modern mind. This is always the case with really great inventions, such as the postal system of the modern world. They are so simple that everybody stares and wonders that they did not occur to somebody in their simple form at once. No practical suggestion, however, had been made when Mr.

Hill's pamphlet, entitled "Post Office Reform: its Importance and Practicability," appeared. The reformer proposed a revolution. According to Mr. Hill's ideas, evolved from a careful study of the vast quantity of material already accumulated, the main cost of postage is incurred in the terminal work of collection and delivery. The distance over which a letter or a bag of letters was sent made no difference. From this arose his theory of uniform charge till then undreamt of. Under the ancient system the labour of collection and delivery was enormous. When a letter reached an old-fashioned post-office its troubles, so to speak, began by inspection and taxing. Weight was, oddly enough, not accepted as a basis of charge. It was too easy a method, and that of charging so much per sheet was employed instead—a system requiring that in every principal post-office there should be a "dark room" supplied at will with strong artificial light, in order that the letters might be "candled," like suspicious eggs, to detect whether more than one sheet was covered by the enclosure. Then came the calculation on distance, the sum was worked out, and the amount of the postage written upon the letter. This was frequently so great as to prevent the delivery of the letter at all. Country folk brought a silver spoon or some such article to leave with the village postmaster till the letter could be redeemed and the natural consequence of a dear postage was a contraband service, carried on between important places by private individuals at half, or less than half, the regulation price. Mr. Hill proposed to clear away the whole mass of absurdity by the imposition of an uniform rate for a certain weight. The cost of taxation would be saved in the first instance, and the major part of the cost of distribution he proposed to get rid of by enforcing the prepayment of letters by stamp.

There was a desperate fight over Mr. Hill's pamphlet in the Postage Committee of 1837-8. There was at first little public opinion to back up the reformer, or rather revolutionist, and the rich members of the Committee were all for trying a two-penny rate of postage to begin with; but in 1839 two thousand petitions were presented to Parliament in favour of Mr. Hill's plan, and in 1840 the penny post was established with the assistance of its inventor, who received an appointment in the Treasury. Mr. Hill next experienced very shabby treatment at the hands of the Government. In 1842 he was removed from his post, on the ground that his work was done; but, inasmuch as his services had been very inadequately requited, a public testimonial in his favour was organized—the amount of which was thirteen thousand six hundred pounds. In 1843 he was engaged in the management of the London and Brighton Railway Company, of which he became chairman in 1845. In the following year he was appointed secretary to the Postmaster-General, and in 1854 Chief Secretary in the room of his old antagonist, Colonel Maberly. In 1860 he was made a K.C.B., and in 1864 retired from his office, the Treasury declaring, in a highly complimentary minute the entire success of his plans, and awarding him for life his full salary of two thousand pounds per annum. In the same year he received a Parliamentary grant of twenty thousand pounds, the first Albert Gold Medal of the Society of Arts and the honorary degree of D.C.L. (Oxon). Sir Rowland Hill also received other flattering testimony of the estimation in which he was held by his countrymen—to wit the freedom of the town of Aberdeen, that of the Fishmongers' Company, a silver salver presented by the town of Liverpool; wine coolers from Glasgow, and vases from Wolverhampton.

In 1827 the late Sir Rowland Hill married Caroline, eldest daughter of the late Mr. Joseph Pearson, of Graisley, near Wolverhampton, by whom he had issue one son, Mr. Pearson Hill, and three daughters two of whom survive him.

Medicine

Medicine has advanced so rapidly over the past two hundred years that it is almost impossible to imagine the medical circumstances in which people found themselves even fifty years ago. Some would say, however, that this advance has become a Frankensteinian monster, a technological extravaganza very nearly out of control: and so either as a tribute to progress or a warning against it, the death is recorded here of **Louis Washkansky**, the recipient, courtesy of Dr. Christiaan Barnard – and donor – of the first transplanted heart. By contrast, the pioneering spirit of medicine as it was before being overtaken by technological expertise would have been represented by Ignaz Semmelweis, who worked out (at first for the wrong reasons) that women were dying of puerperal fever in a Viennese hospital because they were being infected by their doctors – but his death went unrecorded, as did that of George Crile, who performed the first blood transfusion. **Louis Charcot** revolutionalised the treatment of nervous diseases, **Edward Lister** inaugurated the practice of vaccination and innoculation when he began successfully to combat smallpox, at last probably eradicated; and **Emil von Behring** immunology. **Louis Pasteur** discovered bacteria, and, of course, invented pasteurization; and **Alexander Fleming** penicillin. **Robert Philip** pioneered tuberculous treatment and **James Simpson** anaesthesia, bringing to an end the age of "gin and bear it"; and **F. G. Hopkins** discovered the vital role of vitamins, the beginning perhaps of a proper concern with diet as preventive medicine. **Ronald Ross** stands here for all those whose sheer persistence led eventually to the discovery of the cause of a scourge of mankind, in his case malaria. Many others might also have appeared here: Charcot and Hahnemann, for instance.

It would not be heartless to suggest that **Chang** and **Eng Bunker**, the original Siamese twins, might have slotted happily into the Entertainment section. They were great showmen, their physical peculiarity exploited for gain by no one but themselves. But they were also the object of intense interest from surgeons and medical scientists the world over, in life and in death, and it is in no small way due to what the doctors learned about conjoined twins from Chang and Eng that surgical separation is a viable and largely successful possibility today.

News Chronicle
17th September 1932

MAN WHO SAVED MILLIONS OF LIVES

SIR RONALD ROSS DEAD

SIR RONALD ROSS, whose discovery that malaria is transmitted by mosquitoes has saved millions of lives, died last night at the Ross Institute, Putney, of which he was director and chief and which had been founded in his honour.

He was 75 years of age.

Sir Ronald had been ill for a long while, but became worse on Thursday.

His son, Mr. C. C. Ross, was with him yesterday afternoon, and left at 6 o'clock for a short time in the belief that the end was not near. When he reached home he received a telephone message that his father was dead.

In spite of the great benefits which his discovery had brought to civilisation Sir Ronald was in such straitened circumstances that in 1929 a public subscription was raised to provide for his old age.

Less than a week ago it was announced that the fund, contributed to by scientists and institutions in all parts of the world, was closed, the amount subscribed being £15,513.

Sir James Barr (one of the organisers) said: "Thanks to this fund, Sir Ronald's anxiety for the late Lady Ross was removed, and his declining years were made happier."

Sir Ronald Ross was an extraordinary combination of medical scientist, musician, mathematician, poet and novelist. But it was his discovery that malaria was carried by the anopheline mosquito which made him famous.

In the hour of his triumph, Sir Ronald wrote:

This day relenting God
  Hath placed within my hand
A wondrous thing; and God
  Be praised. At his command,
Seeking the secret deeds
  With tears and toiling breath,
I find thy cunning seeds,
  O million-murdering Death.
I know this little thing
  A myriad men will save.
O Death, where is thy sting,
  Thy victory, O Grave!

The son of General Sir C. C. R. Ross, he was born in the Himalayas in 1857, two days after the Mutiny broke out.

In 1881 he joined the Indian Medical Service, but until 1892 he did nothing particular in the domain of medical science, but he studied mathematics, and published two novels "Child of Ocean" and "Spirit of Storm," besides a "Drama in Five Acts."

In 1892 he began studying malaria, which was then responsible for the death of four or five million people in India every year. He had "doubts as to the superstition that the poison emanates from the soil."

Then followed years of the arduous labour which he brought to a triumphal conclusion on August 20, 1897, when he traced the malaria parasite in two large, dappled-winged mosquitoes—a discovery to be followed up by his tracing the life history of the parasite in mosquitoes.

SAVED MILLIONS

As a result of his researches the Canal Zone at Panama was turned from a place of death to a healthy area.

The canal was built; the Gold Coast grows more habitable every year, and in India the death rate from malaria is dwindling.

During the war Ross's labours saved thousands of our men in the Near East. It has already saved millions of lives, and will continue to save more millions.

He was awarded the Nobel Prize for Medicine in 1902 and the Albert Medal in 1923, and the Ross Institute of Tropical Diseases at Putney Heath, was founded in his honour.

For the last five years he has been partly paralysed and had to be wheeled in a bath chair, yet every day he would go to the Ross Institute, and superintend the work of his laboratory.

Lady Ross died in October last year.

The funeral will be at Holy Trinity Church, Putney Hill, and the interment will take place on Tuesday or Wednesday at Putney Hill Cemetery.

Suggestions that Sir Ronald should be interred in Westminster Abbey can have no effect, for Sir Ronald had expressed a wish that his body should lie beside that of his wife, and this wish will be carried out.

Mr. Ramsay MacDonald last night said of Sir Ronald Ross:

"A life of the greatest value has ended. Well does he deserve the gratitude of his generation."

The Daily Telegraph & Morning Post
12th March 1955

DEATH OF DISCOVERER OF PENICILLIN

SIR A. FLEMING

The discovery of penicillin by Sir Alexander Fleming, who has died aged 73, and its development into a most powerful agent against septic infections, ranks as one of the most important in the history of medical science. Penicillin has probably alleviated more suffering, and saved more lives, than any other drug yet known.

Sir Alexander—then Professor—Fleming was pursuing bacteriological researches at St. Mary's Hospital, Paddington, when, in 1929, the accidental contamination by mould of a culture plate of bacteria aroused his interest.

He noticed that the mould appeared to be dissolving the colonies of staphylococci on the plate. Something in the mould, he deduced, was inhibiting the growth of the bacteria. He experimented with cultivations of the mould on liquid broth.

He discovered, with some elation, that while non-poisonous and apparently harmless to white blood-cells, the mixture contained something definitely inimical to many of the most deadly microbes. The mould was identified as Penicillium notatum, and Fleming named the antibiotic it produced, penicillin.

MANY OBSTACLES

Several years elapsed before the great discovery could be put to practical use on the battlefields of the 1939-45 war. The production of penicillin in a purer and more concentrated form was accompanied by many obstacles.

By 1932 research workers had discovered how to grow the mould on a synthetic liquid medium and also how to pass it into ether. Unfortunately, destruction of the ether involved the disappearance of most of the penicillin. Disheartened, the researchers decided that the new antiseptic was too unstable to be practical.

It was not until 1938 that Professor—now Sir—Howard Florey and Dr. E. B. Chain, working at the Oxford School of Pathology with a considerable team of research workers, evolved satisfactory formulas for the production of the new antiseptic.

The next step was production to cope with war casualties. This was achieved by enlisting the aid of American commercial chemists. It remained a matter for regret with Sir Alexander that commercialisation of his product, which he gave freely to the world, entailed payments to American chemists on all subsequent sales.

SON OF FARMER

Alexander Fleming was born in Ayrshire of Covenanting stock. The son of a farmer, he was educated at Kilmarnock Academy, and he worked for five years in a London shipping office before entering St. Mary's Medical School.

Here he came under the wise direction of Sir Almroth Wright, the great bacteriologist. Under his instruction Fleming secured honours in every subject.

He served in the 1914-18 war as a captain in the R.A.M.C., subsequently returning to St. Mary's, where in 1928 he was appointed Professor of the Medical School. Since 1948 he had been Professor of Bacteriology at London University.

He was knighted in 1944 and the world-wide enthusiasm aroused by his discovery was reflected in the international honours bestowed on him. In 1945 he was awarded, jointly with Sir Howard Florey and Dr. Chain, the Nobel Prize for Medicine.

FRENCH HONOUR

In the same year he was appointed a Commander of the Legion of Honour, France's highest honour. In June last year the Duke of Edinburgh presented him with two silver sauce tureens to mark the 25th anniversary of his discovery.

The Times
3rd April 1917

DISCOVERER OF DIPHTHERIA ANTI-TOXIN DEAD

The German newspapers announce the death of Dr. von Behring.

Dr. Emil von Behring's claims to distinction rest upon his introduction of the diphtheria anti-toxin and the tetanus anti-toxin. These discoveries were a great work, for which he deserves the highest credit and for which humanity owes him a debt. His subsequent work was anything but brilliant, and his famous remedy for tuberculosis missed fire sadly. It is said that his reluctance to give this to the profession—which at the time aroused much comment—was due to the fact that he received little or nothing for the discoveries he had made.

The Times
7th May 1870

DEATH OF SIR JAMES Y. SIMPSON.—(By Telegraph.)—Last night, shortly before 8 o'clock, Professor Sir James Y. Simpson died in Edinburgh from disease of the heart, with symptoms of *angina pectoris*. Sir James was born in 1811, and was appointed in 1840 to the Professorship of Midwifery in the University of Edinburgh, for his discoveries in connexion with chloroform, which are well known. Numerous honours were conferred upon him. Among these it may be mentioned that in 1853 he was elected Foreign Associate of the French Academy of Medicine; in 1856 he was awarded the Montyon Prize of 2,000f. by the French Academy of Sciences. About the same time he received the Knighthood of the Royal Order of St. Olaf from King Oscar of Sweden. In 1866 he was created a Baronet; in the same year he received the honorary degree of D.C.L. from Oxford. In October last he was presented with the freedom of the city of Edinburgh, in "recognition of his scientific researches and applications of science to the alleviation of human suffering."

Glasgow Herald
19ᵗʰ May 1947

SIR FREDERICK GOWLAND HOPKINS

Discoverer of Vitamins

The death took place at Cambridge on Friday of Sir Frederick Gowland Hopkins. He was born at Eastbourne in 1861, and after being educated at private schools he studied medicine at Guy's Hospital and London University. For some time he was on the staff of the medical school at the hospital, but he was more strongly attracted to research, and began to investigate the properties of proteins.

His opportunity came when Sir Michael Foster invited him in 1899 to Cambridge, to assist in the new school of physiology, and in 1913 he became Professor of Biochemistry with an independent department.

One of his early studies showed that the pigmentations of certain types of butterflies' wings were derivatives of uric acid, thus indicating that excesses or superfluities which were normally excreted sometimes functioned as ornament.

Hopkins soon proceeded to study the obscure subject of the chemical changes that occur in muscular movements, which led him to inquire into the production of lactic acid in muscle; and about this time an inquiry into the subject of diet laid the foundation of what eventually became the now familiar discovery of vitamins, which has been of immense service to health and incidentally has interested the public in those matters of nutrition which the previous generation took very much for granted.

Sir Frederick was president of the Royal Society from 1930 to 1935. Among the many honours he received were the Order of Merit, the Nobel Prize for Medicine, an honorary D.Sc. from Glasgow University, and LL.D.s from Aberdeen and St Andrews.

The Daily Telegraph
3ʳᵈ December 1967

LOUIS WASHKANSKY died today. But it was not the second-hand heart given to him 18 days ago that killed him.

It was his lungs, both affected by patches of pneumonia, caused, in spite of all precautions, by a virulent form of germ.

A post-mortem examination established this, and soon after the findings were revealed Professor Chris Barnard, leader of the 30-strong team that carried out the historic operation, declared:

"As soon as the occasion arises we will do the next heart transplant."

There's no evidence . . .

Professor Barnard, 44, son of a missionary and father of a teenage boy and girl, went on to say:

THERE IS NO clinical evidence to suggest that rejection played a part in the death.

THERE IS NO evidence for human heart transplants to be discontinued.

The official bulletin announcing the death was issued shortly before a weary and saddened Professor Barnard spoke. It said simply: "Mr. L. Washkansky died at 6.50 a.m. (4.50 London time) this morning. Clinically the cause of death was respiratory failure due to bilateral pneumonia. This was confirmed at post-mortem by Professor J. G. Thomson."

Professor Thomson is a pathologist at Groot Schuur Hospital.

'Not an experiment'

The first question Professor Barnard was asked to answer was whether Washkansky's death "negated the experiment?"

He answered: "Firstly, I would not consider it an experiment—it was a treatment for a sick patient. The problem of infection was loaded against the surgical team.

Washkansky had an infected leg and diabetes. The diabetes probably made him more susceptible to infection.

Transplant anaesthetist Dr. Ozinsky said that to the very end the grafted heart—from a girl who died in a road crash—had worked very well.

There was nothing wrong with the heart or the features of the operation, and the post-mortem were "a vindication of the principle of heart transplants."

Washkansky's wife, Ann, a 41-year-old short, buxom woman, and his 15-year-old son Michael were called to the hospital during the night.

They left the bedside only a few moments before the death. Just after eight o'clock Mrs. Washkansky returned with her brother, Solly Sklar, and Washkansky's elder brother, Tevia.

People outside the hospital entrance surged around the car, and she cried out, "Oh, for God's sake, for God's sake."

A male nurse held people back to allow her to enter and told her: "Don't say anything, don't say a thing."

Mrs. Washkansky stayed at the hospital about 15 minutes.

Her sister, Mrs. Helen Klugman, said afterwards: "My sister has been prety wonderful. She is, of course, terribly upset.

"The doctors tried very hard; they never stopped trying to save his life. Nobody could have done anything more."

THE SAD DOCTORS

It was a death which saddened all the doctors and nurses at Groote Schuur, where Washkansky made miraculous progress in the first 14 days after the operation.

At one stage doctors had said he might be home for Christmas.

But five days ago ne developed pneumonia. Though he rallied briefly from time to time, his newfound life ebbed steadily away.

Treatment with massive doses of penicillin failed to improve the lung condition, which was followed by a drastic slump in the number of white blood cells.

A bulletin around midnight, said he had rallied slightly. Thre ehours later a hospital spokesman reported him in critical condition and his family were called.

Professor Barnard was also

recalled aftr leaving at mi
to try to snatch a few
sleep.

Throughout the
struggle for his life. Wa
helped his doctors' efforts
indomitable strength of

"The man's will to
fantastic." Professor
said after the operation.

Only a week ago, he
ting in the sunlight, talking
joking with doctors and
reading, listening to the
and even being intervie
radio and television.

● Washkansky's funeral
take place tomorrow
town suburban Pine
Jewish Cemetery.

'Now she is completely dead'

EDWARD DARVALL, father of the girl whose heart was transplanted, speaking today: "I was shocked when I heard that he had died. I really thought he would pull through. I feel very bad about it. Giving my daughter's heart was the best I could do, but it didn't work. I feel completely empty. Now that Mr. Washkansky is dead I have nothing more to look forward to. After the operation there was at least part of my daugher still alive in Mr. Washkansky. But now she is completely dead."

New York Times
2nd February 1874

CHANG AND ENG, THE SIAMESE BROTHERS.

The most remarkable natural curiosity of our time was exhibited in the bodies of Chang and Eng, the Siamese twins, who died the other day at Mount Airey, in North Carolina, and perhaps no other "freak of nature" on record excited so much professional interest among the physiologists. There have been thousands of such cases, some scarcely mentioned or only briefly alluded to, in which nature went out of her way to break her own laws. We are told of twin boys born with united bodies in Normandy in the fifteenth century. They lived to the age of sixteen, and then died almost simultaneously. There were also the Hungarian sisters, who lived about a hundred years ago, joined back to back, and, of course, always looking in opposite directions. They had but one passage leading from the intestines, &c., and they died at the same time, when they were twenty-two years old. Ambrose Paré, the celebrated anatomist, records the case of two other girls, who lived in a somewhat similar state of union to the age of ten, when one of them died. The other was at once separated from the corpse, but she scarcely survived the operation. In all such cases recorded, the death of one twin was followed by the death of the other, as in the case under notice.

Chang and Eng were members of a somewhat monstrous family. Their parents had seventeen children, six of these being twins, of the usual sort and, it is said, three of them coming together at one birth. The family lived by fishing, in a village near the Menara, the chief river of Siam, on which Bangkok is situated, and it is a curious fact that one of the Monghuts or Kings of the country ordered that the twins, Chang and Eng, should live in seclusion with their family, a superstitious kind of order, intended probably to prevent the fashion of such irregular growths among the people. Our twins were born in the year 1811, and were brought up to get their livelihood by catching fish from a boat. In their eighteenth year they were purchased from their mother by Capt. Coffin and Mr. Hunter, and brought to Europe in 1830, after which they came to this country. During their visit to Boston Dr. John C. Warren, the most eminent physician of that city, was called on to see and examine them, for the purpose of giving a guarantee that they were genuine monsters, and for the rest not in any way in-

decorous or unfit for exhibition—the main purpose, of course, of those who brought them from Siam. His description and the lithograph accompanying it removed any scruples on that score, and at the same time showed that the twins were distinct in every way except one, that is the narrow, tough ligament which kept them together at the breast where it touched the stomach. This cord, as it was called, was about four inches broad and two inches in thickness, and its length from one body to the other measured from two inches at the upper side to five at the lower, just allowing them to stand side by side when they strained the ligament, and leaving them, in their usual position, standing half facing one another in the attitude so familiar to the public in general. At the lower edge of the ligament was a single umbilicus, through which passed a single cord, the medium by which, before birth, came the natural nourishment of the two children. Dr. Warren found, by touch, that a cartilage extended along the upper edge of the short connection, and had an elastic way of opening or stretching whenever the twins wished to turn outward. He could not distinguish any pulsating vessel in this ligament, which was naturally so strong that the boys allowed a cord to be brought round it on board ship and pulled, without feeling pain. It allowed them to run about the deck and even to leap simultaneously over an open hatchway, or climb a ladder. They were cheerful, in those days, and learned to play draughts, first with the men of the ship and then with one another. The doctor was of opinion that a very minute network of blood-vessels and nerves passed from one body to the other, though he found that, except near the middle of the *nexus*, the puncture of a knife or pin did not affect both at the same time. A touch at either side, two inches or so from the centre, only affected the person on that side. The vascular and nervous communications, as has been observed, were very slight; but the doctor made the important discovery that the heart pulsations of Chang and Eng went together. This he found by touching the arm of each boy. At the same time he perceived that a sudden movement of one of them quickened his pulse, while that of the other remained in its normal condition. This showed, of course, that their breathing was simultaneous; a fact of most significant import, and one which must have proved to the twins themselves the vital nature of their connection.

In England they were visited by crowds, and also invited by some leaders of the "fashion" to their houses on reception nights. They also visited France, and everywhere had the good sense to save the greater part of their earnings. From 1850 to 1855 they sojourned in this City with Mr. Barnum, at the corner of Ann street and Broadway; and then at the age of forty-four they negotiated, by means of letters and mutual friends, for wives. These they found in two lasses of Lancashire, whom they had seen apparently during their English tour, and who came over to accept their very extraordinary destiny. To make the matter still more extraordinary the young women were sisters, whose name has not sufficiently transpired to make the public very sure of it ; and this, no doubt, was just as they would have it, since they would probably have rather married a couple of English yeomen with the same amount of cash in bank. The happy party now went to settle on the purchased plantation of Mount Airey, in North Carolina, where the brothers employed slave hands in the cultivation of cotton and other products, and where, in due course of time, they had families reckoning up, it is stated, eleven children. The first-born of Chang was a deaf-mute, but none of the offspring had any of the strong abnormal features of their Siamese parentage. Dr. Warren, making his diagnosis at Boston, in 1830, supposed that the more luxurious food and habits of civilized life would co-operate with the original defect of nature to shorten the lives of the twins in a very few years. But they falsified his prophecy, and were probably the longest-lived "monsters" of the sort on record. Their lives for the last quarter of a century belonged to themselves more than to the public, and in the mastership of their families and plantation they must have found some relief from their self-consciousness, that always weighed upon them except when they were asleep. They had their differences, too, and would often quarrel as vehemently as if they were free to part from one another in anger. From their birth they were sombre and silent, by nature, and in their youth it was observed that while they conversed with others they hardly seemed to address one another. Their experience of life must have been dreadful enough ; and it is wonderful to think they could have worried through to the age of sixty-three. But custom is one of the strongest laws of life, and they grew callous with regard to a hundred things which untried nature shrinks from contemplating. Their wives, like those of Brigham Young, lived in separate buildings with their re

...have households, and in this way the discomforts of such a family must have been diminished in some degree. One of the twins was stronger and more intelligent than the other, but *which* of them it is not easy to understand. Some say Chang was the strong, domineering fellow—the one who died first; though one would suppose he had the strongest hold on life, and would be the survivor. The doubt shows how little is really known about the lives of these strange Asiatics. No one has stated that they knew how to read or write our language; and if they remained ignorant in this respect, it is hard to understand how they could hold much intercourse with others or know the nature of passing events. There was one event, however, which they understood—the secession of the Southern States; and, holding slaves, they held naturally by the "Confederacy." At the end of the war they found their property greatly reduced, and then came North once more for the purpose of recruiting their finances. In New-York, a few years ago, they were exhibited at Wood's Museum, though without being able to "draw" as they did of old. At that time they went also to England and France, where there were many consultations on the subject of the ligament. Dr. Nélaton, of Paris, was for cutting it, but the American doctor, Mott, and a number of other physicians were opposed to such an experiment on bodies so advanced in years, and as this decision fell in with the secret apprehensions of the brothers themselves, the idea was given up, and Chang and Eng were resigned to wait on the ultimate decision of nature. This came on the 17th of January in this year at their North Carolina home. Chang, who had suffered from an attack of paralysis some months ago, died somewhat suddenly in the night when the brothers were unattended. Eng, finding that his life-long companion had ceased to breathe, and probably feeling some deadly sympathy creeping over himself, called for assistance. When help came he said, "I suppose I must die too;" after which began a mental and bodily agony which ended in his death less than two hours subsequently. The bodies of the brothers have been embalmed and buried under their dwelling-house, and their wives, knowing the general wish for a post-mortem examination, are naturally disposed to receive a consideration—some say of $10,000—before they permit it. The money should be paid as freely as money was ever paid to examine the persons of the living twins. Dr. Hollinsworth, of Mount Airey; Dr. Pencoast, and others are managing the treaty, and it is hoped they will succeed. Chang and Eng, though dead, owe something to the intelligent curiosity which did so much for them. The fate of their existence need not follow them in the grave. As it cannot be said "they were lovely in their lives," it need not be said of them that "in death they are not divided," when the "dividing" would be such a boon to the men of science and the general public.

Chang and Eng, the Siamese twins in their late fifties.

D.N.B Biographies
1931 - 1940

PHILIP, SIR ROBERT WILLIAM (1857–1939), physician and founder of tuberculosis dispensaries, was born at Glasgow 29 December 1857, the youngest son of George Philip, a minister of the Free Church of Scotland, whose charge was the Union church at Govan, by his wife, Margaret Josephine, daughter of Joseph Robertson. Educated at the Royal High School, Edinburgh, and at Edinburgh University, he graduated M.B., C.M. in 1882 and M.D. (gold medal) in 1887.

The life of Philip covers the first fifty-seven years of an era in the history of tuberculosis that began with Robert Koch's discovery of the tubercle bacillus in 1882. In that year, Koch communicated his discovery to the Berlin Physiological Society. At this time Philip was engaged in post-graduate study in Vienna, where he saw the tubercle bacillus for the first time. He was so much impressed by the potentialities of this discovery that 'Embryology, gynaecology, and all the other specialities that had drawn me to Vienna got the go-by', and, having decided to devote special attention to tuberculosis, he returned to Edinburgh in 1883. On confiding his intention to the professor of medicine, he was told: 'Don't think of such a thing. Phthisis is worn to a thin thread. The subject is exhausted.'

Undaunted, Philip established, with the assistance of his *fiancée* and of a few friends, what became in 1894 the Royal Victoria Hospital for Consumption, at Craigleith, near Edinburgh. Its out-patients' department in Bank Street, in the heart of the city, opened in 1887, was the first tuberculosis dispensary in the world. It was a centre for the treatment of ambulant cases, for the examination of contacts, and later a clearing house for the open-air school, the sanatorium, the tuberculosis colony, and the hospital for advanced cases, these being the essential components of what became known throughout the world as the co-ordinated Edinburgh system. In 1909 the first

tuberculosis dispensary in England was established at Paddington through the work of Edith McGaw (later Lady Philip), who devoted herself for over thirty years to the prevention of tuberculosis.

In 1890 Philip joined the staff of the Edinburgh Royal Infirmary, becoming lecturer on chest diseases. When the new chair of tuberculosis was founded in Edinburgh in 1917, Philip was elected to fill the post, which he held until his death. He was an inspiring teacher although not a great clinician. Seldom are these gifts combined. His conception of pulmonary tuberculosis as a visceral lesion in a systemic disease was a conspicuous contribution to medicine. He was author of *Pulmonary Tuberculosis, Etiological and Therapeutic; based on an Experimental Investigation* (1891), and in 1911 *A Selection of Writings* appeared; he wrote *The Actual Position of Tuberculosis To-day* (1923) and *Collected Papers on Tuberculosis* (1937). Twelve of his former pupils, and many specialists in other lands, prepared a *festschrift*, *The Control and Eradication of Tuberculosis; a series of International Studies* (1911).

In 1912 Philip's conception of a uniform tuberculosis service was adopted by the British government, and in 1913 he was knighted. He was elected F.R.C.P. Edinburgh in 1887, was president from 1918 to 1923, and for fourteen years (1923–1937) he was curator of the research laboratory of the college; he was elected F.R.C.P. London in 1933. He was president of the British Medical Association in 1927. He received the honorary degree of LL.D. from the universities of Glasgow and Wales and that of M.D. from the university of Egypt. He was elected F.R.S. Edinburgh in 1889 and received several foreign medals and prizes.

Philip had a clear business head and was unrivalled as an organizer and administrator; as a chairman he was unsurpassed. He had leisure to cultivate culture; and was an excellent companion and an admirable host, not above the art of flattery; a diplomat in English, French, and German. His formal manner, often mistaken for vanity, was really the expression of a profound sense of occasion. He was an egoist, but having an ego that others could admire; an epicurean of the original school and one to whom millions will be indebted who will never hear his name.

Philip was twice married: first, in 1888 to Elizabeth (died 1937), youngest daughter of John Fenton Motherwell, of co. Sligo; secondly, in 1938 to Edith Josephine (died February 1939), eldest daughter of Joseph McGaw, of Kooba, New South Wales. Both marriages were without issue. He died in Edinburgh 25 January 1939.

A portrait of Philip by Sir James Guthrie is in the Royal College of Physicians, Edinburgh. A portrait of Edith McGaw by Hugh de T. Glazebrook (1900) is in the Paddington Tuberculosis Dispensary.

The Times

18th August 1893

Our Paris Correspondent, telegraphing last night, says that the sad news has reached Paris of the sudden death of Dr. Charcot from a cardiac affection while on a pleasure trip in company with his two well-known pupils, Drs. Debove and Strauss. On Wednesday morning he was found dead in his bed. With the death of Dr. Charcot disappears one of the glories of French science. He was born in Paris on November 29, 1825, and was received as doctor in 1853. In 1856 he was appointed physician of the Central Hospital Bureau. In 1860 he became professor in the University of Paris, and in 1862 was attached to the Salpêtrière as a specialist in nervous diseases. In 1873 he became a member of the Academy of Medicine. He was appointed in 1880 clinical professor of nervous diseases, the chair being created especially for him. At this time he founded the *Archives de Neurologie*. In 1883 he was elected member of the Institute. His publications, of which it would be hazardous here to attempt to give a list, are known throughout the scientific world. The *Temps* thus refers to the special field in which M. Charcot was most widely known, the study of hypnotism and the different forms of hysteria :—" Without endeavouring to show whether the conclusions drawn by the master in this order of ideas were always characterized by the most impeccable science, and without entering upon the discussion waged so long between the school of the Salpêtrière and those who were opposed to him, our impartial duty to-day is to note our gratitude to Dr. Charcot for having been the first of the orthodox *savants* who dared to cross the threshold of the mystery, and who succeeded in making simple and comprehensible certain mysterious phenomena which are only for the most part the natural consequences of affections having to do with nervous or mental pathology. Whatever the truth may be, the name of Dr. Charcot calls up a doctrine, and the name will survive by reason of the admirable works which make the uncontested glory of their author." M. Charcot married the daughter of M. Latrend Richard, and had three children, two girls and one son, M. Grean Charcot, already a distinguished practitioner, an *interne* of the Salpêtrière Hospital. As a lecturer Professor Charcot was admirable. " His warm and often vibrating utterance," says the *Temps*, " underlined by his peculiar, quick, decisive gesture, carried weight wherever it was heard, whether in a congress of *savants* or in the foreign countries which he took pleasure in visiting." The *Lancet* says :—" Whilst awaiting particulars of the sad event, which will be profoundly deplored by the whole medical world, and reserving for a more fitting time a full account of the great physician, we may remind our readers of his claims to the position he will occupy in medical history. He was, in the first place, a man of wide acquirements, not limited to professional pursuits alone. His knowledge of the literature of his own and of foreign countries was very extensive. His linguistic accomplishments are well known to those who have frequented medical congresses both in this country and abroad. He was great as a clinical observer, and worthy to be ranked with such masters as Trousseau and Laennec. He was great, also, as a pathologist, and in this regard it may be said that he did not let the advance of age dull his keen interest and love for science. But what is indeed the touchstone of the original mind, no man in medical science has inspired his pupils with greater enthusiasm and regard. Witness the large audiences assembled at his clinique at the Salpêtrière and the volumes of his invaluable Leçons, which we owe to his pupils' devotions. Our readers will recall the scientific precision and the truly marvellous power of ' word-painting ' which characterize all his published writings—from his early thesis on chronic pneumonia down to the latest contribution on the difficulties and abstruse psychological rather than neurolgical problems with which he was mainly concerned of late years. Professor Charcot was an artist as well as a man of science, and to him is owing in very large measure the position occupied by neurology in the present day. He had many friends in this country, and often came to England, and it may be remembered that quite recently he was sent on a visit to Bournemouth on a mission from the French Government. His striking personality will be missed at the coming congress at Rome."

The Times
30th September 1895

DEATH OF M. PASTEUR.

PARIS, Sept. 29.

M. Pasteur died yesterday at Garches, near St. Cloud.

Seldom have the benefits conferred by science upon humanity been more direct and more patent than has been the case with the long series of researches conducted by Louis Pasteur. As has almost invariably been the case when science has conferred a lasting boon on humanity, this eminent chemist began his work with no thought of anything but his science ; but, as so often has happened in the disinterested pursuit of knowledge, the results have been far-reaching and beneficent. The world at large has only recently heard of Pasteur in connexion with his famous " cure " for one of the most terrible afflictions of mankind—hydrophobia. But this was only the culmination of a lifelong series of researches into the lowest forms of life. Pasteur's work was long ago well known to brewers, to sericulturists, to stock-rearers, to viticulturists and the followers of other industries, and by them he was universally recognized as a benefactor. To the chemist and biologist his name, it need hardly be said, was a household word.

Louis Pasteur was born nearly 73 years ago—in December 27, 1822—at Dôle in the Jura, the son of a tanner, who had fought his country's battles with honour. Shortly after Louis's birth the family removed to Arbois, and here Louis was educated at the Communal College. Thence he went to the College of Besançon, and in 1843 was admitted to the École Normale at Paris. Chemistry had become his favourite subject even at Besançon, and under Dumas at Paris, as may be imagined, his devotion was intensified. Pasteur worked hard both at chemistry and physics. He took his doctor's degree in 1847, and in the following year was appointed Professor of Physics at Strasburg University. In 1854 he removed to Lille, where he was appointed Dean of the Faculty of Science. Three years later he returned to Paris as Scientific Director of the École Normale, and in 1867 he was appointed Professor of Chemistry at the Sorbonne. In recent years his headquarters have been at the Pasteur Institute, founded for him for the purpose of carrying out his invaluable bacteriological investigations.

Pasteur's earliest original researches, undertaken at the suggestion of M. Delafosse, who was specially interested in molecular physics, dealt with crystals. These were connected with an investigation of extreme delicacy into the differences which existed between the tartrate and the paratartrate of soda and ammonia. Into the technicalities of Pasteur's discoveries as to the nature and relations of these two isomeric bodies it would be out of place to enter here. A great anomaly was explained and a great problem solved. Moreover, the elaborate research, which occupied Pasteur six years, led him on to researches in other and more practical directions—researches which would scarcely have been possible if this initial problem had not been solved. So long ago as 1856 Pasteur's reputation had spread beyond France ; in that year our Royal Society awarded him its Rumford medal for his researches on the polarization of light, &c.

His next great scientific undertaking, with a practical end in view, was suggested by the chief industry at Lille, where, it has been seen, he was Dean of the Faculty of Science. The manufacture of alcohol from beetroot and corn was of the first importance to Lille. The methods followed seem to have been of a somewhat empirical character, and Pasteur saw that great improvements were possible, not only in this particular industry, but in the brewing of beer, of which, so far as the French market was concerned, Germany and Austria had the monopoly. This naturally led Pasteur to make an exhaustive investigation into the great and complicated subject of fermentation. The result was not simply important to the manufacture of spirits at Lille, but initiated the creation of what may be regarded as a new industry in France, the manufacture of beer on scientific principles. Certainly in this respect Pasteur was a great benefactor to his country, though as a matter of fact it is doubtful if beer of native manufacture has ever been so highly appreciated in France as that imported from the country of the enemy. But it was not only France that benefited by the results of Pasteur's researches, they have become the common property of brewers all the world over. In these investigations he was led from one stage to another, always bringing the microscope to the aid of his chemical methods, until he was convinced that all forms of fermentation were due to the action of minute living organisms. Only those who are familiar with the history of chemistry will recognize the magnitude of the innovation on accepted doctrines involved in Pasteur's theory. But the irresistible logic of facts convinced all impartial students of the essential truth of what is popularly known as the germ theory. It explained many obscurities in science, both in chemistry and biology, and its practical bearings soon became evident. Of course, others had been working in this direction before Pasteur —Appert, Caignard-Latour, Schwann, Helmholtz—but it may with truth be said that it was Pasteur who put his finger on the real secret, who discovered nature's actual method of work in all those processes of which fermentation may be regarded as the typical example. To quote the words of Sir James Paget :—

" He proved the constant presence of living microorganisms, not only in yeast, in which Caignard-Latour and Schwann, especially, had studied them, but in all the fermenting substances that he examined ; he proved the certain and complete prevention of fermentation, putrefaction, and other similar processes in many substances, however naturally subject to them, by the exclusion of all micro-organisms and other germs, or by their destruction if present ; and he proved the constant presence of various micro-organisms and their germs in the air, in the water, in the earth, in dust and dirt of every kind—their abundance " everywhere."

The discovery of this vast hidden field of activity in nature has been fruitful in the most remarkable discoveries and the most beneficent applications. A whole world of obscure phenomena has been explained to science ; diseases of various kinds have been traced to their birthplaces ; much suffering has been spared to men and animals, and multitudes of lives have been saved. It was seen how these germ-diseases could be met and prevented ; and Lister, carrying out Pasteur's discoveries into practice, devised the method, known by his name, and now all but universally applied in surgery. Pasteur carried his war against disease into the enemy's country, so to speak ; he fought the battle against the foes of life and health with disease's own weapons. He found that every form of what may be called putrefactive diseases had its own particular bacillus, which could be separated from all others and cultivated. If allowed to work in their own way, and at their normal strength, the micro-organisms which produce contagious diseases work havoc upon living beings. But Pasteur found they could be attenuated and diluted, and when administered in their attenuated form by means of inoculation, the strength being gradually increased, the disease was contracted in a mild form, and all its deleterious consequences avoided. Of course, the fact that small-pox could be fought in this way is an old discovery ; but it remained for Pasteur to discover the great principle which underlies such diseases, and to show how widely applicable was the preventive method which had been so effective in small-pox. To the agriculturists he did eminent service by showing how certain diseases in fowls and sheep could be met more than half way. His researches in splenic fever fully confirmed the discovery of Davaine. Koch's application of the principle to phthisis is well known. Less cautious and patient than Pasteur, he can hardly be said to have yet succeeded. Pasteur's greatest achievement in this direction—an achievement which drew upon him the attention and the blessings of all the world—was the discovery of an antidote to hydrophobia. Into the discussion of the absolute validity of this antidote we cannot enter ; the evidence in its favour is so strong that in the opinion of impartial and competent judges Pasteur has been able to rob one of the most appalling afflictions of humanity of much of its terror.

It is not possible to recount in detail all the services rendered by Pasteur through the application of scientific discoveries, to industry and humanity. For a time (1865 onwards) he was diverted from his own special researches to cope, at the request of his master Dumas, with the disease which had been rendering havoc among silkworms, and affecting the silk industry of France to the extent of millions annually. He found that the minute "corpuscle" found among the silkworms was really a disease germ, and by a careful series of experiments demonstrated that its havoc could be greatly diminished if not stopped by taking measures to prevent the propagation of diseased eggs. While carrying out this good work Pasteur spent several months every year for four years in a little house near Alais, where he watched every step in the life of silkworms bred by himself and others. Unfortunately, in 1868, he had a paralytic attack, from which he recovered, but which left him for life comparatively powerless on the left side. Again, the sad events connected with the Franco-German war interrupted his work, but for the past 20 years he has been constantly active in developing in many directions the great principle to which he may be said to have been the first to give precise and manageable form. "It would be useless," again to quote Sir James Paget, "to imagine the probabilities of what will now follow from the researches that have already followed the discoveries of Pasteur." He surely deserves to be ranked among the greatest benefactors of humanity.

On December 27th, 1892, Pasteur's 70th birthday was celebrated in the Sorbonne in a manner which, as *The Times* Correspondent stated at the time, affected all present. It was a great international gathering. England was represented by Sir James Lister, and the gold medal which was presented to the veteran investigator was subscribed for by representatives of science of various countries. On that occasion the most illustrious of Pasteur's English disciples said :—

There is certainly not in the entire world a single person to whom medical science is more indebted than to you. Your researches on fermentation have thrown a flood of light which has illuminated the gloomy shadows of surgery and changed the treatment of wounds from a matter of doubtful and too often disastrous empiricism into a scientific art, certain and beneficent. Owing to you surgery has undergone a complete revolution. It has been stripped of its terrors, and its efficiency has been almost unlimitedly enlarged. But medicine owes as much to your profound and philosophic studies as surgery. You have raised the veil which had for centuries covered infectious diseases. You have discovered and proved their microbic nature ; and, thanks to your initiation, and in many cases to your own special labour, there are already a host of these destructive diseases of which we now completely know the causes. This knowledge has already perfected in a surprising way the diagnosis of certain plagues of the human race and has marked out the course which must be followed in their prophylactic and curative treatment. Medicine and surgery are eager on this great occasion to offer you the profound homage of their admiration and their gratitude.

If ever a man deserved a great international monument, it is surely this modest, unassuming, gentle, and humane French chemist, who has done more than most men to initiate the millennium. In his own science he ranks amongst the highest. The variety and multitude of his researches may be learned by a glance at the Royal Society List (where the titles of 137 papers are given), or into the pages of the *Comptes-Rendus* of the Academy of Sciences. Among his books are works on fermentation, on wine and its diseases, on the diseases of silkworms, and on beer. It need hardly be said that honours were showered upon Pasteur. He was a Grand Officer of the Legion of Honour. He was early elected to the Paris Academy of Sciences, and some 13 years ago to the Institute. Of our own Royal Society he was a medallist and a foreign member. He held the Albert Medal of the Society of Arts. The French Government long ago recognized his services by an annuity of 12,000f. The Pasteur Institute in Paris was built at a cost of £100,000, and since its completion both the French public and the French Government have contributed handsomely to the maintenance of an institution which, through the genius and disinterestedness of its chief, waged war not only against hydrophobia, but also against many other deadly foes of the human race and the domesticated animals. Similar institutes have been founded in other countries ; in London the British Institute of Preventive Medicine is conducted on the same lines as the Pasteur Institute under the able direction of Dr. Ruffer, and has more than justified its existence by the good work it has done in connexion with the anti-toxin treatment of diphtheria. It may with more truth be said of Pasteur than can be said of most eminent men that his death is a very great loss to humanity. His work will be taken up by others ; let them follow his method and advice – "N'avancez rien qui ne puisse être prouvé d'une façon simple et décisive."

The Times
12th February 1912

Lord Lister.

In LORD LISTER. whose death we announce this morning, a great man has passed away from the company of the living. If true worth be measured by work accomplished for the benefit of mankind, very few worthier have lived and died. It is no figure of speech to say that the whole civilized world will feel his loss and revere his memory, for every part of it has shared in the benefits he conferred on the human race. He may be called the great life-saver. More than ten years ago, as the full memoir we publish on another page reminds us, it was computed that he had then already saved more human lives than all the wars of the nineteenth century had sacrificed ; and the record has been steadily rolling up ever since. It is a most wonderful achievement for one man and not easy to grasp. But there is probably little or no exaggeration in the statement. Nor does the saving of life—with all that it implies, in the relieving of anxiety, the conversion of sorrow into joy, and the enrichment of mankind—cover the whole story. The lives saved through LISTER's art are those which would have ended, in the vast majority of cases, in grievous pain. He has prevented not less suffering than premature

Continued

death. How this has been brought about is explained in our memoir. The general public, though familiar with LISTER's name and aware that he was a great surgeon, has probably but a vague idea of what he actually did. It may be summed up thus: he discovered the principles and established the practice of scientific cleanliness and applied them to surgery. Thus stated, it does not sound much, and indeed the whole thing is now so self-evident, so simple and complete, that we have considerable difficulty in realizing the state of ignorance which prevailed when he began his researches. Speaking generally, surgeons had then no conception of cleanliness as it is now understood. Some were, no doubt, more particular than others in the avoidance of gross uncleanliness in connexion with their work, and here and there men were groping their way towards a better order of things. But the profession in general accepted as part of the regular process of nature results from injuries and operations which we know to be due to nothing but dirt and wholly avoidable. They had always seen such results and took them for granted as deplorable, of course, but inevitable.

Into this field of conventional, orthodox practice, with its frightful tale of suffering and death, entered the man of genius, the pioneer. He began, as all the great lights of science have begun, by observing the facts before him. He observed them more closely than his colleagues, and sought to explain them. He noticed the great mortality following operations and injuries in which the skin was broken and the tissues exposed to the air; and in attempting to remedy this prevalent evil, which was emphasized by the expansion of operative surgery due to the introduction of anæsthetics, he was led to search for the cause. While pursuing the quest with open eyes and alert mind he learnt of PASTEUR's final proof that the processes of fermentation and putrefaction were caused by the presence and growth of living organisms. This gave him the clue he was looking for He at once perceived the possible bearing of PASTEUR's demonstration upon his own inquiries and set to work methodically to follow it up. It was by no accident or easy path that he had reached this point and pressed onward. The Huxley Lecture, which he delivered in 1900 and devoted by request to an account of some of his earlier experiments, revealed an unsuspected or forgotten background of preliminary work; and the two large quarto volumes of his collected papers published in 1909 by the Clarendon Press contain the record of innumerable observations and experiments in physiology, pathology, and bacteriology, proving once more that the road to success in research is the laborious path of patient and gradual but purposeful exploration. The hackneyed saying that genius is an infinite capacity for taking pains is a sort of half-truth. The man of genius—at any rate in science—possesses that capacity, but it is because he is inspired by an idea. He sees the object of his quest before him like a light which he must follow. He is intensely possessed by it, and cannot desist from the search until he finds it. He is forced to take infinite pains

by the fire within, and that is his real genius. Thousands of other men who are without it may take equal pains and find nothing, because they know not what they are seeking. Hence the grand discoveries made with the most meagre means on the one hand, and the enormous amount of academic research resulting in nothing on the other.

LISTER was of the true type of scientific genius. He had the idea and the capacity to work it out with infinite pains. He brought an unwearied patience to bear. He was not abashed by failure or mistakes, nor was he moved by ridicule. Yet he made mistakes and encountered ridicule. The spray was a mistake, as he acknowledged with perfect readiness and equanimity. He was far too sincere and too intent on the truth to mind such small matters. Like DARWIN, he was too deeply absorbed in his search to have time or inclination for controversy. He went on his course steadfastly, and was rewarded by such full and complete success as falls to the lot of few men in any walk of life. He saw surgery revolutionized. He saw all the old evils of his youth—the dreadful festering wounds, the gangrene, blood-poisoning, and fever that decimated the hospitals—swept away; he saw operative mortality diminished to a fraction of what it had been; he saw limbs and lives saved which would formerly have had no chance, and vast new regions of surgery opened up. His dream had come true, and more, and it was his doing. It did not in the end take exactly the form he had at one time favoured. It became "aseptic" instead of "antiseptic" surgery; and to a certain extent the critics who had ridiculed antisepticism were justified. But that did not detract in the least from the achievement, nor has any man been found to deny him his due. It must have been a supreme happiness for him to contemplate the results. They are pre-eminently results which can be contemplated. His work differed from most scientific research in having a directly practical aim and one, moreover, that is of universal application. In every nation his name is known and honoured by the learned;

and if it is not blessed by the poor the omission is only due to ignorance. The boon of modern surgery is given to all classes alike, but it is the poor who have most reason for gratitude to LISTER. The worker in mine and factory and furnace, the soldier on the battlefield, the woman in child-birth—these and their like suffered most from the old ignorance which he dispelled for ever. He saw his work completed long before he died, full of years and honours, after a serene and peaceful, but intensely full and satisfying, life. Truly a rare and happy lot. That it has been rounded off in the fulness of time by the gentle hand of death is no matter for regret.

Music

As with literature, so with music – how could one possibly come to an agreement about whom to include in any even half-plausibly definitive list? What follows, therefore, must be largely whimsical. **Wolfgang Amadeus Mozart**, also representing all the child prodigies there have ever been, and who have served either as inspiration or as awful warning, carried on where Bach left off, developing western music from the baroque to the modern scale (*sic*). The process is considered by many to have attained its apotheosis in the work of **Ludwig van Beethoven**, the deaf genius of what is now "classical" music. **Richard Wagner** is here for his flamboyance; **Piotr Illyich Tchaikovsky** for his personality; while Chopin, the greatest exponent of the piano, was insufficiently noted in Britain to be accorded an obituary. **Toscannini** is chosen as an outstanding conductor, **Verdi** for light opera. As representative of the contemporary direction of the classical form, **Arnold Schoenberg** seems at least as apposite as anyone else. **Enrico Caruso** and **Maria Callas** must do duty for all the great classical performers. **Paderewski** neatly combined two outstanding careers. **George Gershwin** and **Johann Strauss**, in their quite different ways, have brought pleasure to millions, and along with **Glenn Miller** must suffice to represent that vast region of aural experience which is neither classical, nor popular, nor ethnic – beloved by some and despised by others as "light music". **Edith Piaf** and **Billie Holiday** both vocalised their hearts into music, with rather different results, and lived the kind of tragic personal lives that produce music "with soul". The blues are here in the person of "Leadbelly", and jazz in that of **Charlie Parker**: for these two not only did more than most to bring their sort of music to a wider audience, but also have some claim to be regarded as focal. **Elvis Presley** epitomises the American Pop Star as well as being the herald of rock and roll. **Jimi Hendrix** the rebel of the sixties. Finally, **The Beatles**, the group which died in 1970 – with them, pop music was elevated to new heights, musical and social.

The Daily Telegraph
17th September 1977

TO CALLAS, LIFE WAS PERFORMED FORTISSIMO

MARIA CALLAS, who died yesterday, aged 53, rose from the back streets of New York to become the most brilliant soprano of modern times, thrilling operagoers the world over with a voice which spanned more than three octaves.

The American-born singer, who had a much-publicised love affair with the late Aristotle Onassis before the Greek shipping magnate married Mrs Jacqueline Kennedy, had not appeared on stage since 1973.

The liaison with Onassis followed the break up of her marriage to Giovanni Meneghini, the wealthy Milan industrialist, who had discovered an ungainly, overweight girl with a magnificent lyric soprano voice and guided her to stardom.

Miss Callas told a television interviewer in 1974 that Onassis had been the big love of her life but that she was not sorry she hadn't married him because: "I think love is so much better when you're not married."

She said she harboured no ill feelings for anyone after Onassis married Mrs Kennedy, she said she could "take that in stride."

Voice problems

Declining health and voice problems forced Miss Callas into an eight-year retirement in 1965, but she returned briefly in 1973 with a tour of European capitals and a gala performance in Paris which won her the acclaim of ecstatic audiences and the attacks of critics, who said her voice had lost its sparkle.

Deeply stung by the critics' remarks, Miss Callas never sang in public again, withdrawing to a life of privacy in her homes in Paris and Monte Carlo.

Born Maria Anna Sofia Cecilia Kalogeropoulos in the Flower Hospital, Manhattan, four months after her parents arrived as emigrants from Greece, her potential as a singer was discovered at a very early age.

She was stout and spectacled (in later life she wore contact lenses) and was the ugly duckling of the family, but she became a swan before she was 30.

Sang for troops

In 1938 her mother took her back to her native Greece, and in Athens she sang for the occupying troops in return for sugar and macaroni for her family.

She also studied opera and in 1942 sang in the Athens National Opera Company. At that time she was weighing 14 stone.

When the war was over she returned to New York with an opera company which ran into difficulties, and, with the sole exception of an offer to sing the lead in "Madame Butterfly," for which she was far too bulky, no management would look at her. Two frustrating years passed in New York without a single engagement.

In desperation, she returned to Europe and managed to land a contract to sing at Verona for the equivalent of 20 guineas a performance.

Then came the turning point. Giovanni Meneghini married her, became her manager and, above all, persuaded the 77-year-old Serafin to coach her relentlessly.

After this her first appearance as Aida at Turin was a sensation. The Italians raved about her creamy three-octave voice. They did not mind her figure and even La Scala sent for her.

This was sheer bliss. Less than three years previously she had been accused of having many faults. But now she sang like an angel.

Thereafter she was to have many feuds with the management. As she said at the time, "I understand hate, I respect revenge."

She made a triumphal tour of Italy and another of South America. She queened it at the Metropolitan in New York. She sued a nephew of Pope Pius XII for claiming that his specially prepared pasta was responsible for reducing her weight dramatically from 14 to nine stone and even less.

For the time being at any rate, her loss of weight did not interfere with her voice. According to her, perfect control of breathing was all that mattered.

Nevertheless, it became apparent later on that her future lay as a mezzo soprano, though she could breathe more life into stodgy operatic characters than anyone before her, with the possible exception of Lotte Lehmann.

Nothing mediocre

She certainly lived up to her reputation for tempestuousness. Once she refused to sing unless she was summarily acquitted of a parking offence. On another occasion she walked out of a gala performance after the first act, though the President of Italy was present. "I will never make a pact with mediocrity," she cried.

JIMI HENDRIX

A key figure in the development of pop music

Jimi Hendrix, the pop musician, died in London yesterday, as reported elsewhere in this issue.

If Bob Dylan was the man who liberated pop music verbally, to the extent that after him it could deal with subjects other than teenage affection, then Jimi Hendrix was largely responsible for whatever musical metamorphosis it has undergone in the past three years.

Born in Seattle, Washington, he was part Negro, part Cherokee Indian, part Mexican, and gave his date of birth as November 27, 1945. He left school early, picked up the guitar, and hitch-hiked around the southern States of America before arriving in New York, where he worked for a while with a vaudeville act before joining the Isley Brothers' backing band. He toured all over America with various singers, including Sam Cooke, Solomon Burke, Little Richard, and Ike and Tina Turner, until in August, 1966, he wound up in Greenwich Village, New York, playing with his own band for $15 a night. It was there that he was heard by Chas. Chandler, former bass guitarist with the Animals, who became his manager and persuaded him to travel to England. Once in London he put together a trio with drummer Mitch Mitchell and bass guitarist Noel Redding, called the Jimi Hendrix Experience. The guitarist's wild clothes, long frizzy hair, and penchant for playing guitar solos with his teeth quickly made him a sensation.

His playing was rooted in the long-lined blues approach of B. B. King, but was brought up to date through the use of amplification as a musical device, and his solos were often composed of strings of feedback sound, looping above the free flowing bass and drums. The whole sound of the group, loose and improvisational and awesomely loud, was quite revolutionary and made an immediate impact on his guitar playing contemporaries.

As a singer and composer he was one of the first black musicians to come to terms with the electronic facilities offered by rock music, and his songs and voice, influenced considerably by Dylan, created perhaps the first successful fusion of blues and white pop.

After his phenomenal success in Britain he returned to America, where he was banned from a concert tour by the Daughters of the American Revolution, who considered his onstage physical contortions obscene. That served only to increase interest in him and he rapidly became one of the world's top rock attractions. Then, at the beginning of 1969 and at the height of his fame, he disappeared and spent more than a year in virtual seclusion, playing at home with a few friends. Early in 1970 he unveiled a new trio, the Band of Gipsies, and returned to Britain last month to play at the Isle of Wight festival. In his last interview he was quoted as saying that he'd reached the end of the road with the trio format, and was planning to form a big band.

In direct contrast to the violence and seeming anarchy of his music, Hendrix was a gentle, peaceful man whose only real concern was music. His final public appearance was when he sat in with War, an American band, at Ronnie Scott's club in London last Wednesday, and it was typical of the man that it was he who felt honoured by being allowed to play.

The Times
29th March 1943

M. RACHMANINOFF

COMPOSER AND PIANIST

M. Rachmaninoff, the famous composer and pianist, died yesterday from pneumonia at Beverly Hills, California, telegraphs our New York Correspondent.

Sergei Vassilievich Rachmaninoff was one of the most talented of the Moscow school of composers and a distinguished pianist. He belonged to the old Russian landed gentry and was born on April 1, 1873, in a large country house in the government of Novgorod. His grandfather had been an amateur composer and pianist; his father was a retired cavalry officer. He had piano lessons from the age of four; at the age of 10 he was sent to the Conservatoire of St. Petersburg, but his slow progress impelled his mother to send him as a pupil to Tchaikovsky's friend, Zvierev, at the Moscow Conservatoire, who soon made him work. Arensky's harmony lessons proved to be a great help to him, and after four years he began to give music lessons for a living. He composed an opera, *Aleko*, for his final examination. He obtained in 1892 the gold medal, and Tchaikovsky helped him to produce *Aleko* in the Great Moscow Theatre.

His most original works at that time were his songs and his Prelude in C sharp minor—which was soon acclaimed all over the world. But the failure of his first symphony, when played in St. Petersburg, depressed him, though his visit to England in 1899 came as a bright interval. He conducted in London his " fantasia for orchestra," " The Rock," and played several of his pianoforte pieces. His success gave him some courage, but back in Moscow despondency again seized him, until in 1901 he was cured by treatment. It was then that he wrote his Second Concerto in C minor, the Preludes for Pianoforte, and 12 songs.

The 12 songs were written in great haste, for he needed money for his honeymoon. He married in 1902 his cousin Nathalie Satin, and had two daughters. In 1906 the couple moved to Dresden and spent there three years; there Rachmaninoff composed his Second Symphony, E minor, the first Sonata for Pianoforte, the Symphonic Poem for Orchestra, and the Third Concerto for Pianoforte and Orchestra. In 1909 he went to America as a pianist and as a conductor with the Boston Symphony Orchestra.

During the last war he stayed in Russia and gave many concerts, handing over the receipts to war charities. After the Bolshevist Revolution he left Russia and went to the United States, where he worked chiefly as a pianist and conductor. In his memoirs his estimate of his own work was given as follows:—" The Bells " (a choral symphony), on which I worked with feverish ardour, is still the one I like best of my works, after that comes my Vesper Mass—then there is a long gap between it and the rest." For years he gave a concert annually in London. He would say that it was a pleasure to play in England, as nowhere else, except Russia, did he meet with such appreciative sympathy.

The Sun
11th April 1970

POP GO THE BEATLES

Break-up that really marks end of the 60s

THE NEWS that there will be no more Beatles—that Paul McCartney has decided, in his own parlance, to split the scene—is, in its own peculiar way, pretty shattering.

All over the world, reactionary old spoilsports will be rubbing their hands, airing their superiority complexes and declaring: "About time, too. About time that decadent bunch of no-good layabouts bit the dust."

Others of us will be sad to see the end of a whole slice of our lives. Because the Beatles were something more than simply pop stars.

And I speak as one who was no teenager when the Beatles arrived on the pop scene.

The Beatles were the catalyst of the 60s. They fused off a whole new way of thinking, changed a generation and, in a way that enrages the diehard Tory, put Britain on the map not as the Biggest Little Country in the World, whose influence was supreme, but as the country where people had fun and new things were happening.

Because they were the 1960s, almost single-handed, perhaps it is as well they should fizzle out right at the beginning of the 1970s.

Normal

They were famous collectively and as individuals. Paul, the one with charm, who could be relied upon to smooth things over when the others had put their foot in it.

Ringo, the one with the beautiful eyes, who seemed pretty dumb but could come out with devastatingly perfect squelches if he felt like it.

George, the most complicated; a veritable ocean of still waters running deep.

John, the nut-case whose nuttiness and excesses have an underlying deep truth.

But they weren't always as they are now. Six years ago the Americans called them "the four mopheads." They were beguiling, neat as little tailor's dummies in their Cardin-styled suits and long-haired in a way that seems positively normal now.

Upset

They were also curiously innocent and childishly easy to please.

The loss of that innocence hurt and upset their public when they began to do their own thing and go their own ways.

What now? They are unlikely ever to be poor, though the way John is going, he may even manage that. Paul will become smoother and sleeker. Ringo may retire happily into obscurity—or continue acting. George will go on seeking elusive truths.

The music from John and Paul will go on.

The Beatles are four individuals again. But they are already part of history, and not just show-business history.

THE ROAD FROM YEAH TO 'NO'

THE BEATLES were responsible for the biggest revolution pop has known.

No one could have guessed in the early 60s that four Liverpool lads would shatter America's domination of the pop world.

It was America's music. Jazz, pop, blues. It went with chewing gum and Coca Cola.

The biggest compliment to a British singer or musician was to be told he sounded like an American.

Tommy Steele had half-inched a bit of the thunder. But most of his contemporaries were happy trying to step into Elvis Presley's blue suede shoes.

Brash

The Beatles were rebels. They saw their music as something belonging to youth. Thousands of fans besieged Liverpool's Cavern Club to hear them.

In 1962 London cottoned on. The Beatles made their first record, Love Me Do.

Thousands ignored it. The new thing was bossa nova.

But as the bossa nova faded, pop fans said Yeah! Yeah! Yeah! to the Beatles and Please, Please Me soared to No. 1. Three months later, in May 1963, they put From Me To You at the top for six weeks.

When people said they were finished, they came up with Sgt Pepper. Once again they set the pace. Every new LP set new standards in imaginative pop.

Albums

By March 1964, British beat was the thing. And the eatles, who triggered it off, were up there in the stratosphere.

In under three years the world bought 300 million Beatle tracks. Lennon and McCartney became the Cole Porter-Rodgers and Hammerstein of the post-war era. Their song writing was prolific.

But last week the Beatles' latest single, Let It Be, slipped in the charts without reach No. 1.

The Beatles were finished. Even before Paul McCartney decided to cut the ties.

New York Herald Tribune
15th March 1955

'Yardbird' Parker, 53, Dies; Famed as Jazz Saxophonist

Charles ("Yardbird") Parker, fifty-three, the jazz and bebop saxophonist, died Saturday night in the Stanhope Hotel suite of a long-time friend, Baroness Nica Koenigswater. She said Mr. Parker had come to visit her last Wednesday night, en route to a playing date in Boston.

She said he became ill a short time after he arrived, and a physician she called ordered him to a hospital. But when Mr. Parker objected, she said, she "did not have the heart to force him to go." He was treated at the apartment several times between

Wednesday and Saturday, and collapsed about 8:15 p. m. Saturday.

A hotel physician ascribed the death to a heart attack. He was taken to Bellevue Morgue and a spokesman there said relatives had called to say they would make funeral arrangements.

At Birdland, jazzmen's hangout at 1678 Broadway, the owner, Oscar Goldstein, said he had named the establishment in honor of Mr. Parker when it opened five years ago. Mr. Goldstein described Mr. Parker as "the greatest alto-saxophonist in the world; he was a musical genius."

Mr. Parker had played with some of the greatest names in the jazz world, such as "Dizzy" Gillespie, "Flip" Phillips, Lionel Hampton and Teddy Wilson.

Baroness Koenigswater said she is married to a French diplomat, and that her home is in Mexico. She said her husband came to this country in September.

Her brother, the Baroness said, is Lord Victor Rothschild, British biochemist, jazzophile and amateur pianist—a descendant of the Rothschild banking family.

With her last night was told of Mr. Parker's death was an attorney, Chauncey Olman, of 545 Fifth Ave., who said he had represented the musician several times in the past.

Mr. Olman said the saxophonist is survived by a wife, Chan; a son, in the Air Force, and two younger children. He did not know where they lived.

At Birdland, musicians said they believed Mr. Parker made his home in Greenwich Village. Lately, they said, Mr. Parker had traveled from place to place, playing with local bands. In the past, he had run bands of his own.

The Times
3rd August 1921

DEATH OF SIGNOR CARUSO.

A MASTER SINGER.

RISE FROM HUMBLE ORIGINS.

(FROM OUR CORRESPONDENT.)

NAPLES, AUG. 2.

Signor Caruso had a serious relapse and died this morning at 9 o'clock in the Hotel Vésuve, Naples.

(FROM OUR OWN CORRESPONDENT.)

ROME, AUG. 2.

Signor Caruso, who had been convalescing at Sorrento, suddenly had a very grave relapse, suffering from a severe attack of peritonitis, which necessitated an immediate operation. The heart action was very weak and he was only kept alive by constant injections. He was brought to Naples on Sunday by steamer for the operation.

The relapse was quite unexpected, as only a week ago he went to the famous Sanctuary of Our Lady at Pompeii and made a thank-offering of £250 for his recovery. He had been living very quietly at Sorrento, and even of his oldest friends he asked only to be left in peace. A few weeks ago, however, he sang in private, showing that his voice had not suffered during his illness.

MEMOIR.

Enrico Caruso stood out by himself among the tenor singers of this century, dominating the lyric stage just as Jean De Reszke had done before him. Curiously enough, he came to the front almost immediately after De Reszke had retired.

Two artists, in turn holding the first place, could scarcely have been more unlike. Caruso was the more abundantly gifted by nature. It is quite safe to say that no tenor voice equal to his in its combination of power and extreme beauty of quality has been heard in this generation. De Reszke's voice, though also beautiful, was not so exceptional an organ.

Apart from mere voice, however, De Reszke was by many degrees the greater artist of the two. He had a charm of style and a sense of romance to which Caruso could not pretend, his varied gifts reminding old opera-goers of Mario in his prime. Caruso was a very fine singer, with true Italian warmth, but if blessed with no more than De Reszke's natural endowment he would not have risen to his unapproachable position in the world of opera.

Like nearly all the famous Italian tenors, with the exception of Mario, Caruso was a man of humble origin. Born in Naples in 1873, he was one of a large family of working people. He began to study singing seriously as a lad of 18, his master being Guglielmo Vergine, and in 1895 he made his first appearance on the stage. Then came four years of strenuous endeavour. There was in his case no sudden jump to fame. His great chance came in 1899, when he created at Milan the part of Loris in Giordani's *Feodora*. He was also the first to sing the tenor parts in Cilèa's *Adriana Lecouvreur*, Franchetti's *Germania*, and other operas.

Whether his potential greatness was then realized in Italy it is hard to say, but about this time, or a little earlier, a young Englishman travelling abroad wrote home to his friends that he had heard a singer who was sure to become the first tenor in the world. Such a case of fulfilled prophecy certainly deserves to be placed on record. In these early days of his career Caruso also sang at Milan the part of Faust, in Boïto's *Mefistofele*, and, though to the best of one's knowledge no notice concerning the performance reached this country, some Italian critics felt sure that a voice altogether out of the common had been discovered.

RISE TO FAME.

Caruso's fame really dated from 1902. In the spring of that year he sang with brilliant success at Monte Carlo with Mme. Melba in *La Bohème*, and forthwith he was engaged for Covent Garden. He came to London unheralded, appearing on May 14 as the Duke in *Rigoletto*. It was Mme. Melba's first night at Covent Garden that season, and to a certain extent the soprano diverted attention from the tenor. In one London paper, which need not be particularized, the readers were informed next morning that "the part of the Duke was carefully sung by M. Caruso." Just that, and nothing more. On the other hand, another critic, with a true *flair* for the first-rate, wired to the North the same night, without the smallest hesitation or qualification, that Caruso had the finest Italian tenor voice that had been heard in London for 30 years.

Caruso's success with the London public was never in doubt, and all through the season of 1902 it went on increasing. Still, he did not make himself such an attraction as to sell out Covent Garden whenever he sang. It was in 1904—an engagement in America kept him away from London in 1903—that he became a real power at the box-office. From that time he sang regularly at Covent Garden till

Evening Standard
5th October 1963

Edith Piaf, the songstress of postwar Paris, died here today aged 47. Her husband, former hairdresser turned singer, 27-year-old Theo Sarapo, was at her bedside. Known as the "Little Sparrow" of the French music hall—Piaf, an adopted name, is Paris slang for sparrow—she rose from street singer to international star, but had for years battled against ill-health.

She was taken ill yesterday at her Riviera home near Grasse—where she had gone recently to recuperate—and returned to Paris by ambulance last night. Her doctor was called about dawn, but nothing could be done to save her.

Death was due to an internal haemorrhage.

Edith Piaf's waif-like charm and tremulous voice gave her a mastery over Paris audiences which no French musical star since Maurice Chevalier has achieved

According to her autobiography she was born on the pavement of a Paris slum street after her mother set out to walk to a maternity home, and two gendarmes acted as midwives.

the end of the season of 1907, every part he undertook adding to his fame and popularity. Incidentally, he and Mme. Melba first made *La Bohème* a real success in this country, rendering Puccini incalculable service. In 1905 Caruso sang—in association with Mlle. Emmy Destinn, as she was then called—the part of Pinkerton at the first performance in London of *Madama Butterfly*. In appearance he was not much like an American naval officer, but he sang the music to perfection.

In one of the autumn seasons at Covent Garden Caruso sang with extraordinary success as Des Grieux in Puccini's *Manon Lescaut*. This was one of his finest performances. The force and abandon with which, without the smallest sacrifice of vocal beauty, he sang in the scene when Manon is going away in the convict ship can never be forgotten by his fortunate listeners. An old operagoer of vast experience told the present writer he had heard nothing of its kind so brilliant since Mario was at his best.

Caruso's connexion with Covent Garden came to a stop after the season of 1907. He had become the main attraction at the Metropolitan Opera House in New York, and was bound down by the terms of the contract he had signed with Conried. The result was that in 1908 the Covent Garden Syndicate would not pay the extremely high terms demanded for his services. He was in London during the season, but, apart from a charity concert at the Albert Hall, was only heard at private entertainments. Leaving aside his Des Grieux in *Manon Lescaut*—an opera not often put on—one may say that Caruso's most memorable work at Covent Garden, his voice being then at its very best, was done as Rodolfo in *La Bohème*, Radames in *Aïda*, and Canio in *I Pagliacci*.

A THOROUGH ARTIST.

Towards the end of the American season of 1908-9 Caruso met with the first check in his career of success. His voice failed him, and on returning to Europe he had to undergo an operation for the removal of a small growth on one of his vocal cords. The operation was perfectly successful, and he was soon singing again. Still, when, terms having been arranged, he reappeared at Covent Garden he was not quite the same as he had been. He had gained in vocal finish and was a better actor than before, but his high notes had lost something of their old triumphant ring. A well-known English tenor said of him that he was not entirely his old self, but was still much better than anyone else. The slight falling-off was probably only temporary, as all through the war and right on to the end he remained the chief prop of the Metropolitan Opera House in New York. Of late years, however, one gathered from the American papers that he was in better voice one night than another. In his early seasons in New York, as at Covent Garden, he had no inequalities. His voice could do all he asked of it, no matter how severe the demands.

Caruso was born for the stage, but, unlike some opera singers one could name, he did not in the concert-room disappoint his admirers or destroy illusion. His vocal tone was just as fascinating as in the theatre. As regards material success Caruso must have been the most fortunate of all male singers. Renewing his American contract from time to time he had tremendous terms, and his gramophone royalties furnished in themselves an ample income. He made endless records, so that thousands of people who never saw him in the flesh know something about his exceptional voice. Still, in the reproductions, excellent as they are, one misses something of the tone which, for want of a better word, is called velvety. It was that peculiar quality, allied of course with abundant power, that lifted Caruso above his fellows. Apart from his voice nature had not been specially kind to him. Heavy in figure and plain in face he could not look his parts as Mario and de Reszke did. Still, over and above his one superlative gift, he was a thorough artist. He had a passion for efficiency and a limitless capacity for taking pains.

Signor Caruso, who had of recent years made his home in New York, married, in August, 1918, Miss Dorothy Benjamin, of that city. He had a daughter, who is named Gloriana. During the last year Caruso has suffered constantly. In December last he broke a small blood vessel in his throat while singing in Brooklyn. A few days later, while singing in *Samson and Delilah* in New York, part of a pillar collapsed and fell on him as he was pulling down the temple. Not long afterwards he slipped and strained himself during a performance. The result of these accidents was a severe attack of pleurisy which nearly killed him. He underwent two operations and his life was despaired of, his friends being summoned to his bedside to take farewell. But, bearing up with great courage, he recovered slowly, and a few weeks ago left New York for his native Italy in search of health.

She was abandoned by her mother, went blind and regained her sight after her grandmother had taken her on a pilgrimage. With her father, a tumbler, she travelled from fair ground to fair ground as a child.

She was a street singer when a cafe proprietor gave her her first chance to sing to his customers at the age of 14.

Promoted to a suburban music-hall, she became an instant success.

Her emotional life was tempestuous. She was in love with French boxing champion Marcel Cerdan, and after he was killed when his Paris-New York airliner crashed in the Azores in 1949 she said: "My universe fell in. . . . I thought I could never again be happy, never again laugh."

Her first influential patron, night club owner Louis Leplee, was murdered and she became known as "the woman in the case," though she was not in any way connected with the crime.

Ill-health and emotional instability somehow combined to give her a ferocious, almost self-destructive energy.

Her recent appearances in Paris seemed liked triumphs of will-power, and left her audiences almost as exhausted emotionally as she appeared to be herself.

Her records sold in millions—3,000,000 of La Vie en Rose alone—and she was reputed to be one of the richest women in France.

Her first husband was Jacques Pills, also a singer. They were married in New York in 1952, with Marlene Dietrich as a bridesmaid. They were divorced in 1957.

The Times
9th April 1827

The German papers which arrived last night, mention that the celebrated composer, Beethoven, died at Vienna on the 27th ult., at six o'clock in the evening. The loss to the musical world is irreparable, and will be heard without doubt with universal regret.

Chicago Daily Tribune
17th January 1957

TOSCANINI, 89, GENIUS OF THE PODIUM, DEAD

Born Poor, Achieved Fame as Conductor

New York, Jan. 16 (P)—Arturo Toscanini, 89, hailed by many in the world of music as "the greatest conductor of all times," died peacefully in his sleep today at his home in Riverdale, the Bronx.

Toscanini, who was said to love music better than food, who broke his batons into splinters in temperamental outbursts, and lacerated his musicians in the most volcanic Italian, died without awareness that the end was near. He felt no pain, his son said today.

Retired after nearly 70 years of music in which his baton had shaped the scores of countless operas and symphonies, Toscanini, born to an impoverished tailor and his wife in Parma, Italy, suffered a stroke on New Year's day from which he never recovered.

Body to Lie in State

His body was to be taken to the Frank E. Campbell funeral home in Manhattan, where it will lie in state for public viewing all day tomorrow and Friday.

There will be a solemn requiem mass in St. Patrick's cathedral at 10 a. m. Saturday.

His body will later be flown to Italy for burial in the family chapel in Milan.

Millions, in this country and abroad, have sat breathless as Toscanini led orchestras to the heights of musical expression.

A modest and gentle man in private, the little, white haired Toscanini was a professional despot beloved by his musicians. He shepherded them to grand performances that whispered with the voice of angels or crackled with the thunder of volcanoes.

Last U. S. Concert in 1954

After a lifetime of conducting here, in his native Italy and other European countries and on road tours of America, he gave his last concert on April 4, 1954.

This was at Carnegie hall with the National Broadcasting company symphony orchestra, which had been formed especially for him and which he led since Christmas night, 1937.

None knew then that it was his farewell performance, but it had closed with poignant drama.

"Life an Inspiration"

"His life is an inspiration to everyone, and, indeed to many he stands as the symbol of music."

Toscanini's musical "birth" goes as far back as the age of 9 when he entered the conservatory at Parma.

Actually, it was a whim of fate that made young Toscanini a conductor after he was graduated in piano and cello, winning honors in composition.

He had taken a job with a touring opera company headed for South America. That was in 1886 when he was 19.

There in Rio De Janeiro, the Brazilian conductor got into a quarrel with some of the Italian artists before a performance of Verdi's opera "Aida."

The Daily Telegraph & Morning Post
1st July 1941

M. PADEREWSKI

Ignace Jan Paderewski, pianist, patriot and first Prime Minister of free Poland, whose death is announced, aged 80, was born at Kurilowka, in Russian Poland. After the 1863 rebellion his father was sent into exile in Siberia, and young Paderewski grew up in an atmosphere of hatred for Russia and Germany. In later years he refused to play in either country.

He entered the Warsaw Conservatory at 12, made his first public appearance at 16 and was appointed professor at the Warsaw Conservatory at 19. He married about this time, and soon after suffered a grievous loss—his young wife died and their child survived only as a life-long invalid.

His first concert in London in 1890 was at the St. James's Hall, Piccadilly, and the takings were only £10. However, he was soon the vogue, and in 1891 made his first journey to America. There his success was sweeping, and by 67 concerts in 27 cities he made £37,000.

With the outbreak of war in 1914 Paderewski devoted all his energies to the cause of Poland. He played little, and then only for charities. He devoted his private fortune to founding the force of volunteers known as the Polish Army in France, and was officially recognised in Washington as the spokesman of the Polish people.

When war ended he hurried to Europe and then travelled to Danzig in a British cruiser. The Poles had gained their liberty, but their country was devastated. Paderewski arrived at the critical moment. He was hailed as a saviour, and within a fortnight had become Prime Minister.

His aims were to establish closer relations with the Allies and ensure an economic revival of the country. In November, 1919, 11 months after taking office, he resigned. He felt keenly attacks made by political adversaries.

He retired to Switzerland, but in 1922 again took up his virtuoso's career and immediately regained his old prestige.

In January, 1940, Paderewski was elected President of Poland's Provisional Parliament in Paris. Towards the end of the year he went to America, where he continued his propaganda work for Poland.

The Brazilian audience, out of loyalty to the conductor, hissed the orchestra's Italian conductor off the stage when he sought to take over the baton. The orchestra's chorus master met the same fate. Confusion reigned.

Too Moved to Reappear

The last concert was an all-Wagner program and ended with the Act 1 prelude to "die Meistersinger." As the last note faded, Toscanini dropped his baton to the floor. An orchestra member picked it up and handed it to him. With head bowed, Toscanini walked away.

The audience—unaware that it was his farewell—stood, clapped and cheered. But Toscanini did not reappear. NBC said later that he did not return because he was too moved.

After that concert, his retirement was announced thru the release of a letter he had written a few days earlier to David Sarnoff, chairman of the board of the Radio Corporation of America. Because of shyness, Toscanini had objected to any advance notice of retirement, it was said.

"Now the sad time has come when I must reluctantly lay aside my baton and say good-by to my orchestra," Toscanini wrote.

Children at Bedside

At Toscanini's side at his death were his son, Walter; his daughter, the Countess Wally Castelbarco, and Anita Colombo, former director of singers at Milan's famed La Scala opera.

Another daughter, Wanda, wife of the noted pianist, Vladimir Horowitz, and three grandchildren, also survive him. His wife, the former Carli Di Martini whom he wed in 1897, died in 1951.

Words of grief and tribute came swiftly from friends and notables of the musical world.

Toscanini has "already gone into history as the outstanding musician of our time," said Rudolph Bing, general manager of the Metropolitan opera.

He Arrives Late

Toscanini, then a cellist with the touring orchestra, had thought once that evening he wouldn't even show up for the performance.

But he changed his mind at the last moment and arrived late—slipping into his usual chair unnoticed.

Women in the company's chorus became greatly worried, for fear they would be stranded far away from home. One spied the tardy Toscanini and set up a cry: "He will save us! He knows all the operas by heart!"

Fellow musicians, snatching at the last straw, handed Toscanini a baton. He went to work in the masterly fashion.

When the performance was concluded, the audience rose with resounding cheers. Toscanini's fortune was made.

He came to the United States in 1908. In this country he swept on to the heights.

For seven seasons he conducted at the Metropolitan opera in New York.

Subsequently, he directed the New York Philharmonic symphony and the NBC symphony orchestra.

TOSCANINI

Los Angeles Times
17th August 1977

Elvis Presley Dies at 42; Legend of Rock 'n' Roll Era

Presley Stood as a Symbol

BY ROBERT HILBURN
Times Pop Music Critic

Elvis Presley didn't invent rock 'n' roll but he was its most important figure and its primary symbol.

The 12-day tour that he was to begin today had been sold out for weeks. It didn't matter to Presley's audience whether he had a hit on the charts; they flocked to see him. He represented a link with their youth and their dreams.

Depending on who is estimating, Presley sold between 250 and 300 million records. But sales are not really important in his case. Neither are sold-out shows. Legends in pop aren't made by music alone. His original impact was so spectacular that his audience remained fiercely loyal.

Presley served as a catalyst for a generation of Americans seeking to express themselves in the changing sociological structure of the 1950s. His music was wild, defiant, challenging, adventurous. His long hair, sideburns, loud clothes and uncompromising manner offered a symbol for teen-agers desiring to state their own identity.

Presley's musical influences were simply the natural outgrowth of the working-class heritage of his Mississippi childhood. It was a synthesis so original and strong that radio stations did not know how to handle it. Country music stations dismissed it initially as too "black" sounding. Black stations figured it was too country in tone. Pop stations, used to the slick sounds of Eddie Fisher and Perry Como, just ignored it.

But Presley developed a regional following and, with the help of manager Tom Parker, began an assault on a wider audience. His early 1956 appearances on Tommy and Jimmy Dorsey's "Stage Show" TV program made him a star. His "Heartbreak Hotel" went almost immediately to No. 1.

Rock was never the same. Even those, like Bob Dylan and the Beatles, who would help push the music in still new directions, have cited Presley's influence.

"Nothing really affected me until Elvis," John Lennon once said.

But Presley's artistry wasn't recognized for years. He was first dismissed as a fad, novelty, freak. "Elvis the Pelvis," sneered commentators, referring to his hip-swinging movements on stage.

When rock criticism came of age in the mid-'60s, Presley still didn't receive the credit he deserved. His music, by then, was subdued, bland, without passion. Much of his attention was devoted to a series of largely unambitious, formula-coated films.

Presley's serious reentry came in 1969. Through a highly acclaimed NBC-TV special and then a series of shows in Las Vegas, he reestablished himself. The new records—"Suspicious Minds," "In the Ghetto," "Burning Love"—made him important all over again. The music bristled with the old energy and bite. It wasn't unusual to see mothers and daughters both cheering him in concerts.

But gradually the passion began to leave his work. Perhaps there was no longer a challenge. The records were uneven. The concerts often were sloppy. Some complained about his increased weight. But there was rarely a night when he didn't show signs somewhere during the concert of his greatness.

One night in Las Vegas, Phil Spector, the most respected record producer of the rock era, chided someone at the table for criticizing Presley's performance.

"Hey, he's doing us a favor being up on that stage," Spector said. "He may be overweight and he may not move like he used to, but he doesn't have to be there. He doesn't need the money. We're lucky to be able to see him. Some day we're all going to say, 'Damn, I wish I could still see him.'"

New York Times
7th December 1949

'Lead Belly,' Who Won International Fame As Interpreter of Negro Folk Songs, Is Dead

Huddie Ledbetter (Lead Belly), the Negro minstrel from the deep South who attained international fame as an interpreter of his people's folk songs, died of a bone infection yesterday in Bellevue Hospital. He was 60 years old.

For fifteen years Lead Belly strummed his guitar and sang Negro spirituals, work songs and ballads to audiences in night clubs and concert halls. Some were his own compositions and others anonymous works indigenous to his race. He was acclaimed by critics and untutored music lovers, a tribute to the universality of his art.

His origins were humble and his later years marked by sporadic violence. Lead Belly was born in the bayous of Louisiana, but he left the swamplands early and became a wanderer through the South. He worked as a cotton picker and laborer, learned to play the guitar and became an expert singer of the songs he heard in his travels.

John A. Lomax, an authority on American folk songs, heard Huddie Ledbetter sing in 1933, when the minstrel was serving a sentence in the Louisiana State Prison. He was instrumental in obtaining Lead Belly's pardon and brought him to New York, where he won immediate renown.

The singer found it difficult to shed the habit of quick anger he had acquired during his years as a roustabout. In 1939 he was sentenced to serve a year in a New York State prison for stabbing another man. He resumed his musical career upon his release.

He is survived by his widow, Mrs. Martha Ledbetter of 414 East Tenth Street; a daughter, A. Mae Richardson of Kansas City, Mo., a sister and two nieces.

The Times
14th February 1883

The world is poorer by another great man. RICHARD WAGNER died yesterday at Venice, in his seventieth year ; and thus suddenly, almost without warning, and in a city which, however full of poetical associations, is entirely alien to his genius, the greatest musician of our time disappears from the scene of his struggles and his triumphs. To us of the present day, whose experience of WAGNER's music is that of a theatre filled with a rapt and enthusiastic crowd, it is difficult to recall the time when his name was one to be generally met with derision, and when, among some classes in Germany, and in England as well as in France, his musical ideas were commonly denounced as not so much revolutionary as nonsensical. One has to remember, however, how long it is since WAGNER began to compose. It was in 1841 that he began " Rienzi," in Paris, and " The Flying Dutchman " followed immediately, while " Tannhäuser," which remains to this day his best-known opera, was composed in 1845. At this early date, and even for many years before it, he was possessed with the revolutionary ideas that found expression in his music, but which were based on a much broader foundation than a mere dissatisfaction with existing art. It happens that we possess an authentic account of WAGNER's mental history in the record, which he contributed some three years ago to the *North American Review*, of what he calls " The Work and " Mission of my Life." From this interesting but high-pitched narrative it would seem that WAGNER, very early in the day, set himself to reform not only German music, but German civilization as a whole. With characteristic German thoroughness he went below the outward symptoms, and aimed at a cure that should be radical. " I " could not conceive of a national art entirely " separated from the basis of our national culture ; " and this culture, the sum total of all the " elements of Germany's political and social state, " appeared to me, from an early point in my study " of it, to be something unnatural, narrow, weak, " and incapable of producing the true realization of " any great national idea." In a word, WAGNER, like so many of his generation, hated from the bottom of his soul the order of things that prevailed in Germany between 1815 and 1866—in the period when, as he said, " there was no true " German life, no real German history." His insurrectionary fervour was stimulated by the events of 1830, while his musical sense was stirred by BEETHOVEN's symphonies and by the romantic melodies of WEBER. Then came a time when he began to despair of Germany and German art ; when MEYERBEER ruled the stage and a number of retrograde Princes kept intelligence under severe control. He went to Paris, " the centre of " modern life," hoping to find there both stimulus and encouragement. Alas ! he found neither ; and after a time of struggle, during which he had to support himself by accepting work of any kind'

he joyfully received the summons to return. His " Rienzi " had found favour at the Saxon Court, and he went home again, carrying with him the sketch of many of the operas which are now so familiar to our ears. After 1848 he had again to leave Germany—this time as an involuntary exile ; and in his Swiss home, " finding full " opportunity for the uninterrupted contem- " plation of his ideals," he produced not only two or three more operas, but a complete literary presentment of his theory both of music and of life. The great cycle of the " Ring " of the Nibelungen " was the work of this period of retirement from the world.

For many years the exile tried in vain for leave to return, even for only so long as to direct the performance of one of his own operas in his native land. He went again to Paris in 1860, and there the stormy reception of his " Tannhäuser " convinced him that in the capital of civilization convention was too strong for him. Nor were things much better when the home authorities at last relented and he was allowed " to show himself again in " Germany, and as a German." " I felt more " than ever," he characteristically says, " after my " experience in (Imperial) Paris, the special curse " of the German artist ; that of having no power " behind him—of finding that his effort for the " elevation of his art is taken only for personal " ambition." After having had the authorities so decisively against him, he longed, in fact, to have them decisively on his side ; and in 1864 his wish was gratified. The young KING of BAVARIA took possession of him, and from that moment WAGNER's future was secure. He set to work to finish his " Nibelungen," and, as every one knows, produced it in 1870 in a special theatre at Baireuth, the leaders of the musical world

crowding to hear it from every country of Europe. But from long before 1876 his works have been a staple entertainment in every German concert-room and theatre, and there is no composer, not even the greatest of past times, whose works are so eagerly listened to and so loudly applauded in the opera-houses of Germany. Nor is Germany alone Wagnerian. Last season, as every English music-lover remembers, the cycle was played in London, and was the great musical event of the year. Of the crowds which heard it, many no doubt found it a severer exercise than they could have wished ; but on the whole its success was unquestioned, and every one recognized it as a work of art of the highest and rarest kind.

WAGNER had his full share of the egotism of genius, and the reader of his autobiographical notes is somewhat painfully amused to see how plainly he lays it down that the great object of forming a national German school of music should be to qualify the students for the proper performance of his own works. They may be trained on the symphonies of HAYDN and BEETHOVEN, but the training is all to lead up to the perpetual and faultless performance of " Parsifal." Yet there is, after all, something sublime in self-assertion of this degree. Any creative artist, if he is worth anything, must believe in himself, as MICHEL ANGELO did, and MILTON, and TURNER. On the strength of WAGNER's creations, we may pardon him the immensity of his self-confidence. For there can be no doubt as to the magnitude, and, in the main, as to the beauty, of his creations. His object was to make music more profoundly real, and at the same time more widely appreciable, by bringing it closer to the other recognized modes of expressing human emotion. To do this he rejected at once the falsity of MEYERBEER and the traditional mannerism of the whole school of Italian opera—BELLINI, VERDI, and the rest. To his mind, a performance which was half spoken, while the characters at set intervals came forward to the footlights and trilled a lay to the audience, was worse than useless ; it was simply silly. Music, he said, if it is to be seriously cared for, if it is to have any relation to the deeper interests of life, must be seen to be in close relation to feeling ; it must be wedded to the words in indissoluble bonds, for both music and words are but different methods of communicating feeling. It is a theory which has already had a hard fight on its way to general acceptance, and even now it is far from being admitted universally. But none who sat and listened to " Siegfried " last year, or to the glorious closing scenes of the " Götter-" dammerung," can doubt the reality of music in WAGNER's sense, or can question its power, as he himself expresses it, " to unite mankind by an " ideal bond." The man who first consciously held the theory, and who did so much to carry it out, deserves to be ranked among the great masters of the art of the world.

New York Times
25th December 1944

Major Glenn Miller Is Missing On Flight From England to Paris

Former Orchestra Leader Had Been Conducting Bands of the Army Air Forces Since Enlistment—Won Many Honors

PARIS, Dec. 24 (P)—Maj. Glenn Miller, director of the United States Air Force Band and a former orchestra leader, is missing on a flight from England to Paris, it was announced today.

Major Miller, one of the outstanding orchestra leaders of the United States, left England Dec. 15 as a passenger aboard a plane. No trace of the plane has been found.

His Air Force Band had been playing in Paris. No members of the band were with him on the plane. He last led his band in a broadcast Dec. 12. His band, scheduled to broadcast over BBC tomorrow at 7 P. M. [2 P. M., Eastern war time] in the "AEF Christmas Show," will be conducted by Sgt. Jerry Gray, deputy leader.

Was Top-Rank Leader

Bespectacled and scholarly looking, Glenn Miller was one of the nation's top-ranking orchestra leader before entering the Army as a captain in 1942. He not only established box-office records with his band but several times achieved first place in national popularity polls. In 1940 his gross income was $800,000. Almost 3,000,000 copies of his records were sold in 1940.

He was a trombonist and an arranger of exceptional talents. His theme song, "Moonlight Serenade," was internationally known.

Two-time winner of The Billboard's Annual College Music Survey, he was one of the earliest to understand the scoring of a swing arrangement. He contributed prolifically to the libraries of the nation's outstanding bands.

Born at Clarinda, Iowa, thirty-five years ago, his family moved to a homestead at Nebraska when he was five years old. Later, the family moved to North Platte, where Miller attended school. The roving family settled for a time at Grant City, Mo.; where he became a butcher's helper, and began toying with the butcher's battered trombone. The local town tailor purchased a new trombone for the boy and he worked for nothing until the price of the trombone was paid.

The family kept moving, finally settling at Fort Meyers, Col., where Miller finished high school, took music lessons, and worked his way through the State University by playing in the school dance band. When out of college he decided on the career of a musician and joined the Ben Pollack orchestra, playing at the side of Benny Goodman.

His reputation as a "hot" trombone player spread, and he went east to make records with the Dorsey brothers. While making records he continued his musical education and at the same time played with Red Nichols and his band. Then followed his position with Ray Noble when the latter organized his first band.

He left Noble to organize his own band. His first two bands were not up to his technical standards. His third and final orchestra earned him a nationwide reputation. The third band came into existence in 1939, first playing two engagements at the Paradise Restaurant here and then became a success at Frank Dailey's Meadowbrook, Cedar Grove, N. J., and the Glen Island Casino, New Rochelle, N. Y.

Was in Motion Pictures

His recordings were in great demand, and he was engaged to play at the Hotel Pennsylvania, which culminated in his first radio commercial on CBS, which was renewed several times. He and his band also played several long-term return engagements at the Hotel Pennsylvania. He made several transcontinental trips with his band, making one-night stands at colleges, theatres and ballrooms. His widespread popularity and musical appeal earned for him a motion-picture contract with Twentieth Century-Fox in which he co-starred with Sonja Henie.

In 1942 he enlisted in the Army and was commissioned a captain. He trained and directed service bands, and entertained American troops here and abroad. He was commissioned a Major several weeks ago.

His wife, the former Helen Burger, was a university classmate. They were married on Oct. 6, 1928. They have two adopted children, a three-months old daughter and a two-year-old son. He resided at Tenafly, N. J., with his family.

New York Times
15th July 1951

Schoenberg, Composer, Dies at 76; His Atonal Music Caused a Furor

Special to The New York Times.

LOS ANGELES, July 14—Arnold Schoenberg, composer and teacher, who invented the controversial twelve-tone system in music, died at his home in suburban Brentwood, late last night at the age of 76. He had been ill for some time and only last month canceled a teaching engagement because of his health.

A revolutionary in the music field, Mr. Schoenberg, who became a United States citizen in 1940, was recognized as a leading composer. However, he himself felt that many years, possibly fifty, would be required before he would be completely understood, basing his view on the delayed appreciation of famous compositions of other leaders.

About the lively diminutive and intellectual figure of Arnold Schoenberg the wildest storms of twentieth-century music raged. Hostile demonstrations marked most of the first performances of his work. Pitched polemical battles — as fiercely favoring his revolutionary atonal twelve-tone compositions as opposing—swept central Europe in the early Nineteen Hundreds and then, in turn, the rest of the musical world.

Yet at his death there were few —no matter how little they warmed to his music itself—who could deny either the importance of his influence or that he was a great musical theorist and teacher. And there were many voices who predicted that the Austrian composer's music would finally be accepted in much the same way as the later work of Stravinsky and the compositions of Bela Bartók.

It was Schoenberg's contention that the old dynamic laws of music, tonic to dominant to tonic, were no longer valid, that the next natural step in music was the breaking away from the established harmonic rules and the formulation of a twelve-tone system, by which all twelve tones of the chromatic scale were of equal value.

This revolutionary type of formal structure consists primarily in the use of a "basic series," comprised of all of the twelve tones, with none repeated. The tones may be placed in order and at any intervals desired, and from this series all of the themes are derived. Regular recourse to the contrapuntal devices of inversion, "canzicrans" (reversal) and others are essential features of the polyphonic structure, and symmetrical patterning is banned.

Method Called Artificial

Many have protested that such a method of composition is self-conscious and artificial. But the composer and his followers asserted that the twelve-tone composition existed in practice before it was developed in theory.

It is of interest to note that the term, "atonality" to describe the Schoenbergian school of composition—which was given to the music by the composer's opponents— has never been accepted by him, since atonality in music, as he once remarked, is an impossibility. The composer went on to point out that his music had tones like any other and that it was the arrangement that made the difference. He preferred his method to be known merely as a system of composing with twelve tones.

Mr. Schoenberg also maintained that none of his works was at variance with the principles taught by the old masters and that ultimately it will be their music which will prove how right his path has been.

One American estimate of the work the composer was trying to accomplish appeared as early as January, 1913. At that time the noted critic, James Gibbons Huneker, who had heard the first performance of Schoenberg's important "Pierrot Lunaire" in Europe and had subsequently studied his published scores, wrote the following in The New York Times:

"His mission is to free harmony from all rules. A man doesn't hit on such combinations, especially in his acrid instrumentation, without heroic labors. His knowledge must be enormous, for his scores are as logical as a highly-wrought mosaic; that is, logical, if you grant him his premises. He is perverse and he wills his music, but he is a master in delineating certain moods, though the means he employs revolts our ears."

Arnold Schoenberg was born in Vienna on Sept. 13, 1874. Attracted to music from his earliest years, he already played the violin by the time he was 12 and had composed a number of duets for the instrument. He later taught himself the 'cello and composed several trios and a quartet for a group of school mates with whom he played chamber music.

His father died during his boyhood and left the youth in impoverished circumstances, but he persisted in his self-study of music. He remained entirely untaught in composition until a friend showed some of his work to Alexander von Zemlinsky, who knew Brahms and was considered an authority. Zemlinsky offered to teach him counterpoint, the only musical instruction Schoenberg ever received.

At the age of 23, in quite needy circumstances, the young composer made a piano arrangement of Zemlinsky's opera, "Sarema," and then composed a string quartet, which along with a number of his songs, was presented in Vienna. Many of these stirred opposition.

In 1899 he composed the sextet for strings, "Verkläerte Nacht," one of his few works to achieve any real popularity. The sextet clearly reveals the composer's strong romantic strain springing from, such of his acknowledged masters as Brahms, Wagner and Mahler.

The next year he began work on his "Gurre-Lieder" in Vienna and by 1901 they had been sketched completely. The orchestration, however, was constantly interrupted by the scoring of operettas of other composers—6,000 pages in all—so that he might meet his day-to-day debts.

At about this time he married Mathilde von Zemlinsky, the sister of his friend, and soon left Vienna for Berlin in hopes of improving his fortunes.

Taught at Conservatory

On the basis of the score of the first part of his "Gurre-Lieder," Richard Strauss used his influence to obtain a teaching position and a scholarship for Mr. Schoenberg at the Stern Conservatory in Berlin.

In 1903 the composer returned to Vienna, where he made the friendship of Gustav Mahler, then a power in the musical life of that city, who thought highly of him and the future, even though he did not wholly accept all of the youth's transformations.

It was through the assistance of the older composer that many of Mr. Schoenberg's compositions were performed in Vienna. These include his first string quartet in D minor, the "Kammersymphonie," the symphonic poem, "Pelleas und Melisande," after Maeterlinck; the "Songs for Orchestra," the second string quartet, the "George-Lieder" and the Pieces for Piano.

It is with these compositions that Mr. Schoenberg marked his steady movement away from tonality and began his groping search for the new form which finally developed into the twelve-tone system.

In 1911, Mr. Schoenberg removed to Berlin once more and began to teach privately. There gathered about him a small group of enthusiastic pupils, many of whom later became famous in their own right, the most prominent among them being Alban Berg. Some of the others included Anton von Webern, Egon Wellesz, Karl Horwitz, Heinrich Jalowitz and Erwin Stein.

During the first World War the composer was called to service twice, but, being over 40, did only garrison duty in Vienna and after a time was excused from this. In 1925 he was invited to assume the chair in Berlin that had been occupied by Busoni.

Mr. Schoenberg remained in Berlin until May, 1933, when he left of his own accord because of Hitler's oppression of the Jews. In November he came to the United States to teach at the Malkin Conservatory in Boston, eventually settling in Los Angeles, where he taught at the University of California until his retirement in 1944. He continued to teach privately after his retirement and usually had about eight pupils.

Important Schoenberg compositions not previously mentioned include his operas, "Erwartung," "Die Glueckliche Hand," and "Von Heute auf Morgan"; his Quintet for Winds, Variations for Organ, Variations for Wind Band, Second Chamber Symphony, and "Ode to Napoleon Bonaparte." His "A Survivor From Warsaw" was played last season by the Philharmonic-Symphony, conducted by Dimitri Mitropoulos.

In 1947, Mr. Schoenberg was the recipient of the Award of Merit for Distinguished Achievement given by the National Institute of Arts and Letters to "an eminent foreign artist, composer or writer living in America." The award carried a $1,000 prize.

The composer's first wife died in 1923. They had two children, Mrs. Gertrud Greissle and Georg. In August, 1924, he married Gertrud Kolisch, the sister of the well-known violinist, Rudolf Kolisch, who was once one of his pupils. They had three children, Nuria, Ronald and Lawrence.

COMPOSER VERDI DEAD.

He Had Been Suffering in Milan from Congestion of the Brain.

ROME, Jan. 26.—A special dispatch to Patria announces that Verdi the composer is dead. He had been ill in Milan with congestion of the brain.

Giuseppe Verdi was born in Roncole, near Busetto, in the Duchy of Parma, Oct. 9, 1814. His father was an innkeeper and his first instruction in music was given him by an obscure organist. In 1833 he was placed under the instruction of Lavigna, a member of the orchestra of La Scala. After studying operatic composition for six years Verdi produced, in 1839, his first work, "Oberto di San Bonifazio." "Un Giorno di Regno," written in 1841, was his next work. A year later he produced "Nabucco," which established his fame.

In 1843 he produced "Lombardi," and in 1844-5 he wrote four grand operas—"Ernani," "I due Foscari," "Giovanna d'Arco," and "Alzira." For a time "Ernani" was the most popular of his works. It was first presented in Venice, in March, 1844.

"Attila" was produced in Venice in 1846 and "Macbeth" in Florence in 1847. The same year he visited London and produced there "I Masnadieri." "Il Trovatore" was written in 1853 for production in Rome, and the same year he brought forward "La Traviata." Other of his well-known works are "Un Ballo in Maschera," "Don Carlos," "Aïda," "Otello," and "Falstaff." Verdi in 1859 was a member of the National Assembly of Parma and in 1861 of the Italian Parliament. In November, 1874, the King made him a Senator

New York Herald Tribune
18th July 1959

Billie Holiday, 44, Dies; Famed as Blues Singer

'Lady Day' of Jazz Sang With Top Bands, Had Own Revue; Narcotics Her Big Enemy

Billie Holiday, forty-four, one of the greatest blues singers, died early yesterday in Metropolitan Hospital of congestion of the lungs complicated by a heart ailment.

The Negro entertainer, who lived at 26 W. 87th St., had been brought to the hospital on May 31 in an unconscious condition, suffering from liver and heart ailments. She was reported to have made progress against her illness but her condition worsened several days ago. Her husband and manager, Louis McKay, had been at her side constantly for the last two days and was with her when she died at 3:20 a.m.

Among Greatest Blues Singers

Miss Holiday was one of the most distinctive blues singers in the history of jazz. Her voice had been described in many ways: "a petulant, sex-edged moan"; "incredibly unresonant, whining and hoarse"; "a cerebral lamentation in suggestive pastel shades." But, as some one once said, "Billie Holiday's singing is her own, and although many have tried, none can do quite what she does."

Her greatest enemy, however, was narcotics. She was convicted twice of using drugs and in 1947 she spent nearly a year in a Federal reformatory as an addict. Once she said, "There isn't a soul on this earth who can say for sure that their fight with dope is over until they're dead."

A solemn requiem mass will be held at 11 o'clock Tuesday morning in St. Paul's Roman Catholic Church, Columbus Circle and 60th St. Miss Holiday will be at the Erskine Funeral Parlor, 1341 Bedford Ave., Brooklyn, until tomorrow morning, when she will be taken to the Universal Funeral Parlor, Lexington Ave. and 52d St. She will be buried in the Evergreen Cemetery in Brooklyn.

First Recordings in 1933

She wrote the words of "Fine and Mellow," "God Bless the Child" and "Don't Explain." Miss Holiday, who made her first recordings in 1933, cut her last record this spring, a long-playing disc with twelve of her old numbers, called "Lady Sings the Blues." Her last public appearance here was at a concert at the Phoenix Theater shortly before her illness. Her last major jazz concert appearance was last Sept. 13 at Town Hall.

"A Hep Kitty"

Miss Holiday called herself a hep kitty, and from her autobiography, "Lady Sings the Blues," published in 1956, it was easy to see why. "Mom and Pop were just a couple of kids when they got married," the book began. "He was eighteen, she was sixteen and I was three."

Born Eleanora Fagan in Baltimore, Md., on April 7, 1915, she was baby-sitting and scrubbing steps at five cents a step when she was six. At the same time, she was running errands for call girls in a near-by "establishment"—and listening to records by Louis Armstrong and Bessie Smith in the girls' sitting room. She was raped when she was ten.

Her mother took her to Harlem and opened a restaurant where Billie, then thirteen, sang for tips. A year later, she applied for a job as a chorus girl at a night club called Pod's and Jerry's—later to become famous as the Log Cabin Club—and it was found that while she couldn't dance, she could sing.

She caught on, and soon she was touring the country with the bands of Count Basie and Artie Shaw. She came back to New York, opened at the old Cafe Society, and stayed there two years. She was topping the polls as the nation's blues singer when, in 1947, she was arrested for dope addiction.

Arrested in Hospital

On June 12, twelve days after she entered the hospital, in fact, she was arrested on narcotics charges after a nurse assertedly found a deck of heroin in her handbag. Police suspected smuggling but Miss Holiday insisted she had the drug in her handbag when she entered the hospital. A police guard was briefly placed at her bedside but was removed and she was paroled in the custody of her attorney who told the court, in her absence, that the singer would "never leave her bed."

But in spite of addiction, arrests, police bans on her appearance in night clubs and a life of general unhappiness, Lady Day, as she was known throughout the world of jazz, sang her way to the front ranks of modern American music. Her singular style made memorable such renditions as "Strange Fruit," "Lover Man," "Travelin' Light," "I Cover the Waterfront," "Good Morning, Heartache" and "All of Me."

Miss Holiday was married three times—to Jimmy Monroe, Joe Guy and Louis McKay.

New York Times
12th July 1937

GEORGE GERSHWIN, COMPOSER, IS DEAD

Master of Jazz Succumbs in Hollywood at 38 After Operation for Brain Tumor

WROTE 'RHAPSODY IN BLUE'

Also Composed 'Porgy and Bess,' 'Of Thee I Sing' and Many Musical Comedies

Special to THE NEW YORK TIMES.

HOLLYWOOD, Calif., July 11.— George Gershwin, 38-year-old composer, died today at 10:35 A. M. at the Cedars of Lebanon Hospital. He succumbed five hours after being operated on for removal of a brain tumor. The operation was decided upon when the composer's condition became critical at midnight.

Dr. Gabriel Segall of Los Angeles and Dr. Howard Nafsziger, University of California Professor of Surgery, performed the operation at 5 o'clock this morning.

Dr. Walter E. Dandy, Baltimore brain surgeon, turned back at Newark today upon learning that Mr. Gershwin's condition had changed suddenly and he would be operated on at once. Dr. Dandy had been summoned from Chesapeake Bay, where he was cruising over the week-end with Governor Harry W. Nice of Maryland.

Ira Gershwin, who wrote lyrics for his brother's music, was at his side when he died.

Two weeks ago Mr. Gershwin collapsed at the Samuel Goldwyn studios, where he had been working on nine compositions for "The Goldwyn Follies." He had completed five songs before his breakdown. Taken to the hospital for observation, the composer, when released last week, was in an extremely nervous condition. Yesterday he was returned to the hospital in a coma.

Also surviving are his mother, Mrs. Rose Gershwin; a sister, Mrs. Leopold Godowsky Jr. and another brother, Arthur.

He was a member of the American Society of Composers and Publishers, the Lambs Club and the Bohemians.

Child of the Jazz Age

George Gershwin was a composer of his generation. What he wanted to do most, he said, was to interpret the soul of the American people. Thus in the tempo of jazz he jabbed at the dignities of American life, while he won the plaudits of the musical élite with the classic qualities of "A Rhapsody in Blue." With his brother Ira and that master of gentle satire George S. Kaufman he set the nation laughing at the foibles of its government; but, in more serious mood, he found time to write music that the great conductors of his time were glad to present.

Mr. Gershwin was a child of the Twenties, the Age of Jazz. In the fast two-step time of the years after the war he was to music what F. Scott Fitzgerald was to prose. Four years after that mad decade began, Paul Whiteman sent the strains of his Rhapsody cascading far beyond Broadway and the music they called Jazz had come of age. Serge Koussevitzky of the Boston Symphony Orchestra played his work and the capitals of Europe called for more.

For the musical comedy stage, the vaudeville act, the Hollywood lot, he made his music. He had grown up on the streets of Brooklyn and he had served his apprenticeship in Tin Pan Alley. He had turned out tunes with all the tricks of the dove that rhymed with love. He had woven the cadences of Broadway into his songs and he had given America the plaintive Negro music of Porgy and Bess.

What he wrote was always provocative, often distinctive. Some have doubted that his inspiration and craftsmanship kept up with his ambition to use the forms of jazz in the classical manner. Some have claimed that his real contributions were his saucy, tuneful dance and musical comedy tunes. But upon one thing all are agreed—from the scholarly Philip Hale to the man in the street—that his music will not soon be forgotten.

Mr. Gershwin was born in Brooklyn, Sept. 26, 1898. His early boyhood gave no indication of a bent toward music, nor was his own attitude toward his music-practicing playmates anything more than contempt. "Little Maggies," he called them.

But when he was 12 years old two things happened that were to awaken a fateful unrest in the boy's mind. First, his mother bought a piano; second, he heard the violinist, Max Rosen, give a recital at school. This started young George on his musical career. The piano proved such an attraction that his parents arranged instruction with a young woman teacher of the neighborhood. In the next few years he turned to several teachers until he met Charles Hambitzer, who is credited by some as having "discovered" Gershwin.

Mr. Hambitzer, teacher of piano, violin and 'cello, versatile orchestra musician and composer of light music, found his new pupil a genius. It was Mr. Hambitzer who gave Mr. Gershwin his first rudiments of harmony, and initiated him to the wonder of the classics. At a crucial point in the boy's studies Mr. Hambitzer died. Mr. Gershwin was later to study piano with Ernest Hutcheson, and some composition and orchestration with Edward Kilenyi and Rubin Goldmark.

Worked as a 'Plugger'

Mr. Gershwin's real learning came from experience, and his course therein started at Remick's music-publishing house. The boy was 16 then, and had passed two years in the High School of Commerce. His new position was that of "plugger," and it netted him $15 a week. His duties, like those of a corps of other "pluggers," were to tour the haunts of Tin Pan Alley as a floor pianist to a song-and-dance performer, in order to note which songs were best received. For his future work it was invaluable experience.

It was about this time that, sensing his limitations as a concert pianist, he began to write tunes of his own. After two years at Remick's he left to make his first contact with the theatre. It was a job as rehearsal pianist for "Miss 1917," by Victor Herbert and Jerome Kern. His ability was evident immediately and he was retained after the opening of the show by Ned Wayburn at a salary of $35 a week. It was at one of the Sunday concerts that were part of the run of "Miss 1917" that some of Gershwin's songs had first important hearings, for Vivienne Segal sang "You—Just You" and "There's More to a Kiss."

Then followed a rapid succession of events. He went on the Keith Vaudeville Circuit as accompanist to Louise Dresser; he was hired by the publishing firm of Harms as staff composer; he toured as pianist with Nora Bayes and, his muse becoming more and more fertile, his songs were being heard in revues and other shows.

Continued

Wrote "Scandals" Music

When he was 20 he received his first musical comedy commission from Alex Aarons. The product was "La La Lucille," given in 1919. He was then introduced to George White, with the result that Gershwin wrote the music for the "Scandals" of five successive years, beginning in 1920.

His renown spread rapidly. In the next decade he was to turn out such musical comedy hits as "Our Nell" (1922), "Sweet Little Devil" (1923), "Lady Be Good," "Primrose" (1924), "Tip-Toes," "Song of the Flame" (1925), "Oh, Kay!" (1926), "Strike Up the Band," "Funny Face," "Shake Your Feet" (1927), "Rosalie," "Treasure Girl" (1928), "Show Girl" (1929), "Girl Crazy" (1930), "Of Thee I Sing" (1931) "Pardon My English" (1932), "Let 'Em Eat Cake" (1933).

America was ripe for "Of Thee I Sing" when its characters cavorted across a Boston stage for the first time just before Christmas, 1931. Washington had become a stuffy place in the past few years and the Messrs. Kaufman and Gershwin hit upon the exact psychological moment to present Alexander Throttlebottom and the dancing graybeards of the Supreme Court.

To this gay satire of love in the White House, George Gershwin contributed the catchy tunes. His brother, Ira, wrote the lyrics, and many felt that it had at last developed the Gilbert and Sullivan of the new age. The music, especially that of the finale: "Of thee I sing —baby!" caught the spirit of the book exactly.

To some extent, Mr. Gershwin recaptured the vibrancy of this play in "Let 'Em Eat Cake," its successor, but critics felt, in the words of Mr. Brooks Atkinson, that there was more style than thought. Both scores, however, were hailed as masterpieces of modern light opera composition.

But he brought the artistic haut monde to his feet with the "Rhapsody in Blue," for piano and orchestra. It was written at the suggestion of Paul Whiteman and was first performed in the first concert of jazz music given by Mr. Whiteman's band Feb. 12, 1924, in Aeolian Hall. Mr. Gershwin himself played the solo part.

The next large work was the orchestral piece "An American in Paris," first heard at the hands of the Philharmonic-Symphony, under Dr. Damrosch, in Carnegie Hall. Serge Koussevitzky and the Boston Symphony Orchestra, with Gershwin as soloist, introduced the Second Rhapsody in January, 1932.

Mr. Gershwin often appeared at the Lewisohn Stadium concerts of the Philharmonic-Symphony, as soloist, composer and conductor. One program devoted entirely to his own works, given Aug. 16, 1932, attracted an audience that set a record for the stadium. He appeared with all the leading orchestras in this country and with many in Europe.

Perhaps his most ambitious work was the opera "Porgy and Bess," based on the dramatized novel of Dubose Heyward. Lyrics were by Ira Gershwin and Mr. Heyward. Described as something "between grand opera and musical comedy," it made a sensation at its world première performance in Boston, Sept. 30, 1935, by the Theatre Guild.

It reached the Alvin Theatre in New York Oct. 10 of the same year, and repeated its triumph.

A new light comedy by the Gershwin brothers and Mr. Kaufman had been briefly in the making a short time before the composer died. After going to Hollywood to write the score for the projected "Goldwyn Follies"—on which he was at work when he died—Mr. Gershwin, his brother and Mr. Kaufman had spent about a fortnight on their projected piece.

It was to have been a typical satire, not on government this time, but upon that world they all knew so well—"show business." They were forced to halt operations, however, because of the exacting nature of composing songs for Mr. Goldwyn. Into this work Mr. Gershwin threw himself whole heartedly and advance reports were that those of his tunes already completed for the motion picture were quite in his best manner.

Mr. Gershwin was a talented painter, and some of his works were placed on exhibition. He was also an enthusiastic collector of art objects and his apartment on Riverside Drive contained some notable items.

GERSHWIN CAUSED NEW JAZZ VALUES

His Place in American Music Is Held Unique Due to His Gifts and Circumstances

DID NOT IMITATE MASTERS

Struck Vein of His Own Which Was Fresh, New and Natural in Characteristic Scores

By OLIN DOWNES
Special to THE NEW YORK TIMES.

ASBURY PARK, N. J., July 11.— George Gershwin had a unique position in American music, one due in part to his wholly exceptional gifts and in part to a special set of circumstances which raised him in less than five years from the rank of a song plugger in Tin Pan Alley to that of a composer whose works invaded symphony concert programs and operatic auditoriums and made him internationally famous.

In some respects, and partly by virtue of the immense amount of publicity he received, his value may have been exaggerated. It remains that the composer of the "Rhapsody in Blue" and certain other representative compositions gave jazz itself a new importance and consideration as a musical medium, and proved that significant creation was possible in the terms of this popular national idiom.

Gershwin was not the first to realize these possibilities. Serious American composers such as Henry F. Gilbert, John Alden Carpenter and Aaron Copland of the younger generation had employed jazz motives in ways of their own in symphonies and symphonic poems. But Gershwin, in the first place, had the popular ear. In the second place, while he never was an intellectual composer, he had an extraordinary musical instinct and capacity for assimilation.

Composer of Limitations

He naturally grafted upon his own Broadway style harmonies and progressions he had heard in the works of classic masters. He did not imitate these masters, but naturally absorbed what he wanted of their expression, in a way to make his own richer and more significant than otherwise would have been the case, and without becoming unnaturally "high brow" or slavishly imitative.

He never passed a certain point as a "serious" composer. It was not in him to do what Dvorak did for Bohemian music, or even for America in the "New World" symphony, or what Grieg did for Norway in his art. Gershwin had too limited a technic for that, and the greater forms, because of his beginnings, were never really natural to him.

But in his most characteristic scores he struck out a vein of his own, sufficiently fresh, new, natural, and racy to command wide attention and to refresh enormously the ears in a period which offers

little that is new and original in musical creation.

Some would see in his rise a manifestation of a certain phase of democracy and American opportunity. His emergence from the stage of a highly promising purveyor of popular entertainment to the higher realms of his art began when one day the singer Eva Gauthier walked into Harms Music Shop and asked the young Gershwin if he would play her accompaniment while she sang some American popular songs by him in Boston and New York, offering him for this special service something more than his accustomed $2 an hour.

Gershwin's Playing Effective

At first the young man at the piano did not understand the proposition, but he finally accepted, and soon was famous. The songs, by their swing, their wit, their original rhythmic and harmonic settings of the texts, made an absolutely novel sensation when they fell on ears habituated to, but also perhaps fatigued by, overintellectualized products of certain cerebral modern European composers. It may be added that no small part of the effect was furnished by Gershwin's playing.

Those who have not heard him accompany his songs do not suspect their full flavor. These accompaniments have never been fully written down. They cannot be. Gershwin had a tone, a touch and a rhythm not easily described. The accompaniments were themselves tone-pictures, however trivial or merely topical the character of the song might be. And they possessed one of the most distinctive characteristics of our American jazz—the element of improvisation. They also constituted an extraordinary commentary on Ira Gershwin's texts. These texts have not received their proper praise. They were made for George's special musical gift as George had precisely the style to set off the verses of Ira.

This was the beginning of Gershwin's reputation. Then came a greater success. It occurred when Paul Whiteman played the "Rhapsody in Blue" at the concert of "Ten Years of Jazz" which took place in Aeolian Hall in the early part of 1924.

Then Dr. Walter Damrosch invited Mr. Gershwin to compose a concerto in three movements for first performance by the New York Symphony Society. This was done. For a concerto by a man who had only passed the day before from successful popular song and operettas to a medium which required extensive technical knowledge of composition the piece made a very good showing.

It solidified the composer's position, at the same time that it showed his limitations. Gershwin added to these laurels with his orchestral "American in Paris," a work of a humorous sort which came later, but he never equaled in sheer creativeness the originality and the unprecedented confidence and gusto of the rascally theme which opens the "Rhapsody in Blue" and the best of the pages that follow.

Sometimes it seems that Gershwin was given too great a responsibility by musicians and critics so eager to see a real school of American composition developed that they encouraged him to more serious paths than those he was born to follow. But certainly he pointed the way, even though the first act of "Of Thee I Sing," and passages from his best light operas will rank much higher than any part of his attempted "folk opera" "Porgy"; and though some of his topical or risqué little songs carry a lilt of melody and a wealth of innuendo that outshine more serious attempts in real life and individuality.

A new step was taken by Gershwin for American music, a step that more pretentious composers were unable to execute. The sum of his achievement will make him live long in the record of American music.

The Times
7th November 1893

A Reuter telegram from St. Petersburg states :— M. Tschaikowsky, the famous composer, died here at 3 o'clock this morning from the effects of cholera. On Saturday evening he dined at a restaurant in the city, and drank some water which had not previously been boiled. Symptoms of cholera showed themselves on Sunday, and, although every effort was made by the doctors in attendance to stay the progress of the disease, M. Tschaikowsky's condition became rapidly worse. He lost consciousness yesterday afternoon. During his short illness numerous bulletins regarding his condition were sent to the Tsar at his Majesty's request. The news of M. Tschaikowsky's death has been received with general regret throughout the country. He composed several operas. Peter Ilitsch Tschaikowsky, according to a notice in the "Dictionary of Musicians," was "born in 1840 at Wotkinsk, in the government of Wiatka (Ural district), where his father was engineer to the Imperial mines. In 1850 the father was appointed director of the Technological Institute in St. Petersburg, and there the boy entered the School of Jurisprudence, into which only the sons of high-class Government officials are admitted. Having completed the prescribed course in 1859, he was appointed to a post in the Ministry of Justice. In 1862, however, when the Conservatoire of Music was founded at St. Petersburg, he left the service of the State and entered the new school as a student of music. He remained there till 1865, studying harmony and counterpoint under Professor Zaremba, and composition under Anton Rubinstein. In 1865 he took his diploma as a musician, together with a prize medal for the composition of a cantata on Schiller's ode ' An die Freude.' In 1866 Nicholas Rubinstein invited him to take the post of Professor of Harmony, Composition, and the History of Music at the new Conservatoire of Moscow. He held this post, doing good service as a teacher, for 12 years. Since 1878 he has devoted himself entirely to composition, and has been living in St. Petersburg, Italy, Switzerland, and Kiew." The author of the notice, Mr. Edward Dannreuther, adds—" M. Tschaikowsky makes frequent use of the rhythm and tunes of Russian people's songs and dances, occasionally also of certain quaint harmonic sequences peculiar to Russian church music. His compositions more or less bear the impress of the Slavonic temperament—fiery exaltation on a basis of languid melancholy. He is fond of huge and fantastic outlines, of bold modulations and strongly-marked rhythms, of subtle melodic turns and exuberant figuration ; and he delights in gorgeous effects of orchestration. His music everywhere makes the impression of genuine spontaneous originality."

The Times
24th December 1791

On the 5th inst. at Vienna, Wolfgang Mozart, the celebrated German Composer.

The Standard
5th June 1899

JOHANN STRAUSS.
Composer, died 1899.
On receiving advice to get some sleep...

DEATH OF JOHANN STRAUSS.

THE MUSICIAN'S LAST HOURS.

(FROM OUR CORRESPONDENT.)
VIENNA, SUNDAY NIGHT.
Johann Strauss, one of the greatest in the realm of music, died yesterday afternoon at a quarter past four in his house in Vienna.

Johann Strauss was a Freeman of the town of Vienna, and it is supposed that the town, even under an Anti-Semitic *régime*, will accord him a grave of honour, probably by the side of that of his intimate friend, Brahms, though the fact that he went over from Roman Catholicism to Protestantism, and that, as his third wife, he married a Jewess, exposed even the greatest and most representative of Viennese to violent reproaches, and to certain loss of popularity, and even of Court favour. When his father died, a few weeks after his return from London, on September 25, 1849, fully a hundred thousand persons followed the hearse to the cemetery. It will be seen whether the Greater Vienna of to-day will bestow the same honour on the far greater son. Up to the present the mourning for Johann Strauss is, in Vienna, restricted to expressions of sorrow in newspapers, and to the heartfelt sympathy of the educated classes. No Viennese was better known or held in greater honour among a music-loving people. He had been before the public since 1844, quickly surpassing the fame of his father, the creator of the waltz. He was born in Vienna in 1825, and early exhibited the possession of musical talent. His father wished him to take up commercial pursuits, and he had to get what music teaching he received despite parental wishes and commands. The opposition of Strauss the elder, was withdrawn after the successful *début*, and the son was permitted to join the famous orchestral band.

Independent compositions soon made him something more than a successor to his father's reputation. His first operetta, *Indigo*, was performed in 1871, and among his numerous works the best known are *Das Fledermaus*, *Ritter Pazman*, and the *Carnival in Rome*. His Jubilee was celebrated in Vienna on October 15, 1894, amid enthusiasm such as was possible only in the city where he had made his career. In honour of this event a new operetta from his pen, *Jabuka, or the Frost of Apples*, was performed.

For his "Donau" waltz, which was composed in 1873, and met with cold reception in Vienna, like his best operetta *Das Fledermaus*, Johann Strauss received only two hundred and fifty florins, or about twenty pounds; but the publisher made tens of thousands of pounds by it. When young Strauss got only three to four pounds for one composition, which accounts for the comparatively small fortune the most popular of all composers has left. "The lot of a musician is a hard one," said Johann Strauss, the father, to his youthful son, "and you must strive for an honest living; you must study for a profession. Take my case. In my calling I have attained the highest perfection, and have nothing from it, and I know for certain neither you nor your brothers have a scrap of musical talent." He was totally wrong, this first waltz king, who, with his friend Lanner, introduced the speciality of the Vienna waltz, but he was to be excused, because what was the life of even the most popular conductor and composer of dance music in the first half of the present century in Vienna? He had to wander with his band from one Beergarden to another in Summer, and from one public ballroom to the next in Winter, and to send round the hat in Vienna (in reality the plate) or to go with it himself; and Johann Strauss, the first who was a real artist, suffered not only under this indignity, but still more under the impossibility of keeping up his popularity by always composing something new, or, as he expressed it of filling the poor eight or twelve-bar phrases of a waltz with something taking and novel. He strenuously opposed his oldest son Johann occupying himself with music, and sent him for two years to the Polytechnic Institute to learn bookkeeping and other commercial knowledge. In consequence of his separating from his wife and the boys, who remained with the mother, and thereby obtained full freedom, Johann, at the age of eighteen, ventured on the bold undertaking of forming his own band; and when, on the memorable October 14, 1844, the *début* at Dommayer's Casino, with four of his own compositions, proved to be a really remarkable success, the father became jealous of the son—jealous because he feared the material competition, and

still more because he felt that the new composer would soon surpass him in talent, and, consequently, in popularity.

The young Strauss had, indeed, from the beginning the idea of reforming the dance music to which he devoted his life, of filling the waltzes, and polkas, and marches with something more than rhythmical music to which people could dance—namely, with the expression of feelings and ideas answering the momentary impressions of persons of all classes, describing the passions of love and of despair, of patriotism, and of ambition, painting with musical colours the languid abandonment, the sweet hopeful expectation and the joy of fulfilment. For everyone of the feelings and impressions here mentioned, as well as for dozens of others in the endless variety of human moods, one or more of the odd four hundred and fifty compositions of light music by Johann Strauss could be mentioned as examples. He introduced sentiment as well as thought, and ideas, and in the first place he introduced temperament and musical colouring into dance music, and he conquered by it not only the Viennese, who soon found that their temperament and their passions were the objects of the fertile musical imagination of Strauss, but also the entire world, his name being, without any doubt, the only one of whom every civilised person on our globe must have heard, the young as well as the old.

It is strange that Johann Strauss, the son, had never danced. The great musician once told me that he could not dance; but dance music and melodies applicable to dance music flowed to his last day as easily from his peculiarly musical brain as verses are supposed to flow from the pen of great poets. Passionately fond of card playing as a recreation, he, nevertheless, composed, even when playing. Once being asked whether composing was difficult, he naively remarked, "Not at all; only something must occur to one." To him it occurred day and night. Richard Wagner called his the most musical skull of our age; Brahms regretfully wrote that the "Blaue Donau" was not by him. Rubinstein and Joachim, and, in fact, the greatest musicians of our time, had the deepest admiration for the "Waltz King"; and it was Offenbach himself who induced Strauss to write operettas, of which he finished fourteen, amongst which the *Fledermaus* had the most lasting success. Even the failures, as *Ritter Pazman*, the comic opera he wrote for the Imperial Opera house, are mines of beautiful melodies, which are still to be dug up and to be coined for the musical world. A third Johann Strauss is not likely to arise, in Vienna at least. The easy, pleasure-loving, half gay, and half sentimental race, which adored the two Strausses seems to have completely died out. But not only is a popular musician no longer living in Vienna; the man who will be conducted to the grave on Tuesday was also the last Viennese, and, in fact, the last Austrian, beside the popular Emperor, whose name is familiar to other nations. I am afraid I must say he was the last great Austrian known to our generation.

Politics

No doubt it says something about our values and interests that none of the politicians considered for inclusion here died anonymously. **William Pitt** (the younger) was suitably lauded for his contribution to the establishment of Britain as a world power in the nineteenth century. Likewise **Robespierre**, without whose energy the French Revolution might have provided a very different example for later leaders — although it must be said that the reporting of his demise was hardly a model of objectivity. Nor perhaps, although for quite different reasons and in a quite different way, was that of **Otto von Bismarck**, the creator of Germany. **William Gladstone**, the epitome (with Disraeli of course) of C19th. Britain, was treated with all suitable respect, to say the least. Coming to the present century, it may or may not be of some significance that, apart from Senator **Joe McCarthy** — representing the political possibilities, and, hopefully, limitations, of sheer fear-mongering quite unsupported by even a veneer of positive ideas — no British or American politician has found himself in purely political circumstances in which he could individually either influence or epitomise world politics in the way the following notables have done. **Lenin**, **Stalin**, and **Hitler** between them directed the course of the world in the first half of the century: they of all politicians must be the favourites of the "great individual" school of historical explanation. On a rather different scale, **Franco** does duty for all the sordid dictatorships of the century, from Papa Doc to the Somozas, from the Greek colonels to Mr. Bokassa; and **Verwoerd** for those who evidence the infinite stupidity of which mankind is capable. By contrast, **Salvador Allende**, whatever one's politics, is here as a tribute to all those, or rather to those few, who have genuinely tried and failed to improve the lot of their country for its, rather than any other, sake — the figures of the Prague Spring of 1968 for instance.

Haile Selassie, **Nasser** and **David Ben-Gurion** all shaped their countries in a fundamental way for the twentieth century, though the "Lion of Judah", as Emperor Selassie liked to call himself lost the gratitude of his people in his old age. **Franklin Roosevelt** and **Konrad Adenauer** are responsible for the reconstruction of two of the world's major industrial powers following rather different traumas. "Papa Doc" **Duvalier** epitomises banana — republic tyranny, while **Warren Harding** is (or at least *was* before Watergate) destined to go down in history as the archetypal corrupt politician of a so-called "developed" society — amazingly the American press spurned him on his death, and it is left to a British newspaper to provide us with his obituary.

Harry Truman is the ordinary, undevious man who can still make a success of politics, while **Eva Perón** must be the consummate, guileful politician.

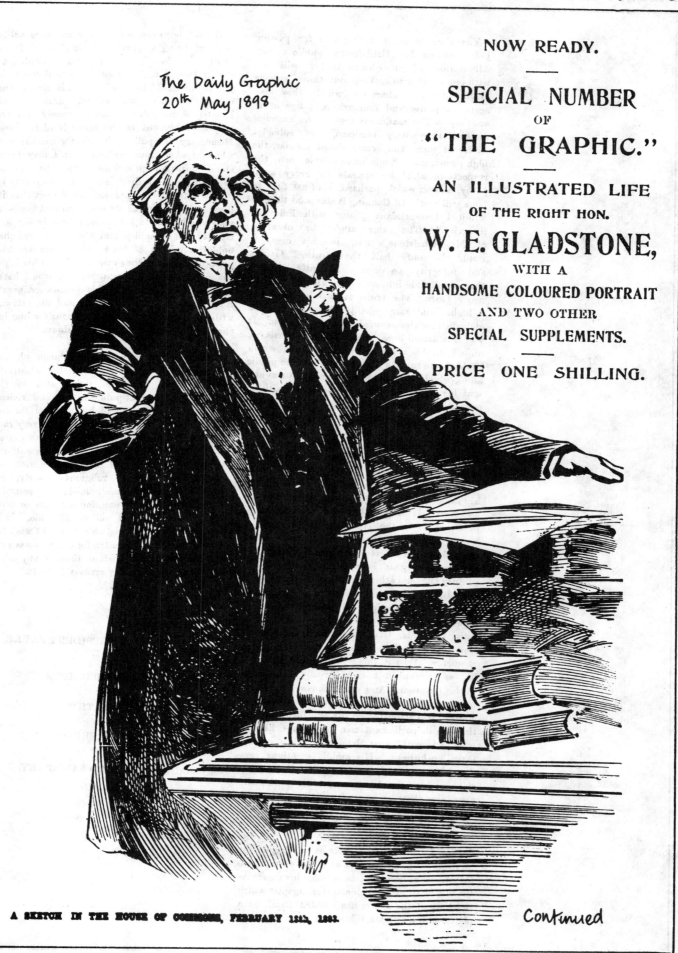

The Daily Graphic
20th May 1898

NOW READY.

SPECIAL NUMBER
OF
"THE GRAPHIC."

AN ILLUSTRATED LIFE
OF THE RIGHT HON.
W. E. GLADSTONE,
WITH A
HANDSOME COLOURED PORTRAIT
AND TWO OTHER
SPECIAL SUPPLEMENTS.

PRICE ONE SHILLING.

A SKETCH IN THE HOUSE OF COMMONS, FEBRUARY 13th, 1882.

Continued

The time is not a fitting one for passing judgment on Mr. Gladstone's public career. All sections of Englishmen to-day will vie with one another in seeking out those aspects of his life and character which they may agree to praise and honour. And how many are they! The matchless orator, the consummate Parliamentary tactician, the splendid leader of men, the accomplished scholar, the high-principled Englishman—these are the respects in which he appeals to every sympathy, and on which, perhaps, his final title to fame will rest. Of Canning it was said that he "united transcendant genius with inflexible integrity." The same might be observed of Mr. Gladstone, but, in his case, it would be only half the truth. Genius and integrity do not sufficiently explain the wonderful influence he wielded for so many years. The truth is that he possessed a higher and rare quality than either. He embodied an almost mediæval enthusiasm. It was his astonishing capacity for enthusiasm, united to his other phenomenal gifts, which enabled him to fill so large a place in the public mind, which attracted him to noble causes and sent his voice in moments of crisis with so magnetic a sympathy from end to end of the country. And yet, with it all, it may be doubted whether he was an epoch-making statesman. The most successful of the great causes with which he was identified found their chief protagonists in other men. The most conspicuous political campaigns in which he figured as leader will not go down to history as successes. It is probable that Lord Beaconsfield's share in the Treaty of Berlin will be longer remembered than Mr. Gladstone's noble crusade on behalf of the Balkan Christians; that in the great Liberal movement of the century the solid achievements of Cobden, Peel, and Bright will count for more with the historian than the lofty impulses, the glowing speech, the magnificent courage and untiring activity of Mr. Gladstone, albeit their superior in every grace of mind and element of character. Why is this? The problem of his life, as we read it to-day, is really summed up in this question. And yet the answer is not far to seek. With all those remarkable practical abilities which made him the first financier and the ablest parliamentarian of his age, he was weighted with the defects of his phenomenal enthusiasm. His mobile emotions rendered him peculiarly susceptible to the impressions of his immediate environment, and the result was that he was often out of harmony with the prevailing spirit of his times. He commenced life far behind it; he ended his political career far in advance of it. In the days of the first reformed Parliament he made his political *début* as a duke's nominee for a pocket borough; he closed his career as the idol of an extreme democracy, against which the bulk of the nation has banded itself on a platform of moderate Whiggism.

A man, however, may be a great personality without being a great historic force. It is probable, although it may seem a paradox to say so, that Mr. Gladstone's political work is yet to come. The magic of his name, the echoes of his unparalleled oratory, the lessons of his political strivings may conceivably mark him out as the Messiah of the new Democracy, the political Teacher whose life and whose spoken and written words may be a standing inspiration and instruction to unborn generations of his disciples. That, however, is for the future. The present only knows that it has lost in him one of its most brilliant sons—a man who battled manfully and bravely for his country and humanity, and who incarnated the noblest impulses of his epoch. Whatever his political mistakes, they cannot blemish his high character, nor can the most rabid political hate belittle the splendour of his genius. A great Englishman he was before all, and the nation, without distinction of party, mourns for him in affection, in pride, and in thankfulness.

The most conspicuous Englishman of our times is now numbered with the illustrious dead. Rich in years, richer still in the splendour of a great public career, and richest of all in the affection of his compatriots and the admiration of his fellow men of every race and creed, William Ewart Gladstone has passed away. One of the moving dramas of our national history is closed, and the close, with its dignity, its serene religious beauty, its wealth of years undimmed by senility, leaves, happily, little occasion for tears or wailing. It is a noble and well-rounded life. It is an end such as all Christian men might wish for themselves—fitting guerdon for one who was perhaps greater as a Christian than in any other relation of his singularly many-sided life.

SYMPATHY FROM PRESIDENT FAURE.

TRIBUTES FROM ABROAD.

THE NATION'S SYMPATHY.

MESSAGES FROM AMERICA.

MESSAGE FROM LORD SALISBURY.

The passing bell at Hawarden Church was tolled, and the news spread through the village with great rapidity.

Messages were at once despatched to the Queen and the Prince of Wales.

The Queen sent immediately a touching message of condolence to Mrs. Gladstone.

In the natural course of things the funeral will be at Hawarden. Mr. Gladstone expressed a strong wish to have no flowers for his funeral, and the family will be grateful if this desire is strictly respected.

OFFICIAL ACCOUNT OF THE ILLNESS.

The following is the official record of Mr. Gladstone's illness and death:—

"Although at an early stage of Mr. Gladstone's long and painful illness the possibility of a grave and insidious case was entertained and discovered, the remarkably favourable course of the outward trouble during the first part of his visit to Cannes led to a reasonably sanguine view of his ultimate restoration to health. The continuance of a severe neuralgic pain, and the spread of the disease from one nerve to another led to grave anxiety, however, though it was not until Mr. Gladstone was at Bournemouth that local developments of the disease occurred, and indicated its true character.

"The announcement of the fatal character of the malady was a source of great comfort to Mr. Gladstone, worn as he was with suffering and distress. There was no question of resigning himself to the inevitable, but rather of a fervent desire to be at peace. For some time before this he had been giving up his ordinary habits of life one by one. On his return to Hawarden at the end of March this feature became more marked as his strength failed, although until within a month of the end he came down to dinner every night.

"The altered view of Mr. Gladstone's illness brought altered views as to treatment, and it was now considered justifiable to endeavour to remove the severe pain that had been so constant a feature of the early months by the most potent measures. These were so far successful on his return home that his suffering was greatly assuaged, but he still had fitful twinges of some severity. Gradually, with waning strength, the pain became less and less, and for quite a fortnight before his death it hardly ever made itself felt.

"Though he ceased to come downstairs after April 18th, Mr. Gladstone got up for an hour or two every day and lay on the sofa in his room. Even this short walk told a tale of diminishing power in the increasing feebleness of his steps. On May 12th he was noticed to be very much tired by this exertion, and his circulation, which had been wonderfully well preserved up to that time, showed signs of grave disturbance. The next day this was so much marked that it was decided to keep him entirely in bed lest syncope might occur. What had only been foreshadowed up to this time, namely, that he would die of the increasing infirmity of his years, and not of his illness nor its complications, was now apparent. Confined to bed without pain, taking nourishment at intervals, his heart failing little by little, Mr. Gladstone's end grew appreciably nearer and nearer. Once or twice it seemed likely to come sooner than was eventually the case, but on Tuesday morning, May 17th, it was evident that life was ebbing very fast.

"He was asked about this time by one of his attendants if he had any pain. He replied, 'Oh, no. I am quite comfortable. I am only waiting, only waiting.'

"Nor did he have long to wait. The last three days he was scarcely conscious, and except when roused to take a spoonful or two of nourishment he lay very quiet and restfully. He ceased making to those around him the acknowledgments that were so dear to them, but during his last days he would often say, 'Kindness, kindness, kindness; nothing but kindness on every side.'

"After Tuesday evening he was too weak to speak coherently or audibly. The warning given by these symptoms had been sufficiently ample to allow of his relatives being summoned, and all those immediately with him were present to the last. At half-past three on Wednesday morning he seemed to be very near the end, and his family gathered round his bed. He rallied, however, towards five o'clock, and lay fluctuating between life and death for the next twenty-four hours. He remained upon his back, being now too weak to turn, but moving his arm from time to time, or returning the pressure of a hand. His breathing was very irregular, his hands and feet chilly, and his lips and cheeks tinged with a cyanotic line. Peace—perfect peace—was limned in every feature.

"There was a slight temporary improvement on the morning of the 18th, breathing became steadier, and the duskiness of his face was replaced by a more natural colour. He roused a little on being spoken to, and an occasional glimmer of consciousness was shown once or twice by some slight change of expression or the barely articulated recognition of some trivial attention.

"Thus he remained until half-past two on Thursday morning, when a change took place that made it obvious that the end was very near. Reverently and on bowed knees prayers were offered and his favourite hymns read. At ten minutes to five the pallor of death and a few laboured respirations led to the recital of the commendatory prayer. Before it was finished quietly and peacefully Mr. Gladstone passed away."

THE LAST HOURS.

In describing the last hours of Mr. Gladstone one who spent the night by the dying statesman says that it became only a question of endurance. Mr. Gladstone could take no nourishment. His lips could merely be moistened with diluted spirits. At midnight all the members of the family gathered for the parting, Mrs. Gladstone stricken with grief. She had passed the previous night wholly in the sick room, and again sat at Mr. Gladstone's bedside grasping his hand and occasionally pressing and kissing it. The Rev. Stephen Gladstone read Litanies and other prayers. Day had just dawned when the medical men saw that death was to be a matter of moments. On the stroke of five o'clock Mr. Gladstone had passed away. The end came so peacefully that the fact had to be announced to the distressed members of the family by the medical attendants. It was a passing from the sleep of life to that of death, so gentle was it. All the family were painfully distressed, and Mrs. Gladstone was led away to another chamber. Mr. Gladstone's features wear a most beautiful expression of repose. There is really no disfigurement of the face. His hands lie crossed upon his breast as in sleep. Dr. Dobie on leaving the Castle left Mrs. Gladstone in what appeared to be a refreshing sleep. The other members of the family also sought rest. The Rev. Stephen Gladstone was an exception. It was Ascension morning, and he drove over to Hawarden Church, where he conducted early morning service at seven o'clock. On the previous evening there had been a choral service there, when a special prayer was offered up for Mr. Gladstone, and his favourite hymn, "Praise to the Holiest in the Highest," was sung.

Continued

IN HAWARDEN VILLAGE.

(FROM OUR SPECIAL CORRESPONDENT.)

HAWARDEN, Thursday Night.

The death of Mr. Gladstone has left a strange quiet behind. Mourning there is, and the signs of mourning are many, but the most complete tribute to his memory is the silence. Even the rumours are spoken in whispers. Hawarden Castle, wrapped in the peaceful sunlight of a glorious Ascension morning, has made no sign all day. The blinds of the chamber of death are drawn. There is no sight nor sound from any part of the village. The windows are shuttered, the blinds are drawn, and on the pretty church a flag has floated all day at half-mast. The news was early abroad in the village this morning, and many who had waited up all night gathered in respectful sympathy to watch those members of the Gladstone family who went to early service in the church. Mrs. Drew, Miss Helen Gladstone, the Dean of Lincoln, and Mrs. and Miss Wickham, Mrs. Stephen Gladstone, and Mr. Dumaresq. attended early communion, which was conducted by the Rev. Stephen Gladstone. The ordinary form of service was prefaced by one or two selected prayers from the burial service, and included also the Collect for All Saints' Day. To and fro in the village all day have hurried the telegraph messengers. Telegrams expressing sympathy and condolence have continued to arrive in ever increasing numbers. The first, which was received from Cork, arrived at the Castle an hour after the announcement of the death. Beyond these tokens of mourning the chief sign of the momentous event has been the muffled peals ringing at intervals all day from the church belfry, solemn, pathetic, continuous.

THE PLACE OF BURIAL.

No definite arrangements for the funeral had been announced last night, but it appears to have been the expressed desire of Mr. Gladstone to rest in Hawarden Church in a grave near the remains of his eldest son, the late W. H. Gladstone; and this, it is understood, is the only place of repose which would meet with the approval of Mrs. Gladstone. The probability of a State funeral at Westminster Abbey is therefore remote. The day had not been fixed, but Tuesday was spoken of as being very likely.

ROYAL CONDOLENCES.

In addition to the message sent by the Queen, telegrams of condolence were received at Hawarden from the Prince of Wales, the Duke of Cambridge, the Prince and Princess Christian, and the Duke and Duchess of Saxe Coburg-Gotha.

Quite a feature of the sorrowful event of yesterday was the enterprising promptitude with which the leading illustrated weeklies appeared with their elaborate and exhaustive special numbers. Within a few hours of Mr. Gladstone's death the *Illustrated London News*, for instance, published his life and political career in a number which included thirty-eight pages of abundantly-illustrated matter, together with a large presentation portrait in colours, after the original painting by H. Weigall. The life itself has been written by Mr. H. W. Massingham, and the portraits, which naturally take a prominent part in the illustrations, include reproductions of the comparatively little-known family portraits at Hawarden Castle. The price of the work is half-a-crown. Equally prompt was the publication of the special shilling number of the *Graphic*, with its thirty odd pages of fully-illustrated letterpress and its three supplements, dealing with Mr. Gladstone's private life at Hawarden. The supplements are all from pictures by Mr. Sydney P. Hall, and give us a charming glimpse of how the aged statesman spent the peaceful evening of his days at home. Besides the life of Mr. Gladstone himself and the story of his illness right up to the time of his death, there are "Personal Recollections" by Mr. Henry W. Lucy, and an interesting article on Mr. Gladstone's contemporaries, as well as their portraits.

The Times
24th January 1806

MR. PITT.

By the account which we gave in yesterday's Paper, our readers were led to expect the afflicting event which has since taken place. Mr. PITT died at half-past four yesterday morning. On Tuesday, the Physicians declared their opinion, that he would not survive eight and forty hours; and it was thought adviseable to communicate that circumstance. He was not aware of the danger of his situation, but he received the communication with his characteristic firmness. He then desired to be left alone with the Bishop of LINCOLN, who had been the preceptor of his youth, and was now the companion of his sick chamber, and a long conference ensued, with the nature of which we are not acquainted. Whether it was devotional or testamentary, whether it related to the concerns of this world, or in immediate preparation for another, has not yet transpired, and perhaps never will transpire. It has indeed been mentioned, but we do not vouch for its truth, though we think it by no means improbable, that the Right Reverend Prelate is the repository of Mr. PITT's last opinions. He continued, after this trying moment, to be perfectly calm and serene, and his debility continued to increase till he was incapable of receiving the least nourishment, and fatally fulfilled the predictions of his physicians. It is also said, that previous to his dissolution, his brother, the Earl of CHATHAM, and Lady HESTER STANHOPE, took their final leave of him; a ceremony which, as it was altogether unnecessary, and must have been inexpressibly afflicting to the parties themselves, we should hope did not take place.

This great man, for such he has been considered even by the parties who opposed him, had not exceeded his forty-eighth year, a period, when the body and mind are frequently in a very high state of activity and enjoyment. We shall speak of him with the truth and the freedom of history; and in that spirit, we are ready to acknowledge the splendor of his talents, the powers of his eloquence, and his indefatigable attention to the objects of his Administration. He began his career with a prematurity of talent, which has no example, and in a time of difficulty, which required the most determined resolution, the utmost vigour of exertion, and a mind of the most potent grasp, and unbounded comprehension; he not only possessed them all, but applied them with incomparable energy and effect, to the advantage of his country. Thus this bright Orb appeared in the ascendant, and rose in a regular and resplendent course to meridian brightness; but in that position, while he filled the eye of his country and the world, he closed his first Administration, by removing from its duties, and for reasons which have never yet been clearly understood or explained, sought a comparative state of retirement and privacy. Of his motives for such inexplicable conduct, we do not pretend to judge; they might be the best, and we do not mean to controvert the position. But the manner in which he regained the seat of power was not equally honourable with his former possession of it. His second Administration was attended with circumstances which lessened the splendour of his distinguished name; and the nation has to regret that his sun should have set amid clouds and storms, instead of descending temperately to a serene and brilliant horizon.*

* WILLIAM PITT was born May 28, 1759, at a time when his father's glory was at its zenith; and when, in consequence of the wisdom of his councils, and the vigour and promptitude of his decisions, British valour reigned triumphant in every part of the globe.

Mr. PITT was, after the usual course of study in the University of Cambridge, entered a student of Lincoln's-inn, and made so rapid a progress in his legal studies, as to be soon called to the Bar with every prospect of success. We understand, that he once or twice went upon the Western Circuit, and appeared as junior Counsel in several causes. He was, however, destined to fill a more important station in the government of his country, than is usually obtained through the channel of law. At the general election, 1780, he was nominated by some of the most respectable persons in Cambridge as a candidate to represent that University; but notwithstanding the high character he had obtained there, he found very few to second his pretensions. In the following year, however, he was returned for the Borough of Appleby, by the interest of Sir J. Lowther. On taking his seat in the House of Commons, he enlisted himself under the banner of the party which had constantly opposed the Ministry, Lord North, and the American war, and which regarded him with a degree of veneration; recognising in his person the genius of his illustrious father revived, and acting, as it were, in him. His first speech was in favour of Mr. Burke's bill; and one of the first acts in which he took the lead in that House, was admirably well calculated to increase his popularity; this was his motion for a Committee, to consult upon the most effectual means to accomplish a more equal representation of the people in Parliament. His propositions were, indeed, rejected; but he continued to repeat and renew them from time to time; and thus kept up the public attention to this great object, which was, consequently, more generally canvassed than it ever had been before.

On the death of the Marquis of Rockingham, the old Whig party fell into a state of dissension, nearly bordering upon dissolution. A new arrangement took place soon after, and Lord Shelburne became the First Lord of the Treasury, assisted by Mr. Pitt, who astonished the country, and, indeed, all Europe, by the phenomenon of a Chancellor of the Exchequer at the age of twenty-three!

His popularity at this period effectually screened him from every charge, which his youth and inexperience might justly have warranted, and which were strongly urged against him by the adverse faction. The situation of the country was extremely critical. The American war had become generally odious; and all hearts panted for a cessation of hostilities. This object was, therefore, the first consideration with the new Ministry.

The Combined Powers had recently experienced great humiliations, and consequently the opportunity was not to be lost. A general peace accordingly took place; but the terms of it were reprobated by a considerable part of the nation. On this occasion, Mr. PITT delivered a most masterly defence of himself and his colleagues, which produced a corresponding, though not successful, effect. The Administration, of which he was one of the most distinguished members, was, therefore, short-lived. On its dissolution, the young Statesman withdrew into retirement, and afterwards went abroad for some time, visiting Italy, and several of the German Courts.

On the Coalition-ministry coming into place, Mr. MANSFIELD's seat for the University became vacant, by accepting the office of Solicitor-General, and Mr. PITT determined to oppose him: with this view he went down to Cambridge; but was treated with contempt by the Heads and Senior Members. From such a scene he retired in a few days, in disgust; though the assurance of support from several independent Masters of Arts, kept alive the scanty hopes of future success. A few months, however, changed the scene; the Coalition-ministry was thrown out; he repaired in triumph to the University, was received with open arms, carried his election by means of a considerable majority, and was able, also, by his influence, to make Lord EUSTON his colleague. For a time, the tergiversation of the Senate was a theme of conversation; the most notorious of the gown who had changed sides were marked by the contempt of the unsuccessful, but they laughed at their own disgrace, being gratified by the rewards of the successful Candidate; mitres, and stalls, and livings, became the portion of the Cambridge Men. But few of the independent Masters, who would have supported him when out of power, and did so on his accession to the Ministry, were to be found among his voters at the next election; they considered him as having receded from those principles of liberty on which he had first acted; for he had now become cool in his zeal for that reform of Parliament, which had, in conjunction with his great talents, first entitled him to their notice.

An occasion, as we have just remarked, suddenly offered, for bringing Mr. PITT forward once more on the great theatre of politics, as a candidate for fame and power. The British dominions in India had long been in an alarming situation, and it was generally admitted, that an immediate remedy was indispensably necessary to preserve them. With this view, Mr. Fox, then Secretary of State, formed, digested, and brought forward his famous India Bill, which he carried through its several stages with a high hand.

The Coalition-ministry, composed of such an heterogeneous mixture, notwithstanding their majority in the House of Commons, were generally obnoxious to the nation, and this measure was particularly offensive to the great body whom it immediately affected. Lord NORTH and his new allies, were accordingly dismissed, and Mr. PITT, the new Premier, was assisted by the advice of Lord THURLOW, as Keeper of the Great Seal—arrangements which, at that time, were, however, only considered as temporary!

He now astonished the commercial and political world, by his own India Bill! He had, however, the mortification to find the majority of the House of Commons against him; and he was placed in the peculiar situation of a Minister acting with a minority, and that too in opposition to the strongest conflux of talents ever combined against any administration. He, however, remained firm in his seat amidst a general confusion; and though the House had petitioned his MAJESTY to dismiss

Continued

him and his coadjutors, our young Premier ventured to inform the Representatives of the nation, that their Petition could not be complied with.

This struggle between the Commons and the Crown was of the greatest importance; but the people at large were of opinion, that the former encroached upon the regal prerogative; on the question being, in a manner, thrown into their hands, by a dissolution of Parliament, a new one was returned, which changed the majority, and preserved the Premier in his office.

The commercial treaty with France was a bold scheme, and evinced deep political and mercantile knowledge. One of the most critical circumstances in the annals of Mr. PITT's administration, was the period when the regal powers were, in a manner, unhappily suspended, and all the wisdom of the Legislature was required to form a Regency. It was a crisis not only novel, but of extreme magnitude, as likely to become the precedent for future times; no such incident having, till then, occurred in the annals of our history. Some statesmen would have worshipped the rising sun; Mr. PITT, however, pursued a different course, and thereby added greatly to his popularity, and essentially secured himself in power.

When the Revolution took place in France, the situation of the Prime Minister of this Kingdom became once more extremely critical. The aspect of Europe had assumed a new face, since the Monarchy of France was shaken from its ancient basis. A war ensued, totally different from all former wars. In judging, therefore, of the merits of those who were concerned in managing the affairs of the nation, it was impossible to have recourse either to precedents, or to old political principles. A new mode of action, a new scheme of politics, was to be devised, and adapted to the circumstances of the day.—If any merit be due to boldness of invention, to vigour of execution, to wide extension of plans, and to firmness and perseverance of conduct, certainly the Administration of that day had an undoubted claim to public gratitude, however unsuccessful their councils and plans proved.

New York Times 13th April 1945

Roosevelt Regime, From '33, Longest in Nation's History

Started in Economic Depression—Saw Us Faced With Gravest Problems and the World With Its Worst War

Chronology of Active Life

A chronology of important events in the life of Franklin Delano Roosevelt follows:

Jan. 30, 1882—Born at family estate, Hyde Park, N. Y.
1904—Graduated from Harvard University.
March 17, 1905—Married Anna Eleanor Roosevelt.
1910—Elected to New York State Senate his first public office.
1913—Appointed Assistant Secretary of the Navy.
1920—Was the Democratic nominee for the Vice Presidency, as the running mate of James M. Cox.
August, 1921—Stricken with infantile paralysis.
Nov. 6, 1928—Elected Governor of New York State.
Nov. 8, 1932—Elected President of the United States.
March 4, 1933—Inaugurated President.
Nov. 3, 1936—Elected to a second term.
Jan. 20, 1937—Inaugurated for a second term, the first to take office on the new date specified by the Twentieth Amendment.
Nov. 5, 1940—Elected to a third term, shattering a precedent as old as the Republic.
Jan. 20, 1941—Inaugurated for his third term.
Aug. 14, 1941—Issued, jointly with Prime Minister Winston Churchill of Great Britain, an eight-point statement of principles for peace which became known as the Atlantic Charter.
Dec. 8, 1941—Appeared before a joint session of Congress and asked a declaration of war against Japan.
Nov. 28-Dec. 1, 1943—Conferred at Teheran, Iran, with Prime Minister Churchill and Marshal Joseph Stalin of Russia.
Nov. 7, 1944—Elected to fourth term as President.
Jan. 20, 1945—Inaugurated at simple ceremony in Washington.
Feb. 4-11, 1945—Conferred at Yalta, Crimea, with Marshal Stalin and Prime Minister Churchill.
April 12, 1945—Died at Warm Springs, Ga.

Strategy of Football Applied to High Office

President Franklin D. Roosevelt's philosophy for meeting sudden changes in the course of events once was illustrated by him when he cited the role of a football quarterback, who must alter his decisions to fit the changing course of a game. Discussing his attitude toward the economic crisis at a press conference on April 19, 1933, he said:

"It is a little bit like a football team that has a general plan of game against the other side. Now the captain and the quarterback of that team know pretty well what the next play is going to be and they know the general strategy of the team; but they cannot tell you what the next play is going to be until the next play is run off. If the play makes 10 yards, the succeeding play will be different from what it would have been if they had been thrown for a loss. I think that is the easiest way to explain it."

Franklin Delano Roosevelt, the thirty-first President of the United States, held that title longer than any man in history, and dealt, during his time, with the gravest problems, internal and external, which had faced the nation, and the world.

The internal crisis which existed at the time of his first inauguration, on March 4, 1933, when the nation's economic system was faltering and its financial organism paralyzed by fear, was followed in his third term by the global war, during which he and Winston Churchill emerged as leaders of the English-speaking world, and of much of the rest of it as well, regardless of language or customs.

The years between were packed with swift and drastic social and economic changes, to make Mr. Roosevelt the most controversial figure in American history. Beloved by millions, hated, admired, feared and scorned by countless adversaries, he did more to mold the future of the nation he headed, and the world he lived in, than anyone else. His character and his policies dominated.

The ultimate verdict of history upon Franklin D. Roosevelt will depend largely on the eventual outcome of the courses he selected—economic reforms at home, and the fight for democracy in the world, even when the latter involved a course that led to war.

Chose to Defy Dictators

So far as the war was concerned, with the bold confidence that was characteristic of him, he chose a policy of defiance of the dictators and aggressor nations, denunciation of efforts at appeasement and the unflinching extension of all-out material and moral support to the embattled democracies, which were locked in a death-grapple with the Axis powers that led to the attack on Pearl Harbor by the Japanese on Dec. 7, 1941.

It placed upon Mr. Roosevelt the responsibility of being Commander in Chief of the armed forces of the United States, of being, with Churchill and Stalin and Chiang Kai-shek, one of the guiding genii of the United Nations, when the responsibility was greatest, and the armed forces the largest, and the alliance the most widespread, in history up to that time.

But had this last and greatest crisis of his life never arisen, there was still far more than enough in the life and deeds of Franklin D. Roosevelt to have filled a library of books. He had been prepared for his final ordeal by a public career of more than thirty years, which had given him an almost unrivaled schooling in the workings of government and a deep insight into the thought processes of the democratic masses of the country.

A State Senator Before 30

As a young New York State Senator who won nation-wide acclaim before he was 30 by a successful fight against Tammany; as Assistant Secretary of the Navy before and during our participation in the first World War; as the unsuccessful Democratic nominee for the Vice Presidency in 1920; and as Governor of New York for two terms beginning in 1928, he had achieved unusual honors even before his accession to the Presidency.

His public career was interrupted for several years by a sudden disaster that seemed at the time to have shattered it irretrievably. While he was swimming near his summer home at Campobello, N. B., in August, 1921, he was stricken with infantile paralysis. For months his life was in danger and it was almost a year before he could begin to get about on crutches. He never fully recovered the use of his lower limbs.

Mr. Roosevelt fought his ailment with the same courageous coolness that he displayed years later when, a few weeks before his first inauguration, he narrowly escaped assassination in Miami, Fla. He devoted his years of enforced leisure to wide reading, especially in the fields of American political and naval history, in which he was unusually well versed, and to carrying on an extensive correspondence with fellow-Democrats all over the United States.

Despite his physical handicap, which compelled him to lean on the arm of an aide while he was walking, Mr. Roosevelt enjoyed robust and vigorous health during most of his years of heavy burdens in his terms of office. Tall and broad-shouldered his weight varied only from 184 to 188. The cares of office put added lines into his handsome face, but never for long banished his smile from it.

A characteristic of the President that was remarked by all who were closely associated with him was his never-failing ability to dismiss from his mind even the gravest problems, once he had reached a decision. It was this capacity for relaxing as soon as the day's work was done that enabled him, his physicians said, to assume the burdens of presiding in wartime in at least as fine physical condition as he had known when he first entered the White House until comparatively recently.

Mr. Roosevelt was fortunate in other ways that helped his extraordinary career. He possessed unusual personal charm, which held to him many associates who questioned the wisdom of some of his policies. His distinguished bearing, made familiar to millions of people by countless news reel and newspaper pictures, was an asset. So was his richly timbred speaking voice, carried by radio into millions of American homes in countless fireside chats and formal addresses.

Gift for Vivid Phrases

He had a gift for vivid phrases that crystallized his policies for the multitude. In accepting his first nomination for the Presidency at the Democratic National Convention in Chicago on July 2, 1932, he pledged himself to "a new deal for the American people." Henceforth,

through four Presidential campaigns and many stirring legislative battles, the term New Deal symbolized for his friends and foes alike the domestic policies he favored.

In the field of foreign relations he coined an almost equally well-known phrase when in his first inaugural he declared he would dedicate the nation to the policy of "the good neighbor." Eight years later, when he grimly resolved that this nation should furnish arms to Britain with which that country might fight for its life, he turned again to the simile of the good neighbor lending a garden hose to fight a fire, to justify his arms-loan plan to the American people.

In his bitterness, when the Supreme Court invalidated the National Recovery Act, he declared at a press conference that the court sought to relegate this country to "a horse and buggy age." His efforts on behalf of legislation designed to improve the social and economic lot of the less fortunate sections of the country were waged to the declaration that "one-third of this nation * * * is ill-fed, ill-clothed and ill-housed."

One of his battles with Congress in which he was defeated was in his attempt to reorganize the Supreme Court soon after his second inauguration. This precipitated a Congressional controversy unmatched in bitterness and in tense public interest since the fight over the League of Nations. And even in that instance his partisans asserted that he had won the substance if not the form of victory, when the court took a friendlier attitude toward New Deal legislation.

Won by Large Margins

Although the popularity of the New Deal with the people, as measured by mid-term Congressional elections and public opinion polls, waxed and waned, there never was any room for argument about the phenomenal and continuing personal popularity of Mr. Roosevelt. This was best illustrated by his success as the standard-bearer for the Democratic party, which, before his advent, had been the minority party in American politics for more than half a century.

In 1932, as the Democratic nominee opposing President Herbert Hoover, he carried forty-two States with 472 electoral votes, to six States with fifty-nine votes for his opponent. The popular vote was: Roosevelt 22,813,786, Hoover 15,759,266. In 1936 he carried every State but Maine and New Hampshire in defeating Governor Alfred M. Landon of Kansas. The electoral vote was 523 to 8; the popular vote was Roosevelt 27,751,612, Landon 16,681,913. In 1940 he defeated Wendell L. Willkie by an electoral vote of 449 to 82, and a popular vote of 27,243,466 to 22,304,755. In 1944 he defeated Governor Thomas E. Dewey of New York by an electoral vote of 432 to 99 and a popular vote of 25,602,505 to 22,006,278.

Even a brief recapitulation of the historic events of his Presidency would be a lengthy recital. The State papers and other documents of his public life alone fill a memorial library, erected at a cost of $250,000 on the Roosevelt family estate at Hyde Park, N. Y., as the gift of the historically minded President to the nation.

The Times
1st August 1898

THE LATE PRINCE BISMARCK.

In the course of his sermon yesterday afternoon at St. Paul's Cathedral, the Archdeacon of London made the following reference to the death of Prince Bismarck :—I would speak a word of sympathy to our Teutonic kinsfolk in the great Fatherland on hearing in England of the death of their most illustrious statesman. Perhaps we should have to be Germans ourselves in order to attempt to appreciate his methods of action. But, at any rate, we can all admire distinctness of aim, firmness of purpose, the resolute will, the dauntless courage, the immense capacity, the indomitable patriotism. The unity of Germany is a fact which we view with unmixed satisfaction ; it was a life-long aspiration of our far-sighted and high-minded Prince Consort ; and it is the maker of Germany who is dead. Surely it is a striking instance of the power of death in the most unexpected ways to level and to harmonize, that the two most prominent figures in German and in English politics during the last half-century, so utterly unlike in their ideas, characters, and careers as Bismarck and Gladstone, should within the same quarter of a year pass into the great Temple of Silence. We trust that what was good in the work of both will be very fruitful for the benefit of each of these two great nations. We view the progress of the German Empire with heartfelt goodwill. No country except the United States is so near to ourselves in religion, in blood, in civilization, in home life. The philosophy, the poetry, the literature, the music of the two races are the common property of each. In view of such potent ties of kinship and common interest, petty commercial jealousies sink into insignificance. If it be true that Christian nations, like Christian individuals, should desire each the good of the other, and that each should share the other's sorrows and joys, then we are right in making the passing away of a majestic and predominant German personality the occasion for the expression of our affection and esteem for the German people. May God bless the Fatherland !

DEATH OF PRINCE BISMARCK.

(FROM OUR OWN CORRESPONDENT.)

BERLIN, JULY 31.

Prince Bismarck died at Friedrichsruh at 11 o'clock last night.

LATEST INTELLIGENCE.

Prince Bismarck's fall, signal and unforeseen, but already remote, will have had for him the immense advantage of raising his career into the domain of history while he was still living. He thus now escapes the fury of his enemies, while his admirers can extol him without encountering the formidable opposition which they must have faced had he died in full political activity. And yet in spite of all the passion which he may excite, in spite of all attempts that may be made to disparage him, one thing remains certain—namely, that he will share the century with Napoleon. The first half belongs to the one, the second half to the other. Round these two men other nations will group their great warriors, writers, philosophers, statesmen, artists, and scientists who form the grand procession of the century, and above them will be imprinted in historic memory those two already legendary names, Napoleon and Bismarck. There has of late years been in France the strange phenomenon of the outburst of the Napoleonic legend at the very moment when the Bonapartist cause seems irreparably lost. The legend developed all the more vigorously as it seemed no longer capable of creating a national danger. So, also, will the Bismarckian epos grow and spread under the pens of manifold writers because it is known that no narrative, however glowing, will resuscitate the Iron Chancellor now struck down by death. *continued*

There is, however—and this is the most curious problem enforced on the attention of thinkers—a wonderful difference between the work of Napoleon and that of Bismarck. Nothing has survived of the conquests of the former. France after her fall found her territorial power lessened and saw herself an object of suspicion and a prey to everlasting dissensions, having lost, so to speak, the sense of concord, whereas what has survived of his work is the Code, to which he devoted only secondary attention, the Moscow decree on the Théâtre Français, which remains a constant anachronism, and that formidable centralization which resists the progress of the age and renders the nominal Democracy of a Republic a purely Cesarian Democracy, ready to serve as an instrument to any nocturnal adventurer who may succeed in stifling the very name of liberty by denouncing the licence substituted for it. The work of Bismarck, on the contrary, survives him in the material results which it has procured for Germany. The German Empire, which, if he was not the only person to create it, was nevertheless his conception, exists and survives him. That country, formidably aggrandized, has attained a prosperity and power which the ancient German Empire had never known. On the contrary, the feudal spirit which he had endeavoured to maintain and develop in spite of modern tendencies, the absolute power which was his dream, are melting away, and the Empire which issued from his brain is governing itself more and more according to laws absolutely opposed to those which he had conceived.

This curious and striking parallel is evoked by the death of this man who has dominated the second half of the century. One involuntarily compares him with the formidable personality who has left on the first half his indelible imprint. But just for this reason those who have had close glimpses of the man who has just died are bound to tell what they have seen and felt, because the Napoleonic renaissance of which I have spoken proves that generations to come receive with avidity at a given moment any information, even the most modest, which the contemporaries of great historical figures can offer them. It is in this light, but in this light only, that I claim a right to sum up my personal knowledge of the Chancellor, not so long ago omnipotent, whom the hand of death has now laid low.

I saw him but once, though for five consecutive hours, during almost the entire period of which, with very rare intervals, I listened to his talk. But it was at the apogee of his greatness. The old Emperor, wounded by the hand of a regicide, was confined to the apartments of the Royal Palace. Hardly was he allowed to come to the window to see what was going on outside. The most sinister rumours were in circulation. One evening I beheld at a reception at Lord Odo Russell's a lady in tears, who announced that the Emperor was dying—and every such alarm added to the uncontrolled authority of the Chancellor who presided over the Berlin Congress. At that moment no journalist had ever been received by Prince Bismarck, and Prince Hohenlohe, who had given me hope of a possible interview, showed daily that he was more and more convinced of the futility of his efforts. "He is so hard pressed," said he to me, "that he really fears to be submerged if he does not maintain the dike which he has raised to keep out those asking for an audience." Moreover, there then prevailed in Berlin a kind of idolatrous superstition. Everybody, almost without exception, bowed to the Chancellor's will, and with few exceptions the members of the Congress deferred to him more deeply and humbly than any. It was not servility, it was abnegation, and it was patriotism. It was known that the entire Congress was, almost without resistance, at his disposal. It was known that on him, almost on him alone, depended the favours to be obtained or wrested for the Fatherland whose interests each was defending. Men sacrificed themselves in order to make their country triumph.

When on July 1 Prince Hohenlohe came to inform me at that reception by Lord Odo Russell that the Chancellor invited me to dinner for the next day "en famille" and in morning dress, he seemed as surprised as I was—even more so, for I, for my part, knew too well that the invitation was not to me but to the Correspondent of The Times, and that it was the journal which I had the honour of representing which enjoyed this unexpected and unprecedented exception. This, however, did not overcome my emotion, and for the first time, perhaps, in my career I felt very nervous at the approach of the moment when I was to wait on the Chancellor. It could not really be otherwise. Everybody was hanging on the lips of this dreaded judge. I knew that he had strongly resented a letter on "A French Scare" published in The Times three years previously, and I knew that it was quite open for him, the day after receiving me, to pass the most unfavourable judgment on me, thus avenging himself on me and on The Times without a voice being raised in protest against an opinion which would have been eagerly endorsed by the entire Press, naturally ruffled by the exception made in favour of the envoy of The Times. This, happily, was not realized, but it was with a real tremor that I saw enter the room where I was waiting with his family the giant, with stiff eyebrows, dressed in his blue uniform, before whom I played pretty much the part of a David without his sling on the approach of a formidably armed Goliath.

Now, this man whom fame unmeasuredly extolled is one of the few whom I then found equal to and above their reputation. He struck me with profound admiration by the terrible simplicity of the means employed by him for carrying on his diplomacy after his own fashion. Dinner was immediately served, and even before we had seated ourselves, turning to me, he said:—"I am glad to see you, and I hope that, with the help of The Times, we shall be able to smooth over this Batum question which threatens to disturb the work of the Congress." Once seated at table and placing me on his right, he gave me the never-to-be-forgotten spectacle of the fascination which a man can exercise when bent on winning over anybody to whom he attaches some interest or importance. This assumed quite the proportions of an art, and I did not even attempt to resist it. He told me simply what he thought should be made known to England and Europe. He explained to me that the English plenipotentiaries had to prepare the country for the concessions imposed on it by their desire for peace, and he asked, with admirably feigned modesty, in what shape I thought proper to give the reflections which he had just communicated. Then, satisfied with my answer, he dropped Batum as a settled question, and set himself to charm and seduce his auditor.

Never have I seen such a Jupiter changing himself into a gentle rain, so formidable a personage assuming a tone of graciousness and charm. At a certain moment he turned to me and said:—"Perhaps you would like a glass of beer? My old Munich friend brews it expressly for me," and he poured me out a glass. I began laughing, and he asked the reason. "Because in my childhood a kind of lunatic said to me:—'Thou wilt rise in the world and princes will offer thee drink,' and behold his prophecy is fulfilled in a glass of beer." The Prince assumed a serious air. "Well," he said, "it is a true prophecy, for I do not offer drink to everybody," and pouring out a second glass he said:—"It is better to fulfil the prediction twice over!" After some minutes he resumed:—"I saw you on the day of your arrival unter den Linden. You entered one grand bazaar, and I said, 'It is flattering for Berlin that a man coming direct from Paris should buy something on arriving in Berlin.'" "Your

Highness," I rejoined, " would have been still more surprised if you had known what I went to buy, for at the hotel there is not a single——." The Prince burst out laughing. " I quite understand," he said, " and you ask yourself what has become of all those which we took in France ! "

I quote these traits because they show the extreme simplicity and extraordinary affability of this omnipotent being towards so simple a mortal as myself, and because they explain the Bismarck who knew how to win the good graces and gain the confidence of Napoleon III. They also explain how he could entrap Count Benedetti into the fatal snare into which he fell, for they show one of the phases of this figure carved out of granite, who could cover himself with velvet when the desire to gain his cause led him to substitute mildness for force, seduction for dictation. This man, in truth, at the height of his power was an elemental force. Nature had given him that which makes leaders of nations—the art of neglecting nothing which may conduce to the end, of disdaining nothing which may serve the object, the resolution of accomplishing the welfare of his nation because it is identified with himself, and also, as a consequence of all this, the abandonment of these great qualities at the moment of fall, the moment when the prestige of power vanishes, leaving only the man confronted by a hard ordeal. The Emperor would have done him an immense service in dispensing with his services if he had not caused himself much greater injury than was done to him ; for if he had known how to remain wrapped in silence like the demigods buried in the mystery of intentional oblivion there would rise up to-day throughout Germany a formidable clamour and the young Emperor would be called upon to explain the audacity with which he ventured to lay a hand on him who, even now, would still be the idol of the German masses. But in spite of this I must confess that the Germans whom I have seen and talked with to-day seem inclined to think that William II. will for some time find it difficult to make his Empire forget the blow dealt by him at its chief founder. There is such a general feeling of resentment for the moment as has not been experienced since the Chancellor's fall. Moreover, it is now too late for Bismarck to compromise his glory and grandeur. Death has rendered henceforth impossible the blunders of utterance which might compromise him and has flung round him that veil of mystery which appals the popular soul.

As for France, she reproaches Bismarck, it is true, with the artifice which he employed to drag her into a war and to expose her to calumnious accusation, but she acknowledges his greatness as a type of human genius, she admits that she was vanquished by the most formidable conception of an unparalleled brain, and, in a word, she has ended by seeing—after having been irritated against him because she was beaten and just because it is France—that she should understand that history will judge him not merely one-sidedly—that is, in his relations with her—but from the point of view also of the achievement of Germany unity, of that great Empire, rescued from poverty and dismemberment ; perhaps, also, she will consider that the moral sufferings which he has endured since his fall are a well-deserved but sufficient expiation for the circuitous means which he employed to precipitate war, that everlasting curse which weighs on the sons of men and is the everlasting expiation which they must undergo.

The Paris papers, while acknowledging Prince Bismarck's great abilities, naturally condemn some of his acts. Thus, the *Débats* says :—

" In spite of the bitterness of a cup almost drained to the dregs, Prince Bismarck must have died self-satisfied. He had realized his plan. He had foreseen and stated that blood and iron would be necessary for it. Although he was in many respects quite modern, the old methods, the procedures of another age, were not repugnant to him. He employed them without hesitation, perhaps even with a secret preference. The pure and simple right of conquest was for him the most unquestionable of all, and he took care that it should not be questioned. All his life is there. Germany has certainly gained much by it, and owes him gratitude. Europe, which for some years he really governed, owes him only an admiration mingled with many reserves. As for France, irrespective of her own misfortune, she has been too long the champion of civilization and right not to protest against the retrogression which Prince Bismarck's policy has enforced on some of the noblest causes which honour mankind."

In like manner the *Temps* says :—

" In France there are still minds which desire to be generous and know how to be just. Just we should in any case have tried to be for him who was one of the great victors of the century, the founder of an Empire, one of the masters of the world. Generous it will not be difficult for us to be for him who dies, as it were, vanquished, overthrown, not merely from the power which he thought to possess for life, but from that pedestal of glory the glitter of which so long prevented men from seeing the feet of clay of that statue of precious metal and from perceiving how many littlenesses contributed to such a greatness. If France owes sincere tears for the Washingtons and Gladstones, those great benefactors of mankind, she knows how to join respectfully in the mourning for her great adversaries, for those who have done her much ill. She did not disturb the solemnity of the funeral of William I., that soldier-Emperor who bore away with him a whole century of history and legend. She will not break the thrilling silence of the funeral given by a whole people to the founder of its unity. If she needed a revenge, would she not find it by listening to the immense rumbling of that sea of Socialism which is ever rising and which threatens the work of the great statesman ? "

The Royalist *Gazette de France*, making party capital, as usual, out of everything, styles Prince Bismarck the founder of the French Republic, and says that grateful Republicans ought to mourn for him. Nothing, it adds, would have been more regretted by " that old malefactor " than the fall of the Republic. M. Tavernier, in the Catholic *Univers*, says :—" To tear Europe to pieces in order to reconstruct Germany there under the hegemony of Prussia—this could be only the work of a powerful brain and arm. Let us not be wanting in justice towards our enemy and our conqueror, although he scorned that same justice."

The Glasgow Herald
23rd January 1924

DEATH OF LENIN

RUSSIA'S REVOLUTIONARY LEADER

THE DRIVING FORCE OF COMMUNISM

Reuter's Agency is officially informed by the Russian Soviet Trade Delegation in London that M. Lenin, President of the Council of the People's Commissaries, died suddenly on Monday. For the past eight months Lenin had been too ill to attend in any way to public business. As long ago as September it was realised that his activities were definitely over, as the overstrained brain after six years had given way, and although every effort was made to help him in his village retreat all were unavailing, the end coming, as is usual in such cases, suddenly. For a year the Red leaders have lacked his counsel, and now his death robs Bolshevism of the prestige of a great name, and leaves it facing an increasingly difficult situation.

SOVIET COMMUNIQUE

"A MOST PAINFUL BLOW"

A communication from the Russian Trade Delegation states:—Lenin died on January 21 (Monday) at 6.50 p.m. in the hills near Moscow. The doctors' bulletin said—"On January 21 the state of the health of Vladimir Ilich suddenly took a sharp turn for the worse. At 5.30 p.m. the breathing became difficult. He lost consciousness, and expired at 6.50 p.m. from paralysis of the respiratory centres."

A Government communiqué says:—There was no indication that the end was near. Of late there had been a considerable improvement in the state of health of Vladimir Ilich. All the signs were that his health would continue to improve. Quite unexpectedly yesterday (the 21st) there was a sharp change for the worse, and some hours later he breathed his last. The All-Russian Congress of Soviets, now sitting in Moscow, and the Union Congress of Soviets, which opens in a few days, will take the necessary decisions to ensure the further uninterrupted work of the Soviet Government. This most painful blow which has overtaken the workers of the Soviet Union since the time of the conquest of power by the workers and peasants of Russia will be a profound shock to every workman and peasant not only in our Republic but in every country. The widest masses of the toilers of the whole world will lament the loss of their greatest lead . He is no longer amongst us, but his work mains unshakable. Expressing the will of the toiling masses, the Soviet Government will continue the work of Vladimir Ilich, marching steadily upon the path he traced out. The Soviet Government stands firm at its post, watchful over the conquests of the proletarian revolution.

The body arrives in Moscow to-morrow (Wednesday), and will lie in state in the Trade Union Palace until the funeral, which has been fixed for Saturday next. The whole population will have access to the coffin.

AN EVENTFUL CAREER

Vladimir Ilich Lenin was born at Simbirsk on April 10, 1870. His father, a director of primary schools, belonged to the higher class of Government officials, and there with the title of State-Councillor, and there seems little truth in the story that his mother was a Jewess. By birth, therefore, he belonged to the hereditary nobility, and

should in ordinary circumstances have been entitled to be called "Excellency." He was educated at the local gymnasium, whose head was Dr Kerenski, the father of Lenin's greatest opponent, A. F. Kerenski, and who gave the youthful revolutionary an excellent character for phenomenal hard work and an excellent report on all subjects except logic. While he was still at school an event occurred which materially affected his whole life. This was the execution in 1887 of his elder brother Alexander, a leader of the terrorist group of the Narodnaia Volia, for complicity in a plot to assassinate Alexander III. From that moment Vladimir Ulianov was a revolutionary.

Leaving school he entered the law faculty in the University of Kazan, and immediately joined himself to the revolutionary group of students, powerful at Kazan as at all the universities. The prevailing tendency was anarchist, but while at school Vladimir had come under the influence of Marx, and in 1886 was even contemplating a translation of some of Marx's essays. Marxist and anarchist were, however, equally suspect, and it was no long time before he was "sent down." He went to Petrograd, and there passed the examinations which entitled him to practise as a lawyer. In Petrograd he encountered the real working class and their tentative endeavours at Socialist organisation. He was quickly admitted into the Marxist ranks, and was sufficiently active as a member of the strike-organising "Union of Struggle for the Deliverance of the Workers" to draw upon himself the attentions of the police, with the result that no long time after he had abandoned the law for the career of a professional revolutionary. He was arrested in 1899 and exiled.

A PROFESSIONAL REVOLUTIONARY

Outside he met for the first time the great leaders of Russian Socialism, and quickly became well known among them. With two colleagues of the Social Democratic Party (Marxist, founded 1898), Martov and Potressov, he founded in 1901 the "Iskra," which had so great an influence on Russian revolutionism, and next year published the first of his well-known writings "What to do," a sort of ha' tbook of revolution, in which he advocated the creation of professional revolutionaries. His previous writings, narrowly polemical, had been little noticed outside revolutionary circles, but they are worth recording:—"On Fines" (1894), a brochure addressed to Petrograd factory workers; articles written under the nom de plume of Toulin against the Narodnaia Volia policy (1894-1895), in which the Bolshevik doctrine is foreshadowed; "The Persecutors of the Zemstvos" (1901), a criticism of his colleague Struve; "The Development of Capitalism in Russia," and the "Problems of the Russian Social Democrats," with a flattering preface by Axelrod, which won him a certain notoriety in international Socialism.

All these writings are marked by a pedantic narrowness worthy of Marx at his worst. Constitutionally incapable of compromise in theory he brought disruption on a purely technical point into the party and final rupture in 1903 when he defeated Plekhanov and was left as leader of the majority (Bolsheviki) in contradistinction to the minority (Mensheviki). The new party immediately held a conference in which one can see the origin of the future Communist Party, though no one then thought of calling it by that name. It laid down the position that a republic can only be established in Russia by an armed rising and the formation of a revolutionary government which would convoke a constituent assembly. The chance to act on this came in 1905. Whenever the revolutionary movement reached its climax, the Bolsheviks from London organised the armed rising in Moscow and in the opinion of their Socialist opponents by their tactics destroyed all hope of a change of régime. With the Petrograd Soviet on the other hand Lenin had little to do. That was the work of the Mensheviks, notably of Trotsky, then one of Lenin's bitterest opponents. Lenin arrived in Petrograd early in 1905—he did not go to Moscow—and watched the Soviet in session from the gallery. He wished to sit at the final meeting after the order for arrest had been given, but according to M. Zinoviev was interdicted from doing so by the party.

He remained in Russia till 1907 in hiding and then again returned to exile, dividing his time between London, Paris, and Switzerland, writing constantly and spending fifteen hours again according to Zinoviev in libraries every day reading and studying. Before he left Russia there appeared his "Two Tactics for Social Democracy," which is still one of the Bolshevik bibles and contains the main theory of Bolshevism. The later years saw a constant stream of articles all on theory, of which the best known is "Materialism and Empiriocriticism" (1909) published under the name of W. Iline. In 1912, with his devoted follower Zinoviev, he established himself at Cracow to be near Russia and from there directed the party activities, and waged fierce war with the rival Socialists. His chief assistants were Malinovski and the editor of "Pravda," Tchernomisov, both of whom were exposed as police spies by Burtzev, a fact which considerably lessened Lenin's influence outside his own party.

THE RETURN TO RUSSIA

The war found him still at Cracow. He was promptly arrested by the Austrian police, and then, on the chance of his revolutionary activities proving helpful to the German cause, was permitted to go to Switzerland, where with Zinoviev and Lunatcharski he commenced a furious propaganda against the war and for a proletarian uprising, the first condition of which he held to be the military defeat of Russia.

On these lines he took a prominent part in the Zimmerwald and Kienthal conferences of Left Socialists, where he was distinguished for fanatic defeatism and advocacy of immediate revolution. "Peace and revolution" were his watchwords, to be attained by any means, and, that being so, the German Government raised no objection to his traversing Germany to gain Russia, when the revolution broke out in March, 1917. There is no proof that he was a German agent in the strict sense of the term, but it is clear from Ludendorff's statements that the decision to let him go to Russia was due to German Headquarters, who saw in him a force that would paralyse the military action of the new Russia.

On his arrival he was little known in Russia except by his pen-name and solely as a polemist, not as a man of action, with the reputation of being an intransigeant, narrow sectarian, who would be content with nothing but the full Marxist revolution, but so obscure and with so small a following that the Government could safely permit his entry into Russia and ignore him otherwise. The Bolshevik Party was extremely tiny, but it was composed not so much of able as of determined men, and its very intransigence and claims of orthodox Marxism brought over to it many of its opponents, of whom the most important was Lenin's old enemy, Leo Trotzki, with whom he now formed a fighting front and found in him the man of action and the organiser the party lacked.

A DRAMATIC COUP

From March the story of Lenin's life is practically that of the Russian revolution. He went into opposition at once to the idea of a coalition Government, and seizing on the existence of the Soviets put forward his plea for a Socialist State in Russia under the watchword of "All power to the S viets." At first the suspicion entertained of the Bolsheviks on account of their notorious defeatism prevented any headway being made. Thanks to the patriotic leanings of the great Socialist leaders, Kerenski, Plekhanov, Axelrod, Tseretelli, Tchidze, and even of the anti-war Soviet Revolutionaries under Tchernov and Spiridonova, Russian Socialism stood firm for the prosecution of the war and a democratic peace. It was on the question of what was a democratic peace that the coalition with the Liberals broke down. From the Kchesinski Palace and through the "Pravda" Lenin pressed his point, accusing the Government of treachery to the democratic ideals, alternating cries of "All power to the Soviets" with demands for the Constituent Assembly and gradually winning over the Left parties to the view that to accept anything short of a Socialist State was to betray the revolution into the hands of the bourgeois. In July the Bolsheviks felt themselves strong enough to attempt an armed rising. It was easily disposed of by Kerenski, and Lenin had to flee to Finland, but Kerenski had not the courage to take sedition by the throat. Content with the proof that the Bolsheviks had not captured the Left parties, all of whom remained true to the Government, he permitted the subversive propaganda to go on, and in the chaotic state to which Russia was reduced, break up of the front, failure of the Coalition Government, absence of a clear-cut policy in home and foreign affairs, failure of the Allies to clarify their position, and the breaking away of the nationalities and constant peasant risings, it made steady headway, simply because it did embody a clear-cut policy. In September that was evident from the Bolshevik victories on the Soviets—the Petrograd Soviet went practically completely Bolshevik—and a working agreement with the Left Social Revolutionaries, who had captured the country Soviets, left Lenin at the head of a strong party. He returned in the end of October, and found Kerenski facing a military revolution and a bourgeois coalition, and so risked the coup of November 7. It was dramatically successful. Resistance collapsed, Kerenski fled, and the Bolsheviks and their allies proclaimed the Federative Soviet Republic under a Council of Commissaries, of whom Lenin was president.

BREST-LITOVSK AND DICTATORSHIP

In its first phase the Bolshevik revolution was not a Communist dictatorship. It was a coalition of Bolsheviks, revolted Mensheviks, Anarchists, Left Social Revolutionaries, and some intellectuals like Gorki. The first task was to liquidate the war, and on the precise means of doing so there was considerable difference among the leaders. Round Lenin gathered the peace-at-any-price party, peace in which to develop the Communist experiment. The dissolution of the Constituent Assembly by force on January, 1918, got rid of parliamentary opposition, and after stormy debates and private discussions in which Trotzki, Madame Kollontai, and the Social Revolutionaries were prominent on the war side, the decision was taken to sign the humiliating peace of Brest-Litovsk. It is characteristic of Lenin that he saw clearly that there was no immediate prospect of world revolution and that he frankly regarded the peace as a truce, a necessary truce to give the revolution a chance of life.

The development of Bolshevism led to the defection of the Anarchists and the Social Revolutionaries. In April, 1918, the anarchist clubs were forcibly suppressed, and Lenin then tackled the Revolutionaries on land reform and on foreign policy. The Revolutionaries used the German occupation of the Ukraine as far as Caucasia to denounce Lenin as an opportunist and a traitor, while the rising of the "Whites" further embarrassed the Government. It was at last a Communist one. While the undisciplined Red Guards were being driven in on Muscovy, the Revolutionaries seized the chance of the Soviet Congress in July, 1918, to attack the Brest peace. They lost their majority in the Congress, but on July 4 signalised the first session by a violent demonstration against the Germany envoy, Count Mirbach. On July 6 Revolutionaries assassinated Mirbach in the Embassy, and next day Lenin retaliated by arresting the Revolutionary leaders. The Revolutionary rising was easily crushed, and the Bolsheviks at last were firmly seated in the dictator's saddle.

THE RED TERROR

A timely apology and the situation in the West prevented German action, but the White armies were becoming really dangerous. Of the negotiations with the Allies this is not the place to speak, but it seems certain that Lenin was in no mind to co-operate with anyone. To have done so would have been to postpone the advent of pure Communism, and the confused conflicting policies of the Entente gave him ample reason for refusing an agreement. The first thing to be done was to crush all opposition at home. On September 5 Lenin was hit by two shots fired by a Right Revolutionary, Dora Kaplan, at Moscow, while Volodarski and Uritzki were murdered in Petrograd. This was enough, and on September 7 the Terror was proclaimed, which admitted officially 16,000 executions in less than sixteen months. The Armistice in November further cleared the situation. The Allies, terrified by the Red menace, which seemed to be ready to flood Europe, began to aid regularly the White armies. It was now the Communists against the world. Dangerously ill, Lenin rose to the occasion, and ably seconded by a now united party he waged pitiless war by arms, police, and propaganda in front and rear. Never, indeed, were the Reds so really formidable as when by all the laws of war they should have been crushed in a few weeks. The campaigns lasted a year, attended by many excesses and a prodigious waste in men and resources, while in the rear Bolshevism was firmly established. The last vestiges of democracy disappeared, and every position of authority was filled either by a Communist or by a creature of the party. Many of the opposition fled or accepted the dictatorship, and as Koltchak, Judenitch, Denikin, and, finally, Wrangel were defeated, the Communist hold strengthened, till the Polish offensive in the spring of 1920 permitted Lenin to summon Russia to a national war. By the Riga Treaty, finally signed on March 18, 1921, Bolshevism was formally at peace with the world.

THE COMPROMISE WITH CAPITALISM

By that time two events had occurred. Russia was exhausted, paralysed and stricken with famine and Communism had been fully realised. But each event caused and counteracted the other. The conditions necessary for so great an experiment had not been present and the end was ghastly failure. To Lenin the formidable work of carrying out the experiment had largely fallen and it was characteristic of him that he was the first to realise the failure. Hence the sudden return from pure undiluted Communism to semi-capitalism and to relations with the bourgeois States. Negotiations were opened up with the various Powers, but it was now evident that Lenin was by no means the dictator he had been. The new risings against him were not political but economic and inside the party the ring of fanatic "no-compromisers" went into violent opposition. Bolshevik policy ceased to be coherent. It breathed peace and war not alternately but together, conducted Imperialistic campaigns while denouncing imperialism, intrigued in the very States with which it was seeking to open up friendly relations. It is possible that only the famine prevented a civil war that would have ended Bolshevism for ever, for the famine caused men to turn to the only government that seemed able. It unlikely to do anything, and when the great project of the Genoa Conference was mooted Lenin was more nearly head of a national government than ever he had been. He himself fell ill with cancer in the throat caused by

the Kaplan attempt two years previously and was unable to go, but from a sick room controlled Tchitcherin from first to last.

LENIN'S GENIUS

No biography of Lenin, however short, would be complete without a reference to the Third International. Its creation is thoroughly characteristic of Lenin's genius. The aim of Communism is world revolution through class war. That war it is the duty of the Socialist International to wage. But the Socialist International was not red enough to satisfy the hierophants of Communism, so another organisation had to be set up. That organisation could not be the Bolshevik Government of Russia which would then be at war with the world, so the Third International was set up (created October, 1918; first congress March, 1919), but at its head and kept there by its constitution were the actual members of the Russian Government. Thus there were two Lenins — M. Lenin the Russian statesman prepared to make Russia re-enter the comity of nations and Comrade Lenin of the International, prepared to wreck that comity for good. The distinction is worthy of the man who threw as much energy into the international movement as he did into the purely Russian one and split the Socialist parties throughout the world in a formidable schism.

Of Lenin's work and doctrine there is little room to speak. Both have experienced innumerable modifications, and both will survive him. He was not the prophet of Communism so much as its driving force. Personally an ascetic and a tireless worker, he assimilated other men's thought rather than created new thought. His books are commonplace, pedantically logical and formal, even dull, and as an orator he was only a qualified success, a clever debater rather than a great speaker. But of his power to lead there is no doubt. His gift for tactics amounted to genius. A fanatic, he found all means justifiable—German gold, Red terror, treachery, murder, and crime. That, in itself, is not exceptional, but he wedded to it an uncanny sense of reality so that he was that almost unique being, a fanatic who could compromise. The French proverb, "reculer pour mieux sauter," he understood and practised as few have done, and time and again, when a less supple man would have been crushed, Lenin carried the day even at the expense of a temporary defeat in principle. His one aim was to retain power so that when the chance came it could be used for Communism, and few have been so successful. He was, indeed, the perfect revolutionary type, with all its virtues and less of its failings than any other, and the cause of Red revolution in him loses an unchallenged master.

Daily Telegraph
20ᵗʰ April 1967

ADENAUER: 'ONE OF THE GREAT MEN OF OUR TIMES'

DR. KONRAD ADENAUER, who died yesterday, aged 91, retired in October, 1963, after 14 years as West Germany's Chancellor.

Sir Winston Churchill, who also died at the age of 91, once described him as the greatest German statesman since Bismarck. Mr. Macmillan, then Prime Minister, called him "one of the great men of our times."

He was not only a "great leader," for Germany, but a "great statesman and partner in the consolidation of Europe and the Atlantic community."

In 1963, Dr. Adenauer signed the Franco-German treaty of consultation and co-operation just after the French President had closed the Common Market door on Britain. The climax and formalisation of his efforts for reconciliation, it marked the beginning of increasing irritation and frustration in Franco-German relations.

Dr. Adenauer became Chancellor when he was 73, and for some years was also Foreign Minister. He finally emerged as one of the shrewdest and most dominating —some thought too dominating— figures in the Western European political and diplomatic scenes.

His steadfast faith in, and Herculean efforts to achieve, the incorporation of Germany in the Western European defence scheme reached a notable climax in 1954 with the London nine-Power conference and the signing of the Paris Treaties.

These revised the five-Power Brussels Treaty to include West Germany and Italy, and permitted German rearmament and entry into the North Atlantic Treaty Organisation. One of their most notable provisions was West Germany's solemn undertaking never to manufacture or possess nuclear weapons.

They were followed by talks between Dr. Adenauer and M. Mendes-France, the then French Prime Minister, which ended in complete agreement on the vexed question of the Saar.

OFFICIAL'S SON
Work for Cologne

The son of a Cologne municipal official who was commissioned on the field of Königgrätz for bravery, Konrad Adenauer was educated locally and grew up a devout Roman Catholic. It was intended that he should become a bank clerk, but preferring to study law, he attended the Universities of Bonn, Munich and Freiburg.

He failed to complete his studies, worked as a law clerk in Cologne from 1902 to 1904, and then transferred to the city's law department. Three years later he was appointed the Lord Mayor's chief assistant.

In 1917 he became Lord Mayor, an office he continued to hold during the years of occupation and under the Weimar Republic. He contributed much to the replanning of the city; its wide green belt, its university, its annual trade fair, the new Rhine bridge and, presaging future events, the autobahn to Bonn, were largely due to his interest and enthusiasm.

As Mayor, he became a member of Prussia's first Chamber and the Rhenish Provincial Diet, and was president of the Prussian State Council. He played a leading part in the Catholic Centre party, and at one point in 1926 declined an offer of the Reich Chancellorship of a coalition government.

But he had made no secret of his hostility to the rising Nazi party, and within a few days of Hitler's assumption of power in 1933 he was dismissed from office.

For 12 years he held himself aloof from politics, living mostly at the family villa at Rhöndorf, near Bonn, on a pension, but did not escape the attention of the Gestapo. He was arrested, and detained for short periods, including the "Night of the Long Knives" in 1934, and the attempt to assassinate Hitler 10 years later.

U.S. CHOICE
Christian Democrat post

After the capitulation of Germany the Americans found in him the answer to their search for a man of wide municipal experience, untainted by Nazi associations, who could act as Lord Mayor of Cologne.

They re-installed him in office. Accused of "obstruction and non-co-operation" by the British authorities when they took over control of the city, he was dismissed for a second time.

Although Dr. Adenauer often joked in later years over this incident, bitterness at the humiliation never entirely left him. It was to prove a recurring undertone in troubled Anglo-German relations.

But within a few months, undeterred by this setback, and only too conscious of the troubled years ahead for Germany, he helped to found the Christian Democrat Union in the British zone, and became the party's first chairman. The strength of the new party, which was later to win five successive general elections, was the parity ensured for Catholic and Protestant interests.

By 1948, when the three Western Military Governors invited political leaders to work out a West German Constitution, Dr. Adenauer was pre-eminent in his party, and his only political rival of importance was the late Dr. Schumacher of the Social Democrats.

On Sept. 15, 1949, the Bundestag elected him Chancellor by a single vote, sometimes jokingly assumed to be his own. During the early years of office he did not escape criticism even within his own party.

He was accused of dictatorial methods, of subservience to the Allied High Commissioners, and of favouritism in appointments. Unmoved, he continued with a policy which he was convinced was the only one which would lead to the salvation of his country.

Bonn, for which Dr. Adenauer himself was the Member, became the federal capital, and by the formation of Ministries and the re-establishment of a Civil Service, and by the drafting of new laws, Dr. Adenauer set Germany on the road to sovereignty.

In 1949 he secured the end of Allied dismantling of war-potential factories, and two years later obtained the first revision of the Occupation Statute which enabled him to enter into normal relations with countries other than the three main Western Powers.

In Paris in the same year he signed the six-nation Schuman Plan Treaty which established a European Coal and Steel Community, and shortly afterwards took his seat in the Committee of Ministers of the Council of Europe.

In 1952 he signed, with the Western Foreign Ministers, the Bonn Conventions which gave almost complete sovereignty to Western Germany, and the ill-fated European Defence Community Treaty.

Perhaps the most controversial and ill-managed event in Dr. Adenauer's long career came in the spring of 1959.

UNREST IN PARTY
Resignation threat

Then, piqued by unrest in his own Cabinet and party as well as sharp criticism of his policies in the British Press, which he believed to be officially inspired, he announced his impending resignation from the Chancellorship and his candidature for the Presidency.

West Germany was preoccupied with the problems of reunification and Berlin, and more than any other Western leader Dr. Adenauer stood for a firm and uncompromising attitude towards the Russians on these questions.

Dr. Erhard, his eventual successor, was not, in Dr. Adenauer's eyes, likely to preserve continuity of policy. Nor did the Chancellor hesitate to express his disparaging views of his deputy's capabilities.

Six weeks after his original announcement, Dr. Adenauer cancelled his candidature for the Presidency. Despite his age, his enormous authority was enough

his life, he faced problems of appalling complexity with characteristic energy. The exodus of East Germans to the West, the Communist wall in Berlin, and the overriding necessity for an honourable settlement with Russia were dilemmas that would have daunted a statesman many years younger.

ACTIVE RETIREMENT
de Gaulle meeting

Undismayed, "Der Alte," "The Old Man," flew to Washington for talks with President Kennedy. The triumphal tour of Germany by the President, with whom the Chancellor formed a warm relationship, in June, 1963, was the last great event of the "Adenauer era."

Dr. Adenauer, though retaining the influential chairmanship of the Christian Democrat party, largely vanished from the limelight in the first months of his retirement to start his memoirs. Extracts from these appeared in *The Sunday Telegraph* in 1965. But by mid-1964 he had shown, in speeches and interviews critical of the new Government's attitude towards France, that he was by no means a spent force.

In November, 1964, he went to Paris to be installed as a member of the French Academy of Political and Moral Sciences. He had discussions with Gen. de Gaulle on Franco-German relations, which helped to ease friction with the Erhard Government.

Dr. Adenauer in January, 1966, received the world's homage on his 90th birthday. Ambassadors, politicians, bishops and leaders in other walks of life went to Bonn to do him honour at a reception in the Parliament house. In the following March he stepped down as chairman of the Christian Democratic Union.

In his farewell speech he called for a politically united Europe. He was elected honorary chairman of the party for life.

Dr. Adenauer maintained his campaign against Dr. Erhard, his successor, right up to the fall of the Erhard administration in the autumn of 1966. "Der Alte's" controversial interviews became rarer after Dr. Kiesinger's Grand Coalition took office last December.

But he maintained his pro-French tone to the last, never hesitating to criticise America. For instance, he urged the United States to break off the Vietnam war and concentrate on preventing a Russian take-over in Europe.

SHARPEST BARBS
Nuclear opinion

Dr. Adenauer reserved some of his sharpest barbs for the nuclear non-proliferation treaty, which he called a " new Versailles."

He also gave his blessing to the growing sense of national consciousness which developed in the Germany of 1966-67. Despite the electoral gains of the Right-wing National Democrats, Dr. Adenauer said that this sense of nationhood had nothing to do with Nazism.

He visited Israel in May, 1966, and last February went to Spain and saw Gen. de Gaulle in Paris.

Dr. Adenauer, who was married twice, is survived by four sons and three daughters and more than 20 grandchildren.

to quell the rebellion threatening in his own party.

He continued as Chancellor. Towards the end of 1959 he had talks with Mr. Macmillan in London and with Gen. de Gaulle in Paris.

At Christmas time he was confronted by an outbreak of swastika-daubing which, beginning in Dr. Adenauer's native Cologne, rapidly spread to many other countries, including Britain. His recommendation that the " louts " responsible should be thrashed on the spot aroused almost as much comment as the offence itself.

More talks with President Eisenhower in New York, with President de Gaulle in Paris, and with Mr. Macmillan in Bonn followed during 1960. It became clear that Dr. Adenauer was anxious to draw Britain into a closer political relationship that would strengthen the European countries vis-à-vis Washington and Moscow.

He retained, however, his latent mistrust of British efforts to achieve a reduction of tension and of armaments in Central Europe, and particularly of the British Labour party.

FOURTH ELECTION
Kennedy talks

Two months before his 86th birthday he was elected Chancellor for the fourth time, but only by a narrow majority. The shock of the Communist wall in Berlin on Aug. 13, 1961, caused the CDU to lose its absolute majority, and Dr. Adenauer was forced to promise to retire well before the next election.

Nevertheless, in the evening of

SHREWD POLITICIAN

Dr. Adenauer, former West German Chancellor, who died yesterday, aged 91.

Manchester Guardian
7ᵗʰ March 1953

JOSEPH STALIN

Joseph Vissarionovitch Djugashvili, whose death was announced yesterday, early in life became known alike to revolutionaries and to the Russian political police as "Stalin." He was the son of a Georgian peasant and was born in 1879 at Gori, not far from Tiflis. In 1892 he entered a seminary, from which six years later he was expelled for holding undesirable political opinions and taking an active part in the organisation inside and outside the seminary of groups that shared these opinions. The same year, 1898, he joined the Social Democratic organisation in Tiflis, and though thereafter he worked as a bookkeeper and in other capacities his profession became that of a revolutionary. At the end of 1901 the police searched his lodgings, whereupon he moved to Batum and helped in the founding of the first illegal Marxist group in that town. The next year he was arrested on account of his activities in connection with the Batum strikes. He spent rather over a year in the prisons of Batum and Kutais, and was banished in 1903 to Eastern Siberia.

He then began a notable series of escapes, in the number and variety of which he was unrivalled by any other revolutionary. He first escaped from banishment in Eastern Siberia. In 1908 he was arrested and banished to Vologda. He escaped and was rearrested in Baku, imprisoned, and exiled for six years to Solvytchegodsk. He escaped and was rearrested in Petrograd, imprisoned for some months, and exiled to Vologda. He escaped and was rearrested in St Petersburg. In April, 1912, he was exiled to the Narym district in the Altai Mountains. He escaped, and in September of the same year was again in St Petersburg. In March, 1913, he was rearrested, and perhaps with a view to making an end of him, this Southerner from the Caspian was exiled beyond the Arctic Circle. This was the only exile from which he failed to escape. He was freed from it by the Revolution of 1917

Saving the Empire

In 1917 he was engaged in editing "Pravda" and other revolutionary newspapers. As a member of the Central Committee of the Bolshevik party he shared in the organisation of the Bolshevik Revolution of November. But he did not play any very decisive rôle in it—though Russian histories have falsely claimed that he did. He became People's Commissar for Affairs of Nationality, a post for which his own origin, his intimate knowledge of the Caucasus (where national feeling in the various races had often found the clearest and most violent expression) particularly fitted him. To him was due a great deal of the policy whereby Russia, while going far to meet and in some cases giving more than the demands of hitherto subject races, contrived, in circumstances in which a general dismemberment seemed inevitable, to preserve as an economic and administrative whole all but a few fragments of the old Russian Empire. Poland and Finland had been promised independence before the Revolution. It was largely due to the policy insisted on by Stalin that Russia did not lose much more than the little Baltic States.

Stalin took an active part in the civil war, distinguishing himself especially by his organisation of the defence of Tsaritzin. When things were going wrong on the Ural front against Kolchak he and Dzerzhinsky, the head of the famous Cheka, were sent there to stiffen things up. The two were complementary to each other: Stalin working in the party organisation, weeded out the unreliable elements, while his colleague, with characteristic ruthlessness, got busy with the firing squad. From here he was rushed to the Petrograd front to defeat Yudenitch. Then to the southern front, where Denikin had broken through in the autumn of 1919 and was within 100 miles of Moscow. It was here that important differences first developed between him and Trotsky in the field of strategy. Trotsky wanted to advance against Denikin by a flanking move via the Cossack Steppes Strategically, no doubt, this was sound, but Stalin knew Russia too well not to realise that this move would arouse intense feeling against the Revolution among the Cossacks, who

'EMPTY SHOES'

STALIN

MALENKOV

BERIA

LOW

were at that time in a state of uncertainty. He recommended the more daring frontal attack on Denikin because he knew that in Kharkov and the Don coal basin was an industrial population politically friendly

For his exploits in the war he earned the Order of the Red Flag. For some years after this he was People's Commissar of Workers' and Peasants' Inspection, and became in 1920 a member of the Revolutionary Military Council of the Republic. After the civil war Lenin started to liquidate "military communism" and to launch the New Economic policy. Stalin was very much opposed to this. He did not like Lenin's tendency to compromise with the peasants. He was a militant revolutionary, who was more impatient with the backward rural elements of the population than was Lenin. Later, after Lenin's death, he started the drive against the "kulaks" which initiated the "collective" farms and the agricultural side of the Five-year Plan. In foreign affairs Stalin took the view that compromise with the Western world was possible, while waiting for the inevitable breakdown of the West through internal contradictions. On this he earned Trotsky's scorn as a compromiser.

Breach with Trotsky

It was clear now that only the powerful personality and immense prestige of Lenin prevented an earlier breach between Stalin and Trotsky. Not only were basic differences in political theory there to divide the two men but also there was a clash of two ambitious personalities, which fact in itself seems to show that even in a Marxian State the individual is a factor in politics. It was around the post of general secretary of the Central Committee of the Communist party that the conflict of the two men developed. Stalin was responsible for the political discrediting of Trotsky that threw the latter into the shade at the moment when, to those who did not know, it seemed that Lenin's death had left Trotsky alone in the field. He used for that purpose Zinoviev's extremist tendency, and thus contrived to be himself among the extremists when it came to the question of what disciplinary measures were to be used against the heretic. He was left with Zinoviev and Kamenev at the centre of affairs. Two years later he manœuvred these two together into opposition, and Trotsky had the satisfaction of seeing them treated as heretics and being reminded of the measures they had used against himself. The elimination of Kamenev and Zinoviev left Stalin obviously head and shoulders above all others, and, in so far as a man of ability can succeed to a man of genius, he thenceforward held undisputed Lenin's old position as leader of the Communist party.

All through this it was possible to notice the difference in character between Lenin and Stalin. Lenin was in many respects more British. When he saw that opponents were determined he tried to find out their point of view and compromise with them, at least temporarily. Gradually he would try to assimilate them to his ideas. Stalin was more of an Oriental in the cunning

of his tactics. He would provoke opponents to quarrel and then play them off against each other, leaving himself as sole dictator. Trotsky, doctrinaire revolutionary that he was and international in his outlook, looked on Stalin as a stupid barbarian from the Caucasus and underrated his quiet Tatar cunning. The struggle between these two Titans is probably best summed up in Lenin's political testament which was read to the Central Committee of the party after his death. Referring to the two men, he wrote: "Comrades Trotsky and Stalin

are the two most able men on the Central Committee. Their rivalry might quite innocently lead to a split. Comrade Trotsky is perhaps the most talented of the leaders, but he is too conceited, and then he is not a Bolshevik." It was the last sentence that finished Trotsky. In other passages Stalin was rebuked for roughness but not for conceit, or for unsoundness of doctrine to boot.

On the other hand, Stalin was a leader of a very different kind from Lenin. One never heard him spoken of with affection in the early days of the revolution. No one dreamed of calling him intimately by any other name than that which he had made his own, Stalin (steel). Lenin used to be called Ilyitch even by those who did not know him personally. Stalin was steel for everybody. Exuberance was impossible to him. He had three gifts: abounding physical strength (he was never known to be tired), unrelenting determination, and an extremely clear and orderly mind. His reports to congresses might have been used as models in teaching the classification and arrangement of material. They were vertebrate things, and it was a pleasure to dissect them and admire their beautifully articulated skeletons. Yet he was a man of action, not of words, for which he cared nothing at all. He was, if anything, afraid of them, weighing them carefully and keeping them chained lest they might turn upon him. In action he could trust himself absolutely, and it was part of his strength that he knew so well that a man of action may weaken by speech.

The Agrarian Revolution

Undoubtedly the first serious crisis in Stalin's career began in 1929 when a decision had to be taken in regard to agricultural policy. As secretary to the Central Committee of the Communist party he had now acquired a position of great strength, at least behind the scenes. Now he saw what Lenin saw, that Russia was agriculturally and industrially backward, that she had not yet the economic background to support a powerful army for the defence of the Union. But he also saw that European affairs were degenerating into anarchy with a resurgent Fascism and a League of Nations deserted by the Western Powers. It was vitally necessary for Russia to have a strong war industry, and moreover the new industries must be sited in areas farther removed from the German frontiers than Poland and the Ukraine, otherwise Russia would be in the same position as she was in after the German invasion of 1915. So a shift of industry eastwards to the mining areas of the Urals was needed and Stalin followed Lenin's original idea and put it into effect.

But in order to bring this about it was necessary that there should be a big increase in agricultural production in order to feed the new and rising centres of metallurgy and mining. This was impossible under the old and antiquated system of agriculture in Central Russia with its long strip system of cultivation. The amalgamation of the tiny peasant plots into large farms, collectively run and worked by tractors, would raise the general standard of farming and provide the food for the new factories.

In 1930 Stalin and his colleagues decided to act. They first tried propaganda and persuasion with the peasants, but this produced no effect. So Stalin decided to be ruthless. By a series of decrees he forcibly amalgamated the peasants' holdings and created a whole series of collective farms all over Russia. Communist workers were sent into the villages and for a time in some areas chaos and bloodshed prevailed. During this period Stalin had sometimes to intervene to stop the more extreme activities of

some of his own party workers. In the end Stalin got his way, the second agrarian revolution by 1933 had become an accomplished fact, and Russia was on the way to becoming a modern agricultural State

The October Revolution of 1917 had swept away the relics of feudalism from the Russian village. But the real constructive agrarian revolution did not come till 1933. It may be said that Stalin's titanic energy accomplished what Lenin had originally planned in the early days of the revolution. It was not a moment too soon. If he had failed then the agricultural background for the new war industries would not have been there to meet the crisis of 1941.

The Treason Trials

This accomplished, Stalin now turned to meet another danger. He knew that the new Soviet State would not be safe until its internal enemies were silenced. The doctrinaire revolutionaries, the romantic Bolshevik Old Guard, and Trotsky's followers were irreconcilable. They saw Stalin building up a modern State in Russia, concentrating on her national greatness and ignoring the drive for the world revolution. Being revolutionaries who had been brought up in the atmosphere of plotting and conspiracy, they conceived the idea of removing Stalin and his colleagues by force and setting up a new regime and restoring the old ideals of the October Revolution. Being Russians, moreover, they found it hard to compromise, and Stalin, too, being of the same fundamental make-up, could not compromise either. It was this simple clash of personalities rather than a melodramatic plot on the part of the anti-Stalinites to betray Russia to Hitler and the Prussian generals that was the real background of the famous treason trials of 1936-7.

Thus in this second great crisis of his career Stalin won through as leader of the Soviet State in the years immediately preceding the Second World War. For he had now built up for himself a position of unassailable power as head of the inner circle of Communist leaders that control the apparatus of government in the Kremlin. No Romanov Emperor ever wielded greater power, but none had half the popular support that he had.

As 1939 approached and the Nazi aggression in Europe became ever more daring and impudent, Stalin had to decide on the line that Russia must take in the coming war. His foreign policy had become by now strictly nationalist and realistic. He knew that Germany was the enemy, but he had reasons to suspect Great Britain and he had little faith in French powers of resistance. He knew that Russia needed more time to build up her own war industries and any breathing-space that she could get would be welcome.

Whether a British Government friendly to Russia could have prevented her from signing the Russo-German Treaty in 1939 is a question which only the historian will one day be able to decide. But, like Alexander I's Treaty of Tilsit with Napoleon, it was short-lived and served a temporary purpose. Meanwhile Stalin decided to strengthen Russia's western approaches by the occupation of strategic points in the Gulf of Finland. This resulted in the Russo-Finnish War. But the event proved that Stalin's foreign policy of national realism had not altered. He merely acquired the strategic points and otherwise left the Finns to themselves.

Continued

The idea of fostering internal revolutionary movements in Finland was completely absent.

When the clash finally came in June, 1941, Stalin's role became more and more that of a popular war leader. His previous military experience, when he had held posts as political commissar in the cadres of the Red Army in the early days of the revolutionary wars, now stood him in good stead. Moreover, he set about getting round him young and competent generals who had come to the front, thanks to the system of popular education and selection to posts in the Soviet Union. His acceptance of the title of " Marshal of the Soviet Union " marked a period in his career in which his capacity for the leadership of the nation in the hour of tragedy and crisis followed by triumph, was acclaimed by all.

Nor had he let slip his hold on policy. His famous Red Army Order of the Day in 1942 showed that he contemplated a Germany some day freed from the Nazi system with whom Russia could deal. Moreover, it is hardly conceivable that the agitation for a second front in Western Europe could have been carried on without his agreement or, indeed, his instigation. This and various utterances attributed to him revealed the Tartar cunning in his make-up which always sought a way to keep Russia on a line of her own, although in the meantime he had signed in 1942 the Anglo-Soviet Treaty of Friendship for 25 years.

The continual see-saw of Russian foreign policy, which can be traced through the centuries, of collaboration with the West at one time but always leaving the door open to a return to semi-Asiatic isolation at another time, is here seen brought up to date.

Tehran and Yalta

As the campaign developed in the summer of 1943 with the liberation of the greater part of the Ukraine, the need of Russia to draw closer to her allies and prepare for the peace which was to follow on the defeat of Germany became ever more urgent. In the work which led up to and successfully accomplished an agreement between Russia, Britain, and the United States, first in the Moscow Conference in the autumn, and then in the Tehran Conference in the winter of 1943, and later still at Yalta, Stalin played a decisive part.

He was now Marshal of the Soviet Union and the supreme commander of her armed forces. With his close co-operation, therefore, the plans were laid in Tehran for the great offensives of 1944. He had never had a military training such as that of a professional soldier, but he knew how to handle the professional soldiers under him. Above all, he knew how to select the young and able men whom the war had brought out. Moreover, his practical military experience which he had acquired during the revolutionary wars now stood him in good stead and undoubtedly qualified him for the high post which he now held.

Throughout 1944 the military plans of the Allies, which he had played such a big part in preparing, matured in resounding victories, both in the East and in the West. But the political problems which followed in the wake of victory began to give rise to some uneasiness. This was particularly the case over Poland, which had only been superficially dealt with at Tehran. During 1944 Stalin pursued a policy of building up a Polish authority in Russia friendly to Russia which would be able to take over the administration of Poland as it was liberated by the Red Army. He also organised and equipped

a Polish Army on Russian soil, which co-operated with the Red Army in the Polish campaign of 1944. The awkward question of the Polish Government in London remained, but this was largely dealt with by the Crimea Conference of February, 1944, which set the final seal on the military and political plans of the Allies for finishing the war and laying the foundations of peace. As the war reached its final stage Stalin was clearly bent on carving out as large a slice of Western and Central Europe as he could in order to form a future defence zone and extend the Soviet system as far as he could in Europe.

In the years following the war Russia's foreign policy under Stalin's guidance swung from one of apparent readiness to co-operate with the Western Powers to one of veiled hostility. He was not and never had been an influence friendly to the West in the councils of the Kremlin. On previous occasions he had exhibited a degree of Oriental cunning and readiness to ride two horses at the same time. In internal affairs he apparently thought that the war-time veneration of popular generals had gone far enough, and he got them down off their high pedestals and appointed reliable Communists both in the Army and in important administrative posts.

Honeymoon with the West

His idea at first seems to have been to build up a defence zone for the Soviet Union by a chain of satellite States in Eastern Europe. During 1945 and 1946 he took the realistic line that for the moment Western Europe, backed by American economic help, would be able to stand firm and that Russia had better come to at least temporary agreement with it. During 1946 he gave press interviews in which he stressed the possibility of the Soviet system and Western capitalism living side by side. He even talked about Russia being interested in an American loan. It seems that this was the mood under which the Paris Conference in 1946 finally got agreement in the peace treaties for South-east Europe.

Russia was then suffering from the effects of a disastrous drought in the Ukraine and U.N.R.R.A. was even allowed to work in Russia. But with the deepening of the dollar crisis early in 1947, the coal crisis in Great Britain, and the growing evidence that without American help Western European economy might lapse into chaos, all the old Bolshevik theories of Marxist dialectic gained ground again. Stalin's friendly interviews ceased, and Russian opposition at conferences and United Nations Organisation proceedings stiffened. It is not to be supposed that Stalin was out of sympathy with this new line. He had defeated Trotsky among other things on the grounds that two systems could live side by side. But if one of these systems showed signs of collapse Stalin could be as ready as Trotsky was in his day to take advantage of this, so that Communist or Communist-controlled Governments should come to power in the West. Stalin now showed the true nature of the Communist doctrine, which postulates the inevitable decay of the capitalist world and the expansion of communism.

From 1948 onwards Russia withdrew rapidly into isolation. At home and in the satellites those who had had contact with the West or who seemed in any way to subscribe to Western ideas in the arts and sciences or who showed any independence of the Moscow line were liquidated or forced to sing another tune. The absorption of Czechoslovakia into the Communist system, the flat rejection of the Mar-

shall Plan, the rising temper of propaganda against the West and against the steps it took in reaction to the Prague coup, its corollary the peace campaign, and the formation of the Cominform marked the end of the honeymoon with the West. The change had one serious result—the revolt of Marshal Tito at Stalin's own misguided attempt to impose on Yugoslavia the same discipline which had been forced on the other satellites. Here Stalin's arrogance proved too much for his cunning, as it did when he advised the Chinese Communists to go slow at a time when he himself was flirting with the West and Chiang Kai-shek—advice which they sensibly rejected.

Elder Statesman

How large a part he played in the shaping of these policies can only be guessed (though the breach with Tito is clearly attributable to his own clumsy over-confidence). In recent years he had made few public appearances and rumours of ill-health circulated from time to time. He seems to have taken less and less part in the details of State administration but, as elder statesman, to have been consulted when differences of opinion arose among his colleagues.

In 1949, however, he published " Problems of Leninism," in which he set forth the theory on which communism is founded. It showed an iconoclastic outlook and a grim acceptance of the inevitability of war within the " capitalist " world which the world revolution can make use of. The " semi-proletarians and small cultivators in the more developed lands and the freedom movements in the colonies " were declared to be Russia's best allies. Again in 1952 just before the meeting of the Nineteenth Congress of the Soviet Communist party he published in " Bolshevik " a long article developing the theme of the inevitability of war between the capitalist Powers and forecasting the revolt of Germany and Japan against American imperialism.

The policy which seemed to emerge from Stalin's pronouncement and from the Congress and the Five-Year Plan was one of further tightening-up at home and the development of self-sufficiency (military and economic) within the Soviet block. Inefficient and disloyal Communists were to be routed out of the party and Zionism (the most obvious and dangerous form of cosmopolitanism) was to be attacked. The Army and the marshals appeared to be coming back into favour. And from the Five-Year Plan it seemed as if Russia was looking forward to a long cold war in which her strength relatively to the West's would grow, while the West would be weakened by internal dissension. In all this could be seen perhaps the realistic and opportunistic mind of Stalin himself, who had no doubt appreciated that neither the Communist parties of the West nor open aggression could win quick victories, and that time might well be on Russia's side.

On his seventieth birthday there were great celebrations all over the Soviet world. Mountains in the Union were named after him, special coins struck, and presents and adulatory messages sent to him from all over the Union and the satellite countries. The publications which appeared at this time inside Russia seem to indicate that Stalin had reached the state of an almost mythical person with supra-natural powers. The Russian inclination to adore saints and holy men had been translated from the ritual of the Orthodox Church to the new Communist mythology.

Daily Telegraph
3rd December 1973

Thousands pay tribute to 'father of Israel'

DAILY TELEGRAPH REPORTER

BY late yesterday afternoon about 200,000 people had filed past the coffin of David Ben-Gurion, who announced to the world in May, 1948, the birth of Israel as the first independent Jewish State for 2,000 years. The country was mourning its "father."

His body was flown to Jerusalem from Tel Aviv where he died on Saturday, aged 87.

Then it was placed in the forecourt of the Knesset (Parliament) in a coffin draped with Israel's white-and-blue flag. Those who waited in drizzling rain for their turn to file past included old people, children, and soldiers on leave from the Egyptian and Syrian fronts.

Beside his wife

By his own wish there will be no grave-side ceremony when Mr Ben-Gurion is buried today alongside his wife Paula in the Negev desert settlement where he spent many years writing and studying. A funeral service will be held in the Knesset today.

In Mr Ben-Gurion's will his many thousands of books, many of them bought by him in Oxford are given to the Israeli Government. It has already been decided to make his Tel Aviv home a museum.

From 1948 until 1963 Mr Ben-Gurion was Prime Minister of Israel except for an interlude between December, 1953, and October, 1955, occasioned by a voluntary retirement.

The two keynotes of his life were his intense Jewish nationalism and his deep socialist convictions. But he was never an extremist so much as a person who held moderate views with extreme tenacity.

One of his most critical and controversial decisions was the launching in 1956 of the attack against Egypt across the Sinai peninsula. Israeli forces drove the Egyptians back to the Suez Canal in a five-day campaign.

Once described as "the Moses of the new Israel," he will always be associated with the late Dr Chaim Weizmann as the founder of modern Israel. If Weizmann made Israel possible, Ben-Gurion made it actual. He was one of the Eastern European pioneers who laboured in the desert to make their dream a reality.

Expelled by Turks

Ben-Gurion was born in Plonsk, Poland, son of Avigdor Green, a lawyer and a pioneer Zionist. On entering Palestine in 1906 he became a farm worker and trade union organiser. He had studied law in Turkey.

During the 1914-18 war he was expelled from Palestine by the Turks for pro-Allied sympathies and fled to America. There he helped to organise a Jewish volunteer force; later he served with Allenby's army in Palestine.

He became Secretary of the Federation of Jewish Labour and soon rose to the front. As chief member of the Jewish Agency Executive in Jerusalem, he had largely succeeded to the mantle of Dr Chaim Weizmann when the first Palestine crisis broke out in 1936.

His ambitions for Palestine were thwarted by the British White Paper of 1939, which rejected the idea of an exclusively Jewish State in Palestine.

When Jewish resistance to this policy flared up after the 1939-45 war, during which 20,000 Palestine Jews had served with units attached to the British forces, Ben-Gurion, as Chairman of the Jewish Agency in Jerusalem, was naturally the central figure of the conflict.

Into the wilderness

After this stormy period he resigned because of mental fatigue and went into the wilderness of Negev to work as a shepherd. This action, in December, 1955, was more in the nature of a crusade, than a withdrawal from the world. For he believed that unless the Negev was developed there was no future for Israel.

In February, 1955, he returned to the Government as Defence Minister. The following October he again became Prime Minister and held the post until 1963.

In 1965, Israelis, electing their new Knesset (Parliament), rejected Ben-Gurion's attempt at a political come-back. Mr Eshkol, the then Prime Minister, was able to claim "a great victory" for his Left-wing coalition.

Mr Ben-Gurion resigned his seat in the Knesset after 22 years as a founder member, in May, 1970.

The Gentleman's Magazine
28th September 1794 Vol 62

28. At Paris, aged 35, under the guillotine, with near 70 of his party, members of the Convention, — —— Robespierre. This emulator of Cromwell was short in stature, being only five feet two or three inches in height: his step was firm; and his quick pace in walking announced great activity. By a kind of contraction of the nerves, he used often to fold and compress his hands in each other; and spasmodic contractions were perceived in his shoulders and neck, the latter of which he moved convulsively from side to side. In his dress he was neat and even elegant, never failing to have his hair in the best order. His features had nothing remarkable about them, unless that their general aspect was somewhat forbidding: his complexion was livid and bilious; his eyes dull and sunk in their sockets. The constant blinking of the eye-lids seemed to arise from convulsive agitation; and he was never without a remedy in his pocket. He could soften his voice, which was naturally harsh and croaking, and could give grace to his provincial accent. It was remarked of him, that he could never look a man full in the face. He was master of the talent of declamation; and as a public speaker was not amiss at composition. In his harangues he was extremely fond of the figure called *antithesis*; but failed, whenever he attempted irony. His diction was at times harsh, at others harmoniously modulated, frequently brilliant, but often trite, and was constantly blended with common-place digressions on *virtue, crimes*, and *conspiracies*. Even when prepared, he was but an indifferent orator. His logick was often replete with sophisms and subtleties; but he was in general sterile of ideas, with but a very limited scope of thought, as is almost always the case with those who are too much taken up with themselves. Pride formed the basis of his character: and he had a great thirst for literary, but a still greater for political, fame. He spoke with contempt of Mr. Pitt; and yet, above Mr. Pitt, he could see nobody unless himself. The reproaches of the English journalists were a high treat to his vanity: whenever he denounced them, his accent and expression betrayed how much his self-love was flattered. It was delightful to him to hear the French armies named the "armies of Robespierre;" and he was charmed with being included in the list of tyrants. Daring and cowardly at the same time, he threw a veil over his manœuvres, and was often imprudent in pointing out his victims. If one of the Representatives made a motion which displeased him, he suddenly turned round towards him with a menacing aspect for some minutes. Weak and revengeful, sober and sensual, chaste by temperament, and a libertine by the effect of the imagination; he was fond of attracting the notice of the women, and had them imprisoned for the sole pleasure of restoring them their liberty. He made them shed tears, to wipe them from their cheeks. In practising his delusions, it was his particular aim to act on tender and weak minds. He spared the priests, because they could forward his plans; and the superstitious and devotees, because he could convert them into instruments to favour his power. His style and expression were in a manner mystical; and, next to pride, subtlety was the most marked feature of his character. He was surrounded by those only whose conduct had been highly criminal, because he could with one word deliver them over to the punishment of the law. He at once protected and terrified a part of the Convention. He converted crimes into errours, and errours into crimes. He dreaded even the shades of the martyrs of liberty, whose influence he weakened by substituting his own. He was so extremely suspicious and distrustful, that he could have found it in his heart to *guillotine* the dead themselves. To enter into a strict analysis of his character, Robespierre, born without genius, could not create circumstances, but profited by them with address. To the profound hypocrisy of Cromwell he joined the cruelty of Sylla, without possessing any of the great military and political qualities of either of these ambitious adventurers. His pride and his ambition, far above his means, exposed him to ridicule. To observe the emphasis with which he boasted of having proclaimed the existence of the Supreme Being, one might have said, that, according to his opinion, God would not have existed without him. When, on the night of the 27th of July, he found himself abandoned by his friends, he discharged a pistol in his mouth; and, at the same time, a *gens d'arme* wounded him by the discharge of another. Robespierre fell bathed in blood; and a *Sans Culotte*, approaching him, very coolly pronounced these words in his ear, *there exists a Supreme Being*. Previous to his execution, the bandage being taken off his head, his jaw fell down, in consequence of the wound which he had given himself.

Manchester Guardian
11th May 1957

TRAGEDY OF JOSEPH McCARTHY

Ever since he was censured by the Senate in December, 1954, Senator McCarthy (whose death was reported yesterday) had been without power. He came to the Senate only rarely, seemed totally uninterested in the debate, and almost invariably spoke to an empty chamber. His support for any bill was always an embarrassment and sometimes was enough to kill it. His last test of strength came recently when he opposed the promotion of General Zwicker, who was so important a figure in the Army-McCarthy hearings. Only one other Senator stood at McCarthy's side in the debate and General Zwicker received his promotion on an overwhelming vote. So it went always in recent years.

But it once was different. There was a time when McCarthy was the most powerful man in Congress, able indeed to threaten and demoralise the Administration itself. His first four years in the Senate, from 1946 to 1950, were inconspicuous. Then he went to Wheeling, West Virginia, and made a speech alleging that he had documentary proof that the State Department was employing numerous known Communists and agents of Russia. He never provided this proof. But he became the leading Republican spokesman in the campaign alleging that the Democrats were "soft on Communism." Later McCarthy formalised this indictment in the spectacular charge that the Democratic party had been guilty of "twenty years of treason." Even responsible Republicans like Senator Taft and Senator Flanders (who later became the man responsible, by his counter-attack, for the vote of censure) were willing to sanction McCarthy's campaign though they found his methods utterly abhorrent. Their argument was that anything which would bring the Republicans into power would clearly serve the national interest after the Democratic party's unbroken rule of twenty years.

In victory the Republicans could discipline and restrain McCarthy. That was the theory, and it prevailed even with Mr Eisenhower. In the 1952 Presidential race, Mr Eisenhower, not fully aware of his great popularity in the country, heeded the advice of his campaign strategists and publicly endorsed Senator McCarthy and Senator Jenner to avoid offending Right-wing Republicans. Moreover, he deleted a paragraph from a speech in praise of General Marshall whom McCarthy had once denounced as a "front for traitors." This surrender has rankled in Mr Eisenhower's memory ever since. It is probably the one act of his public career which he most deeply regrets.

When the Republicans won in 1952, they found that McCarthy had grown so powerful that he was utterly indifferent to party discipline. At this point came the most controversial decision in the Eisenhower Administration. It was decided that President Eisenhower should refrain from any direct challenge to McCarthy, who should instead be allowed to destroy himself by his own excesses. Mr Eisenhower claim: that his policy has been justified by results. So it was, if one is thinking only of the eclipse of McCarthy. But there was a tragic price exacted for these cruel months of delay and temporising. Countless Americans were subjected to unjust attack; the machinery of Government was thrown into confusion; the standards of legislative investigations were brutalised; and an ugly caricature of America was exported to the world.

The man of destiny who destroyed himself

The Republican Administration struck back only when McCarthy, at the very height of his power, began to attack it with the same vigour which he had shown in denouncing Mr Truman and Mr Acheson. His downfall came when the Democrats regained control of Congress in 1954. Senator Lyndon Johnson, the Democratic leader, set himself the task of destroying McCarthy, and he did it with matchless skill. McCarthy, it should be remembered, was never asked to face judgment for his shameful abuse of power: instead, he was asked to defend himself against the soft impeachment of having broken the rules of the Senate. But Senator Johnson knew exactly what he was doing. He knew that no Senator, after being found guilty by his fellow Senators of conduct unworthy of a member of the United States Senate, has ever again been worth his weight in sawdust as a political figure. So it proved with Senator McCarthy.

It took many agonising months before the decent American majority understood the perils of McCarthyism and decided to do battle with it. For a long time many Americans were willing to forgive McCarthy's brutal methods so long as his enemy seemed to be the Communist conspiracy. But when he began to attack Americans totally removed from any association with communism, and of unblemished patriotism, the margin of tolerance which he had enjoyed soon vanished. He was struck down by his colleagues in the Senate on a technicality but he never recovered. The arrogant man of destiny soon dwindled into a forlorn figure in the shadows. Most Americans are now deeply ashamed when they are reminded of the power once exerted by this evil man. McCarthy never showed any mercy when he was dominating the Washington scene and therefore he now deserves justice rather than charity in the final judgment pronounced upon him.

McCARTHYISM

Senator's road to notoriety

Joseph Raymond McCarthy, son of Irish-American stock, was born on a Wisconsin farm in 1909. His schooling ended at 14 and he soon left the farm for jobs in the nearest town. Realising his educational defects, he took a high school course when he was 20, and then passed quickly through college and law school. The law soon turned McCarthy's mind to politics, and as an Irish-American, he naturally joined the Democratic party. But this was the wrong party for an ambitious young politician in Wisconsin, so McCarthy turned his coat and at the age of 30 he was rewarded with a circuit judgeship. McCarthy's ideas of justice were, to say the least, eccentric and it was not long before he fell foul of the Supreme Court for an "abuse of judicial power."

During the war he had a brief career—and gained a captaincy—in the United States Marines, but while still a circuit judge (and still wearing his captain's uniform) he stood in 1944 as a Republican candidate for the United States Senate—another breach of the law. As a serving judge he was disqualified, but he won the election; and although the Supreme Court declared his candidature a clear violation of the Constitution he retained his seat, and held it six years later by a huge majority

It was in 1950 that McCarthy embarked on the campaign that was to make him internationally notorious and to add the word "McCarthyism," with its ugly meaning, to the language. The moment, of course, was ripe for the man. There had been sensational disclosures of treason and the air was full of rumour and suspicion. There had been the Nunn May and Fuchs cases and the twice-tried case of Alger Hiss. There is little doubt that the Truman Administration handled the situation unwisely; it was at times evasive and at others it attempted too lightly to brush aside the Republican charges as a "red herring." McCarthy seized his opportunity greedily and ruthlessly.

The ugliest part of the business was McCarthy's chairmanship of the Senate Subcommittee that investigated "security" charges. Day after day McCarthy grilled his victims behind closed doors and at the day's close gave to the press his own account of what witnesses were alleged to have said. McCarthy's ferret went deep into the ground. Even the disclosure of a donation for the relief of the Republicans in the Spanish Civil War, was enough to secure the smear of communism—and put a man's livelihood in peril. The victim might be cleared of any "un-American activities," but the smear of McCarthy's inquisition was a disfigurement that only time could heal.

The attack on the Army for "coddling Communists" was perhaps the most dramatic chapter. It began with the case of an Army dentist who was given an honourable discharge after displaying Left-wing tendencies. McCarthy summoned the dentist's commanding officer, General Zwicker, told him he was unfit to wear his uniform and that he ought to be dismissed. Mr Stevens, then Army Secretary, made an angry intervention and said he would not allow loyal officers to suffer such treatment. McCarthy did in fact burn his fingers badly over the Army inquisition. The Pentagon produced a report suggesting that Mr Cohn, who was McCarthy's chief counsel, was trying to secure preferential treatment for Private Schine, who had been associated with Mr Cohn before being called up for Army service.

In September, 1953, McCarthy married Miss Jean Kerr, a former research assistant in his office. The wedding took place in Washington and among the 2,000 guests were Mr Dulles and Vice-President Nixon. President Eisenhower himself had another engagement.

Daily Telegraph
7th September 1966

DR. H. VERWOERD, SOUTH AFRICAN PREMIER

INTRODUCED 'BANTU' BILL

DR. VERWOERD, Prime Minister of South Africa, who was assassinated yesterday, aged 64, was the chief architect of apartheid, aiming at complete segregation of the races.

He will also go down in history as the man under whose government the South African people chose to become a Republic and found it impossible to stay in the Commonwealth.

Hendrik Frensch Verwoerd was born in Holland. When he was aged one his parents emigrated to South Africa and settled in Brandfort, Orange Free State.

He went to the Milton Boys' High School in Bulawayo, Southern Rhodesia, where his father moved after becoming a Dutch Reformed Church Minister. He obtained a Master of Arts degree in psychology and philosophy at Stellenbosch University and became a lecturer there in 1923.

Later he studied at Hamburg, Leipzig and Berlin, and graduated as a Doctor of Philosophy.

STELLENBOSCH POST
Introduction to politics

Appointed Professor of Applied Psychology at Stellenbosch in 1928, he became Professor of Sociology and Social Work, a post which, he said, introduced him to politics.

He came into prominence in South Africa in 1936 when he led a small group of Stellenbosch professors in a protest against the admission to South Africa of Jewish refugees from Germany.

The following year, when a new Afrikaans-language daily, *Die Transvaler*, was established in Johannesburg as a Nationalist party organ, he became its editor-in-chief.

During the last war he spoke through his newspaper for the anti-war section of the Afrikaner people and sued the rival Johannesburg *Star* for libel in asserting that his "spiritual home was nearer to Berchtesgaden" than South Africa. He lost his case.

Meanwhile, he had begun to play an active part in politics. He worked hard for the victory that the Nationalists won at the first post-war general election in 1948, though he himself was defeated in the Alberton constituency of the Transvaal.

SEAT IN SENATE
Ministerial appointment

Later in the year, after South Africa's first Nationalist Government was formed under the late Dr. Malan, he ran successfully for the Senate and in 1950 entered the Government as Minister for Native Affairs.

One of his first actions as Minister was to put a summary finish to a dispute between the Government and the Natives' Representative Council, by abolishing the Council.

To replace it Dr. Verwoerd laid the foundation for the establishment of Native Tribal Councils in Native areas under the Bantu Authorities Act.

The Bantu Education Act of 1953 transferred control of education of Africans from the provinces to the Minister of Native Affairs.

Its effects were to change the whole character of African education and to shift control of the country's numerous mission schools from the churches to the Department of Native Affairs.

While Dr. Verwoerd was responsible for improvements in African housing, he increased African rents in Government-subsidised housing schemes, claiming that the Africans' earnings had increased while the White taxpayers were carrying the burden of housing and other services for them.

In March, 1958, Dr. Verwoerd intimated his resignation but agreed to be reappointed after the elections the same month at the request of the Prime Minister, Mr. Strijdom.

DEATH OF STRIJDOM
Nationalists' leader

In this election Dr. Verwoerd, who had resigned his senatorship, was elected to the House of Assembly for the Heidelberg constituency near Johannesburg.

At a party caucus after the death of Mr. Strijdom three months later he was elected leader of the Nationalists over both the acting Prime Minister, Mr. Swart, and the Minister of the Interior, Dr. Donges.

On becoming Prime Minister Dr. Verwoerd, in a broadcast to the nation, announced that he would devote all his energies to the establishment of a republic, which he said was the only way to bring about unity between the English-speaking and Afrikaans-speaking people of the Union.

Six months after assuming office Dr. Verwoerd introduced the promotion of the Bantu Self-Government Bill, probably the most far-reaching and controversial legislation for which he was directly responsible.

The Bill, which became law in 1960, provided for the division of the African population into tribal units, the abolition of the existing representation of natives in Parliament and the creation of self-governing Native states.

MASS ARRESTS
State of emergency

In 1960, Dr. Verwoerd announced in the House of Assembly that legislation would be introduced during the session to provide for the holding of a referendum on whether the Union should become a Republic.

Soon afterwards politics took a violent turn with mass arrests, shootings, declaration of a state of emergency and finally an attempt on the Prime Minister's life.

In March a militant African splinter group of the African National Congress, the Pan-Africanist Congress, called for a nationwide campaign against the pass-laws under which all African males since the 19th century had been required to carry passes for purposes of identification.

The Congress asked all Africans to discard their passes or reference books, and present themselves for arrest at the nearest police station.

On March 21, the date arranged for the beginning of the campaign, thousands of Africans answered the call, mainly peacefully. But at Sharpeville, an African township near Vereeniging, a grave incident took place when police fired on Africans, killing 67 and wounding 183.

Official statements maintained that the police had fired in self-defence after an armed crowd of 20,000 had tried to storm the police station.

As Dr. Verwoerd was opening a trade fair in April, 1960, a white man fired two shots at his head. His alleged assailant was Mr. David Beresford Pratt, an English-born farmer.

He was charged with trying to kill Dr. Verwoerd, but a Supreme Court judge found him to be mentally ill and he was removed to a mental hospital. He subsequently committed suicide.

Dr. Verwoerd left hospital after six weeks, but returned to undergo a plastic operation to repair the drum of his right ear.

PEAK OF POWER
Hammarskjoeld visit

In 1961, the year of the declaration of the South African Republic, Dr. Verwoerd was at the summit of his power.

In January, he had talks with the then Secretary-General of the United Nations, Mr. Hammarskjoeld, who flew to South Africa from New York and spent a week in the country investigating South Africa's race policies.

Two months later Dr. Verwoerd flew to London to play a leading role in the crucial meeting of the Commonwealth Prime Ministers' Conference that led to South Africa's withdrawal from the Commonwealth.

Though the decision was received with dismay by the opposition United Party, Nationalists hailed it as the only one possible in the circumstances and on his return gave him a hero's welcome.

They felt that through his personal charm and obvious sincerity he had done much during his London stay to dispel the popular conception of him as an evil man cynically imposing an unjust racial policy for the benefit of a White minority.

PRESTIGE HIGH
Sound economy

His popularity and influence were such that in August, 1962, the most implacable of his Parliamentary critics, Mrs. Helen Suzman, the only MP of the Progressive Party, a party to the left of the United Party but to the right of the Liberals, said of him:

"His prestige among his own followers and, alas, among certain sections of the English-speaking population, has never been higher."

This position, she said, was immeasurably helped by three factors: the unshakable soundness of the country's economy; the turmoil in the rest of Africa; and the failure of the official opposition (the United Party) to put forward any real alternative to apartheid.

Since then he had been content to allow the spotlight to fall more and more often on his younger colleagues, in particular on his Minister of Justice, Mr. B. J. Vorster, architect of the 90-day detention clause and other legislation ruthlessly designed to maintain and advance apartheid in the face of growing pressures from without and within.

But behind the scenes Dr. Verwoerd had remained firmly in control, just as, in the country at large, he had been seen by English-speaking as well as Afrikaner voters as white South Africa's natural leader in the circumstances of the day.

At the General Election in March this year his party increased the number of its seats from 106 to 126, and reduced the ranks of the United Party from 49 to 39.

SANCTIONS IGNORED
Defence· budget raised

The Rhodesian crisis served only to confirm Dr. Verwoerd's leadership. He decided on a policy of "normal" trading relations, which meant refusing to take part in economic sanctions, and allowing Rhodesians to buy oil from the Republic.

He increased the budget for defence and left no doubt in anyone's mind that, if, through the agency of the United Nations, South Africa were drawn into the conflict, he would lead the white nation in united resistance.

South Africans were astonished last week to see him photographed with Chief Jonathan, Prime Minister of Basutoland, which is to become independent in a month's time.

This was the first time a coloured African leader had met a South African Prime Minister within South African territory.

Few South Africans, however, perceived the possible implications of Dr. Verwoerd's long-term policies. For the moment he was their "granite leader," and it may be some time before they put the same trust in his successor.

● Dr. Verwoerd carrying a milk can on his farm on the banks of the River Vaal, Transvaal. He took an active interest in the farm and had a fine herd of Friesland cattle and extensive crop-lands.

Daily Telegraph
26th August 1975

Haile Selassie, elder statesman of Africa

IF Haile Selassie, the deposed Emperor of Ethiopia, who has died aged 83, had abdicated last year when military discontent made his rule untenable, his reputation as a statesman might have remained untarnished.

Many years earlier he had won a special niche in the affections of the British people by his dignified bearing in adversity. He was driven into exile in 1936 by the Italian invasion, and chose to settle in England at Bath.

Exactly five years later British troops paved the way for his return to Addis Ababa.

He was the last representative of the world's oldest surviving monarchy and had ruled Ethiopia since 1916. He held absolute power and it was a paradox that he was held in high honour by democratic leaders.

But since his deposition last September, when the former "Lion of Judah" was driven to a three-roomed mud hut in an Army barracks, accusations against his régime have grown.

He was accused of indifference to the poverty-stricken plight of most of his subjects and accused of having salted away millions of pounds in foreign banks and sent abroad tons of gold mined by the slave labour of political prisoners of his regime.

Clung to power

His 80th birthday in 1972 was celebrated on a scale not seen in Addis Ababa since his return from exile 31 years earlier. But there was unrest among younger men at the way he clung to power in a country where more than 90 per cent of the people were still illiterate.

The famine of 1973 in Wollo district, where up to 200,000 people are believed to have died, helped to spell the death knell

A man of great gifts and striking personality, his colourful titles included Elect of God, King of Kings, Conquering Lion of Judah. These were reminders of the country's Christian tradition for the rulers claimed descent from King Solomon and the Queen of Sheba.

After the 1939-45 war he emerged as an elder statesman of the African continent. He took a prominent part in the Organisation of African Unity which embraces the developing African-ruled countries.

According to orthodox calculations, Haile Selassie belonged to the 111th generation in descent from King Solomon and the Queen of Sheba.

Daily Express
4th August 1923

FARM HAND TO PRESIDENT.

President Harding—Warren Gamaliel Harding, to give him his full name—was a typical product of American soil. He began his career as a farm hand, became a journalist, entered political life in 1899, became a Senator in 1914, and was elected President of the United States in November 1920.

Mr. Harding came of good old Republican stock, Scottish on his father's side and with some infusion of Dutch blood on his mother's. He was born on November 2, 1865, at a farm in Morrow County, Ohio, where his father was a doctor with a scanty practice and a small farm.

He worked on the farm for some years, and later on literally worked his way through a small school known as the Ohio Central College, where he blacked boots, washed plates, served at table, and was a farm hand during the holidays.

HIS NEWSPAPER.

When he left school he entered a printing-office and learned the trade, and at nineteen, with the aid of his father, acquired in the small town of Marion, in the same State, a struggling weekly newspaper called the "Star." He did everything for this little sheet, from setting the type to writing the editorials, and in the course of a few years he had the satisfaction of making it a daily and a highly prosperous property.

In 1899 he was elected to the Ohio Senate, where he represented Marion until 1903. Then he was for two years Lieutenant-Governor of the State and, in 1914, became a member of the United States Senate, gaining a majority of more than 700,000 over the next candidate on the list.

He became famous in the Senate as an orator, and not less so in a political sense for his unswerving allegiance to the Republican cause. In 1912, when Mr. Roosevelt broke with the party and led the Progressives, it was Mr. Harding who nominated Mr. Taft.

IN THE WAR.

During the war he came again into prominence for his denunciation of Mr. Wilson's delay in taking part in the European conflict, and in 1917 he joined Mr. Roosevelt in his efforts to arouse the President to a sense of America's position.

He was the first professional journalist to become President of the United States, and he still carried with him as a mascot the printers' "make-up" rule which he used daily in his little newspaper office in Marion, Ohio.

In 1891 Mr. Harding married Miss Florence Kling, the daughter of a Marion banker.

The Guardian
13th September 1973

Dignity of the improbable revolutionary

SALVADOR ALLENDE was an improbable revolutionary. A dapper, impeccably dressed figure, fond of strong drink and cigars, he had many of the explosive mannerisms of an apoplectic colonel.

But beneath this undeniably bourgeois facade was a man of political passion, steeped in Chilean history, who saw himself as the last in a long line of upper middle class radical Presidents, men who have helped transform Chile from its nineteenth century status as a virtual British colony into an independent State with considerably more regard for its poorer inhabitants than many other Latin American countries.

Allende never cared to dwell too long on the parallel with Juan Manuel Balmaceda, a predecessor who took his life in comparable circumstances in 1891.

The parallel closest to Allende's heart was that of Pedro Aguirre Cerda, the radical reforming President of a Popular Front Government in the 1930s that provided much of the legislation on which Allende was able to build when he embarked on comparable structural changes in the country's economy in the 1970s.

Aguirre Cerda was Allende's political mentor, and so closely did Allende model himself on this reforming President that John Gunther's description of him in 1940 can be used to describe Allende without a word changed : "The President is an affable, optimistic, and highly confident and astute politician in his early sixties. His manner is jovial.

"He likes to laugh and make mild jokes. He is no great orator, no magnetic personality ; but his political acumen, his shrewdness and adroitness in negotiation, are considerable. The extreme Left calls him a 'bourgeois' and a 'catspaw of the Right.' The Right calls him a Bolshevik. Nowhere else in Latin America did I hear any President so bitterly, so personally, attacked.

Aguirre Cerda, like Balmaceda, did not finish his term of office. But he died less dramatically. He passed on to his young Minister of Health, Salvador Allende (described with foresight by Gunther as "obviously a man marked to rise") all the tricks of his trade.

For more than 30 years, albeit in opposition, Allende dominated Chilean politics. Four times presidential candidate, he won the Presidency in 1970 when all but he had despaired of a Left-wing victory.

Allende, of course, was a Marxist, but he wore his ideological garb lightly. He believed, with Engels, that "it is possible to conceive of peaceful evolution from the old society to the new in countries where the representatives of the people have concentrated in their hands all the power." In Chile — he said in his inaugural speech in November, 1970 — "here, at last, Engels's vision is to be fulfilled."

The possibility of a peaceful transition to socialism was warmly welcomed by many progressive groups on a continent which had witnessed a decade of disastrous experiments with the theories of armed struggle. Many Left-wingers, in Chile as elsewhere, believed that Allende's "Chilean road to socialism" was doomed to failure, but there must have been few who did not wish it well.

From the start, Allende was beset with internal and external enemies. The American copper companies that he nationalised sought to obstruct the country's copper sales. The United States made sure that the international aid agencies suspended new loans to Chile. Even the progressive wing of the Opposition party lifted not a finger to assist him. The "peaceful road" never had much of a chance.

Yet Allende will long be remembered in Latin America as a man who (as he himself once said of Balmaceda) "conscious of his duties and protecting the national interest, acted with dignity." — R. G.

The Daily Mail
21st November 1975

FRANCO THE UNIVERSAL OUTCAST WHO REFUSED TO GO AWAY

TODAY with the death of General Franco we lose an interesting link with the past: thus the obituary columns—and not without reason.

In 1892, the year Franco was born, Alfonso XII's widow Maria Cristina was still Queen Regent of Spain: Benjamin Harrison was in the White House, Kruger was in the Transvaal and the Khalifa was in Gordon's still unavenged palace at Khartoum; Sadi Carnot presided in the Elysée, Leo XIII sat on the Papal throne, and Alexander III was Tsar of all the Russias.

Gladstone was beginning his fourth ministry and Queen Victoria had still to celebrate her Diamond Jubilee. It was the year of the Matabele War, the year of the death of Tennyson, the year before the opening of the Corinth Canal, two years before the Dreyfus trial.

More than 80 years later, quietly tenacious in the Pardo Palace of the Spanish Kings, Franco had outlived them all: Hitler and Horthy; Mussolini and Pétain; Roosevelt, Churchill, Stalin, Khruschev and de Gaulle; Salazar and Adenauer; Eisenhower, Truman and Kennedy; Pius XII and John XXIII; Trujillo, Nehru, Peron, Chiang Kai-shek and de Valera: at the last even Haile Selassie—friend and foe alike, all had predeceased him.

Man and country were indivisible

For a third of a century, Franco was Spain: and Spain was Franco. Although, perhaps, only a lesser milestone in the history of Europe, for Spain Franco's passing is the end of an epoch. Profound changes must now face the Spanish people who have for so long—some enthusiastically, others with bitter aversion, few with indifference—perforce regarded Spain and the Caudillo as one.

Did Franco do well or ill by his country? The question can only evoke a partisan reply. To some he stood for harsh repression and a long denial of all spiritual rights: to others he stood for the salvation of Spain and a chicken in the pot every Sunday.

Both views, presumably, are right — according to the angle from which you saw, or suffered, the regime. But how will history say that Franco served Spain?

Will the spiritual, intellectual, philosophical, political—in brief the abstract shortcomings of his long rule weigh heavier, or lighter in the balance than the material services which he undoubtedly rendered to his country?

No Spaniard can answer the question: perhaps no foreigner should try. But still let us make the attempt: and, like the White Rabbit, begin at the beginning.

Francisco Franco Bahamonde was born on the 4th of December, 1892, in El Ferrol, a small naval town in the north-western corner of Spain. The family was modest middle-class professional. Gossip gives them, as it gives so many Spanish families, a measure of Jewish blood.

Franco père was a naval paymaster of no great distinction who dealt with (and allegedly fiddled) the supplies, living to a ripe, bibulous and disreputable 90. Franco grandpère was also a Naval Officer and passed the 100 mark.

To Morocco and a bright future

In 1907 the young Francisco having failed, largely on social grounds, to get into the Navy, entered the Infantry Academy at Toledo. In 1912 finding himself temperamentally unsuited to garrison life, the ambitious young officer volunteered for active service in Morocco.

This was to prove the foundation of a brilliant military career, in which Franco distinguished himself by his sangfroid, organising skill, ruthless discipline and bravery under fire.

Franco was a born soldier. His rate of promotion was phenomenal: he was the youngest captain in the Army at 22, the youngest major at 23, the youngest brigadier-general at 33.

At 30, he took command of the Foreign Legion, the élite volunteer force then just formed under Millan Astray, the brilliant necrophilous cripple more than half mad, who led his men into battle under the slogan of *Viva la Muerte*—Long Live Death!

At the head of the Legion Franco fought a series of costly but eventually successful campaigns against the Moroccan rebels. Severely wounded once, twice decorated for distinguished conduct in the field, in 1923 the dashing Moroccan colonel, home on leave, at last won the hand of Carmen Polo, the daughter of a prosperous Asturian businessman in his home-town of El Ferrol.

It had taken all Franco's professional success to break down the Polo family's upper-middle-class prejudice against the young officer's humble origins.

In 1925 on the final pacification of Morocco, Franco returned to Spain, a brigadier-general and clearly marked for the future. Largely on his advice Primo de Rivera in 1928 set up the General Military Academy at Zaragoza, with Franco as its first head.

Two years later Primo de Rivera fell, dying within a few weeks in Paris of a broken heart. His ungrateful sovereign Alfonso XIII soon followed the old dictator into exile and in 1931 the Second Republic was inaugurated. The Zaragoza Academy was closed and Franco was relegated to the command of the insignificant garrison at La Coruña.

For the next five years, Franco's career was subject to the ebb and flow of the Republic's calamitous politics, amidst whose murky eddies the Army found itself cast in an uncertain, ineffectual and professionally unhappy role.

In the first three years of the Republic, from 1931 to 1934, when mass retirements were being forced on the officer corps, Franco kept his head down and stayed carefully clear of the recurrent plots against the Government. As late as February 1936, begged by Army dissidents to step in with a *pronunciamiento* against the Popular Front and annul the elections, Franco still refused to be moved.

No compromise through disloyalty

Although out of sympathy with the Liberal reformists of the Second Republic, by nature opposed to the politics of the Popular Front and since 1935 associated through his brother-in-law Ramon Serrano Suñer (later first his Home then his Foreign Minister) with CEDA, the short-lived Conservative Catholic party, until late in the 11th hour Franco would still not compromise himself in any overt disloyalty to the legally established government of the day.

This infinitely cautious reaction to events was to be the hallmark of Franco's long career. All his life Franco was a faithful disciple of the old Duke of Cambridge, whose best, indeed whose only, remembered dictum was: "There is a time and a place for everything; and the time for reform is when it can no longer be resisted."

In 1934, under the slightly more stable premiership of the Radical Lerroux, Franco's star moved once again into the ascendant. He was made Chief of the General Staff and played a leading part in the brutal repression of the Asturian miners' revolt.

Next year he was promoted major-general but when in February, 1936, the Popular Front Government came to power Franco was once again relegated to obscurity, this time to the then remote Canary Islands as commander of the backwater Tenerife garrison.

Given Franco's decisive role from this point on, it is hard to realise that in the preceding years he had appeared a virtually apolitical animal. Never a "joiner" or a café-politician he had been the model of the correct sober dedicated professional soldier, strictly minding his own business and showing a marked distaste for the political intrigues that were the daily bread of his fellow officers.

Marooned in the Canaries

One must at this point stop to remember two things. First that in 1936 Franco, for all his Moroccan successes, was by no means one of the most senior generals in Spain: he was in fact much junior to several national figures of established military reputation such as Queipo de Llano, Yagüe, Mola and Sanjurjo. The last named was indeed the initiator and first leader of the rising: but he was killed in an aircraft crash on the first morning, leaving the way open to the young Major-General Franco.

Secondly, marooned out in the Canaries Franco possessed no troops worth speaking of, no ships, no aircraft, no cash, no Press, no radio. He made his final commitment contingent upon being given command of the Moroccan regiments, whose 32,000 men were at that time the most efficient fighting force under the Spanish flag.

It was indeed his very lack of political identification that brought Franco to the leadership of that motley collection of uneasy fellows that slept together in the wide Nationalist bed. The only common denominators to the forces at his command were an ultra-conservative reaction against Reform: a desire to see the State return to a concept of Law and Order essentially traditional, Catholic, and authoritarian: and an atavistic fear of Communism and Anarchism. Spain, it must be remembered was the one country where Bakunin ever achieved a real following.

In July 1936 after weeks of hedging and prevarication, Franco was finally prevailed upon to join the revolt: and on July 9 Captain Bebb flew briefly into history on the Dragon Rapide hired from Croydon to take Franco on his clandestine journey from the Canaries to Morocco.

This was the beginning of the revolt. There followed the rallying of the garrisons: and then the first insurgent foot on the sacred soil of the peninsula. And thus, ironically enough, after 4½ centuries, the Moors returned to Spain.

The Nationalists most active political support was drawn from the Falange, the Spanish Fascist Party founded in 1933 by José Antonio Primo de Rivera, which owed its inspiration to Mussolini, d'Annunzio and a half-baked sort of proprietary populist national socialism.

More practically the Carlist Requetés of Navarra furnished the Nationalist cause with 60,000 courageous young men in scarlet berets, sworn to defend their own peculiar brand of conservative monarchist Catholicism.

Fighting with dumb discipline

The legitimist Monarchists sided with Franco in the blind hope of restoration — *Amo mi patria, adoro Dios y espero al Rey* — I love my country, I worship God and I await the King — as did the Civil Guard, who in many an isolated barracks over the next few months were to fight with the dumb discipline of Louis XVI's Swiss, frequently sharing the fate of those devoted mercenaries.

The small standing Army was much divided. The Navy, was early taken over by its incompetent Republican crews and thus effectively neutralised for the duration. There was virtually no Air Force. The Church elevated the Army's revolt to the level of a Crusade.

The Republicans were equally divided—Socialist against Communist, Radical against Anarchist, Basque and Catalan separatists against any centrist regime. The Popular Front was a kaleidoscope of divergent loyalties, the doctrines of Karl Marx its only common factor. Neither side was in the remotest sense monolithic. Affiliation was by no means always conscientious or deliberate. In many cases a man simply found himself perforce fighting for the side that controlled the area where he happened to be living when the war broke out.

The Nationalist cause was in particular marked by an overall lack of coherent political ideology. This fundamentally negative attribute was to be of the greatest convenience to Franco during the Civil War but a source of much weakness in the difficult years of reconstruction that followed. The mere fact of fighting the Republicans—usually and over-simply referred to as "los Rojos," the Reds—relieved Franco of the need to produce any positive or coherent political creed.

The "Crusade" served to subsume all differences in the amorphous general cause of Catholicism and Conservatism, anti-Communism and—perhaps most practically important of all right up to the present day —a sweeping anti-Liberalism. It was later when the cold, starving, recriminatory peace set in that Franco's ideological cupboard was shown to be so desperately bare.

Mere permanent improvisation

This lack of political purpose, principle or theory has carried its own long-term intellectual and social bankruptcy. Franco was never able to avoid the charge that his regime stood for scarcely anything positive and was little more than permanent improvisation writ large.

How, then, after Franco, is this fragile house of cards to be preserved by Ministers (and a King) who have no political ideology, who have never known an Opposition, have never had any collective responsibility and whose only loyalty has been to one man? Where can they turn now?

But we are outrunning our history. The one-party corporative State as founded in 1939 never changed in its curiously woolly essentials, practically the only definable feature of which was a basic anti-democracy. In 1945 the "Law of the Rights of the Spaniards" was promulgated, a loose concoction of alleged civil liberties heavily balanced by minatory references to civic duty and the beauty of unquestioning obedience to authority. Parliament as re-constituted by Franco in 1943 had nothing in common with that romantic child of the French Revolution, the Cadiz Cortes of 1813.

The members of today's Assembly are almost literally Conscript Fathers, taking their seats either by direct appointment or by collegiate election. The new Cortes was conceived by Franco as a rubber stamp: and has remained little else.

In 1947 a "Law of Succession" was passed by "plebiscite," re-establishing Spain as a Kingdom and laying down Franco's right, within certain limits, to nominate the successor to the throne.

In 1966 in response to mounting uncertainty and anxiety at his failure to prepare for the future, Franco introduced his "Organic Law" which, in itself almost a new Constitution, laid the basis for the post-mortem division of his powers among various institutions of the State. Notable among these were the Council of the Realm and the Council of Regency. The law was approved by referendum.

It made only the most formal of concessions to individual liberty and democratic rights. In practice it added up to little more than a legislative foundation for the indefinite extension of the existing authoritarian system, under other management.

In 1969 Franco placed the final stone in his pyramid by nominating Prince Juan Carlos to be his successor as Head of State, thus shrewdly side-tracking the legitimate but over-adult and over-liberal Pretender, his father Don Juan. During Franco's last years a campaign, by no means unsuccessful, was waged to popularize the Prince —who has indeed shown gifts of character, balance, hard work and public touch with which few people had earlier been prepared to credit him.

The intrigue and blanket-tugging

But at the end the old King-maker found himself sadly torn between the rival claims of his constitutionally established Dauphin and those of his own newly ennobled family. One could have wished him spared those last unseemly and painful months of intrigue and blanket-tugging.

Franco's long reluctance to deal frankly or in detail with the succession was understandable. The cornerstone of his rule had always been his own position. No successor could hope to claim anything remotely approaching the authority that was sure to die with him.

To draw attention to the succession was to strip away the pretensions of the constitution, to reveal the starkly personal basis of all authority and to unleash a whole flock of worrying question-marks about the future.

But Franco never had any intention of stepping down before his Maker beckoned him away. Only the eventual collapse of his health pushed him into pronouncement on the succession.

Franco was never a Fascist in the proper sense. José Antonio and Mussolini had, it is true much in common and for its half-baked principles the Falange drew heavily on National Socialism.

True, too, there were real Fascists among the motley company which found shelter under the many-coloured golf-umbrella of Franco's régime. The heavy-handed authoritarianism of that regime reflected many of the less endearing characteristics of the Axis dictatorships.

But to its credit, Franco's botch-job constitution incorporated several of the better populist and less reprehensible elements of its German and Italian prototypes.

Total security of employment

The Spanish worker to this day enjoys almost total security of employment: whilst Anti-Semitism was never approved or tolerated, (although since 1492 there have been few Semites in Spain for anybody to be anti.)

The Falange was always a many-feathered, many-fathered sort of bastard. And any way by the time of Franco's death it had under its reformed title of Movimiento Nacional, withered to ridicule and insignificance.

Continued

How fundamental in fact was Franco's tie-in with the Axis? For a while the Berlin-Madrid-Rome alignment plainly appeared to him to be directly serving the international interests of Spain, while the "ideologies" which he borrowed from it suited his immediate domestic needs.

In the first part of the Second World War, though Spain was officially neutral, Franco made no attempt to hedge his bet on an early Axis victory. After the German invasion of Russia, neutrality became non-belligerence and the despatch of the 20,000 Blue Division "volunteers" to starve and freeze on the Russian front was the high-water mark of Spanish collaboration.

Based on a hard-headed calculation of the likely outcome of the war and its meaning for his country, Franco's sole and entire preoccupation at a time when Spain, exhausted by the Civil War was totally incapable of resistance, was to be invaded neither by the Axis nor by the Allies.

Better than anyone Franco knew that to join (or be occupied by) either side would spell immediate blockade, attack and probably occupation by the other. In this all-important balancing act, Franco succeeded to the full.

But moral or emotional commitment there was none. Sir Alexander Cadogan in his Memoirs (p.208) notes, in June, 1940: "Gen. Franco, whose hostility might have rendered the Straits of Gibraltar impassable, declared Spanish neutrality a n d continued throughout the war to show scant gratitude to Hitler and Mussolini."

Franco could at that time have had Gibraltar as a gift from the Germans.

His reasons for refusing such a gift were peculiarly Spanish—but fundamentally admirable and indeed not without their benefit to us. Even in later years Franco never considered the idea of taking Gibraltar by force.

When the Russian campaign turned sour before Stalingrad, Franco saw the writing on the wall. He had the Blue Division withdrawn, reconsidered his policy on the export of wolfram, tightened up on German intelligence activities in Spain and began edging carefully back towards centre. The abrupt dropping of Serrano Suñer redressed the balance both of his foreign policy and of his domestic political manoeuvring.

Franco will have his place in history if only for one thing. At a time when Hitler had tricked, bullied and mesmerised half the leaders of Europe, Franco stood out as the one man who ever, so far as we know, took Hitler for a ride.

Why did the Germans not drive on down through Spain in the autumn of 1940 when they had the finest Panzer army ever known poised fit and fresh on the Pyrenean frontier with the Peninsula open at their feet?

Even Hitler was dismayed

The answer is to be found in the meeting of October 1940 at Hendaye — the famous meeting after which Hitler is reported to have said, that he would rather have two teeth out than go through that again.

If Franco has written his memoirs, they will be worth reading for this passage alone. At present all we know for sure is that Franco talked Hitler out of it. Had he not done so, the course of the war might have been radically (and for us disastrously) different.

The Germans would have rolled on down through Spain, taken Gibraltar overnight, blockaded the Mediterranean and foreclosed any subsequent possibility of an Allied landing in North Africa.

So Franco's nimble war-time footwork saved his regime from being toppled by either one or other of the belligerents, as it would surely have been had he joined either side. But it was also of course the direct cause of Spain's long and painful isolation in the post-war period.

Nor did her eventual return to the international fold derive from any change of heart on Franco's part, being simply the product of the Cold War and the consequent demands of American nuclear strategy.

In 1953 the Spanish Government signed a treaty of economic assistance and military co-operation with the United States which, re-negotiated every ten years, has been the basis of Spain's security ever since. It also proved the immediate pre-

Other Obituaries—P16
Editorial Comment—P18

lude to massive American economic investment, where 10 years before there had, alone in Europe, been no Marshall Aid.

World Bank loans followed, membership of the United Nations and other international bodies, the signing of a Concordat with the Vatican, the return to formal diplomatic relations with all Western Europe and all Latin America except Mexico.

Even so Franco was never able to achieve that complete and unreserved international rehabilitation he so dearly coveted.

His aspirations were always fatally flawed by the crying discrepancy between Spain's external pretensions and her domestic realities. Although Franco could put anything across in Spain, nobody could ever put Franco across in Westminster.

It could all, of course, be put down to the "Black Legend" and Franco would have died sooner than admit the slightest hurt. But it was the enduring London blackball that rubbed the worst.

For all the early ostracism of the United Nations, the Visitors' Book at the Pardo soon showed a gratifying collection of callers. Starting with such early, modest and expectable prizes as Kings Abdullah, Hussein, Feisal and Saud, Presidents Trujillo and Carmona,

Evita Peron and the Sultan of Morocco, by 1959 Franco had landed his first big democratic fish in the beaming shape of President Eisenhower.

From there he graduated steadily through such catches as the Shah of Persia, Nasser, Salazar, Bourguiba and Haile Selassie to his record season of 1970-71 when he hooked, gaffed and landed the major trophies of Erhardt and Nixon. In the same year he caught de Gaulle—but only a retired de Gaulle. His final score was President Ford.

With world records such as these mounted on his gunroom wall Franco had little cause for distress over the absence of lesser specimens from the smaller democracies of Western Europe. For all that, the old sportsman would have dearly loved to see a Lion and a Unicorn among his trophies of the chase.

Post Franco, propter Franco. In what measure will that praise and that blame be allocated?

Franco entered—and emerged from—the Civil War with little apparent understanding of the social tensions that had caused it. He appeared ignorant alike of political theory and of the impact of economic forces on human society.

To him Spain's problem was simply one of order or disorder: victory in the Civil War, public discipline and a sense of civic duty thereafter were to be the end of the matter. Everything else—in particular social peace and material prosperity—would follow automatically.

This simpliste approach was the underlying ethos—clear, comfortable and undemanding: single-track, blinkered, incurious and admitting of no questions: but, let us face it, by no means unsuccessful.

Materially most Spaniards—particularly the urban bourgeoisie—are of course infinitely better off today than they have ever been. Illiteracy, prevalent in 1936, is now near to elimination. There are comprehensive social services which bear comparison with those of most countries in Western Europe.

An inevitable degree of progress

There has been constant and rapid economic growth. Common (as opposed to political) crime, vandalism, dope-addiction, student unrest and strikes are all successfully contained: whilst pollution, traffic congestion and the urban decibel count are up to the highest European standards!

But all this would have come anyway in the natural course of events. Many fundamental weaknesses which lay at the root of the Civil War still obtain—in particular extreme class polarisation and a heavy imbalance in the distribution of wealth.

Franco did nothing to reduce either. Indeed, it probably never occurred to him that this might be a desirable or a necessary process.

To justify his anaesthetic regime he could always rely on the Spanish people's long memory, the traumatic impact of the Civil War and the steady subsequent rise in the country's standard of living. That this was largely due to the healing action of time was not to worry him: and anyway it was he who had kept the ring for time to do its work.

Nor was it in his character to worry about the reverse of the coin—the heavy curtailment of personal liberty, the gagging of the Press, the absence of political debate or democratic institutions, the executive's encroachments on the judiciary, the unhealed scars of war and the deep wounds of regional separatism.

If he ever gave these things a thought Franco probably dismissed them as the Marxist-inspired grumblings of a foreign-misled minority against those small prices which every right-thinking element in the country was wholeheartedly ready to pay for its delivery, its revival and its continued material well-being.

A visit to the National Civil War monument in the Valle de los Caídos, near Madrid even today will not reveal a single Republican buried there. War-disabled who fought against Franco still get no pensions. If you see two one-legged men walking down a Madrid street and one has an artificial limb, you know which side each fought on in the Civil War.

As for "abroad," the picture was much the same. Franco had little direct knowledge or understanding of the outside world. His foreign journeys were few and far between.

As a young man he visited the Military Academy at St Cyr: the only time he came to England was in 1936 as a member of the Spanish delegation to the funeral of King George V. In 1941 he went to Montpellier to visit Pétain: he met Mussolini at Bordighera in 1941 and Hitler at Hendaye in 1940.

At heart, a shrewd peasant

Franco's was not a very complex character. Basically all his life he remained the shrewd, calculating, reserved Galician peasant. (The rest of Spain says that if you meet a Gallego on the stairs, you will never know whether he is going up or coming down!)

Power came to him at the early age of 44. Lacking the education or experience necessary to a statesman, he made up for it as he went along by a cool head, lack of personal vanity and sheer inborn, native cunning.

An infinitely cautious reaction to events, neat calculation of the odds, a highly developed sense of the pragmatic, instinctive understanding of the demands of *realpolitik* and complete freedom from the inhibitions of any established political or intellectual philosophy. Join to these characteristics a quick eye and a cold heart, and you have the ingredients for your successful dictator.

But, however you look at it, Franco's was a most remarkable career. An unquestioning sense of personal vocation was of prime importance. Franco always knew that he was the chosen instrument.

A genuine, if narrow, patriotism, an unquestioning belief in the rightness of a certain settled way of things, a paternalist, unimaginative authoritarianism: an aloofness from personal material gain, a settled family life, a conventional sort of formal piety; the unquestioned moral certainty that Providence had used him to guide Spain back to the paths of righteousness—it was the combination of these convictions that enabled Franco to fulfil his destiny.

Perhaps indeed Spain needed Franco at that moment in history. After the brutal obscenities of the Civil War, he had the luck to coincide with an unprecedented economic boom which created a new middle class with a stake in the maintenance of his political status quo and its concomitant prosperity.

This is a very long requiem for a very short dictator. But Franco's was a long life which cannot but leave a deep mark on Spain. Did he serve his country well or ill? Materially he brought undoubted benefits: but spiritually he left a desert.

Franco's apologists will say that he saved his country from Communism, kept it out of the Second World War and gave it 40 years of peace and prosperity. His detractors will reply that he and his likes by gratuitously starting the Civil War brought upon Spain those very disasters from which they then professed to be saving her. Seen in the immediate aftermath of his departure, Franco's creation hardly has the stamp of durability upon it.

Material prosperity bought at the cost of spiritual suffocation is not the stuff on which futures are built.

And, as Sir Thomas Malory observed. " Time hath an art to make dust of all things."

Daily Telegraph
29th December 1972

The shopkeeper from Missouri great American President

HARRY S. TRUMAN, who has died, aged 88, automatically succeeded, as Vice-President of the United States, to the White House on the death in 1945 of Franklin D. Roosevelt.

There were few at the time who foresaw that he would, three years later, re-assume office as President in his own right.

Probably even fewer realised that in the post-war years he would handle, with great credit, problems as grave and as complex as any that faced his brilliant predecessor.

His own misgivings of his suitability for the tasks which faced him in such a tragically unexpected way in 1945 were reflected not only in America but in many parts of the world.

Yet this mild-mannered little man was to decide on the only use of the atom bomb in war-time, against Hiroshima and Nagasaki in Japan in 1945; to astound his Republican opponents by defeating the popular Governor Dewey for the Presidency; to revolutionise American foreign policy by providing cash and arms for anti-Communist countries, and to launch the life-saving Marshall Plan for the aid of Western Europe.

His Greek-Turkish aid programme, under the Truman Doctrine, had gradually set his country on a new path away from pre-war isolationism.

He was also personally responsible for prompt intervention by American forces, acting on behalf of the United Nations, following the Communist invasion of South Korea in 1950.

Not the least bold, politically, of his actions was his dismissal in 1951 of Gen. MacArthur, regarded as a national hero by millions of Americans, from his post of Commander in the Far East.

The President courted the widest personal unpopularity by this step, but acted unhesitatingly once he had decided that MacArthur's policies could end only in a third world war. His action was subsequently endorsed by the Chiefs of Staff.

Mr Truman's desire for the closest co-operation with Western Europe, and with the British Commonwealth in particular, appeared to gain in strength as his term of office drew to a close.

Courage and shrewdness

As President Harry Truman lacked neither courage nor shrewdness. Yet he was limited in experience, training and outlook. Genial and rather colourless, he lacked intellectual subtlety, and all the poise implied in " background." He never ceased openly to regret what he called the " terrible inadequacy" of his education.

Although he had special instruction in elocution, he was never more than a mediocre speaker. His hurried stumbling delivery from a closely followed script was the reverse of inspiring.

Yet he had a wise, practical attitude and a certain pedestrian sincerity which many found reassuring. He was believed, in his early days, to be " safe " if not brilliant.

His aphorisms were famous, one being " 'If you can't stand the heat, get out of the kitchen."

While in the White House Mr Truman had occasion to reprove some members of his administration for " passing the buck ". He had a sign made and put over his desk which said: " The buck stops here ".

In the White House he soon disabused the minds of those who imagined that he would be content to " ride out " his term of office.

In 1946 he swept away practically all price controls except those on rent, took direct and forceful action to end serious coal and rail strikes, and ousted Mr Henry Wallace from office because of a speech which conflicted with America's foreign policy. He was present at Fulton, Missouri, to hear Churchill's historic speech on Anglo-American relations.

He made the first State visit of an American President to Canada when he visited Ottawa in 1947. In the same year he announced that he had been seeking, without success, to secure another " Big Three " Conference in Washington.

His election victory in the following year took the world by surprise. He secured 24,104,030 votes to Mr Dewey's 21,970,986, and 303 electoral votes to 189, and was assured of a comfortable majority in both Senate and House.

Of several grave decisions he had to take in 1950, none was more momentous, or far-reaching in its effects, than that demanded by the invasion of South Korea in June.

His reaction was swift and courageous. He ordered into immediate action American sea, land and air forces, and also instructed the American Navy to prevent a Communist invasion of Formosa, refuge of the Chinese Nationalists.

His action was regarded as a landmark in the history of the United Nations, and met with the practically unanimous approval of the United States Congress and people.

He had earlier been called upon to determine whether the hydrogen bomb, with its fearful powers, should go into production, and whether American military aid to Western Europe should be extended. He decided, in view of the increasing deterioration of the world situation, in favour of both.

He declared that America's policy was based on full support of the United Nations and economic and military collaboration with Western Europe. He signed a Bill providing £436,600,000 to arm the Atlantic Pact countries and friendly nations of the Middle and Far East; subsequently Congress approved an additional £1,428 million for this purpose.

For some time it had appeared that the Far Eastern policies of Gen. MacArthur commanding United Nations forces in the Korean War, were at conflict with those of Mr Truman. With characteristic forthrightness the President flew to Wake Island, in the Pacific, for a conference with MacArthur. The General's dismissal followed soon after the President's return.

Sir Winston Churchill, who had a great respect for Mr Truman, has been credited with describing him as the man who had done more than anyone else since the end of the war to save Western civilisation.

In 1955 the first of his two-volume memoirs, already serialised in *The Daily Telegraph*, was published. It was " Year of Decisions," and covered the first 12 months of his Presidency. In a preface he wrote, " To be President of the United States is to be lonely, very lonely, at times of great decisions."

Daily Telegraph
22nd April 1971

EXQUISITE CRUELTY OF PAPA DOC'S DICTATORSHIP

NO one likes to write ill of the dead. In the case of Francois Duvalier, dead at 64 in his white palace in Port-au-Prince, an exception is perhaps permissible with no abandonment of humanitarian principles.

Tyrants before " Papa Doc " have shed more blood and imposed their despotism on greater numbers. But, given the wretched state of the Haitian people, and the relative ease with which a genuine reformer could have bettered their lot with sincere use of aid from abroad, the 14 years of dictatorship Duvalier imposed on his people was a period of exquisite cruelty.

It was an horrendous memorial to Black man's inhumanity to Black man.

Whether or not Duvalier was mad is a moot point. I have met or observed him a number of times over the past 11 years and it was his evilness rather than any controlled psychosis that left the lasting impression.

Good qualities once

I grant that Duvalier had some good qualities when he first came to world attention as the American-trained country doctor who won the Presidency of the hemisphere's poorest country.

Born in Port-au-Prince a pure Negro, he served at the Hospital of St Francis de Sales and was attached to the United States Medical Mission as director of malaria control.

As a country doctor he gave free treatment to the poorer Haitians.

Corrupted by power

But power quickly corrupted him. By the mid-1960s he had become not simply a dictator but also a sadist, a gangster and a common crook.

Recently I was privileged to see photostatic copies of one of several bank accounts Duvalier maintained in New York. There were others in Paris and Switzerland, nest-eggs put together in the event that he might be able to leave the country safely after a change of leadership.

The New York account revealed that a courier from Port-au-Prince regularly every fortnight deposited about $14,000 (£5,800) in his account. We can only guess at how much went into other private accounts.

In this same period, with starvation facing a quarter of a million of his five million subjects, and perhaps 90 per cent. of the population suffering the effects of malnutrition, Papa Doc established a " nutrition bureau." He allocated from Government funds the magnanimous sum of £125 a month to run it.

Piquant timing

There is some piquancy in the timing of his end. His death was announced on the 22nd, the day of the month that Papa Doc had always regarded as his most auspicious.

He assumed the presidency on Sept. 22, 1957, had himself declared " president-for-life " on a 22nd, opened the Francois Duvalier jet airport on a 22nd, and made many of his important moves on the 22nd of any month.

When President Kennedy was assassinated on Nov. 22, 1963, Papa Doc did a dance of joy in his palace.

It had been Kennedy who had ordered the cutting of almost all aid money to the Duvalier régime after American observers brought back proof that practically all of it was finding its way into the pockets of Duvalier and his cronies.

At the time of the assassination in Dallas, Duvalier is said to have confided to associates that he had put a death curse on the President and was delighted that it had taken effect on the 22nd of the month.

But any day of the month was appropriate for the murder of an opponent, usually accompanied by the liquidation of the man's entire family, or for a political bloodbath.

Papa Doc sometimes liked to advertise his butchery. For one grisly week, the bullet-ridden body of an opponent was propped up in an armchair in the centre of one of the most heavily-used traffic roundabouts in Port-au-Prince.

The chair had been taken from the dead man's home. The Ton Ton Macoutes spread the word that it had been his favourite chair.

Little Red Book

Duvalier autographed for me his Little Red Book of revolutionary thoughts. It must surely have been inspired by another little red book of thoughts.

In fact, this preposterous little man often publicly compared himself with such revolutionary giants as Mao Tse-tung, Lenin, Ataturk and Nkrumah. I also had the impression during our meeting that Papa Doc saw himself as a black De Gaulle.

Papa Doc was a special sort of megalomaniac. He regarded the Opera Bouffe mismanagement of his country's economy and the Hieronymus Bosch nightmare he had imposed on his people as an authentic revolution.

He saw himself as the reincarnation of the fabled Negro leaders, the " Black Jacobins " who drove out the French in 1803 and gave the modern world its first lesson in Black Power.

He proclaimed himself "t h e Haitian flag, one and indivisible, the Haitian revolution, the Haitian soul." He had read all the works of the early Haitian leaders.

Bue he had also devoured the works of Machiavelli. And it was Machiavelli, rather than Dessalines and Toussaint, who became his political mentor.

Among Duvalier's own writings is a book on Voodoo, published in 1944. Although a Roman Catholic by upbringing, he became a devoted student of Voodoo in his late teens.

That he used Voodoo as a political instrument is beyond question. He would spread the word that Voodoo had made him and his family " bullet proof," that even spirits living in animals and plants were working for " Duvalierism."

The prayer now of all those who feel for the Haitian people is that something good will stem from Duvalier's death. Admittedly, the portents are not good.

But at least Papa Doc, in whatever purgatory he has been consigned to, Christian or Voodoo, will not be manipulating the course of events with his wicked mind.

New York Herald Tribune
27th July 1952

Eva Peron Dies; Fabulous Life Is Ended at 30

Modern Cinderella

Maria Eva Duarte de Peron, the twentieth-century Cinderella of South America, was one of the most hated and loved, powerful and capricious women in Argentina and the world. Her rise to power was meteoric and her use of that power ruthless in support of her husband's regime. But history may remember her not only as the dictator's wife who crushed democratic institutions to satisfy her personal pique, but also as the ardent feminist who gave Argentine women suffrage and a social worker whose generosity knew no bounds.

Her origins were best forgotten by those who sought favor with the Peron regime. The daughter of Juana Ibarguron, a coachman's daughter, and Juan Duarte, a small landowner who had deserted his legal wife, she was born in the pampas town of Los Toldos, on May 7, 1919—although she later claimed to have been born in 1922—the youngest of their five children born out of wedlock.

The children found small relief from social stigma and snobbery even when, after their father's death, their mother took them to the near-by city of Junin, where she operated a boarding house. At sixteen, after eight years of schooling, Eva left home to travel the 170 miles to Buenos Aires to seek a career on the stage.

Favorite of Military

The next eight years brought personal rather than professional success. Five feet five inches tall, with a well endowed figure, her dark brown eyes and brunette complexion set off by artificially honey-colored hair, Eva Duarte was a favorite with various members of the increasingly powerful military clique.

She was earning 150 pesos a month, about $45, as a minor actress for Radio Belgrano, in 1943, when she met Col. Juan Domingo Peron, then an under secretary in the Ministry of War. As she was seen more frequently in the company of the dark, handsome widower, who subsequently became Vice-President, War Minister and Secretary of Labor and Social Welfare in the government of Edelmiro Farrell, her salary rose to 1,500 pesos and before long she was getting $7,500 a month and roles befitting such a wage.

Installed in a luxurious apartment adjoining that of the politically successful colonel, who was twenty-four years her senior, Eva Duarte was soon the most gossiped-about woman in Buenos Aires. Their mutual success seemed boundless until, in a pre-dawn raid on his apartment, Peron was arrested and forced to resign his government posts. She was immediately dismissed by Radio Belgrano.

Presidential Campaign

Eva Duarte came through this first test of loyalty. She organized a mass demonstration of Peron's supporters, "Los Descamisados," the shirtless ones who were to become her own political province, that turned into a howling riot in front of the federal Government House resulting in Peron's release. A few days later, on Oct. 21, 1945, they were married in a secret civil ceremony in Junin, followed by a public religious ceremony at La Plata on Dec. 10.

Immediately Mrs. Peron set out with her husband on his presidential campaign tour, a thing unheard of for an Argentine woman.

and kissed babies—she had none of her own—posed for pictures with peons and distributed gifts like a seasoned politician. When the ballots were counted, she was the First Lady.

Her first acts as First Lady were typical: she banished the nation's leading radio and screen actresses who had snubbed her in her early days; made it illegal for the Ladies of Beneficence, women from the country's oldest and richest families who had scorned her as a social upstart, to continue their charity work, and established the Maria Eva Duarte de Peron Social Aid Foundation which was soon dispensing $12,000 a month to the needy.

Established in the Ministry of Labor, Mrs. Peron showed political keenness and personal drive. She interviewed hundreds of persons a day, from diplomats to dishwashers, spoke at rallies and dedications and soon became the patroness of labor with her strong stand for higher wages and appeal to the masses.

With a $40,000-a-year bill from Paris couturiers alone, a jewel collection reputed to have been exceeded only by Cleopatra's and three rooms of her home serving as storage space for her furs, suits and hats, she nevertheless became the heroine of the poor and needy. She did not hesitate to wear a mink wrap and diamond earrings when addressing her beloved "descamisados," for she would depict herself simply as a shirtless one who had made good in Peron's Paradise, where she and her husband were working to provide such benefits for all.

$4,500,000 a Year

Her foundation, supported on "voluntary" contributions from public employees, labor contracts that provide that workers donate a day's pay each year, and labor unions, provides lavish homes for the aged and for working women in Buenos Aires. On a personal basis she dispensed about $4,500,-000 in charity a year. Soon "Evita," as she urged the workers to call her, was being hailed as "The Madonna of the Humble" and "The Lady of Hope," with her picture—and that of her husband—displayed side by side with religious pictures in the humblest homes of the land.

In 1947 she was invited to Spain by Generalissimo Francisco Franco, who offered her the Order of Isabel la Catolica. In a four-engined plane, accompanied by a lady-in-waiting, a dressmaker, a hairdresser, a physician, secretary and numerous relatives and friends, Mrs. Peron set out on a seventy-eight-day tour that was among the most controversial in political history. It was highlighted by her giving the Falange salute in Spain, having an audience with Pope Pius XII in Rome, being received by the President of France and witnessing the signing of a Franco-Argentine commercial treaty. She was honored at a reception on her way home via Brazil at which the then Secretary of State George C. Marshall proposed a toast to her. But it was also marked by the wolf-whistles of American G. Is who saw the striking blonde arrive in Italy, left-wing demonstrations in Italy, a shower of stones and over-ripe tomatoes in Switzerland and a complete snub from the British King and Queen, who thwarted her ambition to be a house guest in Buckingham Palace.

The richness of her costumes, her distribution of more than $100,000 to the poor of the countries she visited and her discourses on her feelings for the lower classes brought such caustic comment from the press that "Time" magazine was barred from Argentina for four months because of a cover story on her trip.

She returned home, however, in a blaze of local glory, to be met by a cheering horde of 100,000, including 10,000 draftees who had been told to doff their uniforms and mingle with the masses to fill out the crowd. She turned her attention to safer ground and won approval for women's suffrage, to be effective in the 1952 elections, with an amendment providing that no woman need reveal her age when she registers.

Her personal business sense was as keen as her political judgments. She was known to control three newspapers, "Democracia," "Laborista" and "Noticias Graficas," to have a registered trademark under her own name for an agricultural product company and to own an instrument company. She was reported to have purchased a home and established a large bank account in Switzerland, for an eventuality she may have anticipated when she once said, "If I ever go down, watch out for the crash. There won't be anybody else standing up either."

Her personal philosophy which she frequently expressed at public meetings was, "I have three loves —the fatherland, the descamisados and Peron." Apparently the driving force behind her husband, it was said of her that she knew what they both wanted and never let him forget it for long. The role she chose for herself, as she put it to a conference of Argentine governors last year, was, "I try to be a bridge of love and of hope between the people and the leader."

Her brother, Juan Duarte, is secretary to President Peron and thus in a good listening post at the Casa Rosada, or Pink House, where Peron has his offices in downtown Buenos Aires.

Last February, as head of the Peronista Women's party, Mrs. Peron humbly called on her husband, presented him with a watch and urged him to run for re-election to a second six-year term in 1952. It followed logically that in a matter of days there was a boom on for her to run as vice-presidential candidate, in view of women voting for the first time.

A mammoth rally on Aug. 22, attended by 250,000 although planned for 2,000,000, provided the occasion for the government-sponsored General Confederation of Labor to offer the Perons leadership of the ticket for the Nov. 11 elections. They both agreed to bow to the will of the people.

Nine days later Eva Peron, the most politically powerful woman in the Western Hemisphere, declined, in a nation-wide broadcast, the nomination she had maneuvered to get. She had no higher goal in life, she told the nation, than to serve her country and her husband. "I am not resigning my work," she said, "but just the honors."

It was generally known that her candidacy had caused a split in the command of the Peronist party and that the army was a strong opponent, both because of its displacement in power by the labor unions under her guidance and because of the possibility of a woman becoming President and commander-in-chief. Her husband remained loyal, however, announcing a few days later that "in recognition of her self-denial," in refusing to run, she would be awarded the Grand Peronist Medal, Extraordinary grade.

Daily Express
29th September 1970

THERE were two Nassers. One the reasonable man who could coo as sweetly as any sucking dove. The other a ranter, a raver . . . a swayer of the masses.

For Gamal Abdel Nasser was possessed of two demons. One always seemed to be trying to get in, the other to get out.

One made him appear the man seeking a free and happier life for the fellahin. The soft words, the soulful countenance gazing so frankly into the tele-prompter, the p h i l o s o p h i c serenity, contrived to calm the sceptical, lull the suspicious.

Then demon No. 2 took over, and Nasser would go out on to a alcony and sway the mob with breakable pledges, mouthing hatred against Jews, fellow-Arabs, colonialists, imperialists, capitalists, Communists.

Whatever the rights and wrongs of the Jew-Arab conflict, Nasser may be seen in history as a tinhorn dictator who unlocked the Middle East to the Russians.

Schizophrenics of his type can be found everywhere in the Moslem world.

Yet Nasser stood head and shoulders above them all. By his death the 30 million people of Egypt, who venerated him as a god, have lost their deliverer.

Unhappily the *folie de grandeur* which he inspired in simple folk—soil workers, nomadic Bedouin and Nubians alike—was rooted in ill-will, deceit, self-deception and lying propaganda.

Nasser was born on January 15, 1918, ten months before the Great War ended. That war ended in the liberation of the Arabs from centuries of Turkish oppression.

CHARM
Ambition fired

Egypt stayed under British control. With its international canal it was the gateway to Britain's rich Indian empire. Nasser grew up surrounded by evidences of British power. The Sirdar legend was still very much alive.

The future dictator's father was sub-postmaster in the Assiut village of Beni Mur. When RAF biplanes sputtered across the sky the small boy would rush out and scream at them. He was still quite young when he resolved to push these "imperialists" out of his country.

He tried to enter an army officers' academy, but failed. Then he turned to law. In this

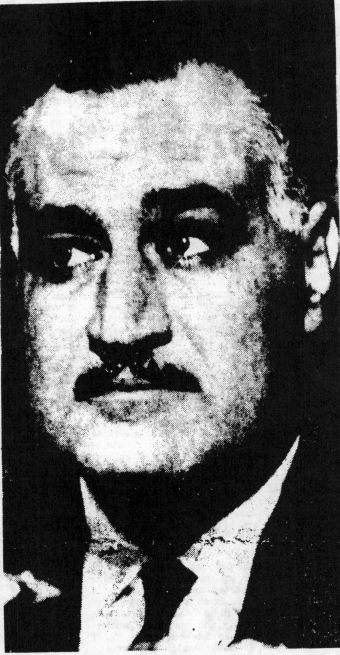

PRESIDENT NASSER: died of a heart attack

subject, too, he failed. Turning back to the army he managed to make the grade at his second attempt.

Nasser was now 19, stood 6ft. 2in., oozed infinite charm, his handsome, if rather Mephisto-phelian, features and black crinkly hair offset by a set of white teeth which he could flash in pleasure or bare angrily as his mood changed.

Military service at home and in the Sudan fed the fires of his ambition to oust the British. But first he must get rid of King Farouk and the corrupt regime which was sucking Egypt's lifeblood.

Corruption had settled on the Army. Nasser blamed it for the failure of the Arabs to win the war against Israel in 1948-49. The "great men" he said he met inside the army turned out to be egoists. "I could hear nothing from them save the word I," he wrote. It was all "utterly futile."

He used to say to himself, "What is important is that someone should come who

should come"—the Deliverer who should liberate his country "from all fetters and shackles."

That is what he wrote in his *Mein Kampf*, which he called *The Philosophy of the Revolution,* and he went on:

"I used to walk amidst the ruins all around me, which were left after the bombardments of the enemy. There I travelled far in my imagination. My voyage took me to the sphere of the stars where I would regard the whole area from my great height above."

KINGS
Two deposed

From that war he conceived the notion of one region, one Arab force, one Arab general staff, one Arab brotherhood. With himself as its leader, of course. Why, he asked, should we dissipate our efforts?

He returned from the war, slightly wounded, ready to remove Farouk and the army leaders. Nasser chose his friends carefully. They included Hakem Amer, Salah Salem—he who danced in his underpants in later years to impress the Sudanese—and others.

A " Free Officers' " movement was formed, with secret printing press and all the other paraphernalia of plotting. But before they struck they had to have a respectable front man.

They chose the middle-aged General Mohammed Neguib. Under his aegis they struck on July 23, 1952. Nasser asked himself, as he wondered whether anyone would have to be killed: "Which is more important ?. That someone should pass away who should pass away, or that someone should come who should come ? "

Reassured by this rhetoric, Nasser and his fellow officers took the palace. Farouk was deposed with unexpected ease. His infant son, Ahmed, was proclaimed king in his place.

Nasser found it more convenient to have the little king deposed, too, after a 'reign' of 11 months. About a year after that he removed Neguib as well.

Now he was uncrowned King of the Nile—and he busily set about removing the 'imperialists.' Britain obligingly withdrew her 80,000 troops from the Suez Canal base in 1954.

Before 1956, as President, he was a fully fledged dictator who could claim that he had been elected by the free vote of his people.

MIXTURE
Faith and doubt

Now he started playing off East against West. John Foster Dulles was very impressed by this up-and-coming young man. He presented him with a silver-plated pistol.

He forced King Hussein of Jordan to sack General John Glubb, who had trained the Arab Legion. He helped Algerian terrorists against France. He began to envisage a United Africa under his own dominion.

Mass hysteria carried him on and on . . . and then the Americans lost patience and withdrew a promise of dollars to build the Aswan High Dam, one of Nasser's early dreams.

The rest is history. Nationalisation of the Suez Canal in July 1956, followed by the Suez war. In the same year he had made a covert attempt to bring Sudan under his control.

There he was striking the posture of the Deliverer the day he chose to take on the Israelis . . . again.

As Nasser said a long time ago, he recognised himself as a " mixed confusion of the factors of nationalism and religion, faith and doubt, knowledge and ignorance." That could be his epitaph.

Nasser had a last triumph before his death. In all the hatred and confusion of the Jordan crisis, he succeeded in getting the two chief protagonists, King Hussein and guerilla leader Yassir Arafat to Cairo for talks.

Daily Express
2nd May 1945

OBITUARY

THE Daily Express rejoices to announce the report of Adolf Hitler's death. It prints today every line of information about the manner of his death.

It wastes no inch of space upon his career. The evil of his deeds is all too well known.

It gives no picture of the world's most hated face.

It records that Hitler was born Schickelgruber at Braunau, Austria, on April 20, 1889, and that his days upon the earth he sought to conquer were too long.

Science

The distinction between scientist and inventor, engineer, or medical innovator is of course somewhat arbitrary: consider **Marie Curie**, the dedicated researcher, and **Wilhelm von Röntgen**, who actually discovered the existence of the X-Rays which pointed in Curie's direction. As representatives of what has for better or worse come to be seen as the epitome of twentieth century science, namely nuclear research, we have three rather different figures. Pre-eminent is of course **Albert Einstein**, The scientist, whose attitude to and concern about the results of his work is perhaps the last instance of the humanist scientist, and whose Theory of Relativity epitomises the mystery of science. **Ernest Rutherford**'s work on splitting the atom helped us develop the atomic bomb; whereas that of **Niels Bohr** provides a peculiarly twentieth century model for understanding the structure of things. By complete contrast, the other end of the scale perhaps, the memory of Monsieur **Mesmer** has not gone unnoticed. **Malthus**, perhaps the first of the futurologists, with his predictions about world population, is of course the forerunner of much of today's practical scientific concern. **Pavlov** exemplifies the scientist who reduces – to his own satisfaction if to no one else's – man to the status of object, differing from other constituents of the universe in complexity only. **Charles Darwin** enthroned biology with his revolutionary account of how we got to be who and where we are, making not only Pavlov possible but Genesis impossible. (The first geneticist proper, incidentally, Mendel, failed to raise forth a British obituary, as did Linnaeus, the great classifier.) Representing veterinary science there is **Robert Stroud**, the Birdman of Alcatraz – jailed for life, he wrote what is still the classic work on the diseases of birds. Finally, **Otto Hahn** the father of nuclear physics, whom we may yet come to thank or blame for his work.

News Chronicle
5th July 1934

MADAME CURIE'S SECRETS

MME. MARIE CURIE, the greatest woman scientist in the world, and co-discoverer, with her husband, of radium, is dead. She was 67.

The end came at a mountain sanatorium near Sallanches, in Upper Savoy, to which she was taken on Thursday. Her daughters, Eve and Irene, were at her deathbed.

She had worked in her laboratory to the last moment that her health permitted, and actually on her deathbed she was giving directions, to be imparted to her assistants at the Curie Institute, to secure the continuation of her experiments.

KNEW END WAS NEAR

It is understood that Mme. Curie had taken one assistant completely into her confidence some time ago, acting on the knowledge that she herself had not long to live.

Although the actual cause of death was pernicious anæmia, her constitution had suffered from the effects of those experiments by which she conferred so many benefits on the art of healing.

The scientist's funeral to-morrow will be a simple ceremony, as she wished, and she will be buried beside her husband in Paris.

Madame Curie was born in Warsaw, her family name being Sklodowska. Her family were poor, and she began to earn her living as a governess in a Russian home. At this time Poles were subjected to persecution by the Russian Government, and Marie Sklodowska determined to flee abroad.

"MISS PROFESSOR"

One night, disguised as an old woman and wearing spectacles, she crept out of the house, crossed the frontier and fled to Paris.

"Miss Professor," as her father called her, went from laboratory to laboratory looking for a job, and at last Professor Lippman appointed her his assistant.

That was the first step on the road to her position as the greatest woman scientist in the world At the Sorbonne she met a fellow student, Pierre Curie. They worked together and opened a new road in scientific thought that led to the discovery of radium.

ROMANCE ENDED

They fell in love and married. But their work went on. They experimented with pitch-blende, a dark brown substance found in Austria.

The Austrian Government sent them 400 tons of pitch-blende, from which they extracted a speck of radium salt no bigger than a pin's head. This was the first speck of the world's most wonderful metal, and its rays could penetrate 15 inches of solid steel.

The great discovery was announced in 1898, and the whole world marvelled. In 1906 the romance of the Curies' lives was shattered.

Pierre, on his way to a lecture, was run over in the street and killed. His wife succeeded him at the Sorbonne, where she carried on till she was appointed Professor of Radiology at Warsaw in 1919.

Working alone in the laboratory, Madame Curie found that radium could be extracted from several natural minerals, and this made its production relatively cheaper

On no woman scientist did honours fall so lavishly, two of her most distinguished awards being the Davy Medal of the Royal Society and the Nobel Prize for Chemistry.

NEVER RICH

In 1921 she returned from the United States with a gramme of radium presented to her by the women of America. The gift was handed to her personally by President Harding.

She again visited the States in 1929 and received a gift of £10,000 from the American women for the purchase of another precious gramme for use in the Radium Institute at Warsaw.

Although she benefited suffering humanity so greatly—the radium being used extensively in medicine for skin diseases as well as cancer—Mme. Curie remained comparatively poor.

In 1931 she took one of her daughters, Mme. Irene Curie-Joliot, into her laboratory as an assistant. Her other daughter is a talented musician.

MME. CURIE.

The Times
1st January 1835

We see with regret the announcement of the death of Mr. Malthus, the eminent writer—a man whose private virtues were not, and could not be, disputed by those who were most hostile to his views of social economy.

The Times
20th June 1815

MESMER, the discoverer of animal magnetism, died lately, in the 81st year of his age, at Mersburg, on the lake of Constance.

The Times
29th July 1968

PROFESSOR OTTO HAHN

Professor Otto Hahn, the man who got so near to discovering the effect that made nuclear weapons and power stations inevitable that he received a Nobel award for his search, died in Göttingen yesterday at the age of 89. The effect was nuclear fission, the splitting of uranium nuclei into fragments of not greatly different masses when a neutron enters the uranium nucleus and causes it to divide in two as in a droplet of water. This was a completely unexpected effect. Scientists in other laboratories had done similar experiments, but had been misled by pitfalls in their evidence. Hahn and his colleague, Fritz Strassmann, sorted out the evidence correctly and carried the problem to a point when the conclusion was bound soon to be drawn. Indeed, they all but drew it themselves. Early the next year Dr. Lise Meitner and Dr. (now Professor) O. R. Frisch did it for them and quickly confirmed the conclusion by further experiment which showed directly that large amounts of energy would be released.

The implication of Hahn's discovery was passed on to Allied scientists who built the atomic bomb. Hahn himself detested the bomb. He was reluctant to allow an atomic weapon to be developed under Hitler. "If Hitler gets an atomic bomb" he is reported to have said, "I shall kill myself." Hitler's mind, fortunately, was by this time arrogantly closed against new and strange ideas. When the Postmaster-General tried to interest him in the idea, the Führer cut him short with "Here we all are wracking our brains how to win the war; and now the Postmaster-General of all people is going to tell us."

Hahn was in the forefront of movements to warn the world of the dangers of atomic weapons and pleaded for peaceful uses of the atom. In 1957, he signed a declaration by 18 leading German atomic physicists who said they would refuse to cooperate if asked to work on atomic arms.

Hahn, the son of a master glazier, was born at Frankfurt am Main on March 8, 1879. He studied at Marburg and Munich, initially intending to be an industrial chemist; gained his doctorate, on a problem in organic chemistry, working under the supervision of Professor T. Zincke, and in 1904, after a period as assistant to Professor Zincke, travelled to London to study under Sir William Ramsay at University College. Here he was introduced to the new field of radioactivity. Within a year he succeeded in identifying the new radioactive species, radiothorium. Ramsay was impressed by his ability and suggested he should extend his knowledge of this new field by joining Professor Ernest Rutherford in Montreal, where he was successful in identifying radioactinium.

On Hahn's return to Europe at the end of 1906, Professor Emil Fischer, then one of the most influential German chemists, supported his appointment to a post at the University of Berlin. It is interesting to note that Fischer himself only half believed the interpretation of the new discoveries in radioactivity. In Berlin Hahn became first professor extraordinarius and later, in 1912, professor at the Kaiser Wilhelm Institut für Chemie at Dahlem, where he remained until the latter part of the Second World War and where most of his important work was carried out. Hahn's outlook on nuclear science was always that of a chemist, but in 1907 he was joined by Lise Meitner, a physicist. Together they made a very successful partnership and they collaborated in their investigations for the next 30 years, as well as becoming close friends for the rest of their lives. In 1919 they completed the identification and characterization of the new radioactive element protactinium, and in 1921 their discovery of UZ led to the idea of nuclear isomerism.

In the years between the world wars, Hahn's researches laid the foundations of a new branch of chemistry called radiochemistry. Among the more important themes of research during this period may be mentioned the study of codeposition reactions, the development of the emanation method for the study of solids, the separation of radioactive decay products by mechanical recoil and several novel applications of radioactive tracers in physical chemistry.

Besides nearly a hundred papers recording these studies, Hahn summarized the results of his work in a book entitled Applied Radiochemistry which appeared in 1936. In 1928, he became director of the Kaiser Wilhelm Institut and in 1933 he spent a year at Cornell University, United States of America, where he was appointed George Fischer Baker visiting lecturer.

In 1935, he became interested in the effects on uranium and thorium of the recently discovered thermal neutrons. This study culminated in January, 1939, in his greatest achievement, the recognition of fission. In this work he was associated with his pupil Professor F. Strassmann. The importance of his work on fission was quickly acknowledged; indeed, seldom have the repercussions of a major scientific discovery been felt so quickly. In 1944, he was awarded the Nobel prize for Chemistry. Two years later, after the war had ended, he was appointed president of the newly established Max Planck Institute at Göttingen. He made Göttingen his home for the rest of his life, although he retired from the presidency in 1960. Two years later he published A Scientific Autobiography. In the post-war period, Hahn received many honorary degrees and other honours including foreign membership of the Royal Society; and in 1966, a share of the United States Atomic Energy Commission's Fermi award.

Hahn was an excellent teacher, so that his research school inspired a numerous progeny.

The Daily Telegraph
19th November 1962

PROF. NIELS BOHR

Prof. Niels Bohr, who died yesterday aged 77, was a Nobel Prize winner and one of the great pioneers of the atomic age. He was the first winner of the "Atoms for Peace" award in 1955, and was often described as the father of atomic physics.

Dr. Bohr was Professor in Theoretical Physics in the University of Copenhagen since 1916.

Prof. Bohr had many links with Britain. He studied at Cambridge and Manchester under J. J. Thomson and Rutherford, and developed Rutherford's theories on the structure of the atom.

His work, "On the Constitution of Atoms and Molecules," which appeared in 1913 had already won him a wide reputation as a brilliant theoretical physicist. In 1922 he was awarded the Nobel Physics Prize for "services in the investigation of the structure of atoms."

Sir John Cockcroft, president of the British Association, said at Cambridge last night: "His death is a very great loss to nuclear physics. He was the most distinguished of living physicists, and he was also a great personal friend."

WARTIME ESCAPE
Flight in bomb bay

OUR SCIENCE CORRESPONDENT writes: One of the most remarkable events of Bohr's life was his escape from Denmark during the war. From 1940 to 1943 the Germans had let him work on at his Copenhagen laboratory. He appreciated the theoretical possibility of a nuclear bomb, but he did not believe it was practical.

In 1943, when it was thought he was to be arrested, he escaped in a boat to Sweden. Then, fitted into the bomb bay of a Mosquito, he was flown to Scotland.

He was one of the first men to be involved with the political implication of the bomb. He proposed, for instance, to Sir Winston during the war that its secrets should be shared with Russia. But his suggestions were not well received.

The Times
12th February 1923

Röntgen Rays.

Few names occupying the highest honour in the world of science can be better known among the common mass of humanity which picks up its science, or such of it as it possesses, at second-hand, than that of the German physicist, WILHELM VON RÖNTGEN, whose death, at the age of seventy-eight, we announce to-day. Many physicists have made contributions to exact knowledge equal to or even greater than those of RÖNTGEN ; but it was RÖNTGEN'S fortune that his discovery of " X "-rays became a new and potent weapon in the healing art, and the foundation of a new era in physical science. In 1895 he found that the emanations from a Crookes vacuum tube, glowing under an electric current, had qualities more opposed to current views of matter than telegraphy or wireless telephony. The phosphorescence of what he called " X-rays," but what are now known by his own name, penetrated substances opaque to other forms of light. Flesh and skin became transparent and revealed the skeleton in the living human frame ; photographic shadow prints of coins could be taken through wooden boxes. Soon it was discovered that in the transparency of substances to the Röntgen rays there were degrees varying almost inversely in the order of their density, and there followed the applications of the rays to diagnosis in surgery and medicine. The nature of fractures, the position of foreign bodies, the effects of disease on internal organs could be ascertained without exploratory operation ; the surgeon's knife could be restrained or directed, and the physician's skill concentrated. But the new knowledge was not without its tragic side. If the exposure were prolonged and frequent, the rays were found to have a disastrous effect on human tissues. By the sufferings and heroism of many doctors, the conditions of danger were ascertained, and means of circumventing them were devised. It was found possible, moreover, to employ the destructive effect of the rays to the benefit of man by taking advantage of their selective action, with the result that some superficial lesions, such as rodent ulcers, can now be healed by their skilled application, and there is more than a hope that cancer itself in time may come to be subdued. The rays have also found a practical application in the detection of flaws in castings and machinery, and in many surprising ways. They have led, indeed, to undreamed advances in our knowledge of the fabric of the universe and of the intimate constitution of matter. No longer isolated phenomena, they have taken their place in an orderly series of disturbers, or disturbances, of the aether, ranging through electric rays, chemical rays, and visible light rays, up to the long rays of wireless telegraphy. By using them in spectroscopy, MOSELEY was able to arrange the elements in a new series depending on the structure of the atom. By them BRAGG has explained the structure of crystals and made it throw light on the structure of atoms. By them also RUTHERFORD has broken down the coherence of atoms, and has accomplished the modern miracle of the transmutation of the elements. RÖNTGEN'S discovery was one of the great crises in the history of science. It marked the attainment of a new peak, from the summit of which the ground already painfully traversed seemed flat and insignificant, and it revealed a new horizon resplendent with shining, but dangerous, mountains.

Manchester Guardian
12th April 1882

It is no exaggeration to say that there is no living scientific man whose death would cause so great a shock throughout the civilised world, or produce so widespread and profound a sense of personal loss, as will follow the announcement which we make in another column that Mr. DARWIN is no more. Of all the sciences there is none which has become so popular as that of which he was so lately the most eminent living professor, and it is not difficult to understand why this is so. Even CARLYLE felt its pleasant influences. " For " many years it has been one of my constant " regrets," he wrote twenty years ago to a friend at Edinburgh, " that no schoolmaster of mine " had a knowledge of natural history, so far " at least as to have taught me the grasses " that grow by the wayside and the little winged " and wingless neighbours that are continually " meeting me with a salutation which I cannot " answer." The study is associated with all the charms of grand and picturesque scenery, and it is pursued under the healthful stimulus of fresh air and novel surroundings. It has been the work of Mr. DARWIN to systematise this science; to give its various parts and innumerable phases a coherence which, while it awakens new interest in every detail, enables the mind more easily to grasp the whole. True Mr. DARWIN did not originate the great doctrine of descent with modification, any more than SHAKSPERE originated the story of HAMLET. He himself has done full justice to his predecessors and to his great contemporary WALLACE in the historical chapter prefixed to the " Origin of Species." But, after all, it was Mr. DARWIN who definitely lifted the idea from the region of mere conjecture, gave it form and substance, and impressed it upon the mind of the age as a working hypothesis. And it will not be merely the naturalists who will feel conscious of the magnitude of his work now that death has removed him from our midst. Rarely in the history of science has a hypothesis had so wide an influence or proved so fruitful in results. In Mr. DARWIN'S own special department, that of natural history, it has been the means of adding vast domains to our knowledge. We have only to remember the results of deep-sea dredging, the disclosure of the remarkable analogies between ancestral and embryonic forms, to cast our eyes over any modern manual of cryptogamic botany, to feel how influential it has been in opening up new lines of investigation and throwing light on previously unknown regions. Even those who have sought to modify Mr. DARWIN'S extreme conclusions have recognised the value of his fundamental conception by adopting his line of thought. The researches of RAY LANKESTER on degeneracy and of SEMPER on the influence of the environment, the latter emphatically opposed in many of their bearings to classification based on DARWIN'S theory of descent, rest on the principle of evolution. We see the fruitfulness of the same doctrine in archæological and geological science, and in astronomy we recognise its influence in the revival of the Kantian hypothesis of the origin of the universe. It is making medicine into a science; to those who are not content except with practical results we may point to the revolution it has effected in the study and treatment of zymotic disease. Nor has its influence ended here; in psychological, sociological, political, and even economic investigation its influence as a method has been equally apparent. It would be erroneous to assume that the value of Mr. DARWIN'S work depends upon whether the extreme and special conclusions which he drew from his original hypothesis are eventually substantiated or not. The vast body of new facts which have accrued through the application of his doctrine, and the higher wisdom developed from them, remain as a heritage for all time, whatever may have been the origin of man. But it is not merely as the practical author of a brilliant generalisation or the apostle of a fecund idea that Mr. DARWIN'S memory will be preserved. The example of scientific caution and accuracy which he set in an age when there is too great a tendency in scientific investigation to endeavour to make a sensation rather than to advance science is not the least of his services. Only lately in a letter to a German friend he told again how long he resisted the theory of descent until forced against his own predisposition, by the constant accumulation of facts, to definitely adopt it; and no one who has read his latest books on the movements of plants and on earthworms could fail to be impressed with the continued industry and carefulness of his late years. It is doubtless in consequence of a recognition of these high qualities in the man that the subsidence of the religious animosity which greeted the appearance of his great work must be attributed. Truth has nothing to fear from the truth, and theologians may well feel that so painstaking and conscientious a worker could not at bottom be inimical to anything they need value.

News Chronicle
28th February 1936

GRAND OLD MAN OF SCIENCE

HATED BOLSHEVISM BUT HONOURED BY SOVIET

PROFESSOR IVAN PETROVITCH PAVLOV, "grand old man of Russia," and perhaps the greatest of the world's physiologists, died yesterday in Leningrad at the age of 86—a victim of the influenza epidemic which is raging in Russia.

With the possible exception of Stalin, Pavlov was the best-known man in the Republic, where he was the object of a double pride.

Russians were proud of his scientific record and his worldwide reputation.

They were proud also of the fact that, despite his well-known critical attitude to the Bolshevik regime, he was not merely tolerated, but honoured and fêted by the heads of the State.

REFUSED TO CELEBRATE

When it was proposed in 1929 to celebrate officially his eightieth birthday, he emphasised his refusal to accept this by addressing to the authority concerned a letter in which he spoke of revolution as "the most deplorable event in history."

Nevertheless, he received a gift of £3,600.

Pavlov's earliest work was on the physiology of the circulation and the nerve supply of the blood vessels.

Latterly, he had conducted a series of experiments on dogs, and it was claimed that he had elaborated a technique by which he spared his subjects all pain.

Beginning with the fact that a dog's mouth will water when food is given it, he rang a bell every time the animal was fed.

MAKING THEIR MOUTHS WATER

After a time the dog so associated the food with the sound that its mouth would water whenever the bell was rung.

Further experiments showed that a dog could associate fine shades of colour with food, and, on seeing certain shades, its mouth would water without food.

Under the encouragement of the Soviet Government, the Pavlov Laboratory outside Leningrad has been developed into an institute of physiology and pathology for the investigation of higher nervous activity and he was appointed director.

IVAN PAVLOV

Manchester Guardian
19th April 1955

Einstein

Einstein is dead. To say that he was a genius is commonplace. To compare him with other great scientists is not a great help, for there are so few of the right stature. To assess the importance of his achievements is an impossible task, for only a meagre fifty years have passed since he burst like a volcano on the scientific world; the echoes of that revolution reverberate still. In science, in physics, there has never been anything quite like that year of 1905. It was a time of confusion. For twenty years people had been collecting evidence that the old classical scheme of things had to go. The world was not as simple as the great Victorian physicists, the Maxwells and the Rayleighs, said it was. For Thomson at Cambridge had made electrons; Lorentz in Holland had found it necessary to introduce into the theory of electricity assumptions that were quite unwarrantable then; and Planck, in Germany, had made a revolutionary postulate in his theory of the way in which heat was radiated from hot bodies that gave the right answer for no reason that was apparent. Yet the new generation of scientists was undismayed; it was a time of great adventure; but a time that needed a guiding hand, a unifying imagination. This was Einstein's task and achievement. His theory of relativity, for example, made Lorentz's assumptions intelligible in terms of much simpler ideas which carried their own conviction. But he did more than make sense out of confusion; he provided the tools, the instructions, and the ideas that have guided physicists ever since.

Einstein has often been analysed in one way or another—among scientists the occupation is as common as Shakespearean criticism is elsewhere. Some have sought the sources of his work in Jules Mach's famous book; others have searched his manuscripts for statements that appeared contradictory (and have found surprisingly few); still more have interpreted his work in different ways, making his theories suitable for one application or another. This will go on for many years. Yet he was more than a scientist; he was a humanitarian. His horror of war was born of the delight in human relationships that those who met him remember. This and his conviction that scientific discoveries could be used for the profit of all mankind were so strong that he overcame his distaste for public affairs and became an unofficial elder statesman. He was a pacifist and a Jew and got into trouble with the Kaiser and with Hitler. He was as frank in his condemnation of certain Russian restrictions on individual freedom as he was when the United States fell sadly short of its liberal traditions. He believed in the international control of atomic energy and continually urged the United States Administration and international bodies of scientists to work towards this end. (There is every reason to suppose that he could not have found a job with the Atomic Energy Commission!) Yet his statements on policy were not characterised by that pontifical smugness that often comes from laboratories. He was a reasonable man and could state his case in reasonable terms. No doubt this quality was as effective as his scientific work in making him so revered wherever science is done. There is a handful of scientists in England who have met him, and a few more who have worked alongside his pupils. Yet all workers everywhere in this vast field have benefited from the awareness that in Princeton there has been this great figure brooding over the progress of science and looking after its place in human affairs. When H. G. Wells died young people recognised that one of their prophets had gone. It will be the same for scientists now.

Glasgow Herald
20th October 1937

DEATH OF LORD RUTHERFORD

Pioneer in Modern Physics

PROBED SECRETS OF THE ATOM

Lord Rutherford, one of the world's foremost scientists, and Cavendish Professor of Experimental Physics and director of the Cavendish Laboratory at Cambridge University since 1919, died at a nursing home in Cambridge yesterday. He was aged 66.

A bulletin issued at 5 p.m yesterday stated that Lord Rutherford had passed a restful day, but that his condition still gave rise to great anxiety. He died a few hours later.

He went through a serious abdominal operation a few days ago, and the doctors we e to have operated again on Monday night, but decided that it would be too dangerous

Lord Rutherford sp nt his life toiling quietly and unobtrusively at experiments into radio-activity transmutation of the elements and the " splitting " of the atom.

NATIVE OF NEW ZEALAND

Ernest Rutherford was born at Nelson, New Zealand, in August, 1871, and educated at Nelson College and Canterbury College, Christchurch. After graduating M.A. B.Sc. at the University

Lord RUTHERFORD.

of New Zealand, he went with a scholarship to Trinity College, Cambridge In the Cavendish Laboratory there, under Sir J J Thomson, he began the career of research which has had such important results His early work was done in connection with the conduction of electricity through gases, and won him the B.A. research degree and the Coutts-Trotter Scholarship in 1897

Next year he was appointed Macdonald Professor of Physics at M'Gill University, Montreal It was there that he carried out, in conjunction with Soddy, the researches which established the nature of radio-active transformations.

BRILLIANT STUDENTS

Elected a Fellow of the Royal Society in 1903 he succeeded Sir A Schuster in 1907 as Langworthy Professor of Physics at Manchester University, attracting a number of brilliant students interested in the investigation of radio-activity These included Hans Geiger, Darwin Chadwick, and, most notable of all, the Dane, Niels Bohr. With the aid of these men this branch of science was rapidly developed

The production of helium and niton as the outcome of the disintegration of radium was shown spectroscopically Rutherford examined the spectrum of the emanation (niton), and counted the number of charged helium atoms (or Alpha particles) produced during the disintegration. The properties of numerous further radio-active products and the radiations produced in their formation were also examined.

Rutherford, to account for the scattering of the Alpha and Beta particles and the radio-active changes, postulated the existence of a nuclear atom consisting of a heavy, positively charged central part surrounded by an atmosphere of electrons (negative particles) rotating in orbits.

KEY TO ATOMIC PHYSICS

One of the most important achievements in his laboratory was the experimental demonstration of the nuclear nature of the atom and the electrical structure of matter. This was the key to what is named " atomic physics."

Rutherford having provided the model for the atom (which could not work according to accepted mechanical principles) Bohr discovered the mechanics by which it could work. Armed with the Rutherford-Bohr conception of the atom, physicists started a campaign for the investigation of matter, which continues with unabated success.

Rutherford was knighted in 1914, and in 1919 he succeeded Sir J. J. Thomson as Cavendish Professor of Experimental Physics at Cambridge and Professor of Natural Philosophy at the Royal Institution In May, 1930, he became chairman of the Advisory Council of the Department of Scientific and Industrial Research. He was raised to the peerage in January, 1931, as Lord Rutherford.

ORIGIN OF GAMMA RAYS

He and his associates were engaged in a detailed study of the atomic nucleus. For a number of years new knowledge was accumulated without any striking discovery.

But in December, 1931, he stated that a problem which had defied investigators for years had been solved—the question of the origin of the Gamma rays (high-frequency X-rays). They were found to arise from the Alpha particles in the nucleus of the atom and had nothing to do with the electron. This discovery had a fundamental effect on the theories of the constitution of the atom.

Then in 1932 came the announcement from his laboratory that Chadwick had discovered the neutron. A few weeks later Cockcroft and Walton announced the first disintegration of the atom by a machine of human construction, and after some months Blackett stated that he had definitely confirmed the discovery of the positive electron by Anderson of Pasadena.

In January, 1933, Lord Rutherford announced that by the method being used in his laboratory it was possible to project millions of particles at enormous speed on to the nucleus of an atom in order to change its composition. He was sure that in this way they could add largely to the knowledge of the possibility of changing one atom into another. The idea that enormous power could be derived from the disintegration of the atom he regarded as quite erroneous.

MANY HONOURS

Lord Rutherford received a great number of honorary degrees—including LL.D. from Glasgow and Edinburgh Universities—and other distinctions at home and abroad. These included the Rumford Medal of the Royal Society, the Barnard Medal, the Bressa prize of Turin, the Copley Medal, the Franklin Medal, and the Albert Medal of the Society of Arts. In 1908 he was awarded the Nobel Chemistry Prize, and in 1925 the Order of Merit. He was president of the British Association in 1923, and of the Royal Society in 1925. His writings include works on radioactivity etc., and numerous papers in the Royal Society's Transactions " and in other scientific journals. Lord Rutherford's energy was astonishing. Students who read the papers he published between 1896 and 1907 must have wondered how such a multitude of experiments could have been done in the time.

Lord Rutherford's work was recognised in a practical way in 1936 when Lord Austin made a donation of £250,000 in order to build a modern research laboratory at Cambridge and for the purchase of costly apparatus. In that year, too, Lord Rutherford became director of the Royal Society Mond Laboratory at Cambridge.

He was married in 1900 to Miss Mary G. Newton, of Christchurch, New Zealand. There is one child, a daughter, who was married in 1921 to Mr R. H. Fowler, a lecturer in mathematics at Trinity College, Cambridge.

San Francisco Chronicle
22nd November 1963

The 'Birdman of Alcatraz' Is Dead

Robert Stroud, who found strange and lonely fame as "The Birdman of Alcatraz," died in his sleep early yesterday at the U. S. Medical Center for Federal Prisoners at Springfield, Mo.

Stroud, who spent 54 of his 73 years in three Federal penitentiaries, succumbed to what Warden J. D. Harris described as the "infirmities of age."

Dr. Harris said the self-educated linguist, lawyer, mathematician, and internationally known authority on bird life was found dead in his cell bed at 5:45 a. m.

APPEAL

The stooped, hawk-nosed Stroud, in whom violence and tenderness were perpetually at war, never ceased his efforts to gain his freedom.

Last May he applied to the courts for parole, claiming he had successfully demonstrated that his years behind bars—43 of them in solitary confinement — had effected his complete rehabilitation. His plea, like the scores before it, was turned down.

And just two weeks ago he went into Federal Court in Springfield to obtain Government permission to publish his book "Penology and Rehabilitation." His complaint on the Bureau of Prison's handling of his million-word manuscript was pending before U. S. District Judge William Becker when he died.

SLAYING

Stroud's prison career dated back to 1909 when, at 19, he killed a bartender at Juneau, Alaska, in a wild brawl over a woman.

He was found guilty of manslaughter and sentenced to a 12-year term at McNeil Island. There he knifed a prisoner and was transferred to Leavenworth Penitentiary in 1912, where four years later, he killed a guard.

For this he was tried three times and sentenced to be hanged. On plea of his mother, Elizabeth, President Woodrow Wilson commuted the sentence to life imprisonment but Stroud was ordered isolated for the rest of his existence.

ACCIDENT

When Stroud entered prison, he had had only three years of schooling and could barely read and write. It was an accident that triggered his interest in birds and transformed an illiterate into an intellectual.

A nest of baby sparrows was blown into his small exercise yard during a storm. Stroud cradled the birds in his hands and carried them to his cell to revive them.

The Leavenworth warden, noticing Stroud's interest in the birds, presented him with a pair of canaries.

Then began a 20-year study of birds that won him international fame. First he bred canaries, selling them outside the prison walls and earning enough to support his mother. At a time when his bird business was at its peak, the canaries contracted a mysterious disease that could not be diagnosed.

STUDIES

Stroud soon discovered that the known facts about contagious diseases in birds were negligible, and began his own inquiry. He studied bacteriology. He built a microscope and devised a microtome that would cut tissue slices 1/12,000 of an inch thick.

For years his work was carried out in secret and without implements except those of his own invention. And at the same time he wrote a monumental and unique work, "Stroud's Digest of Bird Diseases," published in 1939. It was 500 pages in length and was hailed by scientific institutions, bird hospitals, breeders, and bird fanciers throughout the world.

In 1942, suddenly and inexplicably, Stroud was spirited into Alcatraz, island fortress for the Nation's most dangerous prisoners. What he left behind at Leavenworth were 22 live birds, 44 boxes of microscopic slides and half a ton of laboratory, office and bird equipment.

In the move to Alcatraz, Stroud lost the right to continue his bird studies. But in his solitary cell he mastered five languages and wrote a six-volume work on a history of the United States penal system.

He became known far beyond the world of bird fanciers in 1955 when Thomas E. Gaddis, now co-director of Reed College's graduate school of education, published Stroud's biography, called "The Birdman of Alcatraz."

The book became a motion picture starring Burt Lancaster who joined the hundreds of thousands of Americans and Europeans who vainly petitioned the Government for Stroud's parole.

His attorneys cried "cruel . . . unusual . . un-Constitutional punishment" throughout the years, but Stroud was profoundly unpopular with prison officialdom. He never was permitted to read the book written about him nor to see the movie based on it.

TRANSFER

In July of 1959, the then Alcatraz Warden Paul J. Madigan admitted that some weeks before Stroud had been transferred to the U.S. Medical Center at Springfield, known as the "country club" of Federal prisons.

Weary and sick, he worked in the institution's book binding shop until poor health halted even that. But he had a sunny private room and freedom to roam the grounds and general wards.

At no time during his more than half a century behind bars did Stroud claim he was innocent of the two homicides for which he was convicted, or that he had been wrongfully tried.

"But," he repeatedly told judge after judge, "I think I have successfully demonstrated that I have been rehabilitated."

PROBLEMS

Last February film star Lancaster went to the medical center to visit the man whom he had portrayed. Later the actor said Stroud discussed the problems that prevented his parole, among them the fact he was an admitted homosexual.

Lancaster quoted Stroud as saying: "Let's face it. I am 73 years old. Does that answer your question about whether I would be a dangerous homosexual?"

What has happened to the money Stroud received as royalties (40 per cent) from the book "Birdman of Alcatraz" and the 40 per cent of the $35,000 fee paid for the movie rights is not yet known. Much of it went into costly legal fees and court battles, but some of it is believed to be in a trust fund Stroud established for a brother, Al G. Marcus of Honolulu, and a sister, Mamie Stroud of Metropolis, Ind.

Stroud's body was taken to a mortuary in the nearby community of Ozark and prison officials said if it is not claimed, it will be buried in the prison's cemetery in Springfield.

Thomas Gaddis, Stroud's biographer, spoke the Birdman's epitaph in Portland.

"Stroud," he said, "has actually won his battle." His spirit triumphed over his cage. He will be remembered long after his captors are forgotten."

Social Activism

Charles Booth, reminding us of a whole nineteenth-century line, may be thought of as symbolising concerned reaction to the consequences for the individual of the motivating spirit of our society. **Elizabeth Fry** (and **Florence Nightingale**) are here as tributes to all those whose individual efforts to ameliorate the condition of society's outcasts lead eventually to the sort of institutional change which alone can prevent such conditions arising. Working in a quite different way, for her whole effort was from the beginning aimed at producing a change in consciousness, **Marie Stopes** has made unquantifiable differences to people's dealings with each other. Perhaps she is at least as much the forerunner of Women's Lib as **Emily Pankhurst**. **Albert Schweitzer**, (whose obituary appears elsewhere) by contrast, is the European genius (doctor, scientist, musician, theologian) who gave everything up to found a hospital in Lamberene, was until recently regarded as the very model of the enlightened activist, and is now under a shadow. The **Webbs** championed trade unionism, **Beveridge** founded the welfare state. **Abraham Lincoln** not only marked a turning point in the affairs of the world's most powerful nation to be, but is one of the very few politicians whose social conscience survived a term of office. **Billy Sunday** was the original "hell and fire" evangelist. Representing the moralist, perhaps the British moderate moralist *par excellence*, **Keir Hardie** is recorded here, having founded the Labour Party in response to what he saw as the necessary inadequacy of the piecemeal efforts of the individual reformer, but who built into the movement he founded just such a piecemeal approach. Finally, we have **Malcolm X**, the new leader who by example seeks to get people to change their own lives rather than improving their lives for them.

New York Times
7ᵗʰ November 1935

BILLY SUNDAY DIES; EVANGELIST WAS 71

Former Ball Player Induced Thousands to 'Hit Sawdust Trail' to Conversion.

WIFE TELLS OF HIS DEATH

End Came Quickly, as He Had Prayed It Would—Gave Last Sermon Oct. 27.

Special to THE NEW YORK TIMES.

CHICAGO, Nov. 6.—The Rev. William A. (Billy) Sunday, one of the most noted evangelists of the old "sawdust trail," died suddenly to-night of a heart attack in the home of his brother-in-law, William J. Thompson, a florist. He had been in poor health since February, 1933, but had remained moderately active until last night when he went to bed complaining of "queer pains."

The evangelist's wife, Mrs. Helen Sunday, was with him at the end.

"The pains he complained of were in his arms and elbows," she said. "We had a doctor for him and he told me what to do. Tonight I brought Billy his dinner, and even got him some special ice cream. He seemed all right. But suddenly at 8 o'clock he said: 'Oh, I feel so dizzy.' Then he died. I'm glad it came like that because Billy always used to pray: 'O Lord, when I have to go, please make it quickly.'"

Preached on Oct. 27.

She has not yet made any funeral arrangements, Mrs. Sunday said, but the services will probably be held in Chicago. She had tonight telephoned her two sons, William A., Jr., and Paul T., in Los Angeles. They made preparations to leave at once for Chicago by plane.

Mr. and Mrs. Sunday left their Summer camp at Winona Lake, Ind., a week ago yesterday to visit her brother here. On Oct. 27 Mr. Sunday preached his last sermon at a Methodist Church in Mishawaka, Ind. Mrs. Sunday said he still had his old fire then, and that between thirty and forty converts came up to the altar.

"My husband was stricken with a heart attack while preaching in Des Moines, Iowa, in February, 1933," said Mrs. Sunday tonight. "He was forced to rest for six months and has never been well since then, although he continued in the service of the Lord.

"Last May in Chattanooga, Tenn., he had another bad attack. After that he made only a few public appearances."

Ball Player at Early Age.

Measured in terms of claimed converts and net profits the Rev. Dr. William Ashley Sunday, who preferred to be known plainly as Billy Sunday, was the greatest high-pressure and mass-conversion Christian evangel that America, or the world, has known.

The simple chronology of his life, in the statement of dates, does not begin to tell his story, but it does plot the course he followed. He was born in Ames, Iowa, on Nov. 19, 1863, the son of William and Mary Jane Cory. Several months before his birth, his father marched away to the Civil War and did not return.

As a youngster he was fleet of foot, lithe of carriage, capable of orderly coordination of ligaments and muscles, and these things made him what sportsmen call a natural athlete. Therefore he played baseball, and played it well. He began in the Soldiers' Orphans' Home, where he and his brother Edward spent part of their boyhood, at Glenwood, Iowa. He continued playing through his high school days in Nevada, Iowa. For a time he was a student at Northwestern University.

In 1882 he was playing what was probably semi-professional baseball with a team of Marshalltown, Iowa, when Adrian Anson, more widely known as Pop, signed him on for the Chicago White Sox of the National League. In his time he was the fastest baserunner in the circuit and an excellent outfielder.

He was still playing ball when, in 1886, he dropped into a Salvation Army meeting in Chicago and experienced conversion. He continued as a ball player as a member of the Pittsburgh and Philadelphia National League teams until the end of the season of 1890, when he became an assistant Y. M. C. A. secretary in Chicago.

His job in those days consisted largely of organizing Sunday schools, staging meetings in the Y. M. C. A. and, for about three years, serving in the vanguard of the evangelistic organization of the late Rev. Dr. J. Wilbur Chapman.

In 1896 he was invited to conduct a revival by the people of Garner, Iowa, a little hamlet of about 1,000 souls spread out around the spot where the Milwaukee Railroad crossed the Rock Island. It was his first solo flight and its success led to others.

Even in those days Billy Sunday was not precisely an untried and lay fledgling edging into his own power. Of course, he was a fledgling, but he had taken the customary course in the only school of revivalism that the nation boasted. He was directly descended in the theocratic dynasty founded by Dwight Lyman Moody.

Moody began in the early years after the Civil War. His principal contribution to the technique of revivalism was the development of the large choir through Ira David Sankey, the singing member of the famous team of Moody and Sankey.

Now, even though Moody was the "straight Gospeler," his revivals began to demand organization. Among his corps of workers was the Rev. Dr. B. Fay Mills and Dr. Chapman. The latter, incidentally, gave up the pastorate of John Wanamaker's Bethany Presbyterian Church in Philadelphia to join the Moody organization.

After Moody died, Mills climbed to the fore. It was Mills who developed the technique along mass-production lines, with advance agents, capable press agents, financial guarantees from the cities in which he appeared, and the rest. Dr. Chapman continued on his staff.

Then Dr. Chapman branched out on his own. He was, like Moody, Reuben Archer Torrey and Mills before him, notably successful. So it was under Dr. Chapman that Billy Sunday first enlisted in the militant service of the Lord.

Sunday Forms a Team.

It was in 1896 that Dr. Chapman returned to his Philadelphia pastorate and Billy Sunday formed his own team. His beginning was modest, and his organization then consisted of only himself. It was not until two years later, in Oneida, Ill., that he took on a singer. His first tent (Moody had been the first to have tabernacles built in preparation for his appearance, but in the small towns this was impossible, and even a tent was fairly handsome) differing from the tent of a small circus only in that pews replaced the familiar three rings, was pitched in Hawkeye, Iowa.

Billy Sunday was not long, however, in seeing the advantages of a tabernacle. This belief was made a certainty for him in 1900 when his tent pitched in Salida, Col., succumbed to a gale and all but smothered several hundred of the faithful.

In 1898 he had married Miss Helen Thompson, whom he met in Chicago. In later years she became Ma Sunday, the astute business manager of the organization.

Turning, however, to tabernacles, Billy Sunday persuaded the church people of Perry, Iowa, a town of 3,000 to build him a tabernacle which would hold one-third of its population. He was beginning to come into his power, now, and in three weeks the people of Perry piled up a free-will offering of $550.

In 1903 Dr. Chapman preached the sermon at the ceremony in Chicago by which the Chicago Presbytery ordained Billy Sunday a minister. On June 13, 1912, Dr. R. M. Russell, president of Westminster College at New Wilmington, Pa., conferred upon Sunday the honorary degree of Doctor of Divinity.

In the intervening years he had climbed from an obscure evangelist to a figure of national prominence. He had formed an alliance with Homer Rodeheaver, whom he called Rody, whereby the latter managed the choir and led the singing, and the record of his claimed conversions was stretching to unbelievable lengths.

Even so, he was not even then at the height of his climb. Somewhere during the period Billy Sunday had been transformed from the revivalist of dignity carrying on the dignified tradition of Moody, to the acrobatic dervish of evangelism.

A Typical Sunday Revival.

What was a typical Sunday revival like?

Perhaps the best illustration was that which began on April 1, 1917, in New York City. Beginning as early as 1915, when he was staging a revival in Philadelphia, a group of pastors in New York began making overtures to Billy Sunday to come here. He assured them that he would not think of it until all of the Protestant churches lined up behind the revival.

In lieu of complete unanimity among the pastors, the name and influence of John D. Rockefeller Jr. were enlisted. Mr. Rockefeller actively pushed the plan and it began taking shape. A fund was set up and incorporated under the name of the William A. Sunday Evangelistic Association, Inc. Subscriptions were being taken as far as three months before the revival.

Then there was an influx of advance agents. Throughout the city "revival prayer meetings" were held. It was estimated that 20,000 of these were held before the opening night. As the money came in, a tabernacle was set up on the plot where the Presbyterian Hospital Medical Centre now stands.

The task of recruiting a choir and a staff of ushers was begun long in advance. The estimated, and later actual, cost of the whole undertaking came to a round $350,-000. The sum had to be spent or contracted for before the first meeting was held. The tabernacle, a low, rambling structure of brick and wood, was capable of seating 20,000. Behind the platform from which Billy Sunday was to preach rose the seats of the choir.

The opening night. Homer Rod-

heaver, short, stout, dark, persuasive, out in front. The choir begins on "Stand Up for Jesus," the hymn of pseudo-martial spirit which George Duffield had written for the revivals of 1857. This is followed with "Brighten the Corner Where You Are," the tune of which might best be described as pre-syncopation jazz. One, perhaps two more hymns with Rody leading both choir and audience. Then an introduction or two, and Billy Sunday walks simply and straightforwardly into his bout with the devil.

The simplicity, however, was but an opening gesture. The evangel, in height about 5 feet 8 inches, weighing about 145 pounds, and kept at the peak of athletic condition by a physical trainer who forms part of his retinue, gets down to business. His dark, seamed and square face is wreathed in a winning smile. His first routine step is to make his audience laugh with him.

Dances Like Shadow Boxer.

He begins to dance like a shadow boxer. He slaps his hands together with a report like a broken electric lamp. He poses on one foot like a fast ball pitcher winding up. He jumps upon a chair. In the stress of his routine he may stand with one foot in the chair and another on the lectern. All the while he is flaying the "whisky kings," the German war lords, slackers, suffragettes or the local ministry. And, if his story of the sinner come home to salvation fits the gesture, he may emphasize the moral by throwing himself on the floor with an outstretched arm groping for the home plate like a baserunner sliding safely in with a stolen run.

Naturally, it is not pantomime. All the while he is telling a story. It is perhaps, as a typical example, the story of the country boy who went to a "fancy dress ball—I ought to call it a fancy undress ball."

There he was approached by a Jezebel with "hair like a raven's wing, a neck like a swan, teeth like a ledge of pearl in a snowdrift, wearing just enough clothing to pad a crutch, who, with difficulty, persuaded the young man to take his first glass of champagne."

So the night wears on. Midnight, one o'clock, two A. M. and travelers see an agitated young man, "wearing a linen duster over his clothes, walking up and down the station platform, taking a drink every once in a while from a pint flask and moaning. 'What will mother say? My God, what will mother say?'

"Four months later he died of delirium tremens and before he died he attacked his feeble and dear old mother and broke a chair over his father's head, and it took four strong men to hold him down on his deathbed."

"Sawdust Trail" the Climax.

Sunday's exhortations usually lasted about an hour. At the climax, the willing and the indifferent hit the "sawdust trail" together. The willing came with the merest prompting, fluttering in emotional states of tears or joy, to shake the hands of the evangelist and to sign the convert's card. The indifferent were usually locked in the arms of one or more herders, experts who discharged their duties in the task of swelling the ranks of those who came forward, whether they signed up or not.

And, all the while, the choir rendered, over and over, a hymn such as:

Just as I am, without one plea,
But that Thy blood was shed for me,
And that Thou bid'st me come to Thee,
O Lamb of God, I come, I come——

which dragged out in its slow, dirge-like tune with tremendous effect.

The figures on the Billy Sunday revivals are almost staggering. In 1916, before the revivals of that year in Boston and Buffalo, and before the appearance in New York, The Baptist Watchman-Examiner prepared the following table of results.

City.	Converts.	Thank Offering
Philadelphia	41,724	$51,136
Baltimore	25,797	46,000
Pittsburgh	25,979	45,000
Trenton	16,810	32,358
Syracuse	21,155	23,255
Scranton	16,999	22,398
Wilkes-Barre	16,594	22,185
Columbus, Ohio	18,137	20,939
Omaha	13,022	19,000
Paterson	14,255	14,388
Wheeling	8,300	17,450
Toledo	7,686	15,423
Johnstown	11,829	14,000
McKeesport	10,023	13,438
Des Moines	10,200	13,000
East Liverpool	6,354	12,554
Canton, Ohio	5,640	12,500
Springfield	5,312	11,567
Erie	5,312	11,356
South Bend	6,398	11,200
Wichita	6,209	10,111
Denver	8,100	10,000
Kansas City	20,646	32,000

Claimed 68,000 Converts Here.

The figures in Boston late in 1916 were 40,000 converts and $51,000 free-will offering; in Buffalo, 34,-709 converts and $42,204 offering. In New York Billy Sunday claimed 68,000 converts. The offering in New York, figures for which are not of record, was given to the Red Cross. The totals, however, for the few years included in the table are 464,978 converts and $539,670 in cash and gifts which were for the evangelist.

When the Federal Council of Churches and others, in the aftermath of the New York revival, which was the peak in the career of the evangelist, pointed out that of the 63,000 only about 200 had been found to be permanent converts, Billy Sunday replied with a candor that he had never before approached and never since equaled:

"I never yet have been satisfied with the results of any campaign I have ever conducted. No business

house does as much business as it would like to."

The appearance in New York of the evangelist marked the end of his rise. Since then he had continued to conduct revivals with considerable success, but the cities in which they were conducted continuously diminished in size. And, although a wave of revivalism has swept the country on the heels of every economic depression in its

history, there has not yet been any indication of an evangelist to even approach the records set by the old-time ball player of Winona Lake, Ind.

Preached Here Last Year.

After an almost complete absence from New York of sixteen years, Billy Sunday returned here in January, 1934, for four weeks of "real preaching," divided equally between the Calvary Baptist Church, 123 West Fifty-seventh Street, and the Cornell Memorial Methodist Church, 231 West Seventy-sixth Street.

In his first sermon he declared: "I have got just as much ginger and tabasco sauce for God as ever," and he showed his old command of picturesque epigram.

A newspaper interviewer described him at the time as "mellowed by personal tragedy but undefeated, with the same old ripsnorting challenge to the devil in his clear blue eyes." But signs of waning vigor began to appear. In August, 1933, he announced:

"I can't continue to preach prohibition and preach the gospel. I'm not as young as I used to be and the load is too heavy. So I'm returning to my first love—preaching the gospel."

A member of his audience in Kansas City last June wrote that his eyes still flashed but that his voice was strangely softened.

In an interview last May in Rochester, Minn., he expressed his disapproval of the New Deal, saying that "Washington brainstorms cause more trouble than dust storms in the West."

As recently as January, 1934, Mr. Sunday believed that repeal would not endure.

"Prohibition will be back and back to stay," he said. "I hope I'll be here to see it within a decade. I don't give a hoot for these synthetic saloon bars. No, I haven't had a drink. Let 'em have the old rail to put their feet on if they've got the booze. If a girl brings me a drink it's just as bad as if I stand up and talk to the bartender. I can get just as drunk in one of those dumps they call restaurants here today."

Last year he was asked for his All Time Baseball team, and after considerable figuring produced this line-up:

First base, Hal Chase or Lou Gehrig; second base, Tony Lazzeri; third base, —; shortstop, Hans Wagner; pitchers, Christy Mathewson, John Clarkson, Rube Waddell; catcher, Buck Ewing; outfielders, Babe Ruth, Ty Cobb, Tris Speaker; extra, Chuck Klein.

He said he couldn't think of a third baseman. When his wife said he ought to put himself down for the outfield he replied:

"No. I was a good base runner. I could circle the bases in fourteen seconds, touching each bag, and from a standing start. No one ever beat that. But there were better hitters. One year with the White Stockings I had an average of .356, and I was only fourteenth in the National League when Cap Anson led it with an average of .420."

The Guardian,
18th March 1963

The Times
15th August 1910

Ld. BEVERIDGE

Welfare State pioneer

LORD BEVERIDGE, who has died aged 84, provided by means of his wartime Report on Social Security, the basis of what he preferred to call the Welfare Society, rather than the Welfare State.

The present system of comprehensive insurance grew out of the Report, which was instituted by Sir Winston Churchill's Coalition Government in 1941.

He later presided over committees which investigated unemployment, broadcasting and the work of voluntary social services.

Born in Bengal, the son of an Indian civil servant, William Henry Beveridge was educated at Charterhouse and at Balliol. From 1903-05 he was Sub-Warden of Toynbee Hall.

LEADING ARTICLES
Churchill attention won

He became a casual leader-writer on the *Morning Post*, specialising in social problems, and attracted the attention of Sir Winston Churchill, then President of the Board of Trade.

Sir Winston later made him the first chairman of the Employment Exchanges Committee, an appointment which was to have a profound effect on the rest of his career.

He remained at the Board of Trade until 1916, when he moved to the Ministry of Munitions. He also worked at the Ministry of Food, and was created a K.C.B. in 1919.

Director of the London School of Economics, and a senator of London University from 1919-37, he was chairman of the Unemployment Insurance Statutory Committee from 1934-44.

HEAD OF COLLEGE
"Beveridge plan"

He was also Master of University College, Oxford, 1937-45.

The "Beveridge Plan," as it was first known, developed from his chairmanship in 1941-42 of the committee on Social Insurance and Allied Services.

His only experience of Parliament was as Liberal M.P. for Berwick-on-Tweed from 1944-45.

A prolific writer for nearly 50 years, he wrote, among many books, "Unemployment: A Problem of Industry," "Insurance for All," "Planning Under Socialism" and "Full Employment in a Free Society."

He was created a baron in 1946. From 1947 until 1953 he was chairman of the Development Corporation of Aycliffe, Co. Durham.

DEATH OF MISS NIGHTINGALE.

We deeply regret to state that Miss Florence Nightingale, O.M., the organizer of the Crimean War Nursing Service, died at her residence, 10, South-street, Park-lane, on Saturday afternoon.

MEMOIR.

In Miss Florence Nightingale there has passed away one of the heroines of British history. The news of her death will be received to-day with feelings of profound regret throughout not merely the land of her birth, but in all lands where her name has been spoken among men.

THE CRIMEAN WAR.

On September 20, 1854, the battle of Alma was fought, and it is not too much to say that the accounts published in the columns of *The Times* from our Correspondent, the late Dr. (afterwards Sir William Howard) Russell as to the condition of the sick and wounded sent a feeling of horror throughout the length and breadth of the land. There is no necessity to dwell here in detail on the harrowing stories he related. Suffice it to say that he showed how the commonest accessories of a hospital were wanting; how the sick appeared to be tended by the sick, and the dying by the dying; how, indeed, the manner in which the sick and wounded were being treated was "worthy only of the savages of Dahomey"; and how, while our own medical system was "shamefully bad," that of the French was exceedingly good, and was, too, rendered still more efficient because of the sisters of charity who had followed the French troops in incredible numbers.

On October 12, 1854, a leading article appeared in *The Times* in which it was pointed out that while "we are sitting by our firesides devouring the morning paper in luxurious solitude . . . these poor fellows are going through innumerable hardships"; and the article went on to suggest that the British public should subscribe to send them "a few creature comforts." On the following day we published an extremely sympathetic letter from Sir Robert Peel, starting a fund with a cheque for £200, and so generally and so liberally was his example followed that £781 was received by us within two days, £7,000 within seven days, and £11,614 by the end of the month, when the fund was closed. But, in the meantime, the terrible cry from the East had met with a response which was of even more effectual service to the suffering soldiers than the thousands of pounds thus promptly and generously contributed. On October 15, Miss Nightingale wrote to Mr. Sidney (afterwards Lord) Herbert, Secretary at War, offering to go to Scutari, and, as it happened, her own letter was crossed by one to herself from Mr. Sidney Herbert. Medical stores, he said, had been sent out by the ton weight, but the deficiency of female nurses was undoubted. Lady Maria Forrester had proposed to go with or to send out trained nurses, "but there is," Mr. Herbert went on to say, "only one person in England that I know of who would be capable of organizing and superintending such a scheme. . . . A number of sentimental and enthusiastic ladies turned loose in the hospital at Scutari would probably, after a few days, be *mises à la porte* by those whose business they would interrupt and whose authority they would dispute. My question simply is, Would you listen to the request to go out and supervise the whole thing?"

Miss Nightingale, as we have seen, had already answered this question, and preparations could thus be set on foot without a moment's delay. But, as showing how little she was known to fame at that time, we may mention as a curious fact that in *The Times* of October 19, 1854, there appeared the announcement—"We are authorized to state that Mrs. (*sic*) Nightingale" had undertaken to organize a staff of female nurses, who would proceed with her to Scutari at the cost of the Government. Not, indeed, until several days had elapsed does it seem to have been realized that "Mrs." Nightingale was really "Miss" Nightingale, and even then the *Examiner* found it necessary to publish an article, headed "Who is Miss Nightingale?" setting forth who she really was, and bearing eloquent testimony to her accomplishments, her experience, and the nobility of her character.

Within a week Miss Nightingale had selected from hundreds of offers received from all parts of the country, a staff of 38 nurses, including 14 Anglican sisters, ten Roman Catholic sisters of mercy, and three nurses selected by Lady Maria Forrester. It may be interesting to recall that among the ladies forming the gallant little band was Miss Erskine, eldest daughter of the Dowager Lady Erskine, of Pwll-y-crochan, North Wales. Miss Nightingale and her nurses left London on October 21, passing through Boulogne on October 23 on their way to Marseilles; and a letter which appeared in *The Times* some days afterwards, written by a correspondent who had been staying at Boulogne, related how the arrival of the party there caused so much enthusiasm that the sturdy fisherwomen seized their bags and carried them to the hotel, refusing to accept the slightest gratuity; how the landlord of the hotel gave them dinner, and told them to order what they liked, adding that they would not be allowed to pay for anything; and how waiters and chambermaids were equally firm in refusing any acknowledgment for the attentions they pressed upon them.

ARRIVAL AT THE FRONT.

From Marseilles the party proceeded to Constantinople, where they arrived on November 4, the eve of the battle of Inkerman. They found there were two hospitals at Scutari, of which one, the Barrack Hospital, already contained 1,500 sick and wounded, and the other, the General Hospital, 800, making a total of 2,300; but on the 5th of November there arrived 800 more who had been wounded in the course of that day's fighting, so that there were close on 3,000 sufferers claiming the immediate attention of Miss Nightingale and her companions. In the best of circumstances the task which the nurses thus found before them would have been enormous; but the circumstances themselves were as bad as the imagination can conceive, if, indeed, imagination, unaided by fact, could call up so appalling a picture. Neglect, mismanagement, and disease had "united to render the scene one of unparalleled hideousness." The wounded, lying on beds placed on the pavement itself, were bereft of all comforts; there was a scarcity alike of food and medical aid; fever and cholera were rampant, and even those who were only comparatively slightly wounded, and should have recovered with proper treatment, were dying from sheer exhaustion brought about by lack of the nourishment they required.

Miss Nightingale, as "Lady-in-Chief," at once set to work to restore something like order out of the chaos that prevailed. Within ten days of her arrival she had had an impromptu kitchen fitted up, capable of supplying 800 men every day with well-cooked food, and a house near to the Barrack Hospital was converted into a laundry, which was also sorely needed. In all this work she was most cordially supported by Mr. MacDonald, the almoner of *The Times* Fund, the resources of which were, of course, freely placed at her disposal. But in other directions Miss Nightingale had serious difficulties to encounter. The official routine which had sat as a curse over the whole condition of things continued as active, or, rather, as inefficient, as ever. Miss Nightingale was at first scarcely tolerated by those who should have co-operated with her. She had, at times, the greatest possible difficulty in obtaining sufficient Government stores for the sick and wounded; for though, as Mr. Sidney Herbert had written, medical stores had been sent out by the ton weight, they were mostly rotting at Varna instead of having been forwarded to Scutari. On one occasion, when she was especially in need of some that had arrived, but were not to be given out until they had been officially "inspected," she took upon herself to have the doors opened by force and to remove what her patients needed.

But her zeal, her devotion, and her perseverance would yield to no rebuff and to no difficulty. She went steadily and unwearyingly about her work with a judgment, a self-sacrifice, a courage, a tender sympathy, and withal a quiet and unostentatious demeanour that won the hearts of all who were not prevented by official prejudices from appreciating the nobility of her work and character. One poor fellow wrote home :— " She would speak to one and nod and smile to a many more ; but she could not do it to all, you know. We lay there by hundreds ; but we could kiss her shadow as it fell, and lay our heads on the pillow again, content." Mr. MacDonald, too, wrote in February, 1855 :—

Wherever there is disease in its most dangerous form and the hand of the despoiler distressingly nigh, there is that incomparable woman sure to be seen. Her benignant presence is an influence for good comfort even amid the struggles of expiring nature. She is a " ministering angel " without any exaggeration in these hospitals, and as her slender form glides quietly along each corridor, every poor fellow's face softens with gratitude at the sight of her. When all the medical officers have retired for the night and silence and darkness have settled down upon those miles of prostrate sick, she may be observed alone, with a little lamp in her hand, making her solitary rounds. The popular instinct was not mistaken which, when she set out from England on her mission of mercy, hailed her as a heroine. I trust she may not earn her title to a still higher though sadder appellation. No one who has observed her fragile figure and delicate health can avoid misgivings lest these should fail. With the heart of a true woman, and the manners of a lady, accomplished and refined beyond most of her sex, she combines a surprising calmness of judgment and promptitude and decision of character.

It was also written of her :—

She has frequently been known to stand 20 hours on the arrival of fresh detachments of sick, apportioning quarters, distributing stores, directing the labours of her corps, assisting at the painful operations where her presence might soothe or support, and spending hours over men dying of cholera or fever. Indeed, the more awful to every sense any particular case might be the more certainly might be seen her slight form bending over him, administering to his ease by every means in her power, and seldom quitting his side till death released him.

CRITICISM AT HOME.

Meanwhile the reports which Miss Nightingale made both to Lord Raglan, the Commander-in-Chief, and to the War Minister at home were of invaluable service in enabling them to put their finger on the weak spots of the administration. On the other hand, it is painful to recall the fact that while, in all these various ways, Miss Nightingale was doing such admirable work in the East, sectarian prejudices at home had led to unscrupulous attacks being made alike on her religious views and on her motives in going out.

" It is melancholy to think," as Mrs. Herbert wrote to a lady correspondent, " that in Christian England no one can undertake anything without these most uncharitable and sectarian attacks. . . . Miss Nightingale is a member of the Established Church of England, and what is called rather Low Church ; but ever since she went to Scutari her religious opinions and character have been assailed on all points. It is a cruel return to make towards one to whom all England owes so much." Happily a check was put to this campaign of slander and uncharitableness by a letter written by Queen Victoria from Windsor Castle, dated December 6, 1854, to Mr. Sidney Herbert, asking that accounts received from Miss Nightingale as to the condition of the wounded should be forwarded to her, and saying :—

" I wish Miss Nightingale and the ladies would tell these poor noble wounded and sick men that no one takes a warmer interest, or feels more for their sufferings, or admires their courage and heroism more, than their Queen. Day and night she thinks of her beloved troops. So does the Prince. Beg Mrs. Herbert to communicate these my words to those ladies, as I know that our sympathy is much valued by these noble fellows."

The eminently tactful indication conveyed in this letter of her Majesty's complete confidence in Florence Nightingale did much not only towards silencing the ungenerous critics at home, but also towards strengthening the position of the Lady-in-Chief in meeting the difficulties due to excessive officialism in the East.

GROWTH OF THE WORK.

In January, 1855, Miss Nightingale's totally inadequate staff was increased by the arrival of Miss Stanley with 50 more nurses ; and how greatly they were needed is shown by the fact that there were then 5,000 sick and wounded in the various hospitals on the Bosporus and the Dardanelles, 1,000 more being on their way down. By February there was a great increase of fever, which in the course of three or four weeks swept away seven surgeons, while eight more were ill, twenty-one wards in the Barrack Hospital being in charge of a single medical attendant. Two of the nurses also died from fever. Miss Nightingale told subsequently how for the first seven months of her stay in the Crimea the mortality was at the rate of 60 per cent. per annum from disease alone, a rate in excess, she added, of that which prevailed among the population of London during the Great Plague. By May, however, the position of affairs had so far improved at Scutari, thanks mainly to the untiring energies and devotion of Miss Nightingale, that she was able to proceed to Balaclava to inspect the hospitals there. Her work at Balaclava was interrupted by an attack of Crimea fever, and she was afterwards urged to return home ; but she would go no further than Scutari, remaining there until her health had been re-established. Thereupon she again left for the Crimea, where she established a staff of nurses at some new camp hospitals put up on the heights above Balaclava, and took over the superintendence of the nursing department, herself living in a hut not far away. She also interested herself in organizing reading and recreation huts for the army of occupation, securing books and periodicals from sympathizers at home. Among the donors were Queen Victoria and the Duchess of Kent. Another institution she set up was a café at Inkerman, as a counter-attraction to the ordinary canteens. Then she started classes, supported the lectures and school-rooms which had been established by officers or chaplains, and encouraged the men to write home to their families. Already at Scutari she had opened a money-order office of her own, through which the soldiers could send home their pay. She thus set an example which the Government followed by establishing official money-order offices at Scutari, Balaclava, Constantinople, and elsewhere. Some £70,000 passed through these offices in the first six months of 1856.

Continued

THE END OF THE WAR.

Florence Nightingale remained in the Crimea until the final evacuation in July, 1856, her last act before leaving being the erection of a memorial to the fallen soldiers on a mountain peak above Balaclava. The memorial consisted of a marble cross 20ft. high, bearing the inscription, in English and Russian—

LORD, HAVE MERCY UPON US.
GOSPODI POMILORI NASS.

Calling at Scutari on her way home, Miss Nightingale left that place in a French vessel for Marseilles, declining the offer made by the British Government of a passage in a man-of-war, and reached Lea Hurst on August 8, 1856, having succeeded in avoiding any demonstration on the way.

Before returning to England Florence Nightingale had received from Queen Victoria an autograph letter with a beautiful jewel, designed by Prince Albert; the Sultan had sent her a diamond bracelet; and a fund for a national commemoration of her services had been started, the income from the proceeds, £45,400, being eventually devoted partly to the setting up at St. Thomas's Hospital of a training school for hospital and infirmary nurses and partly to the maintenance and instruction at King's College Hospital of midwifery nurses. For herself she would have neither public testimonial nor public welcome. She was honoured by an invitation to visit the Queen and Prince Consort at Balmoral in September, and addresses and gifts from working men and others were sent or presented privately to her. But though her fame was on every one's lips, and her name has ever since been a household word among the peoples of the world, her life from the time of her return home was little better than that of a recluse and confirmed invalid. Her health, never robust, broke down under the strain of her arduous labours, and she spent most of her time on a couch, while in the closing years of her life she was entirely confined to bed.

LATER REFORMS.

But, though her physical powers failed her, there was no falling off either in her mental strength or in her intense devotion to the cause of humanity. She was still the "Lady-in-Chief" in the organization of the various phases of nursing which, thanks to the example she had set, and the new spirit with which she had imbued the civilized world, now began to establish themselves; she was the general adviser on nursing organization not only of our own but of foreign Governments, and was consulted by British Ministers and generals at the outbreak of each one of our wars, great or small; she expounded important schemes of sanitary and other reforms, though compelled to leave others to carry them out, while at all times her experience and practical advice were at the command of those who needed them.

Almost the entire range of nursing seems to have been embraced by that revolution therein which Florence Nightingale was the chief means of bringing about. Following up the personal services she had already rendered in the East in regard to Army nursing, she prepared, at the request of the War Office, an exhaustive and confidential report on the working of the Army Medical Department in the Crimea as the precursor to complete reorganization at home; she was the means of inspiring more humane and more efficient treatment of the wounded both in the American Civil War and the Franco-German War; and it was the stirring record of her deeds that led to the founding of the Red Cross Society, now established in every civilized land. By the Indian Government also she was almost ceaselessly consulted on questions affecting the health of the Indian Army. On the outbreak of the Indian Mutiny she even offered to go out and organize a nursing staff for the troops in India. The state of her health did not warrant the acceptance of this offer; but no one can doubt that, if campaigns are fought under more humane conditions to-day as regards the care of wounded soldiers, the result is very largely due to the example and also to the counsels of Florence Nightingale.

But advance no less striking is to be found in other branches of the nursing art as well. In regard to general hospitals, the pronounced success of the nursing school established at St. Thomas's as the outcome of the Nightingale Fund led to the opening of similar schools elsewhere, so that to-day hospital nursing in general occupies a far higher position in the land than it has ever done before, while this, in turn, advanced the whole range of private nursing in the country. Then, again, the system of district nursing, which is now in operation in almost every large centre of population, has had an enormous influence alike in bringing skilled nurses within the reach of sufferers outside the hospitals, and of still further raising the *status* of nursing as a profession. "Missionary nurses," Florence Nightingale once wrote, "are the end and aim of all our work. Hospitals are, after all, but an intermediate stage of civilization. While devoting my life to hospital work, to this conclusion have I always come—viz., that hospitals were not the best place for the sick poor except for severe surgical cases."

DISTRICT NURSES.

District nursing was really set on foot in this country by the late Mr. William Rathbone, who, in compliance with the dying request of his first wife, started a single nurse in Liverpool in 1859 as an experiment. The demand for district nurses soon became so great that more were clearly necessary, and Miss Nightingale was consulted as to what should be done. She replied that all the nurses then in training at St. Thomas's were wanted for hospital work, and she recommended that a training school for nurses should be started in Liverpool. The suggestion was adopted, and in November, 1861, on being consulted about the plans, she wrote to the chairman of the training school committee :—

God bless you and be with you in the effort, for it is one which meets one of our greatest national wants. Nearly every nation is before England in this matter—viz., in providing for nursing the sick at home ; and one of the chief uses of a hospital (though almost entirely neglected up to the present time) is this—to train nurses for nursing the sick at home.

By about 1865 there was a trained nurse at work among the poor in each of the 18 districts into which Liverpool had been divided for the purposes of the scheme. The example of Liverpool was speedily followed by Manchester, where a district nursing association was formed in 1864 : the East London Nursing Society was established in 1868, and the Metropolitan and National Association followed in 1874. In the organization of the last-mentioned society Florence Nightingale took the deepest

interest, sending to *The Times* a long letter, in which she expressed her gratification at the idea of the nurses having a central home, set forth in considerable detail the nature and importance of the duties the district nurses were called upon to perform, and appealed strongly and successfully for donations towards the cost of a home. After these pioneer societies had been successfully started many others followed ; but the greatest development of all was afforded by Queen Victoria's Jubilee Institute for Nurses, the operations of which have been of the highest importance in spreading the movement throughout the United Kingdom. When, in December, 1896, a meeting was held at Grosvenor House for the purpose of organizing a Commemoration Fund in support of the Institute, a letter from Florence Nightingale was read, in which she expressed the heartiest sympathy with the proposal.

Great and most beneficent changes, again, have followed the substitution in workhouse infirmaries of trained nurses for the pauper women to whose tender mercies the care of the sick in those institutions was formerly left. It was a "Nightingale probationer," the late Agnes Jones, and 12 of her fellow-nurses from the Nightingale School at St. Thomas's who were the pioneers of this reform at the Brownlow-hill Infirmary, Liverpool; and it was undoubtedly the spirit and the teaching of Florence Nightingale that inspired them in a task which, difficult enough under the conditions then existing, was to create a precedent for Poor Law authorities all the land over.

Midwifery was another branch of the nursing art which Florence Nightingale ought to reform. She published in 1871 "Introductory Notes on Lying-in Hospital"; and, in 1881, writing on this subject to the late Miss Louisa M. Hubbard, who was then projecting the formation of the Matrons' Aid Society, afterwards the Midwives' Institute, she said, referring to these "Introductory Notes":

The main object of the "Notes" was (after dealing with the sanitary question) to point out the utter absence of any means of training in any existing institutions in Great Britain. Since the "Notes" were written next to nothing has been done to remedy this defect. . . . The prospectus is most excellent. . . . I wish you success from the bottom of my heart if, as I cannot doubt, your wisdom and energy work out a scheme by which to supply the deadly want of training among women practising midwifery in England. (It is a farce and a mockery to call them midwives or even midwifery nurses, and no certificate now given makes them so.) France, Germany, and even Russia would consider it woman-slaughter to "practise" as we do.

No less keen was her interest in rural hygiene. The need of observing the laws of health should, she thought, be directly impressed on the minds of the people, and to this end she organized a health crusade in Buckinghamshire in 1892, employing—with the aid of the County Council Technical Instruction Committee—three trained and competent women missioners, who were to give public addresses on health questions, following up these by visiting cottagers in their own homes and giving them practical advice.

CLOSING YEARS.

In these various ways one sees how Florence Nightingale, though a bedridden invalid and well advanced in years, was still ever ready, as she had been throughout life, to devote her energies to promoting the practical well-being of her fellow-creatures.

Yet, among all these manifold claims upon her attention, she never forgot that unpretending "Home" in Harley-street, W., over which she was still presiding when she went out to the Crimea. In The Times of November 12, 1901, she appealed for further support for this institution, declaring that it was

Doing good work—work after my own heart, and I trust, God's work. There is [she continued] no other institution exactly like this. In it our governesses (who are primarily eligible), the wives and daughters of the clergy, of our naval, military, and other professional men, receive every possible care, comfort, and first-rate advice at the most moderate cost. . . . Every one connected with this home and haven for the suffering is doing their utmost for it and it is always full. It is conducted on the same lines as from its beginning, by a committee of ladies, of which Mrs. Walter is the president, and she will be glad to receive contributions at 90, Harley-street, W. I ask and pray my friends who still remember me not to let this truly sacred work languish and die for want of a little more money.

The Times
3rd October 1958

DR. MARIE STOPES

CONTRACEPTION IN MARRIED LIFE

Dr. Marie Stopes, who died yesterday at her home at Dorking, Surrey, can fairly be said to have transformed the thoughts of her generation about the physical aspects of marriage and the role of contraception in married life. She was 78.

Immediately after the First World War she began to issue the books which made her famous and notorious. In emotional, even rhapsodic, language far removed from the scientific precision in which she had been trained, she preached the gospel of marriage as a partnership of equals, sacramentally expressed both in its physical relations and in deliberate and joyous parenthood.

Attainment of this ideal of married love required the use of contraception to remove the fear of pregnancy at the wrong time and for deliberate family planning.

Her books discussed the methods of contraception she favoured with uninhibited candour, though not always with medical accuracy; and she founded Britain's first birth-control clinic to give practical expression to a mission she pursued with religious fervour.

Addressed not to the learned or scientific public but to ordinary inarticulate men and women, and especially to wives and mothers, her writings at once achieved—and still retain—an enormous circulation. They helped innumerable humble folk to avoid unhappiness and ill-health. Before her advent the birth-control movement had been the preserve of a group of "Neo-Malthusian" intellectuals preoccupied chiefly by a rather academic concern about the balance between population trends and economic resources.

She transformed it into an openly discussed affair of the masses, directly and intimately concerned with the welfare of individual men and women and of their children. Her frontal attacks on old taboos, her quasi-prophetic tone, her flowery fervour aroused strong opposition from those who disagreed with her for religious reasons or felt she overstepped the bounds of good taste; and the launching of her pioneer clinics in London, Leeds, and Aberdeen was sometimes attended by stormy scenes.

Marie Carmichael Stopes was the eldest daughter of the late Henry Stopes, an anthropologist and archaeologist. Educated at St. George's, Edinburgh, and the North London Collegiate School, she went on to University College London with a chemistry scholarship. Having there gained the gold medal in junior and senior botany and her B.Sc. she later took the D.Sc.—she went to Munich and graduated as Ph.D. In 1904 she joined the science staff of Manchester University. In 1907 she travelled to Japan, where she spent nearly two years at Tokyo University and explored the country (including some remote areas) for fossils. She returned to Manchester as a lecturer in fossil botany. She was also a fellow and sometime lecturer in palaeobotany at University College London. During this period she wrote a number of scientific papers, as well as books on plant life and on Japan. An early marriage was, at her suit, annulled.

In 1918, retaining her maiden name, she married Humphrey Verdon Roe, the aircraft pioneer and co-founder with his brother of the firm which made the Avro biplane. In the same year she produced her two best sellers, Married Love and its sequel, Wise Parenthood, forerunners of a series of similar books which sold in hundreds of thousands. With the support of various well-known people she and her husband established "the Mothers' Clinic" in Holloway (now in Whitfield Street, St. Pancras), and used the proceeds of Married Love and their own private resources to keep it going and to promote other clinics through her Society for Constructive Birth Control. In 1930 a play of hers Our Ostriches, forceful propaganda but without dramatic merit, was staged at the Royalty Theatre. Her husband died in 1949.

In later life, after most of the separate birth-control societies had united and achieved acceptance and respectability in the Family Planning Association, the defects of her qualities became apparent. She remained aloof, for she could not co-operate on equal terms with others. Her dogmatism in scientific matters lost her the support of most doctors sympathetic to her aims. The shortcomings of her exuberant style and literary imagination (which could not readily transcend the plane of private bodily rapture) marred the verse she occasionally published.

Her home was near Dorking. She had two sons, one of whom survives her.

The Times
27th September 1915

MR. KEIR HARDIE.

DEATH OF A FAMOUS LABOUR LEADER.

We regret to announce the death of Mr. Keir Hardie, the well-known Labour member of Parliament, which occurred somewhat suddenly yesterday afternoon at a nursing home in Glasgow. Mr. Keir Hardie had been in failing health for some time past, and had laid aside public duties for several months. He resided for a time in Glen Sannox, Arran, but returned to Glasgow a fortnight ago to his brother's house at Clarkston. Pneumonia developed, and Mr. Hardie was removed to a nursing home last Wednesday.

James Keir Hardie had finished with school, or at any rate had begun to earn a livelihood, in 1863, when he was of the mature age of eight. For seventeen years he worked as a miner in the Lanarkshire collieries, and when he left the pit to take up the task of labour organisation he was only twenty-four. Into the campaign for the electoral equalisation of counties and boroughs Mr. Hardie threw himself with the ardour of a convinced and unenfranchised Radical. From 1882 to 1886 he acted as editor of a local paper, resigning the position to continue his work of organisation among the miners of Ayrshire. Of the body thus formed he became president, declining, however, to accept any remuneration, and in the following year, 1887, he attended his first Trade Unions Congress at Swansea, and signalised his entrance on this larger stage by an attack on Mr. Henry Broadhurst, whose attitude on the eight hours question had brought him into conflict with the pioneers of the movement. The incident marked the opening of a new chapter in Mr. Hardie's life. In the words of an admirer, he became "a visionary, an enthusiast, a Socialist, a contender and a fighter for a new society."

A vacancy in the representation of Mid-Lanark drew him in 1888 into his first by-election as a Labour candidate, when, on a poll of over 7,000, he obtained only 617 votes. After an attempt to establish a journal in the interests of the miners he made a more successful effort with the "Labour Leader," which was at first issued once a month and afterwards every week. Then came his return to Parliament at the general election of 1892 for the borough of West Ham, a Conservative stronghold which utterly collapsed under the combined assault of Liberals and Labour men, thanks to whose co-operation Mr. Keir Hardie obtained a majority of over 1,200.

In 1894 the Independent Labour party was formed, with Mr. Keir Hardie as president. The duties of this position, together with his journalistic work and the demands of an incessant platform propaganda, provided Mr. Hardie with plenty of occupation during his five years' exclusion from Westminster. Somewhat unexpectedly, he obtained re-election to Parliament at the general election of 1900, and on this occasion for the first time he was returned avowedly as an Independent Labour candidate.

At the general election of 1906 Mr. Keir Hardie was again elected as Mr. D. A. Thomas's colleague in the representation of Merthyr Tydvil. For the first time Labour candidates were returned to Parliament not in twos and threes but in tens and twenties, forming a party which numbered in all between fifty and sixty members. Although usually acting in concert on nearly all important questions of practical politics, this considerable group promptly divided itself into two rival sections, one of which, allying itself with Liberalism in Parliament as it had done at the polls, sat on the Government benches, while the other, which had a slight advantage in numbers, went nominally into Opposition and sat below the gangway on the other side. Of this second section Mr. Keir Hardie was elected chairman by a small majority at the beginning of the first session of the new Parliament, and re-elected unanimously at the opening of the second session.

The reticence and habits of caution thus imposed on the Labour spokesman in his new position gave some observers an erroneous idea of his essentially rugged personality. It became the custom to speak of him as a sort of reclaimed character, as another instance of the mellowing influence of advancing years combined with constant association with public affairs at their centre, and so forth. In truth Mr. Keir Hardie never reformed in that sense at all. He remained as much an extremist and as rigid and irreconcilable as ever, but, out of loyalty to his party and to his own position of trust in it, he strove almost pathetically, and on the whole with success, to acquire some of the arts of conciliation, especially in his dealings with Sir H. Campbell-Bannerman.

It is partly a testimony to Keir Hardie's real weight that next to Sir Henry Campbell-Bannerman (in whose case it was a similar testimony) he was the best-abused and the most misrepresented man in British politics. It did not spoil him, though he heeded perhaps overmuch the Biblical admonition to beware when men speak well of us. He attacked Liberals and Conservatives pretty impartially, and both sides struck back. Liberals naturally resented his independent policy at elections, which frequently gave seats to the reactionaries. Conservatives disliked him chiefly for what was but a side-feature, although a marked one—his "Little-Englandism," "pro-Boerism," and championship of native races. And it must be conceded that on both lines he sometimes acted with great want of judgment. Nevertheless the first was the secret of his own political success; and the latter proceeded from an all-embracing love of humanity whose depth, genuineness, and moral nobleness were beyond cavil. In person he was singularly unlike the ogre of the newspapers. His manner was gentle, his voice rich and soft; his breadth of sympathy and loftiness of purpose won and compelled. His oratorical periods and careful choice of words showed wide reading and an artistic bent; just as his spare, tight-knit figure and rugged features recorded the tragedy of toil in which he was born and grew up. Anxious though he was to wean Labour from allegiance to Liberals and Conservatives, he was no less anxious to keep the Labour party from a narrow restriction to class interests. He always put in the forefront, side by side with purely Labour demands, the pursuit of international peace, of justice in Imperial affairs, of morality in domestic affairs, the succouring of the nation's children, the political and social emancipation of its women. Sometimes, as in opposing the South African War, he had to face the hostility of most outside his Labour allies; sometimes, as in championing votes for women, the hostility or apathy of many, perhaps most, of those allies themselves. But he never hauled down his flags, and seldom failed in the long run to carry his point with his party. Anyone who heard him speak with others of the party leaders could hardly miss this distinguishing note of largeness of heart and vision. Platform eloquence, self-denying effort, moral earnestness, a first-hand grip of the life of the common people—these are not rare qualities in a Labour movement. What is rare in any movement is their union with an all-embracing yet actual love for human beings and passion for justice, from which no race, colour, age, sex, or class is quite shut out. To have that one must be something of a poet by nature, and that Mr. Keir Hardie was.

The Times
15th June 1928

MRS. PANKHURST.

A PIONEER OF WOMAN SUFFRAGE.

Mrs. Emmeline Pankhurst, whose death is announced on another page, was born in Manchester on July 14, 1858. In her early childhood she was brought into close touch with those who had inherited the spirit of the Manchester reformers. Her father, Mr. Robert Goulden, a calico-printer, was keenly interested in the reform question and the dawn of the movement for woman suffrage; her grandfather nearly lost his life in the Peterloo franchise riots in 1819. At the age of 13, soon after she had been taken to her first woman suffrage meeting by her mother, she went to school in Paris, where she found a girl-friend of her own way of thinking in the daughter of Henri Rochefort. In 1879 she married Dr. R. M. Pankhurst, a man many years older than herself. An intimate friend of John Stuart Mill and an able lawyer, he shared and helped to mould his wife's political views. She served with him on the committee which promoted the Married Women's Property Act, and was at the same time a member of the Manchester Women's Suffrage Committee. In 1889 she helped in forming the Women's Franchise League, which, however, was discontinued after a few years. She remained a Liberal until 1892, when she joined the Independent Labour Party. After being defeated for the Manchester School Board, she was elected at the head of the poll for the board of guardians and served for five years. When her husband died, in 1898, she was left not well off, and with three girls and a boy to bring up. Accordingly she found work as registrar of births and deaths at Chorlton-on-Medlock, but her propaganda activities were considered inconsistent with this official position, and she resigned.

In 1903 her interest in the cause of woman suffrage was reawakened by the enthusiasm of her daughter Christabel, and she formed the Women's Social and Political Union, the first meeting of which was held in her house in Manchester in October of that year. Two years later the militant movement was started as the immediate result of the treatment received by Miss Christabel Pankhurst and Miss Annie Kenney, two members of the union who endeavoured to question Sir Edward Grey on the prospects of woman suffrage at a political meeting held in Manchester. In 1906 Mrs. Pankhurst and her union began a series of pilgrimages to the House of Commons, which resulted in conflicts with the police and the imprisonment of large numbers of the members. In October, 1906, she was present at the first of these demonstrations, when 11 women were arrested. In January, 1908, she was pelted with eggs and rolled in the mud during the Mid-Devon election at Newton Abbot, and a month later she was arrested when carrying a petition to the Prime Minister at the House of Commons, but was released after undergoing five of the six weeks' imprisonment to which she was sentenced. Some months later, in October, a warrant was issued for her arrest, together with Miss Pankhurst and Mrs. Drummond, for inciting the public to "rush" the House of Commons. During her three months' imprisonment in Holloway Gaol she led a revolt of her followers against the rules of prison discipline, demanding that they should be treated as political prisoners. In 1909, the year in which the "hunger strike" and "forcible feeding" were first practised in connection with these cases, she was once more arrested at the door of the House of Commons, and after her trial, and pending an appeal founded on the Bill of Rights and a statute of Charles II. dealing with petitions to the Crown, she went to America and Canada on a lecturing tour; two days before her return her fine was paid by some unknown person, so that she did not go to prison.

As soon, however, as she was back in England, she again devoted her energies to the encouragement of the campaign of pin-pricks and violence to which she was committed and by which she hoped to further the cause which she had at heart. In 1912, for her own share in these lawless acts, she was twice imprisoned, but in each case served only five weeks of the periods of two months and nine months—for conspiracy to break windows—to which she was sentenced. A year later she was arrested on the more serious charge of inciting to commit a felony, in connexion with the blowing-up of Mr. Lloyd George's country house at Walton. In spite of the ability with which she conducted her own defence, the jury found her guilty—though with a strong recommendation to mercy—and she was sentenced by Mr. Justice Lush to three years' penal servitude. On the tenth day of the hunger strike which she at once began (to be followed later on by a thirst strike) she was temporarily released, under the terms of the measure introduced by Mr. McKenna commonly known as the Cat and Mouse Act, because of the condition of extreme weakness to which she was reduced. At the end of five months, during which she was several times released and rearrested, she went to Paris, and then to America (after a detention of 2½ days on Ellis Island), having served not quite three weeks of her three years' sentence. On her return to England the same cat-and-mouse policy was resumed by the authorities—and accompanied by more and more violent outbreaks on the part of Mrs. Pankhurst's militant followers—until at last, in the summer of 1914, after she had been arrested and released nine or ten times on the one charge, it was finally abandoned, and the remainder of her term of three years' penal servitude allowed to lapse.

Whether, but for the outbreak of the Great War, the militant movement would have resulted in the establishment of woman suffrage is a point on which opinions will probably always differ. But there is no question that the coming of the vote, which Mrs. Pankhurst claimed as the right of her sex, was sensibly hastened by the general feeling that after the extraordinary courage and devotion shown by women of all classes in the nation's emergency there must be no risk of a renewal of the feminist strife of the days of militancy. When the War was over it was remembered that on its outbreak Mrs. Pankhurst, with her daughter Christabel and the rest of the militant leaders, declared an immediate suffrage truce, and gave herself up to the claims of national service and devoted her talents as a speaker to the encouragement of recruiting, first in this country and then in the United States. A visit to Russia in 1917, where she formed strong opinions on the evils of Bolshevism, was followed by a residence of some years in Canada and afterwards in Bermuda for the benefit of her health. Since she came home, at the end of 1925 she had taken a deep interest in public life and politics, and had some thoughts of standing for Parliament, though she declined Lady Astor's offer to give up to her her seat in Plymouth.

Whatever views may be held as to the righteousness of the cause to which she gave her life and the methods by which she tried to bring about its achievement, there can be no doubt about the singleness of her aim and the remarkable strength and nobility of her character. She was inclined to be autocratic and liked to go her own way. But that was because she was honestly convinced that her own way was the only way. The end that she had in view was the emancipation of women from what she believed, with passionate sincerity, to be a condition of harmful subjection. She was convinced that she was working for the salvation of the world, as well as of her sex. She was a public speaker of very remarkable force and ability, with a power of stimulating and swaying her audience possessed by no other woman of her generation, and was regarded with devoted admiration by many people outside the members of her union. With all her autocracy, and her grievous mistakes, unselfish she was a humble-minded, large-hearted, woman, of the stuff of which martyrs are made. Quite deliberately, and having counted the cost, she undertook a warfare against the forces of law and order the strain of which her slight and fragile body was unable to bear. It will be remembered of her that whatever peril and suffering she called upon her followers to endure, up to the extreme indignity of forcible feeding, she herself was ready to face, and did face, with unfailing courage and endurance of body and mind.

The Guardian
22ⁿᵈ February 1965

—apostle of violence

Malcolm X, the militant Negro leader who died of bullet wounds at a Harlem rally, yesterday, was a man who often advocated violence as a means of settling racial problems.

It was Malcolm X who suggested that an American Mau Mau was needed to force whites in the United States into giving Negroes first-class citizenship. He also called for the formation of Negro rifle clubs to allow Negroes to defend themselves in the South.

Ever since his first emergence as Elijah Muhammed's right-hand man in the Black Muslim movement in the United States several years ago, Malcolm X has been steeped in controversy. He acted as Muhammed's spokesman, and his fiery statements about Negro-White relations often gained him world-wide publicity.

He broke with the Muslims about two years ago after what was believed to be a power struggle with the elderly Muhammed.

Own organisation

After the break, Malcolm X formed his own organisation—the Organisation for Afro-American Unity—and made frequent speeches advocating his own policy for dealing with racial problems. Since then there has been a running verbal battle between the Chicago-based Black Muslims, who meet in mosques, and Malcolm X, whose headquarters were in a hotel in the heart of Harlem.

Malcolm X blamed the Moslems for the recent petrol-bombing of his home at Astoria in New York State. Of the bombing he said: "It doesn't frighten me. It doesn't quiet me down or in any way shut me up."

Malcolm advocated an apartheid society in the United States. He once demanded that three States be set aside entirely for Negroes. While in Cairo in August he accused the United States of practising a worse form of organised racialism than South Africa.

Little is known about his background. Some reports have said that he was a former convict, an illicit whisky runner, and a university lecturer. The Black Muslims suspended him after he made a speech on the assassination of President Kennedy in which he spoke of "the chickens coming home to roost."

He was in this country last week. He visited Smethwick where, he said, "Blacks are being treated in the same way as the Negroes, were treated in Alabama, like Hitler treated the Jews." On the Congo he said he was for the kind of extremism that the "freedom fighters" of Stanleyville had displayed against "the hired killers."

Manchester Guardian
21ˢᵗ August 1912

General Booth.

THE news of General Booth's death will be heard with emotion by all England, by all America, by almost countless communities in every quarter of the world. He had won this immense, almost unique, position, as usually happens in the case of such leaders of men, by a remarkable combination of gifts—by deep spiritual fervour and an intensity of religious conviction allied to practical gifts which would have carried him to the front rank in almost any line of achievement; immense self-confidence and the faculty of command, together with unaffected simplicity and an absolute devotion to the welfare of mankind. It was a great and a notable combination, and it has produced great and notable fruits—a world-wide organisation which will survive his death and carry on his work and an example of social care and endeavour which has already provoked widespread emulation and may serve as an incentive to much more. We have nothing here to do with his positive teaching or the precise methods by which it was recommended. Judged by their results these must have had in them elements of a universal appeal. But his figure was heroic, his achievements were extraordinary, and he leaves behind him a great and abiding memory.

General BOOTH was no orator, but he spoke with a directness and precision which seldom failed to strike home. He was no philosopher, but he had the sagacity to perceive and the courage always to insist upon the things that really counted. At the outset of his enterprise, in the seventies, he was solicited by the Anglican bishops, and particularly by MACKARNESS of Oxford, to regularise his new society by making it a Brotherhood within the Church. These overtures, and the manner in which they were made, reflect honour upon the Churchmen of that day, but Mr. BOOTH courteously declined them. He had decided, first, to disengage himself from all entanglement with any other organisation, and, secondly, to make no account whatever of traditional Christian ordinances. He would simply aim at changing the hearts and lives of sinners, especially the very worst, and to that end would take whatever means he found the best within the limits of Scriptural belief. Like all great leaders, he was masterful. He was of SPURGEON's mind, that business could best be transacted by a committee of one. But, unlike SPURGEON, he not only thought it, he acted upon it. He was virtually the founder of a religious Order; he was a nineteenth-century counterpart of a DOMINIC or a FRANCIS. It will never be known how far his earlier thoughts had felt the influence of his gifted and saintly wife, but he had a wonderful power of moulding other natures to his views. All that joined his household by marriage seemed to become prophets of the movement. Only in the United States—

that land of religious experiment, where even the Roman obedience has shown symptoms of "Americanism"—did any mutiny break out in his Army. Above all, he was great in the single-hearted zeal with which he and his colleagues, defiant of all religious as well as social conventions, went straight for the rescue of sinners. So strange were the methods, so uncouth the types of dress, design, or music employed, that convention and taste were alike outraged. It is instructive to recollect how, for the first ten years of the Salvation Army's existence, it was never openly alluded to in polite society. Literature turned her face away in pained surprise. Exactly so had Roman society and letters ignored the existence of the Christian Church in its early decades. It would be interesting to discover how early the work of the "Army" found mention in contemporary fiction, and how long it took to make the "Salvation Army Lass" an accepted type in melodrama. Approval began from below. By degrees the devoted lives of the "Captains" (of either sex) brought the "Army" into deserved respect. Well before the close of his long life "the General" was one of the most popular figures in England, and indeed the world over. Public opinion usually deals so with reformers and agitators who are strong enough to live down its opposition. It was with BOOTH as with JOHN WESLEY. When WESLEY began he was often silenced by the mobs that were instigated to insult him. When he was an old man, and visited his own Oxford again, he could hardly preach for the crowds that surged in to see and welcome him. Perhaps the spiritual greatness of General BOOTH was less evident in his later triumphal progresses with a long train of motor-cars filled with secretaries and assistants than in his earlier and humbler journeys in search of the lost and erring.

It was like his practical nature to discover so soon and so decidedly that religious efforts to save the fallen could not avail very far unless accompanied by extensive schemes of social amelioration. The Christian evangelist had to become the social reformer. It is a lesson that all the Churches have been forced to learn. But few, if any, learned it so rapidly as General BOOTH, and his example has undoubtedly helped to stimulate others. His career suggests many questions. How far is a religious movement which ignores all beauty in form, colour, and sound and offers to its converts no ideal of worship or system of doctrine likely to retain its hold upon civilised people? How long can so crude a theology, which takes no account of the light shed by history and criticism upon Scripture, expect to survive the advance of knowledge? Can any religious body go very far or very long upon the path of social reform without taking account of politics and yoking the might of Parliament to advance the general good?   And, again, how long can an immense organisation—created by the genius of one man—retain its power and efficiency after the impulse of his spirit has been withdrawn? Time will show. There have been greater preachers than General BOOTH, as devoted evangelists. There have been many heroic spirits who have wrought equal marvels in saving the lost. There have been quite as capable social students and reformers. But seldom, if ever, have all these characters been united in one man, who has also had the gift of enlisting thousands of helpers, and organising them into military obedience to his will. His career, and the labours of countless others like him, who have never sought or achieved his prominence, afford an inspiring example of the power of spiritual forces and a strong ground of hope for the future progress and sustained moral vigour of our British race.

New York Daily Tribune
18th April 1865

ABRAHAM LINCOLN'S PLACE IN HISTORY.

The tidings of President Lincoln's tragic death will create a greater sensation in Europe than any event that ever before happened on this continent. He filled a larger space in the public eye than any American before him, partly because of the stupendous events in which he bore a conspicuous part, but in good part also because the Democracy of Europe instinctively and early recognized him as a champion of the cause of Popular Rights—of their own cause and that of all Humanity. If one were to enter a European café or clubroom much frequented by the Liberals of no matter what country, and there announce himself a Democrat and an upholder of Slavery, the great majority would suppose him either just escaped from a mad-house, or unacquainted with the language he was trying to speak. There are great varieties and contrasts of opinion cherished among the Progressives of the other hemisphere, but they have no classification for such a monstrosity as a pro-Slavery Democrat, and would not know what to make of him. And, among all the Democrats of Europe, from the orange-groves of Sicily to the eternal ice of Nova Zembla, there is not one who can read that is not instinctively a champion of the Union cause and an enthusiastic admirer of Abraham Lincoln. While the language of panegyric will be exhausted and the power of hyperbole overstrained in American eulogies on our lost leader, we feel sure that the most effective, because most thoughtful and discriminating, tributes paid to his memory will gush from the hearts and be traced by the pens of the Garibaldis, Victor Hugos, John Brights, and Mazzinis, who uphold against mighty odds the standard of Liberty on the soil of the Old World.

The Times
20th October 1845

THE LATE MRS. ELIZABETH FRY.—This distinguished individual expired at Ramsgate on Sunday last, after a long and protracted illness, which she bore throughout with great fortitude and resignation. The subject of this brief memoir was the daughter of the late Mr. John Gurney, of Earlham-hall, Norfolk, and sister to Mr. Samuel Gurney, of Upton-hall, in this county, banker. But few of her own sex stand so pre-eminent for their works of philanthropy and for alleviating the sufferings and promoting the happiness of their fellow-creatures as Mrs. Elizabeth Fry. At the early age of 18, by permission of her father, she converted an apartment in Earlham-hall into a school-room, where she daily gave 24 poor children elementary instruction in reading, writing, and arithmetic. In the year 1800 she married Mr. Joseph Fry (who still survives), a member of the Society of Friends, who materially aided her praiseworthy exertions by appropriating a large sum annually to her use, by which Mrs. Fry was enabled to extend the sphere of her usefulness. In the year 1814 Mrs. Fry succeeded in establishing a ladies' committee for the reformation of the interior of Newgate, and in this laudable undertaking she met with the cordial co-operation of the sheriffs of London, and the governor of the prison. Not more than a year had elapsed before the beneficial effects of Mrs. Fry's committee were exhibited. The prison, which was previously a scene of riot, licentiousness, and filth, was exchanged for order, sobriety, and comparative neatness, in the chambers as well as in the persons of the female prisoners. Prior to the latter date the female inmates were left without any employment—an evil which the discriminating powers of this memoir soon discovered, and instantly set about to remove it by the establishment of a manufactory for the women's tried side, as well as a school for children, which were daily superintended by the ladies of the committee. No sooner were the benefits of the manufactory known than the women on the untried side petitioned the ladies' committee for a similar provision, which was granted, and we may observe the moral results surpassed the most sanguine anticipations of its promoters. We find the grand jury of the City of London, in their report, dated the 21st February, 1818, expressing themselves in reference to Mrs. Fry's exertions as under:—"They cannot," they say, "conclude their report without expressing in an especial manner the peculiar gratification they experience in observing the important service rendered by Mrs. Fry and her friends, and the habits of religion, order, industry, and cleanliness which her humane, benevolent, and praiseworthy exertions have introduced among the female prisoners; and that if the principles which govern her regulations were adopted towards the males, as well as the females, it would be the means of converting a prison into a school of reform; and, instead of sending criminals back into the world hardened in vice and depravity, they would be restored to it repentant, and probably become useful members of society." Similar sentiments were expressed by the London Grand Jury in a letter to Mrs. Fry, enclosing a donation in aid of her laudable design. The subject of this memoir not only elicited the encomiums of the English press, but her name was associated with every philanthropic object in most of the continental nations of Europe. In the slave trade question her exertions were surpassed only by a few of the opposite sex. Such was her humane and benevolent disposition, that her sympathy extended to the whole human family, without reference to country, clime, or religion. She was looked upon as a physician to body and soul; she fed and comforted the poor, supplied them with clothes, and did everything that would administer to their well-being and promote their happiness. In the neighbourhood where she resided (Upton, in this county), her benevolence is too well known to need comment. Her readiness to hear the cause of the distressed and destitute, and alleviate their sufferings, won for her the respect of all classes, and raised for her a name which reflects credit on her sex as well as on the Society of Friends, of which she was so distinguished a member. The funeral of Mrs. Fry took place on Saturday, the 18th inst., when her remains were interred in the Friends' burial-ground at Barking.—Chelmsford Chronicle.

News Chronicle
1st May 1943

Spent Her Life in Seeking Better Life For Others

MRS. SIDNEY WEBB, great Socialist and sociologist, the woman who refused to become Lady Passfield when her husband entered the House of Lords, has died at the age of 85 at her home in Liphook, Hants. She had been ill for 10 days.

Her death has broken up the " famous firm of Webb and Webb "—that was how she and her husband were known as for more than fifty years they worked together for the Socialist cause and fought to expose the horrors of the lives of Britain's sweated workers.

Daughter of a former chairman of the G.W.R., granddaughter of two M.P.s, Mrs. Webb was born into a world of plenty. But she knew that outside the comfortable, secure life she led there was a different kind of world—one in which poverty was the rule and people died young of exhaustion from overwork.

SLIPPED AWAY

She had to use stealth to discover this other world. She slipped away from her family and went to visit cousins who were cotton operatives in Lancashire. What she saw of their lives caused her to make up her mind. She became a Socialist.

Miss Beatrice Potter, as she then was, knew Charles Booth and had through him become interested in sociology.

The break with her comfortable home came in 1877 when the 19-year-old girl became a social investigator in London. Into the East End she carried her inquiries: she who had never worked with her hands became a trouser-hand in a Co-operative Wholesale workrooms. Her training ended, she dressed in working-class clothes, let her hair hang untidily about her face and got job after job in tailoring " sweat shops." Often she was sacked.

Charles Booth sent her into London dockland to survey working conditions and her findings became one of the most important chapters of his great work, " Life and Labour in London."

KEPT SECRET

Her interest in the Fabian Society led to her meeting with Sidney Webb, a famous Socialist writer even in those early days when both were very young.

They fell in love, but Beatrice Potter could not tell her dying father that she intended to marry a Socialist. They married six months after Richard Potter had died.

From that day the " firm of Webb and Webb " began their joint works which were to give form and meaning to much that Socialism stands for.

In their work the Webbs became known as inseparables. They wrote books on trade unionism which will remain models of their kind and, it has been said of them, " have marked an epoch in social science."

Together they embarked on the monumental history of English Local Government, a work of thousands of words which made them even more famous and admitted them into the ranks of great historians of England.

It was the Webbs, in 1909, who shattered the old, dreadful system of English poor law, writing a Minority Report which has been called the most devastating criticism a Royal Commission has ever produced.

They founded the London School of Economics and although they did not form the Fabian Society, they gave it a full blooded vitality and drive which it needed.

When Sidney Webb was raised to the Peerage in 1929 Mrs. Webb refused point-blank to accept the title of Lady Passfield. She did not argue the matter, but never was she prepared to give in on this subject.

When she was 72 Mrs. Webb decided to go to Russia with her husband. The elderly couple travelled thousands of miles through the Soviet Union, studying the lives and labours of the Russian people 18 years after they had formed their Soviet States.

TAUGHT LENIN

Lenin is said to have learned his English' by reading the works of Sidney Webb. The Webbs learned their Russian by reading the works of Lenin. When they returned to England they wrote " Soviet Communism" in two volumes of 1,200 pages. In 1941 they produced volume 3 of the book, " A New Civilisation." The three volumes have presented to thousands of readers an exhaustive survey of the Soviet world and ranks as one of the Webbs' greatest works.

Mrs. Webb was once reported to be writing her autobiography. She said it would be printed only after her death. If it has been completed and is published, it will give the world the whole amazing story of the girl who listened to Gladstone and Disraeli, sitting 12 hours at a stretch in the Commons gallery; the woman who spent her life seeking an improved science of living for the sake of others; the veteran who was not afraid to travel thousands of miles to see something new because she thought it might result in a discovery for the benefit of all people.

G.B.S. TRIBUTE

Yesterday another great Fabian and her close friend, George Bernard Shaw, gave her this epitaph when a News Chronicle reporter spoke to him:

" She was a very extraordinary woman—that's a platitude of course —but what else can I say? She should get a column, even in a four-page paper."

She has.

Mrs. Sidney Webb
From Wealth to Socialism

Society, Scandal & Trendsetting

Doubtless some of those who find themselves in the following pages would take exception to the company imposed on them. Nevertheless they all have – at the very least – one thing in common: stature. **Charles Atlas** (who appears in our Business section), quite literally, **Rasputin** both literally and metaphorically, and **James Dean** simply in terms of personality, the cult figure *par excellence* of the screen. Many others could of course have been included here: Stalin, Freud, and Chaplin, to suggest but a few. However, their resting-places are elsewhere. **Beau Brummel** is here because he showed us that the human male need not think himself inferior to his ornithological counterpart. Lord **Byron** combined, in the most British of ways, the ability to scandalise an entire generation one day and lift them up on clouds of outraged principle the next. I wonder what he would have thought of **Amy Vanderbilt**'s textbooks of etiquette, circumstantial evidence at least for Shakespeare's suggestion that "all the world's a stage"? Or what **Edward VII** really thought of it all, having in his day served as the exception, with a vengeance, that proved the Victorian rules? **Queen Victoria** herself of course not only laid claim to obituaries the length of a short novel, but also gave us that most useful all-purpose label used above: "Victorian". Lady **Astor**'s eminence as the first woman MP has recently acquired a very special significance; while that of Messrs. **Rolls** and **Royce** will probably survive even our present local difficulties. **Alfred Nobel** is here more in hope than anything else – for having invented dynamite he was so appalled that he founded a series of awards dedicated to the peaceful progress of mankind. Finally, **Bogie** is here simply and solely as himself, a language of the cinema.

Daily Express
7th May 1910

An Empire in Mourning.

The King is dead!

These words will be repeated to-day with bitter sorrow and deep misgiving by the highly placed and by the poor, in halls of state and in humble cottages, on the English countryside, by the great lakes of Canada, in Australian cities, and under the blazing sun of India.

The King is dead! As one writes the words, and considers the wondrous realm over which the King ruled, the great heritage that came to him, and the complete devotion with which he has played his part, one feels that only a great lyric poet could write his record and voice his people's sorrow.

The reign of King Edward has been comparatively short. Less than a decade has passed since, mid ancient pomp, he was crowned King of the most modern of Empires. We can all remember the beginning, and yet in a few years the King became so completely and so intimately associated with his people, and represented so thoroughly all that is best and sanest in the national life, that it is almost impossible to think of the British Empire without thinking of King Edward. The words come to our lips—the King is dead!—but we speak them with dazed bewilderment. The blow is so heavy, so unexpected, so tragically inopportune. Never, it seems to us, has the people wanted the King so badly. Never has a crisis occurred where his qualities would have been so priceless. We have looked to him to find a way out of turmoil and misunderstanding. But the King's work is done. He has run his course, and the nation that he has served so well must call to him in vain.

The strength of the English throne is the fact that it is broad-based upon the people's will. The great achievement of the dead King, as it was the achievement of his mother, was that he was able to represent the ambitions and aspirations of his people more fully and more completely than any politician or any statesman. King Edward was Great Britain, and Great Britain mourns as for herself. We have always felt, all of us, Unionists and Liberals, that in the King there was a reserve of wisdom, not to be lightly drawn upon, but always ready when the extreme difficulty arose. And now this national refuge is no longer ours. "Death's inexorable hand draws the dark curtain close." It is something to know that the whole world will sorrow by the bier of the dead King. This is, after all, the finest tribute to his work. He has made friends for his country. Let that be King Edward's epitaph. Misunderstandings have been conjured away by his smile. Friction has become friendship through his influence. Peace has been assured and war has, at least, been postponed. The whole world knows, as we know, how ceaseless and single-minded have been his efforts, and the sorrow to-day in London and the other cities of the British Empire will be echoed in every capital in Europe, and, indeed, in every place where two or three men of good intent are gathered together.

But the King was also a man, and as we think of the nation's loss we think also with keen and respectful sympathy of the bitter personal grief of the gracious lady who shared King Edward's throne and shared also his place in the hearts of the people. It may be some solace to her to know that she is encompassed with the affection of a great people. She may be buoyed to some measure of fortitude by their sympathies and their prayers. It is magnificently true that the good that men do lives after them. Great Britain is the richer and the better for King Edward. The British throne is more secure. The sceptre falls from his hand, but it falls into the hand of his son. The King is dead! Long live the King! It will be no easy task for King George to follow his father, but he inherits a great tradition, and he and his Queen have already won the respect and the affections of their subjects. The new King will rule an Imperial people with Imperial knowledge. A sailor mounts the throne of the Empire of the sea. If it is inevitable that he should begin to reign at a time of bitter sorrow and lamentation, it is also true that he starts his career in the sunset of a glorious day. That is his heritage—his and ours. He need have no fear of his people's loyalty. We have no fear of his devotion.

God Save the King!

Dictionary of National Biographies 1931–1940

ROYCE, SIR (FREDERICK) HENRY, baronet (1863–1933); engineer, was born at Alwalton, near Peterborough, 27 March 1863, the younger son of James Royce, flour miller, by his wife, Mary, third daughter of Benjamin King, farmer, of Edwin's Hall, Essex. His father's death compelled him to earn his own living at the age of ten, and he was in turn selling newspapers, a post office messenger boy, and at the age of fourteen an apprentice in the Great Northern Railway Company's locomotive works at Peterborough. Being unable to complete his apprenticeship for lack of funds, he found employment in 1881 at Leeds in a tool factory, often working for sixteen hours a day. In 1882 he became a tester with the London Electric Light and Power Company, and advanced his wider education by going to the night classes of the City and Guilds Technical College and at the Polytechnic. So full of promise did he show himself that in the same year the London company appointed him chief electrical engineer for its pioneer scheme for the electric lighting of the streets of Liverpool.

In 1884, at the age of twenty-one, Royce, together with E. A. Claremont, founded the firm of F. H. Royce & company (entitled Royce Limited from 1894 until 1933), manufacturers of arc lamps, dynamos, and electric cranes at Cooke Street, Manchester, and later at Trafford Park; their original capital was only £70. In 1903 he bought his first motor-car, a 10 h.p. Decauville, the noise and untrustworthiness of which (as with other cars of the period) determined him to design and make motor-vehicles himself, and at the end of the year he had his first two-cylinder engines running for many hundreds of hours, coupled to dynamos. Every detail of the car, no matter how small, was designed with the same minute care, with ruthless testing, and even in those early days the slender resources of the company were spent on multifarious experiments, metallurgical research, and heat treatment. So when, on 31 March 1904, the first 10 h.p. two-cylinder Royce car was driven out of the factory at Cooke Street, it at once gave an impression of silence, smoothness, and flexibility and so fired the enthusiasm of C. S. Rolls [q.v.] who had a selling agency (C. S. Rolls & company) in London for continental cars of high repute, that late in 1904 he, with his able partner Claude Johnson, contracted to buy the entire output of cars produced by Royce Limited and to sell them under the name of Rolls-Royce. These two firms were combined in 1906.

Royce had soon perceived that it was a mistake to manufacture a wide range of models. He took as his motto 'Organise and specialise' and concentrated entirely on one car, the 40–50 h.p. 'Silver Ghost', the first of which was completed by the end of 1906. This type remained in production, with numerous improvements of detail, until 1925, when it gave place to 'Phantoms' and 'Wraiths'. The qualities of the 'Silver Ghost' so much increased the demand for it that in 1908 the motor section of the firm was separated from Cooke Street and transferred to Derby.

Royce was now at the height of his powers, but habitual overwork and lack of interest in his meals led to a breakdown in 1911 from which he was not expected to recover. Recovery was indeed only partial, but although he was never able to return to the factory, he continued to control the main designs, keeping in close contact with experiments and other activities for another twenty years. In motor-car design the original features of his work are the silent cam form of the valve-gear, the friction-damped slipper flywheel and spring drive for the timing gears, his battery ignition, the Royce expanding carburettor, and the wear-proof steering.

Royce, however, did not confine himself to designing motor-cars. Although Rolls had often pressed him to design an aero engine, he took no practical interest in the matter until the outbreak of war in 1914, when, after investigating various types of air-cooled engines at the request of the government, he at length characteristically made up his mind not to deviate from liquid cooling; so, starting from a 12-cylinder V, he produced the 'Eagle' early in 1915, which played an important part in the war, and was followed by the 'Falcon', the 'Hawk', and the 'Condor'. It was mainly his determination that led the Rolls-Royce Company to enter for the Schneider cup competitions, in which they won the trophy in 1929 and in 1931, setting up the world speed record at 408 m.p.h. Shortly before his death, Royce laid down the prototype designs of the 'Merlin' engine, making use of the experience gained in the Atlantic flight of 1919 and the Schneider cup competitions. True to his principles he here again stood firm in his decision to adhere to a 12-cylinder V engine, and that this type of engine persisted all through the war of 1939–1945 with extensive use on all types of aircraft is a standing witness to the correctness of Royce's policy.

For his services to engineering and the country, Royce was appointed O.B.E. in 1918 and created a baronet in 1930. There was no issue of his marriage, which took place in 1893, with Minnie Grace (died 1936), third daughter of Alfred Punt, of London. He died at West Wittering, near Chichester, 22 April 1933.

At the time of the Schneider cup competition it was said of him that 'Mr. Royce is not a man who prides himself upon inventing things. He likes to perfect things already in existence.' Apart from his

genius as an engineer, Royce's most marked characteristic was an extraordinary modesty. In appearance he resembled a farmer, and his chief recreation was the cultivation of roses and fruit-trees. His remarkable memory he attributed to his night-school education, which 'made it imperative that I should never forget anything worth remembering, and I have never outgrown that habit'.

A life-size bronze statue of Royce by F. Derwent Wood was erected in the Arboretum at Derby in 1923. A bust by William McMillan is in the main offices of Rolls-Royce Limited at Derby. A cartoon by 'Spy' appeared in *Mayfair*, January 1919.

New York Times
1st October 1955

James Dean, Film Actor, Killed in Crash of Auto

PASO ROBLES, Calif., Sept. 30 (P)—James Dean, 24-year-old motion picture actor, was killed tonight in an automobile accident near here.

A spokesman for Warner Brothers, for whom Mr. Dean had just completed "The Giant," said he had no details of the accident except that the actor was en route to a sports car meeting at Salinas. He was driving a small German speedster.

The actor had appeared in "East of Eden," released last April, and in "Rebel Without a Cause," still unreleased.

Mr. Dean was the star of Elia Kazan's film, "East of Eden," taken from John Steinbeck's novel. It was his first starring role in films. The year before he had attracted attention of critics as the young Arab servant in the Broadway production of "The Immoralist." His portrayal won for him the Donaldson and Perry awards.

The Times
12th May 1916

MURDER OF RUSSIAN MONK RASPUTIN.

COPENHAGEN, MAY 11.

The Bucarest correspondent of the *Berliner Tageblatt* learns that the well-known Russian priest Rasputin has been murdered in Petrograd.—*Exchange Telegraph Company.*

. Rasputin, the son of a peasant of Tobolsk, lived a peasant's life till he was 30. Then, seized with a religious mania, he started on pilgrimages from monastery to monastery, which ended in Petrograd, where he created a kind of religious salon. He acquired influence at Court, and the Tsaritsa is believed to have attributed the birth of the Tsarevitch in 1904 to his intercession. His libertinage scandalized Bishops Teofanos and Hermogen, who sought his banishment, but they themselves had to leave the capital. A gross scandal led to his exile to Tobolsk. Before leaving he told the Empress that "something frightful" would follow his banishment and when the Tsarevitch fell ill the Empress entreated the Tsar to recall Rasputin, who still remained an influence at the Court.

New York Times
28th December 1974

Amy Vanderbilt Is Dead at 66 After a Plunge From Window

Miss Vanderbilt's body was reported found near the front door of the town house close by three steps that lead to street level. She was dressed in a light-colored, flower-patterned dress, covered by a blue jacket-type housecoat. Police officer Alfred Swetokas, who responded to the call, said there had apparently been a heavy impact of the left side of the head against the pavement, causing what he thought was instantaneous death.

Detectives said a window was found open in the study. The metal frame of what had been an outer strom window, but which contained no glass, was in a bent state, but this appeared to have been a longstanding condition and was held unrelated to last night's incident, detectives added.

Of Miss Vanderbilt's medical history, the police said it was immediately known only that she had been under treatment for diabetes. No drugs of any kind were found in the room where she was last seen alive, they said.

Etiquette's Arbiter
By ROBERT D. McFADDEN

To Amy Vanderbilt, etiquette was more than a set of social rules or a guide to gracious living. It was, rather, a panoramic view of the world that enabled her to see—and to comment extensively upon—the greatness and smallness of people.

For years, she was the nation's principal authority on the subject, the successor to Emily Post and the arbiter of manners in an increasingly classless society.

Miss Vanderbilt was a celebrity long before the 1952 publication of "Amy Vanderbilt's Complete Book of Etiquette," a 700-page source book of customs, mores and manners that reviewers of the day called a monumental tract for social historians of the future.

The book, revised a number of times in years since, sold millions of copies. Its advice ranged over the behavioral spectrum from the placement of a soup spoon to the running of a mansion full of servants.

She was a prolific writer. In addition to a half-dozen books, she wrote scores of articles for The New Yorker, McCall's, Collier's, This Week, Better Homes & Gardens, American Home and other magazines and wrote for newspapers for more than 30 years.

She was a columnist for the old International News Service in the nineteen-thirties, and from 1954 to 1968 her column for United Features Syndicate was published in more than 100 newspapers in the United States and abroad and had an audience of more than 40 million readers.

In more recent years, she wrote a column for The Los Angeles Times Syndicate, living, working and occasionally entertaining in her century-old brownstone in Manhattan.

Miss Vanderbilt was married four times and divorced three times and had three sons, Lincoln Gill Clark, Paul Vanderbilt Knopf and Stephen John Knopf.

Her marriages were to Robert S. Brinkerhoff in 1929, Morton G. Clark in 1935, Hans Knopf in 1945 and Curtis B. Kellar in 1968.

A strikingly cosmopolitan woman with gray eyes, Miss Vanderbilt enjoyed her craft and her celebrity. She drew up a code of courtesy for New York bus and subway riders about 10 years ago, and lectured a group of taxi drivers here a year ago.

Miss Vanderbilt was a direct descendant of Jan Aoertsen van der Bilt, who settled on Long Island in 1650, and of five generations of antecedents who lived on Staten Island starting in 1715. She was a cousin of Commodore Cornelius Vanderbilt, the shipping and railroad magnate; her great-great-grandfather was one of the founders of the Bank of Manhattan, and her grandfather, Joseph L. Vanderbilt, invented the figure-eight stitch on baseballs.

She was born on July 22, 1908, the daughter of Joseph Mortimer Vanderbilt, an insurance broker, and Mary Estelle Brooks Vanderbilt. While attending Curtis High School, Staten Island, she worked as society and feature writer for The Staten Island Advance, beginning her journalism career at the age of 16.

Studied in Switzerland

After studies in Switzerland and at the Packer Collegiate Institute in Brooklyn, she entered New York University and studied journalism for two years. In the nineteen-thirties and forties, she worked in a variety of jobs, as an account executive in an advertising agency, the business manager of a literary magazine known as The American Spectator, and in public relations for several concerns.

Miss Vanderbilt, an official etiquette consultant for a variety of organizations, including the World Book Encyclopedia and the State Department, traveled widely, lectured frequently and occasionally found time to tend a garden or fish in the Saugatuck River near her Connecticut farm.

She was often the hostess of parties at her town house here, but she once told an interviewer: "I hate big parties. I like simplicity in people and in entertaining. I have met all kinds of people; I like to talk to and hear them talk."

But, she added, "I have no use for people who exhibit manners."

It was in the late nineteen-forties that Doubleday, Inc., approached her to write a book about etiquette. She retired to "Daisyfields," her farm in Westport, Conn., and devoted about four years to the project that was to make her the national authority on the subject of etiquette.

At first, she told acquaintances that she thought it was "almost silly" to describe "such things as the traditional formal dinner for 34 with a butler and several footmen." But she warmed to the task and produced a massive volume that Leo Lerman, in a review for The New York Times, described as "monumental."

"In writing what is obviously the most comprehensive of current manners manuals," he said, "Amy Vanderbilt has, while codifying today's manners for those who wish information on usage, made a large contribution to the future social historian."

Miss Vanderbilt never talked of etiquette as mere rules, but rather as the basis of kindnesses among people. In recent years, she called traditional etiquette out of place in an era of social, philosophical and economic upheaval and war atrocities.

But she noted that formalized behavior had value in some situations, such as at funerals, where people need to mask their disquiet.

She eschewed the feminist "Ms." title, declaring: "Ms. is unbearable. Look it up in the dictionary. It means 'manuscript.'"

In addition to her literary efforts, Miss Vanderbilt also appeared often on Television and radio. From 1954 to 1960, she was the host of a television etiquette program called "It's in Good Taste," and from 1960 to 1962 she had a radio show called "The Right Thing to Do."

Daily Express
4th May 1964

NANCY: SHE TRIUMPHED IN A MAN'S WORLD

By WILLIAM BARKLEY

The Times
9th April 1840

The celebrated Beau Brummell died at Caen, in Normandy, on the 30th ult., at the age of 62. He had been long in distressed circumstances, living on the charity of friends, and latterly had been confined in a madhouse.—*Evening paper.*

SO "Nancy" is dead, the irrepressible, the tense bundle of electric vitality, who did more than anyone else for the practical emancipation of women.

All the pioneers of women's rights, all the suffragettes to whom she was sympathetic, never put on a show like being the First Woman M.P.

When her husband resigned as Tory M.P. for Plymouth, Sutton, on succeeding his father as Viscount Astor, it seemed natural that she should be the candidate.

It was 1919. The terrible war which had ended 12 months earlier would never have been won if women in millions had not torn up traditions, flooding into factories and Services to do men's jobs.

Preserve

Parliament remained the biggest male preserve. Its walls fell on December 2 when a slim, girlish figure (mother of six) set the first woman's foot during sitting hours on the Floor of the House.

And to be the only woman in the close rough-and-tumble of '600 men was an experience which even she found intimidating.

Not for long. Soon she was fighting like a spitfire for her three causes — down with Socialism, down with booze, and up with the rights of women.

She championed and in four years carried a Bill which prevents the sale of liquor to under-18's. (Does it ?)

Guardianship of children, legitimacy laws, women police—such were her interests. She bounced the Baldwin Government into enacting "Votes for Flappers"—the vote for women at 21 on equal terms with men.

She had harried the Home Secretary into a half-promise which Baldwin interpreted as binding.

Trapped

In the Commons she was exasperating, maddening. She kept up a continuous mutter during speeches in a whisper that rang like a bell. A favourite butt of her attacks, a Cockney Irishman Jack Jones, was so infuriated that in this man's place he was trapped into shouting : " I am a better man drunk than you are sober."

Above the laughter the bell voice rang out : " You have never seen yourself drunk."

Winston Churchill silenced her once by turning round and roaring at her : " Yes, Sir !" As all speeches are addressed to the Speaker — never yet a woman—this term was a damper. No one else had thought of it.

I have heard the whole Socialist Party roar with approval when her disturbing presence rose to leave.

She was an unkind controversialist. She said many foolish things which she should have repented later. But she never gave her words a second thought. At times she did not seem to give them even a first thought.

But such gusto ! Such restless, fidgeting joy in life ! And she had the courage of 50 .

Mystery

Lord and Lady Astor were famous hosts in St. James's Square and at Cliveden.

Left-wing writers built up a sinister mystery about these parties and spread suspicions that some of the "Cliveden set" were pro-Nazis. Lady Astor insisted this was all nonsense.

Coming in on the post-war emotions of 1919, "Nancy" feared she might be eclipsed in those of 1945. After 25 years' unbroken service in the House, she retired to Plymouth where her husband and she, as mayor and mayoress, gave great comfort and aid in the bombing and rebuilding.

There have been as many as 27 women M.P.s at one time in a Parliament. But none who followed her pioneer footsteps ever equalled "Nancy" for indestructible femininity.

Less in the public eye of recent years she brimmed with vitality to the end—aged 84.

The Times
31st May 1824

CHARACTER OF LORD BYRON.
[By Sir Walter Scott.]

The following warm-hearted tribute to the memory of Lord Byron is a proof how much liberality is allied to true genius :—

Amidst the general calmness of the political atmosphere, we have been stunned from another quarter by one of those death-notes which are pealed at intervals, as from an archangel's trumpet, to awaken the soul of a whole people at once. Lord Byron, who has so long and so amply filled the highest place in the public eye, has shared the lot of humanity. His Lordship died at Missolonghi on the 19th of April. That mighty genius which walked amongst men as something superior to ordinary mortality, and whose powers were beheld with wonder, and something approaching to terror, as if we know not whether they were of good or of evil, is laid as soundly to rest as the poor peasant whose ideas never went beyond his daily task. The voice of just blame and of malignant censure are at once silenced ; and we feel almost as if the great luminary of heaven had suddenly disappeared from the sky, at the moment when every telescope was levelled for the examination of the spots which dimmed its brightness. It is not now the question what where Byron's faults, what his mistakes ; but how is the blank which he has left in British literature to be filled up? Not, we fear, in one generation, which, among many highly gifted persons, has produced none who approach Byron in originality, the first attribute of genius. Only thirty-seven years old :—so much already done for immortality—so much time remaining, as it seems to us short-sighted mortals, to maintain and to extend his fame, and to atone for errors in conduct and levities in composition ; who will not grieve that such a race has been shortened, though not always keeping the straight path—such a light extinguished, though sometimes flaming to dazzle and to bewilder ? One word on this ungrateful subject ere we quit it for ever.

The errors of Lord Byron arose neither from depravity of heart—for nature had not committed the anomaly of uniting to such extraordinary talents an imperfect moral sense—nor from feelings dead to the admiration of virtue. No man had ever a kinder heart for sympathy, or a more open hand for the relief of distress ; and no mind was ever more formed for the enthusiastic admiration of noble actions, providing he was convinced that the actors had proceeded upon disinterested principles. Lord Byron was totally free from the curse and degradation of literature—its jealousies, we mean, and its envy. But his wonderful genius was of a nature which disdained restraint, even when restraint was most wholesome. When at school, the tasks in which he excelled were those only which he undertook, voluntarily ; and his situation as a young man of rank, with strong passions, and in the uncontrolled enjoyment of a considerable fortune, added to that impatience of structures or coercion which was natural to him. As an author, he refused to plead at the bar of criticism ; as a man, he would not submit to be morally amenable to the tribunal of public opinion. Remonstrances from a friend, of whose intentions and kindness he was secure, had often great weight with him ; but there were few who could venture on a task so difficult. Reproof he endured with impatience, and reproach hardened him in his error—so that he often resembled the gallant war-steed, who rushes forward on the steel that wounds him. In the most painful crisis of his private life, he evinced this irritability, and impatience of censure in such a degree, as almost to resemble the noble victim of the bull-fight, which is more maddened by the squibs, darts, and petty annoyances of the unworthy crowds beyond the lists, than by the lance of his nobler, and, so to speak, his more legitimate antagonist. In a word, much of that in which he erred was in bravado and scorn of his censors, and was done with the motive of Dryden's despot, " to show his arbitrary power." It is needless to say that his was a false and prejudiced view of such a contest ; and if the noble bard gained a sort of triumph, by compelling the world to read poetry, though mixed with baser matter, because it was wit, he gave, in return, an unworthy triumph to the unworthy, besides deep sorrow to those whom in his cooler moments, he most valued.

It was the same with his politics, which on several occasions assumed a tone menacing and contemptuous to the constitution of his country ; while, in fact, Lord Byron was in his own heart sufficiently sensible, not only of his privileges as a Briton, but of the distinction attending his high birth and rank, and was peculiarly sensitive of those shades which constitute what is termed the manners of a gentleman. Indeed, notwithstanding his having employed epigrams, and all the petty war of wit, when such would have been much better abstained from, he would have been found, had a collision taken place between the aristocratic parties in the State, exerting all his energies in defence of that to which he naturally belonged. His own feeling on these subjects he has explained in the very last canto of Don Juan ; and they are in entire harmony with the opinions which we have seen expressed in his correspondence, at a moment when matters appeared to approach a serious struggle in his native country :

" He was an independent—ay, much more,
" Than those who were not paid for independence ;
" As common soldiers, or a common—Shore,
" Have in their several acts or parts ascendance
" O'er the irregulars in lust or gore,
" Who do not give professional attendance.
" Thus on the mob all statesmen are as eager
" To prove their pride as footmen to a beggar."

We are not, however, Byron's apologists, for now, alas ! he needs none. His excellencies will now be universally acknowledged, and his faults (let us hope and believe) not remembered in his epitaph. It will be recollected what a part he has sustained in British literature since the first appearance of Childe Harold,—a space of nearly 16 years. There has been no reposing under the shade of his laurels, no living upon the resource of past reputation ; none of that coddling and petty precaution, which little authors call " taking care of their fame." Byron let his fame take care of itself. His foot was always in the arena, his shield hung always in the lists ; and although his own gigantic renown increased the difficulty of the struggle, since he could produce nothing, however great, which exceeded the public estimate of his genius, yet he advanced to the honourable contest again and again and again, and came always off with distinction, almost always with complete triumph. As various in composition as Shakspeare himself (this will be admitted by all who are acquainted with his Don Juan), he has embraced every topic of human life, and sounded every string on the divine harp, from its slightest to its most powerful and heart-astounding tones. There is scarce a passion or a situation which has escaped his pen ; and he might be drawn, like Garrick, between the weeping and the laughing Muse, although his most powerful efforts have certainly been dedicated to Melpomene. His genius seemed as prolific as various. The most prodigal use did not exhaust his powers, nay, seemed rather to increase their vigour. Neither Childe Harold, nor any of the most beautiful of Byron's earlier tales, contain more exquisite morsels of poetry than are to be found scattered through the cantos of Don Juan, amidst verses which the author appears to have thrown off with an effort as spontaneous as that of a tree resigning its leaves to the wind. But that noble tree will never more bear fruit or blossom ! It has been cut down in its strength, and the past is all that remains to us of Byron. We can scarce reconcile ourselves to the idea—scarce think that the voice is silent for ever, which, bursting so often on our ear, was often heard with rapturous admiration, sometimes with regret, but always with the deepest interest :

" All that's bright must fade,
" The brightest still the fleetest."

With a strong feeling of awful sorrow, we take leave of the subject. Death creeps upon our most serious as well as upon our most idle employments ; and it is a reflection solemn and gratifying, that he found our Byron in no moment of levity, but contributing his fortune, and hazarding his life, in behalf of a people only endeared to him by their past glories, and as fellow-creatures suffering under the yoke of a heathen oppressor. To have fallen in a crusade for freedom and humanity, as in olden times it would have been an atonement for the blackest crimes, may in the present be allowed to expiate greater follies than even exaggerated calumny has propagated against Byron.

The Times
15th December 1896

A correspondent writes :—With reference to the death of Mr. Alfred Nobel, the Swedish engineer and chemist, who was the inventor of dynamite, a brief notice of which event appeared in The Times on Friday, it may be mentioned that the invention of dynamite by him was more or less the result of an accident. Nitro-glycerine, which is the active agent in dynamite, is a liquid, and was formerly known as glonoine oil. Prior to the invention of dynamite several serious and fatal accidents had occurred with nitro-glycerine, both in transport and handling. Impressed with its value and importance as a blasting agent, and with its highly dangerous character as an article of commerce, Mr. Nobel set to work to discover a means of rendering it safe except under the actual conditions of doing work. It is stated that while he was carrying out his researches in this direction he happened to spill some nitro-glycerine on some sand, which absorbed and retained it. Upon experimenting with the mixture thus accidentally formed, Nobel found that the explosive properties of the nitro-glycerine remained unimpaired. He therefore decided to use sand as a carrier for the oil, and at first he adopted this material for absorbing and retaining it, giving to the compound the expressive name of dynamite. The first demonstration of the power and comparative safety of dynamite in this form was given by Nobel personally at the stone quarries at Merstham, Surrey, on July 14, 1868. Certain disadvantages in the use of sand as a carrier for the oil were, however, developed in practice, and this led to further investigations, which resulted in Nobel's substituting Kieselguhr, or infusorial earth, instead of sand. By this means he succeeded in converting one of the most dangerous explosive compounds into a tractable blasting agent, practically inaugurating the era of high explosives of this class, in which he subsequently introduced several useful improvements.

A PEACEFUL END. SURROUNDED BY CHILDREN AND GRANDCHILDREN.

The Daily Graphic 23rd January 1901

DEATH OF THE QUEEN.

PARLIAMENT TO MEET TO-DAY.

TRIBUTES FROM ABROAD.

MESSAGE FROM THE KING.

THE MOURNING EMPIRE.

continued

VICTORIA.

The Great Queen is dead. Full of years and crowned with glories and love incomparable, Victoria has passed into the Shadowland. The Empire is bereaved of its Chief—of her "who ruled over the land that the great Macedonian could not conquer, and over a continent of which Columbus never dreamt, the Queen of every sea and of nations in every zone." A reign has come to an end of which the splendour has no equal ; a life is closed of which the beauty is unsurpassed. There has gone from us one who, for sixty-four happy years, has been not only the venerated Sovereign, but the adored idol of her people, the personification of all they have held dearest in life. From end to end of the vast Empire which has been so long gladdened with her benignant sway, the dread news will bring a sense of acutest loss. Among the daughter nations in America, Australia, and Africa, as among the dusky myriads of Hindostan, whose Imperial crown she wore, the mourning will be not less profound than with us, the bereaved children of the Motherland. Her wealth of wisdom, her inexhaustible gentleness filled even the wide expanse of her matchless dominions, and there is not one of the hundreds of millions of loyal hearts over whom she ruled which will not be stricken with grief to-day.

To say that a glorious reign has closed and that a life of exceeding beauty has ended is to express but faintly the sense of loss which fills the Empire. Queen Victoria was far more to us than a great Sovereign. She was a part of ourselves in a sense that no other monarch ever was. The unaffected graces of her girlhood captivated our hearts long before her proved sagacity as the guardian of the Empire gained for her our implicit trust. That hold on our affections deepened with every year of her long and happy reign— deepened because we felt that we had in her a mirror of our better selves, an embodiment of those virtues of the home and hearth which are the most sacred elements of the English nature. She rescued the Crown from the cold and academic sphere of its constitutional usefulness and made it an integral part of the pulsating life of the masses of the nation. Other patriot monarchs have been hailed as the personifications of a national spirit which has too often been but the creed of a class ; but she stood not only for the honour and greatness of her people, but also and chiefly for the noblest features in their character, for those rules of conduct and homely affections which make the happiness of the cottage as of the palace, for the Puritan virtues which lie at the root of our democratic progress. We have loved and worshipped her as the highest type of the national character, as our Sovereign lady, not only in the domain of politics, but in that domestic field of the national consciousness which finds little direct reflection in Acts of Parliament and diplomatic despatches. "The grand art of reigning," said Montesquieu, "is to love honour and virtue." Queen Victoria realised this maxim in a sense scarcely dreamt of by the French philosopher. She not only loved honour and virtue, but she personified them, she vitalised the whole of our public life with them, and by their means she secured a place in the hearts of her people and in the esteem of the world which no other woman ever enjoyed. But if it was as the Good Queen that she won our adoring allegiance, it is not less as the Wise Queen that she has been honoured by us, and that she will be remembered by history. The moral beauty of her life permeated the whole of her wonderful conduct of public affairs. It gave to her quick intelligence the precious help of a high conception of duty and a rich fund of natural sympathy. Throughout her life she strove to do the right, to understand the good of her people and to achieve it, to keep the ship of State moving ever onward, its helm obedient to the best impulses of the nation. No one needs to be told nowadays that the Queen exercised a vast influence on the political life of her country and that she laboured as hard and as fruitfully as any of her Ministers. If during the last sixty-four years England has been the one country in Europe which has not been torn and weakened by internecine conflict, the one land in which political liberty has peacefully broadened down, leaving the normal activities of the nation free to amass wealth and to extend and consolidate the Empire, it is to the sagacity of the Queen that we have chiefly to be grateful. She vindicated the Monarchy as an indispensable attribute of democratic progress ; she showed how in the fluctuations and conflicts of popular government the Crown, wisely and sympathetically administered, might become the trusted guardian of the people's rights and of the nation's honour. As the liberties of the people have grown, the influence and authority of the Crown have steadily strengthened, and both have become imperishably united by a tradition of wisdom, of sympathy, and of mutual confidence, which it is to be hoped will dominate our history for ages to come.

This is the great tradition she leaves to her exalted successor, to whom the eyes of the nation are now turned. That he will strive to maintain it we do not doubt, and that in his great task he will have all the affectionate help of his subjects he needs no assurance. But it is not of the future that we can think in these first moments of the nation's bereavement.

Our eyes are turned backward to the glorious past, to that Victorian epoch which has now come to an end, and the story of which will live for ever as one of the most fragrant and most splendid pages of human history. It is difficult to realise that the gentle Lady who made it is now no more, that the nation will no longer know her gracious presence, will no longer feel her wise influence on its affairs, will no longer be thrilled by those unaffected messages which in moments of joy and sorrow have touched every heart.

Pride, honour, country, throbbed through all her strain.
And shall we praise? God's praise was hers before,
And on our futile laurels she looks down,
Herself our bravest crown.

The Queen is dead.

No language can express the sense of personal loss which these four words convey to the millions of men and women who form the great Empire over which the beloved Sovereign ruled so wisely and so long. Few of us, perhaps, have realised till now how large a part she had in the life of every one of us; how the thread of her life, in binding and strengthening, like a golden weft, the warp of the nation's progress, has touched and brightened the life of each and all of her subjects. For the moment the sense of public loss is overwhelmed in personal sorrow.

The melancholy news was first made public by the following message to the Lord Mayor :—

"OSBORNE, 6.45 p.m.

"MY BELOVED MOTHER, THE QUEEN, HAS JUST PASSED AWAY, SURROUNDED BY HER CHILDREN AND GRANDCHILDREN.

"ALBERT EDWARD."

To this message the Lord Mayor at once replied as follows :—

Your Royal Highness's telegram, announcing the nation's great loss, I have received with profound distress and grief, and have communicated this most sad intimation to my fellow citizens. Her Majesty's name and memory will live for ever in the hearts of her people. May I respectfully convey to your Royal Highness and all the members of the Royal family the earnest sympathy and condolence of the City of London in your great sorrow.

FRANK GREEN, Lord Mayor of London.

A few hours previously the Lord Mayor had been warned by the following message :—

"My painful duty obliges me to inform you that the life of the beloved Queen is in the greatest danger.—ALBERT EDWARD.

"Osborne, 4 o'clock."
The bulletins issued earlier in the day had also prepared the public to anticipate the worst. They were as follow :—

Osborne, 8 a.m.
The Queen this morning shows signs of diminishing strength, and Her Majesty's condition again assumes a more serious aspect.
JAMES REID, M.D.
R. DOUGLAS POWELL, M.D.
THOMAS BARLOW, M.D.

Osborne, 12 o'clock.
There is no change for the worse in the Queen's condition since this morning's bulletin. Her Majesty has recognised the several members of the Royal Family who are here. The Queen is now asleep.
JAMES REID, M.D.
R. DOUGLAS POWELL, M.D.
THOMAS BARLOW, M.D.

Osborne, 4 p.m.
The Queen is slowly sinking.
JAMES REID, M.D.
R. DOUGLAS POWELL, M.D.
THOMAS BARLOW, MD.

And finally :—

Osborne, Monday, 6.45 p.m.
Her Majesty the Queen breathed her last at 6.30 p.m., surrounded by her children and grandchildren.
JAMES REID, M.D.
R. DOUGLAS POWELL, M.D.
THOMAS BARLOW, M.D.

Shortly after the receipt of the telegram from the King, a letter reached the Lord Mayor from the Home Secretary in the following terms :—

Home Office, Whitehall,
January 22nd, 1901.
MY LORD,—It is my painful duty to inform your lordship of the death of Our Most Gracious Sovereign Queen Victoria.
This melancholy event took place at Osborne at 6.30 p.m. this day.
I have to request your lordship will give directions for tolling the great bell of St. Paul's Cathedral.
I have the honour to be, my lord,
Your lordship's obedient servant,
CHARLES T. RITCHIE.
The Right Hon. the
Lord Mayor of London.

Mr. Balfour telegraphed from Osborne to the Lord Steward of Her late Majesty's household, the Earl of Pembroke :—

The Queen died peacefully at 6.30.
ARTHUR BALFOUR.

New York Times
15th January 1957

Humphrey Bogart Is Dead at 57; Movie Star Had Throat Cancer

HOLLYWOOD, Calif., Jan. 14—Humphrey Bogart died in his sleep early this morning in the bedroom of his Holmby Hills home. The 57-year-old movie actor, an Academy Award winner, had been suffering for more than two years from cancer of the esophagus.

In the latter part of February, 1956, he underwent surgery at Good Samaritan Hospital for removal of a malignant growth. He recovered from the operation and gained back some of the weight he had lost. But, in November, 1956, he was admitted to St. John's Hospital in Santa Monica for treatment of nerve pressure caused by the growth of scar tissue on his throat.

Mr. Bogart leaves his wife, Lauren Bacall, actress, whom he married in 1945. The couple had two children, a son, Stephen Humphrey, born in 1949, and a daughter, Leslie, born in 1952. The actor is survived also by a sister, Frances Rose Bogart of New York.

Miss Bacall was Mr. Bogart's fourth wife. His previous marriages were also to actresses. He married Helen Menken in 1926 and divorced her a year later. His marriage to Mary Philips the next year lasted until 1937. In 1938 he took Mayo Methot as his third wife. The couple was divorced shortly before Mr. Bogart wed Miss Bacall.

Deflated Publicity Balloons

Mr. Bogart was one of the most paradoxical screen personalities in the recent annals of Hollywood. He often deflated the publicity balloons that keep many a screen star aloft, but he remained one of Hollywood's top box-office attractions for more than two decades.

On the screen he was most often the snarling, laconic gangster who let his gun do his talking. In private life, however, he could speak glibly and wittily on a wide range of subjects and make better copy off the cuff than the publicists could devise for him.

He had a large, seemingly permanent following among the mass audience. Yet he said he deplored "mass activities." Furthermore, he did everything he could to confound the popular image of a movie star.

Mr. Bogart received an Academy Award in 1952 for his performance in "The African Queen." Still, he made it clear he set little store by such fanfare. Earlier he had established a mock award for the best performance in a film by an animal, making sure that the bit of satire received full notice in the press.

Proud of Profession

But despite this show of frivolity, he was fiercely proud of his profession. "I am a professional," he said. "I have a respect for my profession. I worked hard at it."

Attesting to this are a number of highly interesting characterizations in such films as "The Petrified Forest" (1936), "High Sierra" (1941), "Casablanca" (1942), "To Have and Have Not" (1944), "Key Largo" (1948), "The Treasure of Sierra Madre" (1948), "The African Queen" (1951), "Sabrina," "The Caine Mutiny" (1954) and "The Desperate Hours" (1955). The actor's last film, "The Harder They Fall," was released last year.

Mr. Bogart's high sense of responsibility toward his profession may have stemmed from the fact that both his parents were highly successful professional persons. His mother was Maud Humphrey, a noted illustrator and artist. His father was Belmont DeForest Bogart, a prosperous surgeon. Their son, born on Christmas Day in 1899, was reared in fashionable New York society.

He attended Trinity School and Phillips Academy at Andover, Mass., but an early note of discord crept into this genteel strain when he was expelled from Andover for irreverence to a faculty member.

Mr. Bogart enlisted in the Navy in 1917 and crossed the Atlantic several times as a helmsman aboard a transport ship. As a civilian he was a tugboat inspector and saw brief service in an investment house.

Next, he had a job with World Films for a short while and then appeared as a stage manager for an acting group. It was an easy step to his first roles in the early Nineteen Twenties. His rise to fame over the next fifteen years, however, was a hard road, often lined with critical brickbats.

He appeared in "Swifty" and plugged on in drawing-room comedies, appearing in "Hell's Bells," "The Cradle Snatchers," "Its a Wise Child" and many others in which he usually played a callow juvenile or a romantic second lead.

He accepted a movie contract with Fox in 1931, but roles in a few Westerns failed to improve matters and soon he was back on Broadway, convinced that his hard-bitten face disqualified him in the close-ups as a matinee idol.

In 'Petrified Forest'

But toward the end of 1934 he used this granite-like face to rebuild, with enormous success, a new dramatic career. Having heard that Robert E. Sherwood's "The Petrified Forest" had a gangster role, he approached Mr. Sherwood for the important part. The playwright referred him to the director, who told Mr. Bogart to return in three days for a reading.

When Mr. Bogart reappeared before the director he had a three-day growth of beard and was wearing shabby clothes. His reading and appearance brought him the supporting role of Duke Mantee, his most memorable Broadway part. Leslie Howard was the star of the play. Mr. Bogart later did the same part for the movie to considerable critical acclaim.

This was the first of more than fifty pictures that Mr. Bogart made, most of them for Warner Brothers. A spate of crime dramas followed, including "Angels With Dirty Faces," "The Roaring Twenties," "Bullets or Ballots," "Dead End," "San Quentin" and, finally, "High Sierra" in 1941.

Mr. Bogart then insisted on roles with more scope. They were forthcoming in such films as "Casablanca," "To Have and Have Not" and "Key Largo," wherein Mr. Bogart's notorious screen hardness was offset by a latent idealism that showed itself in the end.

Won New Followers

In "The Treasure of Sierra Madre," as a prospector driven to evil by a lust for gold, the range of his characterization won him new followers.

A further range of his talents was displayed also in "The African Queen," wherein his portrayal of a tropical tramp with a yen for gin and Katharine Hepburn won him an "Oscar." Another distinguished portrait was that of the neurotic Captain Queeg in the movie version of "The Caine Mutiny." His aptitude for romantic comedy became clear when he played the bitter business man who softens under the charms of Audrey Hepburn in "Sabrina." Mr. Bogart also appeared in "The Barefoot Contessa," made in 1954.

The movie actor made no secret of his nightclubbing. He was also a yachting enthusiast. At one point in his career he reportedly made $200,000 a film and he was for years among the top ten box-office attractions.

Mr. Bogart joined other actors in 1947 in a flight to Washington to protest the methods of the House Un-American Activities Committee, which was investigating communism in the movie colony. He was often a supporter of Democratic political causes.

Sports & Games

It is curious how so many of those responsible for
formally initiating sports which now have massive
following were not accorded notice when they died:
J. C. Thring, for instance, who formulated the rules of
football, or W. W. Ellis, the man who picked up the ball
and ran, thus starting rugby, who has only the famous
plaque in commemoration. Doing duty for all the
initiators – including also Abner Doubleday (baseball),
E. C. Goode (table tennis), and W. C. Wingfield (lawn
tennis) – there is Lord **Derby**, who gave his name to the
greatest of flat races. Playing together has long been
supposed by many to have extraordinarily beneficial
effects, inducing co-operation, friendship, international
understanding, and so on: in tribute to this delightful
optimism, Baron **de Coubertin** is recorded. The rest
evidence personal whim as much as anything else. **Jack
Broughton**, the first of the great prizefighters,
represents whoever the reader's own boxing hero may
be; and **Babe Ruth** similarly for baseball enthusiasts.
More seriously, **W. G. Grace** epitomises British
sportsmanship, as the genius of cricket, itself perhaps
the British genius. Somewhat more sedately, **Horace
Vanderbilt**, the inventor of bridge, is given his due, as is
also **Harry Vardon**, who still has claim to being one of
the greatest golfers we have seen. The **Renshaw**
brothers dominated lawn tennis in its early days,
Elizabeth Ryan held the record for Wimbledon
championship titles for 50 years until 1979. **John L.
Sullivan** was the first generally recognized world
heavyweight boxing champion and certainly the first
international sports personality; **Jack Johnson** the first
negro sportsman to win worldwide acclaim. **Joe Davis**
represents cue games and **William Webb Ellis** is the
legendary "inventor" of rugby. **Abebe Bikila**'s
achievment of winning the Olympic marathon twice in a
row may never be beaten. Finally, standing for romance
and sheer excitement, **Alberto Ascari** is here, to remind
us of a whole host of great racing drivers.

New York Times
21st March 1937

HARRY VARDON, 66, NOTED GOLFER, DIES

British Star's Record of Six Open Championships in Own Country Never Equaled

WON TITLE HERE IN 1900

Beaten by Ouimet in Famous Play-Off—Regarded as the Greatest Master of Form

Wireless to THE NEW YORK TIMES.

LONDON, March 20.—Harry Vardon, generally regarded as one of the greatest of all golfers, died at his home in Totteridge, Hertfordshire, today of pleurisy at the age of 66. He had suffered from chest trouble for many years.

Never Took Lesson

LONDON, March 20 (Æ).—Harry Vardon, who never took a golf lesson in his life, ranked jointly with Bobby Jones as one of the two greatest masters the game ever produced.

Death resulted from a chill he contracted Wednesday evening while walking around the South Herts golf course, which only six years ago he shot in 67 strokes.

His passing removed the only player whom English and Scottish adherents of the game ever were willing to mention in the same breath with Jones. They still are undecided which was the greater Vardon, a member of the Ryder Cup team in 1921, had won sixty-two first-class championships.

While his game was well-rounded, Vardon will remain famous principally for his beautiful iron shots, which those who watched him during his best years say never will be equaled. He gained the reputation of being an indifferent putter, but his admirers declare this was exaggerated.

His clubs were almost the lightest used by a ranking player. His favorite was the cleek, which he used almost to the exclusion of the brassie. He was one of the first golfers to wear plus fours.

One of his last recorded appearances in championship play was in the 1927 open at St. Andrews, which Jones won with what then was a record total of 285.

The fickle public—even at St. Andrews—had forgotten Vardon as 5,000 of them followed Jones onto the rambling fifth green. Vardon, all alone with his caddy, was playing onto the fourteenth, a few yards away. As the crowd threatened to overrun his ball, the veteran was seen standing over it valiantly fighting them off. Nobody recognized him.

HELPED POPULARIZE GOLF

Played Large Role in Making the Game One for Millions

By WILLIAM D. RICHARDSON

The death of Harry Vardon will be mourned wherever the game of golf is played, especially by linksmen who were in the game up to the early 1920's.

No man played a greater part in building up this game, which is now the recreation of millions in almost every nation on earth, than this product of the little village of Grouville on the Isle of Jersey in the English Channel.

Not only will he be remembered for the prodigious feats he performed on the links but for his influence as a master stylist. He won the British open on six occasions, the years being 1896, 1898, 1899, 1903, 1911 and 1914; he was runner-up in 1900, 1901, 1902 and 1912, twice finished third, once fourth and four times fifth—a record of consistency.

He also played a large rôle in the development of golf in America, focusing attention on the game, which was then in its infancy here by his triumph in the national open at the Chicago Golf Club in 1900.

On the occasion of Vardon's first trip here he made a tour of the country playing exhibition matches during which he was on the winning end of fifty, halved two and lost only thirteen, eleven of his losses coming when he played the best ball of two opponents.

Beginning of Exhibitions Here

That tour, made thirty-seven years ago, marked the beginning of golf exhibitions in this country. It was the first serious missionary effort American golf had ever enjoyed and following it golf stocks of manufacturers became rapidly depleted and golf, then confined almost solely to men of means, was here to stay.

Thirteen years later Vardon returned to America, accompanied by Ted Ray, rollicking, pipe-smoking Englishman. That year the open championship was held at the Brookline course and at the end of the seventy-two-hole journey Vardon and Ray had been tied by a mere stripling of a youth whose name was Francis Ouimet.

On the day following this 19-year-old ex-caddie wrote America's emancipation proclamation in so far as golf was concerned when he beat his two noted adversaries. The news of that triumph went all over the world, but its effect was principally on America. Not only did it bring golf into the headlines of newspapers, but it stirred the imaginations of thousands of boys and lifted the game out of the category of a "sissy" pastime, limited in scope to a few old but wealthy individuals.

Vardon returned to America in 1920 and, at Inverness, Toledo, finished second, one stroke behind his traveling companion, Ray.

How Vardon came to learn the game is an interesting story in itself. It appears that on a certain Sabbath morning a party of English gentlemen arrived from the mainland and proceeded to lay out a course on the common. This intrusion was resented until it was learned that permission had been duly granted.

He was the author of many books on golf, such as "The Complete Golfer," "How to Play Golf" and "My Golfing Life."

Vardon and Bobby Jones

ATLANTA, March 20 (Æ).—O. B. Keeler, golf writer of The Atlanta Journal, recalled today Harry Vardon's famous rejoinder to Bobby Jones in the United States open tournament of 1920 at the Inverness Club, Toledo.

"Vardon was 50 years old," Mr. Keeler said. "Bobby Jones, then a kid of 18 and playing in his first open, was paired with Vardon, the oldest player in the field and the most distinguished, for the two medal rounds of the qualifying test. At the seventh hole, a dogleg affair, both fired big drives over the angle, the balls coming to rest near the green and with nothing in the way.

"Vardon played a simple run-up with his mongrel iron, to lay the ball close for a birdie 3. Bobby, for no good reason, essayed the more spectacular niblick pitch, and topped the ball wretchedly. It scuttled across the green into a bunker on the other side.

"As the pair walked off the green toward the next tee, Bobby, his ears flaming, tried to alleviate his embarrassment by conversation with Vardon, who up to this time had not spoken a word.

" 'Mr. Vardon,' said Bobby, 'did you ever see a worse shot than that?'

" 'No,' replied Harry Vardon. And that was all. As Bobby said later, the matter appeared to be closed."

Jones, now an Atlanta lawyer, said Vardon "was the most graceful, the most finished golfer I've ever seen. He was the 'old master,' truly."

Was a Caddy at 7

Within a few weeks the course was in operation and among the lads who carried clubs was the boy Vardon, then 7 years old, son of a gardener and one of a family of eight.

Vardon, his brother Tom, now a professional at the White Bear Club in St Paul, and some of the other youngsters were not content merely carrying clubs for others. They laid out a course of their own. Each hole measured fifty yards, their clubs were crude affairs fashioned out of blackthorn shafts driven into lady oak heads. The balls were marbles.

Observing others for whom he caddied and playing on this course was the only instruction Vardon ever had.

Caddying failed to meet all the necessities of the Vardon family and at 13 Harry became a gardener, to a man named Major Spofford who, being a golfer himself, gave young Harry a set of clubs and often took him with him to play.

His encouragement, plus the fact that brother Tom had left home to learn the art of club-making at St. Anne's, finally led Vardon into a field in which he was to become outstanding.

His first golfing job was as pro and greenkeeper at the Studley Royal Club at Ripon. Later he went to the Bury Club and it was from there he registered when he played in the British open for the first time at Prestwick in 1893.

The following year he finished fifth in the event, but two years later he won the first of six championships—an unequaled record. In that one he and Taylor tied with a total of 316 at Muirfield and Vardon won in a play-off. He scored at Prestwick in 1898 with a total of 307, won at Sandwich in 1899 with 310, registered 300 to win at Prestwick in 1903, scored 303 to win at Sandwich in 1911 and finished first at Prestwick in 1914 with 306.

Took Part in Big Money Matches

At the time Vardon came along, the era of big money matches in which the professionals played either for their own money or money put up by their followers was just coming to an end, but he did participate in many, once beating Willie Park over North Berwick and Ganton for £100 a side (roughly $500). He and Taylor played as partners in many, often opposing the two Scots, J. H. Braid and Alex Herd.

Three of those men, Vardon, Braid and Taylor, formed what was known as the "Great Triumvirate" and dominated British professional golf. There was a period from 1894, when Taylor won his first crown, to 1914, when Vardon won his last, that the open was almost their joint property. Only five times during those twenty-one years did it happen that one of the three did not win the title.

Vardon's pre-eminence as a competitor, coupled with his graceful form, caused him to be looked upon as a model and even today form in golf is "Vardon form." He has left as an everlasting monument to himself the Vardon overlapping grip, which he popularized, and which is used by almost all the topnotch players.

Before his day the popular golf grip was the palm grip, used by baseball players. Vardon, however, proved that the overlapping grip produced greater control than did any other.

The Times
24th October 1834

The Earl of Derby, whose death we announced yesterday, was born in the year 1752, and was consequently in the 82d year of his age. He was the father of the present Earl Edward Smith Stanley, and grandfather of the Right Hon. E. G. Stanley, the late Secretary for the Colonies. His first marriage was with a daughter of the late Duke of Hamilton, and on her death he married the celebrated Miss Farren, the actress, whom he has long survived. His Lordship held the high offices of Lord Lieutenant of the county and Chancellor of the Duchy of Lancaster, the former for a period of 60 years. The Stanley family is one of the most ancient in England, and the earldom is the second in the British peerage. The late Earl was a most inveterate sportsman, and the passion for horse-racing and cock-fighting was the absorbing one of his life. He possessed the reputation of having the best breed of cocks in England. For some years past, indeed ever since Liverpool has had a racecourse, he personally attended the meetings, and took the most lively interest in the matches of his horses and cocks, more especially the latter. General Yates, whose breed of cocks is also celebrated, was his invariable opponent, and they annually decided the question of their respective game by a match of 1,000 guineas aside. So strong was the late Earl's penchant for his favourite sport, that cocks by his desire have been introduced into his drawing-room, armed and spurred, even during the latter days of his life. The noble Earl had long since retired from the arena of politics, but during the time that he appeared on the political stage he was a staunch supporter of the party of which Lords Grey and Holland were the leading members.—*Globe.*

Daily Telegraph
7th July 1979

Record holder dies at Wimbledon

By GODFREY BARKER

ELIZABETH "BUNNY" RYAN, 88, who held the record for Wimbledon championships jointly with Mrs Billie-Jean King, died after collapsing at Wimbledon yesterday—the day before Mrs King seeks to take the record which has stood since 1932.

Miss Ryan, who won 19 doubles championships between 1914 and 1932, watched the ladies singles final from the members' stand and felt ill shortly after the start of the men's doubles final.

Her niece, Miss Elizabeth Partridge, said last night: "She hase been quiet recently and she said she had been feeling deadly tired. I think she knew."

Miss Ryan, an American, has lived in Chelsea for the last seven years to be near her sister. Yesterday was her fourth day at Wimbledon.

Had she lived, she might have seen Mds King win a 20th title in today's ladies doubles final. "My sister and I are deeply thankful that she did not live to see that," Miss Partridge said.

"She would of course, have been gracious — she was a sportswoman to the end — but I am glad it has happened this way. It is much better for her."

One more day

LANCE TINGAY writes: Few deaths have been as touching as that of Elizabeth Ryan.

Miss Ryan held the titles record from 1934, when she won her last womens doubles title, to 1975, when Mrs King took the singles and equalled the 19 championships.

Aht the Wimbledon centenary celebrations in 1977 she insisted, although finding it difficult to walk, on tnurning out to receive her medal on the centre court as one of the old champions.

She was born in California and played in her first British tournament in 1912. It was not long before she was having considerable success in the game.

With the French player, Suzanne Lenglen, she formed a doubles partnership that was never beaten betwen 1919 and 1926.

She won thousands of prizes and had the distinction of being the last champion of Imperial Russia. She won the women's singles title just before the 1914-18 War.

The Times
25th October 1915

THE GREATEST OF CRICKETERS.

AN APPRECIATION OF DR. GRACE.

(By Sir Arthur Conan Doyle.)

The world will be the poorer to many of us for the passing of the greatest of cricketers. To those who knew him he was more than a great cricketer. He had many of the characteristics of a great man. There was a masterful personality and a large direct simplicity and frankness which, combined with his huge frame, swarthy features, bushy beard, and somewhat lumbering carriage, made an impression which could never be forgotten.

In spite of his giant West-of-England build, there was, as it seemed to me, something of the gipsy in his colouring, his vitality, and his quick, dark eyes with their wary expression. The bright yellow and red cap which he loved to wear added to this Zingari effect. His elder brother, the Coroner, small, wizened, dark, and wiry, had even more of this gipsy appearance. I speak, of course, only of the effect produced, for I have no reason to think that such blood was in his veins, though, following Borrow, I am ready to believe that there is no better in Europe. There was a fine, open-air breeziness of manner about the man which made his company a delight and added a zest to the game. He was, of course, a highly educated surgeon, but he had rather the fashion of talk which one would associate with a jovial farmer. His voice was high-pitched, considering the huge chest from which it came, and it preserved something of the Western burr.

DECEPTIVE SLOWNESS.

His style and methods were peculiar to himself. In his youth, when he was tall, slim, and agile, he must have been as ideal in his form as in his results. But as this generation knew him he had run to great size and a certain awkwardness of build. As he came towards the wicket, walking heavily with shoulders rounded, his great girth outlined by his coloured sash, one would have imagined that his day was past. He seemed slow, stiff, and heavy at first. When he had made 50 in his quiet methodical fashion he was somewhat younger and fresher. At the end of a century he had not turned a hair, and was watching the ball with as clear an eye as in the first over. It was his advice to play every ball as if it were the first—and he lived up to it. Everything that he did was firm, definite, and well within his strength.

I have had the privilege of fielding at point more than once while he made his hundred, and have in my mind a clear impression of his methods. He stood very clear of his wicket, bending his huge shoulders and presenting a very broad face of the bat towards the bowler. Then, as he saw the latter advance, he would slowly raise himself to his height, and draw back the blade of his bat, while his left toe would go upwards until only the heel of that foot remained upon the ground. He gauged the pitch of the ball in an instant, and if it were doubtful played back rather than forward. Often he smothered a really dangerous length ball by a curious half-cock stroke to which he was partial. He took no risks, and in playing forward trailed the bottom of his bat along the grass as it advanced so as to guard against the shooter—a relic, no doubt, of his early days in the sixties, when shooters were seen more often than on modern grounds.

COMMAND OF THE OFF BALL.

The great strength of his batting was upon the off side. I should not suppose that there was ever a batsman who was so good at controlling that most uncontrollable of all balls, the good-length ball outside the off stump. He would not disregard it, as is the modern habit. Stepping across the wicket while bending his great shoulders, he watched it closely as it rose, and patted it with an easy tap through the slips. In vain, with a fast bumpy bowler pounding them down, did three quivering fieldsmen crouch in the slips, their hands outstretched and eager for the coming catch. Never with the edge of the bat but always with the true centre would he turn the ball groundwards, so that it flashed down and then fizzed off between the grasping hands, flying with its own momentum to the boundary. With incredible accuracy he would place it according to the fields, curving it off squarely if third man were not in his place or tapping it almost straight down upon the ground if short slip were standing wide of the wicket.

In no shot was he so supremely excellent; and like all great things it seemed simplicity itself as he did it. Only when one saw other great batsmen fail did one realize how accurate was the timing and the wrist-work of the old man. When he was well on towards his 60th year I have seen him standing up to Lockwood when man after man was helpless at the other wicket, tapping those terrific expresses away through the slips with the easy sureness with which one would bounce a tennis ball with a racket. The fastest bowler in England sent one like a cannon-shot through his beard with only a comic shake of the head and a good-humoured growl in reply.

A BOWLER FULL OF GUILE.

Of his bowling I have very clear recollections. He was an innovator among bowlers, for he really invented the leg-theory a generation before it was rediscovered and practised by Vine, Armstrong, and others. Grace's traps at leg were proverbial in the seventies. His manner was peculiar. He would lumber up to the wicket, and toss up the ball in a take-it-or-leave-it style, as if he cared little whether it pitched between the wickets or in the next parish. As a matter of fact this careless attitude covered a very remarkable accuracy. His command of length was absolute, and he had just enough leg spin to beat the bat if you played forward to the pitch of the ball. He was full of guile, and the bad ball which was worth four to you was sent, as likely as not, to unsettle you and lead you on.

Those who knew him will never look at the classic sward of Lord's without an occasional vision of the great cricketer. He was, and will remain, the very impersonation of cricket, redolent of fresh air, of good humour, of conflict without malice, of chivalrous strife, of keenness for victory by fair means, and utter detestation of all that was foul. Few men have done more for the generation in which he lived, and his influence was none the less because it was a spontaneous and utterly unconscious one.

The Times
3rd September 1913

BARON PIERRE DE COUBERTIN

THE OLYMPIC GAMES

Baron Pierre de Coubertin, founder of the modern Olympic Games and honorary president of the Olympic Games Committee, died suddenly yesterday afternoon from apoplexy while taking a walk in the park of La Grange, in Geneva, telegraphs our Geneva Correspondent.

Born in 1862, Baron de Coubertin received a school and university education in France and travelled widely. He studied in English and American universities and specialized in the methods of education practised in other countries. The baron was a descendant of Rubens and Cyrano de Bergerac, and there are those who attribute many of his remarkable qualities to his famous forebears. He made a name for himself as a publicist, as a writer on politics, and as an innovator in athleticism. But his name will always be best remembered in connexion with the Olympic Games, which he revived, and of which it is true to say he was the founder, as they are known to-day.

In the closing years of last century and the early years of the present century few persons did more than the baron to promote the good relations between England and France. He was a prolific writer and contributed many articles to English, French, and German reviews and periodicals, on travel, education, politics, and kindred subjects, and he published in England a book on France. He had been in the early nineties editor of the *Revue Athlétique*, and he took every opportunity that came his way of promoting the adoption in French lycées and colleges of English methods of physical education. He could not raise the French schoolmasters from their lethargy, so he induced pupils to form athletic associations. Of all English games he came to the conclusion that Rugby football was the best and most manly of games, and the high position that Rugby football holds in the French sporting world to-day is in a great measure due to his ardent propaganda. He created the Union des Sports Athlétiques, which soon comprised many hundreds of clubs and thousands of members.

De Coubertin having done so much for the nationalization of sport in France then turned his attention to international sport. He concluded that the best way to achieve his object would be to revive the Olympic Games. He went to Greece and saw the advantages of combining physical education with the education of the mind in the manner of the ancient Greeks. After experiencing great difficulties he found support in England and the United States for his idea and assembled a Congress in Paris in 1894 to settle the amateur question in sport. This Congress gave its support, as a side issue, to his plan and led to the foundation of the International Committee. With the help of the then Greek Crown Prince Constantine, and through Coubertin's own perseverance, diplomatic gifts and tireless industry the first Olympic Games were held in Athens in 1896. The Games were held again in Paris in 1900, at Saint Louis in 1904, in London in 1908, and in Stockholm in 1912. The War brought an interruption till 1920, when the Games were held at Antwerp, but on that occasion the Central Powers were excluded. Since then the Games have been held regularly every four years as before the War. The Olympic Committee also instituted the International Winter Sports, which first took place at Chamonix in 1924, and were last held in 1936 a Garmisch-Partenkirchen in Bavaria.

His success in internationalizing sport induced him to try to do the same with politics. He wrote of France in foreign papers, and of foreign countries in French publications. At five American universities he established prizes for winners in debates on subjects suggested by contemporary French policy. But perhaps his best work was done in this sphere by his able advocacy of the entente between France and England. He was a reformer, too, in education and wrote a book in support of what he termed the analytical method as opposed to the synthetical method. Other works on educational questions followed, and he published books on French history, the chief of which are "L'Evolution Française sous la IIIe République," "La Chronique de France," "Où va l'Europe?" and "Histoire Universelle," which appeared in 1935 in three volumes.

In December, 1928, the Baron received the Nobel Peace Prize for his work in promoting the reconciliation of differences between nations by the pursuit of common ends, and in the same year he founded at Lausanne, where he lived, the International Bureau for Education by Sport. In January this year the 50 years' service of the baron as a scholar, educationist, and athlete was celebrated at Lausanne, and speeches were made, among others, by M. Alphand, the French Ambassador in Berne, a representative of the Canton Vaud Government, and by Baron de Coubertin himself, who recalled the great efforts he had had to put forth when he set about reviving the Olympic Games.

Daily Telegraph
14th July 1886

LAWN TENNIS CHAMPIONSHIP.

About 3,000 spectators were present yesterday afternoon at the All-England Lawn Tennis Club enclosure at Wimbledon to witness the competition for the championship between W. Renshaw (the holder of the title) and H. F. Lawford. The weather was of the finest, and what little wind there was did not interfere with play to any extent. Lawford, winning the toss, served the ball from the station end of the court soon after four, but in the first set could not win a single game, which was carried six to love in favour of Renshaw. The loser played up much better in the next, and made amends by taking the second set by seven games to five, but Renshaw afforded very little opportunity for scoring after this, as he took the third and fourth sets by six games to three and six to four respectively, and thus won the match by three sets to one (6—0, 5—7, 6—3, 6—4).

The Times
4th September 1899

Mr. ERNEST RENSHAW, whose name in connexion with lawn tennis is so widely known, died suddenly on Saturday at the Grange, Waltham St. Lawrence, near Twyford, in his 38th year. He was never so great a player as his brother William, who for so many years easily retained the championship title on the wonderful lawns of the All-England Club at Wimbledon; but Mr. Ernest Renshaw was a brilliant exponent of the game to watch, and he more than once had the distinction of holding the doubles championship with his brother. For many years there were few men to approach the Renshaws in skill at a game which they did so much to make popular. Mr. Ernest Renshaw divided his attentions in lawn tennis as a rule between the English season and Cannes; at the latter place he was particularly well known. The funeral will take place to-morrow at Waltham St. Lawrence at 3.30.

Chicago Daily Tribune
11th June 1946

MACHINE JUMPS ROAD ON CURVE IN N. CAROLINA

Held - Heavyweight Title Seven Years

Raleigh, N. C., June 10 (P)—Jack Johnson, the first Negro ever to become heavyweight boxing champion of the world, died at St. Agnes hospital here today shortly after an automobile accident early this afternoon near Franklinton, N. C. Dr. W. D. Allison said that Johnson, who was 68, died of internal injuries and shock.

Fred L. Scott, a Negro companion, said he was accompanying the former champion to New York from Texas, where Johnson recently had concluded a personal appearance tour.

As the heavy automobile approached the city limits of Franklinton, which is about 20 miles north of Raleigh on U. S. highway No. 1, Scott said that Johnson apparently lost control of the car on a curve. The car went off the road and crashed into a telephone pole, hitting on the left side where Johnson was sitting.

Funeral to Be in Chicago

Both Johnson and Scott were thrown out of the car which was demolished. The two were rushed to St. Agnes hospital. Scott was treated for minor injuries and released from the hospital.

Johnson's widow, Mrs. Irene Johnson of Chicago, has been notified of his death, Scott said. A Raleigh funeral home reported that it had been ordered to send the body to Chicago.

The boxing career of Johnson lasted 29 years. He fought in 109 major fights and exhibitions—two of which made pugilistic history.

The first of these was the successful defense of his title against Jim Jeffries at Reno, Nev., July 4, 1910, the original "Battle of the Century." The second was the much disputed bout at Havanna, Cuba, April 16, 1915, when he lost to Jess Willard.

Many experts classified Johnson as one of the greatest fighters in the history of the ring.

Riches went to his head, he spent lavishly and wound up his years traveling from place to place, picking up a living where he could.

Won 69 Fights

His career began in 1899 and ended in 1928. He won 69 of his 80 decision bouts. In 29 fights and exhibitions there was no decision or draws.

Johnson was coming along fast when he won the heavyweight title from Tommy Burns of Canada on Dec. 26, 1908. The fight was held at Rushcutter's bay, just outside Sydney, Australia. Burns was the favorite but Johnson gave him a sound beating and was declared the winner on a technical knockout in the 14th round after police raided the fight.

Despite the conclusive victory, many considered Johnson's title a tainted one. Burns had won his title from Marvin Hart at San Francisco and Johnson's critics pointed out that Hart had beaten "Li'l Artha" in 20 rounds in the same city in 1905.

Clamor for White Hope

During 1909 Johnson defended his title five times. The sporting world clamored for a white hope. Finally, Jim Jeffries, five years out of the ring, yielded to pressure and signed to fight him at Reno. Tex Rickard promoted the fight and made his first bid for fame as one of the sport's greatest promoters.

Jeffries worked himself down from 260 to 230 pounds for the fight and nearly ruined his health in the process. Johnson, a fine physical specimen of 210 pounds, at his peak, toyed with the burly former champion. He taunted him continuously, hit him at will, and finally knocked him out in the 15th round. The victory was not popular in many sections of the country and there were racial disputes.

Five years later Willard won the crown at Havana and created a controversy that raged for years. Willard, after absorbing terrific punishment for most of the fight, won by a knockout in the 26th round. The pictures clearly showed the Negro shading his eyes from the tropical Cuban sun with a gloved hand as Referee Jack Welch counted him out.

Charge of Fixed Fight

There were cries of a "fixed" fight. It was known that Jack had received $30,000, while Jess got nothing. Later, Johnson confessed he had thrown the fight and still later repudiated the confession.

At the time Johnson was financially embarrassed, a fugitive from the United States, and an "undesirable alien" in many European countries.

During the lush years after the Jefferies fight he had plenty of unsavory troubles. After his first wife divorced him he married a white divorcee of Brooklyn, N. Y. She committed suicide a year later.

In 1911 Johnson opened a cafe in Chicago. The place became notorious. Watch and Ward societies investigated his activities and a year later he was arrested, charged with violating the Mann act.

He tried to forestall prosecution by marrying the principal witness against him, a white woman. That effort failed. He was convicted and sentenced to a year and a day in Leavenworth prison. Pending appeal, he jumped bail of $15,000 and escaped to Paris, via Montreal. He was no stranger to Europe, but the happy days when he could, and did, spend $20,000 a week were gone.

Surrenders After Flight

Johnson made small sums by fighting second raters in Paris. When the world war came along he was asked to join the French army but fled to Spain. While there, he was induced to go to Havana for the Willard fiasco.

In the money again he returned to Spain, went broke again, and fought all comers in Madrid. Followed drifting years to Mexico, the Argentine and Brazil. Finally, he surrendered to United States marshalls at San Diego, Cal., on July 20, 1920, and went to Leavenworth.

In prison he was permitted to train and give boxing exhibitions. Released July 9, 1921, he immediately returned to the ring. But he had passed his prime and seven years later he retired, after a six round fight with Bill Hartwell in Kansas City.

Then he eked out a precarious living in various ways. He operated saloons and night clubs and finally joined a carnival. Once he carried a spear in the opera "Aida" in the old New York Hippodrome.

Born in Galveston

John Arthur Johnson, as he was christened, was born in Galveston, Tex., March 31, 1878, the son of a caretaker at a public school. He was admiringly called "Li'l Artha" when he thrashed a waterfront bully at the age of 16. He left home and wandered about the country, doing odd jobs and sparring in amateur bouts.

Johnson learned his boxing skill by serving as a sparring partner for Joe Walcott. After his first fight, in Chicago, May 6, 1899, when he quit in the sixth round, he developed rapidly. In his prime he was lightning fast, a natural boxer and possessed a powerful punch.

New York Herald
3rd February 1918

SULLIVAN WAS IDOL OF SPORTING WORLD

The old Roman is gone. John L. Sullivan, the last champion under London prize ring rules and unique figure in the sporting world, died with his fighting spirit unbroken.

"John L." was a household word for a generation and even to this day any youngster who shows pugnacious proclivities is called "John L." by his elders. Champions have come and gone since the day of Sullivan but the oldtimers never consider any one but "John L." His name was synonymous with the prize ring game in America, for he was the first to take away the laurels of the Britons, whose game of fisticuffs was supposed to be invincible. He showed the English fighters that in the United States there could be developed men who could do things with their fists just a bit better than anything that was developed on the other side. He was the last of the old school of bare knuckle fighters, and when he went down to defeat there was a new era in boxing.

Sullivan's school was the school of hard knocks. He was essentially a slugger and depended on his wallop to bring the other fellow to terms. He was not a skilful boxer such as we have seen in recent years, but he had a terrific punch, and most of the time his opponents were defeated before they went into the ring just by thinking of what might happen.

Retired from Ring in 1892.

John L. was no shrinking violet. He liked to tell of the days when he beat them all. Sitting out in Reno at the time of the Jeffries-Johnson fight, he told a HERALD reporter about a fight that he had when he nursed a cluster of boils on his neck. He said that in this fight his opponent kept hammering on the sore spot and he finally became so enraged that he picked a punch right up from his shoe strings and knocked his opponent so cold that he didn't recover for a week.

In recent years Sullivan was a very different person from the one who in his hayday were one of the most liberal spenders in the country. He was on the water wagon with a vengeance, and not only lectured about the folly of taking a wrestle with John Barleycorn, but always was willing to give some personal advice about this phase of life. He often said that the only decision he ever lost in his life was to John Barleycorn, and he used to say that this was the one chap no one could ever beat.

Unlike most champions Sullivan never tried to make a come back. When Jim Corbett defeated him in 1892 he retired from the ring forever. Another thing about him different from the modern title holders was that he did not hesitate to fight any one who wanted to take a chance with him. He always was confident of his prowess and was willing to meet all comers.

Fought for Small Purses.

Nowadays when Jess Willard cannot be tempted to defend his title for $50,000 it is interesting to note that when Sullivan was in his prime a purse of $1,000 was considered a fabulous sum. He received only $50 for the bout which won him the right to challenge Paddy Ryan for the championship.

John L. had friends all over the world and one of his admirers was the Prince of Wales, later King Edward VII. of England. When Sullivan was in England he was invited to the royal palace and an American newspaper man asked to go along. When Sullivan reached the palace an attendant at the door told him he could come in but no one else. Sullivan told the attendant that if his friend would not be admitted to the King's presence he would not go in either. Both were admitted after a little investigation. King Edward always was a great admirer of the old Roman thereafter, for John L. showed that he was no respecter of persons of rank, but that he was a true democrat.

Spent a Fortune on Drink.

Sullivan used to say that he spent a million in buying drinks for himself and his host of friends. He said that the "black bottle" was his greatest enemy, but he gave it the knockout wallop in 1905. On the occasion of his decision to down the Demon Rum he stated, "If I take another drink I hope to choke, so help me, God." This was a favorite expression of his in the years when he was hitting the high spots, but this time he meant it, and he kept faith to the end of his days. He never took another drink and kept up a fight for temperance by lecturing on the evils of drink.

"Your truly, John L. Sullivan," was a phrase that was known all over the world. In 1899 he wrote for the HERALD:—"Live and let live has always been my motto. I have had a varied experience and have made many friends, and there is not a friend among them all who will say that John L. Sullivan did not go into his pocket when there was need of assistance, for it has been my pleasure to be a Good Samaritan where I had the chance."

Sullivan realized that pugilism had changed a lot since he first started, and nearly twenty years ago he wrote for the HERALD:—"Fighting is all changed since I was a youngster. It is on a higher plane, and this began when I stood forth as an American and announced my willingness to meet any man in the world. Americans like manly deeds, and they took pride in one of their own countrymen challenging men of all nations."

Always Ready to Fight.

"I was always ready to fight. The preliminaries were always short and quickly settled. Every one knew where to find John L. Sullivan, and every American knew that his heart was true. When I lost the championship I took pride in the fact that I had lost it to an American. I would never have lost to a foreigner. I have had my ups and downs, but wherever I go I still find that I have a warm place in the hearts of my fellow citizens. They knew me to be honest and sincere. They knew that when John L. Sullivan said he would do a thing he would do it."

LEADING FIGHTS IN RING CAREER OF DEAD PUGILIST

Defeated Joe Goss, Boston, 1880, in three minutes.

Defeated George Rook, New York, 1880, in seven minutes.

Defeated Professor John Donaldson, Cincinnati, December, 1880, ten rounds.

Defeated Steve Taylor, New York, March, 1881, in three minutes.

Defeated John Flood on a barge in the Hudson, opposite Yonkers, May, 1881, in eight rounds.

Defeated Paddy Ryan with bare knuckles at Mississippi City, in February, 1882, in nine rounds. This fight was for the championship.

Defeated Jimmy Elliott, New York, July 4, 1882, in three rounds.

Lost to Tug Wilson, Madison Square Garden, July 17, 1882, in four rounds.

Defeated Charley Mitchell, Madison Square Garden, May 14, 1883, in three rounds.

Defeated Herbert Slade (the Maori), Madison Square Garden, August, 1883, in three rounds.

Defeated Alfred Greenfield, Boston, January, 1885, in four rounds.

Fought a draw with Paddy Ryan (police interfering), Madison Square Garden, January, 1885.

Defeated Jack Burke, Chicago, June, 1885, in five rounds.

Defeated Paddy Ryan, San Francisco, November, 1886, in three rounds.

Draw with Patsy Cardiff, Minneapolis, January, 1887, six rounds.

Draw with Charley Mitchell, Chantilly, France, March 10, 1888, thirty-nine rounds.

Defeated Jake Kilrain, Richburg, Mississippi, July 8, 1889, seventy-five rounds.

Lost to James J. Corbett, New Orleans, September 7, 1892, twenty-one rounds.

The Gentleman's Magazine
8th January 1789 Vol 59

At his house at Walcot-place, Lambeth, in his 85th year, the celebrated Jn. Broughton, whose skill in boxing is well known, and will ever be recorded in the annals of that science. He was originally bred a waterman. His patron, the late Duke of Cumberland, got him appointed one of the yeomen of the guards, which place he enjoyed till his death. He was buried in Lambeth church, on the 21st instant; and his funeral procession was adorned with the presence of the several capital professors of boxing. He is supposed to have died worth 7000l.

New York Times
5th July 1970

H. S. Vanderbilt, Yachtsman and Financier, Dies

..., R. I., July 4— Harold Stirling Vanderbilt, famous yachtsman, originator of contract bridge and former railroad financier, died today at his home here, Rock Cliffe, two days before his 86th birthday.

Mr. Vanderbilt had returned last month from his winter home, Eastover, at Manalapan, Fla.

He is survived by his widow, the former Gertrude Lewis Conway of Philadelphia, whom he married in 1933. They had no children.

The funeral will be held Tuesday at 10 A.M. in Trinity Episcopal Church. Burial, in St. Mary's Churchyard, Ports-

... will be private, the family announced.

A Versatile Leader

Harold Vanderbilt chose three widely different fields for his main occupations in an active life, and in each of them he left a deep imprint.

Thrice he successfully defended the America's Cup in the golden days of international yachting.

More than any other man he merited the title of father of contract bridge—a game that in two decades spread to beguile 40 million people around the world.

For four decades he was a director of the New York Central Railroad, which has since become part of the Penn Central Transportation Company, a concern currently in deep financial trouble. Mr. Vanderbilt's great-grandfather, Commodore Cornelius Vanderbilt, had put the Central system together in 1869. Harold Vanderbilt was for many years the financial power behind the Central network, until he was defeated in a titanic battle of proxies in 1954 by a rival financier, the late Robert R. Young.

Commanding Figure

Mr. Vanderbilt, who stood 6 feet tall, was a commanding figure, whether at the helm of a Cup defender or on the tennis court, where he was also an excellent performer. He showed little interest in the social events of Newport. It was only in recent years that there were indications of declining health.

He was born July 6, 1884, in Oakdale, L. I., the youngest of three children of William Kissam Vanderbilt. His father died in 1920, leaving an estate appraised three years later at $54,530,966. His mother, who after a divorce became Mrs. Oliver H. P. Belmont, died in 1933.

In January, 1954, he resigned from the C. & O., announced he was the Central's largest stockholder, with 100,200 shares, and demanded its chairmanship. The Central directors unanimously refused.

A fight for proxies of the Central's 6,447,410 shares began. A key block of 800,000 was owned by the C. & O., which could not vote them. These were bought in February with $20-million in borrowed funds by Clinton W. Murchison and Sid W. Richardson, Texas oilmen favoring Mr. Young. Mr. Vanderbilt, who owned 60,000 shares himself, said later that he had vainly offered $20-million.

As chairman of the Central's executive committee, he formed a committee to solicit proxies for the management. He lost court suits to prevent voting of the Murchison-Richardson shares.

The headlined battle cost each side more than $1-million. On May 26, the votes were cast at an annual meeting in Albany. On June 14, Mr. Young was found to have won the chairmanship, 3,407,512 to 2,340,239—and for the first time since the 1880's, there was no longer a Vanderbilt on the Central board.

At the time, Mr. Vanderbilt had been a director of 27 other railroad enterprises as well as the First National Bank of New York.

Headed University Board

He was a contributor to various philanthropies, notably Vanderbilt University in Nashville, founded in 1873 with $1-million from Commodore Vanderbilt. Harold Vanderbilt served as president of the school's Board of Trust.

Despite his advancing years, he continued his deep interest in the America's Cup as a member of the syndicate that built Interepid for the 1967 defense. She is a candidate for this year's defense as well.

In October, 1969, Mr. Vanderbilt retired from the North American Yacht Union's rules committee, of which he had been a member since it was formed in 1942. Six years earlier he had formulated a major revision of the racing rules following the revisions after World War II. The "Vanderbilt Rules" were adopted throughout the world.

A Cup on the Mantel

He was a former commodore of the New York Yacht Club. Among his other clubs were the Knickerbocker, Racquet and Tennis, Sewanhaka Corinthian Yacht, Brook, National Golf Links, Creek, Meadow Brook, Whist, Garden City Golf, Piping Rock and River.

Besides Rock Cliffe in Newport and his Florida residence, he had a home in New York and a farm in Virginia.

Rock Cliffe houses color prints of all the America's Cup defenders, various Kings Cups won by Mr. Vanderbilt on New York Yacht Club cruises and "The Wheel," which he used on all of his yachts.

On the mantel in his library is a tiny silver America's Cup. It is a copy of the 27-inch-high bottomless silver trophy that has remained in American hands since 1851.

The son, known as Mike to his friends, completed his studies at Harvard College in three years, even while managing the football team. He graduated in 1907, and went on to get a degree at the Harvard Law School in 1910. In January of the next year, he became a legal assistant at the Central. Three years later, he was elected a director, succeeding the banker J. P. Morgan.

In yachting, Mr. Vanderbilt came to be recognized internationally as a formidable strategist and racing helmsman. Last year he was awarded the Nathaniel G. Herreshoff Trophy of the North American Yacht Racing Union "in recognition of his contributions to yachting as a keen competitor and a superior helmsman in international competition and as the architect of a new and improved code of racing rules."

At the age of 12, he already had skippered his own 14-foot sloop. In 1910, he won his first schooner race to Bermuda. In 1913, he sailed from Portland, Me., to Lisbon, Portugal, in 23 days.

During World War I, Mr. Vanderbilt served as a Navy lieutenant on submarine-chasing duty from Queenstown, Ireland. Between 1922 and 1938, he went on to win five Astor Cups and six King's Cups—the banner

trophies of American yachting.

The America's Cup, named for the 101-foot schooner that first won the race in 1851, had been defended 13 times by the New York Yacht Club when Sir Thomas Lipton, British merchant, challenged for a 1930 race. At 80 years of age, Sir Thomas was making his fifth attempt.

Enterprise Innovations

A syndicate built the Enterprise, smallest of four prospective defenders. Mr. Vanderbilt, her skipper, devised a duralumin mast, a wide boom with horizontal slides to obtain a better curve for the mainsail and mechanical devices to handle more of the running rigging below deck than ever before. He trained a crew of 25 to precision performances.

Weetamoe, the Morgan syndicate racer, sailed by George Nichols, had all the best of early trials. But then Mr. Vanderbilt got the Enterprise tuned up, and he won the right to defend. In four consecutive 30-mile races off Newport, Sept. 13 to 17, he easily defeated the challenger, Shamrock V.

In 1934, T. O. M. Sopwith, British airplane builder, challenged with the Endeavor. Mr. Vanderbilt defended with the syndicate-built Rainbow. Endeavor won the first two races starting Sept. 17, and was leading in the third. Rainbow came to life, and won four straight to keep the trophy here.

In 1937, Mr. Sopwith returned with the Endeavor II. Mr. Vanderbilt built the Ranger, paying her entire cost. She won four straight, July 31 to Aug. 5, and was acclaimed the fastest large sloop ever to defend the silver mug. Only one other skipper, Charles Barr, in 1899, 1901 and 1903, had successfully defended the cup three times.

With racing turning to smaller sloops, Mr. Vanderbilt developed new concepts of right-of-way rules after World War II. They were adopted by the North American Yacht Racing Union in 1947 and 1949.

Mr. Vanderbilt, meanwhile, had given a new sport to the card-playing world. He had been an ardent auction bridge player when, on a 1925 cruise from Los Angeles to Havana, he proposed adopting a principle from the kindred French game of plafond. This permitted scoring only of tricks for which a player had bid—or contracted.

He went on to add "vulnerability," assessing increased penalties against the side that had won the first game of a three-game rubber, and large bonuses for slam contracts bid and made. In 1927, the Whist Club of New York issued official rules with the scoring table Mr. Vanderbilt had invented.

The next year, he established the Harold S. Vanderbilt Cup for an annual "national contract bridge championship." In the 1932 tournament, teamed with Waldermar von Zedtwitz, P. Hal Sims and Willard S. Karn, he won his own trophy.

Fight for the Central

Maneuvering for control of the New York Central began after World War II. In 1947, Mr. Young was blocked in a bid for a Central directorship when the Interstate Commerce Commission ruled that this would be destructive of competition. Mr. Young was chairman of the Chesapeake & Ohio Railroad.

The Guardian
11th July 1978

Joe Davis, snooker's man

Joe Davis, who took snooker by the scruff of the neck and through sheer force of his skill and personality, established it as the premier billiard table game, died yesterday in a Hampshire convalescent home. He was 77.

Without him, snooker would never have had a world professional championship. Without him, it would never have graduated from the early venues in which it was staged—a billiard hall in Birmingham, the back room of a pub in Nottingham—to Thurston's, the billiards holy of holies in Leicester Square, and then to larger public venues like the Horticultural Hall, Westminster, when the fortnight-long 1946 championship final, his last, attracted 20,000 spectators and grossed £12,000.

Without him, indeed, it would have been a different game for it was he who transformed it from a somewhat crude potting contest—"the sort of game you play in clogs," as Tom Reece, a senior billiards player of the day acidly put it—into the sophisticated mixture of break-building techniques and tactical complexities which now engages 4,000,000 players in the British Isles alone.

Originally, Joe was a billiards player. Born in Whitwell, a small Derbyshire village, he was Chesterfield champion when he was 13, the only amateur event in which he competed; he was only 25 when he reached his first professional billiards final; and the whole of Chesterfield turned out at the station to welcome him when he came home champion in 1928.

Even so, it was a struggle to make a living. "I can remember," he said a few years ago, "playing a week in London on a percentage of the gate—no fees—staying out at Clapham in a boarding house for £8 to £9 a week and losing money. I've sat up half the night for the milk train and walked two miles from the station to home. If I could have afforded a taxi, there wasn't one."

It was in the context of "scraping and scratching to get a living" that he approached the Billiards Association in 1926 to sanction a world professional snooker championship. He won the event—it rated only three paragraphs in "The Billiard Player"—and retained it until he abdicated in 1946, by which time snooker had overtaken billiards in popularity.

Joe, the Australian Walter Lindrum, the New Zealander Clark McConachy and another Englishman, Tom Newman, achieved between them a unique sporting distinction: they became so good at their game that they killed it as a public entertainment. Through their mastery of repetitive stroke sequences, notoriously nursery cannons with which the three balls were edged along a cushion so skilfully (but to the spectator so tediously) this activity no longer bore much resemblance to the game he played in his own club. Having this exhausted one game, it was time to try another.

Even after his retirement from snooker championship play Joe continued to dominate the scene. He was co-leaseholder of Leicester Square Hall, which had succeeded Thurston's as the home of the professional game; he was chairman of the Professional Players' Association, what he said, went. He continued to play brilliantly. He made the game's first official 147 maximum break and was only beaten three times on level terms, on each occasion by his brother Fred. In his entire career, he won tournaments conceding substantial handicaps and he was unquestioningly accepted as No. 1 long after he had ceased to play in the championship.

During the Second World War, he toured theatres from the Palladium downwards with a variety act of intricate trick shots; early television snooker revolved round him utterly until he ceased public play in 1964. It was always his priority to present snooker with dignity.

No one took more pleasure than he in seeing the world professional championship, which has been at the Crucible Theatre, Sheffield for the last two years, become established, after many ups and downs, as one of sport's great annual events and spectacles. It was there that I last saw him in April, ashen and shaking with the stress of seeing Fred battle out the championship semifinal. But I shall always remember him as my boyish eyes first saw him, imperious, rock steady, immensely self-assured, despatching ball after ball into the pockets. I suppose he must have missed at times—but I can't remember it.

National Biography
26th October 1973

Abebe Bikila, the Ethiopian athlete, who won gold medals for the marathon in successive Olympic Games, died on October 25, 1973 at the age of 46.

Abebe Bikila was the first of the great athletes of Africa to make their mark on the Olympic Games. His victory in the 1960 marathon in Rome was completely unexpected. Even those who had noted, from the entry list, that this unknown Ethiopian had a best time of 2hr. 21min., did not believe he could be a serious threat.

Bikila, then a member of the household guard to Emperor Haile Selassie, gained his victory in Rome by pulling away in the last 1,000 metres after advice from his coach to leave his effort late. What struck the press, waiting by the floodlit Arch of Constantine, was that his final barefoot steps were taken along the Appian Way, up which his Ethiopian ancestors had been brought as prisoners of the Roman Empire. In fact Bikila's father had fought as a guerrilla against the troops of Mussolini in the 1930s.

Four years later, in Tokyo, Bikila again became Olympic marathon champion, this time wearing warm-up shoes; and so determined to prove his freshness at the end of the traditional 26 miles 385 yards that he went through a series of physical jerks, to delight the crowd.

Bikila won that second gold medal on October 21, 1964. On September 16 he had had his appendix removed. Yet his winning time of 2hr. 12min. 11.2sec. in Tokyo was the fastest achieved for the classic event.

Bikila competed in his third Olympics in Mexico in 1968 without winning any medal. He was forced to drop out and instead had to concentrate on the first place of his countryman, Mamo Wolde.

The next year came tragedy. Bikila was injured so seriously in a car accident that he became paralysed. Even after treatment at Stoke Mandeville, he was confined to a wheelchair. His true fighting spirit was underlined when he took up archery and competed in the paraplegic Olympics. Now, at only 46, this quiet, lean man has finished the good fight.

New York Times
17th August 1948

Babe Ruth, Baseball's Great Star

WORLD-WIDE FAME WON ON DIAMOND

Even in Lands Where Game Is Unknown, Baseball's Star Player Was Admired

SET HOME RUN MARK IN '27

First a Talented Pitcher, Then Foremost Batter, He Drew Highest Pay of His Time

Probably nowhere in all the imaginative field of fiction could one find a career more dramatic and bizarre than that portrayed in real life by George Herman Ruth. Known the world over, even in foreign lands where baseball is never played, as the Babe, he was the boy who rose from the obscurity of a charitable institution in Baltimore to a position as the leading figure in professional baseball. He was also its greatest drawing-card, its highest salaried performer —at least of his day—and the idol of millions of youngstehs throughout the land.

A creation of the times, he seemed to embody all the qualities that a sport-loving nation demanded of its outstanding hero. For it has always been debatable whether Ruth owed his fame and the vast fortune it made for him more to his ability to smash home runs in greater quantity than any other player in the history of the game or to a strange personality that at all times was intensely real and "regular," which was the one fixed code by which he lived.

He made friends by the thousands and rarely, if ever, lost any of them. Affable, boisterous and good-natured to a fault, he was always as accessible to the newsboy on the corner as to the most dignified personage in worldly affairs. More, he could be very much at ease with both.

He could scarcely recall a name, even of certain intimates with whom he frequently came in contact, but this at no time interfered with the sincerity of his greeting. Indeed, by a singular display of craft, he overcame this slight deficiency with consummate skill. If you looked under 40 it was "Hello, kid, how are you?" And if you appeared above that line of demarcation it was "Hello, doc, how's everything going?"

How Ruth Aided Small Boy

The story is told of the case of Johnny Sylvester, a youngster whose life doctors had despaired of unless something unusual happened to shock him out of a peculiar malady. The boy's uncle, recalling how fond he always had been of baseball, conceived the idea of sending word to Babe Ruth and asking his aid.

The next day the Babe, armed with bat, glove and half a dozen signed baseballs, made one of his frequent pilgrimages to a hospital. The boy, unexpectedly meeting his idol face to face, was so overjoyed that he was cured—almost miraculously.

A year later an elderly man accosted the Babe in a hotel lobby and, after receiving the customary whole-hearted greeting of "Hello, doc,'" said:

"Babe, I don't know whether you remember me, but I'm Johnny Sylvester's uncle and I want to tell you the family will never forget what you did for us. Johnny is getting along fine."

"That's great," replied the Babe. "Sure, I remember you. Glad to hear Johnny is doing so well. Bring him around some time."

After a few more words they parted and no sooner had the man removed himself from earshot than the Babe turned to a baseball writer at his elbow and asked:

"Now, who the devil was Johnny Sylvester?"

Never Lost Carefree Spirit

Nor must this be mistaken for affection; for there was never a doubt that the Babe at all times was tremendously sincere in his desire to appear on friendly terms with all the world. And though in later years he acquired a certain polish which he lacked utterly in his early career, he never lost his natural self nor his flamboyant, carefree mannerisms, which at all times made him a show apart from the ball field.

Single-handed, he tore the final game of the 1928 world's series in St. Louis to shreds with his mighty bat by hitting three home runs over the right-field pavilion. That night, returning to New York, he went on a boisterous rampage and no one on the train got any sleep, including his employer, the late Colonel Jacob Ruppert.

Such was the blending of qualities that made Babe Ruth a figure unprecedented in American life. A born showman off the field and a marvelous performer on it, he had an amazing flair for doing the spectacular at the most dramatic moment.

Of his early days in Baltimore even Babe himself was, or pretended to be, somewhat vague during his major league baseball career. Thus various versions of his childhood were printed over the years with neither denial nor confirmation from Ruth as to their accuracy.

However, the following account of his boyhood years appeared in a national magazine under Ruth's own "by-line:"

"In the first place I was not an orphan. * * * My mother, whose maiden name was Schanberg, lived until I was 13. My father, George Herman Ruth, lived until my second year in the majors. Few fathers ever looked more like their sons than my pop and I. My mother was mainly Irish, and was called Kate. My father was of German extraction. It is not true that our family name was Erhardt, as has been repeatedly written. Or Ehrhardt, or Gearhardt.

"But I hardly knew my parents.

I don't want to make any excuses or place the blame for my shortcomings as a kid completely on persons or places. * * * Yet I probably was a victim of circumstances. I spent most of the first seven years of my life living over my father's saloon at 426 West Camden Street, Baltimore. * * *

"On June 13, 1902, when I was 7 years old my father and mother placed me in St. Mary's Industrial School in Baltimore. It has since been called an orphanage and a reform school. It was, in fact, a training school for orphans, incorrigibles, delinquents, boys whose homes had been broken by divorce, runaways picked up on the streets of Baltimore and children of poor parents who had no other means of providing an education for them.

"I was listed as an incorrigible, and I guess I was. * * * I chewed tobacco when I was 7, not that I enjoyed it especially, but, from my observation around the saloon it seemed the normal thing to do.

Gaps in School Life

"I was released from St. Mary's in July, 1902, but my parents returned me there in November of the same year. My people moved to a new neighborhood just before Christmas, 1902, and I was released to them again. This time I stayed out' until 1904, but then they put me back again and I was not released again until 1908. Shortly after my mother died I was returned to St. Mary's once more by my father. He took me back home in 1911 and returned me in 1912. I stayed in school— learning to be a tailor and shirtmaker—until Feb. 27, 1914. The last item on my 'record' at St. Mary's was a single sentence, written in the flowing hand of one of the teachers. It read:

"'He is going to join the Balt. Baseball Team.'"

Ruth said he played in the band at St. Mary's and always pointed with pride to this accomplishment, frequently reminding friends that he also was a musician as well as a ball player. Curiously enough, however, no one ever discovered what instrument the Babe played, although he always stoutly denied that it was the bass drum.

Had a Career Both Dramatic and Bizarre

But baseball captivated his fancy most and now began a train of circumstances that was to carry this black-haired, raw-boned youngster to fame and a fortune that has been estimated as close to $1,000,000. It also happened that Brother Benedict, one of the instructors at St. Mary's, was a great lover of the national pastime.

Using baseball, therefore, as the most plausible means to a laudable end in keeping the Babe out of mischief as much as possible, the good Brother encouraged the youngster to play as much as he could. The Babe scarcely needed encouragement. Every hour he was allowed to spare from his classrooms found him on the ball field.

He batted left-handed and threw left-handed. He played on his school team, also on a semi-professional team. He also played pretty nearly every position on the field. At the age of 19 he astounded even his sponsor, Brother Benedict, who now saw a real means of livelihood ahead for the young man, though little dreaming at the time to what heights he would soar.

He recommended the Babe to his friend, the late Jack Dunn, then owner of the Baltimore Orioles of the International League, and Ruth received a trial, alternating in the outfield and in the pitcher's box. That was in 1914. The same summer he was sold to the Boston Red Sox for $2,900, and after a brief period of farming out with Providence was recalled to become a regular.

Under the direction of Bill Carrigan, then manager of the Red Sox, Ruth rapidly developed into one of the most talented left-handed pitchers ever in the majors. He had tremendous speed and a baffling cross-fire curve, which greatly impressed Ed Barrow, later to become associated with Colonel Ruppert as general manager of the Yankees. Barrow became the leader of the Red Sox in 1918 and gave much time to Ruth's development.

But even then he also displayed unmistakable talent for batting a ball with tremendous power and with unusual frequency, and Barrow, one of baseball's greatest men of vision, decided to convert Ruth permanently into an outfielder on the theory that a great hitter could be built into a greater attraction than a great pitcher.

It was quite a momentous decision, for in the 1918 world's series against the Cubs Ruth had turned in two masterful performances on the mound for the Red Sox, winning both his games. He had also turned in one victory for the Red Sox against Brooklyn in the world's series of 1916.

But Barrow had also seen Ruth, in 1918, hit eleven home runs, an astonishing number for that era, particularly for a pitcher, and his mind was made up.

The next year—1919—Ruth, pitching only occasionally, now and then helping out at first base, but performing mostly in the outfield, cracked twenty-nine home runs and the baseball world began to buzz as it hadn't since the advent of Ty Cobb and the immortal Christy Mathewson. This total surpassed by four the then accepted major league record for home runs in a season, set by Buck Freeman with the Washington Club in 1899.

But it was the following year—1920—that was to mark the turning point, not only in Babe Ruth's career but in the entire course of organized baseball. Indeed, baseball men are almost in accord in the belief that Babe Ruth, more than any individual, and practically single-handed, rescued the game from what threatened to be one of its darkest periods. Not only rescued it, but diverted it into new channels that in the next decade were to reap an unprecedented golden harvest.

The first sensation came early that winter when Ruth was sold by the late Harry Frazee, then owner of the Red Sox, to the Yankees, owned jointly by the two Colonels, Jacob Ruppert and Tillinghast L'Hommedieu Huston, for a reported price of $125,000. It may even have been more, for in making the purchase the Yankee owners also assumed numerous financial obligations then harassing the Boston owner, and the matter was very involved. But whatever the price, it was a record sum, and New York prepared to welcome its latest hero prospect.

The Babe did not disappoint. The Yankees were then playing their home games at the Polo Grounds, home of the Giants, and before the close of the 1920 season they were already giving their more affluent rivals and landlords a stiff run for the city's baseball patronage.

Ruth surpassed all expectations by crashing out the unheard-of total of fifty-four home runs and crowds which hitherto had lavished their attention on the Giants now jammed the historic Polo Grounds to see the marvelous Bambino hit a homer.

Crisis in History of Game

But scarcely had the echoes from the thunderous roars that greeted the Ruthian batting feats subsided than another explosion was touched off that rattled the entire structure of baseball down to its sub-cellar. The scandal of the world's series of 1919 broke into print and through the winter of 1920-21 the "throwing" of that series by certain White Sox players to the Reds was on every tongue.

The baseball owners of both major leagues were in a panic, fearful that the public's confidence in what they had so proudly called America's national pastime had been shaken beyond repair. True, they had induced the late Kenesaw Mountain Landis, a Federal judge, to assume the position of High Commissioner with unlimited powers to safeguard against a repetition of such a calamity, but they feared it was not enough.

With considerable misgivings they saw the 1921 season get under way and then, as the popular song of the day ran, "Along Came Ruth."

Inside of a fortnight the fandom of the nation had forgotten all about the Black Sox, as they had come to be called, as its attention became centered in an even greater demonstration of superlative batting skill by the amazing Babe Ruth. Home runs began to scale off his bat in droves, crowds jammed ball parks in every city in which he appeared and when he closed the season with a total of fifty-nine circuit clouts, surpassing by five his own record of the year before, the baseball world lay at his feet.

In addition to that, the Yankees that year captured the first pennant ever won by New York in the American League, and Ruth was now fairly launched upon the first chapter of the golden harvest. With the help of his towering war club, the Yankees won again in 1922 and repeated in 1923, in addition to winning the world's championship that year.

Also in 1923 came into being the "House That Ruth Built," meaning the great Yankee Stadium with its seating capacity of more than 70,000, which Colonel Ruppert decided to erect the year previous in order to make himself clear and independent of the Giants, whose tenant he had been at the Polo Grounds. The right-field bleachers became "Ruthville." Homers soared into them in great abundance and the exploitation of Babe Ruth, the greatest slugger of all times, was at its height.

Idol of Children

The Daily Mirror
27th July 1925

125-M.P.H. CRASH IN THE GRAND PRIX

Famous Racing Motorist Dies on the Way to Hospital

BOTH LEGS BROKEN

Antonio Ascari, the well-known Italian racing motorist, met with a fatal accident while taking part in the French Motor Grand Prix on the Linas-Moutlhery track yesterday.

During the twentieth lap the Italian Alfa-Romeo car which he was driving skidded and crashed into the palisading.

The car overturned, and Ascari was pinned underneath. Both his legs were broken, an arm was fractured, and the motorist also received severe injuries to the head.

It was found necessary to amputate one leg, says Reuter, but Ascari died while being taken to hospital.

According to the Exchange, Ascari struck one of the posts holding up the barrier along the side of the track. His car skidded, struck the barrier a second time, and overturned. It then made five turns on its side.

At this part of the race cars reach 125 miles per hour.

Ascari, who was thirty-six years of age, leaves a widow and two children.

He was the leading driver of the Alfa-Romeo Company, states Reuter, and but for engine trouble would probably have won the Grand Prix on the Lyons circuit last year. He won the Italian Grand Prix at Monza in 1924 and the Grand Prix d'Europe at Spa last month.

He started a strong favourite for yesterday's race.

ITALIANS WITHDRAW

When the news of his death reached the course (states a Central News message) all the Italians withdrew from the race as a mark of respect.

Fifteen cars took part in the race, which (says Exchange) consisted of eighty circuits of the autodrome, the distance being approximately 621 miles.

Segrave, the only British driver, abandoned the race at the thirty-fourth turn, owing to trouble with his carburettor. At this stage Campari was leading.

Campari was forced to retire and Benoist (France) finished first on a Delage. Wagner (France), also on a Delage, was second and Count Masetti, on a Sunbeam, third.

The winner's speed averaged a little over seventy miles an hour.

THIS STONE
COMMEMORATES THE EXPLOIT OF
WILLIAM WEBB ELLIS
WHO WITH A FINE DISREGARD FOR THE RULES OF FOOTBALL,
AS PLAYED IN HIS TIME,
FIRST TOOK THE BALL IN HIS ARMS AND RAN WITH IT,
THUS ORIGINATING THE DISTINCTIVE FEATURE OF
THE RUGBY GAME
A.D. 1823

Stage & Screen

The first true star of the modern stage was **David Garrick**, in whose person the actor became the hero he is today, and whose death filled very many pages of *The Gentleman's Magazine*. **Henry Irving**, whose style seems so extraordinarily exaggerated to us now, was in his way of presenting a role every bit as revolutionary as, say, Marlon Brando in the early 50's. In tribute to the great forerunners of the screen stars, we have **Sarah Bernhardt**, who paved the way for an acceptance of women as actors rather than adornments and, in contrast, **Ellen Terry** who laid the foundations of the "sex goddess", epitomised of course by **Marilyn Monroe**, whose whole life, from waif to Venus, as well as the manner of her death, seem to stand for all the star is about with due deference to Jean Harlow. A somewhat different tradition is given its due in the person of **Mary Pickford**, "America's Sweetheart", the greatest female star of the cinema's early years. If there is a male equivalent of Monroe, then it must surely be **Rudolph Valentino**. The other two great male screen roles — the tough guy and the comic — are represented by the toughest of them all, Mr. America himself, **John Wayne**; and by **Charlie Chaplin**, whose genius transformed screen comedy from entertainment to art.

W. C. Fields and **Boris Karloff**, in their different ways, refined that art of blurring the distinction between performance and reality. Among directors, whose crucial part has only recently come property to be acknowledged, no definitive choice is possible. On grounds of personal taste alone, therefore, we have **D. W. Griffith**, for his realism; **Fritz Lang** for his (earlier) expressionism; and **Sergei Eisenstein** as an outstandingly powerful imagist. **Samuel Goldwyn** is here as mogul-in-chief. Reverting to the stage, and to a more specialized area altogether, **Nijinsky** epitomises the brilliant performer with the impossible life; and **Isadora Duncan** the sytlist. **Anna Pavlova** is the consummate *artiste*. In much of **Shaw**'s work one can detect the origins of modern theatre. Finally, **Bertholt Brecht** is perhaps the one figure who, in the absence of Antonin Artaud, who died unrecognized by the press, or by anyone else for that matter, and in preference to Alfred Jarry, can do adequate duty for the modern theatre, standing both for innovation and politicization.

Samuel Goldwyn Dies at 91

Samuel Goldwyn, one of the last of the pioneer Hollywood producers, died early yesterday at his Los Angeles home at the age of 91. He had been in frail health since 1968 and two weeks ago had been released from a hospital after several weeks of treatment for an undisclosed illness.

In a distinguished career that spanned a half-century, Mr. Goldwyn became a Hollywood legend, a motion picture producer whose films, always created on a grand scale, were notable for those most elusive of traits—taste and quality.

Truly one of the last tycoons, who even looked the part, Mr. Goldwyn was a driving perfectionist, a man with a titanic temperament whose great gift was the ability to bring together, for each of his productions, the very best writers, directors, cinematographers and other craftsmen.

Having assembled these talented professionals, Mr. Goldwyn would dominate their work and their lives like a benign tyrant, praising them, goading them, encouraging them, browbeating them, as he personally supervised even the tiniest details of each of his productions.

This quest for the excellent often enraged Mr. Goldwyn's employes, but more often than not it gave his productions that sheen of quality and good taste that became known in the motion picture industry as "the Goldwyn touch."

Although he was one of the flashiest and most controversial of the independent producers, to the general public he was probably best known for his "Goldwynisms," the malapropisms, mixed metaphors, grammatical blunders and word manglings that included the now classic "Include me out" and "I'll tell you in two words — im-possible!"

Among the more famous Goldwynisms were:

"An oral agreement isn't worth the paper it's written on."

"A man who goes to a psychiatrist should have his head examined."

"This atom bomb is dynamite."

Another one supposedly evolved from a director's complaint that a film script in which Mr. Goldwyn was interested was "too caustic," to which the producer replied:

"Never mind the cost. If it's a good picture, we'll make it."

Until he decided that, as a pioneer and elder statesman of the motion picture industry, the Goldwynisms no longer lent his image the proper amount of dignity, Mr. Goldwyn shrewdly used them to gain publicity for himself and his pictures.

"People say that whenever I have a picture coming out I always start a controversy about something that gets into the papers," he said. "Well, in all sincerity, I want to assure you that, as a general proposition, there's not a single word of untruth in that."

Urged Better Pictures

Among the controversies that swirled about Mr. Goldwyn's bald head were his campaign against double features and his efforts to persuade his fellow producers to make fewer, better pictures. He once said that Hollywood was grinding out 600 pictures a year when "there are not brains enough in Hollywood to produce more than 200 good ones."

Mr. Goldwyn was born Aug. 27, 1882, in Warsaw. Little was known of his family background, but he was the son of poor parents who died when he was young. At the age of 11, the boy left Poland. After spending two years in England, he migrated to Gloversville, N.Y., where he took a job sweeping floors in a glove factory.

The youth already had the drive for which he was to become noted in Hollywood. By the time he was 17 he was the foreman of 100 workers in the glove plant and at 19 he went on the road as a glove salesman. Four years later he became a partner in the company, and before he was 30, Mr. Goldwyn was making more than $15,000 a year.

It was almost by accident that Mr. Goldwyn got into movie making. In 1910 he married Blanche Lasky, whose brother, Jesse, was a vaudeville producer. Mr. Lasky, at the urging of a lawyer, Arthur S. Friend, toyed with the idea of film making and tried to interest his brother-in-law in such a venture. Mr. Goldwyn, who had moved to New York, was cool to the idea until one cold day in 1913, when he stepped into a Herald Square movie house to warm up and, only incidentally, saw a Western starring Broncho Billy Anderson. He was impressed not only with the movie but also with all the dimes the management was raking in.

Enthusiastic Approach

With the enthusiasm that was typical of him, Mr. Goldwyn took up the idea of forming a film company of his very own. He and Mr. Lasky each put up $10,000 and between them Mrs. Goldwyn and Mr. Friend pledged the rest of the $26,500 capitalization for the new Jesse L. Lasky Feature Picture Play Company.

Mr. Friend had his law practice to attend to, Mr. Lasky his vaudeville management chores, and so it was up to Mr. Goldwyn to do most of the work in the new company and get little of the glory. As a friend was to observe years later, "Sam had a self-effacing streak then, but he soon pinned it to the mat for all time."

The company set out to produce long films that told romantic stories, even if they took an hour to unfold. Most "flickers" at the time were two-reelers, lasting about 20 minutes.

The Lasky company's first movie was a milestone in more ways than one. It was a five-reeler, the first feature-length movie, and one of the first films to be made in Hollywood. Called "The Squaw Man," it starred a well-known Broadway actor, Dustin Farnum, and it was directed by a young stage manager and unsuccessful playwright named Cecil B. DeMille, who had never worked on a movie before.

The company's initial success resulted in a sudden intense interest in it from Mr. Goldwyn's partners, which, as it turned out, was exactly what he didn't want. The partners — who by then included Mr. DeMille — battled constantly and Mr. Goldwyn seemed to be in a permanent rage. Shortly after the company merged with

Adolph Zukor's Famous Players Company, Mr. Goldwyn sold out his shares for nearly a million dollars.

A Name Is Born

In 1917 he joined forces with Edgar and Arch Selwyn, who as Broadway producers had built up a library of plays that might make good films.

At that time, Mr. Goldwyn's name was still Goldfish, the nearest equivalent to his Polish name that immigration officials could think of when he came to this country. Goldwyn Pictures Corporation took its name from the "Gold" in Goldfish and the "wyn" in Selwyn.

Mr. Goldwyn liked the name so much that he had his own name legally changed to it, an action that displeased the Selwyns. Two years after the partnership was formed and had gone bankrupt, one of the Selwyns is said to have told Mr. Goldwyn: "Sam, you not only broke us but took half of our good name as well."

Merger With Metro

When the bankrupt Goldwyn company was merged with Metro Pictures, out of which Metro-Goldwyn-Mayer grew, Mr. Goldwyn withdrew with a substantial financial settlement, but he had to agree that he could never use the name of Goldwyn Pictures Corporation on any films he made. Thus, his productions flashed on the screen with "Samuel Goldwyn presents . . ." to identify them.

In 1922, Mr. Goldwyn became an independent producer, convinced that he would never be able to get along with partners or boards of directors. "It's dog eat dog in this business, and nobody's going to eat me," he said.

In 1926 Mr. Goldwyn became a member of United Artists, a cooperative formed by independent producers to distribute their pictures. In 1939 he had a falling-out with Mary Pickford, one of the other members, and in 1941, after a bitter court fight, he sold his stock to the corporation at a reported loss of $500,000.

From the time he became an independent producer, Mr. Goldwyn was noted for the reverence in which he held creative talent. He coddled actors, writers and directors, but when he felt they were not producing what he had expected of them, he switched tactics and heaped invective upon them.

The late Ben Hecht, who worked on the script of "Wuthering Heights," compared Mr. Goldwyn's treatment of writers to "an irritated man shaking a slot machine."

Lavish Spender on Scripts

But Mr. Goldwyn always believed that the story was the thing that made good movies, and he spent lavishly on scripts written for him by writers

His courting of the Belgian poet Maurice Maeterlinck resulted in disaster. Mr. Goldwyn commissioned him to write a scenario based on Mr. Maeterlinck's "Life of a Bee," which the producer had not read. After seeing the finished script, the story goes, Mr. Goldwyn ran from his office screaming, "My God, the hero is a bee!"

One of several great directors with whom Mr. Goldwyn did not get along was William Wyler, yet Mr. Wyler made some of his best films, including "The Best Years of Our Lives," under the Goldwyn banner.

During the filming of "These Three," Mr. Wyler changed a night scene to a daytime shot. A furious Mr. Goldwyn rebuked him with the fiat that "Nobody can change night into day, or vice versa, without asking me first."

Let Cooper's Option End

George Cukor refused to work for Mr. Goldwyn at all, which so exasperated the producer that he is reported to have said: "That's the way with these directors — they're always biting the hand that lays the golden egg."

Among the stars Mr. Goldwyn discovered were Tallulah Bankhead, Robert Montgomery and Gary Cooper. He let Mr. Cooper's option expire, however, and later had to hire him for "The Adventures of Marco Polo" for a hundred times the amount it would have cost him had the actor remained under contract.

Perhaps Mr. Goldwyn's worst talent-finding gaffe was his import of the Polish actress Anna Sten, upon whom he spent hundreds of thousands of dollars to build up as a star. Miss Sten, he felt, had an enigmatic beauty, or, as he put it, "the face of a spink." She failed to pass muster with the public, however, and he was finally forced to admit, to everyone's amusement but his own, that "She's colossal in a small way."

But his judgment was much better in the case of Vilma Banky, whom he teamed with Ronald Colman in a series of highly successful films, among them "The Night of Love" and "The Dark Angel"; Miss Bankhead, whom he discovered in a beauty contest and starred in "Thirty a Week" long before she won Broadway fame; and several of the "Goldwyn girls" —the leggy chorines he personally chose to decorate his musicals—who later attained stardom, among them Betty Grable.

When Sam Goldwyn made a picture, he spent only his own money and never resorted, as do most producers, to big studio or Wall Street financing.

That was one reason he had a hand in every aspect of his productions, from acquiring the story to editing the film to planning its promotion campaign.

So jealously did he guard his reputation for making high-quality pictures that he would stop at no expense to make improvements. In 1947, for example, he halted production of "The Bishop's Wife," starring Cary Grant, Loretta Young and David Niven, after he had spent more than $1-million on it. He simply wasn't satisfied with the way the film was turning out, and started all over again. It was a hit.

A $1-Million Halt

When he wasn't haunting his sound stages, Mr. Goldwyn was out selling his pictures, both in this country and abroad. "I've got a great slogan for the company," he once said — giving birth to another Goldwynism — "'Goldwyn pictures griddle the earth.'"

They not only girdled the earth, they were immensely popular. In a 20-year period before television started giving mass exposure to films, more than 200 million people paid to see Goldwyn productions. Many of the films were nominated for Academy Awards, but Mr. Goldwyn did not receive an Oscar for best picture until 1947, when "The Best Years of Our Lives" won all the major awards. Mr. Goldwyn was also presented, at that time, with the Irving Thalberg Memorial Award for his contributions to the film industry.

"Wuthering Heights" received the New York Film Critics' Award in 1939, the year "Gone With the Wind" swept the Academy Awards.

Mr. Goldwyn's films won dozens of Oscars in several categories — direction, writing, scenic design, music, color and acting. Five were winners for set design, a reflection of Mr. Goldwyn's care in that field. He was the first producer to use realistic, three-dimensional sets rather than painted flats.

Mr. Goldwyn was divorced in 1915 from Blanche Lasky, by whom he had a daughter, Ruth. In 1925 he married Frances Howard, a stage and screen actress. They had a son, Samuel Jr., who is a movie producer. They both survive.

Mrs. Goldwyn gradually became her husband's unofficial second-in-command at the studio. She also did a splendid job of keeping her husband's personal life in order, according to friends. Whenever the couple went out, she paid all restaurant checks and cab fares. She had to, because Mr. Gold-

wyn never carried change or a wallet. He was an extremely careful dresser and believed that his conservatively tailored suits would look lumpy if he put anything in his pockets.

Several years ago Mrs. Goldwyn installed a croquet field on the seven-acre Goldwyn estate in Beverly Hills, and it soon became a mark of distinction in Hollywood to be invited to play croquet at the Goldwyns' huge Georgian mansion.

Made Last Film at 78

Mr. Goldwyn came out of semiretirement in 1959 to make his last film, "Porgy and Bess." Although he was already 78 years old, he held his chesty, 6-foot-tall body erect, and his swinging walk seemed as always to be jet-propelled as he strode through his studio streets. His eyes, deep-set in his rather plain face, could still flash with anger, and his Polish-accented voice had lost little of its deep vibrancy.

In recent years, Mr. Goldwyn rented his studio to independent film and television productions, but he was not pleased with much of the product that emanated from there and other parts of Hollywood. He believed movies and TV had become trashy.

Summing up his career, Mr. Goldwyn said, "I was a rebel, a lone wolf. My pictures were my own. I financed them myself and answered solely to myself. My mistakes and my successes were my own. My one rule was to please myself, and if I did that, there was a good chance I would please others."

New York Times
24th August 1926

VALENTINO'S FAME A TRIUMPH OF YOUTH

Actor Wanted to Be a Gardener and Went to California to Get Work on a Farm.

BECAME "THE SHEIK" AT 26

Once Worked as Laborer in Central Park—Later Got Job Dancing at Maxim's and on Stage.

Rudolph Valentino was born on May 6, 1895, in Tastelameta, Italy, the son of Giovanni Gugliemi, a veterinary doctor. After taking an "agriculturalist's" diploma from the Royal School of Agriculture in Genoa, Italy, he came to this country in December of 1913 to seek work as a gardener.

He did not find what he wanted, he said later, although it is understood he worked a while on the Long Island estate of Cornelius Bliss Jr. His next position was as an apprentice landscape gardener in Central Park. He found something much more attractive to him in the dance halls and cafés of the city, and in them picked up the accomplishment of dancing. For some time he was practically penniless, accepting such odd jobs as shining brass on automobiles, sweeping and the like.

The head waiter at Maxim's first employed him as a dancer, and thus began his professional career. As dancing partner of Bonnie Glass, and later to Joan Sawyer, he attained some reputation. But at that time he still was bent on farming and his fruitful journey to California, he told friends, was made with the idea of becoming a farmer there. He reached the Coast by joining a musical comedy troupe, which stranded him in San Francisco.

Valentino was advised by a friend he had known in the East, Norman Kerry, to try motion pictures, and on the bounty of Kerry he traveled to Los Angeles. He obtained only occasional jobs as an extra about the movie lots of Hollywood until June Mathis selected him for the rôle of Julio in "The Four Horsemen of the Apocalypse." In that he made his first triumph. That was in 1921. A feature of the picture was the Argentine tango as danced by Valentino, for the tango was then enjoying some of the popularity that has since been accorded the Charleston.

He gained his nickname from "The Sheik," a screen version of another best-seller. One of his earlier pictures was "Camille" in which he played opposite Nazimova. Official stardom came to him after "Beyond the Rocks," a Paramount picture from the story of Elinor Glyn in which he appeared with Gloria Swanson. "Blood and Sand" was his first starring vehicle—hitherto he had been a featured player only.

Valentino's last film was "The Son of the Sheik," which opened in New York on July 25 of this year.

Challenged Editorial Writer.

A month ago the "Sheik" became indignant over an editorial appearing in The Chicago Tribune entitled "Pink Powder Puffs." He resented the imputation that he was the cause of American men using face powder, and issued a challenge to the author of the editorial.

When the Chicago editorial writer would not reveal himself, Valentino said he considered the silence vindication.

When Valentino became famous in "The Four Horsemen," many stories began to circulate about his early life. It was popularly supposed that he had supported himself after his arrival in America by working as a bus boy, a dish washer, and even a barber. All of which Valentino rose to deny.

He had, he said, been educated at Dante Alighieri College at Tarento, Italy, and at the military college della Sapienza in Perugia. He tried to enter the Government Naval Academy, but failed to pass the tests owing to a chest that was an inch short of the required measurement. After attending the agricultural school, he came to New York as a first-class passenger on the S. S. Cleveland of the Hamburg-American line.

He knew nothing of the language, and, failing to get work as a gardener, he became the dancing partner of Bonnie Glass and Joan Sawyer. He even appeared on the legitimate stage in minor rôles. His acting in "The Eyes of Youth," a C. K. Young production, attracted the attention of June Mathis, who had just finished her adaptation for the screen of "The Four Horsemen." She decided that Valentino was just the type to play Julio Desnoyers, and with his engagement for the rôle he leaped from obscurity to fame almost overnight.

Wrote Book of Poems.

In 1924 Rudolph evinced activity in another sphere: he published a book of verse. "Day Dreams" was the title and it was brought out by MacFadden Publications. The poems were described as "jig-saw" verses on love, passion, kisses and kindred topics.

New York Times
26th December 1946

W. C. FIELDS, 66, DIES; FAMED AS COMEDIAN

Mimicry Star of the Films Since 1924 Got Start as a $5-a-Week Juggler

RARELY FOLLOWED SCRIPT

PASADENA, Calif., Dec. 25 (AP)—W. C. Fields, the comedian whose deadpan gestures, raspy remarks and "never give a sucker an even break" characterizations made him a showman beloved the nation over, died today at the age of 66.

He was equally well known in show business for his ad libbing and complete disregard for prepared scripts, either in the movies or radio. Once he said that the only lines he followed truly were those of Charles Dickens.

Fields got his first job in show business as a juggler at a summer park in Norristown, Pa., at $5 a week.

Left Home at Age of 11

Few men have contributed as much to the world's merriment as W. C. Fields. The comedian who ran away from home when he was 11 years old, who starved and suffered and was forced to live on his wits, kept his sense of the ridiculous—developing it, indeed, it would seem, with every hard knock he received in his youth.

His capital consisted of a highly expressive face, with a bulbous nose as the main feature, a fine voice for comedy purposes and a profound capacity for punishment. Of earthly goods he had little until he blossomed forth as one of the really great comedians about the year 1924.

His art has been described erroneously as that of the slapstick and clownerie. It is true that he could out-slapstick and out-clown most funny men of stage, circus or screen, but he possessed just a little more than his contemporaries. He was a master mimic, inimitable in his droll asides, an improviser and innovator of new tricks.

Some years ago when a whole cast of screen stars were picked to take parts in "Alice in Wonderland" he easily outshone the others in his conception of Humpty-Dumpty. The voice alone carried him to one of his greatest artistic triumphs in that egg disguise.

Career a Series of Struggles

It took many long years for Fields to reach the top. There are recorded struggles and infinite patience to master the art of juggling hats and saucepans, nights spent sleeping out in the open and often with little or no food. A weaker man would have whined, begged, asked for governmental relief of some sort. Fields fought his fight against tremendous odds and won—and he never lost his humor. Even in life's darkest moments he saw something funny, for he had the true comedian's ability to laugh at himself.

Claude William Dukenfield—for that was his real name—was born in Philadelphia on Jan. 29, 1880. His father was severe, austere and very poor; also he had old-fashioned ideas about using the rod on his offspring.

There was nothing of the sentimental love-your-father complex in the lad's make-up, and the family ties were snapped forever one afternoon when the elder Dukenfield stepped on a toy shovel. The shovel smacked up against his shin. Thereupon the father used it as a paddle on the boy. The next day the lad waited for his father to arrive and then smacked his pater with a heavy wooden box. Then he ran away.

Developed Art of Juggling

The lad was then a homeless waif. His clothes were so many rags, his outlook most desolate. But he began to juggle anything he could find: stones, apples, tennis balls knocked over fences by beflanneled overprivileged youth and adroitly caught by the future star. Fields practiced for hours, gradually acquiring the exact sense of balance, and he finally managed to get himself engaged in his first theatrical venture.

It is recorded that he went abroad and performed juggling acts in Europe, Asia, South Africa, Australia and even at Pago Pago in the South Sea Islands. He was in Johannesburg while the guerrilla end of the Boer War was still on, juggling clubs and other sundry articles.

Dawn of success began to break when he was engaged for the Ziegfeld Follies. He filled in while the beautiful girls were changing costumes and drew plaudits from everybody except Flo Ziegfeld. The "Great Ziegfeld" knew about as much as there is to know about beautiful women, but he lacked appreciation of comedy. Field's act was cut from twenty-five to five minutes and he was more or less out in the cold again.

Soon after he went into motion pictures under the direction of D. W. Griffith. His many years in pantomime proved invaluable. He was an overnight success, and in 1926 he went on the staff of the Paramount-Famous Players-Lasky Corporation.

New York Times
6th August 1962

Brilliant Stardom and Personal Tragedy

The life of Marilyn Monroe, the golden girl of the movies, ended as it began, in misery and tragedy.

Her death at the age of 36 closed an incredibly glamorous career and capped a series of somber events that began with her birth as an unwanted, illegitimate baby and went on and on, illuminated during the last dozen years by the lightning of fame.

Her public life was in dazzling contrast to her private life.

The first man to see her on the screen, the man who made her screen test, felt the almost universal reaction as he ran the wordless scene. In it, she walked, sat down and lit a cigarette.

Recalled 'Lush Stars'

"I got a cold chill," he said. "This girl had something I hadn't seen since silent pictures. This is the first girl who looked like one of those lush stars of the silent era. Every frame of the test radiated sex."

Billy Wilder, the director, called it "flesh impact."

"Flesh impact is rare," he said. "Three I remember who had it were Clara Bow, Jean Harlow and Rita Hayworth. Such girls have flesh which photographs like flesh. You feel you can reach out and touch it."

Fans paid $200,000,000 to see her project this quality. No sex symbol of the era other than Brigitte Bardot could match her popularity. Toward the end, she also convinced critics and the public that she could act.

During the years of her greatest success, she saw two of her marriages end in divorce. She suffered at least two miscarriages and was never able to have a child. Her emotional insecurity deepened; her many illnesses came upon her more frequently.

Dismissed From Picture

In 1961, she was twice admitted to hospitals in New York for psychiatric observation and rest. She was dismissed in June by Twentieth Century-Fox after being absent all but five days during seven weeks of shooting "Something's Got to Give."

"It's something that Marilyn no longer can control," one of her studio chiefs confided. "Sure she's sick. She believes she's sick. She may even have a fever, but it's a sickness of the mind. Only a psychiatrist can help her now."

In her last interview, published in the Aug. 3 issue of Life magazine, she told Richard Meryman, an associate editor:

"I was never used to being happy, so that wasn't something I ever took for granted."

Considering her background, this was a statement of exquisite restraint.

She was born in Los Angeles on June 1, 1926. The name on the birth record is Norma Jean Mortenson, the surname of the man who fathered her, then abandoned her mother. She later took her mother's last name, Baker.

Family Tragedies

Both her maternal grandparents and her mother were committed to mental institutions. Her uncle killed himself. Her father died in a motorcycle accident three years after her birth.

During her mother's stays in asylums, she was farmed out to twelve sets of foster parents. Two families were religious fanatics; one gave her empty whisky bottles to play with instead of dolls.

At another stage, she lived in a drought area with a family of seven. She spent two years in a Los Angeles orphanage, wearing a uniform she detested.

By the time she was 9 years old, Norma Jean had begun to stammer—an affliction rare among females.

Her dream since childhood had been to be a movie star, and she succeeded beyond her wildest imaginings. The conviction of her mother's best friend was borne out; she had told the little girl, day after day:

"Don't worry. You're going to be a beautiful girl when you get big. You're going to be a movie star. Oh, I feel it in my bones."

Nunnally Johnson, the producer and writer, understood that Miss Monroe was something special. Marilyn, he said, was "a phenomenon of nature, like Niagara Falls and the Grand Canyon."

She became famous with her first featured role of any prominence, in "The Asphalt Jungle," issued in 1950.

Her appearance was brief but unforgettable. From the instant she moved onto the screen with that extraordinary walk of hers, people asked themselves: "Who's that blonde?"

In 1952 it was revealed that Miss Monroe had been the subject of a widely distributed nude calendar photograph shot while she was a notably unsuccessful starlet.

Revealed Her Wit

It created a scandal, but it was her reaction to the scandal that was remembered. She told interviewers that she was not ashamed and had needed the money to pay her rent.

She also revealed her sense of humor. When asked by a woman journalist, "You mean you didn't have anything on?" she replied breathlessly:

"Oh yes, I had the radio on."

One of her most exasperating quirks was her tardiness. She was, during the years of her fame, anywhere from one to twenty-four hours late for appointments. Until lately, she managed to get away with it.

Her dilatory nature and sicknesses added nearly $1,000,000 to the budget of "Let's Make Love." The late Jerry Wald, head of her studio, simply commented:

"True, she's not punctual. She can't help it, but I'm not sad about it," he said. "I can get a dozen beautiful blondes who will show up promptly in make-up at 4 A. M. each morning, but they are not Marilyn Monroe."

The tardiness, the lack of responsibility and the fears began to show more and more through the glamorous patina as Miss Monroe's career waxed.

Speaking of her career and her fame in the Life interview, she said, wistfully:

"It might be kind of a relief to be finished. It's sort of like I don't know what kind of a yard dash you're running, but then you're at the finish line and you sort of sigh—you've made it! But you never have —you have to start all over again."

The Times
23rd July 1928

BEAUTY, GENIUS, AND CHARM.

The death of Dame Ellen Terry, announced on another page, has been received with universal sorrow. In the history of the English stage no other actress has ever made for herself so abiding a place in the affections of the nation.

Ellen Alice Terry was born at Coventry on February 27, 1848, and was the second in age of three sisters, Kate (Mrs. Arthur Lewis), Ellen, and Marion, who, with their brother, Mr. Fred Terry, made up a famous theatrical family. Their parents, Mr. and Mrs. Benjamin Terry, were well-known provincial actors in the days of stock companies, and Miss Ellen Terry took early to their calling. At the age of eight she was engaged by Charles Kean to play Mamillius in *The Winter's Tale* at the Princess's Theatre, and she remained in his company for some years, acting, among other parts, Puck in *A Midsummer Night's Dream* and Arthur in *King John*. Even in those early days she appears to have shown the characteristics that made her irresistible in her prime ; roguish comedy in Mamillius and Puck, pathos in Arthur, and personal charm in all three.

Kean gave up the Princess's Theatre in 1860, and Ellen Terry went to the provinces in search of experience. For some time she was in the old-established stock company of the Chutes at Bristol, of which her sister Kate, Madge Robertson (now Dame Madge Kendal), and Henrietta Hodson were also members. She returned to London in 1863, to play the part of Gertrude in *A Little Treasure* at the Haymarket to the Captain Maydenblush of Sothern ; here, too, she first played Beatrice in *Much Ado About Nothing* before a London audience. Another performance in London was that of Desdemona to the Othello of Walter Montgomery. That was in 1863, and soon after it there came a break in Miss Terry's theatrical career. In February, 1864, she was married to G. F. Watts, the great painter, who was nearly 30 years her senior. In June, 1865, they parted.

In 1867 occurred an event pregnant with interest. Having left the stage for two years, Miss Terry accepted an engagement at the now-extinct Queen's Theatre in Long Acre ; and here she first acted with Henry Irving. He and she played Petruchio and Katherine in *The Taming of the Shrew*, or rather in *Katherine and Petruchio*, Garrick's version of that play. Her elder sister, Kate, had married at the height of her career, and retired from the stage. Ellen Terry was looked upon as her worthy successor, but only the next year she retired once more from the stage, and she remained in private life till 1874. Even then she was only 26 years old, and an actress of her talent had little difficulty in making up lost ground. It even seemed that the interval had done her service by ripening the individual characteristics on which the great part of her success depended.

Returning to the Queen's Theatre for a time, she found her first great opportunity in April, 1875, when Mr. and Mrs. Bancroft put on *The Merchant of Venice* at the old Prince of Wales's Theatre, and, being unable to secure Mrs. Kendal for Portia, turned to Miss Terry. A better move could not have been made. Ellen Terry was always the ideal Portia. More than 20 years later, when she was hampered by a distressing lack of memory and some slight loss of vitality, her beauty (she was well compared to a portrait by Veronese), her dignity, and her graciousness were unimpaired, and the bubbling spring of her mirth seemed as fresh as ever : it would be well worth while to be old to have seen her play the part at 27. The revival, admirable though it was, was short-lived, chiefly owing, it is said, to Coghlan's Shylock ; but Miss Terry's reputation was doubled. She remained with the same management for more than a year, playing Clara Douglas in *Money*, Mabel Vane in *Masks and Faces*, and Blanche Haye in *Ours*. On leaving the Prince of Wales's Theatre she joined John Hare's management at the old Court, where, among other parts, she appeared for the first time as Olivia in Wills's adaptation of "The Vicar of Wakefield."

When Henry Irving took over the Lyceum, at the close of the Bateman management in 1878, one of his first steps was to engage Ellen Terry as his leading lady, and for the next 13 years they acted together, almost without a break. Her first part under the new management was Ophelia, and the influence of Irving was apparent at the outset. The part had been thought out as a whole, and one result was that the "mad scene" had a meaning. The phrases no longer appeared to be ungoverned spurts of lunacy ; each proved to have been born of that character in those circumstances ; and the effect of all was not only to intensify the devotion, the tenderness, and the innocence of Ophelia herself ; but to point the tragedy of the whole story. No doubt Irving had found good material to work on ; beauty (as Ophelia, said M. Jules Claretie in *La Presse*, Miss Terry looked like a "living model of Giovanni Bellini"), rare personal charm, intense vitality, and no lack of intelligence ; but it says much for Irving's own power, and for the loyalty of one who might practically be called his pupil, that at her very first appearance under his management a born comedian should achieve a triumph in the part of Ophelia.

Her first season at the Lyceum was typical of the years of hard work that were to follow ; besides Ophelia it included her appearance as Pauline, Lady Anne, Ruth Meadows, and Henrietta Maria. One of the most remarkable features of her career, indeed, is the loyal and patient manner in which she subordinated her own bias to fulfil the demands of her manager and his theatre. She played a great variety of parts, and though she played them not all equally well, she was always able to present a reasoned and consistent interpretation, while her irresistible personal charm went far to conceal the fact that she was frequently out of her depth. Lady Macbeth, for instance, was a part to which her special gifts were totally unsuited ; but to recall her rendering of it is to recall far more than the regally beautiful woman who appears in Sargent's picture. It fell short of the magnificent, perverted nature which Shakespeare conceived, but it displayed a firmness that was an admirable foil to the moral cowardice of Macbeth, and something of the tragedy of a great love unworthily bestowed.

To chronicle all Miss Terry's appearances between 1878 and 1901 would be to chronicle the history of the Lyceum Theatre. In only two plays—*Nance Oldfield* and *The Amber Heart*—did she appear without Sir Henry Irving ; and to these might be added *Olivia*, as distinctly her triumph rather than his. In consecrating her best years to the Lyceum Miss Terry no doubt sacrificed many chances of appearing in plays, new or old, which might have exploited her personal bent ; on the other hand, she was freed from the dangers of an ever-narrowing range and a faulty judgment which too often beset leading actors and actresses ; she gained breadth and knowledge by playing whatever part Sir Henry Irving wished her to play, and she had the satisfaction of knowing herself a member of one of the greatest histrionic partnerships the English stage has seen.

Like Irving, she commanded the attention ; it was impossible to take one's eyes off her—until he appeared on the stage ; unlike him, she commanded by appealing, by charming, rather than by interesting. Womanly, tender, mirthful, witty, graceful, musical, with a clear and melodious enunciation and rhythmical, flowing movements, she made the most perfect foil to her partner that could be imagined. And once or twice, where Irving was least successful, it happened that Miss Terry was most in her element. Her matchless Portia we have referred to ; Irving's Shylock was long unacceptable to the town ; Miss Terry's Viola (a performance unfortunately cut short by illness) was inimitable, one of her finest achievements, while Irving's Malvolio was all in the wrong key. In *Romeo and Juliet* they failed together, and in *Hamlet* they succeeded together. As Beatrice (which was perhaps the very finest of all the adorable performances she gave) she was so enchanting that the memory of her wit and charm leaves Irving's Benedick somewhat dim.

Of all Miss Terry's failures probably her Madame Sans-Gêne was the most outright, and the best deserved. The incarnation of all that was gracious and graceful, an actress whose every movement was a poem, whose speech was music, and whose ebullient spirits were constantly caught and guided into a stream of beauty by some natural refinement, she turned in that part to try to be vulgar. That she failed was only a new proof of the distance that separated her from the realistic school represented by Mme. Réjane, a new illustration of the rare quality of her gifts. Though she lacked great tragic power, in scenes of simple pathos and affection, like those of Olivia or Cordelia, the emotions of her audience were utterly at her command ; her highest moments came in the high-bred raillery of Portia and Beatrice.

Miss Terry left the Lyceum company in 1901, after the end of the run of *Coriolanus*, but appeared as Portia in the performance of *The Merchant of Venice* which closed the history of the theatre in July, 1902. A short season at the Imperial Theatre in 1903 under her own management brought no success. The name of her son, Edward Gordon Craig, was not then so well known in England as it is now, and his theories of scenery and of stage-lighting were even more puzzling to London then than they would be to-day. And so the interesting it might be called the prophetic production of Ibsen's *The Vikings at Helgeland* fell flat. In subsequent years Miss Terry appeared as Mistress Page in *The Merry Wives of Windsor* at His Majesty's Theatre; she played with indescribable fascination Lady Cecily Waynflete in Shaw's *Captain Brassbound's Conversion*; she appeared in *Alice Sit-by-the-Fire* and in *Pinkie and the Fairies*, and she delivered in many towns of England and the United States two series of wilful, witty, very "feminist," and very perspicacious, lectures on Shakespeare's heroines.

In June, 1906, the 50th anniversary of Miss Terry's first appearance on the stage was celebrated at the Theatre Royal, Drury Lane, amid fervent enthusiasm. She had always been idolized by the public; and even the shrewdest critics found their judgment seduced by her supreme vitality and personal charm. At that "Jubilee" public, critics, and the theatrical profession (to whose memories she had endeared herself by her unfailing kindness, consideration, and unselfishness) joined to show her how much she was loved and admired. In spite of advancing years, failing memory, and increasing restlessness, she was always welcome on the stage; and she preserved her gaiety and *verve* to the end.

In May, 1922, Miss Terry received the hon. degree of LL.D. at St. Andrews. In the New Year honours of 1925, to the delight of her countless admirers, she received the Grand Cross of the Order of the British Empire. In celebration of this event she and her sister Dames created at the same time—namely, Dame Millicent Fawcett and the late Dame Louisa Aldrich-Blake—were presented with wreaths of laurel at a reception held by a number of distinguished women. Her 80th birthday was celebrated last February with messages and tributes from her countless admirers, headed by the King and Queen, and it drew from old playgoers an interesting correspondence in *The Times* containing reminiscences of her triumphs. Some day, perhaps, a full and authoritative biography will fill the gaps inevitably left by her modesty and consideration for others in the fascinating book of memories which was her chief contribution to literature. She was a woman of genius; but her genius was not that of the brain so much as of the spirit, and of the heart. She was a poem in herself—a being of an exquisite and mobile beauty. On the stage or off she was like the daffodils that set the poet's heart dancing.

IN *A WINTER'S TALE*.—Another photograph of Ellen Terry in *A Winter's Tale*. It was taken fifty years after her first appearance in this play.

The Times
27th December 1977

CHARLIE CHAPLIN
Comic genius of the cinema screen

Sir Charles Chaplin, KBE. Charlie Chaplin, the comedian, died on Christmas Day. He was 88.

He was the last survivor from among the founding fathers of the American cinema, one of the greatest comic creators in film, and achieved greater, more widespread fame in his own lifetime than perhaps anyone else in the history of mankind. He was the darling of the intellectuals, who loved to theorize on the significance of his comedy, its social responsibility, its relation to the great tradition of commedia del' arte and circus clowning, its anarchic force and vigour. But he also had to a unique degree the common touch—people of virtually any culture were able to respond with laughter to his screen antics, and for generation after generation of children he was the first introduction to the magic world of the cinema.

During the latter part of his long life Chaplin, though loaded with honours and universally regarded as one o. the unshakable monuments of the cinema (whatever controversy his political attitudes might arouse), did begin to suffer from a certain reaction to the excesses of his early admirers. This had something to do with a grudging but progressive disenchantment with his later films, and something to do with the rediscovery and revaluation of the work of his many rivals in silent comedy. As we moved into the 1950s it became permissible to prefer the refined and unsentimental art of Buster Keaton, who was certainly a far more subtle and imaginative film-maker than Chaplin could ever claim to be, or even the totally unpretentious humour of Laurel and Hardy. The time was coming, in fact, for a thorough reassessment of Chaplin's own work, concentrating on aspects of it which

continued

would be more congenial to modern sensibilities: the elements of childlike ruthlessness which had endeared it to the Surrealists, perhaps, rather than the sentimentalizing elevation of the "little man" which had made him a hero to liberal humanists.

As with Chaplin's performannces, so with his career as a whole, the secret of his success lay in his immaculate timing. His genius was essentially pantomimic, and so ideally suited to the silent cinema. He came into films at a period when the various functions of film-making were undefined, so that anyone with a strong idea of what he wanted to do (which Chaplin certainly had, almost from the outset) was free to go ahead and do it. Having got in on the ground floor, he was able, with the aid of extraordinary business acumen, to build at once on his great success with the public in order to become rich and powerful as well as famous—even in these early days Chaplin off-screen, the budding tycoon and central figure in many an over-publicized romantic drama, was sharply differentiated from the somewhat pathetic underdog he played in films, with his cane and baggy pants, his slum-bred cunning, and his understandable tendency to be overlooked by the girl of his dreams. By the beginning of the 1920s he was his own master in films, able to do exactly what he wanted, in exactly the way he wanted—and in his own time.

And with the coming of sound he alone was able to fight a long rearguard action, making what were in effect silent films with the addition of music and sound-effects, and in *The Great Dictator* a little localized speech, until right into the 1940s. He had had the foresight to own outright and control all his mature works, and to withhold them from general release for years at a time, so that each reappearance of a Chaplin film had a sense of occasion all its own. And even his later contretemps with the American authorities over his flirtations with marxism and his staunchly preserved British nationality, which resulted in some years of exile from America, was eventually resolved to the complete satisfaction of both sides.

When he was 17 Charles Chaplin joined Fred Karno's pantomime group, and in 1910 was taken as first comedian on the company's tour of the United States. In 1913 he was seen in New York by Mack Sennett, America's foremost producer of comedy films, playing a drunk in a sketch called *A Night in an English Music Hall,* and was taken on as a film comedian to replace Ford Sterling.

Chaplin was reluctant to leave Karno, and his early days in Hollywood only confirmed these doubts. His first film, in which he appeared in a frock coat and top hat, was a failure. Later he adopted the tramp costume of the baggy trousers and ill-fitting suit, but it was not until the making of *Tillie's Punctured Romance* in 1914, with Marie Dressler and Mabel Normand, that he became famous.

Chaplin made about 40 comedies for Sennett, then made 14 for Essanay, and in 1916 he went over to the Mutual Company after signing a contract for what was, in those days, an unheard-of salary. But by now he was world famous, and was writing and directing his own films. More important still was the fact that the character of "the little fellow", as the tramp was always known to his creator, had become firmly established in his mind.

The 1920s were the golden age of the silent cinema, and Chaplin entered this golden age with wealth, power, authority, and complete freedom as an independent producer of his own work. To this period belongs *The Kid* (1920) with Jackie Coogan, *The Gold Rush* (1925) with Mack Swain, and *The Circus* (1928) with Merna Kennedy. During this period he also startled the film world by writing and directing a picture in which he did not himself appear. This was *A Woman of Paris* (1923), with Adolphe Menjou and Edna Purviance—an interesting and original work, but one that attempted a sophisticated elegance which was not really within Chaplin's province and which Lubitsch was shortly to undertake with much more success in *The Marriage Circle*.

Up to this point in his career there was little room for controversy of any kind: his popularity was unchallenged, and even *A Woman of Paris* enjoyed considerable success, on its own merits rather than as a Chaplin film. It seems likely now that his lasting reputation will rest most securely on the films he made between 1916 and 1928: later reissues of *The Gold Rush, The Kid, Shoulder Arms, Easy Street* and other films of this era in sparkling new prints with musical soundtracks composed by Chaplin himself confirmed their power over new generations of filmgoers, while *The Circus*, which Chaplin had never considered one of his better films, came as a revelation when shown again in this new form. But from the beginning of the sound era things become more arguable. There were many, and are still, who regard *City Lights* (1931) as his finest film. But for others the sentiment in the "little fellow's" love for a blind flower girl becomes cloying and for the first

time a deathly self-consciousness about the character's symbolism and message for the world seems to intrude. In this film Chaplin resolutely turned his back on the talkie, making a silent film with the musical accompaniment on the soundtrack instead of live in the theatre. He used the same approach in *Modern Times* (1936), a would-be satire on the mechanization of man which leaned heavily on René Clair's *A Nous la Liberté* and despite funny moments demonstrated rather clearly that satire and explicit messages were not Chaplin's forte.

It was no doubt inevitable that eventually Chaplin would have to talk on the screen, and he took the plunge at the end of *The Great Dictator* (1940), with a six-minute speech driving home the point of his satire at the expense of Hitler and Mussolini. Most of the film remained speechless, however; it was the swansong of Chaplin's little man character, in the shape of the humble Jewish barber with an uncanny resemblance to a Hitler-like dictator also played by Chaplin. *Monsieur Verdoux* (1947) marked a complete break with the past: a talkative "comedy of murders" suggested by the life and career of Landru, it gave us a suave, middle-aged Chaplin very different from anything we had seen before. For the first time it is unavoidable to see the limitations of Chaplin's skill as a film director rather than as a performer—the film is stiff and stagy in the extreme, and not too well written either, in a context where high style is a necessity. *Limelight* (1952) was something of a return to form, however: unashamedly Victorian and sentimental in its tale of an aging clown's love for a waiflike ballet dancer, it took on an indefinable quality from Chaplin's own nostalgic re-creation of his early days in the London theatre, and at least it did not even try for most of its length to be funny.

Its appearance marked the beginning of an unhappy period in Chaplin's life. When he left America for the European premiere the State Department banned his reentry (which they could do as he had never become an American citizen), and Chaplin took up residence, at first resentfully, in Switzerland. His next film, *The King in New York* (1957), made in Britain and for long unseen in America, was a bitter but ineffectual satire on America and the American way of life, notable chiefly for Chaplin's succumbing to what is supposed to be the classic comic's temptation, that of playing *Hamlet,* with an unfortunate rendition of "To be or not to be" during a New York dinner party. But the anger on both sides, product of those witch-hunting days, gradually subsided as Chaplin moved into an honoured old age.

Daily Telegraph
13th June 1979

Mary Pickford won the world's heart

MARY PICKFORD has died, aged 86. To have reported her death 40 years ago would have cracked the world's heart, for was she not its sweetheart, or at any rate America's?

Who else has ever cast such a spell with innocence for a wand? Well, in fact there have been others. But those who saw Mary in her heyday will assure you they did not count.

What, then, was the nature of the Pickford spell? There's the rub; for she made her last picture (they were always "pictures" then) with Leslie Howard in 1933, and her work is seldom revived.

Much of it has been destroyed or lost; and most of the rest must be unearthed by the privileged in archives.

Not that she has been forgotten, or ever could be, one gathers, by those exposed to her art.

Anyone decently advanced into middle life will have visions of curls and charming heroics and a general verging on cuteness; as well as the impishness of the comedies and the highly creditable ventures into bolder fields of film art, like Kate in "The Taming of the Shrew."

But accuracy is the problem: accounting for the weekly enthralment of those idolising millions to whom Miss Pickford represented, in her terribly endearing, terribly pure little way, all that was best and (who knows?) healthiest in simple escapism.

She once or twice tried to escape from the type the world had cast for her; to get away from the purity, the endearment, and the littleness of stuff like "A Poor Little Rich Girl," "Little Colonel," "Little Princess," "Little Lord Fauntleroy," "Little Annie Rooney" and "The Little American." But, to adapt Johnson:

The pictures' laws, the picture patrons give
For they that live to please, must please to live.

Charming innocence

And please is what Miss Pickford undoubtedly did with her charming innocence and unaffected acting in an age of histrionic flamboyance.

"Mr Griffith," she was once moved to remark of the great and legendary D. W., "always wanted to have me running around trees and pointing at rabbits and I wouldn't do it." Enough, Miss Pickford felt, was enough in a medium of increasing extravagance.

She herself described her career as a temporary and freakish phenomenon; and of all her films she finally concluded: "There isn't one that is halfway right."

Born Gladys Smith in Toronto in 1893, she began acting young. At five she was on the stage in "stock." Within a few years she was a "child wonder" for David Belasco on Broadway; and even then, Little Miss Mary, who had known poverty, sensed where the money was.

She knocked on Biograph's door, Griffith opened it, gave her a chance in a one-reeler, and success soon followed. "Tess of the Storm Country" (1914) made her name, and in 1915 she was receiving half the profits for her work with Famous Players.

When her contract with Famous Players' ended in 1918 she became, at 25., her own producer, beginning with "Pollyanna," a great success.

The next year, when United Artists was formed, she joined Chaplin. Griffith and Douglas Fairbanks, Snr, whom she married, though they never acted together until the talkies, when they co-starred in Shakespeare's "Shrew" with its "additional dialogue by Sam Taylor" (said to be quite tasteful).

At the age of 40 the screen figure who had at one time stood for everything that was "heavenly, radiant, innocent, kind, noble and true" one of the more sober critical assessments), decided to retire. And not only to retire but to stay retired, without threat or promise of come-back.

She kept her word, to concentrate her interests in production, though in 1971 she was persuaded to release some of her films she made 50 years before and Retrospective Seasons were held.

And the key to her spell? Well, the filmgoer was less sophisticated then; awed rather than cynical, and no more critical than your TV goggler bemused by some routine serial.

PICKFORD MILLIONS FOR POOR

MARY Pickford, the first actress to get star billing in films, left her respendent home, Pickfair, and the bulk of her multi-million-dollar estate to the Mary Pickford Foundation for use in charitable purposes, mainly for the poor.

But her two adopted children, Roxanne and Ronald, received only £25,000 each. There was no immediately explanation.

Her third husband, Buddy Rogers, who was with her for 42 years, received £12,500 in cash, some property, art treasures and £24,000 a year from a trust set up for him. Trust funds were also set up for six grandchildren and a niece.

At least £5m

Miss Pickford's will, filed yesterday in Santa Monica, Calif., gave the value of her estate as just over £5 million. But the true value is believed to be far greater and will not be known until all her property is sold.

Miss Pickford, sweetheart of the silent film era, died last week after suffering a stroke at Pickfair in Beverly Hills.

She was born into a poor family in Toronto but became enormously wealthy from shrewd investment in films, land and oil. She asked for her foundation to find ways of giving relief to those who are poor, distressed and discriminated against.

The Times
27th March 1923

DEATH OF MME. BERNHARDT.

FRENCH QUEEN OF TRAGEDY.

A SIXTY YEARS' REIGN.

WORLD TRIUMPHS

We regret to announce that Mme. Sarah Bernhardt died at 8 o'clock last evening at her Paris residence.

Sarah Bernhardt.

"Aye, Madam, it is common: all that lives "must die." To be born and to die were the only common things that MME. SARAH BERNHARDT ever did. It looked as if she would keep the resolution which HAMILTON declared the MARQUIS DE GRAMMONT to have formed— the resolution of never dying. And even now that Death has won the long battle which she fought with him so gaily, so like a sportsman, it is hard to believe that she will not appear again to-morrow under another name, like the people in MR. BERNARD SHAW'S *Back to Methuselah*. If she does, she must not hope to pass unrecognized on the instant. She not only had the vitality; she was compelled by Nature and fate to express it, to force it upon the world. Both on the stage and off she asserted what we call her personality, which, whatever it may involve of mental and spiritual elements, involves, first, the physical exterior— eyes, hands, voice, and next the intensity of being. In her quietest moments, say when she was lying ill or resting after some great display of emotion on the stage, still she asserted her personality. Many a wordy battle has been fought over the relative merits of MME. BERN-HARDT and SIGNORA DUSE. We conceive it easy to pass the great Italian actress in the street without knowing who she was. MME. BERN-HARDT made herself felt always, everywhere.

To suppose that this heroic form of self-assertion concealed a lack of art is to make a grave mistake. She had a marvellous instru-ment to play upon ; and her notion of acting was to bring out of that instrument every variety and degree of emotional tone of which it was capable. To know her Phèdre well was, indeed, to know approximately how the effects were got ; but the effects themselves were never staled by the knowledge. The "voice of gold," the eloquent hands, the sinuous limbs, were great possessions ; but they could never have torn at our heart-strings with tenderness, pity, shame, fury, if the owner of them had not known to a nicety how to use them best. Since her heyday many a new theory of the art of acting has come among us, from Russia and elsewhere. MME. BERNHARDT believed that the duty of acting was to touch the emotions ; and it is among the clearest proofs of her claim to be artist as well as genius that, when robbed of one of her chief assets, her power of movement, she could still hold her audiences in thrall.

An actress on and off the stage for more than sixty years, she had lived, and lived her fullest, into modern times from an age when it was the fashion for artists, and not artists only, to live more flamboyantly than they do to-day. She brought with her the tradition of a time when the individual was less hampered than now by the criticism of public opinion. Little people half-heartedly indulge their caprice, and are ridiculous. MME. BERNHARDT, who would have made the tradition if she had not found it, was too great, both in caprice and in daring, to be ridiculous. When Paris laughed at her, Paris was adoring or detesting her. And in modern England, which has lost its eighteenth-century reputation for producing flavoursome oddities of individuality, she had the joy of finding herself in her later years a heroine among the populace. The epicures of theatrical art may have turned to subtler, newer thrills. The people loved her, not only because on the stage she knew the way to their hearts, but because she had become a great legend of odd and flavoursome individuality. We admired, above all, her courage in the face of illness, pain, and what in anyone else would have been old age. There will be brave women and great actresses yet ; but in the shadow of the loss of "Sarah" we feel that modern times will not give them such opportunities of warming both hands before the fire of life in public as MME. BERNHARDT had and took. She was a great figure of great days that are gone. We shall not look upon her like again.

Manchester Guardian
16th August 1956

BERTOLT BRECHT

Bertolt Brecht, the German playwright and stage director, whose death is reported on page one, was born in 1898 at Augsburg.

The facts of Bertolt Brecht's life are fairly straightforward. What is complicated is to establish how much he really achieved in the theatre. His sudden death will cause difficulties for some of his advocates. They were obviously prepared to declare, when his Berliner Ensemble appeared for the first time in London the week after next, that Brecht was the greatest living European dramatist. They will not find it easy to uphold the view that he is the greatest dead one.

Brecht played a vigorous, but at first subsidiary, part in the German theatre after the First World War (in which he served), being notable more as a disciple of Piscator than as a leader of his own particular sect. He quickly established a polemical line of pacifism and socialism which later hardened into communism, but his dramatic work was the more lively because his enthusiasm was split between trying to reform human behaviour and trying to find new ways of expressing that behaviour in theatrical terms.

If he was an original thinker it is a curious paradox that two out of three of his best-known works were based on other men's achievement. His "Dreigroschenoper" owed almost everything to the music by Kurt Weill and to the original. "The Beggar's Opera," by our own John Gay—which made at least as much of a success when revived, earlier in the twenties, at the Lyric, Hammersmith, as it did in Brecht's later, less gay version. His "Caucasian Chalk Circle" had already been adapted by Klabund from a Chinese original and used effectively as Socialist propaganda (a translation by James Laver did well in this country). Brecht took a single incident from the story and, without weakening the political line, enormously expanded the dramatic effect.

When Brecht began to strike out on his own there was need for a label more precise than "expressionism" to attach to his work, which was without doubt originally a part of the Expressionist movement. He used the term "narrative realism," but in the end the critics fastened on the descriptions "epic" or "epic theatre" to apply to Brecht's work, with as much semantic justification as the word "plastic" was adopted to describe the scenic innovations of Adolf Appia.

In a recently published book "Trends in Twentieth-century Drama," Frederick Lumley cut through a good deal of the obscure writing on Brecht and defined his attitude thus: "Since the stage has inescapable limitations, why, he asks, try to use the 'let's pretend' method of the naturalists; why not show the stage to the audience as a stage? If the theatre is real, there can be no question of trying to strive for the ecstasy and magical elements which were responsible for the hara-kiri of the Expressionist movement; on the contrary, what was required was the theory of 'alienation.' Brecht devised the alienation of emotion in his work, so that the audience should be prevented from identifying itself with an actor, or from losing itself in the supreme moments of theatre, only to be brought down to earth with a bump when it was over. There were to be no supreme moments and consequently no fall. Emotional strait-jackets were once again in fashion."

Much of the special pleading in favour of Brecht, which was so vexing to those who thought it better to wait and see how his work lasted, was based on political rather than artistic standards. Left-wing breast beaters praised him at the top of their voices, automatically and in chorus, so persistently that it became difficult for the serious critic to disentangle the poet, the dramatist, and the stage director from the cynical propagandist of the "people's" East Germany. The echoes of the New Speak will have to die, more of Brecht's work be seen, better translations offered, before it will be possible to place him accurately. For the time being he belongs in the same category as Gordon Craig—an important man of the theatre not so much for what he did as for what he made other people in irritation try to do.

Glasgow Herald
10th April 1950

Genius of the Ballet

Vaslav Nijinsky, the greatest dancer of his generation, who restored the lost reputation of male ballet dancing, died in London on Saturday. In 1919 he became afflicted by a mental illness, and in his last years the man who had been acclaimed throughout the world was, in the words of a close friend, "practically a beggar."

Nijinsky was born at Kiev, South Russia, in 1890. His father was of Polish descent, and was no mean exponent of the art in which his son was to gain world-wide fame, but he was denied admission to the Imperial schools because he was not of Russian birth, and accordingly he organised his own troupe and toured the country.

In such surroundings Nijinsky first found his feet as a dancer. At 10 years of age he passed his preliminary examination, and he developed so rapidly at the Imperial School that by 1916 he had surpassed his masters in their art. This led to his admission as a regular member of the Mariinsky Theatre (the Imperial Opera House of St Petersburg, which belonged to the Czar, and was subsidised by him to the amount of two million gold roubles per annum).

RENAISSANCE OF BALLET

Nijinsky played a prominent part in the renaissance of the Russian ballet when Sergei Diaghileff became its artistic director. Diaghileff was a man of dominating personality, with a fine background of culture, and he found influential backing for the enterprises which carried him triumphantly first through the Capitals of Europe and eventually to London, where his success was no less pronounced. With Michel Fokine as choreographer and artists like Bakst and Benois at his command, Diaghileff had among his interpreters Nijinsky, Anna Pavlova, Tamara Karsavina, and many other dancers who had become as accomplished as the Russian schools could make them.

Yet none ever impressed the public so greatly as Nijinsky. His art was shown to perfection along with Karsavina in "Le Spectre de la Rose," danced to the music of Weber's "Invitation to the Dance."

TECHNIQUE OF SELF-IMPRESSION

But Nijinsky, the interpreter, had the urge to create something different from the traditional style of ballet dancing, and he tried his hand as choreographer. He wanted to make a definite distinction between movement and the dance, and in order to find an adequate vehicle of self-expression he worked out plans which were regarded by the purists of the classical school as revolutionary. The first example of his new method was seen in the use he made of Debussy's "L'Après-Midi d'un Faune," which was hailed by many as a brilliant creative effort and just as soundly condemned by others. But he went on undeterred.

Diaghileff, however, did not view these innovations with favour, and for that and other reasons drifted apart from Nijinsky. For a time Nijinsky carried on with a company he himself organised. He had a series of great receptions in South America and afterwards in the United States, but the strain of incessant travelling impaired his health.

He had married Romola de Pulszky, a Hungarian, who faithfully stood by him in happiness and in misfortune, and after returning to Europe they set up a home in Switzerland. Shortly after the close of the First World War he withdrew from the world. His years of mental darkness were occasionally illumined by the memories of what he had been and by the recollection of the great music to which he had danced at the height of his fame. For some time latterly he and Mme. Nijinsky lived at Virginia Water, Surrey.

Daily Mirror
4th February 1969

THE GENTLE MONSTER

MAYBE if you have been born William Henry Pratt, in Dulwich, the youngest of nine such Pratts, you clutch at any straw — like a family name "Karloff" on your mother's side.

"Boris" was added as an afterthought to clinch the chilling image of a mad Russian monk or, in a more jugular vein, a vampire hooked on the nearest bloodstream.

Boris Karloff, the monster who lisped and plodded through thirty years of delicious cob-webbed horror, died yesterday in a Sussex hospital at the age of eighty-one. His long reign of terror, which began with Frankenstein's wired and heavy-booted fiend, has ended. Unless, of course, the impish Mr. Pratt has other plans.

In a world of slavering bloodhounds, creaking doors, forked lightning and capricious coffin lids, Boris Karloff was the acknowledged master.

Petrified

If Rudolph Valentino dispensed the world's dreams, Karloff manufactured its nightmares. He had the screen audiences of the thirties so petrified, exhibitors took out accident policies as a cautious—or hopeful—insurance against heart attacks among the patrons.

Those who did not swoon, or totally succumb, sat mutely biting their knuckles as our freezing demon did his ugly stuff.

"The Body Snatcher," "Isle of the Dead," "The Strange Door," "Voodoo Island," the "Curse of the Crimson Altar"—Karloff's credits exceed a shuddering 130 horror films.

Corpses that wouldn't lie down, deep moans from the obstreperously un-dead. ("You're becoming hysterical, old man—kindly decompose yourself.") And, of

course, Karloff was, so to speak, the Daddy of all Mummies.

Like the classic Western, Karloff's horror films soon fell into a much-relished pattern. For the opening scene, you could have a choice of:

A howling gale flings open a casement window as a scream splits the darkness of the night; or close-up on the green slime of an open grave as a rat investigates a skeleton's eye-socket; or that old favourite of the storm-bound hero forced to seek shelter at a forbidding mansion as a ghoul of a housekeeper at the East Window drools at the fangs.

But none of these cheerful diversions could equal the petrifying debut of Frankenstein's do-it-yourself monster.

Crudely bolted at the neck, the ashen features brutally hemstitched, the enormous body creaking forward on a child's brain and a stolen heart, the Thing defied you not to love it.

You know that once his inventor's back is turned, lightning will short-circuit those steel fetters and that the amiable brute will lurch out on his own.

But, of course, he only wanted to be loved (doesn't everybody?) and though his embrace could crush an ox, it was merely a gesture of affection.

This hint of tenderness behind the hemstitching and hinged jaw was what gave the monster its subtle appeal. And only an actor like Karloff, educated at Uppingham, with an affection for cricket and butterflies, could convince us that the monster's heart was approximately in the right place.

Like the Tarzans who eventually loathed their loin-cloths, swallowed morosely on their Cry of the Great Ape. Karloff came to dislike his monsters.

Off-screen he resembled a retired Army general, stylishly dressed, his almost white hair neatly brushed at the temples.

Applaud

Hollywood hostesses hoped he would bring a vicarious thrill to their parties. Karloff just wanted to talk about cricket. Or butterflies. Or in later years his reading of fairy tales on children's records.

Although all his success and wealth was won in Hollywood he remained aggressively British. Whether they liked it or not, the studio bosses had to applaud "this crazy Limey" all the way to the wicket. Those moguls who baulked at fielding first slip received the full cold-eyed treatment from their chosen monster.

But they loved him. Not merely because of his genius at giving his monsters "star quality." He was also the complete professional actor — courteous, even-tempered, always on time, word perfect.

He was ear-marked for the Chinese Consular Service. But a chance performance as the Demon King, at the age of nine, determined his career.

He was a stage actor for twenty years before Frankenstein enticed him in 1931. The instant success frightened him, as much as the character scared the audiences.

"But I always saw my monster as something inarticulate, helpless and tragic," he said. "To him Frankenstein was God. Nothing pleased me more than when children wrote expressing great compassion for him. It was revealing and it was a compliment."

Karloff did not care for some of the current horror films which rely largely on shock. "I like them to feel that I'm not such a bad monster once they get to know me—really just like the ghoul next door."

Unique

Ten years ago, stricken by arthritis which later forced him into a wheelchair, Karloff returned to live permanently in England with his wife, Evelyn.

But the offers continued to pour in. He played the role of the professor in "The Curse of the Crimson Altar" in his wheel chair, one leg in a metal brace.

It was a unique monster who could pause while embalming a reluctant corpse to enquire: "Let me know when Craveney is batting."

Other monsters, like the gifted Christopher Lee, will continue to sink their fangs into accommodating necks or pilfer the graveyards of still-warm cadavers. But all will concede that they cannot hold a flickering candle to Karloff.

Doors will creak a little less ominously in movies now that our favourite fiend has gone. But the name Boris Karloff will continue to chill the spine of history.

Which is a little hard on Mr William Henry Pratt. He was such a nice chap.

Daily Express
24th January 1931

DEATH OF MME. PAVLOVA.

"**ANNA** knew she was dying yesterday afternoon, and was prepared for the end. Yet so great was her devotion to her art that she unconsciously performed some of the movements of her famous 'Dying Swan' dance for hours last night while she lay in a coma. It was tragic and yet impressive to watch her."

This remarkable statement regarding the last hours of Mme. Anna Pavlova, the famous Russian ballerina, who died in the early hours of to-day at the Hotel des Indes here, was made to me by Mr. Kraus, the dancer's impresario.

PREMONITION.

The great dancer, Mr. Kraus revealed, had a premonition of her approaching end as far back as last Sunday, when she discussed with him the expenditure of ballet funds on new clothes.

"Anna authorised the expenditure," Mr. Kraus said, "and then turned to me and exclaimed: 'I have a feeling that I am approaching the end. Perhaps it would be better if this money were given to the poor.'

From another member of Mme. Pavlova's company I learn that when M. Pladoweski, the dancer's ballet master, was informed of her death, he became like one possessed, running from room to room of the hotel and gesticulating wildly in his grief.

"WE WORSHIPPED HER."

M. Dandre, Pavlova's husband, is broken-hearted. A former Russian nobleman, he was married secretly to the dancer, and it was many years before their marriage was revealed by Pavlova.

"We almost worshipped her," M. Dandre told me this afternoon, "and her passing has left an ache in our hearts which will take a long time to remove. And yet, if she had taken proper precautions and listened to our advice, she might have been alive today.

New York Times
12th February 1948

SERGEI EISENSTEIN IS DEAD IN MOSCOW

Sergei M. Eisenstein had been widely acclaimed as one of the world's foremost movie directors. He was responsible for such outstanding examples of the cinema art as "Potemkin" and "Alexander Nevsky," and he was said to have successfully brought about in the motion picture a true fusion of all the arts.

That many of his pictures were patently propaganda works was true, but to students of the movie art this appeared not so much to matter as the fact that he developed new techniques, devised camera approaches and sought always to bring out the potential of a still developing form. That he forgot—or overlooked—to bring the Marxist message to one of his films two years ago brought him that fatal kiss of all—the accusation from the authoritative Soviet magazine, Culture and Life, that his productions had been short on the prescribed Soviet requirement of art and interpretation of history.

One of his most striking contributions was the development of the montage and a new method of cutting and mounting film after "shooting" was over to produce a rapid panoramic progression of images that forcefully projected some idea. "A work of art understood dynamically is just the process of arranging images and feelings in the mind of the spectator," he wrote.

He once tried Hollywood. The visit was not a success and ended without his ever having been assigned a single picture. He did, however, go to Mexico, where he collaborated in the writing and directing of "Thunder Over Mexico," which was released here in a heavily edited version.

Work on "Ivan the Terrible"

It was the second part of a trilogy on "Ivan the Terrible" that halted the director in mid-work in 1946. Having failed to portray what an official paper called "contemporary realism" the film expert coincidentally developed a heart attack.

A few months later he was reported to have regretted that he had "permitted a distortion of historical facts, which made our film bad and ideologically defective." Apart from what forces were brought upon him at home he remained to professional and lay filmgoers here a man of great intellectual vigor and unremitting faith in films as an art form.

He was born in 1898, was trained as a civil engineer and architect. During the revolution he built trenches for the Bolsheviki. He was only 26 when he directed "Potemkin," which has been hailed as his greatest picture. It described the revolt of the sailors on the armored ship Potemkin during the abortive revolt of 1905.

The first part of "Ivan the Terrible" was exhibited in New York a year ago. Bosley Crowther, writing in THE NEW YORK TIMES, called it the product of one of the really great artists in the (film) medium and praised it as a story of "awesome and monumental impressiveness in which the senses are saturated with medieval majesty."

The Times
14th October 1905

DEATH OF SIR HENRY IRVING.

We regret to announce that Sir Henry Irving died suddenly at Bradford last night. He had an attack of syncope on returning from the theatre, where he had appeared as "Becket," and expired in his hotel. His death was entirely unexpected, for he had shown no sign of illness and appeared in his usual health when, only two days ago, he was entertained at luncheon by the Mayor of Bradford, and was presented with an address from his admirers in that town.

Henry Irving, whose original name was John Henry Brodribb, was born at Keinton, near Glastonbury, Somerset, on February 6, 1838. His parents, who were of Cornish extraction, came to London during his boyhood, and sent him to Dr. Pinches's school in George-yard, Lombard-street, where Creswick saw him play Adrastus in a school performance of Talfourd's Ion. At the age of 14 he was given a place in the counting-house of Thacker and Co., the East India merchants, of Newgate-street, and he remained there four years, reading a good deal in his spare moments and studying elocution under Henry Thomas in the City elocution class at Sussex-hall, Leadenhall-street. In 1856 he gave up his employment in business and joined the stock company at the Theatre Royal, Sunderland, his first part being that of Gaston, Duke of Orleans, in Richelieu. For the next nine years he worked hard in various stock companies in the provinces, principally at Edinburgh and Manchester, playing a great number of different parts in pieces ranging from tragedy to pantomime. In 1859 he made a brief appearance at the Old Surrey Theatre, but returned to the provinces till 1866, when Dion Boucicault offered him the part of Rawdon Scudamore in Hunted Down, at the St. James's Theatre. His success there both as actor and as stage-manager was sufficient to keep him in London. From the St. James's he passed to the old Queen's Theatre in Long-acre, where, in Katherine and Petruchio, the burlesqued version of The Taming of the Shrew, which was then in fashion, he first acted with Miss Ellen Terry, and increased his reputation in a number of parts, among them Bill Sikes and Falkland. After leaving the Queen's he was out of employment for six months, until his close friend, and in those days his constant benefactor, Mr. J. L. Toole, secured him an engagement at the Gaiety. Here he made a hit as Richard Chevenix in Byron's Uncle Dick's Darling, in 1869, and in the following year at the Vaudeville as Digby Grant in Albery's Two Roses. In 1871 he joined the Bateman management at the Lyceum. The theatre had long been unlucky, and, admirable as it was, Irving's Jingle in Albery's version of "The Pickwick Papers" did nothing to restore its fortunes. The management, almost in despair, allowed him to force upon them The Bells, an adaptation by Leopold Lewis of Erckmann-Chatrian's Le Juif Polonais. It was a desperate measure. The town of that day had no taste for tragedy, for anything, indeed, but farce and opera bouffe of the vulgarest order; the Lyceum Theatre was unpopular and the leading actor in the piece all but unknown. The audience on the first night was scanty, but by the next morning Henry Irving was famous. There is no need to describe here a performance so well known to playgoers of all generations but the very youngest; it is enough to say that it restored the fortunes of the theatre and marked a turning-point in the history of the English drama. Later in the long run of the play the lavish programme of the times included a performance of Jeremy Diddler, in which Irving gave further proof of his powers as a comedian, and The Bells was succeeded by W. G. Wills's Charles I. The two emotions which this unemotional actor could command were terror and pathos. The Bells had illustrated the former, Charles I. was well chosen to exhibit the latter.

It may be questioned whether in his youth, Mr. Irving's Charles I. can have been quite so majestic a figure as it was in later years, but its success was great. Then, as later, the figure that the audience saw had stepped straight from Vandyck's canvas, and gathered up around it all the romantic, pitiful, and tender associations that float about the name of Charles I. Its dignity, its stately melancholy, its tenderness, and its rare bursts of righteous indignation made it one of the most moving parts he ever acted, and entirely concealed the falseness of a one-sided and shallow play. Charles I. was followed by Eugene Aram, which repeated the triumph of The Bells, and Eugene Aram by Richelieu. Here for the first time Mr. Irving definitely pitted himself against Macready, and the school which still looked upon Macready as the last word in great acting. The new methods challenged the old, and the new were championed, not only by the young and ardent Clement Scott, who was then the mouthpiece of the dramatic revival, but by sound and sober critics like John Oxenford, who described Mr. Irving's Richelieu in The Times as "tragic acting in the grandest style." On October 31, 1874, Mr. Irving made a bid for the highest honours by appearing as Hamlet. In spite of the good work he had done, one is tempted to say, and perhaps without much exaggeration, that that evening was as important in the history of the drama as the first night of Hernani. Had Mr. Irving failed, the revival of the stage as a serious factor in the intellectual and social life of the nation might have been put back, though bound to come in time, for many years. There were still people of intelligence—so low had all serious interest in the drama fallen—who were found to ask, "And who is Henry Irving?" For ten years at least people had been content to let Hamlet sleep under the shadow of great names, Charles Kean, Macready, or Fechter. The moment was critical. For the first two acts the audience received the new Hamlet in complete silence. They could not understand what he was at. He made no "points," he never ranted, he was not lugubrious or idiotic or extravagantly dressed; he was nothing that Hamlets traditionally should be, but only a prince and a gentleman, with an engaging tinge of melancholy and a quiet, almost familiar, demeanour. When he came to his parting with Ophelia the house "rose at him," for now they understood. Mr. Irving's Hamlet was not a thing of lightning flashes, but a consistent and reasoned whole; a prince and a gentleman who failed to do the great things demanded of him, not so much from weakness of will as from excess of tenderness. His reading of the character was hotly contested. A war of pamphlets was waged between the supporters of this or that among the Hamlets of the past and the new Hamlet, and, generally, between the champions of tradition and of the young actor who had dispensed so completely with the conventions and thought out an entirely independent reading of his own. That war was renewed over all the Shakespearian productions that followed, more hotly than ever, perhaps, over his Macbeth. It seems a little surprising now, in a generation which accepts Macbeth as a poet, "a man of letters manqué," that such fierce storms should have been raised by the view that he was a moral coward. It is possible that Mr. Irving's lack of "weight" injured his representation of the character, as it certainly ruined his first performance of Othello in 1876, and again, though to a less extent, in 1881, when he and the American actor, Booth, played Othello and Iago alternately. To continue the story of his Shakespearian productions, in 1877 he revived King Richard III.; in 1879 The Merchant of Venice; in 1882 Romeo and Juliet and Much Ado About Nothing; in 1884 Twelfth Night; in 1892 King Henry VIII. and King Lear; in 1896 Cymbeline; and in 1901 Coriolanus. In no single case was his own performance universally accepted as even good. Long after the days had passed when he was a bone of contention between coteries, there were still large numbers of people to whom his acting did not appeal. Some found his marked mannerisms insuperable obstacles to enjoyment or sympathy; some, and these possibly the least thoughtful portion of the audience, objected to an actor who, whatever he did or did not, always insisted upon having his own reading of every part and every play, a determined innovator who went back invariably to his author and himself for guidance. But, whether people liked him or not, they all crowded to see him and discussed him eagerly afterwards. He appealed to their minds; he interested rather than excited them; and he gave them the opportunity of seeing, what possibly had never been seen in England before, a play of Shakespeare's presented, not as series of opportunities for a "star" actor, but as a single and artistic whole. In the words used by Lord Lytton on the 100th night of *Romeo and Juliet*, "he threw the whole force of his mind creatively into every detail of a great play, giving to the vital spirit of it an adequately complete, appropriate, and yet original embodiment." But this is to anticipate a little. We can do no more than mention the production, under the Bateman management, of Tennyson's *Queen Mary*, *The Lyons Mail*, which introduced his astonishing performance of the two characters of Lesurques and Dubose, *Louis XI.*, which is too well known to need comment, and *The Flying Dutchman*, an unsuccessful play in which his performance of the part of Vanderdecken was yet held by some to be almost his finest achievement.

In 1878 Mr. Irving became manager of the Lyceum. One of his first steps was to engage Miss Ellen Terry as his leading lady, and not the least of his triumphs was the making of a tragic actress out of a born comedian. Miss Terry remained in his company until the end of his American tour of 1901-2, and played Portia in the last performance on the stage of the Lyceum Theatre in July, 1902. The names of actor and actress are inseparably connected in the mind, and each owed to the other a great part of the success and fame that rewarded them. It was thus, too, that Mr. Irving first had the opportunity of bringing the arts of the scene-painter, the musician, the designer, and others to reinforce the work of his own mind. It is noteworthy that in his original performance of *Hamlet* the scenery was scanty and shabby, much of it having been used in the preceding plays. Henceforth, there was to be no scantiness nor shabbiness. Recollections of the splendour of Charles Kean's productions were eclipsed by the artistic beauty of Mr. Irving's; and in spite of all the criticisms that were passed on the amount of attention lavished on accessories, it cannot justly be claimed that the mounting was allowed to supersede the acting, so long as the Lyceum was the scene of the Irving productions. Those productions were not very many in point of number. Without reckoning the Shakespeare plays already mentioned, the chief of them were as follows:— 1879, *The Lady of Lyons*, *Daisy's Escape*, by A. W. Pinero, and *The Iron Chest*, by George Colman; 1880, *The Corsican Brothers*; 1881, *The Cup*, by Tennyson, and *The Two Roses*; 1885, *Olivia*, originally produced by Mr. Hare at the Court Theatre, and W. G. Wills's *Faust*; 1887, Byron's *Werner* (at a special *matinée* in aid of a testimonial to Westland Marston); 1889, *The Dead Heart*, rewritten from Walter Phillips's drama by Walter Herries Pollock; 1890, *Ravenswood*, adapted by Hermann Merivale from "The Bride of Lammermoor"; 1893, Tennyson's *Becket*; 1895, *King Arthur*, by J. Comyns Carr, *A Story of Waterloo*, by A. Conan Doyle, and *Don Quixote*, a condensation of a play written by W. G. Wills on the favourite hero of Sir Henry Irving's boyhood; 1896, *Madame Sans-Gêne*, by Sardou; 1898, *Peter the Great*, by Lawrence Irving, Sir Henry's second son, and *The Medicine Man*, by Robert Hichens and H. D. Traill; and 1899, *Robespierre*, by Sardou.

In 1899 Sir Henry nominally gave up management, and in 1902, after a revival of *Faust* and a final performance of *The Merchant of Venice*, his tenancy of the Lyceum Theatre expired, and his only subsequent production in London was Sardou's *Dante* in 1903, a vast spectacular drama, staged at Drury Lane and irresistibly suggestive of pantomime, which did neither author nor actor any credit. Sir Henry Irving was always an indefatigable worker, and the intervals between his seasons in London were filled with provincial tours and long visits to America and Canada, where his popularity and success were enormous.

Whether Sir Henry Irving was or was not a great actor was a question hotly discussed in his lifetime, and one which his lamented death will doubtless revive. There is only one possible answer. A great actor he was, but his greatness sprang from a different source than that of any other actor that can be mentioned. The success of his famous predecessors lay in their power to affect the emotions of their audience through the strength of their own emotions. They watched for opportunities of emotion, and tore the heart-strings of their hearers, without much regard for the cohesion or the general humanity of the characters they represented. Sir Henry Irving was not an emotional actor, or one who touched the emotions. His greatness lay in his brain, not in his feelings; his appeal was to the brain, and not to the feelings. His first care was to read the part and the play, to find out what the author intended, and to build up for himself a conception (and it must be admitted that he preferred a totally new conception, wherever possible) of the character he was to represent. He played not for moments, but for general effects; he was willing to be tedious through half a play rather than sacrifice the unity of his intellectual apprehension. The novelty of idea was an unfailing source of interest, and another was his magnetic personality. His tall figure, his beautiful, intense, ascetic face, threw a spell over his audience, a spell not so much of sympathy as of interest. But a strong personality necessarily implies limitations. Sir Henry Irving's mannerisms, his peculiar pronunciation, his halting gait, the intonations of his never very powerful or melodious voice, the often excessive slowness that grew upon him with the years, were welcome to some as the result and expression of his personality; others they inspired with a feeling that might be described as a desire to laugh if they dared. His personality, again, while, in Charles I., Hamlet, Richard III., Mathias, Becket, and a number of other parts, it gave him extraordinary and impressive power, made him ill-suited to play such characters as Romeo, Claude Melnotte, or even Benedick, the last of whom in his hands became too sardonic and too little merry a person for the gay and witty bachelor. Wherever there was room for his brain to work he was at home; anything approaching the commonplace, the full-blooded, or the sentimental left his peculiar gifts unemployed.

But there was always occupation for those gifts in the play, if not in the part, and they were unsparingly exercised on every new production. His friends used to say that for weeks before a first night at the Lyceum it was impossible to get Sir Henry to answer the commonest question without a reference to his new play. His mind

Continued

was absorbed in it, its period, its atmosphere, its characters, its clothes. The result aimed at, and almost invariably achieved, was just that unity of impression that was a new thing. He regarded a play as a single whole; as a whole, no doubt, of which he himself should be the central point; but still neither merely as a field for the exhibition of his own powers nor as an excuse for beautiful scenery and dresses. Himself and his painters, designers, and musicians were all to be subsidiary to the author's intentions; and a Lyceum production could be counted on to reveal not only ingenuity of invention nor artistic beauty, but propriety and proportion. It was to that end that he swept into his service the revival of interest in art that was contemporary with the revival of interest in the stage. Like most exceptional men, he was partly a product and partly a creator of the progress achieved in his day. He came into prominence at a time when comedy was already beginning to be regenerated, socially, morally, and artistically, by Mr. and Mrs. Bancroft at the Haymarket. Tragedy was waiting for her champion, and found it in Mr. Irving. It will be seen from the list of his productions that he did little for the original work of contemporary English playwrights. His services to the stage came from another source, that of his own brain. By the unsparing use of his intellect he succeeded in recalling to the theatre the intelligent public which had deserted it for ten years, in making play-going fashionable among all classes, and in accustoming the thousands of new and old playgoers, whom he attracted, to look to the theatre for more than empty amusement. To scholars he appealed by his reverent and often acute treatment of the text of Shakespeare, to people of taste by the beauty of his productions, to people of fashion by having become the fashion, and to all classes by the force of his personality. His career was a career of almost unbroken triumph, not only for himself, but for the English stage.

It was in recognition of these services that in 1895 Queen Victoria conferred on him the first knighthood that was ever won by an actor; and among other honours he held the degrees of D.Litt.Dublin, Litt.D.Cambridge, and LL.D. Glasgow. Of the many lectures he was asked to deliver, we may mention those at Edinburgh in 1881 and 1891, at Harvard in 1885, and at Oxford, by the invitation of Dr. Jowett, then Vice-Chancellor, in 1886. These lectures have since been printed, and the Irving edition of Shakespeare, in which he was interested, is widely known.

Sir Henry Irving was married and leaves two sons; Mr. H. B. Irving, the actor, and Mr. Lawrence Irving, who is also on the stage.

New York Times
15th September 1927

ISADORA DUNCAN, DRAGGED BY SCARF FROM AUTO, KILLED

Dancer Is Thrown to Road While Riding at Nice and Her Neck Is Broken.

HAD PREMONITION OF DEATH

"I Am Frightened That Some Quick Accident Might Happen," She Said the Day Before.

TRAGEDY MARKED CAREER

Founder of Modern Classical Dance Gained World Fame, but Often Could Not Pay Debts.

Copyright, 1927, by The New York Times Company.
Special Cable to THE NEW YORK TIMES.

PARIS, Sept. 14.—Isadora Duncan, the American dancer, tonight met a tragic death at Nice on the Riviera. According to dispatches from Nice Miss Duncan was hurled in an extraordinary manner from an open automobile in which she was riding and instantly killed by the force of her fall to the stone pavement.

Affecting, as was her habit, an unusual costume, Miss Duncan was wearing an immense iridescent silk scarf wrapped about her neck and streaming in long folds, part of which was swathed about her body with part trailing behind. After an evening walk along the Promenade des Anglais about 10 o'clock, she entered an open rented car, directing the driver to take her to the hotel where she was staying.

As she took her seat in the car neither she nor the driver noticed that one of the loose ends fell outside over the side of the car and was caught in the rear wheel of the machine.

Dragged Bodily From the Car.

The automobile was going at full speed when the scarf of strong silk suddenly began winding around the wheel and with terrific force dragged Miss Duncan, around whom it was securely wrapped, bodily over the side of the car, precipitating her with violence against the cobblestone street. She was dragged for several yards before the chauffeur halted, attracted by her cries in the street.

Medical aid immediately was summoned, but it was stated that she had been strangled and killed instantly.

This end to a life full of many pathetic episodes was received as a great shock in France, where, despite her numerous eccentric traits, Miss Duncan was regarded as a great artist. Her great popularity in France was increased by the entire nation's sympathy when in 1913 her two young children also perished in an automobile tragedy. The car in which they had been left seated started, driverless, down a hill and plunged over a bridge into the Seine River.

During the war she acquired the further gratitude of the French by turning over her palatial home here for war relief headquarters.

Husband Committed Suicide.

Her love affair with the young poet laureate of Soviet Russia, Serge Essinin, terminated in divorce and Essinin's suicide two years ago. She herself was reported to have made an attempt at suicide in the Mediterranean.

Miss Duncan, reduced in her resources recently, succeeded through the aid of friends in completing plans for a school of aesthetics which she meant to start on the Riviera.

It was recently a current rumor among the friends of Miss Duncan that she would find happiness in a marriage with an American, which was to be celebrated at Nice Oct. 11.

In connection with her fatal accident it is recalled that Miss Duncan for years affected an unusual dress cult and, with her brother, Raymond, often appeared in the streets of Paris and elsewhere garbed in a Roman toga with bare legs and sandals. Roman purple in recent years was her preferred color and she often walked about Nice in flowing scarfs and robes.

Petit Parisien Pays a Tribute.

The Petit Parisien tomorrow will say, in commenting on the tragedy:

"Sad news which will spread consternation through the world of arts and artists arrived today from Nice: Isadora Duncan has been killed in a frightful manner.

"This woman who throughout her life tried to shed grace and beauty about her met with the most tragic end imaginable.

"She danced as rarely, if ever, has been danced before her, with a fervor which seemed to raise her, transport her. She created a style school in her art. In her time she knew the most complete success in interpreting by that sort of mystic fury which filled the scene and put to rout all theories.

"Had she been practical she could have amassed an immense fortune, but she dies poor. Poor; and doubtless disillusioned, for what sorrows had she not suffered?

"Who does not remember the death of her children in an auto which, suddenly starting by itself, rolled into the Seine? And Isadora 'danced' her grief at their funeral, her grief which was profound and sincere. Few could comprehend such a form of grief which, to those who understood, was nothing short of sublime."

Dancer Was Writing Her Memoirs.

NICE, France, Sept. 14 (AP).—The medical examination after Miss Duncan's death here showed that her neck had been cleanly broken by the red silk scarf. No other marks were apparent.

Paris Singer of the sewing machine family, an old friend of Miss Duncan's, and Mrs. Mary Desto Parks, British journalist, who was helping Miss Duncan with her book, are making the arrangements for the funeral.

At the time of the accident Miss Duncan was accompanied by Mrs. Parks, who came to see her with reference to the publication of her memoirs.

The dancer's body was taken to St. Roch Hospital, and then to her studio. In a conversation with a correspondent of The Associated Press yesterday, Miss Duncan said: "For the first time I am writing for money; now I am frightened that some quick accident might happen."

This premonition of her doom was only too true.

Many Accidents in Her Life.

Fate seemed to have caused automobiles to play no small part in the life of Isadora Duncan. On several occasions she was injured, sometimes seriously, in automobile accidents, and in 1913 her two children were drowned in the Seine River, near Paris, when their automobile crashed into the river.

Later in the same year she was seriously injured in an automobile accident, and in May, 1924, was knocked unconscious when her car was in collision with another in Leningrad. On other occasions she narrowly escaped death from drowning. One of these accidents occured at Nice, where she was killed.

Isadora Duncan was the first exponent of the modern version of classical dances and as such won fame and much criticism in this and many foreign countries. She was born in San Francisco in 1880 and made her first stage appearance at Daly's Theatre in this city when she was 15 years old. She appeared as a fairy in Augustin Daly's company giving "A Midsummer Night's Dream."

It was a year or two later that she conceived her idea of interpretative dancing, and so well did she place her offering before the theatregoing public that within a few years she had amassed a considerable fortune and her name was famous on two continents.

She introduced what was then the shocking novelty of dancing with her limbs bare and her body clothed only in wisps of the most translucent material. In Paris and London she soon became the vogue, and she opened a number of dancing schools in different large cities in Europe. Then came the first of the many tragedies that later swept through her life.

Though she had never married she had two children, Patrick, 5 years old, and Deidre, a year younger. She had often said that she despised the institution of marriage, and she would never reveal the name of the father of her children. The children were drowned in the River Seine in France, when the automobile in which they were riding ran over an embankment and plunged into the river.

In 1915 she returned to this country and organized a dancing school, training her pupils on the stage of the Century Theatre. She became ill and her venture here failed. She was about to return to France, but debts of $12,000 detained her. They were finally settled by some of her friends and she was allowed to leave.

After the war she became an ardent advocate of the Soviet Union of Russia, and Lenin invited her to Moscow, where he gave her the mansion of a former nobleman in which to establish one of her dancing schools. While in the Soviet capital she met and married Sergei Essenin, the so-called "poet laureate of the revolution." He was a youth in his early twenties and was subject to fits of epilepsy. The dancer and the poet soon ran out of funds, and they decided to come to this country and appear on the stage.

Forbidden to Appear in Boston.

They were detained at Ellis Island on their arrival in 1922 because Miss Duncan had lost her American citizenship by marrying a foreigner. After considerable controversy they were allowed to land, and Miss Duncan appeared at various theatres and halls in the East.

In Boston on Oct. 22, 1922, she created a sensation when she danced at the Symphony Hall in filmy attire and at the end of her dance advanced to the footlights and shouted a denunciation of her critics. The following day Mayor Curley issued an order prohibiting her from appearing again in the Massachusetts city.

She returned to Paris with her husband and soon afterward there were reports of friction between the couple. She obtained a divorce from him in Russia and last year he committed suicide, cutting his wrists and writing a poem in his own blood.

In 1924 she was in trouble in Berlin owing to her inability to raise funds to pay her debts, and last year her house in Paris was put up for auction in behalf of her creditors. Friends came to her aid by raising 50,000 francs but this only postponed the evil day. The date of Feb. 17 of this year was then set for the sale of the house, but once again her friends pledged themselves to raise sufficient money to save the place.

Her studio and fittings, however, were sold and she went to the Riviera, where a few months ago it was reported that she had attempted to commit suicide by walking into the sea. She was rescued from the water by an English Army officer.

A few days ago it was reported from Paris that she was engaged to marry Robert Chanler, the former husband of Lina Cavalieri, the opera singer. She was one of a large party of guests being entertained on board the Chanler yacht at Nice. Yesterday she was quoted as saying that the report of the engagement was the result of a joke.

Daily Telegraph
16th July 1976

Director Fritz Lang dies

By Alexander Walker

FRITZ LANG, one of the great directors of movie history, died at his Los Angeles home yesterday, aged 85.

He was a master of the melodrama, the thriller and the saga.

In the pre-War days when he was Germany's top moviemaker, his films like Siegfried, Doctor Mabuse, M, Metropolis, filled with shadows, imposing architecture and an atmosphere of perverse machination seemed to forecast the arrival of Hitler and the Nazis who ultimately destroyed that old High German cinema of which Lang was one of the founders.

He was held in such high regard that Doctor Goebbels, ignoring the fact that Austrian-born Lang was part-Jewish, offered him the top controlling job in the German film industry in 1933.

A monocle

Lang said later: "I saw the big clock outside Goebbels's office crawling round to the time when the banks closed and wondered could I get my money out in time to escape from Germany."

That night, leaving behind his wife, who sympathised with Hitler, he took the train to France, his money hidden in the complaints book in the dining car.

Lang's films broke new ground.

In M, which made a star of Peter Lorre, he pleaded for psychological understanding of a child murderer.

In Metropolis, he used his own early training as an architect to envisage a city state where a leisured class ruled robot-like workers.

In his Doctor Mabuse thriller about a mad criminal genius who operated at one point out of that lunatic asylum, that along with the Grand Hotel is a key image in German cinema, Lang created an underworld that is still the model for screen melodrama in which they hang the lights low and the shadows of expressionism overlay the suspense.

Continued

A mascot

Directors like Hitchcock and Kubrick and writers like Orwell and Graham Greene were some of those who have been strongly influenced by Lang's images.

A bulky figure, moving with surprising lightness, Lang wore a monocle—he had lost an eye in the First World War—and affected opera cloaks and canes that made him resemble some power-mad fuere out of his own movies.

In later years he travelled with a lucky toy monkey, a bizarre mascot that used to sit on the pillow in his hotel suite.

His career recovered its momentum when he settled in Hollywood in the mid-1930s with social melodramas like Fury, with Spencer Tracy as a man unjustly accused of a crime, and *films noirs* Scarlet Street and Woman In The Window where men are trapped by *femmes fatales* in labyrinthine plots of fear and fate.

His best film of the post-war years was The Big Heat, a story of corruption and exposure.

Bernard Shaw

The Times
3rd November. 1950

MR. BERNARD SHAW

A PROPHET IN THE THEATRE

After six decades of unsparing creative and controversial activity Mr. Bernard Shaw, who died yesterday at the age of 94, still commanded an eager hearing on both sides of the Atlantic and in some European countries. He addressed himself habitually to the intellect, rarely to the heart; yet he was a master of comedy, and however acidly satirical or deliberately outrageous his opinions, he was able to treat the driest or most delicate subject with a gaiety that disarmed and with a witty lucidity that entertained. Admiration he systematically courted and in abundant measure won, and for the

sprightly patriarchal figure—a sort of intellectual Father Christmas—delightedly pulling important legs and pricking portentous bubbles with, on the whole, such stimulating and diverting effect, the public came also to feel affection.

Like so many of the most formidable critics of Victorianism, Shaw was himself a Victorian, and a fairly early one at that. He was born in the twentieth year of the Queen's reign and was in his middle forties when the reign ended. Before the Golden Jubilee he had written all his novels, he had been converted by Henry George to Socialism, and was making his mark as Fabian pamphleteer and orator. His art and music criticism were behind him, and he was " G. B. S." of the *Saturday Review*, the most dreaded and the most entertaining dramatic critic of the time, as well as the author of 10 plays, when the Diamond Jubilee was celebrated. In the following year he abandoned professional criticism for professional play writing, though he continued his Socialist crusading and gave up much time to platform work and national and local politics. But it was as an Edwardian that he entered the first of the three productive periods on which his reputation as a comic dramatist rests. From 1904 till 1907 he was the ruling creative spirit of the brilliant Vedrenne-Barker management at the old Court Theatre, and there some of his most exhilarating comedies were first seen. His second period was from 1911 until the outbreak of war in 1914, and with one of the plays of this period, *Pygmalion*, he introduced the Shavian comedy to the straitest sect of West End playgoers. The third began with *Heartbreak House*, written during the war, it continued with *Back to Methuselah*, and ended gloriously with *Saint Joan* in 1923. It was a height to which he never afterwards attained, but he continued to write plays of varying merit during the next quarter of a century, and before the end his dramatic compositions numbered nearly 60.

All this while he was the subject of a continually changing legend which, in each of its forms, he vigorously cultivated. In his days as a Fabian orator he was regarded as a saviour of society by his more enthusiastic disciples and as an emissary of the devil by his more frightened opponents; and he rejoiced in, and profited by, the extravagant alternative. During the time of his increasing fame as a dramatist before the 1914-18 war both the hopes and fears implicit in the alternative lost something of their edge, and his writings on the war were merely unpopular. They plunged him into relative obscurity; but within five years of the Armistice he had with *Saint Joan* become in the fullest sense a popular dramatist. Throughout the world the legend changed again and assumed gigantic proportions. Shaw became a benign major prophet, honoured in his own lifetime as Voltaire and Goethe in theirs.

George Bernard Shaw was born in Dublin on July 26, 1856, the third child and only son of George Carr Shaw, an impoverished and feckless Civil servant, and Lucinda Elizabeth, daughter of Walter Bagenal Gurly, the owner of land in County Carlow, which his grandson inherited. His early home was not happy. In it he learned three things: a hatred of the snobbishness by which he suffered; a dislike of Irish Protestantism, in which, as it seemed to him, hypocrisy and genteel pretensions were bound together; and, from his mother, whose consolation it was, a love and a knowledge of music. Such formal education as he received at the Wesleyan Connexional School, afterwards Wesley College, in Dublin, seems to have profited him less than the acquaintance with the works of great composers acquired at home. When still in his teens he entered the office of a land agent, in whose uncongenial service he remained four years.

At the age of 20, after some lonely dilettantism with a piano and amateur renderings of opera in "Irish Italian," he threw up his employment and came to London to join his mother, who had attempted to become a singing teacher. In those days he thought of himself primarily as an evangelist rather than as an artist, and he appears, from contemporary accounts, to have been at that time not only a bad writer but, if the needs of the papers to which he sought to contribute are a standard of judgment, an unadaptable journalist. Consequently he failed in nine years to earn more than £6 by his pen. Afterwards the journalistic incompetence wholly disappeared; so soon as there began to be a Shavian legend, none knew better than Shaw how to feed it; but his preferring in himself the educationist to the artist never forsook him. Indeed, his letters to *The Times* on all sorts of subjects, their serious purpose hardly cloaked by characteristic sallies, were something of a feature of his last years; the last letter appeared only a few weeks ago.

There are in his works, in the plays no less conspicuously than the prefaces, superb pieces of writing, notably in *John Bull's Other Island* and in the last part of *Back to Methuselah*, the concluding speech of which must crown any anthology of Anglo-Irish prose; but he was not primarily a man of letters; his mastery was as a salutary iconoclast. During his first nine years in London he wrote five novels: *Immaturity*, which was refused by Meredith for Chapman and Hall; *Cashel Byron's Profession*, of which Stevenson, who admired it, afterwards wrote: "If Mr. Shaw is below 25, let him go his path. If he is 30, he had best be told that he is a romantic, and pursue romance with his eyes open"; *The Irrational Knot*, later recognized by the proud author as "an Ibsenite novel"; *Love Among the Artists*, a criticism of shallowness in art and in family relations; and *An Unsocial Socialist*, the first genuine blast of the Shavian gale.

At first no publisher could be found for Shaw's five books, but the result of his entry into the Socialistic arena of the eighties was the serialization of some of them in magazines of propaganda such as *To-day* and Mrs. Besant's *Own Corner*. In time they became a rage in America, "free of all royalty to the flattered author." In 1884 he had joined the Fabian Society, one of whose leaders he became. He wrote and worked for them with an impassioned devotion, lecturing every Sunday on some subject that he was unconsciously storing up in his mind for subsequent use in the theatre. The strong and abiding influence on Shaw from his Fabian days was Sidney Webb, through whom he acquired that perhaps exaggerated veneration for blue-book method which was joined to the habit of iconoclasm he seemed to have taken over from Samuel Butler and to his own native love of paradox.

In 1885, thanks to William Archer, he became art critic of the *World*, and proved himself, in this and the other papers he served, one of the most sparkling contributors to contemporary journalism. He wrote on books for the *Pall Mall Gazette*, on music for the *Star* as "Corno di Bassetto," on music for the *World* where the initials "G. B. S." first became famous, and on the theatre for the *Saturday Review*. He wrote also *The Perfect Wagnerite*, which appeared in 1898, and *The Quintessence of Ibsenism*, the most profound of all his essays in criticism.

Meanwhile Bernard Shaw the dramatist had begun to displace the critic and the Socialist orator. His first play was *Widowers' Houses*, begun years earlier in collaboration with William Archer, but completed by Shaw himself for production by the Independent Theatre in 1892. It was a direct offspring of his Fabian activities. *The Philanderer*, a comment on Ibsenism, followed, but was not produced, and *Mrs. Warren's Profession*, a discussion of prostitution, was withheld from public performance by the censorship and was not seen on the stage until given privately by the Stage Society in January, 1902. *Arms and the Man*, a derisive essay on the false romanticism of war, was, and remains, a remarkably good entertainment; *Candida*, *The Man of Destiny*, *You Never Can Tell*, *The Devil's Disciple*, *Caesar and Cleopatra*, and *Captain Brassbound's Conversion* occupied their author during the closing years of the century.

His marriage took place in 1898 to Miss Charlotte Frances Payne-Townshend, whose considerable wealth was of immediate assistance in helping him to consolidate his position as a dramatist and whose steady, clear-minded companionship was of the greatest value to him until her death in September, 1943. Important though his output had been it was not until the Vedrenne-Barker management began to produce a series of his plays at the Court Theatre that Shaw came into his own. *Man and Superman*, which had been published two years earlier, was produced there on May 23, 1905. It definitely established his fame and, together with a group of revivals, led to a collective reconsideration of his earlier work. *John Bull's Other Island* was performed at the Court Theatre at the end of 1904. *How He Lied to Her Husband*, after earlier production in New York, appeared a few months later; *Major Barbara* in November, 1905; and *The Doctor's Dilemma* in November, 1906. Shaw was now established. During the years that remained before the 1914-18 war he was continuously active, and, though *The Shewing Up of Blanco Posnet* fell beneath the ban of the censorship, *Getting Married* (1908), *Press Cuttings* (1909), *Fanny's First Play* (1911), *Overruled* (1912), *Androcles and the Lion* (1913), and *Pygmalion* (1914) regularly increased his fame.

It was with the production in this country, in 1921, of *Heartbreak House*, a play written during 1913-16 that was designed to illustrate "cultured, leisured Europe before the war," that he began to acquire another and deeper reputation. Here was the unmistakable accent of prophecy, even of poetic prophecy. For the first time the visionary in Shaw stood revealed as he sought to bring contemporary history home to the conscience of the English middle classes.

In the summer of 1921 *Back to Methuselah* was published, but had to wait two years for its first English production at Birmingham. This gigantic work, though parts of it were made tedious by the author's powerlessness to resist personal gibes and idiosyncratic divagations, revealed his increasing preoccupation with philosophy as distinct from contemporary social propaganda. Here the puritanism and the poetry in Shaw were fused in an austere vision of human destiny, a vision that drew something of majesty from Shaw's presiding sense of the purpose of the Life Force. From these remote heights he came out to the illuminated landscape of *Saint Joan*, which was produced by the Theatre Guild in New York in the last days of 1923 and at the New Theatre in London in the following March. This play was a summary of Shaw's strength and weakness. He was unable to resist his ancient quips at the expense of Englishmen, which had been good jokes once but now were a little hoary; he damaged an epilogue, not itself unjustifiable, by needless theatricalism; and he punctuated the most serious passages of the play with rather wanton farcical flourishes. But he did succeed in communicating the passion of insight with which he had dug for truth beneath the rigid crust of history. In November, 1926, the Swedish Academy awarded to him the reserved Nobel Prize for Literature for 1925, with the proceeds of which he afterwards set up the Anglo-Swedish Literary Foundation. A long pause in his output followed, explained in the summer of 1928 by the appearance of *The Intelligent Woman's Guide to Socialism and Capitalism*.

What was virtually a new stage in his career began in 1929. *The Apple Cart*, *Too True to be Good*, and *On the Rocks* showed their author adroitly responding to the world's increasing distaste for Parliamentary forms—a distaste which he was the quicker to applaud because in England these forms had been preserved. In 1936 he was 80, as vigorous and as much himself as ever; but his greatest work was done. *The Simpleton of the Unexpected Isles*, *The Six of Calais*, *The Millionairess*, and *Farfetched Fables* were comparatively unimportant. Only in its third act did *Geneva*, produced in 1938, display the old arresting argument and a truly trenchant wit. His fiftieth play, *In Good King Charles's Golden Days*, was quietly entertaining and even seemed to possess an unfamiliar mellowness. And there were no new legends. In the decade before the war Malvern had become his shrine and lamps of his genius were lit there annually. Revivals of his plays here, there, and everywhere were endless. Broadcasting, the films, and even television united in exploiting him.

It was long a habit of Shaw's opponents to question his sincerity. The truth underlying this accusation was, simply, that, having something to say in which he sincerely believed, he allowed no scruple of good art or conventional good manners to influence the means he used to obtain an audience. There is also no doubt that it was his wit, good or bad, shrewd or knockabout, that won Shaw his audience. Thus, little by little, mixing wisdom with what was doubtful wisdom and relying always upon one device or other of merely arresting attention rather than upon the perfection of any work of art, Shaw imposed the reasoned contrarieties, or seeming contrarieties, of Erewhon upon generations younger than his own. Not himself an original thinker, since he drew his ideas from a miscellany of sources—from English Socialist tradition, from Bergson, from Nietzsche, from Butler and Butler's gloss upon Lamarck—he was nevertheless a leaven and stimulant of popular thought whose achievement is so large as to evade calculation. On his ninetieth birthday, an honorary freeman of the city of Dublin and a freeman of the borough of St. Pancras, he was quite unmistakably acknowledged as a freeman of the world also.

There remains the comic dramatist who showed that it was possible to write comedies in which the dramatic tension should be sustained by the conflict, not of living men and women, but of ideas touched by genius into vivid theatrical life. For a while these stage discussions, stimulating and amusing as they were allowed to be, were not recognized for plays, but criticism came in course of time to realize that the excitement they produced was genuinely dramatic and that the apparently formless talk was in fact shaped by a firmly drawn logical line. It was when the logical line weakened, as it did in most of the plays written after *Saint Joan*, that the author's title to dramatist was once again called in question; but by that time the new comedy which Shaw had created rested on a solid basis.

In nearly all his plays he knew how to entertain for at least a part of the time. Some of the plays are already old enough to enable us to perceive that the seasoning of nonsense, which was a sop to their first audiences, is now the least acceptable part of them. So long as it remains serious the speech of Don Juan in Hell is of unswerving interest; the noblest part of Shaw's genius is in it. Together with *Candida*, the best of *The Devil's Disciple* and, at long range, *You Never Can Tell*, it forms an epitome of his claim to survive in the theatre as a comic dramatist who is also the author of *Saint Joan*; while survival, so far as the pleasures of reading are concerned, must surely extend to *John Bull's Other Island*, *Heartbreak House*, and—for all its imperfections—*Back to Methuselah*. If, indeed, the Shavian theatre as a whole lives on it will live as evidence of the influences that divided the twentieth century from the nineteenth, and of the saving poetic temper as well as the extraordinary vitality which enabled a man whose purpose was not consciously aesthetic to create a theatrical form suited to the needs of the artist driving him imperiously from within.

The Gentleman's Magazine
1st February 1779 Vol 49

BIOGRAPHICAL ANECDOTES *of the late Mr.* GARRICK.

He had at school performed the part of Serjeant Kite with applause *; and he was now prompted to employ the talents which he possessed for his immediate support. He therefore went down to Ipswich, under the name of Lyddel, and performed in a strolling company there. The part in which he first appeared was that of Aboan † in Oroonoko; and the approbation he met with in this country excursion encouraged him to pursue his plan in London. He, therefore, after being (as it is reported) rejected by the manager of Covent Garden, to whom he had offered his service, engaged with Mr. Gifford, at the theatre in Goodman's Fields, in the year 1744. The character he then attempted was that of Richard the Third; and he performed it in a manner which fixed that reputation on that basis upon which it stood, as the first actor of the times, during the rest of his life. Two circumstances were observed on his first night's performance; one, that, on his entrance on the stage, he was under so much embarrassment, that for some time he was unable to speak *: the other, that, having exerted himself with much vehemence in the first two acts, he became so hoarse as to be almost incapable of finishing the character. This difficulty was obviated by a person behind the scenes recommending him to take the juice of a seville orange, which he fortunately had in his pocket, and which enabled him to go through the remainder of the character with that degree of excellence which he always afterwards shewed in the performance of it, and which produced the applause which ever after uniformly attended him in it. The person to whom he owed the seasonable relief was the late Mr. Dryden Leach, printer, who used often to tell the story to his friends.

It was during this first year of his theatrical life that he produced the farce of *The Lying Valet*; a performance which has given pleasure to numberless spectators, even after the principal character ceased to be performed by its author. At the end of the season he went over to Ireland, and in that kingdom added both to his fortune and his fame. The next year (1742 to 1743) he performed at Drury Lane, and the year after (1743 to 1744) at the same theatre. At the beginning of this season he was involved in a dispute with Mr. Macklin, who had joined with him in opposing the oppressions of the managers. That gentleman complained that he was deserted in the agreement made with the managers, and published a state of his case, in a pamphlet, intituled, "Mr. Macklin's Reply to Mr. Garrick's Answer. To which are prefixed, all the Papers which have publickly appeared in regard to this important dispute." The next year

(1744 to 1745) he continued at Drury Lane; but the succeeding season (1745 to 1746) he went again to Dublin, and engaged with Mr. Sheridan as joint sharer and adventurer in the theatre there. In May 1746, he returned to London, and performed in six plays at the end of that month at Covent Garden, by which, we are told, he added 300 l. to a great sum acquired in Ireland *. He performed but one year more as an hired actor (1746 to 1747) which was at Covent Garden theatre, where he produced *Miss in her Teens*.

THE mismanagement of the patentees of Drury Lane Theatre after the deaths of Booth and Wilks, and the retirement of Cibber from the stage, had ruined every person concerned in it.

At this juncture the late Mr. Lacy stepped forward, and boldly ventured to engage for the purchase. Having the reputation of a man of integrity, he soon found friends among the monied men to support him in his undertaking; the success of it, he prudently concluded, must depend in some measure on the abilities of the person with whom he should connect himself in the scheme.

Mr. Garrick's reputation, both as a man and an actor, naturally led him to wish for his junction.

The season which began in 1747 was opened with an admirable Prologue, written by Dr. Johnson, and spoken by Mr. Garrick †. From this time Drury Lane Theatre, which had been so fatal to many adventurers, became the source of wealth and independence to both partners, who jointly exerted their several abilities in the management of the undertaking, with a degree of harmony which did credit to their understandings, and with a share of success which in some measure must be ascribed to that good correspondence which subsisted between them ‡.

The theatrical season which commenced in the year 1750 was rendered remarkable by the spirit of rivalship which prevailed at both houses. At the begining of Mr. Garrick's management he had engaged Barry, Macklin, Pritchard, Woffington, Cibber, and Clive; and, with these excellent performers, it may be imagined the profits of the house were very considerable. Soon after, Mr. Barry, who was under articles, refused to continue any longer at Drury Lane, and, when sued for the breach of his contract, escaped from the penalty by means no way redounding to his honour. Macklin and Mrs. Cibber likewise went over to Covent Garden; as did Mrs. Woffington, who is said to have entertained expectations of being united in marriage with Mr. Garrick. With these deserters, aided by the veteran Quin, Mr. Rich opened Covent Garden Theatre. Mr. Garrick, not intimidated by the strength of the opposition, took the field on the

5th of Sept. with an occasional Prologue spoken by himself *; which was answered by another delivered by Mr. Barry; and this again replied to by a very humourous Epilogue, admirably repeated by Mrs. Clive †. These were only preludes to the trial of strength which was soon to follow. The play of Romeo and Juliet had lain dormant many years. This was now revived at both houses: at Drury Lane, with alterations by Mr. Garrick, who performed the principal character; Mr. Woodward playing Mercutio; and Mrs. Bellamy, Juliet: against them at Covent Garden, were Mr. Barry and Mrs. Cibber in the principal characters, and Mr. Macklin in Mercutio. Both houses began on the first of October, and continued to perform it for 12 successive nights; when Covent Garden gave up the contention; and its rival kept the field one night more, with the credit of holding out longer than its opponent, though it is supposed neither side reaped much advantage from the spirit of perseverance which had governed them both in this contest.

The snarlers against Mr. Garrick's management of the theatre had a long time complained that he conducted himself with too strict an attention to œconomy in the ornamental and decorative parts of theatrical exhibitions. They were perpetually throwing out insinuations, that the manager, relying on his own powers, was determined to regulate the entertainments of the stage with an eye only to his own advantage, and without any regard to the satisfaction of the public.—These murmurs had continued some time, when at last Mr. Garrick determined to meet the wishes of his friends, and to silence the discontents of his enemies. For this purpose he applied to Mr. Denoyer, sen. to recommend some person of genius to superintend and contrive a splendid spectacle to be exhibited at Drury-lane. The person fixed upon for that purpose was Mr. Noverre, a Swiss; who immediately received orders to engage the best troop of dancers that could be procured. These he selected from the foreign theatres; and they consisted of Swiss, Italians, Germans, and some French. The entertainment in which they were employed was soon after contrived. It was called THE CHINESE FESTIVAL; and was, in the theatrical phrase, got up with great magnificence, and at a very considerable expence. The expectations of the managers were however wholly disappointed in the success of the performance. Although but few of the French nation were employed in it, yet a report had industriously been spread, that not only French dancers had been sent for over, but French dresses also, and even French carpenters and manufacturers. The nation was then on the eve of a war; and this afforded an opportunity for engaging the passions of those who professed themselves

Antigallicans. They accordingly formed associations, to discourage the several performers, and suppress the obnoxious performance whenever it should appear. At length, after having taken up more than eighteen months in preparing, it was brought before the publick, and received with all the virulence and opposition which might be expected from the violence and heat of the times. The first performance of it was on the 8th day of November 1755, and was honoured with the presence of his late Majesty; yet, notwithstanding that circumstance, it did not even then escape ill-treatment. On the second, third, fourth, and fifth nights the riots continued with increasing strength, though opposed each evening by several young men of fashion, who had determined to support the performance. On the sixth evening the opposition acquired fresh vigour and increasing numbers. They frustrated every attempt to proceed in the exhibition; and committed every excess which a mob, subject to no controul, is apt to indulge itself in. That evening was the last representation.

The business of the theatre went on without interruption; and he continued to acquire both reputation and fortune. In that year, however, he found himself obliged to exert his poetial talents, in order to correct the impertinence of an insignificant individual, a Mr. Fitzpatrick, who, without provocation, and in defiance of decency, carried on a weekly attack against him, in a paper called " The Craftsman." The original cause of the quarrel, we are informed, was grounded on some illiberal reflexions which Mr. Fitzpatrick threw out against Mr. Garrick, and which the latter resented with spirit and propriety, though a considerable time had elapsed before he was provoked to take public notice of him. As Mr. Fitzpatrick's writings are now entirely forgotten, the revenge which Mr. Garrick took of him must, from that circumstance alone, be involved in some obscurity. Those, however, who are unacquainted with either persons or facts will receive pleasure in reading Mr. Garrick's admirable satire published on this occasion, intituled THE FRIBLERIAD *, a Poem, which had the honour of being highly commended by Churchill, who has also given a very severe correction to the same person.

However unequal Mr. Fitzpatrick was to the task of contending with Mr. Garrick in a literary warfare, yet the rancour which his defeat had engendered pointed out a new mode of attack to distress his antagonist. It had been customary, on the representation of a new performance, to refuse admittance at any part of the evening, unless the whole price of the entertainment was paid. This had almost invariably been the rule; and it had hitherto been submitted to, as a reasonable demand from the managers, to compensate for the extraordinary expence which new dresses and scenes occasioned. To gratify his resentment, Mr. Fitzpatrick seized

on this circumstance as a ground to disturb the peace of the theatre, and to involve the managers in a contest with the public. For this purpose hand-bills were dispersed about the coffee houses in the neighbourhood of Drury-lane, recommending a peremptory demand to be made, and requiring an absolute promise to be given that no more than half the usual price should be taken on any evening of performance after the third act, unless at the representation of a new pantomine. A kind of association was entered into by several young men, to obtain a redress of this grievance, as it was called; and Mr. Fitzpatrick put himself at the head of it. The evening on which the attack was made happened to be when *The two Gentlemen of Verona* was performed for the alterer's benefit. The performance accordingly was interrupted, after several attempts to proceed in it; and the proprietors of the House, thinking the requisition an unjust one, and the manner of making it improper to be acceded to, refused to submit to it: in consequence whereof no play was acted that night; and the audience received their money again at the doors, having first amused themselves with doing all the mischief they were able. By this trial, the malecontents had discovered their strength, and determined to carry their point in humbling the pride of the manager. On the next performance, which was at the tragedy of *Elvira*, they collected their whole force, and again prevented the actors proceeding in the play. It was in vain that Mr. Garrick desired to be heard in defence of the ancient customs of the theatre. The opposition insisted on a peremptory answer to their demand in the new regulation; which, after some time, the proprietors of the house were obliged to agree to; and once more peace was restored to the theatre after a considerable loss had been sustained, and obliged to be submitted to *.

This season was the last in which Mr. Garrick could be said to have acted in the regular course of his profession. From this time he declined performing any new characters; and, finding his health declining, by the advice of his physician he determined to give himself some relaxation from care and fatigue. He therefore made the arrangements necessary for carrying on the public entertainments during his absence; and on the 15th of September 1763, the day on which the house opened, he left London, in order to make the tour of France and Italy. To supply his place, he engaged the late Mr. Powell, who had received his instructions the preceding summer, and whose success was equal to the abilities he possessed. To the honour of his employers, it may be added, that his abilities were not higher than the encouragement he received for the exertion of them. Although he was engaged for a term of years at a small salary; yet he was, before the season closed, generously allowed an appointment equal to the first performer in the house. We are credibly informed, the profits that year exceeded even those in which Mr. Garrick performed in the height of his reputation.

He produced the next season several new pieces, and in the beginning of 1766 the excellent comedy of *The Clandestine Marriage*, written in concert with Mr. Colman. He also, at the request of his Majesty, appeared again on the stage; and on that occasion spoke a new prologue, replete with those strokes of humour in which, in that species of composition, he manifested a superiority over all his contemporaries.

THE year 1769 was remarkable for the celebration of a jubilee at Stratford upon Avon, the 6th, 7th, and 8th of Sept. in honour of Shakespeare; a ceremony which very much engaged the public attention, although it was treated by some as a subject worthy only of ridicule, and by others as a compliment due to the great writer whose memory was intended to be honoured by it.

His audience to be present at it in the following terms:

" My eyes till then no sights like this will see,
" Unless we meet at Shakespeare's jubilee.
" On Avon's *banks where flowers eternal blow!*
" Like its full stream our gratitude shall flow!
" There let us revel, shew our fond regard,
" On that lov'd spot, first breath'd our
        " matchless bard;
" To him all honour, gratitude is due,
" To him we owe our all—to him and you."

The manner in which this entertainment was to have been performed, the disappointments it sustained, and the several occurrences which took place at it, are all so recent in the memories of most of our readers, and were so accurately related * at the time they happened, that we shall not recapitulate them here. It is sufficient to observe, that accident deprived those who were present of part of their entertainment; that all which was exhibited gave general satisfaction; and Mr. Garrick, who was a great sum of money out of pocket by it, framed an entertainment, which was performed at Drury-Lane theatre 92 nights with great applause to very crouded audiences. The ode which was spoken by him at Stratford was also repeated at the same theatre, but not with much success, being performed only seven times †.

In the beginning of the year 1776, he entered into an agreement with some of the present patentees, for the sale of his interest in the theatre; but continued to act during the remainder of that season. The last night of his performance was, for the theatrical fund, on the 10th day of June in that year, when he represented the character of Don Felix in *The Wonder*. At the conclusion of the play he came forward, and addressed the audience in a short speech, wherein he said, " it had been usual for persons in his situation to address the publick in an epilogue; and that he had accordingly turned his thoughts that way, but found it as impossible to write, as it would be to speak, a studied composition; the jingle of rhyme and the language of fiction ill suiting his then feelings: that the moment in which he

Continued

then fpoke was an awful one to him: that he had received innumerable favours, and took his leave on the fpot where thofe favours were conferred."

He then faid, " that, whatever the events of his future life might be, he fhould ever remember thofe favours with the higheft fatisfaction and deepeft gratitude; and though he admitted the fuperior fkill and abilities of his fucceffors, he defied them to exert themfelves with more induftry, zeal, and attention, than he had done." This fpeech, which was delivered with all that emotion which the particular fituation of the fpeaker rendered very interefting and affecting, was received with the loudeft burfts of applaufe; and he left the ftage with the acclamations of a numerous and polite audience, who were unable to forbear expreffing the deepeft concern for the lofs of their favourite performer.

Mr. Garrick now retired to the enjoyment of his friends, the moft refpectable in the kingdom, and of a large fortune, acquired in the courfe of more than thirty years: but the ftone, which he had been afflicted with, fome time, had already made fuch inroads on his conftitution, that he was unable to communicate or receive from his friends that pleafure which his company afforded, except at times, and in a very partial manner. It is fuppofed that he injured his health by the application of quack medicines, and often experienced the moft violent torments from the feverity of his diforder. At Chriftmas 1778, he went to vifit Lord Spencer at Althorp in Northamptonfhire, during the holidays. He there was taken ill, but recovered fo far that he was removed to town, where growing worfe, he died in a few days afterwards, at his houfe in the Adelphi, on the 20th day of January laft, at the age of 63 years; leaving behind him the character of a friendly, humane, charitable, and (notwithftanding many idle reports we may add) liberal man; one who felt for diftrefs, and relieved it; a cheerful companion, a pleafing writer, and the firft actor of this or any other age.

Daily Telegraph
23rd June 1979

JOHN WAYNE FADES OUT FIGHTING 'BIG C' TO THE LAST

JOHN WAYNE displayed his " true grit " to the end, denying himself pain-killers for much of the time in his dying days so he could say farewell to his large family.

Wayne, Hollywood's biggest-ever box office attraction, died of cancer at 1.35 a.m. yesterday in the University of California Hospital in Los Angeles. He was 72.

His three sons and four daughters were at his bedside when he lapsed into his final coma.

In recent days he had also been visited by his grandchildren—the hospital lost count of how many, but there are 21 of them.

Wayne's struggle to stay lucid for his last goodbyes was described by Mr Bernard Strohm, the hospital administrator:

" He had not been well since Saturday. There would be periods of wakefulness, then he would sleep for long periods of time and then come out of it.

" He had been having considerable pain for some time and was under medication. But at times he denied himself medication and wanted to be with his children and grandchildren.

Emotional Oscar farewell

" So he would tolerate discomfort just to be with his family."

Sometimes, Mr Strohm continued, as Wayne lapsed in and out of his coma, his vital signs would stabilise: " He would look over and call, often in a loud voice, for his children. When they would appear, he would lapse back into the coma."

Wayne, known to his friends as "Duke," began the biggest battle of his life when he had a cancerous portion of his left lung removed in 1964. He stopped smoking his regular five packets of cigarettes a day and declared: " I have licked the Big C."

He underwent open-heart surgery in April 1978. Friends sailed their yachts past his luxurious, waterfront home in formation to celebrate his recovery.

But, on January 12, he underwent a nine-hour operation during which his gall bladder and stomach were removed after stomach cancer was found.

Last April he had recovered sufficiently to make what was to be his last public appearance. when he went on stage at the Oscar awards.

Visibly moved by a standing ovation from his peers, Wayne said, in a breaking voice, " That's just about the only medicine a fellow ever really needs."

But last month Wayne returned to his old hospital suite after complaining of stomach pains. Doctors removed an intestinal blockage and found cancerous cells in his intestines. He volunteered to undergo a course of new treatment for cancer, possibly including radiation therapy, but doctors never began the treatment.

As it became clear death was approaching honours were heaped upon him. President Carter visited him in hospital, and the Congress and President authorised a special gold medal for him, one of only 84 such awards.

He played in more than 200 films, and embodied the classic legend of the good guys versus the bad guys. He won his Oscar for best actor for " True Grit " in 1969 for his portrayal of Rooster Cogburn, a one-eyed marshal.

Critics sometimes complained of the lack of versatility in his performances. Wayne was fond of saying: "Nobody likes my acting but the public."

Yesterday, tributes from Hollywood began to pour in reflecting the respect and admiration of those who worked with him. One was from Raoul Walsh, who directed Wayne's first major picture, "The Big Trail," in 1931 and also gave him the name John Wayne.

Walsh recalled: "I put him in pictures 50 years ago and he was a very fine man, a really good American. He enjoyed life a lot, working with the crew and the cast.

"He was always on time, paid good attention to his work and everybody loved him. Say something nice for the old boy, I love him."

Despite the financial success of many of his films, Wayne's business investments often floundered and he never amassed the millions of such Hollywood contemporaries as Bob Hope and Bing Crosby. He once lost half a million dollars (£250,000) in a shrimp business in Panama.

Three wives, his large family and a free-spending life-style also meant he had to keep working.

He had been separated from his third wife, actress Pilar Palette, for six years, after 19 years' marriage.

In recent years his holdings became more substantial, including his valuable home and an Arizona cattle ranch.

Last weekend the sale was completed for Wayne's yacht, a 136ft converted minesweeper he named "The Wild Goose." It was bought by a Californian lawyer, reportedly for £375,000.

His other successes included "The Man Who Shot Liberty Valance," and "The Alamo." A staunch Republican, Wayne often played the part of a war hero. But his role as a colonel in Vietnam in "The Green Berets" was criticed by some as giving too much support to America's military role in Vietnam.

He often said he could never retire: "I would go nuts. Work is the only thing I know."

He made his last full-length film. "The Shootist," in 1976. Ironically, he played an elderly gun fighter dying of cancer.

Nineteen days ago — on May 26 — Wayne, joined by his children and grandchildren, cut a giant cake in his hospital suite to celebrate his 72nd birthday. A hospital official described his birthday party as quiet.

His children knew this was the last time they would say father.

Nobody, surely, could have been given a more inappropriate Christian name in view of what he came to epitomise on the screen in more than 200 films, for John Wayne began life as Marion Morrison.

His boyhood friends at Waterloo, Iowa, called him Duke, after the family dog. It was a label that stuck, aptly, for the rest of his life.

A mode for tough guys

The Duke or "Big John" was destined to become a legend on or off the screen. Countless tough guys, whether Marines, budding cowboys or the taciturn types who like to converse with their fists, have tried to model themselves on the man of whom an early drama coach said: "This boy can never be a success."

There will never be agreement over which films were his best. But some obvious candidates are "Sands of Iwojima," "Red River," "The Fighting Kentuckian" and "The Quiet Man."

But it was "True Grit" in which he portrayed a one-eyed fat old man in a rip-roaring spoof of everything he had been in his earlier films which won him an Oscar in 1969. For many the title of the film summed up John Wayne's career.

"Hell, I should have put on that eye patch 20 years ago," Wayne commented as he picked up his Oscar in 1970. He had been nominated once before for "Sands of Iwo Jima."

In a progression which took more than 20 years, he had to show true grit to work his way up from fourth assistant prop man to the top money-making superstar in Hollywood.

His stature on and off screen produced constant challenges. Regularly in bars, or at cocktail parties, somebody would want to beat Wayne in a fight.

He used to say: "My usual way to avoid a fight is to become deadly quiet, stretching to my full height. If this does not work, I have a use of the English language so filthy and insulting that it scares them more than my fist."

When he started in films, he had to learn to use the word "ain't" convincingly because at college he had taken Latin and Romance languages. He had done well at High School but his academic achievements did not reveal themselves on the screen, when he was knocking out all-comers in a Western saloon or storming some beach with a company of Marines.

At school, Wayne was also a football star and this won him a scholarship to the University of Southern California. His football prowess won him a studio summer job and Wayne became a "prop man" for the legendary director, John Ford. It proved to be the most fateful event of his life.

Ford was filming a submarine picture and wanted men to emerge in the ocean near Catalina Island as though they were escaping from the torpedo tubes of a submarine. Stunt men were not keen because the waves were rough but Wayne volunteered.

Then came 'Stagecoach'

Ford was impressed and later gave Wayne other small acting parts. He eventually gave him the leading role in "The Big Trail," which was not a success. Wayne became stereotyped as a Western actor in low-budget films, frequently shot in three or four days.

He even appeared as the screen's first singing cowboy "I always sang when I got mad." he said. They started putting more songs in each film and he quit in disgust. But in 1939, his big chance came when Ford invited him to portray the Ringo Kid in the film "Stagecoach."

It was one of the biggest hits of the year and set a new standard for Westerns. Wayne never forgot the break that Ford gave him, and although he was later making films for various studios (four or five pictures a year) he always "dropped everything and went running" when Ford wanted him for a part.

Befitting his screen image, Wayne was unswervingly Right-wing politically. He was always berating people who criticised him for his politics.

He once said: "That little clique back there in the East has taken great personal satisfaction in reviewing my politics instead of my pictures and they've drawn up a caricature of me. But that doesn't bother me. Their opinions don't matter to people who go to the movies."

At this year's Oscar ceremonies, Wayne—visibly wasted by the terminal stages of his illness—said with typical bluffness: "Oscar came to the Hollywood scene in 1929, and so did I. We're a little weather-beaten but we're still here, and we plan to be around for a whole lot longer."

For the Duke, it was not to be.

New York Times
24ᵗʰ July 1948

DAVID W. GRIFFITH, FILM PIONEER, DIES

HOLLYWOOD, Calif., July 23— David Wark Griffith, one of the first and greatest contributors to the motion picture art, died this morning in Temple Hospital after suffering a cerebral hemorrhage. His age was 73.

The producer of "The Birth of a Nation," and pioneer in such techniques as closeups, fadeouts and flashbacks, was stricken in his rooms at the Hollywood Knickerbocker Hotel, where he lived alone.

Although an erstwhile titan of the industry, Mr. Griffith had been inactive in recent years and lived unostentatiously in relative obscurity working on his memoirs, emerging chiefly for meals in Hollywood restaurants, where he was a familiar figure, and for sessions of reminiscing with his old-time industry cronies.

"Father of the Film Art"

The name of David Wark Griffith, the master producer and director of silent motion pictures, is synonymous with "father of the film art" and "king of directors."

He produced and directed almost 500 pictures costing $23,000,000 and grossing $80,000,000, of which his most famous film, "The Birth of a Nation," has grossed to date more than $48,000,000.

Although Mr. Griffith did not, according to research authorities, originate all of the technical devices formerly accredited to him, he did originate many of them, and he vastly improved others. Chief, perhaps, among his improvements was his development of the close-up, which had first been employed in 1895 in an early American film, "The Kiss," into a dramatic psychological contribution that shaped the entire art of the cinema down to the present day.

Among the multitude of advanced methods which he started and which have long been an established part of film technique were the long shot, the vista, the vignette, the iris or eye-opener effect, the cameo-profile, the fade-in and fade-out, soft focus, back lighting, tinting, rapid-cutting, parallel action, mist photography, high and low angle shots, night photography, and the moving camera.

Fought for Innovations

In making his innovations Mr. Griffith had to contend with the conservatism of the owners, for, despite the fact that the industry was still something of a novelty when he entered it as an actor-director, it was already stereotyped. Great courage, persistence and vision on Mr. Griffith's part were needed to convince cinematic leaders of the rightness of his ideas.

He was the first director to depart from the standard 1,000-foot film. This caused a break between him and the officers of the old Biograph Company. He then made the first four-reeler, "Judith of Bethulia," which had instantaneous success in America and Europe. When Mr. Griffith ordered a close-up shot of a human face his cameraman of long standing, Billy Bitzer, quit his job in disgust. At the first close-up there were some hisses and cries of "Where are their feet?" but soon the Griffith improvement of the close-up emerged triumphant.

It was as a creator of significant content in the films themselves, aside from their technique, that Mr. Griffith was a mighty force in the cinema. Even before "The Birth of a Nation," that epic of the Civil War and the Reconstruction Period, which, directed by a man whose family had been ruined by the fall of the Confederacy, was most biased but was filled with great sweep and movement, he had exercised his bold conception of the exalted purpose which the medium might serve.

Long before the names of Sergei Eisenstein of Russia, Fritz Lang of Germany, Alfred Hitchcock of England, and Frank Capra of Hollywood were heard of, Mr. Griffith brought to the screen important historical and philosophical themes, challenging social questions, visionary prophecies. His films were emotional, dramatic, intellectual and esthetic.

16,000 "Extras" on One Scene

In 1916 his "Intolerance" appeared on a grand scale, with four parallel stories, a stupendous re-creation of the Ancient World and an apocalyptic image-prophecy of the Second Coming of Christ. This film, in which Griffith used 16,000 "extras" in a single scene, still stands as an example of what can be done with masses of people and architecture on the screen.

Mr. Griffith brought lyric poetry and high tragedy to the screen in 1919 in "Broken Blossoms," a passionate plea for a renewal of the Christian ideal in interracial relations. His "Way Down East," a folk-melodrama of New England in the Nineties, produced in 1920, used landscapes and natural backgrounds as vital psychological and dramatic elements of a story. "Dream Street," produced the next year, contained allegoric symbolism, and experimented with talking-film apparatus.

In "Orphans of the Storm," in 1922, Mr. Griffith combined magnificent spectacle with a social theme, using the French Revolution as a platform from which to attack communism and Soviet Russia, and citing the historic fruits of the revolution as a vindication of liberal democracy.

In 1924, Mr. Griffith produced the mammoth "America," another great historical pageant, this time of the American Revolution. In "America" as in "The Birth of a Nation," he set permanent standards, copied by film-makers the world over, in the technique of battle scenes.

His Methods Copied by Europe

His last important film, which came out in 1925, was "Isn't Life Wonderful!" a grim tale of Polish refugees in post-World War I Germany which was a forerunner of the present-day documentary films with the difference that it transcended the latter's frequent flatness. This film, like "America," was studied and copied by the Russian film directors, especially Rudovkin. In 1931 appeared Griffith's first all-talking film, "Abraham Lincoln," and his final film, "The Struggle," a study of alcoholism.

To the world at large Mr. Griffith was hailed for the many fine screen actors and actresses he molded into stars. Mary Pickford and Lillian Gish were outstanding examples of his genius in choosing and training performers for the new art. It was he, also, who induced the famous Douglas Fairbanks to leave the stage for the screen.

Mr. Griffith's judgment of ability was remarkable, as has been said by his biographer, Seymour Stern. He changed careers and destinies overnight, turning workmen into directors and schoolgirls into actresses. He saw more potential drama in wistful maidens than in the plump type of the time, and the millions who composed his audience backed him in this belief.

Born at La Grange, Ky., on Jan. 22, 1875, the son of Colonel Jacob Wark Griffith and Margaret Oglesby Griffith, he started work at the age of 16 on a local newspaper and as correspondent for The Louisville Courier-Journal.

After seeing Julia Marlowe in "Romola," he decided to become an actor, and eventually obtained the role of a dunce in a play presented by the Meffert stock company. His performance won him additional roles, but his pay was so small that he had to work as an elevator boy and later as a clerk and a book salesman in order to make ends meet.

Wrote Play for Stage

Eventually he was taken into John Griffith's Strolling Players and later joined Ada Gray's traveling troupes. After he had worked in half a dozen other stock companies, a play he had written called "A Fool and a Girl" was produced in 1907 by James K. Hackett at the Columbia Theatre in Washington.

After the failure of his play, Mr. Griffith saw his first flickering film and immediately wrote a scenario of the opera "La Tosca." The scenario, although not accepted, won him entry to moving pictures as an actor.

He worked first at the Edison studio in the film "The Eagle's Nest," under Edwin S. Porter's direction, and then shifted to Biograph, where he appeared in "When Knighthood Was in Flower" and other one-reelers.

In June, 1908, he was made an assistant director, and in July of that year made his first film, "The Adventures of Dollie," which was billed as "one of the most remarkable cases of child stealing."

In 1919, with Mary Pickford, Douglas Fairbanks and Charles Chaplin, he formed United Artists Corporation, under whose seal some of the outstanding productions of the screen were released. He sold his United Artists partnership in 1933.

Treason & Espionage

Some would regard this section as a sort of black museum of the modern world – while others as, even if not entirely heroic, at least paying tribute to those without whom the world might have been an even worse place than it is. Excluding perhaps the legendary **Mata Hari** the very greatest spies are, presumably, those about whom we know nothing at all. Doing duty for Fuchs, Burgess, Philby, Maclean and other post-war figures is **Rudolf Abel**, justly considered by many to have been the prince of Cold War spies. **Oreste Pinto**, the Spycatcher, was almost as successful as his adversaries. **Gavrillo Princip** serves here as a reminder of all those successful assassins whose action is at least the trigger for events of considerable moment – and **John Wilkes Booth** of the fact that even the most horrendous assassinations only rarely make much impact on the course of history. In contrast, **Stauffenberg** represents the tradition, if such there be, of the noble failure to whom one would have wished every success. The thinness of the dividing-line between execution and assassination, between treason and revolution, is perhaps best seen in the deaths of **Louis XVI** (doing duty also for that well-known connoisseur of cake, Marie Antoinette) and **Czar Nicholas II** and his family. As tribute to all those who have since imitated his ''suicide'' – to the great convenience of the governments concerned – **Jan Masaryk**, who ''jumped'' from a high window in Prague, symbolizes the methods and morality of power. As is shown by our language itself, **Quisling** has come to be regarded as the exemplar of treachery, the pinnacle of a long tradition.

Francis Gary Powers' flight into the history books will probably ever epitomise the nation caught with its pants down in the game of international ''dirty tricks'' and the assassination a year later of the Dominican dictator **Trujillo** reminds us of the unbridled power of the CIA and its more discreet counterparts throughout the world. Has the quest for national security got out of control? One day the *full* story behind the bizarre **Kennedy/ Oswald/Ruby** chain of events may open our eyes.

The Times
22nd July 1918

EX-TSAR SHOT.

OFFICIAL APPROVAL OF CRIME.

The following news is transmitted through the wireless stations of the Russian Government :—

"At the first session of the Central Executive Committee elected by the Fifth Congress of the Councils a message was made public, received by direct wire from the Ural Regional Council, concerning the shooting of the ex-Tsar, Nicholas Romanoff.

"Recently Ekaterinburg, the capital of the Red Ural, was seriously threatened by the approach of the Czecho-Slovak bands. At the same time a counter-revolutionary conspiracy was discovered, having for its object the wresting of the tyrant from the hands of the Council's authority by armed force.

"In view of this fact the Presidium of the Ural Regional Council decided to shoot the ex-Tsar, Nicholas Romanoff. This decision was carried out on July 16.

"The wife and son of Romanoff have been sent to a place of security. Documents concerning the conspiracy which was discovered have been forwarded to Moscow by a special messenger.

"It had been recently decided to bring the ex-Tsar before a tribunal, to be tried for his crimes against the people, and only later occurrences led to delay in adopting this course. The Presidency of the Central Executive Committee, after having discussed the circumstances which compelled the Ural Regional Council to take the decision to shoot Nicholas Romanoff, decided as follows :—'The Russian Central Executive Committee, in the persons of the Presidium, accept the decision of the Ural Regional Council as being regular.'

"The Central Executive Committee has now at its disposal extremely important material and documents concerning the Nicholas Romanoff affair ; his own diaries, which he kept almost to the last days ; the diaries of his wife and children ; his correspondence, amongst which are letters by Gregory Rasputin to Romanoff and his family. All these materials will be examined and published in the near future."

The Times
22nd July 1918

NICHOLAS II.

MEMOIR.

The ex-Tsar of Russia has been murdered by the Bolshevists. The Russian account of the crime appears in the next page.

Nicholas II., eldest son of Alexander III., and of Princess Dagmar, sister of Queen Alexandra, was born in St. Petersburg on May 18, 1868, when his father was still Heir-Apparent to the Throne. Under the direction of an English tutor, to whom he was much attached, he learned to speak English as fluently and correctly as his mother tongue, and after his marriage it was the language which he habitually used when alone with the Empress. French and German he also acquired perfectly, but, like his father, he avoided using the latter as much as possible. With public affairs he had no practical acquaintance until he succeeded to the Throne.

As Cesarovitch he travelled in Egypt, India, Ceylon, and Japan. When visiting one of the sacred Japanese cities he was attacked by a native fanatic and received in the head a severe sword-cut, which endangered his life. With the timely assistance of his cousin, Prince George of Greece, who was travelling with him at the time, the assailant was prevented from dealing a second blow, which would probably have proved fatal.

On November 1, 1894, Alexander III. died at Livadia, in the Crimea. The young Princess Alix of Hesse was invited to come to Livadia, and there, shortly before his death, Alexander III. gave his paternal blessing to the young couple at their formal betrothal. On November 19 the Tsar was interred with great pomp and ceremony at St. Petersburg, and a week later was celebrated the marriage.

AUTOCRAT BY HEREDITY.

The young Emperor was inclined to follow in the footsteps of his father, for whom he had a profound affection and veneration—and he lost no time in letting his subjects know his views on the question of constitutional reform. Within three months of his accession, when receiving deputies from the nobility, the Zemstvo, and the municipalities, who had come to St. Petersburg to congratulate him on his marriage, he thanked them for the expression of their loyal sentiments, and then, to the astonishment of all present, he added :—

It is known to me that recently, in some Zemstvo Assemblies, were heard the voices of people who had let themselves be carried away by senseless dreams about the Zemstvo representatives' taking part in the affairs of internal administration ; let these people know that I, devoting all my efforts to the prosperity of the nation, will preserve the principles of autocracy as firmly and unswervingly as my late father of imperishable memory.

Though not endowed with much originality or initiative, Nicholas II. appreciated such qualities in the Ministers who gained his confidence. Of these the most prominent for some time were Prince Lobanof and M. de Witte. By temperament and convictions a man of peace, the ex-Tsar sought to steer his great ship in calm waters, and with this object he decided in 1899 to put forward officially, for the consideration of the Powers, the question as to whether the burden of constantly increasing armaments might not be diminished by general consent.

THE HAGUE CONFERENCE.

This unexpected suggestion, which led to The Hague Conference, coming from a Sovereign who was commonly regarded in Europe as an ambitious autocrat, produced much astonishment among foreign Powers, and in certain quarters it was supposed to conceal secret Macchiavellian designs. In reality such suspicions had no foundation.

A deep shadow was cast over the reign of Nicholas II. by the war with Japan, which temporarily diminished Russian prestige all over the world and specially in Asia, and which displayed in a glaring light the political improvidence and administrative incompetency of the Russian Government. For the disastrous results the autocratic Sovereign was, of course, technically responsible, but it is only fair to add that in the matter of political foresight he was not more wanting than his official advisers and his subjects in general. The military disasters were the logical consequence of assuming that the Japanese would never dare to attack Russia, and down to the outbreak of hostilities the officials and the public indulged placidly in this illusion which German diplomacy sedulously encouraged.

The troublous times which began with the Japanese war brought out into startling relief the weaknesses and defects of the Emperor's character. He did not perceive, until it was too late, the necessity of leaving the old ruts of traditional routine, and when this necessity was forced upon him by the irresistible logic of events he had neither the intellectual perspicacity nor the force of will to strike out a new line for himself.

In face of the outburst of political agitation which followed immediately the assassination of M. Plehve in July, 1904, two courses were open to him, either vigorous repression or large concessions to the liberal aspirations of the educated classes. With the painful lack of decision which had characterized him from his youth upwards, Nicholas II. adopted neither of these courses, but wavered between the two. On one occasion he issued within 24 hours a manifesto conceived in the autocratic, reactionary spirit of Nicholas I., and a rescript foreshadowing satisfaction to the liberal demands of the moment. That unfortunate incident convinced the public of all shades of opinion that there was no longer an autocrat in Russia and that the supreme power was being wielded by two conflicting factions alternatively.

In these circumstances it is not surprising that the revolutionary tide rose rapidly. As usually happens in chaotic revolutionary times, the Extremists obtained more and more the control of the movement. The Liberals had to retire into the background, and the Social Democrats came to the front.

The truth is that the Tsar notwithstanding his pacific tendencies, did not desire the conclusion of the war at that moment. In common with some of the best military authorities, he believed that after a long series of disasters the tide of fortune was about to turn, and that by continuing the war indefinitely Russia would exhaust the resources of her antagonist and obtain very favourable conditions of peace. M. de Witte was accordingly instructed to insist on two conditions, which the Japanese seemed determined not to accept—"Not a foot of Russian territory and not a rouble of war indemnity!" To the surprise of all concerned, the Japanese suddenly, at the last moment, accepted these conditions, and peace was concluded on September 5, 1905.

A CONSTITUTIONAL EXPERIMENT.

As soon as Count Witte returned from Portsmouth, U.S.A., where the peace negotiations had been carried on, he was entrusted with extensive powers to deal with the troublous state of things at home; and on October 30 appeared an Imperial Manifesto instructing the Ministers to carry out the following "inflexible resolutions":—

(1) To confer on the population the immovable foundations of civil liberty, including inviolability of person, liberty of conscience, and freedom of speech, together with the right of holding public meetings and forming associations.

(2) To create a State Duma, containing representatives of the unenfranchised classes.

(3) To lay down as an absolute rule that no law should be valid without the approval of the said Duma.

This important pronouncement, together with an explanatory memorandum by Count Witte, was expected to act as oil on the troubled waters, but it produced the opposite effect. The excitement and disorders increased in the capital and many of the provincial towns, and in December at Moscow broke out a formidable insurrection which required for its suppression a large military force. At Sevastopol a section of the Black Sea Fleet hoisted the red flag and fired on the town, whilst a portion of the garrison mutinied and arrested their officers. At the same time, in many of the rural districts, there were serious agrarian disturbances which had to be repressed by the military.

The Reactionary party expected that these widespread disorders, which continued all through the winter of 1905-6, would induce the Emperor to abandon his intention of convoking a Legislative Assembly and return to the old autocratic *régime*, but at this time he showed unwonted firmness, and on May 10, 1906, the Imperial Duma held its first sitting in the Winter Palace.

THE THREE DUMAS.

In its first Session this new Assembly showed itself so irreconcilably hostile to the Government that after a stormy session of 72 days it was dissolved. Its immediate successor, which sat from March 5 to June 16, 1907, was wrecked by the revolutionary agitation of the Social Democrats. Still the Emperor remained true to his new liberal tendencies, and in the third Duma, which met in November, 1907, he was rewarded. Gradually the national representatives came to cooperate amicably with the Cabinet formed by M. Stolypin. Most of the success was due to him, and he unfortunately did not live to carry out the programme in its entirety. In September, 1911, he was assassinated in the theatre of Kieff during a gala performance. Fortunately a capable successor was found in the Minister of Finance, M. Kokovtsov, and for a time the constitutional experiment went on successfully.

With the outbreak of the great war in August, 1914, there was reason to hope that Nicholas II. was about to show himself in a new light. He at once realized the gravity of the situation, his habitual indecision disappeared, and he unhesitatingly put himself at the head of the enthusiastic national movement of determined resistance to the carefully prepared aggression of the Teutonic Powers.

WAR AND REVOLUTION.

Convinced that the pecuniary loss to the Exchequer would be much more than counterbalanced by the good moral effects of the measure, he issued a decree by which nearly all the liquor shops were closed, and the results exceeded the most sanguine expectations. According to the testimony of a very competent observer, "the Russians suddenly became a temperate nation!" But very soon events showed that the country was utterly unprepared for entering on a great war with a reasonable prospect of success. The military reorganization which had been undertaken after the disasters of the Japanese campaign was still merely in its initial stages. The Minister of War, General Sukhomlinov, showed himself very incompetent, and when he at last retired no efficient successor was found to take his place. In the Headquarters Staff some of the officers occupying important positions were discovered to be traitors who had been systematically selling the secrets of their office to the Headquarters Staff in Berlin, and so clearly was this fact established that several of them were tried by Court-martial and promptly executed. In the field most of the Generals were proved by experience to be incompetent, while the supply of arms, ammunition, and food was found to be altogether

Continued

354

inadequate for the requirements of even an ordinary campaign. More and more distinctly were heard complaints that the country was being ruled and ruined by so-called "dark powers" behind the throne, and the prevailing dissatisfaction was intensified by rumours that the Empress hoped to avert a revolution by obtaining the aid of the German Emperor, the Champion of Autocracy in Europe, and by inducing her husband to conclude with him a separate peace. Discontent was still further intensified by revelations of the so-called Rasputin scandal.

At last, in March, 1917, when measures taken by the Government for provisioning Petrograd proved insufficient, grave disturbances took place. The efforts of the Minister of the Interior to quell the revolutionary movement by means of machine-guns merely increased the disorders, and after a certain amount of bloodshed the Autocracy which had ruled Russia for centuries suddenly collapsed.

A CORONATION OMEN.

An incident at the commencement of his reign would have been regarded in a more superstitious age as a portent of evil omen foreshadowing the misfortunes to come, and made a lasting impression on one at least of the few who witnessed it. It occurred on the Coronation day in 1896, when Nicholas II. was returning in State from the Cathedral to the Palace of the Kremlin, near the church in which are buried the old Tsars of Muscovy. Feeling faint from the long Coronation ceremony and the fasting which the religious rite entailed he let his sceptre fall to the ground. In a moment one of the Grand Dukes who was walking immediately behind him picked it up and replaced it in his hand, and a spectator in the front rank of the crowd remarked under his breath "Absit omen!" That inaudible pagan prayer was not granted by the Fates.

The Times
22nd January 1793

EXECUTION
OF
LOUIS XVI.
KING OF THE FRENCH.

By an express which arrived yesterday morning from Messrs. Fector and Co. at Dover, we learn the following particulars of the King's execution:

At six o'clock on Monday morning, the KING went to take a farewell of the QUEEN and ROYAL FAMILY. After staying with them some time, and taking a very affectionate farewell of them, the KING descended from the tower of the Temple, and entered the Mayor's carriage, with his confessor and two Members of the Municipality, and passed slowly along the Boulevards which led from the Temple to the place of execution. All women were prohibited from appearing in the streets, and all persons from being seen at their windows. A strong guard cleared the procession.

The greatest tranquillity prevailed in every street through which the procession passed. About half past nine, the King arrived at the place of execution, which was in the *Place de Louis* XV. between the pedestal which formerly supported the statue of his grandfather, and the promenade of the Elysian Fields. Louis mounted the scaffold with composure, and that modest intrepidity peculiar to oppressed innocence, the trumpets sounding and drums beating during the whole time. He made a sign of wishing to harangue the multitude, when the drums ceased, and Louis spoke these few words. *I die innocent; I pardon my enemies; I only sanctioned upon compulsion the Civil Constitution of the Clergy.*—He was proceeding, but the beating of the drums drowned his voice. His executioners then laid hold of him, and an instant after, his head was separated from his body; this was about a quarter past ten o'clock.

After the execution, the people threw their hats up in the air, and cried out *Vive la Nation!* Some of them endeavoured to seize the body, but it was removed by a strong guard to the Temple, and the lifeless remains of the King were exempted from those outrages which his Majesty had experienced during his life.

The King was attended on the scaffold by an Irish Priest as his Confessor, not choosing to be accompanied by one who had taken the National oath. He was dressed in a brown great coat, white waistcoat and black breeches, and his hair was powdered.

When M. de *Malsherbes* announced to Louis, the fatal sentence of Death. "Ah!" exclaimed the Monarch, "I shall then at length be delivered from this cruel suspense."

The decree imported that Louis should be beheaded in the *Place de Carouzel*, but reasons of public safety induced the Executive Council to prefer the *Place de la Revolution*, formerly the *Place de Louis XV.*

Since the decree of death was issued, a general consternation has prevailed throughout Paris;—the Sans Culottes are the only persons that rejoice.—The honest citizens, immured within their habitations, could not suppress their heart-felt grief, and mourned in private with their families the murder of their much-loved Sovereign.

The last requests of the unfortunate Louis breathes the soul of magnanimity, and a mind enlightened with the finest ideas of human virtue. He appears not to be that man which his enemies reported. His heart was sound—his head was clear—and he would have reigned with glory, had he but possessed those faults which his assassins laid to his charge. His mind possessed the suggestions of wisdom; and even in his last moments, when the spirit of life was winged for another world, his lips gave utterance to them, and he spoke with firmness and with resignation.

Thus has ended the life of Louis XVI. after a period of four year's detention; during which, he experienced from his subjects every species of ignominy and cruelty which a people could inflict on the most sanguinary tyrant. Louis XVI. who was proclaimed at the commencement of his reign THE FRIEND OF THE PEOPLE, and by the Constituent Assembly, THE RESTORER OF THEIR LIBERTIES—Louis, who but a few years since was the most powerful Monarch in Europe, has at last perished on the scaffold. Neither his own natural goodness of heart, his desire to procure the happiness of his subjects, nor that ancient love which the French entertained for their Monarch, has been sufficient to save him from this fatal judgment.

Long in the habit of supporting the virtues of this unhappy Victim of savage Republicanism; and, steady in persevering to declare, THAT HIS HIGHEST AMBITION WAS THE HAPPINESS OF HIS PEOPLE, we hold ourselves justified, from the universal indignation which has marked this last act of cruelty exercised against him, to pay our sorrowing tribute to his memory, and join with the united millions of Europe, in supplicating the wrath of Heaven, and the vengeance of Mankind, to extend to his unnatural murderers the most exemplary punishment.

Posterity, in condemning those infamous Judges who have sacrificed Louis to the fury and ambition of the vilest of men, will extend their censures yet further; and in the warmth of virtuous indignation,

will not refrain from blasting the memory of that Minister (Necker), who, to gratify a selfish vanity, directed the Royal victim to make the first step towards that precipice, from the brink of which he is now precipitated.

Posterity will condemn those Members of the Constituent Assembly, who allured by the meteor of false philosophy, madly burst asunder the bonds of popular subordination; tore down the pillars of Monarchy and Religion, and left Louis defenceless, forsaken, and abandoned to those hordes of Monsters, who under the different appellations of Legislative Assemblies, Clubs, and Sections, have inflicted upon their miserable victim a thousand agonizing deaths and apprehensions, before they delivered him up to the axe of the executioner.

The perpetrators of such crimes may proceed in their career, till they draw down the same punishment on themselves. The virtuous of every country will bedew with sensibility, the memory of a good and pious King; whilst the tardy tears of the first Revolutionists shall blend themselves with the hypocritical complaints of the new Republicans upon the precipitancy of the King's execution.

Unquestionably, the blood of this unfortunate Monarch will invoke vengeance on his murderers. This is not the cause of Monarchs only, it is the cause of every nation on the face of the earth. All potentates owe it to their individual honour, but still more strongly to the happiness of their people collectively, to crush these savage Regicides in their dens, who aim at the ruin of all nations, and the destruction of all Governments. It is not by feeble efforts only, that we can hope to exterminate these inhuman wretches. Experience has proved them to be ineffectual. Armed with fire and sword, we must penetrate into the recesses of this land of blood and carnage. Louis might still have been living, had neighbouring Princes acted with that energy and expedition, which the case required.

San Francisco Chronicle
4th January 1967

Jack Ruby Dies in Dallas

Belli Blames Dallas Cops in Ruby's Death

Paris

Jack Ruby's onetime defense lawyer, Melvin Belli, last night blamed Dallas police for hastening his death by negligence.

Belli told reporters: "I don't see how a man can be on a suicide watch and how they cannot pick out that the man is damn near dead.

"It shows the sloppy, lackadaisical manner in which Dallas treats the underprivileged and unfortunate. I think it is worse that it was the result of carelessness and not a purposeful act."

LIFE

Ruby was born Jacob Rubenstein in the Maxwell street ghetto district of Chicago. The year was 1911, but the precise date was never documented.

He was the sixth of nine children of a Polish immigrant and his wife. His father was frequently without a job and just as often drunk. His mother had delusions, including one that she had a fishbone stuck in her throat.

The child, who was nicknamed Sparky, passed much of his time in street games and in brawling with the neighborhood boys. When his parents separated in 1923 he was placed in a foster home for a time. He dropped out of school at 16 with a reputation for being quick-tempered and disobedient.

He held a variety of jobs — scalping tickets for sports events, vending peanuts, selling horse-race tip sheets. He was on the fringe of the underworld.

In 1933, he and some friends went to San Francisco for a time, where he made a marginal living by selling newspaper subscriptions door-to-door.

Rubenstein (he changed his name to Ruby in Dallas in 1947) was drafted May 21, 1943. After service as a mechanic in air bases in the South, he was discharged in February, 1946, with a rating of "very satisfactory."

Shortly thereafter he went to Dallas at the invitation of his sister, Eva Grant, to operate two clubs, the Vegas and the Carousel.

'CLASS'

In Dallas Ruby began to acquire some of the "class" he yearned for. He dressed nattily, if not exactly soberly. He made friends. He formed a liaison with a blonde divorcee that lasted for 1½ years. "He wanted to be liked — and he was," a friend who knew him in those years said.

At the same time he built a reputation for toughness, and he seldom required police assistance in keeping order in the Carousel. He threw at least one drunken customer downstairs and was embroiled in fist fights from time to time.

He was arrested eight times between 1949 and 1963 on charges that ranged from disturbing the peace and carrying a concealed weapon to selling liquor after hours. He was never convicted of any of the charges.

The contrasts in Ruby's character — he was compassionate in some circumstances and brutal or truculent in others — were remarked on by a number of persons associated with him and by doctors who examined him.

Jack L. Ruby, who shot President Kennedy's assassin before a nationwide television audience, died yesterday at Parkland Memorial Hospital at the age of 55.

It was the same hospital in which Mr. Kennedy and the assassin, Lee Harvey Oswald, died three years ago.

Dr. Earl Rose, the Dallas county medical examiner, said that Ruby, who had extensive cancer, was killed by a blood clot in the lungs.

Ruby was operating a night club with strip-tease dancers in Dallas when President Kennedy was assassinated on Nov. 22, 1963, during a political tour of Texas.

Two days later Ruby walked into the heavily guarded Dallas police station — apparently unnoticed — and shot Oswald in the stomach with a .38-caliber revolver as Oswald was about to be transferred to the Dallas county jail, a mile away.

Ruby said he shot the assassin to spare Mrs. Kennedy the pain of returning to Dallas to testify at his trial.

REVERSAL

During the following three years, all of which he spent in prison until his final hospital stay, Ruby steadfastly denied that he was part of any conspiracy to silence Oswald.

In March, 1964, Ruby was convicted of murder and was sentenced to die.

In October, 1966, the Texas Court of Criminal Appeals reversed the conviction. The court said the trial judge, Joe B. Brown, has allowed illegal testimony. A new trial was set for Wichita Falls, about 100 miles west of Dallas. The case was pending when Ruby died.

Chicago Tribune
23rd November 1963

ASSASSIN KILLS KENNEDY

San Francisco Chronicle
25th November 1963

OSWALD SLAIN IN TEXAS JAIL

National Intelligencer
29th April 1865

THE CAPTURE OF BOOTH.

PARTICULARS OF HIS DEATH.

FULL AND INTERESTING ACCOUNT.

Yesterday morning the city was electrified by the announcement that John Wilkes Booth, the assassin of President Lincoln, had been captured. It was hoped that he had been taken alive, and that offended justice would be avenged by his summary execution in due course of law; but he has paid in a less public manner the penalty of his great crime.

At as early an hour as nine o'clock on Wednesday night, rumors were flying thick and fast that Booth had been captured. The fact was generally believed, and we made careful inquiry and were satisfied that the report was not without foundation. We refrained, however, from making any allusion to the matter, in obedience to the request of the military authorities, as communicated in a circular dated the 21st instant.

The body of Booth was brought to the city on the tugboat Ida, Capt. Wilson, and was in charge of Lieutenant Dougherty and a squad of the 16th New York cavalry.

From an officer high in the confidence of the Government, and who had much to do with the arrangement of the details resulting in the capture of Booth, we gather the following particulars:

At the time of the assassination of President Lincoln, Col. L. C. Baker, Provost Marshal and Chief Military Detective of the War Department, was with his force in New York, attending to important Government business. He was at once summoned to Washington, and was ordered to use all his efforts to effect the capture of Booth and others implicated in the assassination of President Lincoln, and the attempted assassination of Secretary Seward and son. Col. Baker, who arrived here on the Sunday succeeding the assassination, after looking at all the circumstances, refused to pursue a myth. The authorities seemed to have no idea as to where Booth had gone, or the direction he had taken. Col. Baker at once secured a photograph of Booth, of Surratt, of Herrold, and of other parties implicated in the assassination, and by his direction the selling of the photographs was prohibited, except to detectives. As soon as Col. Baker had perfected his arrangements, he sent his detectives throughout all the southern counties of Maryland. In the meantime two negroes had came in, and reported that suspicious characters were seen wending their way in the direction of Marlboro. Detectives of Col. Baker's force, who visited the lower counties of Maryland, report that there were over sixteen hundred cavalry, and about six hundred detectives, from New York, Philadelphia, and elsewhere, scouring these counties. A day or two afterwards Col. Baker applied to Col. Eckert and obtained two telegraph operators to tap the telegraph wires, and a telegraph office was established at Chapel Point, near the Chaptico. A negro, who was brought in at this time, informed Col. Baker that he had seen Booth and a companion cross the Potomac at Swan's Point, which place is on the Potomac, six miles above Leonardtown. Col. B., not having full confidence in the testimony of the negro, questioned him very closely, and, finding the negro correct in his statement, ordered Colonel E. J. Conger and Lieutenant L. B. Baker to proceed to arrest the party. Colonel Baker applied to General Hancock for a guard, and requested that the men detailed for the duty should be willing to do their duty in all particulars. General Hancock, in compliance with the request of Colonel Baker, detailed a detachment of the 16th New York cavalry, under command of Lieutenant Dougherty, to report to Colonel Baker. They reported on Tuesday, and Colonel B. at once inspected the officers and men, and, believing he had a discreet force, despatched them by steamer to the lower Potomac. Colonel Conger and Lieutenant Baker were ordered with the force, with directions to go to Belle Plain and land at any cost. They landed there at half-past eleven o'clock on Monday night, and started up the Rappahannock, and marched all night. At daylight on Tuesday the cavalry brought up twelve or fifteen miles below Port Royal, and they obtained no trace of the assassins until they arrived at Port Royal, sixteen miles below Fredericksburg. At this point there was a ferry, and Lieut. Baker went to the ferryman, an elderly man, and asked him, describing Booth and others, if such parties had crossed. The ferryman appeared loath to answer, when Lieut. Baker leaped from his horse, and grabbing the ferryman by the throat, held up a picture of Booth and asked if that man had crossed. A negro who was standing by responded and said, "I took that man across this morning, and he is now at Garrett's."

The cavalry, under the direction of Col. Conger, proceeded on their way, and passed Garrett's farm house a distance of fourteen miles to the west. At this point they met a negro in a cart, and who had also two men with him answering the description of Booth and Herrold. The cavalry then took the back track, and at one o'clock on the morning of Wednesday reached the rear of Garrett's house. At that hour the elder Mr. Garrett was walking upon his porch. After being questioned, he denied all knowledge of any strangers being in the vicinity. His son, however, informed Lieutenant Baker that two men were secreted in the barn. Baker went to the barn door and rapped. A voice, supposed to be that of Booth, asked, "Who is there?" Baker made no reply. The same voice then asked, "Are you friends or foes? I have five men in the barn here, and will make a desperate resistance. We are all well armed." Baker replied: "I have fifty cavalrymen, and the barn is surrounded. You cannot hope to escape." Booth, as is supposed, asked the question, "Are you Federals or Confederates?" Baker replied: "It matters not to you what we are; we want John Wilkes Booth."

A parley occurred which lasted about an hour and fifteen minutes; the desire being to take Booth alive if possible. In the meantime Colonel Conger moved up towards the barn, and tearing a board from the rear part of it, fired the hay which protruded with a candle, which he had in his hand. The light inside (the doors having been torn down) showed that Booth ran upon the hay and endeavored to extinguish it.

Colonel Conger ran to the front part of the barn with the intention of intercepting Booth as he came out. While standing in the front, Herrold remarked to Booth, "The barn is on fire; we can't hope to escape; I am going to surrender." Booth replied with an oath, using a most opprobrious epithet, accused him of being a traitor, and said he (Herrold) wished to desert him now when he was most needed.

The orders direct to the cavalry were that Booth should not be shot, but should be taken alive if possible. Col. Conger found it necessary to knock down several men in order to prevent them from leaving the ranks to go to the barn and shoot Booth. The excitement was intense, and it was with great difficulty that the men were restrained. Sergeant Boston Corbett left the ranks without orders, and placing the muzzle of his pistol through a crack of the barn, fired, and shot Booth through the neck. It is a singular coincidence that Booth was shot almost in the same place in which he shot President Lincoln, and that he died at twenty-two minutes past seven o'clock, the same hour and minute at which President Lincoln died.

Booth was shot at fifteen minutes past three o'clock, and as soon as the ball had taken effect, Lieut. Baker took the head of the dying man in his lap, and a conversation ensued. Some important developments were made, but it is not deemed advisable to publish them at this time.

In the neighborhood in which Booth was shot there were some five or six hundred paroled soldiers from Lee's army, and it was not deemed advisable to remain very long in the vicinity.

As soon as the shooting occurred Colonel Conger started for Washington, and arrived in this city early in the evening of Wednesday. The body of Booth was brought up on the tugboat Ida, Captain Wilson, and Herrold was brought up a prisoner in the same boat.

The manner of Booth's shooting seemed to paralyze him. Shortly before he died he requested that his hands should be raised up. The request was complied with, and as he looked upon his hands he remarked: "They are useless now. Blood—blood!—blood is upon them!" These were the last intelligible words he uttered. Herrold, who was with Booth, surrendered himself shortly after the barn in which he and Booth were was fired. By this surrender he saved himself from a sudden death.

Booth died, as he had lived, a braggadocio. He asserted positively that he would never be taken alive, and dared the force opposed to him to single combat in detail. He was a walking armory, for upon him were found half a dozen pistols, three large knives, a dagger, and a slung-shot. In his hand he held a carbine. Immediately after being shot, Col. Conger rushed into the barn. Booth was still standing up, but his arms were powerless, and his eyes starting from their sockets, indicated that the assassin had received his death-wound.

Surgeon General Barnes, assisted by eminent medical practitioners, yesterday afternoon made an autopsy of the body of the criminal

The Times
20th September 1961

LIEUT.-COL. ORESTE PINTO

COUNTER-ESPIONAGE IN WORLD WAR II

Lieutenant-Colonel Oreste Pinto, who was one of the most widely known figures among those connected with the work of Allied counter-espionage during the Second World War, died in a London hospital on Monday at the age of 71. It was his task to interrogate refugees coming to this country from the Netherlands, from Scandinavia, and later through the Allied lines in Normandy, so as to pick out those who were trained enemy agents.

A Dutchman by birth, Pinto had lived in Britain since the First World War. In his youth he had been a skilled amateur boxer and was a more than useful bridge player.

He wrote four books outlining his wartime experiences and giving his views on the problems and techniques of counter-espionage —*Spycatcher*, *Spycatcher Two*, *Spycatcher Three*, and *Friend or Foe*. It was his belief that the careful psychological approach was of more value than any brutality in interrogation, quite apart from the moral issues involved.

His name became familiar to a wider public through the television and radio series based on his experiences and memoirs.

The Times
2nd May 1918

ARCHDUKE'S ASSASSIN DEAD.

THE HAGUE, May 1.—It is announced that Gabrilo Princip, who took part in the murder of the Archduke Francis Ferdinand and his wife at Serajevo, died yesterday from tuberculosis at the fortress of Theresienstadt, near Prague.—*Exchange Telegraph Company.*

• Princip, who, it is alleged, shot the Archduke, had been sentenced to 20 years' penal servitude.

Daily Mail
11th September 1945

QUISLING CRIES 'I APPEAL'

QUISLING *hears the death sentence pronounced.—Picture by radio.*

**From RALPH HEWINS,
Daily Mail Special Correspondent**

OSLO, Monday.

IN face of threats of an underground Nazi rising in Oslo if Quisling were sentenced to death, he was found guilty here today on nine charges, ranging from treason and murder to petty larceny.

Judge Erik Solem imposed the death penalty in a quiet court room. Quisling had to be prompted, then cried out that he would appeal to the Supreme Court. If that fails he is expected to appeal to King Haakon.

Police rounded up Nazi underground cells throughout the capital during the night and strong police and military armed guards were posted in and around the court.

Quisling heard the verdict as if he were living in another world. There was no weeping. There was none of the hysteria, none of the bravado which he displayed in his speeches as the judge read the document tabulating his guilt.

Long indictment

The reading lasted 75 minutes. Sometimes Quisling gazed through a window. Sometimes he held his chin in his hand and seemed asleep. Usually he sat motionless in the dock and gazed vacantly at the court.

Quisling was rushed by Black Maria from Akershus prison tower to the judgment hall 35 minutes before the court opened to avoid demonstrations.

It was feared that a bomb attack might be made on the judges by some fanatical Quisling supporter.

The Times
22nd July 1944

HITLER "EXTERMINATING" THE PLOTTERS

The officer who placed the bomb at Hitler's headquarters, Colonel Klaus von Stauffenberg, aged 37, was shot by a firing squad, according to news given out yesterday.

Daily Telegraph
18th November 1971

MASTER SPY ABEL SAID 'I WAS ONLY A RADIO OPERATOR'

By DAVID FLOYD

COLONEL RUDOLF ABEL, whose death in Moscow on Monday was reported yesterday was the most important and experienced Soviet spy captured in the West.

At the time of his arrest in New York in June 1957 he already had behind him nearly 30 years of experience as an intelligence agent, mostly in Western Europe and America.

His importance to Soviet intelligence, even after he had been exposed and sentenced to 30 years in prison, was made clear in 1962 when Abel was exchanged for Francis Gary Powers, pilot of the American U-2 spy-plane shot down over Russia in 1960.

Abel was said to have continued his work for the Soviet espionage system by training younger men in Moscow until shortly before his final illness.

The colonel's arrest by the American counter-intelligence was not due to any fault on his side. He was betrayed by a subordinate, Reino Heyhanen, a colonel in the KGB (secret police) who lost his nerve on being recalled to Moscow and defected to the West.

He revealed Abel's identity as the "resident," or head, of the Russian spy network in America. Abel was arrested in the quiet New York hotel where he lived under the name of "Martin Collins."

Stream of information

He had then been in charge of Russian spying in North America for nine years and had been responsible for transmitting a steady stream of military and scientific information from America to Russia.

Abel later claimed that, when he was arrested, he outwitted the FBI agents and destroyed important evidence of his work.

Although this was disputed by the Americans, there appears to be no doubt that he rejected all offers to "co-operate" with American counter-intelligence.

Staunchness at trial

It was for the staunchness with which he behaved at his trial and under interrogation that he was later awarded high decorations by the Soviet Government and held up as a model for other would-be spies.

Abel disclaimed the title of "master-spy." He told journalists at Moscow Press Club in 1966: "I was not the great master-spy they made me out to be. I was really only the radio operator.

"The man who really masterminded the Soviet espionage network in the United States is still going strong."

But there can be no doubt that he was a highly-professional agent, whose whole life had been devoted to the task of getting hold of other people's secrets and transmitting them to Moscow.

One of the few people who claimed to know Abel personally described him as "a cold-blooded conspirator who believes firmly in the cause of Communism."

Technical education

His professional qualifications were considerable. An early childhood in Western Europe gave him a facility in French and German, to which he later added English and Italian.

A technical education in Berlin gave him valuable knowledge of electronics. In the 1930s he went back to Russia, to perfect his English and become proficient in photography.

One of his first jobs was as commercial attaché in Germany. He used his position to probe the secrets of the Zeiss works at Jena and enable the Soviet optical industry to get on its feet.

In 1941 Abel was working in Switzerland and is said to have reported to Moscow Hitler's plan to attack Russia that summer— a report Stalin disbelieved.

During the war with Germany he was based in Moscow and then went on missions for the secret police in East European capitals. After the war he worked in Germany, Austria and Britain.

Latest techniques

In 1950, after further training in the latest techniques of micro-photography, radio and wire-tapping, Abel was given the job of taking over and putting new life into the Russian spy network in North America.

It was the year that the Americans uncovered a major group of "atom" spies and sentenced two of them, Julius and Ethel Rosenberg, to death.

Abel went first to Canada under the name of Andrew Kayotis and, after getting used to the American way of life, crossed into the United States.

There he moved with great caution, and it was not until 1954 that he was finally established in New York as the Russian "resident," assuming the name of "Martin Collins."

He was also known as "Emil R. Goldfus," the name of a child born in New York in 1902 who had died in infancy.

Posed as artist

He posed as an unsuccessful artist who also ran a photographic studio. In his "studio" police found micro-cameras, radio transmitters and other paraphernalia of the spy's trade. Within the network Abel was known only as "Nark" or "Milton."

Abel remained tight-lipped throughout his trial. His only admission was that he had entered the United States illegally. At the time the Soviet authorities would not acknowledge his role and made no attempt to protect him.

But in 1960, Russia shot down the U-2 and almost immediately the idea of exchanging Powers for Abel was put forward.

After long negotiations the exchange took place on Feb. 10, 1962 at the Glienicker Bridge, Berlin. Abel had served under five years of his 30-year sentence and Powers 18 months of his 10 years.

Damage minimised

Abel's refusal to "co-operate" with the Americans minimised the damage caused to the network he had created. But it led later to the exposure of the two spies Norris and Lona Cohen who, as Peter and Helen Kroger, were arrested in Britain in 1961 and sentenced to 20 years each. Sentenced with them was Gordon Lonsdale, whose real name was Molody, the Soviet "resident" in Britain. He was exchanged in 1964 for Mr Greville Wynne, a British businessman arrested by the Russians.

In 1965 Abel was awarded the Order of Lenin in recognition of his long service in the Russian intelligence service. He received a second Order of the Red Banner in 1969.

Abel's wife, whom he married in 1932, was German. She and a daughter survive him.

SOVIET SPY ABEL LIES IN STATE

By Our Moscow Correspondent

Rudolph Abel, the Soviet master spy who died of lung cancer on Monday, was cremated in Moscow yesterday.

Earlier, journalists were forbidden to wait by the Lubyanka Prison, headquarters of the K G B, the State security police, where Abel's body lay in state. But a queue of mourners waited to pay their last respects to the man said to have controlled Russia's spy network in America for nine years.

The Times
16th October 1927

WOMAN SPY SHOT.

(FROM OUR OWN CORRESPONDENT.)

PARIS, OCT. 15.

Mata-Hari, the dancer, was shot this morning. She was arrested in Paris in February, and sentenced to death by Court-martial last July for espionage and giving information to the enemy. Her real name was Marguerite Gertrude Zelle. When war was declared she was moving in political, military, and police circles in Berlin, and had her number on the rolls of the German espionage services. She was in the habit of meeting notorious German spy-masters outside French territory, and she was proved to have communicated important information to them, in return for which she had received several large sums of money since May, 1916.

Daily Telegraph
13th August 1977

Powers' flight wrecked detente for years

PERHAPS no man in modern history has single-handedly caused his Government such sudden and exquisite embarrassment as Francis Gary Powers did 17 years ago when his U-2 spy plane route over Russia brought him within range of a new, high-altitude Soviet anti-aircraft missile.

For Powers, who died yesterday on an empty baseball field in the crash of a Los Angeles Television station's helicopter, his moment in history began high over the Urals with a blinding orange explosion.

"I can remember feeling, hearing and just sensing an explosion. I immediately looked up from the instruments, and everywhere I looked was orange," he said later.

A top-secret mission in a top-secret aircraft had come to a sudden end in a fashion which was to have a souring effect on East-West relations for several years to come.

Khrushchev's relish

Nikita Khrushchev, then ruling in the Kremlin, used the incident, step by step, move by move, with the relish and cunning of a chess-player who knows he has his opponents in a trap.

He was able publicly to catch Washington officials in a number of big and small lies—lies which then-President Eisenhower later had to admit.

Relations between the two super-powers deteriorated rapidly to the point where the Big Four 1960 summit planned for Paris could not possibly be held.

Khrushchev said he would go to the meeting only if Eisenhower apologised publicly for his Government's actions in invading Soviet airspace with hostile intent. Eisenhower replied only that U-2 flights had been suspended and would not be resumed.

When his sleek black spy plane was stopped by the Soviet rocket, Powers was able to parachute to open country in the Sverdlovsk region. He was quickly captured by a group of workers and farmers.

Death before dishonour

In the view of many Americans, this highly-paid CIA agent should have chosen death before dishonour in the tradition of spies facing imminent capture.

The C I A, too, wondered why he had not blown his U-2 to smithereens with the built-in destruct mechanism rather than let it fall, reasonably intact, with all its electronic and photographic secrets into Russian hands.

Powers soon answered the C I A's question. He said at his trial in Moscow that the destruct mechanism did not work.

According to Powers's own account in a book that was published after his return to the United States, he did consider taking his life as he drifted down to Russian soil. The C I A had supplied him with a curare poison device.

But the spy, who said later that he had "no desire to be a hero—just an average American," decided not to use the curare jab but to take his chances on what might happen to him in Russian hands.

He insisted in his book, "Operation Overflight," that the C I A had never told him to commit suicide in such circumstances.

A native Kentuckian, Powers collected 50,000 dollars in back pay from the C I A when he returned to America. His neighbours gave him a standing ovation while Barbara, his wife, gave him a divorce.

"She was the only person who ever mistreated me while I was in prison in Russia," according to Powers. For her part Barbara Powers claimed that her husband returned "void of all feeling — all he wants is money." The couple had no children.

If money was what the husband was after he soon got it with a highly-paid job as a test pilot for Lockheed. He left several years later and had other jobs before becoming an airborne reporter for Station K N C B.

The Times
1st June 1961

TRUJILLO THE DICTATOR ASSASSINATED
DOMINICAN REPUBLIC UNDER HEAVY GUARD

ALL COMMUNICATIONS CUT OFF

From Our Own Correspondent

WASHINGTON, MAY 31

General Rafael Trujillo, the dictator who has ruled the Dominican Republic with savage efficiency for the past 31 years, was assassinated last night. Reports of his death were confirmed late tonight in a broadcast from radio Caribe, the republic's official radio station.

A decree was read stating that the "benefactor and father of the homeland has fallen the victim of treasonous attack", and that the Army was in control of the country. No details were given of the manner of the assassination nor of who was responsible. Nine days' national mourning was ordered.

Today the country was under heavy military guard and all direct communications were cut off. Aircraft arriving at Ciudad Trujillo, the capital of the republic, had been surrounded by troops and their passengers prevented from disembarking.

TRAP FOR OPPONENTS

During the day there were some doubts about the veracity of reports of the dictator's death, deriving chiefly from the fact that there have been many earlier false reports that the dictator had been killed. On one occasion at least these were deliberately put about by Trujillo himself, who wanted his political opponents to reveal themselves; this they obligingly did, at the cost of their lives.

Generalissimo Trujillo took over absolute control of the Dominican Republic on August 16, 1930. Since then no opposition of any kind has been tolerated, and a suspicion of it has been enough to instigate large-scale arrests, torture, and political execution. The details of the Generalissimo's ruthless dictatorship have never yet been revealed in full, because he guarded his country with a silent rule of fear that has been as effective a barrier to the outside world as the iron curtain itself.

Rafael Leonidas Trujillo Molina was the third child in a family of 11. He began life as a telegraph operator, and entered the National Guard during the First World War. He became a second lieutenant in 1918, and had reached the rank of major by the time the United States forces were withdrawn from the Republic in 1924. His subsequent rise was rapid. Within four years he was Chief of Staff, and in 1930, when the President of the country was imprisoned, he assumed control of the Government. Much blood was shed before he felt securely in command.

VIGOROUS AND VAIN

Though he successfully lifted the Dominican Republic from the depressed economic state in which it was when he took over, and has provided the people with fine hospitals, good roads, an efficient educational system, clean water, and television, the repressive side of his regime has outweighed its social benefits. He himself has assumed a vast control of the economy, in personal monopolies including the salt, beer, and tobacco industries. At 69 he remained a vigorous and alert little man, though a vain one. He tried to overcome his tendency towards stoutness by wearing corsets, and to increase his height by wearing shoes with built-up heels.

Though he has been in absolute control of the country since 1930, Trujillo has not been President all the time. He relinquished the office from 1938 to 1942, and then gave the post to his brother in 1952.

FLASHING SIGNS

It has been accompanied by a cult of enforced Trujillo-worship that will inevitably leave the country unstable for some time after the idol has been smashed. The Generalissimo awarded himself the title of "Benefactor of the Nation". There are, it has been estimated, about 2,000 plaques and monuments to him in the capital alone—the city which used to be known as Santa Domingo, but which was changed to Ciudad Trujillo on his orders. At night, neon signs blink "God and Trujillo", and over the entrances to hospitals that he has built are the words "Only Trujillo Cures You". Even time, in the republic, is calculated from his advent, this year being the thirty-first of the era of Trujillo.

The last years of his era had been filled with attempts to overthrow the dictatorship, the most effective of which took place in January of last year. It was put down, but thousands of innocent people were arrested and maltreated to such an extent that the Roman Catholic Church finally and openly declared its opposition to him.

INFLUENCE OF CHURCH

From that moment, many believe, his ultimate downfall was assured. Certainly the recent history of Latin America supports the view that dictatorships fall once the Church has felt compelled to move into the political field to protect civil rights. When the Roman Catholic hierarchy published its pastoral letter a year ago, publicly listing its objection to the Generalissimo's actions, the people of the Republic had for the first time a base round which to gather their opposition.

Generalissimo Trujillo made many enemies abroad as well as at home. In 1937, after a dispute with Haiti, he ordered his National Guardsmen to attack Haitians living on the border. Some 10,000 were killed before the United States entered the dispute and declared that Trujillo should pay approximately $75 (about £27) to the Haitian Government for each Haitian killed.

The United States broke of relations with the Dominican Republic last year, after the inter-American Peace Commission had charged Trujillo with "flagrant and widespread" violations of human rights. The report said that the violations were continuing and aggravating tension in the Caribbean area.

Visionaries

These are the people who if they differ at all from social activists and/or dissenters, are those whose activities, whether practical or theoretical, are motivated basically by their vision of a future where the world no longer had need of their efforts. Some, like Thomas More, write of utopias; others, like William Blake, the genius whose death was not thought worthy of mention at the time, simply express their essentially individual vision in parable, poem, painting, and whatever other form comes to hand. Some, like **George Orwell**, express their fears, seeking to avoid a certain sort of future; others, like **Karl Marx** write of the past, and of their hopes for the future, seeking to change the world with what they see as the truth about its condition. Some inspire great change, like the multi-faceted **Benjamin Franklin** and **Herzl**, others *make* the changes, like **Garibaldi**, **Kemal Ataturk** and **Joseph Smith**. On the whole though, there is little to be gained by generalising here. The visionary is the great personality who moves mountains, like **Mao-tse Tung**, or who seeks to do so (rather more naively) but fails, like **Woodrow Wilson**; or who more than anything serves as a direct inspiration for others both in word and in deed, like **Mahatma Gandhi**, whose successful use of the weapon of non-violence may yet prove to mark a crucial development. On a rather different scale, more localized and perhaps more personal, **Robert Owen**, the wealthy industrialist who sought to change people's relationships through cooperation, and to that end founded probably the first workers' cooperative in the modern world, stands also for men such as Wilberforce and Shaftesbury. Finally, **Booker T. Washington** and **Martin Luther King** symbolize man's constant struggle for freedom and dignity, which, if it is ever even partially attained, will be thanks to people such as these and to those who have taken inspiration from them.

HOW KEMAL ATATURK CREATED MODERN TURKEY

GREAT EFFORTS FOR BALKAN PEACE

Daily Telegraph & Morning Post
11th November 1938

Kemal Ataturk, President of the Turkish Republic—whose death at Istanbul yesterday at the age of 58 is reported on another page—will go down to history as the man who rid Turkey of her Greek invaders in 1922, who won for his country a position of moral and diplomatic equality with the Great Powers, and who expelled the Christian subjects of the former Sultans from the present-day State.

He will also be remembered as the leader or dictator who completely modified social and religious conditions in an area where the people always have been and still are conservative at heart.

Yet at the time of the Armistice he was hardly known abroad. Within his own country the position was different. The reputation he gained during the war had given him the support of a strong party in Turkey, and he showed that the faith in him was not misplaced when in May, 1919, he was given an important post as Inspector-General of the Turkish Forces in Anatolia.

His choice by the Constantinople Government was approved by the Allies, and from the moment of his arrival in Anatolia he devoted himself to the organisation of forces that would protect Turkish rights.

Some alarm in Constantinople over his rapidly increasing influence led to his being ordered to return to the capital. He bluntly refused, and was outlawed, whereupon he drew up the famous National Pact which formed the battle cry of the Turks for the next few years.

ELECTED PRESIDENT

In 1920 the first Grand National Assembly met at Angora, and Kemal was elected President. He saw to it that the former irregular bands were replaced by a regular army, and he drew up a military convention with Soviet Russia, which supplied him in return with financial assistance and arms. Almost concurrently public opinion was inflamed by the signature of the Treaty of Sèvres by the Constantinople Government and by the renewed Greek advance in Asia Minor.

In 1921 and 1922 things moved apace. The battle of the Sakaria (August-September, 1921), in which Kemal himself took the command, saw the end of Hellenic military successes. Kemal's prestige rose more and more rapidly, and in September, 1922, the Greeks had fled from Asia Minor, the Turks had occupied Smyrna and the late President had been made a Ghazi—an honour reserved for those who have won a striking victory over a Christian enemy.

The Hellenic débâcle marked the completion of the Nationalist military victory. The Western Powers were thereby brought face to face with the necessity of either meeting the Turks on the field of battle or of negotiating with them, and, when France had openly stated her pacific attitude, and the British people had shown their opposition to further fighting, the armistice, signed at Mudania in October, recognised Eastern Thrace and Asia Minor as Turkish.

SULTAN'S FLIGHT

HOW ATATURK BEGAN DICTATORSHIP

Very shortly after Mr. Lloyd George had retired from the Premiership, the Grand National Assembly proclaimed the end of the Constantinople Government, and the Sultan fled to a British warship. His office was abolished and a cousin of the former ruler elected Khalif. After a conference lasting for many months, the Treaty of Lausanne, signed in July, 1923, gave to Turkey practically, if not absolutely, the whole of the conditions claimed in the National Pact.

This, in conjunction with the Allied evacuation of Constantinople, made Mustapha Kemal the creator of modern Turkey.

The Ghazi's régime was a dictatorship; it was supernationalistic and anti-clerical in the extreme. He secured the passage of legislation at will, Ministers depended upon his favour. If Kemal was not himself an actual free thinker, he did everything within his power to decrease the influence of the Moslem imam, and, in April, 1928, he completely laicized the State by bringing about the repeal of the clauses of the Constitution dealing with religion.

UNIFORMS PUT AWAY

The Army was his first care, but, as a large and keen farmer, he devoted his attention to improvements in agriculture. Finally, he improved education, worked hard to purge the administration, and did a great deal to ameliorate the lot of his own Turkish co-nationals.

Nothing was more characteristic of Kemal Ataturk than his refusal to exploit his magnificent career as a soldier. He put away his uniforms as soon as his task as soldier was finished. After becoming President of Turkey he never wore uniform. Peace within his frontiers and abroad was his unswerving policy, and he maintained that for him to continue to wear uniform was undesirable, misplaced, and illogical. Neither did he consider himself a military genius. Military art, he told the foreign Ambassadors who justly attempted to pay him compliments as a tactician, was merely a matter of common sense and timely action.

BRILLIANT TALKER

NEVER AT A LOSS IN CONVERSATION

While he rigidly exercised supreme power himself, he would not permit any misuse of authority by subordinates, however highly placed. If he discovered that some modest employee was being harshly treated he would severely chastise those responsible.

Incapacity and laziness, however, were anathema to him, and he would not tolerate failure unless a very good reason was the cause. He alone is responsible for the reforms which have westernised and revolutionised Turkey, and he was never content to give orders and allow others to do the work.

A man of great ability, he was never at a loss for a subject of conversation, and within the space of two hours he once gave the foreign diplomats a sample of his knowledge by discussing grammar, politics, history, Darwin, Napoleon, and Lloyd George.

EXPERT POKER-PLAYER

At the annual State ball in Angora it was quite common for him to invite diplomatic representatives of countries of diametrically opposed politics into a corner of the ballroom and draw them into discussion on a subject which afforded him great delight, but which to them meant great discomfort.

He could play as hard as he could work, and one of his favourite games was poker. Games with distinguished and expert players often continued through the night and the President almost always won. But if the differences were too great, and he was winning, he had the habit of pushing his counters into the middle of the table and stating that the game had been played only for fun.

His generosity became a by-word in Turkey, though he never advertised his gifts. Many orphans of brother officers owe to him their education and secure positions in life. Kemal Ataturk had no thought for personal gain, and he was the enemy of anyone who tried to make unreasonable gain to the detriment of the country or the people. He was undeniably the greatest factor for peace that his part of the world has ever known, and he was the only dictator who had been able fully to realise his goal and pass on without ruining his work.

He used the mailed fist to set Turkey on its feet again, but once he accomplished his aim no former animosity obscured his vision. He made peace with his greatest enemies—the Greeks—and he would tolerate no persecution of the Jews in Turkey. He determined that Turkey should be made strong for the enforcement of peace, and he succeeded in attaining his goal.

ADMIRER OF BRITAIN

He was a great admirer of Great Britain and desired the ever strengthening of friendship between the two countries. Turkey received a visit from a distinguished peer of the realm some time ago in Istanbul. The question of the fortification of Cyprus cropped up in the conversation and Kemal Ataturk asked, "Why Cyprus? Would not the Turkish coast provide a better naval base?" The peer replied, "Yes, provided our countries are always friends." The President said, "Great Britain and Turkey must not, and cannot, ever again be anything but friends."

Ataturk once said to Sir George Clerk: "When I die there will be a thousand men to replace me," to which Sir George replied, "Your Excellency is exaggerating a thousand times."

But the success he achieved by efficient leadership, coupled with good fortune, could hardly have been attained had it not been for the prestige he won before, and particularly during, the Great War. Born at Salonika in 1880, he graduated at the Military College at Constantinople in 1900. He was opposed to Abdul Hamid, and although he was exiled to Syria and to other parts of the then empire for some years, he managed ultimately to secure a staff appointment at Salonika.

AT THE DARDANELLES

Kemal took part in the Turco-Italian war and in the Balkan campaigns, and at the beginning of the world hostilities he was Turkish Military Attaché at Sofia. He resigned that post, and soon afterwards was sent to the Dardanelles. There he drove our troops back from Chunuk Bair and Chocolate Hill, thus probably saving the Turkish position, and making himself a great national hero.

In January, 1923, and shortly after the death of his mother, who had accompanied him to the new capital, he married Latife Hanoum, the daughter of a prosperous Smyrna merchant. Her Excellency, then only about 20 years of age, had been educated in France and in England, and she speaks English, French and German.

The marriage took place without having been previously announced. Mme. Kemal Ataturk was a prominent advocate of the emancipation of women and she interested herself in the work of her husband. The President divorced her in August, 1925. No official reasons were given for the dissolution of the marriage, of which there were no children.

DEATH OF ADOPTED DAUGHTER
SHOCK THAT SADDENED

In November, 1935, Ataturk's adopted daughter, Mlle. Zihira Mehmed, aged 20, was killed when she fell from the Golden Arrow train between Calais and Paris. The President was saddened and mystified by her death.

When the Duke of Windsor, who, as Edward VIII., was the first British sovereign to visit Turkey, landed in 1936, Ataturk grasped his hand and helped him to set foot in Istanbul, the old capital of the Sultans.

Six months ago a trade agreement was concluded between Great Britain and Turkey which allowed export credits to Turkey for £10,000,000 and a £6,000,000 loan for armaments.

In July the Franco-Turkish Agreement on the Sanjak of Alexandretta — severed for 20 years from the mother country — was signed. Unlike many other of Ataturk's achievements this was accepted calmly as the natural outcome of Turkey's indisputable rights.

In the same month a Turco-German agreement was signed providing for German credits amounting to approximately £12,500,000.

KEMAL ATATURK.

New York Herald
1st July 1944

We received by the afternoon mail yesterday, and issued immediately, in an extra, the intelligence which we give in another column, of the murder of Joe Smith and his brother. This shocking piece of news, we have every reason to believe, is authentic. It excited a great deal of interest in the city.

We certainly have been expecting for some time past the receipt of some such intelligence from the Mormon country. The irrepressible excitement amongst the people of that district, was, it was easy to foresee, soon to result in bloodshed and murder. This occurrence discovers in a very striking manner, the utter impotency of the law, in controlling the passions of an infuriated mob, and, with the recent catastrophe in Philadelphia before our eyes, we of this region cannot very consistently lecture the people of the West on their preference for Lynch law of the most sanguinary description.

The death of the modern Mahomet will seal the fate of Mormonism. They cannot get another Joe Smith. The holy city must tumble into ruins, and the "latter day saints" have indeed come to the latter day. Mormonism from the beginning was a sad delusion, and the violence and folly, which had begun to characterize the movements of the Prophet, leave little room for sympathy in any quarter for its fate, bloody and revolting as it has been.

New York Times
4th February 1924

WILSON HAD LEAGUE IN MIND IN 1914

EUROPE IS STIRRED BY WILSON'S DEATH

Lloyd George Calls Him Glorious Failure Who Sacrificed His Life for His Ideal.

LONDON, Feb. 3.—In common with most of the allied statesmen of Europe and other personalities whom destiny summoned to fill leading rôles in the World War, former Premier Lloyd George sees in Woodrow Wilson an idealist who stood out as perhaps the most remarkable figure of that tremendous cataclysm.

In an interview which THE NEW YORK TIMES correspondent had with him to-day at his new home at Churt, Surrey, concerning the passing of Mr. Wilson, Mr. Lloyd George said:

"Woodrow Wilson was a very great man, and, like all great men, had his defects, but these will be quickly forgotten in the magnitude of his life work. True he was a failure, but a glorious failure. He failed as Jesus Christ failed, and, like Christ, sacrificed his life in pursuance of his noble ideal.

"He was just as much a victim of the great war as any soldier who died in the trenches. He ruined his health in the endeavor to create a better and happier existence for the people of the whole world, and I am sure that the failure of his altruistic inspirations hastened his tragic end.

"It will perhaps be a generation before the greatness of Woodrow Wilson will be appreciated at its real value by his countrymen and the tragedy which closed his life will bring before the world the unselfishness of his ambitions as nothing else could. Like the tragedy which made for your great martyred Lincoln a permanent place in the hearts of the American people—even of those who disagreed with him, as was made very apparent to me in my recent visit to the Southern States—the sad death of this great Statesman, this great American, will indelibly stamp his name among those at the very top of your history.

Had Violent Likes and Dislikes.

"Like Theodore Roosevelt, Mr. Wilson had violent likes and dislikes, and for this, as always is the penalty of greatness, he was violently criticized. I believe I may say that never have I seen such vicious, cruel vituperation as was heaped upon him at home and in Paris at the time of the Peace Conference. Such abuse never was leveled at any man in like position in history and it hurt him terribly.

criticism cut him like a knife. Had he been a lifelong politician he could have overlooked these attacks. Thirty years or so of political life makes one invulnerable, I know. But Wilson's character was such, he was of such fine stuff, that he was immensely sensitive to this public abuse and he suffered more than others would have done. I have no doubt that this helped to bring on his illness.

"Besides, he was a tireless worker. I remember when we were in Paris I would see lights in his room at all hours of the night as he worked at his League idea. The rest of us found time for golf and we took our Sundays off, but Wilson, in his zeal, worked incessantly. Only those who were there and witnessed it can realize the efforts he expended.

His Personality Grew Upon One.

"He was a man whose personality grew upon one. When I first met him here in England I did not understand him, nor did Clemenceau in Paris; but when you spend every day for five months with a man you have opportunity to become well acquainted with him, and when it was over I had learned to appreciate his great gifts and to like him very much personally, and I remember Clemenceau at the time telling me his feelings were similar.

"Yes, Woodrow Wilson was a very good fellow, and I shall mourn his passing.

COOLIDGE ANNOUNCES DEATH

In Formal Proclamation He Calls the Nation to Mourn.

HE LAUDS WILSON'S WORK

Love and Tenderness Were His Outstanding Characteristics, Says Dr. Axson.

Special to The New York Times.

WASHINGTON, Feb. 3.—Dr. Stockton Axson, whose sister was the first wife of Woodrow Wilson, gave tonight to THE TIMES an intimate picture of Woodrow Wilson before and after he became President of the United States.

Dr. Axson revealed that in 1914 the germ of the League of Nations had taken shape in Mr. Wilson's mind in these words:

"It was one morning in 1914, as he was writing at his desk and I sitting near by in the big White House office," said Dr. Axson. "The President finished his work, and, in his systematic way, put up his pen and papers and came to stand near me, before the open fireplace—although there was no fire.

"He said: 'You know I'm very much troubled about this war. I'm troubled lest something shall happen on the high seas that will draw us into this European struggle. For I know we can render a greater service to the world by keeping out of it.

"'I know nothing is ever finally settled by force. Now, when the war is over the real settlement of problems and differences will come. That will mean a new order of international relations—certain things which have to be definitely settled among nations.

"'Four things will have to be settled after this war. I mean these things: First, that small nations shall have equal rights with great nations; second, that never again must it be permitted for a foot of ground to be obtained by conquest; third, that the manufacture of munitions of war must be by Governments and not by private enterprise; and, fourth, that all nations must be absorbed into some great association of nations whereby all shall guarantee the integrity of each so that any one nation violating the agreement between all of them shall bring punishment on itself automatically.'

"Now, there is the germ of the League of Nations in the Fall of 1914," said Dr. Axson. "I have often tried to recollect exactly whether he said 'Association' or 'League,' but I cannot recall definitely.

"Woodrow Wilson was never a pacifist. He wanted to get into the Spanish-American war the worst way. He said the fight to free Cuba was a righteous cause, and he would have joined the army himself, at that time, if he had been free to do so.

"It was in later years, I think, that he became a passionate lover of peace—and an aggressive advocate of peace."

Dr. Axson then went on to tell of the Woodrow Wilson that few people knew, the Woodrow Wilson of the home.

"I first met Woodrow Wilson after he had been engaged to my sister for a year," he said. "My earliest recollections of him are of his great kindliness of manner, his unfailing courtesy and consideration for others and of his high mindedness when discussing national affairs and problems."

Dr. Axson was associated with Mr. Wilson as a professor at Princeton University and knew Mr. Wilson's point of view as well perhaps as any other living man.

"Tenderness, I think, was easily his outstanding characteristic," said Dr. Axson. "Throughout the days of his youth and manhood I knew him and I consider it a great privilege to have enjoyed such constant association with him during the last forty years. We have never been separated for longer than eight months during that time.

"In the intimate family circle no one ever heard him speak a harsh word. I never heard him criticise or use censorious language toward any one at any time except in condemnation of certain outsiders in high official places during his Presidency.

Made Stern at Princeton.

"His family always found him the most wonderful kind of husband and father and every member of his household will ever remember his unfailing thoughtfulness and love.

"Often in the course of long lecturing trips I enjoyed the home circle hours when we gathered about the blazing hearth and enjoyed the play of wit, his bits of wisdom and the tenderness of ripe home life.

"Many critics have condemned him as a cold-natured man, given to harshness and criticism. Undoubtedly the heavy burdens of the Presidency brought increasing sternness into his manner when dealing with difficult situations, but in his home life he was unfailingly a loving father and a devoted husband."

Dr. Axson said there were too many sides to Mr. Wilson's complex nature to give a pen picture of him in a brief appreciation.

"I remember," he said, "that after he had become President of Princeton University, in which position he was obliged to engage in several bitter controversies in order to accomplish the reforms he had set his heart on, Mr. Wilson said: 'Life is getting grimmer for me—a good deal of play spirit has gone out of me.'

"This may account for the ste[...]

which may have been noted in him during the stern days of war making. But aside from these natural changes, I think he has kept as sweet and serene as any man could.

"Within the last month or so, during our visits and talks in S Street, I have found him just as sweet and serene as ever, as he was in the days of his palmiest youth.

"In the matter of religion, I recently discussed the 'Fundamentalists' versus the 'Modernists' with him. I asked him —'If your father, a Presbyterian minister, were living now, which would he be?' He replied with great emphasis, 'He would be a Fundamentalist.'

"I then said, 'The Fundamentalists seem to deny the evolution hypothesis.' His answer was: 'My father accepted evolution, as I did, long ago, but the trouble with Modernists today is that they take all the mystery out of religion. That's why he would be against Modernists, and that's why I'm against them.'

Called His Religion Universal.

"Woodrow Wilson was most regular in his church attendance," continued Dr. Axson. "He was absolutely regular until his health broke down. His father was a Presbyterian minister well known in the South. Woodrow Wilson was brought up in that faith and he has always continued in the faith which he early accepted.

"I remember when he was a young college professor in the '90s, when most professors were going through a period of doubt and skepticism over the doctrine of evolution, Mr. Wilson never seemed to have any period of doubt. He said there was absolutely no contradiction between the modern doctrine of evolution and his Presbyterian creed. He believed religion was a very simple thing. He said his religion could easily be accepted by all, and I have known him to go through many struggles, but never yet a religious struggle.

"In his family life," continued Dr. Axson, "there could be no more devoted father than Woodrow Wilson. He always maintained discipline. Without one suggestion of harshness he simply tried to let his children know how he felt about things, and they, although each had a marked independence of character, were extremely docile to his wishes.

"My sister's last thought as she lay dying was of him, as she asked Dr. Grayson, with a strong pressure of her hand. 'Take care of him, doctor, take good care of Woodrow.'"

San Francisco Chronicle
5th April 1968

The Turbulent Life of Dr. King

A Dream That Inspired Millions

To many millions of American Negroes, the Rev. Dr. Martin Luther King Jr. was the prophet of their crusade for racial equality.

He was their voice of anguish, their eloquence in humiliation, their battle cry for human dignity. He forged for them the weapons of nonviolence that withstood and blunted the ferocity of segregation.

And to many millions of American whites, he was one of a group of educated Negroes who preserved the bridge of communication between races when racial warfare threatened the United States in the 1960's, as Negroes sought the full emancipation pledged to them a century before by Abraham Lincoln.

WORLD

To the world Dr. King had the stature that accrued to a winner of the Nobel Peace Prize: a man with access to the White House and the Vatican; a veritable hero in the African states that were just emerging from colonialism.

In his determined dedication to nonviolence, Dr. King was caught in the crossfire between white and Negro extremists as racial tensions erupted in many of the Nation's cities during the summer of 1967.

His strong beliefs in civil rights and in nonviolence made him one of the leading opponents of American participation in the war in Vietnam. To him the war was unjust and it diverted vast sums that he believed would have been much better spent to alleviate the condition of the Negro poor in this country.

Inevitably, as a symbol of integration, he became the object of unrelenting attacks and vilification. His home was bombed. He was spat upon and mocked. He was struck and kicked. He was stabbed, almost fatally, by a deranged Negro woman. He was frequently thrown into jail.

Through it all he adhered to the creed of passive disobedience that infuriated segregationists.

ADULATION

The adulation that was heaped upon him eventually irritated even some Negroes in the civil rights movement who worked hard, but in relative obscurity. They pointed out — and Dr. King admitted — that he was a poor administrator. They noted that Dr. King's successes were built on the labors of many who had gone before him.

The Negro extremists he criticized were contemptuous of Dr. King. They dismissed his passion for nonviolence as another form of servility to white people.

At the root of his civil rights convictions was profound faith in the basic goodness of man and the great potential of American democracy.

STIRRED

Scores of millions of Americans — white as well as Negro — who sat before television sets in the summer of 1963 to watch the march of some 200,000 Negroes on Washington were deeply stirred when Dr. King, in the shadow of the Lincoln Memorial, said:

"Even though we face the difficulties of today and tomorrow, I still have a dream. I have a dream that one day this Nation will rise up and live out the true meaning of its creed: 'We hold these truths to be self-evident, that all men are created equal.'"

And all over the world, men were moved as they read his words on Dec. 10, 1964, when he became the third member of his race to receive the Nobel Peace prize.

"I refuse to accept the idea that man is mere flotsam and jetsam in the river of life which surrounds him," he said. "I refuse to accept the view that mankind is so tragically bound to the starless midnight of racism and war that the bright daybreak of peace and brotherhood can never become a reality."

Martin Luther King Jr. was born on Jan. 15, 1929, in Atlanta, Ga., on Auburn avenue. As a child his name was Michael Luther King and so was his father's. His father changed both their names legally to Martin Luther King in honor of the Protestant reformer.

PASTOR

Martin Luther King Sr. was pastor of the Ebenezer Baptist church at Jackson street and Auburn avenue.

Young Martin went to Atlanta's Morehouse college, a Negro institution. The president of Morehouse, Dr. B. E. Mays, took a special interest in Martin, who had decided, in his junior year, to be a clergyman.

He was ordained a minister in his father's church in 1947. It was in this church he was to say, some years later:

"America, you've strayed away. You've trampled over 19 million of your brethern. All men are created equal. Not some men, Not white men. All men. America, rise up and come home."

Before Dr. King had his own church he pursued his studies in the integrated Crozier Theological seminary, in Chester, Pa. He became the first Negro class president. He was named the outstanding student and won a fellowship to study for a doctorate. The young man enrolled at Boston College in 1951.

GRADUATE

While he was working on his doctorate he met Coretta Scott, a graduate at Antioch college, who was doing graduate work in music. They were married in 1953. They have two children, Yolanda

Denise, known as "Yoki," was born in 1955, and Martin Luther King 3d in 1957.

In 1954, Dr. King became pastor of the Dexter Avenue Baptist church in Montgomery, Ala. Five years later he and his family moved back to Atlanta, where he became a co-pastor, with his father, of the Ebenezer Baptist church.

As his fame increased, public interest in his beliefs led him to write books. It was while he was autographing one of these books, "Stride Toward Freedom," in a Harlem department store that he was stabbed by a Negro woman.

Dr. King's effectiveness was enhanced and given continuity by the fact that he had an organization behind him. Formed in 1960, with headquarters in Atlanta, it was called the Southern Christian Leadership Conference.

RABBLE

There was little of the rabblerouser in his oratory. He was not prone to extravagant gestures or loud perforation.

What Dr. King did have was an instinct for the right moment to make his moves. Some critics looked upon this as pure opportunism. Nevertheless it was this sense of timing that raised him in 1955, from a newly arrived minister in Montgomery, Ala., with his first church, to a figure of national prominence.

BOYCOTT

Negroes in that city had begun a boycott of buses to win the right to sit where they pleased instead of being forced to move to the rear.

It was Dr. King who dramatized the boycott with his decision to make it the testing ground of his belief in the civil disobedience teachings of Thoreau and Gandhi.

Dr. King was even more impressive during the "big push" in Birmingham, that began in April, 1963. With the minister in the limelight, Negroes there began a campaign of sit-ins at lunch counters, picketing and protest marches.

The entire world was stirred when the police turned dogs on the demonstrators. Dr. King was jailed for five days. Whiel h ewas in prison he issued the now famous 9000-word Letter from a Birmingham Jail that said:"

"I have almost reached the regrettable conclusion that the Negro's great stumbling block in the stride toward freedom is not the white citizens councilor or the Ku Klux Klanner, but the white moderate who is more devoted to order than to justice; who prefers a negative peace, which is the absence o tension, to a positive peace, which is the presence of justice."

Reactions Among Negro Leaders

New York

Major Negro organizations and Negro leaders lamented Dr. Martin Luther King's death last night but expressed hope that it would spur others to carry on in his spirit of nonviolence.

Roy Wilkins, executive director of the NAACP, said his organization was "shocked and deeply grieved."

"Dr. King was a symbol of the nonviolent civil rights protest movement. He was a man of peace, of dedication. of great courage. His senseless assassination solves nothing. It will not stay the civil rights movement: it will instead spur it to greater activity. It is to be hoped that this tragedy will help move the American people to prompt action to expunge racism from our national life. If such action is taken forthwith. the sacrifice of this great and good man will not have been in vain."

Richard Gordon Hatcher, the Negro mayor of Gary, Ind., termed the death of Dr. King "every man's loss. We are all the survivors of this great leader. With the insanely violent acts of one distorted man. we are each shocked. saddened beyond imagination and eternally diminished. I have lost a friend."

Sen. Edward Brooke (Rep.-Mass.), declared: "In our anguish and bitterness of this awful event. we must not lose sight of the meaning of this great man's life. The vindication of Dr. King's historic endeavors can only come through our own renewed dedication of the human goals of brotherly love and equal justice which he so nobly advanced."

Another call for restraint came from James Farmer. former national director of the Congress of Racial Equality. who said:

"Every racist in the country has killed Dr. King. Evil societies always destroy their consciences. The only fitting memorial to this martyred leader is a monumental commitment — now. not a day later — to eliminate racism. Dr. King hated bloodshed His own blood must not now trigger more bloodshed."

An angry reaction came in Washington, D.C. from Julius Hobson. a Negro who heads a militant but nonviolent civil rights group called ACT.

Hobson said: "The next black man who comes into the black community preaching non-violence should be violently dealt with by the black people who hear him The Martin Luther King concept of non-violence died with him."

As Dr. King's words grew more potent and he was invited to the White House by Presidents Kennedy and Johnson. some critics. — Negroes as well as white — noted that sometimes, despite all the publicity he attracted. he left campaigns unfinished or else failed to attain his goals.

Dr. King was aware of this, but he pointed out, in 1964, in St. Augustine, Fla., one o the toughest civil rights battlegrounds, that there were important intagibles.

"Even if we do not get all we should," he said, "movements such as this tend more and more to give a Negro the sense of self-respect that he needs. It tends to generate courage in Negroes outside the movement. It brings intangible results outside the community where it is carried out."

In 1965 Dr. King led a drive for Negro voter registration in Selma. Ala. Negroes were arrested by the hundreds, Dr. King was punched and kicked by a white man when, during this period of protest. he became the first Negro to register at a century-old hotel in Selma.

There was no false modesty in Dr. King's self-appraisal of his role in the civil rights movement.

"History," he said. "has thrust me into this position. It would be both immoral and a sign of ingratitude if I did not face my moral responsibility to do what I can in this struggle."

Daily Mail
4th July 1904

DR. THEODOR HERZL DEAD.

Founder of the Zionist Movement Was Born in Budapest in 1860.

VIENNA, July 3.—Dr. Theodor Herzl. founder of the Zionist movement and President of the Zionist Congress, is dead.

Theodor Herzl was born in Budapest May 2, 1860. When a boy he settled in Vienna, where he was educated for the law, although he afterward devoted his attention almost exclusively to literature and journalism. His early work was in no way related to the Jews. He acted as correspondent to the Neue Freie Press in Paris, and later become literary editor of that paper. He also became a writer for the Viennese stage.

It was in April, 1896, that his "Judenstaat" appeared. He never confessed to what particular incident his "Jewish State" was due, but the fact that he was moved by the Dreyfus affair is supposed to have had much to do with its production. Herzl in 1897 founded Die Welt of Vienna, and it was then that he planned the first Zionist Congress. He was elected President of the Congress, which position he held continuously till his death.

In 1902-3 Herzl negotiated. through Joseph Chamberlain. with the Egyptian Government for a charter for the settlement of the Jews in Al 'Arish. in the Sinaitic Peninsula, adjoining Southern Palestine, but the scheme failed. Last year he submitted proposals at St. Petersburg for the amelioration of the Jews' position in Russia.

DEATH OF "THE NEW MOSES".

VIENNA, Sunday, July 3.
Theodore Herzl died to-day at Edlach, near Reichenur, from inflammation of the lungs.—Reuter.

Dr. Herzl was born in Budapest in 1860. Until 1895 known only to a few as a clever journalist and author of several comedies, he suddenly became famous all the world over. He wrote " Der Judenstadt," in which he propounded a scheme for the reacquirement of Palestine for the Jews by the flotation of a limited liability company. The book caused a sensation, and stern and excited controversy raged round the proposal and its author.

The Zionist movement spread. and for long Herzl has been known as " the new Moses." He never admitted any doubt as to the success of his scheme. " I do not know when I shall die," he said, " but Zionism will never die."

New York Times
31st January 1948

MILLIONS ESTEEMED GANDHI AS A SAINT

Political Opinions About Him Differed, but His Enormous Influence Was Recognized

CAREER ALWAYS STORMY

Techniques of Fasting, Civil Disobedience Played Part in Work for Independence

Mohandas Karamchand Gandhi, Hindu reformer and nationalist leader, was looked upon as a saint by millions of his followers, who bestowed upon him the admiring appellation of "Mahatma," literally "the great-souled one."

As was perhaps inevitable in the case of one who was the center of violent controversies for more than half a century, there were others who had very different views about the Indian leader, even contending that he was no better than scheming demagogue. But, whatever view history may eventually take, there can be no contradiction of the statement that the emaciated little man in shawl and loin cloth made himself the living symbol of India in the minds of most Americans.

He was born on Oct. 2, 1869, at Porbandar, on the Kathiawar peninsula of India, and came of a Bania family with official traditions. His father had been Prime Minister of the little native state. He was officially betrothed three times before he was old enough to realize it. His first two fiancees died; the third engagement, resulting in a marriage that lasted more than sixty years, came when he was only 7. The marriage took place when he was 13.

"I can see no moral argument in support of such a preposterous early marriage as mine," he wrote in his memoirs.

At the age of 19 Gandhi went to London, where he studied at University College and was called to the bar by the Inner Temple. He had a difficult time in London. Too proud to struggle against the snubs not only of white people but also of Brahmins, he retired to cheap lodgings, where he cooked his own vegetarian meals and lived for next to nothing.

Worked in South Africa

Returning to India Gandhi practiced law for a short time in the Bombay High Court, but in 1893 he was called to South Africa on professional business. There he became engrossed in a long struggle for the liberties of Indians who had migrated to that country, which was his principal occupation for more than twenty years. Both in Natal and the Transvaal race feeling against the Indian settlers was strong and discriminations were many.

When, in 1896, after a brief visit to India, Gandhi returned to Durban, he was attacked and badly beaten for his agitations. The South Africans had become incensed at a pamphlet he wrote in India on the conditions of the Indians in South Africa. It was then that his conception of passive non-violent resistance developed. He relinquished his large income as a lawyer and founded a colony, the Tolstoy Farm, near Durban. It was along the lines of the Russian philosopher's estate at Yasnaya Polyana.

He was often imprisoned and more often subjected to indignities, but this neither checked his energies nor deterred him from rendering service of marked loyalty to the British Government.

In 1914, soon after a commission had removed some of the worst sources of injustice to the Indians living in South Africa, Gandhi returned to his native land and threw himself into support of the home rule movement. By 1918 he was busy organizing his Satyagraha (literally "insistence upon truth") movement, which he defined as follows:

"Satyagraha differs from passive resistance as the North Pole from the South. The latter has been conceived as a weapon for the weak and does not exclude the use of physical force or violence for the purpose of gaining one's end, whereas the former has been conceived as a weapon of the strongest and excludes the use of violence in any shape or form."

In the following year the British Government published the Rowlatt Acts, giving the government emergency powers for dealing with revolutionary crimes and conspiracies. Gandhi declared them to be an insult and denounced the bills as "instruments of oppression." His Satyagraha campaign spread with great rapidity throughout India.

Non-Cooperation Movement

Finally, in June, 1920, he formed his celebrated non-violent, non-cooperation movement. The main points of his campaign were the boycott of Government service, of the new Legislatures and of the courts of law; the surrender of all public offices and the withdrawal of children from Government schools. To this was subsequently added the militant boycott of foreign goods, the fighting of the liquor and opium trade, and the furtherance of Hindu-Moslem friendship.

Gandhi adopted the spinning wheel as a sort of symbol of economic independence. He advocated the home manufacture of khaddar, or homespun cloth, to replace the imported goods from the cotton mills of Lancashire. Hartals, or local strikes, were called and there were many burnings of stacks of foreign-made cloth. The general boycott was accompanied by rioting, looting of shops and unrest throughout India.

Partly by his eloquence, partly by his reputation as an ascetic, Gandhi had won enormous prestige in India by this time. The Indian Congress party delegated its full authority to him and empowered him to appoint his own successor. But the non-cooperation movement continued to be accompanied by outbursts of violence; many of them of a racial character.

In March, 1922, Gandhi was arrested and placed on trial on a charge of conspiring to spread disaffection with a view to overthrowing the Government. He pleaded guilty and took full blame.

His Sentence Remitted

He was condemned to six years' imprisonment but was released in January, 1924, after he had undergone an operation for appendicitis, and the rest of his sentence was unconditionally remitted. In 1925 he announced that he would retire from the world for a year. There followed a long period in which he was the apostle of the spinning wheel, and agitated with much energy for the uplifting of the "untouchables," the Hindu pariah caste.

Early in 1930 Gandhi proclaimed his intention of refusing to pay all Government taxes, and particularly the salt tax. On April 5 he set out with a group of followers to march from Ahmedabad to the sea, where they collected salt water in earthen jars, then obtained salt by evaporation of the water. On May 5 Gandhi was arrested at Surat and spirited away to Poona, charged with having been the leader of plans to seize the Government salt depots.

He was still languishing in prison when the first Indian Round-Table Conference began to gather in London. On Jan. 26, 1931, Gandhi was released by order of the Viceroy, Lord Irwin, who later became Viscount Halifax.

There was much criticism in England of Lord Irwin's action. However, the following month Lord Irwin invited Gandhi to a series of conversations at Delhi which resulted in the Delhi Pact of March, 1931, by which the Viceroy lifted the ban on the Indian Congress party and Gandhi in turn called off the civil disobedience campaign.

As the representative of the Congress party, Gandhi went to London to participate in the round-table conference. After much hesitation he undertook the mission, traveling steerage, clad in his shawl and loin cloth, and taking with him two goats. He was a guest, loin cloth and all, of King George V and Queen Mary in London, lunched with Lady Astor, and waited in vain for Mayor James J. Walker of New York to keep a date with him.

Lived in London Slums

In London, he lived in the slums, familiarizing himself with the condition of the poor. He also visited the · Lancashire mill districts, where he was both cheered and booed.

On his way home he ·stopped in Rome and had a conversation with Premier Mussolini, but because of his scanty costume he was not permitted an interview with the Pope.

He lost no time in instituting a new civil disobedience campaign on Jan. 4, 1932, and was promptly sent back to his old Yerovda Jail. From there he sent out the announcement that he would starve himself to death unless the Government reversed its decision to grant separate political representation for seventy years to the Untouchables.

His fast ended after six days, however, when he was told that the British Government had accepted "with great satisfaction" the principal terms of the settlement between the higher caste Indians and the Untouchables. But in April, 1933, he announced that he would fast for twenty-one days to call attention to the situation of the Untouchables. Despite almost unanimous medical opinion that he could not stand such a strain, he refrained from food from May 8 to May 29, and soon regained his health.

Released from jail at the time he began his fast, Gandhi was re-arrested with his wife and thirty followers on July 31, 1933, when he began a new "individual civil disobedience" campaign. He was sentenced to a year in jail as an ordinary political prisoner without the privileges that had formerly been accorded him. A week later he began a new fast to obtain privileges that would enable him to carry on his fight in behalf of the Untouchables.

In April, 1934, Gandhi instructed his followers to abandon civil disobedience and campaign for the forthcoming elections for the Legislative Assembly. Meanwhile the British had been preparing a new Constitution for India, which Gandhi had announced he would give a trial. On April 26 of that year he was attacked and narrowly escaped a beating by a mob of Indians who resented his attitude on the question of the Untouchables.

When the new Constitution was promulgated the following August, Gandhi was bitterly disappointed in it. Although he had been succeeded as leader of the Congress party by Jawaharlal Nehru, he remained active behind the scenes, helping to direct the opposition to the new form of government. He drafted certain conditions regarding the carrying out of the provisions of the India act, and his tactics hamstrung the workings of the new act until July, 1937, when a compromise was reached.

In the spring of 1939, five years after his ostensible retirement from politics, Gandhi openly returned to activity because the Congress party had elected a president whom he did not want, Subhas Chandra Bose. He began the sixth of his famous fasts to force certain reforms from the Thakore Saheb, autocratic ruler of the tiny principality of Rajkot, in northwestern India.

Apprehension swept India. Eight of the eleven autonomous Indian Governments established in the Provinces resigned and hamstrung the Government of India Act, which had been in operation only two years. Markets closed in Bombay. Trade was at a standstill. The mounting public unrest forced the British Viceroy, the Marquess of Linlithgow, to cut short a tour of northern India and return to the capital at New Delhi to protect the interests of the Crown. He informed Mr. Gandhi that the ruler of Rajkot would be forced to grant the reforms.

Gandhi broke his four-day fast with a glass of orange juice, and his millions of followers rejoiced.

The Congress party promptly committed its new president, Mr. Bose, to the guidance of Gandhi, and Mr. Bose resigned. Gandhi's follower, Dr. Rajendra Prasad, was elected to succeed him.

When the second World War broke out, the Viceroy declared India to be a participant in it without consulting the Congress party leaders. Gandhi, although a strong critic of Nazi Germany, demanded the complete independence of India as the price of Indian cooperation.

There followed three months of conversations between Gandhi and the Viceroy. In the last war, Gandhi pointed out, Britain had promised India "self-governing institutions" after victory. He wanted the promise kept by freeing India at once; Indians could not fight for democracy while it was denied to them. Lord Linlithgow answered for the Pritish Government that any constitutional changes must be deferred until after the war and then Dominion status would be gradually extended to India. He said Gandhi must first solve the everlasting problem of protecting the Moslem and other minorities before they were turned over to the Hindus, who outnumbered them three to one—all creeds and sects hating one another. Gandhi insisted that freedom came first; the minorities would then become a domestic problem of no concern to Britain. There the conversations became deadlocked.

Hated Nazis More

For almost three years during the early part of the war Gandhi, in complete control of the Congress party, pursued a cautious policy of enlarging his support among the Hindu millions, and constantly seeking independence from the British.

In March, 1940, the Congress party voted Gandhi full power to direct its future policy and conduct its program. Under his control, the Working Committee, which is the executive body of the party, made a tentative offer of military aid to Britain in June, but withdrew it two months later when Gandhi declared he was convinced Britain had no intention of recognizing Indian independence.

In October, on his seventy-first birthday, he announced that he had no ill-will toward Britain and that there would be no civil disobedience campaign. Two weeks later he announced that there would be a campaign, but in order not to embarrass the British war effort it would be conducted by a few individuals in a symbolic rather than a massive way.

He instructed two members of the Congress party to break the Defense of India Act prohibiting speeches directed to impede the conduct of the war. One of them was his personal servant. The other was the former president of the Congress party, Pandit Nehru. They made speeches urging disregard of the laws and courts, non-cooperation with munitions manufacture, non-contribution of funds and non enlistment. They were jailed forthwith. Pandit Nehru was sentenced to four years.

Thereupon the Working Committee of the party ordered 1,500 individuals to invite arrest in the same way. The jails filled. Gandhi suspended his weekly paper, Harijan, when he was forbidden to publish accounts of the speeches and the arrests. He now kept out of jail, which he had never avoided previously, in order to direct the fight. In August, 1941, Gandhi said that the purpose was "not to force Britain but to convert her."

With the entry of Japan into the war in December, 1941, Gandhi, on Dec. 30, asked the Working Committee of the party to relieve him from leadership. He explained that sympathy for the Axis-overrun countries, rather than for Britain, dictated his second retirement. But he continued to run the Congress party from behind the scenes.

With the threat of Japanese invasion growing daily, Britain made a great effort in the spring of 1942 to unite the Indian factions behind a common policy of defense. Prime Minister Churchill dispatched Sir Stafford Cripps on a special mission to India to try to compose the difficulties of the parties there. He officially offered complete independence and equality for India in the British Commonwealth of Nations as soon as the war was won, with the right of ultimate secession.

Although this was the largest voluntary disbursement of power that Great Britain had ever offered, the warring groups within India refused it. The Moslems and other minority groups rejected it because of their fear of their status under a Hindu majority. The Congress party rejected it because it was not immediate. Gandhi, in April, introduced a resolution closing the door to further negotiations with the British on the issue.

In May, Gandhi called upon the British to quit India.

Terms for an Ally

Shortly thereafter he laid a resolution before the Working Committee of the Congress party giving Britain a last choice: India would be her war ally if immediate freedom was granted; otherwise "full powers to lead a civil disobedience movement against Britain would

Continued

be given to Mohandas K. Gandhi." The Working Committee adopted it unhesitatingly, and only ratification by the All-India Congress party's general assembly was required to launch "open non-violent rebellion."

Campaigning in behalf of the move, Gandhi said that he would not flinch at calling a general strike. He said that there was increasing ill will against Britain in India, and growing satisfaction at Japanese victories. He warned that India might welcome a Japanese invasion, even as many of the people of Burma had done.

In New Delhi, the British directed Government of India made public a copy of a memorandum seized in a raid on the headquarters of the Congress party, which purported to show that Gandhi had proposed conversations with the Japanese four months earlier. The Government charged that he and his followers were appeasers.

On Aug. 9 the Congress party assembly, in plenary session, voted to throw his strength behind the "non-violent rebellion" and the Government announced its intention "to use force as the necessities of the situation might require." Gandhi and some fifty of his followers were arrested as widespread rioting began. As he was taken to jail he left the slogan: "Either we get freedom or we die."

He was imprisoned in the Victorian palace of the Aga Khan in Poona, but the Government's action was not followed by as widespread unrest as had been predicted by some observers. There were demonstrations and acts of sabotage, but the Government's policy was successful in keeping the heavy war industries running.

Gandhi wrote the Viceroy, disclaiming the responsibility of the Congress party for the acts of violence that were occurring, and threatening to begin a new fast, his ninth, unless he was liberated. The Government, which published the correspondence, refused to yield, terming the hunger strike "political blackmail, for which there can be no moral justification."

Gandhi began his fast on Feb. 10, 1943. He announced that it **would not be a "fast unto death,"** but that he would subsist for twenty-one days on a diet of citrus juice mixed with water. There were some disturbances among the Hindu community, but on the fifth day after the fast began THE NEW YORK TIMES correspondent in New Delhi wrote that "it was evident that his move would probably misfire."

Fears were felt for the life of the fasting man for several days, but he astonished the doctors by surviving, even though he was too weak to lift a glass of orange juice. American correspondents in India, pointing out that this was the first time he had failed to win at least a partial victory by a fast, said that his failure seemed to have disappointed and discouraged him.

Disorders marked the first anniversary of Gandhi's arrest, and agitation for his release was continued both in India and abroad. On Feb. 17, 1944, however, Viscount Wavell, who had assumed the position as Viceroy, declared that he and his associates would be held until they showed "some signs" of cooperation.

Mrs. Gandhi, his frail companion through a married life of more than sixty years, died late in February. She had faithfully followed her husband to jail more than once. He was released on parole for a week, and, sitting in the shade of a tamarind tree, he watched the cremation of her remains. Then he went back to prison.

On May 6, after twenty-one months as a prisoner, Gandhi was released by the Government because of his failing health. The official doctors had considered giving him blood transfusions but Gandhi was said to have frowned on the idea, maintaining that the essential life stream of one human, should not be used to extend the life of another. Viscount Wavell was praised for his decision to release the Hindu leader.

In a proposal designed to break the political deadlock over India's independence Gandhi in September, 1944, agreed to discuss with Mohammed Ali Jinnah, head of the Moslem League, the Moslem's long-standing demand that India be partitioned into separate Hindu and Moslem states. It was this basic plan that was finally agreed upon in 1947 when India won her long-sought independence, but Gandhi's conversations with Mr. Jinnah were fruitless.

Gandhi had some time previously made an offer to withdraw his civil disobedience campaign for the duration of the war. By this time the Japanese drive toward India had been turned back and to most observers the cooperation pledge from the Hindu leader seemed a little gratuitous. Nevertheless, Gandhi was hailed for his conciliatory attitude.

A White Paper issued in London in June, 1945, made a new attempt to break the deadlock in India, and Gandhi announced that he would ask Congress party leaders to accept it. The British offer, looking toward Dominion status for India, proposed setting up of a Viceroy's Council to be composed "in equal portions of Moslems and caste Hindus."

Eight months later Prime Minister Clement Attlee offered to India the right to full independence, and a Cabinet mission was dispatched to work out the procedure. Gandhi appealed to his people to be patient and to give the mission a chance, but warned against "fake promises." When the mission had drafted its plan for Indian self-government, Gandhi at first said he regarded it as "seed to convert this land of sorrow into one without sorrow and suffering."

By June, although the proposal had not been altered to any degree, Gandhi, for reasons that remained obscure, developed "vague misgivings," but the Congress party, which he once controlled, accepted the plan, as had the Moslem League.

In the ensuing months it became clear that other political leaders had taken the stage in India, but Gandhi remained the national Government's core and he told a NEW YORK TIMES correspondent that he intended to remain in politics for many years. Asked if he still expected to live to the age of 125, Gandhi, on the eve of his seventy-seventh birthday replied "Yes," in order to serve his people.

In early 1947 the British plan was to quit India by June, 1948, earlier if the Hindu and Moslem communities would compose their differences. Gandhi, in an open break with the Congress party, reversed himself and balked at a Hindu-Moslem partition and the formation of Pakistan as a separate state for the Moslem majority regions of India.

The Gandhi viewpoint was that whether it caused chaos or not, the British must leave India on the promised date and let India work out its own fate. By this time the British were convinced that partition was the only solution that would be accepted and finally Gandhi reluctantly went along, declaring: "Partition is bad. But whatever is past is past. We have only to look to the future."

When, on Aug. 15, 1947, India achieved her independence, Viscount Mountbatten, Viceroy of India, hailed Gandhi as the "architect of India's freedom through non-violence."

Gandhi did not participate in the independence observances held throughout India. At the moment of victory he sat on a wooden cot in a Calcutta hut, scorning the result of his decades of labor and fast. He announced his intention of living with the Hindu minority in Pakistan, the predominantly Moslem state created by partition.

Riots swept across much of India, with scores killed and injured in communal clashes. Gandhi started in Calcutta his first fast in independent India. It would end, he said, only when Calcutta "returned to sanity."

After he had been assured that there would be no more rioting in Calcutta, Gandhi broke his fast. He was credited with having restored peace to India's largest city. Crowds of Moslems and Hindus made their way to his camp and surrendered guns, swords and ammunition they had used in the riots.

"If the peace is broken again I will come back and undertake a fast unto death and die if necessary," he said.

He went to New Delhi, where he continued his efforts to end the communal strife, which had broken out more violently than ever along the Punjab border and in Delhi itself. Daily he exhorted all non-Moslems to accept Moslem neighbors as friends and brothers.

However, on Sept. 16 he told the Hindu Youth Organization that "if the Dominion of Pakistan persists in wrongdoing there is bound to be war between India and Pakistan."

On Oct. 2 he celebrated his seventy-ninth birthday (Hindus are counted a year old at birth), which had been declared a national holiday by the Government of India.

He started a new fast on Jan. 12, 1948, declaring that he would continue until greater unity between Hindu, Sikh and Moslem communities was achieved. This fast was ended after five days, when Hindus and Moslems in Delhi agreed to live in peace.

The Standard
5th June 1882

On Friday night there passed away from the bodily gaze of men one of the most interesting figures of modern times ; one who will, of himself, for ever suffice to redeem the nineteenth century from the reproach so often brought against it by its own children, of being painfully practical and prosaic. At the ripe age of seventy-four, yet older even than his accumulated years by virtue of his long and laborious achievements and his corporal sufferings, Giuseppe Garibaldi has quitted the scene of his famous exploits. We must turn to the pages of poetic romance, or ransack the chapters of remote and semi-mythical history, if we are to find a parallel to this heroic and romantic personage. Indeed, it may be doubted if even the fact that he was born and acted in an age of rigid science, will prevent his memory from becoming associated with supernatural and incredible recitals ; if even the lofty and surprising character of his actual performances will satisfy the cravings and affection of the popular imagination ; and if, despite his being a contemporary of railways, telegraphs, and an all scrutinising Press, he will not stand out from the century to which he belonged, in the eyes of posterity, as large and ambiguous as an Alfred, an Arminius, or a Charlemagne. His very weaknesses will help to magnify his name, since they were the weaknesses which many share and all forgive. It was in subjection to the promptings of sentiment that sense ever and anon forsook him ; and he was brought nearer to humanity by his generous failings, at the same time that he seemed lifted above it, but above it only for its gaze and admiration, by his unquenchable faith, his nervous enthusiasm, and his prompt intrepidity. The world has seen greater and more important enterprises carried to a happy issue than the unification of Italy ; but never has it witnessed an enterprise that excited such wide-spread sympathy, that was executed so dramatically, or whose success so completely responded to the aspirations of mankind. There are four men whose names will be recalled whenever this striking page of history is read—Victor Emmanuel, Cavour, Mazzini, and Garibaldi. It would be easy to underrate the share which was borne by Victor Emmanuel in the liberation and unification of his country ; but neither by character nor by intelligence can he compete with the remaining three. These we will not compare. It is enough to observe that Garibaldi alone combined in himself patriotic sentiment with martial action ; and hence, whether justly or unjustly, the hero of Marsala and Mentana will engage the imaginations of men more forcibly, and for a longer cycle than either the dreaming mystic or the practical statesman.

" Call no man happy till he dies ; " and t is not easy, in the case of most men, to assign them their position in the eyes of posterity till after the grave has closed over them for many years. But Garibaldi's fame is certain, for it reposes on enduring elements in human nature. He has captivated the popular imagination. His name will glitter in the pages of history, and it will resound in the note of song. He was a great man, if the word great is to preserve any solid meaning. He was not a great thinker ; as an author or a legislator he was, perhaps, the very reverse. But he felt greatly, and acted greatly, and it was his good fortune to feel greatly and act greatly in a drama which fascinated the hearts of his contemporaries. He was, moreover, essentially magnanimous. Full of prejudice, suffused with passion, he was never appealed to on his generous side without responding generously. It cannot be said of him that he was a great General, though it is abundantly evident that he possessed tactical and even strategic talents of no mean order. But his real genius was the genius of enthusiasm combined with daring. He was, above all things, a " doer," and he tried at least to transform into reality his most extravagant dreams. His fierce denunciations of the Papacy, carried to a pitch of extravagance which seemed to involve in condemnation all theologies and all priesthoods alike, may be pardoned on the plea that the Italy of his youth and manhood suffered incredible ignominy, and was denied the very right of existence, in deference to certain supposed theocratic necessities. But it is not to be denied that, apart from his action for the political freedom and unity of Italy, his influence was nearly always mischievous. He was too easily duped by flatterers, enthusiasts, and professors of cosmopolitan philanthropy. It was nothing but the reception accorded to him at Bordeaux, of which we have spoken, together with his growing physical infirmities, saved us from the spectacle of Garibaldi fighting behind the barricades of the Paris Commune. There was no cause he was not capable of embracing, provided it talked big of liberty ; no creed he was not in danger of adopting, so long as it denounced priests. He had the good fortune to be born an Italian, at a period when the long yearnings of Italy for unity were to take practical shape and definite aim. In ordinary times he might well have passed through life as little else than a despised fanatic. He was not a Cæsar, a Dante, or a Savonarola. But he had a great soul, which was promptly fired by a great opportunity. His failings will soon be forgotten. His name will be an enduring one, but it will belong, partly to History, partly to Romance.

Mass. Mercury
12th March 1790

" The house being informed of the decease of BENJAMIN FRANKLIN, a citizen whose native genius was not more an ornament to human nature, than his various exertions of it have been precious to science, to freedom, and to his country, do resolve, as a mark of the veneration due to his memory, That the members wear the customary badge of mourning for one month."

The Times
19th November 1858
DEATH OF ROBERT OWEN.

The public will hear without surprise of the death, at an advanced age, of Robert Dale Owen, the founder of that system of political ethics called " socialism," and which in later years assumed the name of its originator in this country, and was known as " Owenism." The news was communicated in a letter from the eldest son of the deceased, the Hon. Robert Dale Owen, resident Minister from the United States to the Court of Naples, who happened to be on a visit to his father at the time of the latter's decease.

" Newtown, Montgomeryshire, Nov. 17.

"My dear Sir,—It is all over. My dear father passed away this morning at a quarter before 7, and passed away as gently and quietly as if he had been falling asleep. There was not the least struggle, not a contraction of a limb or a muscle, not an expression of pain on his face. His breathing gradually became slower and slower, until at last it ceased so imperceptibly that even as I held his hand I could scarcely tell the moment when he no longer breathed. His last words, distinctly pronounced about 26 minutes before his death, were ' Relief has come.' About half-an-hour before, he said ' Very easy and comfortable.' "

Robert Dale Owen married, in 1797, Miss Dale, the daughter of a much respected and influential gentleman in Glasgow, and the superintendent of a large number of Dissenting congregations. He was then about 26 years of age, and about this time became part proprietor and sole manager of the " New Lanark Twist Company," the management of whose mills, upon his own peculiar principles, soon spread his name far and wide. From 1810 to 1815 he published his " Essays on the Formation of Character," which, with his practical exemplification of the text, introduced him to such men as Mr. Wilberforce, Mr. Zachary Macaulay, Thomas Clarkson, the first Sir Robert Peel, Sir Thomas Bernard, and his particular friend Dr. Barrington, Bishop of Durham, and also the Archbishop of Canterbury, and the Bishop of London of that day. About this time, too, he formed friendships with Mr. James Mill, Sir James Macintosh, Mr. Malthus, Colonel Torrens, Mr. Ricardo, Francis Place, and Lord Brougham. As he says himself, " From those political economists, often in animated discussions, I always differed, but our discussions were maintained to the last with great good feeling and a cordial friendship. They were liberal men of their time, friends to the national education of the poor."

Mr. Owen was now fairly launched before the world as a social reformer. In 1817 he addressed memorials to the Sovereigns assembled at the Congress of Aix-la-Chapelle, confiding their presentation to Lord Castlereagh, and became a notoriety. Among his opposing friends he farther mentions the late Joseph Hume, Jeremy Bentham, Joseph Lancaster, Sir Francis Burdett, Mr. Cobbett, and many other of the leading men of the time, with whom he was in constant intimacy. He founded an infant-school at New Lanark, and among other notable persons who visited it was the late Emperor Nicholas of Russia, then the Grand Duke. At that time there was a great commotion about the doctrines of Malthus, and Mr. Owen relates that, "In a two hours' conversation with the Grand Duke, before he left me, he said, ' As your country is over-peopled I will take you, and two millions of population with you, all in similar manufacturing communities.'" This was in reference to New Lanark. Here was an offer ! The greatest and most arbitrary despotic monarch in the world offering to test " liberty, equality, fraternity," in his own dominion and at his own expense. Mr. Owen, however, declined, as he thought his hands were full enough then. He subsequently visited the various European capitals, and America, where he was looked upon with considerable favour. For many years the public have been well acquainted with his career. As his mind began to fail before his advancing years he accepted the doctrine of spirit rapping, and has published his experience of that doctrine. It may not, perhaps, be generally known that the celebrated Robert Fulton, the mechanical engineer, was once in partnership with Mr. Owen for working an invention for raising boats from low to high levels on canals without the aid of locks.

The last public appearance of Mr. Owen was at the late Social Science Congress at Liverpool. He stood between Lord Brougham and Lord John Russell. He spoke for a few minutes, when, his strength failing him, he was removed to the Victoria Hotel, where he remained for several days. He was accompanied by Mr. Rigby, who has acted as his secretary and man of business for the last 30 years. While at the hotel he expressed a determination to see his native town, and started next day, posting from Shrewsbury, as there was no rail. He only remained a few hours, returned to Liverpool, and after transacting some business went back again to Newtown. He told Mr. Rigby on the way, " I shall leave my bones where I got them." He died at the Bear's Head Hotel, and what is strange, there is not a single inhabitant now alive in the place who was there when he left it, a child of 10 years of age. He was a man of ample means, and disposed of a large fortune in promulgating his principles. His wife has been dead some years, most of his family, which consisted of eight sons and daughters, are alive.

Guardian Extra
10ᵗʰ September 1970

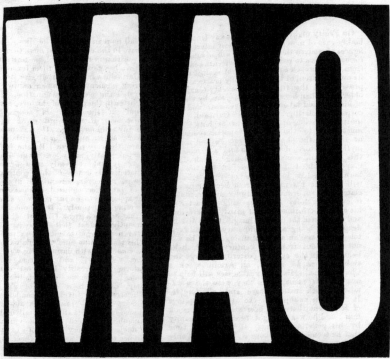

MAO

Even the disorders which Mao deliberately stirred up may turn out to be beneficial

MAO TSE-TUNG was born when the Manchu dynasty still ruled imperial China; grew up in the furnace of Chinese nationalism and anti-imperialist struggle; led his country to make a Communist revolution and saw it become, before his death, an industrialised nuclear Power. Thus his life spanned four generations of change—fast even by twentieth century standards—and it was above all Mao's appreciation of the dialectical advance of history which drove him forward on his confident revolutionary path.

In his later years, as he launched China into the Great Leap Forward and the Cultural Revolution, he left many of his colleagues behind, and he died with China's transition to a fully Socialist society still, in his view, far from complete.

Mao Tse-tung was born on December 26, 1893, in a small village about 40 miles from Changsha, the capital of Hunan. He was the eldest son of a fairly well-off farmer whose two other sons and a daughter gave their lives for the Chinese Communist revolution.

From a village tutor Mao obtained a thorough grounding in the Chinese classics—even though he recalled that, like many other Chinese boys, he much preferred such standard "thrillers" as All Men are Brothers, in which the heroes were rebels.

Later Mao attended a modern school in a neighbouring town where he came into contact with a modern curriculum. Still later he read the writings of the current Chinese political reformers, and embraced their teaching with enthusiasm. But his sense of social injustice had already been aroused over the brutal fate of the starving mobs who were roaming the country, demanding rice from the landlords. Since 1897 Hunan in general and Changsha in particular had been a seething centre of

reformist and radical ideas. These were movements that led up to the 1911 revolution, and Mao was caught in the midst of them.

After the revolution Mao concluded the profession he was best suited for was teaching. Through teaching, he could make China morally, intellectually, and physically fit to survive. So he entered the First Teachers' Training College in 1913, where he remained for five years.

At the age of 25 in 1918, on the completion of his formal education, Mao became an assistant in the library of Peking University under a director who was one of China's foremost Socialist intellectuals; he also joined various radical societies of intellectuals. His Social Darwinian persuasion was being tinted with socialism—from anarchism to Marxism. Thus prepared, when the May 4 Movement started its nationwide protest against the decision at Versailles and the compliance of the Peking Government to concede former German possessions in China to Japan, Mao threw himself into the agitation by giving lectures on Marxism, by editing the radical paper the Hsiang River Review, and by organising strikes and boycotts against Japanese goods.

who became his own god

At the same time his advocacy of provincial self-government led him to a direct clash with the warlords controlling Hunan. Early in 1920 it was provincial politics which caused him to pay another visit to Peking where he was introduced to recent translations of Socialist literature, including the Communist Manifesto. That summer he organised the first Hunan Communist group in his home village. A year later he represented Hunan at the inaugural congress of the Chinese Communist Party in Shanghai.

When the Hunan branch of the party was created, Mao was elected its first secretary.

He moved to Shanghai in 1923 when it and Canton were the two cities where the Russian-instigated alliance between the Nationalist and Communist parties was busily being arranged. Mao was given the task of co-ordinating the policies of the two components of the alliance by working in the organisation departments of both. It was an exhausting and politically taxing task. Before long Mao went back to Hunan to convalesce for six months.

These six months, February to July 1925, witnessed one of the greatest anti-imperialist movement in urban China, and yet Mao "sat it out." Fatefully, it was also during these six months that he discovered the revolutionary zeal of the peasants in his province and began to organise associations for them.

Mao resumed his training of the peasant movement organisers in May. The increasing importance ascribed to the peasant movement by the Communist Party led to the creation of the peasant department

at the party's centre and Mao was appointed to head it. It was in that capacity that he went back to Hunan to investigate the peasant movement there, and made his famous report of 1927. He was elected to the chairmanship of the All China Peasant Union at the end of the fifth congress of the party.

Meanwhile Chiang Kai-shek ignited the campaign which split the two-party alliance: the peaceful competition for revolutionary leadership deteriorated into a civil war. Mao, a member of the newly instituted Politburo of the Communist Party, was given charge of the Autumn Harvest Uprising in Hunan and Kiangsi, an arena familiar to him. He failed. For this he lost his seat in the Politburo and nearly his life. But from the ashes of defeat, many small guerrilla areas sprang up in Central China. One of these was situated at Chingkangshan, a mountain stronghold, between Hunan and Kiangsi. It was led by Mao.

In April 1928, Mao's soviet was strengthened by the arrival of Chu Teh and his troops; still later the rebellion of a government commander, P'eng Teh-huai, helped Mao and Chu to enlarge the area under their control. In the vicissitudes of the early 1930s, the Communist movement in China developed separately among the intellectuals and workers in the cities and among the peasants in the countryside.

To rectify this tendency, the party elbowed Mao out of military power in August, 1932, and out of the party and soviet power in January, 1934. However, his removal from power also freed him from all responsibility for the colossal defeats of 1933 and 1934, when all the soviets in Central China were overrun by Chiang's troops and the Communists were forced to go on the Long March. The urban party leadership, which had been supported and guided by Russia collapsed, and into the vacuum stepped Mao Tse-tung. At the historic Tsunyi Conference in January 1935, he was elected to the chairmanship of the Politburo.

The genius of Mao consisted in his persuading the Communist Party to follow from then on a strategy based entirely on the realities of China, with little reference to the experience of communism in Russia. After the outbreak of the Sino-Japanese war in 1937, the necessities of partisan warfare conducted behind Japanese lines made the Communists adopt a life style indistinguishable from the peasants. Their manner of work, writing and even speech had to be de-Russified and re-Sinicised through their living among and learning from the peasant. "You must be a pupil of the masses before you can be their teacher," Mao exhorted his comrades.

The "rectification" campaign launched by Mao in 1942-3 from the communist capital of Yenan in north-west China gave permanent form to the new "mass line." It

also served to puncture the political ambitions of the pro-Soviet leadership and ensure that Mao was unchallenged at the Seventh Party Congress in April, 1945, when he delivered his report "On Coalition Government." The elevation of Mao (with his own approval) as the party's "great leader" dates from this time, as do his claims to theoretical originality.

Though never prepared to submerge the identity of his party, Mao showed more willingness than Chiang Kai-shek to form a post-war coalition government. Already displaying a degree of flexibility in foreign policy which would bear fruit in the 1970s, Mao even sought American aid in the final months of war against Japan, and offered unsuccessfully to visit Washington for talks with President Roosevelt.

But American mediation after the defeat of Japan was fatally flawed by its preference for Chiang. While some of his colleagues wavered, by mid-1946 Mao was convinced not only that a civil war was inevitable—but that his side would win it. His army of one million was outnumbered five to one, but only on paper, for millions more peasants served in the militia or behind the lines, while Chiang's despotic and corrupt regime had to resort to the press gang to keep its inefficient armies up to strength.

On October 1, 1949, Mao proclaimed the new People's Republic of China from the rostrum in Peking's Tienanmen Square. China had "stood up," he declared, and a glorious future lay ahead. It is unlikely that Mao himself had any idea just how arduous and conflict-prone the task of building socialism would prove to be.

Mao also proclaimed China's intention of "leaning to one side"—the side of the Soviet Union. Though Stalin had remained lukewarm during the civil war, the general configuration of the global cold war left Mao with little choice. And in spite of obvious difficulties—Mao later recalled that he had to struggle for two months with Stalin to secure the Sino-Soviet Treaty of February 1950—the Chinese still regarded Moscow as leader of the socialist camp.

Mao announced that China would

"learn from the Soviet Union," but with the private reservation that it would learn from their "negative" as well as "positive" experiences. Hard pressed by intervention in the Korean War, which Mao did not choose but could not evade, Peking became more dependent on Moscow for military aid and for economic assistance to launch the First Five Year Plan (1953-57).

Yet as soon as China again had room to manoeuvre, under Mao it resumed the search for a Chinese road to socialism at home and

continued

for independence and equality abroad. This course led directly to the Great Leap Forward and was bound to cause conflict with the Russians who, even under Stalin's successors, could not tolerate an independent and equal China.

Unpublished speeches and writings by Mao (which only became available in Red Guard editions during the Cultural Revolution) make it clear that from 1955 onwards Mao actively began to chart a new course for China. In economic policy, he shifted the balance away from Soviet-style emphasis upon heavy industry towards the countryside, and softened the rigid requirements of the plan. Economic development, as explained by Mao in his essay On the Ten Great Relationships (April 1956), was not a matter of priorities but of successfully resolving the dynamic contradictions between the various departments and society.

Against his colleagues, Mao urged a speed-up of the agricultural cooperative movement, which grew into the People's Communes in 1958. Advancing the level of social organisation in the countryside (the "relations of production") took precedence over developing rural mechanisation (the "productive forces").

Not only in agriculture but in society at large Mao had more confidence than some other colleagues in the enthusiasm of the masses for socialism. Politics was the determinant of economics; not the other way around. But the corollary to this view was Mao's conviction—strengthened by developments in the Soviet Union—that the "class struggle" continued even after the revolution and that a small minority of people could pose such a serious threat that the future of socialism itself might be in doubt. Another element in Mao's complex vision in the late 1950s was his determination to "catch up and overtake" the advanced Western powers (including the Soviet Union), which included setting his sights on the development of the Chinese nuclear bomb.

Mao's attempt to advance on all fronts in the Great Leap Forward was a partial failure, and he faced a major challenge to his authority from the Minister of Defence, Peng Teh-huai, at the Lushan Conference in August, 1959. This was surmounted at the price of weakening party unity, and Peng was replaced by Lin Piao. Mao had already resigned from the chairmanship of the People's Republic where he was succeeded by Liu Shao-chi, but remained chairman of the party.

While more cautious economic policies were pursued, Mao turned his attention to foreign policy, again taking a sharper line than his colleagues towards the Soviet Union, where he had decided as early as January, 1962, that the leadership was irredeemably revisionist. The seeds of dispute were nurtured by growing tensions over Peking's attempt to assert autonomy from Moscow and over the emerging US-Soviet détente (which left China out in the cold). But Mao added an extra ingredient, most notably in 1965 when he refused to contemplate even a limited form of united action with Moscow in support of the Vietnamese.

Mao now intervened even more dramatically in domestic affairs, for there would have been no Cultural Revolution without the Chairman. It was in part a power struggle during which Mao settled scores with some of his opponents (real or fancied) since the Great Leap Forward. But it was also a struggle of ideas, principally between those of the party and government apparatus with its inherent bureaucracy and its moderate approach to socialist construction, and those of Mao and a minority of radical followers who sought to create new socialist values and to find in China's youth new successors to the revolution.

But though Mao called on the Chinese masses to "take part in affairs of state," when faced with the contradiction between real democracy and party centralism, he fell back on the latter, and rejected a proposal from the centre of radicalism, Shanghai, to establish popular governments of the Paris Commune type. Mao's use of the People's Liberation Army, where Lin Piao had created a loyal tool with the aid of the "little red book," also helped to enlarge a factional element in Chinese politics which had previously been submerged. First inspired by Mao's call to "make revolution" in July 1966, the Red Guards were disbanded by him two years later and sent to the countryside.

The Cultural Revolution had marked the political death of the man expected to succeed Mao, Liu Shao-chi. Within two years Mao was actively working to diminish the influence of his "chosen successor," Lin Piao, supported by Chou En-lai whose state administration was still in the shadow of the armed forces. Lin Piao's flight and death in September 1971 also removed an obstacle to the rapprochement with the United States. Here, too, Mao took the lead, convinced that the contradiction with Washington was now subordinate to that with Moscow, and cut through the diplomatic knot by inviting President Nixon to Peking.

But while China entered the United Nations and her "moderate" government under Premier Chou was widely welcomed, Mao continued to see the political process as imbalanced and never free from contradictions. The Tenth Party Congress in August, 1973, was followed by the anti-Confucius campaign which sought more fully to eradicate revisionist thinking. And after the National People's Congress in January, 1975, which seemed to promise a long era of stability and economic development, yet another campaign was launched in Mao's name to "study the theory of the dictatorship of the proletariat."

A year later, after the death of Premier Chou, this campaign led to an unprecedented demonstration in Peking's Teinanmen Square, the overthrow of Teng Hsiao-ping, and a major political crisis over the succession.

Mao's theories were logically attractive. His last pronouncements, in which he warned against "the bourgeoisie within the party" and spoke of the threat of "the bureaucratic class," seemed to chime with the realities of state socialist systems elsewhere. Yet the suspicion grew in 1975 and 1976 that the cutting edge of Mao's radicalism was being used by his closest supporters to chop down political opponents, while the real "masses" were not consulted.

Mao's failure in his last years to establish a collective succession seems to have been compounded by a growing quirkiness against his own colleagues or, in terms of his own theory, by a tendency to elevate non-antagonistic contradictions into those of an antagonistic nature. Yet set against this, Mao's achievement in transforming the face of Chinese society is still immense.

The gap between town and countryside has been greatly narrowed; bureaucracy has at least been kept within bounds; the working class has acquired new access to education; medicine has been taken to the villages. All this is in addition to the achievements of the earlier post-Liberation years in promoting full employment, relatively equal distribution, a stable currency, and an increasing standard of living, which are now taken for granted.

The values of the new "socialist man," which Mao asserted during the Cultural Revolution, are widely accepted in China today, though they remain partly an aspiration. Even the disorders which Mao deliberately stirred up in the last decade of his life may turn out to be beneficial, for they have added to the economic and social achievements a current of political assertiveness—especially among the young—to challenge any future leadership. Though Mao has sometimes hesitated to endorse his own slogan that "to rebel is justified," the revolutionary spark which he re-kindled may be his lasting legacy.

The official edition of Mao's writings and speeches up to 1949 has been published in four volumes as his Selected Works. A few post-Liberation works have been published in a single volume of Selected Readings, and Peking has also produced two volumes of Mao's poems in the classical style. Most of these texts have been edited and sometimes toned down to eliminate Mao's colourful and often earthy style. Fortunately a great mass of "unofficial" writings and speeches were popularised by the Red Guards during the Cultural Revolution. Copies of these have found their way abroad, and most can now be found in translation, including the most important documents from the mid-1950s onwards.

Mao is survived by his third wife, Chiang Ching, whom he married during the war against Japan in Yenan. Two sons and two daughters are also believed to be alive, but have been given no publicity, and there has never been a family cult. However, Chiang Ching's own political role is considerable and, with Yao Wen-yuan and Chang Chun-chiao, she formed the radical nucleus around Mao in his last years.

'You must be a pupil of the masses before you can become their teacher,' Mao exhorted comrades

The death of Mao Tse-tung removes one of the most remarkable characters in history. By his ideas and actions the most populous country in the world was transformed from near-feudalism into a modern centralised state.

The Chicago Daily Tribune
15th November 1915

B. T. Washington Is Dead at Scene of His Lifework

Famous Negro Educator and Leader Expires at Tuskegee.

WAS BORN A SLAVE

Tuskegee, Ala., Nov. 14.—Booker T. Washington, leader of the negro people of America and principal of Tuskegee Institute for Negroes, died today. He was 56 or 57 years old, but none knew the exact date of his birth.

Although he had been in failing health for several months, Mr. Washington's condition became serious only last week, when he had a nervous breakdown while in New York. He realized the end was near, but was determined to make the last long trip south, as he had said often. "I was born in the south, have lived there all my life, and expect to die and be buried there."

Accompanied by Mrs. Washington, his secretary, and a physician, Dr. Washington left New York for Tuskegee Friday afternoon. He reached home last midnight and died at 4:40 o'clock this morning. The funeral will be held at Tuskegee institute Wednesday morning at 10 o'clock.

BORN SLAVE IN VIRGINIA.

Booker T. Washington was born on a plantation near Hale's Ford, Va., in 1858 or 1859, a slave. His father, about whom little is known, is believed to have been a slave from a neighboring plantation. As he had no last name, he adopted the name "Washington" when he first went to school.

When the slaves were freed in 1865, Booker went to work in a coal mine to support his mother and himself.

Hearing two coal miners speak of Hampton institute, Virginia, he walked the whole distance, 500 miles, and was admitted to the classes. He did chores and janitor work for his living and worked summers as a waiter.

While in Hampton he conceived the idea, which he worked out in Tuskegee, of an industrial education for the negro race.

Starting with fifty students, he put them to work learning brickmaking, and brick buildings were built on the ground by the students. There now are thousands of pupils and the school's plant is valued at nearly $2,000,000.

Guest at White House.

An incident of Washington's career made him the center of nation-wide discussion during the administration of President Roosevelt. He sat down to lunch with the president at the White House either by formal or informal invitation. There was a storm of protest from many quarters and some hostility was shown toward the educator afterward.

Dr. Washington was honored by Harvard and Dartmouth with honorary degrees and was frequently called on to address educational associates.

PRAISE BY ROOSEVELT.

Oyster Bay, N. Y., Nov. 14.—Col. Theodore Roosevelt made the following statement tonight on the death of Booker T. Washington:

"I am deeply shocked and grieved at the death of Dr. Booker T. Washington. He was one of the distinguished citizens of the United States, a man who gave greater service to his own race than ever had been given by any one else and who, in so doing, also gave great service to the whole country."

The Times
23rd January 1950

MR. GEORGE ORWELL

CRITICISM AND ALLEGORY

Mr. George Orwell, a writer of acute and penetrating temper and of conspicuous honesty of mind, died on Friday in hospital in London at the age of 46. He had been a sick man for a considerable time.

Though he made his widest appeal in the form of fiction, Orwell had a critical rather than imaginative endowment of mind and he has left a large number of finely executed essays. In a less troubled, less revolutionary period of history he might perhaps have discovered within himself a richer and more creative power of imagination, a deeper philosophy of acceptance. As it was he was essentially the analyst, by turns indignant, satirical, and prophetic, of an order of life and society in rapid dissolution. The analysis is presented, to a large extent, in autobiographical terms; Orwell, it might fairly be said, lived his convictions. Much of his early work is a direct transcription of personal experience, while the later volumes record, in expository or allegorical form, the progressive phases of his disenchantment with current social and political ideals. The death of so searching and sincere a writer is a very real loss.

George Orwell, which was the name adopted by Eric Arthur Blair, was born in India in 1903 of a Scottish family, the son of Mr. R. W. Blair, who served in the opium department of the Government of Bengal. He was a King's Scholar at Eton, which he left in 1921, and then, at the persuasion of his father, entered the Imperial Police in Burma, where he remained for five years. After that he was, by turns, dish-washer, schoolmaster, and bookseller's assistant. The name he adopted comes from the river Orwell—his parents were settled at Southwold, in Suffolk, at the time he decided upon it. Orwell preferred to suppress his earlier novels. " Down and Out in Paris and London," his first book, published in 1933, is a plain, observant and, for the most part, dispassionate piece of reporting, which achieves without faltering precisely what it sets out to do. Orwell had starved in a Paris slum and in England had tramped from one casual ward to another, and the lessons of this first-hand acquaintance with poverty and destitution were never afterwards lost on him. Although in time he grew fearful of a theoretical egalitarianism, he made no bones about the primary need of securing social justice. In " The Road to Wigan Pier," which appeared in 1937, he described the lives of those on unemployment pay or public assistance and made his own contribution to Socialist propaganda.

Next year he brought out his " Homage to Catalonia," an outspoken and at times impassioned account of his experience and observation as a volunteer on the Republican side in the Spanish civil war. He had joined not the International Brigade but the militia organized by the small Catalan party—predominantly syndicalist or anarcho-syndicalist in temper—known as P.O.U.M. He was wounded during the fighting round Huesca. With deepening anxiety and embitterment he had noted the fanaticism and ruthlessness of Communist attempts to secure at all costs—even at the cost of probable defeat—political ascendancy over the Republican forces. It was from this point that his left-wing convictions underwent the transformation that was eventually to be projected in " Animal Farm " and " Nineteen Eighty-Four."

First, however, a few months before the outbreak of war in 1939, he published " Coming up for Air," the book which is his nearest approach to a novel proper. It was not his first published essay in fiction. In " Burmese Days," published five years earlier, he had written with notable insight and justice of the administrative problems of the British in Burma and of the conflict of the white and native peoples, though the personal story tacked on to this treatment of his subject was weak and rather lifeless. The book suggested clearly enough, indeed, that Orwell was something other than a novelist. Yet in " Coming up for Air," for all that it sought to present, in a picture of the world before 1914, a warning of the totalitarian shape of things to come, he recaptures the atmosphere of childhood with a degree of truth and tenderness that is deeply affecting. Here was the creative touch one sought in vain in the later books.

Rejected for the Army on medical grounds, Orwell in 1940 became a sergeant in the Home Guard. He wrote spasmodically rather than steadily during the war years. His picture of Britain at war, published in 1941 under the title " The Lion and the Unicorn," was a brave attempt to determine the relationship between Socialism and the English genius. A volume consisting of three long essays, " Inside the Whale," one of which was the entertaining, if occasionally somewhat wrongheaded, study of boys' popular weeklies, preceded the appearance in 1945 of " Animal Farm." In the guise of a fairy-tale Orwell here produced a blistering and most amusing satire on the totalitarian tyranny, as he saw it, that in Soviet Russia masqueraded as the classless society. The book won wide and deservedly admiring notice. In " Nineteen Eighty-Four," published early last year, the premonition of the totalitarian wrath to come had developed into a sense of fatalistic horror. In Orwell's vision of a not too remote future in Airstrip One, the new name for Britain in a wholly totalitarian world, men had been conditioned to deny the possibility of human freedom and to will their subservience to an omnipotent ruling hierarchy. The book was a brave enough performance, though it fell a good way short of the highest achievement in its kind.

Orwell married in 1933 Miss Eileen O'Shaughnessy. She died in 1945 after an operation, and last year he married Miss Sonia Brownell, assistant editor of *Horizon*.

The Times
17th March 1883

Our Paris Correspondent informs us of the death of Dr. Karl Marx, which occurred last Wednesday, in London. He was born at Cologne, in the year 1818. At the age of 25 he had to leave his native country and take refuge in France, on account of the Radical opinions expressed in a paper of which he was editor. In France he gave himself up to the study of philosophy and politics, and made himself so obnoxious to the Prussian Government by his writings, that he was expelled from France, and lived for a time in Belgium. In 1847 he assisted at the Working Men's Congress in London, and was one of the authors of the " Manifesto of the Communist Party." After the Revolution of 1848 he returned to Paris, and afterwards to his native city of Cologne, from which he was again expelled for his revolutionary writings, and after escaping from imprisonment in France, he settled in London. From this time he was one of the leaders of the Socialist party in Europe, and in 1866 he became its acknowledged chief. He wrote pamphlets on various subjects, but his chief work was " Le Capital," an attack on the whole capitalist system. For some time he had been suffering from weak health.

A Reuter's telegram, dated Paris, March 16, says :— " The *Justice*, one of whose editors is a son-in-law of Karl Marx, states this evening that the latter died in London. He spent two months at Argenteuil last summer, but returned to London in October."

War

Again, as might be expected, all the great war leaders of the past two hundred years were accorded the honour of an obituary – though the passing of Clausewitz, the outstanding theoretical strategist, was not regarded as of sufficient interest to the British public. **Nelson** is doubtless well enough known not to require introduction, but is notable as the only naval figure here. Likewise Baron **von Richthofen**, who is the sole aerial representative. Romanticism, especially the rather ludicrous British variety, is symbolized by General **Gordon**, who died trying, of all absurd things, to retain control of Khartoum. **George Custer**, who appears to have been unable to distinguish very clearly between himself and God serves as a reminder of all those generals the world over who have had a similar problem. By contrast, **Ulysses S. Grant** and **Robert E. Lee** were perhaps the last of the classical personal leaders, although Montgomery and **Patton** might also have some claim to this distinction. **Erwin Rommel** is a warning, if it be needed, of how easily many eventually die by the hand they serve. **Winston Churchill**, the senior citizen who had made rather a mess of his chosen career as a politician, became the Churchill we now remember by his leadership. As a genius of rhetoric, an inspirer of men, a figurehead able to hold together his country when things were falling apart, whose ultimate self-expression is war, he is rivalled only by **Ho Chi Minh** – additionally notable for having led a small and poorly armed nation against the world's greatest military power and winning, thanks partly to guerilla, and partly to idological genius.

Sam Houston and Lord **Kitchener** enjoyed the charisma that make men awesome legends in their lifetimes, **Jean Lafayette** was one of the last great soldiers of fortune. **Sitting Bull**'s leadership penetrated every aspect of his followers' lives, while **Napoleon** *was* France in his heyday. The **Duke of Wellington** may well consider himself one of the luckiest of renowned war leaders: if ever a man can be complimented on being in the right place at the right moment of history, the inspirer of the waterproof boot can be said to be he!

New York Times
22nd December 1945

PATTON'S CAREER A BRILLIANT ONE

Germans Admitted He Was the American Field Commander Whom They Feared Most

Gen. George Smith Patton Jr. was one of the most brilliant soldiers in American history. Audacious, unorthodox and inspiring, he led his troops to great victories in North Africa, Sicily and on the Western Front. Nazi generals admitted that of all American field commanders he was the one they most feared. To Americans he was a worthy successor of such hard-bitten cavalrymen as Philip Sheridan, J. E. B. Stuart and Nathan Bedford Forrest.

His great soldierly qualities were matched by one of the most colorful personalties of his period. About him countless legends clustered—some true, some untrue, but all testifying to the firm hold he had upon the imaginations of his men. He went into action with two pearl-handled revolvers in holsters on his hips. He was the master of an unprintable brand of eloquence, yet at times he coined phrases that will live in the American Army's traditions.

"We shall attack and attack until we are exhausted, and then we shall attack again," he told his troops before the initial landing in North Africa, thereby summarizing the military creed that won victory after victory along the long road that led from Casablanca to the heart of Germany.

At El Guettar in March of 1943 he won the first major American victory over Nazi arms. In July of that year he leaped from a landing barge and waded ashore to the beachhead at Gela, Sicily, thus beginning a campaign that, as he himself observed, out-blitzed the inventors of Blitzkreig. In just thirty-eight days the American Seventh Army, under his leadership, and the British Eighth Army, under Gen. Sir Bernard Montgomery, conquered all of Sicily.

But it was as the leader of his beloved Third Army on the Western Front that General Patton staked out his strongest claims to military greatness. In ten months his armor and infantry roared through six countries — France, Belgium, Luxembourg, Germany, Czechoslovakia and Austria. It crossed the Seine, the Loire, the Moselle, the Saar, the Rhine, the Danube and a score of lesser rivers; captured more than 750,000 Nazis, and killed or disabled 500,000 others.

There were times, in those great days when the tank spearheads of the Third were racing across France with almost unbelievable speed and again when they were cutting the dying Nazi armies to pieces in the final spring of the war, that not even Supreme Headquarters itself knew where his vanguards were. Driven by his iron will, his advanced units had to be supplied with gasoline and maps dropped by air.

About such a leader it was inevitable that heroic myths grew up. One eager war correspondent wrote that he jumped onto the Normandy beachhead waving a $1,000 bill and offering to bet it that he would beat Marshal Montgomery to Berlin. When the tale caught up with him, he pithily remarked that he had never seen a bill of that denomination.

One of his men brought back the story that he swam the icy, 150-foot Sauer River in January, 1945, under machine gun and artillery fire, to inspire the men of the Third to follow him. That, too, General Patton denied, but the extent to which the story was believed was eloquent testimony to General Patton's habit of being where the fighting was fiercest.

Called "Old Blood and Guts"

His best-known nickname—"Old Blood and Guts"—was one that he detested, but his men loved. "His guts and my blood," his wounded veterans used to say when they were flown back here for hospitalization. His explosive wrath and lurid vocabulary became legendary wherever American soldiers fought.

General Patton had a softer side to his nature, too. He composed two volumes of poetry, which he stipulated were not to be published until after his death. He was an intensely religious man, who liked to sing in church and who knew the Episcopal Order of Morning Prayer by heart.

He seemed fated to be the center of controversy. Again and again, when his fame and popularity were at their height, some rash statement or ill-considered deed precipitated a storm about his head. The most celebrated of these incidents, of course, was the slapping of a soldier whom he took to be a malingerer but who was actually suffering from battle fatigue in a hospital during the Sicilian campaign.

This episode resulted in widespread demands for his removal from the command of American soldiers, in Congress and in the press, and caused the Senate to delay his confirmation to the permanent rank of major general for almost a year. General Eisenhower sharply rebuked him, but insisted that his military qualifications, loyalty and tenacity made him invaluable in the field.

The turmoil over this incident had hardly died away when he caused another stir by a speech at the opening of a club for American soldiers in London. The original version of his remarks there quoted him as saying that the British and American peoples were destined to rule the world, but after this had evoked an outburst of criticism Army press relations officers insisted that he had actually said that "we British, American and, of course, the Russian people" were destined to rule.

He raised another brief teapot tempest when he came home in June, 1945, and told a Sunday school class that its members would be the officers and nurses of the next war. But this was nothing compared to the furore he caused by an interview he granted American correspondents after his return to Germany. Discussing conditions in Bavaria, where the military government was under his command, he asserted that too much fuss was being made over denazification and compared the Nazi party to the losers in an election between Democrats and Republicans back home.

General Eisenhower promptly called him on the carpet for these remarks. General Patton promised that he would be loyal to General Eisenhower's orders and to the Potsdam agreements prescribing the complete and ruthless elimination of all elements of nazism from German life, but ten days later, on Oct. 2, 1945, he was removed from the command of his beloved Third Army.

Although reports were current that he might retire, General Patton took his transfer in soldierly silence. He assumed command of the American Fifteenth Army, a paper organization devoted to a study of the tactical lessons to be learned from the war just completed, and told friends that this was in line with what had been his favorite mental occupation since he was 7 years old: the study of war.

Although he customarily signed himself George Smith Patton Jr., General Patton was actually the third in line of his family to bear that name. The original George Smith Patton, his grandfather, was a graduate of Virginia Military Institute, and became a colonel in the Confederate Army. He was killed in action at the battle of Cedar Creek.

Expert Horseman From Childhood

General Patton's father went through V. M. I., then studied law, and moved west. He married a daughter of Benjamin Wilson, who was the first Mayor of Los Angeles, and for whom Mount Wilson was named. The future general was born on the family ranch at San Gabriel, Calif., on Nov. 11, 1885, and from childhood was an expert horseman.

At the age of 18 he came east and entered V. M. I., but after a year there he entered West Point with the class of 1909. There is a legend at the academy that he boasted at his entrance that he would be cadet captain, the highest post in the cadet corps, and that he would also be the first member of his class to become a general. Actually, he was cadet adjutant, the second highest post, and was the second member of the class to become a general.

He was a poor student—throughout his life he remained remarkably deficient in spelling—but an outstanding athlete at the Point. He excelled as a sprinter on the track team, and was also an expert fencer, swimmer, rider and shot. He continued his interest in sports and athletics after his graduation as a second lieutenant of cavalry.

In 1912 he represented the United States at the Olympic Games in Stockholm, Sweden, competing in the modern pentathlon, a contest which up to that time had been almost monopolized by

Swedish Army officers. He finished fifth among more than thirty contestants, immediately after four Swedes. Of the five events, swimming, riding, fencing, running and shooting, he made his poorest showing in the pistol marksmanship competition, but he subsequently practiced until he overcame this weakness.

Early in his Army career he established himself as a hell-for-leather cavalry man. His first post was at Fort Sheridan, Ill., but in December, 1911, he was transferred to Fort Myer, Va., where he was detailed to design a new cavalry saber. In 1913 he went to France to study French saber methods, and on his return was made Master of the Sword at the Mounted Service School, Fort Riley, Kan.

He accompanied Gen. John J. Pershing as his aide on the punitive expedition into Mexico after the bandit, Pancho Villa, in 1916, and the next year he went to France with the general as a member of his staff. He attended the French Tank School and then saw action at the battle of Cambrai, where the British first used tanks on a large scale.

The new weapon was one to gladden the heart of a cavalryman, and from that time on his service was closely connected with tanks. He was assigned to organize and direct the American Tank Center at Langres. For his service in that capacity he was subsequently awarded the Distinguished Service Medal. But he was not satisfied with a training command, and sought action.

He took command of the 304th Brigade of the Tank Corps and distinguished himself by his leadership of it in the St. Mihiel offensive in September, 1918. Later that autumn, during the Meuse-Argonne offensive, he was severely wounded in the left leg while charging a pillbox, after 40 per cent of the tanks in his command had been disabled.

His life was saved by Pvt. Joseph T. Angelo of Camden, N. J., who dragged him to safety in a shell hole.

After the first World War he served with tank units and then with the cavalry at various posts in the United States. He was graduated from the Cavalry School, the Command and General Staff School and the Army War College. While on duty in the office of the Chief of Cavalry in Washington, he was detailed as aide to the Prince of Wales on one of his visits to this country. He told the Prince that a game called "craps" was very popular in this country, and taught him to play it.

A Colonel in 1940

When this country began to rearm in the summer of 1940 Patton was a colonel. He was sent to Fort Benning, Ga., for duty as commander of a brigade of the Second Armored Division, then being formed. In April, 1941, he became its commanding officer and made the division famous as a tough and rough-and-ready outfit. Promoted to corps commander, he organized the Desert Training Center in California.

When the North African invasion was planned, General Patton was placed in command of the American forces scheduled to land on the Atlantic coast of Morocco. One of the closest of the many narrow escapes for which he was noted came when a landing boat, into which he was about to step, was sunk. But he got ashore and after a brief but fierce fight took his objectives.

During the Tunisian campaign that followed, General Patton became celebrated for the strictness of his discipline. He punished men who failed to wear their helmets even in back areas.

After the American reverse at Kasserine Pass in February, General Patton took command of the Second United States Corps, which forced the Nazis back into a narrow corridor between the mountains and the sea, up which the British Eighth Army under General Montgomery pursued them. He won the battle of El Guettar in March, but not long thereafter disappeared from the public eye. On April 16 Gen. Omar Bradley succeeded him in command of the Second Corps.

The reason for the shift was not made known at the time and there were rumors that General Patton had fallen into disfavor. Actually, General Eisenhower had withdrawn him from action in order to prepare the American Seventh Army for the invasion of Sicily in July. The invasion was brilliantly successful, and General Patton's troops cut clear across the island to Palermo; then fought their way along the north coast to Messina.

This magnificent feat of arms was marred, however, by the slapping episode, which did not become generally known to the public until the following November. General Patton, who drove himself as hard as he drove his men, visited a hospital not far from the front lines at a time when he had been under prolonged strain and was in an overwrought condition.

There he encountered two men who showed no signs of visible wounds, but who had been diagnosed by medical authorities as suffering from battle neurosis. Losing his temper, General Patton called them "yellow bellies" and other unprintable epithets, and struck one of them so that his helmet liner flew off and rolled on the ground.

General Eisenhower made an investigation and sharply castigated General Patton, although he did not formally reprimand him. General Patton made personal apologies to all those present at the time of the episode, and later sent public apologies to each division of the Seventh Army.

General Patton did not appear during the campaign on the Italian mainland that followed, and some observers thought he had been relegated to a secondary role because of the storm of criticism that his action had caused in this country. Actually, however, General Eisenhower had picked him for a key role in the invasion of Western Europe, and he was then in England preparing for it.

Continued

Whereabouts a Mystery

For almost two months after D-Day, June 6, 1944, General Patton's whereabouts remained a mystery. The fact that he was in England, at the head of an army, was well known, and the inability of the Nazi intelligence to locate him forced their High Command to retain the German Fifteenth Army in the Pas de Calais area, far from the Normandy beachhead, lest he head a landing there.

Instead, the Third Army landed on the beachhead in great secrecy, and deployed behind the First Army. When the First Army broke the German lines between St. Lo and the sea on July 25, the Third Army poured through the breach to exploit it. The opportunity was ideal for a dashing, driving leader of General Patton's talents. His spearheads roared clear across the base of the Breton Peninsula, then turned east toward Paris.

While the Nineteenth Tactical Air Command of the Ninth Air Force protected the right flank along the Loire Valley, General Patton's armor and motorized infantry forced the line of the Seine and smashed clear across France after the badly disorganized Nazis. The pursuit went all the way to the Moselle, with planes dropping supplies to the leading units, before lack of gasoline finally halted the chase and gave the Nazis a chance to make a stand.

In the bitter autumn that followed, General Patton's men made slow but steady headway against the entrenched Nazis. For almost two months—from Oct. 3 to Nov. 22—they carried on a sanguinary attack against Metz, which in 1,500 years of history had never before been taken by assault. They had to fight their way in, fort by fort and street by street, but they eventually took the city.

Early in December the Third Army began an attack on the Saar Basin, but the unexpected success of von Rundstedt's offensive against the First Army's lines to the north forced a swift change. General Patton was ordered to go to the rescue of the crumbling American positions on the south side of the "bulge." He broke off attack and redeployed his with astonishing speed.

Within three days the Third Army had begun to pound at the southern flank of the Nazi wedge. Some of its divisions had traveled 150 miles in open trucks in freezing weather, but they were still full of fight. By Dec. 28 they had fought their way to the relief of Bastogne, and the worst of the danger was over. For another month they hammered away at the bulge, until it was no more.

In February the Third Army broke through the Siegfried Line between Pruem and Echternach and then crossed the Moselle into the triangle bounded by that river, the Rhine and the Saar. Working in perfect cooperation with Lieut. Gen. Alexander M. Patch's American Seventh Army, the Third cut to pieces the Nazi forces in the Saar-Palatinate region. On March it seized Coblenz.

The Third seemed headed for Leipzig when it was diverted to the south toward the so-called Alpine redoubt, where, it had been rumored, the Nazis planned their last stand. On April 18 the Third crossed the border of Czechoslovakia and nine days later it passed the Austrian frontier. Its advance units were in the vicinity of Linz when the cease-firing order came.

On May 26, 1910, General Patton married Miss Beatrice Ayer of Boston. They had two daughters and a son.

In a characteristically brilliant operation, General Patton led the Third Army across the Rhine north of Ludwigshafen on March 22. Attacking without air or artillery preparation at 10:30 P. M., the Third took the Nazis completely by surprise and landed on the east bank without the loss of a single man.

New York Times
20th September 1863

Obituary.

—The Richmond papers record the death of Gen. Sam Houston, of Texas. His decease has been so often reported that its present announcement will be received with many doubts. The event is stated to have occurred at his residence in Texas, on the 25th of July last. It is a little singular that this intelligence was not received long since. Still the report may be correct. The life of Gen. Houston has been a most eventful one, full of strange and stirring incidents. He was born in Rockbridge County, Va., in 1793. His father, an officer in the war of the Revolution, died in 1807, leaving a widow and nine children. Soon after, Mrs. Houston and all her children crossed the Alleghany Mountains and took up their residence near the Tennessee River, then the boundary between white men and the Cherokee Indians. Sam was soon placed in a country store; but was thus employed only a few weeks when he ran off, and spent several months among the Cherokee Indians. When eighteen years of age he enlisted as a private in the United States Army, and was soon made an Ensign. He distinguished himself at the battle of the Horse Shoe, under Gen. Jackson, in 1814, and was dangerously wounded. After peace he was made a Lieutenant, but resigned, and studied law in Nashville. He was soon after elected District-Attorney of Davidson County, Tenn., and Major-General of the State, and in 1823 was sent to Congress. He was reelected in 1825, and chosen Governor in 1827. This latter office, in consequence of a domestic affliction, he resigned in 1829, and again made his home among the Cherokee Indians, with whom he remained for three years, and became exceedingly popular with them. Subsequently he was elected a member of the State Convention which met at San Felipe de Austin in 1833, and after adopting a Constitution, addressed a memorial to the Government of Mexico setting forth the reasons why Texas should be recognized as one of the States of the Mexican Confederacy. The distinguished part Gen. Houston took in the war that followed this movement is well known. He was the first President of the new Republic in 1836, and was again elected to the same office in 1841. On the admission of Texas into the Union, in 1845, he was elected to the United States Senate, where he served several years, and on his final return to Texas he was again chosen Governor of the State. This office he held for a short time after the war broke out, but resigned at the demand of the Secessionists, and has ever since lived in retirement.

SAM HOUSTON.
Texas patriot, died 1863.

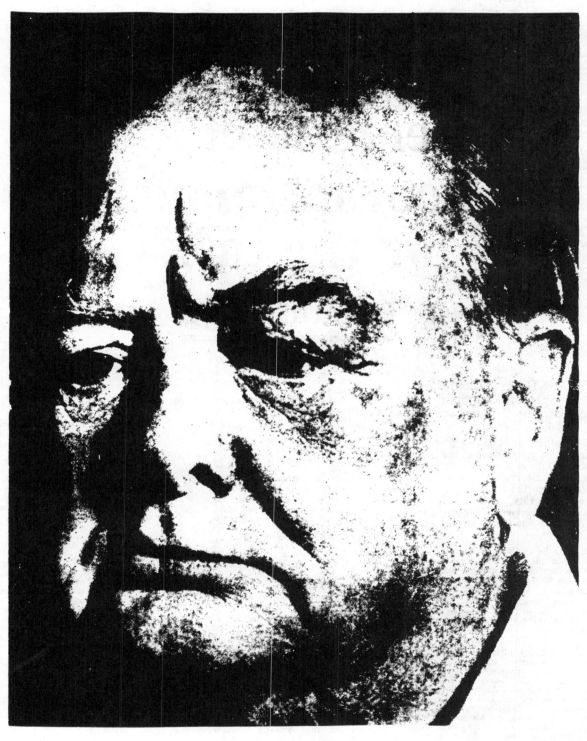

Sir Winston Churchill

The Daily Mail
25th January 1965

The man Providence called in our supreme hour was a tool fashioned for the task

by Quintin Hogg

WINSTON Leonard Spencer Churchill was born on November 30, 1874.

His father, Lord Randolph Churchill, a younger son of the seventh Duke of Marlborough, was the most brilliant, as he later became the most tragic, of contemporary politicians—his mother the lovely daughter of one of the merchant adventurers of New York.

If there be anything in heredity one could predict for this child brains, courage and vivacity. But genius is unpredictable.

Genius does not flow in the accustomed channels. The child was an individualist and, like most individualists, imperfectly appreciated.

Winston Churchill hated school, detested his lessons, and after an unsuccessful academic career scraped into Sandhurst at the third attempt. His Army career was short, brilliant and unconventional. His passion was the profession of arms, but his nature was impatient of peace-time soldiering. He went to Cuba to study guerilla warfare at first hand.

In the height of an Indian summer, his thirst for knowledge drove him to study philosophy and history.

His passion for adventure next took him to the North-West Frontier to join a punitive expedition, then drove him remorselessly to Egypt to see the Battle of Omdurman—the last considerable engagement fought in close order.

Finally, on the eve of the South African War, his natural restlessness drove him from the Regular Army altogether and into politics. He contested Oldham unsuccessfully as a Conservative in 1899.

He had not done with the Army. The South African War had barely begun before Winston Churchill, now war correspondent, suddenly reappeared as a national hero.

Captured by Botha after the ambushing of an armoured train, he escaped from prison, spent a week hidden at the bottom of a coalmine in the company of a host of albino rats, and turned up in Portuguese East Africa concealed in a wagon-load of bales of wool.

On his return to this country he became Conservative Member of Parliament for Oldham after the Khaki Election.

Winston Churchill began in politics where his father left off —a Tory Democrat. He neither forgot not forgave the ingratitude of the party to which, as it seemed to him, Lord Randolph had been all too faithful.

"There remained for me," he afterwards wrote of his father's death, "to pursue his aims and vindicate his memory."

It led him naturally into the Conservative Party, but equally naturally marked him out as a critic of official policy.

When the tariff issue was forced into the open he became one of the most uncompromising of Conservative Free Traders.

At the Ludlow by-election Churchill wrote in support of the Liberal candidate.

The Oldham Conservative Association thereupon repudiated their member, and in March 1904 he was publicly insulted by almost the entire Conservative Party in the House of Commons, who, with Balfour at their head, trooped out in the middle of one of his speeches.

Shortly afterwards he received and accepted from the Liberals of North-West Manchester an invitation to contest the seat in their interest in the General Election. Thus his career was made.

From 1906 to 1914 he was continuously in high places. Always with distinction he held successively the office of Under-Secretary for the Colonies (1906), President of the Board of Trade (1908), Home Secretary (1910), and First Lord of the Admiralty (1911).

As the European situation deteriorated after the Agadir incident Winston Churchill was made First Lord of the Admiralty.

To his initiative and drive was due the readiness of the Fleet to go to war in 1914 and the organisation of the battle-cruiser squadron which played such a decisive part in the victory at the Falkland Islands and in the war at sea.

Churchill's strategy in the first world war was dominated by a desire to utilise British sea-power to further what are now called combined operations.

This desire led him to sponsor first the Antwerp expedition and later the whole Gallipoli campaign.

At the time both these episodes seemed to end in costly failure. In reality the Antwerp expedition was of vital importance in stemming the first German rush, and the failure at Gallipoli was due not to any inherent weakness in the conception of the plan but to the inadequate forces with which it was supported.

The failure at Gallipoli brought his first period in office to a disastrous conclusion.

After a short spell as Chancellor of the Duchy of Lancaster he left the Government at his own request for the trenches, and remained there for the better part of a year as commander of a battalion of the Scots Fusiliers.

In 1917 he was appointed to the Ministry of Munitions—a post which did not carry a place in the War Cabinet; and he returned only to the front rank of responsibility when he became War Secretary in 1919 in order to deal with the crisis on demobilisation—a task which he successfully accomplished.

In 1921 he transferred to the Colonial Office, but in the autumn of 1922 he failed to keep his seat in the General Election.

He was returned as the Constitutionalist member for Epping in 1924 and almost immediately emerged as a fully fledged Conservative and Chancellor of the Exchequer in Mr. Baldwin's new Government.

Winston Churchill's alliance with Mr. Baldwin collapsed early in 1931 over India, and on this Churchill resigned from Baldwin's Shadow Cabinet.

From 1932 onwards Churchill began to issue to the country and its political chiefs a series of increasingly serious warnings concerning Germany.

When the war began on September 3, 1939, Churchill offered his entire support to the war effort. In one of his noblest speeches he referred to the consolation we felt when we recalled our repeated efforts for peace.

"All have been ill-starred but all have been faithful and sincere. Outside the storm may blow and the lands may be lashed with the fury of its gales, but in our own hearts this Sunday morning there is peace. Our hands may be active, but our consciences are at rest."

The next day he again took his seat on the Front Bench as First Lord of the Admiralty.

In May 1940 the disastrous conclusion of the campaign in Norway brought the Chamberlain Government to an end and Winston Churchill was Prime Minister. Was it too late?

The real stature of his national leadership from 1940 to 1945 is only now beginning to emerge.

The man whom Providence had called to direct our affairs in the supreme hour of our destiny was a tool, as it were, fashioned for this very task; a statesman ready of resource; a soldier experienced in the trials of war; an administrator who had held successfully and with distinction each of the higher posts of Government except that of Foreign Secretary; a national hero whose reputation had been kept by long years of opposition untarnished by the failures and compromises of the diplomacy of capitulation.

For my part I cannot conceal my belief that Churchill won the war for Great Britain not by a mere matter of verbal fireworks and moral courage but by the concrete fact of a wise head directing the most complex and intricate of all human plans ever put into practical operation.

Not only in the war, in all its details, did the versatility and abundance of the great man's genius shine.

Victory was the product not only of strategy but of diplomacy.

To achieve any measure of assistance from the United States before her entry into the war, even to ensure perfect harmony after Pearl Harbour, was no light matter; to concert plans with Soviet Russia, herself pressed to the utmost of her endurance, required often the extreme limits of forbearance, infinitely patient ingenuity.

To meet these problems Churchill, overburdened with the direction of our own war effort, over 60 years of age and not in the best of health, undertook journeys all over the world in aircraft operating under conditions of war.

As a leader of the Opposition Churchill was successful neither in the day-to-day conduct of affairs in the House nor in the business of restoring the confidence of the nation in his leadership.

The election of 1951 found Churchill again in with a small majority. In power again, he slowly resumed his ascendancy in Parliament and the country. Coronation year brought fresh honours upon him, for he now felt able to accept the Garter which he refused in 1945.

By 1953 his leadership in the field of foreign politics was beginning to restore to Britain the initiative in international affairs and the absence of war and widespread unemployment largely discredited the attacks upon him.

His illness in 1954, well concealed, gave rise to a remarkable recovery. At the very end of his career his speech on the hydrogen bomb was widely acclaimed as among the finest products of his mind.

He relinquished office of his own free will. He strode off the stage a gigantic figure, with eye undimmed, at the moment of his own choosing.

It would be impossible to conclude this sketch of his life without reference to the abundant and brilliant gift of writing by which he earned his living and enriched his leisure during his years out of office or to omit all mention of the fullness and felicity of his family life.

But his work is ended. The story of Winston Churchill is the epic of an epoch.

Let us now praise this famous man who has passed from us into history. We shall not look upon his like again.

That great man

WHAT can we say of WINSTON CHURCHILL? He is gone, and our grief is profound.

What words can do justice to the life and work of this man of action who was also a master of language? In what phrases can we appraise this career without either extravagance or insufficiency?

He was a great man—that is undeniable. He was one of the outstanding statesmen in our long history. That, too, passes without question. But is it enough?

It has been said that England always finds the right man in her hour of peril. If the man matches the peril, then truly can it be said that this country has never known so great a man as WINSTON CHURCHILL.

There was a time in 1940 when nothing apparent stood between this island and subjugation except our small but resolute Forces.

Warrior

THESE were not enough. They needed to be backed by the unconquerable spirit of an unconquered people. The spirit was there—but even that was not enough. Leadership was also needed—and the leadership was there too.

In that electric moment the soul of England seemed to be caught up in the person of one man. That man was WINSTON SPENCER CHURCHILL.

He was, in appearance, the "typical Englishman." His nature responded like a harpstring to the nobility of our tongue and the wealth of our literature.

He had served this realm on many a field of battle. He had held more offices in the Government than any other man of his time. Was all this not enough for the supreme purpose to which destiny was to call him?

No—not enough. There was something more yet. Through the wasted years his had been the vision; through the era of blindness and complacency his had been the warning voice.

Leader

NOW what he had foretold had come to pass. What he had feared had happened. To him it fell to repair the omissions of his predecessors, and none was more fitted. The Hour had indeed found the Man.

SIR WINSTON's life was a many-sided one. There were light and shade of unusual intensity. Here were the sweets of office and the aloes of the wilderness.

But — we can see it now — everything that had gone before was paving the way for the contest with Hitler.

The downfall of the Nazi power was CHURCHILL's supreme moment — but in the next he was himself dismissed from office.

He was cast for the part of Elder Statesman, a role for which he was temperamentally unsuited. He longed to prove the falsity of the statement that he was a great statesman in war but not in peace.

This he did when, at the age of 76, he became Premier for the second time.

He dies taking with him the admiration and gratitude of free men and women everywhere—this man to whom so many owe so much.

Continued

Perhaps the greatest thing was that the power he had did not corrupt

IT is not the funniest or the most magniloquent story about Winston Churchill, but, in many ways, I think it is most characteristic.

It also has the advantage of being true and not part of the apocrypha which grew up around him.

One evening during the early years of the Labour Government after the war a group of M.P.s stood drinking near the entrance to the Smoking Room in the House of Commons. They included Sir Alan Herbert, who has described the occasion, and Mr. Richard Stokes.

As they talked, Churchill passed them on the way out, and they bowed and bid him "Good night." Churchill walked two or three paces on, then turned and addressed Mr. Stokes. "I must congratulate you, sir," he said, "on the good sense you are talking about Germany." (Mr. Stokes at the time was pleading for a reconciliation.)

Mr. Stokes, who had been one of Churchill's severest critics during the war, thanked him for the generosity of his praise.

Resounding words

Churchill walked away and then turned back once more. "Such hate as I have," he said, looking at Mr. Stokes, "I reserve for the future and not the past."

Yet again he walked away, and yet again turned back: "That, I consider, is a very thrifty and judicious disposal of bile." No one else—and I mean no one—could have uttered those last resounding words, and uttered them, moreover, in a fleeting moment of conversation. "Thrifty," "judicious," "disposal," "bile"; every word stands in the sentence like a picked sentinel.

But the words were not picked: they grew out of the man. If they were large, capacious, generous, it was because the man and his sentiments were large, capacious, generous. Magnanimity: that was there a hundredfold. But there was also wisdom: the deep, unruffled, lightly borne wisdom of experience.

Here, then, was this dominant man of action, impelled by the laws of his own being to take a foremost place in the affairs of men. In what direction were his efforts bent?

The answer is simple. The second important fact about Churchill the politician is that he was really Churchill the historian. He was the historian in action. From the stained records of man's sublimity and man's littleness he drew his nourishment and fertilised it with his own active imagination.

History taught him three things. It gave him, first a profoundly moving vision of man's unceasing struggle against pitiless odds.

In this vision of the indomitable nobility of man lay the source of his hatred of tyranny.

Native audacity

In the same vision was the source of his unfailing magnanimity. At the very beginning of his career he criticised his own commander-in-chief, Kitchener, for desecrating the Mahdi's tomb after Omdurman. At the end of his life he preached to a wartorn France the need for reconciliation with Germany.

Lastly, from this same vision, he drew his own precious conviction that there was nothing that man could not dare if only he would lend wings to his own native audacity.

The second lesson he drew from history was that in the unending march of history Britain had been ordained to play a special part.

The third lesson he took from history was that Britain and Europe should seek their natural ally in America.

But, in the end, the power of Churchill as a politician grew from within himself. Its source in centuries long past when first the temper of Englishmen was first precipitated, its end not yet, for his life and his works will continue to flourish as long as men honour and guard what is audacious within themselves.

One wonders, as I have said before, that there can be such power in a man and that it did not corrupt.

Perhaps, in a world in which power daily accumulates, is daily more concentrated against harmless men, that is the abiding influence of this single man and his greatest glory.

THE BLITZ, 1941 . . . in the bomb-wrecked Commons. He said: "The debt was repaid tenfold, twentyfold."

YALTA, February 1945 . . . with Roosevelt and Stalin. He said :
"Only one link in the chain of destiny can be handled at a time."

The Chicago Tribune
4th July 1855

HE SLEEPS IN PEACE

Beyond the Reach of Care and Pain While a Nation Bows in Grief.

The End of the Sufferings of the Patient Hero at Mount MacGregor.

Gen. Grant Sinks to Rest at 8:04 O'Clock the Morning of July 23.

His Family Grouped Around His Bedside When Life's Spark Went Out.

The Last Word of the Dying Soldier Was a Faint Request for "Water."

Progress of the Funeral Arrangements—Speculation as to the Disposal of the Remains.

On the ninth and tenth pages of this issue appears an extended biographical sketch of Gen. Grant.

THE DEATHBED.

CLOSE OF AN ILLUSTRIOUS CAREER.

MOUNT MACGREGOR, N. Y., July 23.—At 9 last night one of Gen. Grant's physicians conceded with caution that he might survive until July 23. His meaning was that the sick man might yet be living when midnight should mark the new day. The physician's indication (it was not a prognostication) was borne out and more. The General passed into the first hour of the day; he saw its light at sunrise, and through the early morning hours he still survived. The advent of July 23, however, marked a change in Gen. Grant's condition which was significant; the chill at the extremities was increasing, and the use of the hot applications to keep warmth in the extremities and vital parts was resorted to. They were of some avail, but artificial warmth was without power to reach the cause or stay the results of dissolution, which began Tuesday evening, and had been progressing steadily, though gradually. Hypodermics of brandy were frequently given to stimulate the flagging physical powers, but later these failed to affect the patient, whose vitality and whose physical forces were so far spent as to furnish no footing for rebound; indeed, the efforts of the medical men were being made because none could stand by inactive and without the trial of an expedient that might prolong life an hour or a minute. The physicians believed the patient might reach the extreme ebb of his strength at 1 o'clock this morning, and the approach of the hour was anticipated with intense anxiety at the cottage. It passed, however, and the General, lying upon his back and propped by two pillows on the cot bed in the parlor, was yet living, but growing weaker.

The inevitable close of the General's long illness seemed more and more imminent. The feeble pulse-beats wore themselves by their rapidity to a fluttering throb that could not be gauged beneath the finger of the physician. The body was being worn out by its own life-current, so rapid was its coursing through the veins. Repeatedly the brandy was entered beneath the skin of the General's arm, but, despite its waning influence, the respirations had quickened from forty-four to the minute during the evening to a point of labored breathing that was painful to the friends who grouped and bent near the sick man. Two o'clock had been passed, and the evidences of nearing death were multiplying. The increasing respirations were not alone more rapid but more shallow. The lungs and the heart were giving away. So weak had Gen. Grant grown at 3 o'clock that, though he frequently attempted to do so, he was unable any longer to clear the gathering mucus from his throat. It accumulated and remained, and as 4 o'clock drew on and the daylight came, a point had been reached when expectoration was impossible. There was not left enough of strength, and from 4 o'clock on there was in the throat the significant rattle of mucus that was filling the lungs and clogging the throat.

At 3 o'clock the General asked for water, and after that it is not remembered that he uttered any word. At 4 o'clock the breathing was quickened and reached fifty to the minute. An hour later the respirations had reached sixty, and between 5 and 6 o'clock the finger-nails had become blue and the hands further evidenced the progress of numbness at the extremities, and at every breath the mucus clogging in the throat was growing more noticeable.

THE FAMILY SUMMONED.

A few minutes before 8 o'clock Drs. Douglas, Shrady, and Sands stood on the cottage veranda conversing of the condition of Gen. Grant, and discussing the probabilities of his death and the limit of life left the sick man; Mrs. Sartoris and Stenographer Dawson were conversing a little distance away; when Henry, the nurse, stepped hastily upon the piazza and spoke quietly to the physicians. He told them he thought the General was very near to death. The medical men hastily entered the room where the sick man lay and approached his side. Instantly upon scanning the patient's face Dr. Douglas ordered the family to be summoned to the bedside. Haste was made, and Mrs. Grant, Mr. Jesse Grant and wife, U. S. Grant Jr. and wife, and Mrs. Fred Grant were quickly beside the doctors at the sick man's cot. Mrs. Sartoris and Mr. Dawson had followed the doctors in from the piazza, and the entire family was present except Col. Fred Grant. A hasty summons was sent for him, but he entered the sick-room while the messenger was searching for him. The Colonel seated himself at the head of the bed, with his left arm resting on the pillow above the head of the General, who was breathing rapidly and with slightly gasping respirations. Mrs. Grant, calm, but with intense agitation bravely suppressed, took a seat close by the bedside. She leaned slightly upon the cot, resting upon her right elbow, and gazed with tear-blinded eyes into the General's face. She found there, however, no token of recognition, for the sick man was peacefully and painlessly passing into another life. Mrs. Sartoris came behind her mother, and, leaning over her shoulder, so witnessed the close of a life in which she had constituted a strong element of pride. Directly behind Mrs. Grant and Mrs. Sartoris, and at a little distance removed, stood Drs. Douglas, Shrady, and Sands, spectators of a closing life their efforts and counsel had so prolonged. On the opposite side of the bed from his mother and directly before her stood Jesse Grant, and by his side U. S. Grant Jr., and near the corner of the cot, on the same side as Jesse and near to each, was Mr. N. E. Dawson, the General's stenographer and confidential secretary. At the foot of the bed and gazing directly down into the General's face was Mrs. Col. Fred Grant, Mrs. U. S. Grant Jr., and Mrs. Jesse Grant, while somewhat removed from the family circle Henry, the nurse, and Harrison Tyrrell, the General's body-servant, were respectively watching the closing life of the patient, their master. Dr. Newman had repaired to the hotel for breakfast and was not present. The General's little grandchildren, U. S. Grant Jr., and Nellie, were sleeping the sleep of childhood in the nursery-room above. Otherwise the entire family and household were gathered at the bedside of the dying man. The members of the group had been summoned not a moment sooner than was prudent. The doctors noted, on entering the room and proceeding to the bedside, that already the purplish tinge, which is one of nature's signs of final dissolution, had settled beneath the finger nails. The hand that Dr. Douglas lifted was fast growing colder than it had been through the night. The pulse had fluttered beyond the point where the physician could distinguish it from the pulse-beats in his own finger-tips. The respiration was very rapid, and was a succession of shallow, panting inhalations, but happily the approaching end was becoming clear of the rattling fullness of the throat and lungs, and as the respirations grew quicker and more rapid at the close they also became less labored and almost noiseless. This fact was in its results a comfort to the watchers by the bedside, to whom was spared the scene of an agonizing or other than a peaceful death.

IT IS ENDED.

The wife almost constantly stroked the face, forehead, and hands of the dying General, and at times, as the passionate longing to prevent the event so near would rise within her, Mrs. Grant pressed both his hands, and, leaning forward, tenderly kissed the face of the sinking man. Col. Fred Grant sat silently, but with evident feeling, though his bearing was that of a soldierly son at the deathbed of a hero father. U. S. Grant Jr. was deeply moved, but Jesse bore the scene steadily; and the ladies, while watching with wet cheeks, were silent, as befitted the dignity of a life such as was closing before them. The morning had passed five minutes beyond 8 o'clock, and there was not one of the strained and waiting watchers but who could mark the nearness of the life tide to its final ebbing. Dr. Douglas noted the nearness of the supreme moment, and quietly approached the bedside and bent above it, and, while he did so, the sorrow of the gray-haired physician seemed closely allied with that of the family. Dr. Shrady also drew near. It was seven minutes after 8 o'clock, and the eyes of the General were closing. His breathing grew more hushed as the last functions of the heart and lungs were hastened to the closing of the ex-President's life. A peaceful expression seemed to be deepening in the firm and strong-lined face, and it was reflected as a closing comfort in the sad hearts that beat quickly under the stress of loving suspense. A minute more passed and was closing as the General drew a deeper breath. There was an exhalation like that of one relieved of long and anxious tension. The members of the group were impelled each a step nearer the bed, and each waited to note the next respiration, but it did not come then—it never came. There was absolute stillness in the room and a hush of expectancy, so that no sound broke the silence save the singing of birds in the pines outside the cottage and the measured throbbing of the engine that all night had waited by the little mountain depot down the slope.

"It is all over," quietly spoke Dr. Douglas, and there came then heavily to each witness the realization that Gen. Grant was dead. This was at 8:04 o'clock.

Then the doctors withdrew, the nurse closed the eyelids and composed the dead General's head, after which each of the family group pressed to the bedside, one after the other, and touched their lips upon the quiet face so lately stilled.

Dr. Shrady passed out upon the piazza, and as he did so he met Dr. Newman hastening up the steps. "He is dead," remarked Dr. Shrady, quietly. The fact of having been absent from the side of the dying man and his family at the last was a cause of sorrow and sore regret to the clergyman who had waited all night at the cottage. He had been summoned from his breakfast a moment too late and reached the cottage only in time to minister to the family sorrow and gaze upon the scarcely hushed lips of the dead General to whom Dr. Newman's love had bound him in such close ties and relations. Those who saw and knew, and all who learn of the clergyman's absence from the deathbed, quickly speak their impulsive, hearty sympathy.

HIS LAST WORD.

Soon after Drs. Douglas and Shrady left the deathbed they conversed feelingly of the latter hours of Gen. Grant's life. The pulse first had indicated failure, and the intellect was last to succumb its clearness and conscious tenacity, and that after midnight last night, though a circumstance at 4 o'clock indicated cognizance.

"Do you want anything, father?" questioned Col. Fred Grant at that hour.

"Water," whispered the General huskily. But when offered water and milk they gurgled in his throat and were ejected and that one word of response was the last utterance of Gen. Grant.

Dr. Douglas remarked that the peculiarity of Gen. Grant's death was explained a remarkable vitality that seemed to present an obstacle to the approach of death. It was a gradual passing away of the vital forces, and a reflex consciousness, the doctor thought, was retained to the last. The General died of sheer exhaustion and a perfectly painless sinking away.

"Yes," interjected Dr. Shrady, quietly, "the General dreaded pain when he felt he had begun sinking, and he asked that he should not be permitted to suffer. The promise was made, and it has been kept. Since he commenced to sink Tuesday night he has been free from pain."

Toward the last no food was taken, but when a wet cloth was pressed to his lips he would suck from it the water to moisten his mouth. During the General's last night Dr. Shrady was constantly within call, Dr. Douglas was all night at the cottage, and Dr. Sands slept at the hotel after midnight.

Within twenty minutes after the death of Gen. Grant Karl Gerhardt, a Hartford sculptor, who has been making a study here of the General, was summoned to the cottage, at the suggestion of Dr. Newman, to make a plaster cast of the dead man's face. He was highly successful.

THE QUIET SLEEP.

Quietude pervaded the mountain this morning when it was announced that Gen. Grant had ceased his long struggle. This feeling, however, gave place later to a sense of relief that the struggle was ended, and that the tired mind and body were at rest. While there was no heart that warmed not in sympathy toward the General's family, yet there was a strong feeling of gratitude that the man who suffered so bravely and so patiently had earned the quiet of a long rest. The day was a perfect summer's day—warm and clear, and the sun beat down upon the cottage roof just the same as when there was a weak invalid within the house to be more weakened by the heat. Visitors came up the mountain roads, as they did yesterday, and a squad of workmen made some clatter with hammer and adze as they proceeded with the construction of a pavilion to which excursionists might come to be gay and joyous. The cottage was as a deserted house, save that the shutter-blinds at the parlor windows were turned level to allow the light breeze to dally through the room in which the dead General lay. The doors of the cottage were closed, the shutters up-stairs were fastened, and the members of the family were scarcely seen during the day, except as they walked almost silently from the cottage up through the grove on the near-by ridge to luncheon and dinner in a private room at the hotel.

GEN. GRANT DEAD.

In the midst of misfortune not untouched by shameless calumny, weighed down with physical infirmity and mental suffering, the man upon whom the whole country leaned barely a score of years ago has passed away silently and uncomplainingly, leaving behind him an immortal name as a valiant and true soldier who turned the scales for the Union in the most deadly peril which ever encompassed it. Though the representatives of the country which he served and saved neglected him until shame forced them to cancel the obligation, he never complained. Through the dishonesty of others with whom he was associated in business he lost the accumulations of his life, but manfully and dutifully gave all that he had, not sparing the very sword he had drawn for his country, that he might make ample recompense. Though the victim of sharpers, though the target for malice and vituperation, though suffering more keenly in mind and body than any one knows, he sat silently in the shadow of death working faithfully at the task he had assigned to himself to the very last. Knowing that each day brought death nearer to him, he faced fate with as brave a mien as he had ever met it on the battlefield, and at the end, with those near and dear about him, he serenely and courageously passed from the sight of men.

Gen. Grant will be best known in history as the foremost soldier of his time and as the peer of the great soldiers of his century. He was graduated from West Point in the year he entered manhood, and his first service was in Mexico. He entered that war as a Second-Lieutenant and was subsequently made a Captain, earning his promotion by gallant conduct. In 1854 he resigned from the army, and for seven years was lost to the view of the country. During those years great influences were at work in the political world which were destined to gather, accumulate, and break in a terrible storm. The first flash came in 1861. The country was roused to the conviction that civil war was inevitable, and looked about for leaders, not dreaming that the man who was to make history was quietly doing his daily work as a private citizen in Galena. He himself could not have realized the great career which he was to follow. The only call which came to him was that of duty, and that call never came unanswered. He presented himself to the Governor of Illinois as Captain of a company he had raised, but the Governor had other work for him, and commissioned Capt. Grant Colonel of the Twenty-first Illinois Volunteers. Two months later he was made Brigadier-General of Volunteers and assigned to Gen. Fremont's department. From this time his rise was swift and glorious. Belmont, Fort Henry, and Fort Donelson were passed, and he became a Major-General of Volunteers. Then followed Shiloh's bloody days and Vicksburg's surrender, which snatched the Mississippi from Rebel control, and Grant was made a Major-General in the regular army. But greater honors were to come. The whole people and their representatives, and that other Illinoisan, who stood at the head of the Administration—the great Emancipator—already looked upon Gen. Grant as the coming liberator. The country was leaning upon his strong arm and depending upon him to lead it through the dark and troubled waters. The existence of a great Nation, the freedom or bondage of millions of human beings, the integrity of the Union, and the honor of its flag were intrusted to him. After Chattanooga, Mission Ridge, Lookout Mountain, and the other stirring battles of 1863 and the winter months of 1864, he was made the Lieutenant-General of the Army. His word was supreme and his stout arm dealt its blows thick and fast from that terrible campaign of fire and blood in the Wilderness until at Appomattox his work closed. The sword was sheathed, the country was saved, slavery was dead forever, and the Union remained intact. What were the qualities Gen. Grant brought to his work as a soldier? Supreme faith, the necessity of duty, undaunted courage, aggressive energy, iron endurance, and sturdy common sense, which are a better outfit for a long race than emotion, impulse, recklessness, or even brilliancy. His battles were like the steady, resistless blows on a Titan's forge.

He retired from the War with a military reputation which was world-wide and which placed him in the forefront among the great commanders of history, and a few years later the country called him to be its Chief Magistrate. He had previously been made General of the Army, but the call was so imperative that he resigned the position, which was an enviable one in all respects, and accepted the highest civic office in the gift of the people, filling it with such acceptability that he was called a second time. Whatever may have been his mistakes during that eventful period from 1853 to 1870, or his errors in the selection of counselors, he had the satisfaction of serving long enough to witness the restoration of the hostile section which he had conquered to something like harmony and order, to contribute a most important personal part in the complicated work of reconstruction, and to direct the affairs of the country with great skill at a time when all its channels were choked up and obstructed with the débris of a great war. The historian, reviewing the records of these two terms, will find as salient points for comment the reconstruction legislation, the suppression of disorders in the South growing out of the operations of the Ku-Klux-Klan and ballot-box conspirators, the resumption of specie payments, the tariff revision, the constitutional amendments, the San Domingo policy, the reform of the civil service, the Treaty of Washington, the Louisiana imbroglio, the Electoral Commission bill, and numerous other important subjects of legislation. It was a time of transition, as well as of storm and stress, and one which required a man of nerve, coolness, and endurance at the helm.

In 1877 Gen. Grant was once more a private citizen, but before he settled down to the repose which he had so nobly earned he determined to enjoy the pleasures of foreign travel which he had always coveted. He made his famous trip around the world, and was absent from home for two years. During that time he was the guest of every country in Europe, and was the recipient of royal, civic, and social honors such as no American had ever received before. In the midst of all these honors and unusual attentions, the hero of splendid fêtes and glittering pageants, courted and entertained by the aristocracy of position as well as that

continued

of intellect, he comported himself in a manner that won the admiration of his own country. There was not an American citizen who was not elevated in European estimation by the manly bearing of Gen. Grant in whatever situation he was placed. From Europe he extended his journey to the Far East, received the picturesque welcomes of Oriental Princes, and was loaded down with costly gifts. It was a magnificent recognition of the fame of the great soldier, and a significant tribute to the country which he had saved and ruled.

In 1881 Gen. Grant made New York his home and embarked in the business which caused his financial ruin. The sad story is too well known to need rehearsal. The clouds of misfortune were made heavier and darker by the long neglect of the country to do him justice and to restore to him that title which he once wore so grandly and which he only consented to surrender when his country called him to another field of service. Justice was at last done him. His old title was restored, but not until he had been victimized by sharpers, stripped of his fortune, and borne down to the very earth with a load of troubles, in the midst of which the sturdy old hero, stout and silent as some ancient Roman, uncomplainingly labored at his daily task, giving expression to but one wish—that the daughter whom he had loved so tenderly should cross the ocean in time to be with him and remain with him to the end. That wish was granted. All the services he had rendered his country, all the honors he had received at home and abroad, were forgotten in that one aspiration of love for the daughter who had been so much to him. As the spring days passed and warm weather approached, his physicians and family feared that the effect of the hot, stifling atmosphere would be to hasten the progress of his insidious disease, and decided to remove him to a spot where he could have the advantage of pure, bracing air. His sad journey to Mount MacGregor now recalls the equally sad journey which Garfield made to Elberon. It was followed with the prayers of the people that help might come, but the end has been the same. There was no help in the breezes of the sea for the one; no tonic in the mountain air that could strengthen the other. There was no answer to the prayers of the people for either. Then the old soldier, like some ancient knight, waited calmly for the coming of that Presence he had so often faced, and yielded up his soul at its bidding, without complaint, sustained at the last by the presence of those whom he loved, and conscious that his fame was secure. His countrymen may rear monuments to his memory, but the more enduring record will remain in the pages of history and in the hearts of all loyal men and their children's children, who will be inspired with fresh devotion to the Nation as the story of his life is told.

GEN. GRANT AS A MILITARY COMMANDER.

One of Gen. Grant's strongest characteristics as a military commander was the scope, aim, and thoroughness of his work. In no battle which he fought during the War was it his purpose merely to defeat the enemy and drive him from the field, or to kill and wound as many Rebels as possible. He planned his battles and so disposed his forces as to surround and capture the enemy which opposed him, bag and baggage, or "the whole outfit," as military men would say, and thus weaken the Confederacy by successively capturing its armies, guns, ordnance, supplies, and baggage, and withdrawing them from the field. It was never his intention that the Rebel force in his front should be merely beaten and retreat to fight again, but that it should be whipped, captured, and placed where it could not fight again.

His career from the outset illustrates this point. His operations at Fort Donelson were so conducted as to force the Rebels within the works. Although his troops clamored to be led to the assault he held them back until every position was enveloped and there was no line of retreat left open. Then, after some hard fighting on the part of the Rebels to break out, he sent to Gen. Buckner the memorable dispatch: "No terms, except "unconditional and immediate surrender can "be acceptable. I propose to move immedi- "ately on your works." The result was the surrender of the entire Rebel army in the fortifications, 14,500 strong, with all their artillery, arms, supplies, and equipments. He had thus removed one Rebel army entire from the field of operations. At Shiloh the result was different. While Grant was preparing to move on the Rebels in crushing force they stole a march and surprised one-half of his army while the other half was a day's march distant. He made a bloody, desperate drawn battle of the first day's fight, and won the second day's struggle, and when preparing for a vigorous, unrelenting pursuit he was superseded by Halleck, who pursued the Rebels towards Corinth several hundred feet a day, ruined the Tennessee forests by cutting down the trees for breast-works, scarified the surface of the country by digging leagues of trenches, while Gen. Grant was in the rear chafing like a chained lion at enforced inaction. Had he been in command after the second day's fight at Shiloh he would have given Beauregard the liveliest chase ever known in the annals of the Rebellion War. To have escaped bagging and consignment to Camp Douglas the Rebel leader would have made one of the most rapid marches to the rear on record, instead of falling back leisurely while Halleck was hewing down forests and digging up the country with 80,000 men against 35,000.

As soon as Gen. Grant was placed in command of Western Tennessee he again laid his plans for the capture of the Rebel forces, and, with the exception of his mishap at Oxford, his descent of the Mississippi to Vicksburg presents a series of brilliant successes in which large bodies of Rebels were captured en masse. Arkansas Post, Jackson, Raymond, Port Gibson, Champion's Hill, Grand Gulf, one after the other fell, and then Vicksburg passed into his hands. He had weakened the Confederacy to the amount of 50,000 captured men, 55,000 small arms, and

301 cannon, besides supplies and equipments. It was the deathblow to rebellion in the Southwest.

Once more Gen. Grant tried to capture an army and nearly accomplished it, but he defeated it and compelled it to make a precipitate retreat. When Rosecrans was penned at Chattanooga by Bragg and his army nearly starving Grant not only laid his plans to rescue him, but to capture the entire Rebel force which had penned him in, and he disposed his troops with this purpose in view. His army was in three divisions. Gen. Sherman was on the left flank and "Fighting Joe" Hooker on the right. Sherman was to get to the rear of Bragg's army and hold the road over which it would have to retreat after Hooker had smashed it on the right and Grant leading the centre to a grand assault.

Hooker did his part of the smashing, fighting his way up into the clouds and down again, while the centre swept everything before it with the bayonet. The Rebels were forced back, but Sherman had not been so fortunate. He was unable to capture the Rebel line of retreat, tho he made a desperate effort. The back door was open and the Rebels went through it on the double-quick and Grant after them. It was a great victory. Upwards of 6,000 prisoners were taken, besides forty-two pieces of artillery, and 10,000 Rebels were killed and wounded, but the remainder of Bragg's army, some 40,000, got away by rapid running and throwing away their baggage. If Sherman had succeeded in closing the gap they would all have been taken in and sent North. It was the only time during the War when Gen. Grant did not sooner or later bag the army which was opposed to him.

Shortly after the escape of Bragg Gen. Grant was called to Washington and was invested with the command of the armies of the United States, and especially of the Potomac army. He then made his preparations to bag Lee's army, at that time about 80,000 strong. His well-known dispatch to Secretary Stanton, "I propose to fight it out on this line if it takes all summer," rang through the country like a trumpet. The details of that memorable campaign are too well known to need recapitulation. Against tremendous obstacles and the most obstinate resistance behind strong fortifications, Gen. Grant pursued his plans with bull-dog persistence, making new plans when circumstances defeated the original ones, slowly but surely drawing the great anaconda toils about Lee's heroic army, until at last the survivors were surrendered to him at Appomattox, and peace was conquered. With two exceptions, Grant bagged the forces he fought sooner or later. One of these was at Shiloh, when he was prevented from ultimately capturing Beauregard by Halleck's assuming command and superseding him. The other was at Chattanooga, where Bragg escaped because Sherman was unable to close the line of retreat. Both were victories, but they did not result in annihilation of the foe, which was always Grant's purpose and which distinguished him from other Generals. It may be said that

Gen. Sherman captured Johnston's army entire; but it will be remembered that Gen. Grant was in his front, retreat was impossible, and it was only a question whether he should surrender ultimately to Grant or immediately to Sherman. Gen. Grant did not fight battles merely to win victories or to kill the enemy's soldiers, but to capture the opposing army and remove it from the field of hostile action; and in this object he was conspicuously successful, even as compared with Napoleon. When Grant fought a battle he intended it should be a Waterloo and that the army which opposed him should never fight him again. In this respect he was a Cæsar.

GRANT AS A STATESMAN.

Grant as a public man will occupy a higher place in history than has been awarded to him by his contemporaries. He assumed the executive responsibility of government under the most trying conditions. The Rebel States had been whipped back into the Union, but it remained to reëstablish them upon their former footing. The restoration of vanquished Rebels to full and equal rights of citizenship was an untried experiment in government. Grant stood between the unforgiving radicals of the North and the unrepentant radicals of the South; and it must be conceded that his influence was potential in allaying sectional bitterness, shaping wise legislation, and averting acrimonious conflicts. He can be fairly judged during the term of reconstruction only by estimating the full meaning of the difficulties which beset him. The best proof of his success is to be found in the fact that he acquired the respect and regard of the Southern people without forfeiting the confidence of the Northern people.

Gen. Grant's name and influence will always be associated with some of the best achievements in public life during the decade succeeding the Civil War. An enormous public debt and a depreciated and irredeemable paper currency were among the legacies of the War. Demagogs were not lacking in either party who stood ready to tempt the people with schemes of inflation and repudiation. Grant set his face determinedly against all these schemes. His veto of the inflation bill proposing to reissue some 50 millions of greenbacks which had been retired came at a critical moment and turned the scales against depreciated money. In that one action he did more than all the public men of his time to defend the National faith, maintain the National credit, and prepare the way for resumption. With all his personal incapacity for business he had broad and honest ideas of finance and political economy which were of eminent usefulness to his country.

The peaceful settlement of the Alabama claims against England was one of the triumphs of Grant's Administration. The American people were ripe for war with Britain over this bitter controversy. Bitter hostility was entertained against England, and there was a large faction of people who believed that a foreign war would be the most expeditious way to unite the North and South in a bond of patriotism. Grant had the wisdom and force of character to control the hot-headed men and promote the scheme of arbitration, which not only averted war at that time but established a precedent which has proved and will continue to be of great value in other international complications. It will also be remembered to his lasting credit that Grant was the first to give a practical impetus to the movement for civil-service reform. He appointed the first commission to investigate and report on the methods of the proposed reform, and ever afterwards persisted in calling the attention of Congress to its duty in this matter. None of the scandals which occurred during his second Administration were traceable to him, and when the abuses were exposed—especially the operations of the whisky ring and the undervaluation frauds in the New York Custom-House—he adopted the most vigorous policy of prosecution.

Many of his ideas which attracted opposition and censure were of broad and patriotic impulse, notably the proposed acquisition of the splendid Island of San Domingo as an available refuge for the freedmen who were suffering from the race prejudice in the South—a scheme which, if it had been carried out, might have saved much turmoil, injustice, and misery.

There are good reasons for believing that Grant's association with the third-term movement was not due to any consuming desire of his own to assume a new term of executive power, but that he was pushed into it by the importunities of his friends and supporters. His character and entire career furnish a sufficient guarantee that he at no time was actuated by an improper ambition. The cordial and effective support which he gave Garfield during the campaign was the characteristic generosity of a great man. There were undoubtedly mistakes in Grant's political career, but there were also some remarkable performances for which posterity will give him full credit and acknowledge its obligations.

New York Tribune
16th December 1890

SITTING BULL KILLED.

THE FAMOUS SIOUX CHIEF SLAIN IN A FIGHT WITH INDIAN POLICE.

ARRESTED AS HE WAS ABOUT TO STRIKE HIS TENTS AND START FOR THE BAD LANDS—IN AN ATTEMPT TO RESCUE HIM A DOZEN MEN ARE KILLED—HIS SON CROWFOOT AMONG THE DEAD.

Washington, Dec. 15.—Indian Commissioner Morgan this evening received from Indian Agent McLaughlin the following dispatch, dated Fort Yates, N. D., Dec. 15:

"Indian police arrested Sitting Bull at his camp, forty miles northwest of the agency, this morning at daylight. His followers attempted his rescue and fighting began. Four policemen were killed and three wounded. Eight Indians were killed, including Sitting Bull and his son Crowfoot, and several others wounded. The police were surrounded for some time, but maintained their ground until relieved by United States troops, who now have possession of Sitting Bull's camp, with all women, children and property. Sitting Bull's followers, probably 100 men, deserted their families and fled west up the Grand River. The police behaved nobly, and great credit is due them. Particulars by mail."

Commissioner Morgan showed this telegram to the President late this evening. The President said that he had regarded Sitting Bull as the great disturbing element in his tribe, and now that he was out of the way he hoped that a settlement of the difficulties could be reached without further bloodshed.

Chicago, Dec. 15.—At 9 o'clock to-night Assistant-Adjutant-General Corbin, of General Miles's staff, received an official dispatch from St. Paul, saying that Sitting Bull, five of Sitting Bull's men and seven of the Indian police have been killed. The thirteen casualties were the result of an attempt by the police to arrest Sitting Bull. The following official telegram was also received:

"St. Paul, Minn.

"To Colonel Corbin, Assistant-Adjutant-General:
"Sitting Bull was arrested this morning at daylight by the Indian police. Friends attempted his rescue and a fight ensued. Sitting Bull, his son, Black Bird, Catch Bear and four others were killed, also seven Indian police. Captain Fechet arrived just in time with his two troops, Hotchkiss and Gatling guns, and secured the body of Sitting Bull.

"By command of General Miles.
"MAUS, A. D. C."

St. Paul, Minn., Dec. 15.—The news of the killing of Sitting Bull has been confirmed by advices received by General Miles at the military headquarters in this city. He received two dispatches this evening, the first from Pierre, S. D., stating that Sitting Bull and his son had been killed, but giving no further particulars. The other dispatch was from Standing Rock Agency and stated that the Indian police started out this morning to arrest Sitting Bull, having understood that he proposed starting for the Bad Lands at once. The police were followed by a troop of cavalry under Captain Souchet, and infantry under Colonel Drum. When the police reached Sitting Bull's camp on the Grand River, about forty miles from Standing Rock, they found arrangements being made for departure. The cavalry had not yet reached the camp, when the police arrested Bull and started back with him. His followers quickly rallied to his rescue, and tried to retake him. In the melee that ensued the wily old chief is said to have been killed, and five of the best of the Indian police were also killed. One of the police jumped on one of Sitting Bull's horses and rode

back to the cavalry and infantry, telling them to hurry up to the support of the police, and then hurried on to the Agency with news of the battle. Nothing later than this has yet been received, but the death of Sitting Bull and of at least five of those who had captured him seems undoubtedly true.

A VISIT TO SITTING BULL'S CAMP.

OFFICIAL REPORT OF AN AGENT OF THE GOVERNMENT—THE OLD CHIEF'S PROPOSITION.

Chicago, Dec. 15.—The story of the last visit paid by a white man to Sitting Bull's camp prior to the tragic events of to-day is told in a report received this afternoon by Assistant Adjutant-General Corbin. The narrative throws a flood of light on the old chief's wily character, and strongly depicts the circumstances existing in the isolated camp. The document is addressed to Commissioner of Indian Affairs Morgan by United States Indian Agent James McLaughlin, of Standing Rock, and reads in full as follows:

"Having just returned from Grand River District, and referring to my former communication regarding the ghost-dance craze among the Indians, I have the honor to report that on Saturday evening last I learned that such a dance was in progress in Sitting Bull's camp, and that a large number of Indians of the Grand River settlements were participators. Sitting Bull's camp is on the Grand River, forty miles southwest from the agency, in a section of country outside of the line of travel, only visited by those connected with the Indian service, and is therefore a secluded place for these scenes. I concluded to take them by surprise, and on Sunday morning left for that settlement, accompanied by Louis Primeau, arriving there about 3 p. m., and having left the road usually travelled by me in visiting the settlement, got upon them unexpectedly and found a ghost dance in its height. There were about forty-five men, twenty-five women, twenty-five boys and ten girls participating. A majority of the boys and girls were, until a few weeks ago, pupils of the day schools of the Grand River settlements. There were 200 persons, lookers-on, who had come to witness the ceremony, either from curiosity or sympathy, most of whom had their families with them, and encamped in the neighborhood.

"I did not attempt to stop the dance then going on, as in their crazed condition under the excitement it would have been useless to attempt it, but after remaining some time talking with a number of the spectators, I went on to the house of Henry Bull Head, three miles distant, where I remained over night and returned to Sitting Bull's house next morning, where I had a long talk with Sitting Bull and a number of his followers. I spoke very plainly to them, pointing out what had been done by the Government for the Sioux people, and how this faction by their present conduct were abusing the confidence that had been reposed in them by the Government in its magnanimity in granting them full amnesty for all past offences when from destitution and imminent starvation they were compelled to surrender as prisoners of war in 1880 and 1881, and I dwelt at length upon what was being done in the way of education of their children and for their own industrial advancement, and assured them of what this absurd craze would lead to and the chastisement that would certainly follow if these demoralizing dances and disregard of Department orders were not soon discontinued. I spoke with feeling and earnestness and my talk was well received, and I am convinced that it had a good effect. Sitting Bull, while being very obstinate, and at first inclined to assume the role of 'Big Chief' before his followers, finally admitted the truth of my reasoning and said that he believed me to be a friend to the Indians as a people, but that I did not like him personally, but that when in doubt in any matter in following my advice, he had always found it well, and that now he had a proposition to make to me which, if I agreed to and would carry out, it would allay all further excitement among the Sioux over this ghost dance, or else convince me of the truth of the belief of the Indians in this new doctrine. He then stated his proposition, which was that I should accompany him on a journey to trace from this agency to each of the other tribes of Indians through which the story of the Indian Messiah had been brought, and when he reached the last tribe or where it originated, if they could not produce the man who started the story, and we did not find the new Messiah, as described, upon the earth, together with the dead Indians returning to reinhabit this country, he would return convinced that they (the Indians) had been too credulous and imposed upon, which report from him would satisfy the Sioux and all practices of the ghost societies would cease; but that if found to be as professed by the Indians, they be permitted to continue their medicine practices, and organize as they are now endeavoring to do. I told him that this proposition was a novel one, but that the attempt to carry it out would be similar to the attempt to catch up the wind that blew last year."

SITTING BULL'S TURBULENT CAREER.

Sitting Bull (Tatonka, Otanka), who for many years was the cruel and wily leader of the outlaw Sioux, was born in Dakota in 1837, near old Fort George, and was the son of Jumping Bull. When he was fourteen years old he killed an enemy and his name was then changed from The Sacred Stand to Sitting Bull. Sitting Bull's followers were outlaws from all the Sioux bands, and, with few exceptions never entered into treaty relations with the Government. He was not recognized as a chief by such leaders as Red Cloud, Spotted Tail and Young-Man-Afraid-of-His-Horses until about 1868, and prior to that time he was often in open conflict with them. With their recognition his supremacy over the bad Sioux was assured.

Sitting Bull began to figure as a bad chief during the Civil War. After the Spirit Lake massacre in Iowa and the great Sioux massacre in Minnesota, all the more turbulent Sioux banded together. In 1864 General Sully drove them into the Big Horn country. He then followed them to the Yellowstone and established Fort Buford. Upon this post and on the steamboats and immigrants to Montana the Indians kept up an unceasing war, often keeping the garrison at Fort Buford in a state of siege for weeks at a time. An attempt was made to treat with them in 1866, but after accepting the presents and securing some ammunition Sitting Bull broke up the council, and the commissioners escaped to the fort across the river.

In 1867 Sitting Bull threatened the Gallatin Valley in Montana, and in 1868 he attacked the settlement of Muscleshell and suffered defeat. After this defeat he lost prestige. In 1869 and 1870 he devoted himself principally to the slaughter of the Crows, the Mandans, the Rees, the Shoshones and all other tribes friendly to the whites, varying this work by an occasional attack on the Missouri River forts. In 1874 he drove the Crows from their agency and reservation and made war on all peaceable Indians. He spent the summer of 1875 in attacks on the Crow Agency and on Montana settlers.

In 1876 Sitting Bull again took up arms against the whites and friendly Indians. In June of that year he defeated and massacred on the Little Big Horn nearly all of General Custer's advance party of General Terry's column, which was sent against them. He was pursued by General Terry, but with part of his band he escaped into British territory. In 1880, through the mediation of Dominion officials, he surrendered on the promise of pardon, and was taken to Standing Rock Agency, where most of the remaining years of his life were passed. He found that his influence among the Sioux was almost entirely gone, but he was able on several occasions to induce them to refuse to relinquish Indian lands. His hatred of the whites and his desire to regain his lost power led him into several conspiracies, but these were quickly discovered by the authorities, who on several occasions placed him under restraint. In the latest troubles with the Indians Sitting Bull, while not openly engaged in making mischief, undoubtedly did all he could secretly to increase the discontent among red men and nothing that would tend to quiet them.

INDIANS INFLAMED BY BLOODSHED.

TROUBLE FEARED AS THE RESULT OF THE FIGHT WITH COWBOYS—SIGNAL FIRES IN THE BAD LANDS.

Omaha, Dec. 15.—"The Bee" dispatch from Pine Ridge Agency, S. D., says that about 9 o'clock last night a great light suddenly blazed up in the northwest in the direction of the Bad Lands. The light faded to a sullen glow and then rapidly spread along the sky for a distance of a couple of miles. Men posted in Indian signals in the camp said this meant that the Indians in the Bad Lands had determined to fight. It is thought that the conflict between the Indians and the cowboys on Battle Creek, yesterday, in which three of the former were killed, has inflamed the Indians. The Indians in the camp of the friendlies on being asked what the signal meant declined at first to talk, but being pressed finally said it meant that their brothers in the Bad Lands would be on the war-path within one sun, and that all Indians who did not join them would be dogs and enemies forever. The friendlies, however, disclaimed any intention of obeying the signal. The guards here will be doubled, nevertheless, and the friendly camp kept under the closest surveillance. The 6th, 7th and 8th Cavalry and 300 State militia are under marching orders and will start for the Bad Lands either to-night or to-morrow morning. It is the general opinion here that a fight with the hostiles is now inevitable.

A dispatch from Rapid City, S. D., says: "A battery of Hotchkiss guns was sent to-day from Fort Meade to this point, to reinforce General Carr's command at the mouth of Rapid Creek. A number of straggling parties of Indians have been seen going north. They are under the command of Short Bull and Kicking Bear, and say they will not surrender. Short Bull is one of the worst Ind'ans on the reservation. It was he who murdered Agent Appleton in cold blood at Pine Ridge. It is expected that the main body of the hostiles will attempt to follow him. General Carr has orders to intercept and disarm these Indians at all hazards, and it is expected a collision will occur tomorrow in the vicinity of the mouth of Spring Creek or Rapid Creek. Dr. McGillycuddy, surgeon-general of the South Dakota militia, has been ordered to join Colonel Day's command at the front. Several old Indian fighters have volunteered as guides and scouts. A company of Sioux and Crow scouts from the north are on the way to join General Carr. A dispatch from Pine Ridge says that part of the 7th Cavalry have orders to march at midnight."

Chicago, Dec. 15.—A dispatch received at Army Headquarters yesterday from Battle Creek, S. D., stated that a letter had just been received by a courier from Captain Wells at the mouth of French Creek stating that a fight had occurred there December 12 between twenty citizens and a roaming band of Sioux. Five Indians were reported killed, but the loss of the whites was not given.

A dispatch from General Brooke said that reports received by him on the night of December 13 showed a decidedly hostile intent on the part of the Indians in the Bad Lands. He feared that the collision between some citizens and the Indians had turned the scale.

Information from Fort Bennett goes to show that the Indians at Cherry Creek Agency are greatly excited and that under the leadership of Big Foot they are keeping up the ghost dance. The Indians' excitement is increased by the report that bands of Sioux from Rosebud and Pine Ridge are moving in the direction of Cherry Creek.

Colonel Corbin said last night that it was not known whether the fight referred to by General Brooke was the one that occurred at French Creek. "If not," continued the Colonel, "there have been two rows and of the one referred to by General Brooke we know nothing as yet. It is to be feared, now that blood has been shed, that there will be more trouble, for if an Indian knows that some of his tribe have been hurt he will forgo his peaceful intentions. Two Strike was on his way into Pine Ridge and it is to be hoped that he won't turn back when he hears of the French Creek affair. In all probability Kicking Bear and Short Bull are the instigators of such trouble as has occurred."

Washington, Dec. 15.—General Schofield this afternoon received two telegrams from General Ruger, commanding the Department of Dakota, in one of which he says he hopes to get in all the Indians who turned back from the Bad Lands. Two Strike's party are trying to induce them to come along with them. He says that the Indians are moving slowly on account of poor stock. The other telegram includes a dispatch received yesterday from the commanding officer at Oelrichs, Dak., saying that his interpreter, just in from White River, reports that fifty lodges in the Bad Lands are trying to work their way north to the Cheyenne River Agency. General Ruger adds that the necessary steps have been taken to intercept them if possible.

New York Times
13th October 1870

THE LEE MEMORIAL.

Interesting Exercises at Cooper Institute — Speeches, by Hon. John A. Ward, T.

Cooper Inst..... filled last evening by an audience composed of ladies and gentlemen, mostly of Southern birth, who had assembled to pay a tribute to the memory of ROBERT E. LEE. The meeting was presided over by Hon. JOHN A. WARD, and the following gentlemen officiated as Vice-Presidents and Secretaries:

Vice-Presidents—Ex-Gov. E. Lewis Lowe, W. H. Appleton, Esq., Henry Grinnell, Esq., Cyrus H. McCormick, Esq., Norman D. Sampson, Esq., T. A. Hoyt, Esq., James T. Soutter, Esq., W. T. Coleman, Esq., Gen. J. D. Imboden, Gen. Daniel W. Adams, Col. E. C. Caball, John Mitchel, Esq., William Patrick, Esq., M. B. Fielding, Esq., Rev. A. D. Carter, Francis Hopkins, Esq., J. F. Tanner, Esq., Col. Thos. L. Sneed, Esq., Rev. C. W. Marshall, Dr. R. C. Gardner.

Secretaries—Col. Burton N. Harrison, Major Robert Tannahill, Major J. Hamilton Hunt, Major J. F. Cummings, Major J. D. Keley, Jr., Col. George Lemmon.

After prayer by Rev. A. D. CARTER, and an anthem by a quartet from the choir of St. Stephen's Church, Hon. JOHN A. WARD delivered an address. He said the audience had assembled to pay a tribute of respect to one whom the whole South revered with more than filial love and affection. [Applause.] The kind sympathy which had been expressed by the public Press of the Metropolis, the sea of upturned faces which he saw before him, and the presence of those distinguished gentlemen who mingled in their sorrow, testified that the bereaved voice of his affectionate people had calmed down the angry passions excited by that fearful contest of which ROBERT E. LEE was the chosen and beloved leader. There was no cause now for hatred or jealousy; when his cause was lost, and his sword sheathed in surrender he gave his answer that "it were strange, indeed, if human virtue were not, at least, equal to human calamity." The characteristic of his life was devotion to duty. Many believe that he erred in selecting the path of duty when he believed that duty did not command him to draw his sword against his State and his children. He trod the path of duty and left the consequences to God. He taught the Christian world that a man could be a soldier. After his services in the field he assumed the position of instructor to the youth of Virginia, and gained the love of all who were associated to him. The world may have given birth to more renowned warriors, but all must concede that the world never saw a purer man or one who has gone to his grave more lamented. The day is fast approaching when the grave of ROBERT E. LEE will be claimed not by a section, but by the whole people of the nation.

Gen. IMBODEN, Chairman of the Committee, presented a preamble and resolutions as follows:

"In this great metropolitan City of America, where men of every clime and of all nationalities mingle in the daily intercourse of pleasure and of business, no great public calamity can befall any people in the world without touching a sympathetic chord in the hearts of thousands of our fellow-citizens. When, therefore, tidings reached us that Gen. ROBERT E. LEE, of Virginia, was dead, and the people of that and all the other Southern States of the Union were stricken with grief, the great public heart of New-York was moved with a generous sympathy that found kindly and spontaneous expression through the columns of the city Press of every shade of opinion. All differences of the past—all bitter memories—all feuds that have kept two great sections of our country in angry strife and controversy for so long, seems to have been forgotten in the presence of the awe-inspiring fact, that no virtues, no deeds, no honors, nor any position can save any member of the human family from the common lot of all. The universal and profound grief of our Southern countrymen is natural and honorable alike to themselves and to him whom they mourn, and is respected throughout the world. For ROBERT E. LEE was allied and endeared to them by all the most sacred ties that can unite an individual to the community. He was born and reared in their midst—shared their local peculiarities, opinions and traditional characteristics. For his pre-eminent abilities and exalted personal integrity and Christian character he was, by common consent, made their leader and representative in a great national conflict, in which they had staked life, fortune and honor. In Virginia his family name was coeval with the existence of the State, and was emblazoned upon those bright pages of her early civil and military annals that record the patriotic deeds of WASHINGTON and his compeers. By no act of his did he ever forfeit or impair the confidence thus reposed in him by his own peculiar people; and when he had, through years of heroic trial and suffering, done all that mortal man could do in discharge of the high trust confided by them to his hands, and failed, he bowed with dignified submission to the decree of Providence; and from the day he gave his parole at Appomattox to the hour of his death, he so lived and acted, as to deprive enmity of its malignity; and became a bright example to his defeated soldiers and countrymen, of unqualified obedience to the laws of the land, and of support to its established Government. Nay more: With a spirit of Christian and affectionate duty to his impoverished and suffering people, and with a high estimate of the importance of mental and moral culture to a generation of youth, whose earlier years were attended by war's rough teachings, he went from the tented field and the command of armies, to the quiet shades of a scholastic institution in the secluded valleys of his own native Virginia, and entered with all the earnestness of his nature upon the duties of instruction, and there spent the closing years of his life in training the minds and hearts of young men from all parts of the country for the highest usefulness "in their day and generation." By these pursuits, and his exemplary and unobtrusive life since the close of the great war in America, he won the respect and admiration of the enlightened and the good of the whole world. It is meet and natural, therefore, that his own people should bewail his death as a sore personal bereavement to each one of them. Those of us here assembled who were his soldiers, friends and supporters, sharing all the trials and many of the responsibilities of that period of his life which brought him so prominently before the world, honored and trusted him then. We have loved and admired him, and have been guided by his example since; and now that he is dead, we should be unworthy of ourselves, and unworthy to be called his countrymen, did we not feel and express the same poignant grief that now afflicts those among whom he lived and died. Those of us who were not his soldiers, friends and supporters when war raged throughout the land, but who have, nevertheless, met here today with those who were our enemies then, but are now our friends and countrymen, appreciate with them the character of LEE, and admire his rare accomplishments as a great American, whose fame and name are the property of the nation. We all unite over his hallowed sepulchre in an earnest prayer, that old divisions may be composed, and that a complete and perfect reconciliation of all estrangements may be effected at the tomb, where, all alike in a feeling of common humanity and universal Christian brotherhood, may drop their tears of heartfelt sorrow. Therefore without regard to our former relations toward each other, but meeting as Americans by birth or adoption, and in the broadest sense of national unity, and in the spirit above indicated, to do honor to a great man and Christian gentleman who has gone down to the grave, we do

Resolve, That we have received with feelings of profound sorrow intelligence of the death of Gen. ROBERT E. LEE. We can and do fully appreciate the grief of our Southern countrymen at the death of one honored by and so dear to them, and we tender to them this expression of our sympathy with the sorrow that we feel in the contemplation of so sad an event, that we are, and ought to be, henceforth forever, one great and harmonious national family, sharing on all occasions each other's joys and sympathizing in each other's sorrows.

Resolved, That a copy of the foregoing preamble and these resolutions, signed by the President and Secretary, be transmitted to the Governor of Virginia, with a request that the same be preserved in the archives of the State, and that another copy be sent to the family of Gen. LEE.

New York Times
7th July 1876

SKETCH OF GEN. CUSTER.

Major Gen. George A. Custer, who was killed with his whole command while attacking an encampment of Sioux Indians, under command of Sitting Bull, was one of the bravest and most widely known officers in the United States Army. He has for the past fifteen years been known to the country and to his comrades as a man who feared no danger, as a soldier in the truest sense of the word. He was daring to a fault, generous beyond most men. His memory will long be kept green in many friendly hearts. Born at New-Rumley, Harrison County, Ohio, on the 5th of December, 1839, he obtained a good common education, and after graduating engaged for a time in teaching school. In June, 1857, through the influence of Hon. John A. Bingham, then member of Congress from Ohio, he obtained an appointment to the United States Military Academy at West Point, and entered that institution on the 1st of July of the year named. He graduated on the 24th of June, 1861, with what was considered the fair standing of No. 34 in one of the brightest classes that ever left the academy. Immediately upon leaving West Point he was appointed Second Lieutenant in Company G of the Second United States Cavalry, a regiment which had formerly been commanded by Robert E. Lee. He reported to Lieut. Gen. Scott on the 20th of July, the day preceding the battle of Bull Run, and the Commander in Chief gave him the choice of accepting a position on his staff or of joining his regiment, then under command of Gen. McDowell, in the field. Longing for an opportunity to see active service, and determined to win distinction Lieut. Custer chose the latter course, and after riding all night through a country filled with people who were, to say the least, not friendly, he reached McDowell's head-quarters at daybreak on the morning of the 21st. Preparations for the battle had already begun, and after delivering his dispatches from Gen. Scott and hastily partaking of a mouthful of coffee and a piece of hard bread he joined his company. It is not necessary now to recount the disasters of the fight that followed. Suffice it to say that Lieut. Custer's company was among the last to leave the field. It did so in good order, bringing off Gen. Heintzelman, who had been wounded in the engagement. The young officer continued to serve with his company, and was engaged in the drilling of volunteer recruits in and about the defences of Washington, when upon the appointment of Phil Kearny to the position of Brigadier General, that lamented officer gave him a position on his staff. Custer continued in this position until an order was issued from the War Department prohibiting Generals of Volunteers from appointing officers of the regular Army to staff duty. Then he returned to his company, not, however, until he had been warmly complimented by Gen. Kearny upon the prompt and efficient manner in which he had performed the duties assigned to him. At the same time

the General predicted that Custer would be one of the most successful officers in the Army. Nor were these predictions without a speedy realization. With his company Lieut. Custer marched forward with that part of the Army of the Potomac which moved upon Manassas after its evacuation by the rebels. Our cavalry was in advance, under Gen. Stoneman and encountered the rebel horsemen for the first time near Catlett's Station. The commanding officer made a call for volunteers to charge the enemy's advance post. Lieut. Custer was among the first to step to the front, and in command of his company he shortly afterward made his first charge. He drove the rebels across Muddy Creek, wounded a number of them, and had one of his own men injured. This was the first blood drawn in the campaign under McClellan. After this Custer went with the Army of the Potomac to the Peninsula and remained with his company until the Army settled down before Yorktown, when he was detailed as an Assistant Engineer of the left wing, under Sumner. Acting in this capacity he planned and erected the earthworks nearest the enemy's lines. He also accompanied the advance under Gen. Hancock in pursuit of the enemy from Yorktown. Shortly afterward, he captured the first battle-flag ever secured by the Army of the Potomac. From this time on he was nearly always the first in every work of daring. When the Army reached the Chickahominy he was the first man to cross the river; he did so in the face of the fire of the enemy's pickets, and at times was obliged to wade up to his armpits. For this brave act Gen. McClellan promoted him to a Captaincy and made him one of his personal aids. In this capacity he served during most of the Peninsula campaign, and participated in all its battles, including the bloody seven days' fight. He performed the duty of marking out the position which was occupied by the Union Army at the battle of Gaines' Mills. He also participated in the campaign which ended in the battles of South Mountain and Antietam. Upon the retirement of Gen. McClellan from the command of the Army of the Potomac, Custer accompanied him, and for a time was out of active service.

He was next engaged in the battle of Chancellorsville, and immediately after that fight he was made a personal aid by Gen. Pleasonton, who was then commanding a division of cavalry. Serving in this capacity he took an active part in a number of hotly-contested engagements, and marked himself as one of the most dashing, some said the most reckless, officers in the service. When Pleasonton was made a Major General his first pleasure was to remember the valuable services of his Aid de Camp. He requested the appointment of four Brigadiers to command under him, and upon his recommendation, indorsed by Gens. Meade and Hooker, young Custer was made a Brigadier General and assigned to the command of the First, Fifth, Sixth, and Seventh Michigan Cavalry. He did noble service at the battle of Gettysburg. He held the right of line, and was obliged to face Hampton's division of cavalry, and after a hotly-contested fight, utterly routed the rebels and prevented them from reaching the trains of the Union Army, which they hoped to capture. Custer had two horses shot under him in this fight. Hardly had the battle concluded when he was sent to attack the enemy's train, which was trying to force its way to the Potomac. He destroyed more than four hundred wagons. At Hagerstown, Md., during a severe engagement, he again had his horse shot under him. At Falling Waters, shortly after, he attacked with his small brigade the entire rebel rear guard. The Confederate commander Gen. Pettigrew was killed and his command routed, with a loss of 1,300 prisoners two pieces of cannon and four battle flags. For some time after this fight he was constantly engaged in skirmishing with the enemy, and during the Winter which followed in picketing the Rapidan between the two armies. He participated

in the battle of the Wilderness in 1864, and on the 9th of May of the same year, under Gen. Sheridan, he set out on the famous raid toward Richmond. His brigade led the column, captured Beaver Dam, burned the station and a train of cars loaded with supplies, and released 400 Union prisoners. Rejoining Grant's Army on the Pamunkey, he took an active part in several engagements. After the battle of Fisher's Hill, in which he did most important service, he was placed in command of a division, and remained in that position until after Lee's surrender. At the ever-memorable battle of Cedar Creek his division was on the right, and not engaged in the rout of the morning, so that when Sheridan arrived on the field, after the twenty-mile ride, he found at least one command ready for service. His immediate order was "Go in, Custer!" The brave young General only waited for the word, he went in and never came out until the enemy was driven several miles beyond the battle-field. Nearly one thousand prisoners were captured, among them a Major General. Forty-five pieces of artillery were also taken. For this service Custer was made a Brevet Major General of Volunteers. Sheridan, as a further mark of approbation, detailed him to carry the news of the victory and the captured battle-flag to Washington. From this time on his fortune was made, and he continued steadily to advance in the esteem of his superiors and of the American people. When the rebels fell back to Appomattox, Custer had the advance of Sheridan's command, and his share in the action is well described in the entertaining volume entitled *With Sheridan in His Last Campaign*. The book in question says: "When the sun was an hour high in the west, energetic Custer in advance spied the depot and four heavy trains of freight cars; he quickly ordered his leading regiments to circle out to the left through the woods, and as they gained the railroad beyond the station he led the rest of his division pell-mell down the road and enveloped the train as quick as winking. Custer might not well conduct a siege of regular approaches; but for a sudden dash, Custer against the world." After many another dash of the same kind as that described, Custer was mustered out of the volunteer service on the 1st of February, 1866, and on July 28 of the same year he was appointed Lieutenant Colonel of the Seventh United States Cavalry, and since that time has been almost constantly engaged in duty upon the frontier. Recently he has contributed several interesting articles to the magazines. Of his personal appearance Col. Newhall, in *With Sheridan in His Last Campaign*, speaks as follows: "At the head of the horsemen rode Custer of the golden locks, his broad sombrero turned up from his hard, bronzed face, the ends of his crimson cravat floating over his shoulder, gold galore spangling his jacket sleeves, a pistol in his boots, jangling spurs on his heels, and a ponderous claymore swinging at his side. A wild, dare-devil of a General and a prince of advance guards." This description will be recognized by those who knew Gen. Custer as exceedingly true to nature. He was not a great General. He was a great fighter. His place in the Army will not easily be filled.

The Times
4th September 1969

Ho Chi Minh: a leader of Lenin rank

President Ho Chi Minh, President of the Democratic Republic of Vietnam and Chairman of the Vietnamese Workers' (Communist) Party, who died early today, was one of the elder statesmen of international communism. His influence within the communist movement was, for that reason, greater than his position as leader of a small and backward state would seem to justify. Unlike most of today's communist leaders, he had served the movement since the days of Lenin, whom he knew personally.

In the last years of his life Ho remained prominent as the nominal leader of North Vietnam and the father-figure of Vietnamese nationalism in a war represented as being against the Americans. Ho Chi Minh's direct part in policy making throughout the course of this war is not easy to estimate. Some reports of his ill-health would have suggested it was small : on the other hand his name was put to all official communications such as the appeal to the British and other governments in 1965, and replies to American proposals for negotiations, notably the letter addressed to him by President Johnson in February, 1967.

Ho was also glad to meet foreign visitors to Hanoi, it being an assumption of the North Vietnamese that world opposition to the war and especially opposition in the United States was an important factor in bringing it to an end. American correspondents, church delegations from Europe, travellers of all kinds in search of peace were received by him. Yet there is no reason to doubt that Ho's commitment to a communist solution for Vietnam was ever modified by his nationalism. The intervention of the North in the civil war that had developed in South Vietnam was put beyond doubt at the end of 1960, and much other evidence thereafter showed that direction of the war in the south remained under the overall authority of Hanoi.

The Sino-Soviet dispute presented a difficulty to North Vietnam which Ho naturally solved by doing his best to remain neutral between the two. His own past associated him closely with both countries ; so did Vietnam's needs in the war as it developed with the growing American involvement from 1964 onwards. Ideologically it seemed that a pro-Chinese wing was dominant, but Russian aid, and later the vagaries of the cultural revolution in China modified Hanoi's commitment to Maoism. Ho probably could be more independent of both countries than most of his colleagues. Like them he was intransigent. His reply to President Johnson's appeal for negotiations made in 1967 was wooden, filled with jargon, and seemed to show no flexibility whatsoever.

The major portion of his long life was spent as a professional revolutionary, in which capacity he served the Communist International, and even after he emerged as President of North Vietnam he took pains to conceal these earlier activities. Born in or about 1890—his birthday was officially celebrated on May 19—at the village of Kim-lien in Nghe-an province of Vietnam, he was the youngest of three children. His father, Nguyen Sinh Huy, was a minor official dismissed, according to French records, for drunkenness and cruelty, who subsequently supported himself as an itinerant healer. Ho was given the name Nguyen Tat Thanh, but used numerous aliases in adult life. Educated at a Franco-Annamite school, he became an elementary schoolteacher in 1907.

Signing on as a steward in the French liner Latouche Treville in 1912, Ho travelled to Marseilles. Thereafter he worked aboard ship, visiting several countries before finding employment in the kitchens of the Carlton Hotel in London, Towards the end of the 1914-18 War he moved to Paris, where he earned his living by retouching photographs and devoted his free time to politics. Vainly he haunted the corridors of Versailles during the armistice negotiations, seeking to meet President Wilson in order to enlist his aid in improving conditions in Vietnam. About that time he made the acquaintance of such leaders of the French political left wing as Vaillant Couturier, Andre Berton, and Marcel Cachin. He joined the French Socialist Party and formed the Inter-Colonial Union, a body of nationalists from colonial territories living in Paris.

Under the alias which he was then using, Nguyen Ai Quoc (Nguyen the Patriot), he contributed articles to the Socialist paper Le Populaire and edited the Inter-Colonial Union paper Le Paria. The turning point in his life was the 1920 Socialist Congress at Tours, where Ho voted for the Third International and subsequently became a founder member of the French Communist Party. As such he attended the Comintern Congress at Moscow in 1922 and, except for two short visits to France, remained there until 1925 studying at the Toilers of the East University. In that year he accompanied the Borodin Mission to China, ostensibly working as a translator in the Soviet Consulate at Canton under the name of Ly Thuy. There he formed the Vietnamese Revolutionary Youth League, which brought young Vietnamese nationalists for training an indoctrination by Soviet instructors at Whampoa Military Academy. Some, including a number of today's communist leaders, went on to Moscow for further training.

Following Chiang Kai-shek's rupture with the communists in 1927, Ho returned to Russia but was soon back at his revolutionary work in Asia. He founded the Vietnamese—later the Indo-Chinese—Communist Party in 1930 at Hongkong, but was arrested there himself the following year together with a girl, Li Sam, whom he described as a niece. She was more probably his mistress, or possibly his wife, but she disappeared without trace after her release. Defended in Hongkong by a lawyer named Loseby and in Britain by Stafford Cripps, who pleaded his case before the Privy Council, Ho was released in 1932 and was smuggled in disguise to Amoy, in spite of French demands for his extradition.

Ho's whereabouts in the late 1930s remain a mystery. His is believed to have visited Yenan but soon left, apparently finding Mao Tse-tung's personality uncongenial. From there, in 1940, he went to join Vietnamese exiles near the Tonkinese border. In 1941 at Chingsi he formed a communist-dominated political movement later to become widely known by its abbreviated title Viet Minh. Arrested by the Kuomintang in 1942, he spent a year in prison before being released at the insistence of the O.S.S., which wished to use his followers to gather intelligence about the Japanese in Vietnam. It was then that he formally adopted the name of Ho Chi Minh (Ho who seeks enlightenment).

Armed Viet Minh bands in the highlands of Tonkin, supplied by the O.S.S., awaited the defeat of Japan before occupying the capital, Hanoi. In the confused period which followed, Ho's true genius showed itself as he manoeuvred to outwit the Chinese occupation force and the returning French as well as to destroy his nationalist rivals. A keen political sense, utter ruthlessness, and inspired opportunism enabled him to sustain the newly proclaimed Democratic Republic of Vietnam under his own leadership. When his communist affiliations proved a disadvantage,

he took the unprecedented step of dissolving the Communist Party, at least overtly. After protracted negotiations broke down he led his followers into what then appeared a hopeless war in December, 1946, but the eight years of bitter struggle culminated in the defeat of the French at Dien Bien Phu and the convening of the Geneva Conference. Bowing to strong Soviet and Chinese pressure, Ho agreed to the partition of Vietnam and the communists assumed control of the north.

Victory was made possible only by Chinese aid and Ho paid the price by having to submit to Chinese influence in carrying out Maoist land reforms totally unsuited to Vietnam. Peasant revolts resulted, and all of Ho's skill and prestige were needed to avert collapse.

Ho's talents were not for political theory but for political action, in which he outdistanced all his compatriots. He will be remembered as the founder of Vietnamese communism, the leader of his country's struggle against French rule, and the creator of the Democratic Republic of Vietnam. In the simplicity of his dress and manner he resembled Gandhi—the likeness may have been deliberately cultivated—but this mild exterior concealed a shrewd, calculating and ruthless political brain more reminiscent of Stalin. His command of foreign

languages, his sense of humour, and his charm of manner were effective weapons skilfully used to disarm his opponents and to achieve his political ends. With the death of Ho Chi Minh the communist world has lost a man who will rank alongside Lenin, Stalin, and Mao Tse-tung as one of the outstanding figures of the movement.

A message from him, intended to reaffirm his national image among the South Vietnamese, was broadcast last July.

He appeared in 1968 at the May Day celebrations and a poem by him promising greater victories was published for the Tet festival early this year. His last public appearance had been at the May Day celebrations this year.

One of Ho's most passionate concerns—and this is another thing that distinguishes him from a man like Mao Tse-tung—was his determination to win justice for the non-white peoples of the world. Vietnam was the one part of East Asia to be colonized and it proved the most resistant from the earliest days of French rule. A rebellion in 1908 when Ho was already a young man of 18 would have fired his nationalism. But when he travelled abroad he did so not simply as a Vietnamese nationalist seeking the liberation of his country from French rule: what concerned him even more was the liberation of all non-white peoples from the contempt they suffered at the hands of their white dominators.

This incipient international outlook found in the October revolution a challenge to this world of white domination. It was characteristic of Ho's attitude that he consistently emphasized the anti-colonial character of the communist movement and openly attacked those communist parties which were laggard in this respect.

His identification with communism as an international movement lasted until the end. Indeed, one might hazard the view that a political life confined to Vietnam and marred by the growth of the Sino-Soviet dispute must have deeply distressed him. He was not involved at all in Marxist theory. The dispute about revisionism which Mao Tse-tung initiated would not have enlivened him. He was too conscious of China as a country—in which he had lived—ever to think that an affiliation with the Russians to the exclusion of China was possible. But the decline of communism as an international movement resulting from the Sino-Soviet dispute must have darkened his last days.

Perhaps in order to measure up to Mao Tse-tung, Ho Chi Minh's selected works were published in Hanoi in 1960. They have none of the verve of some of Mao's writings: still less of any original political thinking, but the theme of maltreatment of coloured peoples—sometimes illustrated by the treatment of Negroes in the United States which deeply influenced Ho when he was a young man in the first decades of this century—runs consistently through what he wrote.

He is not it must be admitted a man of whom a great deal is known. A natural tendency to secrecy and to a conspiratorial attitude flowered in his early days while working for the Communist International and never left him. He was a man of more pseudonyms than close research has been able to track down. "An old man likes to have a little mystery about himself", he told the late Bernard Fall in an interview in 1962, and he remained unwilling to the last to reveal details of parts of his revolutionary career.

The Times
16th October 1944

SOLDIER AND NAZI

ROMMEL IN SUCCESS AND FAILURE

A MASTERLY TACTICIAN

Field-Marshal Erwin Rommel, whose death was announced by the German wireless yesterday, was an able general, whose spell of success in Africa enabled German propaganda to build him up as a military figure second only to Hitler himself. This exaggerated reputation was exploded in the battle of El Alamein, but Rommel's conduct of the Axis retreat to Tunisia proved beyond doubt his professional competence. Ruthless and resourceful, Rommel had been connected with the Nazi Party since its inception, and was completely identified with its fortunes; his death will be as much a political as a military blow to the enemy.

Erwin Rommel was born in 1891 and was educated at Tübingen University. In the 1914-18 war his career was one of extraordinary distinction for a young and very junior officer. He started off as an ensign in the 124th Infantry Regiment, first came to notice for a brilliant exploit on the French front, and afterwards won the order " Pour le Mérite "—for one of his rank the equivalent of the Victoria Cross—for his skill, leadership, and personal bravery in Italy. After the war he taught at the Dresden Military Academy before joining the National-Socialist Party. He became a storm-troop leader, attached to Hitler's bodyguard, and organized the campaign of terror in Coburg (in which Socialists and Communists were killed) which Hitler described in " Mein Kampf " as the turning-point of his career.

GANGSTER METHODS

Rommel's qualities of leadership—and perhaps also his taste for the methods of a gangster in civil war—brought him the personal favour of Hitler. He took part in the occupation of Austria, the Sudetenland, and Czechoslovakia. In the present war he served in the Polish campaign and in 1940 commanded a Panzer division in France. He received the Knight's Cross for his part in breaking the French front in the region of Maubeuge, and it is believed to have been his division which reached the sea at St. Valery-en-Caux and cut off the British 51st Division.

When Hitler realized that he would have to go to the support of his Italian allies in North Africa or see them driven right out of the continent, he entrusted Rommel with the organization of the Afrika Korps. This force was extremely well trained and equipped, and on being transported to Libya it won an instant success against the depleted and relatively ill-armed British forces. In April, 1941, General Wavell was forced to abandon Benghazi. Advancing with extreme rapidity, Rommel drove his opponent across the Egyptian frontier and laid siege to the isolated garrison which had been dropped in Tobruk.

A long period of comparative lull followed. Rommel—the real commander-in-chief of the Axis forces, though he had a nominal Italian superior—was building up a strong force, but was always short of certain essential supplies. His attacks against Tobruk were fruitless, but he was contemplating one on a bigger scale when he was attacked on November 18, 1941, by the British Eighth Army. The long and extremely confused battle which followed went against Rommel, though the German armoured tactics were, at least to begin with, superior to the British, and the German armour was very much better in quality. By sheer persistence and pluck the British, in spite of almost catastrophic losses in tanks, wore down the enemy, or perhaps rather the enemy's commander. By the end of December, 1941, he had retreated headlong to Jedabia, leaving his forces on the frontier to be mopped up. In all he had lost 20,000 prisoners, but he had saved the personnel of his two crack armoured divisions, which was what he chiefly cared about. Having received some reinforcements in tanks, he succeeded in pushing the Eighth Army back to the line Gazala-Bir Hakeim, some 40 miles west of Tobruk.

BACK AT TOBRUK

This campaign had gone against Rommel on balance, but he made up for it in a resounding victory in May and June, 1942. Outflanking and rolling up the Eighth Army's position from the south, he drove it back in fierce fighting to the frontier, then suddenly turned upon Tobruk, left isolated once again, and carried it by storm. The British were unable to call a halt until they reached El Alamein, 80 miles east of Alexandria. They had lost 50,000 men and vast quantities of material, and were no longer sure of even being able to hold Egypt. Rommel had been aided by superior material, notably in tanks, but his tactics had been masterly. However, he made no headway in his attacks on the El Alamein line; in fact, the Eighth Army began to launch local counter-offensives.

So the stage was set for the final trial, one of the most vital in the war. Rommel's last attack, begun on August 31, failed after sharp fighting. And then, in the last week of October and the first week of November General Montgomery inflicted a heavy defeat upon the Axis forces. Rommel was in hospital in Germany when the offensive began, but hurried back to his post. He succeeded in extricating once more a large proportion of his best German forces, leaving the rest and the Italians to their fate. Though outmanoeuvred in the battle, he conducted the long retreat to Tunisia with skill. But his African career ended with another disaster. His last attack on the Eighth Army at Medenine in March, 1943, was a complete failure, and he then returned home, leaving not only the troops which he had led back across North Africa but also those which had been landed in Tunisia to meet their inevitable end.

His first European appointment after his return, on completing further hospital treatment, was apparently an inspectorship of the western coast defences. But before the allies landed in Normandy on June 6, 1944, he had been made commander of an army group defending the Low Countries and France north of the Biscay coast. He was wholly unable to prevent the landing, which took the Germans largely by surprise, but he made vigorous efforts to confine the allied holding by means of armoured divisions which he concentrated from all points. The Germans have announced that it was on July 17 that he sustained the injuries from which he has now died.

Rommel was undoubtedly a tactician of genius, but with some weaknesses. Restless, arrogant, and difficult to work with, neglectful of the administrative side of the forces which he commanded, he was too apt to repeat himself. But he brought to modern large-scale warfare the methods of bluff and ambush which had begun to appear unattainable in present-day conditions. This strange figure, master of tank warfare without knowing anything about a tank or even understanding the inside of a car, was in fact full of contradictions. Disliked by those with whom he came in contact, he yet exercised an amazing influence over the troops from whom he exacted so much. Brutal in speech and sometimes in action, he treated British wounded prisoners in Africa with consideration. Boundless in daring, it would seem that his nerve was liable to break suddenly. He will be remembered as a brilliant though uncertain and uneven commander in the field rather than as a commander-in-chief.

The Times
23rd April 1918

CAPT. RICHTHOFEN KILLED.

FALL BEHIND BRITISH LINES.

GERMANS' MOST FAMOUS AIRMAN.

(FROM OUR SPECIAL CORRESPONDENT.)

WAR CORRESPONDENTS' HEAD-QUARTERS, APRIL 22.

Yesterday's official German *communiqué* announced that "Cavalry Captain Freiherr von Richthofen, at the head of his trusty 11th Pursuit Flight, has gained his 79th and 80th victories in the air." Before that had been published Richthofen was dead. He was brought down behind our lines not far from the Somme, and is to be buried this afternoon in a village in the neighbourhood where he fell.

While probably not as brilliant as Captain Ball, all our airmen concede that Richthofen was a great pilot and a fine fighting man.

If all the victories credited to him were really personal triumphs and not merely those of the squadron of which he was the leader, then Cavalry Captain Baron von Richthofen was easily the most famous airman that the German Flying Service has produced. Immelmann first, and then Boelke, in whose squadron Richthofen had his first experience of fighting and gained his first success, were accounted great pilots, but their exploits were insignificant compared with those attributed by German Main Headquarters to Richthofen, for while the last-named was reported, as late as Sunday, to have achieved his 80th victory, Immelmann, when he was killed in an air fight in June, 1916, had only 15 "enemy machines" to his credit, and Boelke had brought down, officially, only 38, and unofficially 40, when he met his death in the following October.

Richthofen's official career dates from February 15, 1917, when, as lieutenant, he was said to have won his 20th and 21st aerial victories. His successes followed with almost bewildering rapidity, and by April 9 he was credited with his 40th, his 61st on September 4, and his 70th on March 27 of this year. Between that date and Sunday he was reported to have won 10 further victories. His "star" day was, apparently, April 28, 1917, when it was officially claimed that he had shot down five machines. Lieutenant Wolff, who was a member of Richthofen's squadron, and who was killed last September, was also credited with the same number of victims on the same day. In August last year it was reported, on the authority of statements made by captured prisoners, that Richthofen was wounded in a fight with a British airman, and it may be regarded as some confirmation of the report that his name was absent from the German official *communiqués* for September and October of that year.

Richthofen was appointed commander of the 11th Chasing Squadron after he had brought down his 16th machine—that must have been some time before February, 1917—and two days after his appointment he was decorated with the *Order Pour le Mérite*. On the occasion of his 50th victory, Richthofen received a letter of congratulation from the Kaiser, who is said to have looked with special favour upon the airman, and upon whom this month he conferred the Order of the Red Eagle with Crown and Swords.

In the "Memoirs" which he published in August, 1917, Richthofen, like Boelke before him, paid tribute to the British airman's love of a fight. "He is a dashing fellow," he wrote. "He used to come now and then and pelt Boelke's flying ground with bombs. He simply challenged one to battle, and always accepted it. I hardly ever encountered an Englishman who refused battle." Captain Richthofen claims to have brought down the British airman, Major Hawker, and he gives his brother, Lieutenant Baron von Richthofen, who is also in the German Flying Service on the Western front, the honour of having defeated Captain Ball.

"During my whole life," Richthofen wrote, "I have not found a happier hunting ground than in the course of the Somme battle." And it was on this battle ground that he fought his last fight.

LORD KITCHENER.

The Daily News & Leader
7th June 1916

AN ORGANISER OF VICTORY.

Lord Kitchener from Subaltern to Secretary for War.

MR. ASQUITH'S TRIBUTE: "A GOOD SOLDIER, HE PUT DUTY FIRST."

Field-Marshal Earl Kitchener, G.C.B., G.C.M.G., O.M., was born in 1850 at Ballylongford, in Kerry, and was therefore, as so many British soldiers have been in the past, connected with Ireland, but he was English on both sides. His father, Lieutenant-Colonel H. H. Kitchener, of the 13th Light Dragoons, had his seat at the Manor House, Cossington, Leicestershire, and his mother, Frances Chevallier, was the daughter of the Rector of Aspall, Suffolk.

After passing through Woolwich Academy he offered his services to the French Government during the Franco-German War, and was attached to the Second Army of the Loire, under General Chanzy. He saw some fighting, and made a perilous ascent in a war balloon, but, unfortunately, fell ill with pneumonia and was invalided home.

The early years of his service with the British Army were devoted to civil rather than military pursuits. From 1874-6 he served in Western Palestine in the survey; from 1878-82 he was engaged in the survey of the island of Cyprus; and for a short time acted as Vice-Consul at Erzerum. During these years he acquired a knowledge of Arabic and of the people of the Levant which was later to be of priceless value, and was one of the chief reasons why he was chosen by Sir Evelyn Wood to help create the Egyptian Army.

During Lord Wolseley's advance up the Nile, in 1884, he served in the Intelligence Department and as Quartermaster-General, thus gaining his first experience of providing for the wants of a large expedition. In 1886 he was made Governor of Suakim, where, instead of standing wholly on the defensive, as was the desire of the Egyptian Government, he actively took the part of the friendly tribes against Osman Digna. In January they attacked Osman Digna's camp at Handub, and Kitchener moved up to their support, endeavouring to cover their retreat. In the action he was dangerously wounded in the jaw.

EGYPT.

The Story of Omdurman.

In 1892 Sir F. Grenfell resigned the post of Sirdar to the Egyptian army, and Sir Evelyn Baring (Lord Cromer) appointed Colonel Kitchener to succeed to the command. The next four years were spent in improving the condition of the troops and in preparation for the great struggle with the Mahdi. . . . This was the prologue to the adventure of Omdurman.

From the battle of Atbara (April, 1898) the Sirdar's advance was rapid and unbroken. On the early morning of Sept. 2, the army of the Khalifa Abdullah, 50,000 strong, attacked the Anglo-Egyptian army drawn up to await their onset, but were shot down by the Maxim guns and the long-range rifles before they got to close quarters. But the day was also marked by a gallant charge of the 21st Lancers and a shock between the cavalry of the desert and the British troops in which the conditions of the combatants were more nearly equal. The Sirdar followed up the victory, which was complete before noon, by marching into the city and setting free the European prisoners of the Khalifa from their black and noxious prison.

The enemy's strength had been broken at Omdurman, but the settlement and pacification of the country was a longer business. Two days after Omdurman the Sirdar visited Khartum. His guard of honour took up its position opposite the Palace where Gordon had fallen. The British and Egyptian flags were run up over the ruins, and after cheers had been called for the Queen and the Khedive a short memorial service for Gordon was held. "At the close there were," said a correspondent, "those who said the cold Sirdar himself could hardly speak or see, as General Hunter and the rest stepped out, according to their rank, and shook his hand. What wonder? He had trodden this road to Khartum for 14 years, and he stood at the goal at last."

"INHUMANLY UNERRING."

The general conception of Lord Kitchener at that time was based on the stirring narrative of the campaign written by the late Mr. G. W. Steevens:

Major-General Sir Horatio Herbert Kitchener (he wrote in 1898) is 48 years old by the book, but that is irrelevant. He stands several inches over six feet, straight as a lance, and looks out imperiously above most men's heads; his motions are deliberate and strong; slender, but firmly knit, he seems built for tireless, steel-wire endurance rather than for power or agility; that also is irrelevant. Steady, passionless eyes, shaded by decisive brows, brick-red, rather full cheeks, a long moustache, beneath which you divine an immovable mouth; his face is harsh, and neither appeals for affection nor stirs dislike. All this is, irrelevant too; neither age, nor figure, nor face, nor any accident of person has any bearing on the essential Sirdar. You could imagine the character just the same as if all the externals were different. He has no age but the prime of life, no body but one to carry his mind, no face but one to keep his brain behind. The brain and the will are the essence and the whole of the man—a brain perfect and a will so perfect in their workings that, in the face of the extremest difficulty, they never seem to know what struggle is. You cannot imagine the Sirdar other than as seeing the right thing to do and doing it. His precision is so inhumanly unerring, he is more like a machine than a man.

This was one side of the man; his future record was to prove that he had other qualities than sternness and resolution. Possibly his character mellowed with age. In any case, those who knew him in India hardly recognised the picture of the stern misogynist drawn by the correspondents in the Egyptian campaign.

SOUTH AFRICA.

The Organiser of Victory.

Lord Kitchener was still engaged in the reconstruction of the Sudan when the summons came to him to join Lord Roberts on his way to South Africa as Chief of Staff. It was thought by some that his masterful disposition would make him a difficult subordinate. This was not the case. Lord Kitchener admired and respected Lord Roberts, and accepted the commission with alacrity. He was, he said, ready to black Roberts's boots if required. He left Khartum on Dec. 18, 1899, joined Lord Roberts at Gibraltar on the 26th, and was entrusted by him with the organisation of the transport for the great advance to Pretoria, which he had already planned.

On Feb. 18 Kitchener came into touch with Cronje at Paardeberg after 48 hours of hard manoeuvring. Cronje was strongly entrenched in a laager resembling two villages. With the directness that characterised all that he did, Kitchener determined to annihilate Cronje's force and then make direct for Kimberley. Night fell before anything had apparently been accomplished, except the loss of 1,100 British killed and wounded, and Kitchener reported to Lord Roberts that he hoped to be able to do something more definite on the morrow. On the morrow, however, before anything more had been done, Lord Roberts was himself on the scene, and took a different view of the situation. Under his orders Paardeberg was invested, and the surrender of Cronje was accomplished a week later without further loss of life. The moral effect of this surrender was great, but had Kitchener's original plan been carried out its effect would no doubt have been much greater and might conceivably have shortened the war.

The relief of Kimberley followed, but Kitchener for the present found his work in keeping the line of Lord Roberts's communications, and not in actual fighting. By Nov. 29, 1900, five months after Lord Roberts's entry into Pretoria, it seemed that the war was practically over, and that there was nothing left to do but clear the country of small Boer patrols; it was in this mistaken view of the situation that Lord Roberts relinquished command of the army in Nov., 1900, leaving Lord Kitchener in his place. Two days after Lord Roberts had sailed from Capetown the British outpost at Nooitgedacht was seized, 500 men were taken prisoner, and fighting broke out again in various directions.

General French was set to sweep the Eastern Transvaal clear of the Boers while Methuen was hard at work in the South-West. During the South African winter of 1901 the British position was strengthened by the building of a large number of block houses capable of holding from six to thirty men, and studded along the railway lines at intervals of about 2,000 yards. Meanwhile, Kitchener kept his columns in constant movement, and also entered upon the much-criticised policy of concentration camps. He found by experience that released prisoners left at liberty were apt to rejoin the commandoes; then, too, the British had been driven to denude the country of shelter, and once this policy was adopted it was necessary to provide accommodation for the women and children who were driven from their homes. Public attention was drawn in England to the insanitary and dangerous condition of these camps by Miss Hobhouse, and public feeling was aroused against the General who was responsible for the system. As a matter of fact, the policy of concentration camps was in some ways more to the military advantage of the Boer force than to the British, for once relieved of any anxiety about their wives and children the commandoes were freer in the field.

Impatience in England was rapidly growing, but Lord Kitchener was not to be turned from his policy, and on March 22, 1902, his persistence and resource were rewarded by a request from the Acting-Governor of the Transvaal that facilities should be provided for their coming to Pretoria to discuss terms of peace.

There followed a period of hardly less activity as Commander-in-Chief in India, during which he came into conflict with another strong man, Lord Curzon; then an Empire tour to offer advice on a new scheme of national defence, and finally a rather unexpected return to Egypt as Agent-General in succession to Sir Eldon Gorst.

THE NEW ARMY.

Lord Kitchener's Greatest Task.

Lord Kitchener's appointment to the post of Secretary of State for War was announced on August 6, 1914, in the following terms:

In consequence of the pressure of other duties the Prime Minister has been compelled to give up the office of Secretary of State for War. The King has approved of the appointment of Lord Kitchener as his successor. Lord Kitchener undertakes the duties of the office for the time being in view of the emergency created by the war, and his post in Egypt will be kept open.

In his maiden speech in the House of Lords three weeks later he was able to announce that the first 100,000 recruits for the New Army had already been practically secured, but he added this grave warning: "If the war should be protracted, and if its fortunes should be varied or adverse, exertions and sacrifices beyond any which have been demanded will be required from the whole nation and Empire.

From the first he took a grave view of the probabilities of the situation, and resolutely refused all temptations to underestimate Germany's military power. He was probably the first man in this country to visualise the raising of an Army of millions, and his immense organising ability, coupled with a reputation that appealed as no other could to the imagination of his fellow countrymen, provided him with the power necessary for realising this vision.

"Kitchener's Army" sprang into being with amazing swiftness. Each demand for "Another 100,000," or "Another 500,000" was honoured, and more than honoured, by the men of the Empire. The world was frankly amazed, and for many months Lord Kitchener's name was one to conjure with.

Then, on May 22, 1915, one of the Northcliffe publications came out with the heading:

THE SHELLS SCANDAL.
LORD KITCHENER'S TRAGIC BLUNDER.

The reply of the country was emphatic. The "Daily Mail" was burnt on the Stock Exchange, and in every part of the land resolutions of confidence in the Secretary for War were carried with enthusiasm. The nation refused to throw to the dogs the man who in twelve months had raised Great Britain to the position of a first-class military Power.

Lord Kitchener himself remained entirely unmoved, and steadily continued his efforts to ensure the whole weight of Britain's power being thrown into the scales on the side of the Allies.

In November, 1915, he went to Gallipoli by request of the Cabinet to advise upon the situation there, and it was owing to the soundness of his judgment that the withdrawal of the British forces, so marvellously accomplished, was undertaken.

Still the attacks were continued by a coterie both inside and outside Parliament, and as late as May 31 last a debate in the House of Commons provided an opportunity for further mischief-making of this kind.

Nevertheless, on May 26 the King was able to congratulate his subjects on having raised an army of volunteers numbering over five millions—the final reply to Lord Kitchener's traducers.

THE PREMIER'S TRIBUTE.

Speaking in the House of Commons, Mr. Asquith summed up the significance of the mighty task in these words:

"I think the Army, the country, and the Empire are under a debt which cannot be measured in words to the services Lord Kitchener has rendered since the beginning of the war. . . . He told me in the frankest possible terms of his indisposition, except at the call of duty, to undertake the task which I proposed, with the consent of his Sovereign, to lay on him; but, like a good soldier, he put duty first. Everything else was subordinated to it, and from that moment to this there has not been one single day on which Lord Kitchener has not laboured with an assiduity and a zeal and a patriotic self-devotion which, as I can say from personal observation and daily contact with him, is beyond all praise.

"There is no other man in this country or in this Empire who could have summoned into existence, in so short a time, with so little friction, with such satisfactory and surprising, and even bewildering results, the enormous Army which now at home and abroad is maintaining the honour of our Empire.

"History, I am certain, will regard it as one of the most remarkable achievements of the kind ever accomplished, and I am bound to say, and I say it with all sincerity, that for that achievement Lord Kitchener is personally entitled to the credit."

SOME KITCHENER STORIES.

How He Won Respect and Obedience.

HIS WAY WITH THE DANDY

"Well, Lord Kitchener," a prominent citizen of Capetown is reported to have said to his guest during a crisis in the South African war, "and how do you propose to reorganise the transport?" "Reorganise it?" replied Kitchener drily. "I shall organise it."

Most of the stories about "K. of K."—and he was a man about whose memory stories clustered wherever he went—have the same flavour of mingled irony and self-confidence, but whether they do more than represent a mere fraction of the man may be questioned. Certainly in South Africa he showed that he could be human enough on occasion

HATRED OF THE FOP.

One of the things he hated most was a dandified soldier, though he was very rigorous in his regard for military etiquette. "What is your taste in hairpins?" he is said to have asked a particularly over-groomed and overdressed subaltern. On another occasion he sent for an officer, of whom he had heard good reports, and found that he wore an eyeglass. "Is it necessary for you to wear that?" he inquired. "Absolutely necessary, sir," was the reply.

"What a pity!" exclaimed Lord Kitchener. "I was going to offer you a place on my Staff. But short-sighted men are not wanted here."

Nor had he much patience with physical infirmity. "Sunstroke? What the devil does he mean by having sunstroke?" is the classic instance of his attitude toward the weaker vessels. "I don't profess to be able to win battles without losing men," was his sole contemptuous reply to the criticism levelled against his generalship at Paardeberg.

Men, it used to be said in the Army, did the impossible at a word from him. "Twelve hours in which to carry this despatch! You must do it in six!"—and the officer who had asked for the twelve hours did it in five.

AN ORDER IN EGYPT.

The habit of ordering things to be done at once, like some Eastern potentate, grew upon him in Egypt. One day he wanted to go by motor-car from Cairo to Helouan. At Abidiye the chauffeur stopped, for the simple reason that the road ended there. Lord Kitchener was more than vexed, and ordered the chauffeur to drive him instantly to the great local prison, where he interviewed the Governor.

"Have you got a thousand men," he asked, "to do some work to-morrow morning?" "Four thousand men, sir, if needed," was the reply.

"Then choose a thousand of the best and let them begin to make the road from where it now ends at Abidiye to Helouan. I shall see to tools and material being on the spot by that time."

Some of the Kitchener stories are a trifle grim though not lacking in a certain kind of humour. Such is the statement that when an officer in charge of some works under construction in the Punjab telegraphed to the Commander-in-Chief: "Regret to report killing of twelve labourers by dynamite accident," the reply simply was, "Do you want any more dynamite?"

To an officer in South Africa who reported more than once that during his brushes with the enemy "several Boers were seen to fall from their saddles," he sent the polite inquiry: "I hope when they fell they did not hurt themselves."

BLUE PENCIL RETORT.

A favourite captain of his was once entrusted with an important commission. There was a delay in executing it through his horse casting a shoe. "Very sorry," was Kitchener's comment, "but I cannot rest my plan of campaign on a horse's shoe or an officer's carelessness." Nor had he any mercy on the sort of man who says that a thing "can't be done."

During the course of the South African war he telegraphed to a certain General to know why his force was making no progress. The General replied: "Unless you send me my full complement of mounted troops I can do nothing." Lord Kitchener's note in blue pencil on the telegram filed for reference was the one word: "Poltroon."

But he was by no means always stern and unbending. One of his A.D.C.s in South Africa happened to pick up the gilt-edged Staff cap which usually adorned his Chief's head, and was holding forth to a party of friends. Lord Kitchener missed his hat, and, perceiving its whereabouts through an open door, picked up the A.D.C.'s plumed head-dress, and walked into the room, saying: "How should I have done for Roberts' Horse?" The A.D.C. has since become General Sir John Maxwell—always known as "one of Kitchener's men."

HIS PET STARLING.

While in Pretoria he possessed a tame starling which was the pet of the moment. He spent hours standing in front of the bird's cage as though he expected it to throw light on the problems before him. Presently it occurred to him that the bird was lonely, whereupon the officers of the Staff occupied their spare time hunting up and down Pretoria to find a mate for the Chief's bird. That story, at any rate, seems to suggest another side to the man who has been likened more often than anyone else to a bloodless machine.

His passion for settling things on the spot sometimes led him into difficulties. While he was organising mobile columns on Lord Roberts' line of communications he told off a subaltern to command 200 men. "You will want an adjutant," said Kitchener, and straightway chose a smart-looking man who had just come in by train.

After finding out what his regiment was and introducing him to his commanding officer, he asked, "What is your rank? You mustn't be senior to your commanding officer." "I am a master tailor, sir," replied the man.

The Times
7th November 1805

The LONDON GAZETTE EXTRAORDINARY.
WEDNESDAY, NOV 6. 1805.

ADMIRALTY-OFFICE, Nov. 6.

Dispatches, of which the following are Copies, were received at the Admiralty this day, at one o'clock A. M. from Vice-Admiral Collingwood Commander in Chief of his Majesty's ships and vessels off Cadiz :—

SIR, Euryalus, off Cape Trafalgar, Oct. 22, 1805.

The ever-to-be-lamented death of Vice-Admiral Lord Viscount Nelson, who, in the late conflict with the enemy, fell in the hour of victory, leaves to me the duty of informing my Lords Commissioners of the Admiralty, that on the 19th instant, it was communicated to the Commander in Chief, from the ships watching the motions of the enemy in Cadiz, that the Combined Fleet had put to sea; as they sailed with light winds westerly, his Lordship concluded their destination was the Mediterranean, and immediately made all sail for the Streights' entrance, with the British Squadron, consisting of twenty-seven ships, three of them sixty-fours, where his Lordship was informed, by Captain Blackwood (whose vigilance in watching, and giving notice of the enemy's movements, has been highly meritorious), that they had not yet passed the Streights.

On Monday the 21st instant, at day-light, when Cape Trafalgar bore E. by S. about seven leagues, the enemy was discovered six or seven miles to the Eastward, the wind about West, and very light; the Commander in Chief immediately made the signal for the fleet to bear up in two columns, as they are formed in order of sailing; a mode of attack his Lordship had previously directed, to avoid the inconvenience and delay in forming a line of battle in the usual manner. The enemy's line consisted of thirty-three ships (of which eighteen were French, and fifteen Spanish), commanded in Chief by Admiral Villeneuve: the Spaniards, under the direction of Gravina, wore, with their heads to the Northward, and formed their line of battle with great closeness and correctness; but as the mode of attack was unusual, so the structure of their line was new; it formed a crescent, convexing to leeward, so that, in leading down to their centre, I had both their van and rear abaft the beam; before the fire opened, every alternate ship was about a cable's length to windward of her second a-head and a-stern, forming a kind of double line, and appeared, when on their beam, to leave a very little interval between them; and this without crowding their ships.

The action began at twelve o'clock, by the leading ships of the columns breaking through the enemy's line, the Commander in Chief about the tenth ship from the van, the Second in Command about the twelfth from the rear, leaving the van of the enemy unoccupied; the succeeding ships breaking through, in all parts, astern of their leaders, and engaging the enemy at the muzzles of their guns; the conflict was severe; the enemy's ships were fought with a gallantry highly honourable to their Officers; but the attack on them was irresistible, and it pleased the Almighty Disposer of all events to grant his Majesty's arms a complete and glorious victory. About three P. M. many of the enemy's ships having struck their colours, their line gave way; Admiral Gravina, with ten ships joining their frigates to leeward, stood towards Cadiz. The five headmost ships in their van tacked, and standing to the Southward, to windward of the British line, were engaged, and the sternmost of them taken; the others went off, leaving to his Majesty's squadron nineteen ships of the line (of which two are first rates, the Santissima Trinidad and the Santa Anna,) with three Flag Officers, viz. Admiral Villeneuve, the Commander in Chief; Don Ignatio Maria D'Aliva, Vice Admiral; and the Spanish Rear-Admiral, Don Baltazar Hidalgo Cisneros.

After such a Victory, it may appear unnecessary to enter into encomiums on the particular parts taken by the several Commanders; the conclusion says more on the subject than I have language to express; the spirit which animated all was the same: when all exert themselves zealously Such a battle could not be fought without sustaining a great loss of men. I have not only to lament, in common with the British Navy, and the British Nation, in the Fall of the Commander in Chief, the loss of a Hero, whose name will be immortal, and his memory ever dear to his country; but my heart is rent with the most poignant grief for the death of a friend, to whom, by many years intimacy, and a perfect knowledge of the virtues of his mind, which inspired ideas superior to the common race of men, I was bound by the strongest ties of affection; a grief to which even the glorious occasion in which he fell, does not bring the consolation which, perhaps, it ought: his Lordship received a musket ball in his left breast, about the middle of the action, and sent an Officer to me immediately with his last farewell; and soon after expired.

Having thus detailed the proceedings of the fleet on this occasion, I beg to congratulate their Lordships on a victory which, I hope, will add a ray to the glory of his Majesty's crown, and be attended with public benefit to our country. I am, &c.
(Signed) C. COLLINGWOOD.

The deep impression which the victory and the death of Lord NELSON has made on the mind of the nation, though it is visible to every eye, and is felt in every heart, baffles the efforts of description; and we must borrow the veil of *Agamemnon* to hide the expression of those sensations which we are unable to describe: but the various actions of this great man's heroic life, may be embodied by the Historian; and the readers of *The Times* will expect some general record of them.

HORATIO Lord Viscount NELSON, was born at Burnham Thorpe, in the county of Norfolk, on the 29th day of September, 1758. His father was the Rev. EDWARD NELSON, Rector of that parish, and it was in the Parsonage-house that the Noble Admiral first saw the light. His mother was the daughter of Doctor SUCKLING, Prebendary of Westminster. The first scene of his education was the High School at Norwich, from whence he was removed to North Walsham, in the county of Norfolk.

In the year 1770, when the disputes between Great Britain and Spain, respecting the settlement of Falkland Islands, threatened immediate hostilities, he was received on board the *Raisonable*, of 64 guns, by his maternal uncle Captain SUCKLING; but the storm and the disputes between the two Courts being adjusted, that ship was paid off, and the young sailor was transferred to a West-India merchant ship, belonging to the house of Mess. HIBBERT, PURRIER, and HORTON, and placed under the immediate care of Mr. JOHN RATHBONE, who formerly served in the *Dreadnought* with Capt. SUCKLING.

In July 1787, Captain NELSON returned to England, and the *Boreas* was paid off at Sheerness the 30th of the following November. In the preceding March he had been married to the amiable Lady, who has survived him, Mrs. FRANCES HERBERT NESBIT, widow of Doctor NESBIT, of the island of Nevis, daughter of WILLIAM HERBERT, Esq. Senior Judge, and niece of Mr. HERBERT, President of that Island: and he now retired to the place of his nativity, to enjoy the calm delight of domestic happiness, in the Parsonage-house where he received his birth, and which his father had resigned for his residence. From the age of twelve years to this moment, his life may be said to have been one continued scene of active, perilous, professional duty; which was now succeeded by a contrasted interval of rural amusement, and tranquil occupation.

In 1790, on the disputes between this country and Spain, relative to Nootka Sound, and the preparatory armament, he quitted his retirement to make a tender of his services, which were not then accepted. In the early part of 1793, we, however, find him in possession of the *Agamemnon*, of 64 guns, under the command of Lord HOOD, then appointed to the Mediterranean station; and who, on every service of superior difficulty, never failed to select Captain NELSON. Nay, it was observed in the Mediterranean at this time, that before NELSON quitted his old ship, he had fairly worn her out, and himself, and his crew. At the sieges of Bastia and Calvi, he gave pre-eminent and repeated proofs of his professional skill and personal intrepidity. At the latter he lost the sight of his right eye, from a shot of the enemy, which drove some particles of sand with prodigious violence against his face.

Continued

On June 11, 1779, Captain NELSON obtained his post rank. His first ship was the *Hinchinbroke*, and on the expectation of an attack on Jamaica by Count D'ESTAING, he was entrusted to command the Port Royal batteries.

On his passage from Porto Ferrajo to Gibraltar, with stores, in *La Minerve* frigate, he, on the 19th of December, took the Spanish frigate, *La Sabina*, of 40 guns, 28 eighteen-pounders; and on the 13th of February Commodore NELSON joined the Admiral off Cape St. Vincent. The glorious victory, which immediately followed, over the Spanish fleet, and the share which the Commodore had in it, are in those records which need not be repeated on this page. For his distinguished gallantry in this battle, he was honoured with the Order of the Bath, and the gold medal from his SOVEREIGN, and presented with the freedom of the Metropolis of the British Empire, with every complimentary circumstance of gratitude and respect.

In April 1797, Sir HORATIO NELSON, K.B. hoisted his flag as Rear Admiral of the Blue. On the 27th of May he shifted his flag from the *Captain* to the *Theseus*, and was appointed to the command of the inner squadron at the blockade of Cadiz. July 3, in a successful attack on the Spanish gun-boats, he is said to have transcended even every former display of personal courage: and on the 15th of the same month, he ordered a second bombardment of Cadiz, with great impression on the town and shipping. In this month also he was detached with a small squadron to make a vigorous attack on the town of Santa Cruz, in the island of Teneriffe; but though this enterprise was not crowned with the expected success, it added to the lustre of the British arms. Here it was that Sir HORATIO NELSON lost his arm by a cannon shot.

He now returned to England, and previous to the issuing of a grant, to secure this brave man some remuneration for such a succession of professional duties, his Memorial of Service stated, that he had actually been engaged against the enemy *one hundred and twenty* times, and that, during the then war, he had assisted at the capture of *seven sail of the line, six frigates, four corvettes*, and *eleven privateers*, of different sizes, and taken, or destroyed, near *fifty sail* of merchant vessels.

At this period Sir HORATIO NELSON had done enough for his own fame; his country was satisfied with his services, and he had obtained a place among her Heroes whose names will never die; and yet, with what a stupendous addition of glory has he illuminated the British records! the Battle of the Nile, with all its well-earned honours—the splendid service of Copenhagen—the delivery of the West Indies, and the grand destruction of the Combined Fleets of France and Spain, which closed the long continued and ever varying scene of his unexampled atchievements!

To that unexampled accumulation of honours, which Lord NELSON has provided for himself and his country, no addition is now left for the latter to make, but the magnificent solemnities of interment, the stately sepulchre, the proud inscription, and the eternal name. The nation, alas! must now weave the cypress with the laurel; and while she prepares her eulogy, the tear will glisten in the eye of glory.

New York Times
13th. October 1870

DEATH OF GEN. LEE.

His Final Relapse and Closing Hours at Lexington, Va.—The News at Richmond—Demonstrations of Grief.

The following dispatches relating to the sudden relapse of Gen. LEE were received yesterday afternoon:—

RICHMOND, Va., Oct. 12.—The *Dispatch* has just received the following telegram from Staunton, Va.:

"A messenger arrived here last night from Lexington, bringing the information that Gen. LEE is much worse. His physicians report that his disease has assumed a more serious form, and his friends are alarmed at his condition."

LEXINGTON, Va., Oct. 12, via MILBORO', Va.—Symptoms of an unfavorable character have manifested themselves in the disease of Gen. LEE within the past two days. His condition is not very encouraging; indeed, it begins to excite the grave apprehensions of his friends and physicians. The members of his family living at a distance have been summoned to his bed.

Later in the day the following intelligence arrived:—

Special Dispatch to the New-York Times.

WASHINGTON, Oct. 12.—Private dispatches from Richmond give particulars of the death of Gen. LEE, at Lexington, at 9½ o'clock this morning. He began growing worse on Monday, and continued to sink until the last, dying calmly and gently, with expressions of assured faith in his religion. Business houses in Richmond were closed this afternoon, and great manifestations of grief were made.

LEXINGTON, Va., Oct. 12—10 A. M.—via MILBORO', Va.—Gen. ROBERT E. LEE breathed his last at 9½ o'clock this morning, of congestion of the brain, aged sixty-three years, eight months and twenty-three days.

RICHMOND, Oct. 12.—The *Despatch* has just received the following special telegram:

LEXINGTON, Va., Oct. 12.—Gen. LEE died this morning at 9½ o'clock. He began to grow worse on Monday, and continued to sink until he breathed his last. The places of business are closed, the bells are tolling, and the whole community thrown into the deepest grief.

RICHMOND, Va., Oct. 12.—The telegram received here about noon, announcing that unfavorable symptoms had manifested themselves in Gen. LEE'S disease, had partially prepared our people to anticipate the worst, but notwithstanding this, when later in the afternoon the second dispatch announcing his death was received, the effect was crushing. The news spread around, and in a short time a deep feeling of gloom pervaded the whole community. The city authorities have issued orders that the bells on public buildings be tolled during to-morrow. Gov. WALKER will officially communicate the sad event to the Legislature. There will be a general suspension of business. The City Council will meet to-morrow to take appropriate action.

OBITUARY.

Gen. Robert E. Lee.

Intelligence was received last evening of the death at Lexington, Va., of Gen. ROBERT E. LEE, the most famous of the officers whose celebrity was gained in the service of the Southern Confederacy during the late terrible rebellion. A report was received some days ago that he had been smitten with paralysis, but this was denied, and though it was admitted that he was seriously ill, hopes of his speedy recovery seem to have been entertained by his friends. Within the last two or three days his symptoms had taken an unfavorable turn, and he expired at 9½ o'clock yesterday morning of congestion of the brain, at the age of, sixty-three years, eight months and twenty-three days.

ROBERT EDMUND LEE was the son of Gen. HENRY LEE, the friend of WASHINGTON, and a representative of one of the wealthiest and most respected families of Virginia. Born in January, 1807, he grew up amid all the advantages which wealth and family position could give in a republican land, and received the best education afforded by the institutions of his native State. Having inherited a taste for military studies, and an ambition for military achievements, he entered the National Academy at West Point in 1825, and graduated in 1829, the second in scholarship in his class. He was at once commissioned Second Lieutenant of engineers, and in 1835 acted as assistant astronomer in drawing the boundary line between the States of Michigan and Ohio. In the following year he was promoted to the grade of First Lieutenant, and in 1838 received a Captain's commission. On the breaking out of the war with Mexico he was made Chief-Engineer of the army under the command of Gen. WOOL. After the battle of Cerro Gordo, in April, 1847, in which he distinguished himself by his gallant conduct, he was immediately promoted to the rank of Major. He displayed equal skill and bravery at Contreras, Cherubusco and Chapultepec, and in the battle at the last-mentioned place received a severe wound. His admirable conduct throughout this struggle was rewarded before its close with the commission of a Lieutenant-Colonel and the brevet title of Colonel. In 1852 he was appointed to the responsible position of Superintendent of the Military Academy at West Point, which he retained until 1855. On retiring from the charge of this institution he was made Lieutenant-Colonel of the Second Cavalry, and on the 16th of March, 1861, received the commission of Colonel of the First Cavalry.

Thus far the career of Col. LEE had been one of honor and the highest promise. In every service which had been intrusted to his hands he had proved efficient, prompt and faithful, and his merits had always been readily acknowledged and rewarded by promotion. He was regarded by his superior officers as one of the most brilliant and promising men in the army of the United States. His personal integrity was well known, and his loyalty and patriotism was not doubted. Indeed, it was in view of the menaces of treason and the dangers which threatened the Union that he had received his last promotion, but he seems to have been thoroughly imbued with that pernicious doctrine that his first and highest allegiance was due to the State of his birth. When Virginia joined the ill-fated movement of secession from the Union, he immediately threw up his commission in the Federal Army and offered his sword to the newly-formed Confederacy. He took this step, protesting his own attachment to the Union, but declaring that his sense of duty would never permit him to "raise his hand against his relatives, his children, and his home." In his farewell letter to Gen. SCOTT, he spoke of the struggle which this step had cost him, and his wife declared that he "wept tears of blood over this terrible war." There are probably few who

doubt the sincerity of his protestation, but thousands have regretted, and his best friends will ever have to regret, the error of judgment, the false conception of the allegiance due to his Government and his country, which led one so rarely gifted to cast his lot with traitors, and devote his splendid talents to the execution of a wicked plot to tear asunder and ruin the Republic in whose service his life had hitherto been spent.

He resigned his commission on the 25th of April, 1861, and immediately betook himself to Richmond, where he was received with open arms and put in command of all the forces of Virginia by Gov. LETCHER. On the 10th of May he received the commission of a Major-General in the army of the Confederate States, retaining the command in Virginia, and was soon after promoted to the rank of General in the regular army. He first took the field in the mountainous region of Western Virginia, where he met with many difficulties, and was defeated at Greenbrier by Gen. J. J. REYNOLDS on the 3d of October, 1861. He was subsequently sent to take command of the Department of the South Atlantic Coast, but after the disabling of Gen. JOSEPH E. JOHNSTON at the battle of Fair Oaks, in the Spring of 1862, he was recalled to Virginia, and placed at the head of the forces defending the capital, which he led through the remainder of the campaign of the Chickahominy. He engaged with the Army of the Potomac under his old companion-in-arms, Gen. McCLELLAN, and drove it back to the Rappahannock. He afterward, in August, 1862, attacked the Army of Virginia, under Gen. POPE, and, after driving it back to Washington, crossed the Potomac into Maryland, where he issued a proclamation calling upon the inhabitants to enlist under his triumphant banners. Meantime, McCLELLAN gathered a new army from the broken remnants of his former forces, and met LEE at Hagerstown, and, after a battle of two days, compelled him to retreat. Reinforced by "Stonewall" JACKSON, on the 16th of September, he turned to renew the battle, but after two days of terrible fighting at Sharpsburg and Antietam, was driven from the soil of Maryland. Retiring beyond the Rappahannock, he took up his position at Fredericksburg, where he was attacked, on the 13th of December, by Gen. BURNSIDE, whom he drove back with terrible slaughter. He met with the same success in May, 1863, when attacked by HOOKER, at Chancellorsville. Encouraged by these victories, in the ensuing Summer he determined to make a bold invasion into the territory of the North. He met Gen. MEADE at Gettysburg, Penn., on the 1st of July, 1863, and after one of the most terrible and destructive battles of modern times, was driven from Northern soil. Soon after this, a new character appeared on the battlefields of Virginia, and Gen. LEE found it expedient to gather his forces for the defense of the Confederate capital against the determined onslaughts of Gen. GRANT. In the Spring and Summer of 1864 that indomitable soldier gradually inclosed the City of Richmond as with a girdle of iron, which he drew closer and closer with irresistible energy and inexorable determination, repulsing the rebel forces whenever they ventured to make an attack, which they did several times with considerable vigor. In this difficult position, holding the citadel of the Confederacy, and charged with its hopes and destinies, LEE was made Commander-in-Chief of the armies of the South. He held out until the Spring of 1865, vainly endeavoring to gather the broken forces of the Confederacy, and break asunder the terrible line which was closing around them. After a desperate and final effort at Burkesville, on the 9th of April, 1865, he was compelled to acknowledge his defeat, and surrendered his sword to Gen. GRANT on the generous terms which were dictated by that great soldier. LEE retired under his parole to Weldon, and soon after made a formal submission to the Federal Government. Subsequently, by an official clemency, which is probably without a parallel in the history of the world, he was formally pardoned for the active and effective part he had taken in the mad effort of the Southern States to break up the Union and destroy the Government. Not long after his surrender he was invited to become the President of Washington University, at Lexington, Va., and was installed in that position on the 2d of October, 1865. Since that time he has devoted himself to the interests of that institution, keeping so far as possible aloof from public notice, and by his unobtrusive modesty and purity of life, has won the respect even of those who most bitterly deplore and reprobate his course in the rebellion.

The Times

5th July 1821

DEATH OF NAPOLEON BUONAPARTE.

The following intelligence arrived in town yesterday from St. Helena:—

(From the Courier.)

"ST. HELENA, MAY 7.

"Buonaparte died on Saturday the 5th, at 6 p.m., after an illness of six weeks; the last fortnight only considered dangerous. The body has been opened, and the disease ascertained to be a cancer on the stomach, with a great extent of ulceration.

"He has been lying in state since yesterday afternoon, the Admiral, Governor, and heads of departments having first seen the body."

During the first four weeks of his illness, it did not assume any very dangerous apppearance, though he appeared himself to be conscious that it would terminate fatally. During the last fortnight it was evident to all the medical attendants that he could not recover.

Thus terminates in exile and in prison the most extraordinary life yet known to political history. The vicissitudes of such a life, indeed, are the most valuable lessons which history can furnish. Connected with, and founded in, the principles of his character, the varieties of fortune which Buonaparte experienced are of a nature to illustrate the most useful maxims of benevolence, patriotism, or discretion. They embrace both extremes of the condition of man in society, and therefore address themselves to all ranks of human beings. But Buonaparte was our enemy—our defeated enemy—and as Englishmen we must not tarnish our triumphs over the living warrior, by unmanly injustice towards the dead. The details of his life are notorious, and we omit them. The community of which Buonaparte was in his early days a member, and the military education which he received, may, independently of any original bias of character, have laid the foundation of the greatness to which he attained, and of that mischievous application of unbridled power, through which he fell very nearly to the level whence he first had started. Nothing could be more corrupt than the morals of military society among the French before the revolution—nothing more selfish or contracted than the views (at all times) of a thorough-bred military adventurer. Buonaparte came into active life, with as much (but we have no reason to think a larger share of) lax morality and pure selfishness as others of his age and calling. The public crisis into which he was thrown, gave to profound selfishness the form of insatiable ambition. With talents and enterprise beyond all comparison greater than any against which he had to contend, he overthrew whatever opposed his progress. Thus, ambition in him was more conspicuous than others, only because it was more successful. He became a Sovereign. How, then, was this pupil of a military school prepared to exercise the functions of sovereignty?. An officer, as such, has no idea of divided power. His patriotism is simply love of his troops and his profession. He will obey commands—he will issue them—but in both cases those commands are absolute. Talk to him of deliberation, of debate, of freedom of action, of speech, nay of opinion, his *feeling* is, that the body to which any of these privileges shall be accessible, must fall into confusion and be speedily destroyed. Whatever pretext may have been resorted to by Buonaparte—whatever Jacobin yells he may have joined in to assist his own advance towards power—every subsequent act of his life assures us that the military prepossessions in which he was educated, became those by which he was influenced as a statesman: and we are well persuaded of his conviction, that it was impossible for any country, above all for France, to be governed otherwise than by one sole authority—undivided and unlimited. It may, we confess, be no satisfaction to the French, nor any great consolation to the rest of Europe, to know through what means it was, or by what vicious training, that Buonaparte was fitted, nay, predestined almost, to be a scourge and destroyer of the rights of nations, instead of employing a power irresistible, and which in such a cause none would have felt disposed to resist, for the promotion of knowledge, peace, and liberty throughout the world. In hinting at what we conceive to be the fact, however, we are bound by regard for truth; our business is not to apologize for Buonaparte; but so far as may be done within the brief limits of a newspaper, to analyze and faithfully describe him. The factions also which he was compelled to crush, and whose overthrow obtained for him the gratitude of his country, still threatened a resurrection when the compressing force should be withdrawn. Hence were pretexts furnished on behalf of despotism of which men more enlightened and better constituted than Buonaparte might not soon have discovered the fallacy. Raised to empire at home, his ambition sought for itself fresh aliment; and foreign conquest was at once tempting and easy. Here the natural reflection will obtrude itself—what might not this extraordinary being have effected for the happiness of mankind, and for his own everlasting fame and grandeur, had he used but a moiety of the force or perseverance in generous efforts to relieve the oppressed, which he wasted in rendering himself the monopolist and patron of oppression! But he had left himself no resource. He had extinguished liberty in France, and had no hold upon his subjects but their love of military glory. Conquest therefore succeeded to conquest, until nothing capable of subjugation was left to be subdued. Insolence and rapacity in the victor produced among the enslaved nations, impatience of their misery and a thirst for vengeance. Injustice undermined itself, and Buonaparte, with his unseasoned empire, fell together, the pageant of a day.

His military administration was marked by strict and impartial justice. He had the art, in an eminent degree, of inciting the emulation and gaining the affections of his troops. He was steady and faithful in his friendships, and not vindictive on occasions where it was in his power to be so with impunity.

Of the deceased Emperor's intellectual and characteristic ascendancy over men, all the French, and some of other nations besides the French, who had an opportunity of approaching him, can bear witness. He seems to have possessed the talent, not merely of command, but, when he pleased, of conciliation and persuasion. With regard to his religious sentiments, they were perhaps of the same standard as those of other Frenchmen starting into manhood at a time when Infidel writings had so domineered over the popular mind, that revealed religion was become a public laughing-stock; and in a country where the pure Christian faith was perplexed with subtilties, overloaded by mummeries, and scandalized and discountenanced by a general looseness of morals. Upon the whole, Buonaparte will go down to posterity as a man who, having more good at his disposal than any other potentate of any former age, had actually applied his immense means to the production of a greater share of mischief and misery to his fellow-creatures—one who, on the basis of French liberty, might have founded that of every other state in Europe—but who carried on a series of aggressions against foreign States, to divert the minds of his own subjects from the sense of their domestic slavery; thus imposing on foreign nations a necessity for arming to shake off his yoke, and affording to foreign despots a pretext for following his example.

Daily News
15th September 1852

The Duke of WELLINGTON is dead! The conqueror of NAPOLEON the FIRST is removed from the world, just as NAPOLEON the SECOND is entering upon the scene. The event is the closing one of the greatest cycle of events that has yet been completed in modern history. The pall of the "Great DUKE" covers a terrible past, and the future may now develop itself undisturbed by the shadowy presence of the great soldier who influenced so largely the destinies of the generation just gone by.

It may be said of the DUKE with more truth than even of his great political friend, the late Sir ROBERT PEEL, that he has been fortunate in living so long that the world had time to merge any adverse judgments on some features of his political career in one unanimous verdict upon the wonderful grandeur of his life, taken as a whole. As his uncompromising political opponents on many occasions, we can now well afford to award him the full measure of praise for those qualities of his mind and spirit—and those features of his public conduct—which command respect. If by birth, education, conviction, he was a Tory, he was at least honest, high-minded, and open to fair argument in the discussion of his principles. He maintained his opinions as he would have defended a fortress, precisely as long as they were tenable—and no longer. He gave up the defence of his position in time to make an honourable retreat and while his friends could not with justice complain, his enemies were constrained to respect him.

The Duke of WELLINGTON's life affords one of those few specimens in history—a career thoroughly developed;—a thread spun out to its full and natural length. Many great, original men have been cut off in their activity—thwarted by extraordinary obstacles—and so compelled, in divers ways, to leave imperfect images of themselves in their deeds and in their personal memoirs. WELLINGTON leaves a full length portrait of himself in human history. He had his due and his entire influence, in his generation, at every stage of his life. He entered early in the course for which Nature had peculiarly intended him; had, in due time, his tasks put upon him; achieved everything that he undertook, and was in the best sense, a successful man. His reputation to the last, was the paramount reputation of his day. When he fought a battle, he generally won it, and always made a successful campaign; when he spoke in the House of Lords, his words were received and repeated throughout the country with a peculiar interest and authority such as attached to few other men. As "the DUKE," he was in himself an institution; and to praise him on all due occasions, was one of the natural ways in which many men showed their patriotism.

It has been very commonly—perhaps too invidiously—dwelt on, that he was pre-eminently a great soldier. For the distinctness and uniqueness with which his personality stamped itself on all he said and did, show clearly enough his originality of character. When he spoke or wrote, as well as when he acted, he stamped his image on the work as on a medal. As General—Conqueror—Conservative—Duke—or "noble lord" addressing the Peers, he equally made a distinct, personal impression, sui generis. So that, even when dealing with political ideas which were the ideas of a party, he gave them an entirely new force from giving them his approbation. People concluded that he had found something more in them than they had been able to discover. There was a force of moral integrity about him which extended itself to everything he did, and invested smaller things as well as great ones with veneration. The English people are not so ready as other nations to worship a soldier merely as a great military commander. But everything about WELLINGTON showed that the predominant feeling in his military career was that of the duty which was being performed by the work in progress. The English admired and respected him for that element, more, even, than for his commander's qualities. They felt that if he was a great man among them, he had a man's genuine right to be so; and that it was because he was a great man, that he was a great soldier.

He had—combined in himself—in a singular degree, the national qualities on which the English people pride themselves—clear practical honesty of intellect, patience, probity, fidelity of character. He had the qualities which make Englishmen, not perhaps more personally attractive at first sight, but which make them a historical people, and will keep their name alive in the latest annals of the world. He had the qualities which found colonies—establish commerce—which make great towns, and roads, and canals—which make men suffer hardships, submit to labour, and which make them "pay." You could calculate him like a planet. The comparatively trivial circumstance which we all felt to be so characteristic of him—we mean his formal punctuality in answering all manner of notes, and which people smiled at as the characteristic ways of some old and loved friend was itself a significant symbol of his whole life. He always did what ought to be done, because it was his business. He destroyed an army or took a town with the same punctuality with which he arrived at a dinner party, and marched into a territory as he would have done into the Horse Guards. What else was he there for?—you may fancy to be his first question. It has been admitted that war—was never conducted so purely, so decently, with so much regard to the considerations of the social rectitude of civilization, as under him. Who has done such work, and come away with hands so clean? What soldier could you ever be so safe in expecting to achieve the "came, saw, and conquered"—with the most perfect certainty? The work to be done was with him the primary consideration, for the sake of duty and England; and he expected rigid subordination in others to him, as he acted with rigid subordination to principles himself. He had less of the showy and graceful qualities, which attach romantic interest to great names, than most famous men. But all work in the main is an earnest and grave thing; and fighting, the most earnest and grave species of work. His war bulletins do not read as if they had been written by a novelist; but one may be sure that they are true; and there is no baseness to record. He having done the work—others might let off the fire works.

Continued

He was thus, from his position, his successes, his wealth, and his character, essentially a moral force in this country; and we see accordingly, that after a long peace had removed great prospect of his being again employed in war, the national interest in him, far from abating, was ever on the increase. He had not the dubious fame, the clouded glory, of so many fine soldiers. In the days of RADETZKYS and HAYNAUS, no shudder occurred at the mention of the name of WELLINGTON! No priest shrank from associating it with prayer—no woman from mentioning it with honour. For we know that what he had had to do had been done in all sincerity, and in a cause which he had at heart fully as much as a man as a soldier. His terrible battles were remembered as necessary, if awful, events—and the crop of fame he reaped from his battle-fields was, as stainless as the waving grain that now grows on the plains of Waterloo.

He was a Conservative by instinct and habit, rather than theoretically or speculatively a Conservative politician. Theorising regarding mankind was not his forte. He was not a thinker proper, so much as a man of action, and he acted in politics, from the instinct of "holding fast by the good,"—(or what he believed good)—but with regard to political changes, he disliked them rather instinctively as changes, than from insight into their ultimate tendencies and significance. However, military life had early brought him into contact with fact, and hence when changes became inevitable, no man more decisively conceded to them. His invaluable intellectual sincerity made him see, what dunces could not see, and knaves would not see, to have become part and parcel of the life of England. Hence, he knew when to concede—and conceded, when the time was right, and the concession honourable. He bowed to Catholic Emancipation, and Reform, and Free Trade; and it would, indeed, be a pity, and something worse, to confound this great and fine man, with such "Tories"—as the knot of shufflers and dullards, imposters and quacks, who are now allowed to play at governing the country.

The comparison between the DUKE and the great Sir ROBERT holds with remarkable force when we consider the nature of the political creed with which each entered upon public life, and the mental power which each possessed to correct and modify his creed. Each of these remarkable men had the faculty of reading the great book of the present, and marking accurately where new phases of moral and political life were on the point of appearing. Each recognised the fact that the world is not a dull mechanism to be explained by some few rigid formulæ, and to be kept eternally dependent upon the revolution of the same wheels. Each recognised a principle of growth in the world, a necessity for development. Each was prepared to adapt himself to the change which the fulness of life in the world determined and brought forth. Sir ROBERT probably, and the DUKE certainly, would have preferred the old Tory adjustment. Both would very possibly have been content at one time to wind up the old machine, and provide for its easy working, by a little oiling of the parts. Both, however, saw clearly when the old mechanism must give place to a new form of life. Neither of

them was mad enough to suppose that an oak planted in a porcelain vase would be less certain to develop itself if you changed the porcelain for cast iron! It was the possession by the two of this quality of mind in common which enabled them to be powerful agents in the most extensive reforms recently carried out in this country. Nurtured in the aristocratical faith, both were enabled to command the sympathies of the aristocracy—a sympathy which the one by his intellectual capabilities, the other by the great force of his character, converted into a source of practical power. The oligarchy kicking obstinately and ignorantly against the wall, as long as the mere public opposed them, crouched penitently before the opposition, when Sir ROBERT and the DUKE explained to them the nature of that power which they,—in their dull ignorance of its magnitude, had resisted.

It is the completeness and steadiness of WELLINGTON's character which marks him as one of the true great characters of his age. His rival, NAPOLEON, was perpetually losing his balance. BONAPARTE allowed his belief in himself and his star to degenerate into a superstition. During the later years of his life he was perpetually giving way to the most passionate impulses, if his plans—however wildly conceived—failed. His conduct during the retreat from Moscow, was more like that of a spoiled child than of a great general. He issued orders impossible to be executed, and bewailed his fate at their ill-success,—the same time overwhelming his officers with bitter reproaches. He forgot also, what WELLINGTON never forgot—that the greatest genius, in proportion as the material masses upon which it acts becomes enlarged, loses its power faster and faster as materials stretch away from its own immediate operation.

It was NAPOLEON's mission to carry out the revolution. He accepted it, and by miscalculation of his resources stifled the revolution—and ruined himself.

It was WELLINGTON's mission to oppose the revolution. He also accepted the mission and performed it as far as the spirit of the age would permit him. When he found that he could achieve no more, he bowed to circumstances. No man ever knew so well the extreme capabilities of the forces which he had to manage. No man ever handled those forces with more consummate skill.

The Duke of WELLINGTON has passed away, and at a time when regret for his loss will be mingled with some anxiety. For though the DUKE had passed that time of life when any very active military service could be expected from him, he was yet known to possess—almost in its original clearness and power—that strong common sense—that sagacious prudence and ability for separating essentials from non-essentials which become invaluable at times of danger, emergency, or confusion. Calm, clear, self-reliant, and full of experience, his mind was of an order that secured the confidence of those with whom he acted, and on each occasion when of late years this country has been told that danger surrounded her—the nation always turned with confidence towards "F.M. The DUKE," as one whose judgment in any hour of peril was sure to be equal to the occasion, and whose ripe military genius would successfully direct those younger and more active Englishmen ever ready to sustain the weight

of any personal conflict. To secure this confidence his whole career had tended, and it was natural that England should rest with thorough reliance upon the soldier who had driven the best armies of France before him in the Peninsula, and had finally overthrown NAPOLEON at Waterloo.

The knell that tolls for this great man's death tolls also the death of a remarkable period of history. He was one great spirit in this period, and he leaves us to a future in which we may want such men as he. He leaves us to the working out of principles which he once vainly sought to oppose, but which he had the wisdom afterwards to recognise. He leaves us to the development of serious problems, the solutions of which have been preparing during his eventful life. We shall have our solutions of these problems opposed by our adversaries. Would that they were all like him—grave, courteous, earnest, honest.

His death will occasion a great chasm in that world to which public admiration is directed. With the exception of the sovereign, no one has for years enjoyed so great a share of the national respect. It is impossible not to be in some measure affected by the grief which will take so firm a hold on the minds of thousands. His brothers in arms will have lost the great lodestone which has enchained their admiration for years. His political friends and enemies will each mourn the departure of one who has commanded the irrepressible deference of both. The universal public will mourn one who has carried the military glory of England to a height which has seldom been equalled, never exceeded. Peace to his ashes.

The Times
23rd May 1834

The death of General LAFAYETTE has produced among all the friends of liberty a regret proportioned to their sense of his public and private virtues, rather than to any high estimate formed of the intellectual powers of that revolutionary patriarch. General LA-FAYETTE was a strictly honest man, a brave soldier, a disinterested patriot, an enthusiast in the cause of general liberty, of which there nevertheless appears no evidence that he understood the true nature or theory, which alone would account for his incapacity at the most favourable periods of his political existence to render its principles subservient to the wants and interests of France. The name of freedom, so early as at the outset of the American contest, had no small charms for the ardent spirit of LA-FAYETTE; a war in defence of it dazzled a young soldier's imagination; and a war against England, in a much worse cause, would have inflamed the blood of any genuine Frenchman. As a volunteer for America he had a large field for the display of those popular qualities—vivacity, courtesy, courage, and generosity—by all of which LAFAYETTE was distinguished, and which won for him the personal affection of thousands of individuals among a rude people, not very susceptible of deep impressions from either the showy or the amiable in human nature. The trans-atlantic popularity of M. DE LAFAYETTE followed him to France. When the revolutionary troubles broke out, he was at the top of everything—he was foremost in everything but crime. Successive crises, however, soon arose wherein it was impossible for any but criminals to be leaders, and LAFAYETTE's speedy abdication of a post, which would have required the sacrifice of all his better principles, and all his gentler virtues, was imputed to him as weakness of character. We know that he never made a dishonourable choice, when the question was "weak or wicked?" It is indeed certain that the deceased General had not those qualities which carry men in triumph through the wear and tear of civil conflicts,—where all the resources of sagacity, dexterity, and promptitude of decision under adverse and unlooked for circumstances, are hourly called into play. LAFAYETTE could move confidently along a level road, terminated by a visible and definite object; but the depths and intricacies of a complex and continued revolutionary struggle bewildered him. He could not fathom nor emerge from them. Hence he was extinguished as an actor during the first scene of the tragedy; and the same upright and conscientious spirit which drove him into exile under the Jacobin democracy, condemned him to obscurity under the despotism of NAPOLEON. A republican in word and deed, he never would crouch to BONAPARTE, nor applaud that iron pageant which he miscalled a Government, nor acknowledge the blood and spoils of foreign nations as a sufficient atonement to France herself for the ruin of every institution and every power that could be appealed to by a civilized people as their security against the caprices of a tyrant. LAFAYETTE plunged therefore into deep retirement, and was apparently neglected, though watched with vigilant suspicion, during the whole reign of BUONAPARTE. From the Restoration to the Revolution of 1830, the old apostle of liberty was always at his post—invariably on the side of liberal and national measures, but exemplary in his respect for the laws, and his discouragement of public disturbance. The popular victory which drove the incorrigible BOURBONS of the elder branch from Paris, might have placed LAFAYETTE at the head of a French republic; but good sense, and high principle, alike restrained him from yielding to a seduction which might have cost his country a civil war. He gave with his own hand the crown of France to LOUIS PHILIPPE, and as in former instances the movement, whose first impulse had been directed by him, speedily shaped another course, leaving LAFAYETTE stranded. The fact is, that the worthy General had not ascendancy over others to make them his instruments for any length of time, and was too honest to be theirs when he once disapproved their proceedings. He was ever the first man whom revolution, while it yet wore the aspect of reform, sought as its apologist with the world, and the first who was revolted by its degeneracy. His name will go down to after ages in company with the most portentous events of modern times. But to most of them he was an appendage—they were not his creation. His position made him celebrated—it even made him important, but it could not make him great.

The Standard
17th February 1885

GENERAL GORDON.

The long period of suspense is at last over. The Telegram which will be found in our fifth page sets at rest all doubts as to the fate of Gordon. It is the first authentic narrative that has reached England. The death of General Gordon will come home to the mind of every English man and woman with the sense of a personal and irreparable loss. It seems only the other day that the weight of anxiety which had so long oppressed us with regard to what might be happening at Khartoum was removed by the tidings of General Stewart's successes, and of Sir Charles Wilson's journey to Khartoum, whither it was thought he would carry the certain message of succour and success. This most pleasing supposition had been accepted with a degree of confidence which the suspense of months only served to intensify, and, now that all our hopes are rudely dashed to the ground, the terrible news comes with double force, and almost deprives us of the capacity to measure its significance, or the extent of the deplorable disaster which no activity and no outlay on the part of the Government can now in the smallest degree retrieve or repair. For twenty years the achievements of General Gordon had not merely familiarised his countrymen with his name, but had inspired them with a belief that he could accomplish almost the impossible, and that under his auspices success could be obtained at small cost and less risk. His latest deed was of a character to strengthen this confidence and to confirm all that his greatest admirers had said or written of Chinese Gordon, for, search the annals of history as we may, there is nothing recorded in human experience to equal the magnificent heroism with which he defended Khartoum, and arrested for so many months the advance of the Mahdi. As all the world is aware, the defence of Khartoum was only the latest of a long list of remarkable achievements performed by this wonderful man, each of which would have sufficed to insure the permanent fame of its author. The full narrative of a life which in the span of thirty years' unceasing activity was marked by so many brilliant successes in Asia and Africa would require many volumes. It is only possible here to touch briefly on the more important of them, and by a passing reference to recall events which can never be forgotten, and to point the moral of a career which in its simpler, as well as grander, details must stand for ever as the noblest possible example to future generations of his countrymen.

Index